The Oxford Handbook of Social Influence

OXFORD LIBRARY OF PSYCHOLOGY

*Editor in Chief* PETER E. NATHAN

# The Oxford Handbook of Social Influence

*Edited by*

Stephen G. Harkins

Kipling D. Williams

Jerry M. Burger

OXFORD
UNIVERSITY PRESS

# OXFORD
UNIVERSITY PRESS

Oxford University Press is a department of the University of Oxford. It furthers
the University's objective of excellence in research, scholarship, and education
by publishing worldwide. Oxford is a registered trade mark of Oxford University
Press in the UK and certain other countries.

Published in the United States of America by Oxford University Press
198 Madison Avenue, New York, NY 10016, United States of America.

© Oxford University Press 2017

Library of Congress Cataloging-in-Publication Data
Names: Harkins, Stephen G., 1948– editor. | Williams, Kipling D., editor. | Burger, Jerry M., editor.
Title: The Oxford handbook of social influence / edited by Stephen G. Harkins,
Kipling D. Williams, Jerry M. Burger.
Description: New York : Oxford University Press, [2017] |
Series: Oxford library of psychology | Includes index.
Identifiers: LCCN 2016047130 | ISBN 9780199859870 (jacketed hardcover : alk.paper)
Subjects: LCSH: Social influence. | Interpersonal relations. | Culture—Psychological aspects. |
Influence (Psychology)
Classification: LCC HM1176 .O94 2017 | DDC 302/.13—dc23
LC record available at https://lccn.loc.gov/2016047130

9 8 7 6 5 4 3 2 1

Printed by Sheridan Books, Inc., United States of America

# SHORT CONTENTS

The *Oxford Library of Psychology*, a landmark series of handbooks, is published by Oxford University Press, one of the world's oldest and most highly respected publishers, with a tradition of publishing significant books in psychology. The ambitious goal of the *Oxford Library of Psychology* is nothing less than to span a vibrant, wide-ranging field and, in so doing, to fill a clear market need.

Encompassing a comprehensive set of handbooks, organized hierarchically, the *Library* incorporates volumes at different levels, each designed to meet a distinct need. At one level are a set of handbooks designed broadly to survey the major subfields of psychology; at another are numerous handbooks that cover important current focal research and scholarly areas of psychology in depth and detail. Planned as a reflection of the dynamism of psychology, the *Library* will grow and expand as psychology itself develops, thereby highlighting significant new research that will impact on the field. Adding to its accessibility and ease of use, the *Library* will be published in print and, later on, electronically.

The *Library* surveys psychology's principal subfields with a set of handbooks that capture the current status and future prospects of those major subdisciplines. This initial set includes handbooks of social and personality psychology, clinical psychology, counseling psychology, school psychology, educational psychology, industrial and organizational psychology, cognitive psychology, cognitive neuroscience, methods and measurements, history, neuropsychology, personality assessment, developmental psychology, and more. Each handbook undertakes to review one of psychology's major subdisciplines with breadth, comprehensiveness, and exemplary scholarship. In addition to these broadly conceived volumes, the *Library* also includes a large number of handbooks designed to explore in depth more specialized areas of scholarship and research, such as stress, health and coping, anxiety and related disorders, cognitive development, or child and adolescent assessment. In contrast to the broad coverage of the subfield handbooks, each of these latter volumes focuses on an especially productive, more highly focused line of scholarship and research. Whether at the broadest or most specific level, however, all of the *Library* handbooks offer synthetic coverage that reviews and evaluates the relevant past and present research and anticipates research in the future. Each handbook in the *Library* includes introductory and concluding chapters written by its editor to provide a roadmap to the handbook's table of contents and to offer informed anticipations of significant future developments in that field.

An undertaking of this scope calls for handbook editors and chapter authors who are established scholars in the areas about which they write. Many of the nation's and world's most productive and best-respected psychologists have agreed to edit *Library* handbooks or write authoritative chapters in their areas of expertise.

For whom has the *Oxford Library of Psychology* been written? Because of its breadth, depth, and accessibility, the *Library* serves a diverse audience, including graduate students in psychology and their faculty mentors, scholars, researchers, and practitioners in psychology and related fields. Each will find in the *Library* the information they seek on the subfield or focal area of psychology in which they work or are interested.

Befitting its commitment to accessibility, each handbook includes a comprehensive index, as well as extensive references to help guide research. And because the *Library* was designed from its inception as an online as well as a print resource, its structure and contents will be readily and rationally searchable online. Further, once the *Library* is released online, the handbooks will be regularly and thoroughly updated.

In summary, the *Oxford Library of Psychology* will grow organically to provide a thoroughly informed perspective on the field of psychology, one that reflects both psychology's dynamism and its increasing interdisciplinarity. Once published electronically, the *Library* is also destined to become a uniquely valuable interactive tool, with extended search and browsing capabilities. As you begin to consult this handbook, we sincerely hope you will share our enthusiasm for the more than 500-year tradition of Oxford University Press for excellence, innovation, and quality, as exemplified by the *Oxford Library of Psychology*.

Peter E. Nathan
Editor-in-Chief
*Oxford Library of Psychology*

**Stephen G. Harkins**

Stephen G. Harkins received his Ph.D. at the University of Missouri–Columbia in 1975. Following a two-year postdoctoral fellowship at The Ohio State University, he moved to Northeastern University, where he has been a professor since 1989. He studies the effect of social threat on task performance.

**Kipling D. Williams**

Kipling D. Williams received his Ph.D. at The Ohio State University in 1981. Since 2004, he has been a professor of psychological sciences at Purdue University. His primary research interests are ostracism and social influence. He is editor of the journal *Social Influence*.

**Jerry M. Burger**

Jerry M. Burger received his Ph.D. at the University of Missouri–Columbia in 1980 and has been a professor of psychology at Santa Clara University since 1993. He has conducted extensive research in the areas of obedience, compliance, perception of and motivation for personal control, and social norms.

# CONTRIBUTORS

**Katherine E. Adams**
Department of Psychological Sciences
Purdue University
West Lafayette, IN

**Adam J. Brown**
Department of Psychology
Northeastern University
Boston, MA

**Jerry M. Burger**
Department of Psychology
Santa Clara University
Santa Clara, CA

**Fabrizio Butera**
Institute of Psychology
University of Lausanne
Lausanne, Switzerland

**David Byrne**
New York, NY

**Linda L. Carli**
Department of Psychology
Wellesley College
Wellesley, MA

**Robert B. Cialdini**
Department of Psychology
Arizona State University
Phoenix, AZ

**Linda J. Demaine**
Sandra Day O'Connor College of Law
Arizona State University
Phoenix, AZ

**M. Robin DiMatteo**
Department of Psychology
University of California, Riverside
Riverside, CA

**Juan Manuel Falomir-Pichastor**
Faculty of Psychology and Educational
  Sciences
University of Geneva
Geneva, Switzerland

**Rosellina Ferraro**
Robert H. Smith School of Business
University of Maryland
College Park, MD

**Amber M. Gaffney**
Department of Psychology
Humboldt State University
Arcata, CA

**Rosanna E. Guadagno**
School of Art, Technology, and Emerging
  Communication and School of
  Behavioral and Brain Sciences
University of Texas at Dallas
Dallas, TX

**Andrew H. Hales**
Department of Psychological Sciences
Purdue University
West Lafayette, IN

**Stephen G. Harkins**
Department of Psychology
Northeastern University
Boston, MA

**S. Alexander Haslam**
School of Psychology
University of Queensland
St. Lucia, Queensland, Australia

**Martin Heesacker**
Department of Psychology
University of Florida
Gainesville, FL

**Mary Lynn Miller Henningsen**
Department of Communication
Northern Illinois University
Dekalb, IL

**Bert H. Hodges**
Department of Psychological Sciences
University of Connecticut
Storrs, CT;
Department of Psychology
Gordon College
Wenham, MA

**Michael A. Hogg**
Department of Psychology
Claremont Graduate University
Claremont, CA

**Matthew J. Hornsey**
School of Psychology
University of Queensland
St. Lucia, Queensland, Australia

**Jolanda Jetten**
School of Psychology
University of Queensland
St. Lucia, Queensland, Australia

**Steven J. Karau**
Department of Management
Southern Illinois University
Carbondale, IL

**Allan J. Kimmel**
Department of Marketing
ESCP Europe
Paris, France

**Amna Kirmani**
Department of Marketing
Robert H. Smith School of Business
University of Maryland
College Park, MD

**Leslie R. Martin**
Department of Psychology
La Sierra University
Riverside, CA

**Megan K. McCarty**
Department of Psychology
Amherst College
Amherst, MA

**Gabriel Mugny**
Faculty of Psychology and Educational
    Sciences
University of Geneva
Geneva, Switzerland

**John B. Nezlek**
Department of Psychology
College of William & Mary
Williamsburg, VA;
University of Social Sciences and
    Humanities
Poznan, Poland

**Jessica M. Nolan**
Department of Psychology
University of Scranton
Scranton, PA

**Michael J. Platow**
Research School of Psychology
Australian National University
Canberra, Australian Capital Territory,
    Australia

**Alain Quiamzade**
Faculty of Psychology and Educational
    Sciences
University of Geneva
Geneva, Switzerland;
Distance Learning University, Switzerland

**Stephen D. Reicher**
School of Psychology and Neuroscience
University of St. Andrews
St. Andrews, Scotland, UK

**Dongning Ren**
Department of Social Psychology
Tilburg University
Tilburg, the Netherlands

**Brad J. Sagarin**
Department of Psychology
Northern Illinois University
Dekalb, IL

**Allison E. Seitchik**
Department of Psychology
Merrimack College
North Andover, MA

**C. Veronica Smith**
Department of Psychology
University of Mississippi
University, MS

**Russell Spears**
Department of Psychology
University of Groningen
Groningen, the Netherlands

**Jerry Suls**
Behavioral Research Program
National Cancer Institute
Bethesda, MD

**James M. Tyler**
Department of Psychological Sciences
Purdue University
West Lafayette, IN

**Gerben A. van Kleef**
Department of Psychology
University of Amsterdam
Amsterdam, the Netherlands

**Ladd Wheeler**
Department of Psychology
Macquarie University
Sydney, New South Wales, Australia

**Kipling D. Williams**
Department of Psychological Sciences
Purdue University
West Lafayette, IN

# CONTENTS

The Oxford Handbook of Social Influence

PART 1

# Introduction

# Introduction and Overview

Stephen G. Harkins *and* Kipling D. Williams

**Abstract**

The study of social influence has been central to social psychology since its inception. In fact, research on social influence began in the 1880s, predating the coining of the term social psychology. However, by the mid-1980s, interest in this area had waned. Now the pendulum is swinging back, as seen in growing interest in non-cognitive, motivational accounts. Our hope is that the publication of this volume will aid this movement. The chapters, written by leading scholars, cover a variety of topics in social influence, incorporating a range of levels of analysis (intrapersonal, interpersonal, and intragroup) and both source and target effects. The book also includes chapters on theories that are most relevant to social influence, as well as a set of chapters on social influence in applied settings. Finally, we include a section that considers the future of social influence in social psychology.

**Key Words:** social influence, social psychology, conformity, compliance, obedience, intrapersonal, interpersonal, intragroup, social identity, social comparison

Social influence lies at the heart of social psychology. In fact, in his classic *Handbook* chapter, E. E. Jones (1985) noted that social psychology "can almost be defined as the study of social influence" (1985, p. 79). If anything, this is an understatement, as is shown by a comparison of their definitions. Social influence has been defined as the process "wherein one person's attitudes, cognitions, or behaviors are changed through the doings of another" (Cialdini & Griskevicius, 2010, p. 385) and as "the myriad ways that people impact one another, including changes in attitudes, beliefs, feelings and behavior, that result from the comments, actions, or even the mere presence of others" (Gilovich, Keltner, & Nisbett, 2011, p. 276). Social psychology has been defined as "*an attempt to understand and explain how the thought, feeling, and behavior of individuals are influenced by the actual, imagined, or implied presence of other human beings*" (Allport, 1954, p. 3, italics in original).

The fact that the first experimental work in what would come to be termed "social psychology"

(Allport, 1924) was conducted on topics that would later be placed under the rubric of social influence also demonstrates the crucial role that it has played in the history of social psychology. For example, Binet and Henri's (1894, as cited by Prislin & Crano, 2012) research on suggestibility prefigured Asch's (1951) work on conformity. Féré (1887, as cited by Prislin & Crano, 2012) and Triplett (1898) examined a phenomenon that Allport (1924) would later term "social facilitation." In the 1880s, Ringelmann conducted research on the effect of working with others (published in 1913, as cited by Kravitz & Martin, 1986), which was later extended in work on social loafing (Latané, Williams, & Harkins, 1979).

Given the centrality of social influence in the field, it would be no exaggeration to say that virtually any topic in social psychology, aside, perhaps, from hard-core social cognition, could be included in a handbook of social influence. Certainly there are some topics that form the core of social influence, such as conformity (e.g., Asch, 1951), compliance (e.g., Freedman & Fraser, 1966), and obedience (e.g., Milgram, 1963) that would be included in any such volume. Work in these areas exhibits many of the hallmarks of research on social influence: a high degree of experimental realism; behavioral measures; and real-world settings. As can be seen from the dates of these citations, work in these areas predates the cognitive revolution, and interest in these areas continues to the present day, even in the popular media, as is suggested by the recent release of two films, *The Experimenter* (2015), which depicts Milgram's obedience research, and *The Experiment* (2015), which portrays Zimbardo's prison simulation.

On the other hand, there are other topics that likely would not be included, even though they obviously involve social influence. For example, persuasion clearly represents a means of social influence, but it is typically not included under the rubric of social influence. In fact, research on social influence and attitudes is not even published in the same subsections of the top journal of the field, the *Journal of Personality and Social Psychology*. Research on persuasion is published in the *Attitudes and Social Cognition* section, whereas research on social influence is published in *Interpersonal Relations and Group Processes*.

Prislin and Crano (2012) argue that in the early part of the 20th century, likely as a result of the theoretical influence of people like Dewey (1922/1930) and Mead (1934), attitudes were thought of in terms of group-shared norms. However, they argue that this orientation ran afoul of efforts by psychologists such as Floyd Allport (1919, 1924) to "establish social psychology as a science that uses the individual as a unit of analysis" (p. 332), and "consequently, attitudes were defined in strictly individualistic terms without reference to social influence" (p. 333). Prislin and Crano argue that the domination of the field for the past 50 years by the cognitive orientation has reinforced this divorce of attitudes from social influence.

In addition, persuasion research also tends to use paper-and-pencil paradigms (or, more appropriately in this era, computer-presented paradigms) in laboratories that allow for the measurement of intervening processes. These measures can then be used to assess mediation, the testing of which has been de rigeur in social psychology for the last several decades. Field studies, however, which account for many studies in social influence, are not amenable ⌐ the use of intervening, intrusive questionnaires aimed at assessing possible mediation. In this sense,

classic social influence methods have fallen out of favor in our field, possibly further separating persuasion research and theory from social influence research and theory.

Although these arguments have merit, there may be a simpler explanation. In his 1935 *Handbook* chapter, Gordon Allport noted that "the concept of attitude is probably the most distinctive and indispensable concept in contemporary American social psychology" (p. 798), and, in the 1954 *Handbook*, he noted that the construct of attitude is the "primary building stone in the edifice of social psychology" (p. 63). Perhaps the sheer volume of work on attitudes and its centrality to the field require that it stand alone. Certainly it would be hard to argue that persuasion is not a form of social influence.

In any event, in the current volume we follow historical precedent and devote chapters to topics such as conformity, compliance, and obedience, but we will not include a chapter on persuasion. In fact, consistent with the earlier argument, a treatment of attitudes and attitude change would easily be worth a volume of its own. For the rest of the chapters, we have selected a range of topics that fall under the rubric of social influence. Unlike some reviews that include only research that focuses on the target of social influence attempts (e.g., Cialdini & Trost, 1998), we also include some chapters that focus on influence sources—their motivation and differential effectiveness. The chapters incorporate a range of levels of analysis: intrapersonal, interpersonal, and intragroup. We include two chapters that cover the theories most relevant to social influence effects: social comparison and social identity. We have also included a set of chapters that examine social influence effects in applied settings. Finally, we include a section that considers the future of social influence in social psychology.

## Overview

We begin with a chapter that covers ethical issues in social influence research from Milgram's work in the 1960s, the conduct of which, at the least, served to increase concern about ethical behavior in research, through current work conducted on the Internet (Kimmel). We then move to a pair of chapters on *Intrapersonal Processes*, one on gender and one on personality. In her chapter, Carli compares females and males both as sources and targets of influence. However, as will be seen, although gender differences in influenceability were reported in the 1980s (e.g., Eagly & Carli, 1981), current research shows little evidence of overall differences.

The same is not true for gender differences in source effects: Women are less effective sources of social influence than men. Carli provides evidence for this claim and suggests reasons for it.

Nezlek and Smith's chapter is devoted to the intersection of personality and individual differences with research and theory on social influence. Strangely, the two domains have not enjoyed much overlap; so in addition to covering the existing research in which researchers ask what traits are associated with influence and influenceability, Nezlek and Smith speculate as to why the two areas are not highly interwoven, and they implore future researchers to consider their mutual interaction.

In the next section of the volume we look at social influence as it is reflected in *interpersonal processes*. We begin with a chapter in which Suls and Wheeler review the development of social comparison theory. We do not mean to suggest that social comparison theory (Festinger, 1954) is directly relevant to all of the chapters in this section, but it was a dominant theory in the period of time in which much of the work in this section was begun, and it helped to shape the thinking in this period. For example, the distinction between normative and informational influence in conformity that was made by Deutsch and Gerard (1955) echoes the two aims of social comparison: self-enhancement and self-evaluation. Normative influence stems from our concern about how we appear to others. People want their opinions, beliefs, and attributes to reflect positively on themselves (self-enhancement), but they are also motivated to learn the truth, as is reflected by the effect of informational influence (self-evaluation).

In the next chapters in this section, we cover conformity, compliance, and obedience. We present these topics in this order because this organization reflects an underlying dimension of social control that begins with behavior that is produced by the simple observation of others engaging in the target behavior (conformity), then goes to behavior that is produced by requests (compliance), and ends with behavior that is produced by the orders or demands of someone in authority (obedience).

In his chapter, Hodges describes conformity as a crucial dimension of culture and of human survival. Without it, we would not have survived. However, Hodges argues that equally important is the fact that people have a tendency to diverge. Hodges proposes that traditional experimental social psychology has focused on the former without giving enough weight to the latter. Hodges also argues

that experimental social psychology has focused too much on the molecular level of behavior without situating this behavior in the larger cultural context. In his chapter, he incorporates work from anthropology, as well as social, developmental, and cognitive psychology, arguing for a broader view of the complex interplay of conformity and divergence.

In Guadagno's chapter on compliance, she focuses primarily on how social influence tactics influence others to change their behavior. To many, this focus comprises the core of social influence—a preponderance of field studies in which individuals buy products, commit time, sign petitions, erect posters, or vote, for things, people, and ideas that they were unlikely to buy or endorse before. Relying on Cialdini's (2009) six principles of influence—reciprocity, commitment and consistency, authority, social validation or social proof, and liking and similarity—she organizes her chapter around an examination of the extant research on these six principles, their underlying mechanisms, especially the mindlessness hypothesis, and their application to influence within the newest realm of social influence: social media.

In his chapter, Burger reviews research on how individuals respond to orders or demands from a person or institution in a position of authority. Although there has been some other work, for more than 50 years, research and discussion in this area have been dominated by Milgram's work on destructive obedience. In fact, it would be hard to find any other topic in social influence in which a single program of research has exerted so much influence on the work on that topic dating from its inception to the present. This is particularly surprising given that Milgram's interpretation of his own findings did not find wide acceptance even at the time that it was proposed. Burger provides an account of the development of this area of research and provides suggestions as to how it can move beyond Milgram's pioneering work.

In the next chapter, Nolan discusses social norms as a source of social influence. Although social norms and conformity are closely related topics, there is a key difference. In his chapter on conformity, Hodges notes that conformity is nearly always understood in terms of matching one's behavior with that of others because one observed others engaging in that behavior. In her chapter, Nolan defines social norms as "rules and standards that are understood by members of a group, and that guide morally relevant social behavior by way of social sanctions, instead of the force of laws." Thus, although closely related to conformity, social norms can operate without direct observation of others engaging in the target behavior. In her chapter, Nolan argues that her perspective represents a new way of looking at social norms that emphasizes norm enforcement as an essential component of understanding and defining a behavior as normative. Thus, in addition to the typical review of the literature on social norms as sources of social influence, the chapter discusses how and when individuals enforce norms. Nolan also discusses methods of maximizing the effects of social norm interventions, paying particular attention to combining descriptive and injunctive norms, reference groups, personal relevance, and cognitive resources.

McCarty and Karau define social inhibition as the tendency for behaviors that are typically exhibited to be minimized in the presence of others. In some ways, social inhibition is similar to conformity, in that there need be no intention to influence on the part of the sources: simple awareness of (or belief in) their presence is sufficient to lead to the cessation of the target's behavior. McCarty and Karau argue that, despite its long history, research on social inhibition does not form a cohesive literature. In their chapter, they address this issue by integrating research from several different traditions, including helping behavior, emotional expression, and behaviors that elicit social disapproval. They go on to discuss moderators and mediators of these effects (e.g., arousal, ambiguity, pluralistic ignorance, diffusion of responsibility, feelings of capability, evaluation apprehension, and confusion of responsibility), and to distinguish social inhibition from other related concepts. By so doing, they hope to facilitate the integration of future research on this topic.

In their chapter on social facilitation, Seitchik, Brown, and Harkins note that research conducted for more than a century has shown that the presence of others improves performance on simple tasks and debilitates it on complex tasks, whether these others are audience members or coactors. In their chapter, Seitchik et al. review theories offered to account for how two features of these others, their mere presence and/or the potential for evaluation they represent, produce these effects, and they conclude that we are no closer now to isolating the relevant process(es) than we were 100 years ago. They then consider the molecular task analysis proposed by Harkins (2006) as an approach to attacking this problem, followed by a review of the work testing the mere effort account suggested by this analysis.

Finally, they place the mere effort account in the larger context represented by the threat-induced potentiation of prepotent responses model, which aims to account for the effect of threat on task performance. Seitchik et al. argue that this approach shows great promise, having the potential to integrate the different lines of research that focus on motivated task performance, such as social loafing, goal setting, intrinsic motivation/creativity, achievement goal theory, social facilitation, and stereotype threat.

Hales, Ren, and Williams's chapter examines the universal phenomenon of ostracism—ignoring and excluding—and how it works to guide and influence behavior. A relative newcomer on the social influence research block, this chapter summarizes over 20 years of social psychological research that demonstrates ostracism's power. The authors argue that ostracism—or the threat of it—serves to account for the potency of normative influence. Targets of ostracism experience pain, threatened fundamental needs, and worsened mood. As a consequence, they think and act in ways to fortify their threatened needs, including going along to get along, lashing out, and seeking solitude. The authors also review the research on what motivates sources to use ostracism, as well as examining the impact of ostracizing on the sources who use it. The sources' motives are tied to the functions they think ostracism serves. The authors propose three functions of ostracism: (1) to *protect*—shielding groups from threatening members; (2) to *correct*—signaling to individuals that their behavior needs to be modified to remain in the group; and (3) to *eject*—permanently removing deviant individuals who resist correction.

In a chapter that focuses on source effects, Tyler and Adams consider self-presentation as a social influence tactic. They suggest that past research has characterized people's self-presentations as resulting from conscious and deliberate strategic efforts to influence the impressions that others form of them, and note that this approach results in both theoretical and empirical problems. For example, following this approach has limited the research designs that have been used, thereby ignoring the issue of context cuing. Tyler and Adams argue that the results of the few studies that have examined automatic self-presentation are promising, and they provide the foundation for future work.

In his chapter, Van Kleef examines the interpersonal, rather than the intrapersonal, effects of emotional expression. That is, in contrast to the existing models that focus on the effects that a person's emotions has on him/herself, Van Kleef's theory (emotions as agents of social influence theory) focuses on the effects that one person's emotional expressions has on *another* person's attitudes, cognitions, and/or behavior. Van Kleef proposes a dual process model, which suggests that emotional expressions can exert social influence through an inferential process or through affective reactions. The inferential pathway is used to the extent that the target is motivated and able to engage in thorough information processing and perceives the emotional expression to be appropriate. To the extent that the target's ability or motivation to process the information is reduced and s/he perceives the emotional expression as inappropriate, the affective pathway is used. Van Kleef goes on to discuss differences and commonalities between this interpersonal framework and the more traditional intrapersonal approach.

In the next section of the volume we look at social influence processes as an *intragroup process*. In their chapter on social identity/self-categorization processes, Gaffney and Hogg note that, traditionally, social psychologists have examined social influence processes at an interpersonal level, focusing on the relationship between the individual target and the individual source. However, influence can occur within a group context as well; as a result, accounting for group membership and group identification allows for a more comprehensive understanding of social influence. As was the case for social comparison theory, we do not mean to suggest that social identity/self-categorization is directly relevant to all of the chapters in this section, but it has been highly influential since the early 1990s. In their chapter, adopting a social identity/social categorization perspective, Gaffney and Hogg provide an overview of group-based motivations for influence, including leadership, minority group influence, and political and social movements as examples of social influence taking place in a group context. In later chapters in this section, some of these topics are examined in greater detail (e.g., leadership, minority influence). The Gaffney and Hogg chapter provides an overall context into which these treatments can be placed.

In his chapter on deindividuation, Spears argues that this phenomenon occupies a central place in social influence's pantheon. However, he notes that deindividuation theory's central premise that people lose their sense of self in the group, becoming more likely to engage in mindless aggression, has not received consistent support over the years. In his chapter, Spears makes the case for a social identity account of crowd behavior—that the individual self gives way to the social self; but he also points out that techniques for tapping unconscious states and processes that are now available also provide the opportunity to test the original predictions in more compelling ways than were possible when the original research was conducted.

Hornsey and Jetten, in their chapter on stability and change within groups, examine the psychological tension produced by defending the status quo within groups and engaging in intragroup change. They begin with the same foundational research on conformity covered elsewhere in this volume (e.g., Hodges), but they extend their analysis to the processes at work in interacting groups. They then go on to provide a counterpoint to the analysis that emphasizes pressures toward stability by showing that intragroup change and reform is also an integral part of group life. Finally, they examine the process of change within the group: who is most likely to seek it; who is more effective at seeking it; and what strategies are most effective in producing it.

The next chapter, by Butera, Falomir-Pichastor, Mugny, and Quiamzade, also covers minority influence, but it sets out to explain the ways in which minority points of view may, or may not, influence society at large. Whereas social influence research in the United States tended to focus on the power of majorities, European research reflected their experiences with the power of a persistent minority in effecting important changes. The authors examine the early findings of Moscovici, Nemeth, and others, as well as the critiques leveled against these groundbreaking studies. Always present was a tension between points of view that saw minority influence as derivative of, or qualitatively different from, majority influence. Newer models have sparked a great deal of research that makes this particular topic a lively and growing domain within social influence.

Adopting a social identity perspective, Platow, Haslam, and Reicher propose that leadership, the process of enhancing the contribution of group members to the realization of group goals, essentially represents group-based social influence, emerging from psychological in-group members, particularly highly in-group prototypical ones. The authors argue for a difference between failed and successful leadership, not so much in terms of influence, but in terms of the source of influence. Power over resources can allow a leader to control the behavior of followers, but this is a sign of failed leadership, because in these instances behavior is geared toward gaining reward and avoiding punishment, rather than pursuing a collective vision. Successful leadership depends upon shared social identity, and it is conferred on would-be leaders as much as created by the leaders themselves. This differentiation between successful and failed leadership provides insight into examining research, theory, and application of leadership processes and outcomes.

In the next section of this volume, we include chapters that describe the use of social influence techniques in four *applied fields*: clinical psychology, health, law, and consumer behavior.

Heesacker organizes his chapter on social influence and clinical intervention using Kelman's (1958) tripartite model: compliance, identification, and internalization. In this model, compliance is not defined as behavior in accord with a request, but rather as cooperation motivated by the desire for social acceptance. People are influenced to comply because they wish to avoid negative social consequences or to gain social approval. Heesacker's review suggests that under some circumstances, normative feedback has changed behaviors like drug abuse and gambling. Of course, this work is directly relevant to the work on social norms described by Nolan in her chapter of that name in the current volume, as well as Hodges's chapter on conformity. The second process, identification, is relevant for understanding the effect of the therapeutic alliance between the therapist and client. This alliance strengthens the extent to which the client identifies with the therapist, which Heesacker argues is causally related to clinical outcomes. Finally, Heesacker argues that although a great deal of basic social influence research has been conducted on internalization, this work has had little influence on clinical practice. Much more research has been generated by a clinician-developed approach to internalization: motivated interviewing. Heesacker then bemoans the lack of basic social influence research relevant to clinical practice produced in recent years and describes a number of promising directions that this research could take.

In their chapter on social influence and health, Martin and DiMatteo examine the effects of different sources of social influence on health behavior: parents; peers once one enters adolescence; social networks as one enters adulthood; health care providers; and system-level influences like public health programs, health-related media messages, and educational interventions. Social comparison processes (Suls & Wheeler, this volume), supportive social networks, and social norms (Nolan, this volume) serve as sources of these effects.

In their review, Demaine and Cialdini conceptualize social influence and the law as consisting of three parts: social influence in the legal system; the legal regulation of social influence in our everyday lives; and law as an instrument of social influence. Their review suggests that most psychological research has focused on the first part. For example, the suggestibility of eyewitnesses recounting events underlying litigation and false confessions by crime suspects resulting from police interrogations have each benefitted from long-term, programmatic study, as have several facets of juror decision making. In contrast, the study of the effects of legal regulation of social influence in our everyday lives has received sparse and scattershot attention, as has the third part, law as an instrument of social influence. Demaine and Cialdini argue that the lopsidedness of the attention paid to the three areas does not reflect the importance of or differences in the number of empirical questions in these domains, and that these neglected areas hold great promise for future inquiry.

Kirmani and Ferraro tackle the burgeoning research on social influence in marketing. Marketing and consumer behavior are a perfect fit for social influence because the ultimate goals are behavioral: purchases for self and others, and telling others of their purchases and evaluations of the products. Truly one of the domains in which social influence research has accelerated, the authors focus their review on the research published only in the top journals in marketing and consumer behavior. Recognizing that the research on social influence in marketing borrows from many other disciplines, Kirmani and Ferraro nicely weave theory and research from social psychology, economics, sociology, anthropology, and communication into the field of marketing. The authors also point to some groundbreaking research by consumer researchers—gift giving and word of mouth—that will provide theory and be of interest to these other fields.

In the final section, informed by the chapters of the volume, we speculate about the future of research and theory in social influence. We also include two final chapters: Sagarin and Henningsen's chapter focuses on resistance to persuasion and shows how this research can help to shape the future work that will be required to understand resistance to *behavioral* social influence attempts; and, in recognition of the profound changes coming to the study of social influence, the final chapter, by David Byrne of the Talking Heads, provides an example of how social media can affect the social influence process.

# References

Allport, F. H. (1919). Behavior and experiment in social psychology. *Journal of Abnormal Social Psychology, 67,* 326–333.

Allport, F. H. (1924). *Social psychology.* New York, NY: Houghton Mifflin.

Allport, G. (1935). Attitudes. In C. Murchison (Ed.), *Handbook of social psychology* (pp. 798–844). Worcester, MA: Clark University Press.

Allport, G. (1954). The historical background of modern social psychology. In G. Lindzey (Ed.), *Handbook of social psychology* (Vol. 1, pp. 3–56). Cambridge, MA: Addison Wesley.

Asch, S. (1951). Effects of group pressure upon the modification and distortion of judgments. In H. Guetzkow (Ed.), *Groups, leadership, and men* (pp. 177–190). Pittsburgh, PA: Carnegie Press.

Binet, A., & Henri, V. (1894). De la suggestibilité naturelle. *Revue Philosophique, 38,* 337–348.

Cialdini, R. B. (2009). *Influence: Science and practice* (5th ed.). Boston, MA: Allyn & Bacon.

Cialdini, R. B., & Griskevicius, V. (2010). Social influence. In R. F. Baumeister & E. J. Finkel (Eds.), *Advanced social psychology* (pp. 385–417). New York, NY: Oxford University Press.

Cialdini, R. B., & Trost, M. R. (1998). Social influence: Social norms, conformity, and compliance. In D. T. Gilbert, S. T. Fiske, & G. Lindzey (Eds.), *Handbook of social psychology* (Vol. 2, pp. 151–192). New York, NY: McGraw-Hill.

Deutsch, M., & Gerard, H. B. (1955). A study of normative and informational social influences upon individual judgment. *Journal of Abnormal and Social Psychology, 51,* 629–636.

Dewey (1922/1930). *Human nature and conduct: An introduction to social psychology.* New York, NY: The Modern Library.

Eagly, A., & Carli, L. (1981). Sex of researchers and sex-typed communications as determinants of sex differences in influenceability: A meta-analysis of social influence studies. *Psychological Bulletin, 90,* 1–20.

Féré, C. (1887). *Sensation et movement: Etudes experimentales de psycho-mécanique.* Paris, France: Alcan.

Festinger, L. (1954). A theory of social comparison processes. *Human Relations, 7,* 117–140.

Freedman, J. L., & Fraser, S. C. (1966). Compliance without pressure: The foot-in-the-door technique. *Journal of Personality and Social Psychology, 4,* 195–202.

Gilovich, T, Keltner, D., & Nisbett, R. E. (2011). *Social psychology.* New York, NY: W. W. Norton & Company.

Harkins, S. G. (2006). Mere effort as the mediator of the evaluation-performance relationship. *Journal of Personality and Social Psychology, 91,* 436–455.

Jones, E. E. (1985). Major developments in social psychology during the past five decades. In G Lindzey & E. Aronson (Eds.), *Handbook of social psychology* (Vol. 1, pp. 47–107). New York, NY: Random House.

Kelman, H. C. (1958). Compliance, identification, and internalization: Three processes of attitude change. *Public Opinion Quarterly, 2,* 51–60.

Kravitz, D. A., & Martin, B. (1986). Ringelmann rediscovered: The original article. *Journal of Personality and Social Psychology, 50,* 936–941.

Latané, B., Williams, K. D., & Harkins, S. G. (1979). Many hands make light the work: The causes and consequences of social loafing. *Journal of Personality and Social Psychology, 37,* 822–832.

Mead, G. H. (1934). *Mind, self, and society: From the standpoint of a social behaviorist.* Chicago, IL: University of Chicago Press.

Milgram, S. (1963). Behavioral study of obedience. *Journal of Abnormal and Social Psychology, 67,* 371–378.

Prislin, R., & Crano, W. D. (2012). A history of social influence research. In A. Kruglanski & W. Stroebe (Eds.), *Handbook of the history of social psychology,* (pp. 321–339). New York, NY: Psychology Press.

Ringelmann, M. (1913). Recherches sur les moteurs animés: Travail de l'homme. *Annales de l'Institut National Agronomique, 2e série—tome XIII,* 1–40.

Triplett, N. (1898). The dynamogenic factors in pacemaking and competition. *American Journal of Psychology, 9,* 507–533.

# Ethical Issues in Social Influence Research

Allan J. Kimmel

## Abstract

Social influence researchers encounter a variety of ethical issues in the conduct of their investigations, including those involving deception, privacy, and confidentiality. Facing a growing array of ethical guidelines, governmental regulations, and institutional review, researchers are faced with decisions that often pit the search for scientific knowledge against human welfare. Ethical decisions pertaining to social influence research methodology can have an impact on research participants, organizations, the scientific discipline, and society in general. This chapter surveys ethical issues in the conduct of laboratory, field, online, and applied research; describes remedial efforts (e.g., debriefing) to mitigate adverse research effects; and considers the nature of the ethical review process.

**Key Words:** research ethics, deception, ethical review process, debriefing, ethical dilemmas, ethical decision making

In their pursuit of objectives associated with the betterment of humankind via an understanding of behavior and mental processes, psychology researchers are beholden to high standards of ethical professional conduct. The many challenges associated with the need to balance methodologically rigorous research practice with ethical conduct are especially evident in areas of social influence research. Perhaps more so than any other topical area of social psychology and personality, the scientific investigation of social influence is inextricably bound to ethical considerations and constraints pertaining to the well-being of research participants and the potential impact of research findings on the condition of individuals, organizations, and societies. In fact, many of the early psychological investigations that ultimately gave rise to ethical debate in the behavioral sciences and stimulated movement toward the development of professional principles and governmental guidelines were those focused on social influence areas (Slater, 2004), including landmark research programs on obedience to authority (Milgram, 1963), conformity to group influence

(Asch, 1951, 1955), attitude change (Festinger & Carlsmith, 1959), and the power of authority (Haney, Banks, & Zimbardo, 1973). These research endeavors, among others, ultimately aroused concerns about the use of psychologically or physically risky experimental treatments, the implications of deception and a failure to obtain participants' fully informed consent, the possibility that research findings might be exploited for various political or personal ends to the detriment of certain societal groups, the potential impact of ethical misconduct on public trust in psychologists and perceptions of the scientific process, and the likelihood that mass-mediated accounts of unethical psychological research might tarnish the discipline's public image and jeopardize community support and funding for the research enterprise.

These and related considerations, all of which pertain to the moral dimension of research, form the central subject matter of this chapter. Specifically, the chapter focuses on ethical issues in social influence research, beginning with a brief consideration of the nature and role of ethics and ethical decision making, and the evolution of ethical debate and regulation in the psychology discipline. Next, an overview of issues in the conduct of laboratory, field, and applied social influence research is presented, including a focus on problems relating to deception and informed consent, invasion of privacy, remedial measures, and the ethical review process.

## The Nature of Research Ethics and Ethical Dilemmas

Within the research context, ethics—which pertains to considerations of right and wrong (or appropriate and inappropriate)—refers to the acceptability of one's conduct or, more specifically, appropriateness of one's approach in the pursuance and application of scientific truths. As it has evolved in common usage, the term *ethical* is used to connote rules of behavior or conformity to a code or set of principles (Frankena, 1973). Thus, we can say that *research ethics* comprises principles and standards that, along with underlying values, guide appropriate conduct relevant to scientific decisions (Hunt & Vitell, 1986). In essence, ethics provides researchers with the tools required to determine whether or not a certain action should be carried out and the extent to which a past action was justified. An *ethical dilemma* is apparent in situations in which two or more desirable values present themselves in a seemingly mutually exclusive way, with each value suggesting a different course of action that cannot be maximized simultaneously (Kimmel, 2003; Smith, 1985). Many ethical issues that arise in behavioral research result from conflicting sets of values involving the goals, processes, or outcomes of an investigation. Such issues pose particular difficulties for investigators in unique research situations that lack precedence, when the subject matter of the research arouses strong emotions, or where guidelines are vague or nonexistent (Rogerson, Gottlieb, Handelsman, Knapp, & Younggren, 2011).

One common dilemma in social influence research emerges when investigators attempt to manipulate behavior in laboratory settings by misleading participants about the true nature of the experiment. Such an approach was undertaken in a series of classic experiments on conformity conducted by social psychologist Solomon Asch (1951, 1955). Asch designed his studies to assess what happens when individuals are placed in a situation in which their own judgment conflicts with the majority opinion—even when it is clear that the group judgment is incorrect. In one scenario, a participant had to select from among three comparison lines the one that was the same length as a standard line. Unbeknownst to actual participants, Asch rigged the procedure so that four of his assistants who were pretending to be research participants (i.e., "confederates") would first select the same clearly wrong comparison line on some trials. Consistent with expectation, the actual subject conformed to their opinion on average more than one third of the time. As invaluable as Asch's experiment was from a scientific perspective in demonstrating the power of group influence on individual judgments, the research also raised questions relative to the dishonest treatment of research participants who were deceived about the true parameters of the investigation's purpose and procedure. It is unlikely that much would have been learned about conformity in the face of blatantly incorrect majority opinion had Asch provided participants with accurate details about the study's manipulation and procedure prior to testing. For ethical dilemmas of this sort, researchers must weigh the scientific requirements of validity (i.e., in obtaining an objective and valid measure of behavior) against the ethical importance of informing participants about the research intentions prior to the observation so as to protect individuals' privacy rights.

Ethical decision making encompasses both an intuitive level and a critical-evaluative level, with the former reflecting automatic, nonrational processes linked to personal knowledge and experience, and the latter guided by reasoned judgments based upon moral theory and ethical principles, guidelines, and standards (Kitchener, 1984, 2000). Intuitive decision making is insufficient in and of itself for researchers because it is based on nonrational factors that are subject to emotional influences and cognitive distortions (Rogerson et al., 2011). Authoritative standards, ethical codes, and institutional review procedures have evolved over the years to assist researchers in meeting their ethical responsibilities in a reasoned, objective, and nonbiased manner.

## Influences on Ethical Decision Making

Generally speaking, the researcher has recourse to three sources of guidance for ethical decision making and the resolution of ethical dilemmas: (1) personal, (2) professional, and (3) regulatory.

### Personal Ethical Decision Making

The researcher's decisions about what is appropriate or inappropriate conduct are to a great extent guided by his or her own personal value system, which is shaped by one's upbringing, education, and professional training. Because of these influences, for example, an investigator may decide that it is always wrong to apply the findings derived from research on influence tactics to market potentially harmful products to children, regardless of the incentives for doing so and even if risks have been judged as minimal. This means-oriented approach to ethics reflects a reliance on general principles, rules, or policies to guide behavior (e.g., "do no harm").

By contrast, an ends-oriented approach focuses on the consequences of an action, suggesting that the ends can justify ethically questionable means. This perspective is consistent with a cost-benefit approach to ethical decision making whereby an action is considered acceptable to the extent that it results in a favorable ratio of desirable (or good) outcomes to undesirable (or bad) ones. Consistent with this more utilitarian approach, a researcher may decide that it is ethically acceptable for a firm to apply research findings on influence tactics in a promotional campaign to attract new customers, despite the possibility that some audience members may be led to overestimate the potential benefits of a product.

### Professional Ethical Standards

As a member of the behavioral science profession, the psychology researcher is expected to adhere to the set of ethical standards that have been agreed upon by a majority of the profession's members. Although these standards may be implicit, they often are explicitly presented in the form of ethics codes, which have been adopted by various professional organizations, such as the British Psychological Society (BPS, 2005) and the International Chamber of Commerce/European Society for Opinion and Marketing Research (ICC/ESOMAR, 2008), as well as research institutions where one is employed (e.g., Hogan & Kimmel, 1992). Ethical codes typically are designed to serve as instruments for self-regulation, although they may be used by courts as reference documents within the framework of appropriate, legally binding regulations.

Like many ethics codes adopted around the world, the BPS code is modeled after the guidelines formulated by the American Psychological Association (APA). The current APA code ("Ethical Principles," 2002) includes research guidelines emphasizing voluntary participation and informed consent as fundamental prerequisites for research

with human participants—ethical requirements that date back to the 1947 Nuremberg Code, a general set of standards formulated to prevent atrocities like those perpetrated by Nazi researchers, and the forerunner to all subsequent guidelines governing experimentation with human participants (Schuler, 1982). In 2010, APA created the Committee on Human Research (CHR), whose mission is to facilitate the conduct of human research through discipline-wide education about prevailing ethical principles and governmental regulations (http://www.apa.org).

### Regulatory Mechanisms

In addition to voluntary ethical standards, psychology investigators are required to adhere to legally enforceable regulations guiding research practice. The impact of governmental regulation on human research during recent decades has been substantial. Prior to the establishment of federal regulations, there was very little evidence of any type of required committee review of research projects in university departments in social and behavioral science areas (Reynolds, 1979). Today, ethical review boards are commonplace in most research-oriented institutions, and now extend beyond psychology, sociology, and anthropology to social science fields less typically associated with committee approval, such as history (Shea, 2000). Most universities, hospitals, and other research settings now require some form of review for the approval and monitoring of all human research conducted at those institutions (e.g., Cohen, 2007; Rosnow, Rotheram-Borus, Ceci, Blanck, & Koocher, 1993; Rutecki, Youtsey, & Adelson, 2002).

Ethical review boards are a common feature of human research regulation in numerous countries around the world (Kimmel, 2007; Seligman & Sorrentino, 2002). All members of the European Union adhere to a 2001 European Commission directive (Data Protection Directive 95/46/EC) requiring ethics committees for research. Research ethics committees (RECs) have been in existence in the United Kingdom since the mid-1960s, when they were run on a voluntary basis by the UK National Health Service (NHS). Additional regulations enacted in 2002 gave specific statutory duties to RECs, and in 2004 the United Kingdom Ethics Committee Authority (UKECA) was created by the Medicines for Human Use (Clinical Trials) Regulations to authorize and oversee RECs. For a survey of review procedures in other European members, see Dranseika et al. (2010).

In the United States, significant progress toward the development of guidelines for behavioral research came about with the signing into law of the 1974 National Research Act, creating the National Commission for the Protection of Human Subjects of Biomedical and Behavioral Research and initial requirements for the ethical review of human research by institutional review boards (IRBs). The formal regulations for human research were published by the Department of Health and Human Services (DHHS) in the January 26, 1981 issue of the *Federal Register*. Most noteworthy among the regulations are details concerning proper IRB review for the approval of DHHS-funded research projects, including the exemption of broad categories of research that posed little or no risk of harm. For the approval of research covered by the federal regulations, an IRB must be established at the institution where the research has been proposed, which is to determine whether risks to participants are minimized by sound research procedures and are outweighed sufficiently by anticipated benefits to the participants and the importance of the knowledge to be gained; the rights and welfare of subjects are adequately protected; the research will be periodically reviewed; and informed consent has been obtained. The criteria for informed consent require researchers to provide justification to review boards for the use of deception, unless the investigation entails minimal risk. Currently, recipients of federal research grants are required to complete education and training in ethical guidelines and the protection of human research participants (Breckler, 2009).

Despite the growing prevalence of institutional review, various limitations to this form of ethical regulation have been noted, particularly in terms of what constitutes acceptable use of research deception. Moreover, in addition to the recognition that personal ethical decision making takes place within the context of legal strictures, it also must be acknowledged that ethical practices are governed by the larger system of one's society, with its corresponding set of ethical norms (such as freedom, due process, privacy, and fairness) and cultural values. Rational decision making also is limited by potential heuristics-based biases (Rogerson et al., 2011). Thus, we see that various forces influence the decision-making process for the ethical researcher and, as a result, many questions pertaining to acceptable or unacceptable research practice fall within gray areas, with no easy solutions.

## The Evolution of Research Ethics in Psychology

Although ethical considerations played a minor role, if any role at all, during psychology's formative period, today they have a significant influence on most decisions relative to the planning and conduct of investigations, from the recruitment of participants to the subsequent application of research findings. As far back as 1954, social psychologist W. Edgar Vinacke took issue with psychology experiments in which research participants were deceived and sometimes exposed to "painful, embarrassing, or worse, experiences." However, prior to the 1960s, the idea had not yet taken hold that systematic attention to researchers' moral obligations to study participants and to society as a whole represented an integral element of the research process (Kelman, 1996). The scientific climate was such that considerations related to research ethics were not regarded as representing a critical aspect of decision making in the selection of research design and methods.

A variety of developments ultimately brought greater attention to the moral underpinnings of behavioral research. In retrospect, much of the impetus for ethical progress in psychology was sparked by a significant increase in the employment of deception and other ethically questionable research practices. By the mid-1970s, the practice of deceiving psychological research participants had become commonplace, and public awareness regarding deceptive methods had grown. According to various estimates, the percentage of studies using deception in social psychology alone rose from around 20 percent in 1960 to nearly 70 percent in 1975 (e.g., Adair, Dushenko, & Lindsay, 1985; McNamara & Woods, 1977), with a majority of cases involving the investigation of social influence topics. Vinacke's (1954, p. 155) questions about the "proper balance between the interests of science and the thoughtful treatment of the persons who, innocently, supply the data" were raised anew by Baumrind (1964) and Kelman (1967, p. 2), who lamented the growing frequency with which deceptive procedures had become so firmly a part of psychology's research modus operandi, deftly embedded into studies like a game "often played with great skill and virtuosity."

Although deception arguably proved to be the most pervasive ethical issue in psychological research, other practices also aroused concern, including the invasion of participants' right to privacy, failure to protect the anonymity of respondents or the confidentiality of data, unobtrusive observations of unsuspecting participants, and the use of risky experimental manipulations. The extensive debate surrounding the appropriateness of these practices, aroused by public concerns about some of the more flagrant research cases, sparked a significant movement toward the development of federal and professional research guidelines and the evolution of the institutional review process (see Box 2.1).

## Ethical Issues in Laboratory and Field Research

Investigations into social influence subject areas such as conformity, helping behavior, persuasion, and group influence commonly touch upon a variety of interests and values that are prerequisite and central to ethical decision making. Because of the sensitive nature of these areas of research, the question is not whether ethical dilemmas will be encountered, but rather when and under which circumstances they are likely to pose the most difficult problems for the researcher (and other parties) involved, how such dilemmas can be anticipated before they emerge, and what steps can be taken by the researcher to either avoid or satisfactorily resolve the dilemmas. At the core of most of the ethical conflicts encountered within social influence research are the sometimes

---

**Box 2.1** A Milestone in the Ethics of Social Influence Research: Milgram's Obedience Research

Half a century ago, social psychologist Stanley Milgram initiated his ingenious series of experiments on obedience to authority in the psychology laboratories at Yale University (1960–1964)—research that continues to resonate to this day (Burger, this volume). The research, which involved the bogus delivery of electric shocks to a hapless victim under the guise of a learning experiment, revealed that people are capable of inflicting extreme, potentially deadly punishment on innocent victims if compelled to do so by a malevolent authority figure. The implications of the findings for understanding apparently incomprehensible atrocities ranging from the Holocaust to Abu Ghraib have kept the research salient in our collective consciousness across five decades, and likely will continue to do so as new horrors emerge (Burger, 2009). However, another lasting legacy of Milgram's experiments may well be less about their results than the ethical debate its methodological approach stimulated within the psychology discipline (Kimmel, 2011a).

At the time of the obedience research, deception had not yet become a common fixture in psychological research laboratories, although it certainly was being employed by other researchers. For example, around the same time as Milgram's research, investigators concocted a variety of elaborate research deceptions in order to furnish university students with discrepant information about their sexuality, including one manipulation that led heterosexual males to believe that they had become sexually aroused by a series of photographs depicting other men (Bergin, 1962; Bramel, 1962, 1963). The use of deceptive procedures seemed to grow exponentially from that point forward, yet Milgram's project, perhaps more than any other, aroused concerns about the ethicality of using deception to satisfy research objectives and to a great extent gave impetus to the development of internal standards regulating the use of deception within the discipline of psychology (Benjamin & Simpson, 2009). As Reicher and Haslam (2011, p. 651) observed, "the great field studies of Milgram, and then Zimbardo, were harbingers of their demise. The very power of what they produced raised questions about our right to inflict such experiences upon people in the name of scientific progress."

The ensuing debate over deception and other ethical issues involving the treatment of human participants (such as coercion, exposure to psychological harm, invasion of privacy, and the like) contributed in large part to the codification of ethical standards, which have been substantially strengthened over the years to the point at which it has become increasingly difficult to carry out any more Milgram-type experiments, at least without certain methodological adjustments and ethical safeguards. Public condemnation of some of the more egregious cases of research deception in the biomedical field, such as the Tuskegee syphilis study (a long-term, nontherapeutic experiment in which syphilitic participants were actively deceived about their true medical condition), ultimately led to the enactment of human research regulations and the emergence of ethical review boards in North America and Europe. Milgram himself was something of a pioneer in ethical procedures, having developed what may have been the first structured research debriefings and postexperimental follow-up of participants to systematically assess the impact of participation in his research (Blass, 2009; Reicher & Haslam, 2011).

---

opposing interests of science and the protection of others.

## Informed Consent

Whether a social influence study is conducted within the artificial context of a psychology laboratory, a simulated environment (such as a mock prison), or a natural environmental setting, researchers are obliged to forego the implementation of procedures that are likely (given reasonable estimates of occurrence) to result in psychological or physical harm to participants or others. Arguably, this basic ethical guideline takes priority over all other research practices, and it can be traced back to an underlying principle of the Hippocratic oath, "to do no harm," which dates back to Hellenic times.

Because of the investigator's greater degree of control over the circumstances that take place within settings specifically designated for research purposes, laboratory research provides the opportunity for special steps to be taken to protect participants from experiencing undue harm. Foremost among these steps, and a specific requirement of ethics codes, is the obtaining of *informed consent*, which involves the provision of information to prospective participants that might reasonably influence their decision to take part in the research (e.g., BPS, 2005). Consent to participate typically is viewed as "fully informed" when it includes the following elements: (a) a description of the overall purpose of the research; (b) an explanation about participants' role in the study and why they have been chosen; (c) details about the procedures; (d) a clear statement of the likely risks and discomforts; (e) a description of the anticipated benefits of the research to participants and others; and (f) an offer to answer any questions, along with an assurance that the participant may withdraw at any time without negative consequences (Kimmel, 2007; Levine, 1975).

As an example of informed consent, consider the Stanford prison study, an intensive investigation of the behavioral and psychological effects of imprisonment on the guards who maintain and administer a prison as well as those who experience it as inmates (Haney et al., 1973; Zimbardo, 1973). The researchers hoped to obtain a better understanding of the processes by which prisoners adapt to this novel and alienating environment and how guards derive social power from their status in controlling and managing the lives of others. After being tested for psychological well-being— all applicants underwent extensive psychological testing and psychiatric interviews—volunteers were randomly designated to role-play being guards or prisoners in a mock prison constructed in the basement of the psychology building on Stanford's campus. Prior to the onset of the simulation, each participant signed a "Prison Life Study" consent form explaining that they would be randomly assigned to the roles of either "prisoners" or "guards," that "participation in the research project will involve a loss of privacy," and that participants were expected to continue for the full duration and to follow directions from the research team and others taking part in the study.

Although participants were asked to agree that they were submitting to participation "with full knowledge and understanding of the nature of the research project and of what will be expected of me," certain details—such as the fact that "prisoners" would be "arrested" at their home by local police at an unannounced point in time—nonetheless were withheld (Haney et al., 1973). Given that the provision of all details of an investigation would either be impractical given the study's circumstances or not accessible to participants whose understanding of psychological research practices is likely to be limited, a fully informed consent is often more of an ethical ideal than a realistic practicality.

## Deception

Just as the controlled conditions of the laboratory offer the experimenter a ready opportunity to obtain the informed consent of participants, it also enables the researcher to actively mislead participants about the true nature of the situation and purpose of the investigation or to withhold certain critical details. In this sense, informed consent is something of a double-edged sword in studies of social influence because in many cases, the objectives of the research could not be obtained in an unbiased fashion when participants are fully aware of the research purpose or procedures. For example, in a series of experiments investigating the factors that influence racial stereotypes and attitudes, Stangor, Sechrest, and Jost (2001) first obtained student participants' beliefs about their own and their fellow students' positive and negative stereotypes of African Americans. One week later, the researchers provided false information to the participants claiming that, based on prior research, their beliefs were either more or less favorable than the students had originally estimated, and then had them estimate their racial beliefs again. This was to determine whether their attitudes toward African Americans shifted in the direction of what they presumed to be their fellow students' either more or less favorable stereotypes. This so-called "consensus effect" indeed was confirmed, and it was found to persist when reassessed 2 weeks later. In such studies of attitudes and conformity to group norms, informing participants at the outset about the true purpose of the investigation and the use of false feedback would have negated the possibility of learning anything of interest relative to the objectives of the research. Thus, we see that more than a half century since the early Asch experiments, contemporary social influence researchers continue to face questions about how to reconcile the ethical requirement of informed consent with the methodological necessity to deceive participants.

## WHY USE DECEPTION IN SOCIAL INFLUENCE RESEARCH?

To better understand the methodological rationale for utilizing deception, consider again Milgram's (1963, 1974) experiments on obedience to authority (see Box 2.1). The central deception in the obedience studies involved a misrepresentation of the research as pertaining to the effects of punishment on learning. Volunteers were presented with bogus information about the procedure, having been led to believe that the learner (an experimental confederate) was receiving "punishments" in the form of painful electric shocks for each incorrect response to the learning task. The overheard shouts of protest and, in some variations, the apparent sounds of pounding on the adjoining wall suggestive of the learner's apparent distress, represented other components of the elaborate deception, which together presented the necessary guise to assess whether participants would continue to deliver the apparent shocks as demanded by the experimenter.

Although initially praised for its ingenuity and the insight it provided into an important area of social influence, the research eventually became the target of sharp criticism (e.g., Baumrind, 1964; Kelman, 1967), which centered on the potential adverse outcomes stemming from the deceptive methodology. Specifically, it was argued that Milgram had subjected participants to extreme levels of stress and guilt, that he should have terminated the experiment at the first indications of participant discomfort, and that he alienated participants from future research participation and harmed their image of the discipline. These points typify common ethical arguments against the use of deception in psychological research, which, in one

form or another, suggest that because it involves lying and deceit, its employment in research is morally reprehensible and may have potentially harmful effects on each of the parties involved in the research or implicated by it (Bassett, Basinger, & Livermore, 1992; Christensen, 1988; Kimmel & Smith, 2001; Ortmann & Hertwig, 1997). (For a summary of the methodological considerations related to the use of deception in research, including participant naiveté levels and the impact of suspiciousness of deception on the experimental effect, see Kimmel, 2011b.)

Although there is evidence that Milgram wrestled with these considerations prior to initiating his research (Benjamin & Simpson, 2009; Blass, 2004; Miller, Collins, & Brief, 1995), among his arguments for proceeding is that the study's findings would have been misleading had participants not been deceived; that is, the deceptive procedure provided the necessary "technical illusions" for studying the power of a malevolent authority to elicit obedience. This reasoning suggests that had participants been aware that no shocks were actually delivered, that knowledge likely would have influenced the degree to which they followed the commands of the experimenter. Additionally, Milgram initially doubted that many of the participants actually would follow the experimenter's directives after the first sign of protest from the confederate (Blass, 2004), and he suggested that condemnation of his research procedure may have been fundamentally tied to the disturbing results he obtained. If his results had turned out differently and participants had refused to obey the experimenter-authority, then critics might not have perceived the deception as morally objectionable.

In short, a primary justification for using deception in laboratory settings is that if researchers conformed to the letter of the law regarding informed consent and did not deceive participants at all, then many investigations would be either impossible to conduct or would result in biased findings. It has been shown that informing participants of the true purpose and procedures of a study can exacerbate the problem of research artifacts, distorting participant responses and severely jeopardizing the tenability of inferred causal relationships (cf. Broder, 1998). One can readily imagine how a completely informed consent obtained during investigations into social influence phenomena such as altruism, conformity, and prejudice could cause participants to behave differently so as to present a more socially acceptable (as opposed to a natural or typical) image to the researcher. In this way, informed consent essentially operates as an independent variable—studies conducted with or without it may come up with very different results (Resnick & Schwartz, 1973).

In addition to eliciting more spontaneous behavior from participants than otherwise might be the case, deception can increase the researcher's degree of methodological control over the experimental situation. These advantages were evident in some of the classic studies of helping behavior carried out by Latané and Darley (1970) to determine whether the number of bystanders present during an emergency would influence the likelihood of intervention by any one bystander. Clearly, the researchers could not have expected an emergency to occur repeatedly in a natural setting under precisely the same circumstances with a different number of onlookers present during each occurrence. Instead, it was more feasible for them to conduct their studies in the laboratory, where the number of bystanders present could be systematically manipulated in a series of carefully contrived "emergencies" (such as an apparent fire in an adjoining room or an epileptic seizure experienced by a research confederate). By creating such fictional environments in the laboratory, investigators can manipulate and control the variables of interest with much greater facility than if deception is not used.

One might legitimately question whether the extreme deceptions used in field studies such as the helping experiments or simulations like the Stanford prison experiment can be justified. In addition to moral concerns about misleading research participants, the research paradigms exposed participants to psychological risks, including guilt and a threat to their self-esteem, stress during the research procedure itself, and embarrassment at being duped by the researchers. However, one might defend the procedures by contending that the risks were far outweighed by the importance of the subject matter and potential gain in knowledge about helping behavior during emergencies, the consequences of role taking in prisons, and the like. Deceiving participants about the true nature of the project may have been the only feasible way to collect data to test the hypotheses under study. Thus, for some intended investigations, the decision to be made is not whether to use deception, but whether the research is necessary. The decision *not to do* a study because it would require deception is perhaps as morally problematic as the decision *to do* a study involving deception when one considers the potential loss of knowledge involved (Rosenthal & Rosnow, 1984).

## TYPES OF RESEARCH DECEPTION

Lying involves falsehoods that are intended to deceive, and may vary in everyday usage, from "white lies," which are likely to be viewed as harmless and acceptable social conventions, to blatant falsehoods, which are likely to be considered as morally problematic according to virtually all major philosophical traditions and religions. As in everyday life, deceptions in behavioral research differ in terms of type and severity. In the research context, "active deception" is deception by commission, as when a researcher deliberately misleads the participant about some aspect of the investigation. Research procedures that represent examples of active deception include (a) misrepresentation of the research purpose; (b) untrue statements about the researcher's identity; (c) use of research assistants (confederates) who act out predetermined roles; (d) false promises (including violation of the promise of anonymity or delivery of research incentives); (e) incorrect information about research procedures and instructions; (f) false explanations of scientific equipment and other measurement instruments; (g) false diagnoses and other reports; (h) use of placebos (i.e., inactive medication) and secret application of medications and drugs; and (i) misleading settings or timing for the investigation. Among the examples previously considered, the obedience and conformity studies used various types of active deceptions, including false details about the purpose of the research and the use of confederates. The provision of a false purpose or cover story and making false statements about the procedure or study materials are the most prevalent forms of active deception utilized by investigators (Kimmel, 2001, 2004).

"Passive deception" is deception by omission, as when the researcher purposely withholds relevant information from the participant. With passive deception, a lie is not told; rather, a truth is left unspoken. Deceptions by omission include such research practices as (a) concealed observation, (b) provocation and secret recording of negatively evaluated behavior, (c) unrecognized participant observation, (d) use of projective techniques and other personality tests not identified as such, and (e) unrecognized conditioning of behavior. Withholding information about the research or the procedure, apparent in the aforementioned prison simulation and bystander intervention studies, represents the most common form of passive deception (Kimmel, 2001, 2004; Smith, Kimmel, & Klein, 2009).

Deceptions also differ according to the degree of severity of their potential negative effects, a crucial consideration that must enter into decisions about whether or not to proceed with a study as planned (Lawson, 2001). "Severe deceptions" create false beliefs about central, important issues related to participants' self-concept or personal behavior, as when an experimental manipulation leads participants to believe they lack self-confidence. "Mild deceptions" create false beliefs about relatively unimportant issues peripheral to participants' self-concept, such as misleading them about the research sponsor or purpose (Toy, Olson, & Wright, 1989). Severe deceptions can create negative affect both during and after actual participation in the research (e.g., upset or anxiety linked to a reduced self-image), whereas mild deceptions are unlikely to create negative beliefs and affect until the debriefing at the end of the study (e.g., disappointment that the study was not supported by an alleged sponsor).

The fact that social influence researchers are more likely to employ severe deceptions that are relevant to the fundamental beliefs and values of research participants than are investigators in other research areas, such as marketing and organizational research, to some extent explains why deception has long been such a central issue in this domain of psychology (Smith et al., 2009). Studies involving severe deceptions (e.g., coercing participants into behaving in a way that leaves them feeling guilty or depressed) are harder to justify when ethical principles are applied and are more likely to encounter problems when subjected to committee review.

## DECEPTION IN MINIMAL RISK SOCIAL INFLUENCE RESEARCH

In the present era, social influence researchers have been far less wont to employ the types of severe deceptions that evoked such strong ethical criticisms in the past. To a great extent, research on contemporary topics such as reciprocity, commitment and consistency, social proof, and the like are more apt to require subtle forms of manipulation that involve relatively low levels of risk, both in the laboratory and in the field (cf. Cialdini, 2007). Nonetheless, although mild deceptions are unlikely to cause harm to participants, they can still be morally problematic because they involve misleading participants and risk undermining trust in the research process (Kimmel & Smith, 2001). As an example, researchers have employed some novel approaches to study reciprocity, an influence tactic that pertains to the fact that people inherently want to return favors. The tendency to reciprocate is a common aspect of interpersonal exchanges in which people feel indebted to others from whom they receive something, including goods, services, and information. In natural setting research, researchers have employed the cooperation of restaurant servers to investigate reciprocity tactics that are likely to influence the size of gratuities left by restaurant patrons. In one representative study, servers who left a foil-wrapped piece of chocolate candy with the bill received higher tips than when they did not, and the level of tip further increased when the gift was doubled (Strohmetz, Rind, Fisher, & Lynn, 2002). Although deception was utilized in this investigation, it can be said that the risks were minimal (e.g., inducing customers to spend more than they had intended), and certainly no greater than those that occur in everyday life, where it is a common practice for servers to employ strategies to maximize their gratuities. In the latter case, customers are likely to be aware of such strategies, whereas in the former they are unaware of being manipulated for research purposes. Although the restaurant patrons were not informed of their participation after the fact, we can imagine that some would have voiced resentment toward the researchers for attempting to manipulate the size of the gratuity.

Another influence tactic that has been the focus of recent research pertains to social proof, the proclivity for people to look to others to decide what is desirable and acceptable. If other people are behaving in a particular way, the tendency is to assume that is the correct way or right thing to do, especially under situations marked by uncertainty. Recent field investigations have focused on the factors that influence the cooperation of hotel guests in reducing the number of towels they use during their stays, which cuts costs and benefits the environment by diminishing the use of water, energy, and washing detergent. In one study, Goldstein, Cialdini, and Griskevicius (2008) manipulated the hotel room sign that asks guests to reuse the towels in a mid-sized American hotel. Some guests were informed that "75 percent of the guests who stayed in this room (room 313)" had reused their towels, whereas others were prompted to join their fellow "citizens" or "men and women" by engaging in more environmentally friendly behavior. The signs that cited the guests' room numbers resulted in a significantly higher towels reuse rate than when a standard, more generic sign was used, suggesting the efficacy in persuading people with narrowly directed appeals as opposed to more general characteristics like gender ("men or women"). These findings were replicated in research conducted at two hotels in Swiss and Austrian ski resorts (Reese, Loew, & Steffgen, 2014). Like the reciprocity investigations, the social proof studies also involve low levels of risk (e.g., patrons are led to forego the delivery of freshly cleaned towels) and employ manipulations that mimic those that occur in everyday life. Researchers, however, need to be sensitive to the fact that the withholding of informed consent, even in research employing mild deceptions, may be viewed by some unsuspecting participants as an ethically questionable violation of trust.

From a methodological standpoint, assuming they have any impact at all on participants, the mild deceptions used to study a majority of social influence tactics are unlikely to affect performance in the investigation during which they are employed, but they could influence performance in subsequent experiments. For severe deceptions, performance could be affected in the ongoing study as well as subsequent ones because they have the potential to create negative affect both during and after actual participation in the research (Toy et al., 1989).

## ALTERNATIVES TO DECEPTION

Because of the ethical and methodological concerns related to the use of research deception, various alternative procedures to deception have been proposed, foremost of which are role playing, simulations, and studies conducted in virtual environments (Geller, 1982; Greenberg, 1967; Greenberg & Eskew, 1993; Slater et al. 2006). As an alternative to deception in the laboratory, role play involves the diametrically opposed method of enlisting the participant as an active collaborator in the investigation. Participants are told what the experiment is about and then asked to play a role as if they were actually participating in the experiment. The essence of a role-playing study is for the participant to pretend that a situation is real when in fact it is not (Geller, 1982). In one application of this approach, participants may be asked to passively read a description of an experiment provided by the researcher and to predict how they would respond. In other cases, people may be asked to play a more active role, from the totally improvised to one in which the experimental scenario is acted out with the aid of a script provided by the researcher. For example, to obtain greater insight into consumer reactions to social influence tactics employed by sellers in retail settings, participants may be asked to play the role of a customer in a simulated store setting. The researcher then can observe how the interaction plays out, perhaps by focusing on the factors that lead to a successful or unsuccessful resolution. An alternative to the deceptions utilized in the Milgram obedience experiments, which would have avoided the requirement for a confederate, would have been to conduct a role-play scenario, with participants assuming the role of learner or teacher (Orne & Holland, 1968; Patten, 1977). Whether or not the original obedience research would have been viewed as sufficiently sound in a methodological sense or have generated as much attention had Milgram instead employed a role-play methodology—assuming the research would have been published at all—is certainly open to debate.

Despite the ethical advantages of role playing, there has been much criticism of it as a research tool (e.g., Freedman, 1969; Kimmel, 2007; Miller, 1972; Rosenthal & Rosnow, 1991), and it has not garnered much attention in recent years as an alternative to more traditional experimental procedures in the areas of psychology in which researchers have been most prone to utilize deception (Smith et al., 2009). Critics have claimed that the expectation that role playing would replicate general relationships has not been adequately demonstrated. In the same vein, it is argued that role players often cannot duplicate the most interesting findings that come from true experiments, such as counterintuitive ones.

Similar to the role-play approach, a *simulation* is another alternative to deception in laboratory settings. This technique involves the creation of conditions that mimic the natural environment in some definite way, and participants are asked to act as if the mock situation were real. Simulations require the scaling down of the natural environment to a size that is conducive to analysis in the laboratory but preserves the key elements thought to underlie the dynamics of the real-world phenomenon under study (Rosenthal & Rosnow, 1991). One example of a simulation is the mock jury study, which is intended to closely simulate actual jury procedures and sometimes involves actual cases and real jury candidates and judges. Participants are brought together in groups to read, hear, or see the proceedings of a court case and deliberate as a jury (Bermant, McGuire, McKinley, & Salo, 1974; Lamberth & Kimmel, 1981). The Stanford prison experiment is an example of a *field simulation*, which is characterized by highly realistic staged settings that encourage participants to believe they are participating in natural situations.

As the Stanford prison study illustrated, the simulation alternative to deception is not free of ethical problems. When effectively carried out, such studies can cause intense emotional involvement and distress in participants, risks that some say should not be condoned for research purposes (Baumrind, 1964; Savin, 1973). Additionally, simulations are not always free of intrinsic deceptions (Geller, 1982). This was true of the Stanford prison study in the sense that although the participants had volunteered to role play, they were not told which role they would play (prisoner or guard) until the onset of the study and, as previously mentioned, they also were kept uninformed about the nature and timing of their "arrest."

In general, role play and simulation procedures appear to have limited potential and are unlikely to supersede the use of research deception, at least in the foreseeable future. Indeed, content analyses of psychology journals reveal that despite an apparent gradual decline in the employment of deceptive research procedures in recent years, deception continues to be used within a significant number of studies of human behavior (Kimmel, 2001, 2004; Nicks, Korn, & Mainieri, 1997; Vitelli, 1988). Moreover, there is evidence that the prevalence of deception is increasing in applied areas of behavioral research that have evolved out of the root discipline of psychology, such as consumer research (Kimmel, 2001, 2004; Smith et al., 2009).

In addition to role play and simulations, researchers have begun to develop creative alternative methodologies to overcome some of the ethical concerns linked to deception. Although not "alternatives" in the strict sense of the word, they are used in conjunction with deception to minimize its potential for harm. For example, in his partial replication of the Milgram obedience studies, Burger (2009) incorporated several ethical safeguards. Based on his observation that the 150V level of Milgram's procedure enabled accurate estimates as to whether participants would continue to be obedient or not to the end of the research paradigm (e.g., 79 percent of Milgram's participants who continued past that "point of no return" continued all the way to the end of the shock generator's range), Burger employed a "150V solution"; that is, the study was stopped seconds after participants decided what to do at the critical juncture. This modification did not represent an alternative to deception, but it substantially reduced the risk of harm by eliminating the likelihood that participants would be exposed to the intense stress levels experienced by many of Milgram's participants. Despite some reservations

that Burger's "obedience lite" methodology comes up short in terms of gauging the full breadth of possible participant reactions, his novel approach suggests how researchers can investigate other problematic areas of psychology in a more ethical way (Elms, 2009).

An ingenious nondeceptive alternative to the real-life obedience paradigm utilized by both Milgram and Burger would be to carry out the experiments in a computerized virtual environment, an approach that has been found to replicate the obedience findings while circumventing the ethical problems associated with deception (Cheetham, Pedroni, Angus, Slater, & Jäncke, 2009; Dambrun & Vatine, 2010; Slater et al., 2006). Virtual reality paradigms, whereby visual and auditory stimuli give participants the impression they are in realistic situations (such as a research laboratory), represent viable alternatives to deception methodologies. The promise of this burgeoning approach is apparent in a growing number of psychological research studies (e.g., Bélisle & Bodur, 2010; Rosenberg, Baughman, & Bailenson, 2013; Trawley, Law, Logie, & Logie, 2013). Questions about the ecological validity of virtual reality approaches are tempered by the recognition that virtual technologies and media are increasingly incorporated within our everyday life experiences (Gaggioli, 2004; Vu, 2014).

## Other Ethical Issues

In recent decades, with the emergence of the Internet and other technological developments, ethical issues pertaining to privacy, participant anonymity, and confidentiality of data have become increasingly salient for researchers. In addition to the possibility that research practices may pose a risk of harm directly to individual participants, issues pertaining to the implications of research that go beyond the immediate data-collection setting also have been addressed. For example, the consequences of research could serve to have an adverse impact on the public's image of science or trust in researchers, and there is the possibility that research findings will be inappropriately interpreted or applied in potentially harmful ways. It is essential that judgments pertaining to an investigation's moral dimension take into account the possible effects of the research on all those implicated by it, whether directly or indirectly.

### *Privacy*

Issues related to privacy to some degree are inherent in most of the methodological approaches utilized by social influence researchers, although they are especially likely to emerge in research occurring in naturalistic or online contexts. For example, the circumstances that characterize participation in nonlaboratory research are such that the individual's determination of whether or not to participate frequently is violated. This occurs when people are not informed of their role as research participants and are unaware that a study is in progress. When informed consent cannot be given and participants cannot choose to refuse to participate or leave once the study is in progress, a social contract will not have been established with the researcher. In many cases, it will not be possible to assess the impact of the research on participants or inform them of the results once the study has been completed. Under such circumstances, if researchers obtain or reveal (wittingly or unwittingly) information about attitudes, motivations, or behavior that a participant would prefer not to have revealed, the latter's basic right to privacy will have been breached.

Degree of anonymity is critical in ascertaining whether privacy has been breached. Privacy is clearly maintained when the linkage between the individual and the information obtained for research has been completely severed; conversely, the risk of privacy invasion is high when information can be linked to identifiable persons. Should a researcher choose to unobtrusively observe and record the conversations taking place between a retail salesperson and shoppers, for example, such observations typically can be justified on ethical grounds by the public and anonymous nature of the observations, and by the fact that the risks posed (in this case, having information about a possible transaction revealed to others) were no greater than those encountered in daily experience. Moreover, informed consent will be irrelevant for many research activities that involve observations of ongoing public behavior or the analysis of public records and archives. Another factor in privacy considerations is the nature of the information disclosed during a study. Certain information (e.g., income level, alcohol and drug use, birth control practices) can be expected to raise privacy issues. Ethical judgments should take into account the possibility that disclosed information, particularly when it can be associated with individual participants, may be perceived as an invasion of privacy.

### Internet Research

As an increasing number of behavioral scientists begin to exploit the potential of the Internet and other emerging technologies for research purposes, new ethical dilemmas have been encountered and some familiar ones have been recast in a different light (Birnbaum, 2003). In their analysis of issues pertaining to Internet-based research, Nosek, Banaji, and Greenwald (2002) identified three key differences between Internet research and standard laboratory research: (1) the physical absence of a researcher, (2) the questionable adequacy of informed consent and debriefing procedures, and (3) the potential loss of participant anonymity or confidentiality.

The absence of an investigator to a certain extent reduces the possibility that people will have been coerced into research participation and thus represents an ethical benefit of Internet-based research. However, this also means that the researcher likely will be unable to respond to participant concerns or adverse reactions once the study is underway. Additionally, should the participant choose to withdraw early from a study, this will undermine the possibility that an adequate follow-up can be carried out (see "Debriefing"). Thus, special care should be taken to assure that the informed consent process is thorough and includes clear instructions that will enable those persons who leave the study early to obtain essential information once the investigation is completed. To protect against the possibilities that data may be intercepted by a third party or accessed once stored in files on an Internet-connected server, researchers should take all steps necessary to secure data so as to protect respondent anonymity and confidentiality (Sharf, 1999).

There currently exist few professional and legislative guidelines for the conduct of online research. One notable exception is the 2011 *Guideline for Online Research* developed by ESOMAR, an international market research organization (http://www.esomar.org). The *Guideline* summarizes ethical, regulatory, and methodological issues linked to online research and offers recommended practices for using online technologies in research. On the legislative front, the European Union has in place a directive that requires all member states to restrict the export of data to nations lacking adequate privacy protections, prompting the US Congress to enact similar privacy protections (Collmann, 2007).

Mathy, Kerr, and Haydin (2003) recommend that at a minimum, the Internet researcher must carefully adhere to the basic ethical principles of respect for autonomy and nonmaleficence (i.e., protection from harm). This can be accomplished in large part through the development of appropriate protocols for obtaining the informed consent of participants. For example, persons who are willing to participate in a survey investigation can be required to submit an e-mail request for a copy of the instrument, along with a statement that they clearly understand the study's purpose, risks and benefits, intensity, and duration. In essence, this e-mail could then be accepted as an indication of informed consent. Other precautions can be taken when research instruments are hosted on a Web page: informed consent is provided on the first Web page, which can be designed so that authorized participants must enter a unique password acknowledging that they have read and understand the informed consent protocol. Authorized participants can obtain the password from designated professionals affiliated with the study. According to Mathy et al., one of the keys to protecting participants from harm is the guarantee that they are using a computer and Internet access with proper physical safeguards and password protection locks. These are necessary to prevent unauthorized disclosure of confidential information that can be disseminated via the Internet.

### Applied Research Issues

Applied research is oriented toward the attainment of information that will prove relevant to some practical problem, defined as such from the perspective of the researcher, society, or a specific group (such as a government agency, community association, or business organization). The goal of applied research often is oriented toward modifying or improving the present situation, as would be the case for a study intended to develop an effective advertising campaign for the use of condoms. Among the more serious ethical issues in applied research are those involving the misuse of new scientific knowledge or the improper implementation of widely accepted procedures and principles. The inappropriate utilization of research findings outside clearly stated limiting conditions can have serious and far-reaching consequences, and it raises some important ethical questions when social researchers consult with and report their data to organizations, community agencies, legal and educational officials, and the like. Granted, these considerations also are relevant within the realm of more theoretical research, despite the often-expressed position that nonapplied research is value-free and morally neutral (cf. Kimmel, 1988). However, ethical dilemmas related to the use of research findings are more likely to emerge when the research is conducted in collaboration with others whose goals, interests, and values may be at odds with those of the researcher or the scientific discipline (Mirvis & Seashore, 1982).

Along with the obligation to treat research participants fairly, one must attempt to fulfill the expectations of the client or research user. The researcher also has a responsibility to protect the well-being of the public when the results are put into action. Ethical conflicts may arise as the researcher recognizes that certain duties and responsibilities toward one group are inconsistent with those toward some other group or with one's own values. It may be that the only way to obtain reliable data so as to satisfy certain obligations to a client is by deceiving respondents about the true nature of a study. It thus becomes the researcher's responsibility to clarify and openly communicate from the outset one's own role in the situation and to establish limits in terms of assisting the organization in meeting its anticipated goals.

Ethical dilemmas involving conflicting role expectations should be anticipated prior to carrying out an investigation, especially when entering a relationship with a client whose priorities may subsequently change. As an alternative to foregoing involvement with a troublesome study altogether, a determination should be made as to whether a more ethical procedure for obtaining the desired information or outcomes is available, using an alternative approach. It is important to consider the possibility of potential misuse of scientific knowledge as one weighs potential costs and anticipated benefits prior to conducting the research. To be sure, scientists should not be considered responsible for a misreading or misinterpretation of their work as long as special care has been taken, when publicizing the research, to state boundary conditions pertinent to the usefulness of the research in applied contexts.

### Ethical Safeguards and Institutional Review

Researchers may react with trepidation when confronted with the daunting array of ethical issues associated with social influence research. As described by Rosnow (1997, p. 345), "even experienced researchers often find themselves caught between the Scylla of methodological and theoretical requirements and the Charybdis of ethical dictates and moral sensitivities." In recent decades, the proliferation and increased role of ethics committees, professional standards, legalities, and other external restrictions have already subjected psychologists to a higher level of professional ethical accountability than is found in many other professions (including law, politics, and marketing), where both passive and active forms of deception are commonplace (Rosnow, 1997). Over time, participation in research has become much safer than many of the everyday activities in which people engage (Diener, 2001). There are a variety of practical safeguards that can be incorporated as elements of methodological design so that researchers can strike a reasonable balance between their scientific pursuits and ethical requirements.

## Debriefing

Extant ethical guidelines and external review boards typically require that all participants undergo a full debriefing within a reasonable period following their involvement in a study, to whatever extent possible. *Debriefing* refers to the process by which "psychologists provide a prompt opportunity for participants to obtain appropriate information about the nature, results, and conclusions of the research, and ... take reasonable steps to correct any misconceptions that participants may have of which the psychologists are aware" ("Ethical Principles," 2002, p. 1070). This requirement, which also obliges researchers to minimize any apparent adverse consequences for the participant, is often cited as an important safeguard against some of the potential risks inherent in the use of deception (see Box 2.2).

The debriefing session can serve a variety of functions, foremost of which are to provide researchers with a means of assessing whether participants were adversely affected by the procedures; to serve as an opportunity to eliminate any harm or lasting false impressions about the study; to assess the effectiveness of research manipulations and extent of participants' suspicions; and to serve an educational role through an explanation of the purpose and relevance of the research (Brody, Gluck, & Aragon, 2000; Sharpe & Faye, 2009). In special cases in which confidentiality must be breached (e.g., studies where certain individuals are revealed to be suicidal or intend to harm others), participants can be reminded about any limitations to confidentiality that were agreed upon during the consent procedure, if feasible (cf. Behnke & Kinscherff, 2002, for additional recommendations).

To date, there remain questions about the effectiveness of debriefing in successfully correcting a participant's misconceptions resulting from deception. Effective debriefing may require both "dehoaxing" (i.e., convincing deceived participants that the

information they had been given was in fact fraudulent and relieving any resulting anxiety) and "desensitizing" (i.e., helping deceived participants deal with new information about themselves) (Misra, 1992). An effective debriefing interview should be treated seriously as an essential element of the research process. Thus, it can be argued that an ineffective or incompetent debriefing negatively reflects on the overall quality of the research. The researcher should bear in mind the functions of debriefing as an educational tool as well as a method for identifying and ameliorating any adverse effects. Initially, the researcher should explain the procedures and reasons for them in language that is understandable to participants (which may require pretesting), including a discussion of the importance and relevance of the study. When deception is revealed, the researcher should sensitively explain that the procedure was selected as a last resort and fully explain how the deception was carried out. During the entire process, one needs to carefully monitor and appropriately respond to participants' affective reactions and comments, while encouraging honest feedback about the study.

Debriefing tends to be more difficult to carry out in nonlaboratory settings, especially where participants initially are unaware that they have been studied for research purposes, are no longer accessible to the researcher, or are unwilling to attend to the debriefing. In certain situations, such as naturalistic studies of overheard conversations, debriefing participants once the observations have been made could do more harm than good. The debriefing could serve to raise levels of discomfort or paranoia in other public settings and have a negative impact on the image of scientists in general. A pilot study consisting of interviews with a representative selection of persons from the target group could be conducted to assess feelings about the observations and the appropriateness of debriefing actual participants.

Because of the lack of direct contact with Internet participants, an effective debriefing can be particularly difficult to accomplish for studies conducted online. Nosek et al. (2002) recommended several options for debriefing Internet participants, even in situations where they drop out before the completion of a study. For example, at the outset of the study, participants could be required to provide an e-mail address and debriefing statements could be forwarded to them later; the researcher could include a "leave the study" button on each page, which would direct subjects to a debriefing

**Box 2.2** Postexperimental Ethical Safeguards in the Milgram Obedience Experiments and the Stanford Prison Simulation

Although ethical standards requiring debriefing were not yet in place when Milgram (1963, 1974) conducted his obedience experiments, the researcher took several steps to ascertain the effects of the experience on participants as part of a "postexperimental treatment." The deception was thoroughly explained to participants during a detailed discussion prior to their leaving the laboratory; participants had a friendly reconciliation with the unharmed confederate-learner; and the experiment was explained to both defiant and obedient participants in a way that supported their decision to obey or disobey the experimenter. Once the project was completed, a detailed report was sent to all participants explaining the experimental procedure and research findings, worded in such a way as to dignify their behavior in the study. Finally, Milgram assessed subjects' reactions to their participation via follow-up questionnaires, and conducted thorough interviews with participants one year later.

Similar steps were taken by Philip Zimbardo upon termination of the Stanford prison simulation. Extensive individual and group debriefing sessions were held following the experience, providing participants the opportunity to openly discuss their reactions with members of the research team and with each other. Questionnaires were distributed to participants several weeks after the simulation and at yearly intervals. Interestingly, both Zimbardo (1973) and Milgram (1964) published journal articles in which they discussed the various ethical issues encountered by their research in its design and implementation.

One further point regarding the Stanford prison study is that the study was prematurely terminated by the researchers when it became apparent that participants were experiencing undue psychological distress from the experience. Romanian social scientist Catalin Mamali (2004) dubbed the decision to stop the simulation in advance because of ethical concerns related to the well-being of participants, "Zimbardo's limit"—the critical interval that marks the level or the moment when the experimental procedures, aimed at revealing scientific truths, begin to generate unacceptable consequences and costs for the well-being of participants.

page prior to their dropping out; and the computer program can automatically present a debriefing page if the participant prematurely closes the browser window. Additional components could be added, including the provision of a list of frequently asked questions (FAQs) that address concerns and that emphasize the importance of the research in an engaging way; an e-mail address to which questions about the study can be sent at a later time; and arranging to have the researcher available in an online chat room to respond interactively to participants' comments.

### Forewarning

Another somewhat more uncertain remedy for some of the potential adverse effects of deception is *forewarning*, a type of revised informed consent procedure whereby researchers take steps to brief participants about the study at the outset, informing them that certain information may have to be withheld until the end of the investigation and that they are free to withdraw at any time. The researcher then can carry out the study only with persons who are willing to continue. Forewarning thus addresses the ethical concerns associated with

intentional deception by ensuring the autonomy of participants and fulfilling the researcher's obligation to inform participants of the potential reasonable risks that might be encountered (Smith et al., 2009; Wendler, 1996). It also likely confirms participants' suspicions that a study involves more than meets the eye (Pittenger, 2002), suggesting that some participants may be sensitized by the forewarning to engage in problem-solving behavior so as to identify the nature of the deception (Geller, 1982).

### The Right to Withdraw

Investigators are obligated to respect the individual's freedom to decline to participate in or to withdraw from any stage of the research process. This research protection is included as a basic element of extant ethics codes (Kimmel, 2007) and typically is clarified during the informed consent procedure or as an aspect of standardized instructions. The application of this principle is not always straightforward, and researchers are apt to encounter ethical dilemmas, particularly when they hold power over prospective subjects or otherwise control desired resources. Participants may be reluctant to withdraw from a study for fear of losing promised incentives (such as university course credit or gifts), despite promises to the contrary.

Depending upon the nature of the research procedure and its objectives, certain social influence studies may make it difficult for investigators to adhere to the freedom-to-withdraw requirement, as was apparent in the Milgram obedience research whereby a critical aspect of the procedure included experimenter demands that participants continue despite their desire to quit. During the Stanford prison research, the right to withdraw was temporarily withheld from one distraught prisoner role player when it appeared that the participant was trying to trick the researchers so as to obtain early release from the simulated prison (Zimbardo, 1973).

## Institutional Review

Beyond the decision-making responsibilities of the individual researcher, whose objectivity may be questioned because of a vested interest in conducting a study guided more by methodological and theoretical concerns than ethical ones, there now exists an extensive system of external review for overseeing the ethicality of research.

### THE ETHICAL REVIEW PROCESS

The review process typically includes a determination as to whether risks to participants are minimized by sound research procedures and are outweighed sufficiently by anticipated benefits to the participants and the importance of the knowledge to be gained; the rights and welfare of subjects are adequately protected; the research will be periodically reviewed; and informed consent has been obtained. Although most review boards do not reject the use of deception outright, the criteria for informed consent require researchers to justify the use of deception to review boards, unless the investigation constitutes a minimal risk study (i.e., the study does not include risks greater than those posed in everyday life). During a review the investigator is required to present detailed information about all aspects of a proposed study, including specifics about the characteristics of participants, the procedure and research materials, the nature of any deceptions, confidentiality, risks, and method of debriefing. Certain additional hurdles may have to be passed prior to reaching the review board stage (e.g., departmental approval in academic and organizational settings; parental consent; school, hospital, or prison board approval). Further, review may occur at various intervals once data collection has begun.

The expanded influence of external review has brought with it a growing concern that review boards are overstepping their intended role in an overzealous effort to force behavioral and social research into a biomedical mold, making it increasingly difficult for many researchers to proceed with their studies. Considerations that are not specifically related to the rights and welfare of research participants, such as the study design and methodology, now are routinely included in evaluations of research proposals. Because a poorly designed study can have serious ramifications and costs, one might argue that the technical elements of a proposed investigation in fact should be included as a dimension of ethical review (Rosenthal, 1994). Nonetheless, there is widespread disagreement over whether the scientific aspects of investigations ought to be taken into account by review boards (e.g., Colombo, 1995; Diener, 2001).

### EFFECTIVENESS OF THE REVIEW PROCESS AND RECOMMENDATIONS

Evidence regarding the effectiveness of ethical review committees in protecting research participants from risk and the impact of such committees on research is somewhat mixed (Mueller & Furedy, 2001; Shea, 2000). Moreover, little specific guidance is offered in practice by review committees a priori (e.g., feedback on rejected research protocols may generally refer to problematic use of deception or insufficient informed consent) and researchers are dependent upon the preferences of the individual review board members who possess varying personal norms and sensitivities for assessing costs and benefits. Reviewers can maintain inconsistent standards across time and institutions, such that a proposal that is approved without modification in one institution may require substantial changes, or else be rejected, by a review board at another institution (e.g., Ceci, Peters, & Plotkin, 1985; Rosnow et al., 1993). Further, there are limits on information that can be requested of citizens in varying research contexts.

Several suggestions for improving the review process have been offered (e.g., Diener, 2001; Ilgen & Bell, 2001). The efficiency and fairness of a review board can be maximized when it is comprised of members whose expertise is commensurate with the types of research that the committee typically reviews. Diversity is essential in light of evidence suggesting that differences in individual background characteristics (such as gender, age, professional experience, and moral philosophy) lead to predictable biases in ethical judgments (Kimmel, 1991; Schlenker & Forsyth, 1977). A casebook of actual research protocols that have received extensive review and analysis by both investigators and participants can be provided to review board members (Rosnow et al., 1993). For unique research cases, an advisory board could be created within a discipline's professional association, which would be charged with analyzing and reviewing a review board decision when disagreements emerge. Another approach to improving the review process is to take steps to encourage communication between review boards and investigators (cf. Eisenberg, 2007; Hansen, 2001).

## Conclusion

The need for continued progress in understanding social influence processes has never been more apparent, as issues related to environmental protection, political freedom, violence, the impact of technological advances, and the like gain greater prominence in a complex, rapidly changing world. At the same time, the scope and degree of interest in ethical issues, including those within the context of research, have grown dramatically, consistent with societal, scientific, and technological developments. Although there are a number of safeguards in place for preventing most of the serious breaches of ethics that might occur in social influence research, the first line of defense for the protection of the various interests involved in and affected by the research process are researchers themselves. This point has been emphasized in most ethics codes, which note that researchers have a professional responsibility to evaluate carefully and thoroughly the ethics of their investigations.

In their ethical assessment of deception in consumer behavior research, Smith et al. (2009) derived a set of morally justifiable principles that extend beyond those currently available in extant professional codes. On the basis of an application of social contract theory (Dunfee, 2006; Sayre-McCord, 2000), a normative theory of ethics claiming that binding moral obligations can be identified through the agreement and consent of moral agents, including researchers, participants, and other affected parties, their principles include the following: (1) an adherence to standards on deception, informed consent, and voluntary participation as specified in existing ethical codes and governmental guidelines; (2) the use of deception as a last resort, once all alternative procedures are ruled out as unfeasible; (3) researchers do not expose participants to risks of potential lasting harm or to procedures or risks that they themselves would not submit to if similarly situated; (4) participants be forewarned about the potential use of deception and any known risks, where methodologically feasible; and (5) researchers plan for participant vulnerabilities.

Smith et al.'s principles suggest a set of recommended practical steps for the social influence researcher, which are exemplified by Burger's (2009) replication of Milgram's obedience experiment. Among the safeguards included in the replication, such as the 150V solution (see "Alternatives to Deception"), were a two-step screening process for identifying and excluding vulnerable participants, a repeated assurance to participants that they could withdraw from the study and still receive the monetary incentive, immediate feedback to participants that no shocks were received by the learner, and the choice of a clinical psychologist to run the experiments who was instructed to stop the procedure as soon as any signs of adverse effects became apparent. Prior to running the study, Burger also might have conducted pilot tests to gauge representative participants' reactions to a description of the research procedure, and actual participants might have been asked to agree to participate fully knowing that certain procedural details would not be revealed until the end of the research experience. Although the latter recommendation runs the risk of arousing suspicions, there is evidence that participants typically engage in problem solving about an investigation anyway; by being upfront about withholding certain information, researchers might more effectively gain the cooperation of participants to respond honestly (Kimmel, 2007; Kimmel, Smith, & Klein, 2011).

In short, ethical decision making involves a set of balancing considerations as to how best to contribute to science and human welfare. An important aspect of this decision-making process is the recognition that most research questions in science can be pursued in more than one manner and that the ethical researcher is one who selects the methodological approach that is most likely to satisfy research goals while minimizing potentially negative consequences.

## References

Adair, J. G., Dushenko, T. W., & Lindsay, R. C. L. (1985). Ethical regulation and their impact on research practice. *American Psychologist*, 40, 59–72.

Asch, S. E. (1951). Effects of group pressure upon the modification and distortion of judgments. In H. Guetzkow (Ed.), *Groups, leadership, and men: Research in human relations* (pp. 177–190). Pittsburgh, PA: Carnegie Press.

Asch, S. (1955). Opinions and social pressure. *Scientific American*, 193, 31–35.

Bassett, R. L., Basinger, D., & Livermore, P. (1992). Lying in the laboratory: Deception in human research from psychological, philosophical, and theological perspectives. *Journal of the American Scientific Affiliation*, 34, 201–212.

Baumrind, D. (1964). Some thoughts on ethics of research: After reading Milgram's "Behavioral study of obedience." *American Psychologist*, 19, 421–423.

Behnke, S. H., & Kinscherff, R. (2002, May). Must a psychologist report past child abuse? *Monitor on Psychology*, 33(5), 56–57.

Bélisle, J-F., & Bodur, H. O. (2010). Avatars as information: Perception of consumers based on their avatars in virtual worlds. *Psychology and Marketing*, 27, 741–765.

Benjamin, L. T., & Simpson, J. A. (2009). The power of the situation: The impact of Milgram's obedience studies on personality and social psychology. *American Psychologist*, 64, 12–19.

Bergin, A. E. (1962). The effect of dissonant persuasive communications upon changes in a self-referring attitude. *Journal of Personality*, 30, 423–436.

Bermant, G., McGuire, M., McKinley, W., & Salo, C. (1974). The logic of simulation in jury research. *Criminal Justice and Behavior*, 1, 224–233.

Birnbaum, M. H. (2003). Methodological and ethical issues in conducting social psychology research via the Internet. In C. Sansone, C. C. Morf, & A. T. Panter (Eds.), *The Sage handbook of methods in social psychology* (pp. 45–70). Thousand Oaks, CA: Sage.

Blass, T. (2004). *The man who shocked the world*. New York: Basic Books.

Blass, T. (2009). From New Haven to Santa Clara: A historical perspective on the Milgram obedience experiments. *American Psychologist*, 64, 37–45.

Bramel, D. (1962). A dissonance theory approach to defensive projection. *Journal of Abnormal and Social Psychology*, 64, 121–129.

Bramel, D. (1963). Selection of a target for defensive projection. *Journal of Abnormal and Social Psychology*, 66, 318–324.

Breckler, S. J. (2009, June). The challenges of human research. *Monitor on Psychology*, 40, 38.

British Psychological Society. (2005). *Ethical principles for conducting research with human participants*. Retrieved June 2010, from http://www.bps.org.uk/system/files/Public%20files/bps_code_of_ethics_2009.pdf

Broder, A. (1998). Deception can be acceptable. *American Psychologist*, 53, 85–86.

Brody, J. L., Gluck, J. P., & Aragon, A. S. (2000). Participants' understanding of the process of psychological research: Debriefing. *Ethics and Behavior*, 10, 13–25.

Burger, J. M. (2009). Replicating Milgram: Would people still obey today? *American Psychologist*, 64, 1–11.

Ceci, S. J., Peters, D., & Plotkin, J. (1985). Human subjects review, personal values, and the regulation of social science research. *American Psychologist*, 40, 994–1002.

Cheetham, M., Pedroni, A. F., Angus, A., Slater, M., & Jäncke, L. (2009). Virtual Milgram: Emphatic concern or personal distress? Evidence from functional MRI and dispositional measures. *Frontiers of Human Neuroscience*, 3, ArtID 29.

Christensen, L. (1988). Deception in psychological research: When is its use justified? Personality and Social Psychology Bulletin, 14, 664–675.

Cialdini, R. B. (2007). *Influence: The psychology of persuasion*. New York: Collins.

Cohen, P. (2007, February 28). As ethics panels expand grip, no field is off limits. *The New York Times*. Retrieved March 2015, from http://www.nytimes.com/2007/02/28/arts/28board.html?_r=0

Collmann, J. (2007). Managing information privacy and security in healthcare European Union privacy directive— Reconciling European and American approaches to privacy. *Healthcare Information and Management Systems Society*. Retrieved March 2015 http://www.himss.org/files/HIMSSorg/content/files/CPRIToolkit/version6/v7/D33_European_Union_Privacy_Directive.pdf

Colombo, J. (1995). Cost, utility, and judgments of institutional review boards. Psychological Science, 6, 318–319.

Dambrun, M., & Vatine, E. (2010). Reopening the study of extreme social behaviors: Obedience to authority within an immersive video environment. *European Journal of Social Psychology*, 40, 760–773.

Diener, E. (2001). Over-concern with research ethics. *Dialogue*, 16, 2.

Dranseika, V., Gefenas, E., Cekanauskaite, A., Hug, K., & Mezinska, S. et al. (2010). 20 years of human research ethics committees in the Baltic States. *Developing World Bioethics*, 11 (1), 48–54.

Dunfee, T. W. (2006). A critical perspective of integrative social contracts theory: Recurring criticisms and next generation research topics. *Journal of Business Ethics*, 68, 303–328.

Eisenberg, T. (2007). Enhancing our relationships with IRBs. *Monitor on Psychology*, 38, 5.

Elms, A. C. (2009). Obedience lite. *American Psychologist*, 64, 32–36.

ESOMAR. (2011). *ESOMAR guideline for online research*. Retrieved March 2015, from http://www.esomar.org/knowledge-and-standards/codes-and-guidelines/guideline-for-online-research.php

Ethical Principles of Psychologists and Code of Conduct. (2002). *American Psychologist*, 57, 1060–1073.

Festinger, L., & Carlsmith, J. M. (1959). Cognitive consequences of forced compliance. *Journal of Abnormal and Social Psychology*, 58, 203–210.

Frankena, W. K. (1973). *Ethics* (2nd ed.). Englewood Cliffs, NJ: Prentice-Hall.

Freedman, J. (1969). Role-playing: psychology by consensus. *Journal of Personality and Social Psychology*, 13, 107–114.

Gaggioli, A. (2004). Using virtual reality in experimental psychology. In G. Riva & C. Galimberti (Eds.), *Towards cyberpsychology: Mind, cognitions and society in the internet age* (pp. 157–174). Amsterdam: IOS Press.

Geller, D. M. (1982). Alternatives to deception: Why, what, and how? In J. E. Sieber (Ed.), *The ethics of social research: Surveys and experiments* (pp. 39–55). New York: Springer-Verlag.

Goldstein, N. J., Cialdini, R. B., & Griskevicius, V. (2008). A room with a viewpoint: Using social norms to motivate environmental conservation in hotels. *Journal of Consumer Research*, 35, 472–482.

Greenberg, M. (1967). Role playing: An alternative to deception? *Journal of Personality and Social Psychology*, 7, 152–157.

Greenberg, J., & Eskew, D. E. (1993). The role of role playing in organizational research. *Journal of Management*, 19, 221–241.

Haney, C., Banks, W. C., & Zimbardo, P. G. (1973). Interpersonal dynamics in a simulated prison. *International Journal of Criminology and Penology*, 1, 69–97.

Hansen, C. (2001). Regulatory changes affecting IRBs and researchers. *APS Observer*, 14, 13–14, 25.

Hogan, P. M., & Kimmel, A. J. (1992). Ethical teaching of psychology: One department's attempts at self-regulation. *Teaching of Psychology*, 19, 205–210.

Hunt, S. D., & Vitell, S. (1986). A general theory of marketing ethics. *Journal of Macromarketing*, 6(Spring), 5–16.

ICC/ESOMAR. (2008). ICC/ESOMAR international code on marketing and social research practice. Retrieved March 2015, from https://www.esomar.org/uploads/public/knowledge-and-standards/codes-and-guidelines/ICCESOMAR_Code_German_.pdf

Ilgen, D. R., & Bell, B. S. (2001). Informed consent and dual purpose research. *American Psychologist*, 56, 1177.

Kelman, H. C. (1967). Human use of human subjects: The problem of deception in social psychological experiments. *Psychological Bulletin*, 67, 1–11.

Kelman, H. C. (1996). Foreward. In A. J. Kimmel (Ed.), *Ethical issues in behavioral research: A survey* (pp. xii–xiv). Cambridge, MA: Blackwell.

Kimmel, A. J. (1988). *Ethics and values in applied social research*. Newbury Park, CA: Sage.

Kimmel, A. J. (1991). Predictable biases in the ethical decision making of American psychologists. *American Psychologist*, 46, 786–788.

Kimmel, A. J. (2001). Ethical trends in marketing and psychological research. *Ethics and Behavior*, 11, 131–149.

Kimmel, A. J. (2003). Ethical issues in social psychology research. In C. Sansone, C. C. Morf, & A. T. Panter (Eds.), *The Sage handbook of methods in social psychology* (pp. 45–70). Thousand Oaks, CA: Sage.

Kimmel, A. J. (2004, July 28–August 1). *Ethical trends in psychology and marketing research: An update*. Paper presented at the 112th Annual Convention of the American Psychological Association, Honolulu, HI.

Kimmel, A. J. (2007). *Ethical issues in behavioral research: Basic and applied perspectives* (2nd ed.). Malden, MA: Wiley-Blackwell.

Kimmel, A. J. (2011a). Deception in psychological research–A necessary evil? *The Psychologist*, 24, 580–585.

Kimmel, A. J. (2011b). Deception in research. In S. J. Knapp (Ed.), *APA handbook of ethics and psychology: Vol. 2. Practice, teaching, and research* (pp. 401–421). Washington, DC: APA Books.

Kimmel, A. J., & Smith, N. C. (2001). Deception in marketing research: Ethical, methodological, and disciplinary implications. *Psychology and Marketing*, 18, 663–689.

Kimmel, A. J., Smith, N. C., & Klein, J. G. (2011). Ethical decision making and research deception in the behavioral sciences: An application of social contract theory. Ethics and Behavior, 21, 222–251.

Kitchener, K. S. (1984). Intuition, critical evaluation, and ethical principles: The foundation for ethical decisions in counseling psychology. *The Counseling Psychologist*, 12, 43–55.

Kitchener, K. S. (2000). *Foundations of ethical practice in research and teaching in psychology*. Mahwah, NJ: Erlbaum.

Lamberth, J., & Kimmel, A. J. (1981). Ethical issues and responsibilities in applying scientific behavioral knowledge. In A. J. Kimmel (Ed.), *Ethics of human subject research* (pp. 69–79). San Francisco: Jossey-Bass.

Latané, B., & Darley, J. M. (1970). *The unresponsive bystander: Why doesn't he help?* New York: Appleton-Century-Crofts.

Lawson, E. (2001). Informational and relational meanings of deception: Implications for deception methods in research. *Ethics and Behavior*, 11, 115–130.

Levine, R. J. (1975). *The nature and definition of informed consent in various research settings. Paper prepared for the National Commission for the Protection of Human Subjects of Biomedical and Behavioral Research*. Bethesda, MD: US Department of Health, Education, and Welfare.

Mamali, C. (2004). Lessons from the epistemic, moral and social richness of Stanford prison experiment. *Dialogue*, 19, 22–23, 28.

Mathy, R. M., Kerr, D. L., & Haydin, B. M. (2003). Methodological rigor and ethical considerations in internet-mediated research. *Psychotherapy: Theory, Research, Practice, Training*, 40, 77–85.

McNamara, J. R., & Woods, K. M. (1977). Ethical considerations in psychological research: A comparative review. *Behavior Therapy*, 8, 703–708.

Milgram, S. (1963). Behavioral study of obedience. *Journal of Abnormal and Social Psychology*, 67, 371–378.

Milgram, S. (1964). Issues in the study of obedience: A reply to Baumrind. *American Psychologist*, 19, 848–852.

Milgram, S. (1974). *Obedience to authority*. New York: Harper Colophon.

Miller, A. G., Collins, B. E., & Brief, D. E. (1995). Perspectives on obedience to authority: The legacy of the Milgram experiments. *Journal of Social Issues*, 51, 1–19.

Miller, A. G. (1972). Role playing: An alternative to deception; a review of the evidence. *American Psychologist*, 27, 623–636.

Mirvis, P. H., & Seashore, S. E. (1982). Creating ethical relationships in organizational research. In J. E. Sieber (Ed.), *The ethics of social research: Surveys and experiments* (pp. 79–104). New York: Springer-Verlag.

Misra, S. (1992). Is conventional debriefing adequate? An ethical issue in consumer research. Journal of the Academy of Marketing Science, 20, 269–273.

Mueller, J. H., & Furedy, J. J. (2001). Reviewing for risk: What's the evidence that it works? *APS Observer*, 14, 26–28.

Nicks, S. D., Korn, J. H., & Mainieri, T. (1997). The rise and fall of deception in social psychology and personality research, 1921 to 1994. *Ethics and Behavior*, 7, 69–77.

Nosek, B. A., Banaji, M. R., & Greenwald, A. G. (2002). E-research: Ethics, security, design, and control in psychological research on the internet. *Journal of Social Issues*, 58, 161–176.

Orne, M. T., & Holland, C. H. (1968). On the ecological validity of laboratory deceptions. *International Journal of Psychiatry*, 6, 282–293.

Ortmann, A., & Hertwig, R. (1997). Is deception acceptable? *American Psychologist*, 52, 746–747.

Patten, S. C. (1977). Milgram's shocking experiments. *Philosophy*, 52, 425–440.

Pittenger, D. J. (2002). Deception in research: Distinctions and solutions from the perspective of utilitarianism. *Ethics and Behavior*, 12, 117–142.

Reese, G., Loew, K., & Steffgen, G. (2014). A towel less: Social norms enhance pro-environmental behavior in hotels. *Journal of Social Psychology*, 154, 97–100.

Reicher, S. D., & Haslam, S. A. (2011). The shock of the old. *The Psychologist*, 24, 650–652.

Resnick, J. H., & Schwartz, T. (1973). Ethical standards as an independent variable in psychological research. *American Psychologist*, 28, 134–139.

Reynolds, P. D. (1979). *Ethical dilemmas and social science research*. San Francisco: Jossey-Bass.

Rogerson, M. D., Gottlieb, M. C., Handelsman, M. M., Knapp, S., & Younggren, J. (2011). Nonrational processes in ethical decision making. *American Psychologist*, 66, 614–623.

Rosenberg, R. S., Baughman, S. L., & Bailenson, J. N. (2013). Virtual superheroes: Using superpowers in virtual reality to encourage prosocial behavior. *PLoS ONE*, 8, e55003. doi: 10.1371/journal.pone.0055003

Rosenthal, R. (1994). Science and ethics in conducting, analyzing, and reporting psychological research. *Psychological Science*, 5, 127–134.

Rosenthal, R., & Rosnow, R. L. (1984). Applying Hamlet's question to the ethical conduct of research: A conceptual addendum. *American Psychologist*, 39, 561–563.

Rosenthal, R., & Rosnow, R. L. (1991). *Essentials of behavioral research: Methods and data analysis* (2nd ed.). New York: McGraw-Hill.

Rosnow, R. L. (1997). Hedgehogs, foxes, and the evolving social contract in psychological science: Ethical challenges and methodological opportunities. *Psychological Methods*, 2, 345–356.

Rosnow, R. L., Rotheram-Borus, M. J., Ceci, S. J., Blanck, P. D., & Koocher, G. P. (1993). The institutional review board as a mirror of scientific and ethical standards. *American Psychologist*, 48, 821–826.

Rutecki, G. W., Youtsey, M., & Adelson, B. (2002). The institutional review board: A critical revisit to the protection of human subjects. *Ethics and Medicine*, 18, 135–144.

Savin, H. B. (1973). Professors and psychological researchers: Conflicting values in conflicting roles. *Cognition*, 2, 147–149.

Sayre-McCord, G. (2000). Contractarianism. In H. LaFollette (Ed.), *Ethical theory* (pp. 268–287). Oxford, UK: Blackwell.

Schlenker, B. R., & Forsyth, D. R. (1977). On the ethics of psychological research. *Journal of Experimental Social Psychology*, 13, 369–396.

Schuler, H. (1982). *Ethical problems in psychological research*. New York: Academic Press.

Seligman, C., & Sorrentino, R. M. (2002). The control agenda in Canada's governance of ethical review of human research. *Dialogue*, 17, 22–24.

Sharf, B. F. (1999). Beyond netiquette: The ethics of doing naturalistic discourse research on the internet. In S. Jones (Ed.), *Doing internet research: Critical issues and methods for examining the net* (pp. 243–256). Thousand Oaks, CA: Sage.

Sharpe, D., & Faye, C. (2009). A second look at debriefing practices: Madness in our method? *Ethics and Behavior*, 19, 432–447.

Shea, C. (2000, September). Don't talk to the humans: The crackdown on social science research. *Lingua Franca*, pp. 27–34.

Slater, L. (2004). Opening Skinner's box: Great psychological experiments of the twentieth century. New York: W. W. Norton.

Slater, M., Antley, A., Davison, A., Swapp, D., Guger, C., Barker, C., . . . Sanchez-Vives, M. V. (2006). A virtual reprise of the Stanley Milgram obedience experiments. *PLoS ONE*, 1(1), e39.

Smith, N. C., Kimmel, A. J., & Klein, J. G. (2009). Social contract theory and the ethics of deception in consumer research. *Journal of Consumer Psychology*, 19, 486–496.

Smith, N. L. (1985). Some characteristics of moral problems in evaluation practice. *Evaluation and Program Planning*, 8, 5–11.

Stangor, C., Sechrist, G. B., & Jost, J. T. (2001). Social influence and intergroup attitudes: The role of perceived social consensus. In J. Forgas & K. Williams (Eds.), *Social influence* (pp. 235–252). Philadelphia: Psychology Press.

Strohmetz, D. B., Rind, B., Fisher, R., & Lynn, M. (2002). Sweetening the till: The use of candy to increase restaurant tipping. *Journal of Applied Social Psychology*, 32, 300–309.

Toy, D., Olson, J., & Wright, L. (1989). Effects of debriefing in marketing research involving "mild" deceptions. *Psychology and Marketing*, 6, 69–85.

Trawley, S., Law, A. S., Logie, M. R., & Logie, R. H. (2013). *Desktop virtual reality in psychological research: A case study using the Source 3D game engine*. Unpublished manuscript. Retrieved March 2015, from http://www.psy.ed.ac.uk/res-group/MT/documents/SourceEngine_2013.pdf

Vinacke, W. E. (1954). Deceiving experimental subjects. *American Psychologist*, 9, 155.

Vitelli, R. (1988). The crisis issue assessed: An empirical analysis. *Basic and Applied Social Psychology*, 9, 301–309.

Vu, T. (2014, March 26). Virtual reality is coming to life in research labs and beyond. *Peninsula Press*. Retrieved March 2015, from http://blog.sfgate.com/inthepeninsula/2014/03/26/virtual-reality-stanford/

Wendler, D. (1996). Deception in medical and behavioral research: Is it ever acceptable? Milbank Quarterly, 74, 87–114.

Zimbardo, P. G. (1973). On the ethics of intervention in human psychological research: With special reference to the Stanford prison experiment. *Cognition*, 2, 243–256.

# PART 2

# Intrapersonal Processes

# Social Influence and Gender

Linda L. Carli

## Abstract

This chapter reviews current research on gender and social influence. Overall, men exert greater influence than women do. Women's disadvantage derives from gender stereotypes that characterize men as more competent and agentic than women and that require women to be more selfless and communal than men. Both agentic and communal behaviors predict influence. As a result, women are subjected to a double bind. They may lack influence because of doubt about their competence, or they may lack influence because their competent behavior elicits concern that they are insufficiently communal. In contrast, men have greater behavioral flexibility than women do as influence agents. Men tend to be more resistant to women's influence than women are, particularly when female influence agents behave in a highly competent manner. Resistance to female influence can be reduced in contexts that are stereotypically feminine and when women display a blend of agentic and communal qualities.

**Key Words:** agency, communion, double bind, expectation states theory, gender differences, influenceability, stereotypes, social role theory

Social influence pervades much of social interaction. People influence the opinions and behaviors of others in virtually all personal and professional contexts. Much research on social influence has focused on general principles that facilitate attitude and behavior change, including the importance of source characteristics. According to the elaboration likelihood model (Petty & Cacioppo, 1986), source characteristics such as expertise, power, and personal appeal or likeability are important determinants of social influence. In general, sources who are expert and likeable tend to influence others to a greater degree than inexpert and unlikeable sources (Briñol & Petty, 2009). People trust competent likeable influence agents and yield to their influence.

The contribution of competence and likeability to influence has particular relevance in research exploring gender differences in social influence because gender stereotypes about men and women characterize women as possessing likeable qualities and men as possessing competent ones. In this chapter, I will explore research on gender differences in social influence and the ways in which gender stereotypes underpin those gender differences. In particular, I will show that men exert greater influence than women because of the influence of gender stereotypes, which characterize men as more competent than women. Moreover, because of prescriptive stereotypes requiring women to be communal, people expect women to be warmer and kinder than their male counterparts and consequently resist female influence for not being likeable enough. In this way, influence processes are often tainted by discrimination because the very behaviors that typically enhance influence for men might very well undermine it for women.

Research has revealed that men have an influence advantage. An early meta-analysis of 29 studies examined gender differences in men's and women's influence in task-oriented, mixed-gender groups (Lockheed, 1985). Results revealed that men exerted greater influence and exhibited more leadership behaviors than women did. Subsequent research has confirmed these findings: With a few exceptions (e.g., Foschi & Lapointe, 2002), people are more influenced by men than women, even in experiments where the behavior of the men and women is manipulated to be the same (Carli, 2001, 2006; DiBerardinis, Ramage, & Levitt, 1984; Elias & Cropanzano, 2006; Lee, 2004; Schneider & Cook, 1995; Wagner, Ford, & Ford, 1986). Thus, women's lessor influence does not derive from higher quality male performance. In one vivid illustration of this, Propp (1995) created mixed-sex, four-person groups that were assigned to evaluate a child custody case. In some conditions of the study, one of the male or one of the female participants was assigned at random to contribute a particular piece of information to their groups. Results revealed that the same idea was six times more likely to be used by the groups in forming their decision when the person contributing the idea was a man rather than a woman.

According to Cialdini and Goldstein (2004), social influence is driven by several goals, including motives to make accurate decisions and to establish and maintain good relationships with others. The desire to make accurate decisions likely contributes to the influence of people who appear knowledgeable and competent. Indeed, research has shown an association between the extent to which someone is perceived to be competent and that person's ability to influence others (Driskell, Olmstead, & Salas, 1993; Holtgraves & Lasky, 1999; Rhoads & Cialdini, 2002). This accounts for the frequent use of professional athletes in advertisements for sneakers and energy drinks and for the use of actors portraying physicians in advertisements for medical treatments. Thus, one route to influence is to present oneself as an authority in some domain. But influence can also be achieved by appealing to others' need for affiliation and desire for good relationships. Consequently, another important characteristic of influential people is how likeable they are. Studies have shown that being likeable enhances influence (Carli, 1989; Cialdini, 2001; Wood & Kallgren, 1988).

## Gender Stereotypes

Because influence derives from perceived competence and likeability, stereotypes about social groups can enhance or undermine the influence of those groups. Discriminatory treatment of women occurs because people typically hold different stereotypes about women than about men. Stereotypes reflect people's assumptions that individuals who share membership in some social group are also likely to share common characteristics. In the case of gender stereotypes, there is cross-cultural consensus about what characteristics are thought to distinguish men and women. In one study, across 30 different countries, people considered men to possess traits such as competitiveness, assertiveness, and competence, whereas women were considered kinder, warmer, more supportive, and gentler (Newport, 2001; Williams & Best, 1990a). The constellation of traits that people associate with women are thought to be highly communal and to reflect a concern with the needs and feelings of others. In contrast, the constellation of traits that people associate with men reflect the belief that men are more agentic and status-asserting (Hall & Carter, 1999; Spence & Buckner, 2000). Of course, there is some evidence that stereotypes about women have changed somewhat. Participants asked to characterize women and men of the past, present, and future report that women have become increasingly agentic over time and are likely to continue to increase in agency in the future (Diekman & Eagly, 2000; Diekman & Goodfriend, 2006; Garcia-Retamero, Müller, & López-Zafra, 2011). Nevertheless, participants do not perceive changes in gender differences in communion, and in spite of the perception that women have gained in agency overall, men continue to be judged as generally more agentic than women.

Research examining the evaluation of men's and women's performance provides additional evidence that people credit men with higher levels of agency and competence. Indeed, people recognize agentic behavior more quickly when the behavior is exhibited by men than by women (Scott & Brown, 2006). In addition, research has revealed a double standard in the evaluation of men and women. A number of studies, for example, have shown that when participants are asked to indicate what level of performance would be necessary to conclude that someone had a high level of ability at some task, the performance standards are set higher for women than for men (Biernat & Kobrynowicz, 1997; Foschi, 1996, 2000). The clearest evidence showing male favoritism in perceived competence comes from experimental studies where gender differences in performance are manipulated to be identical or no information about performance is given. College students asked to evaluate the intelligence, general competence, and academic performance of male and female college students solely on the basis of photographs reported higher estimates for men than women (Rashotte & Webster, 2005). Other studies have shown that female managers (Heilman, Block, & Martell, 1995; Heilman & Okimoto, 2007) and undergraduates (Carli, 1990, 2006) are evaluated less favorably than their male counterparts for the same level of performance. Moreover, when participants read about mixed-gender dyads that performed poorly at a management task, they attributed the failure to the woman more than to the man (Haynes & Lawrence, 2012). Similarly, research has documented that for women to receive comparable evaluations to men, participants must be given substantial evidence of female superiority, such as being told that a woman outperformed men on a standardized test (Foschi, Sigerson, & Lebesis, 1995; Shackelford, Wood, & Worchel, 1996; Wagner et al., 1986; Wood & Karten, 1986). For example, when participants read about a work team composed of a man and a woman who had created a successful investment portfolio, they assumed the man had been the primary contributor to the task unless given clear evidence that the woman had made unique contributions to the project or that she had a history of exceptional past performance (Heilman & Haynes, 2005).

Other studies have been conducted in small groups where although objective measures show no evidence of gender differences in performance, participants perceived greater competence in men. In one study, college students assigned to mixed-gender groups worked on a survival exercise in which they were asked to identify whom they believed was the most expert member of their group. Group members chose men more often than women, even though there were no actual gender differences in expertise, and members showed more accuracy in identifying the most expert member when that member was a man, rather than a woman (Thomas-Hunt & Phillips, 2004). In fact, in this study, the more expert the women were, the less expert they were perceived to be. In another study of four-person mixed-gender groups, one member of each group, the "hinter," was given the answer to a group problem and instructed to give the solution to the group. Although the solution was equally likely to be used by the group when given by men or women, the female hinters were judged less likeable and less leader-like than their male counterparts (Watson & Hoffman, 2004).

Likewise, in studies of military cadets (Boldry, Wood, & Kashy, 2001) and college students (Wood & Karten, 1986), men received higher performance evaluations than women, in spite of an absence of objective gender differences in performance. Similar results have been found in research on the evaluation of leaders: A meta-analysis revealed that for comparable levels of performance, female leaders overall receive lower evaluations of competence than male leaders (Eagly, Makhijani, & Klonsky, 1992).

Just as men are perceived to be more competent than women, women are perceived to more communal than men (Bosak, Sczesny, & Eagly, 2008; Deaux & Kite, 1993). But the stereotype about female communion is not merely a description of how women are thought to be but also a demand for women to be especially concerned with the needs of others. Whereas descriptive gender stereotypes reflect everyday beliefs about the characteristics of women and men, prescriptive gender stereotypes reflect how people think men and women ought to be. Thus, prescriptive gender stereotypes reflect social norms about how appropriate or socially acceptable particular characteristics are in men and women. In the case of the stereotype about female communality, people not only believe that women show greater kindness and warmth than men, but they require women to do so (Eagly, 1987; Eagly & Carli, 2007). Moreover, the prescription for female communion includes avoiding behavior that is too dominant or status asserting. Overt attempts by women to seek leadership, status, or authority, or to directly or aggressively attempt to influence others is seen as incompatible with the female communal prescription that women show selflessness and concern for others (Carli, 1999).

Women, but not men, have been found to be disliked for criticizing others (Rudman, Moss-Racusin, Phelan, & Nauts, 2012; Sinclair & Kunda, 2000), disagreeing with others (Carli, 2006), being highly successful in a male-dominated profession (Heilman, Wallen, Fuchs, & Tamkins, 2004; Heilman & Wallen, 2010), or being immodest (Giacalone & Riordan, 1990; Wosinska, Dabul, Whetstone-Dion, & Cialdini, 1996). Because communal behavior is normative for women, evaluations of women are more contingent on perceived communion than are evaluations of men (Biernat, Tocci, & Williams, 2012; Carli, LaFleur, & Loeber, 1995). When women behave in a highly agentic manner, they may risk being judged as lacking communal qualities and as violating gender-role norms that require women to be self-sacrificing and concerned with the needs of others (Carli & Eagly, 1999). Even mere competence may be problematic for women. Highly competent women are sometimes less well liked than competent men or less competent women (Carli, 1991; Falbo, Hazen, & Linimon, 1982; Heilman & Okimoto, 2007; Rudman et al., 2012). Consequently, an unfortunate effect of female gender stereotypes is that highly agentic and competent behavior may be viewed as incompatible with the traditional female gender role.

Indeed, women are penalized for being too agentic and insufficiently communal. For example, studies in which people evaluate exceptionally competent women in leadership or other male-dominated domains have revealed that such high levels of agency are perceived more negatively in women than in men. Specifically, participants perceived highly competent female electricians or engineers (Yoder & Schleicher, 1996) or highly competent female managers to have less desirable personalities than men of equivalent ability (Heilman, Block, & Martell, 1995; Heilman et al., 2004). The penalties against women who succeed in masculine domains result from a perception that such women lack prescribed communal qualities (Heilman & Okimoto, 2007). Similarly, women get less credit than men for exhibiting highly communal behavior. One organizational study found that men received more promotions at work when they were particularly helpful organizational citizens by providing extra help to their colleagues, whereas women who showed equal helpfulness received no increase in advancement (Allen, 2006). In an experimental study assessing reactions to organizational citizenship, participants credited helpful men but not helpful women (Heilman & Chen, 2005).

Given doubts about women's agency and competence and prescriptions that women manifest high levels of communion, women often face competing and contradictory demands. On one hand, women may overcome doubts about their agency by performing exceptionally well and taking command, but such women may be disliked and denigrated for being too threatening and domineering. On the other hand, women may allay concerns about their lack of communion by being especially unselfish, supportive, and kindhearted, but such women may be disrespected and denigrated for being weak and incompetent. Thus, gender stereotypes create a *double bind* for women. To overcome the double bind, women must evince a mix of agentic and communal qualities. The same is not true of men. Men, unlike women, have considerable latitude in their agentic and communal behavior. Unlike female agency, male communion is not penalized (e.g., Allen,

2006; Carli, 2006; Carli, LaFleur, & Loeber, 1995; Heilman & Chen, 2005).

Because of the very different demands placed on women and men, gender stereotypes can be consequential in mediating gender differences in social influence. Women's influence is likely to depend on the ability to overcome the double bind, whereas men experience no pressure to be communal and are presumed to possess agentic competence. Consequently, women's influence is likely to be more dependent than men's on manifesting both communal and agentic behavior.

## Theoretical Explanations for Gender Effects on Influence

Why do people hold different stereotypes about women and men? According to social role theory (Eagly, 1987; Eagly & Steffan, 1984), stereotypes derive from observations of women and men in their everyday social roles. Typically, there are differences in the types of roles held by each gender. There continues to be a traditional division of labor in the family, with women more often than men holding the roles of homemaker and primary caretaker of children, and men more often than women holding roles in the paid workforce. Moreover, even among employed women and men, occupational roles are highly gender segregated: Men's positions on average involve greater authority, power, and income than women's, whereas women's positions often involve support functions. The types of occupational roles characteristic of each gender generally have different demands and requirements. Women's domestic roles and lower status occupational roles often require communal behaviors, such as helpfulness, kindness, selflessness, and nurturance. People then come to expect agentic behavior in men and communal behavior in women.

In contrast, men's higher status occupational roles often require agentic behaviors, such as dominance, assertiveness, leadership, and competition. Thus, by fulfilling the requirements of their respective roles, men and women exhibit very different behaviors. According to social role theory, from observing women and men in these highly segregated roles, people conclude that their different behaviors derive from dispositional gender differences. The extent to which people perceive traits as commonplace in men or women is associated with their perception of the traits as stereotypic of that gender (Krueger, Hasman, Acevedo, & Villano, 2003). Because people perceive a higher percentage of men than women to be agentic and a higher percentage of women than men to be communal, people then come to expect agentic behavior in men and communal behavior in women.

According to social role theory, once descriptive gender stereotypes develop, aspects of the stereotypes become prescriptive—in particular, those that are viewed as most appropriate to fulfilling the roles held by each gender. People view communal traits as important for women and agentic traits as important for men because communal behavior is seen as suited for domestic roles and traditionally female-dominated professions, whereas agentic behavior is seen as suited for the employee role and male-dominated professions (Cejka & Eagly, 1999; Eagly & Steffen, 1984). Thus, communal traits are prescribed for women and agentic traits for men (Williams & Best, 1990b). Moreover, these prescriptions are seen as ideal reflections of male and female personalities. For example, in a recent replication of the classic Broverman studies (Broverman, Broverman, Clarkson, Rosenkrantz, & Vogel, 1970; Broverman, Vogel, Broverman, Clarkson, & Rosenkrantz, 1972), participants identified the characteristics of mentally healthy men and women by selecting primarily communal qualities as desirable in women and agentic qualities as desirable in men (Seem & Clark, 2006). Because possessing influence and authority depends on perceived competence and likeability, women would have more difficulty than men when attempting to influence others. Women's influence, unlike men, would depend on a careful blend of communal and agentic behavior to be successful. In addition, because gender role norms are particularly activated when gender is salient, gender differences in communal and agentic behavior and influence are likely to be pronounced in mixed-gender interactions and highly stereotypically masculine or feminine contexts (Eagly & Wood, 1991).

The demand for female communion exists not only to fulfill the requirements of domestic roles but also to fulfill the type of paid work roles that women hold more often than men—roles that are lower in status and authority. Men's predominance in powerful high-status roles has resulted in men generally possessing higher levels of status than women. Expectation states theory construes gender differences in status as important determinants of gender effects on social influence (Ridgeway & Smith-Lovin, 1999). According to the theory, gender acts as a diffuse status characteristic, one of a number of general attributes of a person that is associated with his or her relative status in society (Berger,

Fisek, Norman, & Zelditch, 1977; Correll & Ridgeway, 2003). Other examples of diffuse status characteristics include race, physical attractiveness, and education. The theory contends that these status characteristics can be used implicitly to form performance expectations that allow people to predict how they and other individuals will perform in various contexts. People presume that higher status individuals have more competence than those of lower status, and consequently, people more often attend to the opinions of high-status persons and yield to their influence, relative to those of lower status (Berger et al., 1977). In the same way, compared with those of lower status, high-status individuals are more likely to behave agentically—making task contributions, exhibiting confidence and authority, and expecting compliance from others. In a self-fulfilling manner, the more high-status individuals make contributions, the more they enhance their status and influence, and emerge as leaders (Hawkins, 1995; Stein & Heller, 1979). As a result, high-status individuals are believed to be more influential and they ultimately do wield more influence.

Like social role theory, status characteristics theory predicts greater communal behavior by women and agentic behavior by men. Because men possess higher status, they have greater legitimacy as influence agents and leaders and are encouraged to behave in an agentic manner, receiving opportunities to make task contributions and exert influence. On the other hand, because of their presumed lower competence, low-status individuals who exhibit agency are unlikely to wield much influence. Instead, their agentic behavior may be perceived as an illegitimate attempt to usurp influence and, as a result, their influence is likely to be resisted (Meeker & Weitzel-O'Neill, 1985; Ridgeway & Berger, 1986). In general, low-status individuals who overtly attempt to influence others risk being ignored or punished, which drops their status further. To overcome this resistance, those of lower status must communicate a lack of interest in personal gain and little desire to take control or lead, but instead convey a collectivist motivation, which can be achieved through communal behavior (Meeker & Weitzel-O'Neill, 1985). The prediction, then, is that women's lower status relative to men makes it difficult for them to influence others unless they demonstrate such a concern for others and a lack of interest in personal gain (Lockheed & Hall, 1976; Ridgeway, 2001). Thus, according to status theorists, communal behavior should enhance the influence of women, whereas assertive and dominant behaviors should reduce their influence. Moreover, because gender-based performance expectations should be evoked when gender is salient, gender differences in agency, communion, and influence should be clearest in interactions between men and women (Ridgeway & Smith-Lovin, 1999).

In summary, based on social role and expectation states theories, because women and men possess different social roles, with men holding more roles that confer status and authority, men have an influence advantage. People presume that men have more competence and other agentic qualities than women and require women more than men to display a selfless concern for others. Consequently, women are held to a higher standard of competence and communion than men, but these demands are sometimes incompatible. This leads to a double bind for women: Because competent and likeable individuals exert greater influence than less competent and likeable ones, women's ability to influence is compromised by a need to be simultaneously agentic and communal, a challenge not faced by men.

## Gender, Agency, and Influence

Given the presumption that women lack agency and the difficulty that women have being recognized as expert, a woman's agentic behavior is less likely to facilitate influence than a man's. Indeed, studies do show a weaker association between agency and influence for women. For example, whereas research on groups has demonstrated that one way to increase one's influence is to contribute more task-related behavior to the group (Hawkins, 1995; Ridgeway, 1978; Stein & Heller, 1979), women's task contributions are more likely than men's to be ignored or ineffective (Butler & Geis, 1990; Walker, Ilardi, McMahon, & Fennell, 1996). An archival study of female and male US Senators revealed similar evidence of women's difficulty in wielding influence through their task contributions (Brescoll, 2011). The study examined the association between the Senators' verbal contributions on the Senate floor to their influence in terms of their (1) assignment to high-powered committees, (2) ability to sway the outcome of votes or congressional agenda, (3) success in obtaining earmarks for their state, and (4) shaping or changing actual legislation. For male Senators, there was a positive association between influence and contributions, but for female Senators no association was found.

Further evidence that male agency enhances influence more than women's comes from mock

employment studies where participants are presented with résumés or job applications that vary only in the gender of the applicant. In these studies, women exert less influence than men in getting hired. Two meta-analyses of such studies revealed that men are rated as more desirable to hire than women with identical qualifications (Davison & Burke, 2000; Koch, D'Mello, & Sackett, 2015). Similar results emerged in a national study of academic psychologists who evaluated curricula vitae of female and male tenure candidates or job applicants for an academic position (Steinpres, Anders, & Ritzke, 1999). Evaluators reported that they would be less likely to vote to tenure or hire female than male applicants. Despite having the same credentials, female applicants were judged to have had weaker research experience, less teaching experience, and less service than male applicants had. Likewise, a recent study examined evaluations by supervisors of female and male junior attorneys at a moderate- to large-sized Wall Street law firm (Biernat, Tocci, & Williams, 2012). Supervisors rated female attorneys as less likely to be promoted to partner; ratings of the attorney's technical competence predicted men's likelihood of promotion to partner but did not predict women's. These studies demonstrate that women's perceived lack of competence relative to men undermines their influence when seeking employment or promotion. Although some recent studies have failed to find a male advantage in hiring when competency cues are controlled (Foschi & Valenzuela, 2008, 2012; Levin, Rouwenhorst, & Trisko, 2005), these studies have asked participants to choose between male and female applicants for the same position, which may highlight gender as an important variable and thereby elicit politically correct responses. When participants are less aware of gender as a variable, they typically favor male job candidates.

Men's perceived competence enhances their influence in other contexts as well. In a mock-jury study, participants reported how likely a defendant was to commit future violence after he or she listened to the testimony of a male or female expert witness who reported that the defendant had a high likelihood of violent reoffending (Neal, Guadagno, Eno, & Brodsky, 2012). The researchers assessed the expert witness's influence when the witness was presented as low in expertise, having minimal professional experience, and little knowledge of the case. Although competency cues were the same for both male and female witnesses, participants were more influenced by the male than the female witness.

Another study presented mock jurors with either a female or male expert witness who gave either simple testimony or complex and more difficult-to-understand testimony about a civil case (Schuller, Terry, & McKimmie, 2005). Previous research had revealed that when testimony is complex and difficult to understand, jurists process the evidence heuristically and rely on the perceived expertise of the witness to yield to the testimony (Cooper, Bennett, & Sukel, 1996). Results revealed that when testimony was complex, and thus perceived expertise would be expected to mediate influence, men exerted more influence than women over the outcome in the case (Schuller et al., 2005).

Research exploring the success rate of male and female scientists submitting manuscripts for publication or post doc fellowship applications has likewise found that women exert less influence. A study examining the peer review scores for postdoctoral fellowships in biomedical research found that a lower proportion of women obtained funding than men because women received lower evaluation scores than male applicants (Wennerås & Wold, 1997). Furthermore, objective evaluation of the applications revealed that women had to be 2.5 times more productive to receive the same score as men. An analysis of publications in a biology journal determined that the acceptance rate for female first-authored manuscripts increased when the journal switched from single- to double-blind review (Budden et al., 2007). Similarly, another study revealed that female musicians were more likely to be hired with blind auditions, where performers work behind a screen that hides their identities, than with open auditions (Goldin & Rouse, 2000).

Although generally men are presumed to have greater competence than women, women are expected to show higher competence than men in stereotypically feminine contexts and, as a result, women have more legitimacy as influence agents in such contexts. Consequently, women's persuasive influence goes up for topics that are stereotypically feminine, such as child care, whereas men's influence increases for masculine topics, such as sports and the military (Chatman, Boisnier, Spataro, Anderson, & Berdahl, 2008; Falbo, Hazen, & Linimon, 1982; Feldman-Summers, Montano, Kasprzyk, & Wagner, 1980; Gerrard, Breda, & Gibbons, 1990; Lee, 2004). In mock jury experiments, a female expert witness exerted more influence over the amount of damages awarded to a plaintiff when the case involved a cosmetics company rather than automobile service business

(McKimmie, Newton, Terry, & Schuller, 2004) or a clothing company rather than a construction company (Schuller, Terry, & McKimmie, 2001). In another study involving a case of a battered woman accused of murder for killing her abuser, participants voted to acquit more often when the expert for the defense was female and not male (Schuller & Cripps, 1998). Nevertheless, men's overall advantage as influence agents is apparent from their greater influence than women in gender-neutral contexts (Carli, 1990; Eagly & Carli, 2007; Lee, 2004; Taps & Martin, 1990).

## Communality, Gender, and Social Influence

It may seem that women could overcome their influence deficit by increasing their agentic behavior. But because women face the double bind, women may lack influence either from too much or too little agency. Women are expected to be communal, and many agentic behaviors, such as assertiveness or competitiveness, are antithetical to communion. Indeed, studies have shown that women's influence is undermined by any signs of dominance or lack of concern for others (Burgoon, Birk, & Hall, 1991; Burgoon, Dillard, & Doran, 1983; Copeland, Driskell, & Salas, 1995; Mehta et al., 1989, as cited in Ellyson et al., 1992). For example, women who seem motivated by a desire for power lack influence relative to men. In one experiment, participants reported being less inclined to vote for a female than a male politician; the woman's perceived desire for power undermined her influence, but the man's desire for power had no effect on his (Okimoto & Brescoll, 2010). Moreover, a second experiment revealed that when politicians' Web sites described them as highly ambitious and power seeking, participants perceived the female politician, but not the male, as less communal, which reduced their willingness to vote for the woman (Okimoto & Brescoll, 2010).

Being too forceful or demanding undermines women's influence in gaining employment. In one experiment, participants viewed a videotape of a job interview in which the applicants described themselves as having felt angry or sad after losing an important account (Brescoll & Uhlmann, 2008). Participants rated female applicants as less deserving to be hired and to have status, power, and independence in the new job when she expressed anger rather than sadness, whereas the reverse was true for men. In another experiment using similar methodology, the male and female applicants described their leadership style as either agentic (i.e., being in charge, leaning on people) or communal (reaching consensus, encouraging people) (Phelan, Moss-Racusin, & Rudman, 2008). There were no differences in how hirable participants judged male and female applicants to be in the communal condition, but in the agentic condition, participants preferred to hire men over women. Other studies have shown that participants rate women job applicants as less hirable than men for being tactless and highly critical of others (Rudman et al., 2012). Likewise, research on negotiation has revealed that asking for a raise, which people perceive as less nice and more demanding than not asking, causes people to especially judge women to be unhirable relative to men (Bowles, Babcock, & Lai, 2007).

Another obstacle to female influence is that self-promotion is perceived differently in women than in men. The goal of self-promotion, of course, is to present oneself as highly competent, and in fact, individuals who self-promote are seen as more competent than individuals who behave more modestly (Carli, 2006; Miller, Cooke, Tsang, & Morgan, 1992; Rudman, 1998). This boon to perceived agency should generally enhance influence, yet because self-promotion lacks social sensitivity (Miller et al., 1992) and is intrinsically noncommunal, self-promoting behavior lessens women's influence. In the mock-jury study in which participants reported how likely a defendant was to commit future violence, participants listened to the testimony of a male or female expert who communicated in a warm likeable style by smiling, conveying modesty, and speaking informally or in a more cold and immodest style by using jargon and appearing arrogant (Neal, Guadagno, Eno, & Brodsky, 2012). Results revealed that there were no gender effects in the warm modest condition, but women's influence was reduced compared with men in the immodest condition. Thus, immodesty hurt women more than men. These findings have been confirmed in other research showing that self-promotion reduces women's influence, but not men's (Carli, 2006; Rudman, 1998).

Even mere competence, without any dominance or aggressiveness, is at times an impediment to women's influence. One investigation examined patients' intention to comply with a physician's advice as a function of the gender and communal and task behaviors of the physician (Christen, Alder, & Bitzer, 2008). Compliance was significantly predicted only by communal behaviors, which female physicians engaged in much more than male physicians did ($d = .80$). Nevertheless, there was no effect of physician gender on compliance. Thus, communal women had about as much influence as noncommunal men. Similarly, corporate executives participating in an organizational study indicated whether they would hire a job applicant after having read the applicant's résumé and a transcript of his or her job interview (Buttner & McEnally, 1996). Applicants communicated in one of three styles, the most competent of which involved being direct and showing initiative. The executives were most persuaded to hire men when they displayed the most competent style and least persuaded to hire women when they displayed the same style.

To overcome resistance to their agentic influence, women can temper agentic behavior with communion. Behavior that might otherwise seem overly demanding can be acceptable in women if there is evidence that it is motivated by communal goals. Evidence of this can be found in organizational research. Studies in which participants negotiated salaries for either themselves or for someone else revealed that women, but not men, had greater influence when negotiating on behalf of others rather than on their own behalf (Bowles, Babcock, & McGinn, 2005). A similar study found that women negotiating for a group exerted just as much influence as men, even though both the men and women used an agentic negotiation style (Amanatullah & Tinsley, 2008, cited in Tinsley, Cheldelin, Schneider, & Amanatullah, 2009). Another negotiation study demonstrated that women seeking higher salaries had more favorable negotiation outcomes when they justified their request either as something they were instructed to do by a team leader or as a means of contributing to the organization (Bowles & Babcock, 2012). Another experiment revealed that women who combined agentic and communal nonverbal behavior increased their influence over those who were merely agentic (Carli, LaFleur, & Loeber, 1995). Similarly, women's somewhat greater reliance on transformational leadership, which blends agentic and communal qualities, may be one way that women can overcome their perceived disadvantage as leaders and influence agents (Eagly, Gartzia, & Carli, 2014).

Unlike women, men have considerable flexibility to behave either agentically or communally without penalty (e.g., Bolino & Turnley, 2003; Carli, LaFleur, & Loeber, 1995; Copeland, Driskell, & Salas, 1995; Heilman et al., 2004; Mehta et al., 1989, cited in Ellyson, Dovidio, & Brown, 1992; Sterling & Owen, 1982). Thus, men have a broader behavioral repertoire as leaders and influence agents. In fact, male communion can be perceived especially favorably (Heilman & Chen, 2005; Meltzer & McNulty, 2011), likely because such behavior is unexpected and unrequired.

## Male Resistance to Female Influence

Women have more difficulty influencing others than men do, but women are at a particular disadvantage when attempting to influence men (Carli, 2001; Lee, 2004), and this is especially true when women behave agentically (Elias & Cropanzano, 2006; Ridgeway, 1981). When male and female college students were asked whether they would comply with the harsh influence tactics of a male or female professor, the condition showing least compliance was that of male students in response to a female professor (Elias & Cropanzano, 2006). Men are also more likely than women to dislike and resist the influence of competent women, instead yielding more to women who communicate in less competent ways (Carli, 1990; Carli et al., 1995; Matschiner & Murnen, 1999; Weiman, 1985). For example, studies reveal that mitigated language, which involves the use of tag questions (e.g., "right?" or "don't you think?"), hedges (e.g., "kinda" or "maybe"), and disclaimers (e.g., "I may be wrong, but... ") can actually increase women's influence with men, despite the fact that use of such language by women is associated with a reduction in women's perceived competence (Carli, 1990; Reid, Keerie, & Palomares, 2003; Reid, Palomares, Anderson, & Bondad-Brown, 2009). Men yield to a less competent woman because they perceive the more competent woman to be threatening or less likeable. Although behaving in a relatively incompetent manner may seem counterintuitive as a social influence tactic, it can be functional in interactions among status unequals. Mitigated language has been shown to be effective at facilitating the influence of relatively low-status individuals in interactions with someone of higher status because it increases their likability (Loyd, Phillips, Whitson, & Thomas-Hunt, 2010).

Other evidence of greater male resistance to female influence comes from hiring studies. Men show a stronger preference to hire male job applicants over female applicants than women do (Koch, D'Mello & Sackett, 2015), even when the female applicants have superior credentials (Foschi, Lai, & Sigerson, 1994; Uhlmann & Cohen, 2005). In one study, when a male candidate was slightly superior to a female candidate, male participants selected the man; however, when the slightly superior candidate was the woman, male participants showed no increased preference to hire the woman (Foschi et al., 1994). Women, on the other hand, selected male and female applicants based on their professional records, preferring the superior candidates.

The general tendency of men to resist female influence is consistent with other research showing that men hold more traditional views about gender. Men endorse traditional gender roles (Twenge, 1997a) and evaluate female leaders more harshly than women do (Eagly, Makhijani, & Klonsky, 1992). Men also associate leadership competence less with feminine characteristics than women do (Koenig, Eagly, Mitchell, & Ristikari, 2011; Schein, 2001).

Research findings suggest that women are particularly disadvantaged as influence agents when interacting in groups where men are in the majority. In one experiment, even though the task was gender neutral, being a token woman reduced women's influence compared with groups that had equal numbers of men and women (Taps & Martin, 1990). Similar findings have been reported in surveys of women in organizational groups, where women reported less influence when they were in the minority than the majority and less influence than men who were in the minority (Izraeli, 1983, 1984). Moreover, men actually experience benefits from a token status. One study revealed that being a token undermined women's influence in a small group discussion task, but actually enhanced men's (Craig & Sherif, 1986). Organizational studies also confirm that men fare better as tokens than women do. Specifically, studies show that token men advance more rapidly than token women do, and they receive greater job benefits and pay (e.g., Hultin, 2003; Smith, 2012; Williams, 1992). These findings show that women in the minority, and token women in particular, may find it especially difficult to be influential, whereas the opposite is true for men. Minority status tends to highlight gender stereotypes and elicit greater gender stereotypical behavior (Yoder, 2002), a condition that favors male influence. One exception has been found to this general pattern, however: Women's token status can enhance her influence concerning stereotypically feminine tasks (Chatman et al., 2008). Female gender stereotypes, which would be particularly salient when women are tokens, would lead to high performance expectations for women in traditionally female domains.

Some scholars have noted that senior women are sometimes more resistant to female agency than men are, a phenomenon known as the queen bee syndrome (Derks, van Laar, Ellemers, & de Groot, 2011; Ellemers, Van Den Heuvel, De Gilder, Maass, & Bonvini, 2004). When does this occur? Senior women are less inclined to support the advancement of other women when they start their careers with relatively little gender identification, have a career in a male-dominated field, and advance while experiencing gender bias, thus experiencing a threat to their identity that can be overcome through denial of gender discrimination (Derks, Ellemers, van Laar, & de Groot, 2011; Derks, van Laar, Ellemers, & de Groot, 2011).

Although the queen bee syndrome does explain differences among women in their support of other women, there is little evidence that women obstruct other women more than men do and no evidence that women resist female influence more than men do. Recent evidence of the queen bee syndrome comes from studies in the Netherlands and Italy, where female faculty rated female doctoral students as less committed to their work than male doctoral students; male faculty did not differ in their ratings of the male and female students (Ellemers, van den Heuvel, de Gilder, Maass, & Bonvini, 2004).

A few studies that have been described in the literature as revealing greater female obstruction actually do not. Specifically, one study found that both men and women reported that an agentic woman was less likeable and had a less desirable personality than a communal woman (Parks-Stamm, Heilman, & Hearns, 2008). There were no gender differences in derogating the woman for being agentic. Instead, women, but not men, rated themselves more favorably when reading about the agentic rather than the communal woman, suggesting that women may have a self-serving motivation to derogate agentic women. A second study described as revealing greater derogation of an agentic woman by women than by men (Mathison, 1986) did not measure derogation. It only showed gender differences in how dynamic the agentic woman was rated to be: Women rated her as more dynamic (i.e., bold, active, emphatic, aggressive, and energetic) than men did. A third study asked participants to evaluate the career prospects of male or female leaders (Garcia-Retamero & Lopex-Zafra, 2006). There were no gender-of-participant effects in rating the performance of the female leader, her character, or her use of transformational leadership. Compared with male participants, female participants did report that for leaders working in a male-dominated field, the woman would be less likely to be promoted than the man when the leaders worked. Thus, women seemed more aware than men of obstacles to promotion for women in male-dominated fields. Thus, although women can sometimes be more resistant to female authority than men, such instances are relatively atypical.

## Gender and Influenceability

Up until this point, I have explored gender differences in men's and women's influence, which reflects contemporary scholarly interest in women's leadership and advancement and the backlash against women as leaders and agents of influence and power. However, early research examining gender and influence effects focused on gender differences in influenceability, the extent to which men versus women yield to the influence of others. Although I was not able to find much current research designed to specifically test for gender differences in influenceability, some recent persuasion and conformity studies with male and female participants have included gender of participants in their analyses. Thus, the results of these studies can be compared to those found 35 years ago and reviewed in a meta-analysis of this literature by Eagly and Carli (1981).

The meta-analysis of gender differences in influenceability revealed small effects, with women being more easily persuaded and more conforming than men; the effects were somewhat larger for conformity than persuasion, particularly when the conformity involved group pressure (Eagly & Carli, 1981). The gender effects, however, were affected by a number of mediators. For persuasion studies, the sex typing of the topics used in the studies was associated with the significance of the gender difference outcomes and marginally associated with the effect sizes of the differences: Studies that included topics that were more interesting to men than to women elicited greater evidence of female persuadability, whereas topics that were more interesting to women than to men elicited greater evidence of male persuadability. This finding is consistent with research discussed earlier in this review showing that women exert greater influence for feminine topics and men exert greater influence for masculine topics. Thus, both genders are more influential and less yielding for topics that stereotypically favor their gender.

In addition to the sex-typing of topics, the Eagly and Carli (1981) meta-analysis revealed that the gender difference in influenceability was also affected by the year of publication and by the gender of the authors of the studies. Studies that had later publication dates were less likely to have significant gender differences in influenceability, suggesting that any gender effect was shrinking over time. Finally, studies authored primarily by women, where 50 percent or more of the authors were female, revealed no gender differences, whereas studies authored by men did. In interpreting this result, Eagly and Carli suggested that the gender of the authors of studies might affect reporting of results, especially when those results reveal nonsignificant gender-of-participant effects. Although reporting of significant findings is considered mandatory, reporting nonsignificant ones remains optional. Possibly, both men and women report nonsignificant findings more often when those results reflect more favorably on their own gender.

To further test this claim, the researchers examined the effect of the gender of the authors on studies included in a review of gender differences in nonverbal decoding ability (Hall, 1978), a literature that revealed a female advantage in decoding skill. Results confirmed that male authors were less likely than female authors to report results showing this female advantage, suggesting that both male and female researchers tend to report results that reflect favorably on their own gender (Eagly & Carli, 1981). Although meta-analytic reviews do not always reveal gender-of-author effects, there is some evidence of authors favoring their own gender: For example, male authors are less likely than female authors to report that men interrupt others intrusively (Anderson & Leaper, 1998) and that there is a female advantage in verbal ability (Hyde & Linn, 1988). In the case of studies on gender and influenceability, the majority of authors were male (i.e., about 80 percent), suggesting that the true gender differences might have been smaller with a greater gender balance among the authors. Overall, gender differences in influenceability were modest, clearer for conformity than persuasion research, and subject to possible reporting biases.

What do more contemporary studies reveal about gender differences in influenceability? With some exceptions (i.e., Mullennix, Stern, Wilson, & Dyson, 2003), most studies examining gender effects in persuasion have found no gender differences (e.g., Carli, 1989, 1990; Carli, LaFleur, & Loeber, 1995; Frey & Eagly, 1993; Meyers-Levy, 1988; Perse, Nathanson, & McLeod, 1996; Petty & Cacioppo, 1984; Pfau, van Bockern, & Kang, 1992; Schouten, 2008; Smith & Stutts, 2003;

Stern, Mullennix, & Yaroslavsky, 2006). Moreover, studies have revealed that both women and men are more persuaded by messages that have greater consistency with the beliefs or values of their gender than the other gender (Delhomme, Chappé, Grenier, Pinto, & Martha, 2010; Wang, Bristol, Mowen, & Chakraborty, 2000). For example, national surveys indicate that women more strongly endorse safe driving practices and drive more safely than men do (US National Highway Traffic Safety Administration, 2003), and, as expected, one study found greater persuasion among women than men to messages advocating safe driving (Lewis, Watson, & Tay, 2007).

Although few studies have revealed main effects of gender on persuadability, there is evidence that gender interacts with other factors. One such factor is whether the persuasive message is sent by computer or conveyed face to face. Studies by Guadagno and Cialdini (2002, 2007) examining same-gender interactions have revealed that women are less likely to be persuaded by computer-mediated communications, such as e-mail, than face-to-face communications; men, on the other hand, are either equally persuaded by both computer-mediated and face-to-face communications or, in some instances, more persuaded by computer-mediated communications. The authors attribute these differences to the women's relative cooperativeness in interactions with other women, which are enhanced in face-to-face interactions, and men's relative competitiveness in interactions with other men, which are attenuated when interactions are conducted electronically. Other research has documented greater communion and cooperativeness in interactions between women than interactions between men (e.g., Carli, 1989; LaFrance, Hect, & Paluck, 2003; Leaper & Ayres, 2007; see Carli, 2013).

Marketing studies have also examined gender effects on influenceability in studies of reactions to advertising. One marketing study revealed that men preferred and were more influenced by simple ads and those that compared one product with another, whereas women preferred and were more influenced by complex ads and those that avoided critical comparisons among products (Putrevu, 2004). Women's persuadability is also more likely than men's to be affected by the wording of the ad. For example, one study found that women, but not men, are affected by the serial position of information in ads (Meyers-Levy & Sternthal, 1991). Another study compared men's and women's reactions to ads that contained claims that varied in objectivity and products that varied in riskiness; women's persuadability and judgments about the ads varied as a function of objectivity and riskiness, but men's did not (Darley & Smith, 1995). Women are also affected more than men by the negative or positive framing in the ad. Putrevu (2010), in a series of marketing studies, found that women were less persuaded than men by ads that used negative frames (i.e., emphasizing avoiding negative consequences), whereas men and women were equally persuaded by ads using positive frames (i.e., emphasizing gaining benefits).

One explanation for these findings is that women, compared with men, engage in more elaborative or relational processing—focusing more on the details within the message and on the similarities and differences in message content between ads—whereas men focus more on particular salient details of a message and the general gist that a message conveys (Darley & Smith, 1995; Meyers-Levey & Maheswaran, 1991; Meyers-Levey & Sternthal, 1991; for a review, see Wolin, 2003). Thus, women pay more attention than men to the details in the message, and, as a result, their persuadability is more contingent on message characteristics than men's persuadability is.

In the Eagly and Carli (1981) meta-analysis, larger gender differences in influenceability were obtained for conformity studies than persuasion studies, suggesting that even if there are no longer overall gender differences in persuadability, there still might be gender effects in conformity settings. Is this the case? Contemporary studies examining gender differences in conformity have often found no gender difference (Amir, 1984; Foschi & Freeman, 1991; Foschi & Lapointe, 2002; Lee, 2005, 2007, study 1). One study reporting a difference measured how often men and women would wait in line to use an ATM when another nearby ATM was free and available (Reysen & Reysen, 2004). The authors reported that women waited in line more often than men and attributed this finding to greater female conformity, but this result could also simply reflect women's greater social awareness and nonverbal sensitivity (see Avtgis, 2005). That is, women may simply have been more likely than men to notice the line and interpret it to mean that the available ATM was out of order.

Other studies have revealed that the direction of the gender difference varies depending on experimental conditions. As found in the meta-analysis (Eagly & Carli, 1981), gender-typed topics continue to affect gender differences in conformity such that men conform more on stereotypical feminine topics (Lee, 2003; Maupin & Fisher, 1989) and women conform more on stereotypical masculine topics (Lee, 2003, 2007, study 2; Maupin & Fisher, 1989).

Kalkhoff, Younts, and Troyer (2008) reported a group composition effect on gender differences in conformity: No gender differences emerged in same-gender groups, but women conformed more in mixed-gender groups. In mixed-gender interactions, gender differences may reflect greater male resistance to female influence or simply greater male influence, overall, rather than greater female conformity. Indeed, expectation states theorists have used mixed-gender conformity studies to specifically test predictions based on the theory that men possess greater status and perceived competence and thus wield more influence than women, and these studies have revealed just such effects (e.g., Hopcroft, 2002; Troyer, 2001). Consistent with this interpretation, another study of conformity in mixed-gender dyads eliminated the gender difference in perceived ability prior to the conformity task. In this study, participants completed a knowledge test and were given fictitious information about their scores relative to their partner's (Maupin & Fisher, 1989). Results revealed no gender differences in conformity when participants were informed that their partner scored as well as they did on the test, but when informed that the female member of the pair had outscored the male member, men conformed more than women. The gender difference was due to an increase in conformity among men in the female-superior condition compared with the equal-ability condition, rather than a drop in conformity in the women.

Finally, two recent studies of computer-mediated communications found no overall gender difference in conformity, but interactions of gender with other variables. Lee (2006) reported that female participants showed greater conformity when they had no information about the other ostensible participants than when they had exchanged personal information with those participants, whereas male participants were equally conforming whether they had exchanged personal information or not. This result was the opposite of that predicted by Lee, who had expected women to be more receptive to influence in more personal interactions because of women's presumed greater attention to social cues. In a second study, participants completed a test of logic and general knowledge while exposed to erroneous answers by other online participants (Rosander & Eriksson, 2012). Counter to the researchers' predictions, men were more conforming than women on logic, but not knowledge questions, and men were more inclined than women to conform as questions increased in difficulty. The implications of these two studies are unclear and their results are idiosyncratic. Without additional research replicating these findings, it is difficult to derive general conclusions about gender and social influence from them.

In summary, research on gender differences in influenceability show little evidence of overall gender differences. Both men and women yield more to persuasive messages that are more consistent with the attitudes of their gender and both genders are less conforming on topics that favor their gender. Women, but not men, respond less to computer-mediated messages than face-to-face messages, and women's influence is affected to a greater degree than men's by the content, wording, and framing of messages because women process messages more elaboratively. Finally, the presence of gender differences in mixed-gender conformity settings is likely a function of men's general greater influence and is consistent with stereotypes associating maleness with agency and authority.

## Conclusion

In summary, women experience an influence deficit. Influence attempts by women are generally less successful than similar attempts by men. Gender stereotypes paint women as especially communal and men as especially agentic, which should create a draw in terms of influence, with men having the competence advantage and women the likability advantage. But people demand more communion from women than men and particularly resist the influence of agentic women—that is, women who are dominant, self-promoting, assertive, and sometimes only merely competent. Thus, the perception that women are more communal than men confers little advantage to women and, instead, creates a double bind: Women may lack influence for being too agentic or not agentic enough. On one hand, people hold women to higher performance standards and judge women more harshly than men, doubting women's competence and agency. On the other hand, women who challenge doubts about their abilities, by performing competently and assertively, may be seen as lacking communion and hence unlikable.

Research indicates that men in particular resist female influence. This is especially true for highly competent women. Although both men

and women dislike dominance in women because dominance is quite incompatible with the selflessness and other-directedness of the female gender role, men react more harshly than women do to female competence. Indeed, women have sometimes been more successful in influencing men by behaving incompetently—for example, by speaking in an uncertain and mitigated manner. Moreover, women's influence deficit increases when they are in the minority, and especially when they have a token status. Men, in contrast, actually benefit as tokens, wielding greater influence and authority.

Gender differences in influence are consistent with predictions based on social role and status characteristics theories. Women's relative absence from high-status roles and men's relative absence from domestic roles help to maintain gender stereotypes and women's disadvantage as influence agents. However, it is likely that as women's roles change, with an increasing proportion of women entering paid employment and higher status occupational roles, gender differences in influence might change as well. Evidence indicates that this is already occurring: Women over time have become increasingly agentic—more assertive, dominant, and masculine (Twenge, 1997b, 2001). Given that throughout the 20th century women's agency has increased and decreased as a function of their career and educational opportunities, it is likely that this trend will continue (Twenge, 2001). Women are increasingly well educated, compared with men, now receiving the majority of bachelor's and advanced degrees (U.S. National Center for Education Statistics, 2010, Table 279). There are also increasing numbers of women in leadership positions and increasingly favorable attitudes toward women leaders (Carli & Eagly, 2011). Furthermore, perceptions of successful leadership have also changed to be more androgynous (Koenig et al., 2011), thereby increasing the association of authority and influence with communal qualities as opposed to agentic ones. These should weaken the double bind, making both female agency and communion more compatible. Thus, although women continue to experience resistance to their influence, there is reason to expect this to change. Women of the future may find that they are no longer constrained by the double bind and that they wield as much influence as men do.

## References

Allen, T. D. (2006). Rewarding good citizens: The relationship between citizenship behavior, gender, and organizational rewards. *Journal of Applied Psychology*, *36*, 120–143. doi:10.1111/j.0021-9029.2006.00006.x

Amanatullah, E. T., & Tinsley, C. H., (2008). *Accepting assertive advocates: The moderation of the backlash effect against assertive women due to advocacy.* Working Paper, Georgetown University.

Amir, T. (1984). The Asch conformity effect: A study in Kuwait. *Social Behavior and Personality*, *12*, 187–190. doi:10.2224/sbp.1984.12.2.187

Anderson, K. J., & Leaper, C. (1998). Meta-analyses of gender effects on conversational interruption: Who, what, when, where, and how. *Sex Roles*, *39*(3-4), 225–252. doi:10.1023/A:1018802521676

Avtgis, T. A. (2005). Sex differences on a measure of confromtiy: Comments on a recent study. *Psychological Reports*, *96*, 306.

Berger, J., Fisek, M. H., Norman, R. Z., & Zelditch, M., Jr. (1977). *Status characteristics and social interactions: An expectation states approach.* New York, NY: Elsevier Science.

Biernat, M., & Kobrynowicz, D. (1997). Gender and race-based standards of competence: Lower minimum standards but higher ability standards for devalued groups. *Journal of Personality and Social Psychology*, *72*, 544–557. doi:10.1037/0022-3514.72.3.544

Biernat, M., Tocci, M. J., & Williams, J. C. (2012). The language of performance evlauations: Gender-based shifts in content and consistency of judgment. *Social Psychology and Personality Science*, *3*, 186–192. doi:10.1177/1948550611415693

Boldry, J., Wood, W., & Kashy, D. A. (2001). Gender stereotypes and the evaluation of men and women in military training. *Journal of Social Issues*, *57*, 689–705. doi:10.1111/0022-4537.00236

Bolino, M. C., & Turnley, W. H. (2003). Counternormative impression manangement, likeability, and performance ratings: The use of intimidation in an organizational setting. *Jounral of Organizational Behavior*, *24*, 237-250.

Bosak, J., Sczesny, S., & Eagly, A. H. (2008). Communion and agency judgments of women and men as a function of role information and response format. *European Journal of Social Psychology*, *38*, 1148–1155. doi:10.1002/ejsp.538

Bowles, H., & Babcock, L. (2012). How can women escape the compensation negotiation dilemma? Relational accounts are one answer. *Psychology of Women Quarterly*, *37*, 80–96. doi:10.1177/0361684312455524

Bowles, H., Babcock, L., & Lai, L. (2007). Social incentives for gender differences in the propensity to initiate negotiations: Sometimes it does hurt to ask. *Organizational Behavior and Human Decision Processes*, *103*, 84–103. doi:10.1016/j.obhdp.2006.09.001

Bowles, H., Babcock, L., & McGinn, K. L. (2005). Constraints and triggers: Situational mechanics of gender in negotiation. *Journal of Personality and Social Psychology*, *89*, 951–965. doi:10.1037/0022-3514.89.6.951

Brescoll, V. L. (2011). Who takes the floor and why: Gender, power, and volubility in organizations. *Administrative Science Quarterly*, *56*, 622–641. doi:10.1177/0001839212439994

Brescoll, V. L., & Uhlmann, E. (2008). Can an angry woman get ahead? Status conferral, gender, and expression of emotion in the workplace. *Psychological Science*, *19*, 268–275. doi:10.1037/0022-3514.89.6.9514

Briñol, P., & Petty, R. E. (2009). Source factors in persuasion: A self-validation approach. *European Review of Social Psychology*, *20*, 49–96. doi:10.1080/10463280802643640

Broverman, I. K., Broverman, D. M., Clarkson, F. E., Rosenkrantz, P. S., & Vogel, S. R. (1970). Sex-role stereotypes and clinical judgments of mental health. *Journal of Consulting and Clinical Psychology*, *34*, 1–7. doi:10.1037/h0028797

Broverman, I. K., Vogel, S. R., Broverman, D. M., Clarkson, F. E., & Rosenkrantz, P. S. (1972). Sex role stereotypes: A current appraisal. *Journal of Social Issues*, *28*, 59–78. doi:10.1111/j.1540-4560.1972.tb00018.x

Budden, A. E., Tregenza, T., Aarssen, L. W., Koricheva, J., Leimu, T., & Lortie, C. J. (2007). Double-blind review favours increased representation of female authors. *Trends in Ecology and Evolution*, *23*, 4–6.

Burgoon, M., Birk, T. S., & Hall, J. R. (1991). Compliance and satisfaction with physician-patient communication: An expectancy theory interpretation of gender differences. *Human Communication Research*, *18*, 177–208. doi:10.1111/j.1468-2958.1991.tb00543.x

Burgoon, M., Dillard, J. P., & Doran, N. E. (1983). Friendly or unfriendly persuasion: The effects of violations by males and females. *Human Communication Research*, *10*, 283–294. doi:10.1111/j.1468-2958.1983.tb00018.x

Butler, D., & Geis, F. L. (1990). Nonverbal affect responses to male and female leaders: Implications for leadership evaluations. *Journal of Personality and Social Psychology*, *58*, 48–59. doi:10.1037/0022-3514.58.1.48

Buttner, E. H., & McEnally, M. (1996). The interactive effect of influence tactic, applicant gender, and type of job on hiring recommendations. *Sex Roles*, *34*, 581–591. doi:10.1007/BF01545034

Carli, L. L. (1989). Gender differences in interaction style and influence. *Journal of Personality and Social Psychology*, *56*, 565–576. doi:10.1037/0022-3514.56.4.565

Carli, L. L. (1990). Gender, language, and influence. *Journal of Personality and Social Psychology*, *59*, 941–951. doi:10.1037/0022-3514.59.5.941

Carli, L. L. (1991). Gender, status, and influence. In E. J. Lawler, B. Markovsky, C. Ridgeway, & H. A. Walker (Eds.), *Advances in group processes: Theory and research* (Vol. 8, pp. 89–113). Greenwich, CT: JAI Press.

Carli, L. L. (1999). Gender, interpersonal power, and social influence. *Journal of Social Issues*, *55*, 81–99. doi:10.1111/0022-4537.00106

Carli, L. L. (2001). Gender and social influence. *Journal of Social Issues*, *57*, 725–742. doi:10.1111/0022-4537.00238

Carli, L. L. (2006, July). *Gender and social influence: Women confront the double bind.* Paper presented at the International Congress of Applied Psychology, Athens, Greece.

Carli, L. L. (2013). Gendered communication and social influence. In M. K. Ryan & N. R. Branscombe (Eds.), *The Sage handbook of gender and psychology* (pp. 199–215). London, England: Sage.

Carli, L. L., & Eagly, A. H. (1999). Gender effects on social influence and emergent leadership. In G. N. Powell (Ed.), *Handbook of gender and work* (pp. 203–222). Thousand Oaks, CA: Sage.

Carli, L. L., & Eagly, A. H. (2011). Gender and leadership. In D. Collinson, A. Bryman, K. Grint, B. Jackson, & M. Uhl Bien (Eds.), *The Sage handbook of leadership* (pp. 269–285). London, England: Sage.

Carli, L. L., LaFleur, S. J., & Loeber, C. C. (1995). Nonverbal behavior, gender, and influence. *Journal of Personality and Social Psychology*, *68*, 1030–1041. doi:10.1037/0022-3514.68.6.1030

Cejka, M. A., & Eagly, A. H. (1999). Gender-stereotypic images of occupations correspond to the sex segregation of employment. *Personality and Social Psychology Bulletin, 25*, 413–423.

Chatman, J. A., Boisnier, A. D., Spataro, S. E., Anderson, C., & Berdahl, J. L. (2008). Being distinctive versus being conspicuous: The effects of numeric status and sex-stereotyped tasks on individual performance in groups. *Organizational Behavior and Human Decision Processes, 107*, 141–160. doi:10.1016/j.obhdp.2008.02.006

Christen, R. N., Alder, J., & Bitzer, J. (2008). Gender differences in physicians' communicative skill and their influence on patient satisfaction in gynaecological outpatient consultations. *Social Science and Medicine, 66*, 1474–1483. doi:10.1016/j.socscimed.2007.12.011

Cialdini, R. B. (2001). *Influence: Science and practice.* Boston, MA: Allyn and Bacon.

Cialdini, R. B., & Goldstein, N. J. (2004). Social influence: Compliance and conformity. *Annual Review of Psychology, 55*, 591–621. doi:10.1146/annurev.psych.55.090902.142015

Cooper, J., Bennett, E. A., & Sukel, H. L. (1996). Complex scientific testimony: How do jurors make decisions? *Law and Human Behavior, 20*, 379–394. doi:10.1007/BF01498976

Copeland, C. L., Driskell, J. E., & Salas, E. (1995). Gender and reactions to dominance. *Journal of Social Behavior and Personality, 10*, 53–68.

Correll, S. J., & Ridgeway, C. L. (2003). Expectation states theory. In J. Delamater (Ed.), *Handbook of social psychology* (pp. 29–51). New York, NY: Plenum Publishers.

Craig, J. M., & Sheriff, C. W. (1986). The effectiveness of men and women in problem-solving groups as a function of group gender composition. *Sex Roles, 14*, 453-466.

Darley, W. K., & Smith, R. E. (1995). Gender differences in information processing strategies: An empirical test of the selectivity model in advertising response. *Journal of Advertising, 24*, 41–56.

Davison, H. K., & Burke, M. J. (2000). Sex discrimination in simulated employment contexts: A meta-analytic investigation. *Journal of Vocational Behavior, 56*, 225–248. doi:10.1006/jvbe.1999.1711

Deaux, K., & Kite, M. (1993). Gender stereotypes. In F. L. Denmark & M. A. Paludi (Eds.), *Psychology of women: A handbook of issues and theories* (pp. 107–139). Westport, CT: Greenwood Press.

Delhomme, P. P., Chappé, J. J., Grenier, K. K., Pinto, M. M., & Martha, C. C. (2010). Reducing air-pollution: A new argument for getting drivers to abide by the speed limit? *Accident Analysis and Prevention, 42*, 327–338. doi:10.1016/j.aap.2009.08.013

Derks, B., Ellemers, N., van Laar, C., & de Groot, K. (2011). Do sexist organizational cultures create the queen bee? *British Journal of Social Psychology, 50*, 519–535. doi:10.1348/014466610X525280

Derks, B., Van Laar, C., Ellemers, N., & de Groot, K. (2011). Gender-bias primes elicit queen-bee responses among senior policewomen. *Psychological Science, 22*, 1243–1249. doi:10.1177/0956797611417258

DiBerardinis, J., Ramage, K., & Levitt, S. (1984). Risky shift and gender of the advocate: Information theory versus normative theory. *Group and Organization Studies, 9*, 189–200. doi:10.1177/105960118400900204

Diekman, A. B., & Eagly, A. H. (2000). Stereotypes as dynamic constructs: Women and men of the past, present, and future. *Personality and Social Psychology Bulletin, 26*, 1171–1188. doi:10.1177/0146167200262001

Diekman, A. B., & Goodfriend, W. (2006). Rolling with the changes: A role congruity perspective on gender norms. *Psychology of Women Quarterly, 30*, 369–383. doi:10.1111/j.1471-6402.2006.00312.x

Driskell, J. E., Olmstead, B., & Salas, E. (1993). Task cues, dominance cues, and influence in task groups. *Journal of Applied Psychology, 78*, 51–60. doi:10.1037/0021-9010.78.1.51

Eagly, A. H. (1987). *Sex differences in social behavior: A social-role interpretation.* Hillside, NJ: Erlbaum.

Eagly, A. H., & Carli, L. L. (1981). Sex of researchers and sex-typed communications as determinants of sex differences in influenceability: A meta-analysis of social influence studies, *Psychological Bulletin, 90*, 1–20. doi:10.1037/0033-2909.90.1.1

Eagly, A. H., & Carli, L. L. (2007). *Through the labyrinth: The truth about how women become leaders.* Boston, MA: Harvard Business School Press.

Eagly, A. H., Gartzia, L., & Carli, L. L. (2014). Female advantage: Revisited. In S. Kumra, R. Simpson, & R. Burke (Eds.), *The Oxford handbook of gender in organizations.* Oxford, England: Oxford University Press.

Eagly, A. H., Makhijani, M. G., & Klonsky, B. G. (1992). Gender and the evaluation of leaders: A meta-analysis. *Psychological Bulletin, 111*, 3–22. doi:10.1037/0033-2909.111.1.3

Eagly, A. H., & Steffen, V. J. (1984). Gender stereotypes stem from the distribution of women and men into social roles. *Journal of Personality and Social Psychology, 46*, 735–754. doi:10.1037/0022-3514.46.4.735

Eagly, A, H., & Wood, W., (1991). Explaining sex differences in social behavior: A meta-analytic perspective. *Personality and Social Psychology Bulletin, 17*, 306–315. doi:10.1177/0146167291173011

Elias, S. M., & Cropanzano, R. (2006). Gender discrimination may be worse than you think: Testing ordinal interactions in power research. *Journal of General Psychology, 133*, 117–130. doi:10.3200/GENP.133.2.117-130

Ellemers, N., van den Heuvel, H., de Gilder, D., Maass, A., & Bonvini, A. (2004). The underrepresentation of women in science: Differential commitment or the queen bee syndrome? *British Journal of Social Psychology, 43*, 315–338. doi:10.1348/0144666042037999

Ellyson, S. L., Dovidio, J. F., & Brown, C. E. (1992). The look of power: Gender differences in visual dominance behavior. In C. L. Ridgeway (Ed.), *Gender, interaction, and inequality* (pp. 50–80). New York, NY: Springer-Verlag.

Falbo, T., Hazen, M. D., & Linimon, D. (1982). The costs of selecting power bases or messages associated with the opposite sex. *Sex Roles, 8*, 147–157. doi:10.1007/BF00287919

Feldman-Summers, S., Montano, D. E., Kasprzyk, D., & Wagner, B. (1980). Influence attempts when competing views are gender-related: Sex as credibility. *Psychology of Women Quarterly, 5*, 311–320. doi:10.1111/j.1471-6402.1980.tb00964.x

Foschi, M. (1996). Double standards in the evaluation of men and women. *Social Psychology Quarterly, 59*, 237–254. doi:10.2307/2787021

Foschi, M. (2000). Double standards for competence: Theory and research. *Annual Review of Sociology, 26*, 21–42. doi:10.1146/annurev.soc.26.1.21

Foschi, M., & Freeman, S. (1991). Inferior performance, standards, and influence in same-sex dyads. *Canadian Journal of Behavioural Science/Revue Canadienne Des Sciences Du Comportement, 23*, 99–113. doi:10.1037/h0078963

Foschi, M., Lai, L., & Sigerson. K. (1994). Gender and double standards in the assessment of job applicants. *Social Psychology Quarterly, 57*, 326–339. doi:10.2307/2787159

Foschi, M., & Lapointe, V. (2002). On conditional hypotheses and gender as a status characteristic. *Social Psychology Quarterly, 65*, 146–162. doi:10.2307/3090098

Foschi, M., Sigerson, K., & Lebesis, M. (1995). Assessing job applicants: The relative effects of gender, academic record, and decision type. *Small Group Research, 26*, 328–352. doi:10.1177/1046496495263002

Foschi, M., & Valenzuela, J. (2008). Selecting job applicants: Effects from gender, self-presentation, and decision type. *Social Science Research, 37*, 1022–1038. doi:10.1016/j.ssresearch.2007.11.002

Foschi, M., & Valenzuela, J. (2012). Who is the better applicant? Effects from gender, academic record, and type of decision. *Social Science Research, 41*, 949–964. doi:10.1016/j.ssresearch.2012.02.001

Frey, K. P., & Eagly, A. H. (1993). Vividness can undermine the persuasiveness of messages. *Journal of Personality and Social Psychology, 65*, 32–44. doi:10.1037/0022-3514.65.1.32

Garcia-Retamero, R., & López-Zafra, E. (2006). Prejudice against women in male-congenial environments: Perceptions of gender role congruity in leadership. *Sex Roles, 55*, 51-61.

Garcia-Retamero, R., Müller, S. M., & López-Zafra, E. (2011). The malleability of gender stereotypes: Influence of population size on perceptions of men and women in the past, present, and future. *Journal of Social Psychology, 151*, 635–656. doi:10.1080/00224545.2010.522616

Gerrard, M., Breda, C., & Gibbons, F. X. (1990). Gender effects in couples' decision making and contraceptive use. *Journal of Applied Social Psychology, 20*, 449–464. doi:10.1111/j.1559-1816.1990.tb00421.x

Giacalone, R. A., & Riordan, C. A. (1990). Effect of self-presentation on perceptions and recognition in an organization. *Journal of Psychology, 124*, 25–38. doi:10.1080/00223980.1990.10543203

Goldin, C., & Rouse. C. (2000). Orchestrating impartiality: The impact of "blind" auditions on female musicians. *American Economic Review, 90*, 715–741.

Guadagno, R. E., & Cialdini, R. B. (2002). Online persuasion: An examination of gender differences in computer-mediated interpersonal influence. *Group Dynamics: Theory, Research, and Practice, 6*, 38–51. doi:10.1037/1089-2699.6.1.38

Guadagno, R. E., & Cialdini, R. B. (2007). Persuade him by email, but see her in person: Online persuasion revisited. *Computers in Human Behavior, 23*, 999–1015. doi:10.1016/j.chb.2005.08.006

Hall, J. A. (1978). Gender effects in decoding nonverbal cues. *Psychological Bulletin, 85*, 845–857. doi:10.1037/0033-2909.85.4.845

Hall, J. A., & Carter, J. D. (1999). Gender-stereotype accuracy as an individual difference. *Journal of Personality and Social Psychology, 77*, 350–359. doi:10.1037/0022-3514.77.2.350

Hawkins, K. W. (1995). Effects of gender and communication content of leadership emergence in small task-oriented groups. *Small Group Research, 26*, 234–249. doi:10.1177/1046496495262004

Haynes, M. C., & Lawrence, J. S. (2012). Who's to blame? Attributions of blame in unsuccessful mixed-sex work

teams. *Basic and Applied Social Psychology, 34*, 558–564. doi:10.1080/01973533.2012.727312

Heilman, M. E., Block, C. J., & Martell, R. (1995). Sex stereotypes: Do they influence perceptions of managers? In N. J. Struthers (Ed.), *Gender in the workplace* (Special issue). *Journal of Social Behavior and Personality, 10*, 237–252.

Heilman, M. E., & Chen. J. J. (2005). Same behavior, different consequences: Reactions to men's and women's altruistic citizenship behavior. *Journal of Applied Psychology, 90*, 431–441. doi:10.1037/0021-9010.90.3.431

Heilman, M. E., & Haynes, M. C. (2005). No credit where credit is due: Attributional rationalization of women's success in male-female teams. *Journal of Applied Psychology, 90*, 905–916. doi:10.1037/0021-9010.90.5.905

Heilman, M. E., & Okimoto, T. G. (2007). Why are women penalized for success at male tasks? The implied communality deficit. *Journal of Applied Psychology, 92*, 81–92. doi:10.1037/0021-9010.92.1.81

Heilman, M. E., & Wallen, A. S. (2010). Wimpy and undeserving of respect: Penalties for men's gender-inconsistent success. *Journal of Experimental Social Psychology, 46*, 664–667. doi:10.1016/j.jesp.2010.01.008

Heilman, M. E., Wallen, A. S., Fuchs, D., & Tamkins, M. M. (2004). Penalties for success: Reactions to women who succeed in male gender-typed tasks. *Journal of Applied Psychology, 89*, 416–427. doi:10.1037/0021-9010.89.3.416

Holtgraves, T., & Lasky, B. (1999). Linguistic power and persuasion. *Journal of Language and Social Psychology, 18*, 196–205. doi:10.1177/0261927X99018002004

Hopcroft, R. L. (2002). Is gender still a status characteristic? *Current Research in Social Psychology, 7*, 339–347.

Hultin, M. (2003). Some take the glass escalator, some hit the glass ceiling? Career consequences of occupational sex segregation. *Work and Occupations, 30*, 30–61. doi:10.1177/0730888402239326

Hyde, J. S., & Linn, M. C. (1988). Gender differences in verbal ability: A meta-analysis. *Psychological Bulletin, 104*(1), 53–69. doi:10.1037/0033-2909.104.1.53

Izraeli, D. N. (1983). Sex effects or structural effects? An empirical test of Kanter's theory of proportions. *Social Forces, 62*, 153–165. doi:10.2307/2578353

Izraeli, D. N. (1984). The attitudinal effects of gender mix in union committees. *Industrial and Labor Relations Review, 37*, 212–221.

Kalkhoff, W., Younts, C., & Troyer, L. (2008). Facts and artifacts in research: The case of communication medium, gender, and influence. *Social Science Research, 37*, 1008–1021. doi:10.1016/j.ssresearch.2007.08.005

Koch, A. J., D'Mello, S. D., & Sackett, P. R. (2015). A meta-analysis of gender stereotypes and bias in experimental simulations of employment decision making. *Journal of Applied Psychology, 100*, 128-161. doi:10.1037/a0036734

Koenig, A. M., Eagly, A. H., Mitchell, A. A., & Ristikari, T. (2011). Are leader stereotypes masculine? A meta-analysis of three research paradigms. *Psychological Bulletin, 137*, 616–642. doi:10.1037/a0023557

Krueger, J. I., Hasman, J. F., Acevedo, M., & Villano, P. (2003). Perceptions of trait typicality in gender stereotypes: Examining the role of attribution and categorization processes. *Personality and Social Psychology Bulletin, 29*, 108–116. doi:10.1177/0146167202238376

LaFrance, M, Hecht, M. A., & Paluck, E. L. (2003). The contingent smile: A meta-analysis of sex differences in smiling. *Psychological Bulletin, 129*, 305–334.

Leaper, C., & Ayres, M. M. (2007). A meta-analytic review of gender variations in adults language use: Talkativeness, affiliative speech, and assertive speech. *Personality and Social Psychology Review, 11*, 328–363.

Lee, E. (2003). Effects of 'gender' of the computer on informational social influence: The moderating role of task type. *International Journal of Human-Computer Studies, 58*, 347–362.

Lee, E. (2004). Effects of gender character representation on person perception and informational social influence in computer-mediated communication. *Computers in Human Behavior, 20*, 779–799. doi:10.1016/j.chb.2003.11.005

Lee, E. (2005). Effects of the influence agent's sex and self-confidence on informational social influence in computer-mediated communication: Quantitative versus verbal presentation. *Communication Research, 32*, 29–58 doi:10.1177/0093650204271398

Lee, E. (2006). When and how does depersonalization increase conformity to group norms in computer-mediated communication? *Communication Research, 33*, 423–447. doi:10.1177/0093650206293248

Lee, E. (2007). Wired for gender: Experientiality and gender-stereotyping in computer-mediated communication. *Media Psychology, 10*, 182–210. doi:10.1080/15213260701375595

Levin, I. P., Rouwenhorst, R. M., & Trisko, H. M. (2005). Separating gender biases in screening and selecting candidates for hiring and firing. *Social Behavior and Personality, 33*, 793–804. doi:10.2224/sbp.2005.33.8.793

Lewis, I., Watson, B., & Tay, R. (2007). Examining the effectiveness of physical threats in road safety advertising: The role of the third-person effect, gender, and age. *Transportation Research Part F: Traffic Psychology and Behaviour, 10*, 48–60. doi:10.1016/j.trf.2006.05.001

Lockheed, M. E. (1985). Sex and social influence: A meta-analysis guided by theory. In J. Berger & M. Zelditch, Jr. (Eds.), *Status, rewards, and influence: How expectations organize behavior* (pp. 406–429). San Francisco, CA: Jossey-Bass.

Lockheed, M. E., & Hall, K. P. (1976). Conceptualizing sex as a status characteristic: Application to leadership training strategies. *Journal of Social Issues, 32*, 111–124. doi:10.1111/j.1540-4560.1976.tb02600.x

Loyd, D., Phillips, K. W., Whitson, J., & Thomas-Hunt, M. C. (2010). Expertise in your midst: How congruence between status and speech style affects reactions to unique knowledge. *Group Processes and Intergroup Relations, 13*, 379–395. doi:10.1177/1368430209350317

Mathison, D. L. (1986). Sex differences in the perception of assertiveness among female managers. *Journal of Social Psychology, 126*, 599–606. doi:10.1080/00224545.1986.9713632

Matschiner, M., & Murnen, S. K. (1999). Hyperfemininity and influence. *Psychology of Women Quarterly, 23*, 631–642. doi:10.1111/j.1471-6402.1999.tb00385.x

Maupin, H. E., & Fisher, R. J. (1989). The effects of superior female performance and sex-role orientation on gender conformity. *Canadian Journal of Behavioural Science/Revue Canadienne Des Sciences Du Comportement, 21*, 55–69.

McKimmie, B. M., Newton, C. J., Terry, D. J., & Schuller, R. A. (2004). Jurors' responses to expert witness testimony: The effects of gender stereotypes. *Group Processes and Intergroup Relations, 7*, 131–143. doi:10.1177/1368430204043724

Meeker, B. F., & Weitzel-O'Neil, P. A. (1985). Sex roles and interpersonal behavior in task-oriented groups. In J.

Berger & M. Zelditch (Eds.), *Status, rewards, and influence* (pp. 379–405). Washington, DC: Jossey-Bass.

Mehta, P., Dovidio, J. F., Gibbs, R., Miller, K., Huray, K., Ellyson, S. L., & Brown, C. E. (1989, April). *Sex differences in the expression of power motives through visual dominance behavior*. Paper presented at the annual meeting of the Eastern Psychological Association Boston, MA.

Meltzer, A. L., & McNulty, J. K. (2011). Contrast effects of stereotypes: "Nurturing" male professors are evaluated more positively than "nurturing" female professors. *Journal of Men's Studies, 19*, 57–64. doi:10.3149/jms.1901.57

Meyers-Levy, J. (1988). The influence of sex roles on judgment. *Journal of Consumer Research, 14*, 522–530. doi:10.1086/209133

Meyers-Levy, J., & Maheswaran, D. (1991). Exploring differences in males' and females' processing strategies. *Journal of Consumer Research, 18*, 63–70. doi:10.1086/209241

Meyers-Levy, J., & Sternthal, B. (1991). Gender differences in the use of message cues and judgments. *Journal of Marketing Research, 28*, 84–96. doi:10.2307/3172728

Miller, L. C., Cooke, L. L., Tsang, J., & Morgan, F. (1992). Should I brag? Nature and impact of positive and boastful disclosures for women and men. *Human Communication Research, 18*, 364–399. doi:10.1111/j.1468-2958.1992.tb00557.x

Mullennix, J. W., Stern, S. E., Wilson, S. J., & Dyson, C. (2003). Social perception of male and female computer synthesized speech. *Computers in Human Behavior, 19*, 407–424. doi:10.1016/S0747-5632(02)00081-X

Neal, T. M. S., Guadagno, R. E., Eno, C. A., & Brodsky, S. L. (2012). Warmth and competence on the witness stand: Implications for the credibility of male and female expert witnesses. *Journal of the American Academy of Psychiatry and the Law, 40*, 488–497.

Newport, F. (2001, February 21). *Americans see women as emotional and affectionate, men as more aggressive*. Gallup Poll News Service. Retrieved February 2015, from http://www.gallup.com/poll/1978/Americans-See-Women-Emotional-Affectionate-Men-More-Aggressive.aspx

Okimoto, T. G., & Brescoll, V. L. (2010). The price of power: Power seeking and backlash against female politicians. *Personality and Social Psychology Bulletin, 36*, 923–936.

Parks-Stamm, E. J., Heilman, M. E., & Hearns, K. A. (2008). Motivated to penalize: Women's strategic rejection of successful women. *Personality and Social Psychology Bulletin, 34*, 237–247. doi:10.1177/0146167207310027

Perse, E. M., Nathanson, A. I., & McLeod, D. M. (1996). Effects of spokesperson sex, public service announcement appeal, and involvement on evaluations of safe-sex PSAs. *Health Communication, 8*, 171–189. doi:10.1207/s15327027hc0802_4

Petty, R. E., & Cacioppo, J. T. (1984). The effects of involvement on responses to argument quantity and quality: Central and peripheral routes to persuasion. *Journal of Personality and Social Psychology, 46*, 69–81. doi:10.1037/0022-3514.46.1.69

Petty, R. E., & Cacioppo, J. T. (1986). *Communication and persuasion: Central and peripheral routes to attitude change*. New York, NY: Springer-Verlag.

Pfau, M., Van Bockern, S., & Kang, J. (1992). Use of inoculation to promote resistance to smoking initiation among adolescents. *Communication Monographs, 59*, 213–230. doi:10.1080/03637759209376266

Phelan, J. E., Moss-Racusin, C. A., & Rudman, L. A. (2008). Competent yet out in the cold: Shifting criteria for hiring reflect backlash toward agentic women. *Psychology of Women Quarterly, 32*, 406–413. doi:10.1111/j.1471-6402.2008.00454.x

Propp, K. M. (1995). An experimental examination of biological sex as a status cue in decision-making groups and its influence on information use. *Small Group Research, 26*, 451–474. doi:10.1177/1046496495264001

Putrevu, S. (2004). Communicating with the sexes: Male and female responses to print advertisements. *Journal of Advertising, 33*, 51–62.

Putrevu, S. (2010). An examination of consumer responses toward attribute- and goal-framed messages. *Journal of Advertising, 39*, 5–24. doi:10.2753/JOA0091-3367390301

Rashotte, L. S., & Webster, M., Jr. (2005). Gender status beliefs. *Social Science Research, 34*, 618–633. doi:10.1016/j.ssresearch.2004.05.004

Reid, S. A., Keerie, N., & Palomares, N. A. (2003). Language, gender salience, and social influence. *Journal of Language and Social Psychology, 22*, 210–233. doi:10.1177/0261927X03022002004

Reid, S. A., Palomares, N. A., Anderson, G. L., & Bondad-Brown, B. (2009). Gender, language, and social influence: A test of expectation states, role congruity, and self categorization theories. *Human Communication Research, 35*, 465–490. doi:10.1111/j.1468-2958.2009.01359.x

Reysen, S., & Reysen, M. B. (2004). Sex differences on a measure of conformity in automated teller machine lines. *Psychological Reports, 95*(2), 443–446. doi:10.2466/PR0.95.6.443-446

Rhoads, K. V., & Cialdini, R. B. (2002). The business of influence: Principles that lead to success in commercial settings. In J. P. Dillard & M. Pfau (Eds.), *The persuasion handbook: Developments in theory and practice* (pp. 513–542). Thousand Oaks, CA: Sage.

Ridgeway, C. L. (1978). Conformity, group-oriented motivation, and status attainment in small groups. *Social Psychology, 41*, 175–188. doi:10.2307/3033555

Ridgeway, C. L. (1981). Nonconformity, competence and influence in groups: A test of two theories. *American Sociological Review, 46*, 333–347.

Ridgeway, C. (2001). Gender, status, and leadership. *Journal of Social Issues, 57*, 637–655. doi:10.1111/0022-4537.00233

Ridgeway, C. L., & Berger, J. (1986). Expectations, legitimation, and dominance behavior in task groups. *American Sociological Review, 51*, 603–617.

Ridgeway, C. L., & Smith-Lovin L. (1999). Gender and interaction. In J. S. Chafetz (Ed.), *Handbook of the sociology of gender* (pp. 247–274). New York, NY: Plenum.

Rosander, M., & Eriksson, O. (2012). Conformity on the internet—The role of task difficulty and gender differences. *Computers in Human Behavior, 28*, 1587–1595. doi:10.1016/j.chb.2012.03.023

Rudman, L. A. (1998). Self-promotion as a risk factor for women: The costs and benefits of counterstereotypical impression management. *Journal of Personality and Social Psychology, 74*, 629–645. doi:10.1037/0022-3514.74.3.629

Rudman, L. A., Moss-Racusin, C. A., Phelan, J. E., & Nauts, S. (2012). Status incongruity and backlash effects: Defending the gender hierarchy motivates prejudice against female leaders. *Journal of Experimental Social Psychology, 48*, 165–179. doi:10.1016/j.jesp.2011.10.008

Schein, V. E. (2001). A global look at psychological barriers to women's progress in management. *Journal of Social Issues, 57*, 675–688. doi:10.1111/0022-4537.00235

Schneider, J., & Cook, K. (1995). Status inconsistency and gender: Combining revisited. *Small Group Research, 26*, 372–399. doi:10.1177/1046496495263004

Schouten, B. C. (2008). Compliance behavior and the role of ethnic background, source expertise, self-construals and values. *International Journal of Intercultural Relations, 32*, 515–523. doi:10.1016/j.ijintrel.2008.06.006

Schuller, R. A., & Cripps, J. (1998). Expert evidence pertaining to battered women: The impact of gender of expert and timing of testimony. *Law and Human Behavior, 22*, 17–31. doi:10.1023/A:1025772604721

Schuller, R. A., Terry, D., & McKimmie, B. (2001). The impact of an expert's gender on jurors' decisions. *Law & Psychology Review, 25*, 59–79.

Schuller, R. A., Terry, D., & McKimmie, B. (2005). The impact of expert testimony on jurors' decisions: Gender of the expert and testimony complexity. *Journal of Applied Social Psychology, 35*, 1266–1280. doi:10.1111/j.1559-1816.2005.tb02170.x

Scott, K. A., & Brown, D. J. (2006). Female first, leader second? Gender bias in the encoding of leadership behavior. *Organizational Behavior and Human Decision Processes, 101*, 230–242. doi:10.1016/j.obhdp.2006.06.002

Shackelford, S., Wood, W., & Worchel, S. (1996). Behavioral styles and the influence of women in mixed-sex groups. *Social Psychology Quarterly, 59*, 284–293.

Seem, S., & Clark, M. (2006). Healthy women, healthy men, and healthy adults: An evaluation of gender role stereotypes in the twenty-first century. *Sex Roles, 55*, 247–258. doi:10.1007/s11199-006-9077-0

Sinclair, L., & Kunda, Z. (2000). Motivated stereotyping of women: She's fine if she praised me but incompetent if she criticized me. *Personality and Social Psychology Bulletin, 26*, 1329–1342. doi:10.1177/0146167200263002

Smith, K. H., & Stutts, M. (2003). Effects of short-term cosmetic versus long-term health fear appeals in anti-smoking advertisements on the smoking behaviour of adolescents. *Journal of Consumer Behaviour, 3*, 157–177. doi:10.1002/cb.130

Smith, R. A. (2012). Money, benefits, and power: A test of the glass ceiling and glass escalator hypotheses. *Annals of the American Academy of Political and Social Science, 639*, 149–172. doi:10.1177/0002716211422038

Spence, J. T., & Buckner, C. E. (2000). Instrumental and expressive traits, trait stereotypes, and sexist attitudes. *Psychology of Women Quarterly, 24*, 44–62. doi:10.1111/j.1471-6402.2000.tb01021.x

Stein, R. T., & Heller, T. (1979). An empirical analysis of the correlations between leadership status and participation rates reported in the literature. *Journal of Personality and Social Psychology, 37*, 1993–2002. doi:10.1037/0022-3514.37.11.1993

Steinpreis, R. E., Anders, K. A., & Ritzke, D. (1999). The impact of gender on the review of the curricula vitae of job applicants and tenure candidates: A national empirical study. *Sex Roles, 41*, 509–528. doi:10.1023/A:1018839203698

Sterling, B. S., & Owen, J. W. (1982). Perceptions of demanding versus reasoning male and female police officers. *Personality and Social Psychology Bulletin, 8*, 336–340. doi:10.1177/0146167282082023

Stern, S. E., Mullennix, J. W., & Yaroslavsky, I. (2006). Persuasion and social perception of human vs. synthetic voice across person as source and computer as source conditions. *International Journal of Human-Computer Studies*, *64*, 43–52. doi:10.1016/j.ijhcs.2005.07.002

Taps, J., & Martin, P. Y. (1990). Gender composition, attributional accounts, and women's influence and likability in task groups. *Small Group Research*, *21*, 471–491. doi:10.1177/1046496490214003

Thomas-Hunt, M. C., & Phillips, K. W. (2004). When what you know is not enough: Expertise and gender dynamics in task groups. *Personality and Social Psychology Bulletin*, *30*, 1585–1598. doi: 10.1177/0146167204271186

Tinsley, C. H., Cheldelin, S. I., Schneider, A., & Amanatullah, E. T. (2009). Women at the bargaining table: Pitfalls and prospects. *Negotiation Journal*, *25*, 233–248. doi:10.1111/j.1571-9979.2009.00222.x

Troyer, L. (2001). Effects of protocol differences on the study of status and social influence. *Current Research In Social Psychology*, *6*, 182–205.

Twenge, J. M. (1997a). Attitudes toward women, 1970–1995: A meta-analysis. *Psychology of Women Quarterly*, *21*, 35–51. doi:10.1111/j.1471-6402.1997.tb00099.x

Twenge, J. M. (1997b). Changes in masculine and feminine traits over time: A meta-analysis. *Sex Roles*, *36*, 305–325. doi:10.1007/BF02766650

Twenge, J. M. (2001). Changes in women's assertiveness in response to status and roles: A cross-temporal meta-analysis, 1931-1993. *Journal of Personality and Social Psychology*, *81*, 133–145. doi:10.1037/0022-3514.81.1.133

Uhlman, E. L., & Cohen, G. L. (2005). Constructed criteria: Redefining merit to justify discrimination. *Psychological Science*, *16*, 474–480.

US National Center for Education Statistics. (2010). *Digest of education statistics, 2010*. Retrieved February 2015, from http://nces.ed.gov/programs/digest/d10/tables_3.asp#Ch3aSub4

US National Highway Traffic Safety Administration (2003). *National survey of speeding and unsafe driving attitudes and behaviors: 2002. Volume 2—Findings report*. Retrieved February 2015, from http://mpdc.dc.gov/sites/default/files/dc/sites/mpdc/publication/attachments/Speed_VolumeII_Findings_Final_1.pdf

Wagner, D. G., Ford, R. S., & Ford, T. W. (1986). Can gender inequalities be reduced? *American Sociological Review*, *51*, 47–61. doi:10.2307/2095477

Walker, H. A., Ilardi, B. C., McMahon, A. M., & Fennell, M. L. (1996). Gender, interaction, and leadership. *Social Psychology Quarterly*, *59*, 255–272. doi:10.2307/2787022

Wang, C., Bristol, T., Mowen, J. C., & Chakraborty, G. (2000). Alternative modes of self-construal: Dimensions of connectedness–separateness and advertising appeals to the cultural and gender-specific self. *Journal of Consumer Psychology*, *9*, 107–115. doi:10.1207/S15327663JCP0902_5

Watson, C., & Hoffman, L. R. (2004). The role of task-related behavior in the emergence of leaders. *Group and Organizational Management*, *29*, 650–685.

Weimann, G. (1985). Sex differences in dealing with bureaucracy. *Sex Roles*, *12*, 777–790. doi:10.1007/BF00287871

Wennerås, C., & Wold, A. (1997). Nepotism and sexism in peer-review. *Nature*, *387*(6631), 341–343.

Williams, C. L. (1992). The glass escalator: Hidden advantages for men in the "female" professions. *Social Problems*, *39*, 41–57. doi:10.1525/sp.1992.39.3.03x0034h

Williams, J. E., & Best, D. L. (1990a). *Measuring sex stereotypes: A multinational study*. Newbury Park, CA: Sage.

Williams, J. E., & Best, D. L. (1990b). *Sex and psyche: Gender and self viewed cross-culturally*. Newbury Park, CA: Sage.

Wolin, L. D. (2003). Gender issues in advertising—An oversight synthesis of research: 1970-2002. *Journal of Advertising Research*, *43*, 111–129.

Wood, W., & Kallgren, C. A. (1988). Communicator attributes and persuasion: Recipients' access to attitude relevant information in memory. *Personality and Social Psychology Bulletin*, *14*, 172–182. doi:10.1177/0146167288141017

Wood, W., & Karten, S. J. (1986). Sex differences in interaction style as a product of perceived sex differences in competence. *Journal of Personality and Social Psychology*, *50*, 341–347. doi:10.1037/0022-3514.50.2.341

Wosinska, W., Dabul, A. J., Whetstone-Dion, R., & Cialdini, R. B. (1996). Self-presentational responses to success in the organization: The costs and benefits of modesty. *Basic and Applied Social Psychology*, *18*, 229–242. doi:10.1207/s15324834basp1802_8

Yoder, J. D. (2002). 2001 Division 35 presidential address: Context matters: Understanding tokenism processes and their impact on women's work. *Psychology of Women Quarterly*, *26*, 1–8.

Yoder, J. D., & Schleicher, T. L. (1996). Undergraduates regard deviation from occupational gender stereotypes as costly for women. *Sex Roles*, *34*, 171–188. doi:10.1007/BF01544294

# Social Influence and Personality

John B. Nezlek *and* C. Veronica Smith

**Abstract**

The study of social influence has been dominated by experimental methods that are not well suited to examine relationships between personality and social influence. Nevertheless, the existing research provided a basis for some tentative conclusions. In terms of susceptibility to influence, it appears that people who depend more on others for guidance are more susceptible to influence than those who depend less on others. Two specific manifestations of this general tendency are authoritarianism and what is called the dependent personality. In terms of sources of influence, relationships between Machiavellianism and influence tactics have received the most attention. It appears that greater Machiavellianism is associated with the use of more and more effective social influence tactics. Understanding relationships between personality and social influence will require research that combines the models and methods of social and personality psychologists.

**Key Words:** social influence tactics, dependent personality, desire for control, compliance proneness, Machiavellianism

We approached writing this chapter with mixed emotions. Social influence has been studied primarily by social psychologists for whom individual differences such as personality tend to be treated more as a source of error variance than as meaningful variance to be analyzed and understood. This suggested to us that we would have difficulty finding a body of research that we could describe or summarize. Noting this, we saw (and were encouraged by the editors to see) a chance to demonstrate the value of understanding the role that personality plays in social influence. Such roles are natural extensions of the traditional social psychological perspective that has emphasized the interaction of the person and the situation as a means of understanding human thought, feeling, and behavior. On the other hand, we were a bit concerned that many social psychologists have paid, and continue to pay, only lip service (if that) to the value of this interaction, and that we would have difficulty putting together a sufficient amount of research on personality and social influence to say anything meaningful. Fortunately, the reality was not as dire as our suspicions suggested it would be, although in our humble opinion, there is certainly room for improvement.

As is evident from the dates of many of the works we cite, relationships between social influence and personality have not been an important focus of research for the past few decades. Although there has been some excellent work done since 2000 (and in other decades), in the past 20–30 years, the vast majority of research on social influence has focused primarily on when, under what circumstances, and how people can be influenced by social sources, with a very broad definition of *social*. Such emphases and a lack of emphasis on relationships between social influence and personality will be evident in the other chapters in this handbook.

When social and personality psychology were more unified, and before Mischel dealt personality research (at least in the United States) a near death blow in the 1960s and 1970s (e.g., Mischel, 1968), experimental social psychologists routinely entertained the possibility that individual differences (including personality traits) needed to be included as part of a full explanation of the phenomena that they were studying. For example, as we note later, even Stanley Milgram, who is probably best known for demonstrating the power of the situation, thought that people's personalities needed to be taken into account to understand obedience to authority. Regardless, his beliefs about the importance of personality to understanding obedience were overshadowed by the strong situational effects he found.

Equally interesting, and perhaps more responsible for the lack of attention to relationships between personality and social influence, has been the neglect of social influence by personality researchers. For example, a search for the term "social influence" in the 30 chapters in the recently published volume of the APA handbook series concerning personality (APA, 2015) produced two hits, and these mentioned social influence only in passing, not as a focus of research. Although personality psychologists may complain that experimental social psychologists do not appreciate individual differences, in the case of social influence, it is social psychologists, not personologists, who are "doing the heavy lifting."

Putting aside issues about who is studying relationships between personality and social influence, we needed to make some assumptions about what constitutes personality. Deciding what constitutes personality is one of the most difficult decisions one needs to make when writing about personality research, defined as broadly as it is for the purposes of the chapter. Although the emergence of the "Big Five" (e.g., John, Naumann, & Soto, 2008) has provided a useful framework for understanding individual differences, this framework is by no means universally accepted as gospel; for example, witness the existence of the HEXACO model—the Big Six (e.g., Ashton & Lee, 2001). One way to address this issue would be to list all the major theories of personality and attempt to explain how they relate (or might relate) to social influence, but there are too many models and theories to do this in one chapter, and we would also have to decide what constituted a major theory and what did not—not an easy task.

Nevertheless, for present purposes, we will rely upon a more or less classic Allportian trait-based approach. Within such a context, personality is conceptualized as a collection of individual differences in people's tendencies to respond. For example, people who are more agreeable are presumed to behave in ways that are different from people who are less agreeable. They may argue less with others, cooperate more, acquiesce more often, and so forth. Given the paucity of research on the topic, we chose not to limit coverage to social influence as it relates to formal, comprehensive models of personality; rather, we included research on specific traits that might not fit neatly into the universe of individual differences covered by comprehensive models. At the end of the chapter, we address the challenges to the trait approach posed by Mischel's influential Cognitive Affective Processing System (e.g., Mischel, 1973; Mischel, & Shoda, 1995).

We will also consider individual differences in motivation as part of personality. Particularly when considering the relationships between personality and social influence, we think it is essential to take individual differences in motivation into account. Why do people try to influence others? What types of goals do people have in mind? What needs does exercising social influence meet and for whom? When considering what motivates people to influence others, we will rely upon Deci and Ryan's Self Determination Theory (Deci & Ryan, 1985a) and its various components.

The other side of the coin for us is social influence. As indicated by the richness of the research discussed in the chapters of this handbook, social influence can be conceptualized in many ways. For present purposes, we will use a very inclusive definition that encompasses most any type of change that is elicited by most any type of action or activity as long as the source of influence is social in nature; however, we will not include persuasion per se. Most important perhaps, we will consider relationships between personality and social influence in terms of both the *target of influence* and the *source of influence*. In the simplest terms, this dual emphasis can be represented with two questions: What personality characteristics are associated with being more readily or easily influenced by social sources, and what personality characteristics are associated with being able to more readily or easily influence others?

In terms of research that has been described as being about social influence, the first question (who is influenced) has received much more attention. This emphasis is probably due to the fact that most of the research on social influence has been done within the context of experiments that have focused on how much people arc influenced. Nevertheless, we think it is important to consider how personality might shape or be related to how influential people are, and so we cover this topic separately.

## Susceptibility to Being Influenced by Others: Who Can Be Influenced More Readily or Easily?

In this section we summarize research that has examined relationships between individual differences in traits and how easily or readily people can be influenced by social sources. We have organized this description using two schemes that overlap somewhat. First, we summarize research by the type of influence that was studied (conformity, compliance, and obedience). Second, we describe those personality characteristics that appear to be more robustly associated with the susceptibility to influence.

### *Conformity*

Of the various ways in which social influence can be manifested, conformity has received a good deal of attention (see Hodges, this volume). In part, this is due to the fact that conformity is a "classic" topic in social psychology and was the focus of attention early in the development of what is now considered to be social psychology. Moreover, as noted earlier, there was a time when experimental social psychologists were interested in individual differences, and studying individual differences in conformity dates back to this time, at least 60 years ago. For example, based on research using his original conformity paradigm, Asch recognized that some people conformed more consistently than others. In his initial study, approximately 25 percent of participants did not conform on any of the trials, and he was curious about how these differences could be explained. Although he did not research such differences per se, he acknowledged that there might be individual differences in how readily people conformed (e.g., Asch, 1956).

Among the first to examine individual differences in conformity explicitly was Crutchfield (1955), who devised a variant of the Asch paradigm known as the "question booth." The question booth technique allowed testing larger groups of participants more quickly than Asch's original paradigm and did not require the use of confederates. When using the question booth, participants are asked to indicate whether a series of statements projected on a screen are true or false. At the bottom of the screen, the answers of other participants are provided. Conformity is measured by the number of times participants agree to obviously incorrect answers. This procedure produced rates of conformity that were similar to those found in the original paradigm developed by Asch. After the conformity trials, a series of personality tests was administered to the participants. Relationships between conformity and the individual difference measured by these tests led Crutchfield to conclude that those who conformed were intellectually less effective, submissive, inhibited, and had stronger feelings of inferiority compared to those who conformed.

This study led some to assume that there were individual differences in the tendency to conform (or confirmed such beliefs), and individual differences in conformity were examined. Unfortunately, the results of this research were far from consistent. One of the earliest studies on the topic found no differences between "yielders" (those who conformed) and "independents" (those who did not conform) on the Minnesota Multiphasic Personality Inventory (Barron, 1953), but a later study found that people who conformed were more dependent (as measured by the Thematic Apperception Test) than those who did not (Kagan & Mussen, 1956). In Appley and Moeller (1963), a sample of undergraduate women took part in a study that followed the original Asch paradigm closely, and they completed a battery of personality questionnaires, measuring 38 individual differences (e.g., self-control, femininity, affiliation). Only one significant relationship was found between yielding and personality (a positive correlation with abasement).

Further research examining the other individual differences has yielded contradictory results. Studies examining locus of control have concluded that those with a more external locus of control are more likely to conform than those with a more internal locus of control (e.g., Larsen, Triplett, Brant, & Langenberg (1979), but other studies found no relationship between locus of control and conformity (e.g., Williams & Warchal, 1981). Similar mixed findings have been found for need for approval, with some studies indicating that those who have higher need for approval are more likely to conform (e.g., Strickland & Crowne, 1962), whereas studies of children (Dodge & Muench, 1969) and Japanese participants (Frager, 1970) found no relationships between conformity and need for approval.

Some research examining relationships between conformity and individual differences as measured by Eysenck's model of personality (1958) have also produced conflicting results. In their discussion of extraversion and neuroticism and conformity, Singh and Akhtar (1973) described studies that reported that conformity was positively related to introversion (e.g., Crutchfield, 1955), as well as studies that reported that conformity was positively related to extroversion (e.g., Barron, 1953). They also reviewed studies that found no link between conformity and neuroticism, a positive link between these two (e.g., Crutchfield, 1955), and a negative link between them (e.g., Barron, 1953). Their own study of conformity and personality in an Indian undergraduate sample using the Hindi version of Eysenck's Personality Inventory found a positive relationship between conformity and extraversion and a negative relationship between conformity and neuroticism.

## Compliance

Although relatively little research has been done examining individual differences in susceptibility to compliance techniques compared to the research done on situational determinants of compliance (Gamian-Wilk & Lachowicz-Tabaczek, 2007), there are some individual differences that have been studied.

Rather than examining a specific personality trait, several studies have examined people's implicit theories of personality. Based on research by Carol Dweck and colleagues (e.g., Dweck, Hong, & Chiu, 1993), individuals either believe that personality is fixed (entity theorists) or malleable (incremental theorists). In terms of social influence, individuals with entity beliefs may be less resistant to social influence, perhaps because of their tendency to prefer easier tasks with certain success over more difficult tasks with less certain outcomes. When faced with a social influence attempt, particularly if the requested task is easily accomplished, entity theorists may be readily compliant. By contrast, incremental theorists enjoy challenge and are not fearful of failure. When faced with a social influence attempt, they may feel that there are fewer negative consequences for noncompliance, or they may be receptive to such attempts if the request offers them an opportunity to be challenged.

Gamian-Wilk and Lachowicz-Tabaczek (2007) examined relationships between people's implicit theories of personality and susceptibility to influence by studying individual differences in susceptibility to the foot-in-the-door technique (Freedman & Fraser, 1966). Across four studies, the authors used both "easy" foot-in-the-door requests (e.g., completing a short questionnaire and then being asked to complete another, longer questionnaire) and more "difficult" requests (e.g., completing a questionnaire and then being asked to donate 2 hours of time to work with a research assistant). As predicted, entity theorists were more likely to comply with an easy request than incremental theorists were, whereas incremental theorists were more likely to comply with a difficult request than entity theorists were.

This research was extended by Gamian-Wilk and Lachowicz-Tabaczek (2009), who examined relationships between implicit theories of personality and compliance with foot-in-the-door techniques compared to compliance with door-in-the-face techniques. An important difference between the two techniques is that the foot-in-the-door technique can be construed as more difficult or challenging because someone is being asked to do something more involved than what has already been asked. As discussed previously, this may be appealing to those who believe that personality is more malleable and flexible. To contrast, the door-in-the-face technique may convey a greater sense of success because by definition, the subsequent (and target request of the technique) is "easier" than the original request. Across four studies, these predictions were supported; incremental theorists are more susceptible to foot-in-the-door compliance techniques, and entity theorists are more susceptible to the door-in-the-face compliance techniques.

A second line of research has examined an individual's preference/need for consistency and compliance. Originally proposed by Festinger (1957) as an individual difference related to dissonance tolerance, Cialdini, Trost, and Newsom (1995) proposed the need for consistency as an explanation for the lack of replication in research on phenomena that involve the need for consistency. In the validation of a measure of one's preference for consistent responding in situations, Cialdini et al. (1995) found that the foot-in-the-door technique (compared to a control condition with just one request) elicited more compliance but this was only true for those with a high preference for consistency. For people low in consistency, they were equally likely to comply regardless of condition. The pattern of means was such that those high in consistency in the control condition complied more than participants in the other three groups, who did vary from one another. In subsequent research by Guadagno, Asher, Demaine, and Cialdini (2001) and consistent with Cialdini et al. (1995), individuals who were high in preference for consistency complied more to a foot-in-the-door request compared to a control request. In addition, individuals with low preference for consistency again showed no difference in compliance between foot-in-the-door methods and control methods. A review of research on the need for consistency can be found in Guadagno and Cialdini (2010).

## Obedience

Although Milgram's original study on obedience was published over 50 years ago, the nature of obedience to authority still generates considerable interest, if not in the scientific discipline per se, certainly in the public at large (see Burger, this volume). In his review of the role of personality in understanding obedience, Blass (1991) highlights that Milgram (1974) was uncertain of the role of personality, quoting him as saying, "I am certain there is a complex personality basis to obedience and disobedience. But I know we have not found it" (p. 205). Further, Milgram (1974) asserted, "The disposition a person brings to the experiment is probably less important a cause of his behavior than most readers assume. For the social psychology of this century reveals a major lesson: often, it is not so much the kind of person a man is as the kind of situation in which he finds himself will determine how he will act" (p. 205).

Nevertheless, Blass argues that some type of individual differences play a role in obedient behavior because the behavior of participants varies no matter what conditions are studied. In some conditions where obedience should be minimal, some people obey. In conditions where obedience should be great, there are people who do not obey. Blass asserts "that there are individual differences in obedience is a fact because in most obedience studies, given the same stimulus situation, one finds both obedience and disobedience taking place" (p. 402).

In his review, Blass (1991) reviews research that has examined the role of personality in predicting obedience. The two most consistent relationships he described were positive relationships between obedience and authoritarianism and hostility. Blass also highlights the fact that not all individual differences should be correlated with obedience, such as introversion-extraversion. He also mentioned that although there is broad agreement among social and personality psychologists that human behavior is a function of the interaction between characteristics of the person and characteristics of the environment, such interactions were examined in only eight studies of obedience, and four of those examined sex differences in obedience.

Since Blass's review, research on individual differences in obedience has continued but has produced conflicting results, particularly in terms of the factors of the Five Factor Model. For example, Bocchiaro and Zimbardo (2010) found no relationship between any of the factors of the Five Factor Model and obedience, measured by how much participants, acting as "coaches," would yell increasingly insulting statements to "learners" who failed to perform. In contrast, Bègue and colleagues (2014) found that agreeableness and conscientiousness were positively related to obedience as measured by the level of shocks administered in a study modeled after Milgram, although they found no relationships between obedience and neuroticism, extraversion, or openness. Adding to this complexity, Zeigler-Hill, Southard, Archer, and Donohoe (2013) also using a design modeled after Milgram found no relationships between scores on the Five Factor Model and obedience, as measured by blasts of noise administered to "learners" (instead of electric shocks). It should be noted, however, that the sample in this study was small ($n = 33$), and there was virtually no variance on the prime dependent measure (only 2 participants out of 33 did not fully obey). Nevertheless, when the number of prods (verbal encouragements) given by the authority figure to elicit obedience was considered, neuroticism interacted with negative affect, such that people low in neuroticism required more prodding when they were experiencing high levels of negative affect.

## Traits That Have Been Consistently Linked to Susceptibility to Social Influence

Although research has examined relationships between social influence and a wide variety of individual differences (and types of influence), there are some traits (or clusters of traits) that have been consistently found to be related to the susceptibility to social influence. We describe these traits next.

### DESIRE FOR CONTROL

One individual difference that has been found to be related consistently to conformity is the desire for control (Burger, 1992). Desire for control is defined as the extent to which people prefer to have control over the events in their lives and is typically measured using the Desire for Control scale (Burger & Cooper, 1979). The Desire for Control scale consists of 20 items, and although these 20 items have been found to constitute a reliable and valid scale (e.g., Burger, 1992), some have suggested that it is useful to distinguish the desire to control *others* as a distinct subfactor (e.g., Gebhardt & Brosschot, 2002).

The explanatory power of the Desire for Control scale is illustrated by the results of Burger (1987). Across three studies, Burger (1987) found that participants with a lower desire for control were more likely to conform compared to those with a higher desire. In Study 1, when information was provided about what other students thought, individual differences in desire for control were negatively related to how much student participants agreed that NCAA athletes should be treated semiprofessionally (the opinion of other students). In contrast, when no information about the opinions of other students was provided, desire for control was not related to agreement. In Study 2, participants rated the humor of cartoons in a group of three other confederates or alone. Participants rated cartoons as funnier when the confederates thought they were funny compared to a condition in which the confederates did not find the cartoons funny, but the difference between the two conditions was moderated by desire for control: The difference between the conditions was stronger for those who had less desire for control. These finding were replicated in Study 3, which added a not funny cartoon condition. Compared to the ratings of participants high in the desire for control, the ratings of participants low in the desire for control corresponded more closely to confederates' ratings in both the funny and not funny conditions.

### THE DEPENDENT PERSONALITY CONSTRUCT

Another construct, represented by a constellation of measures, is what Bornstein (1992) described as the "dependent personality." Bornstein concluded that "The etiology of dependency appears to lie in overprotective, authoritarian parenting. In social settings, dependency is associated with suggestibility, conformity, compliance, interpersonal yielding, affiliative behavior, and sensitivity to interpersonal cues" (p. 3). Bornstein discusses dependency within the context of psychodynamic approaches (including attachment style) and social learning theory, and he concludes that "dependency-related cognitions are the key to understanding the diverse behaviors that are exhibited by dependent people in various situations and settings" (p. 6). We return to the issue of cross-situational consistency later.

Bornstein also discusses different measures of dependency, classifying them along two dimensions: *format* (objective vs. projective) and *content* (interpersonal vs. oral). Despite these differences, Bornstein concludes that the results of studies do not vary systematically as a function of how dependency is measured. Based on a substantial body of research, Bornstein concluded: "First, dependency is associated with a general tendency to be influenced by the opinions of others, to yield to others in interpersonal transactions, and to comply with others' expectations and demands. However, when placed in a position in which they must choose between pleasing a peer or pleasing a figure of authority, the dependent person will typically opt for pleasing the authority figure" (pp. 10–11). It is important to note that a dependent personality is also a diagnosable disorder characterized by a pervasive psychological dependence on other people. Individuals who are diagnosed with dependent personality disorder are, by definition, readily and easily influenced by others.

### COMPLIANCE PRONENESS

A substantial body of research has been done using the Gudjonsson Compliance Scale (Gudjonsson, 1989, 1997). This 20-item true/false self-report measure gauges the susceptibility of people to comply with the requests of others, particularly others in positions of authority, such as parents. Sample items include, "I give in easily when I am pressured" and "I find it very difficult to tell people when I disagree with them." Higher scores indicate a higher likelihood of compliance in general. Similar to other traits, Compliance Proneness is assumed to be relatively stable across time and circumstances.

Scores on the Gudjonsson Compliance Scale have been found to be related to compliance across various situations. For example, Gudjonsson, Sigurdsson, Einarsson, and Einarsson (2008) found a positive correlation between Gudjonsson Compliance Scale scores and the reported likelihood of participants to comply with both impersonal (e.g., those from a salesman) and personal compliance requests (e.g., those from a friend) for both men and women. Furthermore, regression analyses that included other personality traits (psychoticism and neuroticism as measured by the Eysenck Personality Questionnaire) and self-esteem as predictors found that Gudjonsson Compliance Scale was a significant and unique predictor in predicting likelihood of compliance (both for impersonal and personal requests) for both men and women and was the largest predictor in each model.

This measure has been used extensively in the area of false confessions and other forensic contexts. For example, when compared to people who falsely confess, those who maintain their innocence have lower levels of compliance (Gudjonsson, 1991). Additional studies have found that people with higher tendencies to comply are more likely to make false confessions (Sigurdsson & Gudjonsson, 2001), are more likely to take the blame for antisocial acts that they did not commit (Gudjonsson, Sigurdsson, & Einarsson, 2007), and are more readily led to participate in crimes (Gudjonsson & Sigurdsson, 2007).

In addition, research has also examined the personality correlates of the tendency to comply as measured by the Gudjonsson Compliance Scale. This research has found that the compliance proneness is negatively related to self-esteem (Gudjonsson & Sigurdsson, 2003) and is positively related to attachment anxiety and avoidance (Gudjonsson, Sigurdsson, Lydsdottir, & Olafsdottir, 2008). Such results suggest that a general sense of insecurity may underlie or contribute to the tendency to comply with the requests/desires of others. Research has also examined relationships between compliance tendencies and psychopathic personality tendencies, although such relationships seem to vary as a function of facet of psychopathy being considered (Ray & Jones, 2012). Recent research has also found significant positive correlations between the Gudjonsson Compliance Scale responses and agreeableness and neuroticism and negative correlations with openness as measured by the NEO-Five Factor Inventory (Larmour, Bergstrøm, Gillen, & Forth, 2015).

## Susceptibility to Being Influenced by Others: A Summary

Given the variety of types of social influences and individual differences that have been examined, it is difficult to provide a neat and tidy summary of this research. Nevertheless, one theme may provide a foundation or basis for a summary is dependency. In terms of broad concepts, as described by Bornstein (1992), the dependent personality seems to be the construct that best represents how susceptible people are to social influence. By definition, people high in dependency depend upon and look to others more than those low in dependency. Extending this to susceptibility to social influence is a small step.

Although not discussed as such, the specific characteristic of Compliance Proneness can be considered as a specific manifestation of the more general trait of Dependency. The items on the Compliance Proneness Scale concern the ease or difficulty people have in acting in opposition to others' request—that is, the ease or difficulty they have in acting independently. Authoritarianism can also be understood in similar terms. Individuals high in Authoritarianism follow the dictates of authority figures and norms more closely than those who are low in Authoritarianism. Although authoritarians may see themselves as strong and people of action, weakness and insecurity underlie the authoritarian personality, and it is these characteristics that make authoritarians susceptible to social influence.

From a different perspective, dispositional independence, as measured by the Desire for Control scale, is negatively related to the susceptibility to social influence. As suggested by its title, the Desire for Control measures how much people want to control others, but inspection of the scale reveals that it measures (at least to a degree) how important it is for someone to think and behave independently of the influences of others. Such items include the following: "I try to avoid situations where someone else tells me what to do," and "Others usually know what is best for me." In this sense, the Desire for Control is a manifestation of dispositional independence, the polar opposite of dependence.

## Influencing Others: How Do People Try to Influence Others and Who Does This Effectively?

When considering people as a source of social influence, we focus on relationships between personality and the methods people use to influence others, usually referred to as social influence tactics and on the personality characteristics associated with how easily or readily people can influence. Interestingly, research on tactics has tended to ignore effectiveness (how easily or readily someone can influence another), and research on effectiveness has tended to ignore tactics.

### Tactics

One of the widely cited taxonomies of influence tactics is that proposed by Buss, Gomes, Higgins, and Lauterbach (1987). Although Buss et al. examined what they called "manipulation tactics," and they did this within the confines of romantic relationships, the tactics they proposed have been studied outside of the confines of romantic relationships. Buss et al. identified six tactics: charm, silent treatment, coercion, reason, regression, and self-abasement. They found a variety of relationships between how often these tactics were used and measures of personality (too many to list here). We mention a few of these relationships to illustrate their findings. Neuroticism, as measured by the Eysenck Personality Questionnaire (Eysenck & Eysenck, 1975), was positively related to the use of the silent treatment and regression (pouting and sulking). Finally, scores on the calculating subscale of the Interpersonal Adjective Scales (Wiggins, 1979) were positively related to how often each of the six tactics was used. More calculating people were more tactical in their interactions with others.

This line of research was extended by Buss (1992), who broadened the focus to include manipulation tactics within the context of close personal relationships (e.g., with family members), and six additional tactics labeled as responsibility invocation, reciprocity, monetary reward, pleasure induction, social comparison, and hardball. Personality was measured using a measure of the Five Factor Model based on Goldberg (1983). Again, there were numerous relationships between personality and use of tactics, and Buss summarized these results. "Among the major findings were that persons high on Surgency tended to use Responsibility Invocation and Coercion; persons low on Surgency used Debasement; Disagreeable persons tended to use Coercion and Silent Treatment; Conscientious persons tended to use Reason; Emotionally Unstable persons tended to use Regression; persons high on Intellect-Openness tended to use Reason; and those low on Intellect-Openness tended to use Social Comparison" (p. 497).

## Machiavellianism

We focus on Machiavellianism per se because it is an individual difference that explicitly concerns influence tactics, and because of this it is probably the individual difference that has received the most attention in research on social influence. Machiavellianism refers to the extent to which people behave in a manner that is consistent with the advice offered by Niccolo Machiavelli, a 16th-century Italian writer. In his book, *The Prince*, Machiavelli (1532/1961) proposed that in political dealings, the ends justify the means and that leaders should seek to be feared rather than loved. The most widely used measure of Machiavellianism was developed by Christie and Geis (1970). The scale consists of 20 statements, and respondents indicate the degree to which each statement characterizes them. The scale is meant to be unidimensional.

People who score higher on the Machiavellian scale tend to be more dominant, manipulative, and strategic than those scoring lower in Machiavellianism (Paulhus & Williams, 2002; Rauthmann & Kolar, 2012). In a study of MBA students and their propensity to use various social influence techniques in work contexts, Vecchio and Sussmann (1991) found that Machiavellianism was associated with the use of only one technique— blocking (e.g., threatening to stop working). Machiavellianism scores were positively related to how often people used blocking. Falbo (1977) found that people high in Machiavellianism used techniques such as manipulating people's emotions and deceit to get what they wanted; those with more moderate Machiavellianism scores reported using social influence techniques, such as persuasion and threat; and those lower in Machiavellianism used persistence and assertion.

Research also suggests that Machiavellianism is positively related to external locus of control (Fehr, Samson, & Paulhus, 1992). At first glance, a positive relationship between Machiavellianism and external locus of control might seem to contradict the commonsense notion that people high in Machiavellianism believe they can change other people's behaviors to suit their needs, beliefs that would be more consistent with an internal locus of control. To clarify this issue, Paulhus (1983) examined locus of control as a domain-specific construct and distinguished control in three domains: personal achievement, interpersonal control, and sociopolitical control. When examining Machiavellianism in terms of these domains, Paulhus found that externality was related to Machiavellianism only for sociopolitical control. In contrast, Machiavellianism was positively related to internality in terms of interpersonal control. There were no relationships between Machiavellianism and control in the personal achievement.

Machiavellianism represents a style or way of thinking about social influence, which leaves open questions about exactly how Machiavellianism is manifested in terms of social influence. To address this issue, Jonason and Webster (2012) examined relationships between the use of social influence tactics and Machiavellianism. They measured Machiavellianism using the Dark Triad Dirty Dozen (Jonason & Webster, 2010), which also provides measures of the two other traits that comprise what is called the Dark Triad, narcissism and psychopathy (Paulhus & Williams, 2002). Self-reports of the use of influence tactics used tactics based on those proposed by Buss (1992), modified to refer to different relationships. In Study 1, when all three traits were regressed on different influence tactics, Machiavellianism was the sole predictor of using the techniques of hardball (e.g., deception, violence, threats) and seduction (flirting, use of sex) in social influence. In contrast, in Study 2, which differentiated influence as a function of the relationship people had with those whom they were influencing (e.g., friends vs. family members), Machiavellianism was positively related to using all of the 13 strategies being studied. In Study 3, using a forced-choice paradigm, Machiavellianism was positively related to the preference for using charm (e.g., using compliments) for influencing same-sex friends.

Aside from the issue of how Machiavellianism is related to the use of different tactics, there is the question of effectiveness. Is Machiavellianism related to the ability to influence others? The available research is somewhat inconsistent. In a study examining people's perceptions of Machiavellianism, participants viewed videotaped interviews of people high or low in Machiavellianism (Cherulnik, Way, Ames, & Hutto, 1981). The results indicated that it was somewhat easier for people to identify those low in Machiavellianism than those high in Machiavellianism, suggesting that those high in Machiavellianism may mask this disposition to reduce suspicion in others. Individuals high in Machiavellianism were seen more positively than those low in Machiavellianism, particularly in terms of characteristics that would be associated with social influence, for example, being dominant and confident. It is important to note that Cherulink et al. did not study relationships between Machiavellianism and how influential people were.

Relationships between Machiavellianism and how influential people were examined by Sheppard and Vidmar (1980: Study 2). Using a role-playing paradigm, they had a group of participants, either high or low in Machiavellianism, pretend to be attorneys who then examined another group of participants who had witnessed a fake crime. High Machiavellian "attorneys" were able to elicit testimony from witness participants that was more in line with the needs of their client. In addition, judges attributed less blame to the clients of these "attorneys." In contrast to these results, in a study examining the political influence of United States senators, ten Brinke, Liu, Keltner, and Srivastava (2016) found that senators who embodied a Machiavellian style (coded from videos of them speaking in the Senate) did not have more political influence than those who embodied a non-Machiavellian ethical style. Influence in this case was measured by how often senators were able to "enlist colleagues as collaborative cosponsors on bills that he or she originated in a given Congress" (p. 88).

Taken together, the available research suggests that Machiavellianism is associated with the use of manipulative strategies, and these strategies may be more effective than the strategies used by those lower in Machiavellianism. Nevertheless, neither of the questions has been answered definitively.

### Self-Presentation

Although it may not be widely recognized as such, as noted by Leary and Allen (2011a), "At its heart, self-presentation is a means of achieving desired goals, a social influence strategy designed to lead other people to respond to the person in particular ways" (p. 1203; see also Tyler & Adams, this volume). People may use self-presentation to influence others, and by extension, relationships between personality and self-presentation can help us understand relationships between personality and social influence per se. Despite the fact that Leary and Allen noted that "the list of goals that may influence the content of people's self-presentations is virtually endless," they were able to provide some conclusions. They organized the existing research in terms of two broad goals: "fitting in versus standing out" and "acquisitive and protective self-presentation."

In terms of the first category of goals—fitting in versus standing out—Leary and Allen (2011b) studied the extent to which people presented the same persona to different targets (e.g., friends, coworkers, family members). Somewhat surprisingly, agreeableness was positively related to how consistent people's presentations were across targets. Leary and Allen reasoned that more agreeable people might be more authentic and that they tend to display more positive qualities across different situations. They also found that Machiavellianism was negatively related to consistency of the personas displayed and that authenticity (Kernis & Goldman, 2006) was positively related to consistency. Interestingly, Leary and Allen (2011a) concluded that relationships between self-monitoring and the strength of self-presentational motives of this type were inconsistent, at best.

In terms of acquisitive versus protective goals (a distinction akin to approach/avoidance), Leary and Allen concluded that "Whether people approach self-presentation acquisitively versus protectively depends primarily on their self-presentational confidence" (p. 1206). They further suggested that self-esteem was an important determinant of this, such that people who are low in self-esteem may be more likely to present themselves self-protectively compared to those high in self-esteem. The other determinant was social anxiety. They concluded that people who are high in social anxiety may be more likely to present themselves self-protectively compared to those low in social anxiety.

For better or worse, research on relationships between personality and the tactics people use to influence others has been dominated by the study of Machiavellianism. This should not be surprising because Machiavellianism is an individual difference that explicitly concerns a style of social influence. Noting this, it appears that Machiavellianism is positively related to how often people use social influence tactics, and there are suggestions that it is also positively related to how effective people are. Whether "practice makes perfect" or the traits that accompany Machiavellianism are those that are associated with effective influence remains an unanswered question. Although relationships between social influence tactics and other individual differences have been studied, the research is not sufficiently broad to provide a basis for a coherent summary.

### Personality and Individual Differences in Influence in Daily Life

Our thinking about the role of personality in understanding individual differences in how influential people are is grounded in our assumption that social influence is a form of influence similar to the influence people have (or think they) in the nonsocial world (e.g., task achievement). Within the present framework, social influence is a manifestation or aspect of a larger construct of control or mastery over one's environment. To be able to influence other people is to be able to control them, which is conceptually similar to controlling other aspects of one's environment such as task completion. The social and nonsocial domains are not the same (recall Freud's Lieben und Arbeiten, Love and Work), but mastery in the social domain is a form of mastery nevertheless.

Such thinking brings into consideration a large body of research that relies in part on White's (1959) classic paper on competence. White described competence as "an organism's capacity to interact effectively with its environment." We include other people as a part of the environment, an essential part of the environment, assuming Baumeister and Leary's (1995) and others' emphasis on the importance of feeling accepted for humans is indeed the case.

White's conceptualization formed part of the basis for Deci's (1975) introduction of intrinsic motivation, which in turn developed into Deci and Ryan's Self-Determination Theory (1985a; see also Ryan & Deci, 2000). Research based on Bandura's concept of self-efficacy (Bandura, 1986) is in a similar vein. Although these approaches are not identical, they share the assumption that the ability to influence and control the environment is associated with well-being (broadly defined): More control leads to enhanced well-being.

Although the ability to influence others can be considered as a manifestation of a general "mastery" motive, the ability to influence others has not received that much attention per se. For example, within Self-Determination Theory, interpersonal needs/motives are considered separately as one of three constructs: autonomy, competence, and relatedness. Although some research has focused on these needs within close relationships (e.g., La Guardia, Ryan, Couchman, & Deci, 2000), most of the work in this tradition has examined these three needs within work contexts (Basic Psychological Needs Scale, n.d.).

We are not the first to suggest that being influential provides rewards. Bourgeois, Sommer, and Bruno (2009) discussed this topic and provided a compelling rationale for why the effects of exerting influence should be examined from the perspective of the source. Moreover, they explicitly acknowledged the contribution Self-Determination Theory might make to such research. Following up on this, Sommer and Bourgeois (2010) reported the results of two studies in which positive relationships were found between various measures of well-being and the exertion of social influence. Although this work does not involve personality per se, it does highlight the importance of studying individual differences in how much people influence others.

We conducted some preliminary analyses of an experience sample study to provide insight into relationships between personality and how much people feel they can influence others. Participants in the study, 98 undergraduates, answered a series of questions at the end of each day for approximately 2 weeks. Two of these questions concerned how much autonomy and control participants felt they had over the social domain in their lives:

1. Thinking back on your day today in terms of social events that occurred and the relationships

you have with others, to what extent did you feel that you had a choice about what you did and to what extent did things happen the way you wanted them to happen?

2. Thinking back on your day in terms of social events that occurred and the relationships you have with others, to what extent were you able to control the outcomes of these events?

Based on reliability analyses described in Nezlek and Gable (2001), we averaged responses to these two questions to create an outcome measure. Participants also completed the BFI-44 (John & Srivastava, 1999), a widely used measure of the Five Factor Model of personality. Analyses of these data found that only neuroticism was significantly related to daily perceived control over social activities. The more neurotic people were, the less control they felt they had over daily social activities. The estimated correlation between daily mean social control and neuroticism was −.27. These results suggest that perceived control/influence over the social domains of one's life are related to only one aspect of personality (neuroticism), at least as defined within the contexts of the Five Factor Model. Given the nature of this study (size of sample, operational definitions of influence, etc.), these results cannot be taken as "the last word" on this topic. More research is clearly needed.

These results are similar, but not identical, to those reported by Olesen, Thomsen, Schnieber, and Tønnesvan (2010) in that Olesen et al. found that scores on the General Causality Orientation Scale (Deci & Ryan, 1985b) and five-factor model were relatively independent. For reasons that they did not state, Olesen et al. did not calculate correlations between the scores on the Five Factor Model and scores on the three subscales of the General Causality Orientation Scale (autonomy, control, and impersonal); rather, they examined how items on the General Causality Orientation Scale subscales cross-loaded on the Five Factor Model factors in a factor analysis. The apparent rationale for this procedure was that the extent to which items from the General Causality Orientation Scale loaded on factors of the Five Factor model would indicate the extent to which the two sets of constructs were similar or overlapped conceptually.

They found that autonomy items did not cross-load on any factor, and that control and impersonal orientation items cross-loaded on conscientiousness and neuroticism, respectively. The implications of this result for understanding sources of social influences are a bit unclear because Olesen et al. did not take into account the distinction between social and nonsocial domains.

### Personality and Individual Differences in Influence in Day-to-Day Social Interaction

Another, perhaps more direct, way to examine relationships between personality and how much social influence people have is to examine individual differences in people's experiences in everyday social interaction. Most people spend time with others, and the extent to which they can influence the course of these interactions is a prima facie example of social influence. We report the results of preliminary analyses of data that were collected for another purpose to illustrate such a possibility.

In Nezlek and Smith (2005) and Nezlek, Schütz, Schröder-Abé, and Smith (2011), participants used a variant of the Rochester Interaction Record (Wheeler & Nezlek, 1977) to describe the social interactions they had for 2 weeks. Social interactions were defined as social encounters that lasted for 10 minutes or more (see Nezlek, 2012, for a more detailed description of the RIR method). As part of their descriptions of their interactions, participants described how influential they felt during the interaction. Participants also completed a measure of the Five Factor Model of personality and the self-construal scale (Singelis, 1994).

The analyses reported in Nezlek et al. (2011) found that perceived influence was positively related to how conscientious and open to experience people were in a US sample, and in a German sample how dominating people felt was positively related to conscientiousness. Given the lack of relevant theory and research on this topic, any explanation is speculative. With this caveat in mind, it could be that more conscientious people are more organized and are better prepared to make decisions in interactions.

For openness, assuming that social life (particularly among the US undergraduates who constituted one sample) is not as norm bound or structured as interactions in other environments such as work contexts, being flexible and open-minded might allow an individual to be more influential. If this is so, then being open to new experiences, that is, being prepared to accept the unexpected, might provide a basis for controlling the course of an interaction, particularly if others are not as willing to accept new experiences. Nezlek et al. suggested that the lack of relationships between influence and openness in the German sample may have been due to the fact that social interactions in Germany are more formal or structured than interactions in the United States. If this is the case, then openness might not have the value in Germany as it does in the United States.

The analyses reported in Nezlek and Smith (2005) examined relationships between self-construal and influence and found that independent self-construal was positively related to influence, whereas interdependent self-construal was not. Such a relationship is consistent with definitions of the two types of construal. Independent self-construal refers to the extent to which people define themselves autonomously, that is, independently of the thoughts of others. Such a tendency would be realized in being less prone to follow the lead of others and being more prone to act independently. Moreover, these relationships varied somewhat as a function of whether people were interacting with members of their in-group. See Nezlek and Smith (2005) for details.

### Influencing Others: A Summary

In terms of models and theories that emphasize the importance of control over one's environment, the ability to influence others should be positively related to well-being, and the available research supports this. Nevertheless, well-being is not personality per se (although it may be a part of personality). As discussed earlier, the tactics that people use to influence others have been studied primarily in terms of Machiavellianism, and the roles that other individual differences may play remain somewhat open questions. Less is known, however, about relationships between personality and how influential people are (irrespective of tactics). This lack is due in large part to the fact that research has not focused on such relationships. For example, research on relationships between personality (defined in terms of the Five Factor Model) and influence in daily life is limited and inconclusive.

### General Conclusions and Recommendations

As is perhaps evident from what we presented in this chapter, we have found the study of relationships between social influence and personality to be a bit disjointed. Different researchers have studied different aspects of social influence and different aspects of personality, without any overarching or unifying model or structure. To our knowledge, there has been no ongoing long-term systematic effort to examine these relationships. We will not be so bold to propose such a unifying entity here and now, but we think such a structure or structures is/are needed to provide a framework for moving forward.

One possible exception to our generalization about a lack of a long-term systematic effort is the work of David Buss, who has been studying social influence (primarily) within the context of close relationships for some time (30+ years). Although his work does not focus exclusively on the role of personality, he has certainly focused on the topic as part of his larger interest in evolutionary models and explanations of behavior. Moreover, although evolutionary models may not be "everyone's cup of tea," Buss and Penke (2015) make a convincing case that personality psychology needs to incorporate some of what evolutionary psychology has to offer (and vice versa). By extension, this suggests that the study of individual differences in social influence would benefit from incorporating some of the insights offered by evolutionary psychologists, for example, thinking about social influence as an evolved mechanism to solve recurring adaptive problems. Note that we are not proposing that evolutionary psychology become *the* framework for understanding relationships between personality and social influence. Rather we are suggesting that it could and does provide a useful context.

Regardless, as suggested by Burger (2010), it appears that the situation versus person debate is either over or at least not as important as it once was. Whether this means that social influence, which has been studied most often by experimentally inclined social psychologists, will now become the focus of attention by personologists (or those so inclined) is an open question. Although many scientists who were formally trained and label themselves as social psychologists are functionally personality psychologists (JBN being one), it seems unlikely that studying relationships between personality and social influence will become a mainstream interest of social psychologists, some, perhaps many, of whom simply do not believe that personality exists or that it is important. Regardless of who studies this topic, we believe that certain issues need to be addressed. Two of the most important of these is the nature of personality and the types of research methods that are appropriate to study social influence and personality.

In this chapter we have relied upon a definition of personality defined in terms of traits, following more or less the classic definition of traits offered by Allport (e.g., Allport, 1937). Such a definition includes the assumptions that traits guide and direct behavior and that they are relatively stable over time. We relied upon such a definition because it is the definition relied upon by most researchers, although few state this explicitly (see Funder, 1991, for an informed discussion of the trait approach).

Although popular, trait-based approaches to personality (and Allport's is only one of many) were sharply criticized by Mischel (e.g., Mischel, 1968), who argued that trait approaches were not particularly informative, helpful, or scientific. His argument was based in part on what he perceived to be the failure to find relationships between personality traits and various behaviors on a reliable or consistent basis. Although the concept of traits might be appealing in some ways, if traits cannot explain or are not related to behavior (or other outcomes of interest), then they have no place as part of the science of psychology.

To his credit, Mischel simply did not say the traits were not useful; he proposed an alternative model that he named the Cognitive Affective Processing System (e.g., Mischel, 1973; Mischel, & Shoda, 1995). In broad terms, Mischel has proposed that personality consists of regularities of "if-then" relationships, not pure behavioral consistency across situations as some might think trait theories would predict or assume. For example, assume that one person consistently reacts to anger from a peer with anger, but consistently reacts to anger from a superior with fear, whereas a second person consistently reacts to anger from a peer with anger but consistently reacts to anger from a superior with anxiety, and a third person consistently reacts to anger from a peer with fear but consistently reacts to anger from a superior with sadness or disappointment. Within the Cognitive Affective Processing System, these three patterns of consistent responses represent these individuals' personalities, and differences in such patterns are the individual differences that psychologists should seek to understand.

The Cognitive Affective Processing System model is much more elaborate than the thumbnail description provided here. Regardless, it may suffice to note (with apologies to Mischel) that in some senses the Cognitive Affective Processing System defines personality as the "consistency of inconsistency." As described earlier, people may behave inconsistently across situations, something that Mischel interpreted as being inconsistent with trait approaches, but the differences in how they react to different situations are stable, that is, consistent.

Such an approach seems to be well suited to the study of social influence. Researchers seem to assume (or suspect) that influence strategies vary across situations. For example, Buss (1992) and Jonason and Webster (2012) examined influence tactics across different interpersonal contexts, and similarly, Leary and Allen (2011b) studied self-presentation across different interpersonal contexts. Relying upon a trait-based model, each of these studies examined consistency across the contexts they studied. Patterns of inconsistency were not examined or modeled as they would be for analyses within the Cognitive Affective Processing System.

Regardless of whether one is more interested in inconsistency (e.g., the Cognitive Affective Processing System) or consistency (e.g., traits), researchers need to collect data on multiple occasions. Without multiple assessments it is not possible to model inconsistency. Moreover, the lack of multiple assessments in studies relying upon trait models might have been responsible (at least in part) for the failures Mischel described so forcefully.

Traits are typically defined, or at least measured, in terms of broad tendencies. Trait measures often ask "how typically," "how well," "how often," and so forth a person feels, thinks, or behaves a certain way. In contrast, in many studies, particularly the "one-shot" experiments that are the norm for experimental social psychology, outcomes are very specific. For example, did a person conform at this time, under these circumstances, measured in this way? Failures to find relationships between traits, when they are defined as general tendencies, and behaviors, when they are measured in specific circumstances, may be due to incompatibilities in the levels of generality of the measures of the two constructs.

A similar situation existed in the study of attitude–behavior relations. Ajzen and Fishbein (1977) and Wicker (1969) explained that weak relationships between attitudes and behaviors were due (at least in part) to differences in the generality of measures of attitudes and to which they were meant to correspond. For example, a study might ask a people about their attitudes toward organized religion and find that these attitudes were unrelated to whether people attended a religious service that week. To Wicker and to Ajzen and Fishbein, such a study is flawed (or limited in what it can say about attitude–behavior relations) because the attitudinal measure is nonspecific, whereas the behavioral measure is quite specific. They further discuss how relationships between attitudes and behaviors become stronger as the levels of generality of measures of the two constructs correspond more closely. Interestingly, in footnotes both Wicker (p. 44) and Fishbein and Ajzen (p. 890) suggest or mention (respectively) how the problem of a lack of correspondence between levels of measurement also characterizes the study of relationships between personality and behavior—the very point we are making here.

Okay, now what? The simplest recommendation we have is a methodological one. Understanding relationships between personality and social influence will require studies in which outcomes are measured over multiple occasions or situations. For dyed-in-the-wool trait theorists, multiple measures are needed to ensure that the levels of measurement of outcomes correspond to the levels of measurement of traits. Moreover, multiple assessments provide more reliable measures, which increases the ability of a study to detect relationships. For interactionists, those who believe that the person and the situation combine, multiple assessments are needed to provide the data needed to determine if interactions exist. For devotees of Mischel's Cognitive Affective Processing System, multiple assessments are needed to model the "if-then" relationships that are at the core of the system. These multiple assessments do not have to be across time, although they can be. They simply need to occur.

At a more global level, understanding the relationship between personality and social influence is going to require a *rapprochement* between social and personality psychology and psychologists. Social psychologists are going to need to recognize the value of the personological approach and stop thinking of personality theory as a collection of possibly attractive ideas that are nice to talk about at cocktail parties but have no scientific value. For their part, personologists will need to recognize the value of the sometimes more specific models and theories upon which social psychologists rely. The precision of experimental social psychology is not merely elegant trivia. Will such a *rapprochement* occur? The study of social influence is certainly an area that could benefit from this. One can only hope.

## References

Ajzen, I, & Fishbein, M. (1977). Attitude-behavior relations: A theoretical analysis and reveiew of empiorical research, *Psychology Bulletin, 84*, 888–918.

Allport, G. W. (1937). *Personality: A psychological interpretation.* New York, NY: Henry Holt & Co.

APA (2015). *APA handbook of personality and social psychology, Volume 4: Personality processes and individual differences* (edited by M. Mikulincer, P. R. Shaver, M. L. Cooper, & R. J. Larsen).

Washington, DC: American Psychological Association. http://dx.doi.org.proxy.wm.edu/10.1037/14343-000

Appley, M. H., & Moeller, G. (1963). Conforming behavior and personality variables in college women. *Journal of Abnormal and Social Psychology, 66*, 284–290.

Asch, S. E. (1956). Studies of independence and conformity. A minority of one against a unanimous majority. *Psychological Monographs, 70*, 1–70.

Ashton, M. C., & Lee, K. (2001). A theoretical basis for the major dimensions of personality. *European Journal of Personality, 15*, 327–353.

Bandura, A. (1986). The explanatory and predictive scope of self-efficacy theory. *Journal of Social and Clinical Psychology, 4*, 359–373.

Barron, F. (1953). Some personality correlates of independence judgment. *Journal of Personality, 21*, 287–297.

Basic Psychological Needs Scale (n.d.). Retrieved from http://www.selfdeterminationtheory.org/basic-psychological-needs-scale/

Baumeister, R. F., & Leary, M. R. (1995). The need to belong: Desire for interpersonal attachments as a fundamental human motivation. *Psychological Bulletin, 117*, 497–529.

Bègue, L., Beauvois, J-L., Courbet, D., Oberlé, D., Lepage, J., & Duke, A. A. (2014). Personality predicts obedience in a Milgram paradigm. *Journal of Personality, 83*, 299–306. doi: 10.1111/jopy.12104

Blass, T. (1991). Understanding behavior in the Milgram obedience experiment: The role of personality, situations, and their interactions. *Journal of Personality and Social Psychology, 60*, 398–413.

Bocchiaro, P., & Zimbardo, P. G. (2010). Defying unjust authority: An exploratory study. *Current Psychology: A Journal for Diverse Perspectives on Diverse Psychological Issues, 29*, 155–170. doi: 10.1007/s12144-010-9080-z

Bornstein, R. F. (1992). The dependent personality: Developmental, social, and clinical perspectives. *Psychological Bulletin, 112*, 3–23.

Bourgeois, M. J., Sommer, K. L., & Bruno, S. (2009). What do we get out of influencing others? *Social Influence, 4*, 96–121.

Burger, J. M. (1987). Desire for control and conformity to a perceived norm. *Journal of Personality and Social Psychology Bulletin, 53*, 355–360.

Burger, J. M. (1992). *Desire for control: Personality, social, and clinical perspectives.* New York, NY: Plenum.

Burger, J. M. (2010). Participants are people too: Introduction to the special issue on individual differences and social influence. *Social Influence, 5*, 149–151.

Burger, J. M., & Cooper, H. M. (1979). The desirability of control. *Motivation and Emotion, 3*, 381–393.

Buss, D. M. (1992). Manipulation in close relationships: Five personality factors in interactional context. *Journal of Personality, 60*, 477–499.

Buss, D. M., Gomes, M., Higgins, D. S., & Lauterbach, K. (1987). Tactics of manipulation. *Journal of Personality and Social Psychology, 52*, 1219–1229.

Buss, D. M., & Penke, L. (2015). Evolutionary personality psychology. In M. Mikulincer, P. R. Shaver, M. L. Cooper, & R. J. Larsen (Eds.), *APA handbook of personality and social psychology, Vol. 4: Personality processes and individual differences* (pp. 3–29). Washington, DC: American Psychological Association. doi: 10.1037/14343-001

Cherulnik, P. D., Way, J. H., Ames, S., & Hutto, D. B. (1981). Impressions of high and low Machiavellian men. *Journal of Personality, 49*, 388–400.

Christie, R., & Geis, F. (1970). *Studies in Machiavellianism.* New York, NY: Academic Press.

Cialdini, R. B., Trost, M. R., & Newsom, J. T. (1995). Preference for consistency: The development of a valid measure and the discovery of surprising behavioral implications. *Journal of Personality and Social Psychology Bulletin, 69,* 318–328.

Crutchfield, R. S. (1955). Conformity and character. *American Psychologist, 10,* 191–198.

Deci, E. L. (1975). *Intrinsic motivation.* New York, NY: Plenum.

Deci, E. L., & Ryan, R. M. (1985a). *Intrinsic motivation and self-determination in human behavior.* New York, NY: Plenum.

Deci, E. L., & Ryan, R. M. (1985b). The general causality orientations scale: Self determination in personality. *Journal of Research in Personality, 19,* 109–134.

Dodge, N., & Muench, G. A. (1969). Relationship of conformity and the need for approval in children. *Developmental Psychology, 1,* 67–68.

Dweck, C. S., Hong, Y., & Chiu, C. (1993). Implicit theories: Individual differences in the likelihood and meaning of dispositional inference. *Personality and Social Psychology, 19,* 644–656.

Eysenck, H. J. A. (1958). A short questionnaire for the measurement of two dimensions of personality. *Journal of Applied Psychology, 42,* 14–17.

Eysenck, H. J., & Eysenck, S. B. (1975). *Eysenck Personality Questionnaire manual.* San Diego, CA: Educational Testing Service.

Falbo, T. (1977). Multidimensional scaling of power strategies. *Journal of Personality and Social Psychology, 35,* 537–547. doi: 10.1037//0022-3514.35.8.537

Fehr, B., Samsom, D., & Paulhus, D. L. (1992). The construct of Machiavellianism: Twenty years later. In C. D. Spielberger & J. N. Butcher (Eds.), *Advances in personality assessment* (Vol. 9, pp. 77–116). Hillsdale, NJ: Erlbaum.

Festinger, L. (1957). *A theory of cognitive dissonance.* Stanford, CA: Stanford University Press.

Frager, R. (1970). Conformity and anticomformity in Japan. *Journal of Personality and Social Psychology, 15,* 203–210.

Freedman J., & Fraser, S. (1966). Compliance without pressure: the foot-in-the-door technique. *Journal of Personality and Social Psychology, 4,* 195–202.

Funder, D. A. (1991). Global traits: A Neo-Allportian approach to personality. *Psychological Science, 2,* 31–39.

Gamian-Wilk, M., & Lachowicz-Tabaczek, K. (2007). Implicit theories and compliance with the foot-in-the-door technique. *Polish Psychological Bulletin, 38,* 50–63.

Gamian-Wilk, M., & Lachowicz-Tabaczek, K. (2009). The belief to have fixed or malleable traits and help giving: Implicit theories and sequential social influence techniques. *Polish Psychological Bulletin, 40,* 85–100.

Gebhardt, W. A., & Brosschot, J. F. (2002). Desirability of control: Psychometric properties and relationships with locus of control, personality, coping, and mental and somatic complaints in three Dutch samples. *European Journal of Personality, 16,* 423–438. doi: 10.1002/per.463

Goldberg, L. R. (1983, June). The magical number five, plus or minus two: Some conjectures on the dimensionality of personality descriptions. Paper presented at the Gerontology Research Center, National Institute on Aging, Baltimore, MD.

Guadagno, R. E., Asher, T., Demaine, L. J. & Cialdini, R. B. (2001). When saying yes leads to saying no: Preference for consistency and the reverse foot-in-the-door effect. *Personality and Social Psychology Bulletin, 27,* 859–867.

Guadagno, R. E, & Cialdini, R. B. (2010). Preference for consistency and social influence: A review of current research findings. *Social Influence, 5,* 152–163.

Gudjonsson, G. H. (1989). Compliance in an interrogation situation: A new scale. *Personality and Individual Differences, 10,* 535–540.

Gudjonsson, G. H. (1991). The effects of intelligence and memory on group differences in suggestibility and compliance. *Personality and Individual Differences, 12,* 503–505.

Gudjonsson, G. H. (1997). *The Gudjonsson suggestibility scales manual.* Hove, UK: Psychology Press.

Gudjonsson, G. H., & Sigurdsson, J. F. (2003). The relationship of compliance with coping strategies and self-esteem. *European Journal of Psychological Assessment, 19,* 117–123.

Gudjonsson, G. H., & Sigurdsson, J. F. (2007). Motivation for offending and personality. A study among young offenders on probation. *Personality and Individual Differences, 43,* 1243–1253.

Gudjonsson, G. H., Sigurdsson, J. F., & Einarsson, E. (2007). Taking blame for antisocial acts and its relationship with personality. *Personality and Individual Differences, 43,* 3–13.

Gudjonsson, G. H., Sigurdsson, J. F., Einarsson, E., & Einarsson, J. H. (2008). Personal versus impersonal relationship compliance and their relationship with personality. *The Journal of Forensic Psychiatry and Psychology, 19,* 502–516.

Gudjonsson, G. H., Sigurdsson, J. F., Lydsdottir, L. B., & Olafsdottir, H. (2008). The relationship between adult romantic attachment and compliance. *Personality and Individual Differences, 45,* 276–280.

John, O. P., Naumann, L. P., & Soto, C. J. (2008). Paradigm shift to the integrative Big-Five trait taxonomy: History, measurement, and conceptual issues. In O. P. John, R. W. Robins, & L. A. Pervin (Eds.), *Handbook of personality: Theory and research* (pp. 114–158). New York, NY: Guilford Press.

John, O. P., & Srivastava, S. (1999). The Big-Five trait taxonomy: History, measurement, and theoretical perspectives. In L. A. Pervin & O. P. John (Eds.), *Handbook of personality: Theory and research* (Vol. 2, pp. 102–138). New York, NY: Guilford Press.

Jonason, P. K., & Webster, G. D. (2010). The Dirty Dozen: A concise measure of the Dark Triad. *Psychological Assessment, 22,* 420–432.

Jonason, P. K., & Webster, G. D. (2012). A protean approach to social influence: Dark Triad personality and social influence tactics. *Personality and Individual Differences, 52,* 521–526. doi: 10.1016/j.paid.2011.11.023

Kagan, J., & Mussen, P. H. (1956). Dependency themes on the TAT and group conformity. *Journal of Consulting Psychology, 20,* 29–32.

Kernis, M. H., & Goldman, B. M. (2006). A multicomponent conceptualization of authenticity: Research and theory. In M. P. Zanna (Ed.), *Advances in experimental social psychology* (Vol. 38, pp. 284–357). San Diego, CA: Academic Press.

La Guardia, J. G., Ryan, R. M., Couchman, C. E., & Deci, E. L. (2000). Within-person variation in security of attachment: A self-determination theory perspective on attachment, need fulfillment, and well-being. *Journal of Personality and Social Psychology, 79,* 367–384.

Larmour, S. R., Bergstrøm, H., Gillen, C. T. A., & Forth, A. E. (2015). Behind the confession: Relating false confession, interrogative compliance, personality traits, and psychopathy. *Journal of Police and Criminal Psychology, 30,* 94–102. doi: 10.1007/s11896-014-9144-3

Larsen, K. S., Triplett, J. S., Brant, W. D., & Langenberg, D. (1979). Collaborator status, subject characteristics, and conformity in the Asch paradigm. *The Journal of Social Psychology, 108*, 259–263.

Leary M. R., & Allen, A. B. (2011a). Personality and persona: Personality processes in self-presentation. *Journal of Personality, 79*, 1191–1218. doi: 10.1111/j.1467–6494.2010.00704.x

Leary M. R., & Allen, A. B. (2011b). Self-presentational persona: Simultaneous management of multiple impressions. *Journal of Personality and Social Psychology, 101*, 1033–1049. doi: 10.1037/a0023884

Machiavelli, N. (1961). *The prince* (G. Bull, trans.). London, UK: Penguin Classics. (Original work published 1532).

Milgram, S. (1974). *Obedience to authority: An experimental view.* New York, NY: Harper & Row.

Mischel, W. (1968). *Personality and assessment.* New York, NY: Wiley.

Mischel, W. (1973). Towards a cognitive social learning reconceptualization of personality. *Psychological Review, 80*, 252–283. doi: 10.1037/h0035002

Mischel, W., & Shoda, Y. (1995). A cognitive-affective system theory of personality: Reconceptualizing situations, dispositions, dynamics, and invariance in personality structure. *Psychological Review, 102*, 246–268.

Nezlek, J. B. (2012). Diary methods for social and personality psychology. In J. B. Nezlek (Ed.), *The SAGE library in social and personality psychology methods.* London, UK: Sage Publications.

Nezlek, J. B., & Gable, S. L. (2001). Depression as a moderator of relationships between positive daily events and day-to-day psychological adjustment. *Personality and Social Psychology Bulletin, 27*, 1692–1704.

Nezlek, J. B., Schütz, A., Schröder-Abé, M., & Smith. C. V. (2011). A cross-cultural study of relationships between daily social interaction and the Five Factor Model of personality. *Journal of Personality, 79*, 811–840.

Nezlek, J. B., & Smith, C. V. (2005). Social identity in daily social interaction. *Self and Identity, 4*, 243–261.

Olesen, M. O., Thomsen, D. K., Schnieber, A., & Tønnesvan, J. (2010). Distinguishing general causality orientations from personality traits. *Personality and Individual Differences, 48*, 538–543.

Paulhus, D. L. (1983). Sphere-specific measures of perceived control. *Journal of Personality and Social Psychology, 44*, 1253–1265.

Paulhus, D. L., & Williams, K. M. (2002). The Dark Triad of personality: Narcissism, Machiavellianism, and psychopathy. *Journal of Research in Personality, 36*, 556–563.

Rauthmann, J. F., & Kolar, G. (2012). How "dark" are the Dark Triad traits? Examining the perceived darkness of narcissism, Machiavellianism, and psychopathy. *Personality and Individual Differences, 53*, 884–889. doi: 10.1016/j.paid.2012.06.020

Ray, J. V., & Jones, S. (2012). Examining the relationship between self-reported compliance and psychopathic personality traits. *Personality and Individual Differences, 52*, 190–194.

Ryan, R. M. & Deci. E. L. (2000). Intrinsic and extrinsic motivations: Classic definitions and new directions. *Contemporary Educational Psychology 25*, 54–67. doi: 10.1006/ceps.1999.1020

Sheppard, B. H., & Vidmar, N. (1980). Adversary pretrial procedures and testimonial evidence: Effects of lawyer's role and Machiavellianism. *Journal of Personality and Social Psychology, 39*, 320–332.

Sigurdsson, J. F., & Gudjonsson, G. H. (2001). False confessions: The relative importance of psychological, criminological and substance abuse variables. *Psychology, Crime and Law, 7*, 275–289.

Singelis, T. M. (1994). The measurement of independent and interdependent self-construals. *Personality and Social Psychology Bulletin, 20*, 580–591.

Singh, U. P. & Akhtar, S. N. (1973). Extraversion, neuroticism, and conformity. *Manas: A Journal of Scientific Psychology, 20*, 125–132.

Sommer, K. L., & Bourgeois, M. J. (2010). Linking the perceived ability to influence others to subjective well-being: A need-based approach. *Social Influence, 5*, 220–244.

Strickland, B. R. & Crowne, D. P. (1962). Conformity under conditions of simulated group pressure as a function of the need for social approval. *The Journal of Social Psychology, 58*, 171–181.

ten Brinke, L., Liu, C. C., Keltner, D., & Srivastava, S. B. (2016). Virtues, vices, and political influence in the U.S. Senate. *Psychological Science, 27*, 85–93. doi: 10.1177/0956797615611922

Vecchio, R. P., & Sussmann, M. (1991). Choice of influence tactics: Individual and organizational determinants. *Journal of Organizational Behavior, 12*, 73–80.

Wheeler, L., & Nezlek, J. (1977). Sex differences in social participation. *Journal of Personality and Social Psychology, 35*, 742–754.

White, R. W. (1959). Motivation reconsidered: The concept of competence. *Psychological Review, 66*, 297–333.

Wicker, A. W. (1969). Attitudes vs. actions: The relationship of verbal and overt behavioral responses to attitude object. *Journal of Social Issues, 25*, 41–78.

Wiggins, J. S. (1979). A psychological taxonomy of interpersonal behavior. *Journal of Personality and Social Psychology, 37*, 395–412. doi: 10.1037/0022–3514.37.3.395

Williams, J. M., & Warchal, J. (1981). The relationship between assertiveness, internal-external locus of control, and overt conformity. *The Journal of Psychology: Interdisciplinary and Applied, 109*, 93–96.

Zeigler-Hill, V., Southard, A. C., Archer, L. M., & Donohoe, P. L. (2013). Neuroticism and negative affect influence the reluctance to engage in destructive obedience in the Milgram paradigm. *The Journal of Social Psychology, 153*, 161–174. doi: 10.1080/00224545.2012.713041

# PART 3

# Interpersonal Processes

# On the Trail of Social Comparison

Jerry Suls *and* Ladd Wheeler

**Abstract**

Social comparison, a major source of social influence, refers to the selection and utilization of information about other people's standings and opinions to make accurate self-assessments or to protect or enhance self-esteem. We survey the development of comparison theory over six decades, its ambiguities, and reformulations based on the psychology of attribution and social cognition. Selective comparisons allow people to gauge how well they have fulfilled their potential and capacity to accomplish important tasks, and whether their beliefs, values, and actions are appropriate and worthwhile. Exposure to superior and inferior targets shifts self-evaluations toward (assimilation) or away (contrast) from the targets, depending on the kinds of information made cognitively accessible by the situation or by individual differences. To illustrate comparison's effects on social influence, applications, such as the effects of academic tracking on self-esteem and effects of large social networks on mental and physical health outcomes, are described.

**Key Words:** social comparison, self-evaluation, relative standing, self-enhancement, contrast, assimilation

Social comparison refers to the search for and utilization of information about other persons' opinions, beliefs, and performance for assessing one's own opinions, beliefs, and capabilities (Festinger, 1954a,b; Wood, 1996). Virtually any personal attribute, such as physical attractiveness, income, sense of humor, or the ability to ride a bucking bronco, can be the object of comparison. Observations and speculations about this core aspect of human social experience can be found as early as Aristotle. Prior to the time it was formally referred to as "social comparison," its effects were documented in the conformity experiments conducted by Sherif (1936) and studies of status by Hyman (1942). The first systematic scientific perspective, however, was advanced in 1954 by Leon Festinger. Aside from a gap between 1967 and the mid-1970s, social comparison has been actively researched for six decades (Suls & Miller, 1977; Suls & Wheeler, 2000). This chapter provides an updated and integrated version of theory and research, which acknowledges

modifications and extensions inspired by developments in related areas of social psychology. Social comparisons play a major role in social influence. Conformity, as demonstrated in Sherif's (1936) and Asch's (1951) classic paradigms, is dependent in part on comparing with other people's judgments and behaviors in response to the same social or physical stimuli. Relative standing in comparison with the performance of peers on academic tests or in athletic competitions plays a major role in self-concept, self-esteem, and subsequent actions (e.g., Morse & Gergen, 1970). Belief in fads and hearsay seems to be strongly affected by comparison with the opinions of others (e.g., DiFonzo et al., 2013).

Although scientific inquiry often is depicted as a series of ascending steps, "old hands" know that every scientific enterprise encounters weedy paths, parched lands, blind canyons, and occasional picturesque vistas until the clouds roll in. Social comparison is no exception. Although neither of us was present at the birth of social comparison studies, one of us (LW) hit the trail in the late 1950s and the other (JS) in the early 1970s. By the 1990s, we saddled up together to pursue social comparison. Like the two cowboys, Lefty and Dusty, from the radio program, "Prairie Home Companion," we followed the trail, rustled steers, organized a couple of rodeos, were hoodwinked by a snake-oil salesman, shook off the dust, traded bad jokes ("Why was the cowboy arrested for wearing a paper bag? Answer: Rustling"), and continued on our way.

Although some elements of our story may resemble *Blazing Saddles* more than *High Noon*, we promise to tell no tall tales. In the interests of brevity, this chapter is intended as a contemporary perspective with modest bows to the past. (See Suls & Wheeler, 2012; Wheeler, 1991, for extended histories.)

## Functions of Social Comparison

Festinger (1954a,b) wrote about social comparison shortly after he concluded his stint as the leader of research on the dynamics of social influence in informal (leaderless) groups at MIT and at the University of Michigan. The preceding work, summarized in his informal social communication theory (Festinger, 1950), emphasized the actions of social pressures, such as communication between group members and the rejection of deviates, to attain agreement or uniformity in the group. Uniformity of opinion was considered desirable because it provides confidence in one's opinion or facilitates group goals. When Festinger turned his attention to social comparison, he moved from a focus on the power of the group over the individual to how individuals use groups to evaluate themselves. Although he thought people prefer to assess themselves relative to objective standards, these frequently are unavailable or nonexistent. In their absence, social comparison serves as a substitute to reduce uncertainty.

Festinger proposed that people are driven by a motivation to acquire accurate assessments of their abilities and to hold correct beliefs/opinions. He perceived that without an accurate appraisal, a person could not survive effectively. This came to be known as the "self-evaluation motive." To serve this motivation, Festinger proposed that comparisons should be selective because only comparisons with certain kinds of people can reduce uncertainty. His hypothesis was that comparison with similar others provides the strongest feelings of subjective confidence. (Because of another motive relevant for abilities, he offered a more nuanced prediction for them than for opinions; see later.) Unfortunately, Festinger was not precise about what he meant by "similar."

Some of his examples referred to other people who performed at the same level or who shared the same beliefs or opinions, but other examples suggested something more was required for a comparison to provide clarity. Subsequent researchers adopted the "same ability/same opinion" examples, but further down the trail the ambiguity associated with the similarity hypothesis created problems about how researchers should proceed. (More about that later.)

The self-evaluation motive, which was supposed to direct the comparison process to learn the unvarnished truth, seemed straightforward, but subsequent researchers were skeptical about this motive being the only force instigating comparison. For example, Hakmiller (1966) found evidence that subjects, who were made to feel that their score might reflect negatively on themselves (hostility toward one's parents), compared with someone whose score was worse than their own. Presumably, this "downward comparison" was made so subjects could feel better about themselves. In a performance situation where threat was minimal (cognitive flexibility), Wheeler (1966) reported that subjects preferred to learn the score of other subjects whose ranking was just above their own (i.e., upward comparison). Selecting someone ranked higher does not seem enhancing unless one anticipates scoring closely to that person. In fact, subjects expected they scored close to the person ranked just above them. Both empirical studies offered evidence that comparisons were chosen to yield a positive (or less negative) outcome. Both studies used the rank-order paradigm that became popular in the 1960s and 1970s.

By the 1980s, there were many empirical instances of social behavior that seemed to serve self-enhancement, whereby people selectively searched, interpreted, or acted in ways to confirm social information that reflected positively on the self. In keeping with this emphasis, Wood (1989) posited there were two distinct motives—self-evaluation and self-enhancement—in social comparison. Both the selection and effects of comparisons were perceived to vary depending on which motive was dominant.

Although in abstract terms, the two motives can be distinguished, it seems doubtful to us that they work independently. "Evaluhancement" is a mouthful (like "Hank herded heifers"), but there appears to be no conventional term that conveys our meaning better that people are motivated to learn the truth, but they also want their opinions, beliefs, and attributes to reflect positively on themselves. Only when the domain is of little interest and not self-defining, comparisons probably pass with little notice. In most circumstances, the appraisal and cognitive elaboration of comparison information is skewed toward a positive result. This may be manifested in the way people selectively search for comparisons and how they interpret their implications. With the advent of social cognition and particularly recognition of implicit and automatic cognitive processes, neither the search nor interpretation need be conscious or deliberate.

In his theory, Festinger had little to say about the valence of comparison, so his original theory has tended to be associated with the self-evaluation motive. However, Festinger noted there was a cultural value set on doing better and better in terms of abilities, which he referred to as the "unidirectional drive upward." He recognized this drive would conflict with uniformity or agreement as a goal, so a balance is struck for orienting toward someone who was better, but not too superior. He restricted this prediction to abilities, but more contemporary research indicates that when there is a favored side, it is perceived to be better to lean somewhat further in that direction than do other people (Jones & Gerard, 1965). For example, Jellison and Riskind (1970) found that advocating more polarized decisions is interpreted as a reflection of personal ability. This was demonstrated in decision making about risk and caution (see also Baron & Roper 1976), but comparable effects are seen in political attitudes (Moscovici & Zavolloni, 1969). Moderate polarization with respect to abilities, opinions, and beliefs would seem to be the default position.

Another way to think about how self-enhancement and self-evaluation are joined pivots on recognition that comparison simultaneously addresses two sources of uncertainty. One source pertains to the specific opinion/belief or ability (i.e., "Am I correct?" "Am I able to do X?"). However, unless the opinion or ability is only of slight importance, comparative standing has an added implication: "Am I a worthwhile person?" Learning one is correct (by finding others agree) and capable of mastering life tasks (by comparing with "a similar other") carries meanings beyond any purely epistemological need; these beliefs confer a feeling of self-worth that subsumes specific opinions or attributes.[1] In sum, people strive for the truth, but they prefer it to be self-affirming.

## Related Attributes and Similarity

We have already alluded to a difficulty in Festinger's hypothesis that the best comparison person is someone who is similar. If a woman wants to evaluate her ability in a certain area, she should compare herself to someone who has similar ability (or slightly better). But if she already knows that she and the comparison target have similar ability, what would she learn from making the comparison? Goethals and Darley (1977) attempted to clarify this ambiguity by proposing what has become known as the "related attributes hypothesis" (Wheeler & Zuckerman, 1977). The related attributes hypothesis is as follows: "Given a range of possible persons for comparison, someone who should be close to one's own performance or opinion, given his standing on characteristics related to and predictive of performance or opinion, will be chosen for comparison" (Goethals & Darley, 1977, p. 265). In other words, a woman wanting to evaluate, say, her leadership skills should compare her skills to those of another woman who has had the same degree of training and experience in leadership, the same intelligence, and the same social skills. These are all probably related to and predictive of leadership skills. If she discovers that she has superior skills, she should feel the glow of achievement and high self-esteem. If she discovers her skills to be inferior, she would be unhappy (however, depending on other factors, being below par might increase her efforts to be a better leader or ruminate and spiral downhill). If, as is most likely, she discovers that her skills are equal to those of the other woman, she would feel that she is as good as she ought to be, given her relative standing on the related attributes.

Note that she would probably compare with another woman rather than with a man. Why is that? First, there has been a great deal of discussion about different leadership styles of females and males, suggesting that a female should evaluate her skills in the context of other females. (Of course, an astute woman might well also make cross-sex comparisons to test the hypothesis of different leadership styles for males and females.) Secondly, there are some characteristics such as gender and age and perhaps ethnic background that so deeply permeate society that they constrain social comparisons. People rarely compare themselves to others of the opposite sex. When they do, it is likely to be a group comparison rather than an individual comparison. That is, women as a group may compare their income to men as a group and work to remove the injustice they see. But individuals are more likely to make same-sex comparisons in evaluating most things.

The related attributes hypothesis has much to recommend it theoretically and there is substantial empirical support (Gastorf & Suls, 1978; Goethals & Nelson, 1973; Gorenflo & Crano, 1989; Miller, 1982; Suls, Gaes, & Gastorf, 1979; Suls, Gastorf, & Lawhon, 1978; Wheeler, Koestner, & Driver, 1982; Wheeler & Koestner, 1984; Zanna, Goethals, & Hill, 1975). The question it allows us to ask is simply, "Am I as skilled as I ought to be given my resources?" That is an important question and has profound emotional and self-concept effects. To discover that one is better than one "ought" to be makes a cowboy feel a foot taller. However, it is not the only or necessarily the most important question that social comparison answers. In the next section, we will explore an entirely different question.

## The Proxy Model

In the late 1960s and early 1970s, much of the research on social comparison used the rank-order paradigm to investigate the selection of comparison others. As described earlier in this chapter, participants in this research knew their own rank and score in a group and could choose to see the score of another person at another rank selected by them. Jones and Regan (1974) argued that this research did not have much to say about accurate self-appraisal and was instead concerned with enhancing self-esteem or defending against self-derogation. Jones and Regan (1974, p. 134) noted that "the appropriate realm for testing and applying Festinger's conception of ability evaluation is in situations in which decisions involving an ability evaluation and leading to actions utilizing the ability are anticipated."

Indeed, Festinger did stress action possibilities. "Persons also try to find out what they can and cannot do in the environment in which they live. . . . the human being attempts to know what exists in the world around him and to know what his possibilities of action are in that world" (Festinger, 1954b, p. 193). Festinger gave the example of a person who wants to know how intelligent he is. Simply knowing his score on an intelligence test would allow him to label himself as above or below average, as genius or slow, or as average, but it would not tell him what he is capable of accomplishing intellectually. It would, however, allow him to compare himself to others of similar intelligence and to conclude that he can accomplish the same things that they can accomplish. If the person compared to others of divergent intelligence, either lower or higher, he would perhaps learn something, but it would be negative

knowledge, and he would not know exactly what he could accomplish.

Jones and Regan (1974) conducted two experiments to show that (1) people are more interested in comparison information before making a decision concerning that ability than after the decision has been made, and (2) comparison is preferred with someone similar ability who has had experience on the same task that is about to be undertaken rather than someone who has not had such experience.

Unfortunately, the Jones and Regan (1974) paper did not mesh with the zeitgeist, and its message was almost totally ignored. Independently, and with much more research to rely upon, we proposed the proxy model of social comparison for self-assessment of ability (Wheeler, Martin, & Suls, 1997). The proxy model describes how people use social comparison information to answer the question "Can I do X?" Or to put it more formally, the question is "Do I have sufficient ability to perform a specific task successfully?" The individual looks for a person (a proxy) who is as similar as possible on the abilities required for the task and has already performed the task. If the individual and the proxy are quite similar on the required abilities, and if the proxy has successfully performed the task, the individual can feel more confident that he can also.

The proxy model assumes that we can accurately evaluate the abilities of other people in order to compare them to our abilities. This is not always an easy task, because we usually have only witnessed the performances of others, and performances are affected by other variables in addition to ability (Kelley, 1967). One way to view the proxy model is to think of Task 1 (a preliminary task) and Task 2 (the crucial task), both requiring the ability. If the individual and the proxy perform the same on Task 1, the assumption is that they would perform the same on Task 2. However, it is possible that the individual has been misled by the proxy's Task 1 performance and that the proxy's ability is actually far greater than the individual knows (perhaps the proxy was sick or hung over during Task 1 and so performance suffered). In that case, the individual might use related attributes to make the necessary adjustments (Martin, Suls, & Wheeler, 2002). For example, if the proxy's related attributes suggest a higher ability than implied by the Task 1 performance, the individual should proceed with caution.

People often wonder if they can accomplish something but are deterred from trying because of the possible costs of failure. Knowing that someone similar to you has come through more or less successfully reduces the restraints against your making the attempt. This is clearly a strong and frequent type of social influence.

Empirical confirmation of the proxy theory predictions have been obtained in laboratory studies involving physical (i.e., grip strength) and intellectual tasks (i.e., puzzle solving) (Martin et al., 2002). (Insufficient extramural funding prevented our choosing cattle roping.) Smith and Sachs (1997) also provided support with two laboratory studies. The proxy model also provides a coherent explanation for some previously reported results in a different domain. Kulik and Mahler (1989) were interested in patients awaiting coronary artery bypass surgery (CABG), a situation that elicits both uncertainty and threat. Earlier research by Schachter (1959) suggested these patients should prefer to affiliate with other patients awaiting the same procedure (i.e., similar others) to assess whether their feelings about the upcoming surgery are appropriate. Kulik and his associates reasoned that patients might have a greater need for cognitive clarity about how they will get through this arduous procedure. These are questions addressed in the proxy model: "What will I experience? "Can I do X?" "How will I respond?"

Kulik and Mahler (1989) asked men hospitalized for CABG whom they would prefer to be assigned as a roommate: a patient awaiting the procedure like themselves, a patient who was back on the ward recovering after CABG, or no preference. Patients most often preferred a roommate who was already recovering from the surgery. Consistent with the proxy model, patients reported, "It's more helpful for me to talk to someone who's already had it." Subsequently, Kulik, Moore, and Mahler (1996) examined how CABG patients adapted to rooming with another preoperative patient, a post-CABG patient, or a patient with a noncardiac diagnosis. Not only did the participants ask more questions of the post-CABG roommate, they also exhibited less anxiety, recovered faster, and had a shorter hospital stay than participants assigned to the other kinds of roommates. The implication is that being exposed to an appropriate proxy (i.e., someone who succeeded at the same task) resolves uncertainty and anxiety and facilitates better performance.

## Opinion Comparison

The related attribute approach, described earlier, devoted some attention to opinion comparison. In contrast to Festinger, who treated opinions generically, Goethals and Darley (1977) distinguished between beliefs versus values (Goethals &

Nelson, 1973). Beliefs refer to potentially verifiable facts, whereas values are personal preferences. Comparisons with similar others on related attributes, such as background and general worldview, are of most utility for value assessment. For beliefs, however, someone who is dissimilar on related attributes was hypothesized to be more useful because he or she provides another perspective to "triangulate on" the truth. If they concur, albeit coming at things from a different direction, then your confidence should be enhanced (Kelley, 1967).

Our triadic model (Suls, Martin, & Wheeler, 2000) concurs with Goethals and Darley's prediction about values, but to assess facts, people should prefer to compare with someone who is superior on related attributes (more expertise or experience)—not just dissimilar per se. Since few facts are completely value-free, however, someone who has more expertise and also shares the same basic values (i.e., worldview) is probably most preferred. The triadic model refers to such a person as a "similar expert" and is illustrated by the finding that gay men are more likely to adopt safe-sex practices when someone promotes them who is both more knowledgeable and shares their sexual orientation (Kelly et al., 1991).

A real-life example comes from "the violence interrupters" who work for "Save Our Streets Crown Heights" (Brooklyn, NY). These are community members who step in and mediate between neighbors, store-owners, and so on, who are in a conflict that could escalate into violence. One such worker is Rudy Suggs, an ex-gun-toting drug dealer and ex-con. "Mr. Suggs says his message works because he is what Save Our Streets calls a 'credible messenger': someone who has been there" (Yee, 2012, p. A22).

The model is called "triadic" because it adds a third kind of opinion comparison, which concerns predictions about affective responses to future situations (e.g., will I like that new bean recipe at supper?). Like the proxy model, action possibilities also figure here because you probably want to think there is a reasonable likelihood you will like the new recipe before you try it. The model also borrows the concept of proxy. I can predict my future response with some confidence by learning about the response to "X" of a proxy who has already sampled the beans. The proxy should be considered appropriate if he or she shares related attributes or past pattern of agreement with respect to other similar foods.

The triadic logic for preference prediction is similar to the "collaborative filtering" used by Amazon.

com and other Internet retailers. This refers to recommendations about future purchases of compact disks, books, and other products that are based on what other people, with similar past preferences and/or demographics, purchased or rated highly.

## Contrast

A social comparison should induce changes in the person's evaluation of a personal ability or opinion, but does it shift toward (i.e., assimilation) or away (i.e., contrast) from the comparison target? Wheeler's (1966) results, described earlier, are suggestive of assimilation with someone who performed better (originally Wheeler called the phenomenon "assumed similarity"). However, results for contrast also have been reported. A well-known example is Morse and Gergen's (1970) "Mr. Clean-Mr. Dirty experiment," where the self-esteem of subjects increased after being exposed to a disheveled, disorganized student but decreased after exposed to a well-dressed, very competent college student. In the 1980s, the potential for comparison to produce contrast was foremost for researchers (see Brickman & Bulman, 1977). In addition to the evidence reported in the field, the related areas of relative deprivation and other social judgment theories (Pettigrew, 1967) long emphasized how exposure to persons or groups of higher standing, via contrast, created distress in lower ranked members of society.

Research on contrast came even more to the forefront with the publication of downward comparison theory. Inspired by Hakmiller's (1966) earlier evidence, Wills (1981) (originally from the prairies of Hawaii) proposed that people under threat should compare with others who are worse off, and such downward comparisons should lead them to feel better about themselves—a contrast effect. An additional prediction was that low-self-esteem individuals would be most likely to compare downward under threat. These ideas received empirical support in an inventive field study; cancer patients, who were interviewed, seemed to benefit from making or imagining strategic comparisons with other patients who were worse off, such as "At first [the scar] was gross. . . . Now I don't think it's so bad, especially after you've seen my friend; she just had two radiation implants put in," (Wood, Taylor, & Lichtman, 1985, p. 1176).

A flurry of experimental and correlational research followed, which featured medical patients and other samples experiencing threats to self-esteem (Gibbons & Gerrard, 1991). We speculate that researchers were very active partly because some downward comparisons are compelling and memorable in a way other kinds of comparisons tend not to be. For example, after two national tragedies—the havoc created by Hurricane Sandy in the Northeast and the murder of elementary school children in Newtown, Connecticut—this excerpt from a journalist's interview with a resident of the hardest hit beach town in New Jersey appeared: "There really isn't any comparison. . . . We lost things and we can replace those things. They lost children and lives. Those are irreplaceable" (Applebome, 2012).

As evidence accumulated, however, the empirical landscape became complicated; some studies found downward comparison, but others found upward comparison (Molleman, Pruyn, & van Knippenberg, 1986). The correlational evidence from medical patients, a frequently studied group because of the presumed threat they experienced, was very mixed (see Arigo, Suls, & Smyth, 2014 for an extensive review) and, due to the limitations of correlational design, could not identify the direction of causation. Also, many of these studies relied on participants' reports about comparisons in the past or over extended periods. Recall biases could not be ruled out, and we questioned how well people are able to make precise estimates over lengthy time intervals. Especially interesting or impactful comparisons may come to mind and tend to dominate the estimate.

Independent of these problems, Lefty and Dusty had conceptual reservations about downward comparison theory. Whereas Hakmiller's (1966) threatened participants were more interested in seeing the score of someone worse off than themselves, most of the subsequent evidence found avoidance of the highest scorers (e.g., Smith & Insko, 1987). Wheeler (2000) observed that reluctance to compare with the most fortunate is not equivalent to seeking someone worse off. Suls and his coauthors found students who received academic feedback that they had performed poorly preferred to affiliate with superior performers and learn what the highest performance scores were (Suls & Miller, 1978; Suls & Tesch, 1978). Wheeler and Miyake (1992) had college students record details of all their social comparisons as they occurred over a 2-week period. Contrary to the prediction of downward comparison theory, precomparison negative affect (threat) led most frequently to upward comparisons rather than to downward comparisons. This result is consistent with an affect-cognition priming model in which dysphoria primes negative thoughts about the self (Bower, 1991; Forgas, Bower, & Moylan,

1990). In addition, high-self-esteem students engaged in more self-enhancing comparison behavior, either by making more downward comparisons or by responding with more positive affect to lateral and upward comparisons. Downward comparison theory predicts that low-self-esteem students would do these things. On the whole then, downward comparison theory is not supported empirically. On the other hand, the Wheeler and Miyake (1992) research showed that upward comparisons on average decreased feelings of happiness and encouragement, whereas downward comparisons increased such feelings. There is then strong evidence for contrast in social comparison.

## Assimilation *and* Contrast Back on the Range

One thing we did not fully appreciate at the time was that both upward and downward comparison may potentially lead to assimilation or contrast. (As cowboys, who were frequently on the trail, we were quite aware of a *physic*, as a purgative, but *psychophysics*—not so much.) Buunk et al. (1990), however, described four possible outcomes of comparing with superior or inferior others: upward contrast (i.e., negative feelings from feeling different and inferior) or upward assimilation (i.e., positive feelings because one may improve and become more like the comparison other) in response to a superior target, downward contrast (i.e., positive feelings because one is different and better than the other) or downward assimilation (i.e., negative feelings because one identifies with the inferior other and is concerned about faring poorly oneself) in response to an inferior target.

Evidence for these four different consequences was obtained in surveys that inquired about the degree to which cancer patients and married individuals experienced both positive and negative effects of making upward and downward comparisons (Buunk et al., 1990). The newsworthy result was that direction of comparison was not intrinsically associated with positive or negative affect. (Contrary to common sense, upward comparisons did not necessarily make people feel bad nor did downward comparisons make people feel good.) In fact, sometimes upward comparisons were perceived as positive and downward comparisons as negative. The researchers concluded that affective responses depend less on the direction and more on the salient implication of the comparison—usually hinging on "Will I get better or worse?" The key to using comparison to cope with threat seems to

hinge on a person's belief about the likelihood of change in a favorable or unfavorable direction. We appreciated Buunk et al.'s insights, although we were not as impressed with the data because they were based on correlations of small magnitude and global recollections about past social comparisons.

Becky Collins (1996), one of the cowgirls involved in the Buunk et al. research, expanded on the insights. She argued that upward comparison could lead to either contrast or assimilation, depending upon whether the comparison is construed as indicating similarity to, or difference from, the comparison person. Which conclusion one draws depends, at least in part, upon expectations, just as Buunk's subjects construed the outcome of comparison based on their expectations about getting worse or better. Drawing upon the work of Manis (Manis, Biernat, & Nelson, 1991; Manis & Paskewitz, 1984), Collins noted that "people may expect some similarity to any comparison target who is within their own range of ability, leading to some amount of assimilation in all or most comparison judgments. In many cases, contrast processes overwhelm assimilation processes. However, whenever situational or dispositional factors (e.g., direction of comparison, self-esteem, and shared distinctiveness) strengthen the expectation of similarity, assimilation may have the stronger effect" (Collins, 1996, p. 62). The inclusion of "direction of comparison" as one of the factors influencing the expectation of similarity refers to Collins's belief that people assume upward similarity more readily than downward similarity. This idea is consistent with our comments about people desiring the truth but wanting it to be positive.

There are several potentially relevant studies bearing on Collins's (1996) analysis, but the vast majority have serious design limitations. (Significant differences in responses to superior versus inferior targets demonstrate a shift in self-evaluation, but not whether a superior and/or inferior target repelled or attracted self-evaluations; for that, the addition of a no-comparison control condition or a pre-post-test design is required; Wheeler & Suls, 2007). The main problem is that neither no-comparison conditions nor pre-post-test designs have been used. In the typical between-group designs, if responses to superior targets (in one experimental condition) were more negative than to inferior targets (in another condition), it was impossible to determine whether the superior and/or inferior target repelled or attracted self-evaluations (Wheeler & Suls, 2007). All one can definitively conclude is that superior targets produced different responses from inferior targets. Two experiments, however, are notable because they had designs capable of detecting the nature of the shift.

Brown, Novick, Lord, and Richards (1992; Study 3) used a pre-post design and analyzed change scores in self-ratings. They found that women who had the same birthday as an attractive female comparison target assimilated their own attractiveness toward the target. If they did not have the same birthday, however, they contrasted their attractiveness ratings away from her. Presumably, sharing the same birthday created the "shared distinctiveness" with the target that promoted upward assimilation, as Collins (1996) predicted.

The other experiment (Lockwood & Kunda, 1997) included a no-comparison control group. In this research, first-year or senior college students read a description of a very successful senior who had a matching major and gender. The first-year students reported feeling inspired by the "superstar" and made higher self-ratings on traits related to career success (i.e., assimilation) than participants who had not been exposed to any target (control group). The rating by participants who were seniors (and hence the same age as the superstar) did not differ from those in the control group, however. The reasoning was the seniors no longer had time, and hence no reasonable expectation they could attain the same success as the superstar senior, which prohibited upward assimilation. We are a little surprised that they showed no evidence for upward contrast; however, perhaps it was blocked by self-esteem concerns.

Dusty and Lefty were impressed with Collins's (1996, 2000) proposal, but they perceived its contribution as distinct from the proxy model. In the process of formulating the proxy model, we had an inkling that there was a kind of identification occurring when someone assumed there was sufficient similarity to the proxy to expect the same outcome if "X" was attempted. However, we did not refer to the process followed in the proxy model as "assimilation." In hindsight, we recognize a stronger connection between Collins's assimilation model and the proxy model. If I am wondering whether "I can do X," that implies I am probably motivated to do it. If comparison is prompted, in part, to confirm a positive identity, as we propose, then people should want to assume similarity with someone who has succeeded at X. This is more likely when performance is modifiable, when the target's superior standing is not extreme, and the target has similar (related) attributes. In this way, Collins's model is mutually compatible with the proxy model.

Collins's perspective is rooted in ideas about expectations and social psychophysics. Thomas Mussweiler (2003) introduced another approach emphasizing contrast and assimilation, but with stronger ties to research on priming and hypothesis-confirmation in social cognition. For the most part, we see Collins and Mussweiler's approaches as complementary. His selective accessibility theory (SAM) is based on selective accessibility of the cognitions that are elicited during the comparison process. As in all perceptual processing, immediately after exposure to a novel stimulus, people make rapid, holistic impressions based on salient features. In the comparison scenario, a person makes a tentative and rapid judgment of similarity or dissimilarity to the (superior or inferior) comparison target. Salient features (such as gender, race, or age) of the comparison target determine this initial impression. Then there is a cognitive search for information *consistent* with the preliminary judgment (or hypothesis) of similarity or dissimilarity. This kind of hypothesis confirmation can be deliberative or automatic and has been demonstrated in many cognitive scenarios (e.g., Klayman & Ha, 1987). In the case of self-other comparisons, whether one searches for similarity information or dissimilarity information, it should be easy to find information that is consistent because self-concepts are remarkably rich and complicated. (People who hold negative self-concepts may be an exception, a topic elaborated later in this chapter.) That information then becomes selectively accessible when we make judgments about ourselves. If we have searched for information that we are similar to the standard, we are likely to assimilate our self-evaluations toward the target. If we have searched for information that we are dissimilar to the target, we are likely to contrast our self-evaluations away from the target.

Several forms of evidence support SAM. For example, having participants first compare themselves to a superior (e.g., a highly athletic celebrity) versus an inferior (e.g., a highly unathletic celebrity) comparison target led to faster times deciding a letter string was a word (i.e., lexical decision task) when the word was target consistent (e.g., dynamic, in good shape) versus inconsistent (e.g., weak, plump). Such evidence confirms that priming a comparison standard makes standard-consistent or standard-inconsistent information more cognitively accessible and hence faster to access in lexical decision making (Mussweiler & Strack, 2000, Exp. 1).

To demonstrate priming similarity or dissimilarity affects reactions to comparison targets, Mussweiler (2001) first had participants focus on similarities versus differences in pictorial scenes (this is referred to as procedural priming; Smith & Branscombe, 1987) to prompt either similarity or dissimilarity testing. A supposedly separate experiment immediately followed in which all participants read about another college student described as adjusting well or poorly at college. Those who had been previously primed to focus on similarities listed more social activities and friends after comparison with a well-adjusted target than after a poorly adjusted target. But those primed for finding differences reported having fewer social activities and friends after comparison with the well-adjusted target (than a poorly adjusted target). Consistent with SAM, whether assimilation or contrast occurred depended on whether participants were primed to look for similarities or differences (see Mussweiler, 2003, for related evidence.)

Additional experiments confirm predictions derived from SAM: Contrast is more likely if the standard is extreme or unattainable, or if the standard belongs to an outgroup—both manipulations should lead to an initial hypothesis of dissimilarity. Assimilation is more likely to occur if there is psychological closeness with the standard, which would lead to a search for similarity.

SAM is both elegant and explains a wide variety of empirical results. It also has features that are not found in Collins (1996). The conventional dependent variables in social comparison research mainly have been selection measures and responses to subjective rating scales about performance, self-concept, and affect. SAM, however, prefers absolute measures to subjective ratings because selective accessibility is supposed to operate directly on the mental representations of self-evaluation. To illustrate the difference between absolute and subject measures, asking subjects how many push-ups they can do or how tall they are in feet and inches are absolute measures (sometimes referred to as *common-rule scales*; Biernat, Manis, & Nelson, 1991), whereas rating how good one is at push-ups or how tall on seven-point scales (e.g., with "very tall" to "very short" as end points) are subjective ratings. The weakness of subjective ratings is they are subject to the meaning or interpretation of the judgmental scale. This could be a problem if the comparison target acts as an anchor, which alters the meaning of the judgmental scale. For example, Dusty and Lefty might rate themselves

as "very poor riders" in the context of Buffalo Bill, although objectively they might think they are average. For the rating, Buffalo Bill might serve as a reference point that changes the interpretation of the points on the scale, so "average" and "poor" assume different meanings. Absolute ratings, which presumably tap into mental representations (rather than only the language or descriptions used), avoid that; the vast majority of SAM research relies on these rather than rating scales.

Absolute measures are a welcome addition, but we are not sure they are superior to subjective scales. The language that people use to describe their talents and opinions both to themselves and to others matters. Although the scale points or language we choose involves a more "downstream" cognitive process, (a) the language may alter the high-level mental representation (presumably there is cross-talk); and (b) the language we use to describe ourselves may determine our aspirations, advocacies, and behavior. Ideally, experiments should collect both absolute and subjective measures, but that has not happened yet. This should be a task for the future.

Another corollary in SAM is that similarity testing is assumed to be the default when people have not been primed. This is based on the idea, from judgment and decision making, that presence of a standard (a comparison target) increases cognitive activation of features that the standard and the self have in common; hence, people are apt to look for similarities, rather than differences (e.g., Chapman & Johnson, 1999). We are agnostic, however, about similarity being the default, which would suggest that assimilation, rather than contrast, should be the more common outcome of comparison (unless it is self-enhancing to assimilate). Many demonstrations for contrast can be found in the empirical literature (e.g., Gibbons & Gerrard, 1991; Morse & Gergen, 1970; Wheeler & Miyake, 1992). The field is lacking observational or diary studies that assess the degree to which the social world offers extreme targets, that is, highlights ingroup and outgroup membership or other situational features that may prime dissimilarity versus features priming similarity. Whether similarity seeking is the default option in social experience remains to be assessed.

A limitation of the empirical evidence for SAM is the missing control group problem (Wheeler, 2000; Wheeler & Suls, 2007). As mentioned earlier, few experiments have included no-comparison groups or pre-post comparison designs, making it impossible to identify whether an upward or downward target is attracting or repelling or both are influencing the self-evaluation. In other words, where is the action? We hope future researchers will include the appropriate designs to be able to parse the effects.

A second matter concerns SAM's emphasis on cognitive processes, which leads it to predict that upward assimilation and downward assimilation are just as likely depending on whether a similarity or a difference search is instigated. Indeed, some of the evidence (Mussweiler, 2001) suggests cognitive search grinds away, disinterested in the outcome. (But in the absence of a no-comparison control group, those results are ambiguous.) As we have discussed, and in agreement with Collins (1996), we maintain people want to keep a positive self-concept. Consistent with this view, we found no evidence for downward assimilation in a review of the empirical literature (Wheeler & Suls, 2007). Exposure to a low standard may instigate dissimilarity testing to preserve self-esteem.

Our initial response to SAM, like the one to Collins (1996), was very positive, despite the misgivings mentioned earlier. A new *Kuhhirt* (German word for "cowboy") arrived in town, and given the opportunity, we would buy him a drink. However, the thing that was bothering us, like flies swarming around a horse, was whether SAM and the proxy model were compatible. A comprehensive vision of social comparison would be desirable.

Again, with the advantage of hindsight, we think SAM and the proxy model are not only compatible but also integrative. In most instances, if I ask myself, "Can I do X?" I probably am motivated to do it. Now suppose I see Amarillo Slim doing X. The default is to find similarities with him. I probably find similarities and conclude that he is a good proxy and I also can do X. The alternative scenario is I see Amarillo not doing X. My first assessment is we are dissimilar because he is not doing what I want to do. This prompts a search for dissimilarity that leads to the judgment he is not a good proxy. In fact, Amarillo may be a negative proxy, who increases my belief that I can do X. We like this synthesis because it is parsimonious and suggests that information about related attributes may be the cognitive grist for similarity or differences search posited by SAM. If combining insights from the related attributes hypothesis, priming, and social comparison offers a cohesive answer to questions "über cowboy" Leon Festinger posed several decades ago, this is both an intellectually and emotionally satisfying outcome.

Before we become too overjoyed, the story has a sad sidelight. Along the trail, the field did meet up with another theory and a bushel of empirical data with an alternative perspective. Like SAM, it was premised on knowledge accessibility, but it made some distinctive predictions and reported some astounding effects of subliminal social comparisons. As it turns out, however, the perpetrator, made up most, if not all, of the data (unbeknownst to his coauthors). He was found out, he admitted to his fraudulent actions, and most of his work has been redacted (Levelt Commission, 2012) The commotion may inspire higher standards of evidence, more respect for replication, and better documentation (a good consequence). We gave this person great play in a chapter for another book (Suls & Wheeler, 2012). One of our reasons for writing this chapter was to describe the progress of social comparison study, excluding the fraudulent ideas and results. The lesson, we suppose, is to be vigilant on the trail and keep one eye open while sleeping when cattle rustlers and snake-oil salesmen are roving the territory.

## Exceptions to "Evaluhancement"

Most people have a rosy view of their attributes and rate themselves of at least moderate self-worth, but some minority has low-esteem (Baumeister, Campbell, Kruger, & Vohs, 2003). Approximately 20 percent of the population experience strong and frequent negative emotions, such as irritation, sadness, frustration, and anxiety, that are closely related to low self-esteem (Watson & Clark, 1984). This significant minority, described as "negatively affective" or "neurotic," may be less motivated to seek or appraise comparisons in a positive light. If anything, it may be more important for them to seek and accept information that confirms their negative self-conceptions (Swann, 1990; Swann, Wenzlaff, Krull, & Pelham, 1992). Thus, such individuals should tend to socially compare somewhat differently than we described earlier.

In one of the better studies of individual differences and social comparison, Van der Zee, Oldersma, Buunk, and Bos (1998) provided cancer patients in treatment with special computer devices that allowed them to access information about other cancer patients. The patients also had completed an inventory assessing neuroticism. In general, the average patient chose to read more interviews with better-functioning patients and exhibited more positive responses to this information—which looks like upward assimilation. Those patients who had high scores on neuroticism, however, read more interviews about better- and worse-functioning patients and responded more negatively to both kinds of comparison. In the terms we used previously, they seemed to do both upward contrast and downward assimilation (although this is ambiguous because of the absence of no-comparison controls). Notwithstanding this ambiguity, persons of low self-esteem or high neuroticism seem unable to perceive their situation in a more positive light.

The implication is that the majority of people probably adopt an optimizing social comparison strategy (similarity- or dissimilarity-search that would most likely confirm a positive image). However, there are other persons whose self-conceptions of themselves and the social world are more concerned with maintaining a stable view of self, even if it is not a positive one.

## Local Dominance and Comparison

Before closing, we describe some comparison phenomena of recent vintage that have spruced up the trail. Would your evaluation of your verbal reasoning skills be more affected by comparison with 1,500 people randomly selected from your cohort or by comparison with five drinkers in your local saloon? This apparently silly question could be fleshed out as follows: You and your fellow drinkers take a test of verbal skills that is self-scored and that has normative scores. You discover either that (a) you are the best in the group of five but at the 32nd percentile in the larger group, or (b) you are the worst in the group of five but at the 84th percentile in the larger group. The surprising result (Zell & Alicke, 2009, Study 4) was that Group (a) participants rated their skills higher than did Group (b) participants. Local standing in a group of five was more important to self-evaluations than was aggregate standing in a group of 1,500. The same was true for the emotions they felt in connection with their performance. It is not that people ignore their standing in larger groups: When they were not given local comparison information, those who were at the 84th percentile had higher self-evaluations and affect than those at the 32nd percentile. When, however, local comparison information is provided, it overrides the aggregate information. People, however, not to be aware of how important local comparison is. For example, participants completed a verbal task in groups of five and were then asked whether they preferred information about their standing in the group of five or their standing among 1,500 others. Over 80 percent claimed

they preferred learning about 1,500 people and thought it was more useful for self-evaluation (Zell & Alicke, 2009, Study 5). But information about the five group members had more influence on ratings of personal performance. Local dominance is a robust effect, having been demonstrated in numerous experiments (Alicke, Zell, & Bloom, 2010; Buckingham & Alicke, 2002; Zell & Alicke, 2009, 2010, 2012).

The researchers of the local dominance effect believe that humans began in small groups in evolutionary history so we might have tendencies to compare in small groups. Also, the effect might "derive largely from the habitual experience of making social comparisons in small groups such as those that occur early in development among family members, schoolmates, and friends" (Zell & Alicke, 2010, p. 373). We accept these explanations but also wonder if the effect would be even greater if the members of the smaller comparison group were well known to one another so that related attributes could have an effect. Knowing the related attributes of the members of the local group should make local comparisons even more potent.

The local dominance effect has recently been extended to the perception of risks of illness and accident (Zell & Alicke, 2012). The accurate assessment of risk is necessary for people to take steps to minimize susceptibility to accident and illness. Students were tested in small groups for their (alleged) risk of becoming diabetic. In the high general risk condition, they were told that they were at the 68th percentile in a group of 400 students previously tested. In a low general risk condition, they were told that they were at the 32nd percentile in the group of 400. Half of the high general risk participants were told that they were at the lowest risk in their current test group, and half of the low general risk participants were told they were at the highest risk in their current test group. In their subsequent rating of their risk of becoming diabetic, those at high general risk showed higher risk perceptions than those at low general risk, as we would certainly expect. However, the contradictory local comparison manipulation eliminated the difference between high and low general risks. In a second experiment, the risk of a serious automobile accident replaced the risk of becoming diabetic, and the same results were obtained.

We should note that the results are consistent with local dominance but are not exactly the same as reported earlier for verbal reasoning ability (Zell & Alicke, 2009). In that research, local comparison information completely dominated self-evaluations in that high local/low aggregate was higher than low local/high aggregate. In this diabetes/accident research, the two groups were equal. The local comparison information was as powerful as the aggregate information, but not more powerful. Nevertheless, it is a nice demonstration of the power of local comparisons in influencing risk perceptions.

## The Frog Pond Effect

The frog pond effect was the first demonstration of the power of local comparisons. Davis (1966) demonstrated that it was better to be a "big frog in a small pond" than a "small frog in a big pond." College students of any level of academic ability got worse grades in highly selective colleges than in less selective colleges, which led to lower self-evaluations and career aspirations. This was thought to be due to comparisons with fellow classmates, who were all intellectually talented enough to be in the selective schools, rather than with the larger society. For a number of years now, Marsh (1987) and colleagues (Seaton, Marsh, & Craven, 2009) have shown this to be an incredibly robust cross-cultural phenomenon known as the big-fish-little-pond effect (BFLPE). (We are unaware of the reasons the "frog" was transformed into a "fish." We would opt for the "big steer in the small corral.") Marsh and colleagues, following Davis, have always argued that the effect is due to social comparison, but until recently there has been no direct evidence for the involvement of social comparison. Huguet et al. (2009) obtained strong evidence of the involvement of social comparison. Participants were 2,015 students in their first year of secondary school from 99 classes across 16 French public schools. Student ability data (standardized test scores) were collected at the beginning of the first trimester, and all other measures were collected at the end of the second trimester. Schools were chosen to be of high, medium, or low ability based on standardized test scores. All analyses controlled for initial ability. Math and French were analyzed separately and always produced the same results.

The higher the class-average ability, the more students felt inferior to their class in both Math and French, and the more students felt inferior to their class, the lower their academic self-concepts. Thus, the BFLPE was replicated: Students in the higher ability classes had lower academic self-concepts than those in lower ability classes. Class size averaged just over 20 students, and it was this local comparison with 20 students that strongly influenced academic

self-concept. However, controlling for perceived relative standing in class eliminated the BFLPE. Thus, local contrastive comparisons with classmates seem to be responsible for the lower academic self-concepts shown in the BFLPE.

These local comparisons with classmates were forced upon the students just by virtue of being in the class. Students were also asked to nominate the classmate with whom they preferred to compare their grades and to indicate how frequently this classmate got the same grades as theirs. When nominating the classmate with whom they preferred to compare, the students nominated classmates who were on average somewhat better than they were (according to the standardized test scores), replicating previous research by Blanton et al. (1999) and Huguet et al. (2001). To the extent that students made these voluntary upward comparisons, they also had higher academic self-concept. Students felt, moreover, that these objectively superior classmates were similar to them in grades obtained. This set of results provides a nice demonstration of upward assimilation discussed earlier. Students who compared upwardly construed themselves as similar to the objectively superior comparison targets, and they experienced high academic self-concepts. Note that these assimilation effects of voluntary comparisons are in the opposite direction of the forced contrast effects of the BFLPE and should work against the BFLPE. Indeed, when the assimilation effects are controlled for, the size of the BFLPE increases significantly.

The local dominance and frog pond research begin to answer questions about the effects of multiple comparisons—something Festinger (1954a, 1954b) and subsequent researchers had not considered. This topic may open up a rich frontier. Multiple comparisons, which would seem to be the rule rather than the exception in the Wild West that is the social world, probably simultaneously exert push (i.e., contrast) and pull (i.e., assimilation) on the individual. Sorting out their effects is likely to be an important priority in the future.

## Related Social Influence Phenomena

In this chapter, our emphasis has been on the effects of social comparison on self-evaluation, in keeping with the lion's share of contemporary research. As noted earlier, social comparison, however, played a role in Sherif's (1936) seminal studies demonstrating that subjects' judgments tended to converge with the estimates of other subjects when evaluating ambiguous stimuli. Comparison was also implicated in Asch's (1951) conformity experiments (Allen, 1965). Virtually any type of conformity phenomenon or persuasion effect (Hovland, Janis, & Kelley, 1953; Petty & Cacioppo, 1981) involves some element of comparison, but parsing of comparison from other processes has not been an important priority in social psychology (except in the group polarization effect; Burnstein & Vinokur, 1977; Sanders & Baron, 1977). With the increasing balkanization of subfields, persuasion and comparison have run in separate streams for decades, despite the fact that both are concerned with beliefs and values. Attitude change researchers manipulate the effects of variables, such as source credibility, message extremity, quality of arguments, and so on. Comparison researchers manipulate the perception of relative standing on personal attributes, opinions, and behavior. This has been a sound strategy because it is essential to strip persuasive argumentation from relative standing to identify the pure effects of comparison (Suls et al., 2000). By now, however, comparison processes may be sufficiently well understood that it may be timely to examine how comparison operates in combination with other influence processes.

## On the Horizon

Another relatively unexplored area concerns multiple comparisons among members of social networks. A network may comprise a proximal worksite, neighborhood, church, or club; or connections and communications by e-mail, Facebook, or other social media. The critical factor defining a network is not proximity, but existence of social ties. The neighbor next door is not part of a person's network if they have no relationship. How information, such as rumors and fads, and social influence spread across networks has been more extensively studied by sociologists, political scientists, and economists (Latané & Bourgeois's [1996] dynamic social impact theory and Crandall's [1988] research on contagion of eating disorders among sorority members are conspicuous exceptions until recently; also see Mason, Conray, & Smith, 2007; DiFonzo et al., 2013). All of these approaches emphasize communication, persuasion, and conformity among network members. Surprisingly, social comparison is not explicitly mentioned in this context, although it surely is involved. Further, comparison theories have not considered the effects of successive comparisons (Amarillo compares with Lefty, then with Dusty, followed by Becky and Thomas). Since social life probably involves multiple successive comparisons more than one-time occasions, this seems like a topic ripe for study.

Contemporary research on social networks has yielded fascinating phenomena while simultaneously treating social influence as something of a "black box." One study evaluated a social network of over 12,000 people whose body mass indexes were assessed repeatedly from 1971 to 2003 (Christakis & Fowler, 2007). Statistical modeling was used to test whether weight gain in one person was associated with weight gain in his or her friends, siblings, spouse, and neighbors. The probability of becoming obese increased substantially (between 37 and 57 percent) if a person had a friend, an adult sibling, or a spouse who became obese in a given interval. These effects did not appear, however, among neighbors in the immediate geographic location. These effects have been described as a "contagion," analogous to the spread of a virus. This kind of influence is not restricted to obesity, as the same researchers found that depression (Rosenquist, Fowler, & Christakis, 2011) also is a network phenomenon. Such influence also extends to positive changes; for example, quitting smoking also seems to spread across connected persons (Christakis & Fowler, 2008).

The viral contagion metaphor used by network researchers does not seem apt to us, however. Unless a person is vaccinated or unusually healthy, mere contact will lead to an infection. Network research indicates something more than contact is needed to see opinion or behavior change across connections; persons who are influential have relationships with us. One possible reason is that friends, siblings, and spouses most commonly serve as our proxies and similar experts. Their experiences and their related attributes make them relevant and appropriate comparisons. Further (and related to an earlier discussion), even if such individuals are not geographically close by, they are both concrete and "local" via modern forms of communication, such as the telephone and the Internet (Onnela et al., 2011). Elaboration of the process of social influence via social comparison across large social networks may help us to better understand the spread of rumors, fads, and collective behaviors.

## No End of the Trail

We hope that we have communicated both the excitement and insights gathered about social comparison in the last 60 years. As a core element of social influence with connections to persuasion, conformity, educational and health outcomes, and so on, comparison represents an area that has conceptual and practical appeal. We have proposed how three basic perspectives—the proxy/triadic models, Collins's upward assimilation model, and Mussweiler's SAM—clarify and extend Festinger's seminal statement and also can be blended together to their mutual benefit. As we indicated throughout, questions remain, however, that may entice the next generation to saddle up. But we have said enough. As the American cowboy and social commentator Will Rogers quipped, "Never miss a good chance to shut up."

## Author Note

The opinions and assertions herein are those of the authors and do not necessarily represent those of the National Cancer Institute.

## Note

1. A small portion of the population does not have positive feelings of self-worth, and hence these individuals do not want to obtain confirmation that they have desirable attributes (Swann, 1990; Watson & Clark, 1984); like the song from the 1930s, "Glad to Be Unhappy." For them, self-enhancement should not be operative. In a subsequent section, we devote some attention to the social comparisons of such persons.

## References

Alicke, M. D., Zell, E., & Bloom, D. L. (2010). Mere categorization and the frog-pond effect. *Psychological Science, 21*, 174–177.

Allen, V. (1965). Situational factors in conformity. In L. Berkowitz (Ed.), *Advances in experimental social psychology* (Vol. 2). New York: Academic Press.

Applebome, P. (2012, December 31). We lost things and we can replace those things. *The New York Times*.

Arigo, D., Suls, J., & Smyth, J. M. (2014). Social comparisons and chronic illness: Research synthesis and clinical implications. *Health Psychology Review*, 8, 154-214.

Asch, S. (1951). Effects of group pressure upon the modification and distortion of judgments. In H. S. Guetzkow (Ed.), *Groups, leadership and men* (pp. 177–190). Pittsburgh, PA: Carnegie Press.

Baron, R. S., & Roper, G. (1976). Reaffirmations of social comparison views of choice shifts: Averaging and extremity effects in an autokinetic situation. *Journal of Personality and Social Psychology, 33*, 521–530.

Baumeister, R. F., Campbell, D. D., Krueger, J. I., & Vohs, K. S. (2003). Does high self-esteem cause better performance, interpersonal success, happiness, or healthier lifestyles? *Psychological Science in the Public Interest, 4*, 1–44.

Biernat, M., Manis, M., & Nelson, T. F. (1991). Stereotypes and standards of judgment. *Journal of Personality and Social Psychology, 60*, 485–499.

Blanton, H., Buunk, B. P., Gibbons, F. X., & Kuyper, H. (1999). When better-than-others compare upward: Choice of comparison and comparative evaluation as independent predictors of academic performance. *Journal of Personality and Social Psychology, 76*, 420–430.

Bower, G. H. (1991). Mood and memory. *American Psychologist, 36*, 129–148.

Brickman, P., & Bulman, R. J. (1977). Pleasure and pain in social comparison. In J. Suls & R. Miller (Eds.), *Social comparison processes: Theoretical and empirical perspectives* (pp. 149–186). Washington, DC: Hemisphere.

Brown, J. D., Novick, N. J., Lord, K. A., & Richards, J. M. (1992). When Gulliver travels: Social context, psychological closeness, and self-appraisals. *Journal of Personality and Social Psychology, 62*, 717–727.

Buckingham, J. T., & Alicke, M. D. (2002). The influence of individual versus aggregate social comparison and the presence of others on self-evaluations. *Journal of Personality and Social Psychology, 83*, 1117–1130.

Burnstein, E. & Vinokur, A. (1977). Persuasive argumentation and social comparison as determinants of attitude polarization. *Journal of Experimental Social Psychology 13*, 315-332.

Buunk, B. P., Collins, R. L., Taylor, S. E., VanYperen, N. W., & Dakof, G. A. (1990). The affective consequences of social comparison: Either direction has its ups and downs. *Journal of Personality and Social Psychology, 59*, 1238–1249.

Chapman, G. B., & Johnson, E. J. (1999). Anchoring, activation, and the construction of values. *Organizational Behavior and Human Decision Processes, 79*, 115–153.

Christakis, N. A., & Fowler, J. H. (2007). The spread of obesity in a large social network over 32 years. *New England Journal of Medicine, 357*, 370–379.

Christakis, N. A., & Fowler, J. H. (2008). The collective dynamics of smoking in a large social network. *New England Journal of Medicine, 358*, 2249–2258.

Collins, R. L. (1996). For better or for worse: The impact of upward social comparisons on self-evaluations. *Psychological Bulletin, 119*, 51–69.

Collins, R. L. (2000). Among the better ones: Upward assimilation in social comparison. In J. Suls & L. Wheeler (Eds.), *Handbook of social comparison: Theory and research* (pp. 159–171). New York: Kluwer Academic/Plenum.

Crandall, C. S. (1988). Social contagion of binge eating. *Journal of Personality and Social Psychology, 55*, 588–598.

Davis, J. A. (1966). The campus as a frog pond: An application of the theory of relative deprivation to career decisions of college men. *American Journal of Sociology, 72*, 17–31.

DiFonzo, N., Bourgeois, M. J., Suls, J., Homan, C., Stupak, D., Brooks, B. P., . . . Bordia, P. (2013). Rumor clustering, consolidation and confidence: Dynamic social impact and self-organization of hearsay. *Journal of Experimental Social Psychology, 49*, 378–399.

Festinger, L. (1950). Informal social communication theory. *Psychological Review, 57*, 271–282.

Festinger, L. (1954a). A theory of social comparison processes. *Human Relations, 7*, 117–140.

Festinger, L. (1954b). Motivation leading to social behavior. In M. R. Jones (Ed.), *Nebraska symposium on motivation* (pp. 191–218). Lincoln: University of Nebraska Press.

Forgas, J., Bower, G., & Moylan, S. J. (1990). Praise or blame? Affective influences on attributions of achievement. *Journal of Personality and Social Psychology, 59*, 809–818.

Gastorf, J. W., & Suls, J. (1978). Performance evaluation via social comparison: Related attribute similarity vs. performance similarity. *Social Psychology, 41*, 297–305.

Gibbons, F. X., & Gerrard, M. (1991). Downward comparison and coping with threat. In J. Suls & T. A. Wills (Eds.), *Social comparison: Contemporary theory and research* (pp. 317–346). Hillsdale, NJ: Erlbaum.

Goethals, G., & Darley, J. (1977). Social comparison theory: An attributional approach. In J. Suls & R. Miller (Eds.), *Social comparison processes: Theoretical and empirical perspectives* (pp. 259–278). Washington, DC: Hemisphere.

Goethals, G. R., & Nelson, R. E. (1973). Similarity in the influence process: The belief-value distinction. *Journal of Personality and Social Psychology, 25*, 117–122.

Gorenflo, D. W., & Crano, W. (1989). Judgmental subjectivity/objectivity and locus of choice in social comparison. *Journal of Personality and Social Psychology, 57*, 605–614.

Hakmiller, K. (1966). Threat as a determinant of social comparison. *Journal of Experimental Social Psychology*, Suppl. *1*, 32-39.

Hovland, C. I., Janis, I. L., & Kelley, H. H. (1953). *Communication and persuasion: Psychological studies of opinion change.* New Haven, CT: Yale University Press.

Huguet, P., Dumas, F., Marsh. H., Seaton, M., Wheeler. L., Suls, J., . . . Nezlek, J. (2009). Clarifying the role of social comparison in the big-fish-little-pond effect (BFLPE): An integrative study. *Journal of Personality and Social Psychology, 97*, 156–170.

Huguet, P., Dumas, F., Monteil, J.-M. & Genestoux, N. (2001). Social comparison choices in the classroom: Further evidence for students' upward comparison tendency and its beneficial impact on performance. *European Journal of Social Psychology, 31*, 557–578.

Hyman, H. H. (1942). The psychology of status. *Archives of Psychology, 269.*

Jellison, J. M., & Riskind, J. (1970). A social comparison of abilities interpretation of risk taking behavior. *Journal of Personality and Social Psychology, 15*, 375–390.

Jones, E. E., & Gerard, H. B. (1965). *Foundations of social psychology.* New York: Wiley.

Jones, S., & Regan, D. (1974). Ability evaluation through social comparison. *Journal of Experimental Social Psychology, 10*, 133-146.

Kelley, H. (1967). Attribution theory in social psychology. In D. Levine (Ed.), *Nebraska symposium on motivation* (pp. 192–240). Lincoln: University of Nebraska Press.

Kelly, J., St. Lawrence, J., Diaz, Y. E., Stevenson, L. Y., Hauth, A. C., Brasfield, T. L.,. . . . Andrew, M. E. (1991). HIV risk behavior reduction following intervention with key opinion leaders of the population: An experimental analysis. *American Journal of Public Health, 81*, 168–171.

Klayman, J., & Ha, Y.-W. (1987). Confirmation, disconfirmation and information in hypothesis-testing. *Psychological Review, 94*, 211–228.

Kulik, J. A., & Mahler, H. (1989). Stress and affiliation in a hospital setting: Preoperative roommate preferences. *Personality and Social Psychology Bulletin, 15*, 183–193.

Kulik, J. A., Moore, P., & Mahler, H. (1996). Social comparison and affiliation under threat: Effects on recovery from major surgery. *Journal of Personality and Social Psychology, 71*, 967–979.

Latané, B., & Bourgeois, M. J. (1996). Experimental evidence for dynamic social impact: The formations of subcultures in electronic groups. *Journal of Communication, 46*, 35–47.

Levelt Commission. (2012). Flawed science: The fraudulent research practices of social psychologist, Diederik Stapel.

Retrieved September 2014, from http://www.commissie-levelt.nl.

Lockwood, P., & Kunda, Z. (1997). Superstars and me: Predicting the impact of role models on the self. *Journal of Personality and Social Psychology, 73*, 91–103.

Manis, M., Biernat, M., & Nelson, T. F. (1991). Comparison and expectancy processes in human judgment. *Journal of Personality and Social Psychology, 61*, 203–211.

Manis, M., & Paskewitz, J. R. (1984). Judging psychopathology: Expectation, assimilation and contrast. *Journal of Personality and Social Psychology, 20*, 363–381.

Marsh, H. W. (1987). The big-fish–little-pond effect on academic self-concept. *Journal of Educational Psychology, 79*, 280–295.

Martin, R., Suls, J., & Wheeler, L. (2002). Ability evaluation by proxy: The role of maximum performance and related attributes in social comparison. *Journal of Personality and Social Psychology, 82*, 781–791.

Mason, W. A., Conrey, F. R., & Smith, E. (2007). Situating social influence processes: Dynamic, multidirectional flows of information within social networks. *Personality and Social Psychology Review, 11*, 279–300.

Miller, C. (1982). The role of performance-related similarity in social comparison of abilities: A test of the related attributes hypothesis. *Journal of Personality and Social Psychology, 18*, 513–525.

Molleman, E., Pruyn, J., & van Knippenberg, A. (1986), Social comparison processes among cancer patients. *British Journal of Social Psychology, 25*, 1-13.

Morse, S., & Gergen, K. J. (1970). Social comparison, self-consistency, and the concept of the self. *Journal of Personality and Social Psychology, 16*, 148–156.

Moscovici, S., & Zavalloni, M. (1969). The group as a polarizer of attitudes. *Journal of Personality and Social Psychology, 12*, 125–135.

Mussweiler, T. (2001). "Seek and you should find": Antecedents of assimilation and contrast in social comparison. *European Journal of Social Psychology, 31*, 499–509.

Mussweiler, T. (2003). Comparison processes in social judgment: Mechanisms and consequences. *Psychological Review, 110*, 472–489.

Mussweiler, T., & Strack, F. (2000). The "relative self": Informational and judgmental consequences of comparative self-evaluation. *Journal of Personality and Social Psychology, 79*, 23–38.

Onnela, J.-P., Arbesman, S., Gonzalez, M. C., Barabasi, A. L., & Christakis, N. A. (2011). Geographic constraints on social network groups. *PLoS ONE, 6*, e16939.

Pettigrew, T. (1967). Social evaluation theory: Convergences and applications. In D. Levine (Ed.), *Nebraska symposium on motivation* (Vol. 15, pp. 241–311). Lincoln: University of Nebraska Press.

Petty, R. E., & Cacioppo, J. T. (1981). *Attitudes and persuasion: Classic and contemporary approaches.* Dubuque, IA: Wm. C. Brown.

Rosenquist, J. N., Fowler, J. H., & Christakis, N. A. (2011). Social network determinants of depression. *Molecular Psychiatry, 16*, 273–281.

Sanders, G. S, & Baron, R.S. (1977). Is social comparison irrelevant for producing choice shifts? *Journal of Experimental Social Psychology, 13*, 303-314.

Schachter, S. (1959). *The psychology of affiliation.* Stanford, CA: Stanford University Press.

Seaton, M., Marsh, H. W., & Craven, R. G. (2009). Earning its place as a pan-human theory: Universality of the big-fish-little-pond effect across 41 culturally and economically diverse countries. *Journal of Educational Psychology, 101*, 403–419.

Sherif, M. (1936). *The psychology of social norms*. New York: Harper and Brothers.

Smith, E. R., & Branscombe, N. R. (1987). Procedurally mediated social inferences: The case of category accessibility effects. *Journal of Experimental Social Psychology, 23*, 361–382.

Smith, R., & Insko, C. (1987). Social comparison choice during ability evaluation: The effect of comparison publicity, performance feedback and self-esteem. *Personality and Social Psychology Bulletin, 13*, 111–122.

Smith, W.P., & Sachs, P. (1997). Social comparison and task prediction: Ability similarity and the use of a proxy. *British Journal of Social Psychology, 36*, 587-602.

Suls, J., Gaes, G., & Gastorf, J. (1979). Evaluating a sex-related ability: Comparison with same-, opposite- and combined-sex norms. *Journal of Research in Personality, 13*, 294–303.

Suls, J., Gastorf, J., & Lawhorn, J. (1978). Social comparison choices for evaluating a sex- and age-related ability. *Personality and Social Psychology Bulletin, 4*, 102–105.

Suls, J., Martin, R., & Wheeler, L. (2000). Three kinds of opinion comparison: The Triadic Model. *Personality and Social Psychology Review, 4*, 219–237.

Suls, J., & Miller, R. L. (Eds.). (1977). *Social comparison processes: Theoretical and empirical perspectives*. Washington, DC: Hemisphere.

Suls, J. M., & Miller, R. L. (1978). Ability comparison and its effects on affiliation preferences. *Human Relations, 31*, 267–282.

Suls, J., & Tesch, F. (1978). Students' preferences for information about their test performance: A social comparison study. *Journal of Applied Social Psychology, 8*, 189–197.

Suls, J., & Wheeler, L. (Eds.). (2000). *Handbook of social comparison*. New York: Kluwer/Plenum.

Suls, J., & Wheeler, L. (2012). Social comparison theory. In P. van Lange, A. Kruglanski., & E. T. Higgins (Eds.), *Handbook of theories of social psychology* (pp. 460–482). Los Angeles: Sage.

Swann, W. B., Jr. (1990). To be adored or to be known: The interplay of self-enhancement and self-verification. In R. S. Sorrentino & E. T. Higgins (Eds.), *Foundations of social behavior* (Vol. 2, pp. 404–448). New York: Guilford Press.

Swann, W. B., Jr., Wenzlaff, R. M., Krull, D. S., & Pelham, B. W. (1992). Allure of negative feedback: Self-verification strivings among depressed persons. *Journal of Abnormal Psychology, 101*, 293–306.

Van der Zee, K., Oldersma, F., Buunk, B., & Bos, D. (1998). Social comparison among cancer patients as related to neuroticism and social comparison orientation. *Journal of Personality and Social Psychology, 75*, 801-810.

Watson, D., & Clark, L. A. (1984). Negative affectivity: The disposition to experience aversive emotional states. *Psychological Bulletin, 96*, 645–690.

Wheeler, L. (1966). Motivation as a determinant of upward comparison. *Journal of Experimental Social Psychology, 1*(Suppl.), 27–31.

Wheeler, L. (1991). A brief history of social comparison theory. In J. Suls & T. A. Wills (Eds.), *Social comparison: Contemporary theory and research* (pp. 3–22). Hillsdale, NJ: Erlbaum.

Wheeler, L. (2000). Individual differences in social comparison. In J. Suls & L. Wheeler (Eds.), *Handbook of social comparison* (pp. 141–158). New York: Kluwer Academic/Plenum.

Wheeler, L., & Koestner, R. (1984). Performance evaluation: On choosing to know the related attributes of others when we know their performance. *Journal of Experimental Social Psychology, 20*, 263–271.

Wheeler, L., Koestner, R., & Driver, R. (1982). Related attributes in the choice of comparison others: It's there, but it isn't all there is. *Journal of Experimental Social Psychology, 18*, 489–500.

Wheeler, L., Martin, R., & Suls, J. (1997). The proxy social comparison model for self-assessment of ability. *Personality and Social Psychology Review, 1*, 54–61.

Wheeler, L., & Miyake, K. (1992). Social comparison in everyday life. *Journal of Personality and Social Psychology, 62*, 760–773.

Wheeler, L., & Suls, J. (2007) Assimilation in social comparison: Can we agree on what it is? *International Review of Social Psychology, 20*, 31–51.

Wheeler, L., & Zuckerman, M. (1977). Commentary. In J. Suls & R. Miller (Eds.), *Social comparison processes: Theoretical and empirical perspectives* (pp. 335–357). Washington, DC: Hemisphere/Wiley.

Wills, T. A. (1981). Downward comparison principles in social psychology. *Psychological Bulletin, 90*, 245–271.

Wood, J. V. (1989). Theory and research concerning social comparison of personal attributes. *Psychological Bulletin, 106*, 231–248.

Wood, J. V. (1996). What is social comparison and how should we study it? *Personality and Social Psychology Bulletin, 22*, 520–537.

Wood, J. V., Taylor, S., & Lichtman, R. (1985). Social comparison in adjustment to breast cancer. *Journal of Personality and Social Psychology, 49*, 1169–1183.

Yee, V. (2012, December 25). A onetime drug dealer, now working to combat a plague of gun violence. *The New York Times*, p. A22.

Zanna, M., Goethals, G. R., & Hill S. (1975). Evaluating a sex related ability: Social comparison with similar others and standard setters. *Journal of Experimental Social Psychology, 11*, 86–93.

Zell, E., & Alicke, M. D. (2009). Contextual neglect, self-evaluation, and the frog-pond effect. *Journal of Personality and Social Psychology, 97*, 467–482.

Zell, E., & Alicke, M. D. (2010). The local dominance effect in self-evaluation: Evidence and explanations. *Personality and Social Psychology Review, 14*, 368–384.

Zell, E., & Alicke, M. D. (2012): Local dominance in health risk perception. *Psychology and Health*. doi: 10.1080/08870446.2012.742529

# Conformity and Divergence in Interactions, Groups, and Culture

Bert H. Hodges

**Abstract**

Humans have a natural affinity for conformity and coordination that is essential to culture, to groups, and to dialogical relationships. It is equally true that the dynamics of relationships, groups, and culture depend on tendencies to diverge, to differentiate, and to dissent. Evidence from anthropology, as well as social, developmental, and cognitive psychology, reveals remarkably convergent accounts of the complex interplay of divergence and convergence in an array of contexts. Conversational alignment, synchrony, mimicry, imitation, majority-minority dynamics, dissent, trust, intra- and cross-cultural diversity, social learning, and the formation and development of cultures all reveal complex patterns of selectivity and fidelity that continue to surprise researchers. The general pattern is one illustrated by young children: They are most willing to be guided by those who tell the truth and those who care about others. Issues of convergence and divergence are fundamental social phenomena, and they deserve fresh attention.

**Key Words:** alignment, anticonformity, conformity, dissent, divergence, imitation, mimicry, minority dynamics, social learning, synchrony

What makes humans special among other animals? There have been many answers to this question (e.g., large brains, intelligence, language), but one of the most compelling is rarely recognized. Humans have extended their habitat to more places on Earth than virtually any other animal, and their ability to do so has depended on their ability to engage in social learning, using others as guides for directing their actions, emotions, and thinking. As Boyd, Richerson, and Henrich (2011) put it: "We [humans] owe our success to our uniquely developed ability to learn from others. This capacity enables humans to gradually accumulate information across generations and develop well-adapted tools, beliefs, and practices that are too complex for any single individual to invent during their lifetime" (p. 10918). Facing strange new geographies with hostile climates and unfamiliar food sources, humans would have quickly succumbed, had they not learned to trust, to imitate, and to conform.

Thus, conformity is a crucial dimension of culture and of human survival. Tomasello (2008), for example, argues that without the emergence of caring and sharing in humans in ways that led to the emergence of social norms that are unprecedented in other apes, humans would never have been able to interact in ways that allowed linguistic practices (e.g., grammars) to be constructed and stabilized. The existence of complex languages shared by many people over long periods of time is a testament to the power of conformity.

However, there is another side to the story. Learning from others and conforming to the practices of one's elders and peers must be selective, if it is to be adaptive. Neither social learning nor individual learning alone is capable of sustaining cultures; what is required is "critical social learning" (Enquist, Eriksson, & Ghirlanda, 2007). Critical social learners do not imitate or conform indiscriminately; rather, they abandon unsatisfactory practices and learn to choose sources of information that are likely to provide accurate, reliable, and useful information. Another way to describe this second side of the story is to say that humans not only converge in actions, thoughts, and feelings; they also diverge. Thus, although copying and conforming are crucial aspects of being a member of a language community, "Any language spoken by more than a handful of people exhibits this tendency to split into dialects, which may differ from one another along many dimensions ... vocabulary, pronunciation, grammar, usage, social function, artistic and literary expression" (Francis, 1983, p. 1). On balance, people not only conform to each other; they also dissent, differentiate, refrain, and resist.

This chapter will survey a broader array of ways people conform than most such overviews, and it will focus the interplay of divergence and convergence rather than treating them as separate phenomena. The range of disciplines and specialties considered is broader as well. Taking this more comprehensive approach provides a richer, more coherent account of conformity and its place and purpose in the cultural life of humans. It also reveals exciting new directions that research on conformity has taken in the 21st century. A representative sampling is offered, with new directions being highlighted.

Although definitions of conformity vary within and across research traditions, it is nearly always understood in terms of the matching or aligning of one individual's behavior with that of others. However, the matching cannot be coincidental or due to an impersonal source. It requires that someone do something because she or he observed others doing it. Sometimes only two people are ostensibly involved; other times, there are several or many. Sometimes the matching is a response to an explicit or implicit request; other times, it appears uninvited. Sometimes the alignment is self-consciously chosen after careful deliberation; other times, it seems unselfconscious or even counterintuitive. Sometimes the alignment or matching takes the shape of skilled action, while other times it is emotional expression or a choice expressed in words or other symbolic activities. The chapter begins with culture and conformity, moves to the dynamics of groups and individuals, and finishes with the matching of actions in imitation, mimicry, and synchrony. These divergent perspectives reveal a remarkably convergent and intriguing story.

## Social Learning and the Evolution of Culture

### Farmer's Dilemma, Hunter's Dilemma

Imagine a prehistoric farmer who knows of two crops but does not know which one yields more food, given all the variations in climate, soil, rain, and light. The farmer can do his own experimenting, but determining the better yielding crop will be difficult. One good strategy might be to choose the crop grown by most other farmers, especially if they have already done some experimenting of their own. Conforming to local practices or inherited practices (e.g., planting what his father planted) will often lead the farmer to making a better choice than if he had depended only on his own experience. The argument here is a simple statistical one: In a variable environment, having data from a broader sample than just your own experience is likely to lead to a truer judgment, a "wisdom of crowds" effect (e.g., Surowiecki, 2004). But what if our imaginary farmer has copied the behavior of farmers who were simply copying others before them, and they have not really been doing their own experimenting? Now conformity as a strategy for learning is shakier (Sperber et al., 2010). Learning from others works if they are tracking the environment (i.e., discerning what is true), or if they are copying others who have tracked the environment. Of course, the fact that the farmers are alive at all suggests that their prior choices of what to plant have been at least minimally sufficient.

Social psychological processes are central to cultural evolutionary theories (Mesoudi, 2009), yet "social psychologists have not considered cultural transmission to be worthy of study ... and cultural anthropologists have not considered experiments to be particularly relevant to their work" (Mesoudi & Whiten, 2008, p. 3499). However, this situation is rapidly changing. An excellent example of research on conformity and divergence is Mesoudi and O'Brien's (2008) study of arrowhead design. Arrowheads from prehistoric Nevada differ systematically from those found in nearby California, showing much less diversity (Bettinger & Eerkens, 1999). A plausible account for this difference is that in California different individuals each developed their own way of designing and creating arrowheads, while in Nevada there was a tendency for individuals to adopt the designs used by others. How might anthropologists try to evaluate the validity of this hypothesis? Mesoudi and O'Brien (2008) conducted experiments in which people designed "virtual arrowheads" in a computer simulation with feedback that indicated how well their designs worked. They could try improving their designs by individual, trial-and-error learning or by altering their designs to be more like other members of their group whose designs were more successful. Individual learning led to increasing diversity of design, while social learning converged on the most successful design. Thus, the experimental simulation supports the view that California arrowheads were mostly the product of individual learning strategies and Nevada ones emerged from individuals changing their designs to fit the designs of others in their group.

Does this mean that conforming one's actions to others leads to better learning and better outcomes? Mesoudi and O'Brien say that the answer to this question depends on the adaptive landscape underlying arrowhead fitness. If there is one best arrowhead design, then individual and group learning are not very different in their outcomes. If, however, there are a variety of arrowhead designs that are somewhat effective, but some variants are more effective, social learning is likely to converge on the superior designs faster. Individual learners will stick with good-enough designs. What decides what is good enough? This is an ecological, values-realizing question. It seems that the ecological conditions of Nevada were much harsher than those of California at the time. Mesoudi and O'Brien argue that when a population is under environmental stress, it is better to stick together, learn from each other, and conform one's practices to those that are judged most successful. Where the environmental demands are more lenient, greater variety and individuality are possible.

### What Is Conformity and What Does It Accomplish?

Cultural anthropologists define conformity in terms of population trends, based on an individual adopting a behavior because it is the most frequently witnessed in others (Claidière & Whiten, 2012). This yields four different possibilities, three kinds of conformity and anticonformity. Suppose 70 percent of Britons support the monarchy and 30 percent do not. If 10 undecided new Britons (e.g., immigrants, children) are influenced by the views of those around them, four things could happen. If 8 out of 10 come to favor the monarchy, it would be an example of *strong conformity*; the majority view is growing stronger. If 7 out of 10 favor the monarchy,

it is *linear conformity* (i.e., no change in the population probability), and if 6 in 10 favor the monarchy, it is *weak conformity* (i.e., the population preference is still biased in the same direction but is weaker). *Anticonformity* is the other option. Perhaps people attend to frequency distribution information, but they choose the less popular option, because it is rarer. Examples of this might be "snob appeal," a "progressive bias," or being an "early adopter." Eriksson et al. (2007) have pointed out that linear conformity is really *unbiased* social learning: It maintains but does not strengthen, weaken, or challenge existing patterns of action.

Which of these patterns enhances the quality of individual decision making and the fortunes of culture as a whole? Efferson et al. (2008, p. 57) suggest there is no simple answer: "Theoretically, conformity can be a valuable way to make decisions under uncertainty. Importantly, however, conformity is neither good nor bad by itself. It merely exaggerates existing biases in individual decision making." For example, if an increasing number of individual farmers who study their crop yields move away from planting barley toward planting rye, then conformity will have the effect of strengthening this bias toward rye. Whether that is a good thing or not depends on many things. There are now vigorous debates going on within the decision-making sciences about what are the right criteria by which to evaluate the goodness of such choices (e.g., Bennis, Medin, & Bartels, 2010). Wisdom does not come easily.

### Is Convergence Crucial to Culture or Divergence?

One of the most interesting approaches to making an ecological judgment about the value of conformity is the work of Richerson and Boyd (2005). They claim that conformity, imitation, and other forms of social learning lead to greater homogeneity within groups, which leads to greater differences between groups. They believe this helps to answer a basic question of anthropology: How are there so many different cultures, and why are these cultures so stable? Furthermore, they believe that conformity and imitation have contributed to the development of prosocial tendencies within humans, opening up vast new possibilities for cultural enrichment through cooperative action. Other anthropologists, while acknowledging the power and appeal of the Richerson and Boyd thesis, have noted that the picture is more complicated. For the

Richerson and Boyd thesis to work, strong conformity is required. The first problem for the thesis is that there is remarkably little evidence that strong conformity occurs, especially on the scale needed to sustain their theoretical scenario. The second problem is increasing evidence of the pervasiveness and potency of diversity, novelty, and other forms of nonconformity. Third, there are increasing theoretical questions concerning Richerson and Boyd's claims about ingroup homogeneity and between-group heterogeneity.

Efferson et al. (2008) provided a strong test of people's willingness to use social information to guide their own choices. Participants played a game, making choices between two different technologies, one of which was better (i.e., led to a higher payoff). Those who learned from others and followed the majority made the most money. However, Efferson et al. were surprised to find that 30 percent of those playing did not follow the majority and, as a consequence, "left money on the table." They also found even those participants who claimed they had taken other peoples' choices into account tended to choose the less common option (anticonformity) some of the time. They concluded that there is evidence for "mavericks" as well as conformists even in conditions highly favorable to conformity. Similar difficulties have emerged from studies by McElreath et al. (2005) and Eriksson et al. (2007) in which they evaluated people's choices of better and worse technologies (e.g., hammers) when they could learn from others. Even Richerson and Boyd (2005) have revised their earlier hypothesis, suggesting that there may be a "success bias" that exists along with conformity. Perhaps people start with individual learning, and only if this is unsuccessful are they attracted to imitating successful individuals or adopting the practices of the majority. However, a study of Bolivian high plains herders (Efferson et al., 2007) found that they largely relied on their own personal histories and experience for guidance, making little use of either imitation or conformity. Some researchers have argued that individually acquired information generally has a greater impact than socially acquired information (e.g., Eriksson & Coultas, 2009; Eriksson & Strimling, 2009). However, people are more willing to make use of social information when the environment is stable (Toelch et al., 2009). Claidière and Whiten (2012) conclude that the evidence for strong conformity is particularly weak when people are motivated to be accurate. They suggest that conformity generally does little better that random (unbiased) copying of others, and it does even less well than selective copying, in which one pays attention to the accuracy or effectiveness of others.

Thus, there is weak evidence for conformity, especially strong conformity, on the one hand, and on the other, clear evidence that people often depend on individual learning and sometimes engage in selective imitation or make maverick choices. In addition to these empirical difficulties, a number of theoretical critiques of strong conformity have been proposed. Based on mathematical modeling, Eriksson and Coultas (2009) argued that within-group similarity is not as general a phenomenon as Boyd and his colleagues (Henrich & Boyd, 1998; Richerson & Boyd, 2005) have claimed. They argue for a nonconformist hypothesis: The general outcome of social learning is within-group diversity, not within-group homogeneity. A conformist bias, they suggest, might actually be maladaptive for humans, because it would undermine cumulative effects of culture. "Conformist-biased social learning is not, in general, evolutionarily stable, and often leads to lower fitness than unbiased social learning ... individuals' ability to discriminate between cultural variants ... seems more important ... than frequency-based choice rules" (Eriksson et al., 2007, p. 85). Mesoudi (2011) has made the intriguing suggestion that perhaps it is not conformity, imitation, or any other social learning strategy that makes humans so culturally competent and successful, but rather the capacity of humans to *switch* strategies, allowing them to adopt new, improved technologies, skills, and knowledge.

Overall, the arguments and evidence suggest that both convergence and divergence contribute to learning and cultural development. The appeal of conformity is that it speeds up learning, allows one to learn from others' mistakes, especially when those mistakes have large-scale consequences (e.g., death), and conserves energy. However, the most potent argument for conformity is its potential for supplying the individual learner with a broader array of strategies and a greater knowledge of outcomes that any one learner will be able to sample effectively. It is this power to improve accuracy and thus effectiveness that allows other advantages (e.g., time and energy saved) to accrue to conformity. What seems to be most effective is selectivity and flexibility. As valuable as conformity can be, it can also lead a group astray, as even its advocates (e.g., Richerson & Boyd, 2005) acknowledge. It is the potential for going astray that has most intrigued psychologists, and it is to their investigations we turn next. However, they too seem to be moving toward a more balanced portrait of conformity and divergence.

## The Social Dynamics of Groups and Individuals
### Accounting for Asch's Dilemma

A touchstone for most psychological discussions of conformity is a series of experiments by Solomon Asch (1951, 1956). The standard story told is that the studies show individuals blindly following mistaken majorities for fear of being wrong or for fear of being ridiculed (e.g., Cialdini & Trost, 1998; Gilovich, Keltner, & Nisbett, 2010). Despite the popularity of this account, there is reason to be deeply dubious. Asch presented participants with simple factual questions about lengths of lines, which were easily answered correctly if one looked carefully. What made the experimental task demanding, though, was that Asch arranged for all the other members of the group to give the same incorrect answer on 12 of 18 questions. Asch (1952) thought people would not agree with wrong answers when they had clear information of their own. However, 74 percent of participants gave at least one wrong answer, and 28 percent did so 7 or more times out of 12 (Asch, 1951). The other side of the coin is that two thirds of all answers were dissents, 26 percent of participants never agreed with wrong answers, and over 70 percent of participants dissented all or most of the time. The median response to Asch's dilemma was to dissent from the unanimous majority nine times and to agree three times on critical trials, and if a single other person gave the correct answer, as they did in another version of the experiment, participants dissented 95 percent of the time (Asch, 1951).

Early commentary on the studies suggested they provided dramatic evidence that people "stick to their guns" when confronted with mistaken majorities (Ceraso, Gruber, & Rock, 1990), but "with the passing years … the central point of Asch's work has become not only drastically weakened, but reversed" (Friend, Rafferty, & Bramel, 1990, p. 30). Asch (1956) noted the diversity of his results, suggesting that they demonstrated "the love of truth as a psychological reality, and the power it can command" (Asch, 1990, p. 55), but he also worried about people's susceptibility to being misled. Most subsequent researchers have focused only on explaining agreement with wrong answers. The most influential explanation offered is Deutsch and Gerard's (1955, p. 629): People take others' actions

as good evidence about what is true and real (informational influence), and/or because they want to fit "the positive expectations of others" (normative influence). Despite their intuitive appeal, neither of these reasons explains Asch's results adequately. Informational influence could explain the results, if people agreed when they were confused about what the right answers were, but that was not true for most participants (Allen, 1965). Normative explanations, which assume people are motivated by a "desire not to appear deviant" (Bond & Smith, 1996), cannot explain why 70 percent of participants dissented all or most of the time. Ironically, a set of studies, famous for demonstrating conformity and a lack of courage, provide compelling evidence of people's willingness to stand alone, speaking truthfully when no one else has (Hodges & Geyer, 2006).

There have been more sophisticated and nuanced attempts to address the complexities of divergence and convergence in Asch-type dilemmas. Two of the more insightful are Ross et al.'s (1976) attribution account and Campbell's (1990) "moral epistemology" account. Ross et al. claim the majority's incorrect answers challenge participants' sense of competence and sanity, but if they disagree, their dissent will seem equally bizarre to the majority. As a consequence, most people will be unwilling to offer such a challenge; however, agreeing with wrong answers is costly too because the task is so simple and compelling. Participants are trapped: They must acknowledge either weakness or incompetence. Although people are far more willing to dissent than Ross et al. grant, they capture nicely the phenomenology of frustration that defines the situation. Campbell's (1990) analysis of the dilemma is in terms of epistemic responsibility. He argues that humans are utterly dependent on each other for learning about the world, but when there is a conflict between our own individual view and what others tell us, three virtues serve as guideposts. First, it is quite appropriate to *trust* the testimony of others; it is ordinarily an ecologically valid assumption. Second, we should *respect* our own perceptions and beliefs, as well as those of others, and work to integrate the two, in the hope that greater depth of understanding will emerge. Third, while it might be most rational to believe the majority is right in an Asch situation, we should report our own individual perspectives as *honestly* as possible, since it is only through multiple independent reports that greater understanding can emerge. In sum, Campbell is audacious: He suggests there are occasions in which behavior and belief will be inconsistent for the sake of finding the truth and protecting the group and its members.

Hodges and Geyer (2006) reworked the insights of Campbell (1990) and Ross et al. (1976) into a more comprehensive account, one framed in terms of multiple values that jointly constrain action, perception, and cognition. Their values-realizing account suggests a complex array of relationships and obligations are at stake in the Asch situation: "How does one speak the truth in a complex, tense, and frustrating situation ... in a way that simultaneously honors one's peers, the experimenter, one's own perception, and the situation in which all are embedded?" (Hodges, 2004, p. 344). One could, as Campbell suggested, honestly dissent from the majority every time. However, Hodges and Geyer noted that if a person always dissented from others' views, then, from a conversational point of view (i.e., *pragmatics*, as linguists call it), it would be easy for that person to be seen as disrespecting others' views. It would likely be a conversation stopper. Another option would be to take Campbell's advice about belief, and Ross et al.'s concern for how others would react to a challenge, and agree with others in the group most of the time. This approach, however, risks being dishonest, not respecting one's own insights sufficiently. Finally, one could mostly dissent from others' views, making plain one's disagreement, but occasionally agree with others' answers as a pragmatic signal of one's trust and respect. To repeat wrong answers of others is to acknowledge that one hears and understands their point of view, even while disagreeing with it. Although one could be accused of being inconsistent, taking this approach shows a commitment to taking others' views seriously and to continued "conversation" about the situation in the service of truth and social solidarity. The actual pattern of responses in Asch (1956) indicates that something like these three strategies were adopted: Roughly half of participants mostly disagreed but occasionally agreed with wrong answers, about a quarter never agreed, and the remainder agreed more often than they disagreed.

Hodges and Geyer (2006) proposed that the varying patterns of dissent and agreement, both within and across participants, reflect participants' attempts to realize multiple values in an inherently frustrating situation. From this perspective Asch (1956) was wrong to assume that an individual, speaking to others with whom he or she has a sharp disagreement, should say exactly the same thing he or she would have said when alone with the experimenter. What is appropriate to say in a situation marked by sharp disagreement differs from what is fitting to say in a more ordinary, less contentious situation. The situation calls for people to speak truthfully, but in a way that reveals something of the awkwardness and tension of the situation. Understood in this way, truth is larger and more complex than answering correctly, and agreeing with wrong answers functions as a way of staying engaged rather than as a way of avoiding ridicule. This account captures the frustration and risk that Ross et al. highlight, as well as Campbell's concern to respect others' views, even if it produces apparent inconsistencies.

Another approach that might contribute to explaining Asch's results is social identity theory. One version of the theory, which has been applied to Asch (Abrams et al., 1990), focuses on the relation of the participant to his or her peers: People are more likely to conform to ingroup than outgroup members. Another application of the theory, looking at social dilemmas other than Asch's (Reicher, Haslam, & Smith, 2012), focuses on whether participants would identify more with the experimenter or with their peers. If the former, they will tend to give correct answers, and if the latter, they will tend to give agreeing answers. Like values-realizing theory, social identity theory points to the diversity and complexity of interpersonal relationships in social dilemmas. A situation that might differentiate the theories is one in which the group is composed of friends. Social identity theory predicts greater agreement with ingroup members, at least on identity-related issues, while values-realizing theory predicts it is easier to express truthful dissent to friends than strangers, since trust and social solidarity are already well established. Available evidence (Matsuda, 1985; McKelvey & Kerr, 1988) supports the values-realizing claim, although there may be cross-cultural differences (Hodges & Geyer, 2006; Takano & Sogon, 2008).

### Moving Beyond Dilemmas: Ordinary Fashions and Decisions

Despite what has been argued earlier, what makes Asch's results seem compelling to many observers is this: If people will yield, even occasionally, on simple basic truths, how much more will they yield on more difficult or more ambiguous issues and practices. There is, in fact, some evidence that this is the case (Baron, Vandello, & Brunsman, 1996). Thus, in domains such as cultural tastes and fashions, it is very easy to presume that conformity reigns supreme. However, even here divergence is as crucial as convergence. Culture is not a fixed pattern, but a constantly evolving one. As Berger and Heath (2008) observe: "Divergence is pervasive in social life" (p. 593). They argue that groups engage in identity signaling, such that distinctive dress, possessions, actions, and attitudes are adopted in order to make it easier for others to identify whether that group affords a productive and satisfying relationship for the observer. A "Live Strong" wristband sends one signal, a Rolex watch another. However, groups can abandon markers if the marker loses its signal value (i.e., its ability to distinguish the group and its affordances for others). This divergence is not based simply on status or on liking. Shifts in group tastes and styles are selective: Groups are happy to share many things in common with other groups, but certain domains are seen as important to identifying the group to itself and to others. For example, consumers felt threatened if another person imitated their purchasing choices on items that signaled their distinctiveness (White & Argo, 2011).

One of the most powerful arguments in favor of conforming to group judgments is evidence of "wisdom of the crowd" effects (Surowiecki, 2004). However, these effects also indicate the importance of each person making an independent judgment and then sharing what he or she knows with others. When an individual is uncertain about what is true, and he or she receives many independent estimates of the correct answer from others, the average of the estimates made by the group approaches the true value. This group wisdom is often better than even experts' estimates (Larrick, Mannes, & Soll, 2012). Social influence, though, can undermine the wisdom of crowds: People's confidence goes up as they influence each other and come to agree, but accuracy goes down, except on easier questions about which people actually know something (Lorenz, Rauhut, Schweitzer, & Helbing, 2011). This suggests that herding effects (and a loss of wisdom) are mostly confined to social procedures that undermine diversity, to problems that are very difficult, or to situations where correct answers are not yet known. It has been shown that an individual can simulate the wisdom-of-crowds effect by deliberately taking different perspectives on a problem and generating different answers from those perspectives, then averaging all those answers (Herzog & Hertwig, 2009). Finally, research indicates that people frequently "rely too much on their own judgments and miss the opportunity to learn from others" (Larrick et al., 2012, p. 228). Some

people, in fact, appear to make almost no use of others' views.

Groupthink (Janis, 1972) is one widely discussed form of group dynamics that can undermine the wisdom of the group. Packer (2009) has argued that a powerful antidote to groupthink is for groups to deliberately adopt the viewpoint that divergence and deviance are not threats to group integrity but an important means of collective truth finding and problem solving. What seems to be required is strongly identified members who are committed to the good of the group rather than being focused primarily on their own individual good. It is weakly identified members who tend to be silent and contribute to groupthink, not those who are most strongly identified. Thus, conformity to group norms is not blind. Strongly identified members have the most freedom to dissent from the group, and they sometimes use this freedom to try to redirect their groups toward better beliefs or practices (Packer & Chasteen, 2010). This evidence for "loyal deviance" challenges social identity theory's assumption that strongly identified members are most likely to conform to group norms. Other research (e.g., Falomir-Pichastor, Gabarrot, & Mugny, 2009 has also found evidence that conformity to group norms is selective, sometimes leading strongly committed members to undermine ingroup norms in an effort to defend the ingroup against what they see as outgroup threats. Thus, for example, a member of a group favoring tolerance of others may be relatively intolerant of outsiders who are seen as threatening.

As this sampling of research reveals, ordinary situations in which people observe others' actions and hear their judgments and claims, produce patterns of conformity and divergence much like those seen in more dramatic scenarios such as Asch's dilemma. Very often people take their own path, much more than psychologists might have assumed, and sometimes less than might be optimal for making well-informed decisions. These studies also illustrate how quickly the dynamics of converging and diverging become complex, even in ordinary situations.

### Developments in the Dynamics of Agreeing and Disagreeing

Asch's studies generated a large literature (see Allen, 1965; Bond & Smith, 1996), but new questions and perspectives have emerged, several of which are briefly noted, with two being highlighted. One of the most important shifts that occurred in the decades after Asch's work was the recognition that conformity was not a one-way street.

Minorities influence majorities, as well as the reverse (Moscovici, 1976; Nemeth, 1985). Arguments and evidence suggest that within-group disagreement generates uncertainty, which opens up the possibility for all members of the group to be influential, even those initially in the minority (David & Turner, 2001). In some cases, minority views may not lead to immediate changes on focal issues, but their influence may be felt on related issues, which over time may lead to new majority positions (Crano & Seyranian, 2009). A second, related shift has been increasing attention to nonconformity (Allen, 1975), including dissent, resistance, and differentiation (e.g., Griskevicius, Goldstein, Mortensen, Cialdini, & Kenrick, 2006; Hornsey, Majkut, Terry, & McKimmie, 2003; Packer, Fujita, & Chasteen, 2014). For example, Schulz-Hardt, Brodbeck, Mojzisch, Kerschreiter, and Frey, (2006) found that dissent during discussion increased the quality of group decision making, even when the dissent came from those not favoring the correct solution. A third trend related to nonconformity emphasizes motivation and identity. Numerous researchers have proposed that people look for ways to identify themselves as distinctive with respect to others, both within and across groups, which balances their concern for interdependence and social solidarity (e.g., Brewer & Roccas, 2001; Hornsey & Jetten, 2004; Imhoff & Erb, 2009).

A fourth trend is the development of increasingly complex and comprehensive descriptive schemes for identifying various phenomena related to conformity and nonconformity. As an example, Nail and his colleagues (2000) have identified at least 16 possible ways of responding to arguments or actions of others. These possible responses are based on the congruence or incongruence between one's private and public views, and ones' agreement or disagreement with the group's view, both before and after the group expresses its view. According to Nail et al.'s model, there are four types of conformity: conversion, compliance, convergence, and paradoxical compliance. One of the interesting results emerging from this work has been the identification of new phenomena, such as *anticompliance*, that is, publicly disagreeing with a claim that one privately agrees with, both before and after having learned of others' views. This counterintuitive possibility has recently been demonstrated and explored by Hodges et al. (2014). They found that individuals placed in a position that prevented them from seeing clearly, but who heard others in better positions identify answers correctly, often chose to make up their own incorrect answers, instead of repeating the correct answers of others. This *speaking from ignorance effect*, which was predicted by Hodges and Geyer (2006), can be explained with the same values-realizing dynamics used to explain Asch's agreeing-with-wrong-answers finding. Surprisingly often, participants intentionally answered incorrectly, truthfully revealing the ignorance of their position, a finding which challenges claims that people are motivated to achieve goals of being correct and being agreeable (Cialdini & Goldstein, 2004).

A fifth development has been the emergence of models that treat convergence and divergence as related aspects of a single dynamical system. This work grew out of early work on group size and its effect on tendencies to conform, particularly on Asch-type tasks. Latané and Wolf (1981) proposed a social force field model that tried to capture the joint effects of the number, strength, and proximity of sources of influence, which predicted that a dissenter could sometimes have a larger effect on group decision making than a majority member. Several other models have since been proposed, but none seem to be sufficient to account for existing findings concerning conformity (Bond, 2005). Latané (1996) proposed a dynamical systems version of his theory, which predicts that randomly assorted views or practices within a group will tend over time to cluster into self-similar, self-reinforcing groups, but which make it possible for selected minority positions to survive despite an overall decrease in diversity. Others (Bond, 2005; Campbell & Fairey, 1989) have argued that no single model is likely to be adequate because conformity emerges from multiple motives and processes. A simple finding, first noted by Asch (1951), remains: Group size does have a slight effect on conformity, but the magic number seems to be three. The impact of additional sources of influence is minimal.

A sixth issue of note is accountability. Although Asch's task is sometimes seen as lacking in importance or in moral weight, studies that have highlighted these have usually found more conformity, not less (e.g., Baron et al., 1996). Tetlock (2002) suggests that increasing accountability fosters a concern for justifying one's views, which encourages increased self-criticism and increased sensitivity to others' views. Others (e.g., Quinn & Schlenker, 2002) have argued there are conditions where accountability reduces susceptibility to misleading sources.

A seventh development, related to accountability, is the rise of morally charged studies growing out of Asch's work (Haney, Banks, & Zimbardo, 1973; Milgram, 1963), which have helped to create a larger narrative that has been widely influential, particularly among textbook writers (Friend et al., 1990). Along with Sherif's (1935) and Asch's (1951) earlier work, this narrative casts conformity in a strongly negative light, often, in fact, as an evil to be resisted. A counternarrative of resistance and responsibility has begun to emerge (e.g., Haslam & Reicher, 2012; Krueger & Massey, 2009; Reicher et al., 2012), which explores more complicated and balanced approaches to understanding dramatic circumstances.

Finally, four other developments deserve attention. Two that can only be mentioned are studies of collaborative remembering (e.g., Jaeger, Lauris, Selmeczy, & Dobbins, 2012) and experiments on conformity using various brain imaging techniques (Schnuerch & Gibbons, 2014). Two others, cultural issues and developmental issues, are briefly highlighted next.

### Cross-Cultural Issues

Are there important variations in tendencies to converge and diverge across cultures, or is the balance of social learning and individual experimentation relatively stable? Perhaps the most cited finding is Bond and Smith's (1996): "collectivist countries tended to show higher levels of conformity than individualist countries" (p. 111). There is reason for caution, however. Bond and Smith themselves note that agreeing with incorrect answers of a majority in Asch-style dilemmas can be understood in various ways. In cultures that stress harmony rather than self-expression, avoiding public disagreements may reflect tact and sensitivity. This may be true even in American contexts (e.g., McCauley & Rozin, 2003). Similarly, there are differences in how truth, trust, and social solidarity are understood across cultures as well, but evidence indicates these differences also exist within cultures, leading to situational differences that parallel cross-cultural differences (Hodges & Geyer, 2006). Takano and Sogon (2008) argue that conformity in Asch-style tasks is quite comparable in Japan and the United States, with about 25 percent of answers agreeing with incorrect group answers. More generally, they dispute the common claim (e.g., Heine, 2007) that Japanese are collectivist, that is, "willingly conforming to the group and sacrificing themselves for the sake of the group" (Takano & Sogon, 2008, p. 237). This is particularly interesting since an earlier study by Sogon (Williams & Sogon, 1984) is often cited

to support such claims, but Takano and Sogon argue the earlier findings were based on an unusual sample (i.e., military training groups) that would be relatively intolerant of dissent.

Fischer and Schwartz (2011) found more variability within than across cultures in people's ratings of verbally expressed values. Along these lines several studies have found that subtle social pragmatics determine when participants in any particular culture converge or diverge in their actions or judgments. Fu et al. (2007) observed that individuals with a high need for closure who immigrated alone tended to assimilate more to their new culture, but those who immigrated as part of a group did not. Several studies have challenged earlier findings claiming that Americans preferred the unique and Asians the more common option. Japanese are as desirous of a unique colored pen as Americans, but they will forego their preference for the sake of others (Hashimoto, Li, & Yamagishi, 2011). Yamagishi, Hashimoto, and Schug (2008) provide evidence that Japanese are more reflexively careful of others than Americans, but just as capable of wanting to be unique. They also found that if Americans were aware that choosing a pen would have negative implications for other people's choices, they picked a majority-color pen, just as Asians did. Mok and Morris (2009) found that priming one of two cultural identities for Asian Americans shifted behavior in the direction of that identity for those who were culturally integrated, but for those more conflicted about their identity, it shifted their behavior away from the primed culture.

While cultural concerns usually focus on existing cultural groups, coevolutionary theories have opened up interesting avenues for considering historical as well as regional patterns and differences. Murray, Trudeau, and Schaller (2011) have found circumstantial evidence supporting their hypothesis that cultures based on agriculture and subject to greater threat from disease-causing pathogens have stronger norms for conformity. They note that human cultures value both conformity and deviance, and their theory attempts to identify one possible constraint on how the dynamics of conformity and divergence are likely to play out in various ecological settings. Others (e.g., Hruschka et al., 2014) have challenged the pathogen stress hypothesis, suggesting that group norms for sharing depend on a wide array of threats (e.g., food insecurity), not just pathogen prevalence, and how those threats interact with social structures (e.g., poor governmental services). The larger lesson remains,

however: Conformity and divergence vary with ecological settings and dynamics.

## The Development of Trust

If there is anyone we would expect to be conformists, it is children. Children are expected to
learn from parents and older siblings. But how do
children actually proceed in assessing what is true
and false about the world? Whom do they trust and
when? An impressive array of studies during the past
decade has painted the following picture. Children
tend to trust their own perceptions, but they take
into account information provided by others as
well. Furthermore, the way in which they make use
of this information shows considerable epistemic
sophistication, even by adult standards. Children
track the prior accuracy of informants and prefer
accurate ones (Pasquini, Corriveau, Koenig, &
Harris, 2007), but 4 year olds monitor sources for
both accuracy and inaccuracy, while 3 year olds
monitor only for inaccuracy (Corriveau, Meints, &
Harris, 2009). More generally, children seem sensitive to expertise. When seeking information about
nutrition, game rules, or naming a novel object,
children prefer an adult to a child informant; however, they are likely to ask another child about how
a toy functions (Rakoczy, Hamann, Warneken, &
Tomasello, 2010; VanderBorght & Jaswal, 2009).
Children not only take into account the relative
expertise and prior histories of informants, they
adjust for the current activity of the informant and
the likelihood that his or her information is reliable.
Despite prior experience with two people, one inaccurate, the other accurate, 4- to 5-year-old children
believed the claim of the one who had looked in the
appropriate place (in a particular box) to see what
was true or not (Brosseau-Liard & Birch, 2011).
Children tend to trust firsthand evidence over sec-
ondhand evidence, not only when it is their own
perceptual experience but also when another person
has seen for herself rather than relying on another's
testimony (Einav & Robinson, 2011). These studies indicate that children are relatively careful judges
of others' testimony. In general, they value truth,
and they exercise trust with considerable care and
diligence.

Children do tend to conform to majority viewpoints on novel issues, about which they have no
other information (e.g., naming an object with
which the child is unfamiliar); that is, they prefer consensus viewpoints rather than a dissenter's
claim (Corriveau, Fusaro, & Harris, 2009). Thus,
children ordinarily take consensus to be a marker
of the truth. What happens, though, when there is
a direct conflict between the child's direct perception of a situation and what others say about it? Two
recent studies (Corriveau & Harris, 2010; Haun &
Tomasello, 2011) have successfully presented Asch-
type dilemmas to 3- to 4-year-old children. Despite
using somewhat different methods (e.g., a majority of peers or adults), both studies yielded remarkably similar results: Children overwhelmingly
dissented from incorrect answers. For example, in
the Corriveau and Harris study 76 percent of 4 year
olds and 58 percent of 3 year olds answered correctly every time. A minority of the time (20 percent in one study, 34 percent in the other) children
agreed with incorrect answers, and in both studies
agreement with wrong answers decreased over trials.
In an interesting variation, Corriveau and Harris
presented children with a game in which they had
to choose a bridge of the right length so that a rabbit
could cross safely, winning a prize for the child. In
this situation, children never erred, dissenting from
the majority every time. Overall, then, developmental research indicates that children demonstrate
action patterns similar to adults when evaluating
whether to follow the lead of others, although these
patterns emerge over time. Children are rarely gull-
ible; rather, for the most part, they are trusting and
prudent.

## Matching Others in Action and Interaction: Selectivity, Fidelity, and Dialogue
### Imitation

Much of the research described so far has
involved matching choices of others. In this section,
the focus is on more fine-grained matching of the
actions of another, both spatially and temporally.
Imitation, mimicry, and synchrony are less a matter
of agreement and more a matter of replicating or
matching movement patterns of a model, teacher,
or partner. In what follows, each of these is considered in turn, including a brief look at linguistic
alignment.

Imitation can be defined as "matching the
behavior of a model after observing it" (Over &
Carpenter, 2012, p. 183), which is virtually the
same as conformity, except that it involves one
model rather than many. It is a change in a person's movements and intentions based on his or her
observation of another's actions. Imitation is also
like mimicry and synchrony—some authors use
the terms almost interchangeably. However, imitation tends to focus on tasks with objects and the

movements used to engage them; by contrast, mimicry and synchrony focus on the body as an object and what is done in terms of gesture, posture, and expression. It is tempting to assume that imitation is intentional while mimicry and synchrony are not, but that proves to be too simple. Although imitation research has blossomed among developmental researchers, mimicry among social researchers, and synchrony among cognitive researchers, this reflects the eccentricities of disciplinary boundaries as much as anything. All are forms of conformity, and while many substantive issues and findings are remarkably similar, they should not be confused.

Although it is often overlooked, imitation is selective. Human infants and children tend to imitate models that have imitated them (Over, Carpenter, Spears, & Gattis, 2013), who are warm and friendly (Nielsen, 2006), who have previously been reliable (Pasquini et al., 2007), and who are ingroup members (Kinzler, Corriveau, & Harris, 2011). However, when 4- to 5-year-old children are confronted with ingroup and outgroup members (i.e., native and foreign accented speakers) who vary in reliability, they imitate previously accurate speakers, regardless of their accent; that is, "accuracy trumps accent" (Corriveau, Kinzler, & Harris, 2013). Together, these findings indicate that children tend to imitate those who give evidence of caring about them and who provide reliable, accurate information.

Children are also selective about what actions of others they imitate and when. They tend to copy intentional actions of others, but not their mistakes or their failed attempts. If, for example, a child sees an adult attempt to pull a cap off a pen, but not succeed, then the child is likely to pull the cap off, imitating the adult's intention rather than the adult's effort (Meltzoff, 1995). Imitative copying does not require a pedagogical context, and it does not require the model to use normative language (e.g., Schmidt, Rakoczy, & Tomasello, 2010). Children who are uncertain about how to solve a problem, who have failed in previous attempts, or who have been primed with social exclusion tend to imitate models more closely (Over & Carpenter, 2009; Williamson, Meltzoff, & Markman, 2008). When tasks are causally transparent, children imitate less precisely. If an adult turns on a light switch in a strange manner (e.g., with his or her head), the child will imitate this way of turning on the light, if the adult's hands were free to use the switch, but not if the adult's hands were occupied, carrying something. In the latter case children turn on the light,

but they use their hands (Gergely, Bekkering, & Király, 2002). Horowitz (2003) has argued that the meaning of imitation is often vague. She found that imitation was partial and selective, even when there was an explicit intention to imitate. One important reason is that it can be difficult to know what will be counted as relevant by the experimenter. This ambiguity of what constitutes imitation has emerged most dramatically in comparisons of humans with other species.

Both children and chimpanzees imitate actions relatively exactly if they cannot see how a puzzle is solved, but if the demonstrator includes several movements that are not essential to achieving the solution, chimps tend to drop the unnecessary actions, while many children do not (e.g., Lyons, Young, & Keil, 2007). Some view children's more precise copying as excessive and lacking intelligence (Whiten, McGuigan, Marshall-Pescini, & Hopper, 2009). Others (e.g., Nielsen & Tomaselli, 2010) have argued that the fidelity of imitation in children reflects the trust that is distinctive of humans, and that is far from being maladaptive. They believe that children copy faithfully because they come to appreciate that physical causality can be complex and opaque, requiring guidance from others to understand, and also because it allows them to identify with members of their culture. Recent work (Nielsen, Mushin, Tomaselli, & Whiten, 2014) suggests that precise imitation increases the speed and success with which children can flexibly adapt to new learning situations. Finally, Nielsen and Tomaselli propose that high-fidelity imitation may be one way in which humans learn to engage in actions that go against their individual wishes or preferences. Haun, Rekers, and Tomasello (2014) provide an illustration of this possibility: They explored whether children (2 year olds), chimpanzees, and orangutans would switch from an individually acquired way of solving a puzzle to gain a reward to a different way that was demonstrated by conspecific peer demonstrators. Children imitated the new way of solving the puzzle about half the time; the other two species did not. As noted earlier, switching strategies may be a peculiarly human tendency.

The great puzzle facing imitation researchers, according to Over and Carpenter (2012), one they claim no existing theory can accommodate adequately, is how imitation is both faithful and selective. The existing evidence is deeply inconsistent with the view that imitation is some hard-wired tendency to copy what is observed, but it is also inconsistent with views suggesting that imitation is only directed toward making learning more efficient and functional. Over and Carpenter's critique is constructive, especially in highlighting how imitation is a way of relating socially to others, as well as a way of learning skills. However, the challenges facing imitation researchers are larger still. Children do not imitate everything they observe a model do, even in circumstances where they might be expected to (e.g., Buttelmann, Zmyj, Daum, & Carpenter, 2013). For example, 14-month-old children observe someone who speaks in a familiar way or a strange way turn on a light in an odd manner. While the researchers were interested in whether the familiar or stranger model would be imitated more often, the majority of children imitated neither model, but turned on the light in their own way. Children appear to be seeking an understanding of the world that is larger than simply detecting physical causality and/or adhering to social norms (Hodges, 2014).

Reddy (2008) outlines a larger context for understanding the function of imitation, suggesting that imitating and being imitated is a primitive dialogue between an adult (often a parent) and the child. As a dialogue, imitation is a two-way street, not simply a conduit for passing on expertise. Infants attempt to provoke caretakers as well as imitating them (Nagy & Molnar, 2004). What seems most important in imitation, according to Reddy, is *engagement*: It is essential that the child and the adult see the other as caring what the other does, and as being open to what the other has to offer. It is this promise of learning *together* that appears to generate the provoking, copying, and sharing seen in young children.

## Mimicry

Mimicry has been defined as "the tendency to imitate facially, vocally or posturally people with whom we are interacting" (Bourgeois & Hess, 2008, p. 343). It is a variant of conformity, but it focuses on nonverbal actions that are often assumed to be irrelevant to ongoing intentional actions (e.g., how often two people touch their hair while talking to each other). However, there are many cases in which mimicry is clearly relevant to the content of the interaction (e.g., mimicking one another's emotions). Mimicry is also a form of imitation, but the content of what is copied is the bodily movements of the other without respect to an instrumental task (e.g., solving a puzzle box, choosing a toy). Thus, a child could smile after making a choice between two toys, just as the model did when she made her

choice, but the child could make a different choice than the model. In this case, the child has mimicked but not imitated. Few, if any, studies have considered this level of complexity.

Mimicry is often described as an automatic, nonconscious form of imitation (Chartrand & Lakin, 2013) that increases rapport and liking, so that it "promotes smooth and harmonious social interactions and strengthens social relationships" (Leighton, Bird, Orsini, & Heyes, 2010, p. 905), facilitating social learning, group cohesion, and the development of culture (Chartrand & van Baaren, 2009). Recent studies, however, have painted a far more complex picture. Mimicry is not irresistible and unintentional; rather, it is context dependent and selective, for those mimicking, those being mimicked, and others observing the interaction. While mimicry often increases liking and improves rapport (e.g., Chartrand & van Baaren, 2009), there are a variety of situations in which this is not the case. Mimicry is absent or seriously attenuated if the situation is a competitive one (Weyers, Muhlberger, Kund, Hess, & Pauli, 2009), if the other person is disliked (Stel, van Dijk, & Olivier, 2009), or if the other person is an outgroup member (Yabar, Johnston, Miles, & Peace, 2006). Particularly interesting are studies indicating that the participants take into account the social and moral implications of relationships in modulating or eliminating tendencies to mimic. There is a tendency to mimic attractive others, but participants in romantic relationships mimic an attractive stranger less than those who are not in relationships, and those in committed relationships mimic even less (Karremans & Verwijmeren, 2008). Given that mimicry might have encouraged unfaithfulness, participants demurred. Hofman et al. (2012) found that the smiles of a person who was perceived as acting unfairly were not mimicked, while anger expressions were heightened. Participants' facial activity appears to be tuned more to the moral direction of the activity and the relationship than to a simple matching of others' expressions. Similarly, pride seems to attenuate mimicry (Dickens & DeSteno, 2014), while gratitude facilitates it (Jia, Lee, & Tong, 2015). More generally, people tend to imitate people they believe are acting appropriately. Mimicking others who are unfriendly, egocentric, or incompetent does not yield positive social benefits (e.g., Kavanagh, Suhler, Churchland, & Winkielman, 2011; Stel, Rispens, Leliveld, & Lokhorst, 2011). Other negative consequences of indiscriminate mimicry are reduced creative thinking (Ashton-James & Chartrand, 2009) and a reduction in one's ability to evaluate critically the claims of others (Maringer, Krumhuber, Fischer, & Niedenthal, 2011).

Overall, the story emerging from mimicry studies is similar to the pattern emerging elsewhere. Conforming to others is intentional (although often unconscious), selective, and situationally sensitive. Mimicry is natural, but not generally irresistible, and marks the human tendency to work together with others. Imitation of another's actions tends to lead to a perception of increased social solidarity. This is often quite positive in its effects on the relationship of the partners involved and on their social coordination, but what its effects are depends very much on the content of the joint task in which they are engaged and the concerns and proclivities that partners bring to the interaction.

### Synchrony

Mimicry and synchrony are often treated as synonymous, but they are usefully distinguished for two reasons. First, mimicry is *copying* of bodily actions; synchrony is closer to being *temporal matching* (i.e., simultaneous). Second, the tighter focus on timing in synchrony has led researchers to place it in the context of studies of physical coordination (e.g., Marsh, Richardson, & Schmidt, 2009) as well as social influence. While mimicry is compared to animals adapting to their surroundings, synchrony is compared to physical and biological systems that are self-organizing. Thus, mimicry studies tend to describe the action of one person conforming his or her movements to another's, while synchrony studies focus on partners working together to conform to the demands of a common task. Since synchrony refers to correlated patterns occurring across participants, it demands methodologies that treat the dyad (or group) as the unit of measurement (Paxton & Dale, 2013b). Despite these differences, there are important similarities in the stories that have emerged from research.

One theme, often noted, is that synchrony functions to create a sense of purpose that contributes to coordinated, goal-directed activities (Valdesolo & DeSteno, 2011), leading to increased positive affect, empathy, and identification with the group and its purposes (Tschacher, Rees, & Ramseyer, 2014). Some have suggested that synchrony contributes to more prosocial behavior and to greater self-esteem (Lumsden, Miles, & Macrae, 2014; Marsh et al., 2009). This relation between synchrony and concern for others may be reciprocal: Lumsden, Miles, Richardson, Smith, and Macrae (2012) found that participants with prosocial motivation synchronized with their partners more than those with proself motivation.

A second theme is that synchrony and asynchrony occur, depending on the complexities of the varying contexts and tasks within which social interactions occur. For example, participants who were made to wait for someone who was late failed to coordinate their actions (e.g., in-phase walking patterns) with their tardy partner compared to those arriving on time (Miles, Griffiths, Richardson, & Macrae, 2010). Similarly, Paxton and Dale (2013a) found that participants who engaged in a conversation about a topic about which they strongly disagreed did not converge in the timing of their bodily movements. In short, the nature of the social interaction and its evaluative direction affects whether movements tend to converge or not.

A third theme, perhaps the most interesting, is a theoretical paradox: Synchrony seems to be a lawful, self-organizing process that is common across many physical, biological, and social phenomena, yet it varies with social factors that seem to be matters of evaluation and choice (Lumsden et al., 2014). Synchrony is observed not only in social interactions (e.g., matching stride rates while walking together) but also in other species (e.g., fireflies flashing in unison) and in physical and biological activities (e.g., metronomes finding a common rhythm; cardiac pacemaker cells). There are strong physical attractors that pull components into synchronicities, and yet those dynamics are relatively easily modulated by social, personal, and situational factors. The patterns of variability and stability seem to be ones that make sense evaluatively. For example, there is reduced symmetry with someone who acts in a careless way, and there is increased symmetry when prosocial dispositions or situational demands are operative. If one considers the consequences of synchronizing with another, it tends to yield relatively more cooperation and compassion in appropriate circumstances (Valdesolo Ouyang, & DeSteno, 2010; Valdesolo & DeSteno, 2011; Wiltermuth & Heath, 2009). On the other hand, synchronizing with another who acts in unkind or aggressive ways can lead to greater conformity to similar actions (Wiltermuth, 2012). Thus, synchronicity appears to be nested in larger activities that can be judged as either good or bad, so Lumsden et al.'s (2012, p. 750) warning is well-taken: "casting synchrony solely as an attribute of pro-sociality appears a questionable theoretical proposition." The act of synchronizing itself seems to encourage the coherence of the actors and their situations, such that larger scale social-moral activities, for good or ill, are intensified in their forcefulness.

Finally, a particular form of synchrony that has drawn special attention is *conversational alignment*. This is the tendency of people to converge spontaneously to each other on a variety of physical and linguistic parameters, such as rate, intensity, pitch, dialect, word choice, and sentence structure (e.g., Pickering & Garrod, 2004; Tollefsen, Dale, & Paxton, 2013). The range of alignment is impressive: Overall body sway is synchronized when two people are discussing a picture they are looking at together (Shockley, Santana, & Fowler, 2003), and pragmatic choices (e.g., using irony) are often aligned as well (Roche, Dale, & Caucci, 2012). Niederhoffer and Pennebaker (2002) found style matching (e.g., word classes), but the matching did not relate to participants' or judges' ratings of the exchange, which were focused on content. They proposed their findings were best explained by coordination and engagement, not by nonverbal rapport, since there is some alignment in angry arguments as well as in pleasant chitchats. "People can converge on some communicative features to meet social needs, but diverge on others" (Niederhoffer & Pennebaker, 2002, p. 358). Although some researchers (e.g., Pickering & Garrod, 2004) believe alignment is general, and spreads across all dimensions, others disagree. As Fusaroli et al. (2012) point out, if participants in a conversation were being automatically primed to align on all aspects of linguistic functioning, no real conversation would happen. What is required is selective, complementary coordination of various parameters, not complete alignment. They found evidence for selective alignment; in fact, indiscriminate alignment actually had a deleterious effect on task effectiveness.

Although "the vast majority of existing approaches to the psychology of language focus exclusively on the workings of individual minds and brains" (Fusaroli, Rączaszek–Leonardi, & Tylén, 2014, p. 148), "humans are 'designed' for dialogue rather than monologue" (Garrod & Pickering, 2004, p. 8). Conversational activity is fundamentally dialogical. It has less to do with some sort of automatic structural priming, and more to do with an emerging self-organization in which the various parties to the conversation are integrated into a larger scale social unit, with abilities and sensitivities not available to the parties as separate individuals. Thus, the pattern that emerges is familiar: There is divergence as well as convergence, and what gives shape to those dynamics are the physical, social, and moral challenges facing conversation partners.

## Conclusion

Humans have a natural affinity for conformity. Using others to guide or modify one's own actions is a crucial feature of human existence, as is coordinating the direction and pace of one's movements to align with others with whom one is interacting. Without this conformity and coordination, human culture and its many forms of learning and sharing would not be possible. Equally, however, people have a tendency to diverge: Often, they dissent from majorities, imitate models selectively, and trust their own learning over that of others. Without the tension of disagreement, differentiation, and resistance, the dynamics of relationships, groups, and cultures would cease. The complementary dynamics of divergence and convergence are essential.

The array of evidence and perspectives presented in this chapter emerging from social, developmental, and cognitive psychology, as well as anthropology, has revealed a remarkable set of convergences that has taken us far past the simple stereotypes that often dominate our thinking about these topics. First, what is often treated as a single choice point or categorical decision—toward convergence, toward divergence—is better described as dynamical, and multilayered. Within and across tasks, there is ongoing variability and tension. Second, children and adults demonstrate both selectivity and fidelity in following others' actions. Both the sophistication of selectivity and the specificity of fidelity have been surprising to researchers. Third, while people routinely use others' experience and instruction to guide their own social learning, they exercise considerable epistemic and ethical vigilance in ways that defy conventional accounts of people's willingness to conform, obey, and follow. The use of social information is almost never blind, automatic, or complete. In fact, there are clear cases where people trust themselves too much, and others far too little. Fourth, there has often been a tendency to valorize convergence or divergence within a domain in simplistic ways (e.g., mimicry is good; following majorities is bad). Conformity is neither good nor bad by itself; in fact, conformity does not exist by itself. The same is true for divergence. Fifth, the ways in which humans coordinate their interactions and learn from and with each other are remarkable in many ways, but one of the most puzzling and profound is the way they often demonstrate care, trust, and concern for truth and other values. Finally, despite tendencies to complacency generated by decades of reflection on famous studies, the issues of conformity, dissent, imitation, trust, complementary alignment, and their allies are more vital than ever. They deserve fresh attention, both for what has already been discovered, but even more because they are fundamental issues at the heart of the social sciences.

## Acknowledgments

Thanks to Katharine Adamyk, Kelly Burton, Jonathan Gerber, Alexander Haslam, Kerry Marsh, Benjamin Meagher, Zsolt Palatinus, Vasudevi Reddy, Stephen Reicher, and Colwyn Trevarthen for helpful suggestions on earlier versions of this chapter. Thanks especially to the editors for their encouragement and suggestions.

## References

Abrams, D., Wetherell, M., Cochrane, S., Hogg, M. A, & Turner, J. C. (1990). Knowing what to think by knowing who you are: Self-categorization and the nature of norm formation, conformity, and group polarization. *British Journal of Social Psychology*, *29*, 97–119.

Allen, V. L. (1965). Situational factors in conformity. In L. Berkowitz (Ed.), *Advances in experimental social psychology* (Vol. *2*, pp. 133–175). New York: Academic Press.

Allen, V. L. (1975). Social support for nonconformity. In L. Berkowitz (Ed.), *Advances in experimental social psychology* (Vol. *8*, pp. 1–43). New York: Academic Press.

Asch, S. E. (1951). Effects of group pressure upon the modification and distortion of judgments. In H. Guetzkow (Ed.), *Groups, leadership, and men* (pp. 177–190). Pittsburgh, PA: Carnegie Press.

Asch, S. E. (1952). *Social psychology*. Englewood Cliffs, NJ: Prentice-Hall.

Asch, S. E. (1956). Studies of independence and conformity: I. A minority of one against a unanimous majority. *Psychological Monographs*, *70*(9), (Whole No. 416).

Asch, S. E. (1990). Comments on D. T. Campbell's chapter. In I. Rock (Ed.), *The legacy of Solomon Asch: Essays in cognition and social psychology* (pp. 53–55). Hillsdale, NJ: Erlbaum.

Ashton-James, C. E., & Chartrand, T. L. (2009). Social cues for creativity: The impact of behavioral mimicry on convergent and divergent thinking. *Journal of Experimental Social Psychology*, *45*, 1036–1040.

Baron, S. R., Vandello, A. J., & Brunsman, B. (1996). The forgotten variable in conformity research: Impact of task importance on social influence. *Journal of Personality and Social Psychology*, *71*, 915–927.

Bennis, W. M., Medin, D. L, & Bartels, D. M. (2010). Perspectives on the ecology of decision modes: Reply to comments. *Perspectives on Psychological Science*, *5*, 213–215.

Berger, J., & Heath, C. (2008). Who drives divergence? Identity signaling, outgroup similarity, and the abandonment of cultural tastes. *Journal of Personality and Social Psychology*, *95*, 593–607.

Bettinger, R. L., & Eerkens, J. (1999). Point typologies, cultural transmission, and the spread of bow-and-arrow technology in the prehistoric Great Basin. *American Antiquities*, *64*, 231–242.

Bond, R. (2005). Group size and conformity. *Group Processes and Intergroup Relations*, *8*, 331–354.

Bond, R., & Smith, P. B. (1996). Culture and conformity: A meta-analysis of studies using Asch's (1952b, 1956) line judgment task. *Psychological Bulletin*, *119*, 111–137.

Bourgeois, P., & Hess, U. (2008). The impact of social context on mimicry. *Biological Psychology*, *77*, 343–352.

Boyd, R., Richerson, P. J., & Henrich, J. (2011). The cultural niche: Why social learning is essential for human adaptation. *Proceedings of the National Academy of Sciences USA*, *108*, 10918–10925.

Brewer, M. B., & Roccas, S. (2001). Individual values, social identity, and optimal distinctiveness. In C. Sedikides & M. Brewer (Eds.), *Individual self, relational self, collective self* (pp. 219–237). London: Taylor & Francis.

Brosseau-Liard, P. E., & Birch, S. A. (2011). Epistemic states and traits: Preschoolers appreciate the differential informativeness of situation-specific and person-specific cues to knowledge. *Child Development*, *82*, 1788–1796.

Buttelmann, D., Zmyj, N., Daum, M., & Carpenter, M. (2013). Selective imitation of in-group over out-group memebers in 14-month old infants. *Child Development*, *84*, 422–428.

Campbell, D. T. (1990). Asch's moral epistemology for socially shared knowledge. In I. Rock (Ed.), *The legacy of Solomon Asch: Essays in cognition and social psychology* (pp. 39–52). Hillsdale, NJ: Erlbaum.

Campbell, J. D., & Fairey, P. J. (1989). Informational and normative routes to conformity: The effect of faction size as a function of the norm extremity and attention to stimulus. *Journal of Personality and Social Psychology*, *57*, 457–468.

Ceraso, J., Gruber, H., & Rock, I. (1990). On Solomon Asch. In I. Rock (Ed.), *The legacy of Solomon Asch: Essays in cognition and social psychology* (pp. 3–19). Hillsdale, NJ: Erlbaum.

Chartrand, T. L., & Lakin, J. L. (2013). The antecedents and consequences of human behavioral mimicry. *Annual Review of Psychology*, *64*, 285–308.

Chartrand, T. L., & van Baaren, R. B. (2009). Human mimicry. In M. P. Zanna (Ed.), *Advances in experimental social psychology* (Vol. *1*, pp. 219–274). San Diego: Academic Press.

Cialdini, R. B., & Goldstein, N. J. (2004). Social influence: Compliance and conformity. *Annual Review of Psychology*, *55*, 591–621.

Cialdini, R., & Trost, M. (1998). Social influence: Social norms, conformity, and compliance. In D. Gilbert, S. Fiske, & G. Lindzey (Eds.), *The handbook of social psychology* (4th ed., Vol. *2*, pp. 151–192). New York: McGraw-Hill.

Claidière, N., & Whiten, A. (2012). Integrating the study of conformity and culture in human and nonhuman animals. *Psychological Bulletin*, *138*, 126–145.

Corriveau, K. H., Fusaro, M., & Harris, P. L. (2009). Going with the flow: Preschoolers prefer nondissenters as informants. *Psychological Science*, *20*, 372–377.

Corriveau, K. H., & Harris, P. L. (2010). Preschoolers (sometimes) defer to the majority in making simple perceptual judgments. *Developmental Psychology*, *46*, 437–445.

Corriveau, K. H., Kinzler, K. D., & Harris, P. L. (2013). Accuracy trumps accent in children's endorsement of object labels. *Developmental Psychology*, *49*, 470–479.

Corriveau, K. H., Meints, K., & Harris, P. L. (2009). Early tracking of informant accuracy and inaccuracy. *British Journal of Developmental Psychology*, *27*, 331–342.

Crano, W. D., & Seyranian, V. (2009). How minorities prevail: The context/comparison-leniency contract model. *Journal of Social Issues, 65*, 335–363.

David, B., & Turner, J. C. (2001). Majority and minority influence: A single process self categorization analysis. In C. K. W. De Dreu & N. K. De Vries (Eds.), *Group consensus and minority influence: Implications for innovation* (pp. 91–121). Malden, MA: Blackwell.

Deutsch, M., & Gerard, H. B. (1955). A study of normative and informational social influences upon individual judgment. *Journal of Abnormal and Social Psychology, 51*, 629–636.

Dickens, L., & DeSteno, D. (2014). Pride attenuates nonconscious mimicry. *Emotion, 14*, 7–11.

Efferson, C., Lalive, R., Richerson, P. J., McElreath, R., & Lubell, M. (2008). Conformists and mavericks: the empirics of frequency-dependent cultural transmission. *Evolution of Human Behavior, 29*, 56–64.

Efferson, C., Richerson, P. J., McElreath, R., & Lubell, M., Edsten, E., Waring, T. M., Paciotti, B., & Baum, W. (2007). Learning, productivity, and noise: an experimental study of cultural transmission on the Bolivian Altiplano. *Evolution and Human Behavior, 28*, 11–17.

Einav, S., & Robinson, E. J. (2011). When being right is not enough: Four-year-olds distinguish knowledgeable informants from merely accurate informants. *Psychological Science, 20*, 1–4.

Enquist, M., Eriksson, K., & Ghirlanda, S. (2007). Critical social learning: A solution to Roger's paradox of nonadaptive culture. *American Anthropologist, 109*, 727–734.

Eriksson, K., & Coultas, J. C. (2009). Are people really conformist-biased? An empirical test and a new mathematical model. *Journal of Evolutionary Psychology, 7*, 5–21.

Eriksson, K., Enquist, M., & Ghirlanda, S. (2007). Critical points in current theory of conformist social learning. *Journal of Evolutionary Psychology, 5*, 67–87.

Eriksson, K., & Strimling, P. (2009). Biases for acquiring information individually rather than socially. *Journal of Evolutionary Psychology, 7*, 309–329.

Falomir-Pichastor, J. M., Gabarrot, F., & Mugny, G. (2009). Group motives in threatening contexts: When a loyalty conflict paradoxically reduces the influence of an anti-discrimination ingroup norm. *European Journal of Social Psychology, 39*, 196–206.

Fischer, R., & Schwartz, S. (2011). Whence differences in value priorities? Individual, cultural, or artifactual sources? *Journal of Cross-Cultural Psychology, 42*, 1127–1144.

Francis, W. N. (1983). *Dialectology.* London: Longmans.

Friend, R., Rafferty, Y., & Bramel, D. (1990). A puzzling misinterpretation of the Asch "conformity" study. *European Journal of Social Psychology, 20*, 29–44.

Fu, J. H., Lee, S., Morris, M. W., Chao, M., Chiu, C., & Hong, Y. (2007). Epistemic motives and cultural conformity: Need for closure, culture, and context as determinants of conflict judgments. *Journal of Personality and Social Psychology, 92*, 191–207.

Fusaroli, R., Bahrami, B., Olsen, K., Roepstorff, A., Rees, G., Frith, C., & Tylén, K. (2012). Coming to terms: Quantifying the benefits of linguistic coordination. *Psychological Science, 23*, 931–939.

Fusaroli, R., Rączaszek–Leonardi, J., & Tylén, K. (2014). Dialog as interpersonal synergy. *New Ideas in Psychology, 32*, 147–157.

Garrod, S., & Pickering, M. J. (2004). Why is conversation so easy? *Trends in Cognitive Science, 8*, 8–11.

Gergely, G., Bekkering, H., & Király, I. (2002). Rational imitation in preverbal infants. *Nature, 415*, 755.

Gilovich, T., Keltner, D., & Nisbett, R. E. (2010). *Social psychology* (2nd ed.). New York: Norton.

Griskevicius, V., Goldstein, N. J., Mortensen, C. R., Cialdini, R. B., & Kenrick, D. T. (2006). Going along versus going alone: When fundamental motives facilitate strategic (non)conformity. *Journal of Personality and Social Psychology, 91*, 281–294.

Haney, C., Banks, C., & Zimbardo, P. (1973). Interpersonal dynamics in a simulated prison. *International Journal of Criminology and Penology, 1*, 67–97.

Hashimoto, H., Li, Y., & Yamagishi, T. (2011). Beliefs and preferences in cultural agents and cultural game players. *Asian Journal of Social Psychology, 14*, 140–147.

Haslam, S. A., & Reicher, S. D. (2012). When prisoners take over the prison: A social psychology of resistance. *Personality and Social Psychology Review, 16*, 154–179.

Haun, D. B. M., Rekers, Y., & Tomasello, M. (2014). Children conform to the behavior of peers; other great apes stick with what they know. *Psychological Science, 25*, 2160–2167.

Haun, D. B. M., & Tomasello, M. (2011). Conformity to peer pressure in preschool children. *Child Development, 82*, 1759–1767.

Heine, S. J. (2007). *Cultural psychology.* New York: Norton.

Henrich, J., & Boyd, R. (1998). The evolution of conformist tranmission and the emergence of between-group difference. *Evolution and Human Behavior, 19*, 215–241.

Herzog, S. M., & Hertwig, R. (2009). The wisdom of many in one mind: Improving individual judgments with dialectical bootstrapping. *Psychological Science, 20*, 231–237.

Hodges, B. H. (2004). Asch and the balance of values. *Behavioral and Brain Sciences, 27*, 343–344.

Hodges, B. H. (2014). Rethinking conformity and imitation: Divergence, convergence, and social understanding. *Frontiers in Psychology: Cognitive Science, 5*, 726.

Hodges, B. H., & Geyer, A. L. (2006). A nonconformist account of the Asch experiments: Values, pragmatics, and moral dilemmas. *Personality and Social Psychology Review, 10*, 2–19.

Hodges, B. H., Meagher, B. R., Norton, D. J., McBain, R., & Sroubek, A. (2014). Speaking from ignorance: Not agreeing with others we believe are correct. *Journal of Personality and Social Psychology, 106*, 218–234.

Hofman, D., Bos, P. A., Schutter, J. L. G., & van Honk, J. (2012). Fairness modulates non-conscious facial mimicry in women. *Proceedings of the Royal Society B, 279*, 3535–3539.

Horowitz, A. (2003). Do humans ape? Or do apes human? Imitation and intention in humans (homo sapiens) and other animals. *Journal of Comparative Psychology, 117*, 325–336.

Hornsey, M. J., & Jetten, J. (2004). The individual within the group: Balancing the need to belong with the need to be different. *Personality and Social Psychology Review, 8*, 248–264.

Hornsey, M. J., Majkut, L., Terry, D. J., & McKimmie, B. M. (2003). On being loud and proud: Non-conformity and counter-conformity to group norms. *British Journal of Social Psychology, 42*, 319–335.

Hruschka, D., Efferson, C., Jiang, T., Falletta-Cowden, A., Sigurdsson, S., McNamara, R., ... Henrich, J. (2014). Impartial institutions, pathogen stress and the expanding social network. *Human Nature, 25*, 567–579.

Imhoff, R., & Erb, H-P. (2009). What motivates nonconformity? Uniqueness seeking blocks majority influence. *Personality and Social Psychology Bulletin, 35*, 309–320.

Jaeger, A., Lauris, P., Selmeczy, D., & Dobbins, I. G. (2012). The costs and benefits of memory conformity. *Memory and Cognition, 40*, 101–112.

Janis, I. L. (1972). *Victims of groupthink: A psychological study of foreign-policy decisions and fiascos.* Boston, MA: Houghton-Mifflin.

Jia, L., Lee, L. N., & Tong, E. M. W. (2015). Gratitude facilitates behavioral mimicry. *Emotion, 15*, 134–138.

Karremans, J. C., & Verwijmeren, T. (2008). Mimicking attractive opposite-sex others: the role of romantic relationship status. *Personality and Social Psychology Bulletin, 34*, 939–950.

Kavanagh, L. C., Suhler, C. L., Churchland, P. S., & Winkielman, P. (2011). When it's an error to mirror: The surprising reputational costs of mimicry. *Psychological Science, 22*(10), 1274–1276.

Kinzler, K. D., Corriveau, K. H., & Harris, P. L. (2011). Children's selective trust in native-accented speakers. *Developmental Science, 14*, 106–111.

Krueger, J. I., & Massey, A. L. (2009). A rational reconstruction of misbehavior. *Social Cognition, 27*, 786–812.

Larrick, R. P., Mannes, A. E., & Soll, J. B. (2012). The social psychology of the wisdom of crowds. In J. I. Krueger (Ed.), *Frontiers of social psychology: Social psychology and decision making* (pp. 227–242). Philadelphia: Psychology Press.

Latané, B. (1996). Dynamic social impact: The creation of culture by communication. *Journal of Communication, 46*, 13–25.

Latané, B., & Wolf, S. (1981). The social impact of majorities and minorities. *Psychological Review, 88*, 438–453.

Leighton, J., Bird, G., Orsini, C., & Heyes, C. (2010). Social attitudes modulate automatic imitation. *Journal of Experimental Social Psychology, 46*, 905–910.

Lorenz, J., Rauhut, H., Schweitzer, F., & Helbing, D. (2011). How social influence can undermine the wisdom of crowd effect. *Proceedings of the National Academy of Science USA, 108*, 9020–9025.

Lumsden, J., Miles, L. K., & Macrae, C. N. (2014). Sync or sink? Interpersonal synchrony impacts self-esteem. *Frontiers in Psychology, 5*, 1064.

Lumsden, J., Miles, L. K., Richardson, M. J., Smith, C. A., & Macrae, C. N. (2012). Who syncs? Social motives and interpersonal coordination. *Journal of Experimental Social Psychology, 48*, 746–751.

Lyons, D. E., Young, A. G., & Keil, F. C. (2007). The hidden structure of overimitation. *Proceedings of the National Academy of Science USA, 104*, 19751–19756.

Maringer, M., Krumhuber, E. G., Fischer, A. H., & Niedenthal, P. M. (2011). Beyond smile dynamics: Mimicry and beliefs in judgments of smiles. *Emotion, 11*, 181–187.

Marsh, K. L., Richardson, M. J., & Schmidt, R. C. (2009). Social connection through joint action and interpersonal coordination. *Topics in Cognitive Science, 1*, 320–339.

Matsuda, N. (1985). Strong, quasi-, and weak conformity among Japanese in the modified Asch procedure. *Journal of Cross-Cultural Psychology, 16*, 83–97.

McCauley, C., & Rozin, P. (2003). Solomon Asch: Scientist and humanist. In G. A. Kimble & M. Wertheimer (Eds.), *Portraits of pioneers in psychology* (Vol. 5, pp. 249–261). Mahwah, NJ: Erlbaum.

McElreath, R., Lubell, M., Richerson, P. J., Waring, T. M., Baum, W., Edsten, E., ... Pacioti, B. (2005). Applying evolutionary models to the laboratory study of social learning. *Evolution and Human Behavior, 26*, 483–508.

McKelvey, W., & Kerr, N. H. (1988). Differences in conformity among friends and strangers. *Psychological Reports, 62*, 759–762.

Meltzoff, A. N. (1995). Understanding the intentions of others: Reenactment of intended acts by 18-month-old children. *Developmental Psychology, 31*, 838–850.

Mesoudi, A. (2009). How cultural evolutionary theory can inform social psychology and vice versa. *Psychological Review, 116*, 929–952.

Mesoudi, A. (2011). An experimental comparison of human social learning strategies: Payoff-biased social learning is adaptive but underused. *Evolution and Human Behavior, 32*, 334–342.

Mesoudi, A., & O'Brien, M. J. (2008). The cultural transmission of Great Basin projectile point technology I: an experimental manipulation. *American Antiquities, 21*, 350–363.

Mesoudi, A., & Whiten, A. (2008). The multiple roles of cultural transmission experiments in understanding human cultural evolution. *Philosophical Transactions of the Royal Society B, 363*, 3489–3501.

Miles, L. K., Griffiths, J. L., Richardson, M. J., & Macrae, C. N. (2010). Too late to coordinate: Contextual influences on behavioral synchrony. *European Journal of Social Psychology, 40*, 52–60.

Milgram, S. (1963). Behavioral study of obedience. *Journal of Abnormal and Social Psychology, 67*, 371–378.

Mok, A., & Morris, M. W. (2009). Cultural chameleons and iconoclasts: Assimilation and reactance to cultural cues in biculturals' expressed personalities as a function of identity conflict. *Journal of Experimental Social Psychology, 45*, 884–889.

Moscovici, S. (1976). *Social influence and social change.* London: Academic Press.

Murray, D. R., Trudeau, R., & Schaller, M. (2011). On the origins of cultural differences in conformity: Four tests of the pathogen prevalence hypothesis. *Personality and Social Psychology Bulletin, 37*, 318–329.

Nagy, E. & Molnar, P. (2004). Homo imitans or homo provocans? Human imprinting model of neonatal imitation. *Infant Behavior and Development, 27*, 54–63.

Nail, P. R., MacDonald, G., & Levy, D. A. (2000). Proposal of a four-dimensional model of social response. *Psychological Bulletin, 126*, 454–470.

Nemeth, C. (1985). Compromising public influence for private change. In S. Moscovici, G. Mugny, & E. Van Avermaet (Eds.), *Perspectives on minority influence* (pp. 75–90). Cambridge, UK: Cambridge University Press.

Nielsen, M. (2006). Copying actions and copying outcomes: Social learning through the second year. *Developmental Psychology, 42*, 555–565.

Nielsen, M., Mushin, I., Tomaselli, K., & Whiten, A. (2014). Where culture takes hold: "Overimitation" and its flexible deployment in Western, Aboriginal, and Bushmen children. *Child Development, 85*, 2169–2184.

Nielsen, M., & Tomaselli, K. (2010). Overimitation in Kalahari bushman children and the origins of human cultural cognition. *Psychological Science, 21*, 729–736.

Niederhoffer, K. G., & Pennebaker, J. W. (2002). Linguistic style matching in social interaction. *Journal of Language and Social Psychology, 21*, 337–360.

Over, H., & Carpenter, M. (2009). Priming third-party ostracism increases affiliative imitation in children. *Developmental Science, 12*, F1–F8.

Over, H., & Carpenter, M. (2012). Putting the social into social learning: Explaining both selectivity and fidelity in children's copying behavior. *Journal of Comparative Psychology, 126*, 182–192.

Over, H., Carpenter, M., Spears, R., & Gattis, M. (2013). Children selectively trust individuals who have imitated them. *Social Development, 22*, 215–224.

Packer, D. J. (2009). Avoiding groupthink: Whereas weakly identified members remain silent, strongly identified member dissent about collective problems. *Psychological Science, 20*, 546–548.

Packer, D. J., & Chasteen, A. L. (2010). Loyal deviance: Testing the normative conflict model of dissent in social groups. *Personality and Social Psychology Bulletin, 36*, 5–18.

Packer, D. J., Fujita, K., & Chasteen, A. L. (2014). The motivational dynamics of dissent decisions: A goal-conflict model. *Social Psychological and Personality Science, 5*, 27–34.

Pasquini, E. S., Corriveau, K. H., Koenig, M., & Harris, P. L. (2007). Preschoolers monitor the relative accuracy of informants. *Developmental Psychology, 43*, 1216–1226.

Paxton, A., & Dale, R. (2013a). Argument disrupts interpersonal synchrony. *Quarterly Journal of Experimental Psychology, 66*, 2092–2102.

Paxton, A., & Dale, R. (2013b). Frame differencing methods for measuring bodily synchrony in conversation. *Behavioral Research, 45*, 329–343.

Pickering, M. J., & Garrod, S. (2004). Toward a mechanistic psychology of dialogue. *Behavioral and Brain Sciences, 27*, 169–190.

Quinn, A., & Schlenker, B. R. (2002). Can accountability produce independence? Goals as determinants of the impact of accountability and conformity. *Personality and Social Psychology Bulletin, 28*, 472–483.

Rakoczy, H., Hamann, K., Warneken, F., & Tomasello, M. (2010). Bigger knows better–young children selectively learn rule games from adults rather than from peers. *British Journal of Developmental Psychology, 28*, 785–798.

Reddy, V. (2008). *How infants know minds*. Cambridge, MA. Harvard University Press.

Reicher, S. D., Haslam, S. A., & Smith, J. R. (2012). Working toward the experimenter: Reconceptualizing obedience within the Milgram paradigm as identification-based followership. *Perspectives on Psychological Science, 7*, 315–324.

Richerson, P. J., & Boyd, R. (2005). *Not by genes alone: How culture transformed human evolution*. Chicago, IL: University of Chicago Press.

Roche, J. M., Dale, R., & Caucci, G. M. (2012). Double up on double meanings: Pragmatic alignment. *Language and Cognitive Processes, 27*, 1–24.

Ross, L., Bierbrauer, G., & Hoffman, S. (1976). The role of attribution processes in conformity and dissent: Revisiting the Asch situation. *American Psychologist, 31*, 148–157.

Schmidt, M., Rakoczy, H., & Tomasello, M. (2010). Young children attribute normativity to novel actions without pedagogy or normative language. *Developmental Science, 14*, 530–539.

Schnuerch, R., & Gibbons, H. (2014). A review of neurocognitive mechanisms of social conformity. *Social Psychology, 45*, 466–478.

Schulz-Hardt, S., Brodbeck, F. C., Mojzisch, A., Kerschreiter, R., & Frey, D. (2006). Group decision making in hidden profile situations: Dissent as a facilitator for decision quality. *Journal of Personality and Social Psychology, 91*, 1080–1093.

Sherif, M. (1935). A study of some social factors in perception. *Archives of Psychology, 27*(187), 17–22.

Shockley, K., Santana, M. V., & Fowler, C. A. (2003). Mutual interpersonal postural constraints are involved in cooperative conversation. *Journal of Experimental Psychology: Human Perception and Performance, 29*, 326–332.

Sperber, D., Clément, F., Heintz, C., Mascaro, O., Mercier, H., Origgi, G., & Wilson, D. (2010). Epistemic vigilance. *Mind and Language, 25*, 359–393.

Stel, M., Rispens, S., Leliveld, M., & Lokhorst, A. M. (2011). The consequences of mimicry for prosocials and proselfs: Effects of social value orientation on the mimicry-liking link. *European Journal of Social Psychology, 41*, 269–274.

Stel, M., van Dijk, E., & Olivier, E. (2009). You want to know the truth? Then don't mimic! *Psychological Science, 20*, 693–699.

Surowiecki, J. (2004). *The wisdom of crowds: Why the many are smarter than the few and how collective wisdom shapes business, economies, societies and nations*. Boston: Little, Brown.

Takano, Y., & Sogon, S. (2008). Are Japanese more collectivistic than Americans? Examining conformity in in-groups and the reference-group effect. *Journal of Cross-Cultural Psychology, 39*, 237–250.

Tetlock, P. E. (2002). Social functionalist frameworks for judgment and choice: Intuitive politicians, theologians, and prosecutors. *Psychological Review, 109*, 451–471.

Toelch, U., van Delft, M. J., Bruce, M. J., Donders, R., Meeus, M. T. H., & Reader, S. M. (2009). Decreased environmental variability induces a bias for social information. *Evolution of Human Behavior, 30*, 32–40.

Tollefsen, D. P., Dale, R., & Paxton, A. (2013). Alignment, transactive memory, and collective cognitive systems. *Review of Philosophical Psychology, 4*, 49–64.

Tomasello, M. (2008). *Origins of human communication*. Cambridge, MA: MIT Press.

Tschacher, W., Rees, G. M., & Ramseyer, F. (2014). Nonverbal synchrony and affect in dyadic interactions. *Frontiers in Psychology, 5*, 1323.

Valdesolo, P., & DeSteno, D. (2011). Synchrony and the social tuning of compassion. *Emotion, 11*, 262–266.

Valdesolo, P., Ouyang, J., & DeSteno, D. (2010). The rhythm of joint action: Synchrony promotes cooperative ability. *Journal of Experimental Social Psychology, 46*, 693–695.

VanderBorght, M., & Jaswal, V. K. (2009). Who knows best? Preschoolers sometimes prefer child informants over adult informants. *Infant and Child Development, 18*, 61–71.

Weyers, P., Muhlberger, A., Kund, A., Hess, U., & Pauli, P. (2009). Modulation of facial reations to avatar emotional faces by nonconscious competition priming. *Psychophysiology, 46*, 328–335.

White, K., & Argo, J. J. (2011). When imitation doesn't flatter: The role of consumer distinctiveness in responses to mimicry. *Journal of Consumer Research, 38*, 667–680.

Whiten, A., McGuigan, N., Marshall-Pescini, S., & Hopper, L. M. (2009). Emulation, imitation, over-imitation and the scope of culture for child and chimpanzee. *Philosophical Transactions of the Royal Society B, 364*, 2417–2428.

Williams, T. P., & Sogon, S. (1984). Group composition and conforming behavior in Japanese students. *Japanese Psychological Research, 26*, 231–234.

Williamson, R. A., Meltzoff, A. N. & Markman, E. M. (2008). Prior experiences and perceived efficacy influence 3-year-olds' imitation. *Developmental Psychology, 44*, 275–285.

Wiltermuth, S. S. (2012). Synchronous activity boosts compliance with requests to aggress. *Journal of Experimental Social Psychology, 48*, 453–456.

Wiltermuth, S. S., & Heath, C. (2009). Synchrony and cooperation. *Psychological Science, 20*, 1–5.

Yabar, Y., Johnston, L., Miles, L., & Peace, V. (2006). Implicit behavioral mimicry: investigating the impact of group membership. *Journal of Nonverbal Behavior, 30*, 97–113.

Yamagishi, T., Hashimoto, H., & Schug, J. (2008). Preferences versus strategies as explanations for culture-specific behavior. *Psychological Science, 19*, 579–584.

# CHAPTER 7

# Compliance: A Classic and Contemporary Review

Rosanna E. Guadagno

### Abstract

This chapter reviews the literature on compliance, a type of social influence that occurs when a person changes their behavior in response to a direct request. Specifically, I review research on compliance organized by the six classic principles of social influence (Cialdini, 2009)—reciprocity, commitment and consistency, authority, social validation or social proof, and liking and similarity, and examine how they are used to change peoples' behaviors. Furthermore, this chapter reviews the mechanisms that underlie these principles, particularly mindlessness. Finally, this chapter concludes by examining whether this framework for understanding compliance applies to the new realm of social influence—social media—and calls for more research on the effectiveness of the principles of influence when the mode of interpersonal interaction is software based rather than in person.

**Key Words:** compliance, commitment and consistency, reciprocity, authority, social validation, scarcity, liking and similarity, social media

How do people influence others to change their behavior? This is a question that has been studied by social scientists for well over 50 years. Although it varies by individual, some people are markedly adept at getting others to behave in accordance with their desires. Thus, social influence occurs when people alter their attitudes, beliefs, and behaviors as a function of real or imagined pressure from others (Cialdini, 2009). Cialdini proposes that there are two main types of social influence: persuasion—a change in attitude or belief; and compliance—a change in behavior. In this chapter, I review the literature on the latter form of social influence: compliance. This review covers social influence appeals ranging from classic studies conducted at the nascence of this field to contemporary research. Furthermore, for each type of compliance tactic reviewed, I have two secondary aims: (1) to review the extant literature on compliance in the context of social networking; and (2) to explore the notion that mindlessness is an underexplored mechanism

that may underlie the effectiveness of compliance tactics as a means of social influence.

### Overview

Cialdini (2009) spent 2 years conducting observational research on the methods used by influence practitioners in real-life settings such as advertising, fundraising, recruiting, and sales. Based on these observations, he theorized that compliance tactics generally organized into six underlying conceptual categories that he refers to as principles of influence: scarcity, reciprocity, commitment/consistency, authority, social validation, and liking/similarity. Whereas the different principles have varying underlying mechanisms (to be discussed in detail later), they all work best under situations in which an influence target uses heuristics rather than deep thought to guide decision making. This framework has been widely embraced by social influence researchers and serves as the foundation for this review.

## The Six Principles

*Scarcity* is used when a product, opportunity, or item is not widely available either because of low quantity or because the offer is only available for a limited period of time. For example, the home shopping networks use this approach when they introduce a product with limited available quantities or by placing a countdown clock in the corner of the television screen indicating that the opportunity to purchase the product will be lost soon.

*Reciprocity*, the next principle of influence, works because the influence practitioner has provided a favor for or made a concession to the person she or he is attempting to influence. Targets of influence are more likely to agree with the request and change their behavior because they feel they "owe" the influence agent and respond by either repaying the favor or making a concession in response to the influence agent's concession. Most American adults who have received free address labels in the mail along with a request for a donation to a charity should be familiar with reciprocity tactics. Research shows that these "free" address labels dramatically increase donations to the charity and indicates that these address labels are not really free at all (Cialdini, 2009).

*Consistency and commitment* compliance techniques are intended to first secure an initial commitment from the influence target. Once a commitment has been made, the influence agent changes the terms of the agreement. This is a common tactic used by unethical salespersons. When the influence target and agent agree on a price, the salesperson then reveals that the price does not include certain features (e.g., an already installed car alarm or air conditioning in a new car). To be consistent with their initial commitment, the typical customer follows through with the purchase agreement, getting the "low ball" and paying more than the purchase price originally agreed upon.

*Authority* figures or experts on a topic can influence people as well. For example, many actors who have played an authority figure (e.g., doctor, president, police chief) on television have successfully used their status on TV to endorse products and services. The actor Robert Young, who played the physician Marcus Welby on TV, parlayed his role into a successful advertising campaign. To reinforce his authority, he started the ads off with "I am not a doctor but I played one on TV."

*Social validation*, also called *social proof* (and related to conformity, see Hodges, this volume), refers to the influence that actions of others and social norms have on us. This type of social influence is most impactful when people are uncertain about the appropriate course of action. This typically leads people to observe the behavior of others to guide them. Car companies use social validation in advertisements in which the popularity of a particular car model is emphasized. Hotels are adopting this approach to convince people to reuse their towels (see Goldstein, Cialdini, & Griskevicius, 2008).

Finally, *liking and similarity* techniques produce compliance through the portrayal of an influence agent as likable or similar to their target. For example, celebrity endorsements of products, such as actor Jennifer Anniston's endorsement of SmartWater, take advantage of this principle to increase purchases of the product.

### Social Interaction and Social Networking

Technological advances stemming from the Internet have changed the way people live. Broadly construed, social media applications (e.g., Facebook, SnapChat, WeChat, Twitter), networked virtual worlds (e.g., World of Warcraft, ArcheAge, Second Life), and networked discussion forums (e.g., Reddit, Yelp, Meta-Critic) have become popular across the globe, particularly in first-world nations. Through these different social networking sites (SNSs), people discuss topics and ideas, form and maintain relationships, play video games, and find employment opportunities. Although the specifics of the various SNSs vary by time (Boyd & Ellison, 2007; Guadagno, Muscanell, & Pollio, 2013), culture (Kim, Sohn, & Choi, 2011), purpose (social support, gaming, dating, news, employment opportunities), and population (Guadagno, Muscanell, & Pollio, 2013), they all leverage the ever-increasing ubiquity of the Internet to facilitate social interaction. Furthermore, SNS use facilitates both positive experiences (e.g., feeling connected and less lonely; Deters & Mehl, 2012) and negative experiences, including declines in subjective well-being (Kross et al., 2013).

Although the literature on compliance in the networked digital world is still in its nascence, reviews of the emerging research suggest that the compliance tactics translating from the physical world to the digital world will vary in effectiveness as a function of the underlying mechanism behind the influence principle. Specifically, owing to the decreased salience of others inherent in the use of modern technology as portals for social interaction (Bargh, 2002; Guadagno & Cialdini, 2005), evidence suggests that influence principles that are successful in gaining compliance through processes internal to the individual (rather than interpersonal processes) will generalize to the online context (Guadagno, 2013).

## The Mindlessness Hypothesis

Implicit in the aforementioned influence principles is the notion that they successfully increase compliance because people mindlessly process information, a theme I will explore as I review each influence principle. A classic study that illustrates the power of mindless information processing to increase compliance with requests is the well-known "photocopy" study in which a confederate attempted to cut to the front of the line at a library photocopy machine (Langer, Blank, & Chanowitz, 1978). Depending on the experimental condition, the confederate asked to make either 5 or 20 copies and used one of three phrases that varied in the validity of the confederate's explanation: "May I use the copy machine?," "May I use the copy machine because I am in a rush?," or "May I use the copy machine because I need to make copies?" When the confederate made the small request—to make five copies—there were no differences in compliance between conditions that included an explanation starting with the word "because." When the confederate did not use the word "because" in the request to make five copies, participants were far less compliant. The authors reasoned that most participants complied when "because" was included in the request regardless of the validity of the confederate's explanation as a result of heuristic processing. Specifically, the authors reasoned that the word "because" served as a heuristic, or cognitive shortcut, leading nearly all participants to mindlessly process the confederate's request. However, when the request was larger (i.e., 20 copies), the condition in which the confederate provided a legitimate reason for needing to cut in line ("because I am in a rush") garnered more compliance with the request than did the other conditions. This too was consistent with predictions as the authors expected mindless processing of the request only when the request was small enough that an effortful response was not required. Thus, this early study supports the mindlessness hypothesis, suggesting that people comply with Cialdini's (2009) six influence principles without carefully considering the request.

Another test of the mindlessness hypothesis utilized the pique technique, a compliance tactic that is successful because the request is unusual (e.g., asking for 17 or 37 cents results in more compliance than asking for 25 cents; Santos, Level, & Pratkanis, 1994). To examine mindful processing, the researchers tracked whether participants asked the requestors why they needed the money (Burger, Hornisher, Martin, Newman, & Pringle, 2007). As in the photocopy study, requestors varied the response to the pique technique such that they provided either a valid or mindless reason to comply with their request. Results across two studies supported the notion that participants engaged in mindless processing when evaluating the confederate's explanation, as the reason did not matter. Participants who responded to the request by asking the confederate why she or he needed the money were more likely to comply with the request than were those who did not ask. Furthermore, regardless of the answer they received, the inquisitive participants also gave more money to the confederate. Thus, the literature supports the notion that mindlessness is a mediating factor in compliance (Cialdini, 2009) and is the widely accepted mechanism underlying the effectiveness of compliance tactics (Burger et al., 2007; Burger, Messian, Patel, del Prado, & Anderson, 2004).

## Compliance Tactics: What They Are and Why They Work

In the following section, I review the research on the six tactics, the role of mindlessness for the tactic (when it has been investigated), and the applicability of the tactic in social media. Some tactics have not yet been examined with respect to the mediating role of mindlessness; these include authority, social validation, and liking.

## Scarcity

In the United States, each Christmas is preceded with the introduction of a toy that all children find desirable but is limited in availability. Movies have been made about parents fighting to obtain such a toy for their child, television shows have mocked the holiday toy search, and many parents of young children have fallen prey to this perceived scarcity. In a field study examining the role of scarcity in increasing compliance, researchers incorporated information about an impending shortage of Australian beef into the sales script of employees at a meat supplier (Knishinsky, 1982). To examine this, the research team crafted three different versions of the sales script: (1) standard: customer orders were taken as usual—no mention of the impending shortage; (2) scarcity: customers were informed of the impending shortage; and

(3) scarcity plus exclusivity of information: customers were informed of the impending shortage and also informed that this information was generally unknown in the market. Compared to the control condition, participants ordered more than twice the amount of beef in response to the scarcity script. When both scarcity and the exclusivity of the information were made salient, participants ordered more than six times more beef than participants in the control condition. Overall, these results demonstrate the influence of scarcity on compliance and further indicate that the effect is stronger when scarcity occurs on more than one dimension (i.e., scarce information plus a scarce product).

What about conceptualizing scarcity as a unique opportunity? To examine this question, researchers varied uniqueness on a range of dimensions such as participant characteristics and product availability (Burger & Caldwell, 2011). Across four studies, they found that uniqueness significantly increased compliance with a request and that this finding was mediated by the perceived uniqueness of the offer. Thus, scarcity can be conceptualized as a shortage of supply or access to unique or exclusive information.

#### SCARCITY AND SOCIAL NETWORKING

Despite scant research on scarcity and compliance, there has been speculation that scarcity plays a role in the outcome of online auctions (Reynolds, Gilkeson, & Niedrich, 2009). For instance, one study examined the role that scarcity and perceived control over the price played in consumer satisfaction in an online auction (Dunn, 2001). Perceived control over the price was operationalized as setting a fixed price in the high-control condition or as an auction (in which the highest bidder wins the right to purchase the item) in the low-control condition. Scarcity was operationalized by varying the quantity of identical items—tickets to an event—available such that in the no-scarcity condition, all interested parties could purchase tickets, while in the scarcity condition, only a handful of tickets were available. The number of prospective buyers was constant across conditions. Results indicated that in the scarcity condition, participants reported more satisfaction with the purchase experience when perceived control was high relative to low. When the tickets were not scarce, perceived control did not affect participant satisfaction.

#### SCARCITY AND MINDLESSNESS

As indicated earlier, an underlying assumption of the research on scarcity-based influence attempts

is that scarcity is effective in increasing compliance with a request because the influence target is peripherally processing the message and thereby makes his or her decision based on a heuristic indicating that something scarce is valuable. Researchers tested this assumption by asking participants to evaluate a study skills program that either had a limited number of student slots (scarcity condition) or no scarcity in the availability of slots (Grant, Fabrigar, Frozley, & Kredentser, 2014). Basing their work on the theoretical perspective of the elaboration likelihood model (ELM; Petty & Cacioppo, 1986), the authors also varied participants' available attentional resources by putting half the participants under cognitive load. The cognitive load manipulation affected participants' ability to process the message such that those in the load condition engaged in peripheral processing of the message, whereas those in the no-load condition had full access to their attentional resources and could centrally process the message. After reading about the program, participants indicated their intention to join the program and recorded their cognitive responses to the message. Results indicated that, as initially theorized, when peripherally processing under cognitive load, scarcity functioned as a heuristic cue and increased participants' intentions to join the program. This was not the case when participants centrally processed the message.

### *Reciprocity*

According to the norm of reciprocity, it is appropriate for individuals to return favors (Gouldner, 1960). This norm, also called the Golden Rule, conveys the expectation that we give to those who have given to us. Thus, when someone does a favor for an individual, she or he feels beholden to that person until she or he can return the favor. Reciprocity is typically conceptualized as a prosocial action or behavior but can also manifest as retaliation (Parks, 1997). Influence practitioners will take advantage of the norm of reciprocity to obtain compliance with their requests.

For instance, researchers examined the influence of favor-doing on subsequent compliance with a request. They found that, across three studies, reciprocal favors increased compliance (Burger, Ehrlichman, Raymond, Ishikawa, & Sandoval, 2006). They reasoned that reciprocal favors invoke both the obligation inherent in the Golden Rule as well as the friendship heuristic, which indicates to an influence target that she or he ought to do favors for friends. Similarly, other research has reported that reciprocity increases compliance even when the influence agent is a business rather than an individual (Goldstein, Griskevicius, & Cialdini, 2011). For example, in one study, the authors found that hotel guests who were informed that the hotel had made a charitable donation to an environmental cause on behalf of the hotel and its guests were more likely to recycle towels as requested by the hotel. Thus, reciprocity works interpersonally or by proxy.

Reciprocity is also a compliance-gaining tactic that works well when an influence agent employs a series of requests as a means to influence their target. Next, I review some of the well-known reciprocity-based sequential request (i.e., requests that follow one another in order to increase compliance) compliance tactics.

## THE-DOOR-IN-THE-FACE TECHNIQUE

The door-in-the-face (DITF) technique is a sequential request compliance tactic in which influence agents present their target with a request that is so large that most people would not even considering complying with the request (Cialdini et al., 1975). The influence practitioner intends for the influence target to reject this request. Once the target unwittingly reacts as expected and rejects the enormously large request, the influence practitioner then concedes by presenting the target with a smaller, more reasonable target request. More people will agree with the second request when it is preceded by the large request than if they are presented with the second request alone. Scholars maintain that, because the DITF is produced by the normative pressure to reciprocate, the concession on the part of the influence agent is essential for the DITF to work (Cialdini, 2009).

In the initial research on the DITF, experimenters asked college students to volunteer as chaperones for juvenile delinquents on a daylong trip to the zoo (Cialdini et al., 1975). All participants received this request. However, for participants in the DITF condition, this seemingly large request was the second request—the concession. First, participants in the DITF condition were asked to volunteer as counselors to juvenile delinquents with a time commitment of 2 hours a week for 2 years. Once participants refused to comply with this initial request (and they all did), they were then asked to volunteer for the trip to the zoo. Participants in the control condition only received the request to chaperone delinquents to the zoo. The results supported the effectiveness of the DITF: 50 percent of participants who received the large request in the DITF condition agreed to chaperone the trip to the zoo as compared to 17 percent of participants in the control condition.

Another study on the door-in-the-face technique demonstrated that making a large, yet rejected request first was more successful than the target-request-only control condition at leading individuals to comply not only verbally but also behaviorally (Cialdini & Ascanti, 1976). After refusing a request to donate a unit of blood every 6 weeks for 2 years, participants in the DITF condition received the target request to donate just one pint of blood. These participants were more likely to agree to donate a pint of blood than were participants in the target-request-only control condition. Furthermore, the DITF participants who agreed were also more likely than control participants to follow through on their agreement and actually donate the blood.

More recent research has demonstrated the effectiveness of the DITF in nonstudent samples (e.g., professors, Harai, Mohr, & Hosey, 1980), as well as the importance of reciprocity in the effectiveness of the DITF (Millar, 2001). In this latter instance, the benefit for complying with the target request varied in two different DITF conditions. When the participant or a third party benefitted, results revealed that the DITF technique significantly increased compliance relative to the control condition. However, when the influence agent benefitted from the request, the DITF procedure was ineffective. This suggests that when there is a clear advantage for the requestor, the target individual may not feel it is necessary to reciprocate the concession.

In the years since the initial demonstration of the DITF, five meta-analyses have examined the effectiveness of this compliance tactic (Dillard, Hunter, & Burgoon, 1984; Feeley, Anker, & Aloe, 2012; Fern, Monroe, & Avila, 1986; O'Keefe & Hale, 1998, 2001). The most recent of them reviewed the first 35 years of research on the door-in-the-face technique (Feeley et al., 2012). Consistent with the previous meta-analyses, the overall effect size for the DITF was small for verbal compliance with the target request. Moderators that did not affect compliance rates included: whether the target request was a reduction of the initial request (as opposed to novel), the type of behavior requested in the target request (monetary, research/volunteer, personal health, or miscellaneous), the beneficiary of the request (same or different across the two requests), the cause (prosocial or not), whether there was a delay between the initial and target requests, and the difficulty level of the request. The results also revealed several significant moderators of verbal compliance with the target request: same requestor (as opposed to different), the source of the sample (students were more susceptible than nonstudents), communication mode (face-to-face requests resulted in more compliance than mediated requests). Finally, the effectiveness of the DITF was far weaker for the subsets of studies that also assessed behavioral compliance with the target request. In this case, the overall effect size was not significantly different from zero and only one moderator proved significant, indicating that behavioral compliance rates were higher when the same party benefitted from both the initial and target requests.

A common theme across all the DITF meta-analyses conducted is the question of underlying mechanism(s). Although the initial reciprocal concessions explanation of the DITF was supported by some of the earlier studies, meta-analyses that examined the size of concession between the initial and target requests reported that this was not a significant moderator of the DITF (Dillard et al., 1984; Fern et al., 1986; O'Keefe & Hale, 1998, 2001). This null finding has been interpreted as evidence against the reciprocal concessions explanation. However, in a more recent meta-analysis, the concession size was not examined (Feeley et al., 2012). Instead, as in previous meta-analyses (Fern et al., 1986; O'Keefe & Hale, 1998, 2001), the finding that the effect sizes were larger when the requestor was the same across both requests supports the reciprocal concessions interpretation because the pressure to accept the target request would be more intense if the concession was from the person initially refused by the influence target.

## THE THAT'S-NOT-ALL TECHNIQUE

The that's-not-all technique works as follows: The influence practitioner offers the influence target a product at a specific price (Burger, 1986). Then, before the target has a chance to respond, the influence practitioner "sweetens" the offer by either adding a free gift or lowering the price. Reciprocity is a factor in this technique. By lowering the price or adding additional "free" items, the influence practitioner is doing the target individual a favor. This favor increases the normative pressure on the target individual to reciprocate and make the purchase. This technique also works because the initial anchor point—the initial value establishing the worth of an item—is adjusted. Once the initial price point establishes the item's value, the free extra items or

the reduced price makes the second offer appear as a bargain in contrast to the first.

The initial examination of the that's-not-all technique occurred at a university campus bake sale (Burger, 1986). Participants in the "that's not all" condition were presented with a specific price for the cupcake. Then, before they could respond, the experimenter asked them to "wait a second," and then sweetened the offer by including a free small bag of cookies with the cupcake. These participants were significantly more likely to buy the cupcake and cookies package than were participants in the control condition who received the price for the cupcake plus cookies package at the outset of the interaction.

Additional research has established limits to the effectiveness of this reciprocity-based compliance tactic. For instance, one such study demonstrated that the that's-not-all technique backfires if the initial offer is too large (Burger, Reed, DeCesare, Rauner, & Rozilis, 1999). Participants in this study were offered free coffee mugs in exchange for a charitable donation. After a short pause, participants in the "that's-not-all" condition were told that the minimum donation to receive a mug had been reduced. Some of these participants were informed that the minimum donation had been dropped from $10 to $3, whereas those in another condition were told the reduction was much smaller: from $5 to $3. Compared to the control condition in which participants were only asked to make the minimum $3 donation, the $5-to-$3 manipulation produced a significant increase in donations. However, participants in the larger reduction (from $10 to $3) gave significantly less money than the control condition. The researchers argued that the large initial request produced an immediate rejection of the request. Thus, the experimenters were unable to alter the participants' anchor point, and the effectiveness of the that's-not-all manipulation was lost. However, this line of reasoning is inconsistent with the null meta-analytic results on the concession size as a potential moderator of the DITF. This may be because the reciprocity invoked by the technique is not a concession but is instead seen as a free gift with purchase by influence targets. This is an issue that should be further examined in future research.

## SOCIAL NETWORKING AND RECIPROCITY

Finally, evidence—both meta-analytic cited earlier (Feeney et al., 2012)—and empirical indicates that the DITF works successfully in mediated environments (see Ewell, Minney, & Guadagno, 2014).

One such study demonstrated that the DITF was successful in the virtual world of Second Life (Eastwick & Gardner, 2009). There was, however, one notable caveat: When the skin tone of the virtual male requestor was manipulated, participants complied with the request of a light-skinned avatar but not that of a dark-skinned avatar. The authors suggested that these results reflect behavior akin to that seen in the "real" world and that influence targets may have made different assumptions about the person behind the avatar as a function of the apparent "race" of the avatar. Other research indicates that reciprocity in interactions via Twitter affects consumers' intentions to patronize a restaurant (Sardos, Guadagno, & Kimbrough, 2016). Specifically, across two studies, the researchers found that when a consumer tweets a company—in this case a restaurant—women (but not men) were more interested in dining at the restaurant when the restaurant's Twitter account replied to the tweet with an original message of their own relative to conditions in which the restaurant re-tweeted the message or ignored it.

**MINDLESSNESS AND RECIPROCITY**

Need for cognition (NFC), an individual difference characteristic related to mindlessness (Cacioppo, Petty, & Kao, 1984) is one way to assess mindlessness as a moderator of compliance tactics. Although NFC has been widely examined as a moderator of mindlessness in the context of persuasion (e.g., low NFC—as compared to high NFC—people have a higher propensity for mindless or peripheral message processing; Petty & Cacioppo, 2012), the literature on NFC and compliance is far more limited. With reciprocity-based phenomena, the extant research is contradictory in nature. For instance, two unpublished studies examined whether NFC moderated the DITF. In one study, the researcher reported that, contrary to predictions, people high in NFC were marginally more compliant compared to those low in NFC (Kassner, 2011). A second study found the opposite trend: High NFC participants were far less compliant in response to the DITF than controls (Guadagno, Harris, & Strack, 2012). One notable difference is that the former study employed research-related requests, whereas the latter study employed prosocial requests oriented toward helping victims of a tornado. Thus, it may be that the extent of mindless processing in response to the DITF varies as a function of the type of request—something that future research in this area should address.

In support of the mindlessness hypothesis, one study examined the mindlessness hypothesis and the that's-not-all technique (Pollock, Smith, Knowles, & Bruce, 1998). To examine this, the authors added an explanation for sweetening the deal as part of the that's-not-all script in some conditions. Similar to previous research on mindlessness (Langer et al., 1978), some participants were given a placebic explanation. To further understand the role of mindlessness, the authors also varied the cost of the item (chocolate) they were selling, reasoning that mindful processing would more likely be engaged for a more expensive product. Consistent with predictions, there was no difference between the mindless and placebic reasons when the chocolate was inexpensive—both showed a significant difference relative to the control. With the more expensive box of chocolate, this was not the case. In this condition, participants were not swayed by the placebic reason, purchasing no chocolate in that condition.

### Commitment and Consistency

Research has revealed several influence techniques that operate by obtaining an initial commitment to a behavioral outcome. While these techniques vary by sequence, commitment and consistency explains the success of each tactic. The primary tactics that fall under the commitment and consistency umbrella are as follows: the lowball procedure, the foot-in-the-door technique, and the bait-and-switch tactic. To clarify the differences in the sequence of each tactic, the procedure for each is presented in Table 7.1.

**THE LOWBALL PROCEDURE**

When an individual freely commits to one outcome (i.e., purchasing a specific car for a specific price) and the deal changes to become less desirable (i.e., the sales representative mentions that the agreed-upon price does not include the already installed security system), the individual has been lowballed (Cialdini, Cacioppo, Bassett, & Miller, 1978). Because of the existing commitment, many people will maintain their commitment to the initial course of action. Thus, the lowball technique works because of their compliance with that initial request—a request that influence targets accept because it appears to be advantageous or easy to them. When the influence agent changes the opportunity or agreement into something less desirable for the influence target, targets typically perceive that they have already committed and will follow through on their end of the agreement.

**Table 7.1 Commitment-Based Sequential Request Compliance Tactics**

| Tactic | Initial Request | | Second Request | |
|---|---|---|---|---|
| | Initial commitment objective | Example | How the initial commitment traps the target into a less desirable outcome | Example |
| Lowball | Obtaining target's commitment to a set desirable arrangement | Negotiating a home purchase that appears to be a bargain | After commitment, the terms of the agreement change to be less desirable | Changing the deal due to an error in the purchase agreement so that the house costs more or the closing date is undesirable to the target. |
| Bait-and-switch | Entice the target to engage in a certain behavior or course of action | Upon seeing a new car advertised for an extremely low price, the target travels to the dealer to purchase the car | The choice is unavailable or has defects that make it undesirable. The influence agent proposes an alternative that is not as desirable an outcome for the target | Informing the target that the desired car has been sold and offering an alternate, more expensive one. |
| Foot-in-the-door | Obtaining agreement with a small request | Asking the target to sign a petition advocating government aid to tornado victims | Following up with a request for more assistance on a (usually) related request | Asking to target to volunteer time or donate money to help the tornado victims. |

The initial demonstration of the lowball procedure examined compliance with participation (Cialdini et al., 1978). Participants were invited via telephone to sign up for an experiment, the details of which varied by experimental condition. Those in the control condition were scheduled for 7 a.m., an undesirable time for most college students. Those in the lowball condition were initially asked to commit to participate before learning about the undesirable time. Once they committed, experimental participants were then told about the undesirable 7 a.m. start time. Results demonstrated that, compared to the control condition, participants who were lowballed exhibited higher verbal compliance (56 percent to 24 percent, respectively). Additionally, participants in the lowball condition also demonstrated higher behavioral compliance—95 percent of participants in this condition also followed through and showed up for the 7 a.m. lab study.

The lowball technique has subsequently been replicated many times (e.g., Brownstein & Katzev, 1985; Guéguen, Pascual, & Dagot, 2002; Joule,

1987), and the additional research on this compliance tactic indicates that factors other than commitment affect the success rate of a lowball procedure. One study examined the relationship between the influence target and agent to ascertain whether the commitment is stronger to the person (i.e., the influence agent) or the commitment (Burger & Petty, 1981). Their results indicated that the lowball technique was ineffective when the initial and target requests came from different influence agents. Additional research has shown that to ensure a successful lowball technique, the initial commitment needs to be public and vocalized (Burger & Cornelius, 2003). Specifically, this study found that subjects interrupted prior to verbally committing to the initial request were less likely to comply with the (less desirable) target request compared to subjects in a traditional lowball condition.

More recent research examined whether the social acceptability of the target request affected the effectiveness of the lowball technique (Guéguen & Pascual, 2014). To examine this, the research initially examined the lowball in the context of an illegal behavior. A confederate approached cigarette-smoking French adults and asked for assistance lighting his or her cigarette. In the lowball condition, once participants agreed to light the cigarette (the initial request), the confederate produced a large (and illegal to possess) marijuana cigarette rather than the likely expected tobacco cigarette. Results indicated that, relative to controls, participants in the lowball condition were far more likely to light the joint. In a subsequent field study in which the social acceptability of the target request varied, confederates approached participants and asked them to pose for a photograph holding one of three bottles: mint syrup, beer, or absinthe (which is illegal in France). Relative to control participants who received full details of the request, including the type of bottle, participants in the lowball condition were significantly more likely to comply with the target request across all three products. However, compliance rates were affected by the social acceptability of the request. As a result, compliance was highest when participants were asked to hold mint syrup in the photograph and lowest when they were presented with the bottle of absinthe. Nonetheless, across the board, the lowball condition resulted in higher compliance rates than the control condition. These results reinforce the power of commitment and also reveal an important potential limit to the lowball technique. Given that the lowball technique is most effective when the initial request is public in nature, the social acceptability of the target request is an important consideration.

## THE BAIT-AND-SWITCH

Also called the lure technique, the bait-and-switch works by obtaining an initial commitment to a certain course of action, such as traveling to a store with the intent to purchase an item advertised as a good value (Joule, Gouilloux, & Weber, 1989). Once influence targets make this initial commitment (i.e., takes the "bait"), they find out that the item they intended to purchase is no longer available because it is out of stock or sold out. At this point, the influence practitioner then switches by offering an alternate option, item, or action that is not the good value the influence target was expecting. In this situation, most influence targets accept the alternative despite the poorer outcome it represents. Although conceptually similar to the lowball technique, the bait-and-switch differs from the lowball in that rather than changing an existing agreement to a less advantageous outcome, the bait-and-switch replaces a desirable

outcome with a different and less advantageous outcome.

The initial demonstration of the bait-and-switch technique examined this commitment and consistency process in the context of research participation (Joule et al., 1989). Participants were initially recruited for an experiment that ostensibly involved watching film clips—an interesting study from the perspective of a research participant. Instead, this was the bait (initial request). Once participants arrived, those in the bait-and-switch condition were informed that their scheduled experiment was cancelled. These participants were then switched to the target request. Specifically, they were presented with an alternate study involving the memorization of numbers—a much less interesting assignment relative to the initial task to which participants had committed. Results demonstrated the effectiveness of this tactic: Compared to control participants who were just presented with the memorization task, participants who were baited and then switched were over three times more likely to comply with the target request.

More recently, a replication study using the same general paradigm again demonstrated the effectiveness of the bait-and-switch technique (Marchand, Joule, & Guéguen, 2015a). Another series of studies by the same research team examined potentially moderating factors such as the gender of the influence target and agent, the consistency of the goal across the initial and target requests, the time delay between the initial and target requests, and whether the influence agent was the same person across the initial and target request (Marchand, Joule, & Guéguen, 2015b). Their studies demonstrated a significant increase in compliance in the bait-and-switch condition relative to corresponding control conditions under all of the aforementioned experimental settings except for the time delay. In this case, the researchers found that a delay between the initial and target request did not result in an increase in compliance. Thus, the authors illustrated the importance of timing to successfully increase compliance using the bait-and-switch technique.

## FOOT-IN-THE-DOOR TECHNIQUE

Perhaps the most widely studied commitment and consistency-based compliance tactic is the foot-in-the-door (FITD; Freedman & Fraser, 1966). The FITD increases compliance through the use of a small, initial request involving a minor commitment. Given the small size of the request, most people will comply with the request. Then the influence agent builds upon their initial compliance by asking the target to agree with a larger, target request.

In the first published report demonstrating the FITD, the researchers reported that housewives were more willing to agree to let someone enter their homes to catalog the contents of their pantries after initially answering a few short questions (Freedman & Fraser, 1966). In their follow-up study, the scholars examined the impact of consistency between initial and target requests. As with the initial request, participants were either asked to sign a petition or to display a small card in their window. Both the card and petition promoted either an antilittering message or one that encouraged safe driving. Depending on condition, the target request was either conceptually similar or unrelated. About 2 weeks after receiving the initial request, a different influence agent approached participants with the target request: to erect in their front yards an ungainly sign endorsing safe driving. Results revealed that compliance rates were highest when the initial and target requests endorsed the same concept; however, the FITD condition using different prosocial topics as the initial and target requests also resulted in more compliance than the target-request-only controls.

The initially accepted explanation of the FITD utilized self-perception theory (Bem, 1967). Specifically, early research suggested that even compliance with a small initial request (in this case, to endorse a prosocial cause) produces a change in self-perception such that influence targets start to see themselves as "the kind of person who does this sort of thing" (Freedman & Fraser, 1966, p. 201). As a result, complying with a request so minor that few people would refuse opens the door for compliance with much larger requests.

Despite being widely studied, the FITD effect has been remarkably difficult to reliably reproduce. To explain this, some researchers have taken issue with the self-perception explanation of the FITD (DeJong, 1979). A meta-analysis of 120 studies on the foot-in-the-door technique concluded that the average effect size of the FITD is much smaller than was initially demonstrated and that support for the self-perception theory explanation of the FITD was inconsistent (Beaman, Cole, Preston, Klentz, & Steblay, 1983). Other scholars directly tested the self-perception theory explanation of the FITD by measuring self-perception in between the initial and target requests (Gorassini & Olson, 1995). They found that although participants saw themselves as more helpful in the FITD condition

than in the control condition, this difference in self-perceived helpfulness did not predict compliance with the target request. Taken together, these findings suggest that there are other moderating factors that impact the likelihood of increasing compliance using the FITD, and the argument that the FITD is entirely mediated through self-perception should be reconsidered.

Perhaps the most comprehensive review of the FITD was a meta-analysis, the results of which revealed support for a number of moderators of the FITD (Burger, 1999). First, the results of this meta-analysis provided support for the original self-perception explanation of the FITD. Specifically, the researcher reported that when people perceive their compliance with the initial request as indicative of their character, they are more likely to comply with the target request relative to individuals who do not experience a change in self-perception. Illustrative of this, other research found that providing a momentary reward to people after they complied with the initial request decreased compliance with the target request (Burger & Caldwell, 2003). The authors suggested that financial compensation for compliance undermined the self-perception process because participants explained their initial compliance in terms of external reward rather than internal self-perception processes.

In addition to the self-perception process, the meta-analysis identified other moderators of the FITD (Burger, 1999). For instance, the author of the meta-analysis reported that if an influence target complies with the initial request as a result of reciprocity—that she or he believes she or he owes the influence agent—the influence target is less likely to comply with the target request. This suggests that the perception of reciprocity instead undermines compliance within the FITD paradigm because the influence target attributes her or his compliance with the initial request as repayment of a favor. Thus, providing influence targets with a free gift for their compliance with the initial request undermines the self-perception process.

The meta-analysis also revealed several other moderators of the FITD effect such as the importance of carrying out the initial request (Burger, 1999). Illustrative of this moderator, one study found a stronger FITD effect after subjects elaborated on their answers to questions posed as part of the initial request (Hansen & Robinson, 1980). Labeling compliance with the initial request as helpful also increases the magnitude of a FITD effect (Burger, 1999; Guadagno Asher, Demaine, &

Cialdini, 2001). The meta-analysis also found that linking the initial and target requests such that compliance with the target request is perceived as a continuation of the initial request also increases the FITD. Overall, the results of this meta-analysis both explained why the technique has been difficult to replicate while also providing support for the initial self-perception explanation.

## COMMITMENT, CONSISTENCY, AND MINDLESSNESS

To further examine the mindlessness hypothesis, previous research examined whether NFC moderated a commitment and consistency-based tactic: the foot-in-the-door (FITD) technique (Guadagno et al., 2016). To examine this, participants filled out the NFC scale prior to a FITD attempt. Participants in the FITD condition were asked to sign a petition asking the Governor to help victims of a recent tornado as the initial request. All participants received the target request: to volunteer their time to work with a tornado relief group. The results revealed a significant difference between high NFC and low NFC individuals' susceptibility to the FITD effect in support of the mindlessness hypothesis: Low NFC individuals were more compliant with the target request in the FITD condition relative to the control condition, whereas high NFC individuals did not vary in compliance across the two conditions. These results were further supported by a second study that replicated the results using an Internet sample and a FITD request related to voting behavior. Overall, this research provided evidence for the notion that mindlessness is a mechanism underlying the effectiveness of compliance with commitment and consistency-based requests.

## COMMITMENT, CONSISTENCY, AND SOCIAL MEDIA

Research on the effectiveness of the FITD in mediated settings has shown that even in cyberspace, people are susceptible to this commitment and consistency technique (see Ewell et al., 2014). For instance, one such study reported a significant FITD effect for requestors using dark- or light-skinned avatars as influence agents in the popular three-dimensional virtual world Second Life (Eastwick & Gardner, 2009). Furthermore, other studies have reported significant FITD effects in studies, which tested this phenomenon in chat rooms and via email (Guéguen, 2002; Guéguen & Jacob, 2002; Markey, Wells, & Markey, 2001, Study 3; Petrova, Cialdini, & Sills, 2007). Given the underlying internal processes involved in this compliance tactic, it should come as no surprise that the requestor need not be physically present for the FITD to work.

## *Authority*

From an early age, people learn to follow along with authority figures. Children grow up learning to comply with their parents' requests, and this tendency becomes ingrained in people as they learn and grow (Hepburn & Potter, 2011). People are typically rewarded for following the guidance of an authority figure, and some scholars argue that, in the context of compliance with social influence appeals, the underlying heuristic is that if an authority figure says so, it must be true (Cialdini, 2009). This was illustrated in an early study that demonstrated people were more likely to follow a jaywalker when he wore a suit as compared to when he wore street clothing (Lefkowitz, Blake, & Mouton, 1955). Similarly, another study on authority found that, across a number different of hospitals, the vast majority of nurses who received orders to overdose a patient via a phone call ostensibly from a physician complied with the request (Hofling, Brotzman, Dalrymple, Graves, & Pierce, 1966).

Perhaps the most famous research that illustrates the power of an authority figure was conducted by Stanley Milgram (1963, 1974; see Burger, this volume). As the earlier examples illustrate, the power of an authority figure is very strong. One way in which an authority's status can be conveyed is through trappings, which serve as symbols of authority (e.g., one's title, clothing, or material possessions; Cialdini, 2009). For instance, as the earlier jaywalking study found, clothing can convey status (Lefkowitz et al., 1955). Other research supports this notion and finds that well-dressed people are perceived as more authoritative (Bouska & Beatty, 1978; Bushman, 1988). Similarly, research has also found that titles convey authority (Guéguen & Jacob, 2002), as do material possessions such as luxury brands (Bagwell & Bernheim, 1996; Corneo & Jeanne, 1997) and even the font used to convey written information about groups (Donahue, 2012).

### AUTHORITY AND SOCIAL MEDIA

In one such study, the researchers examined whether trappings of authority could be effectively conveyed via email (Guéguen & Jacob, 2002). To examine this, the authors sent participants an email that came from an authority, operationalized by indicating the title of the influence agent—a professor in the authority condition and a student in the no-authority control condition. Group membership was also manipulated such that half the participants were recruited from the university community and half were recruited from the local community. All participants received the same request to complete a survey on their dietary habits. The authors expected higher compliance when the emailed request came from an authority. Reflective of individuals' preference for in-group members (Brewer, 1979), the authors also expected that compliance would be higher when the influence targets were members of the authority figure's in-group (i.e., the university community). Results were consistent with hypotheses such that 97.5 percent of participants from the in-group complied when the request came from an authority figure, whereas only 65 percent complied when the request came from the student. In the out-group sample, compliance was lower but participants from the community were also more compliant when the request came from an authority.

Other studies have found that, when limited information is available, people preferred the movie reviews of experts (Flanagin & Metzger, 2013). Thus, the extant research suggests authority is effective online.

## Social Validation

Social validation, also called *social proof*, refers to the tendency for people to look to the behavior of others when determining the appropriate response to a given situation (Cialdini, 2009). The power of this heuristic on compliance has been illustrated across a variety of contexts such as bystander intervention (Burger et al., 2015; Darley & Latané, 1968), adherence to social norms or social rules to guide behavior (Green & Gerber, 2010), and the introduction of norms for behavior change (Reynolds, Subašić, & Tindall, 2015). Thus, the evidence indicates that looking to one's social network for information regarding the proper behavior has definite adaptive qualities because the actions of others provide a good indication of what is likely to be approved and effective conduct in a given situation (Cialdini, 2009). This tendency is enhanced when people are uncertain about the appropriate guidelines for behavior. This is particularly the case when the environment is uncertain, the number of others from whom to gauge what is appropriate is large, and those being

observed are similar or successful (Cialdini, 2012; Cialdini & Trost, 1998).

Social validation is an effective social influence technique owing in large part to social norms—the general rules for appropriate behavior (see Nolan, this volume). Cialdini and colleagues (Cialdini, Reno, & Kallgren, 1990) theorized that there are two general kinds of social norms: descriptive and injunctive. Descriptive norms are theorized to describe what most people do in a given situation, whereas injunctive norms are theorized to describe what most people approve or disapprove of in a given situation. These two different types of norms vary in strength and effectiveness across different situations. Generally, the research suggests that descriptive norms are more influential when there is no other normative information available, whereas injunctive norms generalize across context.

### DESCRIPTIVE NORMS

In the first set of studies to test the effectiveness of descriptive and injunctive norms, the researchers examined the impact of descriptive and injunctive norms on littering (Cialdini et al., 1990). These initial studies examined whether descriptive norms could affect littering behavior. In their first study, the authors varied the amount of litter in an environment to convey a pro-littering descriptive norm when the environment was heavily littered. This was compared to a control condition in which the same environment was free of litter. The salience of normative information was also manipulated through the use of a confederate who either littered in the environment as a means of enhancing the salience of the descriptive norm or walked through the same area without littering. As predicted, relative to the clean environment, participants littered more when the environment displayed the pro-littering descriptive norm and was already littered. When confederates also enacted the pro-littering norm by littering themselves, compliance was even higher such that participants littered the most when both the environment was littered and the confederate littered. Thus, the results of this initial study highlighted the impact of descriptive norms as conveyed by both the environment and other people on influencing the behavior of others.

In two subsequent studies, the researchers found that a single piece of litter in an otherwise clean environment served to convey the descriptive norm that most people do not litter (Cialdini et al., 1990). In this condition, participants were far less likely to litter. Taken together, this research demonstrates the power of descriptive norms, as the participants attended to and followed the behavior of others, especially when the norm was made salient to them. These findings are also consistent with earlier work, which found that relative to a sign endorsing water conservation while washing hands, confederates modeling water conservation while hand washing (by turning off the faucet while lathering up with soap) dramatically increased compliance to this norm (Aronson & O'Leary, 1982–1983).

Overall, the utility of descriptive norms has been demonstrated across a variety of contexts ranging from evaluations of facial attractiveness (Zaki, Schrimer, & Mitchell, 2011), safety in the workplace (Fugas, Meliá, & Silva, 2011), the propensity to engage in digital piracy (Cho, Chung, & Filippova, 2015), energy conservation (Bator, Tabanico, Walton, & Schultz, 2014), and physical fitness (Burger & Shelton, 2011).

INJUNCTIVE NORMS

Once Cialdini and colleagues investigated the effectiveness of descriptive norms as a tool for behavior change, the researchers expanded their investigation by comparing the impact of descriptive versus injunctive norms (i.e., what people do versus what behavior is approved; Cialdini et al., 1990). To examine this, the researchers used a fully littered environment that varied by norm condition. In the descriptive norm condition, litter was spread over the full area and conveyed a pro-littering descriptive norm. In the injunctive norm condition, the litter was gathered into piles to convey an antilittering injunctive norm. In each condition, a confederate littered in front of participants. This effectively pitted contradictory injunctive and descriptive norms against one another. In the descriptive norm condition, the authors predicted that, as in their earlier studies, littering would increase when the environment and the confederate both endorsed littering. Conversely, in the injunctive norm condition, the authors expected that having the confederate litter in an environment in which the antilittering injunctive norm was made salient by the piles of litter would actually *decrease* littering among participants. Results were consistent with predictions, and the authors concluded that in this context, people followed the (antilittering) injunctive norm when the two types of norms were pitted against each other.

The researchers conducted additional studies examining the mechanism behind the effectiveness of injunctive norms in increasing compliance (Cialdini et al., 1990). Specifically, the authors reasoned that the antilittering norm conveyed by the piles of swept litter could have primed participants. To examine this, the authors developed a series of flyers with different massages and deployed them on the windshields of cars in a parking lot. These messages varied in their closeness to the antilittering norm by endorsing recycling, energy conservation, voting, or visiting an art museum. They expected that the conceptually similar messages would be more likely to prime the antilittering norm. Results confirmed predictions in that the messages that were more conceptually similar to the antilittering injunctive norm produced the least littering among participants.

In a later study the researchers compared the relative power of injunctive versus descriptive normative information across different situations (Cialdini et al., 1990). Their results indicated that injunctive, but not descriptive, norms affect peoples' behavior across situations. Overall, this line of research provided illuminating information about the power and functionality of social norms and suggests that injunctive norms can be effective at countering undesirable behavior established by a descriptive norm. Other research reported similar results with an examination of descriptive and injunctive norms as a means of decreasing the theft of petrified wood from a national forest (Cialdini et al., 2006). To examine this, the authors paired descriptive or injunctive norms with a message discouraging people from stealing the wood. When paired with the descriptive norm—that most people took the wood—the incidence of theft increased. However, when the message was paired with the injunctive norm—that theft is disapproved—the incidence of theft decreased.

Research has applied the findings of the initial research on injunctive norms (Cialdini et al., 1990) to the development of injunctive norm-based interventions to reduce cell phone use while driving (Lawrence, 2015); to research increasing our understanding of the role of injunctive norms on propensity to engage in extradyadic sex (i.e., sex outside a commitment romantic relationship; Buunk & Bakker, 1995); to interventions targeting misperceived injunctive norms endorsing tanning (Reid & Aiken, 2013); and to antilittering public service announcements (Bator & Cialdini, 2000). In this research, antilittering injunctive information that was presented in a televised message successfully motivated antilittering behavior hours later in a different heavily littered environment in which the descriptive norm was prolittering. This finding supports the power of injunctive norms in their ability to direct behavior across situations. Finally, other research has also provided evidence supporting the notion that together, injunctive and descriptive norms can effectively increase compliance with environmentally friendly practices (Cialdini, 2003).

## SOCIAL VALIDATION AND SOCIAL MEDIA

Research has found that social validation processes also functions on the Internet (Guadagno, Muscanell, Rice, & Roberts, 2013). To examine the role of descriptive norms on subsequent compliance with a prosocial request (in this case, volunteering for a canned food drive), introductory psychology students were asked to evaluate a blog post ostensibly created by another student. In one condition, a prosocial descriptive norm was conveyed by the number of other students complying with the blog owner's request and leaving comments indicating their willingness to help in response to the blog post. An antihelping descriptive norm was conveyed in a second condition in which the same number of students refused to help. To assess baseline compliance with the request, a no-response control group was also examined. As expected, results revealed that descriptive norms affected compliance with the request: Participants were significantly more likely to volunteer when others had already done so and were significantly less likely to volunteer when the descriptive norm indicated that refusing to help was the appropriate response.

Research from the social media behemoth Facebook revealed that when members of people's social media networks "like" a product, people are more likely to click on the ad (Bakshy, Eckles, Yan, & Rosenn, 2012). Similarly other people's consumer product preferences affect people's choices of online consumer products (Zhu & Huberman, 2014).

In a study on social validation in mediated communication, researchers sought to examine videos that "go viral" and spread rapidly online (Guadagno, Rempala, Murphy, & Okdie, 2013). To examine this, the researchers examined the role of video source (in-group vs. out-group) and emotion elicited by videos that were selected from a sample of videos that actually spread virally or did not. The results indicated that strong emotional reactions, particularly but not limited to positive emotions such as happiness, predicted intentions to spread the video. Control videos (i.e., the videos

that did not spread virally) did not evoke strong affective responses nor were likely to be spread. With respect to the source of the video, results revealed that videos that evoked anger and ostensibly came from an out-group member were more likely to be spread than were other videos examined in this study. The authors speculated that receiving an anger-invoking video from a person from an out-group may augment the anger experienced by viewers and increase their desire to share their anger with in-group members. Although additional research is needed to better understand this, taken together, the set of studies pertaining to social validation online indicates that this principle of influence functions online.

## Liking

Myriad studies have demonstrated that likeable influence agents are effective in producing compliance (Cialdini, 2009). People who are likeable are typically perceived as erstwhile providers of information. The liking heuristic suggests, "If a likeable or attractive person says so, it must be true." Thus, likeable communicators are typically perceived as credible and typically gain more compliance with their requests than do unlikeable or dissimilar communicators (e.g., Goei, Massi-Lindsey, Boster, Skalski, & Bowan, 2003). In addition, liking can also be produced by an influence agent who is physically attractive, perceived as similar to the influence target, friends with the influence target, uses touch in conjunction with his or her request, or associates with a successful person or group. In each of these instances, the effectiveness of an influence agent's appeal is enhanced relative to situations in which these factors are absent.

### ATTRACTIVENESS

In a classic study on the impact of attractiveness on impression formation, researchers reported that, relative to unattractive people, attractive people were perceived to be more socially desirable, to have higher status occupations, to be better spouses, to have happier marriages, to have happy social and professional lives, and to be more likely to get married (Dion, Berscheid, & Walster, 1972). In the words of the authors:

> The results suggest that a physical attractiveness stereotype exists and that its content is perfectly compatible with the "What is beautiful is good" thesis. Not only are physically attractive persons assumed to possess more socially desirable personalities than those of lesser attractiveness,

but it is presumed that their lives will be happier and more successful.

*(Dion et al., 1972, p. 289)*

This phenomenon has been termed the *halo effect*, referring to the idea that irrelevant characteristics such as physical attractiveness can radiate like a halo to influence inferences about an individual's personality and other characteristics (Forgas & Laham, 2009; Thorndike, 1920). Similarly, research on the halo effect also demonstrates that characteristics introduced early (relative to later) will more heavily influence subsequent inferences and impressions relative to characteristics introduced later on, even when individuals are unaware of this relationship (Nisbett & Wilson, 1977). As a result of this, attractive individuals can be quite influential.

Because of the positive biases associated with physical attractiveness, influence targets tend to like physically attractive influence agents more than less attractive communicators. Thus, one of the ways in which liking increases compliance is through physical attractiveness. For instance, in research reported across a variety of products, physically attractive individuals were more effective at gaining compliance from influence targets (Reingen & Kernan, 1993). Similarly, research has shown that physically attractive political candidates receive more than double the votes of unattractiveness candidates (Efrain & Patterson, 1974). Other research has shown that physically attractive people are also more likely to receive help. For instance, in a large metropolitan area, researchers left mocked-up graduate applications in public phone booths (Benson, Karabenic, & Lerner, 1976). Attached to each application was a stamped, addressed envelope and a photograph of the ostensible prospective graduate student. Compared to applications depicting an unattractive person, bystanders were more likely to mail the application when the accompanying photograph was of an attractive person.

One caveat to the role of physical attractiveness in obtaining compliance with requests applies when the traits associated with an influence agent contradict the halo effect. For instance, consistent with the halo effect, one study found that an attractive communicator obtained higher compliance rates relative to unattractive influence agent (Messner, Reinhard, & Sporer, 2008). However, this was only the case when the influence agent was honest. When the influence agent was dishonest, the results flipped such that the unattractive influence agent was actually more influential than the attractive communicator.

### FRIENDSHIP

With respect to the effect of friendship on compliance, much research suggests that people are more likely to be swayed by their friends. For instance, one study reported that friendship is more influential than exchange-based influence appeals (Barry & Shapiro, 1992). A popular example of the role of friendship in influence appeals is direct sales, such a Tupperware, Mary Kay Cosmetics, or Pampered Chef. For these products, instead of selling from a store, the companies recruit salespersons that invite friends to their homes to demonstrate and sell these products. These parties are quite common; evidence indicates that more than half of American adults have bought items at such a party (Duffy, 2005). Further evidence indicates that the social bond between the influence agent and target is twice as likely as feelings about a product to predict purchases (Frenzen & Davis, 1990).

In addition, research suggests that people are also more likely to comply with the request of an influence agent who behaves as if she or he is the influence target's friend. In support of this notion, research reported that, relative to listening to a monologue, participants complied at higher rates after a conversation with an influence agent (Barry & Shapiro, 1992). Similarly, other research found that simply asking people how they were doing—a common form of greeting—increased compliance (Howard, 1990).

Researchers have also studied the relationship between mere exposure and compliance (Burger, Soroka, Gonzago, Murphy, & Somervell, 2001, Study 1). To examine this, participants completed a filler task in the same room as a confederate in one of two conditions. In the interaction condition, confederates engaged the participant in conversation after their task was complete. In the mere exposure condition, the confederate sat quietly, focused on her completed work, and did not engage the participant in conversation. Compared to a control condition in which the participant completed the task alone, participants in both experimental conditions were significantly more likely to agree to review and provide the confederate with written feedback on an eight-page essay she had ostensibly written for a class.

The researchers conducted a second study using the same general paradigm but replaced the interaction condition with a condition in which the target request (to review the essay) came from someone other than the confederate (Burger et al., 2001, Study 2). This was intended to rule out two alternative explanations for the results of their first study—that the interaction condition had either primed participants for social interaction or induced a positive mood in participants. In support of the mere exposure explanation, the results of this study revealed that participants who sat in the room with the confederate and received the target request from the confederate were more compliant than were participants in the control condition or the different requestor condition (55 percent vs. 20 percent vs. 22.5 percent, respectively).

## SIMILARITY

Early research on similarity demonstrated its effectiveness in increasing compliance. For instance, one such study examined whether dressing in a manner similar to an influence target would increase compliance with an influence attempt (Emswiller, Deaux, & Willits, 1971). To examine this, members of the research team dressed either as "hippies" or as "squares" and asked unwitting participants to give them a dime. When the influence agent and targets were dressed differently, 46 percent of participants complied with the request; when they matched in clothing style, compliance shot up to 68 percent.

Additional research on the impact of similarity on social influence has shown that when influence targets are led to believe that they share a birthday, their name, their fingerprints, or their responses on a personality measure with an influence agent, they are more likely to comply with requests relative to no similarity controls (Burger et al., 2004; Burger et al., 2012, Study 3). Research also indicates that similarity affects peoples' projections of their future prosperity. For instance, one study reported that the success of a similar other increased participants' own expectations about future wealth (Mandel, Petrova, & Cialdini, 2006).

## TOUCH

Research shows that physical contact is a way in which people express their liking for one another (Burgoon, Walther, & Baesler, 1992; Hewitt, 1982; Seger, Smith, Percy, & Conrey, 2014), and the impact of touch on subsequent compliance has been examined. For instance, research indicates that when waitpersons touch their customers, they get better tips. To examine this, the researchers conducted a study in which waitpersons at a restaurant were told to touch their customers on the shoulder or on the palm of the customer's hand (Crusco & Wetzel, 1984). Relative to a control condition in which waitpersons treated their customers identically but did not touch them, touching a customer resulted in significantly higher tips.

Touch has also been examined in response to compliance with a request for a dance (Guéguen, 2007). In two studies, male confederates in a dance club asked young women to dance. In the experimental condition, this request was accompanied with a light touch on her shoulder. In the control condition, the confederate emitted the same request without touching participants. Results revealed that women were more likely to comply with the male confederate's request when it was paired with a touch. In the second study, the confederate approached a woman on the street and asked for her phone number. As in Study 1, women were significantly more likely to comply when the request was accompanied with a touch. Thus, the extant literature in this area suggests that, when used appropriately, touch facilitates compliance with requests.

## LIKING AND SOCIAL MEDIA

There is, however, research on the relationship between liking and compliance in mediated contexts. For instance, one study found that people weight the preferences of their friends over those of a group of strangers (Lee, Hosanagar, & Tan, 2015). Specifically, in an examination of online movie ratings, the authors found that friends' ratings always lead to group polarization in ratings. When friends' ratings are not available, people's movie preferences are impacted by the popularity of the film and the direction (positive or negative) of stranger's ratings. Another study looked at friends' influence on compliance by making a request—to join a new Facebook group—to members of the research team's Facebook friends (Kwon, Stefanone, & Barnett, 2014). In this design, participants may have received the same request from more than one member of their social networks. Their results revealed that participants were more likely to join the group if they were women, had received more than one group invitation, and members of their social network had also joined the group. Finally, one study found that, while people do discern whether an online interactant is likable, liking was not related to compliance (Guadagno, Muscanell, Rice, et al., 2013). Thus, overall, the limited research on this topic suggests that liking online is influential. However, as the studies reviewed earlier suggest, these results conflate liking with social validation in that people are more influenced when more than one friend makes a request or endorses a topic.

## Summary and Future Research Directions

As social psychology has grown as a field, our understanding of the myriad ways in which people influence one another has also grown. This overview of the literature on compliance sought to review both classic and current research on compliance—essentially the factors that are necessary for a successful social influence attempt. Using Cialdini's (2009) framework, the different compliance tactics were organized into one of the six principles of social influence: scarcity, reciprocity, consistency/commitment, authority, social proof, and liking. This framework has been widely adopted and researched as the primary way in which heuristics function in social interactihyon and has implications for social influence and other interpersonal processes.

With respect to the literature on mindlessness and compliance, this review found limited support for mindlessness as a moderator of compliance. These results were generally consistent with the theoretical framework presented by Cialdini (2009). However, as with the literature on mediated social influence, the existing literature is limited. More research is warranted to further understand the role mindlessness plays in compliance.

Finally, while the knowledge amassed since the nascence of this field has taught us much about the ways in which people influence one another, there are also notable areas in which more research is needed. One area that needs additional study is the role that technology-mediated interaction plays in compliance because there are currently many gaps in the literature. The extant literature reviewed herein indicates that in some cases, these tactics work similarly regardless of the physical proximity of the influence agent, whereas in other instances, online social influence appeals work quite differently (Ewell et al., 2014; Guadagno & Cialdini, 2005). For instance, one study described above found that social validation but not liking affected individuals' willingness to comply with a prosocial online request (Guadagno, Muscanell, Rice, et al., 2013). This illustrates an emerging theme in the science of online compliance: When technology rather than face-to-face interaction is the medium, compliance with requests varies in a different manner than previously observed (see Guadagno, Okdie, & Muscanell, 2013). Nonetheless, as scientific evidence builds over time, scholars and practitioners alike continue to learn more about the factors that compel people to say yes to a request when they were initially inclined to say no.

## References

Aronson, E., & O'Leary, M. (1982–1983). The relative effectiveness of models and prompts on energy conservation: A field experiment in a shower room. *Journal of Environmental Systems, 12,* 219–224.

Bagwell, L. S., & Bernheim, B. D. (1996). Veblen effects in a theory of conspicuous consumption. *The American Economic Review, 86,* 349–373.

Bakshy, E., Eckles, D., Yan, R., & Rosenn, I. (2012, June). Social influence in social advertising: evidence from field experiments. In *Proceedings of the 13th ACM Conference on Electronic Commerce* (pp. 146–161), Valencia, Spain. New York, NY: ACM.

Bargh, J. A. (2002). Beyond simple truths: The human–Internet interaction. *Journal of Social Issues, 58,* 1–8.

Barry, B., & Shapiro, D. L. (1992). Influence tactics in combination: The interactive effects of soft versus hard tactics and rational exchange. *Journal of Applied Social Psychology, 22,* 1429–1441.

Bator, R., & Cialdini, R. (2000). The application of persuasion theory to the development of effective proenvironmental public service announcements. *Journal of Social Issues, 56,* 527–542.

Bator, R. J., Tabanico, J. J., Walton, M. L., & Schultz, P. W. (2014). Promoting energy conservation with implied norms and explicit messages. *Social Influence, 9,* 69–82. doi:10.1080/15534510.2013.778213

Beaman, A. L., Cole, C. M., Preston, M., Klentz, B., & Steblay, N. M. (1983). Fifteen years of the foot-in-the-door research: A meta-analysis. *Personality and Social Psychology Bulletin, 9,* 181–196.

Bem, D. J. (1967). Self-perception: An alternative interpretation of cognitive dissonance phenomena. *Psychological Review, 74,* 183–200.

Benson, P. L., Karabenick, S. A., & Lerner, R. M. (1976). Pretty pleases: The effects of physical attractiveness, race, and sex on receiving help. *Journal of Experimental Social Psychology, 12,* 409–415. doi:10.1016/0022-1031(76)90073-1

Bouska, M. L., & Beatty, P. A. (1978). Clothing as a symbol of status: Its effect on control of interaction territory. *Bulletin of the Psychonomic Society, 11,* 235–238.

Boyd, D. M., & Ellison, N. B. (2007). Social network sites: Definition, history, and scholarship. *Journal of Computer-Mediated Communication, 13,* 210–230. doi:10.1111/j.1083-6101.2007.00393.x

Brewer, M. B. (1979). In-group bias in the minimal intergroup situation: A cognitive-motivational analysis. *Psychological Bulletin, 86,* 307–324.

Brownstein, R. J., & Katzev, R. D. (1985). The relative effectiveness of three compliance techniques in eliciting donations to a cultural organization. *Journal of Applied Social Psychology, 15,* 564–574.

Burger, J. M. (1986). Increasing compliance by improving the deal: The that's-not-all technique. *Journal of Personality and Social Psychology, 51,* 277–283.

Burger, J. M. (1999). The foot-in-the-door compliance procedure: A multiple-process analysis and review. *Personality and Social Psychology Review, 3,* 303–325.

Burger, J. M., Bender, T. J., Day, L., DeBolt, J. A., Guthridge, L., How, H. W., . . . Taylor, S. (2015). The power of one: The relative influence of helpful and selfish models. *Social Influence, 10*, 77–84. doi:10.1080/15534510.2014.926291

Burger, J. M., & Caldwell, D. F. (2003). The effects of monetary incentives and labeling on the foot-in-the-door effect: Evidence for a self-perception process. *Basic and Applied Social Psychology, 25,* 235–241. doi:10.1207/S15324834BASP2503_06

Burger, J. M., & Caldwell, D. F. (2011). When opportunity knocks: The effect of a perceived unique opportunity on compliance. *Group Processes & Intergroup Relations, 14,* 671–680.

Burger, J. M., & Cornelius, T. (2003). Raising the price of agreement: Public commitment and the lowball compliance procedure. *Journal of Applied Social Psychology, 33,* 923–934.

Burger, J. M., Ehrlichman, A. M., Raymond, N. C., Ishikawa, J. M., & Sandoval, J. (2006). Reciprocal favor exchange and compliance. *Social Influence, 1,* 169–184.

Burger, J. M., Hornisher, J., Martin, V. E., Newman, G., & Pringle, S. (2007). The pique technique: Overcoming mindlessness or shifting heuristics? *Journal of Applied Social Psychology, 37,* 2086–2096. doi:10.1111/j.1559-1816.2007.00252.x

Burger, J. M., Messian, N., Patel, S., del Prado, A., & Anderson, C. (2004). What a coincidence! The effects of incidental similarity on compliance. *Personality and Social Psychology Bulletin, 30,* 35–43.

Burger, J. M., & Petty, R. E. (1981). The low-ball compliance technique: Task or person commitment? *Journal of Personality and Social Psychology, 40,* 492–500. doi:10.1037/0022-3514.40.3.492

Burger, J. M., Reed, M., DeCesare, K., Rauner, S., & Rozilis, J. (1999). The effects of initial request size on compliance: More about the that's not all technique. *Basic and Applied Social Psychology, 21,* 243–249.

Burger, J. M., & Shelton, M. (2011). Changing everyday health behaviors through descriptive norm manipulations. *Social Influence, 6,* 69–77. doi:10.1080/15534510.2010.542305

Burger, J. M., Soroka, S., Gonzago, K., Murphy, E., & Somervell, E. (2001). The effect of fleeting attraction on compliance to requests. *Personality and Social Psychology Bulletin, 27,* 1578–1586.

Burgoon, J. K., Walther, J. B., & Baesler, E. J. (1992). Interpretations, evaluations, and consequences of interpersonal touch. *Human Communication Research, 19,* 237–263.

Bushman, B. J. (1988). The effects of apparel on compliance: A field experiment with a female authority figure. *Personality and Social Psychology Bulletin, 14,* 459–467. doi: 10.1177/0146167288143004

Buunk, B. P., & Bakker, A. B. (1995). Extradyadic sex: The role of descriptive and injunctive norms. *The Journal of Sex Research, 32,* 313–318, doi: 10.1080/00224499509551804

Cacioppo, J. T., Petty, R. E., & Kao, C. F. (1984). The efficient assessment of need for cognition. *Journal of Personality Assessment, 48,* 306–307. doi:10.1207/s15327752jpa4803_13

Cho, H., Chung, S., & Filippova, A. (2015). Perceptions of social norms surrounding digital piracy: The effect of social projection and communication exposure on injunctive and descriptive social norms. *Computers in Human Behavior, 48,* 506–515. doi:10.1016/j.chb.2015.02.018

Cialdini, R. B. (2003). Crafting normative messages to protect the environment. *Current Directions in Psychological Science, 12,* 105–109.

Cialdini, R. B. (2009). *Influence: Science and practice* (5th ed.). Boston, MA: Allyn & Bacon.

Cialdini, R. B. (2012). The focus theory of normative conduct. In P. M. Van Lange, A. W. Kruglanski, E. T. Higgins, P. M. Van Lange, A. W. Kruglanski, & E. T. Higgins (Eds.), *Handbook of theories of social psychology* (Vol. 2, pp. 295–312). Thousand Oaks, CA: Sage Publications.

Cialdini, R. B., & Ascanti, K. (1976). Test of a concession procedure for inducing verbal, behavioral, and further compliance with a request to give blood. *Journal of Applied Psychology, 61,* 295–300.

Cialdini, R. B., Cacioppo, J. T., Bassett, R., & Miller, J. A. (1978). Low-ball procedure for producing compliance: Commitment then cost. *Journal of Personality and Social Psychology, 36,* 463–476.

Cialdini, R. B., Demaine, L. J., Sagarin, B. J., Barrett, D. W., Rhoads, K., & Winter, P. L. (2006). Managing social norms for persuasive impact. *Social Influence, 1,* 3–15. doi:10.1080/15534510500181459

Cialdini, R. B., Reno, R. R., & Kallgren, C. A. (1990). A focus theory of normative conduct: Recycling the concept of norms to reduce littering in public places. *Journal of Personality and Social Psychology, 58,* 1015–1026. doi:10.1037/0022-3514.58.6.1015

Cialdini, R. B., & Trost, M. R. (1998). Social influence: Social norms, conformity and compliance. In D. T. Gilbert, S. T. Fiske & G. Lindzey (Eds.), *The handbook of social psychology* (Vols. 1 and 2, 4th ed., pp. 151–192). New York, NY: McGraw-Hill.

Cialdini, R. B., Vincent, J. E., Lewis, S. K., Catalan, J., Wheeler, D., & Darby, B. L. (1975). Reciprocal concessions procedure for inducing compliance: The door-in-the-face technique. *Journal of Personality and Social Psychology, 31,* 206.

Corneo, G., & Jeanne, O. (1997). Conspicuous consumption, snobbism and conformism. *Journal of Public Economics, 66,* 55–71.

Crusco, A. H., & C. G. Wetzel (1984). The Midas touch: The effects of interpersonal touch on restaurant tipping. *Personality and Social Psychology Bulletin, 10,* 512-517.

Darley, J. M., & Latané, B. (1968). Bystander intervention in emergencies: Diffusion of responsibility. *Journal of Personality and Social Psychology, 8*(4 Pt. 1), 377–383. doi:10.1037/h0025589

DeJong, W. (1979). An examination of self-perception mediation of the foot-in-the-door effect. *Journal of Personality and Social Psychology, 37,* 2221–2239.

Deters, F. G. & Mehl, M. R. (2012). Does posting Facebook status updates increase or decrease loneliness? An online social networking experiment. *Social Psychological and Personality Science, 4,* 579–586. doi:10.1177/1948550612469233

Dillard, J. P., Hunter, J. E., & Burgoon, M. (1984). Sequential-request persuasive strategies. *Human Communication Research, 10,* 461–488.

Dion, K., Berscheid, E., & Walster, E. (1972). What is beautiful is good. *Journal of Personality and Social Psychology, 24,* 285–290. doi:10.1037/h0033731

Donahue, J. (2012). A true authoritarian type: How fonts can facilitate positive opinions for powerful groups. *Available at SSRN 2156989:* http://papers.ssrn.com/sol3/papers.cfm?abstract_id=2156989

Duffy, D. L. (2005). Direct selling as the next channel. *Journal of Consumer Marketing, 22,* 43–45.

Dunn, S. A. (2001). Do losers matter? An experimental look at the impact of control and scarcity on satisfaction with an online buying experience. *Dissertation Abstracts International Section A, 64,* 208.

Eastwick, P. W., & Gardner, W. L. (2009). Is it a game? Evidence for social influence in the virtual world. *Social Influence, 4,* 18–32.

Efrain, M. G., & Patterson, E. W. J. (1974). Voters vote beautiful: The effect of physical appearance on a national election. *Canadian Journal of Behavioural Science/Revue canadienne des sciences du comportement, 6,* 352.

Emswiller, T., Deaux, K., & Willits, J. E. (1971). Similarity, sex, and requests for small favors. *Journal of Applied Social Psychology, 1,* 284–291.

Ewell, P. J., Minney, J. A. & Guadagno, R. E. (2014). Social influence online: An updated view. In Mehdi Khosrow-Pour (Ed.), *Encyclopedia of information science & technology* (3rd ed., pp. 6762–6772). Hershey, PA: IGI Global.

Feeley, T. H., Anker, A. E., & Aloe, A. M. (2012). The door-in-the-face persuasive message strategy: A meta-analysis of the first 35 years. *Communication Monographs, 79,* 316–343. doi:10.1080/03637751.2012.697631

Fern, E. F., Monroe, K. B., & Avila, R. A. (1986). Effectiveness of multiple request strategies: A synthesis of research results. *Journal of Marketing Research,* 144–152.

Flanagin, A. J., & Metzger, M. J. (2013). Trusting expert-versus user-generated ratings online: The role of information volume, valence, and consumer characteristics. *Computers in Human Behavior, 29,* 1626–1634.

Forgas, J. P., & Laham, S. (2009). Halo effects. In R. Baumeister & K. D. Vohs (Eds.), *Encyclopedia of social psychology* (pp. 499–502). Thousand Oaks, CA: Sage Publications.

Freedman, J. L., & Fraser, S. C. (1966). Compliance without pressure: The foot-in-the-door technique. *Journal of Personality and Social Psychology, 4,* 195–202.

Frenzen, J. K., & Davis, H. L. (1990). Purchasing behavior in embedded markets. *Journal of Consumer Research, 17,* 1–12.

Fugas, C. S., Meliá, J. L., & Silva, S. A. (2011). The "is" and the "ought": How do perceived social norms influence safety behaviors at work? *Journal of Occupational Health Psychology, 16,* 67.

Goei, R., Massi-Lindsey, L. L., Boster, F. J., Skalski, P. D., & Bowman, J. M. (2003). The mediating roles of liking and obligation on the relationship between favors and compliance. *Communication Research, 39,* 178–197.

Goldstein, N. J., Cialdini, R. B., & Griskevicius, V. (2008). A room with a viewpoint: Using social norms to motivate environmental conservation in hotels. *Journal of Consumer Research, 35,* 472–482.

Goldstein, N. J., Griskevicius, V., & Cialdini, R. B. (2011). Reciprocity by proxy: A new influence strategy for motivating cooperation and prosocial behavior. *Administrative Science Quarterly, 56,* 441–473.

Gorassini, D. R., & Olson, J. M. (1995). Does self-per perception change explain the foot-in-the-door effect? *Journal of Personality and Social Psychology, 69,* 91–105.

Gouldner, A. W. (1960). The norm of reciprocity: A preliminary statement. *American Sociological Review, 25,* 161–178.

Grant, N. K., Fabrigar, L. R., Forzley, A., & Kredentser, M. (2014). The multiple roles of scarcity in compliance: Elaboration as a moderator of scarcity mechanisms. *Social Influence, 9,* 149–161. doi:10.1080/15534510.2013.796891

Green, D. P., & Gerber, A. S. (2010). Introduction to social pressure and voting: New experimental evidence. *Political Behavior, 32,* 331–336.

Guadagno, R. E., Asher, T., Demaine, L. J., & Cialdini, R. B. (2001). When saying yes leads to saying no: Preference for consistency and the reverse foot-in-the-door effect. *Personality and Social Psychology Bulletin, 27,* 859–867.

Guadagno, R. E. (2013). Social influence online: The six principles in action. In C. Liberman (Ed.), *Casing persuasive communication* (pp. 319–344). Dubuque, IA: Kendall Hunt.

Guadagno, R. E., & Cialdini, R. B. (2005). Online persuasion and compliance: Social influence on the Internet and beyond. In Y. Amichai-Hamburger (Ed.), *The social net: The social psychology of the Internet* (pp. 91–113). New York, NY: Oxford University Press.

Guadagno, R. E., Harris, J. N. & Strack, J. (2012). [Need for cognition, mindlessness, and susceptibility to the door-in-the-face technique]. Unpublished raw data.

Guadagno, R. E., Muscanell, N. L., & Pollio, D. E. (2013). The homeless use Facebook?! Similarities of social network use between college students and homeless young adults. *Computers in Human Behavior, 29,* 86–89.

Guadagno, R. E., Muscanell, N. L., Rice, L. M., & Roberts, N. (2013). Social influence online: The impact of social validation and likability on compliance. *Psychology of Popular Media Culture, 2,* 51–60. doi:10.1037/a0030592

Guadagno, R. E., Okdie, B. M, & Muscanell, N. L. (2013). Have we all just become "Robo-sapiens"? Reflections on social influence processes in the Internet Age. *Psychological Inquiry, 24,* 1–9.

Guadagno, R. E., Rempala, D. M., Murphy, S., & Okdie, B. M. (2013). What makes a video go viral? An analysis of emotional contagion and Internet memes. *Computers in Human Behavior, 29,* 2312–2319.

Guadagno, R. E., Strack, J., Harris, J. N., Muscanell, N. L., Kimbrough, A. M., & Wingate, V. S. (2016). [Need for cognition and the foot-in-the-door effect: A test of the mindlessness hypothesis]. Unpublished raw data.

Guéguen, N. (2002). Foot-in-the-door technique and computer-mediated communication. *Computers in Human Behavior, 18,* 11–15. doi:10.1016/S0747-5632(01)00033-4

Guéguen, N. (2007). Courtship compliance: The effect of touch on women's behavior. *Social Influence, 2,* 81–97. doi:10.1080/15534510701316177

Guéguen, N., & Jacob, C. (2002). Solicitation by e-mail and solicitor's status: A field study of social influence on the Web. *Cyberpsychology & Behavior, 5,* 377–383. doi:10.1089/109493102760275626

Guéguen, N., & Pascual, A. (2014). Low-ball and compliance: Commitment even if the request is a deviant one. *Social Influence, 9,* 162–171. doi:10.1080/15534510.2013.798243

Guéguen, N., Pascual, A., & Dagot, L. (2002). Low-ball and compliance to a request: An application in a field setting. *Psychological Reports, 91,* 81–84. doi:10.2466/PR0.91.5.81-84

Hansen, R. A., & Robinson, L. M. (1980). Testing the effectiveness of alternative foot-in-the-door manipulations. *Journal of Marketing Research, 17,* 359–364. doi:10.2307/3150534

Harai, H., Mohr, D., & Hosey, K. (1980). Faculty helpfulness to students: A comparison of compliance techniques. *Personality and Social Psychology Bulletin, 6,* 373–377.

Hepburn, A., & Potter, J. (2011). Designing the recipient managing advice resistance in institutional settings. *Social Psychology Quarterly, 74*, 216–241.

Hewitt, J. (1982). Liking for touchers as a function of type of touch. *Psychological Reports, 50*(Pt 1), 917–918. doi:10.2466/pr0.1982.50.3.917

Hofling, C. K., Brotzman, E., Dalrymple, S., Graves, N., & Pierce, C. M. (1966). An experimental study in nurse-physician relationships. *The Journal of Nervous and Mental Disease, 143*, 171–180.

Howard, D. J. (1990). The influence of verbal responses to common greetings on compliance behavior: The foot-in-the-mouth effect. *Journal of Applied Social Psychology, 20*, 1185–1196.

Joule, R. V. (1987). Tobacco deprivation: The foot-in-the-door technique versus the low-ball technique. *European Journal of Social Psychology, 17*, 361–365. doi:10.1002/ejsp.2420170311

Joule, R. V., Gouilloux, F., and Weber, F. (1989). The lure: A new compliance procedure. *Journal of Social Psychology, 129*, 741–749.

Kassner, M. P. (2011). Personality moderators of the door-in-the-face compliance technique (Unpublished Master's thesis). Purdue University.

Knishinsky, A. (1982). The effects of scarcity of material and exclusivity of information on industrial buyer perceived risk in provoking a purchase decisions (Unpublished doctoral dissertation). Arizona State University.

Kross, E., Verduyn, P., Demiralp, E., Park, J., Lee, D. S., Lin, N., . . . Ybarra, O. (2013). Facebook use predicts declines in subjective well-being in young adults. *PloS One, 8*, e69841.

Kwon, K. H., Stefanone, M. A., & Barnett, G. A. (2014). Social network influence on online behavioral choices exploring group formation on social network sites. *American Behavioral Scientist, 58*, 1345–1360.

Langer, E., Blank, A., & Chanowitz, B. (1978). The mindlessness of ostensibly thoughtful action: The role of "placebic" information in interpersonal interaction. *Journal of Personality and Social Psychology, 36*, 635–642.

Lawrence, N. K. (2015). Highlighting the injunctive norm to reduce phone-related distracted driving. *Social Influence, 10*, 109–118. doi:10.1080/15534510.2015.1007082

Lee, Y. J., Hosanagar, K., & Tan, Y. (2015). Do I follow my friends or the crowd? Information cascades in online movie ratings. *Management Science, 61*, 2241–2258.

Lefkowitz, M., Blake, R. R., & Mouton, J. S. (1955). Status factors in pedestrian violation of traffic signals. *The Journal of Abnormal and Social Psychology, 51*, 704.

Mandel, N., Petrova, P. K., & Cialdini, R. B. (2006). Images of success and the preference for luxury brands. *Journal of Consumer Psychology, 16*(1), 57–69.

Marchand, M., Joule, R., & Guéguen, N. (2015a). The lure technique: Replication and refinement in a field setting. *Psychological Reports, 116*, 275–279. doi:10.2466/17.21.PR0.116k11w0

Marchand, M., Joule, R. V., & Guéguen, N. (2015b). The lure technique: Generalization and moderating effects. *Revue Européenne de Psychologie Appliquée/European Review of Applied Psychology, 65*, 105–113. doi:10.1016/j.erap.2015.02.003

Markey, P. M., Wells, S. M., & Markey, C. N. (2001). Personality and social psychology in the culture of cyberspace. In S. P. Shohov (Ed.), *Advances in psychology research* (Vol. 9, pp. 103–124). Huntington, NY: Nova Science Publishers.

Messner, M., Reinhard, M., & Sporer, S. L. (2008). Compliance through direct persuasive appeals: The moderating role of communicator's attractiveness in interpersonal persuasion. *Social Influence, 3*, 67–83. doi:10.1080/15534510802045261

Millar, M. G. (2001). Promoting health behaviours with door-in-the-face: The influence of the beneficiary of the request. *Psychology, Health & Medicine, 6*, 115–119.

Milgram, S. (1963). Behavioral study of obedience. *The Journal of Abnormal and Social Psychology, 67*(4), 371–378.

Milgram, S. (1974). *Obedience to authority: An experimental view.* New York, NY: Harper.

Nisbett, R. E., & Wilson, T. D. (1977). The halo effect: Evidence for unconscious alteration of judgments. *Journal of Personality and Social Psychology, 35*, 250.

O'Keefe, D. J., & Hale, S. L. (1998). The door-in-the-face influence strategy: A random-effects meta-analytic review. *Communication yearbook, 21*, 1–34.

O'Keefe, D. J., & Hale, S. L. (2001). An odds-ratio-based meta-analysis of research on the door-in-the-face influence strategy. *Communication Reports, 14*, 31–38.

Parks, J. M. (1997). The fourth arm of justice: The art and science of revenge. In R. J. Lewicki, R. J. Bies, B. H. Sheppard, R. J. Lewicki, R. J. Bies, & B. H. Sheppard (Eds.), *Research on negotiation in organizations* (Vol. 6, pp. 113–144). Greenwich, CT: Elsevier Science/JAI Press.

Petrova, P. K., Cialdini, R. B., & Sills, S. J. (2007). Consistency-based compliance across cultures. *Journal of Experimental Social Psychology, 43*, 104–111.

Petty, R. E., & Cacioppo, J. T. (1986). The elaboration likelihood model of persuasion. In L. Perkowitz (Ed.), *Advances in experimental social psychology* (Vol. 19, pp. 123–205). New York, NY: Academic.

Petty, R., & Cacioppo, J. T. (2012). *Communication and persuasion: Central and peripheral routes to attitude change.* New York, NY: Springer Science & Business Media.

Pollock, C. L., Smith, S. D., Knowles, E. S., & Bruce, H. J. (1998). Mindfullness limits compliance with the that's-not-all technique. *Personality and Social Psychology Bulletin, 24*, 1153–1157.

Reid, A. E. & Aiken, L. S. (2013). Correcting injunctive norm misperceptions motivates behavior change: A randomized controlled sun protection intervention. *Health Psychology, 32*, 551–560. http://dx.doi.org/10.1037/a0028140

Reingen, P. H., & Kernan, J. B. (1993). Social perception and inter-personal influence: Some consequences of the physical attractiveness stereotype in a personal selling setting. *Journal of Consumer Psychology, 2*, 25–38.

Reynolds, K. E., Gilkeson, J. H., & Niedrich, R. W. (2009). The influence of seller strategy on the winning price in online auctions: A moderated mediation model. *Journal of Business Research, 62*, 22–30.

Reynolds, K. J., Subašić, E., & Tindall, K. (2015). The problem of behaviour change: From social norms to an ingroup focus. *Social and Personality Psychology Compass, 9*, 45–56. doi:10.1111/spc3.12155

Santos, M. D., Leve, C., & Pratkanis, A. R. (1994). Hey buddy, can you spare seventeen cents? Mindful persuasion and the pique technique. *Journal of Applied Social Psychology, 24,* 755–764.

Sardos, A., Guadagno, R. E. & Kimbrough, A. M. (2016). *[Corporate Twitter use and reciprocity with consumers: A social influence examination].* Unpublished raw data.

Seger, C. R., Smith, E. R., Percy, E. J., & Conrey, F. R. (2014). Reach out and reduce prejudice: The impact of interpersonal touch on intergroup liking. *Basic and Applied Social Psychology, 36*(1), 51–58. doi:10.1080/01973533.2013.856786

Thorndike, E. L. (1920). A constant error in psychological ratings. *Journal of Applied Psychology, 4,* 25–29. doi:10.1037/h0071663

Zaki, J., Schirmer, J., & Mitchell, J. P. (2011). Social influence modulates the neural computation of value. *Psychological Science, 22,* 894–900. doi:10.1177/0956797611411057

Zhu, H., & Huberman, B. A. (2014). To switch or not to switch understanding social influence in online choices. *American Behavioral Scientist,* doi:10.1177/0002764214527089

# CHAPTER
# 8

# Obedience

Jerry M. Burger

## Abstract

Most obedience research is concerned with the kind of destructive obedience demonstrated in Milgram's famous studies. A large number of participants in those investigations followed an experimenter's instructions to administer what they believe to be excruciating if not dangerous electric shocks to another individual. Ethical concerns about Milgram's procedures have forced researchers to develop new methods to study obedience, such as virtual reality procedures and partial replications. A small number of studies suggest that personality may affect obedience, but there is little evidence to date that culture or gender plays an important role. Milgram's interpretation of his findings has been largely rejected, but explanations based on the relationship between the experimenter and the participant and on situational variables that affect social influence processes are promising. The extent to which Milgram's findings help us understand the obedience that contributed to the Holocaust in Nazi Germany remains a topic of debate.

**Key Words:** obedience, authority, Milgram, ethics, Holocaust

Obedience researchers are interested in how individuals respond to orders or demands from a person or institution in a position of authority. There is a long history of research on obedience in the social sciences, with much of the early work concerned with the benefits of obedience, such as children obeying their parents (Benjamin & Simpson, 2009). Later research focused on the dangers of blind obedience that lead to what investigators often refer to as destructive obedience. Much of this work is concerned with the failure to challenge an authority figure's orders even when those orders appear to be in error or could lead to disastrous consequences. Examples include military officers issuing illegal commands to soldiers (Kelman & Hamilton, 1989), doctors ordering nurses to give patients inappropriate medicines (Hofling, Brotzman, Dalrymple, Graves, & Pierce, 1966), and airplane pilots calling for actions that others in the cockpit believe are ill advised (Tarnow, 2000).

However, for more than half a century, discussion and research about obedience have been dominated by one program of research. Between August 1961 and May 1962, Stanley Milgram, a young assistant professor at Yale University, conducted a series of investigations that became known as the obedience studies. The research produced some unexpected and disturbing findings and quickly became immersed in controversy. At an unsettling high rate, participants in these investigations followed an authority figure's instructions to administer what they believed to be painful if not dangerous electric shocks to another individual. The studies became arguably the most well-known psychological research inside or outside of academia and have been incorporated into literature, popular songs, and motion pictures (Blass, 2004). More than five decades after it was conducted, Milgram's work remains the starting point for understanding what social influence researchers know about obedience. Because ethical concerns now limit our ability to replicate Milgram's experimental procedures, a large amount of scholarly work on obedience has been devoted to interpreting Milgram's results rather than generating new data. And although obedience investigators occasionally examine behavior much less dramatic than administering electric shocks (e.g., pedestrian street crossing; Geffner & Gross, 1984), it is a rare obedience paper that does not tie its findings to Milgram's work on destructive obedience. Research on the positive aspects of obedience has become almost nonexistent (Ent & Baumeister, 2014).

## Milgram's Obedience Studies

Milgram (1963, 1965, 1974) examined participants' reactions when an experimenter instructed them to administer increasingly stronger electric shocks to a man they believed to be another participant. In most variations of the study, the man receiving the shocks complained vehemently about the pain and demanded to be released, while the experimenter consistently directed the participant to keep administering shocks. The purpose of the research was to see how long participants would continue with the procedure before they refused to follow the experimenter's instructions any further. To better understand the psychological processes underlying this obedience, Milgram also conducted a series of variations on the basic procedure. In all variations, participants, ages 20–50 years, were recruited from the New Haven, Connecticut, community through newspaper ads and direct mail solicitations. They were paid $4.50 to be part of a study on "memory and learning." The composition of the sample was approximately 40 percent blue-collar workers, 40 percent white-collar workers, and 20 percent professionals. With the exception of one variation, all participants were men.

### The Baseline Procedure

The version of the obedience studies that most people are familiar with is the baseline procedure Milgram (1974) identified as Experiment 5. Each session consisted of one participant, one male confederate posing as a participant, and one male experimenter. The experimenter explained that the research was concerned with the effects of punishment on learning and that the form of punishment to be used in the study would be electric shocks. Through a rigged drawing, the real participant was always assigned the role of "teacher," and the confederate was always the "learner." The learner's task was to remember a list of 25 word pairs, whereas the teacher's job was to administer the test and deliver the punishment for wrong answers.

The teacher watched as the learner was strapped into a chair "to prevent excessive movement," which gave the appearance that the learner would be unable to escape from the chair on his own. An electrode, supposedly connected to a shock generator in the next room, was attached to the learner's wrist. After the experimenter explained the test procedures, the learner said, "When I was at the Westhaven V.A. Hospital a few years ago, they detected a slight heart condition. Nothing serious, but are these shocks dangerous?" The experimenter replied that while the shocks might be painful, they were not dangerous and would cause no permanent tissue damage. The teacher witnessed this exchange.

The experimenter and the teacher then moved to the room next door, where the teacher sat in front of a large metal box identified as the shock generator. In addition to gauges and lights, a row of 30 switches spanned the front of the machine. Each switch was identified with the number of volts it delivered, starting with 15 volts for the switch on the far left and moving in 15-volt increments to the 450-volt switch on the far right. Labels placed underneath the switches described the intensity of the shocks. From left to right, the labels read: Slight Shock, Moderate Shock, Strong Shock, Very Strong Shock, Intense Shock, Extreme Intensity Shock, and Danger: Severe Shock. The last two switches (435 and 450 volts) were simply labeled with three red X's.

The teacher and the learner communicated through a one-way intercom system. The teacher spoke into a microphone, but the learner could give his answers only by pressing one of four buttons barely within reach of his strapped-down hand. Each button lit a number (1, 2, 3, or 4) on the teacher's side of the wall. The test began with the teacher reading a list of 25 word pairs (e.g., *blue-girl*) for the learner to remember. The teacher then gave the first word from a pair (e.g., *blue*) and four options for the word that completed the word pair (e.g., *boy, girl, grass, hat*). After seeing the learner's response, the teacher informed the learner whether he had answered correctly. If the answer was incorrect, the teacher gave the correct answer and pressed one of the switches on the shock generator to deliver the punishment. The teacher was instructed to administer the smallest shock (15 volts) for the first mistake and to move one level higher for each subsequent wrong answer, that is, 30 volts for the second mistake, 45 volts for the third mistake, and so on.

In reality, the learner received no shocks. He also was able to extricate himself from the straps with little effort so that he could easily give his answers and play prerecorded verbal responses that could be heard by the teacher through the thin wall. The learner made many mistakes on the test, which forced the teacher to administer stronger and stronger levels of shock. After the teacher pressed the 75-volt switch, he heard the learner make a noise, what Milgram described as *Ugh*! From that point on, the learner made a similar noise that became louder with each shock and eventually resembled a scream of pain. After the teacher administered the 105-volt shock, the learner's first prerecorded response could be heard through the wall. He said, "Hey, *this* really hurts." When the teacher pressed the 150-volt switch, the learner yelled: "Experimenter! That's all. Get me out of here. I told you I had heart trouble. My heart's starting to bother me now. Get me out of here, please. My heart's starting to bother me. I refuse to go on. Let me out."

The experimenter sat a few feet behind the teacher throughout the session. Whenever the teacher showed any hesitation about continuing the procedure, the experimenter gave instructions to proceed with the test. In Milgram's eyes, the experimenter was the authority figure in this obedience situation and the instructions to continue the shocks were the orders to engage in destructive behavior. Milgram gave the experimenter four prods he could use each time the participant hesitated. In order, the prods were as follows: *Please continue* (or sometimes, *Please go on*); *The experiment requires that you continue*; *It is absolutely essential that you continue*; and *You have no other choice, you must go on*. The experimenter started with the first prod each time the participant hesitated and moved to the next prod if the participant continued to resist. If the participant refused to go on with the test after hearing the fourth prod, the experimenter ended the session.

Milgram gave the experimenter a few additional lines he could use for specific situations, such as reminding the teacher that the shocks might be painful but were not dangerous and explaining that whether the learner likes it or not, they had to continue until all the word pairs were learned. However, we should note that researchers examining transcripts and recordings in the Milgram Papers in the Yale University Library Archives have discovered that the experimenter may have had more leeway in his responses than Milgram's description of the procedures suggests (Darley, 1995; Gibson, 2013a). It is possible that the experimenter used more persuasive tactics than reported, although the extent to which additional comments by the experimenter may have affected the participants' behavior remains a matter of speculation.

If the teacher continued to administer the test after the learner's protests at 150 volts, he heard cries of pain that became louder with each shock and demands to be released that became increasingly more vehement. The learner specifically mentioned that his heart was bothering him on two other occasions. If the session continued to the 300-volt shock, the learner announced that he would no longer provide answers to the test items, which prompted the experimenter to say that no answer should be considered a wrong answer and should be punished. After the 330-volt shock, the learner released an "intense and prolonged agonized scream" followed by a string of loud and frantic demands to be set free. It was the last time the teacher would hear the learner. From that point on, each shock was met only with silence, suggesting that the learner was no longer physically capable of responding. The experiment continued until either the teacher refused to go on or he had administered the strongest shock on the generator (450 volts) three times.

### Predictions and Results

The primary dependent variable in the experiment was the point in the procedure beyond which participants refused to continue. Although that point would almost certainly be higher than we would find if there were no encouragement from the experimenter to continue (which Milgram demonstrated in one of his variations), an interesting question arises: How much obedience would we need to see to consider the results remarkable or even noteworthy? If every participant stopped before reaching, for example, 210 volts, would we have an unsettling demonstration of obedience or a reassuring sign of the participants' resistance to authority?

Most discussions of Milgram's findings implicitly address this question by comparing the actual results with the average person's expectation for what people would do in this situation. Virtually all of us believe that we would resist the experimenter's instructions long before reaching 450 volts. Indeed, when Milgram (1974) asked psychiatrists, college students, and middle-class adults to speculate about what they would do if they were participants in the study, no one said that he or she would continue to anywhere near the highest shock level. Another way to measure expectations is to ask individuals to guess the results of the experiment. When Milgram did just that, he found a near unanimous consensus that no one would continue to administer shocks all the way to 450 volts. The exception to unanimity came from the psychiatrists, who on average estimated that 0.125 percent of the participants would continue to the end, a figure that apparently takes into account the rare sociopath who might make it into the study.

However, the actual results were quite different from these expectations. In the baseline procedure, 26 of 40 participants (65 percent) continued to administer electric shocks all the way to the third press of the 450-volt switch. Far from being the rare exception, fully obeying the authority figure's instructions turned out to be the norm.

The unexpected results challenged many of our assumptions about the nature of destructive obedience and about ourselves. If average citizens can be made to administer excruciating and perhaps lethal electric shocks to an innocent victim, then under the right circumstances each of us may also be capable of engaging in uncharacteristic and unsettling behaviors. People hearing about Milgram's studies for the first time often react by asking, "What's wrong with those people?" But upon reflection, unless we accept that two thirds of the population is made up of brutal, sadistic individuals, we are forced to recognize that the average person's goodness or sense of compassion may not be sufficient to prevent truly deplorable acts.

Milgram was quick to draw parallels between the behavior of his participants and the worst of human behavior—atrocities, massacres, and genocide. In particular, he compared the obedience seen in his experiments to the obedience that allowed the despicable acts committed during the Holocaust in Nazi Germany. "These inhumane policies may have originated in the mind of a single person," Milgram (1963) wrote, "but they could only be carried out on a massive scale if a very large number of persons obeyed orders" (p. 371). Indeed, for several decades, Milgram's work has frequently been invoked to explain atrocious acts and disturbing instances of blind obedience. The examples include the My Lai massacre during the Vietnam War and the abuse of prisoners at Abu Ghraib prison during the Iraq War.

We should also note that expectation numbers Milgram reported have not always been found in subsequent investigations. Whereas Milgram found virtually no cases in which individuals expected participants to continue to 450 volts, one team of investigators reported that 27 percent of their undergraduate participants predicted that the

teacher would continue to the end of the shock generator (Kaufmann & Kooman, 1967). In a review of studies that asked participants to guess the level of obedience in Milgram's baseline procedure, Blass (2000) concluded that the gap between expectations and the participants' actual behavior may not be as large as Milgram believed. Nonetheless, Blass also found that most people still greatly underestimate the level of obedience when trying to predict Milgram's results, and few see themselves continuing for very long in the procedure.

### Variations of the Baseline Procedure

Milgram (1974) conducted at least 17 variations of the experiment, which, including the baseline procedure, he labeled Experiments 1 through 18. In most cases, 40 participants were run in each variation, although occasionally the number was only 20. Some of the more interesting variations will be presented here, and a few additional variations will be described later in this chapter. We should note that although scholars typically interpret each of the variations as if they were conditions in a larger experiment, the research falls short of the usual requirements for a scientific experiment. Rather than randomly assigning participants to different conditions as they arrived, each variation was conducted in its entirety before moving on to the next. As a result, confounds associated with order effects (e.g., changes in the experimenter's or learner's behavior over time) are possible. In addition, as described later, the procedures used in some of the variations opened the door for other confounds. Finally, for the most part, Milgram failed to provide statistical tests of significance or effect size when comparing obedience rates between variations, although these statistics usually can be calculated by the interested reader from the data Milgram did provide. Only once in his two journal articles describing the research did he report the results of a statistical test comparing the rates of obedience between variations (baseline variation versus experimenter absent variation; Milgram, 1965, p. 65).

Milgram was particularly interested in the physical proximity of the teacher and the learner. In Experiment 3, the learner sat in the same room as the teacher, only a few feet away. In Experiment 4, the learner sat near the teacher and received a shock only when he put his hand on a metal shock plate. When the learner refused to cooperate after 150 volts, the experimenter instructed the teacher to force the learner's hand onto the plate to receive the shock, a procedure that was required for each subsequent shock. The increase in physical proximity resulted in a decrease in obedience. Forty percent of the Experiment 3 participants continued to the end of the shock generator, and only 30 percent went all the way to 450 volts in Experiment 4 (both figures are significantly different from the baseline condition).

Milgram (1974) identified several reasons for the lower rates of obedience in these two variations. He suggested that having the learner in the same room made it easier for the teacher to empathize with the learner's suffering and harder for him to deny what was happening to the learner. The teacher also could not easily deny his role in causing the learner's pain. However, placing the learner in the same room as the teacher also introduced a few confounds that make it difficult to interpret the results. For example, in both of these variations the teacher would have been able to see that the learner had neither lost consciousness nor stopped breathing, something he could not be sure of in the baseline procedure. Teachers in Experiment 4 also may have worried about hurting themselves when trying to force the learner's hand onto the shock plate.

Other variations were concerned with the authority figure. In Experiment 6, the experimenter was played by a man Milgram (1974) described as "rather soft and unaggressive." This demeanor contrasted with that of the experimenter who was used in all the other variations. Milgram described the usual experimenter as "impassive" with a "somewhat stern" appearance. Only 50 percent of the participants were fully obedient when the instructions came from the meeker experimenter. Although this finding suggests that characteristics of the authority figure might affect obedience levels, the difference between the conditions falls far short of statistical significance. Moreover, a confound again makes interpretation difficult. Experiment 6 not only included a different experimenter; it also had a different learner. In contrast to the original learner, who "most observers found. . . mild-mannered and likeable," the new learner was a man "possessing a hard bony face and prognothic jaw, who looked as if he would do well in a scrap." Thus, we cannot know whether different outcomes between Experiment 6 and the baseline procedure (albeit small differences) are due to a change in the experimenter, a change in the learner, or both.

Several other variations examined features associated with the experimenter. In Experiment 7, after delivering the initial instructions, the experimenter left the teacher alone in the lab room during the memory test and conducted his interactions with the teacher by telephone. Only 20 percent fully obeyed the experimenter in this variation. To examine the effect of the experimenter's association with Yale University and with academia and science generally, Experiment 10 was conducted in a "somewhat run-down commercial building" in nearby Bridgeport, Connecticut, with no apparent ties to any academic institution. The rate of full obedience dropped to 47.5 percent in this variation. However, the difference between this and the baseline condition falls short of statistical significance. In Experiment 13, the experimenter supposedly was called away shortly after the session started, and a male confederate posing as another participant assumed the experimenter's role. The confederate then came up with the idea to give incrementally stronger shocks for each wrong answer. He also provided the prods and statement usually delivered by the experimenter. Only 20 percent of the real participants followed this ordinary man's instructions to 450 volts. In short, several features related to the authority figure appear to affect obedience. Participants seem more likely to engage in destructive obedience when the authority figure is physically present and when his credentials as an authority are clear.

Milgram also wondered whether the learner could do or say anything to reduce the likelihood that he would be the victim of obedience. Perhaps surprisingly, adding the learner's comments about having a heart condition did not make a difference. In an earlier variation (Experiment 2) that was identical to the baseline procedure with the exception of being conducted in a different lab and including no mention of a heart condition, 62.5 percent of the participants followed the experimenter's instructions to the end of the procedure. In Experiment 9, before signing a general release form, the learner paused and said in front of the teacher, "I'll agree to be in it, but only on condition that you let me out when I say so; that's the only condition." The experimenter agreed to the condition but nonetheless gave the same instructions and prods as in the baseline procedure. Full obedience dropped to 40 percent in this variation (significantly different from the baseline condition), suggesting that there may in fact be something the learner can say that affects obedience.

Investigators have discovered that Milgram conducted at least one other variation that he did not report in any of his writings. According to documents in the Milgram archives, a variation was conducted at the Bridgeport location in which male participants were asked to bring a male friend with them to the experiment (Rochat & Blass, 2014; Rochat & Modigliani, 1997). The friend was always assigned to the learner's role, and a research assistant coached the friend so that he gave responses that matched the learner's scripted responses in the baseline procedure. Of the 20 participants in this variation, only 3 (15 percent) continued to press the shock switches all the way to 450 volts.

## Ethical Concerns

Among the legacies of Milgram's obedience studies is the impact the research had on subsequent standards for and discussions about the ethical treatment of participants in psychological experiments. Shortly after the publication of Milgram's first article on the research in October 1963, the studies were challenged on ethical grounds in academic and mass media outlets (Blass, 2004). It is difficult to know the extent to which the controversy over Milgram's research contributed to the implementation of federal and American Psychological Association guidelines for the ethical treatment of human participants and the requirement for institutional review boards (IRBs) that came into practice in the 1970s. However, Milgram's experiments certainly were part of the conversation when these policies were being developed and today are often presented in textbooks and IRB training modules as an example of why such policies are needed (Benjamin & Simpson, 2009).

### Criticisms of Milgram's Procedures

Much of the criticism of Milgram's research focused on the intense stress his participants experienced (Baumrind, 1964; Kelman, 1967; Mixon, 1976). In Milgram's (1963) own words, "In a large number of cases the degree of tension reached extremes that are rarely seen in sociopsychological laboratory studies. Subjects were observed to sweat, tremble, stutter, bite their lips, groan, and dig their fingernails into their flesh. These were characteristic rather than exceptional responses to the experiment" (p. 375). Although Milgram (1964) claimed that he had not anticipated this high level of stress, critics argued that he should have ended the experiment when the actual degree of emotional discomfort to participants became evident (Baumrind, 1964).

Other observers were concerned with the potential long-term consequences of participating in the research (Baumrind, 1964; Kelman, 1967). Despite the fact that no actual shocks were given, fully obedient participants were left with the knowledge

that they had administered what they believed to be potentially harmful electric shocks to another human being. Critics argued that this awareness could result in long-term negative effects for some participants. Other ethical questions raised about Milgram's studies include the value of the experience for the participant and for society versus the potential harms to the participant, the use of deception, and the lack of informed consent.

In his defense, Milgram was not unconcerned about the welfare of his participants. He pointed to data from a follow-up survey in which the vast majority of participants (83.7 percent) indicated that they were either glad or very glad that they had been a part of the experiment (Milgram, 1964, 1974). Only 1.3 percent said they were sorry or very sorry to have participated. When asked whether more studies of this kind should be conducted, 80 percent said yes and just over 3 percent said no. Seventy-four percent reported that they had learned "something of personal importance" from being in the study. Of course, there are reasons to question the accuracy of the survey data, including the possibility that cognitive dissonance could have caused some participants to remember the experience more fondly than it actually was (Blass, 2004).

### Conducting Post-Milgram Obedience Experiments

It is widely recognized that an exact replication of Milgram's obedience studies would be out-of-bounds by today's ethical standards (Benjamin & Simpson, 2009). This situation places social influence researchers in a difficult position. Milgram left us some intriguing findings on an important topic that, like all good research, generated many questions that cry out for additional experiments. However, because of ethical concerns, these questions cannot be examined using the same procedures Milgram employed.

Researchers have responded to this dilemma with a number of strategies. One approach employs role playing (Geller, 1978). Participants in these studies typically are placed in a setting that resembles Milgram's lab and are asked to imagine themselves in the teacher's role or, in some cases, to imagine what someone in the teacher's role might have done. It is made clear to participants at the outset that the shocks are not real and that the learner and experimenter are actors. Some of these investigations do report findings similar to Milgram's (Geller, 1978; Mixon, 1976; O'Leary, Willis, & Tomich, 1970). However, whether these role-playing participants are as emotionally engaged or go through the same psychological experiences as someone who believes he or she is administering painful and perhaps dangerous electric shocks remains an issue (Geller, 1978; Miller, 1972).

More recently, researchers have created virtual reality versions of Milgram's experimental situation (Dambrun & Vatine, 2010). Like participants in the role-playing experiments, participants in virtual reality studies also understand that the shocks are not real and that they are watching actors and listening to prerecorded sounds. However, the visual and auditory information they receive allows them to better imagine themselves in the teacher's position and to become more emotionally involved than participants in a simple role-playing investigation. Researchers using this methodology often find results similar to Milgram's (Dambrun & Vatine, 2010; Slater et al., 2006), but questions remain about the comparability of the experience with what Milgram's participants went through.

Other investigators have attempted to recreate obedience situations similar to Milgram's that do not require participants to physically harm another individual. One team of researchers instructed teachers to administer what the participants believed to be increasingly unpleasant blasts of noise (Zeigler-Hill, Southard, Archer, & Donohoe, 2013). In another set of studies, participants administered an exam to a person supposedly applying for a job (Meeus & Raaijmakers, 1986, 1995). Instead of electric shocks, the experimenter instructed participants to make negative comments when the applicant made a mistake. The 15 comments participants were told to deliver were increasingly stress-inducing and derogatory (e.g., "If you continue like this, you will certainly fail the test"). The applicant indicated that he found the comments quite distressing and that the comments were causing him to perform poorly on the exam, which meant he would not get the job. The researchers found that 91.7 percent of the participants continued the procedures all the way to the last of the comments. To support the claim that this experience was similar to what Milgram's participants went through, the researchers pointed out that, as in Milgram's studies, the rate of obedience changed as a function of the situation. For example, the investigators found that obedience rates dropped when the experimenter left the room.

Finally, Burger (2009) conducted a partial replication of Milgram's procedures designed to avoid many of the ethical concerns while still placing participants in a situation in which they believed they were administering real electric shocks. Changes to Milgram's procedures included screening participants to eliminate those who might have a negative emotional reaction to the experience, informing participants repeatedly that they could end the study at any time, explaining to participants within a few seconds of ending the study that the shocks were not real, and using a clinical psychologist as the experimenter who was prepared to end the session if he saw signs of excessive stress. Most important, the experimenter ended the session as soon as the teacher gave his or her response following the learner's protests at 150 volts. Burger (2009) refers to this moment in the study as something of a point of no return. In Milgram's basic procedure, nearly 80 percent of the participants who continued past 150 volts went all the way to the end of the shock generator. Thus, knowing how participants respond at this decisive juncture allows researchers to make a reasonable guess about what participants would have done if the experiment had continued.

Seventy percent of the participants in the replication continued the test past 150 volts, compared to 82.5 percent of Milgram's participants. The results suggest that average citizens today are as capable of destructive obedience as they were half a century ago. However, observers have raised questions about the comparability of the partial replication and Milgram's procedures (Elms, 2009; Miller, 2009). For example, Burger eliminated participants who might have had a negative emotional reaction to the experience, but Milgram did not. This step may have created important differences between Burger's participants and Milgram's. In addition, reminding participants that they could end the study at any time could have affected how they responded to the experimenter's instructions. Finally, drawing comparisons from the partial replication to Milgram's studies rests on an untested assumption about how participants would have acted had they been allowed to continue the procedure past 150 volts.

## Individual Differences in Obedience

Milgram's research is often held up as an example of the power of the situation (Benjamin & Simpson, 2009; Blass, 2004). The individuals who participated in the research were most likely decent and compassionate people who, left to their own preferences, would never have thought to administer painful electric shocks to a mild-mannered and likeable man. Nonetheless, two thirds of the participants in the baseline procedure found themselves in a situation that led them to act in seemingly brutal ways.

Discussions of Milgram's results typically focus on the large number of participants who continued to press the switches, but some researchers have taken a different approach. What about the participants who opted to not obey the experimenter? What is it about these disobedient participants that allowed them to resist the experimenter's instructions when so many others could not? Although powerful situational forces no doubt influenced the participants' behavior in Milgram's studies, not everyone reacted to these forces in the same way. A complete understanding of obedience requires that we consider both situational factors as well as individual differences (Blass, 1991; Staub, 2014). Milgram would not have disagreed with this observation. As he and one of his students put it, "(D)ifferences in response suggest strongly that personality variables, as well as situational determinants, influence the degree of willingness to obey authoritative command" (Elms & Milgram, 1966, p. 282).

Identifying differences between obedient and disobedient participants not only provides clues about why people obey or disobey orders, finding these individual differences can also suggest avenues for preventing destructive obedience. It is easy to suggest a number of individual difference variables that could conceivably be related to obedience—age, social class, education, religion, and so on. Unfortunately, we have very little data for most of these variables. At best, we have enough empirical data to make a few reasonable observations for three individual difference variables. These three are culture, gender, and personality.

## Culture

Do obedience levels vary as a function of culture? This question has been a concern of obedience researchers from the outset. While developing his procedures for the Yale University studies, Milgram had ideas about also conducting the research overseas. In a 1960 letter to Harvard psychologist Gordon Allport, he described plans for a "project on German character—in which comparative experimental measures of 'obedience to authority' will play an important part" (Blass, 2004, p. 65). Like many scholars during that time, Milgram apparently believed that something about German culture had made possible the widespread obedience that allowed the atrocities committed during the Holocaust. However, he abandoned the idea after discovering that high rates of obedience could be found in American citizens (Blass, 2012).

Nonetheless, there are reasons to suspect that obedience might be affected by culture. Researchers often divide cultures into individualistic and collectivist categories (Triandis, 1989). People who live in individualistic cultures tend to think of themselves as independent and unique, whereas those from collectivist cultures are more concerned with cooperation and being part of the larger community. It is reasonable to speculate from these descriptions that we might find more obedience in collectivist cultures than in individualistic cultures. Unfortunately, to date this hypothesis has not been tested directly, that is, in an experiment in which individuals from more than one culture are examined under identical experimental circumstances.

However, obedience studies have been conducted in several countries. Blass (2012) located nine methodological replications of Milgram's basic procedure conducted outside the United States. The studies were conducted in eight different nations: Italy, South Africa, Germany, Australia, Jordan, Spain, India, and Austria. Blass compared these investigations to similar studies conducted in the United States (including Milgram's). The average percentage of American participants who followed the experimenter's orders to the end of the procedures was 60.94 percent. The average percentage for the non-American participants was 65.94 percent, not significantly different from the Americans. The conclusions we can draw from this comparison are limited by a number of methodological concerns, such as the inclusion of cultures based on availability rather than theory and the lumping of all non-American cultures into one category. Nonetheless, based on the limited amount of data available, we find no evidence for cultural differences in obedience.

## Gender

All but one of Milgram's variations were conducted exclusively with male participants, an observation that begs the question of whether similar results would be found with female participants. Milgram (1974) identified two gender differences that could have an effect on obedience in his experimental setting. He noted that women were sometimes found to be more compliant than men, suggesting that women might be more willing to go along with the experimenter's instructions. However, he also recognized that women tended to be more empathic and less aggressive than men, which could make women less likely to harm the person on the other side of the wall. To examine the role of gender, Milgram conducted one version of the baseline procedure using only female participants (Experiment 8). Remarkably, the women continued to obey the experimenter all the way to the end of the shock generator at exactly the same rate—65 percent—as the men.

In a review of methodological replications of Milgram's basic procedures, Blass (2000) found nine studies that included both male and female participants. No gender differences in obedience rates were found in eight of the nine experiments. The exception to the rule was a study conducted in Australia by Kilham and Mann (1974), which found higher rates for male participants. Consistent with the general pattern, neither Meeus and Raaijmakers (1986) in their job applicant stress studies nor Burger (2009) in his partial replication of Milgram's procedures found a gender difference in the rate of obedience.

But these findings do not mean that men and women had identical experiences during the experimental sessions. In postexperimental questionnaires, Milgram (1974) asked participants to indicate on a scale how "tense or nervous" they were at the point at which they experienced their highest level of tension. The obedient women reported higher levels of tension than did obedient men in any of Milgram's variations. However, Milgram also reported that this gender difference was limited to participants who continued all the way to the end of the shock generator. Similarly, Shanab and Yahya (1977) recorded visible indicators of tension—"nervous laughter, lip biting, trembling, and the like" (p. 534)—in their obedience study with Jordanian children ages 6 through 16. Although the researchers found no gender differences in the rate of obedience, significantly more girls (42 percent) than boys (16 percent) expressed signs of tension during the session. In short, women may experience higher levels of concern for the learner's well-being during the experiment, but other factors prevent this concern from translating into disobedience.

There are other ways gender could play a role in destructive obedience, none of which have been examined empirically. For example, it is possible that participants would react differently to a female authority figure. Researchers sometimes find that men are more able to resist influence attempts that come from women than those that come from men (Carli, 2001). Similarly, whether the gender of the learner makes a difference remains an open question. And, of course, there are all the possible gender combinations of participants, experimenters, and learners that have yet to be studied.

## Personality

Relatively few obedience studies have included measures of personality, and many of the personality traits that have been examined have only a tenuous theoretical relationship to obedience (Blass, 1991). Nonetheless, data on three personality traits that could play a role in obedience situations are worth mentioning: authoritarianism, personal control, and empathy.

First, early efforts by psychologists to explain the rise of fascism in Nazi Germany focused on a collection of individual characteristics that comprised what researchers called an "authoritarian personality" (Adorno, Frenkel-Brunswik, Levinson, & Sanford, 1950). The characteristics said to make up this personality included, among others, an adherence to traditional beliefs, a preoccupation with violence, and a submissive and uncritical attitude toward authority figures. Subsequent work on this concept led to scales measuring *authoritarianism* or *right-wing authoritarianism* (Altemeyer, 1998).

The first evidence connecting authoritarianism with obedience came from a study conducted by Milgram and one of his students. Elms and Milgram (1966) contacted some of the original participants several months after the obedience studies were completed. Twenty obedient and 20 disobedient participants completed a measure of authoritarianism. As predicted, obedient participants scored significantly higher on this measure than disobedient participants. Similarly, in their virtual reality study of obedience, Dambrun and Vatine (2010) found a positive relationship between the highest shock participants delivered and their scores on a measure of authoritarianism. Participants in another investigation watched a video clip from Milgram's studies and were asked to indicate the extent to which the teacher was responsible for the learner receiving electric shocks against his will (Blass, 1995). Participants high in authoritarianism were less likely than those low in this trait to say the teacher was responsible for delivering the shocks. That is, the high authoritarian participants were more likely to believe that the teacher was simply doing what the authority figure demanded and therefore was not responsible for what happened to the learner.

Second, whether individuals follow or defy orders may depend on the extent to which they feel in control or want to be in control of what is happening in the situation. Measures of *locus of control* identify the extent to which people generally believe that what happens to them is under their control or whether events are more often controlled by external forces, such as powerful others or luck (Rotter, 1966). A few obedience studies have included measures of locus of control, but to date the findings from this research are not entirely consistent and often involve interactions with situational variables (Blass, 1991). Nonetheless, the results tend to support the expectation that those who generally believe they are in control of what happens to them are less likely to go along with the experimenter's instructions than those who believe other people are often in control (Blass, 1991).

We can also look at the extent to which individuals are generally motivated to see themselves in control of the events in their lives, what researchers refer to as *desire for control* (Burger, 1992). In Milgram's experimental setting, we might expect that people who are highly motivated to see themselves in control would be less likely to relinquish control to the experimenter. To test this possibility, participants in Burger's (2009) partial replication completed a measure of desire for control one week before they participated in the study. In the condition designed to resemble Milgram's baseline procedure, participants who refused to continue had significantly higher desire for control scores than those who did not stop. These participants with a high desire for control also tended to require prods from the experimenter earlier in the procedure.

Third, it is common for people encountering Milgram's research to lament the participants' lack of empathy for the learner's suffering. Indeed, Milgram (1974) occasionally described the teacher's dilemma as something of a tug-of-war between a desire to please the experimenter on one side and empathy for the learner's plight on the other. He attributed the lower obedience rates when the learner and teacher were in the same room to "empathic responses" triggered by the arrangement. To examine the role of empathy in obedience, Burger (2009) included in his partial replication a measure of *empathic concern*, the extent to which individuals typically experience compassion and sympathy for people in unfortunate circumstances (Davis, 1994). As expected, empathic concern was related to how participants responded to the learner's discomfort and pain. The higher the participants' level of empathy, the earlier they received their first prod. However, this concern for the learner's suffering did not translate into an increase in disobedience. Mean empathic concern

scores for the disobedient participants were not different from those of the obedient participants.

In sum, we have some evidence that personality traits can affect obedience. Participants low in authoritarianism as well as those who generally see themselves in control and want to be in control are less likely to go along with the experimenter's instructions to administer shocks in Milgram's procedure. However, a strong empathic reaction to the learner's pain may not cause participants to stop administering electric shocks.

## Explaining the Results

One curious feature of Milgram's research is that it has achieved widespread and long-lasting attention despite—or, some might argue, because of—the fact that there is no agreed-upon explanation for the high rates of obedience. From the beginning, Milgram was more interested in demonstrating the effect than in developing a comprehensive theory, and his initial efforts to publish the research were rejected for lack of theory (Blass, 2004). Although the studies were completed in 1962, Milgram's book describing the work in detail did not appear until 1974, a gap that reflects in part the challenge to develop a theory to go along with his data (Elms, 1995). Unfortunately, as described next, the theory he eventually came up with has not held up well to scrutiny. Scholars from various academic disciplines have attempted to fill the subsequent vacuum, proposing accounts that range from mathematical models (Rochat, Maggioni, & Modigliani, 2000) to rhetorical analyses (Gibson, 2013b, 2014). This is not to say that psychologists have no idea why Milgram's participants acted the way they did. On the contrary, at least two fruitful social psychological approaches for understanding obedience have surfaced in recent years. These approaches focus on the relationship between the experimenter and the teacher and on the situational features in Milgram's procedure known to affect social influence processes.

### Milgram's Agentic State Theory

Milgram (1974) proposed that his obedient participants, like individuals who obey orders from authority figures in other situations, had fallen into an "agentic state," that is, an altered state of mind in which the individual "sees himself as an agent for carrying out another person's wishes" (p. 133). After going through this transformation, participants are no longer torn between their concern for the learner and the demands of the experimenter. Rather, they focus their attention on the experimenter "with maximal receptivity to the emissions of the authority, whereas the learner's signals are muted and psychologically remote" (p. 144). Decisions about right and wrong are relinquished to the experimenter and "(p)unishment of the learner shrinks to an insignificant part of the total experience" (p. 143).

Milgram's description of an altered state of consciousness was similar to explanations often invoked by psychologists at that time to explain behavior under hypnosis. Like those explanations, the notion of an agentic state is not widely accepted today (Burger, 2014; Reicher & Haslam, 2011). Some of the problems with Milgram's explanation were immediately evident. The filmed images we have of his participants do not reveal teachers paying attention only to the experimenter and virtually ignoring the learner. Quite the opposite. Participants were keenly aware of the learner's suffering and had strong emotional reactions to the screams and protests they heard through the wall. Milgram's postsession questionnaire data make the same point. His participants, particularly those who continued to the end of the shock generator, reported that they were highly stressed about the situation and not, as the agentic state explanation suggests, indifferent to the learner's pain.

## The Relationship Between Experimenter and Teacher

One promising approach for understanding obedience focuses on the relationship between the experimenter and the teacher. Indeed, the phrase "obedience to authority" implies that the subordinate member in the dyad is responding to the person in power. To better understand this relationship, investigators have turned to some well-established concepts from social psychology.

One of these concepts is impression management or self-presentation. Decades of research have demonstrated that people's actions often reflect a concern for what others think about them (Schlenker & Pontari, 2000). In Milgram's studies, hesitant participants may have been faced with the difficult task of figuring out how to reject the experimenter's instructions in a socially appropriate way (Collins & Brief, 1995; Collins & Ma, 2000). A participant who abruptly refuses to follow the experimenter's instructions could come across as disrespectful, insulting, or rude. Because he was not entirely sure about how he was supposed to act, a disobedient participant would also run the risk of appearing ignorant or foolish. An examination of the experimenter's statements and general demeanor during

the study supports this analysis. The experimenter tended to deflect or dismiss the participant's objections, thereby making it increasingly difficult for the participant to politely get out of the situation (Modigliani & Rochat, 1995).

To test this interpretation, one team of researchers presented participants with a videotape described as a segment from an actual experiment using Milgram's procedures (Collins & Ma, 2000). Participants saw a teacher who either politely obeyed the experimenter, politely disobeyed ("I don't mean to be disrespectful, sir, but . . ."), or defiantly disobeyed ("You gotta be out of your mind if you think I'm going on with this"). Although we might expect the teacher who boldly expressed his convictions to be the most admired, this was not the case. The defiant teacher was seen as less desirable than the teacher who disobeyed politely, a finding that may reflect the thinking of Milgram's participants who struggled to find a socially appropriate way out of the experiment.

Although it is reasonable to believe that self-presentation concerns contributed to the participants' reluctance to defy the experimenter, an explanation of obedience based solely on impression management seems incomplete. Most likely, these concerns may have influenced the participants' behavior during the early stages of the experiment. But it is difficult to imagine that participants would overlook the learner's screams of pain and, at a later point, his apparent physical inability to respond simply because they did not want to appear rude.

A related interpretation of Milgram's findings examines the extent to which the teacher identifies with either the experimenter or the learner (Haslam, Reicher, & Birney, 2014; Reicher & Haslam, 2011; Reicher, Haslam, & Smith, 2012). Borrowing from social identity theory (Hogg, 2012), advocates for this view argue that the teacher is forced to decide between the seemingly reasonable interests of two groups. He can side with the experimenter and the scientific community the experimenter represents and continue with the experiment, or he can side with the learner and the general public the learner represents and stop the painful shocks. When the experimental setting is arranged to make the interests of one group more salient than the other, the teacher is likely to identify with the salient group and make decisions about continuing the procedure accordingly. For example, when much of the imprimatur of science was removed by conducting the study in an office building in downtown Bridgeport rather than at Yale University, rates of obedience fell. Similarly, when Milgram placed the learner physically close to the teacher, thus making the learner's suffering more salient, obedience rates also fell. We should note that Milgram (1974) also attributed this latter effect in part to a change in the relationship between the teacher and the learner. When the experimenter and the participant were alone in the lab room, "(t)here is incipient group formation between the experimenter and the subject, from which the victim is excluded,"... but "(w)hen the victim is placed close to the subject, it becomes easier to form an alliance with him against the experimenter" (p. 39).

Reicher et al. (2012) argue that going along with the experimenter's instructions is not an act of obedience as much as an act of "followership." Like military personnel who carry out the wishes of their leaders, Milgram's participants who identified largely with the experimenter continued the memory test as a way to help the experimenter reach his goal. In support of this interpretation, individuals in one study were asked to read descriptions of 15 of Milgram's variations (Reicher et al., 2012). Participants rated each setting for the extent to which the teacher would likely identify with the experimenter and the scientific community or with the learner and the general public. These ratings tended to correlate with the actual rates of obedience Milgram found in his research. That is, situations seen as making the experimenter and the cause of science salient were associated with increased rates of obedience, and situations seen as making the learner and the rights of the general public salient were associated with lower rates of obedience.

Although intuitively appealing, the social identity explanation has been proposed only recently and is in need of direct empirical tests for many of its assumptions. In particular, investigations that manipulate and measure the extent to which participants identify with either the experimenter or learner are required. In addition, as currently described, the explanation seems to be at odds with findings from some obedience studies. First, Reicher et al. (2012) argue that participants are most likely to resist the experimenter's instructions when they are "committed to the well-being of ordinary members of the community as represented by the learner" (p. 322) and motivated by "a concern with his [the learner's] fate" (p. 323). However, as described earlier, participants who are highly concerned about the learner's plight (empathic individuals, women) are no more likely to defy the experimenter than those who are less concerned. Second, obedient

participants are said to "act as they do to the extent that they believe in, and hence are committed to, the scientific enterprise that the experimenter is leading" (Reicher et al., 2012, p. 322). However, as described later, there is ample evidence that participants are more likely to follow the experimenter's instructions when they are able to psychologically separate and distance themselves from the experimenter. In particular, participants are more obedient when they deny personal responsibility for any harm that comes to the learner and instead attribute that responsibility to the experimenter (e.g., "It's him, not me").

In short, the extent to which individuals identify with the authority figure may play a role in the decision to obey or refuse that person's instructions. However, research in support of this explanation is needed and to date a simple social identity interpretation does not seem to fully account for Milgram's findings.

### Situational Variables and Social Influence

Psychologists sometimes refer to the obedience studies as an example of a "strong situation" (Benjamin & Simpson, 2009). That is, although individual variables like personality and personal values often affect behavior, sometimes aspects of the situation overpower these internal influences. As a result, individuals may engage in surprising and sometimes disturbing uncharacteristic acts.

Researchers have identified several situational features in Milgram's laboratory setting that are likely to have affected the participant's decision about whether to continue the experiment (Burger, 2014). Each of these situational variables has been studied extensively in social influence studies not directly tied to obedience, thus making an empirical case for how the variables might have affected participants in Milgram's experiment.

What are the situational variables that led to the high obedience rates? There are probably several (Burger, 2014), but we will look at three here. First, a large amount of research finds that people who agree to perform a small request are more likely to later agree to a similar but larger request than people presented only with the larger request (Burger, 1999). Milgram took advantage of this "foot-in-the-door" effect by instructing his participants to begin with a 15-volt shock for the first mistake and to increase punishments in 15-volt increments for each subsequent mistake. The procedures were arranged so that participants had already administered 10 shocks before hearing the learner's first demands to be released from the study. Research on the foot-in-the-door effect suggests that each press of a switch made it easier for the participant to press the next switch.

Consistent with this analysis, an examination of Milgram's data finds the most likely point for participants to end the experiment was immediately after hearing the learner's protests following the 150-volt shock (Burger, 2009; Gilbert, 1981). This is the one point in the procedure at which pressing the next switch may not have been seen as a continuation of the same behavior. That is, administering shocks before the protests is a qualitatively (as compared to quantitatively) different act than administering shocks to a protesting learner (Gilbert, 1981). If this was how participants perceived the situation, then the power of the foot-in-the-door effect would have been diminished. On the other hand, participants who decided they were going to follow the experimenter's instructions despite the learner's protests found no other obvious stopping point as they worked their way across the shock generator (Packer, 2008).

Second, Milgram created a situation that made it easy for participants to deny or diffuse responsibility for any harm that came to the learner. Numerous studies demonstrate that individuals often avoid taking responsibility when negative consequences are possible and that people are more likely to engage in harmful and antisocial acts when responsibility for their actions is removed (Bandura, 1999). In Milgram's experiments, participants could tell themselves that the experimenter, the principal investigator, the university, or even the learner himself was responsible for the learner's suffering. Indeed, if participants asked about responsibility, the experimenter stated that he—the experimenter—was responsible. This perception was further reinforced by having the learner direct his demands to be released to the experimenter (e.g., "Experimenter, get me out of here!").

The role of perceived responsibility in obedience was demonstrated by a team of investigators who coded spontaneous comments participants made during Burger's (2009) partial replication of Milgram's procedures (Burger, Girgis, & Manning, 2011). Only 12.5 percent of the participants who continued to the end of the procedures made any comment indicating that they felt some responsibility for what was happening to the learner. In contrast, 66.7 percent of the participants who discontinued the memory test indicated that they felt responsible.

Third, Milgram arranged the experimental setting so that participants had little information about how they were supposed to act in this unusual situation. It is a fair assumption that few of Milgram's participants had ever been in a psychology experiment, and certainly none had ever been in a situation in which they were instructed to administer painful electric shocks to a protesting individual. People who find themselves in a new and unusual situation typically seek information about how they are supposed to act (Cialdini, Kallgren, & Reno, 1991). One way to obtain this information is to observe what others are doing; another is to find an expert who can tell you what to do. Except for one variation, Milgram provided his participants with no direct information about how other participants responded to the dilemma they found themselves in. However, Milgram did provide an expert, that is, the experimenter who presumably knew all about the procedures and had seen many other participants in this situation. The experimenter essentially communicated to the teacher that there was nothing to be alarmed about and that continuing the test was the appropriate thing to do. Thus, participants may have acquiesced to the experimenter's orders not because he was an authority figure, but because he was a source of information. As Morelli (1983) described this distinction, it is the difference between being *an* authority and being *in* authority.

Support for this analysis can be found in two of Milgram's variations. In Experiment 15, two experimenters conducted the study. After hearing the learner's protests at 150 volts, one experimenter instructed the teacher to continue, but the other experimenter said the test should stop. Thus, the experimenters failed to communicate clearly that it was appropriate and normal to continue the study. Of the 19 participants placed in this situation (one had stopped earlier), all but one refused to press any more switches. The one participant who proceeded past this point pressed only one more switch before quitting. In Experiment 17, participants witnessed two other teachers (really confederates) disobey the experimenter. Teacher 1 refused to continue after hearing the learner's protests at 150 volts. Teacher 2 refused to participate at 210 volts. The experimenter then turned to Teacher 3, the real participant, and asked him to continue the test. Only 10 percent of the participants in this variation followed the experimenter's instructions all the way to 450 volts.

In short, in many ways the obedience studies can be seen as a dramatic demonstration of some basic social influence processes that investigators have examined in other research settings. That Milgram designed his procedures before most of this research was conducted suggests he had an intuitive grasp for how the situational variables he built into his experiment could lead to his otherwise surprising results.

## The Holocaust Question

From the outset, Milgram's findings have been used to explain the widespread obedience that contributed to the deplorable acts performed during the Holocaust in Nazi Germany. Presentations of Milgram's work in textbooks and in popular media are often accompanied with images of concentration camps, Nazi soldiers, or Adolf Hitler. It would be easy to get the impression that scholars widely consider Milgram's research an important contribution to our understanding of the horrible events that occurred during that time and place. But in fact, the extent to which the obedience studies tell us something about the Holocaust is the subject of a long-standing academic debate (Miller, 2004; Overy, 2014; Staub, 2014).

Challenges to Milgram's assertion that his work was useful in understanding the Holocaust appeared shortly after his first published article on the research (Baumrind, 1964). Critics argue that a complex phenomenon like the Holocaust was the result of multiple causes that simply cannot be captured in a laboratory experiment. Moreover, the Holocaust took place within a historical and cultural context that evolved over many years. A key feature of that context was the dehumanization of Jews and other persecuted groups (Fenigstein, 1998), which allowed the perpetrators to engage in the cruel treatment of their victims without guilt or remorse (Bandura, 1999).

Critics also point out that Milgram's participants were operating under very different motives than the perpetrators of the Holocaust (Fenigstein, 1998; Helm & Morelli, 1985). Milgram's participants were doing their best to participate in a scientific experiment—a laudable endeavor—and they were clearly upset about the apparent suffering of the man on the other side of the wall. There is no evidence that any of Milgram's participants enjoyed the experience. As Fenigstein (1998) notes,

"the historical evidence on the spontaneity, initiative, enthusiasm, and pride with which the Nazis degraded, tortured, and killed their victims ... has no counterpart in the behavior that Milgram observed in his laboratory studies" (p. 68). Whereas Holocaust perpetrators shared common goals with their commanders and saw their atrocious acts as helping to fulfill those goals, Milgram's participants may have had only a vague idea about what the study was about or how their behavior contributed to the experimenter's goal (Staub, 1989). Those who committed atrocities during the Holocaust typically did so without direct supervision, often creating their own methods for carrying out the inhumane acts. However, Milgram's participants appeared to require a nearby and continually directive experimenter to continue their involvement (Darley, 1995).

Finally, applying Milgram's findings to the Holocaust raises the uncomfortable question of exoneration (Mandel, 1998; Miller, 2004). That is, psychologists widely accept that the obedience demonstrated by Milgram's participants was largely a result of the situation participants found themselves in rather than a reflection of their character. No one blames obedient participants for acting the way they did; they were simply doing what they believed the situation called for. But if we extend this reasoning to the perpetrators of the Holocaust, we come disturbingly close to accepting the "just doing my duty" defense for inhumane acts. One might argue that, like Milgram's participants, the perpetrators of these acts were simply reacting to the situation they found themselves in. It is important to note that no responsible social psychologist has ever used Milgram's research to exonerate those who carried out the deplorable acts that characterized the Holocaust or to condone those acts (Miller, 2004). Nonetheless, many find the possibility of such a defense disturbing (Fenigstein, 1998; Mandel, 1998).

It is unlikely that the debate over the relevance of Milgram's research to the Holocaust will end any time soon. But even if one completely rejects the connection, it would be difficult to deny the importance of the obedience studies. Milgram demonstrated that under the right circumstances average citizens could be made to do something as unexpected and unsettling as administering potentially dangerous electric shocks to an innocent person, a finding that surely has implications for a large number of behaviors.

## Directions for Future Research

Few investigations in psychology have had the shelf life of Milgram's obedience studies. Not only has the work retained a significant presence in social psychology textbooks, but interest in Milgram's research, as indicated by journal citations, has risen in recent years (Reicher et al., 2014). In part because of the ethical concerns that limit our ability to conduct research in this area, many important questions remain unanswered. Briefly, here are some suggested directions for future research.

First, investigators should continue to develop new procedures for studying the kind of destructive obedience Milgram demonstrated in his research. However, this may be easier said than done. The challenge is to create situations that do not cause excessive stress for participants but in which participants nonetheless believe they may be doing real harm. Inherent in this challenge is the implied understanding that genuine "obedience to authority" requires the perpetrator do something he or she would not have chosen to do without the authority figure's orders.

Second, researchers can study obedience by using new operational definitions of their concepts and by conducting their investigations in new settings. Virtually all of the research on obedience in the past half century has relied on a variation of Milgram's procedures. But there are many other situations in which a person in authority gives orders/demands/instructions to individuals of lower status. Doctors, teachers, police officers, bosses, judges, supervisors, parents, elected officials, and group leaders, to name a few, can be authority figures. The orders these individuals give need not be as destructive as administering electric shocks to a protesting victim. Researchers can look at when and why people follow instructions to stay out, don't touch, take their medicine, bend the rules, and so on. Studies conducted outside the laboratory can be especially informative, although this kind of research often raises additional ethical concerns.

Third, investigators need not limit themselves to the destructive side of obedience. In many situations, obeying commands is appropriate and beneficial. In addition to preventing destructive obedience, we should explore how to increase positive obedience; that is, how can we get people to follow instructions from medical professionals, firefighters, lifeguards, and so on? These are among the many questions about obedience in need of investigation but which to date may have been lost in the shadow of Milgram's monumental contribution to the field.

## References

Adorno, T. W., Frenkel-Brunswik, E., Levinson, D., & Sanford, N. (1950). *The authoritarian personality*. New York, NY: Norton.

Altemeyer, B. (1998). The other "authoritarian personality." In M. P. Zanna (Ed.), *Advances in experimental social psychology* (Vol. 30, pp. 47–92). San Diego, CA: Elsevier.

Bandura, A. (1999). Moral disengagement in the perpetration of inhumanities. *Personality and Social Psychology Review, 3*, 193–209. doi:10.1207/s15327957pspr0303_3

Baumrind, D. (1964). Some thoughts on ethics of research: After reading Milgram's "Behavioral study of obedience." *American Psychologist, 19*, 421–423. doi:10.1037/h0040128

Benjamin, L. T., & Simpson, J. A. (2009). The power of the situation: The impact of Milgram's obedience studies on personality and social psychology. *American Psychologist, 64*, 12–19. doi:10.1037/a0014077

Blass, T. (1991). Understanding behavior in the Migram obedience experiments: The role of personality, situations, and their interactions. *Journal of Personality and Social Psychology, 60*, 398–413. doi:10.1037/0022-3514.60.3.398

Blass, T. (1995). Right-wing authoritarianism and role as predictors of attributions about obedience to authority. *Personality and Individual Differences, 19*, 99–100. doi:10.1016/0191-8869(95)00004-P

Blass, T. (2000). The Milgram paradigm after 35 years: Some things we now know about obedience to authority. In T. Blass (Ed.), *Obedience to authority: Current perspectives on the Milgram paradigm* (pp. 35–59). Mahwah, NJ: Erlbaum.

Blass, T. (2004). *The man who shocked the world: The life and legacy of Stanley Milgram*. New York, NY: Basic Books.

Blass, T. (2012). A cross-cultural comparison of studies of obedience using the Milgram paradigm: A review. *Social and Personality Psychology Compass, 6*, 196–205. doi:10.1111/j.1751-9004.2011.00417.x

Burger, J. M. (1992). *Desire for control: Personality, social and clinical perspectives*. New York, NY: Plenum Publishing.

Burger, J. M. (1999). The foot-in-the-door compliance procedure: A multiple-process analysis and review. *Personality and Social Psychology Review, 3*, 303–325. doi:10.1207/s15327957pspr0304_2

Burger, J. M. (2009). Replicating Milgram: Would people still obey today? *American Psychologist, 64*, 1–11. doi:10.1037/a0010932

Burger, J. M. (2014). Situational features in Milgram's experiment that kept his participants shocking. *Journal of Social Issues, 70*, 489–500. doi:10.1111/josi.12073

Burger, J. M., Girgis, Z. M., & Manning, C. C. (2011). In their own words: Explaining obedience to authority through an examination of participants' comments. *Social Psychological and Personality Science, 2*, 460–466. doi:10.1177/1948550610397632

Carli, L. L. (2001). Gender and social influence. *Journal of Social Issues, 57*, 725–741. doi:10.1111/0022-4537.00238

Cialdini, R. B., Kallgren, C. A., & Reno, R. R. (1991). A focus theory of normative conduct: A theoretical refinement and reevaluation of the role of norms in human behavior. In L. Berkowitz (Ed.), *Advances in experimental social psychology* (Vol. 24, pp. 201–234). San Diego, CA: Academic Press.

Collins, B. E., & Brief, D. E. (1995). Using person-perception vignette methodologies to uncover the symbolic meanings of teacher behaviors in the Milgram paradigm. *Journal of Social Issues*, *51*(3), 89–106. doi:10.1111/j.1540-4560.1995.tb01336.x

Collins, B. E., & Ma, L. (2000). Impression management and identity construction in the Milgram social system. In T. Blass (Ed.), *Obedience to authority: Current perspectives on the Milgram paradigm* (pp. 61–90). Mahwah, NJ: Erlbaum.

Dambrun, M., & Vatine, E. (2010). Reopening the study of extreme social behaviors: Obedience to authority within an immersive video environment. *European Journal of Social Psychology*, *40*, 760–773. doi:10.1002/ejsp.646

Darley, J. M. (1995). Constructive and destructive obedience: A taxonomy of principal-agent relationships. *Journal of Social Issues*, *51*(3), 125–154. doi:10.1111/j.1540/4560.1995.tb01338.x

Davis, M. H. (1994). *Empathy: A social psychological approach.* Dubuque, IA: Brown & Benchmark.

Elms, A. C. (1995). Obedience in retrospect. *Journal of Social Issues*, *51*(3), 21–31. doi:10.1111/j.1540/4560.1995.tb01332.x

Elms, A. C. (2009). Obedience lite. *American Psychologist*, *64*, 32–36. doi:0.1037/a0014473

Elms, A. C., & Milgram, S. (1966). Personality characteristics associated with obedience and defiance toward authoritative command. *Journal of Experimental Research in Personality*, *1*, 282–289.

Ent, M. R., & Baumeister, R. F. (2014). Obedience, self-control, and the voice of culture. *Journal of Social Issues*, *70*, 574–586. doi:10.1111/josi.12079

Fenigstein, A. (1998). Were obedience pressures a factor in the Holocaust? *Analyse & Kritik*, *20*, 1–20.

Geffner, R. U., & Gross, M. M. (1984). Sex-role behavior and obedience to authority: A field study. *Sex Roles*, *10*, 973–985. doi:10.1007/BF00288518

Geller, D. M. (1978). Involvement in role-playing simulations: A demonstration with studies on obedience. *Journal of Personality and Social Psychology*, *36*, 219–235. doi:10.1037/0022-3514.36.3.219

Gibson, S. (2013a). "The Last Possible Resort": A forgotten prod and the *in situ* standardization of Stanley Milgram's voice-feedback condition. *History of Psychology*, *16*, 177–194. doi:10:1037/a0032430 (a)

Gibson, S. (2013b). Milgram's obedience experiments: A rhetorical analysis. *British Journal of Social Psychology*, *52*, 290–309. doi:10.1111/j.2044-8309.2011.02070.x (b)

Gibson, S. (2014). Discourse, defiance, and rationality: "Knowledge work" in the "obedience" experiments. *Journal of Social Issues*, *70*, 424–438. doi:10.1111/josi.12069

Gilbert, S. J. (1981). Another look at the Milgram obedience studies: The role of the graduated series of shocks. *Personality and Social Psychology Bulletin*, *7*, 690–695. doi:10.1177/014616728174028

Haslam, S. A., Reicher, S. D., & Birney, M. E. (2014). Nothing by mere authority: Evidence that in an experimental analog of the Milgram paradigm participants are motivated not by orders but by appeals to science. *Journal of Social Issues*, *70*, 473–488. doi:10.1111/josi.12072

Helm, C., & Morelli, M. (1985). Obedience to authority in a laboratory setting: Generalizability and context dependency.

*Political Studies*, *33*, 610–627. doi:10.1111/j.1467-9248.1985.tb01584.x

Hofling, C. K., Brotzman, E., Dalrymple, S., Graves, N., & Pierce, C. M. (1966). An experimental study of nurse-physician relationships. *Journal of Nervous and Mental Disease*, *143*, 171–180. doi:10.1097/00005053-196608000-00008

Hogg, M. A. (2012). Social identity and the psychology of groups. In M. R. Leary & J. Tangney (Eds.), *Handbook of self and identity* (2nd ed., pp. 502–519). New York, NY: Guilford Press.

Kaufmann, H., & Kooman, A. (1967). Predicted compliance in obedience situations as a function of implied instrumental variables. *Psychonomic Science*, *7*, 205–206. doi:10.3758/BF03328540

Kelman, H. C. (1967). Human use of human subjects: The problem of deception in social psychological experiments. *Psychological Bulletin*, *67*, 1–12. doi:10.1037/h0024072

Kelman, H. C., & Hamilton, V. L. (1989). *Crimes of obedience: Toward a social psychology of authority and responsibility.* New Haven, CT: Yale University Press.

Kilham, W., & Mann, L. (1974). Level of destructive obedience as a function of transmitter and executant roles in the Milgram obedience paradigm. *Journal of Personality and Social Psychology*, *29*, 696–702. doi:10.1037/h0036636

Mandel, D. R. (1998). The obedience alibi: Milgram's account of the Holocaust reconsidered. *Analyse & Kritik*, *20*, 74–94.

Meeus, W. H., & Raaijmakers, Q. A. (1986). Administrative obedience: Carrying out orders to use psychological-administrative violence. *European Journal of Social Psychology*, *16*, 311–324. doi:10.1002/ejsp.2420160402

Meeus, W. H., & Raaijmakers, Q. A. (1995). Obedience in modern society: The Utrecht studies. *Journal of Social Issues*, *51*(3), 155–175. doi:10.1111/j.1540-4560.1995.tb01339.x

Milgram, S. (1963). Behavioral study of obedience. *Journal of Abnormal and Social Psychology*, *67*, 371–378. doi:10.1037/h0040525

Milgram, S. (1964). Issues in the study of obedience: A reply to Baumrind. *American Psychologist*, *19*, 848–852. doi:10.1037/h0044954

Milgram, S. (1965). Some conditions of obedience and disobedience to authority. *Human Relations*, *18*, 57–76. doi:10.1177/001872676501800105

Milgram, S. (1974). *Obedience to authority: An experimental view.* New York, NY: Harper & Row.

Miller, A. (1972). Role-playing: An alternative to deception? *American Psychologist*, *27*, 625–636. doi:10.1037/h0033257

Miller, A. G. (2004). What can the Milgram obedience experiments tell us about the Holocaust? Generalizing from the social psychology laboratory. In A. G. Miller (Ed.), *The social psychology of good and evil* (pp. 193–239). New York, NY: Guilford Press.

Miller, A. G. (2009). Reflections on "Replicating Milgram" (Burger, 2009). *American Psychologist*, *64*, 20–27. doi:10.1037/a0014407

Mixon, D. (1976). Studying feignable behavior. *Representative Research in Social Psychology*, *7*, 89–104.

Modigliani, A., & Rochat, F. (1995). The role of interaction sequences and the timing of resistance in shaping obedience and defiance to authority. *Journal of Social Issues*, *51*(3), 107–123. doi:10.1111/j.1540/4560.1995.tb01337.x

Morelli, M. F. (1983). Milgram's dilemma of obedience. *Metaphilosophy*, *14*, 183–189. doi:10.1111/j.1467-9973.1983.tb00307.x

O'Leary, C., Willis, F., & Tomich, E. (1970). Conformity under deceptive and non-deceptive techniques. *Sociological Quarterly*, *11*, 87–93. doi:10.1111/j.1533-8525.1970.tb02077.x

Overy, R. (2014). "Ordinary men," extraordinary circumstances: Historians, social psychology, and the Holocaust. *Journal of Social Issues*, *70*, 515–530. doi:10.1111/josi.12075

Packer, D. J. (2008). Identifying systematic disobedience in Milgram's obedience experiments: A meta-analytic review. *Perspectives on Psychological Science*, *3*, 301–304. doi:10.1111/j.1745-6924.2008.00080.x

Reicher, S. D., & Haslam, S. A. (2011). After shock? Towards a social identity explanation of the Milgram "obedience" studies. *British Journal of Social Psychology*, *50*, 163–169. doi:10.1111/j.2044-8309.2010.02015.x

Reicher, S. D., Haslam, S. A., & Miller, A. G. (2014). What makes a person a perpetrator? The intellectual, moral and methodological arguments for revisiting Milgram's research on the influence of authority. *Journal of Social Issues*, *70*, 393–408. doi:10.1111/josi.12067

Reicher, S. D., Haslam, S. A., & Smith, J. R. (2012). Working toward the experimenter: Reconceptualizing obedience within the Milgram paradigm as identification-based followership. *Perspectives on Psychological Science*, *7*, 315–324. doi:10.1111/j.2044-8309.2010.02015.x

Rochat, F., & Blass, T. (2014). Milgram's unpublished obedience variation and its historical relevance. *Journal of Social Issues*, *70*, 456–472. doi:10.1111/josi.12071

Rochat, F., Maggioni, O., & Modigliani, A. (2000). The dynamics of obeying and opposing authority: A mathematical model. In T. Blass (Ed.), *Obedience to authority: Current perspectives on the Milgram paradigm* (pp. 161–192). Mahwah, NJ: Erlbaum.

Rochat, F., & Modigliani, A. (1997). Authority: Obedience, defiance, and identification in experimental and historical contexts. In M. Gold & E. Douvan (Eds.), *A new outline of social psychology* (pp. 235–246). Washington, DC: American Psychological Association.

Rotter, J. B. (1966). Generalized expectancies for internal versus external control of reinforcement. *Psychological Monographs*, *80*(1), 1–28. doi:10.1037/h0092976

Schlenker, B. R., & Pontari, B. A. (2000). The strategic control of information: Impression management and self-presentation in daily life. In A. Tesser, R. B. Felson, & J. M. Suls (Eds.), *Psychological perspectives on self and identity* (pp. 199–232). Washington, DC: American Psychological Association.

Shanab, M. E., & Yahya, K. A. (1977). A behavioral study of obedience in children. *Journal of Personality and Social Psychology*, *35*, 530–536. doi:10.1037/0022-3514.35.7.530

Slater, M., Antley, A., Davison, A., Swapp, D., Guger, C. Barker, C., . . . Sanchez-Vives, M. V. (2006). A virtual reprise of the Stanley Milgram obedience experiments. *PloS ONE*, *1*, 1–10. doi:10.1371/journal.pone.0000039

Staub, E. (1989). *The roots of evil: The origins of genocide and other group violence.* New York, NY: Cambridge University Press.

Staub, E. (2014). Obeying, joining, following, resisting, and other processes in the Milgram studies, and in the Holocaust and other genocides: Situations, personality, and bystanders. *Journal of Social Issues*, *70*, 501–514. doi:10.1111/josi.12074

Tarnow, E. (2000). Self-destructive obedience in the airplane cockpit and the concept of obedience optimization. In T. Blass (Ed.), *Obedience to authority: Current perspectives on the Milgram paradigm* (pp. 111–123). Mahwah, NJ: Erlbaum.

Triandis, H. C. (1989). The self and social behavior in differing cultural contexts. *Psychological Review*, *96*, 506–520. doi:10.1037/0033-295X.96.3.506

Zeigler-Hill, V., Southard, A. C., Archer, L. M., & Donohoe, P. L. (2013). Neuroticism and negative affect influence the reluctance to engage in destructive obedience in the Milgram paradigm. *Journal of Social Psychology*, *152*, 161–174. doi:10.1080/00224545.2012.713041

# Social Norms and Their Enforcement

Jessica M. Nolan

### Abstract

In this chapter social norms are redefined as "rules and standards that are understood by members of a group, and that guide morally relevant social behavior by way of social sanctions, instead of the force of laws." In line with this revised definition, the chapter includes a discussion of how and when individuals enforce social norms along with the customary review of the literature on social norms as agents of social influence. A discussion of how to maximize the impact of social norms interventions follows with special consideration given to (a) combining descriptive and injunctive norms, (b) reference groups, (c) personal relevance, and (d) cognitive resources. The chapter also includes a discussion of the tendency to underestimate the influence of social norms, both on one's own behavior and the behavior of others. Several conflicting results are identified and suggestions are made for how to resolve them with future research.

**Key Words:** Social norms, social sanctions, enforcement, social norms marketing, focus theory, conformity

Social norms in their broadest context represent the social values of a society (Sherif, 1966). In the context of social influence, social norms represent a tool for influencing people by reminding them, implicitly or explicitly, of these values. This chapter begins by identifying deficiencies in how social norms are defined and understood within the social influence literature and proposes a revised definition that emphasizes the role of norm enforcement. Other academic fields, such as anthropology and sociology, have emphasized identifying the existence and operation of social norms in naturalistic settings using descriptive methods. Although these literatures will not be the focus of this chapter, I will draw on them to provide a more complete picture of social norms, particularly with respect to norm enforcement.

Social influence scholars have approached the study of social norms primarily by manipulating social norms and observing their effects. In the present chapter, the review of the literature is divided into social norms interventions that manipulate the physical or social environment and those that provide social norms information via verbal messages. In both cases, these interventions represent an active attempt to change behavior using social norms as a persuasive tool. A discussion of how to maximize the impact of social norms interventions follows, beginning with a summary of advice for aligning *descriptive* (i.e., norms of "is") and *injunctive* (i.e., norms of "ought") norms. Three key moderators of the influence of social norms are identified and discussed: the group referenced in the social norms message; the personal relevance of the behavior; and the cognitive resources available to process the message. The chapter also includes a discussion of the ability of targets and practitioners to detect the influence of social norms on their own behavior and the behavior of others. The body of the chapter concludes with a discussion of the prevalence of norm enforcement, and how people sanction norm violators. The focus throughout the chapter is on experimental research with true behavioral-dependent variables carried out in the last 10 years. The chapter concludes with a summary of conflicting findings and suggestions for how to resolve them, along with additional ideas for future research.

## (Re) Defining Social Norms

Social influence scholars typically define social norms as "rules and standards that are understood by members of a group, and that guide and/or constrain social behavior without the force of laws" (Cialdini & Trost, 1998, p. 152). In most investigations of social norms, the emphasis then quickly shifts to an important distinction between descriptive and injunctive norms. As the term implies, descriptive norms describe how most people behave in a given setting, while injunctive norms prescribe or proscribe behavior. This distinction between norms of "is" (descriptive) versus "ought" (injunctive) has allowed for important theoretical advancements in our understanding of when norms will guide behavior. Specifically, research conducted under the umbrella of "focus theory" has shown that norms must be salient in order to guide behavior (Cialdini, Reno, & Kallgren, 1990; Kallgren, Reno, & Cialdini, 2000; Reno, Cialdini, & Kallgren, 1993). When there is a conflict between descriptive and injunctive norms, focus theory predicts, and research has confirmed, that the focal norm will guide behavior.

While the importance of distinguishing between descriptive and injunctive norms and the theoretical advancements that it allowed cannot be overstated, the emphasis on this distinction in the extant literature has had two drawbacks. First, emphasizing the distinction between descriptive and injunctive norms has taken the focus away from the overarching construct of social norms and vitiated its true meaning as pertaining to important social "rules and standards." Although the behavior of others undoubtedly serves as a guide for one's own behavior, not all common behaviors constitute social norms. That a majority of students favor a particular campus testing policy or buy a certain brand of toothpaste would be better described as *behavioral norms*, rather than social norms (Blanton & Christie, 2003). Social norms carry moral weight and represent more than "common" or "popular" behavior (Rossano, 2012). Social norms are moral in the sense that they pertain to behaviors that are necessary to maintain order in society. That is, social norms pertain to behaviors that are serious enough, because of their effect on individual or collective outcomes, that one could imagine a law being passed to regulate them. Two examples should help to illustrate this point. Environmental behaviors fall under the umbrella of social norms because they often involve choosing between the long-term good of the group over the short-term self-interest of the individual (Rossano, 2012). As such, some cities have elected to formally regulate behaviors such as recycling using local ordinances (Everett & Peirce, 1993) or market-based incentives (e.g., pay as you throw; Skumatz & Freeman, 2006). Health-related behaviors also fall under the umbrella of social norms because they involve behaviors that have serious consequences for the well-being of the individual. As such, some cities have banned foods connected to obesity such as "big gulps" (Jaslow, 2012). Thus, to qualify as a social norm, common behaviors should meet the additional criterion of being morally relevant.

Second, and perhaps most important, the current definition of social norms underemphasizes the importance of enforcement in defining social norms. Viewing social norms as rules implies that an "if-then" logic is in place: *If* you fail to conform to an agreed upon rule, *then* there will be consequences. These consequences are not imposed by formal authorities (Posner & Rasmusen, 1999). Instead, social norms are enforced using social sanctions. According to Axelrod (1986): "A norm exists in a given social setting to the extent that individuals usually act in a certain way and are often punished when seen not to be acting in this way" (p. 1097). Thus, in addition to being common and morally relevant, enforcement is seen by some scholars, including this author, as a necessary attribute for classifying a behavior as normative.

In light of these previous points, I propose a reformulation of Cialdini and Trost's (1998) definition of social norms as "rules and standards that are understood by members of a group, and that guide *morally relevant* social behavior *by way of social sanctions, instead of* the force of laws." This definition, with its emphasis on the endogenous enforcement of rule breaking, is consistent with those adopted by legal and other scholars (e.g., Ellickson, 2001; Kinzig et al., 2013). Allowing the "group" referred to in the original definition to be vague acknowledges that social norms exist at multiple levels (e.g., societal norms, family norms, norms specific to one's workplace or group of friends, etc.). As defined here, social norms are not limited to those behaviors that represent the cultural universals of a society. Instead, rules and standards that belong to only a subset, rather than a majority of the society, or a peer group, may also be referred to as social norms.

## Social Norms as Agents of Influence

There are two ways in which social norms can be harnessed as agents of influence. First, the social and/or physical environment can be altered so that targets may directly observe the social norms present. Second, social norms can be "marketed" using oral or written messages, typically delivered via mass media outlets. Both methods have the potential to change normative beliefs as well as behavior.

In this section I will review the literature on social norms interventions with an emphasis on experimental research findings that measured actual behavior as the dependent variable. In addition, I will discuss how to maximize the impact of social norms interventions and the extent to which the influence of social norms can be detected. Space does not allow for a full discussion of the (myriad) reasons that people conform to social norms, and so the reader is referred to existing reviews on this aspect of social norms research (see Cialdini & Goldstein, 2004; Cialdini & Trost, 1998; Hodges, this volume).

### Manipulating the Social or Physical Environment

One way that people come to understand the social norms present in a given setting is by observing the social and/or physical environment. Thus, one very powerful way to use social norms as agents of influence is to manipulate the surrounding environment. The plethora of research on the effects of manipulating observable norms has been conducted primarily under the umbrella of the focus theory of normative conduct (for a review, see Cialdini, 2011). Focus theory makes two primary assumptions: descriptive and injunctive norms can operate independently, and only salient norms guide behavior.

The most oft-cited examples of manipulating the physical environment to convey social norms come from research by Cialdini and colleagues on littering behavior (Cialdini et al., 1990; Kallgren et al., 2000; Reno et al., 1993). These studies showed (a) that it is possible to alter the physical environment to convey social norms and (b) that such alterations can have a powerful effect on behavior. Across more than 10 studies, results consistently showed that people used the surrounding environment to infer social norms and that salient norms guided behavior. In the simplest of these experiments, participants exposed to a clean environment (i.e., anti-littering descriptive norm) littered less than those exposed to a littered environment (Cialdini et al., 1990, Study 1). Importantly, the effects were enhanced when a confederate made the prevailing norm salient by littering in front of the participant. These results are important because they support the predictions made under focus theory and rule out alternative explanations. For example, social learning theory (Bandura, 1977) would predict that participants would imitate the behavior of a confederate who littered, regardless of the state of the surrounding environment. Contrary to the social learning based prediction, Cialdini and colleagues (1990) found that observing a confederate litter only increased participants' tendency to litter when the environment was already strewn with litter. When the confederate littered into a clean environment, participants actually littered *less*. Additional research showed that the prevailing descriptive norm could also be made salient using a single piece of noteworthy litter in an otherwise clean environment (e.g., a watermelon rind, Study 3). Descriptive norms for behaviors other than littering have also been manipulated using observable cues and produced similar effects. For example, Burger and colleagues (2010) manipulated the descriptive norm for healthy eating by varying the type of snack wrappers (i.e., healthy snack vs. candy bar) participants saw in a trashcan. Dwyer, Maki, and Rothman (2015) manipulated observable descriptive norms by turning the lights off in a public bathroom, and Bator, Tabanico, Walton, and Schultz (2014), by turning computers off in a public computer lab.

The environment can also be manipulated to convey injunctive norms for behavior. Across multiple studies, activating the injunctive norm against littering by having a confederate pick up a crumpled food bag resulted in lowered littering rates compared to when a confederate just walked by the participant (Reno et al., 1993). Using injunctive norms does not require evidence that most people engage in the behavior, only that the behavior is socially approved or disapproved. In fact, activated injunctive norms can positively influence behavior even when the prevailing descriptive norm suggests that most people are *not* engaging in the prosocial behavior (e.g., Cialdini et al., 1990, Study 5; Reno et al., 1993, Study 1), or when personal norms for engaging in the behavior are low (Cialdini et al., 1990, Study 9). There is also evidence to suggest that the more damaging a behavior is, the less likely it is to be enacted when injunctive norms are focal (Kallgren et al., 2000). For example, dropping two pieces of litter on the ground is more "damaging" to the environment than dropping one. In the study by Kallgren and colleagues, when a confederate activated the anti-littering injunctive norm by picking up a piece of litter, participants were less likely to litter when two handbills were placed on their car windshield (versus one). In addition, Reno and colleagues (1993) found that injunctive norms could influence behavior across locations. Participants who saw a confederate pick up a food bag in one location were less likely to litter, both in that same location as well as in a different setting, compared to the control conditions (Reno et al., 1993, Study 2 & 3). The effect of activated descriptive norms did not persist across locations (Study 3). Thus, the effect of injunctive norms on behavior may be more robust and long lasting than that of descriptive norms.

From a practical standpoint, tacticians might be tempted to activate injunctive norms using signs that prohibit or express disapproval for an undesired behavior (e.g., littering). Signs such as "do not litter," "keep off the grass," and "curb your dog" are prevalent and intuitively appealing ways to try to influence behavior. Indeed, research shows that when the environment is clean, a prohibition sign does decrease the rate of littering, compared to when it is absent (Keizer, Lindenberg, & Steg, 2011). However, posting prohibition signs when the state of the environment communicates that most people have disobeyed the sign may be misguided. For example, Keizer and colleagues (2011) found that in an already littered environment, participants were actually *more* likely to litter when a sign prohibiting littering was displayed, compared to when the sign was absent. Rather than activating the injunctive norm against littering, the prohibition sign essentially served to make the prevailing descriptive norm (i.e., most people litter) salient. This may be because the signs were put in place by an authority and, therefore, were not seen as an expression of what "most people" disapprove. This research extends focus theory by showing that people follow salient descriptive norms, even if the cue that makes them salient is a sign prohibiting the behavior.

Can observing the violation of one norm lead to other norm violations? According to broken windows theory, disorder in society begets more and more serious disorder (Wilson & Kelling, 1982). Broken windows theory predicts that if the windows of a house are broken and remain so, it sends a message that the neighborhood is uncared for and will lead to more serious crimes such as theft. According to Keizer and colleagues: "cues signaling other people's disrespect for a norm, have a negative impact on conforming to that norm and even on conforming to other norms" (Keizer et al., 2011, p. 687). For example, participants who observed that others had violated a sign prohibiting the writing of graffiti were subsequently more likely to litter a handbill that had been attached to their bicycle, compared to those who were not exposed to the graffiti (Keizer, Lindenberg, & Steg, 2008). Furthermore, this negative behavioral spillover was not limited to relatively small infractions such as littering but also more serious infractions such as stealing (Study 5 & 6) and trespassing on private property (Study 2).

From a psychological perspective, the aforementioned findings are also consistent with a priming-based explanation of behavior. Behaviors considered normative are conceptually linked in consciousness such that priming one behavior can influence the occurrence of another. This behavioral spillover can flow in a negative direction, as described in the preceding paragraph, but the reverse is also possible. For example, exposing participants to concepts related to littering, such as recycling (Cialdini et al., 1990, Study 5) or graffiti (Kallgren et al., 2000, Study 1), activated the anti-littering injunctive norm. The more closely related the primed concept was to the target behavior (e.g., littering), the less likely the individual was to engage in the undesired behavior.

Because most of the research discussed so far was conducted in the field, as opposed to a more controlled setting, less is known about how manipulating the environment influences cognitive variables such as normative beliefs. However, a recent study examining harassment behavior in schools showed that having popular high school students publicly endorse, and subsequently model, anti-harassment norms effectively changed normative beliefs about harassment, as well as behavior (Paluck & Shepherd, 2012). By the end of the school year, students with ties to the popular spokespeople perceived that fewer students approved of harassment as a desirable strategy for confronting conflict, and fewer perceived harassment as a normal part of life in high school. In addition, they perceived that more students understood that harassment has serious social consequences compared to before the intervention. Furthermore, students with more ties to spokespeople were more likely to be nominated by teachers as defending other students from harassment and less likely to be nominated by teachers as students who contribute to a negative school environment. They were also more likely to purchase an anti-harassment wristband.

The influence of social norms has also been documented in naturalistic studies. For example, naturally occurring descriptive norms for drinking alcohol influenced both the number of drink offers students received and their compliance with those offers while out drinking with friends (Cullum, O'Grady, Armeli, & Tennen, 2012). That is, when drinking socially, the more drinks those around them were having, the more offers the participant received (a dependent variable), and the more drinks they consumed. Thus, placing oneself in a social environment with harmful descriptive norms might lead to the adoption of those harmful behaviors.

Manipulation of the physical and social environment has been helpful in experimentally testing cause-and-effect relationships between norms and behavior and in making theoretical refinements. This research has shown that making descriptive and injunctive norms salient can guide behavior. However, manipulating the observable environment is often impractical and cost-prohibitive in real-world settings. As an alternative, communicating normative information via mass media outlets represents a more promising tool for social influence. Although it is possible to manipulate observable norms via mass media (e.g., Cialdini, 2003), it is more common to provide information rather than to portray actions.

### Social Norms Marketing

In the last 15 years the power of social norms has been repeatedly harnessed using the technique of social norms marketing. Social norms marketing involves communicating the actual percentage of people who engage in and/or approve of a desired behavior, typically via mass media outlets. Social norms interventions are recommended whenever people overestimate the prevalence of an unwanted behavior or underestimate the prevalence of a desired behavior. The underlying philosophy of social norms marketing is that normative information will correct inaccurate normative beliefs, which will in turn change behavior.

The most prevalent social norms marketing campaigns are those targeting substance abuse. Research has shown that students tend to overestimate campus drinking norms, perceiving heavy drinking as more prevalent than it actually is (Borsari & Carey,

2003; Martens et al., 2006; Werch et al., 2000). Social norms campaigns correct this misperception by providing written information about the actual (lower) percentage and/or frequency of student drinking. These campaigns have been shown to be quite effective at correcting students' misperception of campus drinking norms (Clapp, Lange, Russell, Shillington, & Voas, 2003; Mattern & Neighbors, 2004; Neighbors, Larimer, & Lewis, 2004; Peeler, Far, Miller, & Brigham, 2000; Steffian, 1999; Thombs & Hamilton, 2002).

Social norms interventions can also change normative beliefs off campus. Participants from the United States going to the bars in Tijuana, Mexico, were provided with accurate social norms information indicating how much alcohol previous border crossers had consumed (Johnson, 2012). The results showed that those who were exposed to the social norms intervention changed their normative beliefs about drinking significantly more than those in a control condition. Results showed that the change in normative beliefs was most pronounced for participants who were encouraged to seek out examples of nondrinkers while in Tijuana. Interestingly, highlighting the discrepancy between perceived and actual norms (by providing participants with graphs illustrating this difference) did not impact how much participants' normative beliefs changed from entry to exit at the border crossing. Results also showed that there was a correlation between the change in perceived drinking norms and participants' blood alcohol level. The more a participant's normative beliefs changed in line with actual (lower) drinking norms, the lower the participant's blood alcohol level was upon return to the border crossing.

Social norms marketing has also been used successfully to change behavior. Using printed messages to communicate that a majority of people engage in a desired behavior has served to increase towel reuse among hotel guests (Goldstein, Cialdini, & Griskevicius, 2008; Schultz, Khazian, & Zaleski, 2008), conservation of energy (e.g., Nolan, Schultz, Cialdini, Goldstein, & Griskevicius, 2008; Schultz, Nolan, Cialdini, Goldstein, & Griskevicius, 2007), recycling (Schultz, 1999), use of sustainable transportation options (Kormos, Gifford, & Brown, 2015), and exercising (e.g., Burger & Shelton, 2011). Similarly, communicating that a majority of people does not engage in an undesired behavior has served to decrease theft in a national park (Cialdini et al., 2006) and problematic drinking (e.g., Burger, LaSalvia, Hendricks, Mehdipour, & Neudeck,

2011; Haines & Spear, 1996; Perkins, 2003). Social norms interventions have also been applied on a large scale by electric (Allcott, 2011) and water utility companies (Ferraro, Miranda, & Price, 2011) and have yielded similar positive results. However, these positive results have not been universal (e.g., Wechsler et al., 2003) and failed campaigns may be attributed, in part, to unforeseen problems with how descriptive social norms information is communicated.

Descriptive norm information can be communicated in one of three ways. First, the percentage of people who engage in the desired behavior can be reported (e.g., 77 percent of residents turn off the lights when they leave the room). Alternatively, the frequency with which the majority, or a typical person, engages in the behavior can be reported (e.g., Most students only have 2 or 3 drinks when they party). Lastly, an average can be provided for the behavior (e.g., "the average household in your neighborhood consumed 200 kwh of electricity per month"). The latter is typically combined with individual feedback so that a comparison can be made between the individual's behavior and what is normal for the specified group. While the first option provides few issues in terms of implementation, the second and third options must be used with caution. For example, providing households with comparative feedback indicating that they consumed *less* energy than the average household in their neighborhood actually *increased* their energy consumption in subsequent weeks (Schultz et al., 2007). Fortunately, this undesired boomerang effect was eliminated by adding an injunctive component, expressing approval for those who consumed less than average.

With these caveats in mind, social norms marketing has several strengths as an agent of influence. In addition to being suitable for large-scale implementation, the effects of social norms marketing are robust. Changes in normative beliefs can be sustained for three years with an ongoing campaign (Haines & Spear, 1996) and for at least a month without it (Nolan, 2011). Changes in behavior can also persist after the social norms intervention has ended (e.g., Richetin, Perugini, Mondini, & Hurling, 2014). Participants exposed to a sign indicating that most people used the stairs instead of the elevator in a campus building continued using the stairs a week after the signs were removed (Burger & Shelton, 2011), and Georgia residents provided with one initial dose of feedback about how much water they consumed compared to others in their county consumed less water than residents in a control condition, even 3 years later (Ferraro et al., 2011).

In addition, social norms interventions have cognitive ripple effects, whereby the social norms information presented about one referent group engaging in one behavior spills over to influence beliefs about related behaviors and other reference groups (Nolan, 2011). For example, participants who were told that most other students recycled perceived that a greater percentage of students recycled, as expected, but also perceived that more of their friends, neighbors, faculty, and US citizens recycled, compared to a control group. Thus, social norms information about a moderately close referent spilled over to influence normative beliefs about both more proximal (e.g., friends, neighbors) and more distal (e.g., state residents, United States citizens) groups.

Lastly, social norms interventions can decrease the costs associated with running government programs. Farmers participating in a land conservation program in China (Grain-to-Green Program) expressed more willingness to re-enroll in the program in a scenario in which the majority of their neighbors also planned to do so (Chen, Lupi, He, & Liu, 2009). Furthermore, the more of their neighbors who participated in the program, the less money the participating farmers said they would require to re-enroll themselves.

## Maximizing the Impact of Social Norms Interventions

The extant literature provides helpful suggestions for how to maximize the impact of social norms interventions. Existing research provides guidance for how to combine descriptive and injunctive norms as well as for when social norms are likely to be most effective. Three moderator variables that have been explored in considerable depth will be discussed in this section: (a) the group referenced in the message and identification with that group, (b) the personal relevance of the target behavior, and (c) the depth at which the social norms information is processed.

### ALIGNING INJUNCTIVE AND DESCRIPTIVE NORMS

Cialdini (2003) has argued that descriptive and injunctive norms should be aligned to have the biggest impact on behavior. In line with this prediction, Schultz and colleagues (2008) found that a message communicating that towel reuse was both common (descriptive) and approved (injunctive) among hotel guests increased towel reuse significantly more than either norm message presented alone. In a similar vein, proponents of focus theory have cautioned practitioners not to advertise undesired behaviors as being "regrettably frequent" (Cialdini, 2003; Cialdini et al., 2006; Mollen, Ruiter, & Kok, 2010). However, research on deviance regulation theory suggests that in some cases, low descriptive norms can be used successfully, but only if they are combined with supportive injunctive norms.

According to deviance regulation theory (Blanton & Christie, 2003), individuals regulate others' impressions of them by deviating from norms in ways that will make them stand out in positive ways and avoid deviating from norms when it would make them stand out in negative ways. Proponents of deviance regulation theory advise practitioners to focus on approval of deviants when the prevalence of the desired behavior is low and on disapproval of deviants when the prevalence of the desired behavior is high. According to the authors, "deviant acts stick to one's identity to a greater extent than normative acts" (Blanton & Christie, 2003, p. 121). For example, when a message highlighted students who got a flu shot as considerate and responsible, participants were actually more likely to get a flu shot when told that most students did *not* (versus did) get one (Blanton, Stuart, & VandenEijnden, 2001). The reverse was true when the message highlighted students who did not get the flu shot as inconsiderate and irresponsible. In that case, telling participants that getting the flu shot was normative was more effective than telling them that it was deviant.

### REFERENCE GROUPS

Social identity theory (Tajfel, 1974), self-categorization theory (Turner, 1985), and the theory of planned behavior (Ajzen, 1991) all predict that people will be most likely to follow the norms of groups that are important to them. Research across these theories shows that individuals are more likely to conform to the behavior of in-group versus out-group members. This is true even when the behavior is amoral (e.g., cheating; Gino, Ayal, & Ariely, 2009) and when the in-group is not meaningful (e.g., group H; Abrams, Wetherell, Cochrane, Hogg, & Turner, 1990). Conformity to the behavior of the in-group has been observed for both objective and ambiguous tasks; however, for objective tasks, conformity was only observed when participants made their decisions publicly (Abrams et al., 1990). Individuals are especially likely to conform to the behavior of an in-group in identity-relevant domains, even when (or perhaps because) the in-group is a minority (Berger & Heath, 2007).

Those who identify more strongly with an in-group are more likely to conform to its norms (Phua, 2013) and to experience positive emotions and a feeling of satisfaction with the decision to conform (Christensen, Rothgerber, Wood, & Matz, 2004). Those who are highly identified with a group rely more on norms than low identifiers, while low identifiers rely more on their individual attitudes (Terry & Hogg, 1996). However, low identifiers do rely on normative information when they have to make their decisions quickly versus carefully (Terry, Hogg, & McKimmie, 2000). When multiple reference groups are involved, behavior is likely to be determined by how strongly identified the person is with each group as well as the extent to which the behavior is salient within that group. For example, smoking among college students is influenced most by the descriptive norms of peers, while smoking in adult populations is influenced most by the descriptive norms of family members (Phua, 2013). Interestingly, when there is conflict between the norms of embedded groups (e.g., college students in general versus college friends), individuals are more likely to conform to the norms of the more closely identified group when its norms differ from, versus conform to, societal standards (Blanton & Christie, 2003).

There is growing interest in the use of local, or provincial, norms in social norms interventions. The underlying idea is that norms based on place can influence behavior even in the absence of strong emotional ties (Fornara, Carrus, Passafaro, & Bonnes, 2011). However, the results in this case are mixed. Goldstein and colleagues (2008) found that hotel guests were more likely to reuse their towels when told that 75 percent of guests in that specific room had reused their towels, compared to guests who were told that the same percentage of citizens, men and women, or hotel guests had participated. This was true even though the "guest of a particular room" identity was rated as the least important identity by a separate set of subjects. The specific room message also outperformed the control message that emphasized the environmental benefits of reusing towels but did not provide descriptive normative information. In other studies, however, using local referents had no effect. Most notably, Schultz and colleagues (2008) found that hotel guests who received normative information about the towel reuse behavior of guests who stayed in the same room were no more likely to reuse their towels than those who received descriptive norm information about guests of the hotel in general. Similarly, providing participants with normative feedback about alcohol consumption specific to their race and gender had no effect on behavior and resulted in the same changes in perceived norms as more general feedback (Johnson, 2012).

## PERSONAL RELEVANCE

Personal relevance refers to the extent to which an issue or behavior is relevant to an individual. The more involved individuals are with a cause and the stronger their attitude about an issue, the more personally relevant the issue or behavior is likely to be to them. Across a variety of domains, research consistently shows that the more personally relevant an issue is for a person, the less likely they are to rely on the behavior of others as a guide for their own behavior (Berger & Heath, 2007; Burger et al., 2011; Gockeritz et al., 2010; McDonald, Fielding, & Louis, 2013; Smith & Louis, 2008).

Indirect evidence for the moderating role of personal relevance comes from research on college students' drinking behavior. It has been argued that men are more personally involved with drinking and therefore less susceptible to social norms interventions than are women. In line with this hypothesis, female participants who were told that consuming alcohol before going out to the bars (i.e., "pre-gaming") was uncommon on their campus subsequently reduced the number of times they pre-gamed, while male students exposed to the same social norms intervention showed no change in their pre-gaming behavior (Burger et al., 2011).

Likewise, survey research shows that descriptive normative beliefs are more highly correlated with behavioral intentions when respondents are not personally involved with the behavior. For example, those who are less involved with the issue of energy conservation are more likely to go along with the crowd (Gockeritz et al., 2010). In contrast, for people who care about energy conservation, beliefs about the behavior of others have less influence on their own behavior, as they are likely to have other reasons for conserving. In the consumer choice domain, the more relevant a product category is to a person's identity, the less likely the person is to conform to the majority opinion (Berger & Heath, 2007).

A similar pattern has been found when descriptive and injunctive norms are combined. When an injunctive component was added to a descriptive

norm message, individuals for whom the issue had low personal relevance were only willing to act when the message communicated that a majority of the members of their in-group both approved and performed the target behavior (Smith & Louis, 2008). In contrast, when participants were personally involved in the issue, they were willing to take action even when told that only a minority of their in-group had performed the behavior, so long as most members of the in-group approved of it.

More recent research has shown that the related construct of personal norms can also moderate the norm–behavior relationship (Schultz et al., 2014). Personal norms represent a person's self-expectations for his or her own behavior (Schwartz, 1977). Among households that received an aligned norms message indicating that their below-average consumption was approved or that their above-average consumption was disapproved, only those with low personal norms for water conservation decreased their water consumption.

Personal relevance, in the form of stronger attitudes, can also moderate the impact of norms (McDonald et al., 2013). Specifically, when an individual perceives that the norms of different in-groups conflict, those with stronger attitudes become more likely to engage in the attitude-relevant behavior, while the reverse is true for those with weaker attitudes. For those with strong attitudes, conflicting norms between multiple in-groups highlight the need for action on the part of the individual and increase the perceived effectiveness of engaging in the specified behavior. For those with weak attitudes, conflicting norms reduce perceptions of effectiveness and highlight the futility of taking action.

## COGNITIVE RESOURCES

The term "cognitive resources" refers to the energy and/or willingness an individual has to effortfully process information. The effect of the availability of cognitive resources on social norms has been investigated using cognitive load manipulations that distract the individual from fully processing the information during exposure (Melnyk, Herpen, Fischer, & van Trijp, 2011), as well as manipulations designed to deplete self-control or self-regulatory capacity prior to message exposure (DeBono, Shmueli, & Muraven, 2011; Jacobson, Mortensen, & Cialdini, 2011).

Research on the role of cognitive resources as a moderator of the social norms–behavior relationship has produced mixed results. On the one hand, cognitive resources seem to be required to conform to everyday social norms. Individuals whose self-control had been depleted were more likely to cheat, lie, and behave rudely compared to those who were not depleted (DeBono et al., 2011). Similarly, participants placed under cognitive load while reading a newspaper article that included descriptive normative information indicating that most people purchased environmentally friendly processed potatoes expressed less favorable attitudes toward the potatoes, an increase in negative thoughts, and lower behavioral intentions compared to a control group exposed to the same message, but not under cognitive load (Melnyk et al., 2011). In contrast, participants who were encouraged to deliberate on the same newspaper article were more likely to conform to the descriptive norm. The authors argued that deliberating on the descriptive norm message leads to increased conformity because it provides evidence of the behavior's effectiveness and encourages participants to think about their connections with others.

On the other hand, there is evidence to suggest that conformity to social norms can occur heuristically. For example, participants lowered their voices when the goal of going to the library was activated (Aarts & Dijksterhuis, 2003) and participants who were primed with words related to conformity (e.g., adhere, agree, comply) were subsequently more likely to conform to the opinions of confederates (Epley & Gilovich, 1999). Descriptive norms may provide social proof that serves as a heuristic for behavior (Cialdini, 2001). If so, cognitive resources may not be necessary for descriptive norms to have their effect. Indeed, Jacobson and colleagues (2011) found that depleting participants' self-regulatory capacity actually led to an increase in the effectiveness of a descriptive norm message. Participants who were told that most other students had taken the time to complete optional surveys requested more surveys to complete when their self-regulatory capacity was depleted versus when it was not. People are also more likely to rely on descriptive norms, written or observed, when the target behavior will take place in the future or they are made to think abstractly, perhaps because fewer cognitive resources are devoted to processing information under those conditions (Ledgerwood & Callahan, 2012). The results of research on personal relevance presented in the previous section are also pertinent to the current discussion of cognitive resources. According to the elaboration likelihood model (Petty & Briñol, 2012; Petty & Cacioppo, 1986), people will devote more cognitive resources to processing messages that are personally relevant, while those that are not personally relevant will be processed peripherally. Thus, the greater impact of social norms when personal relevance is low provides indirect support for the heuristic operation of norms.

How do cognitive resources impact the influence of injunctive norms? Cialdini (2003) has suggested that greater cognitive effort is needed to process injunctive versus descriptive norm messages. Partial support for this contention comes from a correlational analysis showing that the injunctive component of an ad promoting recycling indirectly increased intentions to recycle by increasing perceptions of the ad's effectiveness, whereas the descriptive norm component had a direct effect on intentions to recycle. Experimental research also shows that depleting cognitive resources reduces the effectiveness of an injunctive norm message (Jacobson et al., 2011; Melnyk et al., 2011). However, Melnyk and colleagues also found that greater *deliberation* on the injunctive norm message produced less favorable attitudes and lowered behavioral intentions compared to the control condition. They argued that injunctive norms might evoke resistance and that greater deliberation on those messages might lead participants to focus on external reasons for engaging in the behavior. In support of this contention, participants who deliberated on the injunctive norm message did show a decrease in the number of positive thoughts they generated about the target behavior compared to a control condition.

### Detecting (or Not) the Influence of Social Norms

The power of social norms to guide behavior has been well documented. However, there is a growing body of evidence showing that individuals fail to recognize the behavior of others as a causal antecedent for their own actions. This underestimation of the efficacy of social norms marketing has resulted in the underutilization of this technique in promoting solutions to important social problems such as global warming (Griskevicius, Cialdini, & Goldstein, 2008). Indeed, while 55 percent of energy experts reported using appeals to save money to promote conservation, only 17 percent had used a normative message to do so (Nolan, Kenefick, & Schultz, 2011).

Glimpses of the underestimation of the influence of others' behavior on our own behavior came initially from anecdotal reports generated from the debriefing phase of classic studies of social influence. For example, in their study of the bystander effect, Latané and Darley (1970) report that individuals generally denied the impact of the presence of other people on their decision not to help a bystander. Similarly, in his classic study on conformity using the autokinetic effect, Sherif (1966) reported that participants denied that their own judgments of how much the light had moved were influenced by the estimates given by the other people in their group.

More recent research has explicitly investigated people's ability to detect the influence of social norms on behavior. Nolan et al. (2008) explored the ability of California residents to detect the influence of their neighbors' energy conservation efforts on their own conservation behavior. An initial statewide survey showed that Californians perceived the behavior of others to be less important than environmental protection, saving money, and benefiting society as an explanation for why they chose to conserve energy. Despite individuals' self-reported reasons for conservation, descriptive normative beliefs about the behavior of their neighbors were the best predictor of self-reported energy conservation behavior (Nolan et al., 2008, Study 1). A follow-up field experiment confirmed that residents were unable to detect the motivating power of social norms on their energy-conserving behavior. Households randomly assigned to receive a descriptive norm message, indicating that the majority of their neighbors were doing things to conserve energy, consumed less energy per day compared to those who received information about how to conserve (e.g., "use fans instead of air conditioning at night") alone or combined with information about environmental, financial, or societal benefits. However, when the same households were interviewed about how much the messages had motivated them to conserve, the opposite pattern of results emerged. That is, those who had received information about the environmental, financial, or societal benefits of conservation reported being more motivated than those who had received information about the behavior of their neighbors. Even those who received messages with no motivating information reported being more motivated than those in the descriptive norm condition. In sum, those who received descriptive norm information reduced their energy consumption but said that the messages had not motivated them to conserve, while those who received more traditional appeals for conservation rated those messages as highly motivating but did not significantly reduce their energy consumption. Similar findings have also been documented in the domain of healthy eating (e.g., Vartanian, Herman, & Wansink, 2008; Croker, Whitaker, Cooke, Wardle, & Ernest, 2009).

People do seem willing to admit that *others* might be influenced by pressures to conform. People believe that they are less susceptible than the average person to the influence of social norms (Pronin, Molouki, & Berger, 2007). This perception that one is "alone in a crowd of sheep" seems to stem from an asymmetry in how individuals weight personal thoughts versus behavioral information when making assessments about the causes of their own behavior versus that of another. Individuals perceive that their own behavior is influenced more by specific thoughts accessed during the process of introspecting than by the behavior of others, while the reverse is true when they are asked to explain the similar behavior of another person. However, there is some evidence to suggest that people may be more willing to admit to being influenced when the source of influence is an in-group (Abrams et al., 1990).

Targets of influence are not the only ones unable to identify social norms as a potent influence on behavior (Cialdini et al., 2006; Nolan et al., 2011). Energy outreach and education specialists erroneously predicted that the descriptive norm message used in Nolan et al. (2008) would create the smallest decrease in daily household energy consumption, rated it as having the least motivating potential, and said they would be least likely to use it in future outreach (Nolan et al., 2011). In contrast, the influence of the financial appeal was overestimated. Experts predicted that the "save money" message would create the largest decrease in daily household energy consumption, rated it as having the most motivating potential, and were most interested in using it in future outreach. Like targets, practitioners asked to judge the effectiveness of the technique for motivating the behavior of others were also unable to acknowledge the power of social norms. These results suggest that the underestimation of the influence of social norms is not merely the result of not wanting to be seen as a "sheep."

The Persuasion Knowledge Model (PKM) provides a context for thinking about why both targets and practitioners may underestimate the influence of social norms (Friestad & Wright, 1994). According to the PKM, persuasion knowledge is accumulated and revised over the course of a person's lifetime as he or she is exposed to both persuasive attempts and discussions about those attempts.

Research has shown that some fundamental beliefs about persuasion are culturally shared and constitute a commonsense, or naïve, psychology of persuasion (Friestad & Wright, 1995). Naïve psychology refers to the layperson's conception of behavior and mental processes (Heider, 1958). Nisbett and Wilson (1977) referred to these naïve explanations as a priori or implicit causal theories. They concluded that verbal reports explaining the causes of behavior, more often, represented these culturally shared theories that could be generated equally well by an observer (e.g., Nisbett & Bellows, 1977). For example, in the United States, people seem to agree that an ad must stir their interest, perhaps by evoking a strong emotion, to be effective (Friestad & Wright, 1994). This may help to explain why communicating the behavior of others, a subtle strategy, is often unrecognized as a potent influence technique (Cialdini, 2005). The PKM specifies that the disparity between real and perceived effectiveness will be more extreme when "subjects rely on their own conscious reactions to assess effectiveness, but those reactions are not the important psychological mediators that actually govern the ad's overall effects" or when "subjects draw on persuasion knowledge to predict effectiveness but have inaccurate mental models of persuasion" (Friestad & Wright, 1994, p. 18).

If we are at all concerned with ensuring that practitioners abandon ineffective techniques in favor of those that are empirically validated, the logical next question concerns how to persuade the persuaders. There is initial evidence to suggest that exposing experts to supportive empirical research is an effective way to convey the efficacy of social norms messages and to change experts' persuasion knowledge models, at least in the context of home energy conservation (Nolan et al., 2011). Following a talk highlighting the efficacy of social norms messages and showcasing the data from Nolan and colleagues (2008), experts perceived the normative message to be more motivating and were more confident that it would persuade people to reduce their energy consumption compared to before the talk. However, there was no change in the perceived motivating potential of the financial message or confidence in its ability to persuade people to use less energy. Thus, the data were able to convince experts of the efficacy of the norms message, but not of the inefficacy of the financial message. Instead, experts were resistant to revising their persuasion knowledge concerning the efficacy of an intuitively appealing technique.

## Norm Enforcement

Earlier in this chapter it was argued that the enforcement of social norms is crucial for defining, understanding, and upholding them. For centuries, traditional societies have cooperated to maintain social order and/or to preserve the resources upon which the group depends for its livelihood by enforcing social norms (Colding & Folke, 2001; Mahdi, 1986; Ruttan, 1998; Sharma, Rikhari, & Palni, 1999; Wiessner, 2005). In these societies, behavior in the group is dictated by an informal code of conduct and maintained by the threat of social sanctions for those who deviate from the established social norms. By their very existence, these groups illustrate the promise and effectiveness of social norms and social sanctions in sustaining cooperation over multiple generations. In this section, I will review the evidence regarding the prevalence and conditions under which norm enforcement takes place and the specific form that sanctions are likely to take.

### Willingness to Enforce Social Norms

Laboratory experimental games studies conducted within the social dilemma paradigm show that, when given the opportunity, the vast majority of people choose to punish a group member who has violated the norm of cooperation (Bochet, Page, & Putterman, 2006; Fehr & Gächter, 2000, 2002; Henrich et al., 2006; Horne, 2004; Ones & Putterman, 2007). In a given experimental games study, anywhere from 50 to 90 percent of participants will sanction a fellow player at least once for noncooperative behavior. Across a variety of studies, results consistently show that the more a player deviates from the group's average level of cooperation, the more he or she is sanctioned. The power of social norms is most convincingly illustrated when players have to pay to punish, when punishers cannot directly benefit from the punishment they confer (e.g., on the last round of a game), or when the punishments are delivered by third-party observers (Fehr & Fischbacher, 2004; Henrich et al., 2006; Kurzban, Descioli, & O'Brien, 2007). Fehr and Gächter (2002) introduced the term "altruistic punishment" to describe sanctioning that occurs even when it is not in the self-interest of the player to do so.

This willingness to sanction is not just an artifact of laboratory research employing college students. Willingness to sanction has been documented both for nonstudent adults playing laboratory games and in real-world settings. Regarding the former, Henrich et al. (2006) found that adults representing

15 different societies from five different continents showed a strong willingness to punish violations of the norm of fairness in an experimental games context. Furthermore, countries with strong norms and a low tolerance for deviance (Gelfand, 2012) and those that are more collectivistic (Brauer & Chaurand, 2009) tend to be more willing to impose social sanctions on norm violators.

It is also clear from research on preindustrial societies that individuals are willing to enforce social norms that maintain social order and preserve natural resources. In particular, Wiessner (2005) conducted an anthropological case study among the Ju/'hoansi that focused specifically on willingness to sanction. The Ju/'hoansi are a traditional, egalitarian society, living in Botswana, Africa. Within their small villages of 20 to 40 people, sanctioning, and punishment in particular, occurred frequently based on a content analysis of recorded conversations (Wiessner, 2005). The Ju/'hoansi enforce their tribal norms with a full range of verbal punishments: put-downs, mild criticisms, and harsh criticisms (Wiessner, 2005). According to Wiessner, 63 percent of the 308 recorded conversations included some form of sanctioning (positive or negative) and 56 percent were specifically coded as including some form of criticism. Only rarely is physical violence used to punish group members. The majority of sanctioning was targeted at behaviors that impacted social order such as public drunkenness, adultery, and free-riding on the efforts of others.

Finally, willingness to sanction has been observed in modern societies for intrusions into waiting lines (Milgram, Liberty, Toledo, & Wackenhut, 1986; Schmitt, Dube, & Leclerc, 1992), maladaptive coping with negative life events (Weber, 2003), divorce (Kalmijn & Uunk, 2007), and vandalism (Chekroun & Brauer, 2002). Chekroun and Brauer (2002) observed the reactions of naïve bystanders to norm violations. In one setting, a male confederate at a mall joined several shoppers in the elevator, where he proceeded to take out a marker and write graffiti on the elevator wall. Out of 144 observations, 49 percent of naïve bystanders sanctioned the graffiti writer. Similarly, a female confederate who threw a large plastic bottle into the bushes of a public park was sanctioned by 59 percent of naïve bystanders. Like the Ju/'hoansi, the sanctions imposed by the naïve bystanders were usually overt; 10 percent were comments made to another bystander (e.g., "It takes some nerve to do that!"), and 18 percent were comments made directly to the confederate (e.g., "That's not very nice!"). Approximately one quarter of the reactions were more subtle, nonverbal expressions of disapproval (e.g., an angry look; Chekroun & Brauer, 2002). Follow-up research showed that people are most likely to sanction norm violators when they perceive the behavior as deviant (Brauer & Chaurand, 2009) and when they feel that the deviant behavior directly impacts them (Chekroun & Brauer, 2002).

This is not to imply that sanctions are imposed indiscriminately, no matter how great the cost or how little the benefit to the enforcer. Norm enforcement, and punishment in particular, can be costly, and willingness to sanction is affected by changes in the decision environment. For example, although people perceive overt sanctions to be dramatically more effective than subtle sanctions, they are more willing to impose the latter, perhaps because of the greater perceived costs associated with the former (Nolan, 2013). Laboratory research confirms that willingness to impose sanctions decreases as the sanctions themselves become more costly (monetarily) to impose (Horne & Cutlip, 2002; Ostrom, Walker, & Gardner, 1992). Wiessner (2005) notes that in addition to the time and energy costs associated with imposing social sanctions, punishment can lead to the loss of a valued group member, severed social ties, and damaged reputation. However, it also seems that the Ju/'hoansi make accommodations to reduce these potential costs. For example, to reduce the chance for violence, coalitions deliver harsh criticism more often than individuals. Another interesting aspect to punishment among the Ju/'hoansi is that when criticism is delivered by a coalition, usually one or more group members, typically relatives, will abstain from joining the coalition to support the sanctioned group member and reduce the risk of losing him or her from the group. Finally, women were found to punish more often than men. Wiessner interprets this as a way to reduce the potential for verbal criticism to escalate into physical violence, a more costly form of punishment.

## Conclusion

Social norms represent more than typical or common behavior. Social norms emerge naturally to help maintain order and ensure the success of groups at multiple levels. This chapter presented a new perspective on social norms that emphasized norm enforcement as an essential component of understanding and defining a behavior as normative. Research shows that individuals are willing to enforce agreed-upon social norms using a variety of social sanctions, even when it is not in their own direct self-interest to do so. Social sanctions refer to rewards and punishments that are directed at an individual by other people. Social sanctions range on a spectrum from subtle to overt. Subtle sanctions might include nonverbal behaviors such as a dirty look, while overt sanctions typically involve some type of verbal or physical activity such as gossip, criticism, pushing, or shoving.

The social influence approach to social norms has used experimental research to determine how norms can be used as a persuasive tool. Research in this tradition has shown that social norms can be harnessed both by manipulating the physical or social environment as well as by providing normative information via verbal messages. To date, social norms interventions have been used primarily to promote health-related and environmental behaviors. When descriptive norms are communicated using the recommended best practices, these interventions can produce relatively long-lasting changes in beliefs and behaviors and can be implemented effectively on a large scale. Research shows that social norms interventions will have their maximum impact when they target individuals who are not highly involved with the behavior and reference groups with whom the target is highly identified. Although social norms present a powerful tool for changing behavior, both targets and practitioners tend to underestimate their influence.

**Future Directions**

This literature review highlighted several conflicting results that future research should endeavor to resolve. The first conflict relates to the activation of injunctive norms. Past research reveals that cues that might be expected to make an injunctive norm salient, such as a prohibition sign, often fail. Similarly, whereas Schultz and colleagues (2007) found that adding an injunctive norm component prevented an increase in energy consumption among "below average" households, follow-up research by Allcott (2011) documenting the application of this technique on a larger scale did not find a significant effect for the injunctive norm component. In both cases it is plausible that participants perceived the source of the injunctive component of the message to be an authority figure. Thus, one possible explanation is that expressions of approval and disapproval that come from an authority are less indicative of what "most people" approve and are therefore less meaningful to participants. Future research should

explore the role of the source of the injunctive norm message, as well as other criteria that must be met in order to activate injunctive norms. For example, it is not immediately clear why a confederate picking up a food bag or sweeping litter into a pile is more effective as a salience manipulation than are nonverbal signs of disapproval for violating the norm (e.g., the "crying Indian"). In sum, although it is clear that salient injunctive norms guide behavior, clearer guidelines are needed for how to effectively make injunctive norms salient.

The second conflict highlighted in this chapter concerns how to combine descriptive and injunctive norms for maximum impact. On this point, the practical advice derived from focus theory (i.e., to only communicate favorable descriptive norms; Cialdini, 2003) contradicts the advice derived from deviance regulation theory (i.e., to highlight deviant acts; Blanton & Christie, 2003). Future research should directly test these competing predictions. Specifically, when a desired behavior is not normative, is it better not to mention the descriptive norm and focus exclusively on the supportive injunctive norm (focus theory), or to juxtapose the two (deviance regulation theory)? Research conducted under these two theories has utilized different behaviors (e.g., littering versus getting flu shots) as well as different manipulations (e.g., manipulating the observable environment versus a newspaper article description). A reasonable starting point would be to examine each behavior using the alternative theory's manipulation. Additional research should also seek to determine when highlighting deviant acts will work, as Blanton and colleagues have proposed, versus when it will backfire, as Cialdini has argued.

Conflicting results have also been found regarding the effectiveness of local norms. Schultz and colleagues (2008) found no difference between a message that referenced "guests who had stayed in the same room" and a more general message referencing guests of the hotel. However, Goldstein and colleagues (2008) found that the "guest of this room" referent was the most effective. Both studies were conducted in a hotel and both promoted the reuse of bath towels. Why would two seemingly similar studies produce different results? One possible explanation involves differences in the perceived heterogeneity of hotel guests versus guests of the particular room at each of the hotels. Goldstein and colleagues conducted their study at a "midpriced national chain hotel," whereas Schultz and colleagues conducted their research at an "upscale beach resort." A midpriced national chain hotel arguably serves a more heterogeneous clientele compared to an upscale beach resort. Thus, at the midpriced hotel, guests might have perceived themselves to be more similar to other guests who stayed in the same room than to guests in general. In contrast, guests at the upscale beach resort might have perceived themselves to be equally similar to guests of the entire hotel and guests of the specific room. Future research should explore the extent to which perceived heterogeneity of a reference group moderates the influence of local norms.

The last conflict described earlier in this chapter concerns whether the availability of cognitive resources helps or hinders the influence of social norms. While Jacobson and colleagues (2011) found that depleting cognitive resources increased the influence of a descriptive norm message, Melnyk and colleagues (2011) found the opposite pattern. These disparate results might be the result of differences in how and when cognitive resources were depleted. In Jacobson and colleagues' study, cognitive resources were depleted prior to exposure to the normative intervention. Specifically, participants were able to fully attend to the message but may have lacked the ability to fully regulate their subsequent responses. In contrast, Melnyk and colleagues depleted participants' cognitive resources during exposure to the normative message, via a cognitive load task. This task prevented participants from fully attending to the message, which may explain why it was less influential. Thus, a task that depletes a person's ability to self-regulate might increase the influence of descriptive norms, whereas a task that distracts a person from attending to the message might weaken the influence of descriptive norms. Future research should test this proposed explanation, as well as others, so that the parameters for how and when to manipulate cognitive resources to maximize the impact of social norms can be clearly articulated.

The extant research shows that individuals are hesitant to attribute motivational power to social norms. However, to date, all of this research has been conducted in the Unites States, a country known for being individualistic. Given that social norms have a more powerful impact on people from collectivistic countries (Cialdini, Wosinka, Barret, Butner, & Gornik-Durose, 1999) and that conformity is seen as more socially desirable in collectivistic countries, it stands to reason that individuals in collectivistic countries may be more willing and/or able to detect the influence of others' behavior on their own behavior. In fact, they might even

overestimate the influence that others have on their own behavior. Future research should explore potential differences in the detection and estimation of the influence of social norms across cultures. If differences are found, additional research can explore whether they are due to differences in citizens' naïve causal theories/persuasion knowledge, differences in the perceived stigma/desirability associated with conforming, or some combination of the two.

On a practical note, more research is needed to sharpen our ability to transmit research findings to practitioners. For example, park rangers at Arizona's Petrified Forest National Park had been using a sign emphasizing that the integrity of the park was being threatened "a small piece at a time" by visitors stealing the petrified wood. Cialdini and colleagues (2006) tested multiple signs and found that a sign similar to the one already in use was actually most likely to inspire theft among park visitors. Unlike the study by Nolan and colleagues (2011) showing that energy experts were more willing to use a social norms message in their future outreach after being exposed to research about the effectiveness of such messages, Cialdini and colleagues (2006) found that empirical evidence was insufficient to persuade the park rangers. Park rangers' resistance to using the less intuitive normative message seemed to stem from the vivid personal accounts they received from members of the target audience supporting the ineffective message. This story highlights the danger of asking people to predict their own behavior and the need to find ways to promote the greater credibility of empirical inquiry over vivid anecdotes.

Lastly, future research should continue to explore the circumstances under which individuals are willing to sanction norm violators. For example, Wiessner's (2005) empirical observations of the Ju/'hoansi suggests that there may be differences in the causes and consequences of bilateral versus multilateral enforcement of social norms. Bilateral sanctioning occurs when one individual sanctions the norm violator (Posner & Rasmusen, 1999), whereas multilateral sanctioning describes sanctions carried out by a group of individuals. Additional research is needed to understand the conditions under which individuals are willing to sanction alone and when they prefer or require the backing of a group. In a related vein, it would be interesting to explore how social distance between two people affects their willingness to sanction one another. The relationship between willingness to sanction and social distance may best be described by an inverted U-shaped curve. The results of laboratory and field research show that individuals are quite willing to sanction strangers, and anecdotal evidence suggests that it is also quite common to sanction those who are closest to us. However, for acquaintances, with whom one is loosely affiliated, willingness to sanction should be relatively low. With acquaintances, particularly those with whom we expect to have repeated contact, the norm of politeness is likely to prevail, making comments about another's behavior inappropriate or even rude.

In closing, social norms will continue to be a fruitful topic of research for social influence scholars for many years to come. In this chapter several conflicts related to the design of social norms messages were identified as well as general directions for future research. These conflicts must be resolved and areas for future research must be pursued if we are to fully understand and utilize social norms for maximum impact.

## Acknowledgments

The author would like to thank Dr. Jessica Barber and Jed Brensinger for their comments on an earlier version of this manuscript.

## References

Aarts, H., & Dijksterhuis, A. (2003). The silence of the library: Environment, situational norm, and social behavior. *Journal of Personality and Social Psychology, 84*, 18–28.

Abrams, D., Wetherall, M., Cochrane, S., Hogg, M. A., & Turner, J. C. (1990). Knowing what to think by knowing who you are: Self-categorization and the nature of norm formation, conformity, and group polarization. *British Journal of Social Psychology, 29*, 97–119.

Ajzen, I. (1991). The theory of planned behavior. *Organizational Behavior and Human Decision Processes, 50*, 179–211.

Allcott, H. (2011). Social norms and energy conservation. *Journal of Public Economics, 95*, 1082–1095. doi:10.1016/j.jpubeco.2011.03.003

Axelrod, R. (1986). An evolutionary approach to norms. *American Political Science Review, 80*, 1095–1111.

Bandura, A. (1977). *Social learning theory.* Englewood Cliffs, NJ: Prentice-Hall.

Bator, R. J., Tabanico, J. J., Walton, M. L., & Schultz, P. W. (2014). Promoting energy conservation with implied norms and explicit messages. *Social Influence, 9*, 69–82.

Berger, J., & Heath, C. (2007). Where consumers diverge from others: Identity signaling and product domains. *Journal of Consumer Research, 34*, 121–134.

Blanton, H., & Christie, C. (2003). Deviance regulation: A theory of action and identity. *Review of General Psychology, 7*, 115–149.

Blanton, H., Stuart, A. E., & VandenEijnden, R. J. J. M. (2001). An introduction to deviance-regulation theory: The effect of behavioral norms on message framing. *Personality and Social Psychology Bulletin, 27*, 848–858.

Bochet, O., Page, T., & Putterman, L. (2006). Communication and punishment in voluntary contribution experiment. *Journal of Economic Behavior and Organization, 60*, 11–26.

Borsari, B., & Carey, K. B. (2003). Descriptive and injunctive norms in college drinking: A meta-analytic integration. *Journal of Studies on Alcohol, 64*, 331–341.

Brauer, M., & Chaurand, N. (2009). Descriptive norms, prescriptive norms, and social control: An intercultural comparison of people's reactions to uncivil behaviors. *European Journal of Social Psychology, 40*, 490–499.

Burger, J. M., Bell, H., Harvey, K., Johnson, J., Stewart, C., Dorian, K., & Swedroe, M. (2010). Nutritious or delicious? The effect of descriptive norm information on food choice. *Journal of Social and Clinical Psychology, 29*(2), 228–242.

Burger, J. M., LaSalvia, C. T., Hendricks, L. A., Mehdipour, T., & Neudeck, E. M. (2011). Partying before the party gets started: The effects of descriptive norms on pre-gaming behavior. *Basic and Applied Social Psychology, 33*, 220–227.

Burger, J. M., & Shelton, M. (2011). Changing everyday health behaviors through descriptive norm manipulations. *Social Influence, 6*, 69–77.

Chekroun, P., & Brauer, M. (2002). The bystander effect and social control behavior: The effect of the presence of others on people's reactions to norm violations. *European Journal of Social Psychology, 32*, 853–866.

Chen, X., Lupi, F., He, G., & Liu, J. (2009). Linking social norms to efficient conservation investment in payments for ecosystem services. *Proceedings of the National Academy of Sciences USA, 106*, 11812–11817.

Christensen, P. N., Rothgerber, H., Wood, W., & Matz, D. C. (2004). Social norms and identity relevance: A motivational approach to normative behavior. *Personality and Social Psychology Bulletin, 30*, 1295–1309.

Cialdini, R. B. (2001). *Influence: Science and practice.* Boston: Allyn and Bacon Boston.

Cialdini, R. B. (2003). Crafting normative messages to protect the environment. *Current Directions in Psychological Science, 12*, 105–109.

Cialdini, R. B. (2005). Basic social influence is underestimated. *Psychological Inquiry, 16*, 158–161.

Cialdini, R. B. (2011). The focus theory of normative conduct. In P. A. M. Van Lange, A. W. Kruglanski, & E. T. Higgins (Eds.), *Handbook of theories of social psychology* (pp. 295–312). Thousand Oaks, CA: Sage.

Cialdini, R. B., Demaine, L. J., Sagarin, B. J., Barrett, D. W., Rhoads, K., & Winter, P. L. (2006). Managing social norms for persuasive impact. *Social Influence, 1*, 3–15.

Cialdini, R. B., & Goldstein, N. J. (2004). Social influence: Compliance and conformity. *Annual Review of Psychology, 55*, 591–621.

Cialdini, R. B., Reno, R. R., & Kallgren, C. A. (1990). A focus theory of normative conduct: Recycling the concept of norms to reduce littering in public places. *Journal of Personality and Social Psychology, 58*, 1015–1026.

Cialdini, R. B., & Trost, M. R. (1998). Social influence: Social norms, conformity and compliance. In D. T. Gilbert, S. T. Fiske, & G. Lindzey (Eds.), *The handbook of social psychology* (4th ed., pp. 151–192). Boston: McGraw-Hill.

Cialdini, R. B., Wosinska, W., Barrett, D. W., Butner, J., & Gornik-Durose, M. (1999). Compliance with a request in two cultures: The differential influence of social proof and commitment/consistency on collectivists and individualists. *Personality and Social Psychology Bulletin, 25*, 1242–1253.

Clapp, J. D., Lange, J. E., Russel, C., Shillington, A., & Voas, R. B. (2003). A failed norms social marketing campaign. *Journal of Studies on Alcohol, 64*, 409–414.

Colding, J., & Folke, C. (2001). Social taboos: "Invisible" systems of local resource management and biological conservation. *Ecological Applications, 11*, 584–600.

Croker, H., Whitaker, K., Cooke, L., Wardle, J., & Ernst, E. (2009). Do social norms affect intended food choice? *Preventive Medicine, 49*, 190–193.

Cullum, J., O'Grady, M., Armeli, S., & Tennen, H. (2012). Change and stability in active and passive social influence dynamics during natural drinking events: A longitudinal measurement-burst study. *Journal of Social and Clinical Psychology, 31*, 51–80.

DeBono, A., Shmueli, D., & Muraven, M. (2011). Rude and inappropriate: The role of self-control in following social norms. *Personality and Social Psychology Bulletin, 37*, 136–146.

Dwyer, P. C., Maki, A. R., & Rothman, A. J. (2015). Promoting energy conservation behavior in public settings: The influence of social norms and personal responsibility. *Journal of Environmental Psychology, 41*, 30–34.

Ellickson, R. C. (2001). The market for social norms. *American Law and Economics Review, 3*, 1–49.

Epley, N., & Gilovich, T. (1999). Just going along: Nonconscious priming and conformity to social pressure. *Journal of Experimental Social Psychology, 35*, 578–589.

Everett, J. W., & Peirce, J. J. (1993). Curbside recycling in the U.S.A.: Convenience and mandatory participation. *Waste Management and Research, 11*, 49–61. doi:10.1006/wmre.1993.1006

Fehr, E., & Fischbacher, U. (2004). Third-party punishment and social norms. *Evolution and Human Behavior, 25*, 63–87.

Fehr, E., & Gächter, S. (2000). Cooperation and punishment in public goods experiments. *American Economic Review, 90*, 980–994.

Fehr, E., & Gächter, S. (2002). Altruistic punishment in humans. *Nature, 415*(6868), 137–140.

Ferraro, P. J., Jose Miranda, J., & Price, M. K. (2011). The persistence of treatment effects with norm-based policy instruments: Evidence from a randomized environmental policy experiment. *American Economic Review, 101*, 318.

Fornara, F., Carrus, G., Passafaro, P., & Bonnes, M. (2011). Distinguishing the sources of normative influence on proenvironmental behaviors: The role of local norms in household waste recycling. *Group Processes and Intergroup Relations, 14*, 623–635.

Friestad, M., & Wright, P. (1994). The persuasion knowledge model: How people cope with persuasion attempts. *Journal of Consumer Research, 21*, 1–31.

Friestad, M., & Wight, P. (1995). Persuasion knowledge: Lay people's and researchers' beliefs about the psychology of advertising. *Journal of Consumer Research, 22*, 62–74.

Gelfand, M. J. (2012). Culture's constraints international differences in the strength of social norms. *Current Directions in Psychological Science, 21*, 420–424.

Gino, F., Ayal, S., & Ariely, D. (2009). Contagion and differentiation in unethical behavior the effect of one bad apple on the barrel. *Psychological Science, 20*, 393–398.

Gockeritz, S., Schultz, P. W., Rendón, T., Cialdini, R. B., Goldstein, N. J., & Griskevicius, V. (2010). Descriptive normative beliefs and conservation behavior: The moderating roles of personal involvement and injunctive normative beliefs. *European Journal of Social Psychology, 40*, 514–523.

Goldstein, N., Cialdini, R., & Griskevicius, V. (2008). A room with a viewpoint: Using social norms to motivate environmental conservation in hotels. *Journal of Consumer Research, 35*, 472–482.

Griskevicius, V., Cialdini, R. B., & Goldstein, N. J. (2008). Social norms: An underestimated and underemployed lever for managing climate change. *International Journal of Sustainability Communication, 3*, 5–13.

Haines, M., & Spear, S. F. (1996). Changing the perception of the norm: A strategy to decrease binge drinking among college students. *Journal of American College Health, 45*, 134–140.

Heider, F. (1958). *The psychology of interpersonal relations*. New York: Wiley.

Henrich, J., McElreath, R., Barr, A., Ensminger, J., Barrett, C., Bolyanatz, A., . . . Ziker, J. (2006). Costly punishment across human societies. *Science, 312*, 1767–1770.

Horne, C. (2004). Collective benefits, exchange interests, and norm enforcement. *Social Forces, 82*, 1037–1062.

Horne, C., & Cutlip, A. (2002). Sanctioning costs and norm enforcement: An experimental test. *Rationality and Society, 14*, 285–307.

Jacobson, R. P., Mortensen, C. R., & Cialdini, R. B. (2011). Bodies obliged and unbound: Differentiated response tendencies for injunctive and descriptive social norms. *Journal of Personality and Social Psychology, 100*, 433.

Jaslow, R. (2012). *Sugary drinks over 16-ounces banned in New York City, Board of Health votes*. Retrieved February 2013, from http://www.cbsnews.com/8301-504763_162-57512246-10391704/sugary-drinks-over-16-ounces-banned-in-new-york-city-board-of-health-votes/

Johnson, M. B. (2012). Experimental test of social norms theory in a real-world drinking environment. *Journal of Studies on Alcohol and Drugs, 73*, 851.

Kallgren, C. A., Reno, R. B., & Cialdini, R. B. (2000). A focus theory of normative conduct: When norms do and do not affect behavior. *Personality and Social Psychology Bulletin, 26*, 1002–1012.

Kalmijn, M., & Uunk, W. (2007). Regional value differences in Europe and the social consequences of divorce: A test of the stigmatization hypothesis. *Social Science Research, 36*, 447–468.

Keizer, K., Lindenberg, S., & Steg, L. (2008). The spreading of disorder. *Science, 322*, 1681–1685. doi:10.1126/science.1161405

Keizer, K., Lindenberg, S., & Steg, L. (2011). The reversal effect of prohibition signs. *Group Processes and Intergroup Relations, 14*, 681–688.

Kinzig, A. P., Ehrlich, P. R., Alston, L. J., Arrow, K., Barrett, S., Buchman, T. G., . . . Saari, D. (2013). Social norms and global environmental challenges: The complex interaction of behaviors, values, and policy. *BioScience, 63*, 164–175.

Kormos, C., Gifford, R., & Brown, E. (2015). The influence of descriptive social norm information on sustainable transportation behavior: A field experiment. *Environment and Behavior 47*, 479–501. doi:0013916513520416

Kurzban, R., Descioli, P., & O'Brien, E. (2007). Audience effects on moralistic punishment. *Evolution and Human Behavior, 28*, 75–84.

Latané, B., & Darley, J. M. (1970). *The unresponsive bystander: Why doesn't he help?* New York: Appleton-Century-Crofts.

Ledgerwood, A., & Callahan, S. P. (2012). The social side of abstraction psychological distance enhances conformity to group norms. *Psychological Science, 23*, 907–913.

Levy Paluck, E., & Shepherd, H. (2012). The salience of social referents: A field experiment on collective norms and harassment behavior in a school social network. *Journal of Personality and Social Psychology, 103*, 899–915.

Mahdi, N. Q. (1986). Pukhtunwali: Ostracism and honor among the Pathan hill tribes. *Ethology and Sociobiology, 7*, 295–304.

Martens, M. P., Page, J. C., Mowry, E. S., Damann, K. M., Taylor, K. K., & Cimini, M. D. (2006). Differences between actual and perceived student norms: An examination of alcohol use, drug use, and sexual behavior. *Journal of American College Health, 54*, 295–300.

Mattern, J. L., & Neighbors, C. (2004). Social norms campaigns: Examining the relationship between changes in perceived norms and changes in drinking levels. *Journal of Studies on Alcohol, 65*, 489–493.

McDonald, R. I., Fielding, K. S., & Louis, W. R. (2013). Energizing and de-motivating effects of norm-conflict. *Personality and Social Psychology Bulletin, 39*, 57–72.

Melnyk, V., Herpen, E. V., Fischer, A. R., & van Trijp, H. (2011). To think or not to think: The effect of cognitive deliberation on the influence of injunctive versus descriptive social norms. *Psychology and Marketing, 28*, 709–729.

Milgram, S., Liberty, H. J., Toledo, R., & Wackenhut, J. (1986). Response to intrusion into waiting lines. *Journal of Personality and Social Psychology, 51*, 683–689.

Mollen, S., Ruiter, R. A., & Kok, G. (2010). Current issues and new directions in psychology and health: What are the oughts? The adverse effects of using social norms in health communication. *Psychology and Health, 25*, 265–270.

Neighbors, C., Larimer, M. E., & Lewis, M. A. (2004). Targeting misperceptions of descriptive drinking norms: Efficacy of a computer-delivered personalized normative feedback intervention. *Journal of Consulting and Clinical Psychology, 72*, 434–447.

Nisbett, R. E., & Bellows, N. (1977). Verbal reports about causal influences on social judgments: Private access versus public theories. *Journal of Personality and Social Psychology, 35*, 613–624.

Nisbett, R. E., & Wilson, T. D. (1977). The halo effect: Evidence for unconscious alteration of judgments. *Journal of Personality and Social Psychology, 35*, 250–256.

Nolan, J. M. (2011). The cognitive ripple of social norms communications. *Group Processes and Intergroup Relations, 14*, 689–702. doi:10.1177/1368430210392398

Nolan, J. M. (2013). Creating a culture of conservation: Willingness to confront environmental transgressors. *Ecopsychology, 5*, 3–8.

Nolan, J. M., Kenefick, J., & Schultz, P. W. (2011). Normative messages promoting energy conservation will be underestimated by experts . . . unless you show them the data. *Social Influence, 6*, 169–180.

Nolan, J. M., Schultz, P. W., Cialdini, R. B., Goldstein, N. J., & Griskevicius, V. (2008). Normative social influence is underdetected. *Personality and Social Psychology Bulletin, 34*, 913–923.

Ones, U., & Putterman, L. (2007). The ecology of collective action: A public goods and sanctions experiment with controlled group formation. *Journal of Economic Behavior and Organization, 62*, 495–521.

Ostrom, E., Walker, J., & Gardner, R. (1992). Covenants with and without a sword: Self-governance is possible. *American Political Science Review, 86*, 404–417.

Peeler, C. M., Far, J., Miller, J., & Brigham, T. A. (2000). An analysis of the effects of a program to reduce heavy drinking among college students. *Journal of Alcohol and Drug Education, 45*, 39–54.

Perkins, H. W. (2003). The emergence and evolution of the social norms approach to substance abuse prevention. In H. W. Perkins (Ed.), *The social norms approach to preventing school and college age substance abuse: A handbook for educators, counselors, and clinicians* (pp. 3–18). San Francisco: Jossey-Bass.

Petty, R. E., & Briñol, P. (2012). The Elaboration Likelihood Model. In P. A. M. Van Lange, A. Kruglanski, & E. T. Higgins (Eds.), *Handbook of theories of social psychology* (Vol. 1, pp. 224–245). London, UK: Sage.

Petty, R. E., & Cacioppo, J. T. (1986). The elaboration likelihood model of persuasion. *Advances in Experimental Social Psychology, 19*, 123–205.

Phua, J. J. (2013). The reference group perspective for smoking cessation: An examination of the influence of social norms and social identification with reference groups on smoking cessation self-efficacy. *Psychology of Addictive Behaviors, 27*, 102–112.

Posner, R. A., & Rasmusen, E. B. (1999). Creating and enforcing norms, with special reference to sanctions. *International Review of Law and Economics, 19*, 369–382.

Pronin, E., Molouki, S., & Berger, J. (2007). Alone in a crowd of sheep: Asymmetric perceptions of conformity and their roots in an introspection illusion. *Journal of Personality and Social Psychology, 92*, 585–595.

Reno, R. R., Cialdini, R. B., & Kallgren, C. A. (1993). The transsituational influence of social norms. *Journal of Personality and Social Psychology, 64*, 104–112.

Richetin, J., Perugini, M., Mondini, D., & Hurling, R. (2014). Conserving water while washing hands: The immediate and durable impacts of descriptive norms. *Environment and Behavior.* doi:0013916514543683

Rossano, M. J. (2012). The essential role of ritual in the transmission and reinforcement of social norms. *Psychological Bulletin, 138*, 529–549.

Ruttan, L. M. (1998). Closing the commons: Cooperation for gain or restraint? *Human Ecology, 26*, 43–66.

Schmitt, B. H., Dube, L., & Leclerc, F. (1992). Intrusions into waiting lines: Does the queue constitute a social system? *Journal of Personality and Social Psychology, 63*, 806–815.

Schultz, P. W. (1999). Changing behavior with normative feedback interventions: A field experiment on curbside recycling. *Basic and Applied Social Psychology, 21*, 25–36.

Schultz, P. W., Khazian, A. M., & Zaleski, A. C. (2008). Using normative social influence to promote conservation among hotel guests. *Social Influence, 3*, 4–23.

Schultz, P. W., Messina, A., Tronu, G., Limas, E. F., Gupta, R., & Estrada, M. (2014). Personalized normative feedback and the moderating role of personal norms: A field experiment to reduce residential water consumption. *Environment and Behavior.* doi:10.1177/0013916514553835

Schultz, P. W., Nolan, J. M., Cialdini, R. B., Goldstein, N. J., & Griskevicius, V. (2007). The constructive, deconstructive, and reconstructive power of normative feedback. *Psychological Science, 18*, 429–434.

Schwartz, S. H. (Ed.). (1977). *Normative influences on altruism.* New York: Academic Press.

Sharma, S., Rikhari, H. C., & Palni, L. M. S. (1999). Conservation of natural resources through religion: A case study from central Himalaya. *Society and Natural Resources, 12*, 599–612.

Sherif, M. (1966). *The psychology of social norms*. New York: Harper.

Skumatz, L. A., & Freeman, D. J. (2006). *Pay as you throw (PAYT) in the US: 2006 update and analyses*. Retrieved July 2015, from http://www.epa.gov/osw/conserve/tools/payt/pdf/sera06.pdf

Smith, J. R., & Louis, W. R. (2008). Do as we say and as we do: The interplay of descriptive and injunctive group norms in the attitude–behaviour relationship. *British Journal of Social Psychology, 47*, 647–666.

Steffian, G. (1999). Correction of normative misperceptions: An alcohol abuse prevention program. *Journal of Drug Education, 29*, 115–138.

Tajfel, H. (1974). Social identity and intergroup behaviour. *Social Science Information, 13*, 65–93.

Terry, D. J., & Hogg, M. A. (1996). Group norms and the attitude-behavior relationship: A role for group identification. *Personality and Social Psychology Bulletin, 22*, 776–793.

Terry, D. J., Hogg, M. A., & McKimmie, B. M. (2000). Attitude-behaviour relations: The role of in-group norms and mode of behavioural decision-making. *British Journal of Social Psychology, 39*, 337–361.

Thombs, D. L., & Hamilton, M. J. (2002). Effects of a social norm feedback campaign on the drinking norms and behavior of division I student-athletes. *Journal of Drug Education, 32*, 227–244.

Turner, J. C. (1985). Social categorization and the self-concept: A social cognitive theory of group behavior. In E. J. Lawler (Ed.), *Advances in group processes: Theory and research* (pp. 77–122). Greenwich, CT: JAI Press.

Vartanian, L. R., Herman, C. P., & Wansink, B. (2008). Are we aware of the external factors that influence our food intake? *Health Psychology, 27*, 533.

Weber, H. (2003). Breaking the rules: Personal and social responses to coping norm-violations. *Anxiety, Stress and Coping, 16*, 133–153.

Wechsler, H., Nelson, T. F., Lee, J. E., Seibring, M., Lewis, C., & Keeling, R. P. (2003). Perception and reality: A national evaluation of social norms marketing interventions to reduce college students' heavy alcohol use. *Journal of Studies on Alcohol and Drugs, 64*, 484.

Werch, C. E., Pappas, D. M., Carlson, J. M., DiClemente, C. C., Chally, P. S., & Sinder, J. A. (2000). Results of a social norm intervention to prevent binge drinking among first-year residential college students. *Journal of American College Health, 49*, 85–92.

Wiessner, P. (2005). Norm enforcement among the Ju/'hoansi Bushmen: A case of strong reciprocity? *Human Nature, 16*, 115–145.

Wilson, J. Q., & Kelling, G. (1982). The police and neighborhood safety: Broken windows. *Atlantic Monthly, 127*, 29–38.

# Social Inhibition

Megan K. McCarty *and* Steven J. Karau

**Abstract**

Social inhibition is the tendency for behaviors that are exhibited when one is alone to be minimized in the presence of others. Despite the long tradition of research investigating the effects of social presence on behavior, research on social inhibition does not constitute a cohesive literature. This chapter integrates social inhibition research from different traditions, focusing on helping behaviors, emotional expression, and behaviors that elicit social disapproval. We discuss moderators and processes that explain when and why social inhibition occurs: arousal, ambiguity, pluralistic ignorance, diffusion of responsibility, feelings of capability, evaluation apprehension, and confusion of responsibility. Key distinctions between social inhibition and related concepts are presented, helping to establish social inhibition as a central social influence concept. We conclude with an analysis of why social inhibition research has not formed a cohesive literature, and we hope that our review of social inhibition facilitates the integration of future research on the topic.

**Key Words:** social inhibition, social presence, bystander effect, evaluation apprehension, pluralistic ignorance, diffusion of responsibility

People often encounter situations where behaviors that they would otherwise engage in freely or with little thought are somehow constrained, restricted, or inhibited when other people are present. For example, an individual who sings loudly in the shower when home alone may not sing as loudly or as frequently when houseguests are present. Or one might not sing at all in a public shower at the gym. The current chapter focuses on this phenomenon of social inhibition and places it in the context of other social influence phenomena regarding the effects of social presence on behavior. Although previous research has investigated social inhibition, a consensus definition has not been formally developed. *We define social inhibition here as the tendency for behaviors that are exhibited when one is alone to be minimized in the presence of others.* Thus, social inhibition can involve the minimization of behaviors in the presence of others in terms of frequency or intensity, or the complete elimination of these behaviors. The presence of others has the potential to inhibit a wide range of behaviors, from more trivial behaviors like singing and asking for directions to more serious ones like the decision regarding whether or not to help a stranger in distress or to seek medical help for an embarrassing illness. Social inhibition may lead to detriments in performance. For example, not bringing up one's opinions in a group might lead to a poorer group decision. However, performance decrements are not a necessary component of social inhibition.

Despite the long tradition of research investigating the effects of social presence on behavior (e.g., Ringelmann, 1913; Triplett, 1898), research on social inhibition does not constitute a cohesive literature. Thus, a primary contribution of this chapter is to bring together social inhibition research from different traditions. Because our review focuses on social inhibition as an important type of social influence, we examine mostly social psychological research, and our discussion of the domains in which social inhibition has been demonstrated is not intended to be exhaustive.

A primary reason social inhibition does not constitute a cohesive literature is confusion regarding terminology. Research relevant to this phenomenon sometimes does not use the term "social inhibition" but is organized around more general processes that drove the research project in question, such as audience effects, helping, altruism, self-censorship, or social anxiety. Also, the term "social inhibition" has been used to refer to an effect, a process, and a personality trait. In defining social inhibition as the tendency for otherwise apparent behaviors to be minimized in the presence of others, we are treating it as an effect. The advantage of this approach is it focuses on the phenomenon as an outcome that could be influenced by a host of variables, and it does not restrict it to just one or a limited set of processes, situational factors, or personality influences. Thus, social inhibition is a phenomenon that can occur for a variety of reasons, or through a variety of processes. Some prior research has applied the term "social inhibition" to specific processes, such as a fear of embarrassment or negative evaluation when in the presence of others (Latané & Darley, 1970; Latané & Nida, 1981). Social inhibition effects can indeed occur due to evaluation apprehension, but many other processes can also create or contribute to social inhibition. Thus, we use the term "social inhibition" to refer to social inhibition effects regardless of process.

Some previous researchers have also used the term "social inhibition" to refer to a personality trait. In clinical domains, social inhibition is a component of Type D personality (distressed personality) characterized by feelings of insecurity, reduced emotional expressiveness, and withdrawal in social settings (Denollet, 2005; Grande, Glaesmer, & Roth, 2010). Conceptually, the individual difference of social inhibition is related to both introversion and shyness and is measured using self-reported agreement with items such as "I find it hard to start a conversation" and "I am a closed kind of person" (Denollet, 2005). We agree that certain types of people may be more likely to exhibit social inhibition effects than others, but we argue that in certain situations nearly anyone may demonstrate social inhibition. Thus, we do not want to limit the discussion of social inhibition to particular types of people, but we do acknowledge that certain individual differences may increase the likelihood that one will minimize behaviors in the presence of others. In sum, we define social inhibition as an effect rather than solely as the processes or individual differences that may contribute to that effect, and we hope this terminological clarification might help integrate social inhibition research across domains.

We begin our discussion of social inhibition with an overview of the variety of domains in which social inhibition occurs. This is followed by a discussion of processes and moderators that explain why and when social inhibition occurs. The final section demonstrates key distinctions between social inhibition and related social influence concepts. The relationships between social inhibition and these well-studied concepts help establish social inhibition as a central social influence concept in its own right.

## Domains of Social Inhibition

Social inhibition occurs across a wide variety of behavioral domains. In particular, the social inhibition of helping behavior and emotional expression have garnered special attention in the literature. We also discuss a number of social inhibition effects that have been demonstrated across areas of expertise, but that generally concern behaviors that may elicit social disapproval.

### Helping Behavior

Much of the work on social inhibition focuses on the bystander effect, the finding that an individual is less likely to help a person in need as the number of observers or potential helpers increases (Darley & Latané, 1968; Latané & Darley, 1968). Because the bystander effect reduces the likelihood of individual helping behavior when in the presence of others, it represents a specific type of social inhibition, namely the social inhibition of helping behavior. Indeed, the terms "bystander effect" and "social inhibition of helping behavior" are often used interchangeably.

Work on the bystander effect was prompted by the tragic case of Kitty Genovese, who was raped and murdered in 1964 over the course of two attacks and 30 minutes as 38 inactive witnesses looked on, many from a nearby apartment complex. Although the specifics of this incident, including the number of bystanders and their reactions, has been called into question (Manning, Levine, & Collins, 2007), this initial reporting of the incident spurred Darley and Latané's prolific program of research on the social inhibition of helping behavior.

In an initial study, participants completed a group discussion task. They were placed in individual rooms and believed they were interacting with other participants via an intercom system (Darley & Latané, 1968). During the task, participants heard what they thought was another participant having a seizure. The presence of others was manipulated such that participants thought that zero, one, or four other bystanders were available to intervene. The results demonstrated social inhibition of helping behavior. Participants were less likely to help as the perceived number of bystanders increased. The majority (85 percent) of participants in the no bystander condition sought to help, whereas only 31 percent of participants in the four-bystander condition did so. Additionally, participants were slower to help as the number of bystanders increased. The bystander effect has been replicated across many different types of helping situations, including personal injury (e.g., Latané & Darley, 1968), stranded motorists (Hurley & Allen, 1974), stolen property (e.g., Howard & Crano, 1974), technical problems (Misavage & Richardson, 1974), and dropped pencils (Latané & Dabbs, 1975).

These findings seem to run counter to the intuition that we might find safety in numbers, but the bystander effect does not speak to the victim's perspective. Thus, although an individual person may be less likely to help when in a larger group of bystanders, a victim can still have a better chance that at least one person will help him or her in a larger group of bystanders. Initial work on the bystander effect has generated a wealth of research, perhaps due to the seemingly counterintuitive nature of this finding, the fact that it helps to explain real-world tragedies, and the compelling experimental realism of several of the landmark studies (for a review of the bystander effect, see Latané & Nida, 1981; for a meta-analysis of factors influencing the likelihood of a victim receiving help, not the "bystander effect," see Fischer et al., 2011).

Research on the bystander effect has not only produced many empirical demonstrations but also some compelling theoretical insights into social inhibition. In particular, early work by Latané and Darley (1970) proposed a step-wise model outlining what a bystander needs to do in order to ultimately help: notice the situation, recognize the need for help, feel personal responsibility, feel able to help effectively, and make a conscious decision to help. Importantly, this model suggests that the presence of others may inhibit one's likelihood of helping others through multiple processes. For example, the presence of others may impede the development of a personal sense of responsibility to help (diffusion of responsibility), may increase concerns regarding

receiving negative evaluations if one helps, or may even prevent one from recognizing the need for help (e.g., pluralistic ignorance). These ideas will be given more attention when we delve into the processes of social inhibition.

Work on the bystander effect continues to thrive, and it has even been extended to explain virtual helping behaviors (Barron & Yechiam, 2002; Markey, 2000). For example, responses to e-mail requests for help are reduced when many others are included on the message (Blair, Thompson, & Wuensch, 2005). Bystander effects have also been observed in responses to questions posted on message boards (Voelpel, Eckhoff, & Forster, 2008).

Researchers have not only demonstrated the social inhibition of helping others but have also demonstrated the social inhibition of helping oneself, or help-seeking (Williams & Williams, 1983a). Indeed, the presence of others can create a strong enough social situation that it can even decrease the likelihood that one engages in self-beneficial behaviors (Latané & Darley, 1968; Williams & Williams, 1983b). In a classic study by Latané and Darley (1968), participants sat in a waiting room that filled with smoke. Participants were alone, with two other naïve participants, or with two confederates instructed to remain nonresponsive. Social inhibition was demonstrated, as participants were less likely to report the smoke when in the presence of others (38 percent or 10 percent for naïve and confederate conditions, respectively) than when they were alone (75 percent). The social inhibition of help-seeking was also demonstrated in a study where individuals experienced a computer program crash and had to seek help from either one or three experimenters to remedy the problem (Williams & Williams, 1983b). Individuals delayed help-seeking longer and pressed more computer keys in an effort to solve the problem on their own when they had to seek help from a group of three experimenters as opposed to a single experimenter. Petty and colleagues (Petty, Williams, Harkins, & Latané, 1977) also demonstrated that people were less likely to help themselves to a free lunch, in the form of a coupon for a free cheeseburger, as the number of others present in an elevator increased.

### Emotional Expression

Social inhibition has not only been studied in the context of helping behavior. In fact, the social inhibition of emotional expression, or "the tendency to inhibit or attenuate expressive behavior in the presence of others," has also generated considerable research (Kleck et al., 1976, p. 1211). For example, participants who were told they were being observed showed less pain-related facial expressivity when receiving electric shocks than participants who were not told they were being observed (Kleck et al., 1976). People also inhibit facial indicators of embarrassment, such as downward gazes and face touches, when viewing erotic pictures in the presence of others (Costa, Dinsbach, Manstead, & Bitti, 2001). This inhibition of emotional expression consumes cognitive resources and can have negative consequences such as decreased task performance (McCarty, Kelly, & Williams, 2014) and health risks (Denollet, 1997). Social inhibition also occurs with other types of body movements and vocalizations such as laughing and talking (Guerin, 1989).

The research on social inhibition of emotional expression suggests that social inhibition may be due in part to socialization processes and evaluation apprehension. For example, Yarczower, Kilbride, and Hill (1979) found that sixth graders who were told to imitate facial expressions did so more accurately and intensely when alone than when in the presence of an experimenter. Because this effect was not found in first graders, the researchers suggest that the social inhibition of emotional expression is learned through socialization processes, in which individuals discover what types of emotional displays are appropriate. Notably, a follow-up study by Yarczower and Daruns (1982) found social inhibition of emotional expression in both sixth and first graders. This finding suggests that processes other than socialization might motivate social inhibition, but it does not discount the role of socialization processes, as these may occur earlier than first grade (Tobin & Graziano, 2010).

More recent work by Friedman and Miller-Herringer (1991) suggests that social inhibition can be demonstrated for positive emotions in addition to negative ones. Postulating that social inhibition of emotional expression stems from the social consequences of the emotional expression, the researchers suggest inappropriate expressions of positive emotions are also subject to social inhibition. Friedman and Miller-Herringer focused on the modest winner display rule: the social norm suggesting that it is inappropriate to express undue positive emotion in response to one's own success. In this study, participants completed difficult probability questions alone and in the presence of confederates. Participants received positive false feedback that

they performed much better than other participants. Naïve coders rated participants' facial expressions as more positive and expressive when they were alone than when they were in the presence of others. Thus, social inhibition of positive expression was demonstrated. This research not only suggests the role of socialization and evaluation apprehension in social inhibition but also demonstrates that "emotional expression is more than an observable correlate of internal affective states; it also serves important functions in social comparison and social influence processes" (Friedman & Miller-Herringer, 1991, p. 76).

### Behaviors That Might Elicit Social Disapproval

Social inhibition has also been examined, albeit less frequently, for a range of behaviors beyond helping and emotional expression. In general, these findings suggest that social inhibition may often occur when the behaviors in question might elicit some degree of social disapproval. For example, research has shown evidence for the social inhibition of stereotyping and prejudice, such that implicit attitudes indicated less bias when participants were tested in groups as opposed to individually (Castelli & Tomelleri, 2008). Social inhibition can also help explain why students may be hesitant to participate in class (Hudson & Bruckman, 2004) and why people fail to confront others for wrongdoings. For example, the presence of other people can reduce the likelihood that an individual confronts a person who violates a societal norm (e.g., vandalizing property; Chekroun & Brauer, 2002). The presence of others has also been shown to inhibit indulgent eating behaviors (e.g., Herman, Roth, & Polivy, 2003), impulse shopping (Luo, 2005), and physiological responses to stress (Phillips, Carroll, Hunt, & Der, 2006).

### Summary

Social inhibition has been studied widely in the helping domain and has also garnered particular attention in the emotional expression literature. Although social inhibition may not be a primary focus of investigation in other domains, many demonstrations of social inhibition exist for a variety of behaviors that may elicit social disapproval. Indeed, although the studies mentioned here demonstrate the inhibition of behaviors when in the presence of others, the majority of this research does not explicitly use the term "social inhibition." This undoubtedly contributes, at least in part, to the fact that there is not a united social inhibition literature. We hope that our consideration of social inhibition work from multiple areas of research may encourage readers to consider the possibility of additional social inhibition effects that may occur within their areas of expertise.

## Social Inhibition Processes and Moderators

Social inhibition has been studied in diverse contexts and likewise has elicited a diverse set of explanations. There are a number of processes through which social inhibition can occur. Namely, arousal, ambiguity and uncertainty, pluralistic ignorance, diffusion of responsibility, feelings of capability, evaluation apprehension, and confusion of responsibility may all create or contribute to social inhibition, either individually or in combination. These processes are not necessarily in competition with each other. Social inhibition is a complex social phenomenon that is likely determined by multiple processes. Indeed, previous research suggests that multiple processes separately contribute to the bystander effect (Latané & Darley, 1976). However, certain processes may be more likely explanations in certain contexts. An analysis of these processes also lends itself to the identification of likely moderating variables.

Notably, as much of the work on social inhibition has focused on the bystander effect, the theoretical work on social inhibition processes has often been couched in terms of social inhibition and helping. However, many of these processes have either been documented to extend to other domains or have clear potential application beyond helping and bystander intervention.

### *Arousal*

Initial research on the effects of social presence on behavior suggests that arousal is an important mechanism. The presence of others is suggested to increase arousal (Laughlin & Wong-McCarthy, 1975; Zajonc, 1965), which can subsequently affect individuals' behaviors. For example, Middlemist and colleagues (Middlemist, Knowles, & Matter, 1976) conducted a clever, albeit methodologically controversial, field study investigating the effects of social presence on micturition. The study was conducted in a three-urinal lavatory. Social presence was manipulated by the presence of a confederate (at the adjacent urinal or one urinal removed from the subject) or the absence of a confederate. Using a hidden periscope-type apparatus to make measurements from a bathroom stall, researchers

measured the time until the onset of urination and the duration of urination. The presence of others inhibited urination behavior, both onset and duration, providing suggestive evidence for the role of arousal in social inhibition. However, arousal cannot always or fully explain social inhibition effects (e.g., Dickerson, Mycek, & Zaldivar, 2008; Kleck et al., 1976; Laughlin & Wong-McCarthy, 1975), as they have also been demonstrated repeatedly without corresponding increases in arousal.

### *Ambiguity and Uncertainty*

Latané and Darley (1970) made great theoretical contributions to the study of social inhibition in their step-wise model, which posited a variety of psychological explanations for social inhibition. The step-wise model suggests that to help someone in need, one must first notice the situation and recognize the need for help. Thus, the social inhibition of helping behavior stems in part from the fact that the presence of others can impede us from noticing situations and recognizing others' needs for help. Individuals look to those around them to define ambiguous situations, and therefore the presence of other inactive bystanders can indicate that the situation does not necessitate help (Latané & Nida, 1981; Latané & Rodin, 1969). For example, the social inhibition of helping is reduced when participants can both see and hear an emergency (a relatively unambiguous situation) as opposed to only hear the emergency (an ambiguous situation; Solomon, Solomon, & Stone, 1978).

The role of ambiguity and uncertainty in the social inhibition of helping behavior is substantiated by evidence that the severity of the situation moderates the effects (Mason & Allen, 1976). For example, the likelihood that an individual will help in the presence of others is also enhanced in dangerous emergency situations, such as situations involving strong-built, intimidating perpetrators as opposed to skinny, unthreatening perpetrators (Fischer, Greitemeyer, Pollozek, & Frey, 2006). The type of bystander likewise influences the degree of social inhibition, also providing support for the role of ambiguity and uncertainty in these effects. For example, social inhibition is less pronounced when the bystanders are friends, and therefore less likely to misinterpret each other's initial inaction and potential confusion as a sign the situation does not require help (Latané & Rodin, 1969). Additionally, the bystander effect is accentuated when bystanders are confederates explicitly instructed not to respond to an emergency situation as opposed to when bystanders are other naïve participants (Latané & Darley, 1968). Witnessing the inactive confederates as opposed to other uninstructed participants creates a more ambiguous situation, and it decreases the likelihood that participants will notice the emergency situation and interpret the situation as requiring action.

Although the step-wise model was developed to explain bystander intervention, it can also be applied to other social inhibition effects, especially in situations that may involve ambiguity or uncertainty about the situation, its outcome, or how others might view an individual who behaves in a certain manner. For example, an influential self-presentational model of social anxiety by Schlenker and Leary (1982) holds that individuals are more likely to experience anxiety about situations in which they are less certain about whether their actions are likely to lead to positive versus negative outcomes and evaluations from others. Although work in this area has focused mostly on individual differences, situational implications are also readily apparent, given that more ambiguous or uncertain social settings make it hard to know which actions are most appropriate (for a review, see Leary, 2010).

Additional insight into ambiguity and uncertainty emerges from social impact theory (Latané, 1981). The primary assertion of social impact theory is that the influence of social forces on a target's behavior is a multiplicative function of three source factors: strength (S), immediacy (I), and number (N). Hence, I = $f$(SIN). Strength denotes the salience or importance of a source of influence. For example, a high-status other would be a particularly strong source of influence. Immediacy denotes the physical or psychological proximity of the source (such as in space, time, or the richness of the interaction mode). Number denotes how many sources of influence are present. Thus, social impact is increased as the strength, immediacy, and number of sources of influence are increased or enhanced.

Factors related to ambiguity can be couched in terms of strength and immediacy. Increasing the strength of the source by having a more salient, obvious need for help increases the likelihood that a victim will receive assistance (Fischer et al., 2006). Increasing the immediacy of the source by allowing participants to both see and hear the emergency as opposed to only hear it also reduces the bystander effect (Solomon et al., 1978). Social impact theory suggests that increasing the immediacy of the source

through other means, such as how physically close one is to an injured person or whether the injury happened an hour as opposed to a moment ago, should also reduce the likelihood that helping behaviors will be minimized in the presence of others. Moderators related to evaluation concerns may also be situated within this social impact theory framework, even in studies of social inhibition of behaviors other than helping. In these studies, there is no victim, so it is the others present that serve as the source of influence. When the others present are less immediate because they are not able to see and evaluate the actor, social inhibition is reduced (Ross & Braband, 1973). Reducing the strength of the audience in terms of likely intimidation, such as when it is composed of friends or others one is already comfortable with, can also reduce evaluation apprehension and thus diminish social inhibition (Buck, Losow, Murphy, & Costanzo, 1992). Alternatively, social impact theory suggests that increasing source strength, such as by having a high-status person or leader present, may increase social inhibition.

### Pluralistic Ignorance

Pluralistic ignorance, the idea that people may go along with group norms that they privately reject because they falsely believe nearly all others accept them, is also related to the role of uncertainty in social inhibition (Miller & McFarland, 1987). Research on pluralistic ignorance suggests that we believe the fear of embarrassment and evaluation is a more significant determinant of our own behavior than others' behavior. Thus, when individuals are nonresponsive in an emergency situation, they may attribute their own inactivity to a fear of embarrassment and confusion about the correct course of action, but they are less likely to interpret others' inactivity in the same way. Thus, the nonresponsivity of bystanders may be interpreted as an indicator that the situation does not necessitate help, contributing to the social inhibition of helping behavior. Pluralistic ignorance can also lead to an incomplete consideration of alternatives during group decision making and has been identified as a contributing factor to groupthink (Janis, 1982).

Although the roles of uncertainty and pluralistic ignorance have primarily been investigated as mechanisms for the social inhibition of helping behavior, these may play a role in other social inhibition effects as well. For example, uncertainty may also come into play in the social inhibition of emotional expression. In a situation where one is uncertain about whether someone is serious or joking, one may inhibit natural emotional expressions when in the presence of others, like the inclination to laugh.

## Diffusion of Responsibility

However, assuming that someone notices a situation and recognizes the need for a particular behavior, the presence of others can still inhibit this behavior. For this behavior to occur, Darley and Latané (1970) suggest that the person must also assume personal responsibility for the action. The diffusion of responsibility explanation for the bystander effect suggests that individuals feel less responsible to help as the number of other people present increases (Darley & Latané, 1968).

The numerical dynamics of responsibility diffusion are nicely articulated within social impact theory (Latané, 1981; White, 1990; Williams & Williams, 1983b). Specifically, it suggests that the social impact of a single help requestor is divided across all targets of that influence attempt. Thus, the need for help of a single victim is divided or diffused across all available bystanders (Darley & Latané, 1968). Another key assertion of social impact theory is that increases in number should be more impactful when Ns are small rather than large, such that the incremental increase in impact should diminish as N gets larger and larger. Indeed, the bystander intervention research supports this assertion. Although the combined impact of a group of two bystanders is greater than the impact of a single bystander, the social impact of the first bystander is greater than that of the second bystander, and so on (Darley & Latané, 1968; Latané, 1981).

Situational factors beyond number also influence the dynamics of responsibility. Evidence for the role of diffusion of responsibility in social inhibition comes in part from studies that manipulate bystander ability to help. When bystanders are present but perceived as unable to help, the social inhibition of helping is minimized or even absent (Bickman, 1971, 1972). For example, when the emergency is the presence of an odorless smoke, social inhibition of helping behavior is obtained when the bystander can see, but not when the bystander is blind (Ross & Braband, 1973). The bystander effect is also mitigated when the other person present is a child as opposed to an adult (Ross, 1971). More recent research also supports the role of diffusion of responsibility in the bystander effect. Work by Garcia and colleagues (Garcia, Weaver, Moskowitz, & Darley, 2002) found that words associated with the construct of

being unaccountable (e.g., "unaccountable" and "exempt") were more accessible in memory when participants were instructed to imagine the presence of others. Group norms that make salient a responsibility to help can actually reverse the bystander effect. For example, Horowitz (1971) found that if other bystanders were members of a service group, increasing the number of bystanders actually increased the likelihood that an individual would help. Evidence that White participants, especially those high in prejudice, are more likely to succumb to the bystander effect when the victim is Black as opposed to White may also be taken as suggestive of the role of feelings of personal responsibility in the social inhibition of helping behavior (Gaertner, Dovidio, & Johnson, 1982).

Thus, diffusion of responsibility is an important process in the social inhibition of helping behavior and also helps identify important moderators of the effect, such as number of bystanders, perceptions of others' ability to help, perceptions of accountability, and service-related group norms. Notably, the degree of responsibility one feels to help is often only measured through actual helping behavior, and thus the mediating role of diffusion of responsibility is often not empirically assessed. In addition, careful attention to the intended meaning of the phrase "diffusion of responsibility" is important, as in some instances the phrase is used more as a synonym for the bystander effect than as a potential process variable. Generally, the study of diffusion of responsibility has focused on the bystander effect and, unlike some of the other processes we discuss, seems uniquely suited to explain social inhibition in this particular realm, although it should be noted that the construct has also been useful in explaining social influence phenomena other than social inhibition, such as social facilitation and social loafing (see Harkins & Seitchik, this volume).

## Feelings of Capability

Even when individuals recognize the need for a particular behavior and feel a personal responsibility to engage in this behavior, they may not do so if they do not feel capable, especially if they are in the presence of others (Darley & Latané, 1970). Individuals who feel highly capable of helping effectively are less likely to demonstrate the bystander effect. For example, registered nurses helped an injured workman equally frequently regardless of the presence of bystanders, whereas individuals who were not nurses helped the man more frequently when no bystanders were present (Cramer,

McMaster, Bartell, & Dragna, 1988). Similar effects have been obtained when participants underwent a competence manipulation, such as watching videos that included medical information that was relevant to the emergency (Pantin & Carver, 1982).

The role of feelings of capability in the bystander effect may be motivated by a desire not to do harm, especially in more complex medical situations. However, these effects may also be explained by a desire not to look foolish doing something that one does not feel confident doing. In other words, evaluation apprehension and self-presentation concerns contribute to social inhibition.

### Evaluation Apprehension and Concerns for Self-Presentation

Ultimately, individuals may recognize the need for a particular behavior and feel responsible and capable to engage in this behavior but make the decision not to do so. A wealth of evidence suggests that this evaluation apprehension plays an important role in social inhibition, and in contrast to some of the other processes discussed here, it has been used to explain these effects across a number of domains. Engaging in a variety of behaviors in the presence of others, such as intervening in an emergency, expressing emotions, or even eating, comes with the risk that others will perceive these behaviors negatively. This risk can result in the inhibition of these behaviors in the presence of others (Latané & Darley, 1970). Indeed, much of the social inhibition research concerns behaviors that are relatively negative, indicate incompetency, and threaten self-esteem, such as seeking help (Williams & Williams, 1983b) and displaying embarrassment (Costa et al., 2001). Similarly, a number of researchers suggest that evaluation apprehension plays a large role in the social inhibition of emotional expression more generally (e.g., Brody, 2000; Jansz, 2000).

Individuals are motivated to save face and avoid the aversive experience of public embarrassment (Brown, 1968, 1970; Shapiro, 1983). This fear of embarrassment and negative evaluation can decrease the likelihood that individuals perform certain behaviors in public (Leary & Kowalski, 1990). Indeed, there is evidence that the presence of others, imagined or actual, automatically activates concerns for social desirability and the impression others are forming (Puntoni & Tavassoli, 2007). We are socialized to learn what emotional expressions are appropriate and to inhibit those expressions that are not appropriate when in the presence of others (Friedman & Miller-Herringer, 1991). Thus, we

may be more likely to inhibit counterstereotypic behaviors in the presence of others (McCarty et al., 2014), as we fear the negative consequences that accompany these expressions, often called backlash effects (Rudman & Fairchild, 2004). For example, to avoid violating the norm of female modesty, women inhibit their expressions of pride in public by underestimating their GPA achievement when in the presence of others (Heatherington et al., 1993). Indeed, modesty may be a strategic form of social inhibition where certain strengths are downplayed in order to elicit favorable impressions from others (Baumeister, Hutton, & Tice, 1989).

Thus, individuals can engage in social inhibition to pursue self-presentation goals (whether implicitly or explicitly), to use their behavior to communicate desired information about the self to others (Baumeister, 1982), or to manage impressions and shape opinions others form about the self (Leary & Kowalski, 1990). By downplaying behaviors that might elicit negative impressions when in the presence of others, individuals may be able to elicit desired or more positive impressions from others. Leary and Kowalksi's model of impression management makes a distinction between impression motivation, the goal to monitor and influence others' perceptions, and impression construction, the processes through which individuals portray a particular impression. Thus, social inhibition is relevant to the impression construction element of impression management. Theories of self-presentation and impression management suggest a number of variables that influence the ways in which people manage the impressions of others, and these variables may help explain the conditions under which social inhibition occurs. For example, not only may one socially inhibit to portray a generally positive impression, but one may also socially inhibit to portray characteristics associated with specific roles, with one's self-concept, or with one's ideal self (for a review of self-presentation, see Tyler and Adams, this volume).

Evidence for the role of evaluation apprehension and self-presentation concerns in social inhibition comes in part from work demonstrating that the types of people who make up the audience influence the strength of social inhibition effects. Indeed, the impact of evaluation apprehension is often investigated by manipulating not only whether others are present but also whether present others are capable of evaluating or not. For example, audience members may be blindfolded or not (Cottrell, Wack, Sekerak, & Rittle, 1968). Alternatively, no audience members may be physically present, but participants may be under the impression they are being videotaped and evaluated or not (Snyder & Monson, 1975). In general, social inhibition is minimized under conditions where there are less evaluation and self-presentation concerns. For example, social inhibition of helping behavior (Latané & Darley, 1970; Latané & Rodin, 1969) and emotional expression (Buck et al., 1992) are minimized or eliminated when the others present are friends. More generally, social inhibition may be reduced or eliminated when the others present share a social category membership (Levine, Cassidy, Brazier, & Reicher, 2002; Levine & Crowther, 2008; Levine, Prosser, Evans, & Reicher, 2005) or are higher in cohesiveness (Rutkowski, Gruder, & Romer, 1983).

Individual differences can also influence social inhibition. Although this chapter focuses on the phenomena of social inhibition, as opposed to personality traits concerning feeling inhibited and insecure in public (e.g., Denollet, 1997), individuals who are especially susceptible to such feelings should be more likely to minimize some social behaviors. In general, stronger social inhibition effects are demonstrated for those individuals with personality traits associated with increased evaluation apprehension and concern for self-presentation. Individuals who report greater fear of negative evaluation are more likely to demonstrate the bystander effect (Karakashian, Walter, Christopher, & Lucas, 2006). Individuals higher in social monitoring also demonstrate greater social inhibition (Friedman & Miller-Herringer, 1991). Social monitoring concerns the motivation and ability to interpret situational social cues and present oneself in socially acceptable ways. Individuals higher in this trait may be more likely to experience evaluation apprehension (Puntoni & Tavassoli, 2007) and are more likely to demonstrate social inhibition of emotional expression (Friedman & Miller-Herringer, 1991). Masculinity also inhibits public helping behavior, and researchers theorize this is because masculinity can be associated with fear of embarrassment and concerns about demonstrating incompetence (Tice & Baumeister, 1985).

Given the relationship between social anxiety and heightened concerns about self-presentation, social anxiety may also be associated with increased social inhibition (Schlenker & Leary, 1982). However, this relationship may be complicated, especially when it comes to explaining the social inhibition of behaviors that are generally socially desirable, such as helping behavior. When the behavior in question

is something clearly positive that comes at a low risk of embarrassment such as donating to charity, those low in social anxiety demonstrate the typical decreases in helping when in the presence of others, whereas those high in social anxiety demonstrate increases in helping in the presence of others (Garcia, Weaver, Darley, & Spence, 2009). Public self-awareness and accountability can also reverse the bystander effect, encouraging helping (van Bommel, van Prooijen, Elffers, & Van Lange, 2012). Thus, although one may experience evaluation apprehension with regards to performing any behavior in public, variables related to evaluation concerns are particularly likely to increase social inhibition of behaviors that are not socially desirable in the given situation. In this way, evaluation apprehension and self-presentation concerns may not play as strong a role in the social inhibition of helping behavior as in the social inhibition of other sorts of behaviors like emotional expression and prejudice, as helping is generally interpreted positively.

Other individual differences that are related to evaluation apprehension or concerns regarding rejection may also moderate social inhibition effects, such as individual differences in embarrassment and shyness (Miller, 1995; Schlenker & Leary, 1982), the need to belong (Leary, Kelly, Cottrell, & Schreindorfer, 2013), and rejection sensitivity (Downey & Feldman, 1996). Not only may individual differences related to evaluation apprehension moderate social inhibition effects, but so too may individual differences related to other processes that contribute to social inhibition. For example, reducing uncertainty and increasing feelings of personal responsibility and capability should attenuate social inhibition. Therefore, individual differences such as self-efficacy (Paulhus, 1983), competence (Abele & Wojciszke, 2007), and self-esteem (Rosenberg, 1965) may also moderate social inhibition.

### Confusion of Responsibility

Finally, the confusion of responsibility provides another explanation for the role of evaluation apprehension and self-presentation in social inhibition that is specific to the social inhibition of helping behavior. Cacioppo, Petty, and Losch (1986) demonstrate that the bystander effect is due in part to what they call confusion of responsibility, the fact that people who help may be attributed responsibility for the victim's fate. The inhibition of helping behavior in the presence of others may stem in part from a desire to avoid this negative attribution and maintain a positive impression. This concern is warranted, as the researchers demonstrate that helpers are in fact attributed greater responsibility for doing harm to the victim as the number of others on scene increases. Thus, the confusion of responsibility explanation for the social inhibition of helping behavior is consistent with the importance of evaluation apprehension and self-presentation in these effects. However, confusion of responsibility should only occur in those limited circumstances where a passerby could confuse the helper with the perpetrator. For example, confusion of responsibility may occur when someone leans down to help an injured person, but it is unlikely to occur when someone gives a stranger food or money.

### Summary

A number of processes can create or contribute to social inhibition. There is evidence that arousal, ambiguity and uncertainty, pluralistic ignorance, diffusion of responsibility, feelings of capability, evaluation apprehension and concerns for self-presentation, and confusion of responsibility all contribute to social inhibition. A number of moderating variables also influence the conditions under which these processes lead to social inhibition effects of varying magnitude. The diversity of these explanations demonstrates the complex nature of social inhibition.

## Concepts Related to Social Inhibition

Social inhibition is central to the study of social influence, as it concerns the impact that the presence of others has on our behavior. As such, social inhibition is related to other social influence concepts, including social facilitation, conformity, social loafing, deindividuation, and groupthink. However, because the study of social inhibition is distributed across domains of research and not concentrated in a single, focused literature, the relationship between social inhibition and other social influence concepts is not always readily apparent. Although social inhibition can be isolated as a distinct phenomenon, it does have links to these other well-established social influence areas, and these linkages help demonstrate that social inhibition is central to the study of social influence.

### Social Facilitation

Social inhibition and social facilitation are two effects whereby the presence of others can influence an individual's behavior. Social facilitation is sometimes oversimplified and construed as increased task performance when in the presence of others. Likewise, social inhibition is sometimes misunderstood as decreased task performance when in the presence of others. In fact, social facilitation can result in either increased or decreased task performance under public conditions. Social facilitation occurs when the presence of others enhances the emission of dominant responses and inhibits the emission of subordinate responses (Zajonc & Sales, 1966; see Harkins & Seitchik, this volume). In the case of simple or well-learned tasks, the dominant response is correct, resulting in improved task performance in public. In the case of difficult or unfamiliar tasks, the dominant response is incorrect, resulting in decreased task performance in public (Bond & Titus, 1983; Markus, 1978). Although some researchers have used the term "social inhibition" to refer to such decreased performance on complex or unfamiliar tasks, this is clearly a misnomer, given that the reduced performance actually results from enhanced drive. Thus, social facilitation encompasses instances in which social presence results in either increases or decreases in task performance, depending on how familiar versus unfamiliar and how simple versus complex the task is.

There are two key differences between social facilitation and social inhibition. First, social facilitation concerns the effects of social presence on performance. Social inhibition concerns the effects of social presence on behaviors more generally. Thus, social inhibition need not have performance implications. For example, eating, singing, or helping others less in public does not necessarily have implications for task performance. Indeed, social inhibition research has not generally focused on task performance. However, social inhibition may have implications for task performance. Being less likely to express anger in a group might lead to better task performance, whereas being less likely to speak up and introduce new information in a group might lead to worse task performance.

Second, social facilitation concerns the enhancement of the dominant response in the presence of others, whereas social inhibition concerns behavior that is present when one is alone being minimized in the presence of others. In fact, social inhibition can involve the minimization of the dominant response in the presence of others, the opposite of social facilitation. For example, singing in the shower or expressing anger in response to a perceived wrongdoing may be habitual, dominant responses, but these can nonetheless be minimized in the presence of others. Therefore, although social inhibition and social facilitation both involve the effects of social presence on behavior, these are distinct constructs. For a more in depth discussion of social facilitation, see Seitchik, Brown, and Harkins (this volume), Strauss (2002), and Guerin (1986).

## Conformity

Social inhibition also has some conceptual ties with conformity (see Hodges, this volume). Conformity concerns changing one's behavior to match that of others. The majority of conformity research involves individuals changing their behaviors to match the group by engaging in a normative behavior they might not otherwise, also known as "conformity by commission." However, conformity can also occur when individuals change their behaviors to match the group by not engaging in a nonnormative behavior they might engage in otherwise. This second type of conformity has been referred to as "conformity by omission" (Cialdini & Trost, 1998; Sorrels & Kelley, 1984). Sorrels and Kelley (1984) demonstrated conformity by omission in the context of the autokinetic effect, in which a small, stationary light appears to move when in a dark, otherwise empty environment. In this study, participants reported seeing more movement individually than when in groups. This conformity by omission is social inhibition: Individuals minimized their natural responding when in the presence of others. Thus, not all conformity is social inhibition, but social inhibition can be construed as conformity by omission.

Although social inhibition can be understood as conformity by omission, there are important reasons to consider social inhibition separately from conformity more generally. Social inhibition can occur when one inhibits a behavior in the presence of others, but this does not necessarily match the behaviors of others. For example, knowledge that an individual will be evaluated via videotape may result in social inhibition, even though no other people are physically present for this individual to match. Thus, although conformity typically involves interacting individuals, social inhibition can involve the impact of mere social presence.

Although there are instances of social inhibition that are conformity by omission (e.g., Sorrels & Kelley, 1984), there are key distinctions between these effects and the typically studied conformity by commission effects that make it important to consider these phenomena separately. Social inhibition and conformity by omission are different from conformity by commission in that that they involve the suppression of one's natural behavioral inclinations (Smith, Smythe, & Lien, 1972). This suppression makes the conformity process qualitatively distinct, as suppression consumes cognitive resources (Richards & Gross, 1999, 2000). Thus, social inhibition results in different cognitive and performance consequences than other types of conformity (McCarty et al., 2014).

Finally, social inhibition should be considered separate from conformity because there are a number of processes that explain social inhibition, but not conformity. Conformity research focuses primarily on two explanations: informational and normative motivations (Cialdini & Goldstein, 2005). Informational motivations concern the desire to be accurate. For example, one might adjust responses in a difficult task to match those of others (Sherif, 1936). Normative motivations for conformity concern the desire to be evaluated positively and affiliate with others. As previously mentioned, individuals who do not conform and who exhibit deviant behaviors and opinions can face negative social consequences like rejection (Kruglanski & Webster, 1991; Schachter, 1951). Instances in which individuals go along with a group's clearly wrong answer in an easy task provide strong evidence for the role of normative motivations in conformity (Asch, 1956). Like conformity, social inhibition can also occur for informational reasons like uncertainty or normative reasons like evaluation apprehension. However, a variety of other processes may play an important role in social inhibition effects but not in conformity effects, such as arousal, diffusion of responsibility, and feelings of capability.

## Social Loafing

Social loafing occurs when individuals exert less effort and motivation when working collectively as opposed to working alone or coactively (Karau & Williams, 1993, 2001). In collective work, individuals pool their inputs with those of others into a group total or product. Social loafing occurs across a wide variety of tasks, including physical (e.g., clapping and yelling) and cognitive (e.g., brainstorming; Karau & Williams, 1993). One might be inclined to construe social loafing as the social inhibition of effort, the reduction of motivation in the presence of others. Diffusion of responsibility in particular can be an important process involved in both social loafing and social inhibition. However, a closer consideration demonstrates that social loafing and social inhibition are quite distinct phenomena for a number of reasons.

First, social loafing focuses on the motivational effects that working with others on a collective task have compared with working individually, and individual comparisons usually deploy a coactive group to control for group size and related factors across the comparison. In contrast, social inhibition concerns the effects of the presence of others on one's actions (whether performance-related or otherwise), rather than the effects of working with others on a common task.

Second, the collective tasks examined in social loafing typically lead individuals to be less identifiable and less easily evaluated, and they may also serve to reduce arousal. Indeed, social loafing can often be reduced or eliminated when evaluation concerns are strengthened, such as when individual contributions to the group product are identifiable and there are standards of comparison with which to assess performance (Harkins & Jackson, 1985; Williams, Harkins, & Latané, 1981). However, as described earlier, social inhibition typically occurs when evaluation apprehension and arousal are higher in the presence of others, and it is reduced or eliminated when evaluation and arousal are lower. For example, social inhibition is less likely when those present are highly cohesive (Rutkowski et al., 1983), friends (Latané & Rodin, 1969), or report low fear of negative evaluation (Karakashian et al., 2006). Although evaluation apprehension is only one process among many that can contribute to social inhibition, the opposite role of evaluation apprehension in social loafing and social inhibition provides strong evidence that despite surface-level similarities, these are separate concepts. Stated differently, social loafing does not represent an inhibition of effort, but a reduced responsibility, accountability, or efficacy of one's actions when working collectively. In this sense, it represents more of a disinhibition of individuals' general tendencies to only work as hard as the situation requires them to than any type of inhibition.

## Deindividuation

There are also some similarities between social inhibition and deindividuation (see Spears, this volume). Deindividuation occurs when individuals experience loss of self-awareness in groups (Festinger, Pepitone, & Newcomb, 1952). When people are deindividuated, they feel anonymous and act in accordance with group norms, positive or negative (Johnson & Downing, 1979). Often there are no explicit prosocial norms in large groups, and thus deindividuation can result in individuals enacting

more selfish and antisocial behavior (Diener, 1976; Douglas & McGarty, 2001). Key to this experience of deindividuation is anonymity, the sense that one is indistinguishable from the group. Thus, deindividuation may be especially likely in large groups, where anonymity is more likely (Mann, 1981). This anonymity may result in a diffusion of responsibility, encouraging behaviors consistent with group norms, even negative ones like vandalism and violence.

However, there are important distinctions between deindividuation and social inhibition that necessitate the separate consideration of these concepts. First, deindividuation and social inhibition occur in different types of group contexts. Deindividuation tends to occur in large groups, in group situations so strong that one loses the self in the anonymity of the group, or in smaller group situations in which the individual's identity is hidden or disguised. Social inhibition, on the other hand, is most frequently studied in small groups such as the presence of a single bystander, or even the expectation that one is being videotaped. These group situations are rarely the type of strong, cohesive group in which one might lose one's separate sense of identity. In fact, social inhibition is less likely in highly cohesive groups (Rutowski et al., 1983). Second, evaluation apprehension operates differently in deindividuation and social inhibition. Deindividuation occurs in circumstances where one is part of the crowd and is not easily identified or evaluated. On the other hand, social inhibition typically occurs in circumstances where individuals are concerned with the potential reactions or evaluations of others. Notably, there is some evidence that social inhibition may be diminished in strength when group size is very large (250 or more members), perhaps because increases in anonymity protect individuals from the risk of evaluation (Voelpel et al., 2008).

## Groupthink

Groupthink is a phenomenon in which groups pursue premature concurrence seeking on a decision without adequately evaluating the decision alternative. Groupthink occurs in group decision-making situations in which individuals suppress dissenting opinions in the interest of positive group dynamics (Janis, 1971, 1982). Groupthink is often characterized by highly cohesive groups, by an exaggerated sense of confidence or morality, and by members suppressing dissenting opinions, and it may be especially likely to occur in groups that are isolated from different opinions and in which the leader takes a clear position early in the decision-making process. Groupthink has been proposed as a contributor to a number of tragedies, including the Challenger explosion (Moorhead, Ference, & Neck, 1991).

Groupthink is typified by a number of elements that contribute to poor decision making. Particularly relevant to our discussion of social inhibition are the illusion of unanimity, self-censorship, and mindguards. Highly cohesive groups can lead to the mistaken impression that all of the group members feel similarly. This illusion of unanimity can lead individuals who have reservations about the group's proposed course of action to remain silent because they fear negative reactions from others and uncomfortable group dynamics. These processes are quite similar to the pluralistic ignorance processes discussed earlier, in which individuals follow group norms they personally disagree with because they incorrectly assume that everyone else accepts these (Miller & McFarland, 1987). Groups who suffer from groupthink may also have mindguards, individuals who protect the group from information that is inconsistent with the proposed course of action to prevent group disruption. Both self-censorship and mindguarding involve the inhibition of information in the presence of others due to evaluation apprehension or concerns about negative interpersonal interactions more generally. Thus, although groupthink effects occur in specific social contexts not necessary for social inhibition (e.g., highly cohesive groups insulated from outside opinions), social inhibition can contribute to the negative decision-making outcomes associated with groupthink. However, the social inhibition involved in self-censorship and mindguarding are not the sole contributors to groupthink; other factors include rationalization and having stereotyped opinions of the opposing point of view.

As groupthink involves social inhibition and evaluation apprehension effects, it makes sense that some solutions to groupthink effects involve removing the evaluation concerns associated with dissent. For example, normalizing dissent by having an assigned devil's advocate can improve group decision making, and encouraging authentic dissent can be even more beneficial (Kameda & Sugimori, 1993; Nemeth, Brown, & Rogers, 2001). However, the inhibition of information dissemination that occurs in self-censorship and mindguarding may happen implicitly or for reasons other than evaluation apprehension. For example, individuals have a natural inclination to discuss common or shared information with others, often referred to as the shared information bias (Stasser & Titus, 1985, 1987). In addition, other individuals can serve as cues for information recall, and thus they may interfere with the recollection or dissemination of information that might otherwise have been readily available (e.g., transactive memory; Wegner, 1987; Wegner, Giuliano, & Hertel, 1985). In sum, social inhibition is an important contributor to groupthink's patterns of unproductive group decision making, and investigating processes other than evaluation apprehension that promote social inhibition may help improve group performance.

### Summary

Social inhibition is related to other social influence concepts, including social facilitation, conformity, social loafing, deindividuation, and groupthink. Social inhibition is conceptually discrete from these phenomena, but the links between these phenomena and social inhibition help illustrate that social inhibition is central to the study of social influence.

## Conclusions and Future Directions

In this chapter we provided a broad definition of social inhibition and examined social inhibition in helping behavior, emotional expression, and a wide variety of behaviors that might elicit negative reactions from others. Our chapter also identified a number of key processes and moderators of social inhibition, and it provided an analysis of how a number of central social influence concepts relate to social inhibition. Taken as a whole, our review suggests that social inhibition is an important and compelling social influence phenomenon that has been demonstrated in diverse domains from diverse perspectives, and that research has documented a range of key factors influencing these effects. Our discussion also clarifies that social inhibition is a phenomenon distinct from other well-studied social influence concepts, yet it shares some common elements with these other concepts, making it central to the study of social influence. Indeed, investigating the ways in which the presence of others may attenuate or eliminate otherwise naturally occurring behaviors is crucial to an understanding of the ways in which social forces impact our behavior.

It seems odd, though, that an organized social inhibition literature does not exist. As noted earlier, social inhibition has not been defined broadly or consistently, and in some literatures it is used to refer to an individual difference or process. This terminological confusion may prevent researchers from finding connections between social inhibition research in their domain and ongoing research in other domains. In fact, although the research discussed herein involves the inhibition of behaviors in the presence of others, the majority of papers do not explicitly use the term "social inhibition." The somewhat dominant impact of bystander and helping behavior research in this area may similarly contribute to the lack of a social inhibition literature that is readily acknowledged as coherent. Although bystander intervention work has offered tremendous insights into social inhibition, the focus on this domain and the use of the term "bystander effect" as opposed to "social inhibition of helping behavior" may have slowed the integration of this work with social inhibition research in other domains.

We hope that by providing an explicit definition of social inhibition that is not tied to a particular area of study and by bringing together social inhibition work from different areas we may encourage researchers to think about relevant effects in their specific areas of expertise as social inhibition more generally, and to use social inhibition research from other domains of interest to inform their work. In particular, we identified a number of explanations for social inhibition, including arousal, ambiguity and uncertainty, pluralistic ignorance, diffusion of responsibility, feelings of capability, evaluation apprehension and concerns for self-presentation, and confusion of responsibility. This research suggests that social inhibition is a complex, multidetermined phenomenon. However, in certain domains particular explanations have been dominant. Future research may benefit from considering whether explanations for social inhibition that are prominent in one domain of study may also contribute to social inhibition in other domains. Future research might also take a more sophisticated approach to studying the processes of social inhibition by conducting mediational and path analyses and allowing for multiple processes to operate simultaneously.

In conclusion, when it comes to a wide variety of behaviors, including helping, emotional expression, prejudice, and eating, the presence of others can sometimes inhibit the amount and level of behaviors that individuals would otherwise engage in. This social inhibition is a basic social influence phenomenon, but complex in that it can occur through a number of different mechanisms. We hope our review of social inhibition facilitates future work on the topic and further integration of social inhibition research across domains.

# References

Abele, A. E., & Wojciszke, B. (2007). Agency and communion from the perspective of self versus others. *Journal of Personality and Social Psychology, 93*, 751–763.

Asch, S. E. (1956). Studies of independence and conformity: A minority of one against a unanimous majority. *Psychological Monographs, 70* (Whole No. 416).

Barron, G., & Yechiam, E. (2002). Private e-mail requests and the diffusion of responsibility. *Computers in Human Behavior, 18*, 507–520.

Baumeister, R. F. (1982). A self-presentational view of social phenomena. *Psychological Bulletin, 91*, 3–26.

Baumeister, R. F., Hutton, D. G., & Tice, D. M. (1989). Cognitive processes during deliberate self-presentation: How self-presenters alter and misinterpret the behavior of their interaction partners. *Journal of Experimental Social Psychology, 25*, 59–78.

Bickman, L. (1971). The effect of another bystander's ability to help on bystander intervention in an emergency. *Journal of Experimental Social Psychology, 7*, 367–379.

Bickman, L. (1972). Social influence and diffusion of responsibility in an emergency. *Journal of Experimental Social Psychology, 8*, 438–445.

Blair, C. A., Thompson, L. F., & Wuensch, K. L. (2005). Electronic helping behavior: The virtual presence of others makes a difference. *Basic and Applied Social Psychology, 27*, 171–178.

Bond, C. F., & Titus, L. J. (1983). Social facilitation: A meta-analysis of 241 studies. *Psychological Bulletin, 94*, 265–292.

Brody, L. R. (2000). The socialization of gender differences in emotional expression: Display rules, infant temperament, and differentiation. In A. H. Fischer (Ed.), *Gender and emotion: Social psychological perspectives* (pp. 24–47). Cambridge, England: Cambridge University Press.

Brown, B. R. (1968). The effects of need to maintain face on interpersonal bargaining. *Journal of Experimental Social Psychology, 4*, 107–122.

Brown, B. R. (1970). Face-saving following experimentally induced embarrassment. *Journal of Experimental Social Psychology, 6*, 255–271.

Buck, R., Losow, J. I., Murphy, M. M., & Costanzo, P. (1992). Social facilitation and inhibition of emotional expression and communication. *Journal of Personality and Social Psychology, 63*, 962–968.

Cacioppo, J., Petty, R., & Losch, M. (1986). Attributions of responsibility for helping and doing harm: Evidence for confusion of responsibility. *Journal of Personality and Social Psychology, 50*, 100–105.

Castelli, L., & Tomelleri, S. (2008). Contextual effects on prejudiced attitudes: When the presence of others leads to more egalitarian responses. *Journal of Experimental Social Psychology, 44*, 679–686.

Chekroun, P., & Brauer, M. (2002). The bystander effect and social control behavior: The effect of the presence of others on people's reactions to norm violations. *European Journal of Social Psychology, 32*, 853–867.

Cialdini, R. B., & Goldstein, N. J. (2005). Social influence: Compliance and conformity. *Annual Review of Psychology, 55*, 591–621.

Cialdini, R. B., & Trost, M. R. (1998). Social influence: Social norms, conformity, and compliance. In D. T. Gilbert & S. T. Fiske (Eds.), *The handbook of social psychology* (4th ed., Vol. 2, pp. 151–192). New York, NY: McGraw-Hill.

Costa, M., Dinsbach, W., Manstead, A. S. R., & Bitti, P. E. R. (2001). Social presence, embarrassment, and nonverbal behavior. *Journal of Nonverbal Behavior, 25*, 225–240.

Cottrell, N. B., Wack, D. L., Sekerak, G. J., & Rittle, R. H. (1968). Social facilitation of dominant responses by the presence of an audience and the mere presence of others. *Journal of Personality and Social Psychology, 9*, 245–250.

Cramer, R. E., McMaster, M. R., Bartell, P. A., & Dragna, M. (1988). Subject competence and minimization of the bystander effect. *Journal of Applied Social Psychology, 18*, 133–1148.

Darley, J. M., & Latané, B. (1968). Bystander intervention in emergencies: Diffusion of responsibility. *Journal of Personality and Social Psychology, 8*, 377–383.

Darley, J. M., & Latané, B. (1970). Norms and normative behavior: Field studies of social interdependence. In J. Macauley & L. Berkowitz (Eds.), *Altruism and helping behavior (pp. 83–102)*. New York, NY: Academic Press.

Denollet, J. (1997). Personality, emotional distress and coronary heart disease. *European Journal of Personality, 11*, 343–357.

Denollet, J. (2005). DS14: Standard assessment of negative affectivity, social inhibition, and type D personality. *Psychosomatic Medicine, 67*, 89–97.

Dickerson, S. S., Mycek, P. J., & Zaldivar, F. (2008). Negative social evaluation, but not mere social presence, elicits cortisol responses to a laboratory stressor task. *Health Psychology, 27*, 116–121.

Diener, E. (1976). Deindividuation: Causes and consequences. *Social Behavior and Personality, 5*, 143–155.

Douglas, K. M., & McGarty, C. (2001). Identifiability and self-presentation: Computer-mediated communication and intergroup interaction. *British Journal of Social Psychology, 40*, 399–416.

Downey, G., & Feldman, S. I. (1996). Implications of rejection sensitivity for intimate relationship. *Journal of Personality and Social Psychology, 70*, 1327–1343.

Festinger, L., Pepitone, A., & Newcomb, T. (1952). Some consequences of deindividuation in a group. *Journal of Abnormal and Social Psychology, 47*, 382–389.

Fischer, P., Greitemeyer, T., Pollozek, F., & Frey D. (2006). The unresponsive bystander: Are bystanders more responsive in dangerous emergencies? *European Journal of Social Psychology, 36*, 267–278.

Fischer, P., Krueger, J. I., Greitemeyer, T., Vogrincic, C., Kastenmuller, A., Frey, D., ... Kainbacher, M. (2011). The bystander-effect: A meta-analytic review on bystander intervention in dangerous and non-dangerous emergencies. *Psychological Bulletin, 137*, 517–537.

Friedman, H. S., & Miller-Herringer, T. (1991). Nonverbal display of emotion in public and private: Self-monitoring, personality, and expressive cues. *Journal of Personality and Social Psychology, 61*, 766–775.

Gaertner, S. L., Dovidio, J. F., & Johnson G. (1982). Race of victim, nonresponsive bystanders, and helping behavior. *Journal of Social Psychology, 117*, 69–77.

Garcia, S. M., Weaver, K., Darley, J. M., & Spence, B. T. (2009). Dual effects of implicit bystanders: Inhibiting vs. facilitating helping behavior. *Journal of Consumer Psychology, 19*, 215–224.

Garcia, S. M., Weaver, K., Moskowitz, G. B., & Darley, J. M. (2002). Crowded minds: The implicit bystander effect. *Journal of Personality and Social Psychology, 83*, 843–853.

Grande, G., Glaesmer, H., & Roth, M. (2010). The construct validity of social inhibition and the type-D taxonomy. *Journal of Health Psychology, 15*, 1103–1112.

Guerin, B. (1986). Mere presence effects in humans: A review. *Journal of Experimental Social Psychology, 22*, 38–77.

Guerin, B. (1989). Social inhibition of behavior. *Journal of Social Psychology, 129*, 225–233.

Harkins, S. G., & Jackson, J. M. (1985). The role of evaluation in elimination social loafing. *Personality and Social Psychology Bulletin, 11*, 457–465.

Heatherington, L., Daubman, K. A., Bates, C., Ahn, A., Brown, H., & Preston, C. (1993). Two investigations of "female modesty" in achievement situations. *Sex Roles, 29*, 739–754.

Herman, C. P., Roth, D. A., & Polivy, J. (2003). Effects of the presence of others on food intake: A normative interpretation. *Psychological Bulletin, 129*, 873–886.

Horowitz, I. A. (1971). The effect of group norms on bystander intervention. *Journal of Social Psychology, 83*, 265–273.

Howard, W., & Crano W. D. (1974). Effects of sex, conversation location, and size of observer group on bystander intervention in a high risk situation. *Sociometry, 37*, 491–507.

Hudson, J. M., & Bruckman, A. S. (2004). The bystander effect: A lens for understanding patterns of participation. *Journal of the Learning Sciences, 13*, 165–195.

Hurley, D., & Allen, B. P. (1974). The effect of the number of people present in a nonemergency situation. *Journal of Social Psychology, 92*, 27–29.

Janis, I. L. (1971, November). Groupthink. *Psychology Today, 5*(6): 43–46, 74–76.

Janis, I. L. (1982). *Groupthink: Psychological studies of policy decisions and fiascos* (2nd ed.). Boston, MA: Houghton Mifflin.

Jansz, J. (2000). Masculine identity and restrictive emotionality. In A. H. Fischer (Ed.), *Gender and emotion: Social psychological perspectives* (pp. 166–186). Cambridge, England: Cambridge University Press.

Johnson, R., & Downing, L. (1979). Deindividuation and valence of cues: Effects of prosocial and antisocial behavior. *Journal of Personality and Social Psychology, 27*, 1532–1538.

Kameda, T., & Sugimori, S. (1993). Psychology entrapment in group decision making: An assigned decision rule and a group think phenomenon. *Journal of Personality and Social Psychology, 65*, 282–292.

Karakashian, L. M., Walter, M. I., Christopher, A. N., & Lucas, T. (2006). Fear of negative evaluation affects helping behavior: The bystander effect revisited. *North American Journal of Psychology, 8*, 12–32.

Karau, S. J., & Williams, K. D. (1993). Social loafing: A meta-analytic review and theoretical integration. *Journal of Personality and Social Psychology, 65*, 681–706.

Karau, S. J., & Williams, K. D. (2001). Understanding individual motivation in groups: The collective effort model. In M. E. Turner (Ed.), *Groups at work: Theory and research* (pp. 113–141). Mahwah, NJ: Erlbaum.

Kleck, R. E., Vaughan, R. C., Cartwright-Smith, J., Vaughan, K. B., Colby, C. Z., & Lanzetta, J. T. (1976). Effects of being observed on expressive, subjective, and physiological responses to painful stimuli. *Journal of Personality and Social Psychology, 34*, 1211–1218.

Kruglanski, A. W., & Webster, D. M. (1991). Group members' reactions to opinion deviates and conformists at varying degrees of proximity to decision deadline and of environmental noise. *Journal of Personality and Social Psychology, 61*, 212–225.

Latané, B. (1981). The psychology of social impact. *American Psychologist, 36*, 343–356.

Latané, B., & Dabbs, J. M. (1975). Sex, group size, and helping in three cities. *Sociometry, 38*, 180–194.

Latané, B., & Darley, J. M. (1968). Group inhibition of bystander intervention in emergencies. *Journal of Personality and Social Psychology, 10*, 215–221.

Latané, B., & Darley, J. M. (1970). *The unresponsive bystander: Why doesn't he help?* New York, NY: Appleton Century Crofts.

Latané, B., & Darley, J. M. (1976). *Helping in a crisis: Bystander response to an emergency.* Morristown, NJ: General Learning Press.

Latané, B., & Nida, S. (1981). Ten years of research on group size and helping. *Psychological Bulletin, 98*, 308–324.

Latané B., & Rodin, J. (1969). A lady in distress: Inhibiting effects of friends and strangers on bystander intervention. *Journal of Experimental Social Psychology, 5*, 189–202.

Laughlin, P. R., & Wong-McCarthy, W. J. (1975). Social inhibition as a function of observation and recording of performance. *Journal of Experimental Psychology, 11*, 560–571.

Leary, M. R. (2010). Social anxiety as an early warning system: A refinement and extension of the self-presentation theory of social anxiety. In S. G. Hofmann & P. M. DiBartolo (Eds.), *Social anxiety: Clinical, developmental, and social perspectives* (2nd ed., pp. 471–486). San Diego, CA: Academic Press.

Leary, M. R., Kelly, K. M., Cottrell, C. A., & Schreindorfer, L. S. (2013). Construct validity of the need to belong scale: Mapping the nomological network. *Journal of Personality Assessment, 95*, 610–624.

Leary, M. R., & Kowalski, R. M. (1990). Impression management: A literature review and two-component model. *Psychological Bulletin, 107*, 34–47.

Levine, M., Cassidy, C., Brazier, G., & Reicher, S. (2002). Self-categorization and bystander non-intervention: Two experimental studies. *Journal of Applied Social Psychology, 32*, 1452–1463.

Levine, M., & Crowther, S. (2008). The responsive bystander: How social group membership and group size can encourage as well as inhibit bystander intervention. *Journal of Personality and Social Psychology, 95*, 1429–1439.

Levine, M., Prosser, A., Evans, D., & Reicher, S. (2005). Identity and emergency intervention: How social group membership and inclusiveness of group boundaries shape helping behavior. *Personality and Social Psychology Bulletin, 31*, 443–453.

Luo, X. (2005). How does shopping with others influence impulsive purchasing? *Journal of Consumer Psychology, 15*, 288–294.

Mann, L. (1981). The baiting crowd in episodes of threatened suicide. *Journal of personality and Social Psychology, 41*, 703–709.

Manning, R., Levine, M., & Collins, A. (2007). The Kitty Genovese murder and the social psychology of helping. *American Psychology, 62*, 555–562.

Markey, P. M. (2000). Bystander intervention in computer-mediated communication. *Computers in Human Behavior, 16*, 183–188.

Markus, H. (1978). The effect of mere presence on social facilitation: An unobtrusive test. *Journal of Experimental Social Psychology, 14*, 389–397.

Mason, D., & Allen (1976). The bystander effect as a function of ambiguity and emergency character. *Journal of Social Psychology, 100*, 145–146.

McCarty, M. K., Kelly, J. R., & Williams, K. D. (2014). The cognitive costs of the counter-stereotypic: Gender, emotion, and social presence. *Journal of Social Psychology, 154*, 447–462.

Middlemist, R. D., Knowles, E. S., & Matter, C. F. (1976). Personal space invasions in the lavatory: Suggestive evidence for arousal. *Journal of Personality and Social Psychology, 33*, 541–546.

Miller, R. S. (1995). On the nature of embarassability: Shyness, social evaluation, and social skill. *Journal of Personality, 63*, 315–339.

Miller, D. T., & McFarland, C. (1987). Pluralistic ignorance: When similarity is interpreted as dissimilarity. *Journal of Personality and Social Psychology, 53*, 298–305.

Misavage, R., & Richardson, J. T. (1974). The focusing of reasonability: An alternative hypothesis in help-demanding situations. *European Journal of Social Psychology, 4*, 5–15.

Moorhead, G., Ference, R., & Neck, C. P. (1991). Group decision fiascoes continue: Space shuttle challenger and a revised groupthink framework. *Human Relations, 44*, 539–550.

Nemeth, C., Brown, K., & Rogers, J. (2001). Devil's advocate versus authentic dissent: Stimulating quantity and quality. *European Journal of Social Psychology, 31*, 707–720.

Pantin, H. M., & Carver, C. S. (1982). Induced competence and the bystander effect. *Journal of Applied Social Psychology, 12*, 100–111.

Paulhus, D. (1983). Sphere-specific measures of perceived control. *Journal of Personality and Social Psychology, 44*, 1253–1265.

Petty, R. E., Williams, K. D., Harkins, S. G., & Latané, B. (1977). Social inhibition of helping yourself: Bystander response to a cheeseburger. *Personality and Social Psychology Bulletin, 3*, 575–578.

Phillips, A. C., Carroll, D., Hunt, K., & Der, G. (2006). The effects of the spontaneous presence of a spouse/partner and others on cardiovascular reactions to an acute psychological challenge. *Psychophysiology, 43*, 633–640.

Puntoni, S., & Tavassoli, N. T. (2007). Social context and advertising memory. *Journal of Marketing Research, 64*, 284–296.

Richards, J. M., & Gross, J. J. (1999). Composure at any cost? The cognitive consequences of emotion suppression. *Personality and Social Psychology Bulletin, 15*, 1033–1044.

Richards, J. M., & Gross, J. J. (2000). Emotion regulation and memory: The cognitive costs of keeping one's cool. *Journal of Personality and Social Psychology, 79*, 410–424.

Ringelmann, M. (1913). Research on animate sources of power: The work of man. *Annales de l'Institut National Agronomique, 2e serie—tome XII*, 1–40.

Rosenberg, M. (1965). *Society and the adolescent self-image.* Princeton, NJ: Princeton University Press.

Ross, A. S. (1971). Effect of increased responsibility on bystander intervention: The presence of children. *Journal of Personality and Social Psychology, 19*, 306–310.

Ross, A. S., & Braband, J. (1973). Effect of increased responsibility on bystander intervention: II. The cue value of a blind person. *Journal of Personality and Social Psychology, 25*, 254–258.

Rudman, L. A., & Fairchild, K. (2004). Reactions to counterstereotypic behavior: The role of backlash in cultural stereotype maintenance. *Journal of Personality and Social Psychology, 87,* 157–176.

Rutkowski, G. K., Gruder, C. L., & Romer D. (1983). Group cohesiveness, social norms, and bystander intervention. *Journal of Personality and Social Psychology, 44,* 545–552.

Schachter, S. (1951). Deviation, rejection, and communication. *Journal of Abnormal and Social Psychology, 46,* 190–207.

Schlenker, B. R., & Leary, M. R. (1982). Social anxiety and self-presentation: A conceptualization and model. *Psychological Bulletin, 92,* 641–669.

Shapiro, E. G. (1983). Embarrassment and help-seeking. In J. D. Fisher, A. Nadler, & B. M. Depaulo (Eds.), *New directions in helping* (pp. 143–163). New York, NY: Academic Press.

Sherif, M. (1936). The psychology of social norms. New York, NY: Harper.

Smith, R. E., Smythe, L., & Lien, D. (1972). Inhibition of helping behavior by a similar or dissimilar nonreactive fellow bystander. *Journal of Personality and Social Psychology, 23,* 414–419.

Snyder, M., & Monson, T. C. (1975). Persons, situations, and the control of social behavior. *Journal of Personality and Social Psychology, 32,* 637–644.

Solomon, L. Z., Solomon, H., & Stone, R. (1978). Helping as a function of number of bystanders and ambiguity of emergency. *Personality and Social Psychology Bulletin, 4,* 318–321.

Sorrels, J. P., & Kelley, J. (1984). Conformity by omission. *Personality and Social Psychology Bulletin, 10,* 302–305.

Stasser, G., & Titus, W. (1985). Pooling of unshared information in group decision making: Biased information sampling during discussion. *Journal of Personality and Social Psychology, 48,* 1467–1478.

Stasser, G., & Titus, W. (1987). Effects of information load and percentage of shared information on the dissemination of unshared information during group discussion. *Journal of Personality and Social Psychology, 53,* 81–93.

Strauss, B. (2002). Social facilitation in motor tasks: A review of research and theory. *Psychology of Sport and Exercise, 3,* 237–256.

Tice, D. M., & Baumeister, R. F. (1985). Masculinity inhibits helping in emergencies: Personality does predict the bystander effect. *Journal of Personality and Social Psychology, 49,* 420–428.

Tobin, R. M., & Graziano, W. G. (2010). Delay of gratification: A review of fifty years of regulation research. In R. H. Hoyle (Ed.), *Handbook of personality and self-regulation* (pp. 47–63). Chichester, West Sussex, U.K.: Wiley-Blackwell.

Triplett, N. (1898). The dynamogenic factors in pacemaking and competition. *American Journal of Psychology, 9,* 507–533.

van Bommel, M., van Prooijen J., Elffers, H., & Van Lange, P. A. M. (2012). Be aware to care: Public self-awareness leads to a reversal of the bystander effect. *Journal of Experimental Social Psychology, 48,* 926–930.

Voelpel, S. C., Eckhoff, R. A., & Forster, J. (2008). David against Goliath? Group size and bystander effects in virtual knowledge sharing. *Human Relations, 61,* 271–295.

Wegner, D. M. (1987). Transactive memory: A contemporary analysis of the group mind. In B. Mullen & G. R. Goethals (Eds.), *Theories of group behavior* (pp. 185–208). New York, NY: Springer-Verlag.

Wegner, D. M., Giuliano, T., & Hertel, P. (1985). Cognitive interdependence in close relationships. In W. J. Ickes (Ed.), *Compatible and incompatible relationships* (pp. 253–276). New York, NY: Springer-Verlag.

White, E. H. (1990). Social influence: A discussion and integration of recent models into a general group situation theory. *European Journal of Social Psychology, 20,* 3–27.

Williams, K. B., & Williams, K. D. (1983a). A social impact-perspective on the social inhibition of help-seeking. In J. D. Fisher, A. Nadler, & B. M. Depaulo (Eds.), *New directions in helping* (pp. 187–204). New York, NY: Academic Press.

Williams, K. B., & Williams, K. D. (1983b). Social inhibition and asking for help: The effects of number, strength, and immediacy of potential help givers. *Journal of Personality and Social Psychology, 44,* 67–77.

Williams, K. D., Harkins, S. G., & Latané, B. (1981). Identifiability as a deterrent to social loafing: Two cheering experiments. *Journal of Personality and Social Psychology, 40,* 303–311.

Yarczower, M., & Daruns, L. (1982). Social inhibition of spontaneous facial expressions in children. *Journal of Personality and Social Psychology, 43,* 831–837.

Yarczower, M., Kilbride, J. E., & Hill, L. A. (1979). Imitation and inhibition of facial expression. *Developmental Psychology, 15,* 453–454.

Zajonc, R. B. (1965). Social facilitation. *Science, 149,* 269–274.

Zajonc, R. B., & Sales, S. M. (1966). Social facilitation of dominant and subordinate responses. *Journal of Experimental Social Psychology, 2,* 160–168.

# Social Facilitation: Using the Molecular to Inform the Molar

Allison E. Seitchik, Adam J. Brown, *and* Stephen G. Harkins

**Abstract**

Research conducted for more than a century has shown that the presence of others improves performance on simple tasks and debilitates it on complex tasks, whether these others are audience members or coactors. In this chapter, we review theories offered to account for how two features of these others, their mere presence and/or the potential for evaluation they represent, produce these effects, and we conclude that we are no closer now to isolating the relevant process(es) than we were 100 years ago. We then consider the molecular task analysis proposed by Harkins (2006) as an approach to attacking this problem, followed by a review of the work supporting the mere effort account suggested by this analysis. Finally, we place the mere effort account in the larger context represented by the Threat-Induced Potentiation of Prepotent Responses model, which aims to account for the effect of threat on task performance.

**Key Words:** social facilitation, mere presence, evaluation apprehension, motivation, threat, task performance

A chapter on social facilitation would typically begin with the claim that Triplett (1898) published the first experiment on social facilitation. In fact, Triplett's work has often been described as the first experiment published in social psychology. However, given Stroebe's (2012) choleric analysis of this claim, let it suffice to say that there has been interest in the effect that the presence of others has on task performance for well over a century. These effects have been studied in two paradigms. In one, the audience paradigm, the others are present as observers or spectators watching the task performance of the participant. In the other paradigm, coaction, the others are present working independently on the task alongside the participant.

In this chapter, we briefly review the early work on social facilitation. We consider research testing the two features of the presence of others that were hypothesized to produce the performance effects, their mere presence and apprehension concerning their evaluation potential. We review the theories

offered to account for how mere presence and evaluation apprehension produce these effects, and we conclude that we are no closer now to isolating the relevant process or processes than we were 100 years ago. We consider the molecular task analysis proposed by Harkins (2006) as an approach to attacking this problem, followed by a review of the follow-up work done to test the mere effort account suggested by this analysis. Finally, we place the mere effort account in the larger context represented by the Threat-Induced Potentiation of Prepotent Responses model, which aims to account for the effect of threat on task performance.

## A Look Back

Triplett's (1898) work has been interpreted as showing that the presence of others enhanced performance, as was much of the work that followed (e.g., Allport, 1920, 1924), leading Allport (1924) to coin the term *social facilitation*. However, it was also found that the presence of others sometimes debilitated performance, and in his 1935 review, Dashiell was unable to specify when which outcome would be produced. Matters had not progressed by the 1950s when Asch (1952) observed that: "The suspicion then arises that the proffered concepts are simply restatements of the quantitative results" (p. 67). Although this criticism was directed specifically at Allport's (1924) research, it actually summarized the whole line of work for its first 50 years.

Perhaps as a result, interest in social facilitation waned until 1965, when Zajonc's drive interpretation of social facilitation renewed interest in this area. In his extremely influential *Science* article, Zajonc surveyed past research on audience (e.g., Bergum & Lehr, 1963; Dashiell, 1930; Pessin, 1933; Travis, 1925) and coaction effects (e.g., Allport, 1920; Gates & Allee, 1933; Travis, 1928) and suggested that these findings could be organized by the simple generalization that the presence of others, as spectators or as coactors, enhances the emission of dominant responses. By dominant response, Zajonc (1965) meant the response that was most probable in a participant's task-relevant behavioral repertoire. In the early stages of learning to perform a task, Zajonc (1965) argued that this response is likely to be incorrect, but, with practice, correct answers become more probable; that is, they become dominant.

As Zajonc (1965) noted, Spence (1956) had already established that arousal, activation, or drive results in the enhancement of dominant responses. Zajonc (1965) then described indirect, but suggestive, evidence supporting the notion that the presence of others increases a person's arousal level. Thus, his resolution suggested that presence of others produces arousal that enhances the likelihood of the emission of the dominant response. If the task is simple or well learned, the dominant response is likely to be correct, and, as a result, performance will be facilitated, but if the task is complex or the appropriate responses are not yet mastered, the dominant response is likely to be incorrect, and the performance will be debilitated.

This paper had a galvanizing effect on research in social facilitation. In a cumulative graph of research activity in social facilitation, Guerin (1993) showed that following the publication of Triplett's work in 1898, a small number of articles were published each year from 1920 through 1965, but, at this point, the number of articles shot up, and this rate of activity continued through 1983, the endpoint of the graph. Although other interpretations for facilitation effects were offered (e.g., Blank, Staff, &

Shaver, 1976; Duval & Wicklund, 1972), most of the research focused on the drive account. Zajonc (1965) suggested that the mere presence of others was sufficient to increase drive, whereas others argued that it was the evaluation and/or competition associated with the others that produced the drive. For example, Cottrell (1968) argued: "If coaction and performance before an audience usually result in positive or negative outcomes for the individual, then he will quickly come to anticipate these outcomes when he coacts with others or performs before an audience" (p. 104), and Cottrell (1968) proposed that it was these associations that produced the drive effects. This proposal led to a series of studies in which researchers tried to design experiments to pit these explanations against each other (e.g., Cottrell, Wack, Sekerak, & Rittle, 1968; Henchy & Glass, 1968; Paulus & Murdoch, 1971).

Whether it was mere presence or evaluation apprehension that produced drive, the drive theory account of social facilitation remained the dominant theory of the time. For example, in 1977, Geen and Gange wrote: "A review of the literature on social facilitation following Zajonc's advocacy of drive theory as the explanatory principle shows that this theory, in general, provides the most parsimonious explanation of the findings reported over those 12 years" (p. 1283). However, after another 12 years, matters had changed. In his review of the facilitation literature since 1977, Geen (1989) wrote: "Today such a confident assertion of the primacy of the drive theoretical approach is not warranted. Instead, several sophisticated alternatives have found considerable support in experimental studies" (p. 17). Geen (1989) proposed three classes of these alternative approaches.

One set of theories included those approaches that continued to rely on the proposal that the presence of others increased drive (e.g., distraction/conflict [Baron, 1986]; evaluation apprehension [Cottrell, 1972]; social monitoring [Guerin & Innes, 1982]; and compresence [Zajonc, 1980]). The second set was comprised of approaches that proposed "the presence of others creates either explicit or implicit demands on the person to behave in some way" (Geen, 1989, p. 31) (e.g., self-presentation [Bond, 1982]; self-awareness [Carver & Scheier, 1981]). The third set argued that the presence of others affects the focus of attention and information processing (e.g., an information-processing view of distraction/conflict effects suggested as an alternative to his drive account by Baron [1986]). At this point, the controversy concerning mere presence and evaluation apprehension was still unresolved. Each of the theories that Geen (1989) reviewed incorporated mere presence effects, evaluation apprehension effects, or both.

## Tests of Mere Presence

Separating the effects of mere presence and evaluation apprehension was recognized as a daunting challenge early on. For example, in his 1935 review, Dashiell noted, "to get pure 'alone' or pure 'coworking' (and may we add, pure 'spectator' or pure 'competing') situations is extraordinarily difficult" (p. 1115). This difficulty has persisted to the present day. In virtually all social facilitation experiments, the experimenter could represent a potent source of evaluation in the "alone" conditions. There has been some recognition of this problem in its most egregious form. For example, in a review of social facilitation research, Bond and Titus (1983) wrote: "In 96 of 241 studies, the experimenter was in the room with the 'alone' subject, and in 52 of these studies, this 'alone' subject could see the experimenter" (p. 271).

Guerin (1993) raised this issue again in his review of mere presence effects. After excluding studies "if they clearly involved group discussion, imitation or the exchange of reinforcements" (p. 129), Guerin (1993) was left with 313 studies. After applying the 12 criteria that he judged appropriate for a good test of the mere presence hypothesis, including the removal of the experimenter from the room, he was left with 18 studies. Of these 18 studies, Guerin (1993) reported that "eleven found evidence for mere presence effects and seven did not" (p. 137). However, in fact, Guerin's (1993) criteria were not stringent enough. As Markus (1978) noted: "In virtually all experiments with humans, the subject in the alone condition is not 'phenomenologically' alone even when the experimenter is physically removed and out of sight. That is, he is quite aware of the experimenter and knows that his performance is being recorded, presumably, for some present or future evaluation" (p. 391). Guerin (1993) did not exclude experiments that afforded the experimenter the opportunity to evaluate performance in the alone condition at the conclusion of the session because "this might, in fact, remove all mere presence tests since all have used a laboratory task which subjects know will be evaluated by the experimenter" (p. 135). However, the reduction of all sources of evaluation to a minimum is exactly what is required in the "no evaluation" conditions. Of Guerin's (1993) published studies, only four

experiments in which performance was measured met this more stringent criterion. Two are audience experiments (Markus, 1978; Schmitt, Gilovich, Goore, & Joseph, 1986), each of which found evidence consistent with the mere presence hypothesis.

The other two are coaction experiments (Harkins, 1987) in which participants in "no evaluation" conditions were led to believe that their performances could not be evaluated by anyone during or after the experiment. In the 2 (alone versus coaction) × 2 (no-evaluation versus evaluation) design, mere presence was manipulated by asking participants to work alone, or alongside another person working independently on the same task (coaction). Crossed with this manipulation, one half of the participants were led to believe that their performances would be evaluated after their performance, whereas the other half were led to believe that their performances would not be evaluated.

Using two different, simple tasks (use-generation and vigilance), Harkins (1987) found main effects for both mere presence and evaluation in this design. Coactors outperformed participants working alone, a "mere presence" effect, and participants whose outputs could be evaluated outperformed participants whose outputs could not be, an evaluation effect. It is probably not feasible to eliminate all concerns about the possibility of evaluation when participants know that they are taking part in an experiment. However, by minimizing the apparent opportunities for evaluation, Harkins's (1987) research approached this goal more closely than previous coaction experiments in which the most that was done was to remove the experimenter from the room.

Subsequent to Guerin's (1993) review, other attempts have been made to test the mere presence hypothesis. For example, Huguet, Galvaing, Monteil, and Dumas (1999) tested the attentional view of social facilitation effects (Baron, 1986) by examining the effect of social presence on the performance of the Stroop color-word task. They led participants to believe that the computer on which they would be performing the Stroop color-word task had not yet been programmed to record their responses. They were asked to perform the task anyway so that they could give their impressions about this new task at the end of the session. They performed the task alone or in the presence of different types of audience (inattentive, invisible, or attentive). Huguet et al. (1999) found that Stroop interference (that is, the difference in the time taken to identify the ink colors of incongruent words, such as the word "red" printed in green ink, and the ink color of control stimuli, for example, + + + printed in green) was reduced when the audience was invisible or attentive, but not when it was inattentive. Huguet et al. (1999) argued that this finding was consistent with Guerin's (1986) argument that mere presence effects emerge when there is uncertainty about the behavior of the audience (e.g., when the behavior of the audience members cannot be monitored).

However, Klauer, Herfordt, and Voss (2008) proposed that these effects were the result of the fact that to make sense of the fact that they were performing the task on an unprogrammed computer, participants were instructed to try to form a general impression of the task. According to Klauer et al., this instruction led to unusually long reaction times in the alone condition, which produced the interference effect. In response, Sharma, Booth, Brown, and Huguet (2010) noted that their follow-up research "refutes Klauer et al.'s (2008) position. Here the dual task instructions were removed, but the social facilitation remained, at least under long RSI (the time between the response and the following stimulus), as expected" (pp. 56–57, parenthetical phrase mine). Although this change may have eliminated this alternative interpretation, it also reintroduced the experimenter as a potential source of evaluation. That is, whether or not the experimenter was actually in the room, the participants could have believed that she or he would be able to evaluate the participant's performance after the session concluded. As a result, there is no true "alone" condition in these experiments. Thus, while this work (Klauer et al., 2008; Sharma et al., 2010) may show social presence effects, it does not provide an adequate test of mere presence.

Platania and Moran (2001) asked participants, who were either alone or observed by another student, to make verbal judgments on the relative size of stimulus squares as they were presented on a wall. The authors report that they found that the participants in the audience condition responded with their preferred response numbers (responses with the highest habit strength) more often than participants who were alone. They argued that the "socially facilitated dominant responses were personal choices (numerical preferences) that could not be construed as either right or wrong, and, therefore, were irrelevant to evaluative judgments" (p. 196). Thomas, Skitka, Christen, and Jurgena (2002) exposed participants who were either alone or in a group composed of a real participant and two confederates (coaction) to an experimenter who attempted to make a very favorable or very unfavorable impression on them. After completing a phrase-completion task, the ostensible point of the study, participants were asked to anonymously rate the experimenter as part of the departmental research process. The experimenter left the room, and the evaluations were placed into envelopes that the participants put in a box full of other envelopes. Consistent with the mere presence hypothesis, the participants in the coaction condition rated the experimenter who had attempted to make a favorable impression more favorably and the experimenter who had attempted to make a negative impression less favorably than participants who took part alone. In these experiments, the potential for evaluation is apparently eliminated, and, along with the experiments of Markus (1978) and Schmitt et al. (1986), they provide evidence consistent with the mere presence hypothesis (see also Greenier, Devereaux, Hawkins, & Johnston, 2001).

## Tests of Evaluation Effects

Taken together, the findings suggest that mere presence contributes to social facilitation effects. As noted previously, when Zajonc (1965) proposed his drive account, research efforts focused on whether the effects were produced by mere presence or evaluation apprehension. The research reviewed thus far suggests that mere presence is sufficient to produce social facilitation effects, but it does not suggest that mere presence is the only explanation. As pointed out by Markus (1981), both factors could contribute to facilitation effects.

In fact, this is the outcome reported in the Harkins (1987) research. In that research, participants worked alone or coacted, and their performances could be evaluated or not. For two tasks, Harkins (1987) found main effects for evaluation and presence. This research supports an additive model with mere presence and the potential for evaluation each contributing to the social facilitation effects on these simple tasks. And it provides evidence consistent with the mere presence hypothesis: Participants in the coaction/no-evaluation condition outperformed participants in the alone/no-evaluation condition. However, interpretation of the evaluation conditions is problematic in this research and in the great majority of the other research looking at the contribution of the potential for evaluation to social facilitation effects.

For example, in the alone/evaluation condition of the Harkins (1987) research, the experimenter had access to the participants' outputs, and so could evaluate them by comparing them to the performances of previous participants. Because this same opportunity for evaluation existed in the coaction/evaluation condition, it may seem that the improved performance in this condition must be the result of mere presence because the potential for evaluation has been held constant. But, in fact, the potential for evaluation was not held constant. In the alone/evaluation condition, the experimenter could evaluate participants only by comparing their performance to that of their predecessors, but, in the coaction/evaluation condition, there were at least three different ways in which the potential for evaluation could have been increased.

First, participants might feel more evaluation apprehension when they know that the experimenter can compare their performances not only to those of their predecessors but also to those of coactors who are present in the same session (the experimenter evaluation account). Second, participants could feel more apprehension in the coaction setting when they know that they themselves can compare their performances to those of participants who are present in the same session (the self-evaluation account). Third, participants could feel more apprehension when they know that their performances can be evaluated by coactors who are present in the same session (the coactor account).

In Harkins's (1987) research, in the alone/evaluation and coaction/evaluation conditions, there was the potential for evaluation by the experimenter, but in the coaction condition, there was also the potential for coactor and self-evaluation. Latané's (1981) theory of social impact would suggest that when a person is the target of social forces emanating from other people, the magnitude of the effect of these sources *would* be a multiplicative function of the strength, immediacy, and number of people present. Thus, as the number of sources increases, the amount of impact should be increased, resulting in improved performance on a simple task. Of course, social impact theory would only make clear predictions in those cases in which there is a manipulation of the number of *external* sources (for example, increasing the number of coactors, or coactors plus experimenter). It would not make a prediction if one of the sources of evaluation were the self.

In fact, in a series of experiments (Bartis, Szymanski, & Harkins, 1988; Harkins, 2000, 2001a, 2001b; Harkins & Lowe, 2000; Harkins & Szymanski, 1988, 1989; Harkins, White, & Utman, 2000; Seitchik & Harkins, 2014; Szymanski &

Harkins, 1987, 1993; Utman & Harkins, 2010; White, Kjelgaard, & Harkins, 1995), Harkins and his colleagues have found that, when taken alone, the potential for experimenter and self-evaluation each motivates performance, but when both are possible, concern over the potential for experimenter evaluation supersedes interest in self-evaluation. These findings suggest that the potential for self-evaluation may not contribute to facilitation effects, at least in combination with the potential for experimenter evaluation.

Of course, this research leaves open the possibility that the potential for self-evaluation can contribute to facilitation effects in combination with the potential for evaluation by a coactor. However, Szymanski, Garczynski, and Harkins (2000, Experiment 1) found that concern over the potential for evaluation by a coactor appears to supersede interest in the potential for self-evaluation in just the same way as the potential for evaluation by the experimenter. In a second experiment, Szymanski et al. tested the coactor account and found that the motivation stemming from the potential for evaluation by the coactor summed with the motivation produced by the potential for evaluation by the experimenter. Thus, consistent with Latané's (1981) theory of social impact, the combination of these sources (experimenter plus coactor) led to better performance than either one taken alone.

Gagné and Zuckerman (1999) also report findings consistent with this analysis. Their participants were led to believe that no one would be able to evaluate their performance on a use generation task, that the experimenter alone would be able to do so, or that the experimenter and coactors could evaluate them. The linear contrast on these data was significant, showing that the combination of the potential for experimenter and coactor evaluation produced better performance than the potential for experimenter evaluation alone, which produced better performance than when evaluation by no one was possible.

These experiments represent the beginning of what will be required to understand the effects of mere presence and the potential for evaluation in the social facilitation paradigm. In many experiments, researchers leave out conditions that would allow a systematic examination of the effects of evaluation on performance, because these conditions may not bear on the particular question that they are asking. For example, Gagné and Zuckerman (1999) did not include a condition in which there was the potential for coactor evaluation alone. Jackson and Williams (1985) included an alone/evaluation condition along with coaction/evaluation and coaction/no-evaluation conditions, but not an alone/no-evaluation condition. Sanna (1992) included an alone/no-evaluation condition along with coaction/evaluation and coaction/no-evaluation conditions, but no alone/evaluation condition.

In addition, in research in which the potential for evaluation was manipulated, it is not clear what the participants were told or inferred about which source or sources would have access to their performances. The haphazard manipulation of this variable may account for Bond and Titus's (1983) failure to find that evaluation potential had systematic effects in their meta-analysis of social facilitation research. To tie down these evaluation effects will require a set of experiments that focus on each of the potential sources of evaluation in the facilitation paradigm individually (for example, experimenter, self, and coactor), and then in combination with the other sources, along with the appropriate tests of mere presence effects. It is only at this point that we will know how to design performance settings to capture the motivational structure that we want. For example, if we believe that behavior motivated by the potential for self-evaluation will be more likely to be sustained over the long haul than that produced by external evaluation, we may wish to structure situations such that the potential for external evaluation is minimized.

## Mediator(s) of Social Facilitation Effects

However, even if we knew how mere presence and the potential for evaluation combine to produce social facilitation effects, we are still left with the task of specifying which, if any, of the theories incorporated in Geen's (1989) review can account for these effects. It is noteworthy that these theories do not even agree on whether participants subject to evaluation are working hard on complex tasks, but failing nonetheless (or as a consequence), are withdrawing effort leading to failure, or are failing as a result of a cognitive, rather than a motivational process.

Drive approaches suggest that participants are putting out more effort when they work in the presence of others, and this increased effort enhances performance on simple tasks (correct answer high in the habit hierarchy) but debilitates performance on complex tasks (correct answer low in the habit hierarchy). Bond's (1982) self-presentation approach suggests that participants are working hard in the presence of others, but

concern over the embarrassment of potential failure causes cognitive interference. Baron's (1986) focus-of-attention interpretation would suggest that it is not a motivational effect but a cognitive one. Participants working on difficult tasks are working as hard as participants facing easy tasks, but the presence of others leads to a narrowing of attention that debilitates performance on complex tasks because these tasks require attention to a wide range of cues.

In contrast to these approaches, Carver and Scheier (1981) suggested that debilitated performance on complex tasks results from the withdrawal of effort. That is, the presence of others makes participants self-aware, leading them to be "more cognizant of both the level of performance being manifested at the moment and the salient standard" (Geen, 1989, p. 32). When they find that they have little chance of bringing their performance into alignment with the standard, they stop trying.

Twelve years after Geen's review, in their own review, Aiello and Douthitt (2001) described what are essentially the same theories and presented a framework for advancing theory in this area. Unfortunately their advice was not followed. In fact, in looking back over the work done in this area, it appears that, instead of making any progress, the same set of potential explanations are just recycled. For example, Triplett (1898) suggested "brain worry" as one explanation for his findings, which reappeared as "cognitive interference" in the 1980s (e.g., Bond, 1982) and is now termed "working memory deficit" (e.g., DeCaro, Thomas, Albert, & Beilock, 2011). Another explanation, range of cue utilization (Easterbrook, 1959), which was used by Geen (1976) and Baron (1986) to account for performance effects, remains with us but is now termed "focus of attention" (e.g., Muller & Butera, 2007).

One could argue that the mediating process will emerge from an analysis of the psychophysiology of performance. For example, Blascovich has applied his biopsychological model of challenge and threat to the phenomenon of social facilitation (Blascovich, Mendes, Hunter, & Salomon, 1999). Blascovich et al. (1999) found the pattern of cardiovascular reactivity associated with challenge when participants performed a well learned task in the presence of others, whereas on a task that was not well learned (that is, complex), they exhibited the pattern of cardiovascular reactivity associated with threat. In contrast, participants working alone demonstrated no reactivity from baseline, whether the task was well learned or not.

This work identifies precise physiological patterns of cardiovascular reactivity that are associated with the facilitation and debilitation of performance. However, as Blascovich et al. (1999) note, it does not tell us whether the physiological responses are causes, concomitants, or results of the performance effects. In addition, because the timing period was limited to the first minute of the testing period, we know only that the participants performing the unlearned task in front of the audience were displaying the cardiac pattern associated with threat at that point. We do not know whether these participants continued to exhibit this patterning as the timing period continued, nor do we know whether these participants continued their striving in an effort to perform the task successfully or if they withdrew effort. As a result, we are left with the same questions that are left unresolved in the other accounts.

## Mere Effort Account

Harkins (2006) argued that our lack of progress might be a result of the fact that our efforts have focused broadly on theory construction rather than on an analysis of how performance actually unfolds on a given task. Although it would appear that a molecular analysis of task performance would be an integral part of theory development, this type of analysis has not been conducted, and it is possible that the mediating process could be identified through such an approach. To this end, Harkins (2006) undertook a molecular analysis of the effects of evaluation on the performance of a specific task, the Remote Associates Test (RAT).

The RAT requires participants to look at a set of three words (e.g., *lapse, elephant*, and *vivid*) and generate a fourth word that is related to each word in the given triad (in this case *memory*). Harkins (2001b) has shown that the potential for evaluation produces the typical pattern of performance on this task: Participants who anticipate evaluation by the experimenter solve more triads shown by a pretest to be simple than do no-evaluation participants, whereas participants who anticipate experimenter evaluation solve fewer triads shown by a pretest to be difficult than do no-evaluation participants.

Harkins's (2006) analysis suggested the *mere effort* account. This explanation argues that the potential for evaluation motivates participants to want to do well, which potentiates whatever response is prepotent ("dominant," using Zajonc's [1965] terminology) on the given task. For example, when performing the Stroop Color-Word Test

(Stroop, 1935), the prepotent response is to read the color-word, rather than call out the color, which the mere effort account argues is potentiated by the potential for evaluation. On the RAT, Harkins's (2006) analysis showed that the prepotent response is to generate words that are closely related to one of the triad members. Because on simple items the correct answers tend to be a close associate of at least one of the triad members, the greater effort on the part of participants subject to evaluation leads to the production of more close associates and to better performance.

On the other hand, on the complex items, the associations between the triad members and the correct answer are much weaker (i.e., the associates are more remote), and the participants are extremely unlikely to produce the solution by generating associates for the individual triad members. For example, if presented with the triad member *note*, a participant would be extremely unlikely to produce the associate, "bank." Nonetheless, when the participant considers the word *note*, the solution, "bank," is weakly activated. Likewise, the solution "bank" is also weakly activated when the participant considers the other two triad members, *river* and *blood*. If this were the only process operating, this weak activation should accumulate over time, leading to the emergence of the correct answer. However, when participants actively test close associates as solutions for the triads (e.g., "teller" for "bank"), these associates are highly activated, and they strongly inhibit the activation of the remote (weak) associates. Thus, generating close associates, the same behavior that facilitates the performance of participants subject to experimenter evaluation on simple items, debilitates that performance on complex items.

Drive theory (Zajonc, 1965), like the mere effort account, accords a central role to prepotent or dominant responses. Once again, drive theory contends that the presence of others produces arousal, which increases drive, enhancing the probability of the emission of dominant responses. On simple tasks, these responses are likely to be correct; on difficult tasks they are likely to be incorrect. In fact, Cottrell (1968, 1972) argued that this drive was the result of the participants' apprehension about the fact that they could be evaluated.

Thus, both mere effort and Cottrell's (1968, 1972) evaluation apprehension account of social facilitation effects predict that the potential for evaluation will potentiate dominant or prepotent responses. However, in the case of mere effort, this potentiation results from the motivation to perform well, which should also lead to an effort to correct an incorrect response, if the participant recognizes that his or her response is incorrect, knows the correct response, and has the opportunity to make it. In contrast, Cottrell's (1968) modification of Zajonc's (1965) drive theory suggests only that the positive or negative anticipations produced by the presence of others nonselectively energize individual performance (i.e., potentiate the dominant response). On a task like the RAT, one is unable to distinguish between mere effort and evaluation apprehension accounts because even if the participants know that the response is incorrect, they do not know how to correct it. As a result, one cannot see the effect of the motivation to correct on this task.

However, these findings are inconsistent with the other three explanations. For example, Harkins's (2006) findings suggest that on the complex RAT items, participants subject to evaluation do not perform poorly because they withdraw effort (Carver & Scheier, 1981). It is the fact that they are putting out effort that is the source of their difficulty on complex triads. It is also not that worry concerning failure takes up processing capacity (Bond, 1982). Once again, Harkins's (2006) findings suggest that participants subject to experimenter evaluation are engaged in the same behavior on both simple and complex items. It is just that this behavior is effective on simple items but is ineffective on complex ones.

A third explanation, focus of attention, suggests that the potential for evaluation produces an attentional overload that "leads to a restriction in cognitive focus in which the individual attends more to cues that are most central to the task (or alternatively most central geographically in the display) at the expense of more peripheral cues" (Baron, 1986, p. 27). This cognitive explanation does not account for the role that motivation plays in producing the pattern of results on the RAT. That is, participants who are subject to evaluation do not perform better on simple items because the answer candidates that they generate are more closely related to the triad members (central cues) than are the answer candidates generated by the no-evaluation participants. The participants in the two conditions are equally likely to think of answer candidates that are closely related to the triad members. It is the fact that participants subject to evaluation are motivated to *generate and test* more of these closely related candidates that accounts for the fact that they outperform no-evaluation participants. On the complex items, it is this same motivation to test more closely related candidates that inhibits the accumulation of the

activation required for the correct answer to emerge. Thus, no-evaluation participants do not perform better on complex items than do participants who are subject to evaluation because no-evaluation participants are better able to think of more remotely associated answer candidates (i.e., peripheral cues) than are participants subject to evaluation. No-evaluation participants perform better because the same lack of motivation that prevents them from testing enough closely related candidates to come up with correct answers on simple items allows the small amount of activation produced by each triad member to accumulate to the point that the correct answer *pops out* on the complex items.

Although Harkins's (2006) findings are inconsistent with these three accounts, this research was aimed at attempting to identify the mediating process, rather than at pitting this process against these accounts. In addition, this work does not distinguish between the drive/evaluation apprehension and mere effort accounts. McFall, Jamieson, and Harkins (2009) conducted a set of experiments that were aimed at pitting the mere effort account against these other explanations, and, in each case, they found support for the mere effort account.

For example, McFall et al. (2009) used the Stroop Color-Word task to test the focus of attention account as well as to distinguish between the mere effort and drive/evaluation apprehension explanations. Consistent with Baron's (1986) analysis, Huguet et al. (1999; see also Huguet, Dumas, & Monteil, 2004) have found that social presence enhances performance on the Stroop and have argued that this facilitation is a result of the fact that social presence reduces the range of cues used by the participants. As they write, "Narrowing one's focus should indeed allow one to screen out the incorrect semantic cues and focus more exclusively on the letter color cues" (Huguet et al., 1999, p. 1013). That is, these participants see less of the word, and so it interferes less with their response.

In their review of previous work on the Stroop, Huguet et al. (1999) cited work that they suggested shows that "arousal has been associated with *increased* (italics added) Stroop interference in past research" (p. 1012; e.g., Hochman, 1967, 1969; Pallak, Pittman, Heller, & Munson, 1975). They cited other research that shows that "distraction has been associated with *decreased* (italics added) Stroop interference in past research" (p. 1013; e.g., Houston, 1969; Houston & Jones, 1967; O'Malley & Poplawsky, 1971), as well as MacKinnon, Geiselman, and Woodward's (1985) research, which shows that coaction decreases Stroop interference. Huguet et al. (1999) commented on the contradictory nature of these findings and argued that their well-controlled experiments show that social presence reduces the amount of Stroop interference, consistent with the focus of attention interpretation.

However, McFall et al. (2009) argued that the findings of the previous work are not contradictory, and, in fact, are consistent with the mere effort account. Consistent with the mere effort and drive accounts, reading the word is the prepotent (dominant) response. However, on the Stroop, unlike the RAT, the fact that this response is incorrect is quite obvious, as is the correct response. Thus, when given sufficient time, participants who are more motivated can inhibit the prepotent response and still produce the correct response more quickly than can participants who are less motivated.

In the previous research that showed increased Stroop interference, the participants had only 1 second to produce the response (Hochman, 1967, 1969; Pallack et al., 1975), and the dependent measure was the number of errors. Under these conditions, the more motivated participants did not have sufficient time to inhibit the prepotent response to read the word and make the correct response. Thus, the more motivated participants made more errors than did less motivated participants. In the experiments that showed decreased Stroop interference (Houston, 1969; Houston & Jones, 1967; Huguet et al., 1999; MacKinnon et al., 1985; O'Malley & Poplawsky, 1971), the dependent measure was the time required to read a whole list of color-words or the time required to make each individual response. Under these conditions, the motivated participants had sufficient time to inhibit the reading response and still produce the color response more quickly than did the less motivated participants.

This analysis suggests that simply manipulating the amount of time available for the response can produce either facilitation or debilitation. When given a limited response window (e.g., 1 second), participants subject to evaluation should make reliably more errors than participants who are not. That is, the prepotent response is to read the word, and given a brief response period, participants subject to evaluation will not have enough time to inhibit this response and generate the correct response. When more time is made available for the response (e.g., 2 seconds), few mistakes should be made and participants subject to evaluation should name the colors more quickly than participants who are not subject to evaluation.

In contrast, the focus of attention account predicts better performance by participants subject to evaluation at each response window. Reducing the amount of time available for a response should not diminish the advantage afforded by a restricted focus of attention. In fact, if anything, one could argue that the restricted focus would lead to a greater performance advantage at the brief exposure period because these participants only see, and only need to see, part of the color word to respond correctly.

Finally, the drive/evaluation apprehension account (Cottrell, 1972; Zajonc, 1965) would predict that the presence of others simply increases drive, energizing the dominant response, reading the word. Thus, this account would predict that participants subject to evaluation would perform more poorly than participants in the no-evaluation condition, regardless of the time available for a response.

McFall et al. (2009) tested these predictions in two experiments. They found that when the response window was brief (1 second or 750 ms; Experiment 3), participants subject to evaluation performed more poorly than no-evaluation participants. However, with the 2-second response window (Experiment 2), the finding was reversed: Participants subject to evaluation performed better than no-evaluation participants.

Finding that participants subject to evaluation make more errors on color-words than do no-evaluation participants is consistent with mere effort and drive/evaluation apprehension predictions. Each of these accounts would contend that reading color-words is the prepotent (dominant), but incorrect, response and that the motivation produced by the potential for evaluation potentiates this response. However, the drive/evaluation apprehension account only predicts this energization, whereas the mere effort account also predicts that participants subject to evaluation will be motivated to produce the correct answer. At the brief response windows (Experiment 3), these participants do not have sufficient time to inhibit the prepotent response and produce the correct response, and, as a result, they perform more poorly than no experimenter evaluation participants. However, at the longer response window (Experiment 2), they are able to inhibit the incorrect response and produce the correct response faster than no experimenter evaluation participants.

Finding that participants subject to evaluation perform better than do participants in the no-evaluation condition at the 2-second window is consistent with the focus of attention prediction.

However, finding that they perform worse when brief response windows are used is not. If anything, a briefer display period should represent an advantage for participants with a narrowed focus of attention. Instead, we find that participants subject to evaluation make more errors than do participants who are not. Thus, in this test of the focus of attention and mere effort explanations, we find support for the mere effort account, but not focus of attention.

Recently Augustinova and Ferrand (2012) reported other findings that are inconsistent with Huguet et al.'s (1999) focus of attention account. In addition to the standard Stroop items (e.g., the word "blue" printed in green), these investigators included "color-associated" items (e.g., the word "sky" printed in green) in a replication of Huguet et al.'s (1999) research and found interference effects on both types of items in both their social presence condition and their alone condition. However, they also found that, unlike on standard Stroop items, social presence did not affect the magnitude of this effect for "color-associated" items. Of course, the "color-associated" items could only produce an interference effect if the participants were processing the semantic content of the words, suggesting that the participants, regardless of social presence condition, are reading the words, not focusing "exclusively on the letter color cues" (Huguet et al., 1999, p. 1013).

Augustinova and Ferrand (2012) argue that this finding suggests that "social presence simply influences response competition" (p. 1216), not the semantic processing of the color-words. Augustinova and Ferrand speculate about how inhibitory processes suggested by Sharma et al. (2010) could work under these circumstances, but neither their findings nor the findings of Sharma et al. are inconsistent with the potentiation process proposed by the mere effort account.

However, Augustinova and Ferrand's (2012) finding that social presence did not produce facilitation on either control or "color-associated" items is inconsistent with the mere effort account. Mere effort would argue that the social presence effect that Huguet et al. (1999) and Augustinova and Ferrand found on standard Stroop items stems from the fact that these participants are motivated to perform well and have the time required to correct for the prepotent response (reading the word) as in Experiment 2 of McFall et al. (2009). Reflecting this motivation to perform well, in Experiment 2, McFall et al. also found that participants subject to evaluation responded more quickly to the Stroop

control stimuli than no-evaluation participants. They also found this facilitation effect on the prosaccade task (Hallett, 1978), a control task used with another inhibition task, the antisaccade task (McFall et al., Experiment 4), and this facilitation effect on control stimuli has been found in other research in this line of work (e.g., Stroop: Jamieson & Harkins, 2011; antisaccade task: Jamieson & Harkins, 2007, 2011; Jamieson, Harkins, & Williams, 2010). Of course, in some cases, floor effects could account for the failure to find effects for control stimuli, but this would be much less likely to occur for stimuli that produce interference effects, like those found by Augustinova and Ferrand on the "color-associated" items. Additional research will be required to resolve this issue.

Recently, building on previous work by Muller and Butera (2007), Normand, Bouquet, and Croizet (2014) tested an elaborated version of the focus of attention account. They propose that when participants are under evaluative pressure, they implement a stronger attentional set than when they are not, which allows them to filter out stimuli that are not critical for task performance. Thus, a distractor that does not match the attentional set produced by the task will lead to better performance by participants subject to evaluative pressure than those that are not, whereas a distractor that does match the attentional set will lead to poorer performance by these participants.

To test this account, Normand et al. (2014) first replicated an experiment by Muller and Butera (Exp. 5, 2007) with minor modifications. Participants were asked to look at a fixation point that was displayed for one of four durations ranging from 850 to 1,500 ms. A dot then flashed for 30 ms approximately 7° from the screen's center in one of four locations forming a square followed by a 50 ms blank, and a display of four letters (three Qs and one O) in the same square. The participants' task was to identify the location of the O. On one third of the trials, the dot flashed in the location where the O would appear. On one third of the trials, the dot flashed in a location where a Q would appear, and on one third, dots flashed in all four locations. In other words, one third of the time the dot was a valid cue as to the location of the O, one third of the time the dot was an invalid cue, and one third of the time the four dots comprised control cues. Ordinarily, one would expect that a cue with a sudden onset would capture participants' attention (e.g., Yantis & Jonides, 1990), but according to Normand et al., the dot does not match the task demands (identifying the location of the letter O) and is, therefore, irrelevant. As a result, participants subject to evaluative pressure should be able to filter out its effects, making them faster on the trials when the cue is invalid but slower on the trials when the cue is valid than participants not subject to this pressure.

Consistent with this prediction, Normand et al. (2014) reported that they replicated Muller and Butera's (2007) finding: a smaller cueing effect (i.e., the difference between the reaction times for invalid and valid cues) for participants subject to evaluative pressure than for those that were not. This finding stands in contrast to the prediction that they ascribe to the mere effort account. The mere effort account argues, "evaluative pressure increases the emission of the 'prepotent' response, that is the response that is dominant for a given task" (p. 2). "In accordance with this account, research indicates that individuals under evaluative pressure are more prone to attentional automatisms, for example, they show higher propensity to reflexive saccades in the antisaccade task" (p. 2). This logic would suggest that participants who are subject to evaluative pressure should look at the abrupt onset cue more, not less, than participants who are not, and, as a result, the cueing effect should be larger, not smaller.

Normand et al.'s (2014) finding that participants subject to evaluation exhibit a smaller cueing effect than those who were not would appear to favor their focus of attention account over the mere effort account. However, this conclusion does not take into account the fact that the mere effort account incorporates correction. That is, as McFall et al. (2009) showed, when participants subject to evaluation know what the correct answer is (as on the Stroop), and are given adequate time, they outperform no-evaluation participants. Clearly on Normand et al.'s task, participants know the difference between the correct (O) and the incorrect (Qs) answers. In addition, Normand et al. gave participants as much time as they required to make their responses. As a result, participants subject to evaluation could look at the abrupt onset cue more than no-evaluation participants and still have faster reaction times than these participants.

As a result, finding a smaller cueing effect in reaction times alone does not allow us to distinguish between these two accounts. The most straightforward test would simply require the replication of Normand et al.'s (2014) experiment with eye tracking, which would allow us to determine whether participants subject to evaluative pressure look at the cue more or less than participants who are not. As a first step in this test, we have collected data from a baseline sample of 21 undergraduate participants (i.e., experimenter evaluation was not manipulated) in Normand et al.'s paradigm, while also collecting eye-tracking data.

The participants in this baseline sample showed the typical cueing effect in their reaction time (RT) data, such that invalid RTs were longer than valid RTs. More important, participants looked at the cue on only 24.6 percent of the invalid trials. We would argue that this percentage represents our best estimate of the potency of the cue. Participants responded to valid "cues" on 49.8 percent of the trials, but on these trials we cannot distinguish between eye movements to the cue and to the target, because they occupy the same space. Consistent with the argument that eye movements on valid trials consist of these two different responses, we find that the launch times for eye movements to invalid cues are faster than movements to valid cues. As a result, in this paradigm, our best estimate is that the cue attracts an eye movement approximately 25 percent of the time. Clearly this is not a prepotent response, and, as a result, we cannot distinguish between these two accounts using these stimulus parameters. Furthermore, the eye-tracking data revealed that the letters in the stimulus display were so large that participants did not need to make an eye movement at all to respond correctly. In fact, participants did not make eye movements on 30 percent of all trials in which they correctly identified the location of the letter.

More generally, these findings emphasize the importance of understanding the characteristics of one's task prior to using it to examine the effect of evaluation, or any other social variable, on performance. Clearly, using a terminal measure, like reaction time, is not sufficient to draw any conclusions about the processes that produce any differences that are found. These results indicate that the stimulus conditions used by Normand et al. (2014), as well as Muller and Butera (2007, Experiment 5), while producing an effect of evaluation on overall RTs, cannot be used to pit the focus of attention and mere effort accounts against each other. It will be necessary to replicate Normand et al.'s visual cueing experiment with eye tracking to determine what process is producing their evaluation effect. Going forward, the size of the stimuli could be reduced such that eye movement is required, but it would be necessary to demonstrate in a baseline experiment that looking at the cue is the prepotent response in this paradigm. For example, in this focus of attention work, the cues are displayed for very brief periods of time (e.g., 30 ms), and this short exposure time may affect the potency of the cue.

Normand et al. (2014) use other tasks in this set of experiments that provide evidence consistent with the focus of attention account, but, once again, the evidence consists only of reaction times. Without evidence about the underlying processes, we are unable to draw any firm conclusions about the source of these effects.

However, we can pit the focus of attention account against mere effort by using a visual attention task that has a well-established prepotent response and also requires that participants make eye movements to perform the task. The antisaccade task (Hallett, 1978) serves this purpose well. On the antisaccade task, a participant is asked to fixate on a cross that appears in the center of the visual display and to respond to a target presented randomly on one side of the display or the other. However, before the target appears, a cue (a white square) is presented on the opposite side of the display. Participants are instructed to ignore this cue and look to the opposite of the display where the target will appear. However, there is a reflexive-like, prepotent tendency to look at the cue that must be inhibited to optimize performance. Thus, this task shares many features with the visual cueing task used by Muller and Butera (2007) and Normand et al. (2014). For instance, both tasks begin with the presentation of a central fixation, followed by an abrupt onset peripheral cue, and then the target (central cue). Also, attention to the peripheral cue is not necessary for target identification in either task, and each task requires that participants shift their visual attention to the target's location to respond accurately. However, unlike the visual cueing task, on the antisaccade task, the peripheral cue is always on the side opposite to the one on which the target will appear.

Jamieson and Harkins (2007) used this task to test a mere effort account of the effect of stereotype threat on performance. Stereotype threat, like the potential for evaluation, arouses participants' concern about their ability to perform well on tasks relevant to the stereotype. Thus, the mere effort account argues that stereotype threat should produce the same basic pattern of findings on the antisaccade task as is produced by the potential for evaluation on other inhibition tasks like the Stroop. When not given sufficient time to correct

for the prepotent tendency (i.e., at a brief display time), the participants subject to stereotype threat should be less accurate than controls in their ability to correctly identify target orientation. However, when the display time is increased enough to allow enough time for correction, stereotype threat participants should be able to respond to the target more quickly than controls, as a result of increased motivation to perform well, and this is exactly what Jamieson and Harkins (2007) found.

Jamieson and Harkins (2007) used an eye tracker to conduct a more fine-grained analysis of performance on this antisaccade task at a display time that permitted correction. Under these conditions, the mere effort account predicted that the participants under threat would look the wrong direction, toward the cue, more often than would participants in the control group, because the motivation to perform well potentiates the prepotent response. At this point, if the participants have failed to inhibit the reflexive saccade, their eyes are at the cue and they must launch a corrective saccade to get to the target site. If they have successfully inhibited the saccade, they must launch a correct saccade to the target site from the fixation point. Because correct and corrective saccades are each an "extreme example of a voluntary saccade" (Sereno, 1992, p. 92), the motivation to correct should reduce the latency to launch each type of saccade, and, as a result, the evaluation participants should launch these saccades faster than control participants. Finally, after the participants' eyes arrive at the target area, the participant must determine the target's orientation and press the appropriate response key. When the participants see the target, the mere effort account predicts that the greater motivation of participants subject to stereotype threat would lead them to respond more quickly than would participants in the control condition. Jamieson and Harkins (2007) found support for each of these predictions.

McFall et al. (2009, Experiment 4) replicated this experiment with an evaluation manipulation. Overall, evaluation participants reported target orientation more quickly than no-evaluation participants with no sacrifice in accuracy. Of course, these findings are consistent with the predictions of both the focus of attention and the mere effort accounts. The accounts can only be pitted against each other when the processes that culminate in the terminal performance measures are examined. In each case, the eye-tracking measures are consistent with the mere effort predictions but not the focus of attention predictions. Participants subject to evaluation made more, not fewer, reflexive saccades. However, they also launched correct and corrective saccades faster than no-evaluation participants, as well as produced faster adjusted reaction times (times adjusted for the time of arrival of the participants' eyes at the target site).

As a result, even though evaluation participants looked the wrong way more often than no-evaluation participants, evaluation participants ended up outperforming the no-evaluation participants. These findings do not support the focus of attention account. Instead of focusing on the central cue (the target), the participants subject to evaluation looked toward the peripheral cue (the box) more, not less, than no-evaluation participants. The focus of attention account also cannot account for the motivated behavior reflected in the faster saccade launches for correct and corrective saccades, nor can it account for the faster adjusted reaction times. These findings are consistent with the mere effort account and replicate the pattern of findings that Jamieson and Harkins (2007) report in their research on stereotype threat.

It should be noted that the mediating process that Muller and Butera (2007) and Normand et al. (2014) invoked could lead to a different set of predictions for performance on the antisaccade task. That is, the focus of attention account argued that self-evaluation threat leads participants to ruminate about the discrepancy between their performance and the participants' standards, which takes up attentional capacity, leading to a restricted focus of attention. Similarly, Schmader and Johns (2003) have argued that when under stereotype threat, participants expend cognitive resources that could be devoted to task performance on processing information resulting from the activation of the negative stereotype. Thus, in each case, participants are using processing capacity to ruminate about their task performance. However, instead of leading to reduced focus of attention, Schmader and Johns argued that the reduction in working memory capacity directly produces the performance debilitation reported in the stereotype threat literature (e.g., Cadinu, Maass, Rosabianca, & Kiesner, 2005; Croizet et al., 2004).

More specifically, Schmader and Johns (2003) argued that the executive attention component (central executive) of working memory (Engle, 2001, 2002) is impaired by the ruminations. The central executive is essential for effective performance on inhibition tasks, like the antisaccade task. Thus, if evaluation potential produces ruminations, which interfere with working memory, participants subject to evaluation should produce more reflexive saccades than controls because participants subject to evaluation have less ability to inhibit their tendency to look at the cue. They should also launch correct and corrective saccades more slowly than control participants because the capacity to launch these eye movements also requires the central executive (Kane, Bleckley, Conway, & Engle, 2001; Roberts, Hager, & Heron, 1994; Stuyven, Van der Goten, Vandierendonck, Claeys, & Crevits, 2000; Unsworth, Schrock, & Engle, 2004). However, as described previously, McFall et al. (2009, Experiment 4) found that participants subject to evaluation generated more reflexive saccades than control participants; they also launched correct and corrective saccades faster than control participants, and had faster adjusted reaction times. Each of these effects indicates that participants' central executive processes were not impaired by the potential for evaluation. Thus, these findings are consistent with the mere effort account but with neither the focus of attention account nor with Schmader and Johns's (2003) working memory account.

Taken together, McFall et al.'s (2009) research supports the mere effort account over these alternative explanations for social facilitation effects (withdrawal of effort, focus of attention, processing interference [aka working memory deficit]). In three other research traditions in psychology, it has also been found that the potential for evaluation tends to facilitate performance on simple tasks but to debilitate it on complex ones: social loafing (e.g., Jackson & Williams, 1985), creativity (e.g., Amabile, 1979), and achievement goal theory (e.g., Elliott, Shell, Henry, & Maier, 2005). Within these traditions, process models have been proposed to account for these findings, but a review reveals no agreement across, or even within, these traditions (Harkins, 2001b). In fact, the explanations that have been proposed to account for the performance effects are the same ones suggested to account for social facilitation effects: concern about failure leads to withdrawal of effort (achievement goal theory [Elliott et al., 2005]; social loafing [Harkins, 2001b]; creativity [Hennessey, 2001]); concern over failure diminishes processing capacity (achievement goal theory [Elliott et al., 2005]); and attentional overload restricts focus of attention leading to poor performance on complex tasks, which often require use of a wider range of cues than simple tasks (creativity [Hennessey, 2001]). Thus, to the extent that mere effort can provide a plausible account for social facilitation effects, this account is likely to also apply to these other areas of research.

As noted earlier, Jamieson and Harkins (2007, 2009, 2011) have extended the analysis to the effects of stereotype threat on performance. Of course, when one is subject to stereotype threat, there is not only the possibility that one will fail to measure up as an individual, as is the case for the potential for evaluation, but also the possibility that one will confirm the negative stereotype, which is also hypothesized to motivate participants to perform well. As noted previously, Jamieson and Harkins (2007) found support for the mere effort account on the antisaccade task, and they have also found support in research using GRE quantitative problems (Jamieson & Harkins, 2009; Seitchik, Jamieson, & Harkins, 2014) and the Stroop task (Jamieson & Harkins, 2011). Additional research has found support for this account using horizontal subtraction problems, modular arithmetic (Seitchik & Harkins, 2015), and a virtual ball-bouncing task (Huber, Seitchik, Brown, Sternad, & Harkins, 2015).

## Threat-Induced Potentiation of Prepotent Response Model

The research conducted thus far suggests that mere effort can account for performance on a range of tasks across domains. However, we would argue that these effects are best understood as part of a more encompassing account, the Threat-Induced Potentiation of Prepotent Responses (TIPPR) model. The TIPPR model builds on the mere effort account, arguing that the potential for evaluation and stereotype threat impacts task performance by potentiating prepotent responses, but they do so because they represent social *threats*, and it is the threat that produces the potentiation.

Consistent with this analysis, research suggests that exposure to social threats like stereotype threat and the potential for evaluation can produce a pattern of physiological arousal that is characterized by the activation of one or both of the two primary stress systems: the HPA (hypothalamus, pituitary, adrenal) axis; and the SAM (sympathetic adrenal medullary) axis. For example, in a meta-analysis of studies examining cortisol levels in response to acute stressors, Dickerson and Kemeny (2004) found that exposure to social-evaluative threat was associated with heightened levels of cortisol, which is released in response to HPA activation. Rohleder, Wolf, Maldonado, and Kirschbaum (2006) found that a psychosocial stressor increased levels of salivary alpha amylase (sAA), a protein found in saliva that

has been used as a proxy for catecholamines (specifically epinephrine and norepinephrine), which is released as part of the activation of the SAM axis. Blascovich and Mendes (2010) have summarized work in this area as showing that social threat, among other variables (e.g., effort and distress, striving for control, uncertainty, fear), is associated with moderate to high levels of activity in the HPA and SAM axes.

Furthermore, increases in arousal have been argued to be associated with the potentiation of prepotent (dominant) responses in both the evaluation (e.g., Cottrell, 1968, 1972) and stereotype threat (e.g., Ben-Zeev, Fein, & Inzlicht, 2005; O'Brien & Crandall, 2003) literatures. However, the TIPPR model argues that not just social threat but any environmental event that is perceived as a threat potentiates prepotent responses, and research on nonsocial threats is consistent with this argument. For example, Grillon, Ameli, Woods, Merikangas, and Davis (1991) have shown that the startle reflex produced by a loud auditory stimulus is potentiated by the threat of shock. Lang and his colleagues (e.g., Lang & Bradley, 2008) have shown that the viewing of unpleasant (threatening) stimuli also potentiates the startle reflex. Valls-Solé and his colleagues (e.g., Queralt et al., 2008) have shown that auditory startle speeds up obstacle avoidance. In this case, the researchers argue that the participants have prepared the motor program necessary for avoidance (i.e., it is prepotent), and the auditory startle (the independent variable in this case) potentiates this behavior. Similar effects have been found for walking, gait initiation, and sit-to-stand.

The potentiation of responses like these could have been adaptive in our ancestral past because responses to threat would likely require "flight or fight" or some other relatively simple behavior that would be facilitated by such potentiation. However, given the range of tasks that now confront us, this potentiation may help or hurt performance, as depicted in Figure 11.1.

If the prepotent response is correct, performance is facilitated. Thus, it is prepotency, not the fact that the task is "easy," that determines whether or not performance is facilitated. As it happens, on most "easy" tasks, the prepotent response is correct. However, one can decouple prepotency and task difficulty and see the primacy of prepotency.

For example, the GRE-quantitative test includes two types of problems: *solve problems*, which require the application of a formula; and *comparison problems*, which require logic and estimation. Previous

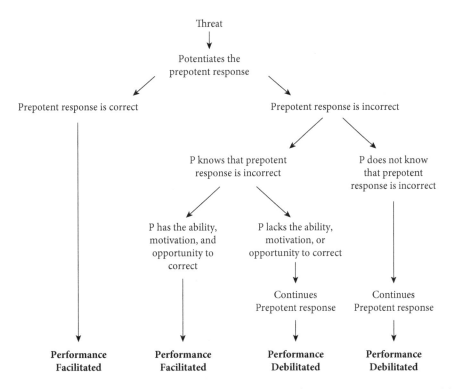

**Figure 11.1** Summary of findings for research on the Threat-Induced Potentiation of Prepotent Responses (TIPPR) model.

work shows that participants' prepotent tendency when given math problems is to take a conventional or solving approach (i.e., compute the answer using a rule or an equation) (Gallagher & De Lisi, 1994; Gallagher et al., 2000; Jamieson & Harkins, 2009; Quinn & Spencer, 2001). Using these types of problems, Jamieson (2009) found the same pattern of performance whether GRE-Q items were more (50 percent average solution rate in the population) or less difficult (75 percent average solution rate). In each case, when the prepotent response (using the solving approach) is correct, participants subject to stereotype threat performed better than no-threat participants.

Likewise, McFall et al. (2009, Experiment 1) found that participants subject to evaluation outperformed no-evaluation participants on an anagram task when the words began with consonants (prepotent response is to try consonants as the first letter; Witte & Freund, 2001), whether the words to be solved were low frequency (difficult) or high frequency (easy). Thus, regardless of task difficulty, if the prepotent response was correct, performance on the task was facilitated. On other tasks, like the Remote Associates Task (RAT), however, task difficulty is confounded with prepotency. Harkins (2006) found that on the "easy" RAT items, the

prepotent response (producing close associates of the triad members) was correct, and its potentiation facilitated performance.

If the prepotent response is incorrect, the outcome depends on whether or not the participant knows that this is the case. In many cases, the participant will not know that the prepotent response is incorrect. Under these circumstances, once again, it is prepotency, not task difficulty that determines the outcome. For example, on comparison-type GRE-Q problems, the prepotent response (the conventional, or solving approach) tends to be incorrect, and threat participants perform more poorly than control participants whether the problems are harder (50 percent solution rate) or easier (75 percent solution rate). On anagrams, the prepotent response, trying consonants in the first position of the word, is incorrect on words that begin with vowels, and participants anticipating evaluation perform more poorly than no-evaluation controls, whether these words are low frequency (harder) or high frequency (easier). On the RAT, on "difficult" items, participants do not know that producing close associates of triad members, the prepotent response, is actually reducing the likelihood that activation of the correct answer will accumulate to the point that the correct answer "pops out" (Harkins, 2006), and potentiation debilitates performance.

Although, on many tasks, participants will not know that the prepotent response is incorrect, on some tasks, they do know, and performance on these tasks is informative as to the underlying processes. For example, on inhibition tasks, like the Stroop and the antisaccade task, the prepotent response is incorrect, but it is quite obvious to the participant that this is the case. Under these circumstances, performance depends upon whether the participant has the ability, motivation, and opportunity to correct for the incorrect, prepotent tendency.

On inhibition tasks like the Stroop and the antisaccade task, participants certainly have the ability to make the response, and the TIPPR model argues that the potential for evaluation and stereotype threat motivate participants to perform well. Given ability and motivation, the model predicts facilitation if participants have the opportunity to make the correct response, and this is what we find on the Stroop for evaluation and stereotype threat (McFall et al., 2009, Experiment 2; Jamieson & Harkins, 2011, respectively) and on the antisaccade task for evaluation and stereotype threat (McFall et al., 2009, Experiment 4; Jamieson & Harkins, 2007, Experiments 2 and 3, respectively). In each of these cases, even though the incorrect prepotent response is potentiated, participants subject to evaluation or stereotype threat outperform control participants.

We have also found that if participants are motivated to perform well, have the requisite ability, and the opportunity to make the response, simple instructions are enough to make up for the fact that participants do not know that the prepotent response is incorrect. For example, Harkins (2006) told all of his participants that their performance on the RAT would be subject to evaluation. One third of these participants were told that if they wanted to succeed, they should refrain from generating close associates. Instead they were to simply register the triad members, and then wait for the answer to "pop up." Another third were told that if they wanted to succeed, they should generate as many close associates as possible. The final third, a control condition, were told nothing. Harkins (2006) found that participants who were told not to generate close associates, but to wait for the answer to emerge, outperformed the other two groups, which did not differ from each other.

Jamieson and Harkins (2009, Experiment 2) attempted to improve the performance of stereotype threat participants on the GRE-Q by providing instructions designed to reduce their reliance on the solving approach on comparison problems. This manipulation had a significant impact on performance, as the difference between threat and no-threat participants in the percentage of comparison problems solved was eliminated. A mediation analysis showed that threat participants' improvement on comparison problems resulted from the fact that threatened females took the instructions into account and reduced their reliance on the solving approach when they tried to solve comparison problems (see also Seitchik et al., 2014).

Even if participants know that the prepotent response is incorrect, if they lack the ability, motivation, or the opportunity to correct for the prepotent response, performance will be debilitated. For example, we have found that even when the participants are motivated and have the ability to make the response, if the time to respond is too brief (no opportunity to correct for the potentiation of the prepotent response), performance is debilitated on the Stroop (McFall et al., 2009, Experiment 3) and on the antisaccade task (Jamieson & Harkins, 2007, Experiment 1).

We have also found that performance is debilitated if threatened participants are not motivated to correct for the potentiated response, even if they have the requisite ability and the opportunity for correction. In the case of stereotype threat and evaluation, the effects of threat and motivation to do well cannot be separated. For instance, there is no stereotype threat without the concern that one's performance may confirm the stereotype. However, this is not the case for another social threat, ostracism. If one was ostracized, and then performed the antisaccade task, the experience of ostracism represents a threat. However, ostracized participants have no reason to be motivated to perform well unless their performance could serve to fortify their fundamental needs (belonging, self-esteem, control, and meaningful existence; Williams, 2009). In the absence of instructions suggesting this possibility, there is no reason for them to believe that the antisaccade task would serve this purpose. Under these conditions, the TIPPR model argues that the threat resulting from the experience of ostracism should potentiate the prepotent response, looking the wrong way at the cue. However, ostracism should have no effect on the measures of motivated behavior (volitional saccade launch times and reaction time adjusted for the time of arrival of the eyes at the target site) because the participant's needs cannot be fortified. This prediction was confirmed

(Jamieson et al., 2010, Experiment 1) and shows that performance was debilitated if participants lacked the motivation to perform well, even though they had both the ability and the opportunity to make the correction.

In a second experiment, an evaluation manipulation either directly linked performance on the antisaccade task to the experience of ostracism or did not (Jamieson et al., 2010, Experiment 2). When there was no link, the first experiment's findings were replicated (performance debilitated as a result of potentiated prepotent response: looking the wrong way at the cue), but when ostracized participants believed that their performance would be seen by their ostracizers, they were motivated to perform well on the antisaccade task, as reflected in faster volitional saccade latencies and adjusted reaction times, resulting in faster terminal reaction times, even though the ostracized participants also produced more reflexive saccades, the prepotent response. Once again, in this case, the participants had the ability to make the response, they had the opportunity, and they were motivated to do so.

## Summary

Research relevant to understanding the effect that the presence of others has on task performance has been conducted for over a century (Stroebe, 2012). Taken together, this research has shown that mere presence and the potential for evaluation improve performance on simple tasks and debilitate it on complex tasks, whether the others are audience members or coactors. However, there is no agreement as to what process or processes mediate(s) these effects. In fact, the same explanations that were suggested in the early twentieth century are still with us today (e.g., focus of attention, working memory deficits, withdrawal of effort, drive theory).

Harkins (2006) suggested that a molecular analysis of performance on a single task might reveal a mediating process that could then be tested on other tasks. This analysis has led to the development of the Threat-Induced Potentiation of Prepotent Reponses (TIPPR) model, which is aimed at accounting for the effect of threat on task performance. This model builds on Harkins and his colleagues' (Harkins, 2006; McFall et al., 2009) mere effort account of social facilitation effects, which was then extended to stereotype threat (Huber et al., 2015; Jamieson & Harkins, 2007, 2009, 2011; Seitchik et al., 2014; Seitchik & Harkins, 2015). Other work (e.g.,

Jamieson et al., 2010) suggests that the mere effort account is best understood in the broader context provided by the TIPPR model.

The TIPPR model argues that threat potentiates prepotent responses. This potentiation could have been adaptive in our ancestral past because responses to threat would likely require "flight or fight" or some other relatively simple behavior that would be facilitated by such potentiation. However, given the range of tasks that now confront us, this potentiation may help or hurt performance. If the prepotent response is correct, the model predicts that threat will facilitate performance. If the prepotent response is incorrect, and participants do not know, or lack the ability, motivation, or opportunity for correction, performance will be debilitated. However, if participants are able to recognize that their prepotent tendencies are incorrect and have the ability, motivation, and opportunity required for correction, performance will be facilitated. In previous work, Harkins and his colleagues have found support for this model using three different manipulations of social threat (the potential for evaluation: Harkins, 2006; McFall et al., 2009; stereotype threat: Jamieson & Harkins, 2007, 2009, 2011; and ostracism: Jamieson et al., 2010), and a variety of tasks (anagrams, antisaccade task, Remote Associates Task, GRE-quantitative problems, Stroop, horizontal subtraction problems, modular arithmetic, a virtual ball-bouncing task).

In 1935, Dashiell noted the difficulty of conducting research in this domain and then commented: "But this is no counsel of despair: Before solid findings can be achieved in any science a great amount of grub-work must needs be done in the way of clarification of problems and trying-out of techniques" (p. 1115). It is clear that much grub work remains both with respect to work that has already been done (e.g., accounting for the inconsistency with Augustinova and Ferrand's (2012) findings; see also Wuhr and Huestegge, 2010) as well as to extensions of the account. However, even with the many issues that remain to be tackled, we believe that this approach has promise. The TIPPR model has relevance for any line of research that focuses on motivated task performance, such as social facilitation, social loafing, goal setting, intrinsic motivation/creativity, achievement goal theory, and stereotype threat, to name a few. It has the potential to integrate research across these areas by suggesting a common process through which threat affects performance. In addition, the work suggests that this process can be located within a more general model of reactions to both social and physical threat.

## Acknowledgments

This work was funded in part by the U.S. Army Research Institute for the Behavioral and Social Sciences (Contract W5J9CQ-12-C-0046; PI: Stephen G. Harkins). The views, opinions, and/or findings contained in this report are those of the authors and shall not be construed as an official Department of the Army position, policy, or decision, unless so designated by other documents.

## References

Aiello, J., & Douthitt, E. (2001). Social facilitation from Triplett to electronic performance monitoring. *Group Dynamics: Theory, Research and Practice, 5*, 163–180. doi:10.1037/1089-2699.5.3.163

Allport, F. H. (1920). The influence of the group upon association and thought. *Journal of Experimental Psychology, 3*, 159–182. doi:10.1037/h0067891

Allport, F. H. (1924). *Social psychology.* New York, NY: Houghton Mifflin.

Amabile, T. M. (1979). Effects of external evaluation on artistic creativity. *Journal of Personality and Social Psychology, 37*, 221–233. doi:10.1037/0022-3514.37.2.221

Asch, S. (1952). *Social psychology.* Englewood Cliffs, NJ: Prentice-Hall, Inc. doi:10.1037/10025-000

Augustinova, M., & Ferrand, L. (2012). The influence of mere social presence on Stroop interference: New evidence from the semantically-based Stroop task. *Journal of Experimental Social Psychology, 48*, 1213–1216. doi:10.1016/j.jesp.2012.04.014

Baron, R. (1986). Distraction-conflict theory: Progress and problems. In L. Berkowitz (Ed.), *Advances in experimental social psychology* (Vol. *19*, pp. 1–40). New York, NY: Academic Press. doi:10.1016/S0065-2601(08)60211-7

Bartis, S., Szymanski, K., & Harkins, S. G. (1988). Evaluation and performance: A two-edged knife. *Personality and Social Psychology Bulletin, 14*, 242–251. doi:10.1177/0146167288142003

Ben-Zeev, T., Fein, S., & Inzlicht, M. (2005). Arousal and stereotype threat. *Journal of Experimental Social Psychology, 41*, 174–181. doi:10.1016/j.jesp.2003.11.007

Bergum, B. O., & Lehr, D. J. (1963). Effects of authoritarianism on vigilance performance. *Journal of Applied Psychology, 47*, 75–77. doi:10.1037/h0043188

Blank, T. O., Staff, I., & Shaver, P. (1976). Social facilitation of word associations: Further questions. *Journal of Personality and Social Psychology, 34*, 725–733. doi:10.1037/0022-3514.34.4.725

Blascovich, J., & Mendes, W. B. (2010). Social psychophysiology and embodiment. In S. T. Fiske, D. T. Gilbert, & G. Lindzey (Eds.), *Handbook of social psychology* (5th ed., Vol. *1*, pp. 194–227). Hoboken, NJ: John Wiley & Sons Inc.

Blascovich, J., Mendes, W. B., Hunter, S., & Salomon, D. (1999). Social "facilitation" as challenge and threat. *Journal of Personality and Social Psychology, 77*, 68–77. doi:10.1037/0022-3514.77.1.68

Bond, C. F. (1982). Social facilitation: A self-presentational view. *Journal of Personality and Social Psychology, 42*, 1042–1050. doi:10.1037/0022-3514.42.6.1042

Bond, C. F., & Titus, L. J. (1983). Social facilitation: A meta-analysis of 241 studies. *Psychological Bulletin, 94*, 265–292. doi:10.1037/0033-2909.94.2.265

Cadinu, M., Maass, A., Rosabianca, A., & Kiesner, J. (2005). Why do women underperform under stereotype threat? Evidence for the role of negative thinking. *Psychological Science, 16*, 572–578. doi:10.1111/j.0956-7976.2005.01577.x

Carver, C., & Scheier, M. (1981). The self-attention-induced feedback loop and social facilitation. *Journal of Experimental Social Psychology, 17*, 545–568. doi:10.1016/0022-1031(81)90039-1

Cottrell, N. B. (1968). Performance in the presence of other human beings: Mere presence, audience, and affiliation effects. In E. C. Simmell, R. A. Hoppe, & G. A. Milton (Eds.), *Social facilitation and imitative behavior* (pp. 91–110). Boston, MA: Allyn & Bacon.

Cottrell, N. B. (1972). Social facilitation. In C. G. McClintock (Ed.), *Experimental social psychology* (pp. 185–236). New York, NY: Holt, Rinehart & Winston.

Cottrell, N. B., Wack, D. L., Sekerak, G. J., & Rittle, R. H. (1968). Social facilitation of dominant responses by the presence of an audience and the mere presence of others. *Journal of Personality and Social Psychology, 9*, 245–250. doi:10.1037/h0025902

Croizet, J. C., Després, G., Gauzins, M. E., Huguet, P., Leyens, J. P. & Mèot, A. (2004). Stereotype threat undermines intellectual performance by triggering a disruptive mental load. *Personality and Social Psychology Bulletin, 30*, 721–731. doi:10.1177/0146167204263961

Dashiell, J. F. (1930). An experimental analysis of some group effects. *Journal of Abnormal and Social Psychology, 25*, 190–199. doi:10.1037/h0075144

Dashiell, J. F. (1935). Experimental studies of the influence of social situations on the behavior of individual human adults. In C. Murchison (Ed.), *A handbook of social psychology* (pp. 1097–1158). Worcester, MA: Clark University Press.

DeCaro, M. S., Thomas, R. D., Albert, N. B., & Beilock, S. L. (2011). Choking under pressure: Multiple routes to skill failure. *Journal of Experimental Psychology: General, 140*, 390–406. doi:10.1037/a0023466

Dickerson, S. S., & Kemeny, M. E. (2004). Acute stressors and cortisol responses: A theoretical integration and synthesis of laboratory research. *Psychological Bulletin, 130*, 355–391. doi:10.1037/0033-2909.130.3.355

Duval, S., & Wicklund, R. A. (1972). *A theory of objective self-awareness.* Oxford, England: Academic Press.

Easterbrook, J. A. (1959). The effect of emotion on cue utilization and the organization of behavior. *Psychological Review, 66*, 183–201. doi:10.1037/h0047707

Elliott, A. J., Shell, M. M., Henry, K. B., & Maier, M. A. (2005). Achievement goals, performance contingencies, and performance attainment: An experimental test. *Journal of Educational Psychology, 97*, 630–640. doi:10.1037/0022-0663.97.4.630

Engle, R. W. (2001). What is working memory capacity? In H. L. Roediger, J. S. Nairne, I. Neath, & A. M. Suprenant (Eds.), *The nature of remembering: Essays in honor of Robert G. Crowder* (pp. 297–314). Washington, DC: American Psychological Association. doi:10.1037/10394-016

Engle, R. W. (2002). Working memory capacity as executive attention. *Current Directions in Psychological Science, 11*, 19–23. doi:10.1111/1467-8721.00160

Gagné, M., & Zuckerman, M. (1999). Performance and learning goal orientations as moderators of social loafing and social facilitation. *Small Group Research, 30*, 524–541. doi:10.1177/104649649903000502

Gallagher, A. M., & De Lisi, R. (1994). Gender differences in Scholastic Aptitude Test: Mathematics problem solving among high-ability students. *Journal of Educational Psychology, 86*, 204–211. doi:10.1037/0022-0663.86.2.204

Gallagher, A. M., De Lisi, R., Holst, P. C., McGillicuddy-De Lisi, A. V., Morely, M., & Cahalan, C. (2000). Gender differences in advanced mathematical problem solving. *Journal of Experimental Child Psychology, 75*, 165–190. doi:10.1006/jecp.1999.2532

Gates, M. F., & Allee, W. C. (1933). Conditioned behavior of isolated and grouped cockroaches on a simple maze. *Journal of Comparative Psychology, 15*, 331–358. doi:10.1037/h0073695

Geen, R. G. (1976). Test anxiety, observation, and range of cue utilization. *British Journal of Clinical and Social Psychology, 15*, 253–259. doi:10.1111/j.2044-8260.1976.tb00032.x

Geen, R. G. (1989). Alternative conceptions of social facilitation. In P. B. Paulus (Ed.), *Psychology of group influence* (2nd ed., pp. 15–51). Hillsdale, NJ: Lawrence Erlbaum Associates, Inc.

Geen, R. G., & Gange, J. J. (1977). Drive theory of social facilitation: Twelve years of theory and research. *Psychological Bulletin, 84*, 1267–1288. doi:10.1037/0033-2909.84.6.1267

Greenier, K. D., Devereaux, R. S., Hawkins, K. C., & Johnston, M. D. (2001). Social facilitation: The quest for true mere presence. *Journal of Social Behavior and Personality, 16*, 19–31.

Grillon, C., Ameli, R., Woods, S. W., Merikangas, K., & Davis, M. (1991). Fear-potentiated startle in humans: Effects of anticipatory anxiety on the acoustic blink reflex. *Psychophysiology, 28*, 588–595. doi:10.1111/j.1469-8986.1991.tb01999.x

Guerin, B. (1986). Mere presence effects in humans: A review. *Journal of Experimental Social Psychology, 22*, 38–77. doi:10.1016/0022-1031(86)90040-5

Guerin, B. (1993). *Social facilitation.* New York, NY: Cambridge University Press. doi:10.1017/CBO9780511628214

Guerin, B., & Innes, J. M. (1982). Social facilitation and social monitoring: A new look at Zajonc's mere presence hypothesis. *British Journal of Social Psychology, 21*, 7–18. doi:10.1111/j.2044-8309.1982.tb00506.x

Hallett, P. E. (1978). Primary and secondary saccades to goals defined by instructions. *Vision Research, 18*, 1279–1296. doi:10.1016/0042-6989(78)90218-3

Harkins, S. G. (1987). Social loafing and social facilitation. *Journal of Experimental Social Psychology, 23*, 1–18. doi:10.1016/0022-1031(87)90022-9

Harkins, S. G. (2000). The potency of the potential for experimenter and self-evaluation in motivating vigilance performance. *Basic and Applied Social Psychology, 22*, 277–289. doi:10.1207/15324830051035983

Harkins, S. G. (2001a). The role of task complexity, and sources and criteria of evaluation in motivating task performance. In S. G. Harkins (Ed.), *Multiple perspectives on the effects of evaluation on performance: Toward an integration* (pp. 99–131). Norwell, MA: Kluwer Press.

Harkins, S. G. (2001b). The three-variable model: From Occam's razor to the black box. In S. G. Harkins (Ed.), *Multiple perspectives on the effects of evaluation on performance: Toward an integration* (pp. 207–259). Norwell, MA: Kluwer Press.

Harkins, S. G. (2006). Mere effort as the mediator of the evaluation-performance relationship. *Journal of Personality and Social Psychology, 91*, 436–455. doi:10.1037/0022-3514.91.3.436

Harkins, S. G., & Lowe, M. D. (2000). The effects of self-set goals on task performance. *Journal of Applied Social Psychology, 30*, 1–40. doi:10.1111/j.1559-1816.2000.tb02303.x

Harkins, S. G., & Szymanski, K. (1988). Social loafing and self-evaluation with an objective standard. *Journal of Experimental Social Psychology, 24*, 354–365. doi:10.1016/0022-1031(88)90025-X

Harkins, S. G., & Szymanski, K. (1989). Social loafing and group evaluation. *Journal of Personality and Social Psychology, 56*, 934–941. doi:10.1037/0022-3514.56.6.934

Harkins, S. G., White, P. H., & Utman, C. H. (2000). The role of internal and external sources of evaluation in motivating task performance. *Personality and Social Psychology Bulletin, 26*, 100–117. doi:10.1177/0146167200261010

Henchy, T., & Glass, D. C. (1968). Evaluation apprehension and the social facilitation of dominant and subordinate responses. *Journal of Personality and Social Psychology, 10*, 446–454. doi:10.1037/h0026814

Hennessey, B. A. (2001). The social psychology of creativity: Effects of evaluation on intrinsic motivation and creativity of performance. In S. G. Harkins (Ed.), *Multiple perspectives on the effects of evaluation on performance: Toward an integration* (pp. 47–75). Norwell, MA: Kluwer Press.

Hochman, S. H. (1967). The effect of stress on Stroop color-word performance. *Psychonomic Science, 9*, 475–476.

Hochman, S. H. (1969). Stress and response competition in children's color-word performance. *Perceptual and Motor Skills, 28*, 115–118. doi:10.2466/pms.1969.28.1.115

Houston, B. K. (1969). Noise, task difficulty, and Stroop color-word performance. *Journal of Experimental Psychology, 82*, 403–404. doi:10.1037/h0028118

Houston, B. K., & Jones, T. M. (1967). Distraction and Stroop color-word performance. *Journal of Experimental Psychology, 74*, 54–56. doi:10.1037/h0024492

Huber, M., Seitchik, A. E., Brown, A., Sternad, D., & Harkins, S. G. (2015). A mere effort account of the effect of stereotype threat on performance of a racket task. *Journal of Experimental Psychology: Human Perception and Performance, 41*, 525–541. doi:10.1037/xhp0000039

Huguet, P., Dumas, F., & Monteil, J. M. (2004). Competing for a desired reward in the Stroop task: When attentional control is unconscious but effective versus conscious but ineffective. *Canadian Journal of Experimental Psychology, 58*, 153–167. doi:10.1037/h0087441

Huguet, P., Galvaing, M. P., Monteil, J. M., & Dumas, F. (1999). Social presence effects in the Stroop task: Further evidence for an attentional view of social facilitation. *Journal of Personality and Social Psychology, 77*, 1011–1025. doi:10.1037/0022-3514.77.5.1011

Jackson, J. M., & Williams, K. D. (1985). Social loafing on difficult tasks: Working collectively can improve performance. *Journal of Personality and Social Psychology, 49*, 937–942. doi:10.1037/0022-3514.49.4.937

Jamieson, J. P. (2009). The role of motivation in blatant stereotype threat, subtle stereotype threat, and stereotype priming.

Psychology Dissertations. Paper 10. Retrieved from http://hdl.handle.net/2047/d20000007

Jamieson, J. P., & Harkins, S. G. (2007). Mere effort and stereotype threat performance effects. *Journal of Personality and Social Psychology*, *93*, 544–564. doi:10.1037/0022-3514.93.4.544

Jamieson, J. P., & Harkins, S. G. (2009). The effects of stereotype threat on the solving of quantitative GRE problems: A mere effort interpretation. *Personality and Social Psychology Bulletin*, *35*, 1301–1314. doi:10.1177/0146167209335165

Jamieson, J. P., & Harkins, S. G. (2011). The intervening task method: Implications for measuring mediation. *Personality and Social Psychology Bulletin*, *37*, 652–661. doi:10.1177/0146167211399776

Jamieson, J. P., Harkins, S. G., & Williams, K. D. (2010). Need threat can motivate performance after ostracism. *Personality and Social Psychology Bulletin*, *36*, 690–702. doi:10.1177/0146167209358882

Kane, M. J., Bleckley, M. K., Conway, A. R. A., & Engle, R. W. (2001). A controlled-attention view of working memory capacity. *Journal of Experimental Psychology: General*, *130*, 169–183. doi:10.1037/0096-3445.130.2.169

Klauer, K. C., Herfordt, J., & Voss, A. (2008). Social presence effects on the Stroop task: Boundary conditions and an alternative account. *Journal of Experimental Social Psychology*, *44*, 469–476. doi:10.1016/j.jesp.2007.02.009

Lang, P. J., & Bradley, M. M. (2008). Appetitive and defensive motivation is the substrate of emotion. In A. J. Elliott (Ed.), *Handbook of approach and avoidance motivation* (pp. 51–65). New York, NY: Psychology Press.

Latané, B. (1981). The psychology of social impact. *American Psychologist*, *36*, 343–356. doi:10.1037/0003-066X.36.4.343

MacKinnon, D. P., Geiselman, R. E., & Woodward, J. A. (1985). The effects of effort on Stroop interference. *Acta Psychologica*, *58*, 225–235. doi:10.1016/0001-6918(85)90022-8

Markus, H. (1978). The effect of mere presence on social facilitation: An unobtrusive test. *Journal of Experimental Social Psychology*, *14*, 389–397. doi:10.1016/0022-1031(78)90034-3

Markus, H. (1981). The drive for integration: Some comments. *Journal of Experimental Social Psychology*, *17*, 257–261. doi:10.1016/0022-1031(81)90026-3

McFall, S. R., Jamieson, J. P., & Harkins, S. G. (2009). Testing the generalizability of the mere effort account of the evaluation-performance relationship. *Journal of Personality and Social Psychology*, *96*, 135–154. doi:10.1037/a0012878

Muller, D., & Butera, F. (2007). The focusing effect of self-evaluation threat in coaction and social comparison. *Journal of Personality and Social Psychology*, *93*, 194–211. doi:10.1037/0022-3514.93.2.194

Normand, A., Bouquet, C. A., & Croizet, J. (2014). Does evaluative pressure make you less or more distractible? Role of top-down attentional control over response selection. *Journal of Experimental Psychology: General*, *143*, 1097–1111. doi:10.1037/a0034985

O'Brien, L. T., & Crandall, C. S. (2003). Stereotype threat and arousal: Effects on women's math performance. *Personality and Social Psychology Bulletin*, *29*, 782–789. doi:10.1177/0146167203029006010

O'Malley, J. J., & Poplawsky, A. (1971). Noise-induced arousal and breadth of attention. *Perceptual and Motor Skills*, *33*, 887–890. doi:10.2466/pms.1971.33.3.887

Pallak, M. S., Pittman, T. S., Heller, J. F., & Munson, P. (1975). The effect of arousal on Stroop color-word task performance. *Bulletin of the Psychonomic Society*, *6*, 248–250.

Paulus, P. B., & Murdoch, P. (1971). Anticipated evaluation and audience presence in the enhancement of dominant responses. *Journal of Experimental Social Psychology*, *7*, 280–291. doi:10.1016/0022-1031(71)90028-X

Pessin, J. (1933). The comparative effects of social and mechanical stimulation on memorizing. *American Journal of Psychology*, *45*, 263–270. doi:10.2307/1414277

Platania, J., & Moran, G. P. (2001). Social facilitation as a function of the mere presence of others. *Journal of Social Psychology*, *141*, 190–197. doi:10.1080/00224540109600546

Queralt, A., Weerdesteyn, V., van Duijnhoven, H., Castellote, J., Valls-Solé, J., & Duysens, J. (2008). The effects of auditory startle on obstacle avoidance during walking. *Journal of Physiology*, *18*, 4453–4463. doi:10.1113/jphysiol.2008.156042

Quinn, D. M., & Spencer, S. J. (2001). The interference of stereotype threat with women's generation of mathematical problem-solving strategies. *Journal of Social Issues*, *57*, 55–71. doi:10.1111/0022-4537.00201

Roberts, R. J., Hager, L. D., & Heron, C. (1994). Prefrontal cognitive processes: Working memory and inhibition in the antisaccade task. *Journal of Experimental Psychology: General*, *123*, 374–393. doi:10.1037/0096-3445.123.4.374

Rohleder, N., Wolf, J. M., Maldonado, E. F., & Kirschbaum, C. (2006). The psychosocial stress-induced increase in salivary alpha-amylase is independent of saliva flow rate. *Psychophysiology*, *43*, 645–652. doi:10.1111/j.1469-8986.2006.00457.x

Sanna, L. J. (1992). Self-efficacy theory: Implications for social facilitation and social loafing. *Journal of Personality and Social Psychology*, *62*, 774–786. doi:10.1037/0022-3514.62.5.774

Schmader, T., & Johns, M. (2003). Converging evidence that stereotype threat reduces working memory capacity. *Journal of Personality and Social Psychology*, *85*, 440–452. doi:10.1037/0022-3514.85.3.440

Schmitt, B. H., Gilovich, T., Goore, N., & Joseph, L. (1986). Mere presence and social facilitation: One more time. *Journal of Experimental Social Psychology*, *22*, 242–248. doi:10.1016/0022-1031(86)90027-2

Seitchik, A. E., & Harkins, S. G. (2014). The effects of nonconscious and conscious goals on performance. *Basic and Applied Social Psychology*, *36*, 99–110. doi:10.1080/01973533.2013.856785

Seitchik, A. E., & Harkins, S. G. (2015). Stereotype threat, mental arithmetic, and the mere effort account. *Journal of Experimental Social Psychology*, *61*, 19–30. doi:10.1016/j.jesp.2015.06.006

Seitchik, A. E., Jamieson, J., & Harkins, S. G. (2014). Reading between the lines: Subtle stereotype threat cues can motivate performance. *Social Influence*, *9*, 52–68. doi:10.1080/15534510.2012.746206

Sereno, A. B. (1992). Programming saccades: The role of attention. In K. Rayner (Ed.), *Eye movements and visual cognition* (pp. 89–107). New York, NY: Springer.

Sharma, D., Booth, R., Brown, R., & Huguet, P. (2010). Exploring the temporal dynamics of social facilitation in the Stroop task. *Psychonomic Bulletin & Review*, *17*, 52–58. doi:10.3758/PBR.17.1.52

Spence, K. W. (1956). *Behavior theory and conditioning*. New Haven, CT: Yale University Press. doi:10.1037/10029-000

Stroebe, W. (2012). The truth about Triplett (1898), but nobody seems to care. *Perspectives on Psychological Science, 7*, 54–57. doi:10.1177/1745691611427306

Stroop, J. R. (1935). Studies of interference in serial verbal reactions. *Journal of Experimental Psychology, 18*, 643–662. doi:10.1037/h0054651

Stuyven, E., Van der Goten, K., Vandierendonck, A., Claeys, K., & Crevits, L. (2000). The effect of cognitive load on saccadic eye movements. *Acta Psychologica, 104*, 69–85. doi:10.1016/S0001-6918(99)00054-2

Szymanski, K., Garczynski, J., & Harkins, S. G. (2000). The contribution of the potential for evaluation to coaction effects. *Group Processes & Intergroup Relations, 3*, 269–283. doi:10.1177/1368430200033003

Szymanski, K., & Harkins, S. (1987). Social loafing and self-evaluation with a social standard. *Journal of Personality and Social Psychology, 53*, 891–897. doi:10.1037/0022-3514.53.5.891

Szymanski, K., & Harkins, S. (1993). The effect of experimenter evaluation on self-evaluation within the social loafing paradigm. *Journal of Experimental Social Psychology, 29*, 268–286. doi:10.1006/jesp.1993.1012

Thomas, S. L., Skitka, L. J., Christen, S., & Jurgena, M. (2002). Social facilitation and impression formation. *Basic and Applied Social Psychology, 24*, 67–70. doi:10.1207/153248302753439146

Travis, L. (1925). The effect of a small audience upon eye-hand coordination. *Journal of Abnormal and Social Psychology, 20*, 142–146. doi:10.1037/h0071311

Travis, L. (1928). The influence of the group upon the stutterer's speed in free association. *Journal of Abnormal and Social Psychology, 23*, 45–51. doi:10.1037/h0074512

Triplett, N. (1898). The dynamogenic factors in pacemaking and competition. *American Journal of Psychology, 9*, 507–533. doi:10.2307/1412188

Unsworth, N., Schrock, J. C., & Engle, R. W. (2004). Working memory capacity and the antisaccade task: Individual differences in voluntary saccade control. *Journal of Experimental Psychology: Learning, Memory, and Cognition, 30*, 1302–1321. doi:10.1037/0278-7393.30.6.1302

Utman, C. H., & Harkins, S. G. (2010). The effect of increasing ego-involvement on the potency of the potential for self-evaluation. *Journal of Applied Social Psychology, 40*, 1579–1604. doi:10.1111/j.1559-1816.2010.00630.x

White, P. H., Kjelgaard, M. M., & Harkins, S. G. (1995). Testing the contribution of self-evaluation to goal-setting effects. *Journal of Personality and Social Psychology, 69*, 69–79. doi:10.1037/0022-3514.69.1.69

Williams, K. D. (2009). Ostracism: A temporal need-threat model. In M. Zanna (Ed.), *Advances in experimental social psychology* (pp. 279–314). New York, NY: Academic Press. doi:10.1016/S0065-2601(08)00406-1

Witte, K. L., & Freund, J. S. (2001). Single-letter retrieval cues for anagram solution. *Journal of General Psychology, 128*, 315–328. doi:10.1080/00221300109598914

Wuhr, P., & Huestegge, L. (2010). The impact of social presence on voluntary and involuntary control of spatial attention. *Social Cognition, 28*, 145–160. doi:10.1521/soco.2010.28.2.145

Yantis, S., & Jonides, J. (1990). Abrupt visual onsets and selective attention: Voluntary versus automatic allocation. *Journal of Experimental Psychology: Human Perception and Performance, 16*, 121–134. doi:10.1037/0096-1523.16.1.121

Zajonc, R. B. (1965). Social facilitation. *Science, 149*, 269–274. doi:10.1126/science.149.3681.269

Zajonc, R. B. (1980). Compresence. In P. Paulus (Ed.), *Psychology of group influence* (pp. 35–60). Hillsdale, NJ: Lawrence Erlbaum Associates, Inc.

# Protect, Correct, and Eject: Ostracism as a Social Influence Tool

Andrew H. Hales, Dongning Ren, *and* Kipling D. Williams

**Abstract**

Ostracism—ignoring and excluding—is an evolutionarily adaptive response that protects groups from burdensome members either by correcting the misbehavior while promoting sameness and civility, or, if correction is not achieved, then ejecting the member, resulting again in a homogeneous, albeit smaller, group. Over 20 years of research demonstrates that ostracism is a powerful tool of social influence. Being the target of ostracism activates brain regions associated with pain, threatens fundamental needs, worsens mood, and causes behavior changes aimed at fortifying threatened needs. We review research showing three functions of ostracism: (1) to protect—shielding groups from threatening members; (2) to correct—signaling to individuals that their behavior needs modification to remain in the group; and (3) to eject—permanently removing deviant individuals who resist correction. Although ostracism is a powerful and effective social influence tool, it can cause unintended and potentially dangerous consequences for those who employ it.

**Key Words:** ostracism, social exclusion, rejection, Cyberball, social susceptibility, aggression, solitude, social pain

Classic approaches to social influence acknowledge the important role that social rejection can play in the social influence process, often assuming that fear of rejection is an important force behind processes such as conformity (e.g., Schachter, 1951). This is especially apparent in the distinction between normative and informational social influence. Normative influence, thought to account for at least a portion of conformity in the Asch line paradigm, was described as producing "alienation rather than solidarity" when resisted (Deutsch & Gerard, 1955, p. 629; see also, Hodges, this volume). In the past 20 years, social psychologists have turned their attention to the phenomenon of ostracism—being ignored and excluded—directly. In line with the assumptions of classic social influence research, there is now considerable evidence that ostracism, or its anticipation, plays a crucial role in social influence processes.

Our goal in this chapter is to review and organize contemporary research on ostracism as (1) a tool used by *sources* of social influence, and (2) as an experience felt by *targets* of social influence. After providing context by reviewing the temporal need–threat model of ostracism, which guides research in this area, we give an overview of how and when ostracism affects the social influence process. The use of ostracism is functional for groups, and the efficient detection of ostracism is functional for individuals. The behavior of ostracizing others, and also the feelings generated by being ostracized, serve three broad functions: to protect, to correct, and to eject. That is, groups will use ostracism to (1) *protect* their members and their group identity; (2) signal to targets that they must *correct* deviant or burdensome behavior; and lastly, (3) to *eject* members who are a lost cause. Evidence for each of these functions of ostracism is available both from examining the circumstances under which ostracism occurs (the source's perspective) and the ways in which people react to being ostracized (the target's perspective).

The boundaries between these purposes of ostracism are sometimes fuzzy, but we find this to be a useful structure to organize the literature on ostracism and social influence.

## Temporal Need–Threat Model of Ostracism

According to the *temporal need–threat model of ostracism* (Williams, 2009), responses to ostracism unfold over three sequential stages: reflexive, reflective, and resignation.

### Reflexive Stage

In the first, *reflexive stage*, the individual detects cues that he or she is being ostracized and experiences immediate pain, negative affect, and threat to four basic human needs: belonging, self-esteem, control, and meaningful existence. The strong immediate reaction to cues of ostracism is thought to have evolutionary origins (Wesselmann, Nairne, & Williams, 2012). When an organism is ostracized, the fitness cost is drastic; the organism forfeits the benefits of cooperative group living, loses mating opportunities, and becomes vulnerable to predators. It follows that ancestral humans who were sensitive to the pain of ostracism would be motivated to adjust their behavior accordingly or seek affiliation with new groups. From an evolutionary perspective, humans should therefore have evolved a highly sensitive pain-detection system (Eisenberger & Lieberman, 2005; Gardner, Pickett, & Brewer, 2000; Kerr & Levine, 2008; Spoor & Williams, 2007).

Just as a properly functioning fire detector will be biased toward false positives, and away from misses (Nesse, 2005), so too should humans overdetect ostracism. Indeed, research suggests that people are highly reactive even to subtle cues of ostracism (see also *error management theory*; Haselton & Buss, 2000). Being denied acknowledgment by a passerby is sufficient to threaten one's need for belonging (Wesselmann, Cardoso, Slater, & Williams, 2012), and being denied eye contact threatens both explicitly and implicitly measured self-esteem (Wirth, Sacco, Hugenberg, & Williams, 2010). Further evidence of sensitivity to ostracism comes from the widely employed *Cyberball* paradigm (Williams, Cheung, & Choi, 2000; for a meta-analysis of Cyberball studies, see Hartgerink, van Beest, Wicherts, & Williams, 2015). Cyberball participants engage in a short online ball-tossing game with virtual confederates who throw the ball to the participant a fair 33 percent of the time (in the inclusion condition) or throw the ball only once

or twice in the beginning of the game, but not at all after that (in the ostracism condition). The virtual confederates, who are thought by participants to be complete strangers, typically ostracize Cyberball participants for only a few minutes. Despite the logical ease with which one could dismiss such an experience, Cyberball-ostracized participants reliably and strongly report threatened basic needs satisfaction and negative affect (Williams, 2009).

If, contrary to the evolutionary reasoning just outlined, people tend to immediately distinguish between ostracism events that pose serious versus trivial threats to basic needs, then we would expect the immediate negative effects of ostracism to be highly dependent on contextual factors. If, on the other hand, people overdetect ostracism and respond indiscriminately (like a sensitive fire detector), then we would expect the immediate effects of ostracism to occur regardless of contextual factors. Research tends to support the conclusion that people tend to be indiscriminant in responding to ostracism. Cyberball-induced ostracism is threatening even when the other players are thought to be members of a despised outgroup (Gonsalkorale & Williams, 2007), when there is a financial incentive to being ostracized (van Beest & Williams, 2006), and even when the other players are known to be controlled by a computer (Zadro, Williams, & Richardson, 2004). Even witnessing an episode of ostracism directed at someone else is sufficient to threaten basic needs (Wesselmann, Bagg, & Williams, 2009; Wesselmann, Williams, & Hales, 2013). This is not to say that reflexive responses to ostracism are never moderated (see, for example, participants high in personality disorder traits; Wirth, Lynam, & Williams, 2010); only that such responses are highly resistant to moderation.

### Reflective Stage

Ostracism's immediate impact is strong, but not irreparable. In the second, *reflective stage*, people begin the recovery process. It is here that personality and situational factors play an important role in either speeding or slowing recovery from the ostracism episode. For example, the immediate impact of ostracism has been found to be just as distressing for those who were low and high in social anxiety (Zadro, Boland, & Richardson, 2006). Following a period of delay, however, participants high in social anxiety had recovered significantly less than their less-anxious counterparts.

Similar findings have been reported in regards to situational factors affecting rates of recovery.

Participants recover more quickly from ostracism when it is perpetrated by members of a temporary and minimalistic outgroup (players wearing a certain color shirt) than a permanent outgroup (gender; Wirth & Williams, 2009). Similarly, attributing ostracism to prejudice is associated with slower recovery (Goodwin, Williams, & Carter-Sowell, 2010).

One particularly important situational factor affecting recovery is the opportunity to self-distract. Following ostracism, participants who were distracted by a change detection task showed significantly greater recovery than those who were allowed to ruminate (Wesselmann, Ren, Swim, & Williams, 2013). Similarly, interventions such as self-affirmation or prayer also lead to greater recovery compared to conditions where participants are allowed to ruminate (and among participants who prayed, those who were more religious experienced more recovery; Hales, Wesselmann, & Williams, 2016).

While in the reflective stage, people are motivated to restore their basic needs and to behave in ways that promote this goal. Often this leads to visibly prosocial behaviors that suggest a heightened susceptibility to social influence for the purpose of being liked and included. For example, ostracism can lead to the trifecta of social influence outcomes: increased *conformity* (to unanimous, incorrect group responses; Williams, Cheung, & Choi, 2000), *compliance* (Carter-Sowell, Chen, & Williams, 2008), and *obedience* (Riva, Williams, Torstrick, & Montali, 2014). Additionally, ostracism leads to better memory for social information (Gardner et al., 2000; Pickett, Gardner, & Knowles, 2004), increased ability to distinguish between sincere smiles and faked smiles (Bernstein, Young, Brown, Sacco, & Claypool, 2008), and greater nonconscious mimicry of an interaction partner's behaviors (Lakin, Chartrand, & Arkin, 2008), which is known to lead to greater liking (Chartrand & Bargh, 1999). Further, ostracism leads females to work harder collectively than individually (Williams & Sommer, 1997). All of these behaviors suggest that ostracized individuals try to fortify belonging and social self-esteem by *going along to get along*.

In sharp contrast to prosocial behaviors, many studies have documented that ostracism can produce aggression (Twenge, Baumeister, Tice, & Stucke, 2001). Williams (2009) proposed that the type of response produced by ostracism depends largely on which needs the individual is motivated to restore. If the individual is motivated to restore the *inclusionary* needs of belonging and self-esteem, he or she will respond prosocially. Alternatively, if the individual is motivated to restore the *power/provocation* needs of control and meaningful existence, he or she will lash out aggressively. In support of this resolution, Warburton, Williams, and Cairns (2006) observed that ostracism led to aggression, but not when participants were given the opportunity to restore their need for control.

Finally, new research suggests a third type of behavioral outcome: solitude seeking (Ren, Wesselmann, & Williams, 2016). In some cases and for some people, the preferred method for coping is to hunker down alone and lick one's wounds. This choice serves a few purposes: It preempts further rejection by removing oneself from others altogether; and it allows the individual to regroup and plot out an effective thoughtful response.

### Resignation Stage

Finally, if ostracized individuals are continuously ignored and excluded, and they are unable to repair their threatened needs, they enter the final *resignation stage*. Individuals in this stage are theorized to succumb to feelings of alienation, depression, helplessness, and unworthiness (Williams, 2009).

Because this stage entails long-term ostracism, it cannot be studied experimentally in humans. Various other approaches have been taken to understand this stage. First, researchers have conducted qualitatively rich interviews with targets and sources of long-term ostracism (see Williams, 2009, for excerpts). The feelings victims express in these interviews are consistent with the predictions that long-term ostracism produces serious negative consequences. Second, using animal models, researchers have examined the results of experimentally isolating prairie voles and found that isolated voles exhibit signs of learned helplessness (Grippo, Wu, Hassan, & Carter, 2008). Finally, researchers can study marginalized groups, or individuals who are often ignored and excluded (e.g., the homeless). The practice of incarceration, an institutional form of punitive ostracism, also offers insight into the effects of long-term ostracism. Research shows that, compared to those in the normal prison population, inmates exposed to solitary confinement are more depressed and are at greater risk for suicide (Haney, 2003; Haney & Lynch, 1997).

To summarize, the temporal need–threat model of ostracism has produced many research findings relevant to the study of social influence processes.

We turn to those after briefly considering the question of why ostracism is so common.

### Why Is Ostracism So Common?

Given that ostracism is plainly unpleasant, we might expect it to be a rare experience. However, this does not seem to be the case. Evidence from event-contingent diary studies documents the fact that the typical person experiences ostracism on a daily basis (Nezlek, Wesselmann, Wheeler, & Williams, 2012). Not only is ostracism ubiquitous, in that individuals encounter it frequently, but it is also common across generations, cultures, and even species (Gruter & Masters, 1986; Zippelius, 1986). Given this apparent paradox, scholars have raised the question of why it is that we ostracize (Wesselmann, Wirth, Pryor, Reeder, & Williams, 2013).

Perhaps people ostracize because they are unaware of the pain that ostracism causes others. There is evidence that people systematically underestimate the social pain of ostracism (Nordgren, McDonnell, & Loewenstein, 2011, Study 1; O'Reilly, Robinson, Berdahl, & Banki, 2015; Nordgren, Banas, & MacDonald, 2011, but see van Dijk, van Dillen, Seip, & Rotteveel, 2012, for an experiment showing that peoples' affective forecasts of ostracism can also *overestimate* the anger and sadness of Cyberball). However, even if people tend to underestimate the pain of ostracism, they are still aware that it does cause pain. This is apparent from research documenting the effects of vicarious ostracism on observers (for a review, see Wesselmann, Williams, et al., 2013). For example, after viewing a 10-minute scene depicting ostracism in a children's movie, people report threatened needs satisfaction (Coyne, Nelson, Robinson, & Gundersen, 2011). The vivid and engaging depictions that one would expect from a movie are not necessary to elicit these effects; merely watching another person be ostracized in Cyberball threatens people's needs satisfaction (Wesselmann et al., 2009). It seems then that obliviousness to the pain of ostracism cannot account for the ubiquity of its use.

Perhaps people are aware of the pain of ostracism, but use it because it can provide them direct psychological benefits, at least temporarily. This possibility is hard to reconcile with anecdotal reports that confederates who administer in-person ostracism in laboratory research find it difficult to do so (Williams & Sommer, 1997; Williams, 2009). More systematic research has explored this possibility; ostracism has been documented to cause negative effects such as decreased needs satisfaction, mood, self-regulation, and even self-dehumanization (Bastian et al., 2012, Study 1; Ciarocco, Sommer, & Baumeister, 2001; Legate, DeHaan, Weinstein, & Ryan, 2013; Poulsen & Kashey, 2012; see Zadro & Gonsalkorale, 2014, for a review, and Grahe, 2015, for a special issue on this topic). It is important to note, however, that there may be cases in which people do benefit from ostracizing others, particularly if it is seen as deserved (Gooley, Zadro, Williams, Svetieva, & Gonsalkorale, 2015; Sommer & Yoon, 2013).

Ostracism hurts. People know it hurts, and they do not always enjoy using it. So why is ostracism so common? The answer lies in the functional nature of ostracism. Ostracism serves to protect, correct, and eject. That is, by using ostracism, groups can *protect* their members from real or symbolic threats. Because individuals experience ostracism as immediately aversive, groups can also use ostracism to *correct* the behavior of individuals within the group. Finally, by using ostracism, groups can *eject* individuals whose problematic behavior is resistant to correction.

### Protect

Humans are social animals, with a fundamental need to belong (Baumeister & Leary, 1995). However, they are not indiscriminately social. Evolutionary theorists have argued that ostracism serves a protective function for groups. Kurzban and Leary (2001) argued that selective social exclusion can be highly functional for groups, serving to protect groups from individuals who exploit the group from within, from individuals who threaten the group from without, and from individuals who might pose a risk of introducing pathogens. Similarly, Baumeister and Tice (1990) argued that groups use ostracism to ensure that they are free from incompetent, deviant, or unattractive members. Buss (1990) also notes that the factors thought to lead to social exclusion are evolutionarily important; someone is likely to ostracize other people when those people engage in behaviors that threaten the fitness of the ostracizer (e.g., sexual infidelity, violent aggression, cheating, etc.).

If ostracism really does serve the purpose of protecting groups, then we would expect the following to be true: (1) Ostracism should be selectively targeted at individuals who pose threats to a group, and (2) groups should function more successfully when ostracism is available as an incentive against freeriding. As shown in the following, existing evidence supports both propositions.

## OSTRACISM IS SELECTIVELY TARGETED

One of the earliest studies examining social exclusion asked the question of how a group reacts to a deviant member. In this classic study, Schachter (1951) examined groups' reactions to a member who persistently argued in favor of an unpopular opinion (in this case, the position that a juvenile delinquent, Johnny Rocco, should be treated with the harshest punishment possible). Schachter observed that, following failed attempts at converting the group member to the majority opinion, groups rejected the deviate by discontinuing communication with him, and by choosing to exclude him from future group meetings (see Wesselmann et al., 2014, for a recent replication of these findings). These actions were not taken against other confederates who either matched the majority opinion the entire time or who initially disagreed with the majority but eventually succumbed.

More recent research shows that group ostracism is not only directed at opinion deviants but also at other types of deviants as well. For example, Szczurek, Monin, and Gross (2012) explored the circumstances under which individuals reject *affective deviants*: individuals who either fail to display emotion in response to evocative events or who display an emotion that is incongruent with evocative events. They found that participants not only rated affective deviants more negatively but also desired greater social distance from affective deviants (a form of ostracism). This effect was mediated by a decrease in the perception that the target shared the moral values of the participant, suggesting that people use ostracism as a tool to protect themselves from others who do not share their moral values (in this case, people who display deviant affect).

In addition to selectively ostracizing targets that are deviant, groups can be expected to also direct ostracism toward those who are likely to take advantage of the group's cooperative efforts. Evidence for this comes from social dilemma and public goods experiments in which participants can choose to maximize group well-being by behaving cooperatively or instead maximize their own well-being by behaving selfishly (e.g., Cinyabuguma, Page, & Putterman, 2005). In one such experiment (Feinberg, Willer, & Schultz, 2014), participants engaged in a public goods game in which they could choose how many of 10 tokens to contribute to a group fund which would be doubled and distributed equally to the group members. Under some conditions, prior to each trial, participants could exchange information about the other players (gossip) and vote to exclude another player from the upcoming trial. Participants availed themselves of the opportunity to ostracize low-contributing others (i.e., those who benefit from the group fund but do not contribute to it).

Because ostracism functions as a means of protecting groups from individuals who exploit collective group efforts, we recently tested whether people who are disagreeable are more likely to be ostracized (Hales, Kassner, Williams, & Graziano, 2016). The personality trait of agreeableness has been conceptualized as the motivation to maintain positive relations with others (Graziano & Eisenberg, 1997). As such, people who are disagreeable are less helpful, cooperative, and socially mindful (for a review, see Graziano & Tobin, 2013). Because disagreeable people make poor exchange partners, they should be especially vulnerable to ostracism from others. Indeed, our data revealed that people who report being chronically ostracized tend to be disagreeable. To assess whether disagreeable targets are actually more likely to be ostracized (as opposed to the alternative causal pathway that ostracism's callusing effect produces disagreeableness), we asked participants to read a description of a classmate and imagine that the person was trying to join a group to which they belong. They then reported the extent to which they would ignore and exclude the target individual. Participants rated a greater willingness to ignore and exclude a disagreeable target (described as "cold, untrusting, and uncaring") than an agreeable target (described as "warm, trusting, and caring"). This was the case both when participants read that the target had refused to help a friend move and when they read that the target agreed to help a friend move, suggesting that a specific antisocial behavior is not necessary to provoke ostracism of disagreeable others. A follow-up experiment included a control condition and found that differences in willingness to ostracize disagreeable versus agreeable targets were produced by a desire to ostracize the disagreeable target, rather than a desire to affiliate with the agreeable target. Mediation analyses showed that the disagreeable targets were trusted less, which predicted intentions to ostracize the target. Not surprisingly, how much participants liked the target was a strong predictor of ostracism intentions. However, the mediational effect of trust significantly predicted ostracism intentions after controlling for liking.

The preceding research establishes the tendency of groups to ostracize individuals who behave (or are likely to behave) in an exploitative manner. That is, they consume group resources for their own benefit. In these cases, targets are ostracized for violating the principle of *fairness*, a fundamental dimension of moral judgment (Graham et al., 2011). This raises the question of whether people would be ostracized for being merely burdensome to a group, without actually benefiting in an exploitative or unfair fashion. Is mere burden sufficient to elicit ostracism? Experiments conducted by Wesselmann, Wirth, et al. (2013) address this question. In this research, participants played Cyberball with three other virtual confederates. Two of the virtual confederates were programmed to either ostracize or include the third virtual confederate, depending on condition. Of interest is whether participants compensate for the ostracism by throwing a greater proportion of tosses to the player who is being ostracized. Under normal circumstances, participants did in fact compensate by throwing extra tosses to the target. However, when the target was a burden to the group (taking three times as long to return a typical ball toss), then participants joined in with the confederates and ostracized the target. It seems then that a potential target of ostracism does not have to be unfairly benefiting from the group's efforts to find himself/herself being rejected; merely being a burden to the group is sufficient.

Finally, even when individuals do not directly harm the group through exploitation or by being a burden, there are circumstances under which individuals pose a *symbolic* threat to group identity. A *black sheep effect* occurs when individuals are more punitive and hostile toward an ingroup member who commits and infraction than they would be toward an outgroup member that commits the same infraction. This tendency has been described as "an attempt to insure a positive social identity when such identity is threatened from inside one's group" (Marques & Paez, 1994, pp. 38–39). In this sense, the black sheep effect represents an effort to use ostracism to protect group esteem.

Although the black sheep effect seems to run counter to the prevailing tendency to favor ingroup members over outgroup members, Otten and Gordijn (2014) explain that the black sheep effect and ingroup favoritism are two routes to the same end: protecting group esteem. The strategy one chooses to protect group esteem will depend on the situation. For example, if it is ambiguous whether the individual is guilty of a misdeed, ingroup members are given the benefit of the doubt, but if the individual is clearly guilty, the ingroup member is judged more harshly (van Prooijen, 2006).

In a prototypical experimental demonstration of the black sheep effect, participants are asked to consider a target individual whose behavior is somehow deviant or unlikable. The target is presented as either as an ingroup member or an outgroup member. Participants are asked to report their reactions to this target. The typical finding is that ingroup members are regarded more negatively, met with stronger disapproval, and receive higher recommended punishments than outgroup members who commit the same infraction (Marques & Paez, 1994).

The existing black sheep literature is highly suggestive of the possibility that groups use ostracism not just to rid themselves of disadvantageous members but also to protect their identities and images. This is an interesting possibility, but to our knowledge, no experiments have directly tested it. Instead, the literature has focused mostly on how deviance committed by an ingroup member leads to negative evaluation (e.g., Marques and Yzerbyt, 1988) or recommended punishments (e.g., van Prooijen, 2006) toward the deviant individual. It seems ostracism would be an extremely effective method for establishing distance between the deviant ingroup member and the ingroup itself.

To summarize, based on these research findings, it is reasonable to argue that ostracism is used as a tool to protect its sources from a wide range of real threats (such as cheaters or violent criminals) and symbolic threats (such as black sheep who harm the group's image and threaten the social identities of its members). But does it work? Next we consider evidence that the looming possibility of ostracism can be used to lead to more harmonious group interactions, thereby succeeding in protecting the group from threat.

## OSTRACISM CAN IMPROVE GROUP FUNCTIONING

If groups use ostracism to protect themselves from exploitation, it follows that groups in which ostracism is a viable possibility will enjoy greater cooperation. Existing research supports the proposition that the threat of ostracism can motivate cooperative behaviors.

Kerr and colleagues (2009) demonstrated the beneficial effects of ostracism for groups using a social dilemma task similar to the one described earlier (Feinberg et al., 2014). In conditions where ostracism was not an available tool for group members to use in response to noncooperative members, group members showed a greater tendency to follow the lead of a "bad apple" and contribute fewer resources to the shared group account. However, in conditions in which participants believed that they could be ostracized from the game, participants overrode the temptation to imitate the bad apple. Other studies have demonstrated similar positive effects of the threat of ostracism on cooperative behaviors (Cinyabuguma et al., 2005; Maier-Rigaud, Martinsson, & Staffiero, 2010).

Just as ostracism (or threat of ostracism) can protect groups from the effects of exploitative members, so too can it protect groups from the effects of burdensome members. In collective group tasks in which individual input is not identifiable, people tend to engage in *social loafing* by relaxing their individual efforts (Karau & Williams, 1993). However, at least for women, being ostracized can lead to *social compensation* by enhancing individual efforts on anonymous group tasks (Williams & Sommer, 1997). Presumably ostracized women were more committed to the *group*'s success, even though their individual inputs would not be known.

Together, these findings speak to the important first function of ostracism: group protection. Initially groups use ostracism to protect themselves from others who are exploitative, burdensome, or threatening to group identity. Based on the findings that group members behave more cooperatively when the social influence tactic of ostracism is a viable threat, it seems that it can be an effective strategy for promoting cooperation.

## Correct

The research reviewed so far has focused on ostracism that is largely preemptive in nature. Groups are motivated to avoid even initial contact with others who pose a threat to the group. However, to function optimally as a tool for social influence, ostracism should also have an effect on individuals who are already members of a group but stray away from group norms. This is where the second function of ostracism comes into play. Ostracism can serve as a tool to entice group members to *correct* their behavior (assuming here that misbehavior was the force that elicited the ostracism, as opposed to other factors such as pathogen threat). If this is the case, then ostracism should lead to a series of prosocial behaviors that will help the individual regain standing within the group. In terms of the temporal need–threat model, ostracism motivates individuals to refortify their threatened needs. This can be accomplished by engaging in corrective

behaviors that re-establish standing within a group. For example, recall that in a multitrial public goods game, exploitative participants were more likely to be ostracized (Feinberg et al., 2014). The researchers also found that ostracized participants sizably increased their contributions on trials immediately following ostracism, relative to trials immediately preceding the ostracism. In line with the corrective function of ostracism, people who experience ostracism should be generally sensitive to social influence, especially while in the reflective stage of recovery. Indeed, the research reviewed next supports this conclusion.

### CONFORMITY, COMPLIANCE, AND OBEDIENCE

Traditionally, the study of social influence has emphasized three related but distinct forms of influence: conforming to the behaviors of others (Asch, 1956), complying with the requests of others (Cialdini, 2008), and obeying the commands of authority figures (Milgram, 1974). In recent years, research has accumulated showing that ostracism can lead to greater susceptibility to conformity, compliance, and obedience: the "social influence trifecta" (Riva et al., 2014, p. 215).

The first study to employ the Cyberball paradigm not only tested the effects of ostracism on basic needs satisfaction but also tested whether ostracism would lead to an increase in conformity (Williams et al., 2000). In an Asch-style paradigm, participants who had just played Cyberball online were asked to make simple perceptual judgments (identifying simple shapes embedded within other shapes) after preceding participants appeared to make unanimously incorrect judgments. On average, ostracized participants conformed on more trials than included participants. Given the power of ingroups, one might expect ostracism to only increase conformity to an ingroup. However, ostracism increased conformity whether the other players were members of an ingroup or members of an outgroup (mac versus PC users).

The effects of ostracism on conformity have also been observed with a novel paradigm in which a brief conversational silence serves as a subtle rejection signal to an individual (Koudenburg, Postmes, & Gordijn, 2013). In this research, participants engaged in a structured in-person discussion of a controversial topic with two confederates. In the experimental condition, after the participants stated their position on the topic, the confederates waited 4 seconds before continuing the conversation. In the control condition, confederates did not include a pause, but continued with the conversation in an otherwise equivalent manner. Conceptually replicating the original Cyberball experiment, the conversational silence led to greater attitudinal shifts in the direction of the group's position, but only among participants who expressed a high motivation to belong. This study can be viewed as the auditory counterpart to Wesselmann and colleagues' (2012) finding that remarkably subtle visual cues of rejection can have a measurable impact. Just as groups use ostracism to protect themselves from deviant members, individuals use the pain of ostracism as motivation to be less deviant.

To test whether ostracism creates susceptibility to compliance tactics, Carter-Sowell et al. (2008) had participants play Cyberball prior to being confronted with a compliance request. Specifically, as participants were in the waiting room, they were approached by a confederate who appeared to be a member of the local university marching band and requested that they pledge to make a donation to the band. Participants who were ostracized were more compliant, as evidenced by their agreements to pledge larger amounts of money. Interestingly, the degree of compliance did not depend on whether the requester employed a known compliance technique (foot-in-the-door technique or door-in-the-face technique) or simply made a direct request. Thus, special compliance techniques are not necessary for ostracism to make people more likely to go along with a request.

Finally, completing the trifecta, there is also evidence that being ostracized makes people more obedient to authority figures (Riva et al., 2014). Specifically, after playing Cyberball, participants were instructed by the experimenter (authority figure) to go outside in the cold of winter (in the American Midwest, with average temperatures of 20°F) and take creative photographs. Ostracized participants were more obedient than included participants, as indicated by the creativity ratings of their photographs.

The corrective function of ostracism does not just make people more susceptible to the three major types of social influence. It also produces a cluster of perceptual and cognitive processes that result in better and more thorough processing of social information. For example, when people are asked to recall an experience of being socially rejected (which reactivates the original pain; Chen, Williams, Fitness, & Newton, 2008), they are better at distinguishing between sincere smiles and fake smiles (Bernstein et al., 2008), and they express a

greater desire to work with those expressing sincere smiles (Bernstein, Sacco, Brown, Young, & Claypool, 2010). They also show an improved memory for socially relevant information (Gardner et al., 2000; Pickett et al., 2004). These alterations in attention and memory are thought to promote reaffiliation.

Extending this reasoning, Claypool and Bernstein (2014) asked whether ostracism would cause people to *individuate* others, rather than stereotype them. On the one hand, other research has shown that ostracism reduces complex cognitive functioning (Baumeister, Twenge, & Nuss, 2002), and it should thus increase people's reliance on stereotypes, which allows for less effortful processing. Claypool and Bernstein (2014) discovered, however, that this is only the case for nonsocial processing, or processing of targets that are not viable sources of affiliation. When an ostracized person considers possible sources of affiliation, on the other hand, that person will tend to rely more on individuating information rather than stereotypes (Claypool & Bernstein, 2014).

Susceptibility to social influence, and extra processing of social information, can be viewed as mechanisms by which people achieve reaffiliation with groups and fulfill their threatened needs satisfaction. If this is the case, then ostracism should produce a greater desire to affiliate with others. Accordingly, following social exclusion experiences, people report greater interest in making new friends and working with others (rather than alone; Maner, DeWall, Baumeister, & Schaller, 2007).

Similarly, recent correlational and experimental research has shown that this desire for affiliation is not limited to socially normative groups. Ostracism also motivates people to be more interested in extreme groups that would otherwise be seen as unappealing. People who are chronically ostracized reported greater interest in joining Mormonism, Scientology, the Westburo Baptist Church, and (oddly) Alcoholics Anonymous (Hales & Williams, 2015). When ostracism was induced experimentally through Cyberball, participants reported greater openness to gang membership, and in another experiment, greater interest in attending meetings of a campus organization dedicated to advocating tuition reduction through extreme actions such as blockading campus (Hales & Williams, 2015).

As noted earlier, responses to ostracism are not uniformly prosocial. In fact, a sizeable literature attests to the power of ostracism in provoking aggression toward both the ostracizers and also uninvolved bystanders (Williams & Wesselmann, 2011). Research continues to explore the factors that determine whether people respond to ostracism prosocially versus antisocially; however, a number of important moderators have been identified. Ostracism leads to less aggression when the targets have an opportunity to restore their need for control (Warburton et al., 2006) or belonging (Twenge et al., 2007). Ostracism leads to greater aggression when it comes without warning (Wesselmann, Butler, Williams, & Pickett, 2010) or when it is particularly unjust (Chow, Tiedens, & Govan, 2008).

All together, there is strong evidence that the experience of ostracism motivates individuals to behave in ways that are essentially corrective, in the sense that they increase the likelihood that individuals will be reincluded and therefore able to refortify threatened needs satisfaction.

## Eject

The three functions of ostracism are not merely different uses of ostracism but form a logical sequence, in which ostracism may occur at any point. Insurgent disagreeable newcomers to a group may be denied membership as the group seeks to protect itself. Alternatively, supportive well-intentioned newcomers might be welcomed into the fold (Moreland & Levine, 1982). As individuals navigate within the group, they may from time to time receive subtle cues of ostracism for unwelcomed or burdensome behavior, which should motivate them to correct their behavior. Finally, if such cues are insufficient to motivate individuals to correct their behavior, they may reach a critical threshold or duration of misbehavior, at which point the group will eject them. This sequence is plausible and follows logically from the literature reviewed in this chapter. However, research has yet to directly test whether the use of ostracism unfolds in this manner. Specifically, in contrast to the other two functions of ostracism, far less is known about ostracism being implemented as a tool to eject unwelcome members from groups (possibly because of methodological difficulties associated with permanently excluding group members). However, the existing literature does offer intriguing clues as to when groups will resort to more permanent forms of ostracism.

The most interesting feature of the ejection function of ostracism is that it seems not to be the first resort of groups when dealing with a troublesome member. Recall that in Schachter's (1951) research, groups only excluded the opinion deviate after attempts to *correct* the deviate's behavior by winning him over to the majority position. Using a highly similar procedure, Miller and Anderson (1979) replicated Schachter's finding that opinion deviates are rejected by the groups. However, they found this to only be the case when the deviate was able to interfere with the group's ability to arrive at the favored position: when the deviate was assigned to be a *chairperson* who made the final decision or when the decision was required to be unanimous. In other words, groups are willing to tolerate a deviate so long as it does not interfere with group functioning. It is sensible that groups would be reluctant to fully eject members—they need to maintain membership. Ejecting individuals for minor violations is hardly a practical way for groups to function. Not only would an overly sensitive ejection system cause groups to bleed members, but it could also likely damage the trust among the remaining members.

This reasoning suggests an interesting asymmetry in the decision-making processing of targets and sources of ostracism. As described, targets of ostracism are heavily biased toward false positives (or overdetection) in deciding whether or not a certain behavior is a cue for forthcoming ostracism. In contrast, groups are fairly conservative in administering ostracism. That is, when individuals are deciding whether a behavior is ostracism, they have an *over*detection bias. When groups are deciding whether a group member's actions are deserving of ostracism, they have an *under*detection bias (against false positives). This arrangement would be advantageous for both targets of ostracism and the groups who may deliver it. Future research should explore these speculations.

As the literature currently stands, there are a number of other unexplored questions relevant to the ejection function of ostracism. The first and most basic is its prevalence. How often is ejection the primary goal of ostracism? The foregoing analysis suggests that often ostracism is used in an escalating fashion (e.g., begin with decreased eye contact, then reduce the number of comments made to the target, and eventually stop responding to the target altogether if necessary). It follows that most often the purpose of ostracism should be to screen poor interaction partners or motivate the individuals to correct their behavior. Of course, contextual factors almost certainly moderate the extent to which groups rely on ejection-focused ostracism as opposed to correction-focused ostracism. A second, related, question is whether ostracism takes different forms when it is being utilized for different purposes. It is reasonable to expect that when ostracism is employed to eject an individual, it is particularly strong, whereas when ostracism is used in the service of correction, it manifests itself in a subtler fashion. Finally, under what circumstances does ejection-based ostracism work? There is anecdotal evidence of individuals persisting through years of ostracism to accomplish desired goals (for example, Cadet James Pelosi endured nearly 2 years of ostracism from his West Point classmates after he violated the honor code by continuing to work on an exam after time expired; Williams, 2001). Future research should explore the factors that enable people to reject a group's ostracism.

## Conclusions

We have observed that some of the most captivating demonstrations of social influence implicitly assumed that fear of rejection motivated people to be highly sensitive to group pressure (Williams, 2001). The research reviewed in this chapter has largely confirmed this assumption. For sources, ostracism is perhaps the most powerful tool of social influence available. In its most extreme form, it is the proverbial "nuclear option." It is, when used in this way, the denial of any and all social interaction. For targets, ostracism is an important signal that their belonging has been jeopardized, and that a change of behavior is in order.

In this chapter, we have shown that ostracism is a complicated social influence tool that can be used for three main functions. First, groups use ostracism to protect. It is used as an initial screening to (1) filter out members who are threats to the group or (2) create an incentive to not take advantage of group resources. Second, groups use ostracism to correct. It is used to signal to group members that their behavior is in need of modification. Indeed, research shows that the detection of ostracism triggers a series of cognitive and behavioral processes aimed at correcting behavior and fortifying basic needs. Third, groups use ostracism to eject. Rehabilitation is not always feasible, and when individuals are highly resistant to correcting their behavior, they may be met with more extreme forms of ostracism.

Though the protective and corrective functions of ostracism are well supported by existing research, there is much to be learned about the use of ostracism to permanently eject members from groups. We hope that researchers turn their attention to this largely unexplored use of ostracism. Those attempting to use ostracism to eject, however, should heed a cautionary warning. As reviewed in this chapter,

attempts to correct and protect the group through the use of ostracism may result in unwanted consequences: to the extent that the ostracized individuals feel there is little chance to maintain membership within the group, or to find membership in another group, then other needs, like control and meaningful existence, might trump attempts to fortify belonging and social self-esteem. This may lead the individuals to provoke attention and impact through aggression and violence. Clearly, ostracism can be an important socializing tool, but it can also have unexpected dangerous consequences. To ostracize with the goal of ejection and absolute permanent exclusion is likely to punish not only the ostracized individual but also the ostracizing group.

## References

Asch, S. E. (1956). Studies of independence and conformity: I. A minority of one against a unanimous majority. *Psychological Monographs, 70*, 1–70.

Bastian, B., Jetten, J., Chen, H., Radke, H. M., Harding, J. F., & Fasoli, F. (2012). Losing our humanity: The self-dehumanizing consequences of social ostracism. *Personality and Social Psychology Bulletin, 39*, 156–169. doi:10.1177/0146167212471205

Baumeister, R. F., & Leary, M. R. (1995). The need to belong: Desire for interpersonal attachments as a fundamental human motivation. *Psychological Bulletin, 117*, 497–529. doi:10.1037/0033-2909.117.3.497

Baumeister, R. F., & Tice, D. M. (1990). Anxiety and social exclusion. *Journal of Social and Clinical Psychology, 9*, 165–195. doi:10.1521/jscp.1990.9.2.165

Baumeister, R. F., Twenge, J. M., & Nuss, C. K. (2002). Effects of social exclusion on cognitive processes: Anticipated aloneness reduces intelligent thought. *Journal of Personality and Social Psychology, 83*, 817–827. doi:10.1037/0022-3514.83.4.817

Bernstein, M. J., Sacco, D. F., Brown, C. M., Young, S. G., & Claypool, H. M. (2010). A preference for genuine smiles following social exclusion. *Journal of Experimental Social Psychology, 46*, 196–199. doi:10.1016/j.jesp.2009.08.010

Bernstein, M. J., Young, S. G., Brown, C. M., Sacco, D. F., & Claypool, H. (2008). Adaptive responses to social exclusion: Social rejection improves detection of real and fake smiles. *Psychological Science, 19*, 981–983.

Buss, D. M. (1990). The evolution of anxiety and social exclusion. *Journal of Social and Clinical Psychology, 9*, 196–201. doi:10.1521/jscp.1990.9.2.196

Carter-Sowell, A. R., Chen, Z., & Williams, K. D. (2008). Ostracism increases social susceptibility. *Social Influence, 3*, 143–153. doi:10.1080/15534510802204868

Chartrand, T. L., & Bargh, J. A. (1999). The chameleon effect: The perception–behavior link and social interaction. *Journal of Personality and Social Psychology, 76*, 893–910. doi:10.1037/0022-3514.76.6.893

Chen, Z., Williams, K. D., Fitness, J., & Newton, N. C. (2008). When hurt will not heal: Exploring the capacity to relive social and physical pain. *Psychological Science, 19*, 789–795. doi:10.1111/j.1467-9280.2008.02158.x

Chow, R. M., Tiedens, L. Z., & Govan, C. L. (2008). Excluded emotions: The role of anger in antisocial responses to ostracism. *Journal of Experimental Social Psychology*, *44*, 896–903. doi:10.1016/j.jesp.2007.09.004

Cialdini, R. B. (2008). *Influence: Science and practice* (5th ed.). Boston: Allyn & Bacon.

Ciarocco, N. J., Sommer, K. L., & Baumeister, R. F. (2001). Ostracism and ego depletion: The strains of silence. *Personality and Social Psychology Bulletin*, *27*, 1156–1163. doi:10.1177/0146167201279008

Cinyabuguma, M., Page, T., & Putterman, L. (2005). Cooperation under the threat of expulsion in a public goods experiment. *Journal of Public Economics*, *89*, 1421–1435.

Claypool, H. M., & Bernstein, M. J. (2014). Social exclusion and stereotyping: Why and when exclusion fosters individuation of others. *Journal of Personality and Social Psychology*, *106*, 571–589. doi:10.1037/a0035621

Coyne, S. M., Nelson, D. A., Robinson, S. L., & Gundersen, N. C. (2011). Is viewing ostracism on television distressing? *The Journal of Social Psychology*, *151*, 213–217. doi:10.1080/00224540903365570

Deutsch, M. & Gerard, H. B. (1955). A study of normative and informational social influences upon individual judgment. *The Journal of Abnormal and Social Psychology*, *51*, 629–636.

Eisenberger, N. I., & Lieberman, M. D. (2005). Why it hurts to be left out: The neurocognitive overlap between physical and social pain. In K. D. Williams, J. P. Forgas, & W. von Hippel (Eds.), *The social outcast: Ostracism, social exclusion, rejection, and bullying* (pp. 109–127). New York, NY: Psychology Press.

Feinberg, M., Willer, R., & Schultz, M. (2014). Gossip and ostracism promote cooperation in groups. *Psychological Science*, *25*, 656–664. doi: 10.1177/0956797613510184.

Gardner, W., Pickett, C. L., & Brewer, M. B. (2000). Social exclusion and selective memory: How the need to belong influences memory for social events. *Personality and Social Psychology Bulletin*, *26*, 486–496.

Gonsalkorale, K., & Williams, K. D. (2007). The KKK won't let me play: Ostracism even by a despised outgroup hurts. *European Journal of Social Psychology*, *37*, 1176–1185.

Goodwin, S. A., Williams, K. D., & Carter-Sowell, A. R. (2010). The psychological sting of stigma: The costs of attributing ostracism to racism. *Journal of Experimental Social Psychology*, *46*, 612–618. doi:10.1016/j.jesp.2010.02.002

Gooley, S. L., Zadro, L., Williams, L., Svetieva, E., & Gonsalkorale, K. (2015). Ostracizing for a reason: A novel source paradigm for examining the nature and consequences of motivated ostracism. *The Journal of Social Psychology*, *155*, 410–431. doi:10.1080/00224545.2015.1060933.

Graham, J., Nosek, B. A., Haidt, J., Iyer, R., Koleva, S., & Ditto, P. H. (2011). Mapping the moral domain. *Journal of Personality and Social Psychology*, *101*, 366–385.

Grahe, J. E. (Ed.). (2015). Investigating how individuals feel ostracizing others [Special issue]. *The Journal of Social Psychology 155*(5).

Graziano, W. G., & Eisenberg, N. (1997). Agreeableness: A dimension of personality. In R. Hogan, J. Johnson, & S. Briggs (Eds.), *Handbook of personality psychology* (pp. 795–824). San Diego, CA: Academic Press.

Graziano, W. G., & Tobin, R. M. (2013). The cognitive and motivational foundations underlying agreeableness. In M. D. Robinson, E. Watkins, & E. Harmon-Jones (Eds.), *Handbook of cognition and emotion*. New York, NY: Guilford.

Grippo, A. J., Wu, K. D., Hassan, I., & Carter, C. S. (2008). Social isolation in prairie voles induces behaviors relevant to negative affect: Toward the development of a rodent model focused on co-occurring depression and anxiety. *Depression and Anxiety*, *25*, E17–E26.

Gruter, M., & Masters, R. D. (1986). Ostracism as a social and biological phenomenon: An introduction. *Ethology and Sociobiology*, *7*, 149–158.

Hales, A. H., Kassner, M. P., Williams, K. D., & Graziano, W. G. (2016). Disagreeableness as a cause and consequence of ostracism. *Personality and Social Psychology Bulletin*, *42*, 782–797. doi: 10.1177/0146167216643933.

Hales, A. H., Wesselmann, E. D., & Williams, K. D. (2016). Prayer, self-affirmation, and distraction improve recovery from short-term ostracism. *Journal of Experimental Social Psychology*, *64*, 8–20. doi: 10.1016/j.jesp.2016.01.002

Hales, A. H., & Williams, K. D. (2015, February). In with the out crowd: Ostracism increases interest in extreme groups. Poster presented at the Society for Personality and Social Psychology, Long Beach, CA.

Haney, C. (2003). Mental health issues in long-term solitary and "supermax" confinement. *Crime & Delinquency*, *49*, 124–156.

Haney, C., & Lynch, M. (1997). Regulating prisons of the future: A psychological analysis of supermax and solitary confinement. *New York University Review of Law and Social Change*, *23*, 477–570.

Hartgerink, C. H. J., van Beest, I., Wicherts, J. M., & Williams, K. D. (2015). The ordinal effects of ostracism: A meta-analysis of 120 Cyberball studies. *PLOS ONE*, *10*. e0127002. doi:10.1371/journal.pone.0127002

Haselton, M. G., & Buss, D. M. (2000). Error management theory: A new perspective on biases in cross-sex mind reading. *Journal of Personality and Social Psychology*, *78*, 81–91.

Karau, S. J., & Williams, K. D. (1993). Social loafing: A meta-analytic review and theoretical integration. *Journal of Personality and Social Psychology*, *65*, 681–706.

Kerr, N. L., & Levine, J. L. (2008). The detection of social exclusion: Evolution and beyond. *Group Dynamics, Special Issue: Evolutionary Approaches to Group Dynamics*, *12*, 39–52.

Kerr, N. L., Rumble, A. C., Park, E. S., Ouwerkerk, J. W., Parks, C. D., Gallucci, M., & van Lange, P. M. (2009). 'How many bad apples does it take to spoil the whole barrel?': Social exclusion and toleration for bad apples. *Journal of Experimental Social Psychology*, *45*, 603-613. doi:10.1016/j.jesp.2009.02.017

Koudenburg, N., Postmes, T., & Gordijn, E. H. (2013). Resounding silences: Subtle norm regulation in everyday interactions. *Social Psychology Quarterly*, *76*, 224–241. doi:10.1177/0190272513496794

Kurzban, R., & Leary, M. R. (2001). Evolutionary origins of stigmatization: The functions of social exclusion. *Psychological Bulletin*, *127*, 187–208. doi:10.1037/0033-2909.127.2.187

Lakin, J. L., Chartrand, T. L., & Arkin, R. M. (2008). I am too just like you: Nonconscious mimicry as an automatic behavioral response to social exclusion. *Psychological Science*, *19*, 816–822.

Legate, N., DeHaan, C. R., Weinstein, N., & Ryan, R. M. (2013). Hurting you hurts me too: The psychological costs of complying with ostracism. *Psychological Science*, *24*, 583–588.

Maier-Rigaud, F. P., Martinsson, P., & Staffiero, G. (2010). Ostracism and the provision of a public good: Experimental evidence. *Journal of Economic Behavior and Organization*, *73*, 387–395. doi:10.1016/j.jebo.2009.11.001

Maner, J. K., DeWall, C. N., Baumeister, R. F., & Schaller, M. (2007). Does social exclusion motivate interpersonal reconnection? Resolving the "porcupine problem." *Journal of Personality and Social Psychology, 92*, 42–55.

Marques, J. M., & Paez, D. (1994). The "black sheep effect": Social categorization, rejection of ingroup deviates, and perception of group variability. *European Review of Social Psychology, 5*, 37–68.

Marques, J. M., & Yzerbyt, V. Y. (1988). The black sheep effect: Judgmental extremity towards ingroup members in inter- and intra-group situations. *European Journal of Social Psychology, 18*, 287–292. doi: 10.1002/ejsp.2420180308

Milgram, S. (1974). *Obedience to authority: An experimental view.* New York, NY: Harper & Row.

Miller, C. E., & Anderson, P. D. (1979). Group decision rules and the rejection of deviates. *Social Psychology Quarterly, 42*, 354–363. doi:10.2307/3033805

Moreland, R. L., & Levine, J. M. (1982). Socialization in small groups: Temporal changes in individual group relations. In L. Berkowitz (ed.), *Advances in experimental social psychology* (Vol. *15*, pp. 137–192). New York, NY: Academic Press.

Nesse, R. M. (2005). Natural selection and the regulation of defenses: A signal detection analysis of the smoke detector principle. *Evolution and Human Behavior, 26*, 88–105.

Nezlek, J. B., Wesselmann, E. D., Wheeler, L., & Williams, K. D. (2012). Ostracism in everyday life. *Group Dynamics: Theory, Research, and Practice, 16*, 91–104.

Nordgren, L. F., Banas, K., & MacDonald, G. (2011). Empathy gaps for social pain: Why people underestimate the pain of social suffering. *Journal of Personality and Social Psychology, 100*, 120–128. doi:10.1037/a0020938

Nordgren, L. F., McDonnell, M. M., & Loewenstein, G. (2011). What constitutes torture?: Psychological impediments to an objective evaluation of enhanced interrogation tactics. *Psychological Science, 22*, 689–694. doi:10.1177/0956797611405679

O'Reilly, J., Robinson, S. L., Berdahl, J. L., & Banki, S. (2015). Is negative attention better than no attention? The comparative effects of ostracism and harassment at work. *Organizational Science, 26*, 774–793. doi.org/10.1287/orsc.2014.0900

Otten, S., & Gordijn, E. H. (2014). Was it one of us? How people cope with misconduct by fellow ingroup members. *Social and Personality Psychology Compass, 8*, 165–177. doi:10.1111/spc3.12098

Pickett, C. L., Gardner, W. L., & Knowles, M. (2004). Getting a cue: The need to belong and enhanced sensitivity to social cues. *Personality and Social Psychology Bulletin, 30*, 1095–1107.

Poulsen, J. R., & Kashy, D. A. (2012). Two sides of the ostracism coin: How sources and targets of social exclusion perceive themselves and one another. *Group Processes and Intergroup Relations, 15*, 457–470. doi: 10.1177/1368430211430507

Ren, D., Wesselmann, E. D., & Williams, K. D. (2016). Evidence for another response to ostracism: Solitude seeking. *Social Psychological and Personality Science, 7*, 204–212. doi: 10.1177/1948550615616169

Riva, P., Williams, K. D., Torstrick, A. M., & Montali, L. (2014). Orders to shoot (a camera): Effects of ostracism on obedience. *The Journal of Social Psychology, 154*, 208–216. doi:10.1080/00224545.2014.883354

Schachter, S. (1951). Deviation, rejection and communication. *Journal of Abnormal and Social Psychology, 46*, 190–207.

Sommer, K., & Yoon, J. (2013). When silence is golden: Ostracism as resource conservation during aversive interactions. *Journal of Social and Personal Relationships, 30*, 901–919. doi: 10.1177/0265407512473006

Spoor, J., & Williams, K. D. (2007). The evolution of an ostracism detection system. In J. P. Forgas, M. Haselton, & W. von Hippel (Eds.), *The evolution of the social mind: Evolutionary psychology and social cognition* (pp. 279–292). New York, NY: Psychology Press.

Szczurek, L., Monin, B., & Gross, J. J. (2012). The stranger effect: The rejection of affective deviants. *Psychological Science, 23*, 1105–1111. doi:10.1177/0956797612445314

Twenge, J. M., Baumeister, R. F., Tice, D. M., & Stucke, T. S. (2001). If you can't join them, beat them: Effects of social exclusion on aggressive behavior. *Journal of Personality and Social Psychology, 81*, 1058–1069.

Twenge, J. M., Zhang, L., Catanese, K. R., Dolan-Pascoe, B., Lyche, L. R., & Baumeister, R. F. (2007). Replenishing connectedness: Reminders of social activity reduce aggression after social exclusion. *British Journal of Social Psychology, 46*, 205–224. doi:10.1348/014466605X90793

van Beest, I., & Williams, K. D. (2006). When inclusion costs and ostracism pays, ostracism still hurts. *Journal of Personality and Social Psychology, 91*, 918–928.

van Dijk, W. W., van Dillen, L. F., Seip, E. C., & Rotteveel, M. (2012). Emotional time travel: Emotion regulation and the overestimation of future anger and sadness. *European Journal of Social Psychology, 42*, 308–313. doi:10.1002/ejsp.1853

van Prooijen, J. (2006). Retributive reactions to suspected offenders: The importance of social categorizations and guilt probability. *Personality and Social Psychology Bulletin, 32*, 715–726. doi:10.1177/0146167205284964

Warburton, W. A., Williams, K. D., & Cairns, D. R. (2006). When ostracism leads to aggression: The moderating effects of control deprivation. *Journal of Experimental Social Psychology, 42*, 213–220.

Wesselmann, E. D., Bagg, D., & Williams, K. D. (2009). "I feel your pain": The effects of observing ostracism on the ostracism detection system. *Journal of Experimental Social Psychology, 45*, 1308–1311. doi:10.1016/j.jesp.2009.08.003

Wesselmann, E. D., Butler, F. A., Williams, K. D., & Pickett, C. L. (2010). Adding injury to insult: Unexpected rejection leads to more aggressive responses. *Aggressive Behavior, 36*, 232–237. doi:10.1002/ab.20347

Wesselmann, E. D., Cardoso, F. D., Slater, S., & Williams, K. D. (2012). To be looked at as though air: Civil attention matters. *Psychological Science, 23*, 166–168.

Wesselmann, E. D., Nairne, J. S., & Williams, K. D. (2012). An evolutionary social psychological approach to studying the effects of ostracism. *Journal of Social, Evolutionary, and Cultural Psychology, 6*, 309–328. doi:10.1037/h0099249

Wesselmann, E. D., Ren, D., Swim, E., & Williams, K. D. (2013). Rumination hinders recovery from ostracism. *International Journal of Developmental Science, 7*, 33–39

Wesselmann, E. D., Wirth, J. H., Pryor, J. B., Reeder, G. D., & Williams, K. D. (2013). When do we ostracize? *Social Psychological and Personality Science, 4*, 108–115. doi:10.1177/1948550612443386

Wesselmann, E. D., Williams, K. D., Pryor, J. B., Eichler, F. A., Gill, D. M., & Hogue, J. D. (2014). Revisiting Schachter's research on rejection, deviance, and communication (1951).

*Social Psychology, 45*, 164–169. doi:10.1027/1864-9335/a000180

Wesselmann, E. D., Williams, K. D., & Hales, A. H. (2013). Vicarious ostracism. *Frontiers in Human Neuroscience, 7*, 1–2.

Williams, K. D. (2001). *Ostracism: The power of silence*. New York, NY: Guilford Press.

Williams, K. D. (2009). Ostracism: Effects of being excluded and ignored. In M. P. Zanna (Ed.), *Advances in experimental social psychology* (Vol. *41*, pp. 275–314). New York, NY: Academic Press.

Williams, K. D., Cheung, C., & Choi, W. (2000). Cyberostracism: Effects of being ignored over the Internet. *Journal of Personality and Social Psychology, 79*, 748–762.

Williams, K. D., & Sommer, K. L. (1997). Social ostracism by coworkers: Does rejection lead to social loafing or compensation. *Personality and Social Psychology Bulletin, 23*, 693–706.

Williams, K. D., & Wesselmann, E. D. (2011). The link between ostracism and aggression. In J. P. Forgas, A. W. Kruglanski, & K. D. Williams (Eds.), *The psychology of social conflict and aggression* (pp. 37–51). New York: Psychology Press.

Wirth, J. H., Lynam, D. R., & Williams, K. D. (2010). When social pain is not automatic: Personality disorder traits buffer ostracism's immediate negative impact. *Journal of Research in Personality, 44*, 397–401. doi:10.1016/j.jrp.2010.03.001

Wirth, J. H., Sacco, D. F., Hugenberg, K., & Williams, K. D. (2010). Eye gaze as relational evaluation: Averted eye gaze leads to feelings of ostracism and relational devaluation. *Personality and Social Psychology Bulletin, 36*, 869–882. doi:10.1177/0146167210370032

Wirth, J. H., & Williams, K. D. (2009). "They don't like our kind": Consequences of being ostracized while possessing a group membership. *Group Processes and Intergroup Relations, 12*, 111–127. doi:10.1177/1368430208098780

Zadro, L., Boland, C., & Richardson, R. (2006). How long does it last? The persistence of the effects of ostracism in the socially anxious. *Journal of Experimental Social Psychology, 42*, 692–697.

Zadro, L., & Gonsalkorale K. (2014). Sources of ostracism: The nature and consequences of ignoring and excluding others. *Current Directions in Psychological Science, 23*, 93-97. doi:10.1177/0963721413520321

Zadro, L., Williams, K. D., & Richardson, R. (2004). How low can you go? Ostracism by a computer lowers belonging, control, self-esteem, and meaningful existence. *Journal of Experimental Social Psychology, 40*, 560–567.

Zippelius, R. (1986). Exclusion and shunning as legal and social sanctions. *Ethology and Sociobiology, 7*, 159–166.

# Self-Presentation and Social Influence: Evidence for an Automatic Process

James M. Tyler *and* Katherine E. Adams

**Abstract**

Self-presentation is a social influence tactic in which people engage in communicative efforts to influence the thoughts, feelings, and behaviors of others as related to the self-presenter. Despite theoretical arguments that such efforts comprise an automatic component, the majority of research continues to characterize self-presentation as primarily involving controlled and strategic efforts. This focus is theoretically challenging and empirically problematic; it fosters an exclusionary perspective, leading to a scarcity of research concerning automatic self-presentations. With the current chapter, we examine whether self-presentation involves an automatic cognitive mechanism in which such efforts spontaneously emerge, nonconsciously triggered by cues in the social environment.

**Key Words:** self-presentation, social influence, automaticity, identity, self, social image

In his classic work, *The Presentation of Self in Everyday Life*, Erving Goffman (1959) popularized the concept of self-presentation, describing social life as a series of behavioral performances that symbolically communicate information about the self to others. Since the publication of this seminal work, research on self-presentation has bourgeoned, emerging as a fundamental topic in social psychology, as well as numerous other disciplines ranging from communication to organizational behavior and management. The breadth of work ranges from examining "the targets of people's self-presentation attempts to the levels of awareness at which self-presentation efforts may be enacted" (DePaulo, 1992, p. 204).

Although theorists frame self-presentation from slightly different theoretical perspectives, there is agreement that the overarching goal of self-presentation falls under the umbrella of social influence, in that people's self-presentations are aimed at influencing how others perceive them and behave toward them. Leary and Kowalski (1990) succinctly capture this goal in their characterization of self-presentation as including "all behavioral attempts to create impressions in others' minds" (p. 39). The

reason *why* people self-present is built on their recognition that the impressions others hold of them have important influences on desired outcomes ranging across a variety of life domains. Conveying desired identity-images provides a framework for people's social relationships, holds direct and indirect implications for the achievement of occupational and financial goals, and satisfies important intra- and interpersonal functions (Leary, Allen, & Terry, 2011; Schlenker, 2003). In all, self-presentation is a social influence tactic in which people engage in efforts to influence the thoughts, feelings, and behaviors of others as applied and related to the self-presenter.

There is abundant research examining various aspects of self-presentation; however, the literature remains replete with a number of entrenched misconceptions. One particularly persistent belief that continues to plague self-presentation research involves the implicit or explicit assumption that most if not all self-presentation involves conscious and deliberate efforts. The definitional words that researchers use to characterize self-presentation typically emphasize and focus on words like *controlling*, *deliberate*, and *strategic*. Self-presentation efforts are also frequently described as people *trying to* or *attempting to* influence the impression others form of them. Even Goffman (1959) defined self-presentation as a process in which people *strategically control* the inferences that others draw about them. We argue that the obvious face value of these types of words are heavily skewed toward controlled and deliberate efforts, and as such have exerted both an unbalanced and inaccurate influence on the resulting direction that most empirical research lines follow.

Although there has been a good deal of theoretical discussion focused on automatic self-presentation, there is a scarcity of empirical work, and the degree to which this work supports the viability of an automatic self-presentational component has not been fully vetted or reviewed. In this chapter, we focus on evaluating the hypothesis that the self-presentation process involves an automatic cognitive mechanism in which people spontaneously engage in automatic self-presentational efforts. We examine whether automatic self-presentations emerge of their own accord nonconsciously triggered by context cues, in the absence of direct instructional prompts. We also seek to actively draw attention to the dearth of empirical work examining automatic self-presentation; by doing so we hope to encourage researchers to more fully explore this vitally important feature of interpersonal behavior. To foreshadow our overall conclusion, although some evidence supports the general tenets of automatic self-presentation, it remains unclear empirically whether such efforts are truly emerging via a nonconscious mechanism. The key elements concerning such a mechanism relate primarily to the *awareness* (i.e., behavior is activated outside of conscious awareness) and *involuntary* (i.e., behavior is initiated by certain cues or prompts in the situation) features of automaticity as described by Bargh (1996).

Our summary to date clearly begs the question: Why is construing self-presentation as primarily involving controlled and strategic actions, while giving short shrift to nonconscious efforts, necessarily a problem? To reiterate, self-presentations are typically described as involving controlled and deliberate actions that are grounded in the implicit or explicit belief that self-presentation includes only conscious efforts that are meant to explicitly influence others' impressions. We argue that characterizing self-presentation as solely deliberate has the negative consequence of fostering an exclusionary research perspective, which results in severely limiting research attention to a narrower bandwidth

of social situations. Such a narrow conceptual approach characterizes self-presentation as primarily occurring only in limited situations in which people are deliberately trying to control the conveyance of self-information to others. Put differently, if people are not consciously trying to communicate a desired image, it is simply assumed they are not engaging in self-presentation at all (see Schlenker, 2003).

These fundamental constraints shape and impact the theoretical and conceptual foundations of most self-presentation research. The majority of paradigms explicitly and directly provide participants with self-presentational instructions, narrowly focusing empirical attention on controlled and deliberate self-presentational efforts. Participants are instructed to consciously think about the particular impression they are trying to convey, and of importance, the impression per se becomes the focal goal, rather than framing the presented identity as a means to achieve another type of valued goal (Leary et al., 2011).

Emphasizing that self-presentations comprise only controlled and strategic efforts also further promotes one of the most widespread misconceptions about self-presentation, which holds that such efforts are inherently false, manipulative, and duplicitous. Although certainly self-presentations can involve deception, for the most part, people's efforts reflect an accurate, if slightly embellished portrayal of themselves (Back et al., 2010; Leary & Allen, 2011; Wilson, Gosling, & Graham, 2012).

Our summary is not meant to suggest that examining controlled self-presentations has been an unproductive strategy; such approaches have generated useful and valuable findings concerning basic self-presentational processes. Nonetheless, we argue that adopting a limited conceptualization of self-presentation as primarily involving controlled efforts results in an artificially narrow empirical framework. This serves to restrict the field of inquiry to arguably only a small and specific slice of self-presentation behavior, while relatively ignoring the broader automatic component (Leary et al., 2011; Schlenker, 2003). Focusing on the strategically controlled aspects of self-presentation has left a lingering theoretical residual, resulting in forceful, but misguided assumptions that continue to reinforce and propagate the common misperception that all, or at least most of self-presentation involves conscious and deliberate efforts.

However, like most other social behaviors, self-presentation has also been characterized in theoretical terms as comprising dual processes involving conscious and nonconscious behaviors (e.g., Leary & Kowalski, 1990; Paulhus, 1993; Schlenker, 2003). In that spirit, theorists argue that self-presentations more often occur in an automatic rather than controlled fashion, and that the intentions underlying the initiation of such efforts do not necessarily have to be conscious. For instance, Paulhus (1993) suggests an automatic path for self-presentation that focuses on people's tendency to communicate overly positive self-descriptions; Hogan (1983) proposed that self-presentational efforts often involve automatic and modularized behavior, unfolding in a nonconscious fashion; Baumeister (1982) posited that the intention behind self-presentation need not be conscious; while Leary and Kowalski (1990) suggest that people nonconsciously monitor others' impressions of them and engage in automatic self-presentation when impression-relevant cues are detected.

Schlenker (2003) also proposed that context cues guide self-presentations outside of conscious awareness and trigger interpersonal goals, behavior, and motivation, and once activated, these nonconscious efforts continue until the desired goal or outcome is achieved. Schlenker goes on to argue that many self-presentations are characteristic of goal-dependent forms of automatic behavior. Evidence concerning social behavior, in general, shows that "goal pursuit can arise from mental processes put into motion by features of the social environment outside of conscious awareness . . . with the assumption that goals are represented in mental structures that include the context, the goal, and the actions to aid goal pursuit, and thus goals can be triggered automatically by relevant environmental stimuli" (Custers & Aarts, 2005, p. 129). The goal activation sequence and the operations to obtain a particular goal can unfold in the absence of a person's intention or awareness.

In much the same manner, self-presentations can be conceptualized as being nonconsciously activated by features of the social environment (Schlenker, 2003). This suggests that self-presentations comprise cognitive structures that include the context, the goal, and the actions to achieve the goal, and like other social behaviors, these efforts can be automatically triggered by environmental stimuli. People strive to achieve a self-presentation goal, although they are often not aware that such efforts have been activated. As a result, they do not characterize their behavior as self-presentation, in that they do not view themselves as self-consciously and purposefully trying to achieve impression-oriented

goals. A key element underscoring automatic self-presentations is the assertion that such efforts comprise "behaviors that consist of modulated, habit-formed patterns of action" or consist of "an individual's most well-practiced set of self-attributes" (Paulhus, 1993, p. 576; Schlenker & Pontari, 2000, p. 205). Characterizing automatic self-presentations as habitual patterns of behavior finds broad conceptual support from the more general theorizing on habitual responding. For example, theorists' perspective concerning the relationship between context-cueing and self-presentational efforts dovetails nicely with the general framework of habit performance as outlined in Wood and Neal's (2007) habit model. We will highlight conceptual areas of relevance where appropriate, focusing attention on propositions drawn from Wood and Neal's model. In summary, theorists argue that self-presentations can unfold in an automatic or habitual manner via a context-cueing process; these efforts are guided outside of conscious awareness when interpersonal goals, behavior, and motivation are automatically triggered by context cues in the social environment. Once activated, people's self-presentations persist until the desired goal is achieved.

Our goal, in the sections to follow, is to examine the degree to which relevant literature supports the proposition of an automatic self-presentational process (for more controlled aspects, see Schlenker, Britt, & Pennington, 1996; Schlenker, & Pontari, 2000). Before delving into the empirical evidence, we first briefly outline one theoretical perspective—the self-identification theory—that provides a succinct and integrative framework to conceptualize and illustrate the processes and mechanisms thought to be involved in automatic self-presentation (Schlenker, 1985, 2003). Although there are other automatic self-presentation models (e.g., Paulhus, 1993), the self-identification theory is arguably the most comprehensive one; areas of overlap with other approaches will be noted where appropriate.

## Self-Identification Theory

Self-identification theory characterizes self-presentation as a common and pervasive feature of social life in which self-identification is broadly described as the process with which people attempt to demonstrate that they are a particular type of person. More formally, self-presentation is defined as a "goal-directed activity in which people communicate identity-images for themselves with audiences by behaving in ways that convey certain roles and personal qualities. They do so in order to influence the impressions that others form of them" (Schlenker, 2003, p. 492). The communication of identity-images provides a framework for people's relationships, holds direct and indirect implications for the outcomes and goals that people receive, and satisfies valued intra- and interpersonal functions. Self-identification theory posits that communicating specific identity-images, via self-presentation, is a key aspect of interpersonal interactions.

Identity-images are desirable in that they typically embody what people would like to be within the parameters of their abilities, appearance, and history. These images often involve beneficial self-identifications that are structured to serve a person's interpersonal goals (Schlenker, 2003). In the parlance of self-identification theory the combination of a desired identity-image and a corresponding behavioral script is defined as an *agenda*, which is activated by context cues in the social environment (Schlenker, 2003).

Although people are frequently motivated to achieve multiple agendas, the limits of cognitive capacity minimize the number of agendas that can simultaneously occupy the foreground of attention (Paulhus, 1993). Some agendas necessarily receive greater attention, effort, and monitoring than others, with those considered more relevant operating in the foreground and those of less concern unfolding in the background. Imagine a computer running numerous programs—some open, contents displayed and attentively monitored and examined, whereas others are minimized, operating behind the scenes, working on tasks but not distracting the operator unless a reason or purpose to check them arises (this metaphor is borrowed from Schlenker & Pontari, 2000). In a similar fashion, agendas focusing on self-presentation concerns, involving the goal of communicating a particular impression to an audience, can be more or less in the foreground of conscious awareness. This leads us directly to an overview of background-automatic and foreground-controlled modes of self-presentation as described in the self-identification theory.

## Foreground Self-Presentation

Self-presentation agendas that operate in the foreground are characterized as involving consciously controlled attention, with people exerting significant cognitive resources to plan and implement their behaviors. Such efforts consume cognitive attention by requiring people to first access self-information, after doing so they must synthesize and integrate the information in a manner relevant to an interaction and prepare it for expression; people make judgments about what to say and about how to communicate it to others. In doing so, people stay more alert and aware, consciously scanning and monitoring the environment to assess their behaviors and audience reactions. They engage in these efforts, in part, to accomplish the goal of communicating desired identity-images. Foreground self-presentations represent those occasions that people are most likely to report being on stage and consciously concerned with the impression they project to others (Schlenker, 2003).

The antecedent conditions that direct self-presentation agendas to operate in the foreground involve broad features of the situation, the audience, and people's interaction goals. People more thoroughly process a social situation when they perceive that the situation is important, in that their performance bears on their desired identity; involves positive or negative outcomes; or is relevant to valued role expectations. The motivation to process a situation is also more likely to increase when people expect or encounter a potential impediment (e.g., critical audience) to achieving their desired self-presentation goals (Schlenker et al., 1996). This outline of foreground self-presentations is consistent with Paulhus's (1993) description of controlled self-presentations; he posits that such efforts require attentional resources to consider one's desired self-presentation goal and the target audience, prior to the delivery of any particular self-description. In summary, self-presentation agendas become salient, moving from the background to the foreground when the context is perceived as important or when obstacles impede the successful communication of a desired identity-image (Schlenker et al., 1994).

## Background Self-Presentation

In contrast and key to the current chapter, self-presentation agendas that operate in the background are conceptualized as automatically guided by goal-directed behavior, operating with minimal conscious cognitive attention or effort. This representation is akin to Bargh's (1996) proposition that "automatic processes can be intentional; well-learned social scripts and social action sequences can be guided by intended, goal-dependent automaticity," which refers to an autonomous process that requires the intention that an action occur, but requires no conscious guidance once the action begins to operate (p. 174). Like Bargh, Schlenker (2003) argues that self-presentations with familiar others, or those involving well-learned behavioral patterns and scripts, are characteristic of an intended, goal-dependent form of automaticity. Here, self-presentations involve an automatic process in which cues in the social milieu direct self-presentations in the absence of conscious awareness and trigger interpersonal goals, behavior, and motivation. Once activated, these efforts are maintained until the desired goal or outcome is achieved (Paulhus, Graf, & Van Selst, 1989; Schlenker, 2003).

Theorists propose that background self-presentation agendas are automatically activated based on overlearned responses to social contingencies. This description is similar to Paulhus's (1993) idea that automatic self-presentation is a residual of overlearned situationally specific self-presentations. These overlearned responses include scripts that provide an efficient and nonconscious guidance system to construct a desired identity-image. Context-contingent cues (e.g., audience) converge in the background to trigger automatic self-presentation agendas. People are often not aware that these efforts have been activated and, as a result, do not characterize their communications or behavior as self-presentation, in that they do not view themselves as self-consciously and effortfully attempting to achieve impression-oriented goals (Schlenker et al., 1996).

While background self-presentation agendas unfold, people nonconsciously monitor their behavior and the audience's responses to ensure a proper construal of a desired impression. For these automatic efforts to be overridden by conscious, controlled processing, at least two requirements need to occur. First, people must be motivated to think or act differently than what occurs automatically, and second, they must have the cognitive resources to support the flexible, relatively unusual sequence of actions (Schlenker, 2003). If a deviation from a social script or an impediment is detected, the agenda can *pop* into the foreground. As a result, attention is drawn to conscious awareness to correct the mis-impression and to achieve one's self-presentation goals, shifting self-presentation agendas from a background to a foreground mode of operation. This attention-drawing process is akin to Paulhus's (1993) automatic self-presentation model, where affect regulates that attention is directed toward any glitch in an activity that is currently unfolding via an automatic process.

Characterizing automatic self-presentation as *habit-like* is also consistent with theoretical descriptions of habits in general, as outlined in Wood and Neal's (2007) habit model. They argue that the "automaticity underlying habits builds on patterns of repeated covariation between the features of performance contexts and responses—that is, habits are defined as learned dispositions to repeat past responses" (Wood & Neal, p. 843). Once the habitual response is created, it can be triggered when an individual perceives relevant cues that are embedded in the performance context. Even though habits are not necessarily mediated by a goal, they can also advance the original goal that first impelled people to repetitively perform the context-response, which in effect resulted in the formation of the habit (Aarts & Dijksterhuis, 2000; Verplanken & Aarts, 1999). Habits and goals interface, in that habit associations are initially formed under the guidance of goals: "goals direct control of responses prior to habit formation, and thus define the cuing contexts under which a response is repeated into a habit" (p. 851). Theorists posit that self-presentations can become so well practiced that they operate like mindless habits that are triggered nonconsciously by environmental cues and unfold in an automatic fashion, similar to the operational processes associated with habit responding as described by Wood and Neal.

Having outlined the theoretical foundation for automatic self-presentations, we now examine research germane to the key question underscoring the current chapter: Do automatic self-presentations emerge of their own accord nonconsciously triggered by context cues, in the absence of direct instructional prompts? Following a review of this evidence, we provide discussion and critical assessment.

### Evidence for Automatic Self-Presentation

Although the self-presentation literature includes a voluminous number of studies, the vast majority does not include measurements or manipulations that can be interpreted as depicting automatic self-presentation. Rather, previous work primarily centered on identifying self-presentation strategies, discerning when self-presentation will or will not occur, and determining whether such efforts communicate self-beliefs accurately or in a self-serving manner, promote self-consistency or maximize self-esteem, or depict self-enhancement or self-protective purposes (see Schlenker et al., 1996). There are a number of studies, however, that either directly involve the manipulation of self-presentational automaticity or focus attention on self-presentation behaviors that can be viewed as unfolding via an automatic process. Review of these studies will be divided into sections; the first four relate to the availability of cognitive resources during self-presentation and its effect on *recall, self-presentation effectiveness, reaction times,* and *self-description,* followed by sections focused on the availability of *self-regulatory resources* during self-presentations and the *implicit activation* of self-presentational efforts.

The first four sections examine the cognitive effects of automatic self-presentation, beginning with the general concept that there is a limit to people's cognitive resources, and effectively attending to simultaneous activities that require cognitive effort is difficult (Bargh, 1996). These limitations in cognitive capacity enable researchers to use empirical methods to investigate the differences between automatic and controlled self-presentations. Introducing a second, cognitively effortful activity generates nominal interference with a concurrent task if a process is automatic; however, this second task significantly interrupts the ongoing efforts if the process is controlled.

### The Availability of Cognitive Resources during Self-Presentation and Its Effect on Recall

Given the proposition that automaticity consumes minimal cognitive resources, it follows that people should be able to more efficiently process information when delivering automatic self-presentations. To override these automatic efforts, however, more controlled self-presentations require an increase in cognitive resources (Schlenker, 2003). As a result, controlled rather than automatic self-presentations may disrupt the processing of information (Schlenker, 1986). To demonstrate empirically the presence of automatic self-presentations, the studies in this first section focus on the differential effects of automatic and controlled self-presentations on subsequent recall.

It is important to preface the studies that address this issue by emphasizing that Western norms typically favor positive self-presentations (e.g., Schlenker, 1980; see also Baumeister & Jones, 1978; Jones & Wortman, 1973). People are far more practiced at conveying a self-promoting identity-image (i.e., automatic self-presentation) rather than a self-depreciating one (i.e., controlled self-presentation). Self-promotion efforts would be expected to leave more cognitive resources available to process information and ultimately should have less negative impact on recall. However, engaging in self-deprecation—a controlled self-presentation—should remove the automaticity of self-presentation, increasing the

demand for cognitive resources. These expectations found support across a series of studies in which participants displayed significantly better recall of interaction details when their social interaction comprised automatic compared to controlled self-presentations (Baumeister, Hutton, & Tice, 1989).

Evidence also indicates that a key determinant of people's self-presentations is whether an interaction involves strangers or friends (Tice, Butler, Muraven, & Stillwell, 1995). From this work we know that certain constraints and contingencies position the communication of a favorable image as the optimal way to self-present to strangers, whereas a more modest identity approach prevails among friends. If these self-presentation patterns are habitually used, they should be relatively automatic, requiring minimal cognitive resources for encoding, leading to more accurate recall. Violation of these patterns, however, should trigger controlled self-presentations, requiring more cognitive resources, consequently impairing accurate recall. Like Baumeister et al., (1989), this work also shows that when participants engaged in automatic self-presentations—*they interacted with a stranger in a self-promoting manner or with a friend in a modest manner*—their recall of interaction details was significantly better compared to when they engaged in controlled self-presentations—*they interacted with a stranger in a modest fashion or with a friend in a self-promoting manner.* Follow-up studies replicated these results and additionally demonstrated that even when recalling a stranger's behavior people made fewer recall errors when engaged in automatic self-presentations rather than controlled ones (Tice et al., 1995).

### The Availability of Cognitive Resources during Self-Presentation and Its Effect on Self-Presentational Effectiveness

The studies in the prior section demonstrate that the automatic-controlled self-presentation process involves the availability of cognitive resources and, in part, familiarity with the self-presentational context. Automatic self-presentations are characterized by familiar and habitual self-presentations, which require minimal cognitive resources. It follows that under low cognitive demand people should be able to engage effectively in the self-presentation of familiar identity-images but also unfamiliar ones as well. In contrast, controlled self-presentations are characterized by unfamiliar and atypical self-presentations, which require increased cognitive resources. It can then be reasoned that under high cognitive demand people's capacity to engage effectively in the self-presentation of unfamiliar identity-images will be negatively impacted, whereas the effectiveness of self-presenting a familiar identity-image should not suffer. To demonstrate an automatic self-presentation process, the studies in the second section focus on the effect that automatic and controlled self-presentations have on people's self-presentational effectiveness.

In this first set of studies, Pontari and Schlenker (2000) interviewed extraverted and introverted individuals under low- or high-cognitive load conditions. As part of the instructions, these individuals were told to convey either an extraverted or introverted identity-image to the interviewer. It was thought that participants who enacted congruent self-presentations, for example, an extravert acting as an extravert, were acting consistently with their self-schemata. They delivered familiar and relatively automatic self-presentations, requiring minimal cognitive resources. In contrast, those who enacted incongruent self-presentations, for example, an extravert acting as an introvert, were acting inconsistently with their self-schemata. They delivered unfamiliar and relatively controlled self-presentations, requiring an increase in cognitive resources.

The results from these studies indicated that for extraverts and introverts alike, the self-presentation of congruent and familiar identities was successfully achieved in both the high- and low-cognitive-load conditions. Extraverts were also successful at self-presenting incongruent identities when they had sufficient cognitive resources available, that is, in the low-cognitive-load condition. However, extraverts were unable to successfully self-present incongruent and unfamiliar identities when they lacked the requisite cognitive resources, that is, in the high-cognitive-load condition. By comparison, an unexpected finding showed that introverts were successful at self-presenting incongruent and unfamiliar identities even when they lacked available cognitive resources. Pontari and Schlenker (2000) posited that the increased cognitive load interrupted introverts' dysfunctional thoughts, which would have otherwise interfered with their capacity to engage effectively in controlled self-presentations. The additional mental tasks in the high-cognitive-load condition may have shifted introverts' attention from negative self-ruminations to more dispassionate thoughts. This shift in attention may have allowed introverts to successfully enact a social performance that was relatively incongruent with their automatic pattern of self-presentational responses.

## The Availability of Cognitive Resources during Self-Presentation and Its Effect on Reaction Times

A set of studies consistent with Pontari and Schlenker's (2000) notion of self-presentations as congruent or incongruent with self-schema were carried out by Holden and colleagues (1992, 2001). These studies focused on reaction times rather than self-presentational effectiveness to demonstrate automatic and controlled self-presentation processes. Participants were instructed to respond quickly to self-descriptive personality items in a manner that would make them appear either very well adjusted or not well adjusted. When participants made responses that were incongruent with a self-schema—conveying a *favorable* impression via *socially undesirable* items or an *unfavorable* impression via *socially desirable* items—their reaction times were slower. When they made responses that were congruent with a self-schema—conveying a *favorable* impression via *socially desirable* items or an *unfavorable* impression via *socially undesirable* items—their reaction times were faster.

These findings show that responding in a manner incongruent with a self-schema requires the availability of cognitive resources, whereas responding in a congruent manner consumes minimal cognitive resources and attention. The data also support the presence of a cognitive mechanism that is fast and efficient, and a cognitive override mechanism that is slower and intentional, which they suggest are consistent with the processes described in Paulhus's (1993) automatic and controlled self-presentation model (Holden, Wood, & Tomashewski, 2001). In Paulhus's work, "automatic processes are those that are so well rehearsed that they are fast, oriented toward positive self-presentations, and operate without attention, whereas controlled processes are much slower and require increased attention" (Holden et al., 2001, p. 167).

## The Availability of Cognitive Resources during Self-Presentations and Its Effect on Self-Descriptions

Other programs of research (e.g., Paulhus & Levitt, 1987) also posit that controlled self-presentations occur when attentional capacity is available, whereas automatic self-presentations emerge when attentional capacity is relatively limited. Controlled self-presentations are thought to involve conscious self-descriptions that are adjusted to fit situational demands with such efforts requiring available cognitive resources and attentional capacity. Automatic self-presentations, in contrast, are posited to involve nonconscious default responses that are characterized by the communication of overly positive self-descriptions. These efforts require minimal cognitive attention and resources, primarily because they consist of well-practiced and chronically activated self-descriptions (Paulhus, 1993).

To examine these ideas, a series of studies were conducted in which participants provided self-descriptive ratings on positive, negative, or neutral traits while in a high- or low-cognitive-load condition (Paulhus, 1993; Paulhus et al., 1989; Paulhus & Levitt, 1987). Results showed that participants in the high-cognitive-load condition endorsed more positive than negative traits. They were also significantly faster at both endorsing positive and denying negative traits when their resources and attention were focused on other tasks. Put differently, when cognitive attention was diverted, only a default set of positive self-descriptions was left available for automatic self-presentations. Paulhus (1993) concluded that increasing cognitive demands can trigger automatic self-presentations in which people are more likely and quicker to claim positive traits and deny negative ones.

In a similar fashion, cognitive capacity is also required for honest trait responding—it takes attentional resources to scan one's memory for accurate responses. If cognitive demands are increased, attention is diverted and honest trait responding can be disrupted. But the subsequent responses are not random; they are systematically more positive and emerge from the positive automatic self. Evidence from a number of studies shows that participants instructed to engage in controlled self-presentations produced more positive self-descriptions in a high- compared to low-cognitive-load condition (e.g., Paulhus & Murphy, unpublished data ). These findings support the assertion that automatic self-presentations are activated when controlled self-presentations are disrupted by an increase in cognitive demands.

To examine this idea further, a second study experimentally created automatic self-presentation patterns and then tested whether these patterns reappeared under cognitive load (Paulhus, Bruce, & Stoffer, 1990). To induce a *new* automatic-self, participants practiced communicating overly positive self-descriptions, negative self-descriptions, or honest self-descriptions by repeatedly responding to a set of 12 traits. Subsequently, participants were told to forget what they did during this practice phase and to instead respond honestly to the 12 traits (i.e., controlled self-presentation). During a first test, participants were given as much time as they wanted to respond, a low-cognitive-load condition, whereas in a second test they were told to answer as fast as possible, a high-cognitive-load condition. Results showed that the automatization effects that were created in the initial practice phase emerged in the high-cognitive-load condition but not in the low-cognitive-load condition. When controlled self-presentations were disrupted, automatic self-presentations appeared, as evidenced by the automatic self emerging only during the high-cognitive-load condition.

Another line of evidence also shows that people positively bias their descriptions of self-associated stimuli, and they do so without conscious awareness (Koole, Dijksterhuis, & van Knippenberg, 2001). Theorists posit that early self-descriptions shape later self-descriptions by structuring self-relevant cognitions and behavior into working models, which can be nonconsciously activated (Mikulincer, 1995). These models are conceptualized as an integral part of automatic self-presentations, typifying people's most well-practiced and chronically activated self-descriptions (Paulhus, 1993). When encountering self-associated stimuli, people's positively biased self-descriptions can be automatically triggered and, as such, can be characterized as automatic self-presentations. If people lack available cognitive capacity, their self-descriptions of self-associated stimuli may reflect implicit and automatic efforts, whereas, if sufficient cognitive resources are available, self-descriptions may reflect more explicit and controlled efforts (Koole et al., 2001).

These ideas were tested in two studies by examining the relationship between implicit self-positivity and explicit self-descriptions. Implicit self-positivity was measured by the name-letter bias (Kitayama & Karasawa, 1997) and explicit self-description by participants' self-ratings on positive, negative, or neutral trait words (Paulhus & Levitt, 1987). With respect to the explicit measure, quickly delivered self-descriptions were characterized as automatic self-presentations, and slowly delivered self-descriptions were characterized as controlled self-presentations, primarily because automatic processing requires less time than controlled processing. It was expected and found that implicit self-positivity only matched the explicit self-descriptions when the trait self-ratings were quickly delivered but not when they were slowly delivered.

A second study mirrored the results of the first by manipulating the availability of cognitive resources rather than the delivery speed of explicit self-descriptions. Specifically, participants under a high cognitive load (vs. low cognitive load) displayed greater congruence between implicit and explicit self-descriptions. When cognitive resources were limited, it increased the self-positivity of explicit self-descriptions, in that the congruence between implicit and explicit self-descriptions only increased when controlled efforts were undermined, that is, in the high-cognitive-demand condition. But when participants were in a situation in which they possessed sufficient cognitive resources, their explicit and implicit self-descriptions did not match. When responding explicitly, participants presumably were aware of the self-presentation implications of responding in an overly positive manner and, as such, managed their responses accordingly. Their responses were far less positive when they were explicitly versus implicitly measured. In contrast, when participants lacked sufficient cognitive resources, they presumably were unable to consciously control the delivery of their explicit self-descriptions, which essentially then became automatic self-presentations. As result, their implicit and explicit self-descriptions were congruent in the high-cognitive-load condition; both showed positively biased self-descriptions, which is characteristic of automatic self-presentations.

Related studies also examined whether the automatic self-descriptions that underlie the self-positivity bias can be inhibited by consciously controlled efforts (Koole et al., 2001). Here, participants were instructed to judge self-associated stimuli while focusing on either *cognitive reasoning*, which was thought to require more controlled efforts, or *feeling*, which was thought to require less controlled efforts. If greater preference for self-associated stimuli results from automatic self-presentation, a positive bias for such stimuli should increase when the focus is on feelings, an automatic response, compared to deliberate reasoning, a controlled response. In line with this reasoning, participants delivered more positively biased judgments for self-associated stimuli when they were focused on feelings rather than reasoning. This suggests that controlled efforts inhibit the emergence of automatic self-presentations. Participants also reported no awareness that they were displaying a positivity bias toward self-associated stimuli. In all, implicit self-positivity responses, based on overlearned

self-descriptions, may be representative of automatic self-presentations.

### The Availability of Self-Regulatory Resources during Self-Presentations

The first four sections focused on studies that essentially involved either low or high cognitive demands as a means to demonstrate, respectively, automatic or controlled self-presentations. We now turn to a set of studies that addressed the relationship between self-presentation and the consumption of self-regulatory resources (Vohs, Baumeister, & Ciarocco, 2005). The logic underlying this relationship basically mimics the argument underscoring how the availability of cognitive resources impacts the degree to which self-presentations emerge via automatic or controlled efforts. When people engage in unfamiliar patterns of self-presentation, it requires increased self-regulatory efforts to override their habitual responses and to effortfully control their behavior. Carrying out "these effortful self-presentations drain[s] more self-regulatory resources compared with presenting oneself in a standard, familiar, or habitual manner of self-presentation" (Vohs et al., 2005, p. 634). In four studies that examined this idea, participants were instructed to present themselves in a manner that was based either on familiar/habitual and less effortful patterns of self-presentations or on patterns that were unfamiliar/atypical, which called for more deliberate and thoughtful efforts.

The results across all four studies consistently demonstrated that engaging in habitual self-presentations demanded less regulatory efforts than carrying out an atypical or unfamiliar self-presentation, which required an increase in regulatory efforts, and subsequently depleted the self's resources. As with cognitive demands, these findings suggest that automatic self-presentations emerge when the situation is perceived as more familiar and routine, and hence does not require exerting an increase in regulatory efforts. In contrast, more effortful and controlled self-presentations emerge when the situation calls for patterns of responding that are not typical or habitual, thus requiring more regulatory resources to be consumed. The results from these studies are consistent with the cognitive demand studies in the previous sections, again demonstrating that self-presentational efforts can assume different forms, and that conveying an image that is in conflict with one's typical, habitual response patterns consumes greater regulatory resources than responses that follow one's familiar self-presentational patterns. Automatic self-presentations require less regulatory resources than controlled self-presentations, which is theoretically consistent with the broad sentiment of the first four sections.

### Cued Activation of Automatic Self-Presentation and Its Effect on Self-Description

For the most part, automatic self-presentations involve the conveyance of relatively favorable identity-images. Paulhus (1993) describes these efforts as "consisting of the individual's most well-practiced, and hence, most chronically activated set of self-attributes," which he posits are typically positive due to a lifetime of practice (p. 576). He argues that there are copious sources that underlie the widespread prevalence of the positivity that follows from a lifetime of practice. From childhood, people actively learn that they should provide more positively oriented self-descriptions and explanations for their social behavior. These ideas fit well with Schlenker's (2003) description of background self-presentation agendas, which involve the construction of desired images of the self and are based on overlearned and habitual responses to social contingencies.

It is also important to note that although the majority of peoples' automatic self-presentations are indeed characterized by positive self-representations, they are not necessarily restricted to just positive images. Certainly not all early life lessons and habits will reflect or result in only positive representations of the self. Some context cues can serve to trigger habit-molded patterns of behaviors that result in the conveyance of a less than favorable image of the self.

These automatic instances of less favorable images emerge from "people's repertoire of relational schemas, or cognitive structures representing regularities in patterns of interpersonal relatedness involving a range of common interpersonal orientations: from expecting that another person will be consistently accepting, for example, to expecting that others will be evaluative or judgmental" (Baldwin, 1992, p. 209). Theorists propose that these relationships become internalized, in part, via the development of relation-oriented schemas. These schemas are thought to represent patterns of interpersonal behavior, consisting of interaction scripts including schemas for self and other as experienced within that interaction, which also include inference processes for communicating self-descriptions (Baldwin, 1992). Researchers suggest, for example,

that an individual can anticipate a negative evaluation because negative memories and knowledge structures have become activated, which influences how one anticipates and interprets a forthcoming or ongoing social interaction (Baldwin & Main, 2001).

Theoretically any cue that has become linked with a particular interpersonal experience can trigger relational constructs and knowledge, and as such it can impact one's current behavior (Baldwin & Main, 2001). It is plausible that these cued activation procedures could impact automatic self-presentations, in that such efforts may involve more positive self-descriptions if the activated relational knowledge is associated with acceptance/favorability, and more negative self-descriptions if associated with rejection/unfavorability.

In a series of studies, researchers examined the idea that cued knowledge activation may differentially impact interpersonal behavior depending on the context of the activated relational schema. Although the direct intent of these studies was not focused on automatic self-presentations, the results, involving participants' self-descriptions, can be construed as such (Baldwin & Main, 2001). At the outset of these studies, participants underwent a conditioning procedure that surreptitiously paired expectations of acceptance and rejection with distinct aural tones (Baldwin & Meunier, 1999). These conditioned tones were later used to nonconsciously activate the knowledge structures associated with acceptance and rejection. Specifically, during an interpersonal interaction one of the two tones from the conditioning procedure was repeatedly emitted from a computer terminal. The results indicated that participants communicated more positive self-descriptions in the acceptance compared to rejection condition and, conversely, more negative self-descriptions in the rejection versus acceptance condition. The conditioned tones to cue acceptance or rejection may have nonconsciously triggered automatic self-presentations, even to the degree that some of these efforts resulted in negative self-descriptions (see Swann, 1983).

In a similar fashion, other studies have examined the implicit motivational effects that significant others can have on automatic self-presentations (e.g., Shah, 2003). This research suggests that people's self-representations incorporate the goals, values, and expectations that close others hold for them, and that the cued activation of these internal representations automatically influences people's behavior via the other's association to a variety of interpersonal goals (Moretti & Higgins, 1999). The implicit effect of close others may extend to goal-directed behavior in which others influence people's interpersonal behavior during ongoing social interactions. In other words, the implicit influence of significant others may serve to trigger automatic self-presentations.

To examine this idea, researchers covertly acquired the names of significant others, either an accepting or a critical other's name (Baldwin, 1994; Shah, 2003). These names were used at a later point to prime subliminally participants' interpersonal goals. Following the priming manipulation, participants completed an ego-threatening task, after which they completed self-descriptive questionnaires. The results indicated that participant's self-descriptions were influenced by the critical and accepting others' name, even though detailed manipulation checks showed that participants were not consciously aware of name exposure. When a critical other's name was primed, self-descriptions were more negative; when an accepting other's name was primed, self-descriptions were more positive. These findings suggest that self-descriptions were nonconsciously influenced by the cued activation of relational schemas that were associated with the accepting or critical other. Subliminally reminding people, for example, of a negative, demanding or positive, friendly other may automatically trigger a *be friendly or be aggressive* goal, as well as the corresponding self-presentation behavior associated with the activated relational schema.

Consistent with the idea of cued activation, Tyler (2012) utilized priming procedures across a set of three studies to assess directly the automatic nature of self-presentational efforts. In the first two studies, participants were primed with words associated with impression-oriented people or with a set of neutral words; the second study also included a condition in which participants received explicit self-presentation instructions to present themselves favorably. In the first study, the self-presentation measure involved participants answering a series of self-descriptive questions put forth by the experimenter. With the second study, each participant engaged in an unscripted conversation with a confederate, which was videotaped and later coded for how favorable the participants described themselves. The results across both studies revealed that participants in the impression condition self-presented a more favorable image compared to participants in the neutral condition. The results from the second study also showed that participants' self-presentations in the

explicit condition mimicked the favorability of participants' self-presentations in the impression prime condition. Put differently, participants' automatic self-presentations were very similar to their efforts when they were explicitly instructed to self-present a favorable persona. The third study was grounded on the idea that the participating audience one is interacting with might serve as a nonconscious self-presentation cue. Here, participants were primed with words associated with friends or strangers. Following the priming procedure, participants were instructed to write a self-description, which was later coded with regard to how favorable participants described themselves. Analysis in the friend prime condition showed that participants self-presented a more modest image, whereas in the stranger prime condition participants self-presented a more self-enhancing image. Taken together, the findings across these studies provide compelling support for the proposition that people's self-presentations can be primed by environmental cues outside of their conscious awareness.

## Critical Assessment and Discussion

The driving logic underlying the proposal of an automatic self-presentational process is the same across all review sections, allowing for a straightforward interpretation of the findings. Recall that the goal of the current chapter is focused on determining if automatic self-presentations emerge of their own accord, triggered outside of conscious awareness by context cues in the absence of direct self-presentational instructions.

## Automatic Self-Presentations and Context Cues

According to a number of influential models (e.g., Leary & Kowalski, 1990; Paulhus, 1993; Schlenker, 1985, 2003), automatic self-presentations are predicated on habitual and routine response patterns that include scripts, overlearned responses, and well-practiced sets of self-attributes. For instance, Paulhus (1993) suggests "the default self-presentation, the automatic self, has it origins in a lifetime of self-presentation practice" (p. 580). Even more directly, Schlenker (1985, 2003) posits:

> Automatic self-presentations reflect modulated
> units of action that eventually "settle in" to become
> habits. These habitual patterns of behavior form self-
> presentation scripts that are triggered automatically
> by context cues and guide action unthinkingly,
> in relevant situations. Such scripts provide a rich

store of knowledge and experience (i.e., relational knowledge), which can be automatically accessed to quickly and effectively communicate desired identity-images. When a script is triggered consciously or unconsciously by context cues, it provides a definition of the situation being encountered, a set of expectations about events, and a set of operations for thoughts and behaviors in the situation.

*(pp. 76, 495)*

A common thread among these models underscores the notion that habitual self-presentation patterns are triggered by context cues and people are not consciously aware that their efforts are influenced by such cues. Although the exact nature of context cues varies from occasion to occasion, in general, "the situation or audience itself cues associated information about the self, social roles, and social expectations in memory and makes salient the context-contingencies between particular self-presentations and relevant outcomes" (Schlenker, 1986, p. 35). This description accentuates the context-contingent nature of the cues that can trigger automatic self-presentations and, as noted earlier, has a straightforward connection with Wood and Neal's (2007) habit model, in that habits are characterized as learned dispositions to repeat past responses and are activated by context cues. In summary, theorists' characterization of automatic self-presentations as habit responses, automatically triggered by context cues, unfolds in much the same fashion as Wood and Neal describe habit performances.

Describing automatic self-presentations as triggered by context cues is also consistent with the characterization of automatic processes as involuntary, such that people's behavior is activated by prompts in the social environment (Bargh, 1996). Schlenker and Pontari (2000) also argue that background self-presentations are guided by an intended, goal-dependent automatic process, characterized as "an autonomous process requiring the intention that it occur, and thus awareness that it is occurring, but no conscious guidance once put into operation" (Bargh, 1996, p. 174). Self-presentational efforts that emerge via an intended, goal-dependent automatic process comprise a well-learned, sequential set of actions that were previously associated with goal accomplishment. People are not consciously aware that context cues influence their social behavior; however, the goal-directed activity of structuring and maintaining a desired identity is nonetheless occurring. In summary, theorists contend that automatic self-presentations are activated nonconsciously by cues in the social situation and are founded on overlearned responses to behavioral-outcome contingencies.

Consistent with self-presentation theories and with support from more general models of habit responding, we argue that cues in the social environment, in and of themselves, are a necessary imperative and represent the fundamental cornerstone with which to establish the validity of an automatic self-presentation process. Although such a process has strong logical and theoretical footing, without corroborating evidence for context cuing, the process would nonetheless remain nothing but a conceptual proposition. If we fail to demonstrate empirically a context-contingent pathway for the nonconscious activation of automatic self-presentations, there is no other logical or clear mechanism with which to build and support an evidentiary foundation for such a process. As a result, we would necessarily be required to accept the notion outlined at the outset of this chapter: that the vast majority of self-presentations involve controlled and deliberate efforts, and as such only emerge during very specific sets of narrowly defined occasions. Without clear and sustaining evidence demonstrating that cues in the social environment trigger automatic self-presentations, identifying a mechanistic pathway for an automatic self-presentational process would be untenable. This leads directly to the key question underpinning our goal for this chapter: Do automatic self-presentations emerge of their own accord, triggered outside of conscious awareness by context cues in the absence of explicit self-presentation instructions? This issue relates to specific features of automatic processes in which self-presentations are thought to be involuntary responses initiated outside of conscious awareness by prompts in the social environment.

To shed light on this question, we look to the studies outlined in the research section. Although the evidence in support is quite limited, the findings suggest that automatic self-presentations are likely to emerge during situations involving familiar and routine patterns of responding, which require minimal cognitive and regulatory resources. Presenting oneself in accord with habitual response patterns required less effort, was delivered with greater speed, and was more likely to involve a favorable presentation of self. For instance, the studies that focused on recall measures demonstrate that automatic self-presentational efforts represent habitual patterns of responding that can be triggered automatically by features of the audience and situation (Schlenker, 2003). To go against habitual patterns requires foregoing the benefits of automaticity, with the resulting use of controlled self-presentations then operating like cognitive load. Faced with the need to make conscious self-presentation decisions, people are then left with diminished cognitive resources, for example, to encode and recall information. The studies addressing the effect of cognitive resources on self-presentational effectiveness also illustrate that habitual self-presentations transpire with minimal resource demands, and they can unfold effectively even if an individual is faced with other cognitively demanding activities. Engaging in controlled self-presentations, however, requires increased cognitive resources and, as such, suffers if an individual is simultaneously engaged in other efforts that diminish his or her resources. These findings are consistent with Schlenker and Pontari's (2000) notion of foreground self-presentations, which require available cognitive resources, and background self-presentations, which require minimal resources, primarily because background efforts are founded on repeatedly used scripts and over time have emerged as habitual aspects of a person's personality and identity. In all, participants prompted to self-present in a typical or familiar manner displayed cognitive effects consistent with an automatic process.

It is important, however, to emphasize that the design of most of the studies involved the efficiency feature of automatic processes, which focused on the influence that available cognitive resources have on self-presentations. Such evidence only demonstrates that automatic self-presentational behavior may occur in the absence of controlled efforts; that is, once consciously activated, self-presentations may unfold in an autonomous manner. For the most part, participants were aware of the goal conditions, in that they received explicit instructions to engage in a specific type of self-presentation, typically one that was either congruent or incongruent with what would be expected in that particular situation, and with the implication that under certain conditions these different self-presentations would consume more or less cognitive resources. These research designs did not just rely on the presence of context cues to nonconsciously trigger automatic self-presentations, and because participants were explicitly given instructions to self-present in a particular manner, it is impossible to tease apart any effects being due to self-presentation instructions or to context cues. We argue that the majority of research cannot unequivocally confirm an automatic process; the data do not allow for definitive conclusions in that we cannot determine whether self-presentations were triggered outside of conscious awareness by context cues in the absence of explicit self-presentation instructions.

However, the few studies outlined in the *cued activation* section may offer plausible evidence supporting the proposition that self-presentation involves an automatic cognitive mechanism in which people's efforts are nonconsciously triggered by context cues. Together, these studies demonstrate that cued knowledge activation, the implicit influence of significant others, and the subliminal priming of self-presentation cues can influence people's self-presentational efforts. For instance, as a context cue, the conditioned aural tones triggered self-presentations outside of conscious awareness, in that positive or negative self-descriptions emerged, respectively, when participants were surreptitiously cued with a tone that had been previously paired with either acceptance or rejection (Baldwin & Meunier, 1999). Results from Shah (2003) also showed that participants' self-descriptions were more negative when primed with a critical other's name and more positive when primed with an accepting others' name. He proffered that this effect occurred because the self-descriptions were nonconsciously influenced by the cued activation of relational schemas, which had become cognitively and emotionally linked over time to an accepting or critical other. In the same vein, Tyler's (2012) data revealed that participants primed with an impression word self-presented a more favorable persona, which not incidentally mimicked self-presentations in an explicit self-presentation control condition. Tyler's findings, which are consistent with Tice et al. (1995), also showed that participants primed with friend-oriented words self-presented a more modest image, whereas those primed with stranger-oriented words conveyed a more self-enhancing image.

The findings outlined in the *cued activation* section are theoretically consistent with the concept of a background self-presentation agenda in which an individual's behavior is automatically guided based on repeatedly used scripts that have been successful in the past. The behaviors that ensue comprise patterns of action that are habit-formed and emerge without conscious awareness. In a background mode, impression-relevant cues prompt or activate self-presentations, although people are not consciously aware that their efforts are, in part, fashioned by the social environment and their activated self-presentation scripts (Schlenker & Pontari, 2000). These automatic self-presentations typically represent positive characterizations of the self, but as the studies in the final review section illustrate, they can also involve more negatively oriented self-descriptions.

Although we tender our comments with a healthy degree of caution, we are optimistic that the results utilizing very subtle or subliminally primed context cues offer the strongest, albeit limited evidence in support of the proposition that self-presentations can be activated by environmental cues outside of conscious awareness. What these few studies seriously lack, however, is an examination of the effect during an actual ongoing social interaction.

Future work is sorely needed to not only conceptually replicate the cued context and priming effects but also to move the examination of these effects into more real-life types of situations (Leary et al., 2011). To do so will require the use of creative designs to offset the fact that in real-life settings the context cues may often exist within the boundaries of people's conscious awareness. People are cognizant of an audience, for instance, and as such, their self-presentations may be guided by an intended, but goal-dependent, automatic process, which is consistent with background self-presentations as proposed in the self-identification theory.

We also emphasize that any research designs utilizing context cues or primes to trigger automatic self-presentations need to take particular care to ensure that the cues/primes are not transparent, and that their influence occurs, indeed via a nonconscious mechanism. Clarifying the mechanism underlying automatic self-presentation is of key import, in part, because research designs may unintentionally neglect cues in the experimental setting that nonconsciously trigger or motivate self-presentational behavior, which of course, would inadvertently affect the subsequent results. This concern has historical precedent; during the 1970s, a significant amount of self-presentation research was aimed at providing alternatives to the currently held explanations for a variety of interpersonal phenomena. Results from numerous studies, spanning wide domains within social psychology, provided evidence demonstrating that people's interpersonal behavior (e.g., helping behavior, conformity, cognitive dissonance, voting behavior) was influenced by their desire that others view them in a particular fashion (e.g., Tedeschi, Schlenker, & Bonoma, 1971; see Leary, 1995). For the most part,

the self-presentation perspective argued, "that the people we use as the sources of behavioral data are active, anticipatory, problem-solving, role-playing, and impression-managing beings (Page, 1981, p. 59; see Adair, 1973). Page further argued that experimental subjects "may feel very much as if they are on stage (Goffman, 1959, ), and they may control and calculate their own behavior so as not to receive what in their own eyes would be a negative evaluation of their performance" (p. 60). At the time, these contentions were directly aimed at participants' consciously, controlled self-presentational efforts and were viewed by traditional social psychology as methodological artifacts that could be ameliorated (see Kruglanski, 1975). The degree to which these issues have actually been remedied is well beyond the scope of the current chapter. If theorists' proposition is correct, however, and automatic self-presentations are a ubiquitous feature of people's daily life, it would behoove researchers to assiduously examine their experimental design and protocols to determine if potential cues in the laboratory setting are unintentionally triggering participants' automatic self-presentational efforts. If this were the case, the concerns are obvious and meaningful, in that such cued behavior would severely confound any subsequent results and data interpretation.

An essential ingredient of the research that directly examines automatic self-presentations is the development of tightly designed control or comparison conditions; at the least, such conditions must demonstrate that the absence of a particular cue leads to less self-presentational efforts compared to the presence of the cue. Such research designs must also keep potential self-presentational motivations, for example, goal importance and audience status, constant across all experimental conditions, while manipulating the context-cued condition. If the design fails to adequately do so, it is nearly impossible to determine if participants' self-presentation efforts are unfolding in a background mode or whether other motivational factors have shifted participants' efforts to the foreground. It is important to evaluate implicit self-presentation cues, not only for their effectiveness at triggering automatic self-presentations, but also to ensure that they are able to do so in a nonconscious manner.

Integrating elements from a number of the reviewed studies may also prove useful in examining automatic self-presentations, particularly during the course of an ongoing interpersonal interaction.

In a number of studies, various self-presentations were characterized as comprising or inducing different levels of cognitive demand, which combined with information processing measures, enabled researchers to infer automatic self-presentations. Much of the evidence indicated that when cognitive attention was diverted only a default set of positive self-descriptions remained available for automatic self-presentations. By turning the notion around that different self-presentations induce high or low cognitive load, one could predict that high- or low-cognitive-load circumstances would lead to automatic or controlled self-presentations, respectively. It would be fruitful to manipulate the level of cognitive demand during an ongoing interpersonal interaction in the absence of any explicit self-presentation instructions, with the expectation that automatic self-presentations (i.e., default set of positive self-descriptions) should emerge in the high- compared to low-cognitive-load condition. Rather than assess self-ratings or recall, it would also be more externally valid and informative to measure and/or code people's self-descriptions or behaviors.

Although Pontari and Schlenker's extravert-introvert study (2000) involved explicit self-presentation instructions, it followed a design similar to the one proposed herein; they directly manipulated cognitive demands during an interaction. Automatic self-presentations were presumed to have occurred under conditions in which participants were instructed to engage in congruent self-presentations in both the high- and low-cognitive-load conditions. One can readily imagine adding another condition in which participants under both cognitive load conditions received no explicit self-presentation instructions. The results from such a condition should mirror the data from the presumed automatic self-presentation condition because participants in either cognitive load condition who received no self-presentation instructions would have no particular reason or motivation to behave in a manner other than the one they are most familiar with—extraverts would act extraverted and introverts would act introverted. If this no-instruction condition replicated the automatic self-presentation condition, it would provide additional support for an automatic component to the self-presentation process. It would also provide much needed evidence to demonstrate that automatic self-presentations emerge spontaneously during interpersonal interactions, in the absence of any direct instructional prompts.

## Conclusion

At the start of this chapter, we argued that characterizing self-presentation in terms that predominantly evoke controlled and strategic efforts is not only theoretically challenging but also empirically problematic. It serves to foster an exclusionary research perspective, severely limiting research attention, leading to a paucity of work examining automatic self-presentations. Following a conceptual approach that positions self-presentation as occurring primarily in limited situations has fundamentally shaped the fabric of most self-presentation research designs, in that participants are often explicitly provided with self-presentation instructions, essentially bypassing the issue of context cuing.

Although the scarcity of empirical work became apparent in the evidence sections, the studies that are available offer some promising avenues for future work. Pontari and Schlenker's (2000) extravert-introvert studies suggest an empirical direction and offer results to build and expand upon. The cued activation and priming studies not only provide the strongest evidence to date for automatic self-presentations, but they also provide a solid empirical foundation with which to design additional work. Nonetheless, the evidence remains very limited, underscoring a palpable and substantive need for further research. Considerable work remains to be done in order to determine empirically whether self-presentations are actually triggered nonconsciously by cues in the social environment, in that people are unaware of the initiation, flow, or impact of their self-presentational efforts.

## References

Aarts, H., & Dijksterhuis, A. (2000). Habits as knowledge structures: Automaticity in goal directed behavior. *Journal of Personality and Social Psychology, 78*, 53–63.

Adair, J. G. (1973). *The human subject: The social psychology of the psychological experiment.* Boston: Little Brown.

Back, M. D., Stopfer, J. M., Vazire, S., Gaddis, S., Schmukle, S. C., Egloff, B., & Gosling, S. D. (2010). Facebook profiles reflect actual personality not self-idealization. *Psychological Science, 21*, 372–374.

Baldwin, M. (1992). Relational schemas and the processing of social information. *Psychological Bulletin, 112*, 461–484.

Baldwin, M. (1994). Primed relational schemas as a source of self-evaluative reactions. *Journal of Social and Clinical Psychology, 13*, 380–403.

Baldwin, M. W., & Main, K. J. (2001). Social anxiety and the cued activation of relational knowledge. *Personality and Social Psychology Bulletin, 27*, 1637–1647.

Baldwin, M., & Meunier, J. (1999). The cued activation of attachment relational schemas. *Social Cognition, 17*, 209–227.

Bargh, J. A. (1996). Automaticity in social psychology. In E. T. Higgins & A. W. Kruglanski (Eds.), *Social psychology: Handbook of basic principles* (pp. 169–183). New York: Guilford Press.

Baumeister, R. F. (1982). Self-esteem, self-presentation, and future interaction: A dilemma of reputation. *Journal of Personality, 50,* 29–45.

Baumeister, R. F., Hutton, D. G., & Tice, D. M. (1989). Cognitive processes during deliberate self-presentation: How self-presenters alter and misinterpret the behavior of their interaction partners. *Journal of Experimental Social Psychology, 25,* 59–78.

Baumeister, R. F., & Jones, E. E. (1978). When self-presentation is constrained by the target's knowledge: Consistency and compensation. *Journal of Personality and Social Psychology, 36,* 608–618.

Custers, R., & Aarts, H. (2005). Positive affect as implicit motivator: On nonconscious operation of behavioral goals. *Journal of Personality and Social Psychology, 89,* 129–142.

DePaulo, B. M. (1992). Nonverbal behavior and self-presentation. *Psychological Bulletin, 111,* 203–243.

Goffman, E. (1959). *The presentation of self in everyday life.* New York: Doubleday Books.

Hogan R. (1983). A socioanalytic theory of personality. In *Nebraska Symposium on Motivation* (Vol. 30, pp. 55–89). Lincoln: University of Nebraska Press.

Holden, R. R., Kroner, D. G., Fekken, G. C, & Popham, S. M. (1992). A model of personality test item response dissimulation. *Journal of Personality and Social Psychology, 63,* 272–279.

Holden, R. R., Wood, L. L, & Tomashewski L. (2001). Do response time limitations counteract the effect of faking on personality inventory validity? *Journal of Personality and Social Psychology, 81,* 160–169.

Jones, E. E., & Wortman, C. (1973). *Ingratiation: An attributional approach.* Morristown, NJ: General Learning Press.

Kitayama, S., & Karasawa, M. (1997). Implicit self-esteem in Japan: Name letters and birthday numbers. *Personality and Social Psychology Bulletin, 23,* 736–742.

Koole, S. L., Dijksterhuis, A., & van Knippenberg, A. (2001). What's in a name: Implicit self-esteem and the automatic self. *Journal of Personality and Social Psychology, 80,* 669–685.

Kruglanski, (1975). The human subject in the psychological experiment: Fact and artifact. In L. Berkowitz (Ed.), *Advances in experimental social psychology* (Vol. 8, pp. 101–147). New York: Academic Press.

Leary, M. R. (1995). *Self-presentation: Impression management and interpersonal behavior.* Boulder, CO: Westview.

Leary, M. R., & Allen, A. (2011). Self-presentational persona: Simultaneous management of multiple impressions. *Journal of Personality and Social Psychology, 101,* 1033–1049.

Leary, M. R., Allen, A., & Terry, M. L. (2011). Managing social images in naturalistic versus laboratory settings: Implications for understanding and studying self-presentation. *European Journal of Social Psychology, 41,* 411–421.

Leary, M. R., & Kowalski, R. M. (1990). Impression management: A literature review and two-component model. *Psychological Bulletin, 107,* 34–47.

Mikulincer, M. (1995). Attachment style and the mental representation of the self. *Journal of Personality and Social Psychology, 69,* 1203–1215.

Moretti, M. M., & Higgins, E. T. (1999). Own versus other standpoints in self-regulation: Developmental antecedents and functional consequences. *Review of General Psychology, 3,* 188–223.

Paulhus, D. L. (1993). Bypassing the will: The automatization of affirmations. In D. M. Wegner & J. W. Pennebaker (Eds.), *Handbook of mental control* (pp. 573–587). Englewood Cliffs, NJ: Prentice-Hall.

Paulhus, D. L., Bruce, N., & Stoffer, E. (1990, August). *Automatizing self-descriptions.* Paper presented at the American Psychological Association meeting, Boston, MA.

Paulhus, D. L., Graf, P., & Van Selst, M. (1989). Attentional load increases the positivity of self-presentation. *Social Cognition, 7,* 389–400.

Paulhus, D. L., & Levitt, K. (1987). Desirable responding triggered by affect: Automatic egotism? *Journal of Personality and Social Psychology, 52,* 245–259.

Page, M. P. (1981). Demand compliance in laboratory experiments. In J. T. Tedeschi (Ed.), *Impression management theory and social psychological research* (pp. 57–82). New York: Academic Press.

Pontari, B. A., & Schlenker, B. R. (2000). The influence of cognitive load on self-presentation: Can cognitive busyness help as well as harm social performance? *Journal of Personality and Social Psychology, 78,* 1092–1108.

Schlenker, B. R. (1980). Impression management. Monterey, CA: Brooks/Cole.

Schlenker, B. R. (1985). Identity and self-identification. In B. R. Schlenker (Ed.), *The self and social life* (pp. 65–99). New York: McGraw-Hill.

Schlenker, B. R. (1986). Self-identification: Toward an integration of the private and public self. In R. Baumeister (Ed.), *Public self and private self* (pp. 21–62). New York: Springer-Verlag.

Schlenker, B. R. (2003). Self-presentation. In M. R. Leary & J. P. Tangney (Eds.), *Handbook of self and identity* (pp. 492–518). New York: Guilford Press.

Schlenker, B. R., Britt, T. W., & Pennington, J. W. (1996). Impression regulation and management: A theory of self-identification. In R. M. Sorrentino & E. T. Higgins (Eds.), *Handbook of motivation and cognition: The interpersonal context* (pp. 118–147). New York: Guilford Press.

Schlenker, B. R., Britt, T. W., Pennington, J. W., Murphy, R., & Doherty, K. J. (1994). The triangle model of responsibility. *Psychological Review, 101,* 632–652.

Schlenker, B. R., & Pontari, B. A. (2000). The strategic control of information: Impression management and self-presentation in daily life. In A. Tesser & R. B. Felson (Eds.), *Psychological perspectives on self and identity* (pp. 199–232). Washington, DC: American Psychological Association.

Shah, J. (2003). Automatic for the people: How representations of significant others implicitly affect goal pursuit. *Journal of Personality and Social Psychology, 84,* 661–681.

Swann, W. B., Jr. (1983). Self-verification: Bringing social reality into harmony with the self. In J. Suls & A. G. Greenwald (Eds.), *Psychological perspectives on the self* (pp. 33–66). Hillsdale, NJ: Erlbaum.

Tedeschi, J. T., Schlenker, B. R., & Bonoma, T. V. (1971). Cognitive dissonance: Private ratiocination or public spectacle? *American Psychologist, 26,* 685–695.

Tice, D. M., Butler, J. L., Muraven, M. B., & Stillwell, A. M. (1995). When modesty prevails: Differential favorability of self-presentation to friends and strangers. *Journal of Personality and Social Psychology, 69*, 1120–1138.

Tyler, J. M. (2012). Triggering self-presentation efforts outside of people's conscious awareness. *Personality and Social Psychology Bulletin, 38*, 619–627.

Verplanken, B., & Aarts, H. (1999). Habit, attitude, and planned behaviour: Is habit an empty construct or an interesting case of goal-directed automaticity? European *Review of Social Psychology, 10*, 101–134.

Vohs, K. D., Baumeister, R. F., & Ciarocco, N. J. (2005). Self-regulation and self-presentation: Regulatory resource depletion impairs impression management and effortful self-presentation depletes regulatory resources. *Journal of Personality and Social Psychology, 88*, 632–657.

Wilson, R. E., Gosling, S. D., & Graham, L. T. (2012). A review of Facebook research in the social sciences. *Perspectives on Psychological Science, 7*, 203–220.

Wood, W., & Neal, D. T. (2007). A new look at habits and the habit–goal interface. *Psychological Review, 114*, 843–863.

# Emotions as Agents of Social Influence: Insights From Emotions as Social Information Theory

Gerben A. van Kleef

## Abstract

Emotion is part and parcel of social influence. The emotions people feel shape the ways in which they respond to persuasion attempts, and the emotions people express influence other individuals who observe those expressions. This chapter is concerned with the latter type of emotional influence. Such interpersonal effects of emotional expressions are quite different from the traditionally studied intrapersonal effects of emotional experience. This calls for a new theoretical approach that is dedicated specifically to understanding the interpersonal effects of emotional expressions. I summarize emotions as social information (EASI) theory, which posits that emotional expressions shape social influence by triggering affective reactions and/or inferential processes in observers, depending on the observer's information processing and the perceived appropriateness of the emotional expression. I review supportive evidence from various domains of social influence, including negotiation, leadership, attitude change, compliance, and conformity in groups. Differences and commonalities with traditional intrapersonal frameworks are discussed.

**Key Words:** emotion, social influence, interpersonal effects, persuasion, compliance, conformity, negotiation, leadership

Social influence is a defining feature of life. Wherever people interact, they influence each other's attitudes, judgments, and behaviors. This is often an emotional enterprise—consider how easily a conversation about politics can turn into a heated debate. Traditionally, theory and research on the role of emotion in social influence have focused on the intrapersonal effects of emotions, considering how people's affective experiences shape the ways in which they respond to influence attempts. Until recently, little was known about the social effects of emotional *expressions*. This is striking if we consider how often people engender social influence by expressing their emotions to others. When two friends discuss the pros and cons of nuclear energy, one friend's enthusiasm may lead the other to reconsider her opinion. When a shopper refuses to donate to a charity collector, the collector's disappointment may lead the shopper to reconsider and offer some change. When a negotiator gets angry upon receiving his counterpart's demands, the counterpart may feel pressured to make a concession. When a manager expresses dissatisfaction about the performance of a work team, the team may become motivated to work harder. When a group of scientists at a conference attempts to decide where to go for dinner, their annoyance with one person's deviating preferences may lead that person to conform to the group's position.

These examples illustrate that emotion is an integral part of the social influence toolbox. Indeed, several theorists have noted that emotional expressions may be used deliberately to influence others. Clark, Pataki, and Carver (1996) reported anecdotal evidence that people strategically use displays of sadness to solicit help. This can be effective (especially in communal relationships), because observers may infer that the expresser is needy and dependent. Likewise, people may express anger to intimidate and influence others (Frank, 1988). For instance, managers have been reported to deliberately feign anger in order to influence their subordinates (Fitness, 2000). Furthermore, people may purposefully express happiness to get others to like them (Clark et al., 1996). Clearly, then, there is much more to emotion than its private experience: Emotional expressions are a potential source of social influence (Van Kleef, Van Doorn, Heerdink, & Koning, 2011).

This chapter is concerned with the ways in which people engender social influence by means of their emotional expressions. The chapter unfolds as follows. First I define what is meant by emotion and how it differs from related concepts. Then I briefly discuss the traditional intrapersonal approach to emotion and persuasion as well as some of the dominant theoretical models in that area. Next I describe a recent theory that aims to explain the interpersonal effects of emotional expressions in social influence, and I explicate how this theoretical approach differs from traditional models. Subsequently, I review empirical work on the interpersonal effects of emotional expressions in various domains of social influence. The first part of my review will focus on well-established and somewhat older research on the interpersonal effects of emotional expressions in negotiation and leadership, two research domains that are highly relevant to social influence yet seldom discussed in the context of social influence research. The second part of my review will address more recent and ongoing empirical investigations of the interpersonal effects of emotional expressions in classic domains of social influence, namely attitude change, compliance, and conformity. Finally, I discuss the emerging conception of emotions as agents of social influence, highlight theoretical implications as well as differences and commonalities between the current interpersonal approach to emotions and traditional intrapersonal accounts, and suggest avenues for future research.

## Conceptualizing the Role of Emotion in Social Influence

The question of what constitutes an emotion has occupied philosophers, psychologists, and other social scientists since the dawn of civilization, and it continues to do so. Countless definitions of emotion have been advanced, attesting to the difficulty of formulating one that is satisfactory to all who are interested in the phenomenon. Instead of inventing yet another definition, I will describe the basic features of emotion about which there is reasonable consensus in the literature.

Most theories of emotion hold that emotions arise as a result of an individual's conscious or unconscious evaluation (appraisal) of some event as positively or negatively relevant to a particular concern or goal (Frijda, 1986; Lazarus, 1991). Emotions are typically characterized by distinct subjective experiences (Scherer & Tannenbaum, 1986), physiological reactions (Levenson, Ekman, & Friesen, 1990), and expressions (Ekman, 1993). Furthermore, emotions are accompanied by a sense of action readiness (Frijda, 1986), in that they prepare the body and the mind for behavioral responses aimed at dealing with the circumstances that caused the emotion.

The term *emotion* is sometimes used interchangeably with *affect* or *mood*. However, these terms carry distinct meanings. According to Frijda (1994), *affect* is an overarching term that may be used to refer to dispositional affective tendencies (e.g., chronic positive vs. negative affectivity), diffuse moods (e.g., cheerfulness or depression), specific and acute emotions (e.g., anger or fear), and chronic sentiments (e.g., positive or negative attitudes). Emotions differ from the various other affective phenomena in that they (a) are directed toward a specific stimulus, such as a person, an object, or an event (unlike moods and dispositional affective tendencies, which have no clear object or identifiable cause); (b) can be differentiated in terms of their associated physiological responses, subjective feelings, expressive patterns, and action tendencies (unlike the other affective phenomena, which only differ in terms of valence); and (c) are relatively short-lived (compared to the other affective phenomena, which tend to be more enduring if not chronic).

In conceptualizing the role of emotion in social influence, it is useful to distinguish between intrapersonal and interpersonal effects of emotions (Morris & Keltner, 2000; Van Kleef et al., 2011). At the intrapersonal level of analysis, scholars seek to understand how people's attitudes, cognitions, and behaviors are influenced by their own emotional states. For instance, researchers explore whether certain emotional states render people more susceptible to influence attempts (e.g., Are happy people more likely than sad people to provide help when asked?). At the interpersonal level of analysis, studies are aimed at uncovering how people are influenced by the emotional expressions of others. In other words, research at the interpersonal level of analysis investigates how the emotional expressions of a source shape the attitudes, cognitions, and behaviors of a target (e.g., Are people more likely to extend help to a person who smiles than to a person who frowns?).

There is a rich tradition of research in social psychology and adjacent disciplines on the ways in which emotional states influence information search and processing, message scrutiny, and susceptibility to persuasion attempts. This research has been inspired in part by various formulations of the elaboration likelihood model (ELM; e.g., Petty & Briñol, 2012; Petty & Cacioppo, 1986), which specifies (among other things) how emotional states influence people's responses to persuasive messages, and how the impact of felt emotions depends on the extent of a person's information processing. Besides the ELM, research has been guided by the affect as information model (Schwarz & Clore, 1983), the affect infusion model (AIM; Forgas, 1995), and the mood as input model (Martin, Ward, Achee, & Wyer, 1993). All of these models speak to the various ways in which people's information processing and responses to persuasive messages are shaped by their *own* affective states. As such, the models are located at the intrapersonal level of analysis when it comes to understanding the role of emotional phenomena in social influence. An in-depth discussion of this literature therefore falls outside the scope of this chapter, which is concerned with the ways in which people are influenced by the emotional expressions of other individuals. I limit the current discussion to a brief summary of the types of emotional influences that have been studied in the intrapersonal tradition.

The ELM identifies a number of different processes through which emotional states may modulate social influence by impacting on basic cognition (Petty & Briñol, 2015). When the likelihood of thorough elaboration is low, emotions may serve as simple cues. This notion is also present, among other things, in research on evaluative conditioning (e.g., De Houwer, Thomas, & Baeyens, 2001).

When elaboration likelihood is high, emotions may be used as arguments, as detailed in the mood as input model (Martin et al., 1993). Under high elaboration, emotions may also influence the direction of thinking, as noted also in the AIM (Forgas, 1995). Finally, when elaboration is not constrained, emotions may influence the degree to which individuals process available information (Wegener, Petty, & Smith, 1995). For a more in-depth treatment of theorizing and research on the intrapersonal effects of emotions in relation to social influence, the reader is referred to a recent review by Petty and Briñol (2015).

The focus of this chapter is on the interpersonal level of analysis, because this is the primary arena of social influence. People continuously influence one another through their emotional expressions, whether deliberately or unconsciously, in personal relationships, in the workplace, and in the political domain. I define the interpersonal effects of emotions in social influence broadly as any effects of one person's emotional expressions—whether expressed through words, via facial displays, through the voice, via bodily postures, or through any combination of these expressive modalities—on (one or more) other individuals' attitudes, cognitions, and/or behavior.

The critical distinction between intrapersonal and interpersonal effects of emotions is that the former pertain to the effects of a person's own emotional experience on his or her cognitions, attitudes, decisions, and behavior, whereas the latter concern the effects of the emotional expressions of one or more other individuals on a person's cognitions, attitudes, decisions, and behavior. A logical corollary of this distinction is that intrapersonal effects of emotions can occur in social isolation, because a person may be influenced by his or her own emotions in the absence of other people. In practice, intrapersonal effects of emotions nonetheless frequently occur in social situations, because other individuals are often the cause of people's emotions (Parkinson, 1996). Interpersonal effects of emotions, however, can by their very nature only occur in social situations, because they require that one person observe an emotional expression of another person. The fact that interpersonal effects of emotions happen between rather than within individuals also means that traditional intrapersonal models of emotion and persuasion cannot account for the interpersonal effects of emotions, except to the extent that the emotions of the expresser become shared by the observer (an issue to which I will return later). The intrinsically social nature of the interpersonal effects of emotions thus calls for a theory that explains under which circumstances and by which mechanisms individuals are influenced by the emotional expressions of others. This call is answered by emotions as social information theory, which I summarize below.

## Emotions as Social Information Theory

Emotions as social information (EASI) theory (Van Kleef, 2009, 2016; Van Kleef, De Dreu, & Manstead, 2010; Van Kleef, Homan, & Cheshin, 2012) was developed specifically to account for the interpersonal effects of emotional expressions. As such, it is highly suitable for analyzing the interpersonal effects of emotions in social influence (Van Kleef et al., 2011). EASI theory is rooted in a social-functional approach to emotion (Fischer & Manstead, 2008; Frijda & Mesquita, 1994; Hareli & Rafaeli, 2008; Keltner & Haidt, 1999; Oatley & Jenkins, 1992; Parkinson, 1996; Van Kleef, 2009). A central tenet of the social-functional perspective is that emotions do not only influence those who experience them but also those who observe them (Fischer & Van Kleef, 2010). EASI theory extends this general notion by specifying two processes through which observers may be influenced (i.e., affective reactions and inferential processes) and identifying two classes of moderating variables that influence the relative predictive strength of these mechanisms (i.e., the target's information processing depth and the perceived appropriateness of the emotional expression).

### *Affective Reactions*

Emotional expressions can evoke affective reactions in observers, which may subsequently influence their behavior. One type of affective reaction is produced by emotional contagion, the tendency to unintentionally and automatically "catch" other people's emotions (Hatfield, Cacioppo, & Rapson, 1994). Emotional contagion can occur when individuals are exposed to others' nonverbal displays of emotion (e.g., facial, vocal, and postural expressions), which may be mimicked and produce congruent emotional states via afferent feedback (i.e., physiological feedback from facial, vocal, and postural movements; e.g., Hess & Blairy, 2001; Neumann & Strack, 2000; Wild, Erb, & Bartels, 2001). Emotional contagion can also occur via verbal expressions of emotion, even in the absence of face-to-face interaction, for instance, through

computer-mediated interaction (e.g., Cheshin, Rafaeli, & Bos, 2011; Friedman et al., 2004; Van Kleef, De Dreu, & Manstead, 2004a). As a result of these processes, individuals tend to catch others' emotions on a moment-to-moment basis.

When people catch others' emotions, the resulting feeling state may influence their judgments and decisions via various types of "affect infusion" (Forgas, 1995). First, individuals may (mis)attribute the affective state to the situation at hand, using their feelings as input to their social judgments and decisions—a "how do I feel about it?" heuristic (i.e., affect-as-information; Schwarz & Clore, 1983). In ELM terms, this would be an instance of emotions biasing processing. Thus, if a person catches another's happiness and thereby comes to experience positive feelings, he or she may judge the situation as benign, which may promote cooperation. Second, the emerging affective state may selectively prime related ideas and memories that are part of an associative network, thereby facilitating their use when planning and executing behavior (i.e., affect priming; Bower, 1981; Isen, Shalker, Clark, & Karp, 1978). Thus, if a person catches another's anger, he or she may selectively focus on negative aspects of that person, which may undermine cooperation.

The emotions individuals catch from others may also influence social behavior through mood maintenance and negative state relief. The core assumption here is that people strive to promote and maintain positive mood states and to avoid experiencing negative mood states (Carlson, Charlin, & Miller, 1988). This basic drive motivates people in a negative mood to engage in behaviors associated with positive feelings (e.g., helping others) in order to relieve their negative feeling state (e.g., Schaller & Cialdini, 1988). Likewise, individuals in a positive mood are motivated to exhibit behaviors that produce positive feelings and to abstain from activities that entail the risk of spoiling the good mood (i.e., positive mood maintenance; Wegener & Petty, 1994). In the current context, this means that when one's interaction partner feels happy, one may catch the partner's happiness and become motivated to maintain the positive feeling by acting in a friendly and generous way. Similarly, when the other expresses sadness, one may become somber through emotional contagion and become motivated to relieve oneself of the negative feelings, for instance, by acting generously.

In addition to emotional contagion, affective reactions may take the form of favorable or unfavorable impressions (Hareli & Hess, 2010;

Knutson, 1996). Expressions of positive emotions tend to inspire positive impressions, and negative emotions negative impressions (Clark & Taraban, 1991). Such impressions may in turn shape social behavior. For instance, we tend to be more willing to help others whom we like and more likely to deny help to others whom we do not like (Clark et al., 1996). These effects are probably more direct and motivational than the effects of emotions on judgments and behavior discussed earlier, which are mediated by cognitive processes such as affect-as-information and affect-priming. Despite these differences, both types of affective reactions to other people's emotional expressions shape our responses to those other people. This notion has important implications for the interpersonal effects of emotional expressions in social influence, as the ensuing review of the literature will show.

### Inferential Processes

Another way in which emotional expressions can wield interpersonal influence is by triggering inferential processes in observers. Because specific emotions arise in response to appraisals of specific situations (Frijda, 1986; Lazarus, 1991), observing a particular emotion in another person provides relatively differentiated information about how that person regards the situation. Note that such specific information is not provided by positive or negative moods, which only indicate whether things are generally going well or not. The implications of an emotional display vary as a function of the situation, but the basic informational value of discrete emotions generalizes across situations (Van Kleef, 2009). For instance, according to appraisal theories (e.g., Frijda, 1986; Roseman, 1984; Scherer, Schorr, & Johnstone, 2001; Smith, Haynes, Lazarus, & Pope, 1993), happiness arises when goals have been met (or good progress is being made toward attaining them) and expectations are positive. Expressions of happiness therefore signal that the environment is appraised as favorable and benign. Anger arises when a person's goals are being frustrated and he or she blames someone else for it. Expressions of anger therefore signal appraisals of goal blockage and other blame. Sadness arises when one faces irrevocable loss and experiences low coping potential. Expressions of sadness therefore signal lack of control and helplessness. Guilt arises when one feels that one has transgressed some social norm or moral imperative. Expressions of guilt therefore

signal that one is aware of (and possibly troubled by) one's misdemeanor (for a detailed account of such appraisals and concomitant inferences, see Van Kleef, De Dreu, & Manstead, 2010).

Because discrete emotions have such distinct appraisal patterns (Manstead & Tetlock, 1989; Smith et al., 1993), they provide a wealth of information to observers (Keltner & Haidt, 1999; Van Kleef, 2009). For instance, emotional expressions convey information about the expresser's inner states (Ekman, 1993), social intentions (Fridlund, 1994), and orientation toward other people (Hess, Blairy, & Kleck, 2000; Knutson, 1996). In addition, emotional expressions inform observers about the expresser's appraisal of the situation (Manstead & Fischer, 2001; Van Doorn, Heerdink, & Van Kleef, 2012). This is illustrated by classic work on social referencing, which revealed that infants are more likely to cross a visual cliff when their mother smiles at them than when she looks fearful (e.g., Klinnert, Campos, Sorce, Emde, & Svejda, 1983). Presumably the mother's emotional display signals that the environment is safe (happiness) or unsafe (fear), thus informing the infant's behavior.

Individuals may thus distill useful pieces of information from others' emotional expressions (Van Kleef, 2009, 2016). For instance, when one is the target of another's anger, one may infer that one did something wrong, and this inference may in turn inform one's behavior (e.g., apologizing, changing one's conduct). When confronted with another person's happiness, one may conclude that things are going well, which may lead one to stay the course. When confronted with another's sadness, one might infer that the other faces a loss and has low coping potential, which may lead one to offer help or consolation. And when one's partner shows guilt after a faux pas, one may infer that he or she cares about the relationship and is willing to make up for the transgression. In short, inferential processes constitute a second set of mechanisms underlying the interpersonal effects of emotional expressions in social influence.

### Competing or Converging Processes

The two sets of mechanisms underlying the interpersonal effects of emotional expressions specified in EASI theory are distinct but mutually influential (Van Kleef, 2009). In some cases inferences and affective reactions lead to the same behavior. For example, the distress of a significant other signals that help is required (inference) but also triggers negative feelings in the observer (affective reaction), both of which may foster supportive behavior (Clark et al., 1996). In other cases, however, inferences and affective reactions motivate opposite behaviors. For instance, when faced with an angry opponent in conflict, one's own reciprocal anger may provoke competition and retaliation, but one's inference that the other is upset because his or her limits have been reached may encourage strategic cooperation (Van Kleef et al., 2004a). Which process takes precedence in guiding social behavior depends on two classes of moderators: factors that influence the observer's information processing depth and factors that determine the perceived appropriateness of the emotional expression.

## Information Processing

Building on the idea that emotional expressions provide information about the expresser, EASI theory posits that the interpersonal effects of emotional expressions depend on the observer's motivation and ability to process the information conveyed by these expressions: The deeper the information processing, the stronger the relative predictive power of inferential processes; the shallower the information processing, the stronger the relative predictive power of affective reactions (Van Kleef, 2009).

To illustrate, imagine you show up 30 minutes late to a meeting with a colleague. Your colleague expresses anger regarding your tardiness. If you are motivated and able to carefully consider the reasons, meaning, and implications of your colleague's anger, you may come to realize that your being late caused the anger, that it is inappropriate to arrive late to a meeting, that you should apologize, and that you should be on time for the next meeting (a series of inferences). However, if you are not motivated and or unable to think through the meaning and implications of your colleague's anger, the anger may upset you and make you dislike your colleague (affective reactions), and possibly cause you to decide not to meet anymore at all.

Information processing depth depends on the individual's *epistemic motivation*, that is, his or her willingness to expend effort to achieve a rich and accurate understanding of the world, including other people (Kruglanski, 1989). Individuals with higher epistemic motivation have lower confidence in their knowledge and experience less certainty. As a consequence, they tend to engage in rather deliberate, systematic information search and processing before making judgments and decisions (De Dreu & Carnevale, 2003; Kruglanski, 1989; Kruglanski & Webster, 1996; see also Chaiken & Trope, 1999).

Epistemic motivation is partly rooted in personality. For instance, individuals with higher need for cognition, lower need for cognitive closure, lower personal need for structure, and higher openness to experience have chronically higher epistemic motivation than their counterparts who score on the opposite poles of these scales, and as a result they engage in more deliberate information processing (De Dreu & Carnevale, 2003; Homan et al., 2008; Neuberg & Newsom, 1993; Van Kleef, Anastasopoulou, & Nijstad, 2010; Webster & Kruglanski, 1994). In terms of the present argument, these individuals are more likely to reflect on their partner's emotions, and therefore the effects of their partner's emotional expressions are more likely to be mediated by inferential processes than by affective reactions.

Epistemic motivation may also vary as a function of the situation. For instance, epistemic motivation is increased when a task is perceived as attractive or personally involving (Eagly & Chaiken, 1993; Petty & Cacioppo, 1986); when one is held accountable for one's judgments and decisions (Tetlock, 1992); when outcomes are framed as losses rather than as gains (De Dreu, Carnevale, Emans, & Van de Vliert, 1994); and when a situation is competitively rather than cooperatively structured (Van Kleef, De Dreu, & Manstead, 2010). Conversely, epistemic motivation is undermined by factors such as environmental noise (Kruglanski & Webster, 1991), mental fatigue (Webster, Richter, & Kruglanski, 1996), time pressure (Van Kleef, De Dreu, & Manstead, 2004b), and power (De Dreu & Van Kleef, 2004; Fiske & Dépret, 1996; Keltner, Van Kleef, Chen, & Kraus, 2008). By influencing epistemic motivation, these factors influence the relative predictive strength of affective reactions and inferential processes.

## Perceived Appropriateness

The relative predictive strength of inferential processes and affective reactions also depends on social-contextual factors that influence the perceived appropriateness of the emotional expression (Van Kleef, 2016). Such factors include (cultural) norms regarding emotion expression, the way the emotion is expressed, relative status, and dispositional preferences for social harmony, among other things. EASI theory posits that inferential processes become relatively more powerful in shaping responses to emotional expressions to the extent that observers perceive the emotional expressions as appropriate. Although inappropriate emotional expressions could be argued to trigger information processing because they violate expectations (Hamilton & Sherman, 1996; Stern, Marrs, Millar, & Cole, 1984), evidence indicates that negative affective reactions to expectancy violations are primary (Bartholow, Fabiani, Gratton, & Bettencourt, 2001; Olson, Roese, & Zanna, 1996). Consider the case of a person who starts laughing out loud during a funeral ceremony. Even though other attendants may at some level be curious about what caused the person to laugh, their sense that the amusement is entirely inappropriate for the situation is likely to make them experience strong negative affective reactions. Accordingly, EASI assumes that the tendency toward additional information seeking that may be triggered by expectancy violations is outweighed by the strong negative affective reactions that are typically evoked by inappropriate displays of emotion (Shields, 2005; Van Kleef & Côté, 2007).

One factor that influences the perceived appropriateness of emotional expressions is culture. For example, in individualistic cultures, expressions of anger tend to be relatively acceptable. In the United States, expressions of anger are more likely to be interpreted as a sign of assertiveness and individuality than as a sign of aggression. In collectivistic cultures, however, expressions of anger are not appreciated. In Japan, expressing anger is perceived as highly inappropriate (except perhaps when the anger is directed at an outgroup) because anger poses a threat to group harmony (Kitayama, Mesquita, & Karasawa, 2006; Markus & Kitayama, 1991). Such "display rules" also vary across social groups and organizations. For instance, some organizations have explicit guidelines regarding emotional expressions (e.g., service with a smile; Rafaeli & Sutton, 1987), whereas others do not.

Personality factors also influence to what extent emotional expressions are perceived as appropriate. For instance, some people have a strong desire for social harmony (e.g., individuals who score high on agreeableness; McCrae & Costa, 1987), whereas others have less of such a desire. Individuals with a strong desire for social harmony are more likely to perceive expressions of anger as inappropriate and to respond negatively to such expressions because they may create hostility and conflict and thus undermine social harmony (Graziano, Jensen-Campbell, & Hair, 1996; Suls, Martin, & David, 1998). In addition, the perceived appropriateness of emotional expressions depends on characteristics of the interactants that may be (partly) unrelated to personality, such as status. People tend to accept more from high-status others than from low-status others (Porath, Overbeck, & Pearson, 2008), and therefore expressions of anger from low-status others are more likely to arouse negative affective reactions than expressions of anger from high-status others.

## Summary

EASI theory provides a social account of emotion by focusing on the interpersonal consequences of emotional expressions. As such, it complements existing models that attempt to explain the *intra*personal effects of emotions on cognition, judgment, and behavior (e.g., Forgas, 1995; Martin et al., 1993; Schwarz & Clore, 1983; for a recent review, see Petty & Briñol, 2015). EASI theory moves beyond the valence approach that characterizes many other theories and posits that each discrete emotion conveys specific social information (for a detailed account, see Van Kleef, De Dreu, & Manstead, 2010). The theory specifies two processes through which emotional expressions exert social influence (inferences vs. affective reactions), and it identifies two classes of moderators (information processing and the appropriateness of the emotional expression) that determine which of these processes takes precedence. The predictive strength of the inferential pathway increases to the extent that the target is motivated and able to engage in thorough information processing and perceives the emotional expression as appropriate; the predictive strength of the affective reactions pathway increases to the extent that the target's information processing is reduced and he or she perceives the emotional expression as inappropriate.

## Interpersonal Effects of Emotional Expressions in Social Influence: Empirical Evidence

This section provides an overview of empirical work on the interpersonal effects of emotional expressions in various domains of social influence. The first part of the review is devoted to established work in the adjacent fields of negotiation and leadership. The second part of the review addresses more recent and ongoing investigations into the interpersonal effects of emotions in classic areas of social influence, including attitude change, compliance, and conformity.

### Evidence From Neighboring Fields of Inquiry

Research on the interpersonal effects of emotions in social influence has only recently started to emerge. As a result, the current empirical record is modest. However, there is a lot to learn from adjacent areas of inquiry that are not traditionally seen as prototypical for social influence research yet contain clear processes of social influence. One such domain is negotiation. Negotiation is defined as a discussion between two or more parties aimed at solving a (perceived) divergence of interests (Pruitt & Carnevale, 1993). Social influence is central to this process. Typically, parties in negotiation attempt to persuade each other to make concessions using a variety of strategies. In that sense, negotiation can be seen as a sequence of reciprocal requests (akin to compliance). The main difference between negotiation and a request is that the former situation is typically characterized by competitive incentives, whereas the latter is not (Van Kleef, De Dreu, & Manstead, 2010). Nevertheless, research on the interpersonal effects of emotional expressions in negotiations reveals a lot about the ways in which emotions engender social influence.

In a first study of the interpersonal effects of emotions in negotiation, Van Kleef and colleagues (2004a) investigated the interpersonal effects of anger and happiness using a computer-mediated negotiation task. In the course of the negotiation, participants received emotional messages from their (simulated) opponent (e.g., "This negotiation pisses me off"). Negotiators who received angry messages estimated the opponent's limit to be high, and to avoid costly impasse they made relatively large concessions. Conversely, negotiators who received happy messages judged the opponent's limit to be low, felt no need to concede to avoid impasse, and therefore made smaller concessions. A later study showed that the inferences that negotiators draw from their counterpart's emotions continue to influence behavior in subsequent encounters with the same person. In a second encounter with an opponent who had previously expressed anger, negotiators conceded again because they believed that the other had ambitious limits, even when that person expressed no emotion during the second encounter (Van Kleef & De Dreu, 2010).

In line with the idea that emotions provide relevant information, research has shown that the tendency of negotiators to concede more to angry opponents than to happy ones is moderated by the extent to which individuals are motivated and able to systematically and deliberately process information during the negotiation. Thus, negotiators with a low dispositional need for cognitive closure, those who were under low time pressure, and those who depended strongly on their counterpart were influenced by their counterpart's expressions of anger versus happiness. In contrast, those with a high need for closure, those who were under high time pressure, and those who did not depend on their counterpart were uninfluenced by the counterpart's emotional expressions (Van Kleef et al., 2004b). Other studies showed that the interpersonal effects of anger and happiness are similarly moderated by power, with low power negotiators being more strongly affected by their counterpart's emotions than high power negotiators (Sinaceur & Tiedens, 2006; Van Dijk, Van Kleef, Steinel, & Van Beest, 2008; Van Kleef, De Dreu, Pietroni, & Manstead, 2006b).

Several other moderators of the interpersonal effects of anger and happiness in negotiations have been identified. Inspired by the classic advice to "separate the people from the problem" (Fisher & Ury, 1981), Steinel, Van Kleef, and Harinck (2008) differentiated between emotions that are directed toward a negotiator's *offer* and emotions that are directed toward the negotiator *as a person*. When emotional statements were directed at the participant's offer, participants used the opponent's emotion to assess his or her limits, and consequently they conceded more to an angry opponent than to a happy one. However, when the emotions were directed at the negotiator as a person, negotiators conceded *less* to an angry opponent than to a happy one. In this case, participants did not find useful information in their opponent's emotions, but instead felt affronted by the angry remarks (see also Lelieveld, Van Dijk, Van Beest, Steinel, & Van Kleef, 2011). Other work has demonstrated that expressions of anger may be effective when they are perceived as appropriate but elicit negative affective reactions and retaliation when they are deemed inappropriate, for instance because they violate a display rule (Van Kleef & Côté, 2007).

Another recent study also illustrates how the social context shapes the perceived appropriateness of emotional expressions and subsequent behavioral responses to those expressions. Adam, Shirako, and Maddux (2010) examined the interpersonal effects of verbal expressions of anger across cultures. They found that European American participants conceded more to angry than to neutral opponents, whereas Asian American participants conceded *less* to angry than to neutral opponents. This reversal could be explained in terms of different cultural norms about the appropriateness of anger expressions in negotiations. Asian American participants deemed expressions of anger inappropriate, and therefore they responded negatively to such expressions.

Relatively few studies have addressed the effects of emotions other than anger and happiness. In one such study, Van Kleef, De Dreu, and Manstead (2006a) found that participants whose opponents expressed guilt or regret developed a positive impression of their opponents but were nonconciliatory in their demands. By contrast, participants whose opponents expressed disappointment or worry rated their opponents less positively, but they made larger concessions. Additional experiments revealed that another's expressions of guilt are interpreted as a sign that the other has claimed too much, whereas disappointment is taken as a signal that the other has received too little. Furthermore, the effects of guilt and disappointment were eliminated when the target had low trust, because lack of trust undermined thorough processing of the implications of the opponent's emotional expressions. Finally, another study revealed that the effects of disappointment on concessions are especially prominent when the perceiver is sensitive to the strategic implications of the other's emotion, namely that his or her personal interests are jeopardized by a looming impasse (Van Kleef & Van Lange, 2008).

In sum, these studies show that expressing emotions can be a powerful influence strategy in negotiation, but success depends on which emotion is expressed under which circumstances. In line with EASI theory, expressions of anger help to elicit concessions when targets are motivated to engage in thorough information processing, because this increases the relative predictive strength of inferential processes compared to affective reactions. Conversely, expressions of anger evoke retaliation when targets deem the anger inappropriate, because this increases the relative predictive strength of affective reactions.

Another area of inquiry that is not traditionally seen as representative of social influence research yet contains the key ingredients of social influence processes is leadership. Leadership refers to the process of influencing others to accomplish a goal (Yukl, 2010). Following a leader shares resemblances with obedience—a special type of compliance that occurs in response to orders by an authority figure (Cialdini & Goldstein, 2004). In the past 20 years, researchers have started to explore the effects of leaders' emotional expressions on followers. Early studies focused on the effects of leader emotional displays on follower ratings of leadership quality (e.g., Glomb & Hulin, 1997) and charisma (Bono &

Ilies, 2006), showing that positive emotional expressions of leaders generally elicit more favorable ratings from followers than negative expressions.

More recently, researchers started to focus on actual follower behavior as a function of leaders' emotional expressions. Sy, Côté, and Saavedra (2005) studied the effects of leader moods on team functioning. They invited groups of participants to the lab and randomly selected one of them to play the role of leader. This person then saw a film clip that induced either a positive or a negative mood. The leader then joined the rest of the group and coached them as they built up a tent together while blindfolded. Teams that were exposed to a leader in a positive mood developed a positive mood themselves, and as a result they exhibited better coordination than teams with a leader in a negative mood. Teams with a leader in a negative mood expended more effort, presumably because they interpreted the leader's negative mood as a signal that performance was unsatisfactory. A potential caveat of this study is that it is unclear whether the mood induction may also have influenced the leader's behavior (an intrapersonal effect), which could in turn have influenced participants' responses—a limitation that is inherent to studying the interpersonal effects of emotions in real social interactions. Later studies circumvented this issue by using alternative procedures.

Van Kleef and colleagues examined the effects of expressions of anger versus happiness by a leader on team performance as a function of followers' information processing motivation (Van Kleef et al., 2009). Four-person teams collaborated on a task, during which they were supposedly observed by their leader via a video camera setup. After a while, the leader (a trained actor) appeared on a video screen and provided standardized feedback and tips to the team, expressing either anger or happiness by means of facial expressions, vocal intonation, and bodily postures. Teams consisting of members with low information processing motivation (measured in terms of need for structure; Neuberg & Newsom, 1993) performed better when the leader expressed happiness, because they experienced positive emotions themselves and developed favorable impressions of the leader. Teams consisting of members with high information processing motivation, in contrast, performed better when the leader expressed anger, because they inferred from the leader's anger that their performance was suboptimal and that they needed to expend more effort.

Another study addressed the moderating role of followers' desire for social harmony, operationalized in terms of individual differences in agreeableness (Van Kleef, Homan, Beersma, & Van Knippenberg, 2010). In a first experiment, participants read a scenario about a leader who expressed anger or no emotion about their performance, with emotion being manipulated via pictures of emotional expressions. Participants high on agreeableness reported lower motivation in the anger condition compared to the neutral condition, while those low on agreeableness reported higher motivation in the anger condition than in the neutral condition. In a second experiment, participants performed a task in four-person teams and they received angry or happy feedback from their leader, as described earlier. Teams consisting of followers with high levels of agreeableness performed better when the leader expressed happiness, while teams consisting of low-agreeable followers performed better when the leader expressed anger. Additional analyses revealed that agreeable followers experienced high levels of stress when confronted with an angry leader, which undermined their performance on the task.

These studies indicate that the emotional expressions of leaders are an important source of influence. Although leaders who express negative emotions such as anger tend to receive poorer evaluations than leaders who express positive emotions, in some cases expressing anger appears to be an effective way to motivate followers and to get them to perform—at least in the short run. In line with the predictions of EASI theory, the effects of leader emotional displays on follower performance are mediated by both affective reactions (emotional contagion and impressions of the leader) and inferential processes (inferences about performance quality), and the relative predictive strength of both processes depends on followers' information processing motivation and their desire for social harmony.

### Emerging Evidence From Research in Classic Domains of Social Influence

Recently, research on the interpersonal effects of emotions has started to address some of the more classic domains of social influence, such as attitude change, compliance, and conformity in groups. Research in this area is still very much in progress, but initial findings are consistent with the basic tenets of EASI theory.

Perhaps the "oldest" documented form of social influence is attitude change (sometimes called persuasion). Attitude change refers to a change in an individual's attitude(s) resulting from exposure to information from others (Olson & Zanna, 1993). Aristotle (350 BC/2004) already advocated the use of emotion in the process of influencing others' attitudes and beliefs. Interestingly, however, until recently theory and research with regard to emotional influences on attitude formation and change have been limited to intrapersonal effects. For instance, one class of models posits that message recipients' affective states influence their processing of persuasive arguments (Petty & Briñol, 2015), with some models postulating that negative affect increases processing and other models suggesting that positive affect increases processing (see Côté, 2005b; Schwarz, Bless, & Bohner, 1991; Wegener et al., 1995). Other relevant accounts maintain that the role of a message recipient's affective state in shaping persuasion is determined by the depth of his or her information processing (e.g., Briñol & Petty, 2009; Forgas, 1995). For instance, Briñol and Petty argued that under high elaboration, information about the source that is presented *after* the persuasive message determines how people weigh their initial reactions to the message. The interpersonal approach advocated by EASI theory is notably different from these perspectives, because it focuses on the effects of the emotional expressions of a source rather than on the emotional state of a recipient.

Building on EASI theory, Van Kleef, Van den Berg, and Heerdink (2015) investigated the interpersonal effects of the emotional expressions of a source on the attitudes of a target. In a first experiment, they investigated attitudes about a popular Dutch television show called *Lingo*. Around the time of the study, there were plans to discontinue the show. Participants read a reaction to these plans from a source in the broadcasting business, which was manipulated to contain verbal expressions of sadness, happiness, or no emotion, while the content of the message was held constant. Participants reported considerably more favorable attitudes toward *Lingo* after reading a sad reaction to the intended discontinuation than after reading a happy reaction. In a second study, the effect was replicated in the context of a different attitude object. In the aftermath of the terrorist attacks of 9/11, plans had been proposed to rebuild identical replicas of the Twin Towers in New York. Shortly before the study was run, these plans were aborted. Participants read a sad, happy, or neutral emotional reaction to the abortion of the replica plans. They reported more favorable attitudes toward the initial plan to rebuild the Twin Towers after reading the sad reaction than after reading the happy reaction.

These patterns suggest that the interpersonal effects of emotional expressions on attitude formation in these studies were driven by inferential processes rather than affective reactions. If affective reactions had been dominant, affect infusion (Forgas, 1995) should have led to more favorable attitudes after seeing happy rather than sad reactions. However, the opposite was found. Presumably, participants inferred from the source's negative emotional reactions to the intended discontinuation of *Lingo* and the abortion of the Twin Tower plans that *Lingo* and the Twin Tower plans were important and should be continued. Indeed, additional studies provided more direct evidence for the role of inferential processes (Van Kleef et al., 2015). For instance, one experiment showed that nonverbal expressions of sadness versus happiness only influenced targets' attitudes when targets had ample cognitive resources available; when they were put under cognitive load, the effect disappeared. This finding suggests that other people's emotional expressions are not processed as peripheral cues but are used as relevant pieces of information upon which to base judgment and behavior provided that sufficient cognitive resources are available.

These studies demonstrate that EASI theory can be meaningfully applied to attitude change. It appears that targets used the emotional expressions of a source as information, which shaped their attitudes about various topics. The effects occurred both for verbal expressions of emotion and for nonverbal expressions of emotion. That these effects were only observed when the target had sufficient cognitive resources suggests that the effects are carried primarily by inferential processes rather than affective reactions. Even though these studies contained no direct measures of information processing, the patterns are consistent with such an interpretation.

Another classic domain of social influence is compliance. Compliance can be defined as "a particular kind of response—acquiescence—to a particular kind of communication—a request" (Cialdini & Goldstein, 2004, p. 592). As is the case for attitude change, most research on emotion and compliance has focused on intrapersonal effects. For example, the experience of emotions such as gratitude (Goei & Boster, 2005), guilt (Carlsmith & Gross, 1969), and embarrassment (Cann & Blackwelder, 1984) has been found to increase compliance. Other research has shown that people in positive moods tend to be more willing to comply with requests than people in

a neutral mood (Carlson et al., 1988; Isen, Clark, & Schwartz, 1976).

Shifting this focus, Van Doorn, Van Kleef, and Van der Pligt (2015) investigated the interpersonal effects of emotional expressions on compliance with requests. In a first experiment, participants read a scenario about a man who expressed anger or disappointment about the fact that several bicycles were blocking the sidewalk, one of which belonged to the participant. Verbal expressions of anger versus disappointment were accompanied by pictures of matching facial expressions. Participants read that the man was moving heavy furniture and asked for help moving the bikes out of the way. Participants indicated that they were willing to move more bikes after the man had expressed disappointment rather than anger.

In a second study, participants were asked to imagine that while out shopping they encountered a charity collector. After the participant had donated a 50-eurocent coin, the charity collector paused in front of the participant, as if he expected an additional donation. Participants were shown a picture of the collector's face, which expressed either anger, disappointment, or no emotion. Participants in the disappointment condition were willing to more than double their initial donation, while those in the neutral and angry conditions did not intend to make an additional donation. In fact, several participants in the anger condition indicated that they wanted to *take back* their initial donation. The difference between the disappointment and anger conditions was mediated by the perceived appropriateness of the charity collector's emotional expression for that situation, which was higher in the case of disappointment than in the case of anger.

A shortcoming of these studies is that they relied on hypothetical scenarios. This limitation was remedied in a third study, in which participants played a computer-mediated donation game with a simulated partner, which involved real behavior (Van Doorn et al., 2015). Participants first made a donation in a practice round. Then they were informed that previous players had on average made either low or high allocations (i.e., a descriptive norm). Then they received a message from their "partner," who asked them to be more generous in the real game than they had been in the trial round. This request was paired with anger or disappointment about the participant's allocation in the trial round, or with no emotion. In the absence of an emotional expression participants conformed to the descriptive norm, giving more or less generously according to what others had given in the past. When the partner had expressed disappointment, participants donated more regardless of the norm; when the partner had expressed anger, participants donated less regardless of the norm. The difference between the anger and disappointment conditions was again mediated by perceived appropriateness.

These studies demonstrate that expressing emotions as part of a request can affect targets' willingness to comply. Interestingly, the predictive value of emotional expressions outweighed that of an explicit descriptive norm, indicating that emotional expressions can be a powerful source of social influence. The studies corroborate the proposition of EASI theory that expressions of anger are more likely to be perceived as inappropriate in cooperative settings (e.g., a request for help) than in competitive settings (e.g., negotiation), and this helps to explain why expressions of anger undermined the effectiveness of a request for help, compared to expressions of disappointment, which were perceived as more appropriate.

A final line of research that has recently emerged aims to understand how emotional expressions shape conformity processes in groups. Conformity refers to the act of changing one's behavior to match the responses of others (Cialdini & Goldstein, 2004). People may publicly accept a majority's position to avoid being ridiculed or ostracized (without necessarily accepting the position in private), or they may privately adopt the group's position because they strive for accuracy and the majority position appears to be correct (Deutsch & Gerard, 1955). There has been very little research on emotion and conformity. Similar to most other areas of social influence, the scarce research that has been conducted has focused exclusively on the intrapersonal effects of moods and emotions. For instance, one study showed that positive moods increase conformity relative to negative moods (Tong, Tan, Latheef, Selamat, & Tan, 2008), presumably due to an increased reliance on the consensus-implies-correctness heuristic.

Heerdink, Van Kleef, Homan, and Fischer (2013) performed a first exploration of the interpersonal effects of anger and happiness on conformity in groups. They reasoned that expressions of anger signal that certain behavior is not tolerated by the group and may be sanctioned. Groups fulfill individuals' need to belong (Baumeister & Leary, 1995), and, as research on ostracism has shown, threatened belongingness is highly aversive and motivates behavior aimed at improving acceptance (Williams,

2007). By conforming to the group norm, the deviant can show that he or she is a "good" group member and thus increase chances of acceptance (Steinel et al., 2010; Van Kleef, Steinel, Van Knippenberg, Hogg, & Svensson, 2007). Happiness, on the other hand, is usually construed as a signal of affiliation (Clark et al., 1996) and acceptance (Cacioppo & Gardner, 1999). Targets of happy expressions can therefore be expected to feel safe in the group and to feel free to be unique and deviate from the group's position, as their behavior is unlikely to compromise their group membership.

In a first study testing these ideas, Heerdink and colleagues (2013) asked participants to recall an incident in which their opinion had differed from that of the majority of the group. After describing the situation, they reported which emotions the majority had shown and how this had made them feel. The more anger the majority had expressed, the more the participant had felt excluded; the more happiness the majority had expressed, the more the participant had felt accepted. These feelings of inclusion versus exclusion in turn predicted the extent to which participants felt pressure to conform to the majority position. Although this critical-incidents procedure yields rich data about actual experiences, it does not enable standardization. In follow-up studies, various standardized manipulations of group members' emotional expressions were employed.

In a second study the majority emotion was manipulated using a scenario. Participants read about a situation in which they were attempting to decide on a holiday destination with three of their friends. It turned out that the three friends all had the same holiday destination in mind, but the participant preferred a different destination. The majority did not agree with the participant's proposal. Depending on the condition, the majority expressed anger, enthusiasm, or no emotion about the situation. Heerdink and colleagues (2013) also manipulated the availability of an alternative group with which participants could go on holiday, reasoning that expressions of anger might prompt conformity in the absence of an alternative, but not in the presence of an alternative. Expressions of anger led to greater feelings of exclusion than expressions of enthusiasm, with neutral expressions falling in between. Feelings of exclusion in turn motivated participants to conform when no alternative group was available, whereas they motivated participants to leave the group when such an alternative was available.

In a third study, Heerdink et al. (2013) explored these mechanisms in the context of a computer-simulated group discussion (see Homan, Greer, Jehn, & Koning, 2010) on aesthetic preferences. In one condition, participants learned that their responses on several questionnaires indicated that they were very prototypical members of the group, meaning that their personality overlapped strongly with the personalities of the other group members. In the other condition they learned that they were rather peripheral members of the group, because their personality structure was different from that of the other group members (Steinel et al., 2010; Van Kleef et al., 2007). Participants then privately rated a number of abstract paintings. To generate discussion, their ratings were supposedly sent to the "other group members," who were preprogrammed to express different preferences than the participant. All group members then sent a few messages to the rest of the group to initiate the discussion. Depending on the condition, participants received messages expressing anger or happiness about their deviating opinion. Then participants rated the paintings for a second time, and this time their ratings could supposedly be seen by the rest of the group. Participants who occupied a peripheral position in their group exhibited conformity after receiving angry reactions, but not after receiving happy reactions. Participants with a prototypical position in the group were not influenced by their group members' emotional expressions, because they experienced little fear of social exclusion and, consequently, little pressure to change their opinion.

These studies indicate that the emotional expressions of group members may be interpreted as signals of future acceptance or exclusion, which in turn influence conformity depending on the security of the target's position in the group and on the extent to which the target depends on the group. As such, these studies provide initial evidence that emotional expressions can provide a means to engender conformity in groups, lending further support to the conceptualization of emotions as agents of social influence.

## Implications and Suggestions for Future Research

We have seen that emotional expressions can engender social influence by triggering inferential processes and/or affective reactions in targets. We have also seen that the consequences of emotional expressions differ widely. In line with EASI theory, the effects of emotional expressions depend on the target's information processing depth and on the perceived appropriateness of the emotional expression. Evidence for the critical role of processing depth stems from moderating influences of personality characteristics such as need for cognitive closure (Van Kleef et al., 2004b) and personal need for structure (Van Kleef et al., 2009; Van Kleef, Anastasopoulou, & Nijstad, 2010), experimental manipulations of time pressure (Van Kleef et al., 2004b) and cognitive load (Van Kleef et al., 2015), and self-report measures of information processing as well as objective measures of time spent processing (Van Kleef et al., 2004b). Support for the role of perceived appropriateness comes from moderating influences of dispositional differences in the desire for social harmony (Van Kleef, Homan, et al., 2010), situational display rules (Van Kleef & Côté, 2007), the cultural context within which the emotion is expressed (Adam et al., 2010), and self-report measures of perceived appropriateness of emotional expressions (Van Doorn et al., 2015; Van Kleef & Côté, 2007).

### Differences and Commonalities Between EASI and Other Theoretical Perspectives

As noted before, the critical distinction between EASI theory and other theoretical perspectives such as the ELM (Petty & Briñol, 2012; Petty & Cacioppo, 1986), the AIM (Forgas, 1995), the affect as information model (Schwarz & Clore, 1983), and the mood as input model (Martin et al., 1993) lies in the level of analysis: With regard to the influence of emotions, EASI is situated at the interpersonal level of analysis, whereas the other models are situated at the intrapersonal level of analysis (Morris & Keltner, 2000). Unique aspects of EASI concern its focus on the effects of a source's emotional expressions (rather than on a recipient's emotional experience); the role of inferential processes and affective reactions triggered by others' emotional expressions; and the moderating role of the perceived appropriateness of emotional expressions. A commonality between EASI theory and several other models (including the ELM and the AIM) is the importance that is attached to the recipient's information processing. Furthermore, the processes specified under "affective reactions" in EASI theory partly overlap with those featured in other models. Thus, to the degree that a source's emotional expressions are picked up by a target (e.g., through emotional contagion), the target could be influenced by some of the processes specified in the ELM and the AIM, as noted earlier in this chapter. Effects of emotional expressions on inferences and concomitant judgments and behavior cannot be accounted for by other models, however. In short, EASI complements existing models with its unique focus on the interpersonal effects of emotions.

## The Emerging View of Emotions as Agents of Social Influence

Research on social influence aims to uncover the processes through which, and the circumstances under which, individuals come to adapt their attitudes, cognitions, and/or behavior to other individuals. Besides an interest in fundamental processes, the social influence literature reveals a strong interest in tactics that can be used deliberately to influence other people. Classic examples are the foot-in-the-door technique (making a small request that is almost certainly granted and then following up with a larger, related request; Freedman & Fraser, 1966) and the door-in-the-face technique (making an extreme request that is likely to get rejected, so that a subsequent smaller request for a truly desired action is more likely to be granted; Cialdini et al., 1975). These strategies rely on individuals' desire for consistency and reciprocity, respectively. Other strategies capitalize more on emotional processes. For instance, "fear appeals" can be used to frighten targets (e.g., by showing pictures of tar lungs to smokers), which may in some circumstances help to establish behavioral change (Rogers, 1983). The theory and findings reviewed here suggest that interpersonal emotional strategies should be added to the social influence toolbox.

Changing the perspective from the observer to the expresser, the foregoing review also indicates, however, that the use of emotional expressions as a strategy of social influence is a delicate endeavor. A particular emotional expression may work in one situation, but not in the next. The effectiveness of emotional expressions depends on which emotion is expressed to whom and under which circumstances. The many contingencies of the effects of emotional expressions in social influence are perhaps best illustrated by research on anger, which is by far the most studied emotion in this context. For instance, expressions of anger may engender attitude change (Van Kleef et al., 2015), but they also undermine compliance with requests (Van Doorn et al., 2015). Expressions of anger by a leader may increase motivation and performance among followers who are high on epistemic motivation and among those who are low on agreeableness, whereas anger undermines motivation and performance of followers low on

epistemic motivation and high on agreeableness (Van Kleef et al., 2009; Van Kleef, Homan, et al., 2010). Expressions of anger may engender conformity in groups when targets depend on the group and/or occupy a peripheral position in it, whereas anger undermines conformity when targets do not depend on the group and/or occupy a central position in the group (Heerdink et al., 2013). Finally, expressions of anger elicit concessions in negotiation when they are deemed appropriate and the target is motivated to consider the implications of the anger, but they backfire when they are perceived as inappropriate and/or the target is not motivated to process the information that the anger conveys (e.g., Steinel et al., 2008; Van Kleef & Côté, 2007; Van Kleef et al., 2004a, 2004b, 2006b).

The insights arising from these studies have obvious practical implications. It is clear that anger can be a powerful instrument of social influence, but it should be used with care. Expressing anger is only likely to have desired effects on targets when a number of conditions are met, as specified in EASI theory. Future research is needed to illuminate whether the effects of other emotional expressions are subject to the same moderating influences as are expressions of anger. When we learn more about the contingencies of the effectiveness of emotional expressions, we can start to consider how emotional expressions can be used in marketing or incorporated in governmental campaigns to promote desired behavior and discourage undesired behavior.

The present review also indicates that using emotional expressions to engender social influence requires adequate emotion regulation. Individuals who understand which emotional expressions work under which circumstances are likely to be more successful at exerting social influence than those who lack such knowledge. Indeed, Côté and Hideg (2011) argued that the ability to influence others by means of emotional displays should be considered a new dimension of emotional intelligence. Importantly, successful emotion regulation requires not just showing the right emotion at the right time but also showing the right emotion in the right way. In one study, participants felt more trust toward and cooperated more with a person who showed an authentic rather than an inauthentic smile (Krumhuber, 2007). In another study, "deep acted" displays of anger (which appear authentic) elicited concessions in negotiation, whereas "surface acted" anger (which appears inauthentic) had the opposite effect (Côté, Hideg, & Van Kleef, 2013). This difference could be explained in terms of lower levels of trust in the latter condition, which may have fueled reactance. Another recent study revealed that individuals with high emotion regulation ability are more successful than their less emotionally able counterparts in achieving their social goals, whether these are benign or malicious (Côté, DeCelles, McCarthy, Van Kleef, & Hideg, 2011). In short, some individuals are better equipped than others to use their emotions as tools of social influence.

### Valence, Discrete Emotions, and Emotion Blends

There is a pervasive tendency in the literature to conceptualize emotions in terms of their positive or negative valence. The foregoing review challenges this practice. Together with a growing body of research on the intrapersonal effects of emotions (e.g., Bodenhausen, Sheppard, & Kramer, 1994; DeSteno, Petty, Wegener, & Rucker, 2000; Fischer & Roseman, 2007; Keltner, Ellsworth, & Edwards, 1993; Lerner & Keltner, 2001; Tiedens & Linton, 2001), the theory and research reviewed here suggest that there is more promise in conceptualizing emotions in terms of their unique appraisal patterns and action tendencies than in terms of their valence. For instance, the "core relational themes" of anger and guilt are other-blame and self-blame, respectively (Smith et al., 1993), which helps to explain why they have opposite effects in negotiations even though both have a negative valence (Van Kleef et al., 2004a, 2006a). Further, the fact that disappointment does not involve assigning blame to another person whereas anger does helps to explain why expressing disappointment is more effective in securing compliance with a request (Van Doorn et al., 2015). Accordingly, future research would do well to measure or manipulate discrete emotions rather than focusing solely on positive or negative valence.

When it comes to discrete emotions, the preceding review also highlights important gaps in our knowledge. Although we are beginning to understand the effects of happiness, anger, sadness, disappointment, guilt, and regret, the effects of many other emotions have yet to be explored. A focus on other discrete emotions is needed to gain a more complete understanding of the role of emotion in social influence. One question that could be addressed in future research is whether different positive emotions (e.g., happiness, pride, gratitude, relief, hope, compassion, awe) have differential effects, as is the case for negative emotions. For example, it seems plausible that in benign situations

positive emotions with an other-focus (e.g., gratitude, compassion, awe) would be more likely to elicit cooperation than positive emotions with a self-focus (e.g., pride).

Without exception, the studies reviewed here have examined the effects of single emotional states and expressions (e.g., "pure" happiness, anger, sadness, or guilt). However, in everyday life individuals often experience "blends" of emotions (Scherer & Tannenbaum, 1986). These blends may even comprise emotions with a different valence. For instance, individuals reported that they simultaneously experienced happiness and sadness on graduation day (Larsen, McGraw, & Cacioppo, 2001). Little is known about the interpersonal effects of mixed emotional displays, but qualitative evidence suggests that the alternating or simultaneous expression of positive and negative emotions can be an effective instrument of social influence. In a classic study, Rafaeli and Sutton (1991) investigated the use of "emotional contrast strategies" as a social influence tactic. They discovered that criminal interrogators and bill collectors often use combinations of expressed positive and negative emotions to elicit compliance in others, a strategy that may be regarded as a variation of the "good cop, bad cop" technique. Such emotional contrast strategies can be effective in exerting social influence, although it is not clear exactly why such strategies are effective. Further exploration of the mechanisms and contingencies of emotional contrast strategies and other forms of mixed emotional expressions is needed to develop a more complete understanding of the interpersonal effects of emotional expressions in social influence.

### Conclusion

My goal for this chapter has been to demonstrate that emotions are powerful tools of social influence. Building on EASI theory (Van Kleef, 2016), I have argued that emotional expressions exert social influence by triggering affective reactions and/or inferential processes in targets, depending on the target's information processing depth and the perceived appropriateness of the emotional expression. I have applied this framework to several domains of social influence, including attitude change, compliance with requests, negotiation, leadership, and conformity in groups. Although emerging evidence from these domains is consistent with EASI theory, more work is needed to establish the generalizability of the theory to other areas of social influence, such as politics and minority influence. Such research would further solidify the emerging conceptualization of emotions as agents of social influence.

## Author's Note

Preparation of this chapter was supported by a grant from the Netherlands Organisation for Scientific Research (NWO 452-09-010).

## References

Adam, H., Shirako, A., & Maddux, W. W. (2010). Cultural variance in the interpersonal effects of anger in negotiations. *Psychological Science*, 21, 882–889.

Aristotle. (350BC/2004). *Rhetoric*. (W. Rhys Roberts, Trans.). New York: Dover.

Bartholow, B. D., Fabiani, M., Gratton, G., & Bettencourt, B. A. (2001). A psychophysiological examination of cognitive processing of and affective responses to social expectancy violations. *Psychological Science*, 12, 197–204.

Baumeister, R. F., & Leary, M. R. (1995). The need to belong: Desire for interpersonal attachments as a fundamental human motivation. *Psychological Bulletin*, 117, 497–529.

Bodenhausen, G. V., Sheppard, L. A., & Kramer, G. P. (1994). Negative affect and social judgment: The differential impact of anger and sadness. *European Journal of Social Psychology*, 24, 45–62.

Bono, J. E., & Ilies, R. (2006). Charisma, positive emotions, and mood contagion. *Leadership Quarterly*, 17, 317–334.

Bower, G. H. (1981). Mood and memory. *American Psychologist*, 36, 129–148.

Briñol, P., & Petty, R. E. (2009). Source factors in persuasion: A self-validation approach. *European Review of Social Psychology*, 20(1), 49–96.

Cacioppo, J. T., & Gardner, W. L. (1999). Emotion. *Annual Review of Psychology*, 50, 191–214.

Cann, A., & Blackwelder, J. G. (1984). Compliance and mood: A field investigation of the impact of embarrassment. *Journal of Psychology: Interdisciplinary and Applied*, 117, 221–226.

Carlsmith, J. M., & Gross, A. E. (1969). Some effects of guilt on compliance. *Journal of Personality and Social Psychology*, 11, 232–239.

Carlson, M., Charlin, V., & Miller, N. (1988). Positive mood and helping behavior: A test of six hypotheses. *Journal of Personality and Social Psychology*, 55, 211–229.

Chaiken, S., & Trope, Y. (Eds.). (1999). *Dual-process theories in social psychology*. New York: Guilford Press.

Cheshin, A. Rafaeli, A., & Bos, N. (2011). Anger and happiness in virtual teams: Emotional influences of text and behavior on others' affect in the absence of non-verbal cues. *Organizational Behavior and Human Decision Processes*, 116, 2–16.

Cialdini, R. B., & Goldstein, N. J. (2004). Social influence: Compliance and conformity. *Annual Review of Psychology*, 55, 591–621.

Cialdini, R. B., Vincent, J. E., Lewis, S. K., Catalan, J., Wheeler, D., & Darby, B. L. (1975). Reciprocal concessions procedure for inducing compliance: The door-in-the-face technique. *Journal of Personality and Social Psychology*, 31, 206–215.

Clark, M. S., Pataki, S. P., & Carver, V. H. (1996). Some thoughts and findings on self-presentation of emotions in relationships. In G. J. O. Fletcher & J. Fitness (Eds.), *Knowledge structures in close relationships: A social psychological approach* (pp. 247–274). Mahwah, NJ: Erlbaum.

Clark, M. S., & Taraban, C. B. (1991). Reactions to and willingness to express emotion in two types of relationships. *Journal of Experimental Social Psychology*, 27, 324–336.

Côté, S. (2005). Reconciling the feelings-as-information and hedonic contingency models of how mood influences systematic information processing. *Journal of Applied Social Psychology*, 35, 1656–1679.

Côté, S., DeCelles, K., McCarthy, J., & Van Kleef, G. A., & Hideg, I. (2011). The Jekyll and Hyde of emotional intelligence: Emotion regulation knowledge facilitates prosocial and interpersonally deviant behavior. *Psychological Science*, 22, 1073–1080.

Côté, S., & Hideg, I. (2011). The ability to influence others via emotion displays: A new dimension of emotional intelligence. *Organizational Psychology Review*, 1, 53–71.

Côté, S., Hideg, I., & Van Kleef, G. A. (2013). The consequences of faking anger in negotiations. *Journal of Experimental Social Psychology*, 49, 453–463.

De Dreu, C. K. W., & Carnevale, P. J. (2003). Motivational bases of information processing and strategy in conflict and negotiation. *Advances in Experimental Social Psychology*, 35, 235–291.

De Dreu, C. K. W., Carnevale, P. J. D., Emans, B. J. M., & Van De Vliert, E. (1994). Effects of gain-loss frames in negotiation: Loss aversion, mismatching, and frame adoption. *Organizational Behavior and Human Decision Processes*, 60, 90–107.

De Dreu, C. K. W., & Van Kleef, G. A. (2004). The influence of power on the information search, impression formation, and demands in negotiation. *Journal of Experimental Social Psychology*, 40, 303–319.

De Houwer, J., Thomas, S., & Baeyens, F. (2001). Associative learning of likes and dislikes: A review of 25 years of research on human evaluative conditioning. *Psychological Bulletin*, 127, 853–869.

DeSteno, D., Petty, R., Wegener, D. T., & Rucker, D. D. (2000). Beyond valence in the perception of likelihood: The role of emotion specificity. *Journal of Personality and Social Psychology*, 78, 397–416.

Deutsch, M., & Gerard, H. B. (1955). A study of normative and informational social influences upon individual judgment. *Journal of Abnormal and Social Psychology*, 51, 629–636.

Eagly, A., & Chaiken, S. (1993). *The psychology of attitudes*. New York: Harcourt Brace Jovanovich.

Ekman, P. (1993). Facial expression and emotion. *American Psychologist*, 48, 384–392.

Fischer, A. H., & Manstead, A. S. R. (2008). Social functions of emotion. In M. Lewis, J. Haviland, & L. Feldman Barrett (Eds.), *Handbook of emotion* (3rd ed., pp. 456–468). New York: Guilford Press.

Fischer, A. H., & Roseman, I. J. (2007). Beat them or ban them: The characteristics and social functions of anger and contempt. *Journal of Personality and Social Psychology*, 93, 103–115.

Fischer, A. H., & Van Kleef, G. A. (2010). Where have all the people gone? A plea for including social interaction in emotion research. *Emotion Review*, 2, 208–211.

Fisher, R., & Ury, W. (1981). *Getting to yes*. New York: Penguin.

Fiske, S. T., & Dépret, E. (1996). Control, interdependence, and power: Understanding social cognition in its social context. In W. Stroebe & M. Hewstone (Eds.), *European review of social psychology* (Vol. 7, pp. 31–61). Chichester, UK: Wiley.

Fitness, J. (2000). Anger in the workplace: An emotion script approach to anger episodes between workers and their superiors, co-workers and subordinates. *Journal of Organizational Behavior*, 21, 147–162.

Forgas, J. P. (1995). Mood and judgment: The affect infusion model (AIM). *Psychological Bulletin*, 117, 39–66.

Frank, R. H. (1988). *Passions within reason: The strategic role of the emotions*. New York: Norton.

Freedman, J. L., & Fraser, S. C. (1966). Compliance without pressure. The foot-in-the-door technique. *Journal of Personality and Social Psychology*, 4, 195–202.

Fridlund, A. J. (1994). *Human facial expression: An evolutionary view*. San Diego, CA: Academic Press.

Friedman, R., Anderson, C., Brett, J., Olekalns, M., Goates, N., & Lisco, C. C. (2004). The positive and negative effects of anger on dispute resolution: Evidence from electronically mediated disputes. *Journal of Applied Psychology*, 89, 369–376.

Frijda, N. H. (1986). *The emotions*. Cambridge, UK: Cambridge University Press.

Frijda, N. H. (1994). Varieties of affect: Emotions and episodes, moods, and sentiments. In P. Ekman & R. J. Davidson (Eds.), *The nature of emotion: Fundamental questions* (pp. 59–67). New York: Oxford University Press.

Frijda, N. H., & Mesquita, B. (1994). The social roles and functions of emotions. In S. Kitayama & H. S. Markus (Eds.), *Emotion and culture: Empirical studies of mutual influence* (pp. 51–87). Washington, DC: American Psychological Association.

Glomb, T. M., & Hulin, C. L. (1997). Anger and gender effects in observed supervisor-subordinate dyadic interactions. *Organizational Behavior and Human Decision Processes*, 72, 281–307.

Goei, R., & Boster, F. J. (2005). The roles of obligation and gratitude in explaining the effects of favors on compliance. *Communication Monographs*, 72, 284–300.

Graziano, W. G., Jensen-Campbell, L. A., & Hair, E. C. (1996). Perceiving interpersonal conflict and reacting to it: The case for agreeableness. *Journal of Personality and Social Psychology*, 70, 820–835.

Hamilton, D. L., & Sherman, S. J. (1996). Perceiving persons and groups. *Psychological Review*, 103, 336–355.

Hareli, S., & Hess, U. (2010). What emotional reactions can tell us about the nature of others: An appraisal perspective on person perception. *Cognition and Emotion*, 24, 128–140.

Hareli, S., & Rafaeli, A. (2008). Emotion cycles: On the social influence of emotion. *Research in Organizational Behavior*, 28, 35–59.

Hatfield, E., Cacioppo, J. T., & Rapson, R. L. (1994). *Emotional contagion*. New York: Cambridge University Press.

Heerdink, M. W., Van Kleef, G. A., Homan, A. C., & Fischer, A. H. (2013). On the social influence of emotions in groups: Interpersonal effects of anger and happiness on conformity versus deviance. *Journal of Personality and Social Psychology*, 105, 262–284.

Hess, U., & Blairy, S. (2001). Facial mimicry and emotional contagion to dynamic emotional facial expressions and their influence on decoding accuracy. *International Journal of Psychophysiology*, 40, 129–141.

Hess, U., Blairy, S., & Kleck, R. E. (2000). The influence of facial emotion displays, gender, and ethnicity on judgments of dominance and affiliation. *Journal of Nonverbal Behavior*, 24, 265–283.

Homan, A. C., Greer, L. L., Jehn, K. A., & Koning, L. (2010). Believing shapes seeing: The impact of diversity beliefs on the construal of group composition. *Group Processes and Intergroup Relations*, 13, 477–493.

Homan, A. C., Hollenbeck, J. R., Humphrey, S. E., van Knippenberg, D., Ilgen, D. R., & Van Kleef, G. A. (2008). Facing differences with an open mind: Openness to experience, salience of intra-group differences, and performance of diverse work groups. *Academy of Management Journal*, 51, 1204–1222.

Isen, A. M., Clark, M., & Schwartz, M. F. (1976). Duration of the effects of good mood on helping: "Footprints on the sands of time." *Journal of Personality and Social Psychology*, 34, 385–393.

Isen, A. M., Shalker, T. E., Clark, M., & Karp, L. (1978). Affect, accessibility of material in memory, and behavior: A cognitive loop? *Journal of Personality and Social Psychology*, 36, 1–12.

Keltner, D., Ellsworth, P. C., & Edwards, K. (1993). Beyond simple pessimism: Effects of sadness and anger on social perception. *Journal of Personality and Social Psychology*, 64, 740–752.

Keltner, D., & Haidt, J. (1999). Social functions of emotions at four levels of analysis. *Cognition and Emotion*, 13, 505–521.

Keltner, D., Van Kleef, G. A., Chen, S., & Kraus, M. (2008). A reciprocal influence model of social power: Emerging principles and lines of inquiry. *Advances in Experimental Social Psychology*, 40, 151–192.

Kitayama, S., Mesquita, B., & Karasawa, M. (2006). Cultural affordances and emotional experience: Socially engaging and disengaging emotions in Japan and the United States. *Journal of Personality and Social Psychology*, 91, 890–903.

Klinnert, M., Campos, J., Sorce, J., Emde, R., & Svejda, M. (1983). Emotions as behavior regulators: Social referencing in infants. In R. Plutchik & H. Kellerman (Eds.), *Emotion theory, research, and experience* (Vol. 2, pp. 57–68). New York: Academic Press.

Knutson, B. (1996). Facial expressions of emotion influence interpersonal trait inferences. *Journal of Nonverbal Behavior*, 20, 165–182.

Kruglanski, A. W. (1989). *Lay epistemics and human knowledge: Cognitive and motivational bases*. New York: Plenum.

Kruglanski, A. W., & Webster, D. M. (1991). Group members' reactions to opinion deviates and conformists at varying degrees of proximity to decision deadline and of environmental noise. *Journal of Personality and Social Psychology*, 61, 212–225.

Kruglanski, A. W., & Webster, D. M. (1996). Motivated closing of the mind: "Seizing" and "freezing." *Psychological Review*, 103, 263–283.

Krumhuber, E., Manstead, A. S. R., Cosker, D., Marshall, D., Rosin, P. L., & Kappas, A. (2007). Facial dynamics as indicators of trustworthiness and cooperative behavior. *Emotion*, 7, 730–735.

Larsen, J. T., McGraw, A. P., & Cacioppo, J. (2001). Can people feel happy and sad at the same time? *Journal of Personality and Social Psychology*, 81, 684–696.

Lazarus, R. S. (1991). *Emotion and adaptation*. New York: Oxford University Press.

Lelieveld, G-J., Van Dijk, E., Van Beest, I., Steinel, W., & Van Kleef, G. A. (2011). Disappointed in you, angry about your offer: Distinct negative emotions induce concessions via different mechanisms. *Journal of Experimental Social Psychology, 47,* 635–641.

Lerner, J. S., & Keltner, D. (2001). Fear, anger, and risk. *Journal of Personality and Social Psychology, 81,* 146–159.

Levenson, R. W., Ekman, P., & Friesen, W. V. (1990). Voluntary facial action generates emotion-specific autonomic nervous system activity. *Psychophysiology, 27,* 363–384.

Manstead, A. S. R., & Fischer, A. H. (2001). Social appraisal: The social world as object of and influence on appraisal processes. In K. R. Scherer, A. Schorr, & T. Johnstone (Eds.), *Appraisal processes in emotion: Theory, research, application* (pp. 221–232). New York: Oxford University Press.

Manstead, A. S. R., & Tetlock, P. E. (1989). Cognitive appraisals and emotional experience: Further evidence. *Cognition and Emotion, 3,* 225–239.

Markus, H. R., & Kitayama, S. (1991). Culture and the self: Implications for cognition, emotion, and motivation. *Psychological Review, 98,* 224–253.

Martin, L. L., Ward, D. W., Achee, J. W., & Wyer, R. S. (1993). Mood as input: People have to interpret the motivational implications of their moods. *Journal of Personality and Social Psychology, 64,* 317–326.

McCrae, R. R., & Costa, P. T., Jr. (1987). Validation of the five-factor model of personality across instruments and observers. *Journal of Personality and Social Psychology, 52,* 81–90.

Morris, M. W., & Keltner, D. (2000). How emotions work: An analysis of the social functions of emotional expression in negotiations. *Research in Organizational Behavior, 22,* 1–50.

Neuberg, S. L., & Newsom, J. T. (1993). Personal need for structure: Individual differences in the desire for simpler structure. *Journal of Personality and Social Psychology, 65,* 113–131.

Neumann, R., & Strack, F. (2000). "Mood contagion": The automatic transfer of mood between persons. *Journal of Personality and Social Psychology, 79,* 211–223.

Oatley, K., & Jenkins, J. M. (1992). Human emotions: Function and dysfunction. *Annual Review of Psychology, 43,* 55–85.

Olson, J. M., Roese, N. J., & Zanna, M. P. (1996). Expectancies. In E. T. Higgins & A. W. Kruglanski (Eds.), *Social psychology: Handbook of basic principles* (pp. 211–238). New York: Guilford Press.

Olson, J. M., & Zanna, M. P. (1993). Attitudes and attitude change. *Annual Review of Psychology, 44,* 117–154.

Parkinson, B. (1996). Emotions are social. *British Journal of Psychology, 87,* 663–683.

Petty, R. E., & Briñol, P. (2012). The Elaboration Likelihood Model: Three decades of research. In P. A. M. van Lange, A. Kruglanski, & E. T. Higgins (Eds.), *Handbook of theories of social psychology* (pp. 224–245). London: Sage.

Petty, R. E., & Briñol, P. (2015). Emotion and persuasion: Cognitive and meta-cognitive processes impact attitudes. *Cognition and Emotion, 29,* 1–26.

Petty, R. E., & Cacioppo, J. T. (1986). The elaboration likelihood model of persuasion. *Advances in Experimental Social Psychology, 19,* 123–205.

Porath, C. L., Overbeck, J., & Pearson, C. M. (2008). Picking up the gauntlet: How individuals respond to status challenges. *Journal of Applied Social Psychology, 38,* 1945–1980.

Pruitt, D. G., & Carnevale, P. J. (1993). *Negotiation in social conflict.* Buckingham, UK: Open University Press.

Rafaeli, A., & Sutton, R. I. (1987). Expression of emotion as part of the work role. *Academy of Management Review, 12,* 23–37.

Rafaeli, A., & Sutton, R. I. (1991). Emotional contrast strategies as means of social influence: Lessons from criminal interrogators and bill collectors. *Academy of Management Journal, 34,* 749–775.

Rogers, R. W. (1983). Cognitive and physiological processes in fear appeals and attitude change: A revised theory of protection motivation. In J. T. Cacioppo & R. E. Petty (Eds.), *Social psychophysiology: A sourcebook* (pp. 153–176). New York: Guilford Press.

Roseman, I. J. (1984). Cognitive determinants of emotion: A structural theory. In P. Shaver (Ed.), *Review of personality and social psychology* (Vol. 5, pp. 11–36). Beverly Hills, CA: Sage.

Schaller, M., & Cialdini, R. B. (1988). The economics of empathic helping: Support for a mood management motive. *Journal of Experimental Social Psychology, 24,* 163–181.

Scherer, K. R., Schorr, A., & Johnstone, T. (Eds.). (2001). *Appraisal processes in emotion: Theory, methods, research.* New York: Oxford University Press.

Scherer, K. R., & Tannenbaum, P. H. (1986). Emotional experiences in everyday life: A survey approach. *Motivation and Emotion, 10,* 295–314.

Schwarz, N., Bless, H., & Bohner, G. (1991). Mood and persuasion: Affective states influence the processing of persuasive communications. *Advances in Experimental Social Psychology, 24,* 161–199.

Schwarz, N., & Clore, G. L. (1983). Mood, misattribution, and judgments of well-being: Informative and directive functions of affective states. *Journal of Personality and Social Psychology, 45,* 513–523.

Shields, S. A. (2005). The politics of emotion in everyday life: "Appropriate" emotion and claims on identity. *Review of General Psychology, 9,* 3–15.

Sinaceur, M., & Tiedens, L. Z. (2006). Get mad and get more than even: When and why anger expression is effective in negotiations. *Journal of Experimental Social Psychology, 42,* 314–322.

Smith, C. A., Haynes, K. N., Lazarus, R. S., & Pope, L. K. (1993). In search of the "hot" cognitions: Attributions, appraisals, and their relation to emotion. *Journal of Personality and Social Psychology, 65,* 916–929.

Steinel, W., Van Kleef, G. A., & Harinck, F. (2008). Are you talking to me?! Separating the people from the problem when expressing emotions in negotiation. *Journal of Experimental Social Psychology, 44,* 362–369.

Steinel, W., Van Kleef, G. A., Van Knippenberg, D., Hogg, M. A., Homan, A. C., & Moffit, G. (2010). How intragroup dynamics affect behavior in intergroup conflict: The role of group norms, prototypicality, and need to belong. *Group Processes and Intergroup Relations, 13,* 779–794.

Stern, L. D., Marrs, S., Millar, M. G., & Cole, E. (1984). Processing time and the recall of inconsistent and consistent behaviors of individuals and groups. *Journal of Personality and Social Psychology, 47,* 253–262.

Suls, J., Martin, R., & David, J. P. (1998). Person-environment fit and its limits: Agreeableness, neuroticism, and emotional reactivity to interpersonal conflict. *Personality and Social Psychology Bulletin, 24,* 88–98.

Sy, T., Côté, S., & Saavedra, R. (2005). The contagious leader: Impact of the leader's mood on the mood of group members, group affective tone, and group processes. *Journal of Applied Psychology, 90,* 295–305.

Tetlock, P. E. (1992). The impact of accountability on judgment and choice: Toward a social contingency model. *Advances in Experimental Social Psychology, 25,* 331–376.

Tiedens, L. Z., & Linton, S. (2001). Judgment under emotional certainty and uncertainty: The effects of specific emotions on information processing. *Journal of Personality and Social Psychology*, 81, 973–988.

Tong, E. M. W., Tan, C. R. M., Latheef, N. A., Selamat, M. F. B., & Tan, D. K. B. (2008). Conformity: Moods matter. *European Journal of Social Psychology*, 38, 601–611.

Van Dijk, E., Van Kleef, G. A., Steinel, W., & Van Beest, I. (2008). A social functional approach to emotions in bargaining: When communicating anger pays and when it backfires. *Journal of Personality and Social Psychology*, 94, 600–614.

Van Doorn, E. A., Heerdink, M. W., & Van Kleef, G. A. (2012). Emotion and the construal of social situations: Inferences of cooperation versus competition from expressions of anger, happiness, and disappointment. *Cognition and Emotion*, 26, 442–461.

Van Doorn, E. A., Van Kleef, G. A., & Van der Pligt, J. (2015). How emotional expressions shape prosocial behavior: Interpersonal effects of anger and disappointment on compliance with requests. *Motivation and Emotion*, 39, 128–141.

Van Kleef, G. A. (2009). How emotions regulate social life: The emotions as social information (EASI) model. *Current Directions in Psychological Science*, 18, 184–188.

Van Kleef, G. A. (2016). The interpersonal dynamics of emotion: Toward an integrative theory of emotions as social information. Cambridge, UK: Cambridge University Press.

Van Kleef, G. A., Anastasopoulou, C., & Nijstad, B. A. (2010). Can expressions of anger enhance creativity? A test of the emotions as social information (EASI) model. *Journal of Experimental Social Psychology*, 46, 1042–1048.

Van Kleef, G. A., & Côté, S. (2007). Expressing anger in conflict: When it helps and when it hurts. *Journal of Applied Psychology*, 92, 1557–1569.

Van Kleef, G. A., & De Dreu, C. K. W. (2010). Longer-term consequences of anger expression in negotiation: Retaliation or spill-over? *Journal of Experimental Social Psychology*, 46, 753–760.

Van Kleef, G. A., De Dreu, C. K. W., & Manstead, A. S. R. (2004a). The interpersonal effects of anger and happiness in negotiations. *Journal of Personality and Social Psychology*, 86, 57–76.

Van Kleef, G. A., De Dreu, C. K. W., & Manstead, A. S. R. (2004b). The interpersonal effects of emotions in negotiations: A motivated information processing approach. *Journal of Personality and Social Psychology*, 87, 510–528.

Van Kleef, G. A., De Dreu, C. K. W., & Manstead, A. S. R. (2006a). Supplication and appeasement in conflict and negotiation: The interpersonal effects of disappointment, worry, guilt, and regret. *Journal of Personality and Social Psychology*, 91, 124–142.

Van Kleef, G. A., De Dreu, C. K. W., & Manstead, A. S. R. (2010). An interpersonal approach to emotion in social decision making: The emotions as social information model. *Advances in Experimental Social Psychology*, 42, 45–96.

Van Kleef, G. A., De Dreu, C. K. W., Pietroni, D., & Manstead, A. S. R. (2006b). Power and emotion in negotiation: Power moderates the interpersonal effects of anger and happiness on concession making. *European Journal of Social Psychology*, 36, 557–581.

Van Kleef, G. A., Homan, A. C., Beersma, B., & van Knippenberg, D. (2010). On angry leaders and agreeable followers: How leader emotion and follower personality shape motivation and team performance. *Psychological Science*, 21, 1827–1834.

Van Kleef, G. A., Homan, A. C., Beersma, B., van Knippenberg, D., van Knippenberg, B., & Damen, F. (2009). Searing sentiment or cold calculation? The effects of leader emotional displays on team performance depend on follower epistemic motivation. *Academy of Management Journal*, 52, 562–580.

Van Kleef, G. A., Homan, A. C., & Cheshin, A. (2012). Emotional influence at work: Take it EASI. *Organizational Psychology Review*, 2, 311–339.

Van Kleef, G. A., Steinel, W., Van Knippenberg, D., Hogg, M., & Svensson, A. (2007). Group member prototypicality and intergroup negotiation: How one's standing in the group affects negotiation behaviour. *British Journal of Social Psychology*, 46, 129–154.

Van Kleef, G. A., Van den Berg, H., & Heerdink, M. W. (2015). The persuasive power of emotions: Effects of emotional expressions on attitude formation and change. *Journal of Applied Psychology*, 100, 1124–1142.

Van Kleef, G. A., Van Doorn, E. A., Heerdink, M. W., & Koning, L. F. (2011). Emotion is for influence. *European Review of Social Psychology*, 22, 114–163.

Van Kleef, G. A., & Van Lange, P. A. M. (2008). What other's disappointment may do to selfish people: Emotion and social value orientation in a negotiation context. *Personality and Social Psychology Bulletin*, 34, 1084–1095.

Webster, D. M., & Kruglanski, A. W. (1994). Individual differences in need for cognitive closure. *Journal of Personality and Social Psychology*, 67, 1049–1062.

Webster, D. M., Richter, L., & Kruglanski, A. W. (1996). On leaping to conclusions when feeling tired: Mental fatigue effects on impressional primacy. *Journal of Experimental Social Psychology*, 32, 181–195.

Wegener, D. T., & Petty, R. E. (1994). Mood management across affective states: The hedonic contingency hypothesis. *Journal of Personality and Social Psychology*, 66, 1034–1048.

Wegener, D. T., Petty, R. E., & Smith, S. M. (1995). Positive mood can increase or decrease message scrutiny: The hedonic contingency view of mood and message processing. *Journal of Personality and Social Psychology*, 69, 5–15.

Wild, B., Erb, M., & Bartels, M. (2001). Are emotions contagious? Evoked emotions while viewing emotionally expressive faces: Quality, quantity, time course, and gender differences. *Psychiatry Research*, 102, 109–124.

Williams, K. D. (2007). Ostracism. *Annual Review of Psychology*, 58, 425–452.

Yukl, G. A. (2010). *Leadership in organizations* (7th ed.). Upper Saddle River, NJ: Pearson.

# PART 4

# Intragroup Processes

# Social Identity and Social Influence

Amber M. Gaffney *and* Michael A. Hogg

## Abstract

Sitting at the heart of social influence is the relationship of the influencer to the target of influence. Whereas influence can and does occur on an interpersonal level, it often flows from other group members. Social categorizations both within and between groups are paramount in this process, and the dissemination of group norms is the mechanism through which influence occurs in groups. This chapter examines social influence within and between groups, placing self-categorization processes at the center of this analysis. We provide an overview of social influence within and between groups and explore group-based motivations for influence, highlighting leadership, extremist group factions, political movements, and social movements as examples of social influence occurring in a group context. In addition, we examine social context as well as motivational factors for identifying with and accepting group norms.

**Key Words:** social identity, self-categorization, social influence, group processes, norms

The self-identified Islamic State (IS) arose in war-ravaged Syria, a country where an estimated 2.5 million citizens have fled to neighboring countries (syrianrefugees.eu, 2014) and roughly 11 million people are displaced. This organization has rapidly spread to Iraq, intent on enacting an Islamic state and gaining religious and political control of all Muslims. The IS formed in a time of political, religious, and humanitarian crisis. Its self-imposed name change was a conscious attempt to declare a caliphate—an Islamic state for all Muslims. The name change also demonstrates an attempt to encompass something larger than a movement in Syria—this is a movement that can (and does) claim members worldwide, through broadening the physical boundary of the IS but also by giving a very clear and simple identity for its followers: an Islamic State.

Belonging to a group establishes an individual's social identity, and group membership provides a sense of shared belonging and understanding of the self with respect to the group. The benefits of group membership go beyond providing an understanding of similar others (ingroup members) and different others (outgroup members) to defining the individual in terms of the group—that is, the group's norms provide a path for individual members to understand their places both within the group and in the world at large. For people experiencing uncertainty, whether from societal upheaval or from personal struggle, turning to a group with clear norms and distinct boundaries is an effective means for organizing the world into a more certain place (Hogg, 2012). When people claim group membership and identify strongly with a group, they take on the attitudes, behaviors, and norms of the group as their own (Hogg & Turner, 1987). As a result, social influence occurs through a process of categorization of the self as group member.

In this chapter, we provide an account of social influence as it relates to group memberships and social identity. We focus on the social informative nature of norms and when and why group members adhere to their group's norms and when they resist and defy them. Ingroup members, both those occupying central roles within the group and those on the fringes of the group fulfill powerful roles in social influence. Our analysis considers these positions by examining the important role of social context in norm development and social change.

## Social Influence

The study of social influence includes myriad social psychological phenomena, including leadership and followership, minority influence, polarization, attitude change, compliance, and conformity. Whereas individuals influence other individuals, people often make decisions based on the norms and values of their important group memberships. For example, political party identification is by far the largest predictor of voting behavior, including selection of both candidates and issues/measures (see Campbell, Converse, Miller, & Stokes, 1960). It is not presumptive to assume that a proud Democrat voted for Obama in 2012. A single individual was not likely responsible for pressuring the Democrat to vote for Obama—being a Democrat and the knowledge of how fellow Democrats voted were large factors in that person's support for Obama.

While different typologies of social influence define either nuanced differences or outline different routes to influence, they share the common component of relying on others for information on how to act, feel, and respond to social situations. For example, Kelman (1958) identified three forms or responses to social influence: compliance (publically agreeing with a source, but not private acceptance); identification (agreeing with the position of an admired source); and internalization (both publically agreeing with a source and privately accepting that position). Furthermore, Nail (1986) compiled a comprehensive model to systematize the study of influence, accounting for five responses to influence which vary in degree and type of acceptance or denial of influence attempts.

Deutsch and Gerard (1955) outlined the distinction between influence occurring as a result of a need to garner accurate information (informational influence) and a need to fit in (normative influence). These two types of influence need not be competitive or mutually exclusive; in fact, at the core of each is the *social* component of social influence: the relationship of the target to the source. Importantly, the source of influence is often a collection of people; the target's relationship to the group rests upon the extent to which the target identifies as a member of that group.

Many approaches to the study of social influence abide by a two-process dependency model, which makes a distinction between informational and normative influences (Deutsch & Gerard, 1955). Under informational influence, people turn to others for specific information, and as such they change their attitudes to be correct. Under normative influence, people change their attitudes to go along with others and to resist censure. In general, normative influence produces compliance, whereas informational influence produces real change or conversion (see also Nail, 1986, for a summary of compliance and conversion as responses to influence).

Social psychologists have traditionally examined these processes at an interpersonal level, considering how source characteristics such as power (e.g., Raven, 1993), status and trustworthiness (e.g., Hovland, Janis, & Kelley, 1953), and obedience to authority (Milgram, 1963, 1974) produce influence. This interpersonal approach focuses on the relationship between the individual target and the individual influencer, but influence occurs within a group context as well; thus, accounting for group memberships and group identification allows for a broader study of social influence.

## Social Identity and Self-Categorization

The extent to which a group has the ability to exert influence depends on the target's relationship to the group. Social identity theory (Tajfel & Turner, 1979) provides an account of how the self is constructed with respect to group affiliations, encompassing both intragroup and intergroup phenomena. Social identity is the evaluative part of the self-concept through which people define themselves in terms of what their group is (the ingroup) and what their group is not (the outgroup) (Tajfel, 1972; Tajfel & Turner, 1979; see also Abrams & Hogg, 2010; Hogg, 2006)—that is, in terms of group *prototypicality*. Prototypes are cognitive representations of the features that best define a group, both in terms of ingroup norms as well as the attributes that make it distinct from relevant outgroups (see Tajfel, 1959, 1969). Thus, prototypicality refers to the extent to which group members approximate their ingroup prototype.

Social identification occurs through processes of self and social categorization (Turner, Hogg, Oakes, Reicher, & Wetherell, 1987). When group membership becomes salient, people depersonalize their identities, viewing themselves and others in terms of prototypes, which prescribe what it means to be a member of the ingroup. This process creates a sense of intersubjectivity—the ability to feel as another group member feels. For example, when an ingroup member feels pain or even embarrassment, people can vicariously experience these feelings and will change their own cognitions in an attempt to assuage this discomfort (e.g., Cooper & Hogg, 2007). Depersonalization occurs between groups as well, such that outgroup members are viewed not as unique individuals but as representatives of the outgroup prototype (e.g., Hogg, 2006).

Group members determine prototypicality using the *metacontrast* principle, in which group attributes become prototypical to the extent that they maximize intergroup distinction and minimize intragroup variation (Turner et al., 1987). Hogg, Turner, and David (1990) computed ingroup prototypicality using the metacontrast ratio: the average similarity of ingroup members' positions to outgroup members' positions. This provides a mathematical computation of metacontrast; however, this is a dynamic process, which responds to the changing nature of ingroup prototypes with respect to outgroups.

Group members conform to prototypes because they provide invaluable information about their ingroup and thus themselves (see Hogg & Turner, 1987). Hence, prototypes prescribe thoughts, feelings, and behaviors of group members. Prototypicality is context specific, changing with a dynamic social context. For example, the Democrat from the earlier example might think of Democrats as a very liberal political party when thinking about how Democrats *differ* from Republicans. People seek to view their ingroup both favorably and distinct from relevant outgroups; thus. in comparison to Republicans, Democrats view their group as more liberal than when they think about how they personally relate to other Democrats.

### Referent Informational Influence

People who identify strongly with their ingroup accept group norms as personal standards, because norms provide invaluable information about the ingroup and thus the self (e.g., Hogg & Gaffney, 2014). Research on self-categorization and influence suggests that ingroups create both informational and normative influence (see Hogg & Turner, 1987; Turner, 1991). For example, Christensen, Rothgerber, Wood, and Matz (2004) demonstrated that student participants were unconcerned about violating a norm that merely described students at their university; however, students who violated a norm that outlined appropriate behavior of students at their university reported less positive emotions, highlighting a basic difference between accepting information purely based on information and accepting behavior that delineates normative fit with the group. When students were provided the same information about the norms in a context where both types of norms distinguished them from students at a rival school, participants reported negative emotions in both conditions.

Individual group members' convergence on the ingroup prototype occurs through comparison of self to the ingroup prototype. Social comparison is a fundamental component of social influence within groups, because social comparison along an opinion-based dimension holds a strong normative component. Aligning the self with a subjective attitude that is socially grounding tethers a person's own position to that of a group (Crano & Hannula-Bral, 1994, Pérez & Mugny, 1996). Social comparison plays a direct role in the self-categorization approach to social influence (see Turner, 1985; Turner et al., 1987) and more broadly in the social identity analysis of intergroup relations (see Tajfel & Turner, 1979). Festinger's social comparison theory (Festinger, 1954a, b; Suls & Wheeler, this volume) outlines the basic principles of social comparison in an interpersonal setting, but the theory is easily extrapolated to explain social comparison within and between groups (Hogg, 2000a; Hogg & Gaffney, 2014).

People are motivated to understand themselves and the world around them. When they cannot adequately assess the veracity of their own opinions and the extent of their own abilities through objective means, they turn to similar others. The actions and opinions of others are informative because they often tell us the correct path to take or they outline where our abilities stand in relation to others. Festinger (1954a) posited that humans frequently choose similar others as a comparison source because they (as opposed to different others) provide greater information about the self and what a person can hope to accomplish or the level at which the person might actually perform. Comparison with similar others creates a pressure toward uniformity within groups (Festinger, 1954a), because people actively strive to reduce discrepancies between their own opinions and abilities and that of those to whom they are comparing. Group members can achieve this by either changing themselves or by changing similar others.

Tajfel (1972) expanded Festinger's work explicitly to intergroup comparisons as a key component of social identity theory. Social comparison between groups allows for intergroup distinction—a separation of the ingroup from a relevant outgroup (Tajfel, 1972; Tajfel & Turner, 1979; Turner, 1975). Intergroup comparisons allow ingroup members to clearly define group boundaries and, in some cases, maintain or achieve a positive social identity through favorable comparisons to outgroups.

Self-categorization theory (Turner et al., 1987) places intergroup and intragroup comparisons at the heart of social influence (Turner, 1991; Turner, Brown, & Tajfel, 1979). Interpreting and enacting norms are crucial to the group experience and define social influence in groups. As highlighted earlier, group members can achieve metacontrast through social comparison both within (decreasing discrepancies with fellow ingroup members) and between groups (increasing the differences between the ingroup and a relevant outgroup).

It is not always the case that social comparison will create a desire to minimize differences with fellow ingroup members (for a related argument on distinctiveness, see Brewer, 2012). In a context in which the source of comparison is the ingroup (an intragroup context), social comparison might serve to differentiate ingroup factions. Specifically, people can use intragroup comparisons to distinguish themselves from nonprototypical group members or factions. Group members strategically use intergroup and intragroup social comparisons to clarify their identities, whether it means distinguishing the ingroup from a relevant outgroup (i.e., "we are *not* them") or distinguishing factions within the ingroup. Social context dictates the direction of normative acceptance, and other factors, such as uncertainty, can increase the desire for identity clarification, leading to greater acceptance of group attitudes.

Self-categorization theory does not treat movement toward consensus as mere compliance. Through self and social categorization, ingroup attitudes converge through intragroup agreement, which provides validation of group members' attitudes, behaviors, and ultimately self-concepts (Hogg & Turner, 1987). Whereas compliance implies going along with an important reference group for fear of rejection or censure, conformity toward group norms (referent informational influence) refers to accepting ingroup norms as representative of the self. The former does not entail true acceptance of norms, while the latter entails true attitude change and conversion toward the group's prototype. In this analysis, social influence

stemming from the ingroup is both normative and informational because normative cues provide information regarding prototypicality. Support for referent informational influence includes research that demonstrates conformity to ingroup norms in private settings (Hogg & Turner, 1987), evidence of conformity to ingroup norms in Sherif's autokinetic paradigm (Abrams, Wetherell, Cochrane, Hogg, & Turner, 1990), and also the persistence of and adherence to ingroup norms in several historical events (e.g., Reicher, 1984). Because group identification is fundamental to a group's ability to exert influence, contextual factors motivating social identification become prerequisite for understanding when groups create social change.

### Uncertainty-Identity Theory

Contextual factors that predict group identification are important for understanding influence and comparison processes. Social comparison as a means of uncertainty reduction was embedded within Festinger's social comparison theory (1954a, 1954b). When people do not know the extent of their abilities or the correctness of their own opinions, they experience informational uncertainty, and as a result, they turn to others to determine how they fair respectively. Other people are an invaluable source of information when people feel uncertain about how they should act and feel. Indeed, Deutsch and Gerard (1955) found that participants who felt certain about their responses to test questions were less likely to conform to the incorrect responses of others than those subjects who felt uncertain in their own responses. Possessing some amount of uncertainty then, might open people to influence from a valued reference group.

Not all uncertainty is aversive (e.g., Hogg, 2000b), but uncertainties that relate to the self, specifically ones that question the nature of the self, the future, and the ability to successfully navigate life, can create a negative drive state (e.g., van den Bos & Lind, 2002). Uncertainty-identity theory (Hogg, 2000b, 2007a, 2012) posits that group identification is a powerful way to reduce feelings of uncertainty, particularly about a person's own sense of self and identity. Through depersonalization, self-inclusive groups prescribe attitudes and behavior. Empirical research supports uncertainty-identity theory's basic prediction that uncertainty leads to identification with inclusive groups (e.g., Grant & Hogg, 2012) and that uncertainty can be reduced through self-categorization (Mullin & Hogg, 1998). Moreover, uncertainty can lead to ingroup bias (e.g., Grieve & Hogg, 1999; Hogg & Grieve, 1999). Several social psychologists have documented the relationship between uncertainty and group phenomena, highlighting uncertainty as an impetus for supporting cultural institutions (e.g., van den Bos, 2007) and ideological conviction (e.g., Nash, McGregor, & Prentice, 2011). In experimental studies, self-uncertainty is either primed such that participants create a list of the things that make them feel uncertain (e.g., Hohman, Hogg, & Bligh, 2010) or manipulated such that participants perform a task that is meant to make them feel uncertain (e.g., Grieve & Hogg, 1999). Researchers measure self-uncertainty by asking questions which either target a general feeling of uncertainty (e.g., "I am uncertain about the type of person that I am;" Hohman & Hogg, 2015) or target uncertainty intolerance as personality trait (e.g., Sorrentino & Short, 1986).

Groups that have structured norms and are cohesive are particularly attractive when people experience self-uncertainty (Hogg, Sherman, Dierselhuis, Maitner, & Moffitt, 2007). Entitativity is a property that allows a collection of individuals to be perceived as a coherent unit or group (Campbell, 1958). Because groups that are high in entitativity are characterized by cohesiveness, clear and unambiguous norms, well-defined boundaries (i.e., it is clear who is a group member and who is not), and similarity among group members (Hamilton & Sherman, 1996), people assume that such groups and their members are predictable (Rydell & McConnell, 2005). Hogg and colleagues (2007) demonstrated that participants primed to be high in uncertainty increased their identification with their political party, particularly when their party was described as high (but not low) in attributes associated with entitativity.

Many of the processes that occur within and between groups can both cause and alleviate uncertainty, making uncertainty a crucial factor in the study of social influence. This chapter focuses on social identification processes and social influence, outlining how attitudes and behavior are influenced by group memberships and contextual factors that are important to these analyses. Our goal in this chapter is to outline both the purveyors of influence in a group and the situations that open groups to change.

## Leadership

Social identity and self-categorization theories emphasize norms and prototypes in social influence, highlighting group members as a primary source of influence. However, social identity theory does not fully explore the physical vehicle of influence. Which members bring about change? The very nature of leadership implies influence. Leaders can emerge naturally in groups that are not highly organized. For example, a leader will naturally arise in a group of friends that attempts to organize an event, such as a party. In democratic societies, voters formally elect leaders to represent them in government. In other situations, a leader can come into power when a committee or a few individuals holding power within the larger group or nation appoint that person to the position. Regardless of the type of leadership, most leaders enjoy a disproportionate amount of influence in their groups (see Hogg, 2010). They have the ability to enforce, create, and change group norms because of the unique positions they hold in their groups (e.g., Gaffney & Hogg, 2012).

Much of the leadership research is dominated by an individualistic or an interpersonal approach. The former examines the personality characteristics that "make" an individual a leader. This research focuses on characteristics such as charisma (e.g., Avolio & Yammarino, 2003; Bass, 1985) and leadership styles such as transformational leadership (see Antonakis & House, 2003) to demonstrate the qualities that effective leaders possess. Interpersonal work stresses the interpersonal interaction and transaction between leaders and followers (see Hogg, 2010, for a detailed review). While the research examining such characteristics is fruitful for understanding individual qualities and leader–individual follower interactions, in this chapter we focus our analysis on leadership as a social identity process (see also Platow, Haslam, & Reicher, this volume).

The relationship between the leader and followers sets the stage for effective leadership (e.g., Fiedler, 1964, 1967; Thomas, Martin, Epitropaki, Guillaume, & Lee, 2013). A successful leader, one who wields influence and helps the group to achieve its goals, embodies the core elements of the group (Chemers, 2001). In other words, a leader is prototypical of the group (Hogg & van Knippenberg, 2003). People elect and support leaders they believe best embody what it means to be a member of their ingroup. Studying leadership from a group's perspective starts with perceptions and stereotypical representations of leaders, which can lay the foundation for leadership to arise.

Lord's leadership-categorization theory (e.g., Lord, Foti, & DeVader, 1984) focuses on leadership schemas, suggesting that people possess cognitive representations of the traits that they believe leaders possess (e.g., assertiveness, competence). When deciding whether to support a leader, people compare the leader to the schema. If there is sufficient fit between the leader and the schema, they will support the leader.

Leadership-categorization theory suggests the immense challenges that "atypical" or "nontraditional" leaders face when attempting to occupy leadership roles. If the schema to which people compare potential leaders is discrepant from the stereotypes associated with a potential leader's social category (e.g., a woman leader), then occupying this role will be exceptionally difficult (Eagly & Karau, 2002). Stereotypical representations of women, for example, characterize women as warm and incompetent (e.g., Fiske, Xu, Cuddy, & Glick, 1999), which is discrepant from the leader schema. Women who do possess such leadership characteristics tend to be viewed as violating gender roles. In 2008, US voters perceived Hillary Clinton as competent, but lacking warmth—traits associated with men and leadership. However, this perception of lacking warmth predicted voters not voting for Clinton in the Democratic primary election (Gaffney & Blaylock, 2010).

Similarly, expectation states theory or status characterization theory (e.g., Ridgeway, 2003) posits that leadership and influence are a function of group members' perceptions that their leader (or the source of influence) possesses both specific traits that will endow him or her to be successful at a given task and traits that are indicative of high status.

### Social Identity and Leadership

How followers perceive leaders and potential leaders is not only contingent upon the perceived fit of the leader to broad leadership traits and task effectiveness but also on that leader's fit to the ingroup. People compare themselves and fellow ingroup members to their ingroup's prototype to determine normative fit of self and others (e.g., Hogg & Gaffney, 2014). As group identification becomes salient, prototypicality is more important to determining leader effectiveness than broad schemas (e.g., Hains, Hogg, & Duck, 1997; Hogg, Hains, & Mason, 1998).

The social identity theory of leadership (Hogg, 2001, 2008; Hogg & van Knippenberg, 2003) examines leadership as a function of social identification processes. Group members select and deem effective leaders that they believe are prototypical, because prototypical group members best represent the core tenants of their ingroup.

When group membership is salient, prototypical group members become a powerful source of influence (Hogg, 2010). Depersonalization allows people to view ingroup members who approximate the ingroup prototype as an extension of the self and thus people tend to like and be attracted to prototypical ingroup members (see Hogg, 2001). As a result, prototypical group members are a source of conformity, because they best embody what it means to be a member of the ingroup. This endows such members with greater power and influence than less central group members (e.g., Hogg & Reid, 2001). Because group prototypes are consensual, leaders are by and large group members who best represent the ingroup prototype (see Hogg, van Knippenberg, & Rast, 2012, for a review). Sharing a group membership with their leader allows followers to perceive a special bond with their leader, particularly if the leader is prototypical of the ingroup (Steffens, Haslam, & Reicher, 2014).

People tend to trust ingroup members to a greater extent than outgroup members (e.g., Brewer, 1981), particularly those who are prototypical (e.g., Hogg, 2007b). Moreover, appearing prototypical is associated with legitimacy (Platow, Reid, & Andrew, 1998). As a result, ingroup members trust prototypical leaders, even after they fail (e.g., Giessner & van Knippenberg, 2008) and view them as both persuasive and charismatic (e.g., Platow et al., 2006; Steffens et al., 2014).

With all that we bestow upon prototypical leaders, do they deserve it? Research demonstrates that prototypical group members tend to identify with their groups more strongly than less central members (e.g., Hogg et al., 1998), and group identification is positively correlated with enhanced treatment of ingroup goals (see Abrams & Hogg, 2010) and ingroup favoritism (e.g., De Cremer & Tyler, 2005).

Leaders are often the source of influence within a group because people use them to gauge group norms. Given the special positions that leaders occupy within their groups, they are also provided leeway to deviate from group norms (e.g., Abrams, Randsley de Moura, Marques, & Hutchison, 2008). Real-world examples of leaders demonstrate that they have the ability to instigate social change. Steve Jobs, for example, was known for changing Apple into the company that most of us rely on for smartphones, laptops, and tablets. Through design and advertising he changed the identity of Apple.

Obama successfully won the 2008 US presidential election using the platform *Change We Can Believe In*. Obama's 2008 campaign relied heavily on a sense of collective identity, promoting future change.

Abrams and colleagues have deemed a prototypical leader's ability to deviate from group norms "innovation credit" (Abrams et al., 2008). This work importantly shows that group members are more tolerant of a future leader (e.g., "2008 Obama") advocating deviation from the ingroup prototype than a current or past leader. Incumbent leaders might be "bound by an implicit contract of prototypicality" (Abrams et al., 2008, p. 675), which means that deviating from specific norms might be difficult for them, while new leaders might be bestowed belief in their ability to advocate change.

Whereas people usually hold prototypical members to high standards in terms of committing transgressions (Pinto, Marques, Levine, & Abrams, 2010), leaders are given special privileges. People evaluated captains of their net ball and soccer teams more positively after breaking game rules than other team members and opposition when the leader broke the rules (Abrams, Randsley de Moura, & Travaglino, 2013). This work has significant implications for speaking out against leaders who transgress and motivations for not doing so. If a leader defines our group and is acting in the best interest of the group, then we might not question such transgressions.

Leaders have the ability to help us define ourselves in terms of our group (see Hogg, 2010; Hogg et al., 2012). Leaders often communicate social identity through rhetoric, which focuses on transforming and mobilizing the group (Reicher, Haslam, & Hopkins, 2005). Prototypical leaders, because of their influential positions, are entrepreneurs of identity, both crafting and enacting social identity through their rhetoric (Reicher & Hopkins, 2003).

Leaders can use their ability to enact their ingroup's social identity to bridge the boundaries between groups. Nelson Mandela, for example, was able to lead South Africa out of apartheid into National Reconciliation through promoting a "Rainbow Nation." The social identity theory of intergroup leadership (Hogg, 2015; Hogg et al., 2012) posits that leaders can bridge subgroup divides by promoting an identity that encompasses subgroups and is marked by a mutually cooperative relationship (an intergroup relational identity). Successful intergroup leadership must overcome the challenge of threatening subgroup identities through identity embodiment of each faction. Leaders can create a clear identity that defines subgroup relations in such a way that reduces uncertainties that they might have regarding intergroup interactions, allowing for successful intergroup relations.

### Leading Under Uncertainty

Group-based cues that provide identity clarification are particularly attractive under uncertainty (see Gaffney, Rast, Hackett, & Hogg, 2014); thus, leaders who have the ability to clearly define their group and lay forth a clear social identity should be particularly attractive when group members experience uncertainty. Rast, Hogg, and Giessner (2013) showed that among organizational employees, uncertainty was positively correlated with increasing preference for autocratic leaders. In some situations, experiencing uncertainty might promote the "dark side of leadership" (e.g., Rast, Gaffney, & Hogg, 2013), paving the way for authoritarian-type leadership to develop or even extremist leaders to emerge.

By and large the social identity theory of leadership has consistently demonstrated that people prefer leaders who are prototypical; however, this preference might weaken under uncertainty. Rast, Gaffney, Hogg, and Crisp (2012) found that when participants were primed with uncertainty, their preference for a prototypical leader (over a non-protoypical leader) weakened. Presumably, when people experienced uncertainty, they sought out a leader regardless of leader prototypicality—they latched on to ingroup cues rather than cues regarding prototype fit. Similarly, Reid and Hogg (2005) found that when people experience uncertainty, they identify with low-status groups as strongly as with high-status groups—a finding that further illustrates the intricate nature of the relationship between uncertainty and support for the status quo. In some cases then, when people feel uncertain, they look for a group and identify with the available group; and if they need a leader, leadership might be enough to fulfill the identity function needed to reduce uncertainty.

These findings somewhat contradict the work of Cicero, Pierro, and van Knippenberg (2010), which found that participants high in need for closure (a construct related to tolerance for uncertainty) prefer a prototypical to a nonprotoypical leader. Rast and colleagues (2012) examined potential leaders, while Cicero and colleagues examined incumbent leaders, which in light of the research on leader innovation credit might explain some of the differences. Future research in this area will shed light on the differences between incumbent and perspective leaders, as will the cognitive underpinnings of uncertainty and ingroup relevant information. This work highlights the importance of studying when and how nonprototypical group members can gain influence in their groups, because often group members are marginalized for deviating from group norms. Just as leaders serve multiple identity functions within groups, so do peripheral and marginal group members.

## Deviance and Marginalization

While the group tends to elevate prototypical group members even to leadership positions, it often casts norm violators as deviants (Hogg, 2005). Being a member of a group provides members with several benefits. There are clear monetary and extrinsic benefits to belonging to clubs and organizations. Each month, we receive journals and discounts for attending conferences as a part of the benefits of being a member of our professional psychology affiliations. Other groups provide us with a sense of psychological well-being, protection, status, self-esteem, fitness, a sense of who we are—the benefits that our group memberships offer us are endless. Loneliness and exclusion from others are correlated with depression and even illness (see Jaremka et al., 2014; Sugisawa, Liang, & Liu, 1994). Indeed, some scholars have argued that the desire to belong to a group is ingrained strongly in the human psyche because it is a trait that we have developed through evolution (see Kameda & Tindale, 2006).

### Normative Deviants

In parts of southern Ethiopia, children born with physical abnormalities and deformities and children who are born out of wedlock are believed to be evil. As a result, some children and adults have been accused of witchcraft and drowned, or they have been shunned and left to survive alone. While this is a drastic example, deviating from group norms carries a large social cost: often derogation and marginalization. Because individuals are motivated to both view their groups positively and to cultivate and preserve their group's cohesiveness, punishing deviants serves a distinct group function (see Marques, Abrams, Paez, & Marinez-Taboada, 1998). Moreover, ingroup members make a distinct effort to persuade ingroup deviants to accept the normative position (Marques, Abrams, & Serôdio, 2001) before throwing them out (Schachter, 1951; Wesselmann et al., 2014).

Subjective group dynamics theory (Abrams, Marques, Bown, & Henson, 2000; Marques et al., 2001) outlines the social identity-based motivations that lead to ingroup derogation. Ordinarily, other group members are a positive source of social identification to the extent that they uphold the ingroup's positive image and or "distinctiveness" (Marques et al., 1998; see also Brewer, 1991; Leonardelli, Pickett, & Brewer, 2010) from relevant outgroups (e.g., Pinto et al., 2010). People are motivated to see their groups in a positive light, and they achieve this, in part, by maintaining normative distinctiveness from outgroups (e.g., Abrams & Hogg, 1990; Tajfel & Turner 1979). However, the presence of norm violators within the group can cause members to call into question the validity of the ingroup prototype. When people feel uncertain about the superiority of their ingroup, they more harshly derogate fellow ingroup members who violate norms than normative members and even outgroup members (Marques et al., 1998; for a discussion of ostracism as a tool to protect positive group identity, see Hales, Ren, & Williams, this volume).

Research inspired by subjective group dynamics theory reliably demonstrates that ingroup members derogate normatively deviant ingroup members to a greater extent than deviant outgroup members (e.g., Abrams et al., 2000; Marques & Yzerbyt, 1988; Marques, Yzerbyt, & Leyens, 1988; Pinto et al., 2010). In addition, outgroup members who deviate from their own group prototype in such a way that bolsters the ingroup's credibility (i.e., in the direction of the ingroup) are elevated in terms of favorability with respect to ingroup members who deviate away from the ingroup norm (Abrams et al., 2000). This so-called black-sheep effect occurs in situations in which social identity is salient (e.g., Marques, Yzerbyt, & Leyens, 1988) and is enhanced among those who identify strongly with their ingroup (e.g., Abrams et al., 2000).

Whereas a nonnormative position that calls into question the validity of the ingroup prototype can produce uncertainty in the ingroup, the expression of a position that is normatively extreme can also help to validate the ingroup prototype (see Hogg et al., 1990). Thus, ingroup pro-norm deviants are evaluated more positively than ingroup anti-norm deviants, and even outgroup anti-norm deviants are viewed more favorably than ingroup anti-norm deviants (Abrams et al., 2000). For example, in a competitive context where the outgroup is "atheists," members of a particular Christian church might derogate their own members who appear to question the existence of God and upgrade members who espouse extreme zealotry that supports their church's ideology. They might also act more warmly toward a known atheist who admits that God could exist than their own members who question the existence of God. In sum, we like those group members who help us to look different from and better than a relevant outgroup, and we are not threatened by an outgroup member who helps to make our ingroup look positive.

Normative deviants experience derogation because their presence and actions might reflect poorly on the ingroup. Deviants call into question intragroup integrity and entitativity as well as the ingroup's subjective positivity on an intergroup level. How then can ingroup members effect change or stand up against their group's wrongdoings?

### Criticizing the Ingroup

While dissenters can be punished, what happens to group members who point out the ingroup's flaws? Are they marginalized for casting a nonfavorable shadow on their group? According to research on intergroup sensitivity (Hornsey & Imani, 2004), the answer is not necessarily. In general, when something critical is said about the ingroup, people are less defensive about the criticism if it comes from an ingroup rather than an outgroup member (Hornsey & Imani, 2004). People tend to assume that an ingroup member is trying to be constructive to benefit the group, while an outgroup member might be doing so out of animosity or self-interest. Australians received criticism about their country more positively when it came from an Australian and when the ingroup critic appeared to be attached to Australia than from an outgroup member or an Australian not attached to the homeland (Hornsey, Trembath, & Gunthorpe, 2004). People appear to be able to better take criticism from an outgroup source when the source can stress a shared, superordinate identity (i.e., construe itself as part of the ingroup). For the most part, outsiders are not free to criticize the ingroup unless they can cast themselves as doing so from the inside.

### Some Consequences of Marginalization

Excluding and derogating ingroup deviants can cause pain and embarrassment for those who experience ostracism (see Williams, Cheung, & Choi, 2000). Moreover, those who have been excluded to the fringes of the group might feel a need to establish their belongingness to the ingroup (and distinguish themselves from relevant outgroups)

by derogating outgroup members and expressing ingroup bias (see Pickett & Brewer, 2005). In an analysis of gang behavior and social identification processes, Goldman, Giles, and Hogg (2014) argue that members who feel marginalized by a meaningful group are more likely to commit extreme behaviors to gain acceptance into the group relative to their prototypical counterparts (who already feel accepted). It is group members on the fringes who are the most likely to seek out and punish ingroup deviants (Pickett & Brewer, 2005).

Along with the negative implications that ingroup exclusion carries, these processes serve important intragroup functions. The presence of deviants helps to clarify the ingroup prototype—they allow for social comparison, which determines normative fit to the ingroup prototype (see Hogg & Gaffney, 2014). Although those who deviate from their group's norms might produce uncertainty about the viability of the ingroup (see Hogg, 2005, 2010), deviation from the status quo can produce social change when the dissenting voices can, particularly when expressed by a subgroup rather than isolated individuals, overcome specific social-cognitive obstacles and make themselves heard. In other words, against stacked odds, sometimes David overcomes Goliath.

### Minority Influence

Social psychology and leadership provides countless examples prototypical group members (see Hogg & van Knippenberg, 2003) and social norms (see Jacobson, Mortensen, & Cialdini, 2011) exerting influence. Moscovici advocated the idea that social change arises from minorities within society (see Moscovici, 1976; see also Butera et al., this volume). History is replete with examples of successful minority movements and positions: women's suffrage, the US civil rights movement, marriage equality, the Cuban revolution, the German Worker's Party, Al-Qaeda, the Islamic State—societal change, for good or bad, is often initially ignited by a small group.

Moscovici's conversion theory (see Moscovici, 1980) laid the groundwork for the field of minority influence, modern social influence, and persuasion research. When targets question the validity of their perceptions against the position of a source, they experience conflict, which is at the heart of all influence (Moscovici, 1976). Conversion theory posits different processes for minority and majority influence, ultimately suggesting that through a process of verification, targets might think about a minority's message, but through a process of social comparison, targets merely agree with a majority message, giving it little thought. Thinking about a message can eventually lead to conversion (Moscovici, 1980), albeit at a later time or on related attitudes (Crano, 2001). Early work in minority influence anticipated dual-process models of persuasion (Chaiken, Liberman, & Eagly, 1989; Petty & Cacioppo, 1986), which now dominate the study of minority and majority influence (for a comprehensive review, see Martin & Hewstone, 2008).

### Cognitive Processing and Influence

Fruitful research on minority influence and persuasion has sprung from Moscovici's conversion theory, detailing the cognitive processing of minority and majority messages and the elaboration conditions under which each group can be successful (see Martin & Hewstone, 2008). Dual-process models of persuasion posit that conversion occurs as a result of systematic and effortful processing of persuasive messages. This occurs when people have both the ability and the motivation to carefully consider messages (Petty & Cacioppo, 1986). However, when ability and motivation are low, people process persuasive messages at a low level, relying on heuristics such as source characteristics.

If people seek normative approval from the majority, majority source cues might operate as heuristics whereby people outwardly accept the majority position with little consideration of the message. As a result, the change that occurs from this type of normative pressure is short-lived because targets do not carefully consider the message (see Martin & Hewstone, 2008).

True conversion, on the other hand, is lasting and resistant to further persuasion attempts (e.g., Martin, Hewstone, & Martin, 2003; Tormala, DeSensi, & Petty, 2007). Minorities can spark careful consideration of their messages as targets attempt to understand *why* they hold a differing perspective (Moscovici, 1980). That is, under many circumstances, minorities induce systematic processing, and majority source status is a heuristic cue. However, given the social constraints of agreeing with a minority position, attitude change might not readily occur as a result of exposure to the minority. Nonetheless, a persuasive minority has the ability to exert pressure on the whole attitudinal structure and can result in change on a related attitudinal dimension or delayed attitude change (e.g., Alvaro & Crano, 1997). There are several moderators to

these processes, which indicate the conditions under which a minority or a majority can stimulate systematic processing and attitude change (see Martin & Hewstone, 2008). In general, this work suggests that in many influence settings, a minority posing a strong argument elicits greater systematic processing than a majority (see Crano, 2001). On the other hand, the majority often produces a default in which people automatically side with the majority without considering its argument (e.g., Martin & Hewstone, 2008).

Alvaro and Crano's (1997) work suggests that whether or not an influence source can cast itself as part of the ingroup is tantamount for its ability to exert change. The amount of energy that an individual expends thinking about a message is directly related to group membership. That is, outgroups rarely have the ability to change people's attitudes (Mackie, Gastardo-Conaco, & Skelly, 1992; Mackie, Worth, & Asuncion, 1990), while ingroup status can act as a heuristic cue (Mackie et al., 1992). An ingroup can, however, produce systematic processing when information regarding the message is unclear (Mackie et al., 1992), or a persuasive message provides information regarding prototypicality (van Knippenberg & Wilke, 1992).

A message from an ingroup source, particularly one that provides invaluable information about features of the ingroup's prototypicality, has the ability to induce systematic processing (McGarty, Haslam, Hutchinson, & Turner, 1994). Moreover, situations that make social identity salient give people the motivation to focus on and pay attention to group-related cues, and they thus systematically process the messages of ingroup sources. This reflects not just mere compliance with the ingroup's position, but systematic processing of the ingroup's message when it provides information regarding how to think, act, and feel in terms of the ingroup's prototype.

### Minority Influence in Social Context

Minority and majority influence are group processes, grounded in the relations between subgroups and superordinate groups, ingroups, and outgroups. Some minority influence research considers ingroup status as part of its research paradigm, such as Crano's leniency contract (see Crano, 2001; Alvaro & Crano, 1997). However, much of the current work in this area focuses on the persuasion processes stimulated by either a numeric minority or majority. While this research has its roots in group processes, it has studied persuasion somewhat separately from social identification processes. Social identity clearly influences the ways in which people process messages from ingroup and outgroup sources, and it has several implications for how we process information from subgroups and minority groups.

Very little work has examined how specific group relations and social context affect minority influence. David and Turner (1999), however, showed that ingroup minorities do in fact have the ability to induce direct attitude change when adopting the minority position, which allows prototype distinction from a relevant outgroup. Targets in their experiments were moderate feminists, to whom they showed a persuasive message from an ingroup minority ("radical" feminists). When social context was never stated, or was an intragroup context (the comparison was other moderate feminists), the minority was only effective on delayed attitudes—a common finding in minority influence research. However, when the comparison source was antifeminists, creating an intergroup context, targets immediately aligned their attitudes with that of the minority. This research demonstrates that an ingroup minority is a successful influence source when acceptance of its position helps to clarify the ingroup's identity in contradistinction to a relevant outgroup.

Gaffney and colleagues (2014) further demonstrated the importance of social context in identity clarification in acceptance of extreme ingroup positions. They primed moderate American conservatives with either high or low uncertainty and then exposed them to an extremely conservative message from a Tea Party leader. Because the Tea Party is a small faction of the conservative movement in the United States, they might be viewed as an ingroup (numeric) minority for moderate conservatives. Social context was primed such that the comparison source was either ingroup (Republicans) or outgroup (Democrats). Targets demonstrated increased conservatism and support for the extremely conservative Tea Party message only under uncertainty in the intergroup context. Especially when people experience uncertainty, they turn to their ingroups to make sense of the world and to clarify their identities. Similarly, other research shows that members of a numeric opinion minority tend to rate their self-concept as clearer than members of the majority, particularly if they find their opinion group to be value expressive (Rios & Wheeler, 2010). Supporting an extreme position that is pronormative (e.g., Abrams et al., 2000) allows for ingroup members to clearly define their group in contradistinction to an outgroup. This shift occurs through

the fluidity of prototypes, which are malleable in response to changes in the social context (e.g., Oakes, Haslam, & Reynolds, 1999).

Sometimes minorities are successful at getting their point across and might eventually persuade the majority to accept their position (e.g., the fall of the Berlin Wall and German reunification). In many cases, extreme minorities are granted ingroup leniency whereby group members hear out their position because they share a common group (see Crano, 2001). There are, however, instances when a minority faction advocates something so extreme that their position is no longer seen as part of the ingroup. This, of course, might lead to marginalization or attempts to bring the minority back into the fold of the ingroup. When a minority group or subgroup feels that its voice cannot be heard within the superordinate group and that the superordinate group no longer serves a representative identity function, the difficult option can arise for the subgroup to exit the group (e.g., Sani, 2008; Sani & Pugliese, 2008).

## Extreme Group Norms
### Group Polarization

In extreme instances, schisms occur within groups. In general, groups avoid splintering and, as a result, groups can be diverse. Group-based attitudes can and do become more extreme as a result of several factors. Group polarization refers to a tendency toward the extremitization of group attitudes after group discussion (Isenberg, 1980).

Numerous studies in social psychology have demonstrated that when people come together in a group, postdiscussion attitudes become more extreme than prediscussion attitudes in a variety of paradigms (e.g., the "risky-shift" paradigm) and along a variety of different attitudes (e.g., prejudice and egalitarian attitudes; Myers & Bishop, 1970). Social psychological research has offered three distinct (but often overlapping) explanations for group polarization. The social comparison/normative influence approach posits that attitudes become more extreme after group discussion because individuals use other group members' comments as a guide for determining normative acceptance. As a result, they adjust their own attitudes to be slightly "better" than (or more extreme) than what they believe to be the average of the group. This research emphasizes bandwagon effects where individuals demonstrate their virtuosity in terms of group norms by "one-upping" other group members and presenting a slightly different but better position than what most people in the group espoused in the discussion (e.g., Brown, 1974; Myers, 1978). The other emphasis in social comparison research is the removal of pluralistic ignorance where prior to group discussion people underestimate the position of the group and present their own position as less extreme as a result. Group discussion exposes people to arguments that are closer to the actual group norm, and on a second testing, people can present a position that is closer to their own ideal positions (see Isenberg, 1980).

Persuasive arguments/informational influence argues that group discussion exposes individuals to novel pro and con arguments regarding a specific issue. If the group presents arguments that appear both persuasive and valid in a more extreme direction than the members' previously held position, attitudes will polarize. However, persuasive arguments that the group presents in the opposite direction can actually cause group members' attitudes to depolarize (Kaplan, 1977). Isenberg (1980) concluded through a broad meta-analysis of the aforementioned approaches that both normative and informational influence processes are valid explanations of group polarization, with informational influence effects being slightly stronger.

Self-categorization theory has examined polarization in different social contexts. Hogg et al. (1990) examined attitude polarization and the shifting of ingroup prototypes in response to changes in the social context, using the "risky shift paradigm." Participants listened to an ingroup discussion group debate over the course of action that should be taken in a vignette. They also received information regarding how outgroups responded to the vignette, in which an outgroup chose a riskier course of action, a more cautious course of action, or both a riskier and more cautious course (i.e., two outgroups) than the ingroup's choice. Participants' positions extremitized away from the position of the outgroup in all situations, either becoming more cautious, riskier, or converging to the middle of their ingroup distribution (normative) in the case of the outgroups being both risky and cautious. This approach to the study of attitude polarization and norm change implicates the importance of social comparative context in defining and adhering to group norms (McGarty, Turner, Hogg, David, & Wetherell, 1992).

This self-categorization approach to group polarization has been documented across various studies (e.g., Abrams et al., 1990; Mackie, 1986; Mackie & Cooper, 1984); however, Krizan and Baron (2007) failed to find support for intergroup differentiation as a motive for group polarization. Krizan and Baron exposed participants to an actual group discussion in which participants could gauge the views of their fellow ingroup members and, in effect, be influenced and influence the group discussion (see Prislin, 2010). Such interaction could potentially reduce subjective uncertainty, which Hogg et al. (1990) argue is another factor in norm convergence. Future work on polarization should explore this as a possibility and also examine these processes in actual group-based attitudes to give a rich picture of attitude polarization.

The research on attitude polarization illustrates how the presence of extreme ingroup members can (under certain circumstances) lead to a normative shift in which group members come to accept extreme and even radical positions as prototypical of their ingroup. This approach highlights the functionality of extreme ingroup positions—they sometimes allow prototype change to keep the ingroup distinct from relevant outgroups.

### Extremism and Radicalization

The desire to see one's social identity as distinct from a relevant outgroup is magnified by conditions that pose a threat to the ingroup's subjective positivity or which produces uncertainties regarding the individual or group's identity (Hogg, 2015). The world is filled with such threats and uncertainties (e.g., living in a war-ravaged country, facing an uncertain economy). Hence, social identity-related research on extremism tends to focus on how climates that breed intergroup competition or uncertainty can produce a desire to support and engage in extreme behaviors (Hogg, 2014). The term *extremism* varies in its definition and may refer to holding attitudes that deviate from social norms to joining terrorist groups. While we have covered topics that may be defined as "extremism," such as attitude polarization and minority influence, we focus this section specifically on radical support for groups and the adoption of attitudes and behavior that are both antinormative and potentially harmful. Our focus here is a brief account of sociopolitical and ideological extremism as it relates to social identity and social influence. Political and social turmoil often propagate such behaviors and cognitions (e.g., the rise of the Islamic State in Syria and Iraq).

When people experience conceptual self-uncertainty, some groups are more attractive than other groups, particularly those that can prescribe behavior and attitudes (e.g., Hogg, 2014). For example, moderates were more likely to identify with an extreme faction of their group when they experienced uncertainty (Hogg, Meehan, & Farquharson, 2010), particularly if that identification allowed them to distinguish their group from a relevant outgroup (Gaffney et al., 2014). Presumably this occurred because extreme groups with insular group norms are attractive in uncertain times (see Hogg, 2015). Kruglanski and colleagues (2014) have posited that threats to feelings of significance can also induce acts of extremism. Other work has shown that the experience of uncertainty leads to support for cultural institutions (van den Bos et al., 2005), such as religion (Hogg, Adelman, & Blagg, 2010) and social conservatism (Jost, Glaser, Kruglanski, & Sulloway, 2003). Although the bulk of this work has focused on groups that promote "negative" forms of extremism, uncertainty and threats to significance should also promote identification with and support of extremely "positive" group norms such as education and charitable giving (see Crwys, Gaffney, & Skipper, forthcoming; Kruglanski et al., 2014).

Research conducted in the Middle East with Israelis and Palestinians demonstrates that the experience of uncertainty promotes support for military force against an outgroup (e.g., Hogg & Adelman, 2013). In this research, the identity of the ingroup is defined in large part by the presence of the outgroup. In such situations, especially when the ingroup perceives conflict and people believe that their group is deprived with respect to the outgroup (see Pettigrew et al., 2008; Runciman, 1966), they tend to identify more strongly with their group or factions of their group that might be able to bolster the ingroup's ability to succeed over the outgroup. This paints a complex picture of extremism as intertwined responses to competitive intergroup relations and a climate of group and self-related uncertainties.

Showing the interplay of uncertainty and intergroup tensions, Doosje, Loseman, and van den Bos (2013) found that uncertainty, perceived injustice, and threats to the ingroup produced a radical belief system in young Muslims in the Netherlands, such that they were more likely to believe in Muslim superiority over other groups, have feelings of disconnect with Dutch society, and to characterize the Dutch legal system as illegitimate. This radical belief system was also related to support for Muslims committing acts of violence. Similarly, compensatory control theory (Kay & Eibach, 2013) maintains that when people's desire to view the world as orderly is thwarted in some way, they seek orderly social systems and hierarchies that help them to organize their worlds. For example, experiencing a loss of personal control was related to employees perceiving and supporting greater social hierarchy within their workplaces (Friesen, Kay, Eibach, & Galinsky, 2014).

Kruglanski and colleagues (2014) posit that threats to personal and social significance promote collectivism. Collectivism, or group affiliative behaviors that promote the ingroup, do not always promote intolerance or violence. Radical attitudes and behaviors result if they align with the direction of the ingroup's norms. If the ingroup is tolerant and promotes humanitarianism, a threat to one's significance might bring about charitable behaviors; however, when ideological dogma and violence are normative, such a threat will most likely bring about radical attitudes in support of this prototype (e.g., Kruglanski et al., 2014). A movement can become radicalized when group members believe that radical acts and violence are legitimate because they help the group to achieve its goal (Thomas, McGarty, & Louis, 2014).

Not all acts of extremism are directed specifically at political issues (and yet many are the product of the sociopolitical structure). For example, adolescents might join gangs or engage in other risk-taking behavior. Emler and Reicher (2005) suggest that this occurs when children feel that authorities have rejected their identities from important social systems, such as education and the legal system. To protect themselves, these children develop a deviant identity from which they can gain a positive sense of self; their identity is based on rejecting the very system from which they feel rejected. Hogg, Siegel, and Hohman (2011) surmise that such deviance and risk-taking behavior in adolescence is in large part the result of feeling uncertain. Feelings of uncertainty—whether about life transitions or fitting in—leads adolescents to identify with self-inclusive groups, some of which promote risk-taking behavior. Crwys et al. (forthcoming) demonstrated that students experiencing uncertainty prefer to identify with and take on the norms of a group high in entitativity, whether the group promotes "partying" or "studying." This research suggests that while uncertainty produces a desire to identify with and join self-inclusive groups, which are often insular and may cultivate extreme behaviors, it is the quality and structure of the ingroup and the relationships that the group can provide that determines identification and conformity to group norms.

Extremist positions are a "normal" part of group behavior (Abrams, 2012). They help to give clarification and distinction to the ingroup prototype. They tell us who is in our group, who is in the outgroup, and also who is on the fringes of our own group. They clarify who we are by providing definition to our ingroups and distinction from outgroups. Radicalized behaviors and support for authoritarian ideology (e.g., Henry, 2011) can occur in contexts that threaten one's ingroup or make the individual experience uncertainty. While extreme ingroup positions can create discomfort and even uncertainty (see Hogg, 2010), it is extreme views that are also novel and ignite social change. Radicalism, violence, terrorism, and authoritarianism leading to stagnation arise from extremist views, but so can positive social change. The ways in which people understand who they are in sociopolitical contexts and within environments that breed violence and/or uncertainty determine in large part their responses of radicalism or positive change.

## Conclusion

The construction of social influence is at the heart of social identity and self-categorization theories. Group prototypes, self-stereotypes, and our knowledge of our groups are determined by social influence. The history, study, and future of social identity and self-categorization theories cannot be disentangled from social influence. The actions of other people allow us to know who we are within our groups and in the world at large. We often garner our knowledge of group behaviors and attitudes from leaders and group members who typify group membership. Moscovici (1976) hammered into social psychology the philosophy that sometimes marginalized groups and group factions, which appear to have no normative clout, can spark social change and be the sources of influence. Research on deviance, marginalization, and extremist factions demonstrates that such group members and factions can and do influence their groups at large. Moreover, such individuals and groups serve the very important functions of enforcing and displaying group norms as well as changing them.

Where societies are plagued by war, classism, and hierarchical stratification, future work in social identity and influence will continue to examine why and how people's group memberships predict their desire to endorse systems that promote the differential treatment of humans based on their group memberships. What are the conditions and the motivations behind when people are no longer

willing to be a part of such systems and when will people work to cast such systems aside? When and how can peaceful (and sometimes nonpeaceful) demonstrations over the deaths of unarmed African Americans at the hands of police officers lead to systemic change? How can we prevent the marginalization of immigrants? When and how can we stop people from joining extremist organizations such as the Islamic State? Do we target the group or the situation out of which it arose? Our research on targeting group memberships and social identifications as a means for both protest and change will contribute largely to shedding light on such important questions.

Exploring social influence with respect to social identity theory entails both a broad and specific examination of social context. To a certain extent, all social identity and self-categorization work examines social influence, and all work in social influence considers (although maybe not explicitly) social identity. Considering self-categorization, particularly with respect to referent informational influence, allows a nuanced view of social influence, which goes beyond a dual-process approach. Referent informational influence demonstrates that informational and normative influences cannot be distinct from one another in a group context. When social identity is salient, referent groups are both informative and normative. They provide uncertainty-reducing information that is normative. Precisely because this information is normative is *why* it is also informational—it tells group members not only what other group members do but also holds a prescriptive function for enacting the behavior. We listen to and systematically process information that provides us with cues about relevant ingroup prototypes. Our group memberships and our fellow ingroup members have the ability to shape our attitudes and behavior, not only through normative pressure but also through a shared identity and thus a shared reality.

Most human action is embedded within either a small group context (e.g., sports teams) or a larger sociopolitical context (e.g., national identities). A context of social and political turmoil contributes to a willingness to take up arms against other groups and nations in the name of a well-defined and organized groups such as the Islamic State. Thus, the study of how people influence one another must take into account how a diverse landscape of group memberships, political affiliations, social contacts, and political and social systems affect people's ability to enact their identities and engage with their worlds.

# References

Abrams, D., & Hogg, M. A. (1990). Social identification, self-categorisation, and social influence. *European Review of Social Psychology, 1*, 195–228.

Abrams, D. (2012). Extremism is normal: The roles of deviance and uncertainty in shaping groups and society. In M. A. Hogg & D. L. Blaylock (Eds.), *Extremism and the psychology of uncertainty* (pp. 36–54). Malden, MA: Wiley-Blackwell.

Abrams, D., & Hogg, M. A. (2010). Social identity and self-categorization. In J. F. Dovidio, M. Hewstone, P. Glick, & V. M. Esses (Eds.), *The SAGE handbook of prejudice, stereotyping and discrimination* (pp. 179–193). London, England: SAGE.

Abrams, D., Marques, J. M., Bown, N., & Henson, M. (2000). Pro-norm and anti-norm deviance within and between groups. *Journal of Personality and Social Psychology, 78*, 906–912.

Abrams, D., Randsley de Moura, G., Marques, J. M., & Hutchison, P. (2008). Innovation credit: When can leaders oppose their group's norms? *Journal of Personality and Social Psychology, 95*, 662–678.

Abrams, D., Randsley de Moura, G., & Travaglino, G. A. (2013). A double standard when group members behave badly: Transgression credit to ingroup leaders. *Journal of Personality and Social Psychology, 105*, 799–815.

Abrams, D., Wetherell, M., Cochrane, S., Hogg, M. A., & Turner, J. C. (1990). Knowing what to think by knowing who you are: Self-categorization and the nature of norm formation, conformity and group polarization. *British Journal of Social Psychology, 29*, 97–119.

Alvaro, E. M., & Crano, W. D. (1997). Indirect minority influence: Evidence for leniency in source evaluation and counterargumentation. *Journal of Personality & Social Psychology, 72*, 949–964.

Antonakis, J., & House, R. J. (2003). An analysis of the full-range leadership theory: The way forward. In B. J. Avolio & F. J. Yammarino (Eds.), *Transformational and charismatic leadership: The road ahead* (pp. 3–33). New York, NY: Elsevier.

Avolio, B. J., & Yammarino, F. J. (Eds.). (2003). *Transformational and charismatic leadership: The road ahead*. New York, NY: Elsevier.

Bass, B. M. (1985). *Leadership and performance beyond expectations*. New York, NY: Free Press.

Brewer, M. B. (1981). Ethnocentrism and its role in interpersonal trust. In M. B. Brewer & B. Collins (Eds.), *Scientific inquiry and the social sciences* (pp. 345–360). San Francisco, CA: Jossey-Bass.

Brewer, M. B. (1991). The social self: On being the same and different at the same. *Personality and Social Psychology Bulletin, 17*, 475–482.

Brewer, M. B. (2012). Optimal distinctiveness theory: Its history and development. In P. M. Van Lange, A. W. Kruglanski, & E. T. Higgins (Eds.), *Handbook of theories of social psychology* (Vol. 2, pp. 81–98). Thousand Oaks, CA: SAGE.

Brown, R. (1974). Further comment on the risky shift. *American Psychologist, 29*, 468–470.

Campbell, A., Converse, P., Miller, W., & Stokes, D. (1960). *The American voter*. New York, NY: John Wiley & Sons Inc.

Campbell, D. T. (1958). Common fate, similarity, and other indices of the status of aggregates of persons as social entities. *Behavioral Science, 3*, 14–25. doi:10.1002/bs.3830030103

Chaiken, S., Liberman, A., & Eagly, A. H. (1989). Heuristic and systamtic information processing within and beyond the persuasion context. In J. S. Uleman and J. A. Bargh (Eds.), *Unintended thought: Limits of awareness, intention and thought* (pp. 212–252). New York, NY: Guilford Press.

Chemers, M. M. (2001). Leadership effectiveness: An integrative review. In M. A. Hogg & R. S. Tindale (Eds.), *Blackwell handbook of social psychology: Group processes* (pp. 376–399). Oxford, England: Blackwell.

Christensen, P. N., Rothgerber, H., Wood, W., & Matz, D. C. (2004). Social norms and identity relevance: A motivational approach to normative behavior. *Personality and Social Psychology Bulletin, 30*, 1295–1309.

Cicero, L., Pierro, A., & van Knippenberg, D. (2010). Leadership and uncertainty: How role ambiguity affects the relationship between leader group prototypicality and leadership effectiveness. *British Journal of Management, 21*, 411–421.

Cooper, J., & Hogg, M. A. (2007). Feeling the anguish of others: A theory of vicarious dissonance. *Advances in Experimental Social Psychology* (Vol. 39, pp. 359–403). Elsevier Academic Press, San Diego, CA.

Crano, W. D. (2001). Social influence, social identity, and ingroup leniency. In C. W. De Dreu & N. K. De Vries (Eds.), *Group consensus and minority influence: Implications for innovation* (pp. 122–143). Malden, MA: Blackwell.

Crano, W. D., & Hannula-Bral, K. A. (1994). Context/categorization model of social influence: Minority and majority influence in the formation of a novel response norm. *Journal of Experimental Social Psychology, 30*, 247–276.

Crwys, T., Gaffney, A. M., & Skipper, Y. (forthcoming). Uncertainty in transition: The influence of group cohesion on learning. In K. Mavor, M. Platow, & B. Bizumic (Eds.), *Self, social identity, and education*. New York, NY: Psychology Press.

David, B., & Turner, J. C. (1999). Studies in self-categorization and minority conversion. The ingroup minority in intragroup and intergroup contexts. *British Journal of Social Psychology, 38*, 115–134.

De Cremer, D., & Tyler, T. R. (2005). Managing group behaviour: The interplay between procedural fairness, self, and cooperation. In M. P. Zanna (Ed.), *Advances in experimental social psychology* (Vol. 37, pp. 151–218). San Diego, CA: Academic Press.

Deutsch, M. & Gerard, H. B. (1955). A study of normative and informational social influences upon individual judgment. *Journal of Abnormal and Social Psychology, 51*, 629–636.

Doosje, B., Loseman, A., & van den Bos, K. (2013). Determinants of radicalization of Islamic youth in the Netherlands: Personal uncertainty, perceived injustice, and perceived group threat. *Journal of Social Issues, 69*, 586–604.

Eagly, A. H., & Karau, S. J. (2002). Role congruity theory of prejudice toward female leaders. *Psychological Review, 109*, 573–598.

Emler, N., & Reicher, S. (2005). Delinquency: Cause or consequence of social exclusion? In D. Abrams, M. A. Hogg, & J. M. Marques (Eds.), *The social psychology of inclusion and exclusion* (pp. 211–241). New York, NY: Psychology Press.

Festinger, L. (1954a). A theory of social comparison processes. *Human Relations, 7*, 117–140. doi:10.1177/001872675400700202

Festinger, L. (1954b). Motivation leading to social behavior. In M. R. Jones (Ed.), *Nebraska symposium on motivation* (Vol. 2, pp. 121–218). Lincoln: University of Nebraska Press.

Fiedler, F. E. (1964). A contingency model of leadership effectiveness. In L. Berkowitz (Ed.), *Advances in experimental social psychology* (Vol. *1*, pp. 149–190). New York, NY: Academic Press.

Fiedler, F. E. (1967). *A theory of leadership effectiveness*. New York, NY: McGraw-Hill.

Fiske, S. T., Xu, J., Cuddy, A. J. C., & Glick, P. (1999). (Dis) respecting versus (dis)liking: Status and interdependence predict ambivalent stereotypes of competence and warmth. *Journal of Social Issues, 55*, 473–491.

Friesen, J. P., Kay, A. C., Eibach, R. P., & Galinsky, A. D. (2014). Seeking structure in social organization: Compensatory control and the psychological advantages of hierarchy. *Journal of Personality and Social Psychology, 106*, 590–609.

Gaffney, A. M., & Blaylock, D. L. (2010). Hillary Clinton's race: Did she match the presidential prototype? *Advancing Women in Leadership Journal, 30, 1–15*.

Gaffney, A. M., & Hogg, M. A. (2012). Group processes. In W. S. Bainbridge (Ed.), *Leadership in science and technology: A reference handbook* (Vol. *1*, pp. 132–139). Thousand Oaks, CA: SAGE.

Gaffney, A. M., Rast, D. E. III, Hacket, J. D., & Hogg, M. A. (2014). Further to the right: Uncertainty, political polarization, and the American Tea Party movement. *Social Influence, 9*, 272–288.

Giessner, S. R., & van Knippenberg, D. (2008). "License to fail": Goal definition, leader group prototypicality, and perceptions of leadership effectiveness after leader failure. *Organisational Behaviour and Human Decision Processes, 105*, 14–35.

Goldman, L., Giles, H., & Hogg, M. A. (2014). Going to extremes: Social identity and communication processes associated with gang membership. *Group Processes and Intergroup Relations, 17*, 813–832.

Grant, F., & Hogg, M. A. (2012). Self-uncertainty, social identity prominence and group identification. *Journal of Experimental Social Psychology, 48*, 538–542.

Grieve, P., & Hogg, M. A. (1999). Subjective uncertainty and intergroup discrimination in the minimal group situation. *Personality and Social Psychology Bulletin, 25*, 926–940.

Hains, S. C., Hogg, M. A., & Duck, J. M. (1997). Self-categorization and leadership: Effects of group prototypicality and leader stereotypicality. *Personality and Social Psychology Bulletin, 23*, 1087–1100.

Hamilton, D. L., & Sherman, S. J. (1996). Perceiving persons and groups. *Psychological Review, 103*, 336–355.

Henry, P. J. (2011). The role of stigma in understanding ethnicity differences in authoritarianism. *Political Psychology, 32*, 419–438.

Hogg, M. A. (2000a). Social identity and social comparison. In J. Suls & L. Wheeler (Eds.), *Handbook of social comparison: Theory and research* (pp. 401–421). New York, NY: Kluwer/Plenum.

Hogg, M. A. (2000b). Subjective uncertainty reduction through self-categorization: A motivational theory of social identity processes. *European Review of Social Psychology, 11*, 223–255.

Hogg, M. A. (2001). A social identity theory of leadership. *Personality and Social Psychology Review, 5*, 184–200.

Hogg, M. A. (2005). All animals are equal but some animals are more equal than others: Social identity and marginal membership. In K. D. Williams, J. P. Forgas, & W. von Hippel (Eds.), *The social outcast: Ostracism, social exclusion, rejection and bullying* (pp. 243–261). New York, NY: Psychology Press.

Hogg, M. A. (2006). Social identity theory. In P. J. Burke (Ed.), *Contemporary social psychological theories* (pp. 111–136). Palo Alto, CA: Stanford University Press.

Hogg, M. A. (2007a). Uncertainty-identity theory. In M. P. Zanna (Ed.), *Advances in experimental social psychology* (Vol. *39*, pp. 69–126). San Diego, CA: Academic Press.

Hogg, M. A. (2007b). Social identity and the group context of trust: Managing risk and building trust through belonging. In M. Siegrist, T. C. Earle, & H. Gutscher (Eds.), *Trust in cooperative risk management: Uncertainty and scepticism in the public mind* (pp. 51–71). London, England: Earthscan.

Hogg, M. A. (2008). Social identity theory of leadership. In C. L. Hoyt, G. R. Goethals, & D. R. Forsyth (Eds.), *Leadership at the crossroads. Volume 1: Leadership and psychology* (pp. 62–77). Westport, CT: Praeger.

Hogg, M. A. (2010). Influence and leadership. In S. T. Fiske, D. T. Gilbert, & G. Lindzey (Eds.), *Handbook of social psychology* (5th ed., Vol. *2*, pp. 1166–1207). New York, NY: Wiley.

Hogg, M. A. (2012). Uncertainty-identity theory. In P. A. M. van Lange, A. W. Kruglanski, & E. T. Higgins (Eds.), *Handbook of theories of social psychology* (Vol. *2*, pp. 62–80). Thousand Oaks, CA: SAGE.

Hogg, M. A. (2014). From uncertainty to extremism: Social categorization and identity processes. *Current Directions in Psychological Science, 23*, 338–342.

Hogg, M. A. (2015). Social instability and identity-uncertainty: Fertile ground for political extremism. In J. P. Forgas, K. Fiedler, & W. D. Crano (Eds.), *Social psychology and politics* (pp. 307–320). New York, NY: Psychology Press.

Hogg, M. A., & Adelman, J. (2013). Uncertainty–identity theory: Extreme groups, radical behavior, and authoritarian leadership. *Journal of Social Issues, 69*, 436–454.

Hogg, M. A., Adelman, J. R., & Blagg, R. D. (2010). Religion in the face of uncertainty: An uncertainty-identity theory account of religiousness. *Personality and Social Psychology Review, 14*, 72–83.

Hogg, M. A., & Gaffney, A. (2014). Prototype-based social comparisons within groups: Constructing social identity to reduce self-uncertainty. In Z. Križan & F. X. Gibbons (Eds.), *Communal functions of social comparison* (pp. 145–174). New York, NY: Cambridge University Press.

Hogg, M. A., & Grieve, P. (1999). Social identity theory and the crisis of confidence in social psychology: A commentary, and some research on uncertainty reduction. *Asian Journal of Social Psychology, 2*, 79–93.

Hogg, M. A., Hains, S. C., & Mason, I. (1998). Identification and leadership in small groups: Salience, frame of reference, and leader stereotypicality effects on leader evaluations. *Journal of Personality and Social Psychology, 75*, 1248–1263.

Hogg, M. A., Meehan, C., & Farquharson, J. (2010). The solace of radicalism: Self-uncertainty and group identification in the face of threat. *Journal of Experimental Social Psychology, 46*, 1061–1066.

Hogg, M. A., & Reid, S. A. (2001). Social identity, leadership, and power. In A. Y. Lee-Chai & J. A. Bargh (Eds.), *The use and abuse of power: Multiple perspectives on the causes of corruption* (pp. 159–180). Philadelphia, PA: Psychology Press.

Hogg, M. A., Sherman, D. K., Dierselhuis, J., Maitner, A. T., & Moffitt, G. (2007). Uncertainty, entitativity, and group identification. *Journal of Experimental Social Psychology, 43*, 135–142.

Hogg, M. A., Siegel, J. T., & Hohman, Z. P. (2011). Groups can jeopardize your health: Identifying with un-healthy groups to reduce self-uncertainty. *Self and Identity, 10*, 326–335.

Hogg, M. A., & Turner, J. C. (1987). Social identity and conformity: A theory of referent informational influence. In W. Doise & S. Moscovici (Eds.), *Current issues in European social psychology* (Vol. 2, pp. 139–182). Cambridge, England: Cambridge University Press.

Hogg, M. A., Turner, J. C., & David, B. (1990). Polarized norms as social frames of reference: A test of the self-categorization theory of group polarization. *Basic and Applied Research, 11,* 77–100.

Hogg, M. A., & van Knippenberg, D. (2003). Social identity and leadership processes in groups. In M. P. Zanna (Ed.), *Advances in experimental social psychology* (Vol. 35, pp. 1–52). San Diego, CA: Academic Press.

Hogg, M. A., van Knippenberg, D., & Rast, D. E. III. (2012). The social identity theory of leadership: Theoretical origins, research findings, and conceptual developments. *European Review of Social Psychology, 23,* 258–304.

Hohman, Z. P., & Hogg, M. A. (2015). Fearing the uncertain: Self-uncertainty plays a role in mortality salience. *Journal of Experimental Social Psychology, 57,* 31–42.

Hohman, Z. P., Hogg, M. A., & Bligh, M. C. (2010). Identity and intergroup leadership: Asymmetrical political and national identification in response to uncertainty. *Self and Identity, 9,* 113–128.

Hornsey, M. J., & Imani, A. (2004). Criticizing groups from the inside and the outside: An identity perspective on the intergroup sensitivity effect. *Personality and Social Psychology Bulletin, 30,* 365–383.

Hornsey, M. J., Trembath, M., & Gunthorpe, S. (2004). "You can criticize because you care": Identity attachment, constructiveness, and the intergroup sensitivity effect. *European Journal of Social Psychology, 34,* 499–518.

Hovland, C. I., Janis, I. L., & Kelley, H. H. (1953). *Communication and persuasion: Psychological studies of opinion change.* New Haven, CT: Yale University Press.

Isenberg, D. J. (1980). Levels of analysis of pluralistic ignorance phenomena: The case of receptiveness to interpersonal feedback. *Journal of Applied Social Psychology, 10,* 457–467.

Jacobson, R. P., Mortensen, C. R., & Cialdini, R. B. (2011). Bodies obliged and unbound: Differentiated response tendencies for injunctive and descriptive social norms. *Journal of Personality and Social Psychology, 100,* 433–448.

Jaremka, L. M., Andridge, R. R., Fagundes, C. P., Alfano, C. M., Povoski, S. P., Lipari, A. M., . . . Kiecolt-Glaser, J. K. (2014). Pain, depression, and fatigue: Loneliness as a longitudinal risk factor. *Health Psychology, 33,* 948–957.

Jost, J. T., Glaser, J., Kruglanski, A. W., & Sulloway, F. J. (2003). Political conservatism as motivated social cognition. *Psychological Bulletin, 129,* 339–375.

Kameda, T., & Tindale, R. S. (2006). Groups as adaptive devices: Human docility and group aggregation mechanisms in evolutionary context. In M. Schaller, J. A. Simpson, & D. T. Kenrick (Eds.), *Evolution and social psychology* (pp. 317–341). Madison, CT: Psychosocial Press.

Kaplan, M. F. (1977). Discussion polarization effects in a modified jury decision paradigm: Informational influences. *Sociometry, 40*(3), 262–271.

Kay, A. C., & Eibach, R. P. (2013). Compensatory control and its implications for ideological extremism. *Journal of Social Issues, 69,* 564–585.

Kelman, H. (1958). Compliance, identification, and internalization: Three processes of attitude change. *Journal of Conflict Resolution, 1,* 51–60.

Krizan, Z., & Baron, R. S. (2007). Group polarization and choice-dilemmas: How important is self-categorization? *European Journal of Social Psychology, 37,* 191–201.

Kruglanski, A. W., Gelfand, M. J., Bélanger, J. J., Sheveland, A., Hetiarachchi, M., & Gunaratna, R. (2014). The psychology of radicalization and deradicalization: How significance quest impacts violent extremism. *Political Psychology, 35,* 69–93.

Leonardelli, G. J., Pickett, C. L., & Brewer, M. B. (2010). Optimal distinctiveness theory: A framework for social identity, social cognition and intergroup relations. In M. Zanna & J. Olson (Eds.) *Advances in experimental social psychology* (Vol. 43, pp. 65–115). New York: Elsevier.

Lord, R. G., Foti, R. J., & DeVader, C. L. (1984). A test of leadership categorization theory: Internal structure, information processing, and leadership perceptions. *Organizational Behavior and Human Performance, 34,* 343–378.

Mackie, D. M. (1986). Social identification effects in group polarization. *Journal of Personality and Social Psychology, 50,* 720–728.

Mackie, D., & Cooper, J. (1984). Attitude polarization: Effects of group membership. *Journal of Personality and Social Psychology, 46,* 575–585.

Mackie, D. M., Gastardo-Conaco, M., & Skelly, J. J. (1992). Knowledge of the advocated position and the processing of in-group and out-group persuasive messages. *Personality and Social Psychology Bulletin, 18*(2), 145–151.

Mackie, D. M., Worth, L. T., & Asuncion, A. G. (1990). Processing of persuasive in-group messages. *Journal of Personality and Social Psychology, 58*(5), 812–822.

Marques, J. M., Abrams, D., Paez, D., & Martinez-Taboada, C. (1998). The role of categorization and in-group norms in judgments of groups and their members. *Journal of Personality and Social Psychology, 75,* 976–988.

Marques, J. M., Abrams, D., Paez, D., & Martinez-Taboada, C. (1998). The role of categorization and in-group norms in judgments of groups and their members. *Journal of Personality and Social Psychology, 75,* 976–988.

Marques, J. M., Abrams, D., & Serôdio, R. G. (2001). Being better by being right: Subjective group dynamics and derogation of ingroup deviants when generic social norms are undermined. *Journal of Personality and Social Psychology 81,* 436–447.

Marques, J. M., & Yzerbyt, V. Y. (1988). The black sheep effect: Judgmental extremity towards ingroup members in inter- and intra-group situations. *European Journal of Social Psychology, 18,* 287–292.

Marques, J. M., Yzerbyt, V. Y., & Leyens, J. (1988). The "black sheep effect": Extremity of judgments towards ingroup members as a function of group identification. *European Journal of Social Psychology, 18,* 1–16.

Martin, R., & Hewstone, M. (2008). Majority versus minority influence, message processing and attitude change: The source-context-elaboration model. In M. P. Zanna (Ed.), *Advances in experimental social psychology* (Vol. 40, pp. 237–326). San Diego, CA: Elsevier.

Martin, R., Hewstone, M., & Martin, P. Y. (2003). Resistance to persuasive messages as a function of majority and minority source status. *Journal of Experimental Social Psychology, 39,* 585–593.

McGarty, C., Haslam, S., Hutchinson, K. J., & Turner, J. C. (1994). The effects of salient group memberships on persuasion. *Small Group Research, 25,* 267–293.

McGarty, C., Turner, J. C., Hogg, M. A., David, B., & Wetherell, M. S. (1992). Group polarization as conformity to the prototypical group member. *British Journal of Social Psychology, 31*, 1–19.

Milgram, S. (1963). Behavioral study of obedience. *Journal of Abnormal and Social Psychology, 67*, 371–378.

Milgram, S. (1974). *Obedience to authority.* London, England: Tavistock.

Moscovici, S. (1976). *Social influence and social change.* London, England: Academic Press.

Moscovici, S. (1980). Towards a theory of conversion behaviour. In L. Berkowitz (Ed.), *Advances in experimental social psychology* (Vol. *13*, pp. 209–239). New York, NY: Academic Press.

Mullin, B., & Hogg, M. A. (1998). Dimensions of subjective uncertainty in social identification and minimal intergroup discrimination. *British Journal of Social Psychology, 37*, 345–365.

Myers. D. G. (1978). Polarizing effects of social comparison. *Journal of Experimental Social Psychology, 14*, 554–563.

Myers, D. G., & Bishop, G. D. (1970). Discussion effects on racial attitudes. *Science, 169*, 778–779.

Nail, P. R. (1986). Toward an integration of some models and theories of social response. *Psychological Bulletin, 100*, 190–206.

Nash, K., McGregor, I., & Prentice, M. (2011). Threat and defense as goal regulation: From implicit goal conflict to anxious uncertainty, reactive approach motivation, and ideological extremism. *Journal of Personality and Social Psychology, 101*, 1291–1301.

Oakes, P. J., Haslam, S. A., & Reynolds, K. J. (1999). Social categorization and social context: Is stereotype change a matter of information or of meaning? In D. Abrams & M. A. Hogg (Eds.), *Social identity and social cognition* (pp. 55–79). Malden, MA: Blackwell.

Pérez, J. A., & Mugny, G. (1996). The conflict elaboration theory of social influence. In E. H. & J. Davis Witte (Eds.), *Understanding group behaviour* (Vol. *2*, pp. 191–210). Hillsdale, NJ: Laurence Erlbaum Associates.

Pettigrew, T. F., Christ, O., Wagner, U., Meertens, R. W., van Dick, R., & Zick, A. (2008). Relative deprivation and intergroup prejudice. *Journal of Social Issues, 64*, 385–401.

Petty, R. E., & Cacioppo, J. T. (1986). The elaboration likelihood model of persuasion. In L. Berkowitz (Ed.), *Advances in experimental social psychology* (Vol. *19*, pp. 123–205). San Diego, CA: Academic Press.

Pickett, C. L., & Brewer, M. B. (2005). The role of exclusion in maintaining ingroup inclusion. In D. Abrams, M. A. Hogg, & J. M. Marques (Eds.), *The social psychology of inclusion and exclusion* (pp. 89–111). New York, NY: Psychology Press.

Pinto, I., Marques, J., Levine, J. M., & Abrams, D. (2010). Membership status and subjective group dynamics: Who triggers the Black Sheep Effect? *Journal of Personality and Social Psychology, 99*, 107–119.

Platow, M. J., Reid, S. A., & Andrew, S. (1998). Leadership endorsement: The role of distributive and procedural behavior in interpersonal and intergroup contexts. *Group Processes and Intergroup Relations, 1*, 35–47.

Platow, M. J., van Knippenberg, D., Haslam, S. A., van Knippenberg, B., & Spears, R. (2006). A special gift we bestow on you for being representative of us: Considering leader charisma from a self-categorization perspective. *British Journal of Social Psychology, 45*, 303–320.

Prislin, R. (2010). Persuasion as social interaction. In J. P. Forgas, J. Cooper, W. D. Crano, J. P. Forgas, J. Cooper, & W. D. Crano (Eds.), *The psychology of attitudes and attitude change* (pp. 215–227). New York, NY: Psychology Press.

Rast, D. E. III, Gaffney, A. M., & Hogg, M. A. (2013). The tyranny of normative distance: A social identity account of the exercise of power by remote leaders. In M. C. Bligh & R. E. Riggio (Eds.), *Exploring distance in leader-follower relationships: When near is far and far is near* (pp. 215–240). New York, NY: Routledge.

Rast, D. E. III, Gaffney, A. M., Hogg, M. A., & Crisp, R. J. (2012). Leadership under uncertainty: When leaders who are non-prototypical group members can gain support. *Journal of Experimental Social Psychology, 48*, 646–653.

Rast, D. I., Hogg, M. A., & Giessner, S. R. (2013). Self-uncertainty and support for autocratic leadership. *Self and Identity, 12*, 635–649.

Raven, B. H. (1993). The bases of power: Origins and recent developments. *Journal of Social Issues, 49*, 227–251.

Reicher, S., Haslam, S. A., & Hopkins, N. (2005). Social identity and the dynamics of leadership: Leaders and followers as collaborative agents in the transformation of social reality. *The Leadership Quarterly, 16*, 547–568.

Reicher, S., & Hopkins, N. (2003). On the science of the art of leadership. In D. van Knippenberg & M. A. Hogg (Eds.), *Leadership and power: Identity processes in groups and organisations* (pp. 197–209). London, England: SAGE.

Reicher, S. D. (1984). The St. Pauls' riot: An explanation of the limits of crowd action in terms of a social identity model. *European Journal of Social Psychology, 14*, 1–21.

Reid, S. A., & Hogg, M. A. (2005). Uncertainty reduction, self-enhancement, and ingroup identification. *Personality and Social Psychology Bulletin, 31*, 804–817.

Ridgeway, C. L. (2003). Status characteristics and leadership. In D. van Knippenberg & M. A. Hogg (Eds.), *Leadership and power: Identity processes in groups and organizations* (pp. 65–78). London, England: SAGE.

Rios Morrison, K., & Wheeler, S. (2010). Nonconformity defines the self: The role of minority opinion status in self-concept clarity. *Personality and Social Psychology Bulletin, 36*, 297–308.

Runciman, W. G. (1966). *Relative deprivation and social justice.* London, England: Routledge and Kegan Paul.

Rydell, R. J., & McConnell, A. R. (2005). Perceptions of entitativity and attitude change. *Personality and Social Psychology Bulletin, 31*, 99–110.

Sani, F. (2008). Schism in groups: A social psychological account. *Social and Personality Psychology Compass, 2*, 718–732.

Sani, F., & Pugliese, A. (2008). In the name of Mussolini: Explaining the schism in an Italian right-wing political party. *Group Dynamics: Theory, Research, and Practice, 12*, 242–253.

Schachter, S. (1951). Deviation, rejection and communication. *Journal of Abnormal and Social Psychology, 46*, 190–207.

Sorrentino, R. M., & Short, J. C. (1986). Uncertainty orientation, motivation, and cognition. *Handbook of motivation and cognition: Foundations of social behavior* (pp. 379–403). New York, NY: Guilford Press.

Steffens, N. K., Haslam, S. A., & Reicher, S. D. (2014). Up close and personal: Evidence that shared social identity is a basis for the "special" relationship that binds followers to leaders. *The Leadership Quarterly, 25*(2), 296–313.

Sugisawa, H., Liang, J., & Liu, X. (1994). Social networks, social support, and mortality among older people in Japan. *Journal of Gerontology, 49*, S3–S13.

Syrianrefugees.eu (26 July, 2014). *A snapshot of the crisis in Syria and Europe.* Retrieved from http://syrianrefugees.eu.

Tajfel, H. (1959). Quantitative judgement in social perception. *British Journal of Psychology, 50*, 16–29.

Tajfel, H. (1969). Social and cultural factors in perception. In G. Lindzey & E. Aronson (Eds.), *Handbook of social psychology* (Vol. *3*, pp. 315–394). Reading, MA: Addison-Wesley.

Tajfel, H. (1972). Social categorization. English manuscript of "La catégorisation sociale." In S. Moscovici (Ed.) *Introduction à la Psychologie Sociale* (Vol. *1*, pp. 272–302). Paris: Larousse.

Tajfel, H., & Turner, J. C. (1979). An integrative theory of intergroup conflict. In W. G. Austin & S. Worchel (Eds.), *The social psychology of intergroup relations* (pp. 33–47). Monterey, CA: Brooks/Cole.

Thomas, G., Martin, R., Epitropaki, O., Guillaume, Y. & Lee, A. (2013). Social cognition in leader–follower relationships: Applying insights from relationship science to understanding relationship-based approaches to leadership. *Journal of Organizational Behavior, 34*, 63–81.

Thomas, E. F., McGarty, C., & Louis, W. (2014). Social interaction and psychological pathways to political engagement and extremism. *European Journal of Social Psychology, 44*(1), 15–22.

Tormala, Z. K., DeSensi, V. L., & Petty, R. E. (2007). Resisting persuasion by illegitimate means: A metacognitive perspective on minority influence. *Personality and Social Psychology Bulletin, 33*, 354–367.

Turner, J. C. (1975). Social comparison and social identity: Some prospects for intergroup behaviour. *European Journal of Social Psychology, 5*, 5–34.

Turner, J. C. (1985). Social categorization and the self-concept: A social cognitive theory of group behavior. In E.

J. Lawler (Ed.), *Advances in group processes: Theory and research* (Vol. *2*, pp. 77–121). Greenwich, CT: JAI Press.

Turner, J. C. (1991). *Social influence.* Buckingham, UK: Open University Press.

Turner, J. C., Brown, R. J., & Tajfel, H. (1979). Social comparison and group interest in ingroup favouritism. *European Journal of Social Psychology, 9*, 187–204.

Turner, J. C., Hogg, M. A., Oakes, P. J., Reicher, S. D., & Wetherell, M. S. (1987). *Rediscovering the social group: A self-categorization theory.* Oxford, England: Blackwell.

van den Bos, K. (2007). Hot cognition and social justice judgments: The combined influence of cognitive and affective factors on the justice judgment process. In D. de Cremer (Ed.), *Advances in the psychology of justice and affect* (pp. 59–82). Greenwich, CT: Information Age.

van den Bos, K., & Lind, E. A. (2002). Uncertainty management by means of fairness judgments. In M. P. Zanna (Ed.), *Advances in experimental social psychology* (Vol. *34*, pp. 1–60). San Diego, CA: Academic Press.

van den Bos, K., Poortvliet, P. M., Maas, M., Miedema, J., & van den Ham, E. (2005). An enquiry concerning the principles of cultural norms and values: The impact of uncertainty and mortality salience on reactions to violations and bolstering of cultural worldviews. *Journal of Experimental Social Psychology, 41*, 91–113.

van Knippenberg, D., & Wilke, H. (1992). Prototypicality of arguments and conformity to ingroup norms. *European Journal of Social Psychology, 22*, 141–155.

Wesselmann, E. D., Williams, K. D., Pryor, J. B., Eichler, F. A., Gill, D., & Hogue, J. D. (2014). Revisiting Schachter's research on rejection, deviance, and communication (1951). Special issue on "Replications of Important Effects in Social Psychology," *Social Psychology, 45*, 164–169.

Williams, K. D., Cheung, C. K. T., & Choi, W. (2000). Cyberostracism: Effects of being ignored over the Internet. *Journal of Personality and Social Psychology, 79*, 748–762.

# Deindividuation

Russell Spears

## Abstract

Deindividuation is among the classic phenomena researched by the early pioneers of social psychology. Building on the theorizing of LeBon (1895/1985), deindividuation provided an explanation for aggression in the crowd, a concern as relevant today as it was in the previous two centuries. The theory predicts that behavior becomes more antinormative and aggressive under conditions of anonymity, associated with group immersion, and that this occurs because of reduced self-awareness and deregulated behavior. However, close scrutiny of the deindividuation literature provides scant evidence for the deindividuation process. Revisiting the primary literature reveals at best mixed support for the original claims and many contradictions, often belied by accounts in secondary sources and textbooks. Reformulation and refinement of the theory has not helped. I present a reinterpretation, in terms of social influence by group norms, in line with social identity principles, supported by experimental evidence and a meta-analysis of the original deindividuation literature.

**Key Words:** deindividuation, aggression, anonymity, identifiability, self-awareness, accountability, social identity, SIDE model

The concept of deindividuation is one of the most celebrated, compelling but perhaps also most controversial concepts that emerged from the birth of modern social psychology as an empirical science in the postwar era. In what has been called the crowd century (Reicher, 2011), a key political concern that emerged after the defeat of fascism, superseded by the reality of communism in the cold war, was the psychology of the mass and the power of the collective, epitomized by the crowd. Here a driving interest to understand the process of social influence, central to this volume, was not only to find ways to encourage housewives to accept cheaper cuts of meat, but to understand group processes that had the potential to change the world order through riot and revolution. Deindividuation, as an attempt to explain social disorder in the mass, emerged as a concept that seemed to capture this urgency and concern, and although its roots in the seminal publication by Festinger, Pepitone, and Newcomb

(1952) did not acknowledge this, it had its foundation in the writings of Le Bon in the preceding century.

Le Bon's *The Crowd* (1995/1895) was a response to a very similar "crisis of control" which arose during the social upheaval in the wake of the industrial revolution, leading to fears of revolution of a more political kind (Reicher, 1982, 1987, 2011). Indeed the fear of collective power as a threat to both authority and individual freedom is a recurring theme that framed the era from the French revolution to the Paris commune that preoccupied Le Bon, but with no less resonance in the aftermath of World War II. It was against this backdrop that Festinger and others sought an explanation for the apparent power of the crowd and found compelling ideas and answers in Le Bon's writings. One needs to realize that this was an era when social psychology was still in its infancy, and few established texts, still fewer based on solid empirical science, existed.

Indeed, it was the task of this postwar generation of social psychologists to write these texts. Although Le Bon's ideas had little scientific credence (even in their day), this was not seen as a problem as the ideas predated the science of social psychology. Thus, these early theorists saw it as their mission to provide this credence, by testing these ideas in the laboratory, rather than simply observing events in the field. Lewin's (1951) credo that "there is nothing so practical as a good theory" seemed to justify this approach, but in retrospect, theories can sometimes be wrong and begin to live a life of their own, even under empirical scrutiny. I jump ahead, however, and it is the purpose of this chapter to give an account of the deindividuation concept and its literature, which has perhaps both a historical and a scientific perspective.

With this in mind, I deal with this literature in the first instance and for the most part in narrative terms and generally in chronological order. It is useful to see how ideas developed but also how the construct cast a powerful influence (perhaps shadow) over several decades of ensuing research. It is also instructive to see, somewhat in historical perspective also, how deindividuation research was to some extent a child of its time. Methods suitable to testing some of the key assumptions and predictions were often not yet there or insufficiently developed to allow this test (especially in relation to measuring unconscious states). Interestingly, the literature has not been revisited as such methods have become available, but nevertheless some of the myths persist, perhaps because the ideas were so compelling. Deindividuation, as the unruly child, is still very much alive in textbooks and the popular image of the crowd. Toward the end of this narrative review I present some results from a more quantitative (meta-) analysis of the literature that evaluates some of the key ideas. However, rather than cut to the chase, it is instructive first to take the full journey and see how these ideas around deindividuation developed, and persisted, and ponder how and why they captured the scientific as well as the popular imagination.

## Classic(al) Contributions—The First 25 Years of Deindividuation Research

The first study to define and research deindividuation was published in 1952 by Festinger, Pepitone, and Newcomb, in the *Journal of Abnormal and Social Psychology*, and entitled "Some consequences of deindividuation in a group." It had no references (and no abstract), which is perhaps not

surprising given the pioneering nature of this very first study on the topic. As noted earlier, one reference that could have been included (but was not) would have acknowledged the debt to Le Bon's *The Crowd* (1995/1895), which was clearly the source of the basic ideas. The basic premise of the paper is that being in a group allows people to be released from the restraints they feel as individuals and thus indulge their inhibitions. They suggest that crowds create a context in which submergence in the group means that people are not singled out or paid attention to, which loosens and lessens inner restraints, allowing the release of behavior that would typically be restrained. This state of affairs was defined as "deindividuation."

Festinger et al. attempted to gain evidence for these ideas in a series of discussions among groups of four to seven Michigan psychology students. After being engaged in some "small talk" by the observer, the experimenter then read the participants the results of (bogus) research using modern psychiatric techniques that suggested that 87 percent of a representative sample of Americans "possessed a strong, deep-seated hatred of one or both parents," with denial of such impulses a sure sign that they existed (in line with psychoanalytic thinking about denial and defense mechanisms). This last feature was added after pilot research had shown that without it participants were reluctant to admit to any such hostile feeling toward their parents.

This formed the prompt for a group discussion of participants' personal feelings about their parents, lasting for 40 minutes. The observer later coded the comments critical of parents. The researchers took the "extent to which members of the group were unable to identify who said what during the discussion" as a measure of deindividuation. To do this, they computed the errors in identifying who said what, and subtracted from this the errors in correctly identifying statements that were made when presented with foils. This was then correlated with the frequency of expression of negative attitudes about parents as a test of the deindividuation hypothesis ($r = .22$, which became .57 after eliminating an outlier group!). In a second key prediction, this reduction in restraint was also positively correlated with attraction to the group ($r = .36$, albeit only $p < .1$). The authors interpreted the reduction in inner restraints in the group and attraction to the group as support for their deindividuation predictions.

Clearly there are a number of issues with methodology and interpretation in this seminal study. Perhaps a central concern is the strong directive, if not *demand characteristic*, to produce negative comments that were in turn interpreted as a lack of restraint. This set a pattern for much subsequent deindividuation research, which, at least in its heyday, received little comment or concern, but arguably has returned to haunt interpretation of deindividuation research (see Postmes & Spears, 1998). An alternative interpretation not considered was that people were less identifiable for their statements to the extent that they followed the group norms or demand given by the experimenter. Interestingly the excluded outlier group, which they characterized as uninterested in the task (and which included not going along with the experimental demands) showed the lowest degree of identifiability (i.e., defined as deindividuation) but highest levels of restraint in terms of negative attitudes expressed about parents. In short, these participants seemed to reject the demand to be negative about parents but showed no less deindividuation in terms of lack of identifiability.

These issues notwithstanding, this study was extremely important and influential in starting the scientific program that put Le Bonian ideas into action.

Despite the auspicious beginnings, the course of deindividuation research hardly spread like wildfire (in contrast to Festinger's other contributions to the field) with only a couple of papers in the next two decades (Cannavale, Scarr, & Pepitone, 1970; Singer, Brush, & Lublin, 1965).

Singer et al. (1965) developed the deindividuation paradigm and presented the first attempt to manipulate the identifiability factor in terms of clothing. In two studies they manipulated this by asking their women participants (sophomore students) to dress up (dress, high heels, and hose) or to turn up in old/casual clothes. They defined these conditions as high versus low identifiability, respectively. They then presented a paradigm in the guise of a concept learning task in which participants were required to read out and assess whether passages from an erotic literature text that was considered taboo (*Lady Chatterley's Lover*) fit the particular complex concept under consideration (i.e., whether or not it conformed to the definition of being pornographic). In a nontaboo control condition participant reacted to a more neutral text assessing whether or not an education was considered liberal. Singer et al. predicted and found that these women were (inter alia) more likely to use obscene language (an indicator of disinhibited deindividuation) when in less identifiable clothing. However, the prediction

that participants would show more attraction to the group under the deindividuated/taboo conditions was not upheld.

An alternative interpretation of the finding here is that greater use of taboo or obscene language does not so much reflect identifiability of clothing but the norms associated with being "dressed up" (more refined and following social decorum and etiquette standards) and "dressing down," with associated norms being more relaxed and less prudish.

Perhaps the next major milestone in the deindividuation literature was the publication of Zimbardo's (Zimbardo, 1969) provocatively entitled chapter: "The human choice: Individuation, reason and order versus deindividuation, impulse and chaos." This influential and widely cited chapter truly ignited interest in deindividuation. As Zimbardo's other famous work on the Stanford Prison experiment demonstrated, he had the knack for promotion in publicizing a phenomenon (and it is noteworthy that mainstream experimental journals were not the chosen forum in either case). This chapter includes field studies showing mindless vandalism to cars, as well as laboratory experiments, as evidence for deindividuation.

Zimbardo developed a model that sought to further analyze the processes in deindividuation in terms of a sequence of input variables (e.g., anonymity, group size, arousal), inferred subjective changes (reduced self-evaluation, lowered thresholds for expressing inhibited behaviors), and output variables (e.g., impulsive irrational behaviors). The range of input variables and output behaviors in particular is quite extensive and heterogeneous (10 and 11 factors listed, respectively). Moreover, some seemed potentially inconsistent. For example, under output behaviors was listed "perceptual distortion—insensitivity to incidental stimuli . . . " (f), whereas the following item (g) refers to "Hyper responsiveness—'contagious plasticity' to behavior of proximal active others" (p. 253). In short, the cues to which participants might be more or less responsive is not always clear (a theme to which we shall return). Zimbardo then goes on to present two experiments examining the effects of anonymity (one of the input variables) on aggression.

In the first study with women students (coeds), anonymity was induced in half the participants by having them wear large coats and hoods, never addressing them by name, and conducting the study in the dark. In the other condition "their individuality and identifiability were emphasized throughout" (p. 262) by giving them name tags and emphasizing their unique reactions in the instruction (p. 264). Participants then heard a taped interview with the experimenter and a future (female) "victim," one sweet and the other obnoxious (portrayed as conceited and prejudiced toward the Jewish students at their university). They were then provided a rationale for allocating electric shocks to the victims in order to study whether "empathy judgments differ when one is passively or actively involved with the target persons." (Actively involved meant inducing reactions directly from the target, although this was combined with another conditioning experiment.) Ps understood that two of the four in the group would allocate the shocks with the other two serving as observers. After being seated in separate cubicles and receiving a strong test shock to show how this felt, they were shown how this apparatus worked: A light came on when they were required to shock and a green light remained on for the duration of the administered shock. They could see the victim interacting with the experimenter, and also reacting in considerable pain. All Ps were allocated to the shock condition and thought the shock was combined with the shock administered by the other group member through a common system. The main dependent variable was the duration of the shock administered. The duration of shock was twice as long in the deindividuated participants (although the frequency did not differ). Moreover, whereas the shock administered by identifiable participants was reduced for the nice victim and increased for the nasty victim over time, shocks seemed to increase for both targets over trials in the deindividuation condition.

A second study was conducted with soldiers in the Belgian army. In this study participants were seated in separate cubicles and told that the research was concerned with impression formation in which they were asked to judge strangers whom they could see (identifiable) or not (nonidentifiable). Together with the identifiability of the participants themselves, this resulted in a 2 × 2 design. Telling participants that interpersonal judgments can be biased by others helped to justify concealing the Ps' identity, so that Ps so informed wore hoods in the deindividuated condition, whereas those in the identifiable condition just wore their military uniforms.

The task was to control the duration of shock administered to an observed other in order to "judge his reaction to a condition they helped create." Once again the main DV was the duration of the shock administered (again, other judges also delivered shocks independently so the source of

shock could not be ascertained, resulting in diffusion of responsibility). The identifiability conditions contrasted with the deindividuation condition on a number of dimensions (no hoods, name tags, bright lighting), whereas nonidentifiable Ps also knew from observing-closed circuit TV that they were not identifiable as only the backs of others were visible to each other.

Unexpectedly, aggression measured by shock duration was actually *less* under both conditions of own anonymity and deindividuation (i.e., whether or not the victim was also identifiable). Moreover, shock duration increased in the identifiable conditions rather than in the nonidentifiable conditions (in contrast to the earlier experiment). Zimbardo, on the basis of reactions of some of the participants, concluded that their manipulation had not worked because the soldiers indicated that they were uncomfortable wearing the hoods and were self-conscious. Moreover, the military uniforms they were wearing and which were visible in the identifiable conditions made them indistinguishable and thus deindividuated. In other words, Zimbardo was able to reconcile these results with the theory and predictions.

## Some Emerging Questions: Variability, Valence, Cues, and Norms

We have now reviewed enough early classical studies to get a good idea of early research on deindividuation and the experimental paradigms used to test these ideas. The puzzling results of Zimbardo's second study were not an isolated problem in the deindividuation literature. In the 1970s evidence started to emerge that classical deindividuation conditions such as anonymity could sometimes lead to much more positive and prosocial behavior. In particular, a study by Gergen, Gergen, and Barton (1973) showed students put in a darkroom where nobody was identifiable engaged in altogether much more positive "touchy-feely" behavior (participants were not required to administer shocks), more akin to the T-group and love-ins that were part of the zeitgeist at the height of the Hippy era (and presumably no less so at a liberal arts college where this study was conducted). Therefore, Gergen et al. argued, in contrast to Zimbardo's claims that deindividuation generically increases antisocial behavior, that the behavior depends on the nature of the salient cues.

Although the absence of aggression in this study in which people were free to behave could be seen as a strength, the possibility remains that aggression could be stronger under anonymity when the means are available and encouraged (i.e., the typical Buss aggression machine paradigm). This point is nicely addressed even more explicitly in an elegant study by Johnson and Downing (1979) in which they noticed that the hoods and overalls used by Zimbardo (and others) in his deindividuation manipulation were rather reminiscent of the attire of the Ku Klux Klan white supremacists and therefore provided implicit cues to aggression. They tested this idea by using deindividuated clothing designed to reflect these and alternative cues. The experimenter stated of the uniforms to be donned in the deindividuation condition either (a) "I'm not much of a seamstress; this thing came out looking kind of Ku Klux Klannish" or (b) "I was fortunate the hospital recovery room let me borrow these nurses' gowns to use in the study." Results showed no main effect of deindividuation (i.e., wearing of clothing to produce anonymity), but main effects of the *type* of uniforms, reflected in reduced aggression (shocks in a learning paradigm) for nurses compared to KKK-like clothing. An interaction effect also indicated reduced aggression in the nurses' uniforms but marginally more aggression in the KKK uniforms compared to individuated conditions. This study would therefore seem to confirm that it is not deindividuation qua anonymity per se that produces aggression; the nature of the cues seems to be critical.

This notion that there were positive as well as negative sides to the classical deindividuation process was a central theme of Dipboye's (1977) review of the deindividuation literature. Dipboye highlighted two sides of the deindividuation process. The idea that anonymity and group immersion free one from inhibitions leading to negative behavior was only one side; there is also an implicit sense that losing one's inhibitions could be positively liberating. However, Dipboye suggests that because deindividuation implies a loss of identity, it can also be threatening to lose one's sense of self and who you are as an individual (although it is not clear how such threat manifests itself under lack of awareness). This narrative fit also with the then current zeitgeist of self-discovery and self-actualization proposed by Maslow and others. In other words, it seems that deindividuation could be characterized as a liberating state with predominantly negative outcomes or a threatening state that prevented self-expression. In short, which direction liberation lies depends somehow on one's view of human nature and the view of the self. And as we have seen, deindividuation itself could also be associated with positive outcomes. So

how can we explain this? A theory that predicts both positive and negative outcomes, especially when designed to explain the negative, could be seen as problematic.

It is also interesting to note that findings that behavior produced by deindividuating conditions was sensitive to normative cues were used to refine rather than reject deindividuation theory. One potentially plausible and parsimonious explanation for this effect is that people become more sensitive to the (local) group norms under deindividuating conditions. However, for most theories of group influence, following group norms implies a conscious process of conformity or compliance to the group whether this reflects the influence of reference groups, normative (group) influence (Deutsch & Gerard, 1955), or (albeit much later) referent informational influence (RII) in self-categorization theory (SCT; Turner, 1982, Turner et al., 1987). As we will see later, RII is a favored interpretation of social identity-based conceptualization of deindividuation findings.

The (group) norm explanation for deindividuation effects has always been problematic from a deindividuation theory perspective. This is because a central plank of the deindividuation account is that the deindividuation process should result in transgression of norms or antinormative behavior. However, the implicit conceptualization of norms and "normative" within deindividuation theory is rather generic and rigid, associating norms with general moral values ("doing the right thing") rather than with specific norms. In other words, according to this approach, aggression is antinormative by definition. More seriously for deindividuation theory, following norms seems to imply a conscious social process with awareness of social standards, quite the opposite of the mindless process invoking loss of self-awareness and self-regulation. The typical deindividuation theory answer to this conundrum has been to argue that people are more influenced by local *cues* (see Diener, 1980). However, it is not clear that labeling this influence by cue instead of norm solves the conceptual problems. The question simply arises of how to distinguish a situational cue from a local or specific group norm and the role of (self) awareness in this process?

It is worth briefly revisiting some of the classic studies we have considered so far to see whether a (group) normative interpretation can make sense of the earlier findings. A number of studies that used women participants may have inadvertently tapped into normative gender role behavior (e.g., notably women to be less aggressive), especially in the individuated conditions where personal accountability is also typically emphasized. For example, in the study by Singer, Bush, and Lublin (1965), described earlier, it is not hard to imagine that the manipulation that required them to dress up smartly (individuation conditions) conveyed stronger "ladylike" gender norms (especially in that era) than were present when they were asked to dress down.

Similarly the individuated condition in Zimbardo's second study with Belgian soldiers found more evidence of aggression in this condition (contrary to original predictions). But this also seems to fit with a normative interpretation, insofar as aggression is quite consistent with the military role and identity salient when in uniform (which the hoods and overalls arguably only obscured and neutralized). On this interpretation, group norms can also help to make sense of the pattern found in the individuated conditions, and this is arguably problematic for the interpretation that "salient situational" cues will typically have more impact in deindividuating conditions.

Supporting this line of analysis, Carver (1974; also cited in Dipboye's 1977 review) found that when there is a norm or standard for aggression (e.g., that shocks given by a teacher can facilitate learning), lowered self-awareness *decreased* aggression and heightened awareness *increased* it. This goes directly against the deindividuation account of aggression flowing from reduced self-awareness but fits a normative interpretation that behaving aggressively can reflect conscious and regulated goal-directed behavior. We will return to the normative theme later when we consider the social identity reinterpretation of deindividuation effects (the SIDE model). In the meantime these concerns and alternative interpretations made it all the more important to critically evaluate evidence for the deindividuation process and specifically the claim that aggression followed from reduced self-awareness. This was a key objective of the subsequent wave of deindividuation research to which we now turn.

## Process Focus: Reduced Self-Awareness as the Basis for Deindividuated Aggression

By the end of the 1970s much research on deindividuation phenomena had accumulated, but the combination of mixed evidence and alternative interpretations seemed to raise as many questions as provide answers. In an influential review

chapter, Diener (1980), who had conducted many field and lab experiments on deindividuation, made a concerted plea to refocus research on the proposed process involved in deindividuation, namely the absence of self-awareness and self-regulation. Integrating deindividuation theory with Duval and Wicklund's (1972) objective self-awareness theory, he argued that many of the input variables considered by Zimbardo (e.g., anonymity, group immersion) will lead people to become less aware of themselves as individuals, to direct attention outward, and to be more susceptible to influence by external cues to aggression, resulting in disinhibited behavior.

Although he acknowledged that people could be influenced by the "ad hoc" norms in the group, and thereby drew a link with the "emergent norm" account of R. H. Turner (see e.g., Turner & Killian, 1972), he argued that these are "not really norms at all" because they do not follow from internalized and morally correct personal norms (or those associated with their primary reference group) (see Diener, 1980, p. 230). In short, the basic deindividuation account that the deindividuated behavior results from lack of self-awareness, externally directed attention, and a breakdown in self-regulation was maintained.

However, despite this focus on the self-regulation process, hard evidence for this was difficult to find, and it should be acknowledged that techniques to investigate such processes, which often imply lack of awareness and unconscious or implicit processes, were not well developed at this time. Indeed, although such methods have developed dramatically since the 1980s, by then the heyday of deindividuation research had passed and has not since been revisited (perhaps for reasons that will become clearer).

If we examine some of Diener's own representative research on this topic, then once again interpretations of findings could be made in terms of equally plausible mechanisms based on conscious and even rational or norm-following behavior. One example is evident in the research using the "trick or treat" paradigm that Diener and colleagues developed in a series of field experiments (e.g., Diener, Fraser, Beaman, & Kalem, 1976). The key dependent variable in these studies was whether the children took more than one piece of candy (or stole money) when offered at the doorstep, which increased to the extent that the children were in groups, were anonymous, and where responsibility was attributed to another. However, rather than reflecting a deindividuated state (reduced self-awareness and self-regulation), which was nearly impossible to measure in this context, it seems equally plausible that behavior was driven by self-interest, and the (perceived) reduced likelihood of getting caught and being held accountable for such "transgressions."

A series of studies by Beaman, Klentz, Diener, and Svanum (1979) aimed to provide more direct evidence for the role of the self-awareness process by placing a mirror behind the candy bowl in an attempt to manipulate "objective" self-awareness (Duval & Wicklund, 1972). The mirror manipulation indeed reduced transgression rates among those who had been individuated by giving their name and address, but not among those who were anonymous. Unfortunately, however, this finding is also consistent with the argument that people who are less likely to feel recognized and accountable will be more likely to pursue hedonic or self-interested behavior they think they can get away with. In other words, proof of the decreased accountability is not evidence of the *reduced awareness* proposed to drive the effect in the deindividuation condition.

In another equally high impact paradigm, Diener, Dineen, Endresen, Beaman, and Fraser (1975) used a context in which they manipulated aggressive norms, models, and degree of responsibility for a task, labeled elsewhere (Diener, Westford, Dineen, & Fraser, 1973; Diener, 1980) as "beat the pacifist." Participants were instructed that they could do various things to a "role player" sitting on the floor of a dimly lit room. Various materials were provided for this purpose (paper balls for throwing, rubber bands, foam bats, plastic guns, Ping-Pong balls). Factors were manipulated that were predicted to increase aggression (an aggression norm, an aggressive role model, lowered responsibility), all of which had independent effects in the predicted direction. However, no evidence was found for the proposed mediating state of deindividuation through reduced self-awareness.

In later research, Diener further pursued the quest to find evidence for this deindividuated state (e.g., Diener, 1979; Diener, Lusk, DeFour, & Flax, 1980). Unfortunately, these studies are also clouded by questions of interpretation in relation to methodology and measures. For example, in Diener (1979) the deindividuation manipulation consisted of a wide range of group activities, any of which could be responsible for differences with the other contrast conditions (high vs. low self-awareness), and the fact that Ps were told that their data "would be treated as a group, not on an individual basis."

So once again (notwithstanding possible confounds between group and individual identity—see the SIDE model later), there is the problem that differences can be attributed to differences in individual responsibility for action, potentially reflecting the presence of a conscious accountability process in individuated conditions, rather than an unconscious disinhibition process in the deindividuated conditions (see earlier).

Moreover, the measures designed to assess such a process involved a series of self-report scales (e.g., reported self-consciousness), which are far from an ideal means of tapping into a processing involving *lack* of awareness (again this was before the era of implicit measures that would be less open to this criticism). In another series of studies Diener et al. (1980) showed that whereas a number of group factors were related to (reduced) self-consciousness in groups (e.g., group size, number of observers), behavior disinhibition was not related to this lowered self-consciousness, contrary to deindividuation predictions.

To summarize, although Diener and his associates greatly enriched the deindividuation literature and developed a number of colorful and high-impact paradigms to research deindividuation, many questions remain about the evidence and particularly the underlying process. In particular, a key concern that recurs in a number of studies, but which was arguably inherent in the deindividuation concept from the very start (i.e., Festinger et al., 1952), is the problem of reconciling a deindividuated state, premised on lack of self-awareness and reduced self regulation, with the possibility that antisocial behavior resulting from anonymity in the group could also reflect a conscious process in which group members act with the knowledge that they are not accountable and therefore cannot be held responsible for their behavior. This is particularly problematic when such behavior is hedonic or self-interested (e.g., in the trick-or-treat paradigm). But even when it is not, the behavior in question could reflect the behavioral demands of the experiment or experimenter or at least implicit norms within the situation.

In the most recent wave of deindividuation research to date, pioneered by Prentice-Dunn and Rogers (see Prentice Dunn & Rogers, 1989, for a review and model), this central problem was at least (and at last) explicitly acknowledged. These authors further pursued the agenda of previous deindividuation theorists, and particularly Diener, in trying to pin down evidence for the elusive deindividuated state, and, thus, the process underlying aggressive behavior in the group. However, they now recognized explicitly that there was a problem in treating deindividuation manipulations involving anonymity as implicating the deindividuation process qua reduced self-awareness. In contrast, they proposed that anonymity could lead to disinhibited behavior by a different "accountability" route in which transgressions go unpunished. However, rather than relinquishing the link to self-awareness entirely, they introduced a second type of self-awareness originally proposed by Fenigstein, Scheier, and Buss (1975), namely *public* self-awareness (or self-consciousness), to apply to this anonymity route to aggression. Public self-awareness corresponds to how you are seen by a relevant audience and thus involves a degree of conscious metacognition. This is distinct from "private" self-awareness, which is more akin to the original formulation of objective self-awareness (Duval & Wicklund, 1972) and corresponds to awareness of self. It is private self-awareness that is thus reduced in the true deindividuation route, which Prentice-Dunn and Rogers argue follows from immersion in the group and the heightened arousal and externally directed attention that this can evoke. Formulated in this way, many of the effects resulting from reduced identifiability should not be seen as reflecting a process of deindividuation (newly defined), but rather reduced accountability. Although this distinction looks useful and rescues the deindividuation concept from processes where conscious accountability may play a role, it is also a significant concession in the sense that the original conceptualization and test of deindividuation by Festinger et al. (1952), inter alia, would not count as deindividuation.

Although this "bracketing off" of anonymity is to some extent welcome in terms of clarifying the process, it may also be problematic to associate anonymity only with identifiability to others. As diverse theorists have noted, anonymity has different facets and different effects (see Diener, 1980). In particular, in developing the SIDE model (Reicher, Spears, & Postmes, 1995; Spears & Lea, 1994; Spears & Postmes, 2015), we have made a distinction between anonymity "of" (self) and anonymity "to" (others), and both these aspects have played a role in deindividuation theorizing. Thus, the early formulation of Festinger does not simply refer to the ability to be recognized but the possibility of being singled out in general, which includes others as well as the self. This was clearly part of their idea of submergence in the crowd—that others are difficult to distinguish (cf. the concept of "depersonalization" in self-categorization theory). We return to this issue shortly.

Meanwhile, with this conceptual clarification in place, the challenge was now on to find evidence for the deindividuation process more narrowly defined (in our review of the literature, Postmes & Spears, 1998, refer to this as the *contemporary* deindividuation account to distinguish it from the classical definition involving anonymity). However, as we shall see, unfortunately this quest suffered from some of the same problems that Diener had encountered in his program of research.

Prentice-Dunn and Rogers (1980) conducted a study in which they manipulated deindividuated versus individuation cues with aggression models (high, low, no) in a 2x3 design. The experimental procedure ostensibly combined two different experiments concerned with behavior modification and biofeedback. In the biofeedback set-up participants were instructed to administer electric shocks to a participant when his displayed heart rate fell below a certain level. Participants were seated at separate "aggression" machines, blocked from the view of others, and could choose a range of shock intensities, providing a measure of the aggression. In the deindividuated conditions, identifiability was minimized (similar to Zimbardo's paradigm) by *not* addressing participants by name, ensuring they would *not* meet the biofeedback subject afterward, and took place in a dimly lit room with white noise. In the individuated conditions the participants wore name tags, were addressed by name, expected to meet victims, the room was brightly lit, and so on.

The aggressive and less aggressive behavioral models were implemented under the guise of an equipment check. A confederate posing as one of the behavior modification participants then administered a series of test shocks to the biofeedback participants, which were high in intensity (aggressive model), or low (low aggression model), or this procedure was omitted (no model). The mean shock intensities subsequently administered by participants formed the main dependent variable and participants also completed a postsession self-report questionnaire designed to measure the deindividuated state. This measure (19 items) comprising two factors labeled as altered experience (e.g., thinking was somewhat altered, felt aroused, etc.) and self-awareness (e.g., felt self-conscious, heightened sense of individual identity, concerned with what others thought of me), and a combination of both of these was used to define the subjective state of deindividuation.

Results showed predicted main effects of both deindividuation and aggression models manipulations and no interactions. Deindividuating cues resulted in stronger shock intensities (but not longer shock durations) than the individuating conditions. Highly aggressive models produced more intense shocks than low, with the no-model condition in between. Both altered experience and self-awareness (negatively) predicted shock intensity, which was interpreted as providing evidence that the deindividuated state mediated the aggression.

A further experiment (Prentice-Dunn & Rogers, 1981) obtained similar results with a similar paradigm and deindividuation manipulation and an elaborated measure of self-reported states (but with other factors in the design involving the race of target). The self-report measure included altered states, but the self-awareness factor was now labeled as public self-awareness (albeit with many similar items from the earlier study).

From these studies it is clear that Prentice Dunn and Rogers were in the process of shifting to their more refined analysis of public versus private self awareness, and consequently these studies do not resolve the question of the whether the results are due at least in part to the lack of accountability associated with reducing public self-awareness. This interpretation is also consistent with the way in which deindividuation was manipulated (involving reduced identifiability). This issue was more directly addressed in their next publication (Prentice-Dunn & Rogers, 1982), in which they explicitly distinguished the public and private self-awareness dimension and relate these to the accountability and deindividuation routes, respectively. In this experiment they manipulated the variables associated with the two key routes outlined in their two-path model, namely public self-awareness associated with the reduced identifiability and accountability route, and reduced private self-awareness, associated with the deindividuation explanation (cf. Fenigstein et al., 1975). They then present a 2×2 experiment in which they manipulated accountability cues (high vs. low) designed to manipulate public self-awareness, and internal versus external attentional focus designed to manipulate private self-awareness (now defined as the true deindividuation path).

Similar to earlier studies, the cover story described the study as comprising *two* combined experiments, relating to problem solving and memory. The problem-solving experiment allowed the manipulation of deindividuation conditions (e.g., involving distractions to participants, multitasking, etc.), whereas the memory experiment was focused on the effect of "stressful distractions" on memory for the targets (victims), which provided participants the justification to allocate shocks to the victims. Ps (all male) were told that because both studies involved video games, these studies had been combined.

For the critical manipulation (external attentional cues condition designed to reduce private self-awareness and induce the deindividuated state), participants were repeatedly told to focus attention outward and not on themselves, and the study was repeatedly described as concerning group problem solving to enhance group cohesiveness. Ps then solved anagrams collectively in a dimly lit room and while listening to loud rock music (albeit devoid of aggressive lyrics; e.g., Bruce Springsteen). Verbal interaction was encouraged and facilitated by playing color video games. In the internal attentional cues condition, all these features were reversed: Ps were repeatedly instructed to concentrate on their own thoughts and feelings; the anagram and video task (only one game in black and white with less action) were solved individually in a brightly lit room without music.

The accountability cues manipulation was designed to heighten identifiability and public self-awareness. In the high-identifiability/awareness condition, Ps were introduced to the potential targets/victims of the memory experiment and told they would meet them again afterward (i.e., after the shock treatment), whereas in the low-accountability condition they did not meet nor expect to meet the victims later. Public and private self-awareness were measured after critical shock trials, and a retrospective questionnaire (i.e., self-report) was designed to measure any deindividuated state. Once again, this focused on altered experience but also on private self-awareness (linked to the deindividuated state).

In line with predictions, the different components of self-awareness were higher in the conditions where they were manipulated to be high. Moreover, rating of private self-awareness did not differ for the accountability manipulation or public self-awareness for the attentional focus manipulation. In short, the manipulations of the two factors seemed successful in that they had the predicted effects on the two types of self-awareness. Aggression as measured by the shocks (intensity and duration) also had the predicted main effects of manipulations, namely higher levels in low accountability and external attentional focus conditions.

Although these results look promising for the revised deindividuation account, the attempt to show mediation by means of the deindividuated state was less compelling. The attentional focus manipulation had effects on both altered experience and private self-awareness factors, but only altered experience was a reliable predictor of aggression and not the (reduced) private self-awareness (this was blamed on low power). In short, the crucial test of the revised (contemporary) deindividuation theory seemed to fall short in demonstrating the key mediating role for reduced (private) self-awareness. Moreover, although altered experience did seem to play a role, questions remain about what exactly this construct measures (it seems to be a mixed bag of different things) and how central this concept is to the proposed deindividuation process or state. The viability (and validity) of using explicit measures (self-report questionnaire items) to measure a putative absence of self-awareness is also debatable.

In sum, although the authors interpret this research as salvaging the more circumscribed definition of the deindividuation process in terms of reduced private self-awareness, a number of thematic problems remain. Notwithstanding the failure of the crucial mediating role of self-awareness in the process, a number of other features of the research raise questions and point to alternative interpretations of the findings. The manipulations, while high impact, are compound and complex, making it unclear just what process might explain these effects. In particular, the focus on the group in the deindividuation condition and the contrast with individual identity under the inward attentional focus instructions make it unclear whether the role of (individual) responsibility associated with the accountability route has entirely been eliminated from the purer conceptualization of the deindividuation process. Moreover, although the authors were at pains to point out that the additional stimuli such as heavy rock music were devoid of aggressive lyrics, this does not rule out the possibility that the (exclusively male) participants of the sample could have associated rock music with a more male-gendered mindset, priming aggression. A subsequent study by Prentice-Dunn and Spivey (1986) replicated some of the findings but suffered from some similar methodological questions raised here and below. In short, despite these efforts, the jury seems to still be out on whether the deindividuation process has been demonstrated.

## General Problems With Deindividuation: Some Recurring Themes and Questions

We have now considered sufficient deindividuation studies to get a good flavor of the research findings and the paradigms used over several waves of research. By the end of the 1980s, the deindividuation research program seemed to have more or less run its course, with the research program of Prentice-Dunn and Rogers providing the latest statement. However, it was unclear whether this was because there was little left to add, and the phenomenon was convincingly established, or because the claims for the process had remained elusive and unsustained. Whereas the textbooks might suggest the former, emerging critiques in the research literature itself suggested the deindividuation claims remained controversial and disputed. In the emerging era of automatic processes and implicit measurement techniques, one might have hoped that more compelling evidence for the key processes and deindividuated state might have emerged, but this seems not to have materialized.

Looking back at the deindividuation literature, we can discern a number of themes and questions amply illustrated in many of the studies presented here. One key concern is the question of demand characteristics, especially in deploying the Buss aggression machine paradigm used from Zimbardo's work to the research of Prentice-Dunn and Rogers. Despite noble attempts to justify the administration of electric shocks, often by ingenious means (combining experiments on learning, distraction, etc.), too often such instructions can be seen as producing the behavior prompted by the demands of the situation rather than acts of aggression. A key problem here is that aggression is usually defined and understood as the *intention* to do another harm (Averill, 1983), and if any harm done is directed by another, who often takes responsibility for this harm, then it is unclear whether this might not more appropriately be interpreted as conformity or even helping behavior. This criticism is not necessarily eliminated by the argument that it does not explain why participants may choose to shock longer or with greater intensity in key conditions, as this could represent greater willingness to conform or obey.

Indeed, the Milgram obedience to authority paradigm, perhaps the most (in)famous application of the aggression machine, is the elephant in the room that has curiously gone largely unremarked in the deindividuation literature. An exception mentioned earlier is Diener (1980), who tried to explain the difference. Zimbardo did refer to the similarities to the Milgram paradigm but distinguishes between the two: "there was no agent of coercion present to force the girls to act like killers (as in Milgram's obedience studies)." In this case, and unlike his "Frankenstein" moment of epiphany in the Stanford Prison experiment where he realizes the power of his role, Zimbardo curiously fails to acknowledge the power of the experimenter in such contexts (cf. Spears & Smith, 2001).

The deindividuation and Milgram paradigms are actually quite similar, but whereas the shocks in the Milgram studies were interpreted as reflecting a conformity to authority (a conscious process as reflected by the great anxiety experienced by many participants), we are asked to believe that giving shocks in the deindividuation paradigm, as requested by the experimenter, reflects a mindless process inaccessible to social norms and social influence. Thus, what appears to be essentially the same phenomenon (albeit save for the clothing, lighting, and group context) is taken as evidence for almost opposite psychological processes.

As noted earlier, the evidence that deindividuation reflects a process without conscious awareness is not at all clear or proven. Indeed, up until the very latest incarnation of the deindividuation process, lack of accountability resulting from anonymity and lack of identifiability were considered central aspects of the deindividuation process, but ones that Prentice-Dunn and Rogers explicitly noted produced an alternative and consciously mediated explanation for antinormative (i.e., aggressive) behavior. However, even in the latest research, classic deindividuation manipulations typically draw attention to the fact that participants are part of a group and will not be individually distinguished (read also: not be held individually accountable) for what the group as a whole does. This is true of most research by Prentice-Dunn and Rogers (as well as previous deindividuation researchers) designed to separate out deindividuation from accountability.

Moreover, focusing on the group versus the individual introduces a further confound between levels of identity (group vs. individual) and any norms that might be associated with the group in particular (and here gender group norms are sometimes in play). As we shall see shortly, the social identity account attaches central relevance to the level of identity (especially group identity) and its associated norms. Rather than treating the group as a vehicle for losing one's identity, it could be an important source of identity itself. Just as we have seen in the earlier research of Zimbardo and others,

many of the findings of Diener and Prentice-Dunn and Rogers and their associates could also reflect the role of group processes, in terms of group identities and group norms. For example, the male participants, used in perhaps the critical test of the "two paths" model of Prentice Dunn and Rogers, could well have taken the heavy rock music and video games as albeit subtle cues to aggression, especially when urged to focus on their group and lose their individual identity and responsibility. It is now time, then, to consider more directly alternative explanations for deindividuation phenomena that are grounded in group identity and group norms.

## Postdeindividuation Research: The Social Identity Critique and the SIDE Model

Although R. H. Turner's analysis of crowd behavior in terms of emergent norms (e.g., Turner & Killian, 1972) provided a contrasting group-based explanation of behavior in the crowd, the research of Reicher (1982, 1984, 1987) directly tackled the deindividuation approach from a social identity perspective. Reicher made explicit the problems with the LeBonian legacy underlying deindividuation research, and specifically the contrast of the rational individual with the irrational crowd (and thus group members). Using social identity theory (Tajfel & Turner, 1979), and its sister theory, self-categorization theory (Turner et al., 1987), he argued that immersion in the crowd did not represent a loss of identity or reduced self-awareness but rather a switch from individual identity to group identity and its associated group norms (e.g., Reicher, 1987).

This analysis still had to explain the characteristic effects of anonymity/identity found in the deindividuation studies, however. Here the argument was that one effect of anonymity was somewhat similar to the original argument of Festinger et al., namely that anonymity associated with immersion in the group could reduce the tendency to distinguish or "single out" individuals in the group. Self-categorization theory (Turner, 1982; Turner et al., 1987) argues that such a process, referred to as "depersonalization," can occur to the extent that group identity becomes salient: Individuals become seen less in terms of their unique individuality and more in terms of their shared group characteristics (they effectively become *interchangeable* group members). Clearly such a process of depersonalization would only be exacerbated to the extent that individual differences become harder to perceive (e.g., due to wearing masks and overalls, low lighting, etc., that is, the classic anonymity deindividuation manipulations).

However, it cannot be stressed strongly enough that this depersonalization process is radically different from the deindividuation process, both in terms of its cause and effects. Depersonalization reflects not a *loss* of self, but the presence and salience of a group self. This distinction between individual and group self (based on SCT, SIT) is wholly missing from deindividuation theory, which only considers the individual self and sees the group as an external entity in which the self is submerged and lost.

This traditional view of the group, as external to the self, was consistent with the mainstream view of group processes and social influence at the time that deindividuation theory was developed. This is reflected, for example, in the dual-process model of Deutsch and Gerard (1955), which regarded group influence (normative influence) as compliance, motivated by rewards and punishment from the group ("we go along with the group to get along"), rather than true influence (qua "informational influence"), an altogether more individual process, conforming to the notion of individual rationality.

The self-categorization account of social influence, by contrast, regarded the (in)group as perhaps the ultimate source of socially valid information (Turner, 1991). Because the group is part of self (especially for high identifiers, when salient), group influence is internal and willed rather than external and imposed, a process referred to as "referent informational influence" (Turner, 1982, 1991). People who categorize themselves as part of the group are likely to take on and internalize (i.e., be influenced by) what they see as normative for the group. This can be inferred "deductively" from knowledge of group norms, but where this is unclear, as it often is in the crowd, it can also be inferred "bottom up," inductively, from the behavior of others in situ (especially those seen as prototypical for the group; its leaders; see also Postmes, Spears, Lee, & Novak, 2005).

The first attempt to test some of these ideas and apply the self-categorization analysis of group influence to the deindividuation paradigm was conducted in a study by Reicher (1984). This was modeled closely on the classical deindividuation manipulations of group anonymity. A major criticism of the deindividuation approach from the perspective of social identity theorists is that, despite focusing on the group, it neglects the role of group identity and the role of the intergroup context in which crowd behavior typically occurs. Reicher

(1982, 1987) has argued that many crowd events that deindividuation research is intended to model (e.g., protests, riots) actually have a clear *inter*group character. This aspect is often suppressed or denied both in popular media representations of riots, as well as in research that tends to pathologize the crowd and see its behavior as a spontaneous effect of the mass, devoid of context, rather than in reaction to an antagonistic out-group (e.g., the police, the authorities). In the "mad mob" view of the crowd running amok propagated by Le Bon, and perpetuated by deindividuation theory, an analysis of intergroup context and antagonism was not necessary because the problem was the group itself, rather than the intergroup relationship.

Although this antagonistic analysis of the intergroup relation was less central to the current experiment, it is a key theme of the social identity analyses developed later in this chapter. Nevertheless in a departure from much previous deindividuation research, Reicher (1984) used an intergroup context in which science and social science students discussed their attitudes toward vivisection (research on animals) to assess the effects of group immersion and anonymity.

In the experiment, Reicher manipulated group norms in a video presentation such that the science students supported vivisection, whereas social science students were opposed. He predicted that groups would conform to their own group norms, especially when group boundaries and group identity salience was high (by seating the groups at separate tables), and even more so when members were rendered anonymous by virtue of the classical overalls and masks manipulation. Group salience indeed had a strong effect on conformity to the in-group norm, and there was also evidence, albeit only among science students, that under the "deindividuating" conditions of anonymity, their attitudes became more pro-vivisection (in line with the in-group norm) when their group boundaries and identity was salient, but less so when group identity salience was low.

The key point of this first study is that the classical deindividuation manipulations of group immersion and anonymity within the group produced behavior more in line with a group norm. Deindividuation theory, by contrast, would claim that deindividuating conditions would result in the transgression of (generic, prosocial) norms. Thus, using a group influence paradigm, Reicher's study suggests that anonymity within the group may enhance the operation of group norms, rather than simply being mindlessly directed by local cues. Although this paradigm was not focused on the classical aggressive behavior measures, this effect has close parallels to the study of Johnson and Downing (1979), which *did* focus on aggression and showed diveregent effects of the deindividuation manipulation based on the cues contained in the clothes (KKK cloaks vs. nurses uniforms), which could also be interpreted as signaling a contextual norm.

Spears, Lea, and Lee (1990) conducted a conceptual replication of the Reicher study in a paradigm more resembling the typical single group context of the classical deindividuation paradigm. Once again, the focus in this study was on the depersonalizing effects of anonymity in the group, enhancing group salience and thus conformity to group norms. Participants were all psychology students. We used the group polarization paradigm, predicting that group attitudes would polarize in the direction of group norms if this group identity was made salient and individuals were anonymous, resulting in increased depersonalization.

A novel twist in this study was that because all communication within the group was via computers, anonymity could be achieved in a naturalistic way by having people located in separate rooms (vs. together in the same room and therefore visible and individuated), thereby also side-stepping any reactive effects of the clothing (e.g., subtle cues, increased self-consciousness). This manipulation was crossed with an identity manipulation in which we emphasized group identity as psychology students or focused on individual identity by stating that the study focused on personality differences. The results were conceptually similar to the interaction for Science students in the Reicher (1984) study. Responses conformed more to the group norm under conditions of anonymity when group identity was salient (depersonalization). Thus, once again the combination of group identity salience and anonymity seems to lead to more group conformity in line with the self-categorization theory analysis but contra deindividuation theory. When group members are anonymous and their group identity is salient, they conform to these norms (depersonalization). In short, this reflects a shift to group identity, not a loss of individual identity.

Interestingly, attitudes shifted *away* from group norms when individual identity was made salient under visually anonymous conditions (Spears et al., 1990). This is not surprising, however, because conformity to group norms should not be expected if individual identity is salient. Indeed, we argued this result makes sense to the extent that in this context, where group norms are clear, the most effective and perhaps only way to express individuality is in *contrast* to the group norms.

One shortcoming of both these early tests of the social identity/SIDE account is that they lack evidence for the proposed mediating process in terms of group influence and depersonalization. This is important not least because of my critique that classical and contemporary deindividuation research is severely wanting in this respect. In some subsequent research we have provided further evidence for this group influence process.

In one set of studies, Postmes, Spears, Sakhel, and De Groot (2001) used a surreptitious priming procedure to manipulate the group norm in task groups that used computer-mediated communication (CMC) to make decisions in which group members were identifiable or visually anonymous. Specifically groups were tasked to resolve a policy dilemma about a hospital concerning whether patient care versus management efficiency should receive priority. To manipulate the group norm, we used a scrambled sentence procedure, ostensibly linked to another study, in which either efficiency-oriented or more prosocial concepts were made salient (i.e., these concepts were central to the "solved" sentences comprising scrambled words). Anonymity was manipulated by displaying photos of participants on the screen in the identifiable conditions, or not doing so. Consistent with SIDE predictions, groups tended to conform to the primed norm, and this effect *grew stronger over time*, but only in the anonymous condition.

In a second study we aimed to establish that this effect was caused by true intragroup influence and rule out the possibility that this was just an individually based cognitive priming effect. To this end, we created groups of four people of whom only two were primed (the efficiency prime) with the remaining two group members primed with a neutral prime that had nothing to do with the discussion topic. Once again we found that the impact of the norm was stronger in the anonymous condition, and most important the effect transferred just as strongly from the efficiency-primed to the neutrally primed group members. This research also provided evidence that influence was mediated by group identification, a proxy for group salience.

These studies are also important in showing that the social influence process is not confined to the group-polarization paradigm, where some controversy remains as to whether polarization can be explained by conformity to group norms (i.e., where influence can be more extreme than the group average). Other studies have provided additional evidence for greater group influence and group cohesion being mediated by a depersonalization processes (greater self-categorization and ingroup stereotyping) under conditions of anonymity (Lea, Spears, & De Groot, 2001; Lea, Spears, & Watt, 2007; see Spears & Postmes, 2015).

The study by Lea et al. (2001) is also noteworthy here because it provides an interesting exception to the principle that anonymity increases depersonalization effects (e.g., conformity to group norms, group attraction). This turns out to be relevant in (re)interpreting some anomalous findings of classic deindividuation studies (see later). In this research, we made a distinction between social groups and categories that are visually cued and those that are not. By "visually cued," we mean that category membership is evident from visually available features, as in the case of gender and "race" for example. In such cases we argued that visibility (rather than anonymity) could further enhance the salience of such social categories by designating and drawing attention to the category itself. This could then increase depersonalization and related group effects (i.e., in contrast to the prediction that anonymity generally increases depersonalization effects in groups that are not visually cued).

We tested this idea in an experiment in which we had groups of four people discuss various topics via computer. Two group members were male and two female (gender: a visually cued category membership) and two were Dutch (i.e., one Dutch male one female, etc.) and two British (nationality: a non–visually cued category). We also varied the discussion topics to render either gender salient (e.g., "Women make better leaders because they are more in touch with their emotions") or nationality salient ("the British reputation for bad food is justified"). We predicted that anonymity would increase group attraction and group cohesion for the nationality categorization (not visually cued) under conditions of anonymity for high-salience discussion topics. However, for gender (the visually cued categorization) we predicted most group attraction and cohesion on high-salience topics when the discussion group was *mutually visible* (via a computer video link). These predictions were confirmed. Moreover, the attraction and cohesion effects were mediated by self-categorization processes (depersonalization) in both cases.

These studies laid the foundations for a social identity–based analysis of deindividuation effects, and specifically what developed into the social identity model of deindividuation effects (the SIDE model). However, these studies only focus on one aspect of anonymity in the group, namely the tendency to obscure differences between individual group members (or to obscure cues to category membership for visibly cued groups), and thereby influence the salience of the relevant group identity ("depersonalization"). Within the SIDE model this corresponds to just one aspect of anonymity, referred to as "anonymity *of*" group members. This can be contrasted to another key effect of anonymity, also noted in deindividuation theory, namely "anonymity *to*" others, which is relevant to issues of identifiability and accountability (see the second route to aggression in Prentice and Dunn's latest model described earlier). This effect of anonymity relates not to the effects of making group identity more salient (as in "anonymity *of*") but in the ability to express aspects of that group identity that might be sanctioned or punished if held to account (i.e., when identifiable).

For Prentice-Dunn and Roger's model, this accountability is relevant to behavior that might otherwise be seen as antinormative (e.g., aggression, or taking too many candies in trick or treat) by some general audience (the public; hence, public self-awareness) that might view such behavior with opprobrium. For the SIDE model the relevant audience, with the power of sanction, is typically a powerful out-group or authority. For example, in a crowd context where students are demonstrating for some cause, the out-group with power of sanction might be the university authorities or the police. Following this analysis, being anonymous in the mass may reduce identifiability to such out-groups and encourage behavior that could otherwise be punished (e.g., throwing stones). However, one of several key differences with the deindividuation account is that any such behavior would have to be normative for the group to engage in it. For the SIDE model, a contrast with classical deindividuation theory (i.e., which includes anonymity vs. accountability as a key input variable) is that group norms are not determined by some generic prosocial criterion but will vary widely with the group and the context (e.g., for pacifist groups, violent conduct in the crowd is very unlikely). For classical deindividuation theory, and the accountability route of Prentice-Dunn and Rogers (1989), the accountability effect is grounded in self-presentation and impression management concerns relating to the individual self and reputation (Leary & Kowalski, 1990; Schlenker & Leary, 1982). It is perhaps then not so surprising that in this context being accountable means avoiding any behavior that might reflect badly on the individual self, and thus avoiding antisocial behavior. However, once the self is defined more broadly, notably also in terms of group identity, the door is opened to group norms that could cut across such generic prosocial behavior, and behavior should also depend on the nature of the audience to which one is accountable (e.g., in-group vs. out-group).

Anonymity is not the only factor that could encourage behavior that is seen as normative for the group but punishable by the out-group; in principle, any situational factor that empowers the in-group relative to the out-group is likely to foster in-group behavior even when it is punishable. The social support of other in-group members in situ is one such factor typical in crowd contexts: Group immersion is only likely to render people somewhat anonymous in the mass, but perhaps even more important is the empowerment provided by "strength in numbers" (indeed, people may not even feel anonymous in relation to other proximal members of the crowd).

Research using the SIDE model has investigated the empowering effects of both anonymity and the copresence of coacting others. Reicher and his colleagues developed a paradigm in which they used the intergroup context of undergraduate students (the in-group) versus staff (the out-group) to test these ideas. They found that students were more likely to endorse behavior seen as punishable by staff, so long as this was normative for their own student group, to the extent that they were anonymous (Reicher & Levine, 1994a) or had the social support of many other students who were copresent in the situation, as opposed to being isolated (Reicher & Levine, 1994b).

To summarize, anonymity in the group can have at least two different kinds of effects on group behavior, according to the SIDE model. Anonymity "of" group members can render them less individually distinguishable, thereby increasing the salience of a group identity that is already salient in situ, by the process of depersonalization. Salience can also be increased for visually cued groups by visibility (Lea et al., 2007). This is referred to as the "cognitive" dimension of SIDE insofar as it affects the salience and impact of (social) identity. Note that if individual identity is salient (see Spears et al., 1990), anonymity will not accentuate group identity and may increase differentiation from the group.

By contrast, anonymity "to" others, and notably to a powerful out-group, can increase the ability to act in line with group norms that could be sanctioned by that out-group. This is referred to as the "strategic dimension" of SIDE, insofar as behavior, reflecting the agenda of a salient group identity, is only acted out if the group members feel they are empowered to do so, and can thus "get away with" behavior that could be punished by the out-group. This is more likely to the extent that group members are anonymous to the out-group (and thus not identifiable and accountable to them). However, other factors, such as the copresence of like-minded group members, may empower the in-group to act without fear of sanction even when they are not protected by the cloak of anonymity.

Once again these ideas as applied to the crowd can also be applied to other contexts in which anonymity and the social support from others in the group might vary. Just as Spears et al. (1990) applied the cognitive dimension of SIDE to the context of computer-mediated communication (CMC), where visual anonymity is a common feature, Spears, Lea, Corneliussen, Postmes, and Ter Haar (2002) applied the rationale of the strategic dimension to this CMC context. For example, in one experiment, they adapted the paradigm of Reicher using staff and students and distinguishing attitude items that were normative for students but either punishable or not punishable by staff (and also punishable items that were also not normative for students, such as cheating on exams).

The experiment then manipulated two factors orthogonally. The psychology student participants were all located in the same room but were either visible to each other or masked by the use of screens between them (and thus visually anonymous). Second, they either had the ability to communicate with each other by means of computer (CMC) or they did not. We predicted that the visual anonymity manipulation would affect group salience of the psychology student identity and that this would increase conformity to nonpunishable group normative items (e.g., partying) compared to the individuated condition. This was confirmed and is in line with the effects of "anonymity *of*" or cognitive dimension of SIDE. However, the availability of CMC was predicted to provide a key channel in which students could communicate support to resist the out-group also on more *punishable* items normative for the in-group (note that copresence was kept constant here). This prediction was also supported and implicates the strategic dimension of SIDE in which channels of support enabled resistance to the out-group.

Returning to the deindividuation literature, the true test of the SIDE model is whether it is able to make sense of earlier deindividuation research. Revisiting the deindividuation studies discussed earlier and viewing them through the prism of the SIDE model is one approach. To an extent, our narrative review already allows this reappraisal. A key difference between the classic deindividuation approach and the SIDE model is that the SIDE model proposes that classic deindividuation effects reflect the operation of conformity to in-group norms, corresponding to salient social identities, rather than antinormative behavior (primarily aggression) brought on by the loss of identity and reduced self-regulation. A recurring theme of our narrative review is that many of the effects arising from the classic deindividuation manipulations of anonymity and group immersion can be reinterpreted as following from such specific group norms or situational demands in the experiment.

As we have already noted, this was essentially the very argument of Johnson and Downing (1979), who noted the similarities between Zimbardo's classic manipulation and the typical Ku Klux Klan clothing, pointing to the role of normative cues, in addition to the effects of reduced accountability associated with anonymity. However, some of Zimbardo's actual results present more of a puzzle. Recall that the young women of his first study were less likely to shock victims when identifiable and accountable (see also the results of Singer et al., 1965, for a similar effect). This was as predicted by Zimbardo but, in the second study, Belgians soldiers shocked *more* when identifiable (in their uniforms), rather than when disguised by anonymity through masks and overalls. A group normative explanation for both these effects is readily available: Participants seem to be acting in line with group norms when identifiable, resulting in less aggression for the women ("young ladies should just not do this kind of thing") but more aggression for the soldiers ("this is just part of our job"). So far so good. However, recall the cognitive dimension SIDE model predicts more normative behavior (assuming group identity is salient) under *anonymous* conditions. Recall also,

however, the exception to this principle for visually cued categories. Both these categories (women and soldiers in uniform) are strongly visually cued. Indeed, it is possible that these group identities were not even salient under anonymous conditions because they were not referred to as part of the experiment. For visually cued categories, visibility should enhance the salience of group norms (cf. Lea et al., 2007), as seems to have happened in these cases.

This narrative reappraisal of the various effects found is possible for a range of classic studies but also remains somewhat speculative and post hoc. In a more systematic approach to this issue, we conducted a meta-analysis in which, inter alia, we tried to test SIDE model predictions against classic and contemporary deindividuation theories in attempting to account for the data (Postmes & Spears, 1998). To this end we analyzed 60 independent studies comprising the deindividuation literature (including unpublished studies). A key step in this analysis was to employ coders to rate the studies for what they would consider situationally normative had they been participants in the various experiments. In this case the use of psychology students, who represented the overwhelming participant population of the original studies, seems entirely appropriate. Studies were also coded for the key manipulations, such as anonymity (to in-group and out-group where relevant), group size, private self-awareness, and public self-awareness and also the key dependent variables (e.g., administration of shocks, stealing or cheating, antinormative attitudes, failure to act prosocially, etc.).

The first key test was for the predicted overall relation between deindividuation manipulations and antinormative behavior. The overall relation was small ($r = .09$) albeit statistically reliable, but the funnel plot shows a wide range of effects from strongly negative to strongly positive, indicating considerable variability and thus the need to consider moderator variables to explain this. Moreover, excluding three studies involving children (with cheating/stealing as the key measures as in the trick-or-treat paradigm) that showed strong support for deindividuation theory rendered the remaining effects with student and other adult samples as not reliable ($r = .06$, ns). A general societal norm could not account for the variance in effects. By contrast the specific situational norms seen as appropriate conduct in the studies (as rated by the coders) was a highly significant positive predictor of deindividuation effects. Group size was the only other moderator that significantly predicted variance, albeit more weakly. Together these accounted for 50 percent of the variance in effects ($R^2$ = .50). In sum, consistent with the SIDE model, but contradicting deindividuation theory, situational norms *positively* predicted deindividuation effects.

We also examined the small subset of studies that tried to address the deindividuated state as a potential mediator of deindividuation effects. Although none of these studies reported full mediational analyses following the recommendations of Baron and Kenny (1986; most predated this influential paper that introduced the era of mediation testing) in 7 of 12 available studies, we were able to compute relevant regressions to test for mediation. These analyses revealed no evidence for significant mediation of deindividuation effects by the measured states: The small effect of manipulations on antinormative behavior in these studies was not reduced by taking into account the mediator. Moreover, distinguishing the type of self-awareness (public self-awareness vs. private self-awareness) outlined in the most contemporary statement of the deindividuation theory (Prentice Dunn & Rogers, 1989) revealed no reliable differences in their relations with the independent or dependent variables. In short, there is no clear evidence that self-awareness mediated any manipulated effects of deindividuation.

## Summary and Conclusions

Deindividuation theory occupies a central place in the pantheon, and the textbooks, of social psychology alongside other classic phenomena such as Festinger's dissonance experiments and Milgram's obedience studies. Understanding why people misbehave in the crowd has been high on the political agenda and fired the popular view of the crowd. However, it is perhaps interesting to compare the legacy of deindividuation theory against these two comparison examples. Although deindividuation theory reclaimed some history from Le Bon's account of the crowd, it could be argued, based on the evidence presented here, that time has treated the theory less well than these other classic phenomena. This is not to deny that the tradition of research generated by this theory has been rich and enriching. However, in this chapter I claim that much of the evidence for deindividuation theory's central premise that people lose their sense of self in the crowd, and become more prone to mindless aggression, has not stood up well to closer empirical

or theoretical scrutiny. In this chapter I have made a case for a more (group) normative explanation for deindividuation effects, consistent with a social identity explanation of crowd behavior. However, each theory has its own focus and blind spots and I would not claim that this provides the full story of why people behave in crowds as they do. I have also argued that there is an important sense in which the original prediction of deindividuation theory has not been optimally tested, and some of the techniques for tapping unconscious states and processes developed since the heyday of deindividuation research provide hope for better tests of the theory.

On a more conciliatory and integrative note, the basic insight that immersion in the crowd can be intensely arousing and emotional experience is also surely valid (albeit difficult to research in experimental terms) and may well involve unconscious processes. However, the research reviewed here points to the possibility that such processes may be more socially regulated and channeled through group norms, including intergroup emotions, than deindividuation theory would suggest. In this respect this reappraisal locates deindividuation phenomena squarely within the realm of social influence, reflecting social and group processes, central to the focus of this volume.

## References

Averill, J. R. (1983). Studies on anger and aggression: Implications for theories of emotion. *American Psychologist*, 38, 1145–1160.

Beaman, A. L., Klentz, B., Diener, E., & Svanum, S. (1979). Self-awareness and transgression in children: Two field studies. *Journal of Personality and Social Psychology*, 37, 1835–1846.

Cannavale, F. J., Scarr, H. A., & Pepitone, A. (1970). Deindividuation in the small group: Further evidence. *Journal of Personality and Social Psychology*, 16, 141–147.

Carver, C. S. (1974). Facilitation of aggression through objective self-awareness. *Journal of Experimental Social Psychology*, 10, 365–370.

Deutsch, M. & Gerard, H. (1955). A study of normative and informational social influences upon individual judgment. *Journal of Abnormal and Social Psychology*, 51, 629–636.

Diener, E. (1979). Deindividuation, self-awareness, and disinhibition. *Journal of Personality and Social Psychology*, 37, 1160–1171.

Diener, E. (1980). Deindividuation: The absence of self-awareness and self-regulation in group members. In P. Paulus (Ed.), *The psychology of group influence* (pp. 209–242). Hillsdale, NJ: Erlbaum.

Diener, E., Dineen, J., Endresen, K., Beaman, A. L., & Fraser, S. C. (1975). Effects of altered responsibility, cognitive set, and modeling on physical aggression and deindividuation. *Journal of Personality and Social Psychology*, 31, 328–337.

Diener, E., Fraser, S. C., Beaman, A. L., & Kelem, R. T. (1976). Effects of deindividuation variables on stealing among Halloween trick-or treaters. *Journal of Personality and Social Psychology, 33*, 178–183.

Diener, E., Lusk, R., DeFour, D., & Flax, R. (1980). Deindividuation: The effects of group size, density, number of observers, and group member similarity on self-consciousness. *Journal of Personality and Social Psychology, 39*, 449–459.

Diener, E., Westford, K. L., Dineen, J., & Fraser, S. C. (1973). Beat the pacifist: The deindividuating effects of anonymity and group presence. Proceedings of the 81st Annual Convention of the American Psychological Association, 8, 221–222.

Dipboye, R. L. (1977). Alternative approaches to deindividuation. *Psychological Bulletin, 84*, 1057–1075.

Duval, S., & Wicklund, R. A. (1972). *A theory of objective self-awareness.* New York, NY: Academic Press.

Fenigstein, A., Scheier, M. F., & Buss, A. H. (1975). Public and private self-consciousness: Assessment and theory. *Journal of Consulting and Clinical Psychology, 43*, 522–527.

Festinger, L., Pepitone, A., & Newcombe, T. (1952). Some consequences of deindividuation in a group. *Journal of Abnormal and Social Psychology, 47*, 382–389.

Gergen, K. J., Gergen, M. M., & Barton, W. H. (1973). Deviance in the dark. Psychology Today, 7, 129–130.

Johnson, R. D., & Downing, L. L. (1979). Deindividuation and valence of cues: Effects on prosocial and antisocial behavior. *Journal of Personality and Social Psychology, 37*, 1532–1538.

Lea, M., Spears, R., & De Groot, D. (2001). Knowing me, knowing you: Effects of visual anonymity on self-categorization, stereotyping and attraction in computer-mediated groups. *Personality and Social Psychology Bulletin, 27*, 526–537.

Lea, M., Spears, R., & Watt, S. E. (2007). Visibility and anonymity effects on attraction and group cohesiveness. *European Journal of Social Psychology, 37*, 761–773.

Leary, M. R., & Kowalski, R. M. (1990). Impression management: A literature review and 2-component model. *Psychological Bulletin, 107*, 34–47.

Le Bon, G. (1995). *The crowd: A study of the popular mind.* London: Transaction Publishers. (Original work published in 1895).

Lewin, K. (1951). *Field theory in social science; selected theoretical papers.* D. Cartwright (ed.). New York, NY: Harper & Row.

Postmes, T., & Spears, R. (1998). Deindividuation and anti-normative behavior: A meta-analysis. *Psychological Bulletin, 123*, 238–259.

Postmes, T., Spears, R., Lee, A. T., & Novak, R. J. (2005). Individuality and social influence in groups: Inductive and deductive routes to group identity. *Journal of Personality and Social Psychology, 89*, 747–763.

Postmes, T., Spears, R., Sakhel, K., & De Groot, D. (2001). Social influence in computer-mediated groups: The effects of anonymity on social behavior. *Personality and Social Psychology Bulletin, 27*, 1243–1254.

Prentice-Dunn, S., & Rogers, R. W. (1980). Effects of deindividuating situational cues and aggressive models on subjective deindividuation and aggression. *Journal of Personality and Social Psychology, 39*, 104–113.

Prentice-Dunn, S., & Rogers, R. W. (1982). Effects of public and private self-awareness on deindividuation and aggression. *Journal of Personality and Social Psychology, 43*, 503–513.

Prentice-Dunn, S., & Rogers, R. W. (1989). Deindividuation and the self-regulation of behavior. In P. Paulus (Ed.), *The psychology of group influence* (2nd ed., pp. 87–109). Hillsdale, NJ: Erlbaum.

Prentice-Dunn, S., & Spivey, C. B. (1986). Extreme deindividuation in the laboratory: Its magnitude and subjective components. *Personality and Social Psychology Bulletin, 12*, 206–215.

Reicher, S. D. (1982). The determination of collective behaviour. In H. Tajfel (Ed.), *Social identity and intergroup relations* (pp. 41–83). Cambridge, England: Cambridge University Press.

Reicher, S. D. (1984). Social influence in the crowd: Attitudinal and behavioural effects of de-individuation in conditions of high and low group salience. Special Issue: Intergroup processes. *British Journal of Social Psychology, 23*, 341–350.

Reicher, S. D. (1987). Crowd behaviour as social action. In J. C. Turner, M. A. Hogg, P. J. Oakes, S. D. Reicher, & M. S. Wetherell, *Rediscovering the social group: A self-categorization theory* (pp. 171–202). Oxford, England: Blackwell.

Reicher, S. (2011). "The crowd" century: Reconciling practical success with theoretical failure. *British Journal of Social Psychology, 35*, 535–553.

Reicher, S., & Levine, M. (1994a). Deindividuation, power relations between groups and the expression of social identity: The effects of visibility to the out-group. *British Journal of Social Psychology, 33*, 145–164.

Reicher, S., & Levine, M. (1994b). On the consequences of deindividuation manipulations for the strategic communication of self: Identifiability and the presentation of social identity. *European Journal of Social Psychology, 24*, 511–524.

Reicher, S., Spears, R., & Postmes, T. (1995). A social identity model of deindividuation phenomena. In W. Stroebe & M. Hewstone (Eds.), *European review of social psychology* (Vol. 6, pp. 161–198). Chichester, England: Wiley.

Rogers, R. W., & Prentice-Dunn, S. (1981). Deindividuation and anger-mediated interracial aggression: Unmasking regressive racism. *Journal of Personality and Social Psychology, 41*, 63–73.

Schlenker, B. R., & Leary, M. R., (1982). Audiences' reactions of self-enhancing, self-denigrating and accurate self-presentations. *Journal of Experimental Social Psychology, 18*, 89–104.

Singer, J. E., Brush, C. E., & Lublin, S. C. (1965). Some aspects of deindividuation: Identification and conformity. *Journal of Experimental Social Psychology, 1*, 356–378.

Spears, R., & Lea, M. (1994). Panacea or panopticon? The hidden power in computer-mediated communication. *Communication Research, 21*, 427–459.

Spears, R., & Postmes, T. (2015). Group identity, social influence and collective action online: Extensions and applications of the side model. In S. Shyam Sundar (Ed.), *The handbook of psychology of communication* (pp. 23–46). Oxford, England: Wiley-Blackwell.

Spears, R., Lea, M., & Lee, S. (1990). De-individuation and group polarization in computer-mediated communication. *British Journal of Social Psychology, 29*, 121–134.

Spears, R., Lea, M., Corneliussen, R. A., Postmes, T., & Ter Haar, W. (2002). Computer-mediated communication as a channel for social resistance: The strategic side of SIDE. *Small Group Research, 33*, 555–574.

Spears, R., & Smith, H. J. (2001). Experiments as politics. *Political Psychology, 22*, 309–330.

Tajfel, H., & Turner, J. C. (1979). An integrative theory of inter-group conflict. In W. G. Austin & S. Worchel (Eds.), *The social psychology of intergroup relations* (pp. 33–48). Monterey, CA: Brooks/Cole.

Turner, J. C. (1982). Towards a cognitive redefinition of the group. In H. Tajfel (Ed.), *Social identity and intergroup relations* (pp. 15–40). Cambridge, England: Cambridge University Press.

Turner, J. C. (1991). *Social influence*. Milton Keynes: Open University Press.

Turner, J. C., Hogg, M. A., Oakes, P. J., Reicher, S. D., & Wetherell, M. S. (1987). *Rediscovering the social group: A self-categorization theory*. Oxford: Basil Blackwell.

Turner, R., & Killian, L. M. (1972). *Collective behavior* (2nd ed.). Englewood Cliffs, NJ: Prentice-Hall.

Zimbardo, P. G. (1969). The human choice: Individuation, reason and order versus deindividuation, impulse, and chaos. In W. J. Arnold & D. Levine (Eds.), *Nebraska Symposium on Motivation* (pp. 237–307). Lincoln: University of Nebraska Press.

# Stability and Change Within Groups

Matthew J. Hornsey *and* Jolanda Jetten

**Abstract**

This chapter examines the psychological tensions between protecting the status quo within groups and engaging in intragroup change. In the first section we review two research traditions that imply self-reinforcing cycles of stability and preservation of the status quo: (a) research on conformity and the punishment of deviance and (b) research examining biases toward shared knowledge in small decision-making groups. In the second section we provide the counterpoint to these theoretical traditions, exploring several reasons why, despite psychological pressures that appear to favor majority opinions and shared assumptions, intragroup change and reform is a robust reality of group life. In the third and final section of this chapter we move on to examine who within the group is most likely to push for change; who within the group is more effective at pushing for change; and what are the effective strategies for initiating change.

**Key Words:** opinion deviance, dissent, criticism, conformity, groupthink, minority influence, task conflict

A superficial reading of many undergraduate textbooks would lead one to believe that groups are inherently conservative, governed by psychological pressures designed to protect the status quo. For example, there is a well-established assumption in the literature that majorities rule: Their attitudes are seen to be diagnostic proxies of reality; group members fear providing a counterpoint to these attitudes; and shared knowledge and common assumptions tend to prevail over new information and fresh viewpoints. Taken to an extreme, these principles imply a self-reinforcing cycle of stasis, such that majority opinions and shared knowledge perpetually crowd out alternative viewpoints. The general message appears to be that collective improvement will be slow and difficult and that intragroup dynamics aimed at change are the exception, not the rule.

In this review, we acknowledge that there might be important psychological forces that make change difficult, and we review literature relevant to this point in the first section of this contribution. However, there must be escape hatches from these self-perpetuating cycles of stability and

conformity, because groups *do* change. Although not all groups necessarily change as quickly as people might like them to, it is hard to think of a group culture that remains implacably and stubbornly static. Reform, evolution, contemporariness, and positive change are often part of the DNA of groups—part of their declared mission—and intragroup dynamics play an important role in that change. Often in a wish to improve the group, members might seek to overturn a collective decision; campaign to change suboptimal group cultures; engage in constructive intragroup criticism; or simply contribute unique information to influence a group discussion. In the second section we review this empirical body of work and discuss a range of theories and models that help explain why groups change, and the intragroup dynamics that lead to such change.

In the third and final section of this chapter we move on to examine the who, how, and when of social change. Who within the group is most likely to push for change? Who within the group is more effective at pushing for change? And what are the effective strategies for initiating change?

## Intragroup Dynamics Preserving the Status Quo

Here, we broadly cover two social influence phenomena that, on the surface, presume change will be difficult and slow: conformity and common knowledge effects.

### Conformity and Punishment of Opinion Deviance

Asch's research on conformity remains iconic in the field, and for decades it provided the methodological template for subsequent conformity researchers. In his paradigm, participants were asked to judge which of three lines was equivalent in length to a standard line that was presented parallel to it. The task was easy. When tested alone, participants identified the correct line 99 percent of the time. But Asch was interested in what would happen if the naïve participants were surrounded by confederates who called out an incorrect answer. The answer is that people frequently conformed: Roughly a third of the time the naïve participants called out the confederates' incorrect answer. The take-home message was clear: Majorities shape (and sometimes corrupt) the way humans report seeing the world (see Jetten & Hornsey, 2012, for a recent review).

Conformity effects have typically been explained as a function of two independent processes: informational influence and normative influence (Deutsch & Gerard, 1955). Informational influence occurs when people assume that majority opinions are probably grounded in reality. If the majority of people think X or do Y, then it is plausible that they do so because X is correct or because Y is the most appropriate course of action. Normative influence occurs when people presume that failure to conform will lead to punishment. Standing out with a "deviant" opinion can (literally) be a heart-pounding experience (Costell & Leiderman, 1968; Gerard, 1961): It makes you stand out and potentially opens you up to ridicule. It is therefore not surprising that, rather than risking negative attention by calling out an answer they knew to be correct, many participants in Asch's experiments decided the best option was to conform to the majority, even if this meant that they found themselves calling out a clearly incorrect answer (Asch, 1952, 1956).

Does deviance in fact lead to ridicule by others in the group? In the Asch paradigm it certainly did. In one experiment the paradigm was inverted such that many naïve participants called out correct answers in the company of a single confederate

who was trained to call out the incorrect answer. The confederate was mocked, humiliated, and sneered at. There are no shortage of classic studies and phenomena that feed into the same collective wisdom: Deviance results in social punishment. Most famously, Schachter (1951; recently replicated by Wesselmann et al., 2014) introduced confederates into small decision-making groups and, in some cases, instructed them to oppose the emerging consensus. Compared to confederates who were trained to go along with the majority response, dissenters faced an escalating series of communications designed to change their mind, with the "heat" only subsiding when the dissenter conceded to the majority. If the dissenter did not concede, he or she tended to be evaluated poorly and overlooked for desirable committee work in the future.

The spirit of this effect has been replicated so many times that it is often mistaken for being a truism in the field (we critique this notion later). Festinger (1950, 1954) popularized two explanations for why deviants and dissenters might be socially punished. One is that the dissenter interrupts "group locomotion." Often, small groups need to rally behind a single decision in order to move forward and act. Dissenters slow that process down, which can lead to frustration and blame. Second, people tend to use their group memberships as frames of reference that help guide their worldview and prescribe action and attitudes. To the degree that there is intragroup uniformity, the group can provide a satisfying level of certainty, solidity, and assurance about one's beliefs. To have this uniformity punctured by a dissenter can, for some, lead to disorientation and resentment.

The notion that deviants invite punishment is well ingrained early in life. Dominic Abrams and Adam Rutland have pioneered a developmental theory of subjective group dynamics built around the notion of "group nous." Group nous is an implicit understanding of the general ground rules of group membership. According to their model, middle school students have already developed a set of intuitive understandings about how groups operate. They grow to understand, for example, that unity in a group is important, and that being part of a unified group can be satisfying. They also grow to understand that deviance is likely to lead to social exclusion by others. Not only does this insight make them less likely to display deviance themselves, it guides their own treatment of deviants.

Consistent with the group nous idea, school children rate ingroup targets more favorably when they make ingroup-praising comments than when they behave in ways that cast doubt over their loyalty, a preference that increases with age (Abrams, Rutland, & Cameron, 2003; Abrams, Rutland, Cameron, & Marques, 2003). Disproportionate derogation of the deviant ingroup member increases to the extent that children understand that groups differentially include normative over deviant children, and particularly so for participants who have strong identification with the group (Abrams et al., 2003a). Derogation of the deviant ingroup member is also most pronounced when the norms that are being violated are seen to be relevant to the group (Abrams, Rutland, Ferrell, & Pelletier, 2008) and when responses are visible to other ingroup members (Abrams, Rutland, Cameron, & Ferrell, 2007). Consistent with the notion of group nous, children were more likely to differentially include normative over deviant members the higher they rated on a measure of theory of mind (i.e., the more they had a sophisticated sense that other people have desires, perceptions, and intentions different from their own; Abrams, Rutland, Pelletier, & Ferrell, 2009).

The conclusion is that the development of understandings about group processes is a skill; it is something that develops as children get older and more cognitively sophisticated, and it increases with both experience and the ability to perspective-take. The social skill that children learn is that unified groups are good groups (particularly in intergroup situations) and that deviance or disloyalty should be punished with social exclusion.

Furthermore, these childhood understandings of group dynamics extend into adulthood. Research on the "black sheep effect" shows that dislikeable, nonnormative, or disloyal ingroup members are derogated—and to a greater extent than outgroup members who display the same behavior (Marques & Paez, 1994). As for children, the differential derogation of ingroup deviance tends to be greater the more strongly people identify with the group; the more the prescriptive norms are salient; and the more people feel their responses are visible to other ingroup members (Marques, Abrams, Páez, & Martinez-Taboada, 1998). Heightened derogation of ingroup opinion deviance is also more exaggerated when the level of uniformity within the group is in doubt or where there is uncertainty about the relative superiority of the ingroup (Marques, Abrams, & Serodio, 2001). Circumstantial evidence for this ingroup-protection motive is found also at the societal level; a survey of 33 nations showed that the countries with the strongest norms and the lowest tolerance for deviant behavior were those nations that were prone to ecological and historical threats like a history of territorial conflict and disease (Gelfand et al., 2011).

Together, these effects imply that derogation of opinion deviance is a motivated process designed to reinforce the integrity of the ingroup in the eyes of others. Deviance threatens the validity of people's beliefs about the relative superiority of their group over others. The subjective group dynamics model (e.g., Abrams, Marques, Bown, & Dougill, 2002) nuances this insight by making it clear that the same behavior might be seen as normative or deviant depending on the intergroup context and the norms of the outgroup. For example, because group distinctiveness is an important precondition for identification and meaning, deviant opinions that blur the distinction between the ingroup and outgroup are derogated more strongly than those that exaggerate the intergroup difference (Abrams et al., 2002; Abrams, Marques, Bown, & Henson, 2000; Hichy, Mari, & Capozza, 2008). Perhaps as a consequence, group members are more likely to express deviant opinions that accentuate rather than diminish intergroup boundaries (Morrison & Miller, 2008).

Taken to an extreme, the principles of informational influence and normative influence imply a circular psychological process, the end result of which is ongoing stasis within groups. If it is true, for example, that consensus implies correctness (informational influence), then the majority opinion, once formed, should be self-perpetuating. Majority opinions imply authoritativeness and certainty; they create a gravitational pull that sucks in those who are skeptical, doubtful, uncertain, or wavering, and they can do so long after the original opinion holders have left the group (Sherif, 1936).

Adding to the momentum of self-perpetuation is the fact that those who persist in deviating from the majority are punished, ridiculed, or ostracized. Naturally, people grow to fear expressing minority opinions, preferring instead to keep their deviant opinions private while they nod along with the majority. This process has the ironic effect of deepening the perception that people are in a minority with their divergent opinions, thus intensifying normative influence and creating a second psychological cycle leading to preservation of the status quo. This circular effect of normative influence on group dynamics can lead to the phenomenon of pluralistic ignorance (Katz & Allport, 1931), which refers to the tendency for people to overestimate support for the status quo. The perception of pluralistic ignorance can lead to conformity to the (illusory) norm over time or to a sense of alienation among those who do not conform and feel (again, illusorily) like deviants (Prentice & Miller, 1993). A similar circular effect has been proposed among theorists in the literature on communication and media. Spiral of silence theory (Noelle-Neumann, 1993) proposes that, through fear of isolation, individuals who hold minority viewpoints are reluctant to express their attitudes publicly. The consequence is that, in the public discourse and in the media, minority opinions are increasingly marginalized, while majority opinions only gain in strength (although see Matthes, Morrison, & Schemer, 2010, for a qualification of this point).

## Biases Toward Shared Knowledge in Decision-Making Groups

We now move on to a research question that is independent from (but related to) the work on conformity: Given that individual group members have different perspectives and access to different information, how is this information shared within the group to facilitate a decision? Research on this question has been heavily influenced by the "hidden-profile" paradigm developed by Stasser and Titus (1985). In these paradigms certain pieces of decision-relevant information are provided to all group members, while other pieces of information are provided to just one group member. For example, imagine a situation in which a small group of three people are trying to decide which of two candidates (A or B) to hire for a job. There are three pieces of information that are known to all three group members going into the discussion: Two reflect positively on candidate B and one reflects positively on candidate A. Over and above the shared information, each member of the group has a different piece of information that is unique to the particular member, and each of those pieces of information reflects positively on candidate A. Which candidate would the group choose?

Logically, if the group is openly sharing their information, the group should choose candidate A. This is because there are four pieces of information that reflect positively on candidate A and only two pieces of information that reflect positively on candidate B. But more often than not, the group will choose candidate B (Stasser & Titus, 1985). This is because there is a tendency for the group to disproportionately raise, discuss, and elaborate the information that is common to all of them. This favors candidate B because the unique (and flattering) information that group members have about candidate A is less likely to be raised and elaborated. The bias in favor of shared knowledge is particularly pronounced at the beginning of a group discussion, when shared understandings and common ground are being established (Larson, Foster-Fishman, & Keys, 1994).

Not only is shared information more likely to be raised than unshared information, but information that is held by more people is more heavily weighted in terms of making the final decision (the "common knowledge effect"). For example, Gigone and Hastie (1993) conducted a number of studies in which three-person groups estimated the grade that different students would receive in a course based on six independent pieces of data (e.g., entrance exam score, high school GPA). Some pieces of data were provided to all three of the group members; some were provided to just two of the group members; and some were provided to just one. First, group members provided an estimate on the basis of whatever data to which they were privy. The three group members then discussed the data and reached a consensus estimate. Gigone and Hastie were able to show that the more people within the group were privy to the data, the more influential the data were in determining the final estimate. Consistent with Stasser and Titus, there was a tendency for the "common knowledge" to be more likely to be shared. But the effect of prediscussion estimates was significant even after levels of information sharing were statistically controlled for. The conclusion is that individuals form an impression on the basis of their own information, and that this impression provides a lens through which subsequent information is elaborated, processed, and interpreted. The implication is that common (or highly shared) knowledge will be influential even if it is *not* raised in the group discussion.

Wittenbaum and colleagues argue that the bias in favor of shared knowledge is driven, in part, by motivations of acceptance and enhancement. They found that when dyads discussed shared information, they rated both themselves and their partners as more competent than when they discussed unshared information (Wittenbaum, Hubbell, & Zuckerman, 1999). Presumably, raising shared information leads to nods of approval and recognition, providing safe common ground for discussion. Discussing information that everybody owns and is comfortable with is mutually validating. It is also relatively easy and economical; if information is already consistent with shared assumptions, then one needs less time and fewer words to communicate the point. For all these reasons, it can be argued that the process of sticking to common ground is a form of politeness strategy (Kashima, Klein, & Clark, 2007) in that it communicates one's sensitivity and connection to the audience. In contrast, raising unshared information invites more critical scrutiny and skepticism, chews up communication resources, and invites conflict and controversy. This may help explain why group members—and particularly lower status members (Wittenbaum, 1998)—tend to stick to shared information. This is where the work on information sharing dovetails with the work on conformity described earlier: People stick with the status quo because it is more likely to lead to acceptance and, ultimately, to an enhancement of one's standing within the group.

Just like the work on conformity, the work on shared knowledge biases implies a circular, self-reproducing process that some theorists have described as a vicious circle (Klein, Tindale, & Brauer, 2008). First, when groups strive for consensus in the early phases of discussion, they privilege shared over unshared information even when the shared information is more accurate or diagnostic. This shared information then becomes part of the "common ground" of the group, and information that is consistent with that common ground is easier to communicate, perceived to be more polite, and more likely to be met with acceptance. This process further discourages the airing of unshared information, particularly among low-status or otherwise vulnerable members of the group. Finally, common or shared information can be disproportionately influential even when it is not discussed (Gigone & Hastie, 1993). So even if the widely shared information is too taboo or socially unacceptable to declare, it wields disproportionate influence.

## Intragroup Dynamics Promoting Change and Collective Improvement

The literature reviewed to this point all implies that the intragroup dynamics of groups are built to resist change. Clearly, though, these theoretical positions need to be elaborated to account for the fact that groups *do* change, and intragroup dynamics play an important role in that change. In the next section we review a range of theories that help explain why, within groups, the self-reinforcing cycles of stasis rarely eventuate. First, we review evidence showing how dissent, critical engagement,

and deviance can occur *because of* rather than despite group conformity. We then discuss the power of dissenters and attitudinal deviants to neutralize the power of the majority to instill conformity and obedience in their members. In the final part of this section we examine how attitudinal deviants and intragroup critics lead to better decision making and increased motivations for reform (even if it comes at the expense of personal likeability).

### Conformity Can Produce (Rather Than Inhibit) Individualism and Dissent

The standard perspective on norms is that groups provide a frame of reference for their members; as such, they help guide and shape attitudes and behavior. Social identity theorists (e.g., Tajfel & Turner, 1979; Turner, 1991, 1999) would add that this process is more pronounced the more one identifies with that group. Indeed, to the extent that people identify strongly with a group, and to the extent that the group is made salient in the context, people shift their attitudes and behavior to conform to the prototypical expectations of the group. In other words, they are more likely to conform to salient group norms and act in line with group expectations.

On the surface, this process seems to leave little room for constructive criticism, engaged dissent, or group transformation. If high identifiers conform to the group prototype, then by definition they will find themselves reaffirming established norms and practices. What this obscures, however, is the reality that many groups actually *prescribe* deviance, dissent, and individualism as part of their core normative values. If, in the United States, individualism is a core cultural value, then individualism can be seen as an ironic manifestation of conformity. If, in academia, researchers are trained to be skeptical, critical of presumed wisdoms, and attracted to debate, then these qualities are what good, conformist group members will demonstrate. In short, there are many examples where good group members would find themselves under pressure to conform to a group norm of nonconformity.

Jetten, Postmes, and McAuliffe (2002) were the first to demonstrate empirically that individuation can, paradoxically, be a function of group identification. In North America (an individualistic culture), those who identified strongly with their national identity tended to be more individualist than did low identifiers. The reverse was true in Indonesia, a highly collectivist culture. Hornsey, Jetten, McAuliffe, and Hogg (2006) extended this research to include tolerance for dissent. They induced norms of collectivism and individualism in both ad hoc and real-world groups, and then examined participants' evaluations of an ingroup member who displayed selfish or deviant attitudes. Overall, members of individualist groups were more tolerant than were collectivists of the deviant behavior, and *particularly* when they identified strongly with the group. Thus, tolerance for dissent (like individualism) can be an *outcome* of conformity rather than an enemy of it (Hornsey & Jetten, 2004).

A corollary of this process is that groups (in the West) are more likely to recruit members, and are more likely to retain their loyalty, to the extent that they place fewer constraints on their group members' individuality and their ability to express themselves freely. Simon, Aufderheide, and Hastedt (2000) found that members of majority groups felt more like they "fit in" the group when individualization was fostered than when it was not. Sheldon and Bettencourt (2002) found that measures of personal autonomy (e.g., "To what extent does this group membership allow you to express your authentic self?") correlated strongly with how positively people felt about a campus group. It is this quality more than any other group process that predicted recovery within people seeking group psychotherapy for depression and anxiety (Dwyer, Hornsey, Smith, Oei, & Dingle, 2011). Together, these studies suggest that some groups have a vested interest in allowing for authenticity (including deviance and dissent) among their members. To the extent that these qualities become a core part of the group values, conformity and loyalty becomes synonymous with individual expression, critical engagement, and fearless expression.

## Dissenters Have a Transformative Influence on Groups

In the previous sections we have discussed the question of what groups do to dissenters. In this next section we invert that question and ask: What do dissenters do to groups? We separately examine the effects of dissenters on (1) other group members' willingness to conform, (2) the decision-making processes of small groups, and (3) the willingness of groups to accept criticism from within and engage in reform. In each case the literature suggests that dissenters influence groups to grow and develop, that they do so independently of whether they are personally liked, and they do so with disproportionate power. This provides another answer to the question of how and why groups change, grow, and

reform despite psychological processes that produce stasis.

One of the more intriguing lines of research that Asch conducted was his work on partner effects (Asch, 1951, 1955). In these studies, naïve participants again found themselves surrounded by confederates who mysteriously called out the wrong answer in a line judgment task. The twist was that one of the confederates was instructed to call out the correct answer, thus reinforcing the naïve participant's view of the world. Perhaps unsurprisingly the levels of conformity were lower when participants had the support of a partner than when they did not. What is more surprising is the sheer scale of the effects. Without a like-minded partner, participants conformed in more than 1 of 3 trials. With a supportive partner, the levels of conformity were closer to 1 in 18 trials. In other words the "spell" of conformity was shattered by just one person who spoke out against the majority. Dramatic effects like this are evident even when the experimental apparatus is rigged so that the naïve participant believes he or she is the only person in the room to hear the dissenter (Bragg & Allen, 1972). It is not the case, then, that dissenters diffuse the risk and shame associated with deviance. Rather, dissenters seem to genuinely embolden the participant with respect to the correctness of their answer and their right to express that answer confidently.

Not only do the dissenters have a liberating effect on the group, they are also rewarded for it. Like-minded partners are typically liked more than the other confederates; they are rated as warmer, more likeable, smarter, more confident, and better adjusted (Allen & Levine, 1969; Asch, 1955; Darley, Moriarty, Darley, & Berscheid, 1974), and the positive evaluations are greater the more public pressure the dissenting confederate was ostensibly under (Morris & Miller, 1975; Morris, Miller, & Spangenberg, 1977). On the surface this seems inconsistent with the oft-repeated study in which the naïve participants mocked the confederate who called out the wrong answer. But the similarities are superficial. In the Asch study the dissenter was calling out what everyone else in the room knew clearly was the wrong answer. In the partner effect studies the dissenter appears to be the only person in the room who is sane and who sees the world in the same way that the participant does. It is little wonder that this person commands loyalty. These individuals become valuable and diagnostic guides to reality—so much so that in later trials participants find themselves conforming to their fellow dissenters' pronouncements (Darley et al., 1974).

Intriguingly, large drops in conformity are evident even when the partner confederate picks an option that is different from the majority but that is also clearly wrong (what Asch referred to as an "extreme dissenter"). Imagine, for example, that the correct answer was line A, but all the confederates called out line B. As mentioned earlier, participants would give the correct answer (line A) about two thirds of the time, preferring to conform the rest of the time. But if one of the confederates called out line C—an equally incorrect answer—then participants gave the correct answer 91 percent of the time (Asch, 1955). Significant increases in nonconformity even emerged when the extreme dissenter was clearly incompetent (e.g., the dissenter wore thick glasses and pretended to be visually impaired; Allen & Levine, 1971; see also Nemeth & Chiles, 1988). Typically these incorrect or extreme dissenters are rated as neither well liked nor competent (Allen & Levine, 1968). But the results of these studies also suggest that they do not have to be likable or competent in order to deliver you from social pressure. Rather, it is sufficient for the deviant to shatter the sense of unanimity within the group; this alone seems to be enough to disinhibit or liberate people to have the courage to live up to their convictions.

## DISSENT AND ITS EFFECT ON GROUP DECISION MAKING

Research on minority influence (reviewed in detail elsewhere in this handbook) has shown that messages from minorities tend to be processed more carefully and systematically than messages from majorities (although evidence is mixed; see Hewstone & Martin, 2008). The work of Nemeth and colleagues shows that minorities do not just promote different ways of processing the message; they also prompt different (and more creative) ways of thinking about the issue as a whole (see Nemeth & Goncalo, 2011, for a review). According to Nemeth, majorities stimulate thinking among those they seek to influence, but they do so from the majority perspective. In the face of majorities, recipients of influence try to reconcile their point of view with that of the majority (e.g., "If so many people think X, then X must be right. . . . so what am I missing?"). Minorities, on the other hand, stimulate a different type of thinking. Majorities

who are confronted with majority attitudes wrestle with the paradox: "If they are wrong, why are they so persistent and certain?" This triggers a fresh start in people's minds—a setting aside of assumed wisdoms and a fundamental reappraisal of the issue. The result of this may not necessarily be conversion to the minority's point of view (although this may be one outcome). But what *is* predicted to occur is fresher, more divergent, and more creative thinking, which ultimately should lead to better decision making.

There is now a convergence of evidence in favor of this prediction. For example, Nemeth and Rogers (1996) selected university students who opposed the restriction of dormitory life, and then exposed them to what they were led to believe were minority or majority arguments supporting restrictions to dormitory life. Subsequently, participants were exposed to a range of articles on the proposal. Participants who were led to believe they were in the majority primarily chose to read articles that already reinforced their point of view, whereas those who were led to believe they were in the minority chose to read articles from both points of view. In another study, Nemeth and Kwan (1987) exposed participants to a divergent way of solving anagrams, which was presented as a minority or majority strategy. When presented as a strategy used by a majority of people, participants initially stuck with that strategy to the exclusion of other options, which had detrimental effects on task performance. When presented as a strategy used by a minority of people, participants used multiple strategies to solve the anagrams and were more productive as a result. In a separate study, participants tended to adopt the solutions of majority confederates on a hidden figures task, even if the majority was incorrect (Nemeth & Wachtler, 1983). When faced with minority positions, they detected solutions that would otherwise have gone undetected. Other studies show that in the face of minority perspectives, group members also come up with more original word associations (Nemeth & Kwan, 1985) and more creative solutions to a vacation scheduling problem (Nemeth, Brown, & Rogers, 2001) than do majorities. The power of dissent and conflict to trigger creativity seems to be greater than the power of (traditionally uncritical) brainstorming sessions (Nemeth, Personnaz, Personnaz, & Goncalo, 2004), and it seems to be one reason why groups with continually changing memberships tend to produce more creative outcomes than those with stable memberships, even when the group members themselves perceive the opposite (Nemeth & Ormiston, 2007).

Emerging from work on jury decision making and situated within the world of small-group decision making, Nemeth's insights have now been applied and confirmed in organizational settings. For example, van Dyne and Saavedra (1996) formed classroom discussion groups that met and worked on a problem over a 10-week period. In half the groups, a confederate was planted whose job was to serve as a dissenter. The groups that contained dissenters engaged in more divergent thinking and came up with more creative solutions than did the control groups. Others have conducted archival analyses of successful and unsuccessful companies, and concluded that successful companies were distinguished by their willingness to encourage dissent in boardroom meetings (Peterson, Owens, Tetlock, Fan, & Martorana, 1998). Bringing bad news and divergent opinions to the attention of superiors is relatively rare (Morrison & Milliken, 2000) and so needs to be actively encouraged. Active discouragement of threatening or new ideas can be disastrous and has been blamed, among other things, for the collapse of Enron (Tourish & Tourish, 2012).

The power of dissent to facilitate better decision making is consistent with Janis's (1972) formula for what leads groups to make catastrophic decisions. Janis argued that there was a set of psychological conditions that can lead to a decision-making style referred to as groupthink. These conditions include excessive cohesiveness; insulation of the group from the outside; a lack of impartial leadership; ideological homogeneity; and external threat associated with high stress. The symptoms of these conditions typically include feelings of invulnerability; feelings of unanimity; a conviction that the group must be right; ignoring or discrediting information contrary to the group's position; and the active pressuring of dissidents into conforming. These conditions are often characteristic of circumstances in which groups full of smart people make stupid decisions. Janis's insights were seminal in introducing the notion that there is such a thing as too much cohesion, and in highlighting the value of dissent in promoting optimal decision making.

As described earlier, work in organizational psychology and management broadly reinforces this point. However, this literature has also identified important boundary conditions. Central to this is Jehn's (1995, 1997) distinction between task conflict, relationship conflict, and process conflict. Consistent with the experimental work reported

earlier, task conflict (disagreement about the content of a task) on its own seems to be relatively successful in producing divergent thinking and creativity in organizations (Amason & Schweiger, 1994; Jehn, Northcraft, & Neale, 1999; see Butera, Darnon, & Mugny, 2011, for a similar point with respect to educational contexts). On the other hand, relationship conflict (interpersonal incompatibilities) and process conflict (different ideas about how to proceed with a task) tend to have detrimental effects (Greer, Jehn, & Mannix, 2008).

In reality, of course, the three forms of conflict tend to be intertwined, and the emerging picture suggests that the payoffs for introducing dissent may be overwhelmed by the costs in terms of undermined harmony and morale (de Dreu & Weingart, 2003). The power of dissent to create positive change may depend on how sensitively the organization itself manages the competing tensions between harmony and healthy conflict, for example, by maintaining employees' participation in group decision making (de Dreu & West, 2001) or by making clear that the ultimate goal is to build consensus (Dooley & Fryxell, 1999). The fact remains, however, that dissenters are powerful, and when their power is harnessed correctly, it can have a beneficial influence on the health and future direction of a group (see also Jetten & Hornsey, 2014).

### Ingroup Membership Can Provide Protection for Opinion Deviants and Critics

In much of the research reviewed earlier, the dissenter is part of an ad hoc small group charged with making collective decisions. But what if the minority viewpoint is expressed by people who share a social identity with the receiver—somebody who is an ingroup member and part of the same social category? Social identity theory (and its sister self-categorization theory) predict that when people share a social identity, they are more open to social influence (Tajfel & Turner, 1979; Turner, 1991). Consistent with this, there is evidence that minority perspectives are better received when they are presented by ingroup members than when they are presented by outgroup members (Clark & Maass, 1988; David & Turner, 1999).

William Crano and colleagues elaborated this insight and argued that there is a "leniency contract" between majority and minority group members when their disagreement occurs within the boundaries of a shared ingroup membership (Crano, 2001; Crano & Chen, 1998; Crano & Seyranian, 2009). From the majority members' point of view the contract maintains that they will listen to the minority's point of view without derogation or counterargument. From the minority members' point of view the contract maintains that they accept that the group will not actually change. The terms of the contract are nested within a broader politeness strategy that offers voice and respect to minorities, but it is a noninstrumental voice in the sense that neither group anticipates change to be forthcoming. Furthermore, the leniency that majorities offer minorities is contingent on the fact that the minority message does not threaten core group values. If the message is threatening—and particularly if it is expressed by a minority of one—the leniency is withdrawn and the minority will be received in a more derogatory fashion.

Research on ingroup criticism, however, suggests that the extent of leniency may well be more expansive than that envisaged by Crano (see Hornsey, 2005, for a review). This research examines what happens when ingroup members explicitly criticize the group culture—a threatening message that is often designed to provide a catalyst for positive change. This research suggests that there is a surprising amount of tolerance for ingroup critics; relative to outsiders who say the same thing, ingroup critics are viewed as more likeable and their comments arouse less negativity. Ingroup critics are also agreed with far more—and arouse a greater motivation to instigate reform—than when the same comments are made by an outsider. In some cases the support offered to an ingroup critic is equivalent to that offered to an ingroup member who praises the group (Hornsey, Oppes, & Svensson, 2002), and agreement with ingroup criticisms is significantly greater than a control, baseline condition (Hiew & Hornsey, 2010).

The relative acceptance of ingroup over outgroup criticisms—referred to as the *intergroup sensitivity effect*—is driven by trust. According to Hornsey (2005), the first question that people ask themselves when faced with a criticism of their group culture is not "Are they right or wrong?" Rather, the first question is "Why would they *say* that?" Attribution of motive, of course, is an important determinant of how people respond to many communicative acts, but in the case of criticism it might be of paramount importance, wrapped up as it is in issues of threat and defensiveness. It is only after the question "Why would they say that?" is resolved that the question of whether the criticism is right or wrong can be considered. If the answer is a positive one— that the person is making the comments because he or she cares and has the best interests of the group at heart—the message will then be accepted or rejected on the basis of the quality of the argument. But if the answer to the question is negative—that the person is trying to be hurtful or to derogate the group—then even high-quality messages will be rejected (Esposo, Hornsey, & Spoor, 2013).

Of course, one can never get smoking-gun evidence for what a messenger's motives are; recipients are forced to make educated guesses on the basis of context and heuristics. One heuristic, which is well established in the literature on intergroup dynamics, is that people intuitively trust ingroup members more than people not included in their group (Tanis & Postmes, 2005; Yamagishi & Kiyonari, 2000). Several studies confirm that ingroup members are attributed more constructive motives than outgroup members, and it is this attribution that mediates the intergroup sensitivity effect (Hornsey & Imani, 2004; Hornsey, Trembath, & Gunthorpe, 2004).

As shall be seen later, it is not the case that ingroup critics have complete amnesty to say what they want about a group; there are a number of critical errors ingroup members can make that can transform how their criticisms are received (most critically, failing to make clear their ongoing commitment to the group). Another key qualification is that the support for ingroup critics tends to be stronger in private than in public. For example, when participants are led to believe that their responses will be visible to important members of their own group, their reported negativity to the ingroup critic increases dramatically, to the point that the intergroup sensitivity effect is not observable (Hornsey, Frederiks, Smith, & Ford, 2007). This could lead critics themselves to underestimate the level of support they truly have, as group members engage in collective impression management in front of senior colleagues (they pretend to be more resistant than they really are). But the fact remains that privately—in the jury room of people's own minds—ingroup critics are received in a surprisingly positive way, and the trust that flows on from their ingroup membership can shield them from rejection even in the context of the most threatening and painful messages.

## The Who, How, and When of Dissent and Group Change
### Who Within a Group Is Most Likely to Dissent?

There is limited work on the personality variables that predict whether somebody will engage in dissent, conflict, or rebellion. The conclusions drawn from this research are perhaps unsurprising: People who are high in extraversion and low in agreeableness are more likely to voice dissent than others (LePine & Van Dyne, 2001). This research also found that people high in conscientiousness are willing to voice dissent, but Packer (2010) showed that the positive relationship between conscientiousness and dissent only emerges when people are also high in openness to experience, and thus are predisposed to the formation of alternative positions. Rather than taking a personality approach, however, most researchers in this domain have examined contextualized social identity variables as predictors of how likely a group member is to voice dissent or criticism.

One influential model that relates to this question is Dominic Packer's normative conflict model of dissent (Packer, 2008, 2011). According to this model, willingness to engage in dissent can be predicted as a function of (1) the strength of members' identification with the group and (2) the extent to which members experience "normative conflict" (i.e., the norms are viewed as suboptimal, harmful, or immoral). Of most relevance to the current review is what happens in the context of normative conflict. Packer's model argues that it is the high identifiers—the people who really care about the group and are psychologically enmeshed with it—who are most likely to engage in critical dissent. In contrast, low identifiers simply disengage.

This model was surprising at first sight when viewed through the lens of social identity theory, because it is often presumed that high identifiers (a) see their group through rose-colored glasses, meaning that they are less likely to see fault, and (b) are governed by a principle of loyalty and solidarity, so that they will rally behind the group even when there are flaws. However, this would be a misreading of social identity theory (Hornsey, 2006; Packer, 2011), and it seems more consistent with the core premises of the social identity approach that it is the high identifiers who are often most invested in change that has the potential for collective self-improvement. Precisely because they care about the fate of the group, high identifiers are most willing to bear the potential social costs associated with engaging in ingroup dissent. Supporting dissent or expressing dissent thus epitomizes loyalty for those who are highly identified with a group. The empirical work on this model is supportive of this notion: High identifiers are indeed more likely to express dissent in groups, whereas low identifiers are more likely to remain silent in the face of collective problems (Packer, 2009; Packer & Chasteen, 2010).

Packer's model is pragmatic enough to recognize that high identifiers will not always dissent to improve group functioning and the final action will depend on cost–benefit analyses. Depending on the nature of these cost–benefit analyses, certain strategic alternate responses might be preferred. For example, if the risks are seen to be too great, high identifiers may opt for uneasy conformity (see also Nail, MacDonald, & Levy, 2000). On the flipside, high identifiers may express dissent even where there is low normative conflict, in the hope that this devil's advocate position might create more divergent and creative thinking. Packer's model also leaves open the possibility that low identifiers will strategically dissent if it helps bring about personal benefits.

### Who Within a Group Are the Most Effective Dissenters?

Not only are high identifiers more *willing* to engage in dissent, there is evidence they are more *effective* dissenters. As reviewed earlier, there is a tendency for ingroup members to be extended relative generosity and amnesty when criticizing their own group (at least relative to outgroup members). The reason for this is that it is assumed that ingroup critics are making their comments with the best interests of the group at heart. But if group members are given reason to believe that this is not the case, then ingroup critics face as much resistance and negativity as outgroup critics.

For example, Hornsey et al. (2004) exposed Australians to an extract from an interview in which a speaker criticized Australians for being racist and uncultured. All participants knew the speaker's nationality (Australian or non-Australian) and, in those conditions where the speaker was Australian, they also knew his or her responses on a national identification scale. Where the speaker was clearly a patriotic Australian, he or she was received relatively well: Consistent with the intergroup sensitivity effect, highly identified ingroup critics were liked more and aroused less emotional negativity, and participants agreed more with them than with outgroup members who delivered the same message. But if the speaker was revealed as someone with relatively low identification as an Australian, the level of support plummeted and the intergroup sensitivity effect disappeared.

Of course, in real life one is not usually privy to a speaker's responses on an identification scale, and so one must guess at the underlying commitment of a critic to the group. One proxy for that might be the amount of time that the critic has been a group member. Old-timers have proven their commitment to the group through their longevity, whereas newcomers have not had the same chance to build up the reservoir of trust that a critic often needs to draw on. In support of this reasoning, Hornsey and colleagues (Hornsey, Grice, Jetten, Paulsen, & Callan, 2007) showed among allied health professionals that when the ingroup member was an old-timer (i.e., had served for 30 years in this field), the classic intergroup sensitivity effect emerged. But when the critic was a newcomer to the profession, the effect disappeared and the ingroup critic was rejected as strongly as the outgroup critic. Importantly, this effect was mediated by the level of *attachment* the critic had to his or her group. In sum, it is not the outsiders or the disengaged insiders who can effectively criticize the group, but rather the committed insiders; that is, the people who can reasonably claim that they are making these comments because they care and because they want the group to be the best group possible. In this way the findings broadly correspond with Hollander's (1958) classic notion of idiosyncrasy credits: After a long history of conformity and loyalty to group norms, an ingroup member's reward is the freedom to engage in deviance and individual expression.

The pessimistic results regarding the impact of newcomers are concerning because newcomers are often in a unique position to present news ideas, fresh perspectives, or provide ideas that worked well in groups of which they were previously a member (Nijstad & Levine, 2007). For those who have been embedded in a group culture for a long time, a film of dust can settle over their eyes, and it can be difficult to see beyond established and well-rehearsed collective wisdoms about the way things should be done. Newcomers, on the other hand, arrive with fresh eyes, yet the work reviewed herein would suggest that newcomers are least able to have influence in a group.

Fortunately, this negativity toward newcomers is less pronounced when less threatening forms of dissent are examined. For example, work on subjective group dynamics (discussed earlier; Abrams et al., 2002) suggests that deviant newcomers are extended some forgiveness for their attitudes relative to full group members: They are derogated less by established members and, if they do face derogation, it is associated with a socializing intention

(for established members, derogation is more likely to be associated with a punishing intention; Pinto, Marques, Levine, & Abrams, 2010). This is consistent with group socialization models (e.g., Levine & Moreland, 1994) suggesting that groups expect to go through a process of shaping and accommodating new members' individual desires in order to fit in with those of the group.

Work on small-group decision making also provides a relatively optimistic picture about the capacity of newcomers to influence group members. The standard paradigm in this work is to have small groups cooperating on a task for several trials (e.g., the hidden profiles task popularized by Stasser & Titus, 1985), and for a new member to enter the group midsession and to participate in a final, critical trial. Groups that experience the injection of new members are more creative, more innovative, and better decision makers than those who do not receive new members (Choi & Thompson, 2005; Rink & Ellemers, 2009). Acceptance of newcomer input is greater when the group is used to regular membership changes (Ziller, 1965); when the group has a history of failure and is therefore open to new ideas (Choi & Levine, 2004); and when the newcomer has specific skills that are recognized as valuable by the group (Choi & Levine, 2004; Rink & Ellemers, 2009). These latter two conclusions remind us that groups are pragmatic and will sometimes absorb the threat of deviance and normative change if they feel that it will pay off in terms of collective success (Morton, Postmes, & Jetten, 2007).

Interestingly, the influence of some newcomers may be independent of whether they are liked or "accepted" into the group. Rink and Ellemers (2009) examined real teams of interacting students and manipulated whether the input of a newcomer was vital to the solution on a hidden profiles task. Newcomers were told they were either a temporary group member who would soon be rotated out or a new, permanent group member. Newcomers who felt as though they were entering their new, permanent group behaved much like old group members: Presumably to avoid rejection, they generally sat back and did not want to draw attention to themselves. As a result, they contributed suboptimally to the task. Temporary newcomers (perhaps because they had less to lose) were comparatively willing to speak out, and consequently solutions in these groups were better. However, on measures of liking and acceptance, it was the permanent group member who was evaluated more positively than the temporary group member. In this way the temporary newcomers resemble the extreme dissenters that Asch spoke of: Their presence can have a liberating influence but at the expense of their personal acceptance.

One group member who has a particularly delicate but important role to play in driving innovation is the leader. On one hand, leaders often wield their influence as a function of the success with which they embody and epitomize the prototypical norms and values of the group (Hogg, 2001; Hogg & van Knippenberg, 2003). On the other hand, leaders often have a responsibility to transform groups—to engage in constructive change—and this in turn requires them to engage in "constructive deviance" (Fielding & Hogg, 1997).

Some argue that this paradox is so difficult to resolve that leaders only have a small window of opportunity to create genuine change and simultaneously maintain the support of their followers. According to Abrams and colleagues (Abrams, Randsley de Moura, Marques, & Hutchison, 2008), future and incoming leaders are given permission to create change, and that successful change often happens in the "honeymoon period" soon after a leader takes charge. Indeed, a series of experiments made clear that deviance is supported more by future leaders than it is by ex-leaders or current leaders (Abrams et al., 2008).

### What Strategies Allow for More Effective Dissent?

In this chapter, we have built the empirical case that dissent, deviance, and criticism can be valuable to promote creativity, improve decision making, and catalyze the process of reform. If this is the case, then it is in the group's interests to create a culture in which people feel free to express their attitudes without fear of recrimination. Research in the small group and social identity traditions shows that norms of individualism (Hornsey et al., 2006), creativity (Adarves-Yorno, Postmes, & Haslam, 2007), critical engagement (Nemeth et al., 2004), and dissent (Postmes, Spears, & Cihangir, 2001) can indeed succeed in increasing tolerance for dissent, enhancing divergent thinking, optimizing decision making, and removing the destructive influence of groupthink. The importance of these values is increasingly recognized among management theorists (Amabile, 1996; Collins & Porras, 1994) where attention has turned to the micro-strategies that organizations can employ to encourage dissent and fearless expression (Tourish & Tourish, 2012). Some of these strategies are surprisingly simple; for

example, common knowledge effects can be reduced if the task is framed as being about "solving a problem" rather than "making a decision" (Stasser & Stewart, 1992).

One tradition of research that has been particularly energetic in examining the strategies that dissenters can use to maximize influence is the research under the broad rubric of "minority influence." Because this research is reviewed in depth elsewhere in this handbook, we will not spend much time breaking it down here. But several broad principles have stood the test of time: Minorities are more effective if they are consistent in their message (but not so inconsistent they are seen as inflexible); if they can demonstrate their authentic investment in the attitude and shake off notions that their messages stem from vested interest; and if they can convince their audience that they are open-minded and willing to engage in dialogue (Moscovici, 1976, 1980).

Another tradition of research that has examined the rhetorical processes associated with creating change is that of leadership. Earlier we asked: How do leaders embody the prototype of the group while at the same time working to innovate, reform, and change prevailing norms? One strategy is to shift the comparative context. According to self-categorization theory, norms and prototypes are not static properties of groups. Rather, they shift as a function of which relevant outgroups are salient in a particular intergroup context. A strategically skilled leader can manipulate which outgroups members focus on as a way of shifting the normative expectations within the group (Reicher & Hopkins, 2003). The leader creates a new set of norms and conforms to these new normative prescriptions, thus creating change and maintaining prototypicality simultaneously. Reicher and Hopkins (2003) refer to this process as leaders becoming "entrepreneurs of identity."

Another strategy is to shore up one's identity credentials by showing ingroup-favoring behavior. Leaders who have previously demonstrated their willingness to favor the ingroup receive more support from members when pushing for change (Haslam & Platow, 2001) and are more likely to be excused for their own deviation from the prototype (Platow & van Knippenberg, 2001). Similar to the principle of idiosyncrasy credits, leaders who display their loyalty will be given greater scope to push for change and to deviate from those norms. This is also the message that emerges from the work on intragroup criticism: Unless ingroup members can convince their peers that they are committed group members with constructive motives, then a quality argument is unlikely to be enough to win over the group (Hornsey, 2005, 2006). Ingroup critics need to build their identity credentials first and then work on the quality of their argument.

One simple rhetorical strategy for maintaining a sense of ingroup solidarity—with all the attributional advantages that this implies—is to use inclusive, identity-embracing language (e.g., "we," "us"). This is a common rhetorical strategy that leaders use (Reicher & Hopkins, 1996) and appears to be relatively effective, particularly for high identifiers within the group (Hornsey, Blackwood, & O'Brien, 2005). It may also be particularly effective for people who have ambiguous ingroup credentials (Hornsey et al., 2004).

Although it is very important to prove one's loyal, identity-embracing credentials, this ability may not be sufficient for critics and dissenters to have their messages accepted in an open-minded fashion. In addition, critics and dissenters need to be sensitive to the social conventions (or "rules of engagement") associated with intragroup conflict. For example, it is well established that groups are more open to divergent ideas when they are not facing external pressures. Indeed, pressure from an external threat was, for Janis (1972), a key precondition of groupthink. Dissenters and critics are cognitively demanding (in the sense that they require people to think divergently) and emotionally draining (in the sense that they can trigger socioemotional conflict). They also risk fracturing the unity of a group, which in turn can damage group locomotion and reduce the ability of the group to resist external enemies. One message for critics and dissenters, then, is the importance of timing. If the group is relaxed and feeling secure, they will be more receptive to divergent and threatening ideas than when they are under pressure from intergroup conflicts, environmental stressors, or impending deadlines (for empirical demonstrations, see Ariyanto, Hornsey, & Gallois, 2009; Kruglanski & Webster, 1996).

## Conclusion

In this chapter, we discussed two separate lines of research that at first sight aim to understand opposing processes: one is concerned with processes aimed at maintaining the group the way it is (e.g., conformity, groupthink), and the other focuses on processes that can help us understand how groups change (e.g., motives of dissenters, group critics). As discussed, it is probably fair to say that there has been more research attention to the former than the latter type of processes (see Moscovici, 1976,

for a similar point). Unfortunately, this has led some researchers to portray the dynamics within groups as stifling forces that undermine individuals' creativity, performance, and rationality (for a recent analysis, see Jetten & Hornsey, 2011; 2014; Spears, 2010).

It is clear, however, that one can only understand the forces that motivate maintaining the status quo when one understands the dangers and risks associated with pushing for group change. It is equally true that one can only understand why people press for change within groups when one understands their concerns with maintaining the status quo. Because the process of change cannot be understood without an understanding of stability (and vice versa), we recommend that they be treated as two sides of the same coin: Only the study of these processes in combination and in conjunction with each other can help us to develop a better and more comprehensive understanding of *both* stability and change within groups.

## References

Abrams, D., Marques, J. M., Bown, N., & Dougill, M. (2002). Anti-norm and pro-norm deviance in the bank and on the campus: Two experiments on subjective group dynamics. *Group Processes and Intergroup Relations, 5*, 163–182.

Abrams, D., Marques, J. M., Bown, N. J., & Henson, M. (2000). Pro-norm and anti-norm deviance within in-groups and out-groups. *Journal of Personality and Social Psychology, 78*, 906–912.

Abrams, D., Randsley de Moura, G., Marques, J. M., & Hutchison, P. (2008). Innovation credit: When can leaders oppose their group's norm? *Journal of Personality and Social Psychology, 95*, 662–678.

Abrams, D., Rutland, A., & Cameron, L. (2003a). The development of subjective group dynamics: Children's judgments of normative and deviant in-group and out-group individuals. *Child Development, 74*, 1840–1856.

Abrams, D., Rutland, A., Cameron, L., & Ferrell, J. (2007). Older but wilier: Ingroup accountability and the development of subjective group dynamics. *Developmental Psychology, 43*(1), 134–148.

Abrams, D., Rutland, A., Cameron, L., & Marques, J. M. (2003b). The development of subjective group dynamics: When in-group bias gets specific. *British Journal of Developmental Psychology, 21*(2), 155-176.

Abrams, D., Rutland, A., Ferrell, J. M., & Pelletier, J. (2008). Children's judgments of disloyal and immoral peer behavior: Subjective group dynamics in minimal intergroup contexts. *Child Development, 79*(2), 444–461.

Abrams, D., Rutland, A., Pelletier, J., & Ferrell, J. M. (2009). Group nous and social exclusion: The role of theory of social mind, multiple classification skill and social experience of peer relations within groups. *Child Development, 80*, 224–243.

Adarves-Yorno, I., Postmes, T., & Haslam, S. A. (2007). Creative innovation or crazy irrelevance? The contribution of group norms and level of identity to innovative behaviour and perception of creativity, *Journal of Experimental Social Psychology, 43*, 410–416.

Allen, V. L., & Levine, J. M. (1968). Social support, dissent and conformity. *Sociometry, 31*(2), 138–149.

Allen, V. L., & Levine, J. M. (1969). Consensus and conformity. *Journal of Experimental Social Psychology, 5*, 389–399.

Allen, V. L., & Levine, J. M. (1971). Social support and conformity: The role of independent assessment of reality. *Journal of Experimental Social Psychology, 7*, 48–58.

Amabile, T. M. (1996). *Creativity in context*. Boulder, CO: Westview.

Amason, A., & Schweiger, D. M. (1994). Resolving the paradox of conflict, strategic decision making, and organizational performance. *International Journal of Conflict Management, 5*, 239–253.

Ariyanto, A., Hornsey, M. J., & Gallois, C. (2009). United we stand: Intergroup conflict moderates the intergroup sensitivity effect. *European Journal of Social Psychology, 40*, 169–177.

Asch, S. E. (1951). Effects of group pressure upon the modification and distortion of judgment. In H. Guetzkow (Ed.), *Groups, leadership and men* (pp. 177–190). Pittsburgh, PA: Carnegie Press.

Asch, S. E. (1952). Effects of group pressures upon the modification and distortion of judgments. In G. E. Swanson, T. M. Newcomb, & E. L. Hartley (Eds.), *Readings in social psychology* (pp. 393–401). New York: Holt, Reinhart & Winston.

Asch, S. E. (1955). Opinions and social pressure. *Scientific American, 193*, 31–35.

Asch, S. E. (1956). Studies of independence and conformity: A minority of one against a unanimous majority. *Psychological Monographs, 70*, 1-70.

Bragg, B. W., & Allen, V. (1972). The role of public and private support in reducing conformity. *Psychonomic Science, 29*(2), 81–82.

Butera, F., Darnon, C., & Mugny, G. (2011). Learning form conflict. In J. Jetten & M. J. Hornsey (Eds.), *Rebels in groups: Dissent, deviance, difference and defiance* (pp. 36–53). Chichester, UK: Wiley-Blackwell.

Choi, H. S., & Levine, J. M. (2004). Minority influence in work teams: The impact of newcomers. *Journal of Experimental Social Psychology, 40*, 273–280.

Choi, H. S., & Thompson, L. (2005). Old wine in a new bottle: Impact of membership change on group creativity. *Organizational Behavior and Human Decision Processes, 98*, 121–132.

Clark, R. D., & Maass, A. (1988). Social categorization in minority influence: The case of homosexuality. *European Journal of Social Psychology, 18*, 347–364.

Collins, J. C., & Porras, J. I. (1994). *Built to last: Successful habits of visionary companies*. New York: Harper Collins.

Costell, R. M., & Leiderman, P. H. (1968). Psychophysiological concomitants of social stress: The effects of conformity pressure. *Psychosomatic Medicine, 30*, 298–310.

Crano, W. D. (2001). Social influence, social identity and ingroup leniency. In C. K. W. DeDreu & N. K. DeVries (Eds.), *Group consensus and minority influence: Implications for innovation* (pp. 122–143). Malden, MA: Blackwell.

Crano, W. D., & Chen, X. (1998). The leniency contract and persistence of majority and minority influence. *Journal of Personality and Social Psychology, 74*, 1437–1450.

Crano, W. D., & Seyranian, V. (2009). How minorities prevail: The context/comparison–leniency contract model. *Journal of Social Issues, 65*, 335–363.

Darley, J. M., Moriarty, T., Darley, S., & Berscheid, E. (1974). Increased conformity to a fellow deviant as a function of prior deviation. *Journal of Experimental Social Psychology, 10*, 211–223.

David, B., & Turner, J. C. (1999). Studies in self-categorization and minority conversion: The in-group minority in intragroup and intergroup contexts. *British Journal of Social Psychology, 38*, 115–134.

De Dreu, C. K. W., & Weingart, L. R. (2003). Task versus relationship conflict, team performance, and team member satisfaction: A meta-analysis. *Journal of Applied Psychology, 88*, 741–749.

De Dreu, C. K. W., & West, M. A. (2001). Minority dissent and team innovation: The importance of participation in decision making. *Journal of Applied Psychology, 86*, 1191–1201.

Deutsch, M., & Gerard, H. (1955). A study of normative and informational social influences upon individual judgment. *Journal of Abnormal and Social Psychology, 51*, 629–636.

Dooley, R. S., & Fryxell, G. E. (1999). Attaining decision quality and commitment from dissent: The moderating effects of loyalty and competence in strategic decision-making teams. *Academy of Management Journal, 42*, 389–402.

Dwyer, L. A., Hornsey, M. J., Smith, L. G. E., Oei, T. P. S., & Dingle, G. A. (2011). Participant autonomy in cognitive behavioral group therapy: An integration of self-determination and cognitive behavioral theories. *Journal of Social and Clinical Psychology, 30*, 24–46.

Esposo, S. R., Hornsey, M. J., & Spoor, R. (2013). Outsiders critical of your group are rejected regardless of argument quality. *British Journal of Social Psychology, 52*, 386–395.

Festinger, L. (1950). Informal social communication. *Psychological Review, 63*, 181–194.

Festinger, L. (1954). A theory of social comparison processes. *Human Relations, 7*, 117–140.

Fielding, K. S., & Hogg, M. A. (1997). Social identity, self-categorisation and leadership: A field study of small interactive groups. *Group Dynamics: Theory, Research and Practice, 1*, 39–51.

Gelfand, M. J., Raver, J. L., Nishii, L., Leslie, L. M., Lun, J., Lim, B. C.,. . . Yamaguchi, S. (2011). Differences between tight and loose cultures: A 33-nation study. *Science, 332*, 1100–1104.

Gerard, H. B. (1961). Disagreement with others, their credibility, and experienced stress. *Journal of Abnormal and Social Psychology, 62*, 559–564.

Gigone, D., & Hastie, R. (1993). The common knowledge effect: Information sharing and group judgment. *Journal of Personality and Social Psychology, 65*, 959–974.

Greer, L. L., Jehn, K. A., & Mannix, E. A. (2008). Conflict transformation: A longitudinal investigation of the relationships between different types of intra-group conflict and the moderating role of conflict resolution. *Small Group Research, 39*, 278–302.

Haslam, S. A., & Platow, M. J. (2001). The link between leadership and followership: How affirming social identity translates vision into action. *Personality and Social Psychology Bulletin, 27*, 1469–1479.

Hewstone, M., & Martin, R. (2008). Social influence. In M. Hewstone, W. Stroebe, & K. Jonas (Eds.), *Introduction* to social psychology (4th ed., pp. 216–243). Malden, MA: Blackwell.

Hichy, Z., Mari, S., & Capozza, D. (2008). Pro-norm and anti-norm deviants: A test of the subjective group dynamics model. Journal of Social Psychology, 148, 641–644.

Hiew, D. N., & Hornsey, M. J. (2010). Does time reduce resistance to out-group critics? An investigation of the persistence of the intergroup sensitivity effect over time. British Journal of Social Psychology, 49, 569–581.

Hogg, M. A. (2001). A social identity theory of leadership. Personality and Social Psychology Review, 5, 184–200.

Hogg, M. A., & van Knippenberg, D. (2003). Social identity and leadership processes in groups. In M. P. Zanna (Ed.), Advances in experimental social psychology (Vol. 35, pp. 2–55). London: Academic Press.

Hornsey, M. J. (2005). Why being right is not enough: Predicting defensiveness in the face of group criticism. European Review of Social Psychology, 16, 301–334.

Hornsey, M. J. (2006). Ingroup critics and their influence on groups. In T. Postmes & J. Jetten (Eds.), Individuality and the group: Advances in social identity (pp. 74–91). London: Sage.

Hornsey, M. J., Blackwood, L., & O'Brien, A. (2005). Speaking for others: The pros and cons of group advocates using collective language. Group Processes and Intergroup Relations, 8, 245–257.

Hornsey, M. J., Frederiks, E., Smith, J. R., & Ford, L. (2007). Strategic defensiveness: Public and private responses to group criticism. British Journal of Social Psychology, 46, 697–716.

Hornsey, M. J., Grice, T., Jetten, J., Paulsen, N., & Callan, V. (2007). Group directed criticisms and recommendations for change: Why newcomers arouse more resistance than old-timers. Personality and Social Psychology Bulletin, 33, 1036–1048.

Hornsey, M. J., & Imani, A. (2004). Criticizing groups from the inside and the outside: An identity perspective on the intergroup sensitivity effect. Personality and Social Psychology Bulletin, 30, 365–383.

Hornsey, M. J., & Jetten, J. (2004). The individual within the group: Balancing the need to belong with the need to be different. Personality and Social Psychology Review, 8, 248–264.

Hornsey, M. J., Jetten, J., McAuliffe, B. J., & Hogg, M. A. (2006). The impact of individualist and collectivist group norms on evaluations of dissenting group members. Journal of Experimental Social Psychology, 42, 57–68.

Hornsey, M. J., Oppes, T., & Svensson, A. (2002). "It's ok if we say it, but you can't": Responses to intergroup and intragroup criticism. European Journal of Social Psychology, 32, 293–307.

Hornsey, M. J., Trembath, M., & Gunthorpe, S. (2004). "You can criticize because you care": Identity attachment, constructiveness, and the intergroup sensitivity effect. European Journal of Social Psychology, 34, 499–518.

Hollander, E. P. (1958). Conformity, status, and idiosyncrasy credit. Psychological Review, 65, 117–127.

Janis, I. L. (1972). Victims of groupthink: A psychological study of foreign-policy decisions and fiascoes. Oxford, UK: Houghton Mifflin.

Jehn, K. (1995). A multi-method examination of the benefits and detriments of intragroup conflict. Administrative Science Quarterly, 40, 256–282.

Jehn, K. (1997). A qualitative analysis of conflict types and dimensions in organizational groups. Administrative Science Quarterly, 42, 530–557.

Jehn, K. A., Northcraft, G. B., & Neale, M. A. (1999). Why differences make a difference: A field study of diversity, conflict, and performance in workgroups. Administrative Science Quarterly, 44(4), 741–763.

Jetten, J., & Hornsey, M. J. (Eds.). (2011). Rebels in groups: Dissent, deviance, difference and defiance. Chichester, UK: Wiley-Blackwell.

Jetten, J., & Hornsey, M. J. (2012). Conformity: Revisiting Asch's line judgment studies. In J. R. Smith & S. A. Haslam (Eds.), Social psychology: Revisiting the classic studies (pp. 76–90). London: Sage.

Jetten, J., & Hornsey, M. J. (2014). Deviance and dissent within groups. Annual Review of Psychology, 65, 461–485.

Jetten, J., Postmes, T., & McAuliffe, B. J. (2002). "We're all individuals": Group norms of individualism and collectivism, levels of identification, and identity threat. European Journal of Social Psychology, 32, 189–207.

Kashima, Y., Klein, O., & Clark, A. (2007). Grounding: Sharing information in social interaction. In K. Fiedler (Ed.), Social communication (pp. 27–78). Philadelphia, PA: Psychology Press.

Katz, D., & Allport, F. H. (1931). Student attitudes. Syracuse, NY: Craftsman.

Klein, O., Tindale, S., & Brauer, M. (2008). The consensualization of social stereotypes. In K. Fiedler & F. Freytag (Eds.), Stereotype dynamics (pp. 263–292). Mahwah, NJ: Erlbaum.

Kruglanski, A. W., & Webster, D. M. (1996). Motivated closing of the mind: "Seizing" and "freezing." Psychological Review, 103, 263–283.

Larson, J. R., Jr., Foster-Fishman, P. G., & Keys, C. B. (1994). Discussion of shared and unshared information in decision-making groups. Journal of Personality and Social Psychology, 67, 446–461.

Levine, J. M., & Moreland, R. L. (1994). Group socialization: Theory and research. European Review of Social Psychology, 5, 305–336.

Marques, J. M., Abrams, D., Páez, D., & Martinez-Taboada, C. M. (1998). The role of categorisation and in-group norms in judgments of groups and their members. Journal of Personality and Social Psychology, 75, 976–988.

Marques, J. M., & Páez, D. (1994). The black sheep effect: Social categorisation, rejection of ingroup deviates, and perception of group variability. European Review of Social Psychology, 5, 37–68.

Marques, J. M., Páez, D., & Abrams, D. (1998). Social identity and intragroup differentiation as subjective social control. In J. F. Morales, D. Páez, J. C. Deschamps, & S. Worchel (Eds.), Current perspectives on social identity and social categorization (pp. 124–142). New York: Sage.

Matthes, J., Morrison, K. R., & Schemer, C. (2010). A spiral of silence for some: Attitude certainty and the expression of political minority opinions. Communication Research, 37, 774–800.

Morris, W. N., & Miller, R. S. (1975). Impressions of dissenters and conformers: An attributional analysis. Sociometry, 38(2), 327–339.

Morris, W. N., Miller, R. S., & Spangenberg, S. (1977). The effects of dissenter position and task difficulty on conformity and response conflict. Journal of Personality, 45(2), 251–266.

Morrison, K. R., & Miller, D. T. (2008). Distinguishing between silent and vocal minorities: Not all deviants feel marginal. Journal of Personality and Social Psychology, 94, 871–882.

Morrison, E. W., & Milliken, F. J. (2000). Organizational silence: A barrier to change and development in a pluralistic world. *Academy of Management Review, 25,* 706–725.

Morton, T. A., Postmes, T., & Jetten, J. (2007). Playing the game: When group success is more important than downgrading deviants. *European Journal of Social Psychology, 37,* 599–616.

Moscovici, S. (1976). *Social influence and social change.* London: Academic Press.

Moscovici, S. (1980). Toward a theory of conversion behavior. In L. Berkowitz (Ed.), *Advances in Experimental Social Psychology* (Vol. 13, pp. 209-239). New York: Academic Press.

Nail, P. R., MacDonald, G., & Levy, D. A. (2000). Proposal of a four-dimensional model of social response. *Psychological Bulletin, 126,* 454–470.

Nemeth, C., Brown, K., & Rogers, J. (2001). Devil's advocate versus authentic dissent: Stimulating quantity and quality. *European Journal of Social Psychology, 31,* 707–720.

Nemeth, C., & Chiles, C. (1988). Modeling courage: The role of dissent in fostering independence. *European Journal of Social Psychology, 18,* 275–280.

Nemeth, C., & Goncalo, J. A. (2011). Rogues and heroes: Finding value in dissent. In J. Jetten & M. J. Hornsey (Eds.), *Rebels in groups: Dissent, deviance, difference and defiance* (pp. 17–35). Chichester, UK: Wiley-Blackwell.

Nemeth, C., & Ormiston, M. (2007). Creative idea generation: Harmony versus stimulation. *European Journal of Experimental Social Psychology, 37,* 524–535.

Nemeth, C., & Rogers, J. (1996). Dissent and the search for information. *British Journal of Social Psychology. Special Issue: Minority Influences, 35,* 67–76.

Nemeth, C. J., & Kwan, J. L. (1985). Originality of word associations as a function of majority vs minority influence. *Social Psychology Quarterly, 48,* 277–282.

Nemeth, C. J., & Kwan, J. L. (1987). Minority influence, divergent thinking and detection of correct solutions. *Journal of Applied Social Psychology, 17,* 788–799.

Nemeth, C. J., Personnaz, M., Personnaz, B., & Goncalo, J. (2004). The liberating role of conflict in group creativity: A cross-national study. *European Journal of Social Psychology, 34,* 365–374.

Nemeth, C. J., & Wachtler, J. (1983). Creative problem solving as a result of majority vs. minority influence. *European Journal of Social Psychology, 13,* 45–55.

Nijstad, B. A., & Levine, J. M. (2007). Group creativity and the stages of creative group problem solving. In M. Hewstone, H. A. W. Schut, J. B. F. de Wit, K. van den Bos, & M. S. Stroebe (Eds.), *The scope of social psychology: Theory and applications. Essays in honour of Wolfgang Stroebe* (pp. 159–171). New York: Psychology Press.

Noelle-Neumann, E. (1993). *Spiral of silence: Public opinion—Our social skin* (2nd ed.). Chicago: University of Chicago Press.

Packer, D. J. (2008). On being with us and against us: A normative conflict model of dissent in social groups. *Personality and Social Psychology Review, 12,* 50–72.

Packer, D. J. (2009). Avoiding groupthink: Whereas weakly identified members remain silent, strongly identified members dissent about collective problems. *Psychological Science, 20,* 546–548.

Packer, D. J. (2010). The interactive influence of conscientiousness and openness to experience on dissent. *Social Influence, 5,* 202–219.

Packer, D. J. (2011). The dissenter's dilemma, and a social identity solution. In J. Jetten & M. J. Hornsey (Eds.), *Rebels in groups: Dissent, deviance, difference and defiance* (pp. 281–301). Chichester, UK: Wiley-Blackwell.

Packer, D. J., & Chasteen, A. L. (2010). Loyal deviance: Testing the normative conflict model of dissent in social groups. *Personality and Social Psychology Bulletin, 36,* 5–18.

Peterson, R. S., Owens, P. D., Tetlock, P. E., Fan, E. T., & Martorana, P. V. (1998). Group dynamics in top management teams: Groupthink, vigilance and alternative models of organizational failure and success. *Organizational Behavior and Human Decision Processes, 73,* 272–305.

Pinto, I. R., Marques, J. M., Levine, J. M., & Abrams, D. (2010). Membership status and subjective group dynamics: Who triggers the black sheep effect? *Journal of Personality and Social Psychology, 99,* 107–119.

Platow, M. J., & van Knippenberg, D. (2001). A social identity analysis of leadership endorsement: The effects of leader ingroup prototypicality and distributive intergroup fairness. *Personality and Social Psychology Bulletin, 27,* 1508–1519.

Postmes, T., Spears, R., & Cihangir, S. (2001). Quality of decision making and group norms. *Journal of Personality and Social Psychology, 80,* 918–930.

Prentice, D. A., & Miller, D. T. (1993). Pluralistic ignorance and alcohol use on campus: Some consequences of misperceiving the social norm. *Journal of Personality and Social Psychology, 64*(2), 243–256.

Reicher, S., & Hopkins, N. (1996). Seeking influence through characterizing self-categories: An analysis of anti-abortionist rhetoric. *British Journal of Social Psychology, 35,* 297–311.

Reicher, S., & Hopkins, N. (2003). On the science and art of leadership. In D. van Knippenberg & M. A. Hogg (Eds.), *Leadership and power: Identity processes in groups and organizations* (pp. 197–209). Oxford, UK: Blackwell.

Rink, F., & Ellemers, N. (2009). Temporary vs. permanent group membership: How the future prospects of newcomers affect newcomer acceptance and newcomer influence. *Personality and Social Psychology Bulletin, 35,* 764–776.

Schachter, S. (1951). Deviation, rejection, and communication. *Journal of Abnormal and Social Psychology, 46,* 190–207.

Sheldon, K. M., & Bettencourt, B. A. (2002). Psychological need-satisfaction and subjective well-being within social groups. *British Journal of Social Psychology, 41,* 25-38.

Sherif, M. (1936). *The psychology of social norms.* New York: Harper & Bros.

Simon, B., Aufderheide, B., & Hastedt, C. (2000). The double negative effect: The (almost) paradoxical role of the individual self in minority and majority members' information processing. *British Journal of Social Psychology, 39,* 73–93.

Spears, R. (2010). Group rationale, collective sense: Beyond intergroup bias. *British Journal of Social Psychology, 49,* 1–20.

Stasser, G., & Stewart, D. (1992). Discovery of hidden profiles by decision-making groups: Solving a problem versus making a judgment. *Journal of Personality and Social Psychology, 63,* 426–434.

Stasser, G., & Titus, W. (1985). Pooling of unshared information in group decision-making: Biased information sampling during discussion. *Journal of Personality and Social Psychology, 48*, 1467–1478.

Tajfel, H., & Turner, J. C. (1979). An integrative theory of intergroup conflict. In W. G. Austin & S. Worchel (Eds.), *The social psychology of intergroup relations* (pp. 33–47). Monterey, CA: Brooks/Cole.

Tanis, M., & Postmes, T. (2005). A social identity approach to trust: Interpersonal perception, group membership and trusting behaviour. *European Journal of Social Psychology, 35*, 413–424.

Tourish, D., & Tourish, N. (2012). Upward communication in organisations: How ingratiation and defensive reasoning impedes thoughtful action. In R. Sutton, M. J. Hornsey, & K. Douglas (Eds.), *Feedback: The communication of praise, criticism and advice*. New York: Peter Lang.

Turner, J. C. (1991). *Social influence*. Milton-Keynes, UK: Open University Press.

Turner, J. C. (1999). Some current issues in research on social identity and self-categorization theories. In N. Ellemers, R. Spears, & B. Doosje (Eds.), *Social identity: Context, commitment, content* (pp. 6–34). Oxford, UK: Blackwell.

Van Dyne, L., & Saavedra, R. (1996). A naturalistic minority influence experiment: Effects of divergent thinking, conflict and originality in work groups. *British Journal of Social Psychology, 35*, 151–168.

Wesselmann, E. D., Williams, K. D., Pryor, J. B., Eichler, F. A., Gill, D., & Hogue, J. D. (2014). Revisiting Schachter's research on rejection, deviance, and communication (1951). *Social Psychology, 45*, 164–169.

Wittenbaum, G. M. (1998). Information sampling in decision making groups: The impact of members' task-relevant status. *Small Group Research, 29*, 57–84.

Wittenbaum, G. M., Hubbell, A. P., & Zuckerman, C. (1999). Mutual enhancement: Toward an understanding of collective preference for shared information. *Journal of Personality and Social Psychology, 77*, 967–978.

Yamagishi, T., & Kiyonari, T. (2000). The group as the container of generalized reciprocity. *Social Psychology Quarterly, 63*, 116–132.

Ziller, R. C. (1965). Toward a theory of open and closed groups. *Psychological Bulletin, 64*, 164–182.

# Minority Influence

Fabrizio Butera, Juan Manuel Falomir-Pichastor, Gabriel Mugny, *and* Alain Quiamzade

**Abstract**

The aim of the present chapter is to explain the processes through which minority points of view may, or may not, diffuse in society at large. The first section presents the rise in the 1970s of a new stream of research, that of minority influence, and summarizes early conceptions and the initial experimental works that allowed differentiating minority from majority influence. The second part reviews the subsequent criticism to early minority influence research, in particular as regards its differences from majority influence. The third section examines the various models that attempted to reconcile previous controversies, and it organizes the great diversity in results observed over the years in studies on majority and minority influence. The final section points to the liveliness of this area of investigation by reviewing some recent extensions and applications of minority influence research.

**Key Words:** minorities, conflict, consistency, attitude change, conversion, manifest influence, latent influence, information processing

What do Hong Kong's Umbrella Revolution, USA's Occupy Wall Street protest, the Spanish Indignados, and the Slow Food movement have in common? They, as well as many other social movements around the globe, consist of minority groups who have the firm conviction that their action and claims will eventually promote some political, economic, or cultural innovation. In all realms of ideas, beliefs, attitudes, knowledge, or behaviors, innovation implies the emergence of a new point of view almost necessarily held by individuals or groups that represent a minority faction in society. The present chapter presents the various lines of research that have attempted to explain the processes through which such minority points of view may, or may not, diffuse in society at large.

## The Rise of Minority Influence Research

The story began with a question about science (for an historical account, see Moscovici, 1996) that was generalized to society at large: How is it possible that an individual or a school of thought

that has no authority and no credibility can sometimes succeed in convincing other people? From Galileo's revolution in science to the suffragettes' role in promoting vote for women, history is full of examples of isolated individuals or minority groups that brought about great changes. Yet minorities lack the numerical strength that would allow them to exert either informational or normative influences (Deutsch & Gerard, 1955); moreover, they are at first believed to be wrong and do not represent a real possibility to attain a consensus in defining social reality. They instead challenge the prevailing positions and impede the establishment of an undisputable consensual view in their field. Moscovici (1976) was the first to theorize when and why minority influence can arise; his main assumption was that all influence attempts create a conflict, no matter what their origin, and thus minorities too should have an impact because they create a conflict and refuse whatever compromise is proposed to them (Moscovici, 1980; but see the section on "Negotiating Conflict"). History of science suggested the key to such an impact: a rhetoric of tenacity (or consistency).

## Explaining Innovation and Social Change

In Moscovici's (1976) analysis, classical works on social influence and communication did not help understand influence in the direction of innovation: The dominant functionalist approach in social psychology had focused researchers on the reproduction and maintenance of social relations, the status quo. The advocates of this approach were considered as looking essentially at the processes through which social systems become long lasting and protect themselves against social change. Moscovici (1976) criticized the implicit assumption of this line of thought that there is only one correct, ahistorical, and somehow predetermined view of the world and its values. Whenever a norm is defined in such absolute terms, research amounts to searching for the conditions and mechanisms through which individuals and groups adapt to that norm. For the most part, social psychological studies between the 1940s and the 1960s dealt with the mechanisms of conformity and obedience, in short, with social control and its internalization (see Hodges—conformity, and Burger—obedience, this volume). These mechanisms were seen as the constituents of majorities and dominant entities considered to be responsible for maintaining uniformity and consensus. Moscovici proposed instead that norms should be considered as relative (i.e., to be the outcome of compromise or submission) and that emphasis be focused on the mechanisms underlying the spread of innovation, viewed as fundamental to social and historical evolution. At the root of such change are minorities, be they individuals or groups.

As concerns social influence dynamics, Moscovici proposed that minority influence follows a logic that is quite different from majority influence. Majority influence is the consequence of informational and normative pressures that force or motivate people to yield. Conversely, people do not feel compelled by informational and normative pressures when facing minorities and are free to oppose minority's ideas and refuse to adopt them. This does not mean that minorities have no effect: They do not leave their opponents indifferent. They create conflict in presenting their positions as an alternative to existing positions in the field. They gain attention from the majority members, since they attract more communication toward them, even if it is mainly in order to restore the consensus (Schachter, 1951). They are perceived as committed to their position because

they resist social pressures to conform and may even foster courage to resist (Nemeth & Chiles, 1988). Finally, when minorities obtain some influence, it is at the end of a long and painful process, and it takes the form of a hidden, latent internalization that Moscovici (1980) called conversion (hence, the name of conversion theory given to Moscovici's theory). The notion of conversion was introduced to highlight that the change following minority influence consists of—for example, in religious conversion—a profound restructuring of opinions, values, and behaviors.

## From Compliance to Conversion

To conceptualize the distinct dynamics of majority versus minority influence, Moscovici (1976) insisted on the importance to distinguish two general forms of influence, namely manifest versus latent, that is, influence behaviors, beliefs, and attitudes explicitly linked to the responses given by a source versus indirectly linked to the explicit responses. This claim has given rise to methodological innovations in the area of minority influence, because the issue was to measure if influence appears when, for instance, responses are given in public or in private, following the principle that the displacement of influence to a private level is proof of the social costs that influence targets would incur if they explicitly joined up with a minority source. Along the same lines, it appeared important to detect influence either immediately or after a certain delay, having in mind that influence targets might be more prone to change when the relationship with the minority source has become less salient. Yet another method consisted of measuring to what extent an influence source can affect judgments upon which that source has explicitly taken a stand (direct influence) or not (indirect influence). Other developments have led to consider still other forms of indirect influence, such as the greater level of creativity underlying the responses of the target following the influence attempt, the more elaborated level of reasoning, the depth of information processing of the influence content, or even the resistance to counterpersuasion attempts.

Moscovici (1980) argued that, in general, majorities induce a pattern of manifest influence without private acceptance, whereas minorities induce a pattern of latent influence despite a weak or null manifest influence (i.e., a pattern of influences that characterizes conversion)—a dual perspective whose critical examination will be at the core of this chapter. The reasoning is as follows. When the divergence of judgments is the result of a majority—a source believed to be legitimate and to provide valid shared information about reality—individuals compare their own judgment to that proposed by the source without necessarily reconsidering the contents of the divergence. They focus on the relation with the source in an attempt to reduce the disagreement and focus on the respective explicit responses. When required to express their views without further exposure to the majority, their personal judgments then remain unchanged. In this case, a compliance pattern of influence (Kelman, 1958), that is, mostly public submissiveness without private acceptance, would prevail (Moscovici & Personnaz, 1980).

In contrast, the nature of conflict is not the same when divergence of judgment is introduced by a minority. Through its consistency in front of the majority views, the source demonstrates that it is strongly committed to a diverging view of reality and is unwilling to compromise. It then generates both a social conflict and a cognitive conflict that lasts as long as targets consider the minority positions as reflecting an alternative to their own position. The minority's views are considered illegitimate and contrary to reality, and targets most often avoid adopting the minority's responses, since to do so would mean becoming themselves openly deviant. However, when active minorities consistently maintain the social conflict, which they usually do, majority members engage in a validation process by considering that the deviant view might contain some truth and confront minority judgments with the corresponding object, leading to a careful examination of arguments and facts. This conflict triggers an intense cognitive processing in order to assess the adequacy of the minority's judgments to reality, that is, to verify or falsify them, and leads to their internalization.

### Initial Evidence for Minority Influence

In a study using blue slides varying only in luminosity (Moscovici, Lage, & Naffrechoux, 1969), groups of six persons first took a color test showing that everyone had normal vision. Then, four participants were exposed to two confederates who gave a unanimous "green" response (such synchronic consistency was kept constant). Diachronic consistency was manipulated through the proportion of incorrect unanimous answers of the two confederates. In the consistent condition, they always said the color to be green. In the inconsistent condition, they answered green to two thirds of the trials and

blue to the remaining ones. In a control condition, six participants responded privately. In the consistent minority condition, 8.42 percent of green responses were observed compared to 0.25 percent in the control condition, which represents a weak but significant manifest influence. The inconsistent minority induced only 1.25 percent of green responses, which did not differ from the control condition. As for latent influence, after the experimental phase, participants individually took part in a color discrimination test to determine the threshold at which they would give the green response when presented with colors changing gradually from evidently blue to evidently green. Participants exposed to the consistent minority perceived green earlier than participants in the control group, which was not the case for participants in the inconsistent minority condition.

These results suggested that through the systematic repetition of the very same answer the minority manifests a clear-cut recognizable system of responses. However, it should be noted that it is perceived consistency and not repetition in itself that is theorized to be the key element. This was demonstrated in a study (Nemeth, Swedlund, & Kanki, 1974) in which bright blue slides and dim slides were presented at random and participants were instructed to answer all the colors they saw, if they saw more than one color. In a straight green condition, the two confederates always repeated the green response. In two patterned conditions, confederates responded green (versus green-blue) to the bright slides and green-blue (versus green) to the dim slides. Compared to the straight green condition, the confederates in both patterned conditions—where an organizing principle was introduced—were perceived more confident in their judgments and superior in their perception to the naïve participants, and induced more green responses. Mere repetition may sometimes be perceived as rigidity (see later), and the patterning of responses as a function of a salient property of the slides preserved the attribution of consistency.

A critical test showed that this influence pattern was specific to a consistent minority (Moscovici & Lage, 1976). Using the same paradigm, in the majority conditions four confederates were opposed to two participants, whereas in the minority conditions two confederates were opposed to four participants, with a control group without influence. The source was either consistent or inconsistent, as in Moscovici et al.'s (1969) experiment. Results showed that manifest influence varied as a function of both faction size and consistency. The consistent minority induced 10.07 percent of green responses, significantly more than the inconsistent minority (0.75 percent) that did not differ from the control condition (1.22 percent). Manifest influence was much higher for majority, with the unanimous consistent majority inducing 40.16 percent of green responses, more so than the inconsistent majority (12.07 percent). However, as for latent influence, the color discrimination posttest revealed that only the consistent minority condition differed from the control condition. The pattern of conversion (latent but no manifest influence) then appeared to be more typical of a consistent minority, and compliance (manifest but no latent influence) more typical of majorities.

### Beyond Consistency: Negotiating Conflict

If consistency plays a central role in minority influence, it was also evident from the beginning that the minority's intransigence that characterizes consistency may lead to the mere rejection of the deviate (e.g., Schachter, 1951). Indeed, consistent deviates have been shown to obtain less influence in cohesive groups, especially when they can be easily rejected by the group (Wolf, 1979). To solve this problem, Mugny (1982) suggested the need to understand the effect of consistency in terms of negotiation strategies within a more general social context in which *power* and *population* are two distinct actors of the so-called majority position (Mugny, 1982). Contemplating the important controversial social issues in which social change takes place (e.g., ecology, women rights, immigration, and antimilitarism) led to the consideration that, instead of opposing a minority to a unique majority counterpart, a minority influence model should separate *power* and *population* as two distinct components of the majority. On one side there are powerful subgroups or individuals who dictate norms and rules, whereas on the other side there is the population that is submitted to this dominant ideology because it is socialized to do so in various institutions (e.g., family, school, work). A consistent minority then represents a third party that introduces a point of view that is necessarily conflictual in the *antagonistic relation* with power, and in this respect must be intransigent to be recognized as an alternative by the population. However, a consistent minority also generates a conflict in the *influence relation* with the population, and this conflict needs to be negotiated in order to counter the population's resistances. Accordingly, a flexible negotiation style with the population, while maintaining consistency and opposition to power, would be more appropriate for the minority in order to influence the population.

In a series of experiments about significant social issues (Mugny, 1982), participants were exposed to minority positions endorsed by different minority groups (e.g., ecologist, antimilitarist, and xenophobic groups) that were consistent in their counter-normative contents. Negotiation was manipulated through the use of slogans inserted in the text: In the rigid minority conditions the source accentuated the conflict with the population (for instance, by declaring itself "absolutely" in favor of an extreme position on all themes) whereas in the flexible minority conditions it attenuated it (for instance, by declaring itself "rather" in favor on some themes). When the image of the minorities was assessed, both sources appeared to be equally consistent, whereas they differed in perceived flexibility/rigidity. Importantly, more manifest influence was generally observed after exposure to the flexible than to the rigid minorities. Indirect measures, however, showed in general the same influence for rigid and flexible minorities. In some studies, rigid minorities obtained less influence when disagreement with the minority was particularly salient and rigidity could be attributed to specific peculiarities of the minority (e.g., the psychological traits of its members; Mugny & Papastamou, 1980). This model has proven useful for social psychological analyses of the influence strategies used by historical minorities, for instance in Marx and Engels's *Communist Manifesto* (Chryssochoou & Volpato, 2004) or in the evolution of the feminist movement in Italy (Crespi & Mucchi Faina, 1988).

### Evidence for Dual Process

These lines of early research set the stage for a more systematic validation of conversion theory. Indeed, several further studies tested the theory's main hypotheses, in particular that majorities and minorities obtain their influence at different levels, through different focuses of attention, and with different forms of cognitive processing. As far as level of influence is concerned, stringent evidence of the conversion pattern was observed using a sophisticated measure of latent influence. In two studies (Moscovici & Personnaz, 1980), participants first answered a private pretest. In a dark room they had to judge the color of blue slides and the chromatic afterimage that is automatically perceived when the projection of the blue slide is stopped. In a second phase, participants were informed that 81.8 percent of previous participants had seen a green slide and 18.2 percent a blue slide (majority condition), or 18.2 percent and 81.8 percent, respectively (minority condition). Then, they were exposed to the influence of one confederate consistently answering that the slide was green and gave their response publicly. In a control condition (study 1), the participant and the confederate responded privately. The third and fourth phases were similar to the pretest: Participants judged the color of the slide and the chromatic afterimage privately in presence of the source (phase 3) and in its absence (phase 4). Manifest influence was near zero, and experimental conditions did not differ from one another, probably because of the low pressure exerted by the 1:1 faction size. The chromatic afterimage was used to measure latent influence. Given that the color perceived after exposure to a colored stimulus is its complementary color, participants should see the yellow-orange range of the spectrum after a blue slide and the red-purple one after a green slide. If validation of the minority claim (green) changes the majority's perception of the original stimulus, then participants should indicate an afterimage closer to red-purple, the complementary color of green. Such a change was significant for phases 3 and 4 in the minority condition but not in the majority condition (studies 1 and 2), nor for the control conditions (study 1).

More recently, Tafani, Souchet, Codaccioni, and Mugny (2003) compared the influence of a consistent majority and a consistent minority in a series of studies on the social representation of drug consumption. Majority versus minority factions advocated a diverging definition of what drugs are and were manipulated as in Moscovici and Lage (1976), and a control condition without any source was introduced. Manifest influence concerned the number of participants who followed the source at least once. Latent influence concerned the extent of change between individual pretest and posttest measures of the central core of the representation of drugs. In a first study, manifest majority influence was significantly higher than minority influence, but both sources induced influence compared to the control condition. Latent influence was significantly higher in the minority condition than in the other two conditions that did not differ from one another. In a second study the superiority of majority manifest influence was replicated, as was the superiority of minority latent influence. Additionally, minority latent influence was also observed 10 days later, showing a delayed effect of

the minority on the latent measure, an effect that was not significant for the majority. Consistent with these findings, the meta-analysis by Wood, Lundgren, Ouellette, Busceme, and Blackstone (1994) concluded that minorities in general obtain more latent influence (i.e., in private and indirect measures) than manifest influence. However, the prediction according to which majorities only induce manifest influence was not supported.

Moving to focus of attention, conversion theory (Moscovici, 1980) proposes that majority influence proceeds from enhanced focus on social relationships (a social comparison process), whereas minority influence proceeds from enhanced focus on content (a validation process). Evidence for this dual process is reported in Personnaz and Guillon (1985). In a study on abortion, one pro-abortion participant had to discuss with three anti-abortion confederates (majority condition), or three pro-abortion participants were opposed to one anti-abortion confederate (minority condition). The content of the arguments advanced by the confederate(s) was predetermined. The entire discussion was recorded and later presented to the participants who had to express what they thought and felt during the discussion. The thoughts and feelings expressed were coded as either positive or negative, and as referring either to the content advocated by the confederate(s) or to the relation with the confederate(s). The results for the negative thoughts and feelings showed that, when confronted with a minority, participants focused increasingly more, in the course of the discussion, on the content of the confrontation and less on the relational dimension (validation). Confronted with a majority, they increasingly focused more on the relation and less on the content (social comparison).

Indirect evidence for the validation process of minority views may be found in other studies employing alternative methodologies. For instance, ambivalence, that is, the coexistence of positive and negative evaluations, may be a useful construct to study the role of validation, to the extent that validation was conceived as requiring consideration of negative and positive features of a minority's message (Moscovici, 1980). Mucchi Faina and Pagliaro (2008) confronted their participants (university students) with a counterattitudinal minority that proposed the introduction of a final comprehensive exam. Participants were to write either positive outcomes that might follow a meeting with that minority (univalent arguments), negative outcomes (univalent arguments), or both positive and negative outcomes (ambivalent arguments). Direct influence was measured through the attitude toward the introduction of the final comprehensive exam, and indirect influence through attitude toward the introduction of other measures that made the curriculum more difficult. Results showed that the minority message elicited more indirect, but not direct, influence in the ambivalent condition, as compared with the two univalent conditions. This study thus brings support to conversion theory by providing a characterization of the kind of cognitive processes that might occur during the validation process, and an indication that they are linked with indirect influence.

In an experiment using an Asch-like paradigm, the procedure was modified in order to allow for the measurement of latent influence (Mugny, 1984). Compared to a control condition without influence, manifest influence was observed in a majority condition but not in a minority condition. Conversely, latent influence appeared in the minority condition but not in the majority condition. These results are congruent with Moscovici's hypotheses, but, importantly for the present contention, they were observed only in conditions that replicated the usual influence paradigm in which participants are exposed to a dissenting majority or minority without any other specification. Interestingly, the study was also run after informing participants that the task involved optical illusions. Participants were shown optical illusions, using a ruler to demonstrate that apparently different lines were in fact the same length. Under this specification, the influence dynamics were quite different: The majority induced both manifest and latent influence, whereas the minority induced neither manifest nor latent influence. These results suggest that when the divergence may lead to the interpretation that one of the dissenting factions is in error, the majority prevails because the participants can believe that the majority is right (Nemeth, 1986) and they are victims of illusions, allowing for a true informational dependence dynamic to replace the usual relational processing leading to compliance. More important, in such circumstances the minority loses any possibility to achieve influence because it appears as most probably in error, thus impeding the validation process and the conversion dynamic to take place. In other words, validation is necessary for the minority influence to appear.

In more recent studies, Falomir-Pichastor and his colleagues integrated Moscovici's conversion theory and regulatory focus theory (Higgins, 1997) by examining the motivations underlying attitudes with majority (88 percent) versus minority (12 percent) support. Regulatory focus theory holds that goal-directed behavior is regulated by two different tendencies, namely a prevention focus and a promotion focus. Prevention focus is concerned with the fulfillment of security needs and the respect of duties and obligations. Promotion focus is concerned with the attainment of an ideal and the pursuit of aspirations. Falomir-Pichastor and colleagues reasoned that group members should mainly perceive majority positions as personal duties and responsibilities, and they should be more concerned with the presence or absence of negative outcomes such as punishment; in other words, people holding a majority position should concentrate on a social comparison process with a focus on deviance in Moscovici's (1976) terms. Conversely, minority positions are less constraining, and group members endorsing these positions may therefore consider the need to promote them, that is, a proxy of a validation process. Two studies (Falomir-Pichastor, Mugny, Quiamzade, & Gabarrot, 2008) showed that positive attitudes toward foreigners were more strongly related to prevention-related emotions (i.e., agitation versus relaxation) when supported by a majority of the population, and to promotion-related emotions (i.e., dejection versus cheerfulness) when supported by a minority of the population. Furthermore, three additional studies (Falomir-Pichastor, Mugny, Gabarrot, & Quiamzade, 2011) showed that among participants with prior positive attitudes toward homosexuality, prevention-focused participants were more influenced by a majority (i.e., increased their positive attitude toward homosexuality), whereas promotion-focused participants were more influenced by a minority. Overall these findings suggest that majority positions primarily influence people on the basis of their motivation to comply with normative standards, whereas minority positions succeed on the basis of their motivation to provide social validity for valued albeit minority positions.

### Beyond Conversion: Convergent and Divergent Thinking

Nemeth (1986) proposed that differential thought processes characterize majority and minority impact, and they have distinct consequences on the quality of problem solving and decision making. People exposed to a dissenting majority would focus on aspects of the task that are associated with the position of the majority, think in a convergent way with the dominant position, and adopt the solutions proposed by the majority while neglecting potential alternative ones. Their solutions and decisions are thus tied to the correctness or appropriateness of the majority's views. By contrast, people exposed to a diverging minority would attend to more aspects of the task, think in a divergent way, and detect new solutions that can be more correct even if the minority is wrong. The rationale for these hypotheses is as follows.

If one is confronted with a dissenting majority, more stress would ensue than if one is confronted with a dissenting minority: Targets assume that the majority is correct and that they themselves might be wrong, and also experience negative arousal because they fear disapproval from the majority if they maintain their own deviant judgments. Because arousal leads to a narrower focus of attention, the induced stress would increase the focus on the dominant responses, that is, those of the majority, which may be detrimental in particular in complex tasks. Conversely, arousal induced by dissenting minorities is lower, because these are considered to be wrong and are less able to retaliate. Targets then widen their perspective and consider more dimensions and alternative ways of resolving the task. Thus, whereas Moscovici hypothesized that people think more about a minority's position, Nemeth suggested that scrutiny of source position or message-relevant thoughts are more characteristic of the convergent thinking activated by majorities (Nemeth, 2003). The active thought processing stimulated by opposing minority viewpoints is more issue relevant: Targets think divergently by considering more viewpoints than simply the one proposed. The quality of the solution thus would tend to be better because more alternatives are considered and allow novel correct solutions to be detected.

As a direct test of this conceptualization, a study using an embedded figures test illustrates part of these dynamics (Nemeth & Wachtler, 1983). Participants were shown a series of slides comprising a standard figure along with six comparison figures, and had to identify all the comparison figures that contained the standard. Three comparison figures contained the standard and three did not. One comparison figure was rather evident, whereas the others were more difficult. In groups of six persons, a majority (four confederates unanimously giving the same answer) or a minority (two confederates; a control condition was run with only naïve

participants) judged the standard as embedded in the easy comparison figure and in one of the difficult comparison figures; depending on a second independent variable, the confederates were either correct or incorrect in identifying the difficult figure. Independent of the correctness of the source, participants showed more manifest influence, that is, more mere imitation (the same two answers as the confederates) when exposed to the majority than to the minority. However, participants exposed to the minority gave more novel responses (i.e., not given by the confederates) than those exposed to the majority. This effect was not due to a mere differentiation process, since this effect was observed for correct novel responses only, and not for new incorrect ones. In other experiments (for a review, see Nemeth, 2012), as compared to majorities, minorities were also shown to induce more original associations, to allow better recall of tape-recorded lists of words, to promote the consideration of more of the possible strategies and their use in finding more overall solutions, and to stimulate the search for information and facts for all sides of an issue; also, previous exposure to a consistent minority fostered courage in front of a dissenting majority.

In sum, the early research on minority influence demonstrated that whereas minorities might exert some direct influence, they would induce primarily latent influence, more so than the majorities. The role of behavioral styles in these dynamics (consistency/inconsistency and flexibility/rigidity in particular) was emphasized, as well as the importance of social comparison processes in the emergence of majority influence and validation processes in the emergence of minority influence. It should be noted that this research is concerned with minority influence conceived of as change (or lack thereof) toward the minority position. There is, however, a small set of studies that show that minority influence can induce a boomerang effect, that is, change away from the minority position; it has been shown that this is the case when the minority adopts a rigid negotiation style and is construed as dogmatic (Mugny, 1975; Papastamou & Mugny, 1985). As the vast majority of the studies in the minority influence literature investigated influence toward the source's position, we have focused on this approach in the present chapter. The evidence presented here notwithstanding, minority influence research raised critical reactions, and the question then turned to be when and why minorities and majorities induce one pattern of influence or another.

## Controversies About Dual Process

Moscovici's and Nemeth's models relegated majority influence to, at best, the social reproduction of extant and dominant views and convergent ways of thinking, and they rejected the possibility for majorities to induce innovation and social change. As a consequence, these models, and in particular Moscovici's claims regarding the majority being limited to manifest influence, boosted strong negative reactions.

### Looking for the Afterimage Effect

A number of authors questioned Moscovici's conversion theory by undermining the results obtained in the line of research using the chromatic afterimage paradigm (see section "The Rise of Minority Influence Research"). Two immediate replications using exactly the same research paradigm as Moscovici and Personnaz (1980) were published in the same issue of the *Journal of Experimental Social Psychology*. Doms and Van Avermaet (1980) observed that both majority and minority sources produced conversion as assessed by the afterimage effect. In contradiction with the idea that majorities and minorities induce distinct forms of influence, this finding rather suggested an overall improved perception that could have resulted from a heightened level of attention to the stimulus arising from the confederate's deviant response, regardless of its majority or minority status. Sorrentino, King, and Leo (1980) focused on minority influence, and observed the predicted conversion effect only for participants who were suspicious about the experiment. They interpreted this effect in terms of the suspicion that arises when a minority provides a deviant response, which led to a heightened attention to the stimulus.

Martin (1995) also conducted replications of Moscovici and Personnaz's studies and examined several methodological issues. The Moscovici and Personnaz original blue slide had a large portion of its wavelength within the green spectrum, and Martin reasoned that, if afterimages shifted toward the complementary color of green because of the participants' heightened attention to the original slide, afterimages should shift in the opposite direction (i.e., toward the complementary color of blue) when the slide was a pure blue slide. Results confirmed this prediction, again regardless of the numerical support for the source. In five supplementary studies, Martin (1998) examined influence effects in the different posttest phases, as well as the role of the participants' suspiciousness. Afterimage

effects in the direction of the green's complementary color were observed for both majority and minority sources, consistently with Doms and Van Avermaet's (1980) findings, and were stronger for participants who were high in suspicion, consistently with Sorrentino et al.'s (1980) findings. Finally, Martin observed consistent within-phase afterimage effects in those studies with more posttest than pretest trials: Judgments shifted toward the complementary color of green over progressive within-phase trials.

In sum, whereas Moscovici and Personnaz's studies using the afterimage paradigm provided findings in support of the conversion effect, replications of their work suggested that the afterimage effect was prompted by the increased attention to the slide after exposure to a deviant view, regardless of its numerical status. Importantly, these findings not only raised questions about the validity of the afterimage paradigm but also challenged the contribution of the emerging field of minority influence (see section "The Rise of Minority Influence Research") that insisted on different influence patterns and different processes for majority and minority sources. This challenge also came from theories suggesting that influence proceeds from one single process.

### Mathematical Models

Several models consider that minority influence is governed by the same principles and mediated by the same processes as majority influence (Latané & Wolf, 1981; Tanford & Penrod, 1984). Accordingly, social influence is theorized as the result of social forces that apply in a social field and therefore depends, among other quantifiable attributes (source's power and immediacy), on the number of people composing the source of influence (and the target). In particular, each additional source member is expected to add some impact, but less than the preceding one, and each added target in the social field reduces the source's impact, but less than the preceding co-target. Thus, these theories predict a curvilinear function for social influence (a power function in the case of Latané and Wolf, 1981). As a consequence, when the numerical minority target is confronted by a numerical majority source, the source's influence should be greater than when the target is in the majority and confronted by a minority source. Similarly, Mullen (1983) proposed that the larger the source group (and the smaller the co-target group), the greater the source's influence. However, Mullen added that influence proceeds from a focus on the self, which increases as the size of the group decreases, producing an increase of correspondence between behavior and behavioral standards (like values or group norms). The result is that, in heterogeneous group contexts like those with majorities and minorities, the members of the smaller subgroups would match their behavior to the dominant norms to a greater extent, which implies that the larger groups would get more influence. The formal interest of these models notwithstanding, it is important to note that later research has questioned the generalizability of such models, by showing that curvilinear models did not provide a better fit than a linear model, except for studies with very specific features (Bond, 2005).

## Objective Consensus Approach

Another challenge to the idea that minority influence is qualitatively different from majority influence came from research based on the principle of social proof. This principle contends that the greater the number of people who find any idea correct, the more that idea will be considered correct (Cialdini, 1984). Indeed, according to an attributional analysis source numerosity, consensual views are perceived as more correct because, as long as the different sources are perceived as independent, their agreement is less likely the result of personal biases or contextual factors. However, some discrepancies exist about the nature of consensus effects. On the one hand, and consistent with conversion theory, research showed that consensus can work as a heuristic cue (i.e., as a proof of validity), increasing the acceptance of majority views without further elaboration and private change. On the other hand, consensus can increase people's motivation to scrutinize the relevant arguments because the fact that multiple sources converge on the same position may indicate that such a position is valid notwithstanding the diversity of perspectives (Harkins & Petty, 1987).

As a consequence, some scholars argued that disagreement with majority views, as compared to minority views, not only elicits more manifest influence toward the majority position, as suggested by Moscovici, but also more elaboration of relevant information and consequent latent influence. Mackie (1987) was the first to provide support to this argument. In the standard procedure, participants who were initially mildly or strongly supportive of the proposition that the United States of America should maintain a military balance in the Western hemisphere listened to a tape-recorded discussion by two confederates in which one stated four supportive arguments and the other stated four

equally persuasive arguments opposing this position. Participants were then informed that a majority of the students either supported this position (and a minority opposed it) or opposed this position (and a minority supported it). Attitude change was assessed in private through the pretest/posttest differences on a direct item (reproducing the core proposition) and on an indirect item (indirectly related to that proposition). In addition, posttest attitudes were assessed both immediately and 1 week later. Moreover, in order to assess the amount of cognitive elaboration, participants had to write down anything they could recall about the discussion, and two independent judges coded whether participants' responses expressed favorable or unfavorable reactions to the majority or minority position. Across four experiments, results showed that participants opposing a majority position showed greater immediate change toward the statement directly related to the majority position, as well as greater change toward the statement indirectly related to the majority position. Furthermore, this attitude change persisted 1 week later and was associated with participants' cognitive elaboration of majority arguments.

Overall, Mackie's findings provided support for the idea that opposition to majority positions (but not to minority positions) produces attitude change associated with a greater cognitive activity (i.e., internalization). Disagreement with a majority would be likely to provoke systematic processing of the majority's positions because it violates the expectation that opinions are held widely. Conversely, pro-attitudinal messages should be more scrutinized when associated with minority endorsement. Baker and Petty (1994) provided evidence in support of this explanation. They found that the persuasive strength of a counterattitudinal message (i.e., a tuition increase) had a greater impact on students' attitudes when associated with a majority, whereas the strength of a pro-attitudinal message (i.e., a tuition break) had a greater impact on attitudes when associated with a minority. Furthermore, attitude change in the predicted expectancy-violation conditions was positively associated with the issue-relevant thoughts generated while reading the message.

Despite the consistent pattern of findings obtained by Mackie and Baker and Petty as a function of whether the source's position was counter- or pro-attitudinal, a considerable number of studies have observed the opposite pattern of findings (e.g., Martin & Hewstone, 2001). Martin and Hewstone

(2003) proposed an integration of these conflicting findings as a function of participants' self-interest. They highlighted that a pattern consistent with conversion theory emerged in paradigms using topics that were not against the participants' self-interest (Erb, Bohner, Rank, & Einwiller, 2002; Martin & Hewstone, 2001), whereas studies showing a greater processing of majority views employed topics against participants' interests (e.g., Baker & Petty, 1994; Mackie, 1987). In two experiments, Martin and Hewstone (2003) provided empirical support to this integration. For instance, when the message argued for a negative personal outcome for participants (at that time, the introduction of a single currency in Europe), a majority source led to more message elaboration, whereas when the message did not argue for a negative personal outcome (i.e., the legalization of voluntary euthanasia), a minority source led to more message elaboration. Accordingly, what seems to be counterintuitive and leads to cognitive elaboration of the message is a majority arguing for a negative personal outcome, and not merely a majority counterattitudinal position. Further evidence in support to this conclusion comes from studies conducted by Erb et al. (2002) in which the topic was relatively relevant for participants and did not introduce any negative personal outcome. In two experiments, these authors distinguished opposing or moderate premessage attitudes toward the topic, exposed the participants to a majority versus minority message, and assessed the extent of message processing by measuring the differential impact of strong versus weak arguments. A pattern of results consistent with conversion theory appeared when participants held conflicting prior attitudes (i.e., the minority message was processed more extensively than the majority message), whereas a pattern consistent with the objective consensus approach was observed when participants held moderate prior attitudes (i.e., the majority message was processed more extensively than the minority message).

Finally, and importantly, the use of a definition of minority in exclusively numerical terms, as in the objective consensus approach, also appears somewhat controversial, because it reduces the relevance of influence processes that are related to the typical social attributes that characterize minorities. Indeed, Wood et al. (1994) showed in their meta-analysis that studies that defined minorities through membership in a particular, typically deviant social group as related to the broader society, produced stronger conversion patterns (greater indirect than direct effects) than studies defining minorities as statistically infrequent (mere consensus). In other words, an exclusive focus on numerical support when studying minority influence may fail to detect the phenomenon of minority conversion because this phenomenon is also related to the conflict that active minorities elicit in the social space.

### Self-Categorization Theory

Self-categorization theory (Turner, 1991; Turner, Hogg, Oakes, Reicher, & Wetherell, 1987) offers a single explanation of social influence. This theory makes the unambiguous assumption that influence is based on shared social identity (i.e., the categorization of others as similar to the self) and results in individuals shifting their attitudes and behaviors toward those of ingroup members. One only expects to agree with people categorized as similar to self on a relevant dimension, and only disagreement with similar people produces uncertainty (Festinger, 1950). Therefore, people's uncertainty about the validity of their opinions is a direct consequence of the degree of perceived discrepancy between their own views and those of the members of the ingroup. Conversely, discrepancy between one's opinions and opinions of members of an outgroup does not create uncertainty, given that social categorization suffices to explain disagreement. Furthermore, uncertainty can be reduced either by recategorizing the ingroup as an outgroup or by reducing existing discrepancies through social influence. On the one hand, the categorization of dissenting others as members of an outgroup constitutes an alternative to social influence, as rejecting and disqualifying others as different implies that no uncertainty has to be resolved. On the other hand, social influence can entail either attempts to influence other ingroup members or a shift toward their positions.

Applied to majority/minority influence, self-categorization theory explicitly states that both sources can influence only if targets perceive them as an ingroup. Accordingly, self-categorization theory assumes that both majority and minority influence proceed from the same process (target-source similarity). In two studies, David and Turner (1996) employed an ingroup versus outgroup categorization on a dimension related to the influence message (participants' initial attitudes were consistent with an ingroup source's message and in conflict with an outgroup source's message) and showed majority compliance and minority conversion effects only for ingroup sources. Targets strongly rejected messages from outgroup (either majority or minority) sources at the public/immediate and private/delayed levels. Conversely, ingroup majorities obtained more public and immediate than private and delayed influence, whereas ingroup minorities induced exactly the reverse pattern. In a follow-up study, David and Turner (1999) presented their participants with the message from an extreme minority of their group (feminists) and made an intragroup context salient to facilitate the categorization of the minority as outgroup, versus an intergroup context in order to facilitate the categorization of the minority as ingroup. The minority conversion pattern (no immediate but delayed influence) was observed in particular when the minority was expected to be perceived as ingroup, but not when it was expected to be perceived as outgroup.

In sum, David and Turner's findings consistently showed minority conversion only when the source is categorized as an ingroup. Despite the fact that this pattern is consistent with both self-categorization theory and conversion theory, self-categorization theory challenges conversion theory's assumptions in several ways. First, self-categorization theory assumes that both majority and minority influences are affected by the same process (i.e., target-source similarity). Second, self-categorization theory takes issue with the assumption that conversion results from explicitly rejecting the minority message and subsequently validating it. Rather, it assumes that ingroup minority messages are given attention that results in private/delayed influence. However, the reason why this attention results in a conversion pattern specifically for the minority (and not the majority) conditions remains unclear within this framework, and it does not help to integrate past findings showing that outgroup minorities can result in considerable, and sometimes even greater, conversion (see Martin, Hewstone, Martin, & Gardikiotis, 2008; see also the next section).

## Integrative Models of Majority and Minority Influence

In this section, we present models that attempted to integrate previous controversies and demonstrate the existence of dual processing in majority and minority influence, although specific processes are not viewed as strictly paired with each kind of source. For these models it is the context that determines what kind of process each source will elicit.

## Heuristic and Systematic Processing in Majority and Minority Influence

De Vries, De Dreu, Gordijn, and Schuurman (1996) took issue with the contention that minorities always elicit a deeper processing of the message and more private influence than majorities. They proposed that both majority and minority could elicit such a processing depending on specific circumstances. To study the nature of processing, these authors relied on the heuristic-systematic model of persuasion (HSM; Eagly & Chaiken, 1993). According to this model—and to the elaboration likelihood model of persuasion (ELM; Petty & Cacioppo, 1986)—persuasion may follow two routes, namely systematic versus heuristic processing (called central versus peripheral routes by ELM). On the one hand, systematic processing is an analytical form of information processing in which targets judge the validity of a message by scrutinizing the arguments. On the other hand, heuristic processing is a more superficial way to process the information in which targets use simple rules to judge the validity of the message. Majority (versus minority) support may serve as such a rule, since consensus is a cue that easily allows inferring correctness.

De Vries et al. (1996) thus proposed that a majority most often elicits a systematic processing of the message, but not a minority. Indeed, discrepancy with a majority's message would reduce the target's confidence level (a key to elicit systematic processing) more than discrepancy with a minority's message. A majority is thus more likely to lower the confidence below a sufficient threshold, leading to a higher motivation to process the message systematically. Schuurman, Siero, De Dreu, and Buunk (1995) manipulated the availability of cognitive resources by distracting half the participants (i.e., a supplementary task to carry out) that would impede systematic processing. They showed that persuasive arguments produced more attitude change with majority than with minority support, but only when the targets had enough available cognitive resources to process the message. The authors interpreted these results as supporting the proposition that majority sources induce systematic processing.

The discrepancy with a minority is most often insufficient to reduce the target's confidence, and thus would elicit a heuristic processing that leads to the rejection of the minority's position, as minorities suffer from a negative image. However, a minority can elicit more systematic processing than a majority when circumstances make its arguments difficult to neglect. De Vries et al. (1996) suggested that the dimensions that have been found responsible for minority influence—consistency, conflict, threat, ingroup nature of the source—might reduce the target's confidence level enough to elicit systematic processing. In that case, a minority might get more attitude change than a majority.

De Vries et al. (1996) also assumed that majority influence should produce convergent thinking (Nemeth, 1986) mainly on focal issues, whereas minority influence should produce divergent thinking on related issues, when the context asks for systematic processing. De Dreu and De Vries (1993, experiment 2) confronted a sample of students to a majority or a minority, arguing in favor of introducing an admission exam at university. They also manipulated the strength of arguments (strong vs. weak) as well as the mode of evaluation of the source's and own judgments: They used a comparative evaluation of judgments (to distribute a total of 100 points to the source's and own position) to increase motivation to process the source's position, and a noncomparative evaluation of judgments (to distribute 100 points to the source's and 100 points to one's own position) to decrease motivation to process the source's position. Finally, they measured pre/posttest attitude change on the focal issue (the admission exam) and on a related issue (the relation between students' academic achievement and the grant provided to them by the government). They found that attitude change on a focal issue was influenced by quality of arguments (a sign of systematic processing) more for the majority than for the minority under noncomparative evaluations. In other words, they found similar results to those found by Baker and Petty (1994), but specifically on a focal issue. As regards the related issue, they found more influence for the minority than for the majority source under comparative evaluation, thus when the source's position could not be simply neglected.

### Source-Context Elaboration Model

Martin and Hewstone (2008) extended the parallel between dual processing in persuasion and majority/minority influence. Relying on HSM as well as ELM, they distinguished elaborative from nonelaborative processing. Elaborative processing involves attending to the content of the source's argument, generating pro- and counterarguments, evaluating the arguments in the light of preexisting attitudes, assimilating the arguments into attitudes, and being aware of the consequences to identity and group membership. Nonelaborative processing relies more on heuristics cues.

These authors first proposed that the reason why some studies show influence and systematic processing for both majority and minority sources, while others show these effects for minority sources only, is that the effect of the source's status varies along an elaboration continuum, that is, the extent to which the context demands elaboration of the source's message. When the elaboration demand is low (when the topic is of low personal relevance), targets do not process the message and attitudes depend on heuristics; the majority is then expected to obtain more attitude change, but mainly at a manifest level. When the elaboration demand is high (when the topic is of high personal relevance), the target will systematically process a majority's as well as a minority's message, leading to a change in attitude. These authors focused on standard situations in which the elaboration demand is intermediate, based on Petty, Fleming, and White's (1999) statement that "when thinking is not constrained to be high or low by other variables ... source variables can determine the extent of thinking" (p. 20). They hypothesized that it is at this intermediate level that a minority source will elicit more processing of its message than a majority source, leading to Moscovici's conversion pattern. Results supported these predictions (Martin, Hewstone, & Martin, 2007).

The second set of predictions concerns the strength of attitudes following majority and minority influence. Influence through heuristic processing is expected to result in weaker attitudes, whereas systematic processing should lead to stronger attitudes. At the most common level of elaboration demand, the intermediate one, differences in message processing induced by minority and majority sources should lead to disparities in attitude strength. Compared to majority influence, attitudes following minority influence were shown to be more resistant to counterpersuasion (Martin, Hewstone, & Martin, 2003), more persistent over time (Martin, Hewstone, & Martin, 2010), and more predictive of behavior (Martin, Martin, Smith, & Hewstone, 2007), three patterns indicating a stronger attitude.

### Dissociation Theory

Dissociation theory (for a review, see Mugny & Pérez, 1991) aimed to address questions resulting from the aforementioned dissenting views about the very existence of minority influence, in particular the problem that some studies revealed conversion effects, while others showed no influence at all. To take both sets of results into account, Mugny and Pérez reconsidered Moscovici's distinction between social comparison and validation processes. Whereas Moscovici considered these processes as mutually exclusive and specific to, respectively, majorities and minorities, dissociation theory suggests that both processes may characterize minority influence. However, they can operate either in a dissociated way (validation and social comparison are processed separately) or in a nondissociated way (namely, when social comparison contaminates validation).

Dissociation theory states that the social comparison process often results in targets' increased motivation to psychologically distance themselves from the minority source, given that minorities carry negative connotations with them and may be rejected. Accepting minority views implicitly means the self-attribution of minority's negative characteristics, which results in an identity threat that prevents the processing of minority views (Mugny, Kaiser, Papastamou, & Pérez, 1984). In this context, targets are, most of all, preoccupied by the threatening social comparison, and validation processes work in a nondissociated way: The processing of the conflict with a minority is dominated by resistance, and a search for dissimilation is activated to protect social identity. Lack of dissociation is then the consequence of an identification conflict, and it increases when targets focus on a threatening social comparison (Pérez & Mugny, 1989). This explains why minorities may induce no influence at all. As a corollary, dissociation theory assumes that minority influence only occurs when social comparison is nonthreatening and the related self-attribution process does not disrupt the processing of the minority's position—that is, social comparison and validation processes work in a dissociated way—thus allowing for latent influence to take place.

Dissociation theory also contends that a threatening social comparison process mainly occurs within the ingroup boundaries. Ingroup minorities are more threatening because the shared social category suggests a common identity and thus a facilitated self-attribution of the ingroup minority's characteristics. As a consequence, social comparison interrupts the validation of the minority views (i.e., nondissociation), in particular when the source is an ingroup minority opposing the ingroup majority. Conversely, outgroup minorities are often paradoxically less threatening because people do not need to attribute the outgroup minority's characteristics to themselves. Thus, as compared to threatening ingroup minorities, less threatening outgroup

minorities are expected to facilitate to a greater extent dissociation between social comparison and validation, and therefore to obtain as much influence as ingroup minorities (e.g., Martin, 1988), or even more (e.g., Pérez & Mugny, 1985). For instance, Mugny, Kaiser, and Papastamou (1983) found that an ingroup minority obtained more influence than an outgroup minority, but only when it was not associated with negative connotations. Pérez and Mugny (1985) found that if an ingroup minority was associated with negative connotations, an outgroup minority obtained more influence than an ingroup minority. Likewise, although it has been shown that increasing the impression of belonging to a common group with a minority leads to more influence (Mugny & Papastamou, 1982), common membership disrupts conversion when symbolic costs of identification are emphasized (e.g., Mugny, Ibáñez, Elejabarrieta, Iniguez, & Pérez, 1986; Souchet, Tafani, Codaccioni, & Mugny, 2006).

These findings are in apparent conflict with self-categorization theory, which predicts greater influence of ingroup minorities, as compared to outgroup minorities (see section "Controversies About Dual Process"). However, an integration of self-categorization theory and dissociation theory seems possible when considering identity threat (Quiamzade, Mugny, Falomir-Pichastor, & Pérez, 2017). Indeed, ingroup minorities appear to obtain more influence than outgroup minorities when the identity threat resulting from the endorsement of the minority position is relatively low, which is congruent with self-categorization and social identity theory (this was the case with the endorsement of an extreme feminist position by feminist participants; David & Turner,1999). On the contrary, outgroup minorities obtain more influence when such identity threat is relatively high, which is consistent with dissociation theory (this was the case with the endorsement of a minority stance in favor of legalizing abortion by pupils from an all-girls Spanish school; Pérez & Mugny, 1985).

### Context/Comparison Model and Leniency-Contract

The context/comparison model was developed to make predictions about majority and minority influence based on the distinction between weak and central attitudes, source categorization, and the nature of task (Crano & Alvaro, 1998). When attitudes are *weak or unvested*, there is little resistance given the unvested nature of the attitude. An ingroup minority is more distinctive than an ingroup majority and therefore attracts more attention, which stimulates divergent thinking and message elaboration in particular when the task is objective. When attitudes are *central or vested*, the ingroup majority should obtain more influence, in particular in subjective tasks, because shared identity calls for conformity (Alvaro & Crano, 1997, Study 3). However, given that the group serves an important social identity function, when the ingroup minority does not threaten the existence of the group, a tacit *leniency contract* allows targets to be open-minded toward the minority and keep considering it as ingroup (Crano, 2010). Although targets are reluctant to be identified with the minority, they are also reluctant to reject an ingroup and therefore elaborate upon minority views, which results in indirect influence, in particular when the persuasive arguments are strong and the nature of the task is subjective (Alvaro & Crano, 1997, Study 1). Finally, this model contends that outgroups are generally derogated and will not have any influence. However, if the outgroup is viewed positively or at least nonnegatively and its message is strong, it may have an effect, albeit a delayed one (Crano, 2000).

### Conflict Elaboration Theory

Conflict elaboration theory (CET; Pérez & Mugny, 1993, 1996) is a metatheory that focuses on an integrative notion referring to the meaning of divergence in different tasks: *conflict elaboration*. It distinguishes four kinds of tasks depending on underlying lay epistemic knowledge. In *objective nonambiguous tasks* (as in Asch's or Moscovici's paradigms), in which error relevance predominates, targets expect unanimity. CET predicts that mere yielding will follow from a divergence with a majority because it is the easiest way to restore consensus; conversely, the impossibility to yield to a minority leaves unresolved the question why consensus is not reached and calls for object processing. However— and this is an original prediction of this theory—as unanimity is an epistemic requirement, if yielding is impeded (e.g., the source is derogated and presented as victim of optical illusions), divergence is elaborated at a latent level to produce the necessary unanimity (majority conversion), whereas conversion is no longer observed with minorities (Brandstätter et al., 1991; for a review, see Quiamzade, Mugny, Falomir-Pichastor, & Butera, 2010).

*Aptitudes tasks* are tasks in which correct solutions exist but are not easily identified among the various incorrect answers (e.g., problem solving). Uncertainty is then high and dissent most plausible.

Personal identity stakes are high because the main concern is one's level of competence, with wrong answers indicating incompetence. The main factors affecting conflict elaboration are the source's as well as the target's competence level, and the salience of identity threat (Quiamzade, Mugny, & Butera, 2014). Dissent with competent sources (as majorities or experts are believed to be) is often threatening for incompetent targets and resolved through mere imitation, unless the threat is relieved by contextual factors (Buchs, Butera, Mugny, & Darnon, 2004). It is also threatening for competent targets, whose competence is challenged by the source's equal competence and impedes influence; however, the reduction of threat (e.g., through self-affirmation) allows influence to appear (Quiamzade & Mugny, 2009). The divergence with incompetent sources (as minorities or nonexperts are expected to be) leads most probably to the overt rejection of their a priori wrong answers. However, for incompetent targets, fear of self-invalidity is increased, resulting in deep task processing, divergent thinking, and constructivism, specifically when task representation calls for decentering, a context that is favorable to minority (Butera, Mugny, Legrenzi, & Pérez, 1996) and nonexpert sources (Quiamzade, Mugny, & Darnon, 2009).

*Opinions tasks* include values and ideologies and are more akin to Moscovici's general model of social change (see section "The Rise of Minority Influence Research"). Conflict elaboration is shaped by the concern to maintain ingroup agreement and outgroup disagreement (Turner, 1991), and avoidance of negative attributes to the self (Tajfel & Turner, 1986). Majorities here induce dynamics based on positive identification, whereas minority influence follows the logic described in dissociation theory. Finally, in *socially nonimplicating* tasks, error relevance and social anchoring are the lowest. Social interactions would then be guided by conflict avoidance and by the use of available heuristics attached to source characteristics.

## Extensions and Applications

In this section, we report a series of studies that have contributed to research on minority influence by extending the work conducted on some specific mechanisms or studying specific minority groups.

### Specific Mechanisms

Several studies have attempted to uncover specific mechanisms that may enrich minority influence research. We present them as a function of whether they address intraindividual, intragroup, or intergroup mechanisms (Doise, 1986).

## INTRAINDIVIDUAL MECHANISMS

Tormala, DeSensi, and Petty (2007) proposed a metacognitive perspective to explain minority conversion. They suggested that immediate, direct, and public opposition to minority influence may result in targets' negative appraisals of their resistance when they perceive they have resisted simply because of the source's minority status. In this case, targets would conceive their resistance as illegitimate, which may decrease attitude certainty. For instance, undergraduate students were led to believe that either a large majority (86 percent) or a small minority (14 percent) of students supported a new policy under consideration at their university. Results showed more agreement with this policy in the majority condition but a lower attitude certainty in the minority condition (Study 1), a pattern specific to conditions in which participants perceived they had resisted because of the minority source status and believed this was illegitimate (Study 2). Moreover, participants who perceived their resistance as illegitimate showed reduced attitude certainty and were more vulnerable to subsequent persuasion attempts.

Follow-up studies addressed this issue from an expectancy-violation approach (Tormala & DeSensi, 2009) and demonstrated that attitude certainty increases when source status (majority or minority) matches rather than mismatches perceived argument quality. Regarding minority sources, they reasoned that resistance to influence should decrease attitude certainty, in particular when the minority presents strong arguments, against expectations. Conversely, a minority source that presents, as expected, weak arguments, increases attitude certainty. Similarly, attitude certainty decreases with a majority when persuasive arguments are unexpectedly weak.

Finally, Horcajo, Petty, and Briñol (2010) examined the possibility that the majority versus minority source status can not only affect traditional influence outcomes but also the confidence with which people hold their thoughts in response to the persuasive message. Indeed, source status would validate source position when source information precedes the message, whereas source status would validate recipients' cognitive response when source information follows the message. Accordingly, when source information was presented before the persuasive message, a pattern consistent with conversion was observed: Participants' cognitive elaboration of persuasive information was higher (i.e., an argument quality effect) in the minority condition than in the majority condition (Study 2). This finding suggests that the majority status provided anticipatory validity to the source's position, which decreased the need for further information processing, whereas minority status did not validate the source's position, and participants had to engage in effortful thinking in order to validate it (i.e., a conversion effect). A different pattern emerged when source status was induced after the persuasive message (Study 1), where participants' cognitive elaboration of persuasive information was higher in the majority condition than in the minority condition (see also Horcajo, Briñol, & Petty, 2014).

## INTRAGROUP MECHANISMS

Two lines of research represent an extension of minority influence research in that they study the change occurring within the minority group, as opposed to previous research that focused on the change occurring in the targets of minority influence. Prislin and her colleagues (see Prislin & Christensen, 2009, for a review) studied the minority's reactions to gained majority status in terms of identification to the group. In a series of five studies, a participant was part of one of two interacting groups, a majority or a minority, in which the other members were confederates. The two groups debated important social issues, and either all confederates maintained their initial positions—leaving the majority-minority composition unaltered—or some confederates moved to the opposite position—turning the majority group into minority, and the minority into majority. Results revealed that when group composition remained stable, group identification (operationalized as attraction to the group and self-group similarity) was higher for participants in the majority than for those in the minority group. When group composition changed, participants who were in the majority and found themselves in the minority at the end of the debate logically displayed lower group identification than participants in the stable majority condition. However, and most interestingly, although it is assumed that minority groups strive to gain new members and become majorities, participants who were in the minority and found themselves in the majority at the end of the debate did not display any increased group identification. Prislin, Levine, and Christensen (2006) explained this paradox by showing that, even if the minority's goal is to convert their targets, new converts remain suspect, as their reliability needs to be proven.

A complementary line of research, also concerned with changes in group processes following minority influence, studied the effects of the lack of recognition of the minority's role in social change, a phenomenon called "social cryptomnesia" that frequently occurs after the successful influence of minority groups (Mugny & Pérez, 1989). Although this phenomenon has been documented, Butera, Levine, and Vernet (2009) remarked that it was not known what the consequences are for minority groups: Are they satisfied by their success, even if they are not recognized, or, on the contrary, are they motivated to continue the struggle?

In an experimental study, these authors confronted two participants with four confederates who fiercely opposed their point of view in a political debate, and measured the participants' attitudes before, during, and after the interaction. At the end of the discussion, in a first condition the four confederates remained an opposing majority; in a second condition, they changed their point of view and adopted that of the minority, and the experimenter praised the minority for changing the majority's attitude; in a third condition, which corresponds to social cryptomnesia, the confederates changed their point of view and adopted that of the minority, but the experimenter praised the majority for their interesting ideas. The results revealed that the social cryptomnesia condition led the minority members to a more pronounced tendency to prepare for more action than the two other conditions. Participants in the social cryptomnesia condition displayed higher attitudinal consistency and maintained their attitude strength high across the three measurement points, whereas participants in the two other conditions at the end lowered their attitude level with the topic they had been defending. In sum, minorities' goal is not only to convert the majority but also to be gratified for this conversion as a group. When their contribution is overlooked, minorities are motivated to remain active.

## INTERGROUP MECHANISMS

Active minorities have been the focus of research on minority influence since its inception, as discussed in the first part of this chapter. However, Moscovici and Pérez (2009) noted that in the past 20 years intergroup relations between minorities and majorities have changed. Whereas until the 1990s minorities used to be in a relationship of antagonism with majorities and presented themselves as a

source of counterpower (Mugny, 1982), according to the historical analysis of Moscovici and Pérez, in more recent times minorities have turned to a different strategy in their claims: They present themselves as victims and aim at inducing some level of social guilt in the majority. Thus, these authors devised a line of research that allows moving from the study of political relations between majorities and minorities to the study of ethical relations.

In their experiments (Moscovici & Pérez, 2007), participants read a text on the persecutions that Gypsies had to endure in the course of the centuries. In the victimized minority condition, the text was attributed to a Gypsy association and ended with a request for compensation from the State in recognition of past sufferings; in the active minority condition, the text was attributed to a Gypsy political party and ended with a call to mobilize and fight to change society. A thought-listing task revealed that indeed the victimized minority elicited more thoughts related to compensation, suffering, and injustice, whereas the active minority elicited more thoughts related to struggle, conflict, and courage. Finally, two scales measured manifest influence (overt items requesting compensations and resources for Gypsies) as well as latent influence (with items referring to latent racism toward Gypsies). Results revealed that victimized minorities elicited more positive manifest attitudes (in terms of compensation), whereas active minorities elicited more latent influence. In sum, although these findings replicate the classic effect that an active minority may produce latent change, they also reveal that the effect of victimized minorities may be limited to manifest influence.

These results have been extended by a line of research that has studied social guilt through the "guilt for social cryptomnesia," with a view to improving the attitudes toward militant active minorities. In a first experiment, Vernet, Vala, Amâncio, and Butera (2009) asked female participants to express their attitudes toward women's rights and feminist militant groups. Then, participants had to compare their responses to the two scales and—as all of them had a much higher score for women's rights than for feminist groups, that is, the social cryptomnesia effect—the experimenter induced collective guilt: He reminded that feminist militant groups were in fact the very movements that allowed women's rights to gradually penetrate society, and he pointed out that the lack of recognition that the participants just displayed was unfair. Such a conscientization procedure (building some consciousness about social problems; Vernet et al., 2009) thus consisted in making the participants aware of the unjust treatment that they exerted on minority groups. However, creating a conflict may be threatening and block attitude change, and the conscientization came in two kinds, either threatening (the participants' social cryptomnesia was attributed to discrimination) or nonthreatening (it was attributed to mere forgetting), plus a control condition without conscientization. The results showed that in the nonthreatening condition, the conscientization procedure (eliciting guilt for social cryptomnesia) resulted in a more positive change in manifest attitudes toward feminist groups than in the two other conditions. In sum, this research corroborates Moscovici and Pérez's (2009) idea that guilt may be used to induce majority members to grant the minority some resources (in the present research, symbolic recognition); moreover, it specifies that the induction of guilt is a double-edged sword that may hinder social influence when it is too threatening.

## Specific Minority Groups

Several authors have directly or indirectly applied the knowledge derived from minority influence research to study specific minority groups or social phenomena in which minorities intervene. Although many studies have emerged in recent years (see Butera & Levine, 2009), the majority of them are in the domains of politics and work.

### POLITICAL GROUPS

A direct application of minority influence to an important phenomenon is Chen and Kruglanski's (2009) essay on "terrorism as a tactic of minority influence." These authors propose that the framework of minority influence may be useful to understand what gives power to terrorist movements and at which conditions such movements may fulfill their goals. The first element of their analysis is that terrorism provides some power to an otherwise powerless minority. As argued for pacific minorities (Mugny, 1982), minorities may find ways to exert a certain power. Terrorism, with its ability to create great damage with small means, affords such power to minority groups. Second, terrorism may be considered a form of innovation, another crucial factor in minority influence (Moscovici, 1980). Over the last decades, terrorist groups have displayed a certain level of "innovativeness" in the forms of violence they exert, in the type of targets they choose, and in the norms

and taboos that they violate, which contributed to creating an atmosphere of terror. The parallel with minority influence also helps to understand under which conditions terrorist groups may reach their goals. Chen and Kruglanski's analysis first points to consistency and internal coherence (Moscovici & Lage, 1976), as they "convey the image that the minority is committed, undeterred, unwavering, and resolute. These features are part and parcel of the terrorist strategy" (Chen & Kruglanski, 2009, p. 209). As for the zeitgeist, although Pérez, Papastamou, and Mugny (1994) have noted that minorities are most effective when their claims are congruent with the majority's values, norms, and goals, Chen and Kruglanski note that terrorist actions may be in stark contrast with the zeitgeist of the ruling majority, but aligned with that of a dominated minority, such as in the case of groups fighting for oppressed populations. Although classic minority influence research has provided a key to analyze the action of pacific, albeit conflictual minority groups, this essay proves to be useful to understand the action of extreme and violent groups, a particularly valuable endeavor in recent times.

Another line of research investigated an interesting phenomenon that previous minority influence research had not considered: schisms (Sani, 2005). Indeed, a strong emphasis on attitude and behavioral change has led scholars in this area to focus on the minority's success and failure in changing the majority, concluding that change indicated influence and no change the absence of influence. However, it is possible that a failure in minority influence results nevertheless in social change. This phenomenon appears when a minority faction, after attempting in vain to convert the majority, decides to secede from the larger group and create an autonomous and distinct group. Sani (2005) has worked on two historically important schisms, namely that of the Italian Communist Party and that of the Church of England, and has developed a model that identifies the important factors regulating such a phenomenon. When a faction in a group develops the perception that the group's social identity has been subverted by new rules, practices, or norms, then negative emotions emerge, group entitativity decreases, and identification to the group is reduced. As negative emotions increase and identification decreases, schismatic intentions increase. In other words, the impossibility to influence the majority leads the minority to lose a sense of belonging to the larger group as well as a discomfort with membership, which in turn heightens the likelihood for this faction to leave the group.

## WORK GROUPS

Another area in which minority influence research has been applied is work and organizational psychology, in particular with the aim to understand team innovation. In their seminal article, Schulz-Hardt, Frey, Lüthgens, and Moscovici (2000) had shown that introducing a dissenting minority within work groups (among which groups of managers) resulted in the reduction of confirmation bias in exposure to information. Interestingly, this was the case when the minority remained consistent in its dissent throughout the task in accordance with early work on minority influence. Along the same lines, De Dreu and West (2001) showed that teams benefit from minority dissent in terms of emergence of innovative ideas, when participation in decision making is high and allows implementation of ideas.

Among these streams of research, Choi and Levine (2004) proposed that a very common event in the life of teams, namely the arrival of a newcomer, can be interpreted as a form of minority influence. In their experiment, a three-person team either chose or was assigned a task strategy, and either succeeded at its task or failed. At the end of the work shift, one member was replaced by a newcomer (in fact, a confederate) who proposed a new strategy. Results showed that the newcomer influenced the team, especially when the members were assigned their strategy and had failed. Interestingly, in another experiment with a similar paradigm, Hansen and Levine (2009) showed that a newcomer is particularly influential when his or her behavioral style is consistent and assertive, in line with early minority influence research.

## Conclusion

The present chapter has begun with an historical journey through the rise and development of minority influence research. We have discussed the societal and theoretical interest of conceiving that minorities may achieve some social change, as well as the mechanisms that facilitate and hinder such change. This research has been highly controversial and has elicited fierce opposition. We have shown, however, that most of the controversies that have animated this field can be reconciled by building predictive models that integrate the relevant factors accounting for when and why (and at which level) minority influence may occur. The result is an extremely rich theoretical corpus that allows a fine-grained

analysis of the social contexts that allow, or not, the emergence of minority and majority influence, and of the mechanisms involved in multiple influence processes. With such a corpus, minority influence researchers are today well equipped to engage in at least two categories of future directions.

First, minority influence has blossomed at the end of the 1960s, in times of great social unrest, when active minorities were concerned with social justice and social rights issues, when ideals such as gender equality, antiracism, peace, and ecology were some of the driving forces of those minorities. The work conducted on minority influence is today sufficiently refined to apply its findings to emerging minority phenomena. A wealth of movements are currently asking for change in the domain of culture (e.g., the lesbian, gay, bisexual, and transgender movement), economy (e.g., the Tobin Tax initiative), and politics (e.g., antifascist movements in several European countries), fighting with the traditional toolbox of minority movements, that is, with conflict and consistency. However, drawing on Moscovici and Pérez's (2007) distinction between active and victimized minorities, other movements, even if their tactics rely on inducing guilt in the majority (e.g., the movements that oppose or facilitate the unprecedented wave of immigration that Europe is facing as we write), may be worth investigating within the framework of minority influence. In sum, minority influence research is "mature" enough to take up the challenge of studying new forms of minority influence.

Second, it should be acknowledged that in recent years, the analysis of the diversity of social movements has been conducted by sociology, political sciences, geography, and demography; social psychology might profit from joining forces with the other disciplines in an interdisciplinary effort to understand the new trends in minority action. Some attempts have already been made to articulate social psychology with other disciplines to reach a more elaborate understanding of social movements, such as the edited volume by Klandermans and Roggeband (2007); it is now time for minority influence research to integrate the knowledge derived by other disciplines directly into its models and to realize the interconnection of levels of explanation called upon by Doise (1986). This call for more interdisciplinarity in the study of minority influence is not only aimed at encompassing a greater range of phenomena but also at probing the existing models against a wider variety of minorities, which may result in bringing researchers to study new dynamics and mechanisms.

## Acknowledgments

This work was supported by the Swiss National Science Foundation.

## References

Alvaro, E. M., & Crano, W. D. (1997). Indirect minority influence: Evidence for leniency in source evaluation and counterargumentation. *Journal of Personality and Social Psychology*, *72*, 949–964.

Baker, S. M., & Petty, R. E. (1994). Majority and minority influence: Source–position imbalance as a determinant of message scrutiny. *Journal of Personality and Social Psychology*, *67*, 5–19.

Bond, R. (2005). Group size and conformity. *Group Processes & Intergroup Relations*, *8*, 331–354.

Brandstätter, V., Ellemers, N., Gaviria, E., Giosue, F., Huguet, P., Kroon, M., . . . Pérez, J. A. (1991). Indirect majority and minority influence: An exploratory study. *European Journal of Social Psychology*, *21*, 199–211.

Buchs, C., Butera, F., Mugny, G., & Darnon, C. (2004). Conflict elaboration and cognitive outcomes. *Theory into practice*, *43*, 23–30.

Butera, F., & Levine, J. M. (Eds.). (2009). *Coping with minority status: Responses to exclusion and inclusion*. New York, NY: Cambridge University Press.

Butera F., Levine, J. M., & Vernet, J. P. (2009). Influence without credit: How successful minorities respond to social cyptomnesia. In F. Butera & J. M. Levine (Eds.), *Coping with minority status: Responses to exclusion and inclusion* (pp. 311–332). New York, NY: Cambridge University Press.

Butera, F., Mugny, G., Legrenzi, P., & Pérez, J. A. (1996). Majority and minority influence, task representation and inductive reasoning. *British Journal of Social Psychology*, *35*, 123–136.

Chen, X., & Kruglanski, A. W. (2009). Terrorism as a tactic of minority influence. In F. Butera & J. M. Levine (Eds.), *Coping with minority status: Responses to exclusion and inclusion* (pp. 202–221). New York, NY: Cambridge University Press.

Choi, H. S., & Levine, J. M. (2004). Minority influence in work teams: The impact of newcomers. *Journal of Experimental Social Psychology*, *40*, 273–280.

Chryssochoou, X., & Volpato, C. (2004). Social influence and the power of minorities: An analysis of the Communist Manifesto. *Social Justice Research*, *17*, 257–388.

Cialdini, R. B., (1984). *Influence: How and why people agree to things*. New York, NY: Morrow.

Crano, W. D. (2000). Social influence: Effects of leniency on majority- and minority-induced focal and indirect attitude change. *Revue Internationale de Psychologie Sociale*, *15*, 89–121.

Crano, W. D. (2010). Majority and minority influence in attitude formation and attitude change: Context/categorization—leniency contract theory. In R. Martin & M. Hewstone (Eds.), *Minority influence and innovation: Antecedents, processes and consequences* (pp. 53–77). Hove, England: Psychology press.

Crano, W. D., & Alvaro, E. M. (1998). The context/comparison model of social influence: Mechanisms, structure, and linkages that underlie indirect attitude change. In W. Stroebe,

M. Hewstone, W. Stroebe, & M. Hewstone (Eds.), *European review of social psychology* (Vol. *8*, pp. 175–202). Hoboken, NJ: John Wiley & Sons Inc.

Crespi, F., & Mucchi-Faina, A. (1988). *Le strategie delle minoranze attive*. Napoli: Liguori.

David, B., & Turner, J. C. (1996). Studies in self-categorization and minority conversion: Is being a member of the outgroup an advantage? *British Journal of Social Psychology*, *35*, 179–199.

David, B., & Turner, J. C. (1999). Studies in self-categorization and minority conversion: The ingroup minority in intragroup and intergroup contexts. *British Journal of Social Psychology*, *38*, 115–134.

De Dreu, C. K. W., & De Vries, N. K. (1993). Numerical support, information processing and attitude change. *European Journal of Social Psychology*, *23*, 647–663.

De Dreu, C. K. W., & West, M. A. (2001). Minority dissent and team innovation: The importance of participation in decision making. *Journal of Applied Psychology*, *86*, 1191–1201.

De Vries, N. K., De Dreu, C. K. W., Gordijn, E., & Schuurman, M. (1996). Majority and minority influence: A dual role interpretation. In W. Stroebe & M. Hewstone (Eds.), *European review of social psychology* (Vol. *7*, pp 145–172). Chichester, England: John Wiley and Sons.

Deutsch, M., & Gerard, H. B. (1955). A study of normative and informational social influence upon individual judgment. *Journal of Abnormal and Social Psychology*, *51*, 629–636.

Doise, W. (1986). *Levels of explanation in social psychology*. Cambridge, England: Cambridge University Press.

Doms, M., & Van Avermaet, E. (1980). Majority influence, minority influence and conversion behavior: A replication. *Journal of Experimental Social Psychology*, *16*, 283–292.

Eagly, A. H., & Chaiken, S. (1993). *The psychology of attitudes*. Fort Worth, TX: Harcourt Brace Jovanovitch.

Erb, H.-P., Bohner, G., Rank, S., & Einwiller, S. (2002). Processing minority and majority communications: The role of conflict with prior attitudes. *Personality and Social Psychology Bulletin*, *28*, 1172–1182.

Falomir-Pichastor, J. M., Mugny, G., Gabarrot, F., & Quiamzade, A. (2011). A regulatory fit perspective in majority versus minority support to attitudes towards homosexuals. *Group Processes and Intergroup Relations*, *14*, 45–62.

Falomir-Pichastor, J. M., Mugny, G., Quiamzade, A., & Gabarrot, F. (2008). Motivations underlying attitudes: Regulatory focus and majority versus minority support. *European Journal of Social Psychology*, *38*, 587–600.

Festinger, L. (1950). Informal social communication. *Psychological Review*, *57*, 71–282.

Hansen, T., & Levine, J. M. (2009). Newcomers as change agents: Effects of newcomers' behavioral style and teams' performance optimism. *Social Influence*, *4*, 46–61.

Harkins, S. G., & Petty, R. E. (1987). Information utility and the multiple source effect. *Journal of Personality and Social Psychology*, *52*, 260–268.

Higgins, E. T. (1997). Beyond pleasure and pain. *American Psychologist*, *52*, 1280–1300.

Horcajo, J., Briñol, P., & Petty, R. E. (2014). Multiple roles for majority versus minority source status on persuasion when source status follows the message. *Social Influence*, *9*, 37–51.

Horcajo, J., Petty, R. E., & Briñol, P. (2010). The effects of majority versus minority source status on persuasion: A self-validation analysis. *Journal of Personality and Social Psychology*, *99*, 498–512.

Kelman, H. C. (1958). Compliance, identification and internalisation: Three processes of opinion change. *Journal of Conflict Resolution, 2,* 51–60.

Klandermans, B., & Roggeband, C. (Eds.) (2007). *Handbook of social movements across disciplines.* New York, NY: Springer.

Latané, B., & Wolf, S. (1981). The social impact of majorities and minorities. *Psychological Review, 88,* 438–453.

Mackie, D. M. (1987). Systematic and nonsystematic processing of majority and minority persuasive communications. *Journal of Personality and Social Psychology, 53,* 41–52.

Martin, R. (1988). Minority influence and social categorization: A replication. *European Journal of Social Psychology, 18,* 369–373.

Martin, R. (1995). Majority and minority influence using the afterimage paradigm: A replication with an unambiguous blue slide. *European Journal of Social Psychology, 25,* 373–381.

Martin, R. (1998). Majority and minority influence using the afterimage paradigm: A series of attempted replications. *Journal of Experimental Social Psychology, 34,* 1–26.

Martin, R., & Hewstone, M. (2001). Afterthought on afterimages: A review of the afterimage paradigm in majority and minority influence research. In C. K. W. De Dreu & N. K. De Vries (Eds.), *Group Consensus and Minority Influence: Implications for Innovation* (pp. 15–39). Oxford, England: Blackwell.

Martin, R., & Hewstone, M. (2003). Majority versus minority influence: When, not whether, source status instigates heuristic or systematic processing. *European Journal of Social Psychology, 33,* 313–330.

Martin, R., & Hewstone, M. (2008). Majority versus minority influence, message processing and attitude change: The source-context-elaboration model. In M. P. Zanna & M. P. Zanna (Eds.), *Advances in experimental social psychology* (Vol. *40,* pp. 237–326). San Diego, CA: Elsevier Academic Press.

Martin, R., Hewstone, M., & Martin, P. Y. (2003). Resistance to persuasive messages as a function of majority and minority source status. *Journal of Experimental Social Psychology, 39,* 585–593.

Martin, R., Hewstone, M., & Martin, P. Y. (2007). Systematic and heuristic processing of majority- and minority-endorsed messages: The effects of varying outcome relevance and levels of orientation on attitude and message processing. *Personality and Social Psychology Bulletin, 33,* 43–56.

Martin, R., Hewstone M., & Martin, P. Y. (2010). Consequences of attitudes changed by minority influence. In R. Martin & M. Hewstone (Eds.), *Minority influence. Antecedents, processes and consequences* (pp. 175–200). New York, NY: Psychology Press.

Martin, R., Hewstone, M., Martin, P. Y., & Gardikiotis, A. (2008). Persuasion from majority and minority groups. In W. Crano & R. Prislin (Eds.), *Attitudes and Attitude Change* (pp. 361–384). New York, NY: Psychology Press.

Martin, R., Martin, P. Y., Smith, J. R., & Hewstone, M. (2007). Majority versus minority influence and prediction of behavioral intentions and behavior. *Journal of Experimental Social Psychology, 43,* 763–771.

Moscovici, S. (1976). *Social influence and social change.* London: Academic Press.

Moscovici, S. (1980). Toward a theory of conversion behaviour. In L. Berkowitz (Ed.), *Advances in experimental social psychology* (Vol. *13,* pp. 209–239). New York, NY: Academic Press.

Moscovici, S. (1996). Foreword: Just remembering. *British Journal of Social Psychology, 35,* 5–14.

Moscovici, S., & Lage, E. (1976). Studies in social influence III: Majority versus minority influence in a group. *European Journal of Social Psychology, 6,* 149–174.

Moscovici, S., Lage, E., & Naffrechoux, M. (1969). Influence of a consistent minority on the responses of a majority in a color perception task. *Sociometry, 32,* 365–380.

Moscovici, S., & Pérez, J. A. (2007). A study of minorities as victims. *European Journal of Social Psychology, 37,* 725–746.

Moscovici, S., & Pérez, J. A. (2009). A new representation of minorities as victims. In F. Butera & J. M. Levine (Eds.), *Coping with minority status: Responses to exclusion and inclusion* (pp. 311–332). New York, NY: Cambridge University Press.

Moscovici, S., & Personnaz, B. (1980). Studies in social influence V: Minority influence and conversion behavior in a perceptual task. *Journal of Experimental Social Psychology, 16,* 270–282.

Mucchi Faina, A., & Pagliaro, S. (2008). Minority influence: The role of ambivalence toward the source. *European Journal of Social Psychology, 38,* 612–623.

Mugny, G. (1975). Negotiations, image of the other and the process of minority influence. *European Journal of Social Psychology, 5,* 209–228.

Mugny, G. (1982). *The power of minorities.* London, England: Academic Press.

Mugny, G. (1984). Compliance, conversion and the Asch paradigm. *European Journal of Social Psychology, 14,* 353–368.

Mugny, G., Ibáñez, T., Elejabarrieta, F., Iniguez, L., & Pérez, J. A. (1986). Conflicto, identificacion y poder en la influencia minoritaria. *Revista de Psicologia Social, 1,* 39–56.

Mugny, G., Kaiser, C., & Papastamou, S. (1983). Influence minoritaire, identification et relations entre groupes: étude expérimentale autour d'une votation. *Cahiers de Psychologie Sociale, 19,* 1–30.

Mugny, G., Kaiser, C., Papastamou, S., & Pérez, J. A. (1984). Intergroup relations, identification and social influence. *British Journal of Social Psychology, 23,* 317–322.

Mugny, G., & Papastamou, S. (1980). When rigidity does not fail: Individualization and psychologization as resistances to the diffusion of minority innovations. *European Journal of Social Psychology, 10,* 43–61.

Mugny, G., & Papastamou, S. (1982). Minority influence and psycho-social identity. *European Journal of Social Psychology, 12,* 379–394.

Mugny, G., & Pérez, J. A. (1989). L'influence sociale comme processus de changement. *Hermès, 5–6,* 227–236.

Mugny, G., & Pérez, J. A. (1991). *The social psychology of minority influence.* Cambridge, England: Cambridge University Press.

Mullen, B. (1983). Operationalizing the effect of the group on the individual: A self-attention perspective. *Journal of Experimental Social Psychology, 19,* 295–322.

Nemeth, C. J. (1986). Differential contributions of majority and minority influence. *Psychological Review, 93,* 23–32.

Nemeth, C. J. (2003). Minority dissent and its « hidden » benefits. *New Review of Social Psychology, 2,* 21–28.

Nemeth, C. J. (2012) Minority influence theory. In P. A. M. Van Lange, A. W. Kruglanski, & E. T. Higgins (Eds.), *Handbook of theories in social psychology* (Vol 2, pp. 362–378). New York, NY: Sage.

Nemeth, C., & Chiles, C. (1988). Modelling courage: The role of dissent in fostering independence. *European Journal of Social Psychology, 18,* 275–280.

Nemeth, C., Swedlund, M., & Kanki, B. (1974). Patterning of the minority's responses and their influence on the majority. *European Journal of Social Psychology, 4,* 53–64.

Nemeth, C. J., & Wachtler, J. (1983). Creative problem solving as a result of majority vs minority influence. *European Journal of Social Psychology*, *13*, 45–55.

Papastamou, S., & Mugny, G. (1985). Rigidity and minority influence: The influence of the social in social influence. In S. Moscovici, G. Mugny, & E. van Avermaet (Eds.), *Perspectives on minority influence* (pp. 113–136). Cambridge, England: Cambridge University Press.

Pérez, J. A., & Mugny, G. (1985). Influencia minoritaria sobre las opiniones frente al aborto y los anticonceptivos. *Estudios de Psicologia*, *23/24*, 29–54.

Pérez, J. A., & Mugny, G. (1989). Discrimination et conversion dans l'influence minoritaire. In J.-L. Beauvois, R.-V. Joule, & J.-M. Monteil (Eds.), *Perspectives cognitives et conduites sociales* (Vol. 2, pp. 47–66). Cousset: Delval.

Pérez, J. A., & Mugny, G. (1993). *Influences sociales: la théorie de l'élaboration du conflit*. Neuchâtel, Paris: Delachaux et Niestlé.

Pérez, J. A., & Mugny, G. (1996). The conflict elaboration theory of social influence. In E. Witte & J. Davis (Eds.), *Understanding group behavior, Small group processes and interpersonal relations* (Vol. 2, pp. 191–210). Mahwah, NJ: Lawrence Erlbaum.

Pérez, J. A., Papastamou, S., & Mugny, G. (1994). Zeitgeist and minority influence—where is the causality: A comment on Clark. *European Journal of Social Psychology*, *25*, 703–710.

Personnaz, B., & Guillon, M. (1985). Conflict and conversion. In S. Moscovici, G. Mugny, & E. Van Avermaet (Eds.), *Perspectives on minority influence* (pp. 91–111). Cambridge, England: Cambridge University Press.

Petty, R. E., & Cacioppo, J. T. (1986). The elaboration likelihood model of persuasion. In L. Berkowitz (Ed.), *Advances in Experimental Social Psychology* (Vol. 19, pp. 123–205). New York, NY: Academic Press.

Petty, R. E., Fleming, M. A., & White, P. H. (1999). Stigmatized sources and persuasion: Prejudice as a determinant of argument scrutiny. *Journal of Personality and Social Psychology*, *76*, 19–34.

Prislin, R., & Christensen, P. N. (2009). Influence and its aftermath: Motives for agreement among minorities and majorities. In F. Butera & J. M. Levine (Eds.), *Coping with Minority Status: Responses to exclusion and inclusion* (pp. 82–103). New York, NY: Cambridge University Press.

Prislin, R., Levine, J. M., & Christensen, P. N. (2006). When reasons matter: Quality of support affects reactions to increasing and consistent agreement. *Journal of Experimental Social Psychology*, *42*, 593–601.

Quiamzade, A., & Mugny, G. (2009). Social influence and threat in confrontations between competent peers. *Journal of Personality and Social Psychology*, *97*, 652–666.

Quiamzade, A., Mugny, G., & Butera, F. (2014). *Psychologie sociale de la connaissance. Étayage expérimental*. Grenoble: Presses Universitaires de Grenoble.

Quiamzade, A., Mugny, G., & Darnon, C. (2009). The coordination of problem solving strategies: When low competence sources exert more influence than high competence sources. *British Journal of Social Psychology*, *48*, 159–182.

Quiamzade, A., Mugny, G., Falomir-Pichastor, J. M., & Butera, F. (2010). The complexity of majority and minority influence processes. In R. Martin & M. Hewstone (Eds.), *Minority influence and innovation: Antecedents, processes and consequences* (pp. 21–52). Hove, England: Psychology Press.

Quiamzade, A., Mugny, G., Falomir-Pichastor, J. M., & Pérez, J. A. (2017). Multiple categorizations and minority influence: An integration of dissociation and self-categorization theories. In S. Papastamou, A. Gardikiotis, & G. Prodromitis (Eds.). *Majority and minority influence: Societal meaning and cognitive elaboration* (pp. 72–97). London, New York: Routledge.

Sani, F. (2005). When subgroups secede: Extending and refining the social psychological model of schisms in groups. *Personality and Social Psychology Bulletin*, *31*, 1074–1086.

Schachter, S. (1951). Deviation, rejection, and communication. *Journal of Abnormal and Social Psychology*, *46*, 190–207.

Schulz-Hardt, S., Frey, D., Lüthgens, C., & Moscovici, S. (2000). Biased information search in group decision making. *Journal of Personality and Social Psychology*, *78*, 655–669.

Schuurman, M., Siero, F. W., De Dreu, C. K. W., & Buunk, A. P. (1995). Differentiële verwerking van numerieke steun. In N. K. De Vries, N. E. Ellemers, R. Vonk, & C. K. W. De Dreu (Eds.), *Fundamentele sociale psychologie* (Vol. 9, pp. 1–9). Tilburg, The Netherlands: Tilburg University Press.

Sorrentino, R. M., King, G., & Leo, G. (1980). The influence of the minority on perception: Anote on a possible alternative explanation. *Journal of Experimental Social Psychology*, *16*, 293–301.

Souchet, L., Tafani, E., Codaccioni, C., & Mugny, G. (2006). Influence sociale selon le statut numérique et l'appartenance de la source: auto-catégorisation et élaboration du conflit. *Revue Internationale de Psychologie Sociale*, *19*, 35–67.

Tafani, E., Souchet, L., Codaccioni, C., & Mugny, G. (2003). Influences majoritaire et minoritaire sur la représentation sociale de la drogue. *Nouvelle Revue de Psychologie Sociale*, *2*, 343–354.

Tajfel, H., & Turner, J. C. (1986). The social identity theory of intergroup behaviour. In S. Worchel & W. G. Austin (Eds.), *Psychology of intergroup relations* (2nd ed., pp. 7–24). Chicago, IL: Nelson-Hall.

Tanford, S., & Penrod, S. (1984). Social Influence Model: A formal integration of research on majority and minority influence processes. *Psychological Bulletin*, *95*, 189–225. doi:10.1037/0033-2909.95.2.189.

Tormala, Z. L., & DeSensi, V. L. (2009). The effects of minority/majority source status on attitude certainty: A matching perspective. *Personality and Social Psychology Bulletin*, *35*, 114–125.

Tormala, Z. L., DeSensi, V. L., & Petty, R. E. (2007). Resisting persuasion by illegitimate means: A metacognitive perspective on minority influence. *Personality and Social Psychology Bulletin*, *33*, 354–367.

Turner, J. C. (1991). *Social influence*. Pacific Grove, CA: Brooks Cole.

Turner, J. C., Hogg, M. A., Oakes, P. J., Reicher, S. D., & Wetherell, M. S. (1987). *Rediscovering the social group: A self-categorization theory*. Oxford: Blackwell.

Vernet, J. P., Vala, J., Amâncio, L., & Butera, F. (2009). Conscientization of social cryptomnesia reduces hostile sexism and rejection of feminists. *Social Psychology*, *40*, 130–137.

Wolf, S. (1979). Behavioural style and group cohesiveness as sources of minority influence. *European Journal of Social Psychology*, *9*, 381–395.

Wood, W., Lundgren, S., Ouellette, J. A., Busceme, S., & Blackstone, T. (1994). Minority influence: A meta-analytic review of social influence processes. *Psychological Bulletin*, *115*, 323–345.

# The Social Psychology of Leadership

Michael J. Platow, S. Alexander Haslam, *and* Stephen D. Reicher

### Abstract

Leadership is the process of influencing others in a manner that enhances their contribution to the realization of group goals. We demonstrate how social influence emerges from psychological in-group members, particularly highly in-group prototypical ones. Through leader fairness, respect, and other rhetorical behaviors, leaders become entrepreneurs of identity, creating a shared sense of "us." Personality research reveals contextual variability in correlations with leadership outcomes, suggesting that situational parameters exert their own influence over the influence of would-be leaders. Successful transactional leadership is predicated upon a shared social identity, and transformational leadership can help create that identity. Group members have shared beliefs about what makes a leader, with these beliefs themselves fluctuating with changes in the group and intergroup context. Approaching the analysis of leadership from a psychological group perspective allows us to understand leadership literature as an integrated oeuvre that provides insight into leadership's foundation.

**Key Words:** Leadership, psychological group, social identity, in-group prototypicality, transactional leadership, transformational leadership, leader stereotypes

In reviewing the social psychology of leadership in the current chapter, we adopt a working assumption with a long intellectual history in our field, namely that leadership exists "within a group, and not outside of it" (Sherif, 1962, p. 17). For authors such as Sherif, as for ourselves, leadership is an aspect of group processes in general, and not of the individuals who occupy specific roles. This working assumption can be understood through the simple observation that the absence of followers indicates the clear absence of leadership. An individual can enact all the right behaviors derived from the multitude of leadership lists currently available (e.g., Conger & Kanungo, 1987), can have all the right personality characteristics that the empirical work identifies as related to aspects of erstwhile leaders' successes; but if no one follows, there is simply no leadership. Gibb (1947) recognized this over a half-century ago when he observed, "there can be no leader without followers" (p. 270); King (2010)

recently reaffirmed this by noting that "when individuals follow another's actions, they make that individual a leader" (p. 671). Gibb's (1947) and King's (2010) observations (among others, e.g., van Knippenberg, van Knippenberg, de Cremer, & Hogg, 2005) highlight the essential, conceptual linchpin underlying the *process* of leadership: social influence. Indeed, no analysis of leadership is complete without a proper analysis of social influence. This is because *leadership is the process of influencing others in a manner that enhances their contribution to the realization of group goals* (Haslam, Reicher, & Platow, 2011).

## Scope of Analysis: Psychological Groups

As we noted, our positioning of leadership within the domain of group processes is far from unique (e.g., Hogg & van Knippenberg, 2004; Sherif, 1962), despite many analyses seeking to identify or list individual attributes (e.g., Bass,

Avolio, & Goodheim, 1987) and personal developmental experiences (Avolio & Gibbons, 1988) of leaders. For example, Gibb's (1969) analysis of leadership in Lindzey and Aronson's *Handbook of Social Psychology* began with just the same premise, as did Stogdill's (1950) analysis before him. Before even defining leadership, these authors provided theoretical overviews of contemporary understandings of social groups. We briefly do the same, focusing our analysis as social psychologists specifically on *psychological groups* rather than *sociological groups* (i.e., with the latter groups defined by such features as structure, interdependence, and roles, independently of members' subjective representations).

The processes underlying *psychological* group memberships are most clearly outlined in social identity theory (Tajfel & Turner, 1986) and self-categorization theory (Turner, Hogg, Oakes, Reicher, & Wetherell, 1987), as well as other similar theories of psychological group membership and leadership processes specifically (e.g., Lord, Brown, & Freiberg, 1999; Shamir, House, & Arthur, 1993). Self-categorization theory, in particular, assumes, inter alia, that people's self-concepts are comprised of cognitive self-categorizations that vary between personal (i.e., self as a unique individual) and social identities (e.g., self-as-an-Indigenous Australian). When any given social identity is salient, self-perception is that of a group member rather than a unique individual, and people are hypothesized to act in accordance with the norms and values of that salient group. In working from this perspective, we are assuming that people must understand and accept as self-defining specific group memberships before group-based processes, including leadership, will emerge. Leaders do have a role in constructing the boundaries and meanings of these categories, but erstwhile leaders should expect no followers by simple position of a formal role, at least without buying their followership (Haslam et al., 2011).

## Psychological Group Membership and Social Influence

As outlined earlier, central to our analysis is that leadership is essentially group-based social influence (Cartwright, 1951; Turner, 1991). There is strong empirical evidence in support of the hypothesis that social influence—the very basis of leadership—is enabled through shared psychological group membership between the would-be influencing agent and the target of influence. For example, Bond and Smith's (1996) meta-analysis of Asch-like conformity studies (e.g., Asch, 1956) revealed significantly lower levels of influence when the potential influencing agents were likely to be perceived as out-group members. So, when independence was observed in Asch's original studies, it is likely to have emerged from the failure of psychological out-group members to be influential. Abrams, Wetherell, Cochrane, Hogg, and Turner (1990) demonstrate this directly in an Asch-like paradigm. Moreover, there are now many additional experimental tests revealing that it is specifically in-group members who are the ones who affect people's (1) understandings of the reality confronting them (e.g., Platow et al., 2007); (2) actual overt behaviors (e.g., Platow et al., 2005); and (3) promotion of the collective welfare (e.g., Platow et al., 1999). What is more, research examining minority influence—precisely the situation often confronting leaders—demonstrates stronger influence processes emerging from in-group minorities than out-group minorities (e.g., David & Turner, 1996).

## Being One of Us: In-Group Members Are Preferred as Leaders

People may be influenced by fellow in-group members, but will that translate into active placement of themselves into roles of followers? Will they explicitly *trust* and *endorse* the influencing agent to take on a formal leadership position? Trusting would-be leaders is essential to followership (e.g., Burke, Sims, Lazzara, & Salas, 2007), with research demonstrating that successful in-role behaviors are reliably predicted from trust in the leader (Bartram & Casimir, 2007). Moreover, one meta-analysis (Dirks & Ferrin, 2002) showed that trust in a leader significantly predicts a variety of positive individual (e.g., life satisfaction) and group-based outcomes (e.g., job performance). In terms of the group processes pertinent to leadership, shared group membership is a key basis for trust (e.g., Tanis & Postmes, 2005). Not only are fellow in-group members judged to be more trustworthy than out-group members, but people are willing to place their fates in the hands of in-group members over out-group members, at least when these in-group and out-group members also know of the shared group membership (Foddy, Platow, & Yamagishi, 2009). This last point is critical: people's trust in in-group members comes when they know that these in-group members will treat them well *as fellow in-group members*.

As for leadership *endorsement*, a recent laboratory study by Graf, Schuh, van Quaquebeke, and van Dick (2012) revealed stronger endorsement of in-group over out-group leaders. In an earlier study, Gaertner, Mann, Murrell, and Dovidio (1989) directly measured participant *voting* behavior. First, participants completed a task to create a psychological in-group social identity, after which they entered a situation with one of three group structures: maintenance of an original intergroup context, a merging of two groups into a single group, and a complete elimination of groups by focusing on participants' individuality. When participants then voted for a leader, a majority preferred a leader from their original first-phase in-group when either (1) the two groups remained or (2) individual identities were emphasized. Only in the single group condition did a majority of participants choose a leader from a former out-group. In this latter instance, the former out-group became part of a new psychological in-group.

Of course, group processes are not this simple, and merely having a shared superordinate group does not automatically translate into the adoption of that superordinate group as self-defining. This, again, is why analyses of psychological group memberships are important. For example, Duck and Fielding (1999) examined group members' responses to two subgroup leaders, one who had been a member of participants' own organizational subgroup, and the other who had been a member of a different subgroup (yet within the same overall organization). Even in this context, framed by a shared in-group, participants perceived their subgroup in-group leaders as having greater concern for the subgroup out-group, than subgroup out-group leaders were seen to have for the (participants') subgroup in-group. Critically, participants themselves identified more strongly with their subgroup than with the superordinate, organizational group.

So individuals holding formal roles of authority in contexts with multiple subgroups (like many businesses, and the broader nations in which they operate) cannot rely on the sociological, superordinate group as the basis for their followership. Group members' leader preferences are for *psychological* in-group members over psychological out-group members. And, ultimately, the active ceding of authority in this manner is critical to analyses of leadership, as in many (but certainly not all) social contexts, leader legitimacy can be gained only through this means (e.g., Ben-Yoav, Hollander, & Carnevale, 1983).

## Variability in "In-Groupness": Leadership and Relative In-Group Prototypicality

Our argument thus far implies that, to be a leader, all one need to do is be an in-group member. Leadership, of course, is patently not so simple. We share group membership with many people, and not all are equally influential. A key factor that affects the relative degree of influence within a group is the relative in-group prototypicality of a person, idea, or behavior (e.g., Turner et al., 1987). Relative in-group prototypicality represents the degree to which, say, an individual group member contextually represents (e.g., is similar to) other in-group members while being different from contextually relevant out-group members. The greater the ratio of the first to the second of these comparisons, the more in-group prototypical the person will be. Critically for leadership, the more in-group prototypical a group members is, the more influential he or she is hypothesized to be (Turner, 1991). Note that changing the comparative *out-group* can change the relative prototypicality of one's in-group members (Turner & Haslam, 2001). In this way, relative in-group prototypicality—and, hence, leadership—is *not* considered to be a stable characteristic of an individual group member; instead, it is a dynamic outcome of group and intergroup processes (see also Sherif & Sherif, 1969).

One early demonstration of the role of relative in-group prototypicality in affecting ability to influence others was conducted by McGarty, Turner, Hogg, David, and Wetherell (1992). They measured the in-group prototypical attitude among their participants along a variety of attitudinal domains. Participants then had a face-to-face group discussion a week later. In two separate studies, with different attitudes and different participants, significant positive relationships between the postdiscussion attitudes and the in-group prototypical positions were observed. Similarly, van Knippenberg, Lossie, and Wilke (1994) presented students with arguments for and against university entrance exams supposedly written by in-group prototypical or in-group nonprototypical group members. As expected, the participants aligned their own private attitudes more closely with the communication from the in-group prototypical source than with the in-group nonprototypical source, regardless of the position he or she was arguing for (i.e., for or against the exams). Clearly, the most in-group prototypical in-group member displays the greatest degree of leadership (see also Hogg & van Knippenberg, 2004) by being the most attitudinally influential.

## Maintaining the Group via Fairness and Respect

Of course, leadership is not just about being; it is about doing as well. And part of this doing entails the maintenance of the group itself (Cartwright & Zander, 1960), including providing group members with a sense of social identity (including a sense of pride and respect within the group) and bringing people "into the fold." Fundamental to this success is the would-be leader's relative procedural, interactional, and distributive fairness (Skarlicki & Folger, 1997). Indeed, the fairness of leaders is crucial to their abilities to garner support from potential followers; fairness is, after all, a frequent expectation people have of their leaders (e.g., Lord, Foti, & De Vader, 1984). Wit and Wilke (1988), for example, showed that distributively fair leaders received stronger endorsements from fellow group members in the context of a depleting commons dilemma than distributively unfair leaders. So, material outcomes, and the fairness of their distribution, matter to group members.

Beyond material outcomes, however, other research suggests the presence of a separate, *symbolic* component of leaders' fairness behaviors. This was shown, for example, in a study by Rasinski and Tyler (1988), in which Americans' support for presidential candidates was predicted by their perceptions of the candidates' fairness, *above and beyond their perceptions of the material outcome benefits of having that candidate as president.* In Lind and Tyler's (1988) theoretical framework, this symbolic meaning is assumed to take the form of status recognition within the group, so that an authority's fair treatment toward a fellow in-group member provides a symbolic message to that in-group member that he or she is a valued group member in good standing. Moreover, it is *procedural* and *interactional* fairness, more so than distributive fairness, that are assumed to have this effect.

Procedural and interactional fairness are both hypothesized to provide group members with a sense of their standing within the group (Lind & Tyler, 1988). The individual consideration that comes with these forms of fairness has been shown to enhance both personal self-esteem (e.g., Koper, van Knippenberg, Bouhuijs, Vermunt, & Wilke, 1993) and—central to the current analysis—social identification and group commitment. In a sample of California residents, for example, Tyler and Degoey (1995) found that the more procedurally fair water authorities were perceived to be (in the context of a major water shortage), the more the respondents saw these authorities as legitimate *and* the more respondents felt respected within their communities. Tyler, Degoey, and Smith (1996) followed this up with evidence showing that procedural justice judgments within family, school, work, and national contexts all positively and significantly predicted pride in the relevant group.

Leader procedural fairness also encourages commitment to both the leader and to the group as a whole. A study with *Fortune 500* managers, for example, showed that experimentally induced leader fairness was associated with greater commitment to both the leader and to the group (Korsgaard, Schweiger, & Sapienza, 1995). Moreover, in ongoing organizational contexts, employee perceptions of managerial fairness predict not only fewer sick days (Schmitt & Dörfel, 1999) but lower levels of employee turnover both 6 months later (Simons & Roberson, 2003) and a full year later (Allen, Shore, & Griffeth, 2003). Further, Blader and Tyler (2009) observed in employment contexts with both government and nongovernment authorities, procedural fairness predicted both social identification and extra-role behaviors. This follows Platow, Filardo, Troselj, Grace, and Ryan's (2006) earlier demonstration that enhanced extra-role behaviors were predicted from authority voice provision (as a form of procedural fairness) in an experimental context.

The work on the procedural fairness of voice provision helps us to understand the classic leadership research of Lewin, Lippitt, and White (1939). In this work, group members under a leader who provided voice to them (in the authors' terms, a democratic leader) tended to express much less hostility than those under a leader who provided no voice at all (i.e., an autocratic leader). Lewin et al. (p. 290) were quite clear on the implications of this for successful group maintenance, as they noted that the hostility often took the form of intersubgroup aggression; failure to provide voice thus led to a splitting of the original group into subgroups, and then to clear *intergroup* hostilities. At the same time, group members under a voice-providing leader had a higher "we":"I" ratio in their spontaneous speech than group members under a voice-denying leader (White & Lippitt, 1960); and the former also engaged in more frequent mutual praise of each other and higher "readiness to share group property" (White & Lippitt, p. 549). These findings clearly attest to the group maintenance value of procedural fairness and voice provision.

## Maintaining the Leadership Support via *Un*-Fairness

The literature on fairness is substantial, and it demonstrates not only a clear followership for those who are fair but also the absence of active protest and revolt (e.g., Vermunt, Wit, van den Bos, & Lind, 1996). Indeed, Platow, Hoar, Reid, Harley, and Morrison (1997) found that distributively fair leaders received stronger endorsements than did distributively unfair leaders *in an intragroup context*. Critically, however, this effect attenuated, and even reversed, in an intergroup context when the unfairness was in-group favoring. Moreover, the leader's ability to influence fellow group members mirrored this pattern of endorsement (i.e., more influence from fair intragroup leaders, but more influence from unfair, in-group favoring leaders). Haslam and Platow (2001) observed a similar finding with regard to leaders' abilities to influence, with the influence translating into actual work on the leaders' behalf. Of course, as noted earlier, *procedural fairness* also has a symbolic, group membership element. So must leaders always be procedurally fair? Research by Platow, Reid, and Andrew (1998) suggests not: Although fair intragroup voice provision leads to relatively high levels of endorsement, so does in-group favoring voice provision between groups.

Collectively, these patterns of data suggest that a key process underlying successful leadership is that of promoting the group's relative welfare and standing, achieved through the expression of *intragroup* fairness and *intergroup* unfairness (in-group favoring). By pursuing intragroup fairness, leaders are able to maintain relative group harmony (Deutsch, 1975) and affirm group membership (Lind & Tyler, 1988). But by pursuing intergroup unfairness, leaders are able to positively differentiate "us" from "them," clarifying group boundaries, and enhancing relative social identification (Platow, Grace, Wilson, Burton, & Wilson, 2008). Indeed, Castelli and Carraro (2010) showed that these latter effects occur precisely because of the enhancement of the in-group relative to the out-group. This intergroup unfairness, thus, represents a process promoting the in-group relative to a relevant and salient out-group (Tajfel & Turner, 1986).

Of course, these findings are not without qualification. Platow and van Knippenberg (2001) showed that highly in-group prototypical leaders are able to maintain their support even when favoring the out-group over the in-group (at least among highly identified group members); in contrast, non-in-group prototypical leaders *had* to engage in distributive in-group favoritism (even over intergroup fairness) to maintain their following. This is consistent with what people in leadership positions actually do. Leaders whose own positions are under threat engage in higher levels of intergroup competition (Rabbie & Bekkers, 1978), and in-group nonprototypical group members are more likely to pursue intergroup competition than in-group prototypical members (van Kleef, Steinel, van Knippenberg, Hogg, & Svensson, 2007). So the pursuit of relative gain, rather than an even-handed approach in intergroup relations, is particularly strong among leaders (and would-be leaders) who need to establish their in-group credentials by promoting the group's relative intergroup standing.

## Giving "Us" Meaning: Leaders as Entrepreneurs of Identity

Up to this point, we have been writing as if there is a basic consensus among group members over the very meaning of "us," both who we are now and who we will be in the future. This, of course, is patently untrue, and there is a growing body of research outlining the contexts and consequences of *disagreement* over "who we are" and "where we should be heading" (e.g., Sani & Reicher, 1998). Leaders play a prominent role in this process by offering not only visions of possible futures for the group (Halevy, Berson, & Galinsky, 2011) but by offering visions of "who we are" (Reicher, Drury, Hopkins, & Stott, 2001). Leaders (and would-be leaders) actively construe meanings of "us," so that they and their aspirations for the group are, indeed, seen by fellow group members as in-group prototypical. Would-be leaders can strive to enhance their in-group prototypicality through their rhetoric by reconstructing or reframing (1) their own deeds and/or (2) the nature of the group itself and its place in the broader intergroup context. As Reicher and Hopkins (1996, p. 355) observed, language is the "domain in which category definitions are constructed and contested." So, for example, when national politicians vie for positions of leadership, they propose not simply political and economic policies in the abstract, but visions of what the nation is itself (Haslam et al., 2011).

In a detailed analysis of political discourse, Reicher, Hopkins, and Condor (1997) outlined politicians' construals of the meaning of Scottishness as they vied for positions of political representation in Scotland. A candidate from a conservative party, for example, described Scots as "a nation who believe in paying our way in the world" (p. 105). This construal of the group allowed for this candidate, from a party with strongly individualistic and market-driven policies, to place himself as prototypically representing Scots. By contrast, a candidate from the Labour Party claimed that "the Scottish tradition is far more egalitarian" (p. 104). Both of these candidates were clearly creating images in constituents' minds of a particular meaning of the group to be led. They were *creating* as much as *representing* the group. Reicher and Hopkins (1996) similarly observed different category constructions by the then British Prime Minister, Margaret Thatcher, and the opposition Labor leader, Neil Kinnock, in the context of the miners' strike that dominated British politics in the early 1980s. More recently, Augoustinos and De Garis's (2012) analyses of Barack Obama's speeches show how he managed to construe both himself and the category "American" to enable him to garner substantial support, despite his apparent out-groupness to many potential voters based upon his sociological ethnic group.

Of course, there remains one niggling issue in our analysis. Our claim throughout has been that it is in-group members who influence us (i.e., suggesting that the group precedes the act of influence), and yet we are now saying that would-be leaders can influence our understanding of what the group is (i.e., so that influence can precede the group). This contradiction is actually more apparent than real. In the examples we provided, the political debates were, in fact, framed within a superordinate, shared group membership (e.g., American or British). The ability to affect the psychological representations of the group by a complete out-group member would be difficult and would necessitate some other shift in group members' perceptions to enhance the person's in-group prototypicality (Platow, Reicher, & Haslam, 2009). Indeed, this out-group member would ultimately have to engage in other kinds of behaviors and strategies to inveigle his or her way into the psychological group. In the end, as Haslam and Reicher (2007, p. 140) note, "effective leadership facilitates the development of a sense of shared social identity" and the "long term success (and failure) of leadership depends upon the creation of structures and processes through which identity-based projects can be realized." In this way, leaders are not simply entrepreneurs of identity but are also *embedders* of identity (Haslam et al., 2011).

## And What of the Leader?

Our earlier observation of variability in group members' relative influence—and, hence, leadership expression—has ended up being the precise focus of a separate body of leadership research. This latter research often poses its empirical questions at the level of variability against an assumed static contextual background. This has led to an analysis of leadership that focuses on the leader per se and, in particular, personality (e.g., Ng, Ang, & Chan, 2008; Resick, Whitman, Weingarden, & Hiller, 2009). Indeed, a simple PsycInfo search indicates well over 3,000 papers on leadership and personality. We will not review them all here (see, however, Smith & Nezlek, this volume); instead, we will build upon others' substantive integrations.

Two of the earliest reviews of personality correlates of leadership were presented by Stogdill (1948) and Mann (1959), each of which identified a range of correlates, albeit often of small magnitude. Stogdill summarized the key leadership correlates as "capacity, achievement, responsibility, participation, and status" (p. 64). Mann, after limiting his review to a subset of more than 500 personality dimensions available for study, identified intelligence (comparable to Stogdill's "capacity"), adjustment, extraversion, dominance, masculinity, and conservatism (negatively related). Lord, de Vader, and Alliger (1986) subsequently reevaluated Mann's data, showing even stronger relationships between specific personality predictors and specific measures of leadership. More recently still, Ensari, Riggio, Christian, and Carslaw (2011) identified extraversion, emotional stability, openness to experience, masculinity, conscientiousness (comparable to Stogdill's "responsibility"), antagonism, authoritarianism, leadership experience, self-esteem, and creativity all as significant correlates with their operationalizations of leadership.

Several features are striking about these different summaries. First, significant relationships between measures of individual differences and measures of leadership do exist. Second, however, there is considerable variability in the magnitudes of these relationships. Third, there is also considerable variability in the precise characteristics that emerge as reliable predictors of leadership measures. And fourth, the latter two outcomes are likely to be due, at least in part, to the variable nature of the studies examined. Mann (1959) and Ensari et al. (2011) intentionally studied only face-to-face groups, and Lord et al. (1986) focused on leader perceptions held by potential followers (rather than, say, social influence, per se). Moreover, part of the difficulty in identifying a focused set of personality characteristics relates to the field's fluctuating, and often atheoretical, analysis of both personality and leadership. So researchers often study sociological groups, albeit for very good reasons (e.g., their theoretical and applied questions are relevant to these groups). However, within these groups, identifying people holding *roles* that are accompanied by the title or descriptor "leader" need not translate into influence in the manner we have identified. Thus, specific personality characteristics may, indeed, be associated with specific roles, but not necessarily with leadership per se.

Judge, Bono, Ilies, and Gerhardt (2002) advanced the field in their attempt to clarify the theoretical underpinnings of both leadership and personality. For leadership, the authors differentiated between leadership emergence and leadership effectiveness. For personality, they focused their review on those characteristics recognized in the field of personality as fundamental dimensions of personality: the Big Five (e.g., Costa & McCrae, 1988). They also examined the potential correlations across different social contexts (i.e., business, government/military, students). Their meta-analytic results showed that all Big Five characteristics were reliable correlates of leader emergence; but only extraversion and openness were significantly correlated with measures of fellow group members' perceptions of leader influence. There was also variability in which characteristics predicted leadership outcomes in each of the different social contexts; indeed, it was only extraversion that correlated significantly across all three contexts. This latter point is particularly interesting, as DeRue, Nahrgang, Wellman, and Humphrey's (2011) meta-analysis found *no* relationship between leader extraversion and a more behavioral measure of group performance.

Since Judge et al.'s analysis, other authors have also reported meta-analyses of the correlation between Big-Five traits and various measures of leadership (e.g., Bono & Judge, 2004; DeRue, Nahrgang, Wellman, & Humphrey, 2011). Once again, all five traits are variably related to different measures of leadership. So, again, clear correlates of personality and leadership measures can be identified, although variability still exists. This variability suggests that situational parameters exert their own influence over the influence of would-be leaders (Zaccaro, 2012). More specifically, this variability is likely to be the outcome of variability in the meanings and contexts of psychological groups themselves (Platow et al., 2003). The degree to which the observed correlations represent true causal relationships or simply redescriptions of leaders in context remains unclear. For example, if extraversion emerges as a significant correlate with various leadership measures, to what degree are we measuring an aspect of behavior that is effectively isomorphic with what it means for a group member to emerge as relatively in-group prototypical in a particular context? When introverts as a group compare themselves to extraverts, will the most extraverted introvert emerge as the most influential? Possibly, but we predict only if the introverts view extraversion as both an aspirational and attainable goal (Tajfel & Turner, 1986). Otherwise, extraversion will be a leadership liability.

Moreover, interpretation of the correlational variability becomes even more difficult upon recognizing that patterns of Big Five correlations with leadership measures can mirror correlations with other criterion variables, obfuscating any conclusions about leadership per se. For example, Hayes and Joseph (2003) observed a similar pattern of correlations between different traits and subjective well-being as Judge et al. (2002) found with measures of government/military leadership. And Saroglou (2002) observed a similar pattern of correlations between traits and "open, mature religion and spirituality" as Bono and Judge (2004) found between the traits and one measure of leadership behavior (i.e., individualized consideration).

Finally, a personality analysis of leadership implicitly assumes that some aspect of the individual *as an individual* (i.e., personality) is stable and leads to some aspect of successful leadership (that is also stable). This assumption, in its purest form, fails to recognize that leaders and would-be leaders are influenced as well. For example, Foddy and Hogg (1999) found that group members assigned to leadership roles were uniformly more conserving in their commons-dilemma choice behaviors than individual group members in nonleadership positions. Although individual differences were not measured, the very process of being assigned a leadership role appears to have reduced variability in behavior in the direction of promoting the collective welfare. We do not wish to overstate the supposedly simple power of roles in homogenizing behavior (Reicher & Haslam, 2006). However, we do wish to demonstrate that leaders are subject to influence as well, and despite variability in personality there *can* be uniformity in leader behavior.

Ultimately, then, as a group process, leadership is fundamentally relational. It is to analyses of relationships that we now turn.

## Leadership as Resource Control and Exchange

There are a variety of exchange-based analyses of leadership, all of which share several common features (Bass, 1985; Graen & Uhl-Bien, 1995; Hollander, 1964). First, they are, indeed, relational analyses of leadership. They all recognize the futility, if not impossibility, of studying leadership in the absence of studying followership. Second, there is a strong focus on *interpersonal* relationships. Individuals are conceptualized primarily *as individuals*, entering into what is, more or less, a sociological group so as to achieve individual need and goal satisfaction. This does not mean that group-level processes, such as norms, are not considered; indeed, they are. But the fundamental process by which leadership (i.e., influence) is assumed to be enabled is that of group members' successful fulfilment of their goals. And third, toward this end, the primary process through which leadership emerges is resource based (both symbolic and material) rather than identity based.

The now classic French and Raven (1960) typology of power bases presents one of the early theoretical social-psychological accounts of resource-based influence. Two fundamental bases of power are reward and coercive power, each of which involves the control over the positive and negative outcomes afforded to those over whom one seeks influence. But it was authors such as Blau (1964) and Hollander (1964) who developed the exchange analysis of leadership more fully. For both of these latter authors, leaders gain legitimacy through exchange by enabling individuals to achieve the outcomes they seek; and through this legitimacy, the leader can influence individuals to engage in both individual and collective pursuits. Each of these exchange-based analyses represents characterizations of *leadership by buying*. Indeed, in his own exchange-based analysis, Homans (1961) observed that "Influence over others is purchased at the price of allowing one's self to be influenced by others." Of course, if this were the extent of leadership, then, we would not need a separate analysis of leadership. But we know there must be more, if only because of our observations of leadership *failures*—leadership success would be oh so easy, and certainly more frequent, if we could only buy it.

### A Model of Idiosyncrasy Credits

Hollander (1964, 1985) recognized that there was more as well. In doing so, he outlined a model in which leaders and would-be leaders can gain psychological credits in the minds of potential followers. These credits, known as idiosyncrasy credits, are gained through systematic expressions of *competence* in helping achieve the group's goals, and *conformity* to the group's norms. The theoretical and empirical value of the idiosyncrasy credit concept is that it provides an explanation for an apparent contradiction often inherent in leadership: In order to move the group forward, leaders must be deviant, at least descriptively. In Hollander's model, the more idiosyncrasy credits a person gains, the more latitude he or she is given by others to deviate.

Hollander's propositions were confirmed in a series of his own studies, as well as other independent studies. For example, Estrada, Brown, and Lee (1995) found a significant positive relationship between group members' attributions of idiosyncrasy credits to fellow group members and these latter group members' frequency of proposing *new* ideas in a small group setting. Of course, highly competent and conforming individuals are likely to be seen not simply as highly in-group like, but potentially as outright in-group prototypical (Haslam & Platow, 2010). Thus, running through Hollander's exchange analysis is a clear recognition of the importance of establishing one's *in-group credentials* (see also Abrams, de Moura, Marques, & Hutchinson, 2008).

### A Model of Leader-Member Exchange

A line of research and theory paralleling Hollander's (1964) is work conducted under the rubric of leader-member exchange (e.g., Graen & Uhl-Bien, 1995; Schriesheim, Castro, & Cogliser, 1999). This work began with the recognition, as in our analysis, that treatment of sociological group members as if they consensually agree upon the nature and meaning of their group membership is, ultimately, flawed (Dansereau, Graen, & Haga, 1975). To overcome problems in treating sociological groups as homogenous wholes, researchers in this area shifted their analytic focus to dyadic exchanges, contexts in which the researchers believed they could more accurately capture the hypothesized variability between leaders' behaviors, followers' behaviors, and the interplay between the two.

Like Hollander's (1964) work, exchange plays a conceptually important role in this approach, as followers are assumed to enact leaders' will in exchange for valued outcomes (typically, continued employment). Thus, when Scandura and Graen (1984) established experimental training sessions for people in leadership roles, part of the training content was on the nature of resource and expectation exchange. At the same time, measurement of leader-member exchange often takes on a slightly different character. For example, Liden and Graen (1980) asked their participants questions such as "How flexible do you believe your supervisor is about evolving change in your job?" and "To what extent can you count on your supervisor to 'bail you out,' at his expense, when you really need him?" And Graen and Uhl-Bien (1995) recommend items such as "How would you characterize your working relationship with your leader?" and "How well does your leader recognize your potential?" Clearly, what these items capture is not the parameters of the exchange per se (those remain assumed) but the *quality* of the relationship. Indeed, even in Scandura and Graen's experimental training sessions, lessons were also given on active listening (individual consideration in the form of voice provision, perhaps?), a behavior likely to improve the quality of the interaction but also likely to be independent of any resource exchange per se.

This quality ends up being extremely important, as high-quality exchanges are seen to encompass a "high degree of mutual trust, respect, and obligation" (Graen & Uhl-Bien, 1995, p. 227). Interestingly, these high-quality exchanges were originally seen to represent followers' *in-group standing* with the leader (e.g., Scandura & Graen, 1984). This is certainly not an unreasonable labeling, as we noted earlier that respect provision is likely to produce just this effect, and trust is an outcome of shared group membership. Although authors have, more recently, replaced this wording with "partnership" (Graen & Uhl-Bien), we still see conceptual value in the older terminology.

Empirically, a substantive body of work has been conducted examining the quality of leader-member exchanges. Recent meta-analyses have confirmed a range of positive outcomes from high-quality exchanges, including enhanced job commitment, performance, satisfaction, role clarity (Dulebohn, Bommer, Liden, Brouer, & Ferris, 2012; Gerstner & Day, 1997), and organizational citizenship behaviors (Ilies, Nahrgang, & Morgeson, 2007). In terms of clear causal relations, Scandura and Graen's (1984) experiment showed that instantiating

relatively high-quality leader-member exchanges produces enhanced job satisfaction, performance, and productivity. Other research, however, questions the dyadic imperative so fundamental to the leader-member exchange model (e.g., Hogg et al., 2005). This latter work starts from the specific premises of self-categorization theory and questions whether high-quality *interpersonal relations* will necessarily yield the best outcomes.

In a first study conducted by Hogg et al. (2005), perceptions of high-quality interpersonal treatment were associated more strongly with leadership satisfaction and perceived leadership effectiveness when group members perceived the group context (i.e., an employment context) to be one in which people were valued more as individuals than team members. This relationship, however, significantly weakened when group members perceived the context to be one in which *teams* played a more prominent role (e.g., "working in teams is considered very important in this company," p. 995). In a second study, Hogg et al. showed that nonpersonalized (or "depersonalized" in self-categorization terms) treatment actually increased perceptions of leader effectiveness over personalized treatment *specifically among group members who highly valued their group membership*.

Taken together, the results of the last two studies suggest that high-quality *interpersonal* treatment need not be necessary for the favorable outcomes often examined within the rubric of the leader-member exchange model. The dyadic, interpersonal exchange quality seems to be most important when broader groups (e.g., broader work teams, the organization as a whole) are either relatively psychologically nonsalient or unimportant. Simply put, interpersonal processes are causally important when interpersonal processes matter to people. But even this seeming truism may not best characterize Hogg et al.'s findings, precisely because the dyad can still be psychologically represented as a "partnership" or salient in-group. Recalling our fundamental premise that leadership is a group process, Hogg et al.'s work in conjunction with traditional leader-member exchange reasoning suggests successful leader-follower consequences follow from behaviors that correspond most appropriately to the shared salient *social* self-category.

Several conclusions can be drawn from research and theory on exchange models of leadership. First, any instance of influence via pure exchange with no other features to characterize the relationship—that is, any instance of leadership by buying—represents either the nascent forms of true leadership (but not true leadership itself) or, simply, failed leadership. As Graen and Uhl-Bien (1995, p. 238) observe, "When material exchange is the basis for the relationship, the process is not really leadership; it is closer to 'managership' or 'supervision.'" This may well be needed in contexts when there is, indeed, no sense of "us"—contexts that may be predominant in many sociological groups (e.g., employment contexts). In time, however, relationships characterized by material exchange can *transform* into true leadership through the development of a shared social identity, with concomitant respect, trust, and loyalty. This is one of Graen and Uhl-Bien's clearly stated ideals for their model. Second, much of the work highlighting the success of high-quality leader-member exchanges may, inadvertently, be overemphasizing the relative importance of the exchange. Given the shared group membership features of high-quality exchanges, we suggest that their successes are likely to occur *in spite* of the exchange, not because of it. The third, and final, point we want to make about exchange analyses of leadership is that a fundamental assumption (albeit often unstated) remains that individuals' needs and desires to be satisfied through the exchange are necessarily formed exogenously and *brought into* the leadership situation. However, we not only know that individual need satisfaction is not essential to group formation (Tajfel, Billig, Bundy, & Flament, 1971), but we know that leaders can also create new needs and desires as they move group members toward pursuing a future of new realities (Reicher, Haslam, & Hopkins, 2005). Leadership is, thus, often transformational.

## Leadership as Transformation

A major advance in leadership theory and research was made by the recognition that leadership in practice is more than simple exchange (Bass, 1985; Burns, 1978). Instead (or, at least, in addition), leaders often *inspire* and *motivate* fellow group members beyond personal self-interest. This inspirational and motivational leadership was termed "transformational leadership," and it is considered to be a counterpart to exchange-based, "transactional leadership." Bass argued, for example, that "the transformational leader can move those influenced to transcend their own self-interest for the good of the group" (p. 15). Achieving such an outcome is highly valuable, as contingent rewards often come with resource and psychological costs associated with surveillance and monitoring (Turner, 2005), and even group member motivation loss (Deci, Koestner, & Ryan, 1999).

Bass (e.g., 1985; Bass & Steidlmeier, 1999) outlined four primary components in his model of transformational leadership: idealized influence (or charisma), inspirational motivation, individual consideration, and intellectual stimulation. Through idealized influence and inspirational motivation, group members are assumed (e.g., Avolio, Bass, & Jung, 1999) not simply to express and display confidence (often associated with charismatic leadership, e.g., Conger & Kanungo, 1987) but to promote the interests of the group by going beyond their self-interests, emphasizing "the collective mission" (Avolio et al., 1999, p. 450) and framing their talk around shared values. Through individual consideration, leaders and would-be leaders actually pay attention to, and respect, their fellow group members, providing them voice through active listening. And through intellectual stimulation, group members' interpretations of the reality confronting them are expanded so that they see the world in new ways. It represents a "discrete jump in the followers' conceptualization, comprehension, and discernment of the nature of the problems they face and their solutions" (Bass, 1985, p. 99). Bass's model has received broad confirmation in empirical analyses measuring group members' perceptions of leaders, although the first two components often statistically load together on the same factor in formal analyses (e.g., Avolio et al., 1999). These empirical analyses also demonstrate that group members can differentiate between transformational leadership and transactional leadership.

In correlational research, ratings of transformational leadership predict group-level performance in a variety of contexts, including business (e.g., Peterson, Walumbwa, Byron, & Myrowitz, 2009) and military (e.g., Bass, Avolio, Jung, & Berson, 2003) contexts. Moreover, a recent meta-analysis showed that perceptions of transformational leadership were positively related to both individual and collective performance, above and beyond transactional leadership (Wang, Oh, Courtright, & Colbert, 2011). In an attempt to establish causality, training in transformational leadership has led to enhanced (1) perceptions of intellectual stimulation, follower performance, and organizational commitment among bank employees (Barling, Weber, & Kelloway, 1996); and (2) self-efficacy and effort, follower performance, and collective orientation among military personnel (Dvir, Eden, Avolio, & Shamir, 2002).

Additional research has identified at least two self- and identity-related variables that are related to transformational leadership. One is perceptions of self-efficacy. As noted earlier, follower efficacy is one outcome of transformational leadership training (Dvir et al., 2002). Correlational research also suggests that transformational leaders can enhance group members' perceptions of efficacy (e.g., Walumbwa, Avolio, & Zhu, 2008), although some unclarity remains about the role of efficacy as an outcome or a moderator of transformational leadership (Pieterse, van Knippenberg, Schippers, & Stam, 2010). Most likely, it is both.

The second identity-related variable is that of a positive orientation to the relevant psychological in-group. Again, both Barling et al. (1996) and Dvir et al. (2002) showed enhanced follower commitment and collective orientation (respectively) after leader training in transformational leadership. In correlational studies, the positive relationship between perceptions of transformational leadership and group member performance was *mediated* by group members' perceptions of group cohesion (Bass et al., 2003) and social identification (Walumbwa et al., 2008). These psychological group and social identity findings should not be surprising, as components of transformational leadership are very similar to those we have identified previously as promoting a social self-categorization, including voice provision (via individualized consideration) and rhetorically emphasizing the collective (via inspirational motivation). Indeed, as Reicher et al. (2005, p. 563, emphasis added) have already noted, "leaders are not passive onlookers when it comes to identity processes. They actively intervene in creating and redefining identities and thereby in creating and *transforming* their followers."

Indeed, both theory and research highlight how successful transformational leadership is predicated upon a shared social identity. For example, Pawar and Eastman (1997) argued strongly for contextual variability in transformational leadership success. They proposed that the expression of transformational leadership is *less* likely to be successful if the group itself exists in a self-interested, intergroup context (i.e., the market place); here, a transactional style was predicted to be more successful. Transformational leadership may, thus, be best suited for those contexts in which people share a collective orientation toward each other that is not undermined by, say, a broader individualistic reward

structure. In a more recent empirical investigation with teachers, Nahum-Shani and Somech (2011) observed that teacher organizational citizenship behaviors were positively predicted by perceptions of transformational leadership *when the teachers held high collective values and low individualistic values*. Again, being collectively focused effectively enabled transformational leadership to be successful. Complementing Nahum-Shani and Somech's findings are those of Leong and Fischer's (2011) meta-analysis of cultural variations in the expression of transformational leadership. The results of their analysis showed that transformational leadership varied as a function of broader cultural values; in the authors' words, "higher egalitarianism and lower hierarchy values were associated with higher transformational leadership" (p. 169).

In one final observation, shared group membership may not simply be a prerequisite to successful transformational leadership; it may actually create it. This is borne out in two separate experiments conducted by Platow, van Knippenberg, Haslam, van Knippenberg, and Spears (2006). In these experiments, the authors treated perceptions of leader charisma as *outcomes* of self-categorization processes. In their first study, university students rated the charisma of an in-group prototypical leader as greater than that of an in-group nonprototypical leader. This occurred *regardless* of the collectively oriented or exchange-based nature of the leader's communication—although in their second study, in-group nonprototypical group members were, indeed, able to gain in perceived charisma via a collectively oriented communication. Ultimately, Platow et al.'s research suggests that simply embodying who "we are" can be enough for group members to attribute higher levels of charisma to their leader.

Overall, as we noted at the start of this section, the movement of the leadership field into a theoretical and empirical analysis of transformational leadership represents a major advance in the quest to understand leadership processes more fully. The work clearly identifies an interrelationship between transformational behaviors and the creation of a shared social identity. Moreover, much like analyses of transactional leadership, analyses of transformational leadership demonstrate how crucial the presence of this shared social identity is for transformational leadership itself to be most effective.

## Leadership Attributions

We outlined earlier group members' relative willingness to cede authority to fellow in-group members more so than out-group members. But in much of the leadership research to date, including that of both personality-based and transformational leadership, there has been an implicit assumption that potential followers do not simply cede authority; they *make* that authority through their relative attributions of leadership to their fellow group members (or, at least, agents who fill a role in a sociological group nominally referred to as "leader"). This assumption is embedded in the researchers' measurement of leadership by means of followers' (and would-be followers') ratings. This assumption, explicit or not, represents another important insight. Leadership is *attributed* to specific group members from their fellow group members. Leadership, thus, is as much about followers as it is about leaders per se; once again, leadership is fundamentally a group process.

Lord and his colleagues (Lord et al., 1982; see also Lord & Shondrick, 2011 for a recent expansion) developed their *leader categorization theory* to understand more fully this process of follower attributions. They recognized that the concept "leader" is, itself, a social category and, hence, is imbued with shared stereotyped meanings. Lord et al. (1982), thus, proposed that, within a particular social context, there is likely to be relatively high consensus among group members' beliefs about what leadership is and what leaders do. To evaluate this hypothesis, over 200 participants were asked to list attributes that they thought were associated with various leadership and nonleadership roles. Other participants then independently judged the relative "fit" of each of the attributes to their own subjective image of "leader." Through this method, the researchers were able to identify attributes that were relatively high and relatively low in leadership stereotypicality.[1] Attributes that were rated as relatively high in leader stereotypicality mirrored some identified by (1) leader personality research (e.g., intelligent and open minded [openness to experience?]), (2) exchange analyses of leadership (e.g., industrious [competence?]), (3) transformational analyses of leadership (e.g., charismatic and concerned [individual consideration?]), and (4) leadership theory and research more broadly (e.g., persuasive and fair). These findings suggest some congruence between theoretical analyses of leadership and potential followers' expectations.

Lord et al. (1984) followed up their initial study with another in which they presented short descriptions of potential leaders to a new group of subjects. As expected, greater attributions of leadership were made to those targets described with high leader stereotypical qualities than to those with leader non-stereotypical attributes. Perceptions of leadership were, indeed, bestowed upon those whose behavior matched potential followers' leadership expectations. More recently, Epitropaki and Martin (2005) examined these processes outside of the laboratory among employees of British manufacturing companies. In this latter study, respondents indicated the degree to which they believed a series of attributes (e.g., intelligence, dedication, sensitivity) were stereotypical of business leaders, as well as the degree to which they believed the attributes characterized their own direct managers. Results showed that the closer managers were perceived to be to respondents' leader stereotypes, the higher was the quality of their exchange relationship with their manager (following Graen & Uhl-Bien, 1995) *1 year later.*

In a separate line of enquiry, researchers examined attributions of leadership to managers as a function of the relative success of the group (in this case, the business) in achieving its goals (Meindl, Ehrlich, & Dukerich, 1985). Although "success" per se was not among the stereotypical leader attributes identified by Lord et al. (1984), other associated attributes were rated as relatively high in leader stereotypicality, including being industrious, goal oriented, a good administrator, and a high achiever. To examine their hypothesis, Meindl et al. presented participants with descriptions of companies that had slight or substantial increases or decreases in performance. Critically, the descriptions of the performance changes never directly implicated the managers. Nevertheless, participants made stronger leadership attributions to the manager under substantial performance changes compared to slight performance changes. In other words, participants attributed substantial enhancements in company performance directly to the manager; but so, too, did they make person attributions when there were substantial declines. Haslam et al. (2001) showed similar results in attributions of charisma.

Hence, there is very good evidence to support the hypothesis that people hold relatively consensual beliefs about what leaders are, and that these beliefs are associated with the attribution of leadership to specific group members. However, it is important to remember that stereotypical beliefs themselves are highly context dependent (Haslam, Turner, Oakes, McGarty, & Hayes, 1992); their very content *and* degree of consensus changes with changes in the broader comparative context (Haslam, Oakes, Reynolds, & Turner, 1999; Haslam et al., 1998).

This remains true for leader stereotypes as well. In fact, there was enough variability in Lord et al.'s (1984) analysis to lead them to conclude that "leadership is better described as a person-in-situation category" (p. 358). In other words, the content of the leader stereotype, like other stereotypes, is highly context dependent.

Moreover, not only is the content of the stereotypes fluid but the nature of the group (including norms and the relative importance of the group per se) and the intergroup context in which would-be leaders' behaviors are enacted provides variable meanings to the otherwise stereotypical attributes. For example, as predicted by leader categorization analyses, Cronshaw and Lord (1987) observed greater perceptions of leadership among leader-stereotypical than non-leader-stereotypical targets overall. However, this difference emerged primarily when the target's leader-stereotypical behavior was *normative* for the group; behavioral deviation from the group, even via leader-stereotypical behavior, led to lower levels of perceived leadership. Identical attributes thus conveyed different meanings in different group-normative contexts. When leader-stereotypical behavior is normative for the group, the would-be leader is not *only* leader stereotypical but in-group prototypical. Hains et al. (1997) examined this process directly by manipulating the relative leader stereotypicality of targets as well as their relative in-group prototypicality. These authors found that, in contexts that emphasized the group, it was in-group prototypicality that predicted leadership perceptions, not leader stereotypicality. It was only in contexts that *de*-emphasized the group that the broader, societal-based leader stereotypes played any role in leader perceptions.

As for broader *inter*group relations, their relevance becomes significant upon recognizing that much of the content of the leader stereotype is also associated with the masculinity stereotype, as shown in a recent meta-analysis (Koenig, Eagly, Mitchell, & Ristikari, 2011). On the one hand, this may not be too surprising, as we noted earlier that Mann (1959) and Ensari et al. (2011) identified masculinity as a reliable personality correlate of leadership. On the other hand, however, it does bring into question whether it is leadership, per se, that is being examined or whether it is broader societal status characteristics (e.g., Ridgeway, 2001). Indeed, a series of meta-analyses have highlighted this very problem, revealing that men, more than women, are likely to emerge as leaders (Eagly & Karau, 1991) and are evaluated more favorably as leaders (Eagly, Makhijani, & Klonsky, 1992). These findings occurred despite the absence of *overall* differences between men and women's leader effectiveness (Eagly, Karau, & Makhijani, 1995), and women's (slightly) greater employment of both transformational and aspects of transactional leadership behaviors. In light of these data, it is more likely, then, that follower and would-be followers' attributions of leadership are being guided by leader-stereotype expectations that are strongly associated with being male rather than female (indeed, this may even extend to being a white male; Rosette, Leonardelli, & Phillips, 2008).

Overall, the major advances in the study of leader attributions made by researchers such as Lord and his colleagues was the formal recognition that group members (1) hold beliefs (often consensual) about what leadership is and what leaders do, and that (2) these group members ultimately bestowed leadership upon their fellow group members to the degree that these beliefs are confirmed. In other words, there are, indeed, clear leader stereotypes; but, like all stereotypes, they are context dependent and the outcomes of group processes. Moreover, to the degree that contextual variability can alter the salience of different social categories (e.g., Oakes, Turner, & Haslam, 1991), different stereotyped beliefs actually collide (e.g., women vs. leaders). So the process ends up being not one of simple feature matching but one of contextually dependent interpretations of the social reality confronting group members (Oakes, Haslam, & Turner, 1994) and the potential mismatch in stereotype content among variably salient social categories. In the end, however, this work on leader stereotypes reemphasizes the principal assumption that we have followed throughout this chapter: Leadership is fundamentally a psychological group process.

## Summary and Conclusions

Leadership is about influence, and it has been our premise throughout that it is shared psychological group memberships that make this influence possible. Undoubtedly, resource power can be wielded *over* people to force them to bend to one's will (French & Raven, 1960; Turner, 2005). But this is more of a sign of failed leadership, or simply its absence, as people's motivations, goals, and behaviors will be geared toward avoiding punishments rather than pursing a collective vision. Brute force serves only to divide people from would-be leaders (Reynolds & Platow, 2003). This will ultimately create (or at best, maintain) an *inter*group relationship, with its concomitant conflictual social identities that will form the counterforce to oppose—rather than collaborate with—the leader (e.g., Drury & Reicher, 2009). Successful leadership, in contrast, builds upon shared social identities, and it is as much conferred upon would-be leaders as it is created by these leaders themselves. These shared identities can be earned (e.g., via competence at, and conformity to, group tasks) and can be created (e.g., through fair and respectful behavior), all within a fluctuating context of ever-changing meanings of "us" and of "leadership" itself. In this way, simply appointing someone to the role of leader, even if based on what otherwise may seem to be legitimate criteria, may actually yield poorer group outcomes if this role-appointment process breaks down (or, at least, fails to build up) a shared social identity (Haslam et al., 1998).

Our differentiation between successful leadership achieved through shared social identities and the absence of leadership through resource control also provides insight into sociological groups where both are likely to be observed. On the positive side, sociological leaders (e.g., CEOs) may be employing psychological leadership through shared identities with some fellow group members, while working to *develop* these identities with others through high-quality exchange relationships. There is a negative side, however, that we can identify, one that will continue to exist unless we move our analysis from a purely psychological one to a political one.

Consider, for example, a hypothetical situation in which a university vice-chancellor (VC) makes sweeping resource-based changes, even to the point of terminating staff employment. If fellow professors see this as unfair, a clear intergroup divide will be created, with the professors failing to confer leadership upon the VC and failing to follow. How can such a VC maintain his or her position in such a clear case of failed leadership? It comes because the formal, sociological group position is conferred not by all professors, but by a small board of trustees. Alas, we can now see that the shared social identity the VC needs to cultivate is with this small board; resource power can be wielded with impunity over the remaining academic staff. Of course, corporate CEOs also need not harness the followership of general employees, provided they maintain a shared social identity with the corporate board. And dictators need not have the consent of the masses, only of those who will do their bidding to keep the masses in check. In such cases,

rhetoric such as "my fellow colleagues," "we're all on the same team," and "fellow countrymen" are simply empty attempts at conning one's way into the shared identity. And the only way out of this is through political action of protest and social change. So our conceptual focus on psychological group memberships does not mean that the sociological groups are superfluous to analyses of leadership. Indeed, they are often the places in people's lives where both material and symbolic realities play out. Nevertheless, our analysis still informs us that a focus on psychological group memberships allows researchers and practitioners to harness valuable tools to understand the patterns and progress of leadership and would-be leadership as it is played out in real time.

In the end, analyses of leadership are many and varied, all offering insight into what often appears to be (and possibly is) an elusive topic. The current chapter is, thus, one further offering. We have, however, endeavored to thread through our chapter a common premise—grounded in well-established theory and research—that helps to unite a range of these leadership analyses. In this manner, we hope that readers can look afresh at the scope of the extant work and understand it less as a motley collection and more as expression of the underlying reality of the social psychology of leadership (Haslam et al., 2011). Thus, although our analysis adopts a classic assumption that leadership is fundamentally a group process, it is through our specific analysis of psychological group memberships as understood by the principles of social identity and self-categorization theories that we can shine a new light (or maybe just from a different angle) on this perennial question.

## Note

1. Lord et al. (1984) refer to these attributes as leader "prototypicality", as their conceptual work emerges from the same analysis of categorization processes as self-categorization theory (i.e., Rosch, 1978). However, following previous publications in this area that have examined the independent contributions of relative "leader prototypicality" and relative "in-group prototypicality" (e.g., Hains, Hogg, & Duck, 1997), we are currently referring to the former as "leader stereotypicality" so as not to confuse it with in-group prototypicality.

## References

Abrams, D., de Moura, G. R., Marques, J. M., & Hutchinson, P. (2008). Innovation credit: When can leaders oppose their group's norms? *Journal of Personality and Social Psychology, 95,* 662–678.

Abrams, D., Wetherell, M., Cochrane, S., Hogg, M. A., & Turner, J. C. (1990). Knowing what to think by knowing who you are: Self-categorization and the nature of norm formation, conformity and group polarization. *British Journal of Social Psychology, 29,* 97–119.

Allen, D. G., Shore, L. M., & Griffeth, R. W. (2003). The role of perceived organizational support and supportive human resource practices in the turnover process. *Journal of Management, 29,* 99–118.

Asch, S. E. (1956). Studies of independence and conformity: A minority of one against a unanimous majority. *Psychological Monographs, 70,* 1–70.

Augoustinos, M., & De Garis, S. (2012). Too black or not black enough: Social identity complexity in the political rhetoric of Barack Obama. *European Journal of Social Psychology, 42,* 564–577.

Avolio, B. J., Bass, B. M., & Jung, D. I. (1999). Re-examining the components of transformational and transactional leadership using the Multifactor Leadership Questionnaire. *Journal of Occupational and Organizational Psychology, 72,* 441–462.

Avolio, B. J., & Gibbons, T. C. (1988). Developing transformational leaders: A life span approach. In J. A. Conger & R. N. Kanungo (Eds.), *Charismatic leadership: The elusive factor in organizational effectiveness* (pp. 276–308). San Francisco: Jossey-Bass.

Barling, J., Weber, T., & Kelloway, E. V. (1996). Effects of transformational leadership training on attitudinal and financial outcomes: A field experiment. *Journal of Applied Psychology, 81,* 827–832.

Bartram, T., & Casimir, G. (2007). The relationship between leadership and follower in-role performance and satisfaction with the leader: The mediating effects of empowerment and trust in the leader. *Leadership and Organization Development Journal, 28,* 4–19.

Bass, B. M. (1985). *Leadership and performance beyond expectation.* New York: Free Press.

Bass, B. M., Avolio, B. J., & Goodheim, L. (1987). Biography and assessment of transformational leadership at the world-class level. *Journal of Management, 13,* 7–19.

Bass, B. M., Avolio, B. J., Jung, D. I., & Berson, Y. (2003). Predicting unit performance by assessing transformational and transactional leadership. *Journal of Applied Psychology, 88,* 207–218.

Bass, B. M., & Steidlmeier, P. (1999). Ethics, character, and authentic transformational leadership behaviour. *Leadership Quarterly, 10,* 181–217.

Ben-Yoav, O., Hollander, E. P., & Carnevale, P. J. D. (1983). Leader legitimacy, leader-follower interaction and followers' ratings of the leader. *Journal of Social Psychology, 121,* 111–115.

Blader, S. L., & Tyler, T. R. (2009). Testing and extending the group engagement model: Linkages between social identity, procedural justice, economic outcomes, and extra-role behaviour. *Journal of Applied Psychology, 94,* 445–464.

Blau, P. M. (1964). *Exchange and power in social life.* New York: Wiley.

Bond, R., & Smith, P. B. (1996). Culture and conformity: A meta-analysis of studies using Asch's (1952b & 1956) line judgement task. *Psychological Bulletin, 119,* 111–137.

Bono, J. E., & Judge, T. A. (2004). Personality and transformational and transactional leadership: A meta-analysis. *Journal of Applied Psychology, 89,* 901–910.

Burke, C. S., Sims, D. E., Lazzara, E. H., & Salas, E. (2007). Trust in leadership: A multi-level review and integration. *Leadership Quarterly, 18,* 606–632.

Burns, J. M. (1978). *Leadership.* New York: Harper & Row.

Cartwright, D. (1951). Achieving change in people: Some applications of group dynamics theory. *Human Relations, 4,* 381–392.

Cartwright, D., & Zander, A. (Eds.). (1960). *Group dynamics: Research and theory* (2nd ed.). New York: Harper & Row.

Castelli, L., & Carraro, L. (2010). Striving for difference: On the spontaneous preference for ingroup members who maximize ingroup positive distinctiveness. *European Journal of Social Psychology, 40,* 881–890.

Conger, J. A., & Kanungo, R. A. (1987). Toward a behavioural theory of charismatic leadership in organizational settings. *Academy of Management Review, 12,* 637–647.

Costa, P. T., & McCrae, R. R. (1988). Personality in adulthood: A six-year longitudinal study of self-reports and spouse ratings on the NEO Personality Inventory. *Journal of Personality and Social Psychology, 54,* 853–863.

Cronshaw, S. F., & Lord, R. G. (1987). Effects of categorization, attribution, and encoding processes on leadership perceptions. *Journal of Applied Psychology, 72,* 97–106.

Dansereau, F., Graen, G., & Haga, W. J. (1975). A vertical dyad linkage approach to leadership within formal organizations: A longitudinal investigation of the role making process. *Organizational Behaviour and Human Performance, 13,* 46–78.

David, B., & Turner, J. C. (1996). Studies in self-categorization and minority conversion: Is being a member of the outgroup an advantage? *British Journal of Social Psychology, 35,* 179–199.

Deci, E. L., Koestner, R., & Ryan, R. M. (1999). A meta-analytic review of experiments examining the effects of extrinsic rewards on intrinsic motivation. *Psychological Bulletin, 125,* 627–668.

DeRue, D. S., Nahrgang, J. D., Wellman, N., & Humphrey, S. E. (2011). Trait and behavioural theories of leadership: An integration and meta-analytic test of their relative validity. *Personnel Psychology, 64,* 7–52.

Deutsch, M. (1975). Equity, equality and need: What determines which value will be used as the basis of distributive justice? *Journal of Social Issues, 31,* 137–149.

Dirks, K. T., & Ferrin, D. L. (2002). Trust in leadership: Meta-analytic findings and implications for research and practice. *Journal of Applied Psychology, 87,* 611–628.

Drury, J., & Reicher, S. (2009). Collective psychological empowerment as a model of social change: Researching crowds and power. *Journal of Social Issues, 65,* 707–725.

Duck, J. M., & Fielding, K. S. (1999). Leaders and subgroups: One of us or one of them? *Group Processes and Intergroup Relations, 2,* 203–230.

Dulebohn, J. H., Bommer, W. H., Liden, R. C., Brouer, R. L., & Ferris, G. R. (2012). A meta-analysis of antecedents and consequences of leader-member exchange: Integrating the past with an eye toward the future. *Journal of Management, 38,* 1715–1759.

Dvir, T., Eden, D., Avolio, B. J., & Shamir, B. (2002). Impact of transformational leadership on follower development and performance: A field experiment. *Academy of Management Journal, 43,* 735–744.

Eagly, A. H., & Karau, S. J. (1991). Gender and the emergence of leaders: A meta-analysis. *Journal of Personality and Social Psychology, 60,* 685–710.

Eagly, A. H., Karau, S. J., & Makhijani, M. G. (1995). Gender and the effectiveness of leaders: A meta-analysis. *Psychological Bulletin, 117,* 125–145.

Eagly, A. H., Makhijani, M. G., & Klonsky, B. G. (1992). Gender and the evaluation of leaders: A meta-analysis. *Psychological Bulletin, 111,* 3–22.

Ensari, N., Riggio, R. E., Christian, J., & Carslaw, G. (2011). Who emerges as a leader? Meta-analyses of individual differences as predictors of leadership emergence. *Personality and Individual Differences, 51,* 532–536.

Epitropaki, O., & Martin, R. (2005). From ideal to real: A longitudinal study of the role of implicit leadership theories on leader-member exchanges and employee outcomes. *Journal of Applied Psychology, 90,* 659–676.

Estrada, M., Brown, J., & Lee, F. (1995). Who gets the credit? Perceptions of idiosyncrasy credit in work groups. *Small Group Research, 26,* 56–76.

Foddy, M., & Hogg, M. A. (1999). Impact of leaders on resource consumption in social dilemmas: The intergroup context. In M. Foddy, M. Smithson, S. Schneider, & M. A. Hogg (Ed.), *Resolving social dilemmas: Dynamic, structural, and intergroup aspects* (pp. 309–330). Philadelphia: Psychology Press.

Foddy, M., Platow, M. J., & Yamagishi, T. (2009). Group-based trust in strangers: The role of stereotypes and expectations. *Psychological Science, 20,* 419–422.

French, J. R. P., & Raven, B. (1960). The bases of social power. In D. Cartwright & A. F. Zander (Eds.), *Group dynamics* (2nd ed., pp. 607–623). Evanston, IL: Row Peterson.

Gaertner, S. L., Mann, J., Murrell, A., & Dovidio, J. F. (1989). Reducing intergroup bias: The benefits of recategorization. *Journal of Personality and Social Psychology, 57,* 239–249.

Gerstner, C. R., & Day, D. V. (1997). Meta-analytic review of leader-member exchange theory: Correlates and construct issues. *Journal of Applied Psychology, 82,* 827–844.

Gibb, C. A. (1947). The principles and traits of leadership. *Journal of Abnormal and Social Psychology, 42,* 267–284.

Gibb, C. A. (1969). Leadership. In G. Lindzey & E. Aronson (Eds.), *Handbook of social psychology* (2nd ed., Vol. 4, pp. 205–282). Reading, MA: Addison Wesley.

Graen, G. B., & Uhl-Bien, M. (1995). Relationship approach to leadership: Development of leader-member exchange (LMX) theory of leadership over 25 years: Applying a multi-level, multi-domain perspective. *Leadership Quarterly, 6,* 219–247.

Graf, M. M., Schuh, S., van Quaquebeke, N., & van Dick, R. (2012). The relationship between leaders' group oriented values and follower identification with and endorsement of leaders: The moderating role of leaders' group membership. *Journal of Business Ethics, 106,* 301–311.

Hains, S. C., Hogg, M. A., & Duck, J. M. (1997). Self-categorization and leadership: Effects of group prototypicality and leader stereotypicality. *Personality and Social Psychology Bulletin, 23,* 1087–1099.

Halevy, N., Berson, Y., & Galinsky, A. D. (2011). The mainstream is not electable: When vision triumphs over representativeness in leader emergence and effectiveness. *Personality and Social Psychology Bulletin, 37,* 893–904.

Haslam, S. A., & Platow, M. J. (2001). Social identity and the link between leadership and followership: How affirming an identity translates personal vision into group action. *Personality and Social Psychology Bulletin, 27,* 1469–1479.

Haslam, S. A., & Platow, M. J. (2010). Idiosyncrasy credit. In M. A. Hogg & J. M. Levine (Eds.), *Sage encyclopedia of group processes and intergroup relations* (pp. 420–422). Thousand Oaks, CA: Sage.

Haslam, S. A., McGarty, C., Brown, P. M., Eggins, R. A., Morrison, B. E., & Reynolds, K. J. (1998). Inspecting the emperor's clothes: Evidence that random selection of leaders can enhance group performance. *Group Dynamics: Theory, Research, and Practice, 2,* 168–184.

Haslam, S. A., Oakes, P. J., Reynolds, K. J., & Turner, J. C. (1999). Social identity salience and the emergence of stereotype consensus. *Personality and Social Psychology Bulletin, 25,* 809–818.

Haslam, S. A., Platow, M. J., Turner, J. C., Reynolds, K. J., McGarty, C., Oakes, P. J., . . . Veenstra, K. (2001). Social identity and the romance of leadership: The importance of being seen to be "doing it for us." *Group Processes and Intergroup Relations, 4,* 191–205.

Haslam, S. A., & Reicher, S. D. (2007). Identity entrepreneurship and the consequences of identity failure: The dynamics of leadership in the BBC Prison Study. *Social Psychology Quarterly, 70,* 125–147.

Haslam, S. A., Reicher, S. D., & Platow, M. J. (2011). *The new psychology of leadership: Identity, influence and power.* New York: Psychology Press.

Haslam, S. A., Turner, J. C., Oakes, P. J., McGarty, C., & Hayes, B. K. (1992). Context-dependent variation in social stereotyping 1: The effects of intergroup relations as mediated by social change and frame of reference. *European Journal of Social Psychology, 22,* 3–20.

Haslam, S. A., Turner, J. C., Oakes, P. J., Reynolds, K. J., Eggins, R. A., Nolan, M., & Tweedie, J. (1998). When do stereotypes become really consensual? Investigating the group-based dynamics of the consensualization process. *European Journal of Social Psychology, 28,* 755–776.

Hayes, N., & Joseph, S. (2003). Big five correlates of three measures of subjective well-being. *Personality and Individual Differences, 34,* 723–727.

Hogg, M. A., Martin, R., Epitropaki, O., Mankad, A., Svensson, A., & Weeden, K. (2005). Effective leadership in salient groups: Revisiting leader-member exchange theory from the perspective of the social identity theory of leadership. *Personality and Social Psychology Bulletin, 31,* 991–1004.

Hogg, M. A., & van Knippenberg, D. (2004). Social identity and leadership processes in groups. *Advances in Experimental Social Psychology, 35,* 1–52.

Hollander, E. P. (1964). *Leaders, groups, and influence.* New York: Oxford University Press.

Hollander, E. P. (1985). Leadership and power. In G. Lindzey & E. Aronson (Eds.), *The handbook of social psychology* (3rd ed., pp. 485–537). New York: Random House.

Homans, G. C. (1961). *Social behavior: Its elementary forms.* New York: Harcourt, Brace & World.

Ilies, R., Nahrgang, J. D., & Morgeson, F. P. (2007). Leader-member exchange and citizenship behaviours: A meta-analysis. *Journal of Applied Psychology, 92,* 269–277.

Judge, T. A., Bono, J. E., Ilies, R., & Gerhardt, M. W. (2002). Personality and leadership: A qualitative and quantitative review. *Journal of Applied Psychology, 87,* 765–780.

King, A. J. (2010). Follow me! I'm a leader if you; I'm a failed initiator if you don't? *Behavioural Processes, 84,* 671–674.

Koenig, A. M., Eagly, A. H., Mitchell, A. A., & Ristikari, T. (2011). Are leader stereotypes masculine? A meta-analysis of three research paradigms. *Psychological Bulletin, 137,* 616–642.

Koper, G., van Knippenberg, D., Bouhuijs, F., Vermunt, R., & Wilke, H. (1993). Procedural fairness and self-esteem. *European Journal of Social Psychology, 23,* 313–325.

Korsgaard, M. A., Schweiger, D. M., & Sapienza, H. J. (1995). Building commitment, attachment and trust in strategic decision making teams: The role of procedural justice. *Academy of Management Journal, 38*, 60–84.

Leong, L. Y. C., & Fischer, R. (2011). Is transformational leadership universal? A meta-analytical investigation of multifactor leadership questionnaire means across cultures. *Journal of Leadership and Organizational Studies, 18*, 164–174.

Lewin, K., Lippitt, R., & White, R. K. (1939). Patterns of aggressive behaviour in experimentally created "social climate." *Journal of Social Psychology, 10*, 262–299.

Liden, R. C., & Graen, G. B. (1980). Generalizability of the vertical dyad linkage model of leadership. *Academy of Management Journal, 23*, 451–465.

Lind, E. A., & Tyler, T. R. (1988). *The social psychology of procedural justice.* New York: Plenum.

Lord, R. G., Brown, D. J., & Freiberg, R. J. (1999). Understanding the dynamics of leadership: The role of follower self-concepts in the leader-follower relationship. *Organizational Behaviour and Human Decision Processes, 78*, 167–203.

Lord, R. G., de Vader, C., & Alliger, G. M. (1986). A meta-analysis of the relation between personality traits and leadership perceptions: An application of validity generalization procedures. *Journal of Applied Psychology, 71*, 402–410.

Lord, R. G., Foti, R. J., & de Vader, C. L. (1984). A test of leadership categorization theory: Internal structure, information processing, and leadership perceptions. *Organizational Behaviour and Human Performance, 34*, 343–378.

Lord, R. G., Foti, R. J., & Phillips, J. S. (1982). A theory of leadership categorization. In J. G. Hunt, U. Sekaran, & C. Schriesheim (Eds.), *Leadership: Beyond establishment views* (pp. 104–121). Carbondale: Southern Illinois University Press.

Lord, R. G., & Shondrick, S. J. (2011). Leadership and knowledge: Symbolic, connectionist, and embodied perspectives. *Leadership Quarterly, 22*, 207–222.

Mann, R. D. (1959). A review of the relationships between personality and performance in small groups. *Psychological Bulletin, 56*, 241–270.

McGarty, C., Turner, J. C., Hogg, M. A., David, B., & Wetherell, M. S. (1992). Group polarization as conformity to the prototypical group member. *British Journal of Social Psychology, 31*, 1–20.

Meindl, J. R., Ehrlich, S. B., & Dukerich, J. M. (1985). The romance of leadership. *Administrative Science Quarterly, 30*, 78–102.

Nahum-Shani, I., & Somech, A. (2011). Leadership, OCB and individual differences: Idiocentrism and allocentrism as moderators of the relationship between transformational and transactional leadership and OCB. *Leadership Quarterly, 22*, 353–366.

Ng, K-Y., Ang, S., & Chan, K-Y. (2008). Personality and leader effectiveness: A moderated mediation model of self-efficacy, job demands, and job autonomy. *Journal of Applied Psychology, 93*, 733–743.

Oakes, P. J., Haslam, S. A., & Turner, J. C. (1994). *Stereotyping and social reality.* Oxford: Blackwell.

Oakes, P. J., Turner, J. C., & Haslam, S. A. (1991). Perceiving people as group members: The role of fit in the salience of social categorizations. *British Journal of Social Psychology, 30*, 125–144.

Pawar, B. S., & Eastman, K. K. (1997). The nature and implications of contextual influences on transformational leadership: A conceptual examination. *Academy of Management Review, 22*, 80–109.

Peterson, S. J., Walumbwa, F. O., Byron, K., & Myrowitz, J. (2009). CEO positive psychological traits, transformational leadership, and firm performance in high-technology start-up and established firms. *Journal of Management, 35*, 348–368.

Pieterse, A. N., van Knippenberg, D., Schippers, M., & Stam, D. (2010). Transformational and transactional leadership and innovative behaviour: The moderating role of psychological empowerment. *Journal of Organizational Behavior, 31*, 609–623.

Platow, M. J., Durante, M., Williams, N., Garrett, M., Walshe, J., Cincotta, S., . . . Barutchu, A. (1999). The contribution of sport fan social identity to the production of prosocial behaviour. *Group Dynamics: Theory, Research, and Practice, 3*, 161–169.

Platow, M. J., Filardo, F., Troselj, L., Grace, D. M., & Ryan, M. K. (2006). Non-instrumental voice and extra-role behaviour. *European Journal of Social Psychology, 36*, 135–146.

Platow, M. J., Grace, D. M., Wilson, N., Burton, D., & Wilson, A. (2008). Psychological group memberships as outcomes of resource distributions. *European Journal of Social Psychology, 38*, 836–851.

Platow, M. J., Haslam, S. A., Both, A., Chew, I., Cuddon, M., Goharpey, N., . . . Grace, D. M. (2005). "It's not funny when they're laughing": A self-categorization social-influence analysis of canned laughter. *Journal of Experimental Social Psychology, 41*, 542–550.

Platow, M. J., Haslam, S. A., Foddy, M., & Grace, D. M. (2003). Leadership as the outcome of self-categorization processes. In D. van Knippenberg & M. A. Hogg (Eds.), *Leadership and power. Identity processes in groups and organizations* (pp. 34–47). London, UK: Sage.

Platow, M. J., Hoar, S., Reid, S., Harley, K., & Morrison, D. (1997). Endorsement of distributively fair and unfair leaders in interpersonal and intergroup situations. *European Journal of Social Psychology, 27*, 465–494.

Platow, M. J., Reicher, S. D., & Haslam, S. A. (2009). On the social psychology of intergroup leadership: The importance of social identity and self-categorization processes. In T. Pittinsky (Ed.), *Crossing the divide: Intergroup leadership in a world of difference* (pp. 31–42). Boston: Harvard Business School Press.

Platow, M. J., Reid, S., & Andrew, S. (1998). Leadership endorsement: The role of distributive and procedural behaviour in interpersonal and intergroup contexts. *Group Processes and Intergroup Relations, 1*, 35–47.

Platow, M. J., & van Knippenberg, D. (2001). A social identity analysis of leadership endorsement: The effects of leader ingroup prototypicality and distributive intergroup fairness. *Personality and Social Psychology Bulletin, 27*, 1508–1519.

Platow, M. J., van Knippenberg, D., Haslam, S. A., van Knippenberg, B., & Spears, R. (2006). A special gift we bestow on you for being representative of us: Considering leader charisma from a self-categorization perspective. *British Journal of Social Psychology, 45*, 303–320.

Platow, M. J., Voudouris, N. J., Gilbert, N., Jamieson, R., Najdovski, L., Papaleo, N., . . . Terry, L. (2007). In-group reassurance in a pain setting produces lower levels of physiological arousal: Direct support for a self-categorization analysis of social influence. *European Journal of Social Psychology, 37*, 649–660.

Rabbie, J. M., & Bekkers, F. (1978). Threatened leadership and intergroup competition. *European Journal of Social Psychology, 8*, 9–20.

Rasinski, K., & Tyler, T. R. (1988). Fairness and vote choice in the 1984 presidential election. *American Politics Quarterly, 16*, 5–24.

Reicher, S., Haslam, S. A., & Hopkins, N. (2005). Social identity and the dynamics of leadership: Leaders and followers as collaborative agents in the transformation of social reality. *Leadership Quarterly, 16*, 547–568.

Reicher, S., & Hopkins, N. (1996). Self-category constructions in political rhetoric; an analysis of Thatcher's and Kinnock's speeches concerning the British miners' strike (1984–5). *European Journal of Social Psychology, 26*, 353–371.

Reicher, S., Hopkins, N., & Condor, S. (1997). Stereotype construction as a strategy of influence. In R. Spears, P. Oakes, S. A. Haslam, & N. Ellemers (Eds.), *Stereotyping and social identity* (pp. 94–118). Oxford, UK: Blackwell.

Reicher, S. D., Drury, J., Hopkins, N., & Stott, C. (2001). A model of crowd protoypes an dcrowd leadership. In C. Barker, M. Lavalette, & A. Johnson (Eds.), *Leadership and social movements* (pp. 178–195). Manchester, UK: Manchester University Press.

Reicher, S. D., & Haslam, S. A. (2006). Rethinking the psychology of tyranny: The BBC Prison Study. *British Journal of Social Psychology, 45*, 1–40.

Resick, C. J., Whitman, D. S., Weingarden, S. M., & Hiller, N. (2009). The bright-side and dark-side of CEO personality: Examining core self-evaluations, narcissism, transformational leadership and strategic influence. *Journal of Applied Psychology, 94*, 1365–1381.

Reynolds, K. J., & Platow, M. J. (2003). Why power in organizations really should be shared: Understanding power through the perils of powerlessness. In S. A. Haslam, D. van Knippenberg, M. J. Platow, & N. Ellemers (Eds.), *Social identity at work: Developing theory for organizational practice* (pp. 173–188). Philadelphia: Psychology Press.

Ridgeway, C. L. (2001). Gender, status, and leadership. *Journal of Social Issues, 57*, 637–655.

Rosch, E. (1978). Principles of categorization. In E. Rosch & B. B. Lloyd (Eds.), *Cognition and categorization* (pp. 28–49). Hillsdale, NJ: Erlbaum.

Rosette, A. S., Leonardelli, G. J., & Phillips, K. W. (2008). The white standard: Racial bias in leader categorization. *Journal of Applied Psychology, 93*, 758–777.

Sani, F., & Reicher, S. (1998). When consensus fails: An analysis of the schism within the Italian Communist Party (1991). *European Journal of Social Psychology, 28*, 623–645.

Saroglou, V. (2002). Religion and the five factors of personality: A meta-analytic review. *Personality and Individual Differences, 32*, 15–25.

Scandura, T. A., & Graen, G. B. (1984). Moderating effects of initial leader-member exchange status on the effects of leadership intervention. *Journal of Applied Psychology, 69*, 428–436.

Schmitt, M., & Dörfel, M. (1999). Procedural injustice at work, justice sensitivity, job satisfaction and psychosomatic well-being. *European Journal of Social Psychology, 29*, 443–453.

Schriesheim, C. A., Castro, S. L., & Cogliser, C. C. (1999). Leader-member exchange (LMX) research: A comprehensive review of theory, measurement, and data-analytic practices. *Leadership Quarterly, 10*, 63–113.

Shamir, B., House, R. J., & Arthur, M. B. (1993). The motivational effects of charismatic leadership: A self-concept based theory. *Organization Science, 4*, 577–594.

Sherif, M. (1962). Intergroup relations and leadership: Introductory statement. In M. Sherif (Ed.), *Intergroup relations and leadership: Approaches and research in industrial, ethnic, cultural, and political areas* (pp. 3–21). New York: Wiley.

Sherif, M., & Sherif, C. W. (1969). *Social psychology.* New York: Harper & Row.

Simons, T., & Roberson, Q. (2003). Why managers should care about fairness: The effects of aggregate justice perceptions on organizational outcomes. *Journal of Applied Psychology, 88*, 432–443.

Skarlicki, D. P., & Folger, R. (1997). Retaliation in the workplace: The roles of distributive, procedural, and interactional justice. *Journal of Applied Psychology, 82*, 434–443.

Stogdill, R. M. (1948). Personal factors associated with leadership: A survey of the literature. *Journal of Psychology, 25*, 35–71.

Stogdill, R. M. (1950). Leadership, membership, and organization. *Psychological Bulletin, 47*, 1–14.

Tajfel, H., Billig, M. G., Bundy, R. P., & Flament, C. (1971). Social categorization and intergroup behaviour. *European Journal of Social Psychology, 1*, 149–177.

Tajfel, H., & Turner, J. C. (1986). The social identity theory of inter-group behaviour. In S. Worchel & L. W. Austin (Eds.), *Psychology of intergroup relations* (pp. 7–24). Chicago: Nelson-Hall.

Tanis, M., & Postmes, T. (2005). A social identity approach to trust: Interpersonal perception, group membership and trusting behaviour. *European Journal of Social Psychology, 35*, 413–424.

Turner, J. C. (1991). *Social influence.* Milton Keynes, UK: Open University Press.

Turner, J. C. (2005). Examining the nature of power: A three-process theory. *European Journal of Social Psychology, 35*, 1–22.

Turner, J. C., & Haslam, S. A. (2001). Social identity, organizations, and leadership. In M. E. Turner (Ed.), *Groups at work: Theory and research. Applied social research* (pp. 25–65). Mahwah, NJ: Erlbaum.

Turner, J. C., Hogg, M. A., Oakes, P. J., Reicher, S. D., & Wetherell, M. S. (1987). *Rediscovering the social group: A self-categorization theory.* Oxford, UK: Blackwell.

Tyler, T. R., & Degoey, P. (1995). Collective restraint in social dilemmas: Procedural justice and social identification effects on support for authorities. *Journal of Personality and Social Psychology, 69*, 482–497.

Tyler, T. R., Degoey, P., & Smith, H. J. (1996). Understanding why the fairness of group procedures matters: A test of the psychological dynamics of the group-value model. *Journal of Personality and Social Psychology, 70*, 913–930.

van Kleef, G. A., Steinel, W., van Knippenberg, D., Hogg, M. A., & Svensson, A. (2007). Group member prototypicality and intergroup negotiation: How one's standing in the group affects negotiation behaviour. *British Journal of Social Psychology, 46*, 129–152.

van Knippenberg, B., van Knippenberg, D., de Cremer, D., & Hogg, M. A. (2005). Research in leadership, self, and identity: A sample of the present and a glimpse of the future. *Leadership Quarterly, 16*, 495–499.

van Knippenberg, D., Lossie, N., & Wilke, H. (1994). In-group prototypicality and persuasion: Determinants of heuristic and systematic message processing. *British Journal of Social Psychology, 33,* 289–300.

Vermunt, R., Wit, A. P., van den Bos, K., & Lind, E. A. (1996). The effects of unfair procedure on affect and protest. *Social Justice Research, 9,* 109–119.

Walumbwa, F. O., Avolio, B. J., & Zhu, W. (2008). How transformational leadership weaves its influence on individual job performance: The role of identification and efficacy beliefs. *Personnel Psychology, 61,* 793–825.

Wang, G., Oh, I-S., Courtright, S. H., & Colbert, A. E. (2011). Transformational leadership and performance across criteria and levels: A meta-analytic review of 25 years of research. *Group and Organization Management, 36,* 223–270.

White, R., & Lippitt, R. (1960). Leader behaviour and member reaction in three "social climates." In D. Cartwright & A. F. Zander (Eds.), *Group dynamics* (2nd ed., pp. 527–553). Evanston, IL: Row Peterson.

Wit, A., & Wilke, H. (1988). Subordinates' endorsement of an allocating leader in a commons dilemma: An equity theoretical approach. *Journal of Economic Psychology, 9,* 151–168.

Zaccaro, S. J. (2012). Individual differences and leadership: Contributions to a third tipping point. *Leadership Quarterly, 23,* 718–728.

# PART 5

# Social Influence in Applied Settings

# Social Influence and Clinical Intervention

Martin Heesacker

**Abstract**

Kelman's tripartite model organizes advances in research on social influence and clinical outcomes. Recent years have produced important advances in the field's understanding of compliance, identification, and internalization. In compliance research, normative feedback has, under some conditions, altered clinically relevant behaviors, including drug abuse and gambling. In identification research, the therapeutic alliance has predicted 5–30 percent of the variance in clinical outcomes. Evidence suggests a causal relationship between alliance and outcomes, and that ruptured alliances can be repaired. Internalization theories from basic science have generated little recent clinical application research, but a clinician-developed approach to internalization, motivational interviewing, has generated substantial recent research. Though mixed, enough evidence supports motivational interviewing to warrant additional research.

**Key Words:** social influence, psychotherapy, counseling, clinical outcomes, working alliance, persuasion, social norms, compliance, identification, internalization

Since Richard McFall's *Manifesto for a Science of Clinical Psychology* was first published (McFall, 1991), and for many psychologists long before then (see Rogers, 1946, which describes the first psychotherapy outcome study), psychotherapeutic psychology has required a scientific, empirical foundation. The present chapter celebrates and extends this commitment by focusing on how the psychology of social influence has advanced and can advance clinical intervention.

Recent work by Lilienfeld and colleagues underscores why practitioners must embrace scientists in their empirical evaluation of clinical applications (Lilienfeld, Ritschel, Lynn, Cautin, & Latzman, 2014). In a paper destined to become a classic and a mainstay of clinical education, Lilienfeld and colleagues catalogued 26 distinct reasons why ineffective therapies are wrongly concluded to be effective. These reasons fall into three broad categories: (1) misperception that clients have changed when they have not; (2) misattribution of real client

change to treatment when change was caused by extraneous factors, such as regression to the mean; and (3) misattribution of real client change to treatment when it was caused by nonspecific factors, such as novelty or effort justification.

Scientific evaluation is necessary for treatments, to illuminate for practitioners and the public whether evidence supports or fails to support use of those treatments. In addition, several practitioner concerns identified by Heesacker and Lichtenberg (2012), among others, are important for clinical intervention scientists to bear in mind as they do their work because they limit the degree to which practitioners adopt science-based treatments. These include weaknesses in science, practitioners' difficulty understanding scientific presentations of treatments, and differing conceptual foci of practitioners and scientists (practitioners focusing more on individuals, and scientists focusing more upon groups, as a gross generalization; see also Lilienfeld, et al. 2013, for another perspective on therapists' resistance to practice science and how to address that resistance).

An explicit and continuing focus on theory is perhaps the most effective way for science to benefit practice and for practice to benefit science. Why? First, as Kurt Lewin (1951, p. 169) observed, "Nothing is so practical as a good theory." Theories are very useful tools in guiding clinical application because they can guide therapist thoughts and actions in a wide array of circumstances with a wide array of clients and clinical concerns. Second, theory functions as a psychological Rosetta Stone, according to Heesacker and Lichtenberg (2012), creating a common communication pathway for scientists and practitioners, who otherwise often feel like residents of the biblical city of Babel. Finally, theory allows for an iterative process of theory validation, oscillating from theory to laboratory to practical application and back again, a process that Robert Cialdini originally articulated as "full cycle social psychology" (Cialdini, 1980), but which can be applied just as effectively to clinical interventions.

This chapter is science-based, à la McFall's *Manifesto*. It is simultaneously practitioner friendly, à la Heesacker and Lichtenberg's (2012) call for social and behavioral scientists to make every effort to engage and embrace psychotherapy practitioners and to have their scholarship embraced by practitioners. Finally, this chapter is theory driven because theory provides the language that unites scientists and practitioners in a common intellectual discourse.

## Scope of the Review of Research

This chapter will cover reviews of research as well as some selected, original research conducted since the latest review of an area within social influence. The focus will be on social influence research linked to clinically relevant outcomes. Generally, this means clinicians using social influence theories and strategies to improve clinical outcomes for clients, but as the reader will see, it also means social influence theory and research applied *to* clinicians, with the purpose of identifying factors that increase and decrease the degree to which clinicians use scientifically supported social influence scholarship in clinical practice.

Analogue studies, which are studies that use research participants who are not seeking clinical treatment and typically do not represent any clinical population, will not be the focus of this chapter. An example of an analogue study is an investigation of responses from collegiate research participants who are watching videos of others in psychotherapy. This chapter will review clinically relevant laboratory studies and field studies. The laboratory studies reviewed typically provided manualized treatment to research participants in need of clinical intervention, by therapists trained to adhere to the manual. The field studies reviewed often involved research that dealt with people who sought clinical help in traditional treatment settings. This distinction is important because the therapists, therapy, and clients all tend to differ between these types of settings. Some other field studies I review are large-scale studies that used social influence scholarship to alter clinically relevant behavior, such as alcohol abuse, through public media.

I uncovered more clinical research in the laboratory and in media campaigns than in clinical settings. This could be a consequence of the ease with which laboratory studies and media campaigns are conducted, as well as the experimental control that is possible in laboratories, but not in regular treatment facilities. Also, it is challenging to find clients and therapists in traditional settings who are willing to work with researchers. Unlike university clinical laboratories, there is rarely an incentive for research participation in traditional settings. The problem with only studying people in laboratory clinical settings is that the results may not generalize to traditional settings. Without field studies, it is challenging to know which clinical laboratory findings will and which will not transfer to more typical clinical settings. With the scope of research now described, it is time to define the terms "social influence" and "clinical intervention."

### *Defining Social Influence*

Kelman (1958) defined social influence as the change in behavior caused by other people or groups. It is comprised of three components: compliance, identification, and internalization. The review of the literature on social influence and clinical intervention is organized around these components. The first social influence component is *compliance*, which is cooperation motivated by the desire for social acceptance. People are influenced to comply because they wish to avoid negative social consequences and garner positive social consequences (see Hodges's chapter, this volume). Compliance can occur in the absence of identification and internalization, so attitudes may or may not change. An example of compliance social influence is social norm–marketing campaigns on college campuses (e.g., Neighbors et al., 2010), which are attempts to alter high-risk behaviors such as heavy drinking or high-risk sex by indicating that relatively few others engage in these behaviors or that others dislike those behaviors.

Kelman's second social influence component is *identification*, which occurs because of the motive to identify with or relate to a person or group. In identification, people are motivated to be influenced by a person or group so that they can establish or maintain a social connection. Research on the therapeutic alliance exemplifies this category. For example, the strength of the connection between client and therapist has been shown to account for a large portion of psychotherapeutic effectiveness, perhaps as much as 30 percent (Lambert & Barley, 2001).

Kelman's third component of social influence is *internalization*, which is the internal acceptance of norms or beliefs. This internal acceptance generally coincides with the person's existing values. An example of internalization research comes from the central route of Petty and Cacioppo's (1986) elaboration likelihood model, in which clients are persuaded by their therapists to change their thought-based attitudes on a clinically relevant topic, with enduring attitude change and behavior change as a result (see review: Perrin, Heesacker, Smith, & Pendley, 2010).

### Defining Clinical Intervention

Clinical intervention can be defined as "an intervention carried out to improve, maintain or assess the health of a person, in a clinical situation" (Australian Institute of Health and Welfare, 2014). A very broad definition such as this one is appropriate for this chapter because it allows the review of an array of important and promising studies on a range of clinical activities. Any one set of clinical activities (such as individual psychotherapy) may or may not be relevant to a given clinician or clinical researcher, but another set (such as psychoeducation) might. Next, I review this research.

### Review of Social Influence Clinical Intervention Research

The story of social influence clinical intervention research is a story of feast and famine—feast with regard to compliance and identification, and a fascinating combination of feast *and* famine with regard to internalization. Since the last major review of clinical applications of social influence research (Heppner & Claiborn, 1989), a lot of work has been published on normative influence (which is a compliance process in which people's perceptions of

the relevant social norms influence their behavior so that the group will accept or value them), and a lot of research has been published about working alliance (an identification process in which there is a social connection, or alliance, between therapist and client). These relative feasts in clinically useful compliance and identification research stand in contrast to a relative famine of *traditional* internalization research on clinical intervention. The picture for internalization research is of relatively little traditional social influence research, but a great deal of research on an internalization approach developed clinically (motivational interviewing; e.g., Miller & Rollnick, 2002). The lack of traditional internalization research is not only in quantity but also in quality because of a paucity of such research that studies the so-called *strong* measure outcomes praised by Heppner and Claiborn (1989, to be described next). On the other hand, clinically relevant social influence research on motivational interviewing (MI), which is a more recent clinical approach to enhance internalization, is plentiful.

In reviewing the social influence clinical literature, Heppner and Claiborn (1989) made a very useful distinction between strong and weak *outcomes* of social influence. Weak outcomes are self-reports of clients' satisfaction or similar self-report variables. In contrast, strong outcomes are measures of changes in actual behavior (also see Hoyt, 1996, for a similar perspective regarding strong and weak evidence of social influence and data supporting the distinction, though Hoyt valued both kinds of evidence). Their logic for the strong-weak distinction is found in Nisbett and Wilson's (1977) demonstration "that people have difficulty accurately reporting their internal cognitive, sensory, and perceptual processes in ambiguous situations" (Heppner & Claiborn, 1989, p. 383), though people rarely recognize that difficulty.

### Compliance: Social Norms and Clinical Outcomes

The social norms approach to social influence (see Nolan's chapter on social norms, this volume) posits that through three interconnected social norm misperceptions, people are influenced to engage in high-risk or dysfunctional behaviors, such as overdrinking, sexual assault, or excessive gambling, because they believe that to do so is normative, when in fact it is not. There is clear evidence that descriptive norms (describing what is typical) such as these and others do, indeed, influence behavior, accounting for nearly 20 percent of behavioral intention, according to a meta-analysis of over 8,000 participants (Rivas & Sheeran, 2003).

The demonstrated influence of descriptive norms can be contrasted with research on injunctive norms (describing what people typically approve or disapprove of). For example, research on a high-risk group provides evidence that injunctive norms are not very influential (an effect found in several other studies as well) and that descriptive norms, especially the norms of friends, are more influential. In a secondary data analysis of the impact of descriptive and injunctive norms on collegians who had gotten in trouble for violating university alcohol use policies, Carey, Henson, Carey, and Maisto (2010) found that injunctive norms were ineffective in changing drinking behavior, but that descriptive norms strongly predicted drinking reduction. For both male and female participants, changes in their perceptions of how much their friends drink (when delivered by a therapist, not a computer program) was a stronger predictor of participant drinking reductions than either changes in perceived local drinking norms or national norms. Their data also replicated a finding by Suls and Green (2003) that males are more likely than females to model the drinking rates of same-sex drinkers, even if they are strangers.

A. D. Berkowitz (2004) identified pluralistic ignorance, false consensus, and false uniqueness as types of misperceptions about norms that support and encourage dysfunctional behavior. Berkowitz contended that pluralistic ignorance is the most common type of normative misperception. It occurs when people are typical of their peers in some way, yet believe they are not. For example, collegians who drink moderately often assume, incorrectly, that most of their peers drink alcohol heavily (Baer, Stacy, & Larimer, 1991). False consensus, on the other hand, occurs when those who engage in unusually high levels of problematic behavior believe that most people also engage in high levels of these behaviors, when in fact, they do not. For example, collegiate binge drinkers may grossly overestimate how many other collegians are also binge drinkers (e.g., Kypri & Langley, 2003; McAlaney & McMahon, 2007; although there is debate about the magnitude of this overestimation, see Pape, 2012, and commentaries in response). In contrast to false consensus, false uniqueness, which is similar to pluralistic ignorance, occurs among people who engage in relatively unusual behaviors but overestimate how unusual they are. So people who engage in healthy and low-risk behaviors wrongly believe that few if any others in their peer group also engage in these healthy and low-risk behaviors. For example, alcohol abstainers know they are unusual but grossly *under*estimate the number of other abstainers in their peer group.

A longitudinal study by Cullum, O'Grady, Armeli, and Tennen (2013) documents that pro-drinking norms can indeed alter drinking behavior via increased social influence attempts designed to increase the drinking of others. Nonetheless, it remains unclear why or whether only those engaging in problematic behaviors are likely to fall prey to false consensus errors and why only those engaging in healthy or low-risk behaviors would fall prey to false uniqueness errors. Nonetheless, Berkowitz (2004, p. 9) reported that over 55 studies provide support for the operation of pluralistic ignorance and false consensus effects for collegians. In fact, Berkowitz suggested that only a single published investigation has failed to report these collegiate normative misperceptions and that study has been criticized in two other published studies for suffering from methodological problems (2004, p. 10). Moreover, Berkowitz reviewed results of a literature review, five longitudinal studies, and seven other studies, all of which supported the link between norm misperceptions and problematic behaviors, such as underage drinking, DUIs, and other high-risk drinking behaviors. This approach has paved the way for a host of clinical interventions, some of which were effective, though not all.

Though not formally peer reviewed, Berkowitz's (2004) review discusses lots of published research documenting benefits resulting from correcting inaccurate social norms that support such problematic behaviors as alcohol abuse, driving under the influence of alcohol, smoking, and engaging in sexual assault. Often these studies were pre-experiments (pre-post investigations without control groups to rule out such threats to validity as history, instrumentation, or maturation). However, Berkowitz reported that in more recent research, social norms intervention groups have outperformed comparison groups with regard to positive health outcomes (presumably in quasi-experiments, which have control groups to which participants are not randomly assigned) and that in multicomponent interventions, the social norm component outperformed most others (pp. 2–3). Buttressing Berkowitz's enthusiasm, a review of 13 studies of normative feedback alcohol intervention programs on college campuses revealed that over three-fourths reported significant reductions in drinking compared to a control or quasi-control group (Walters & Neighbors, 2005). A meta-analysis of 8,000 participants conducted by Rivas and Sheeran (2003) revealed that descriptive norms correlated $r = 0.44$ with behavioral intentions. In fact, descriptive norms explained an additional 5 percent in behavioral intention variance even after participant attitudes, *subjective* norms, and perceived behavioral control were statistically controlled.

In contrast to the promising future documented in the review by Berkowitz (2004), Walters and Neighbors (2005), and Rivas and Sheeran's (2003) meta-analysis, a review by DeJong et al. (2009) found little evidence for the effectiveness of social norms marketing campaigns. DeJong and colleagues reviewed the published research on university-based social norms public health campaigns. Comparison of the alcohol-related outcome measures of universities that had or had not implemented these campaigns revealed no significant outcome differences.

Work by Cialdini and colleagues on norms (Kallgren, Reno, & Cialdini, 2000) provides a way of reconciling Berkowitz's enthusiasm with the unimpressive results obtained across college campuses. Kallgren et al. pointed out that norms, whether descriptive or injunctive, only affect behavior when they are *salient*. So perhaps campus campaigns provided important normative information but failed to influence behavior because they were too removed in time from when potential drinking behavior occurred. In other words, when students were making their drinking choices, perhaps those campaign-activated norms were no longer salient and therefore had no impact on behavior.

A study that provides another explanation for the failure to find an effect of social norms marketing campaigns on college campuses was conducted by Scribner et al. (2011), who found that when there were fewer drinking outlets for collegians, these campaigns had an effect on the number of drinks consumed. Campuses where there were many drinking outlets showed no effect. These findings suggest that the believability of the norms advocated in these campaigns may have impacted their effectiveness. In a college town where stores that sell alcohol are ubiquitous, it simply is not credible to say that the norm is to drink moderately or not at all. If no one drinks, why do they have all these stores that sell alcohol? In a town where these stores are few and far between, a claim that moderation and abstinence are normative is more believable.

Yet another insight into potential causes of the failure of these social norms campaigns comes from Thombs et al. (2007). In a report on their 2-year study of a residence hall–based social norms campaign, Thombs and colleagues suggested that the very small differences between the social norm group and the control group in average evening blood alcohol level may have been the result of a small number of students reacting *negatively* to the campaign and drinking *more* in reaction to it. They cautioned that "Social norms interventions could provoke some episodes of excessive drinking in students who find these messages objectionable" (p. 325).

A limitation identified in a review by Lewis and Neighbors (2006) involves college students' motives for drinking. In one study, they found that those who drank for social reasons were more likely to be influenced by social norms than those who reported drinking for other reasons, such as to cope with stress. However, this effect may be an artifact of the inherently social focus of norms campaigns. An approach that focused on coping with stress, rather than social norms, might have more impact on those who drink to cope and less on those who drink to socialize.

Another possible explanation for the failure to find social norms marketing reliably affecting clinical outcomes on college campuses comes from research by Cullum, O'Grady, Sandoval, Armeli, and Tennen (2013), who reported that peer affiliation led to reduced influence from social norms. Specifically, when perceived social support was low, the amount participants reported drinking in a daily diary study was strongly influenced by social norms. When perceived social support was high, participants' drinking behavior was not strongly influenced by social norms. The authors suggest that people rely on norms to guide their behavior primarily in the absence of adequate social support. Support for this explanation comes from a large-scale field experiment of groups of young people crossing the border from San Ysidro, California, to Tijuana, Mexico, where the drinking age is lower (Johnson, 2012). As small groups came to the border, researchers randomly assigned each *group* to a different social norm marketing condition. The key point is that all members of the group were kept together for the intervention, which ostensibly preserved the social support function of group membership. Despite creating reliable changes in participants' drinking-related norms, those normative changes were not accompanied by corresponding differences in blood alcohol as measured by a breathalyzer, assessed as they returned to California after an evening in

Tijuana. The data from Cullum et al. (2013) suggest that social support from the group may have made reliance on norms unnecessary.

A final possible explanation for the failure to find social norms marketing effects involves the medium (e.g., face to face, online, public media). Consistent with the perceived social support explanation provided by Cullum et al. (2013), a meta-analysis of 22 social norms marketing studies on young people's alcohol misuse found that social norms marketing effectively altered drinking behavior *only* when delivered online (Moreira, Smith, & Foxcroft, 2009). Presumably, when norms are presented online, the social support effect is minimized because people are probably alone at their computers. This effect may be truer for women than men. In a 2-year randomized control trial, Neighbors et al. (2010) found that Web-based normative feedback was effective for female college student participants, but not males, a finding consistent with the finding by Suls and Green (2003) reported earlier, that male participants were more influenced by drinking rates of other same-sex drinkers, even strangers. Men may be somewhat more prone to adhere to social cues, and women may be somewhat more prone to adhere to normative cues.

Work assessing a social norm explanation for obesity conducted by Hruschka, Brewis, Wutich, and Morin (2011) suggests yet another limitation of social norms marketing for clinical interventions. Changing descriptive norms may not be a promising obesity treatment strategy because less than 20 percent of the variance in obesity in their community sample of 101 women was accounted for by normative explanations (assessed by reviewing input from participants' regular social contacts). This finding is all the more surprising because of the research cited earlier that showed women to be more prone to normative cues than social cues.

One additional limit on social norms marketing campaigns was identified by Perkins, Linkenbach, Lewis, and Neighbors (2010), whose quasi-experimental study focused on drunk driving among drivers aged 21–34 years in Montana. They expressed concern that fear-appeal campaigns focused on drunk driving may in fact thwart social norms marketing campaigns like theirs: "Fear-based media efforts may compete with social norms messages by solidifying misperceptions about the prevalence of impaired driving; thereby potentially reducing the impact of a social norms campaign" (p. 867).

In summary, research documents that descriptive norms influence behavior, whereas injunctive norms are not very influential. There is also evidence that misperceptions about norms support and encourage dysfunctional behavior. Yet, it remains unclear why or whether only those engaging in problematic behaviors are likely to fall prey to false consensus errors and why only those engaging in healthy or low-risk behaviors would fall prey to false uniqueness errors. The norm misperception perspective has led to a host of clinical interventions, some of which were effective, though not all. Over three fourths of normative feedback alcohol intervention programs on college campuses reported significant reductions in drinking compared to a control or quasi-control group, but a review of social norms marketing campaigns on college campuses found little evidence for their effectiveness. These potential boundary conditions may explain these inconsistent findings: Norms may only affect problematic behavior when they are salient, believable, and not objectionable; when motives for engaging in the behaviors are social; when direct peer social support is lacking; when the campaign is delivered online; and when fear appeals do not interfere by making the undesired behavior salient, thereby strengthening misperceptions about its prevalence.

### Identification: Working Alliance and Clinical Outcomes

Many studies have been conducted concerning the working alliance since the term was coined by Greenson (1965; though Horvath, Del Re, Flückiger, & Symonds, 2011, among others, source the term "therapeutic alliance" to Zetzel, 1956, p. 369). The working or therapeutic alliance refers to the relationship between therapist and client. Research on working alliance falls into Kelman's category of identification because the alliance strengthens the client's identification with the therapist. The process of gaining an alliance is preceded by the client's assessment of a therapist's relevant traits, such as attractiveness, credibility, and expertness (Strong & Matross, 1973). The client would be more willing to identify with the therapist if a relationship with the therapist is seen as beneficial. This alliance is not simply an end in itself.

A recent meta-analysis mirrors prior reviews in documenting that the working alliance, which is one aspect of the therapeutic relationship, improves clinical outcomes, accounting for 7.6 percent of the outcome variance, across an array of psychotherapeutic outcomes (Horvath et al., 2011). Several meta-analyses have calculated an overall effect of alliance on therapeutic outcome. For example, Flückiger, Del Re, Wampold, Symonds, & Horvath (2012), found a moderate effect of alliance, generally, on therapeutic outcome ($r = .30$). This finding coincides with findings from a different analysis conducted in 2012 by Horvath et al. ($r = .28$). They found that researcher allegiance (whether or not the researcher had been involved in writing or developing the procedure for testing the alliance or outcome measure) had a moderating effect on the alliance in the beginning stages of therapy. However, the effect disappeared as treatment continued. They also found no effect for different types of outcome measures (e.g., Heppner and Claiborn's strong vs. weak outcomes) and no difference between cognitive-behavioral therapy and other therapies (Flückiger et al., 2012). A meta-analysis of the related skill of therapist empathy suggests a similar result: Therapist empathy was moderately predictive of clinical outcomes ($r = +.31$) across 59 studies that included over 3,500 participants (Elliott, Bohart, Watson, & Greenberg, 2011).

A review by Marshall and Burton (2010) suggests that research on sexual offenders, domestic violence offenders, and other legal offenders who are in psychotherapy show similar associations between alliance variables and psychotherapy outcomes:

> In both the adult and juvenile offending literature, process variables, compared to the effects of specific techniques, account for approximately twice the variance observed in treatment-induced changes. In particular, characteristics of the therapist (e.g., empathy, warmth, support), the quality of the therapeutic alliance, and the nature of the group climate (particularly the cohesiveness of the group, and the level of group expressiveness), are all significantly related to the positive benefits that result from treatment.
>
> (p. 147, though the picture is less rosy when the focus is on violent offenders; see the review by Kozar & Day, 2012)

There are other benefits to having a strong therapeutic alliance, including client retention in therapy. For example, Sharf, Primavera, and Diener (2010) found the weaker the therapeutic alliance, the more likely the client was to drop out of therapy. Their findings, which also controlled for education as a moderating factor, coincided with Wierzbicki and Pekarik's (1993) meta-analysis, which found that the more education the client had, the weaker the relationship between working alliance and dropping out of treatment. Perhaps participants with more education were able to delay gratification from the relationship longer than those with less education. Willingness to delay gratification has been linked to more success in school (Mischel, Shoda, & Rodriguez, 1989). Perhaps those with more education were better able to focus on abstract and intellectual reasons to stay in treatment, to compensate for the inadequacies of the therapeutic relationship. Participants with less education instead may have relied more on their immediate experience of therapeutic relationship in deciding whether to stay in therapy, rather than waiting for the relationship to improve.

Horvath et al. call for the alliance to be accepted as an integral part of the therapeutic process. In their meta-analysis, Horvath et al. offered several prescriptions about how the working alliance should be addressed in therapy. They argued that that alliance is not independent from the clinical processes administered to produce positive outcomes. They view it as an essential part of the clinical process. They argued that developing the therapeutic alliance is a skill, just like other skills clinicians must develop and maintain to be effective. They also argued that developing at least a minimally adequate working alliance early in therapy is crucial to having a successful therapeutic relationship (Horvath et al., 2011).

Haverkamp (2012) reviewed the counseling relationship literature, of which working alliance is an essential part, but not the only part. She reported that in earlier reviews, the counseling relationship was estimated to account for approximately one third of outcome variance, whereas more recent meta-analyses place the outcome variance accounted for much lower, for example in one study, approximately 5 percent of the variance. She suggested that the six-fold difference (5 percent vs. 33 percent) may reflect a difference in the focus of the reviews. The earlier reviews, she suggested, had a narrower focus, whereas the later review assessed the overall working alliance effect across a much broader swath of studies. Regardless of whether the figure is 5 percent or 33 percent, clearly working alliance is accounting for an important part of outcome but nothing approaching the lion's share of the outcome variance. The question is why not?

One answer resides in measurement. Haverkamp (2012) suggested that definitional issues plague this research area, just as Miller and Rollnick (2013) suggested with regard to motivational interviewing, addressed later in this chapter. If a construct is not clearly defined—and according to Haverkamp

(2012) this one is not—its operationalization, which in this case means its reliable and valid measurement, will remain elusive. So one potential answer is that unreliability and invalidity in the measurement of working alliance attenuate the correlation between working alliance and therapeutic outcomes, suggesting that the estimates and especially the lower bound estimates of variance accounted for in outcome are *underestimates*. A second answer resides in the diversity of outcomes. It may be the case that working alliance powerfully affects some outcomes and not others. Here it is instructive to note that Haverkamp (2012) suggested that the *client's* perception of the working alliance, but not that of the therapist or an outside observer, predicted outcomes. This finding suggests that perhaps working alliance functions more like another outcome measure, rather than like an independent variable. If so, the so-called soft outcomes identified by Heppner and Claiborn (1989) would be more likely to be influenced by working alliance. However, a meta-analysis by Del Re, Flückiger, Horvath, Symonds, and Wampold (2012) suggests this is *not* the case. The outcome variance accounted for by therapists in the alliance is actually greater than that for clients, when controlling for a host of potentially confounding factors. In addition, outcomes of different types did not differ in this large-scale meta-analysis, suggesting that the alliance does not primarily influence soft outcomes.

A final possible explanation is that the working alliance is necessary, but insufficient to produce salubrious therapeutic outcomes, an explanation consistent with common factors theory, which posits that working alliance is one of *several* necessary factors. Evidence for this final limitation is provided by a psychiatric nursing study conducted in Britain, in which Hewitt and Coffey (2005) concluded that "Therapeutic relationships are necessary but not sufficient to enable change when working with people with schizophrenia" (p. 561). Hewitt and Coffey called for a more structured approach to therapy, combining the therapeutic relationship (alliance) with cognitive-behavioral therapy. Left out of this analysis is the concept of alliance *ruptures*, which are reductions in the strength of the working or therapeutic alliance.

## ALLIANCE RUPTURES

The concept of ruptures underscores that learning what *not* to do in pursuit of social influence is as important as learning what to do.

According to research reviewed by Norcross and Wampold (2011), empirical evidence points to several social-influence techniques and processes that do *not* work because they rupture alliances. These include confrontations, negative interpersonal processes, assumptions, therapist-centricity, rigidity, and the concept of the Procrustean bed. The Procrustean bed is a metaphor for the habit to force an "identical therapy relationship (and treatment method)" onto all clients (Norcross & Wampold, 2011, p. 101). Many of these alliance-rupturing features were anticipated by Rogerian client-centered therapy, which systematically trained therapists to avoid each of these behaviors long before empirical evidence documented their ill effects on clinical outcomes. To achieve better clinical outcomes, perhaps it is necessary to reiterate these lessons to generations of clinicians largely unfamiliar with Rogers's psychotherapy approach.

The findings from Norcross and Wampold generally mirror results of a review conducted a decade earlier by Ackerman and Hilsenroth (2001; as well as a 2003 review by Marshall et al.), who reported that reviewed studies identified the following therapist characteristics as harmful to the working alliance: rigidity; uncertainty; and being critical, distant, tense, or distracted. In addition, these therapeutic interventions also harmed the working alliance: overstructuring therapy, inappropriate self-disclosure, unyielding use of transference interpretation, and inappropriate use of silence. Regardless of theoretical orientation, psychotherapy training should instruct therapists-in-training (and continuing education should remind practicing therapists) to avoid engaging in these therapeutically dysfunctional behaviors. When therapists engage in these behaviors, the therapeutic alliance is compromised, and so is the client's identification with the therapist.

One especially bright note with regard to alliance ruptures is that they can be repaired, with the result of improved clinical outcomes. Safran, Muran, and Eubanks-Carter (2011) reported the results of two meta-analyses of research on rupture repair. The first meta-analyzed three studies of clinical relationship rupture repairs and showed that repair was associated with better clinical outcomes ($r = +.24$, 148 participants). Their second meta-analysis was of eight studies with 376 participants and revealed a moderately large relationship between training therapists in techniques to repair ruptured alliances and clinical outcomes ($r = +.65$).

Clearly, working or therapeutic alliance is associated with improved clinical outcomes with adult clients, but does this effectiveness extend to children and adolescence? From a Kelmanian perspective, this is an important issue because at the heart of the therapeutic alliance is Kelman's concept of identification. Do children and adolescence identify with psychotherapists (who are after all adults)? The empirical evidence suggests yes (Haverkamp, 2012), but with some limitations. For example, a study of children referred for oppositional and antisocial behaviors found that children higher on social and intellectual competencies formed better therapeutic alliances (Kazdin & Durbin, 2012). A meta-analysis of 16 studies that measured alliance prospectively and later measured outcome in over 1,300 children and adolescents found a correlation of $r = +.22$ between alliance scores on commonly accepted measures and psychotherapy outcome. The effect was marginally stronger for children than for adolescents, which may have reflected developmentally appropriate resistance to adult input by adolescents (Shirk, Carver, & Brown, 2011). In a meta-analysis of 38 studies of children and adolescents, McLeod (2011) found an average effect size of $r = +.14$. The difference in effect size estimates between McLeod (2011) and Shirk et al. (2011) may be the result of McLeod's inclusion of a more heterogeneous set of studies, with regard to measurement of the alliance.

## Internalization and Clinical Outcomes

Readers will recall that the third of Kelman's social influence processes is *internalization*, which is the internal acceptance of norms or beliefs. Internalization stands in contrast to both compliance and identification because the motive is to hold accurate attitudes or beliefs, whether they do or do not garner approval and whether they do or do not strengthen a social connection. In clinical outcome research, two approaches, Petty and Cacioppo's (1986) elaboration likelihood model (ELM) and Miller and Rollnick's (2013) motivational interviewing (MI), have been the most prominent and important.

### ELABORATION LIKELIHOOD MODEL

The elaboration likelihood model was developed in the laboratory by two social psychologists,

Richard E. Petty and John T. Cacioppo, who sought to understand why some attitude changes stand the test of time, whereas others are more easily achieved, but transitory, and why some attitudes strongly influence behavior whereas others do not (Petty & Cacioppo, 1986). These distinctions are just the ones most critical to clinical application, with goals that virtually always include enduring changes in behavior. The ELM not only explains the difference between types of attitude change, but it also has emerged as a comprehensive theory of attitude change. Petty and Cacioppo also sought to explain the diverse and often contradictory findings in the existing attitude change literature, such as the finding that source credibility (for example, the therapist's credibility with a client) could have a wide range of effects, including attitude change, boomerang change (which is attitude change in the direction *opposite* to the direction of the influence attempt), and no change. Again, these are just the kinds of issues that are directly relevant to clinical interventions.

According to the ELM (Petty & Cacioppo, 1986), there are two routes to processing, the central route and peripheral route. Whereas the *central* route produces deep, thoughtful cognitive processing, resulting in internalization (using Kelman's language) and behavior change, the ELM's *peripheral* route is based on superficial or heuristic cognitive processing. For example, superficial processing could be based on the client's perception of the therapist's attractiveness or credibility, or based on the use of other heuristics. This could include the therapist's use of big words as a social influence attempt to convey a sense of expertness (see the review of this literature by Hoyt, 1996, which concludes that therapist credibility does significantly predict clinical outcomes—more strongly for weak than strong measures of outcomes, but it is not sufficient to account for social influence in clinical outcomes). The ELM has been nominated by a number of applied scientists as an approach that can account for the variability of client change in counseling, as well as serve as an effective bridge between social influence theory and clinical intervention (e.g., McNeill & Stoltenberg, 1989).

The ELM is not the only depth-of-processing model of attitude change that has garnered substantial empirical support. Both Russell Fazio's MODE model (Motivation and Opportunity as DEterminants of the attitude-behavior relation; Fazio, 1990) and Shelly Chaiken's systematic vs. heuristic model of persuasion (Chaiken, 1980) are important depth-of-processing (or dual-process) theories. Space limitations and the fact that I uncovered fewer clinically relevant studies based on these two models keep me from discussing them further, but both have important implications for clinical practice, implications generally in line with those of ELM and MI.

The ELM's central route represents Kelman's (1958) internalization process of social influence. For central route attitude change to occur, Petty and Cacioppo (1986) posited that certain conditions must be met. First, the person (in this case, the client in the clinical intervention) must be motivated to think about the persuasive message that the speaker (in this case, the therapist) is giving. Second, the client must have the ability to process this message. Third, the nature of the client's thoughts (or cognitive responses) triggered by the therapist's message needs to be mostly favorable toward the position advocated by the therapist. Finally, these message-triggered thoughts must be stored in memory so that they are readily accessible in the future. When these four conditions have been met, the result is ideal for clinical interventions; these changed attitudes endure over time, are resistant to counterpersuasion, and influence subsequent behavior. This is every clinician's dream! So it is no surprise that a number of articles and book chapters have been written for clinicians about this model (see review by Perrin et al., 2010).

Given its obvious relevance, published research on the application of the ELM to clinical practice has had a curious pattern of growth. In 1981, Petty and Cacioppo published their first comprehensive presentation of the ELM (Petty & Cacioppo, 1981). However, research on clinical applications of the ELM was not immediately forthcoming, with the first clinical application publications occurring 5 years later (Heesacker, 1986; Stoltenberg, 1986). By the early 1990s a few additional studies and book chapters had been published on the use of the ELM in clinical applications, including an outstanding paper by McNeill and Stoltenberg (1989). Research continued throughout the 1990s but never seemed to gain momentum and in recent years has lost momentum, despite publication of a book chapter in 1991 by Petty, Cacioppo, and their colleagues outlining a program of research for clinical applications of the ELM (Cacioppo, Claiborn, Petty, & Heesacker, 1991). Perrin et al. (2010) discussed possible reasons for this decline, which include a change in the psychotherapy culture that views

persuasion by a health care professional as culturally insensitive. Perrin et al. proposed a more culturally sensitive approach using the ELM.

Recently, Luttrell, Briñol, and Petty (2014) have written a chapter linking a very popular clinical application, mindfulness and mindful living, with the ELM. Likewise, a few years ago Green and Brock (2005) wrote a chapter on the links between persuasion and personal narratives, which are an important part of many psychotherapies. This novel approach of linking existing basic social influence theory and research to an already popular and widely used clinical application holds real promise for greater application of this social influence approach in clinical settings. On the other hand, there has already been an explosion of research in another internalization social influence approach to clinical application: motivational interviewing (MI; Miller & Rollnick, 2013).

## MOTIVATIONAL INTERVIEWING

MI is a therapy approach developed by practitioners, and it has been found effective on several fronts. Miller and Rollnick (2013), the developers of motivational interviewing, argued that even their book-length treatment is inadequate to cover all of the research conducted on and about the motivational interviewing approach. What follows is an overview based largely on their 2013 book and on the most recently published meta-analyses.

In contrast to the disappointing lack of research conducted on the promising clinical applications of the ELM and other dual-processing models, recent research on MI is abundant and continues to grow. MI is "a collaborative conversation style for strengthening a person's own motivation and commitment to change" (Miller & Rollnick, 2013, p. 12). Whether the focus is behavior change or emotional change, MI focuses on the outcome of client change. Miller and Rollnick asserted that MI is never done "to" a person, but rather "with" or "for" a person (2013, p. 15). Though MI was originally developed for alcohol and drug abuse, it is not a specific treatment model. It takes a decidedly client-centered approach, acknowledging that the therapeutic process, especially the part that involves the internalization change, requires active therapist–client collaboration. Some have even suggested that MI might best serve as a pretreatment preparation (e.g., Westra, Arkowitz, & Dozois, 2009), rather than as a stand-alone treatment.

Although it generally reflects a client-centered approach, MI provides clear directives and focuses on client change (Miller & Rollnick, 2013, p. 37). One of the first directives of MI is to develop a working alliance, a phase Miller and Rollnick (2013) entitle *Engaging* (p. 37). Initially, the therapist establishes a working relationship or alliance with the client. Similar to research described regarding factors that harm the working alliance, Miller and Rollnick (2013) described a few "don'ts" in the *Engaging* phase. Miller and Rollnick's (2013) Assessment Trap, Expert Trap, Premature Focus Trap, Labeling Trap, Blaming Trap, and Chat Trap (pp. 40–45) are all labels for ways in which therapists could weaken the working alliance and thereby limit psychotherapy outcomes. These traps largely mirror alliance research findings that have already been reviewed in this chapter.

Though the *Engaging* stage of MI reflects Kelman's concept of identification, MI goes further than identification, by facilitating the internalization process in later stages. After the engaging phase, MI therapists shift to *Focusing*, in which the therapist attempts to establish, with the client, specific goals or outcomes to direct their remaining work together (Miller & Rollnick, 2013, p. 101).

After the focusing phase comes the phase where Kelman's internationalization processes should operate, called *Evoking*. In this phase, the therapist listens for and supports the client's change talk, or expressed desire to behave differently, while accepting and expecting client ambivalence with regard to making changes (Miller & Rollnick, pp. 155, 166). Following their exploration of the motivation to change, client and counselor shift to the phase called *Planning*, in which a specific plan for change is developed, implemented, and supported (Miller & Rollnick, 2013, pp. 255–301).

Because MI was first developed as a treatment for substance abuse disorders, the earliest outcome research overrepresented these disorders. However, MI has been applied to many other therapy concerns, including gambling and eating disorders, unhealthy behaviors, parenting, and emotional well-being (Lundahl & Burke, 2009).

In a randomized clinical trial, Larimer et al. (2012) found that a personalized feedback intervention (PFI), which is feedback delivered to a participant in a motivational interviewing style, lowered perceived gambling norms. PFI and cognitive-behavioral therapy (CBT) both led to decreases in gambling related problems, but only PFI led to a reduction in perceived gambling norms. Also, multiple doses of CBT had less of an effect on frequency and perceived norms than just one dose of PFI. This may indicate that CBT, while having the right content focus, may not have targeted fundamental attitude change, or internalization, as well as MI does.

In Chapter 27 of their 2013 book, Miller and Rollnick summarized the research literature on motivational interviewing. Among the most relevant and important findings and conclusions are those that follow. A meta-analysis conducted by Vasilaki, Hosier, and Cox (2006) found that approximately an hour and a half of MI was more effective than no treatment in the short run (approximately 3 months). Vasilaki and colleagues also reported that an hour of MI was more effective than other treatments. MI was not compared directly to *each* specific treatment, but instead to the *group* of non-MI treatments, potentially masking the superiority of one or more of the comparison treatments because it was averaged with others.

Miller and Rollnick (2013, p. 280) reported wide variability in the research findings about MI's effectiveness and explored the nature of this variability in some detail. Some reviews reported no substantial treatment effect, whereas some reviews reported small to medium-sized treatment effects (e.g., Carey, Scott-Sheldon, Carey, & DeMartini, 2007; Lundahl & Burke, 2009), and some reviews reported showing substantial variability in MI's effectiveness as a function of who was doing therapy, the site in which therapy was conducted, and the researchers who conducted the studies.

Regarding therapist skill, many reviewed studies did not include measures assessing the degree to which the therapist actually followed MI directives. On the other hand, overadherence to those directives violates MI's warning against overrigidity. According to Miller and Rollnick (2013), adhering too rigidly to manualized treatment directives would not allow for a therapist to respond in a fluid manner, thus reducing the effectiveness of MI-based therapy, a prediction supported empirically in a meta-analysis by Hettema, Steele, and Miller (2005), who reported that manualized MI treatment was half as effective on average as MI treatment that allowed for greater variability in application.

Finally, one key to the success of MI is its explicit avoidance of confrontational treatments that often have been used in addiction therapy. One of MI's early goals is to gain a working alliance within which to foster and direct change talk. However, it is not clear whether MI therapists consistently adhere to this nonconfrontation directive (Miller & Rollnick, 2013, pp. 26–27). This concern about adherence to directives in MI is part of the larger issue just discussed, which is that Miller and Rollnick have not provided explicit standards for MI practice because they are concerned that overly codifying an approach that evolved naturally might be counter-productive. On the other hand, not doing so raises questions about (a) whether research on MI reflects standard or idiosyncratic practice, and (b) whether deviating *from* MI actually *improves* outcomes. From the evidence available, it is difficult to assess whether MI therapists are applying MI faithfully but flexibly or whether, instead, they are improving outcomes by applying interventions that are not part of MI. A meta-analysis of MI as a treatment for adolescent substance abuse by Barnett, Sussman, Smith, Rohrback, and Spruijt-Metz (2012) suggests a preliminary answer. They found no difference for the effectiveness of interventions that adhered exclusively to MI versus those that included elements of other treatment approaches, suggesting that flexibility in application of MI, and not introduction of non-MI treatment elements, best accounts for the finding that rigidly manualized MI was less effective than flexibly applied MI. Future research should specify and assess the conditions under which MI is effective and those under which it is less effective or ineffective (see Vasilaki et al., 2006).

## Social Influence on the Adoption of Clinical Interventions

An important, but very different, perspective on social influence and clinical intervention involves understanding when and why practicing clinicians adopt or fail to adopt a particular clinical intervention. A battle is underway about which therapies and therapeutic technologies are adopted by practicing psychotherapists and why. This battle is about social influence in clinical practice, no less than social influence processes that influence clients directly. No social influence technology can be clinically effective unless it is adopted by clinicians.

This issue can be conceptualized as having two threads: a process thread and a content thread. The process thread involves research on the processes that are more likely versus those less likely to result in clinicians adopting a particular clinical approach or intervention. This process thread reflects that age-old tension between scientists (who believe their research is relevant to clinical science, and who are frustrated with practitioners ignoring the scientific literature and instead engaging in what these scientists fear is non–scientifically supported clinical practice) and practitioners (who report finding

journal articles difficult to follow and largely irrelevant to practice, and who find scientific conclusions difficult or impractical to implement). A review of these process factors by Heesacker and Lichtenberg (2012) is instructive. They reported that these four challenges affect the process by which clinicians adopt treatments and technologies: (a) epistemic style differences between scientists and practitioners, with some studies indicating that practitioners select treatments based on the compatibility with their epistemic style (e.g., rationalist versus constructivist), whereas scientists advocate that selection is based on the degree of empirical support for the treatment; (b) weaknesses in science, with concerns raised about over focus on statistical significance and under focus on clinical significance (a concern mirrored in the scientific community starting with a 1960 *Psychological Bulletin* paper by Rozeboom and continuing through 2014, with a *Psychological Science* article by Cumming entitled *The New Statistics*), with concerns raised about the failure of psychological clinical science to follow established protocols for randomized clinical trials, and too much focus on linear effects when clinicians frequently conceptualize clinical causes recursively; (c) difficulty in understanding science, with the concern that scientists typically write to other scientists, rather than practitioners, and that as quality of the communications about clinical science improves, so does the understanding and implementation of that science by practitioners; and (d) practitioners and scientists lack a common conceptual focus, with scientists typically maintaining a *problem* focus (e.g., social influence or depression) and practitioners typically maintaining a client focus (e.g., this particular individual or couple).

The content thread involves the very active current debate among clinical scientists over what constitutes acceptable evidence in support of a particular approach or intervention. To simplify a complex debate, the major rift here is between adherents to a common factors model (e.g., Wampold, Imel, & Miller, 2009) and adherents to a specific ingredients or medical model (e.g., Barlow, 2010; Lilienfeld et al., 2014). A common factors model holds that the factors that particular therapies have in common, and not the specific treatment ingredients posited by the authors of the therapies as curative, are responsible for the well-documented effectiveness of psychotherapy. Evidence in support of this view comes from a series of meta-analyses showing that most of the major and commonly accepted psychotherapies are similar in their effectiveness for most problems (beginning with Smith & Glass, 1977) and evidence that there is little or no dose–response relationship between the putative active ingredient in most major therapies and outcome success (Messer & Wampold, 2002). A specific ingredients model holds that effective treatment results from particular theoretically relevant components being delivered in psychotherapy. Chambless and Ollendick (2001), for example, provided what at the time was viewed as a comprehensive list of specific treatments that were proven best to treat various disorders; for example, applied relaxation and cognitive-behavioral therapy were listed as the proven treatments of choice for generalized anxiety disorder (p. 692).

Clearly, it cannot be the case both that all major therapies are similarly effective in treating the range of mental disorders and that some major therapies are more effective than others in treating specific disorders. Though it cannot be the case, credible evidence exists on both sides of the issue. Unless and until this contradiction is resolved, the battle for the hearts and minds of clinicians will rage on, with the scientific credibility of psychotherapy with the public the clear victim (see Begley, 2009, for an example of threats to the scientific credibility of psychotherapy).

## Conclusions

Kelman's tripartite model of social influence remains a useful one for conceptualizing social influence and clinical outcomes. Each of Kelman's three categories, compliance, identification, and internalization, has seen important clinical application advances in recent years, exemplifying the Allen and Sager song lyrics "Everything old is new again." In compliance, although the evidence is complex and mixed, the concept of normative feedback to reduce clinically problematic behaviors has, under some conditions, altered people's clinically relevant behaviors, including drug abuse and gambling. Future research should be devoted to identifying the conditions under which normative feedback is effective in influencing clinically relevant behavior. Existing research points to a number of promising leads, which must be explored and unified in ways that practitioners and policy makers can readily use.

In identification, research on the working or therapeutic alliance (which, from Kelman's perspective, is about clients identifying with therapists) has clearly shown that perhaps over 30 percent of the variance in clinical outcomes is predicted by the quality of the alliance between therapist and client.

Indeed, substantial evidence exists that the relationship is a causal one. One of the most important recent findings is that when this alliance is damaged or ineffective, it can be repaired and clinical outcomes and therapy are improved.

In internalization, a curious state of affairs exists, in which internalization theory and research by basic scientists (e.g., dual-processing models such as the elaboration likelihood model of attitude change and the MODE model) in recent years have generated relatively little published science in clinical applications, despite their indisputable promise. Renewed scientific interest in improving clinical outcomes through these basic-science theories may prove to be the single most beneficial focus of future research in this area. In contrast to internalization scholarship from basic scientists, clinician-developed motivational interviewing (Miller & Rollnick, 2013) has generated a great deal of research on clinical applications in recent years. Although, like the social norms interventions research discussed under compliance, the evidence about the effectiveness of MI in improving clinical outcomes is mixed and complicated. Nonetheless, there is sufficient support for the effectiveness of MI that scholars will be wise to pursue research on MI as a social influence tool for improving clinical outcomes.

Finally, a burgeoning interest area related to social influence involves a different target audience, namely clinicians. Clinicians are, indeed, a very important target audience for social influence related to clinical application because the best clinical applications of social influence will remain ineffective unless they are widely adopted and implemented by clinicians. The field has, in recent years, begun a debate regarding the criteria to be used for the adoption of clinical interventions by therapists, as well as a greater focus on identifying factors that advance, and factors that impede, adoption of clinical application technologies by practitioners.

## Future Directions

Arguably *the* most important future direction in this area is refocusing the efforts of social influence scholars back onto clinical applications of social influence theory and research. A review of all articles published since 2009 in the *Journal of Social and Clinical Psychology*, the one major scholarly journal devoted to clinical applications of social psychology, uncovered only two articles directly relevant to this review, suggesting that social influence scholars may not be producing much publishable research related to clinical applications, or if they are, it is not appearing in the one journal devoted to this type of research. This finding is consistent with a review of part of this literature by Perrin et al. (2010), in which they documented a major decline in published attitude change and persuasion research applied to clinical outcomes. It is also consistent with the pattern of publications reviewed in this chapter, in which most of the reviewed scholarship appears to have come from clinical scientists rather than from social psychologists. This trend represents a major concern, because, as Paul Meehl (1978, p. 806) wrote years ago, "Theories in 'soft' areas of psychology lack the cumulative character of scientific knowledge. They tend neither to be refuted nor corroborated, but instead merely fade away as people lose interest." These publishing trends support the concern that this group of basic social influence theories—promising though they are—may be fading away from psychological clinical science. The public, and those in need of psychological services in particular, will pay the price in interventions that are less influential and therefore less effective in improving mental health. Arguably, the most critical future direction is to reactivate interest in this interface among this generation of social influence scholars and their graduate students. What follows is a brief description of factors that may facilitate this reactivation and those that may hinder it.

Several factors may have led to a decline in social psychologists contributing to clinical applications of social influence research. These same factors may also hinder a reactivation of their interest in this research. One of these is the very heavy focus in recent psychological clinical science on manualized treatments and randomized clinical trials (RCTs). Social psychologists generally have not engaged in the extensive codification required of manualized treatments and have not generally involved themselves in extensive training programs for clinicians who provide experimental clinical treatments. Likewise, though extensively trained in experimentation, social psychologists are unlikely to be trained in RCT procedures. So they may not generally think of RCT designs for their studies, and therefore their studies are less likely to focus on clinical applications. If they do focus on clinical applications, they are less likely to do so in ways that garner favorable reviews from journals specializing in clinical applications. A closely related concern was articulated by Levenson (2007) in a chapter on the future of the clinical science movement in psychology, "Clinical science is highly time consuming" (p. 355). Social psychologists can often conduct nonclinical studies more quickly, which also deters them from researching clinical applications. Another factor that may deter social influence research on clinical applications is that approaches that directly and unapologetically focus on influencing clients are increasingly viewed as incompatible with multicultural psychology's sensitivity to domination of members of marginalized groups by those in power, such as psychotherapists and scientists. This multicultural perspective is embraced more in counseling psychology than clinical psychology, but it is also increasingly being embraced in both psychotherapy specialties. So the concern is that when social influence clinical application research is published, there may be no substantial practitioner constituency championing its use.

Despite these deterrents, a number of factors may *facilitate* this reactivation. These include the fact that this is a relatively uncontested scientific area, which favors the chances of success for scholars who choose to work in it. In contrast to basic social influence research, social influence clinical application is an area with relatively little scientific competition, and yet it is, undoubtedly, important scholarship. This perspective mirrors a TED Talk by Edward O. Wilson (2012), in which he urged young scientists who wish to make an immediate impact on science to avoid the highly populated research areas, in favor of relatively unplowed scholarly ground. Another facilitating factor is federal funding priorities. Clinical applications fall squarely within the funding priorities of the National Institutes of Health (including, for example, the National Institute of Mental Health, the National Institute on Drug Abuse, and the National Institute on Alcohol Abuse and Alcoholism), which provided $20 billion in research funding in fiscal 2013 (National Institutes of Health, 2013). In contrast, the budget of the National Science Foundation, which focuses more on basic research, in fiscal 2013 was only a third that size, $6.9 billion (National Science Foundation, 2013). In this climate of tight funding for social and behavioral science, pursuing funding for clinical application gives social psychologists access to a much larger pool of funds than pursuit of basic science funding. A third and related facilitating factor is the emphasis on federal funding (from both NSF and NIMH) for *translational* science (versus basic science). In translational science, the emphasis is on translating basic science into real-world applications that have benefit for citizens. Clinical applications of basic social influence research are clearly consistent with the priorities of the NSF (2010) and the NIMH (2014). One hallmark of translational research is that it is collaborative (vs. traditional silo science). This collaborative element is yet another facilitating factor. Social psychologists can readily sponsor and participate in collaborative projects on social influence in clinical practice, where they can serve as the experts in basic social and behavioral science who collaborate with applied scientists and health care providers to develop fundable translational science research proposals to support their applied science.

A second and related future direction is to avoid an exclusive focus on traditional one-on-one psychotherapy when applying social influence theory and research to clinical outcomes. Other fruitful application areas include telehealth (e.g., Hanley & Reynolds, 2009), test interpretation (e.g., Claiborn & Hanson, 1999), and supervision of psychotherapy (e.g., Claiborn, Etringer, & Hillerbrand, 1995), as well as group therapy, psychoeducation, and prevention, which have all been mentioned earlier in the chapter.

A third promising future direction involves a conceptual replication and extension of research by Houser, Feldman, Williams, and Fierstien (1998), who asked mental health counselors to identify what, if any, persuasion and social influence tactics they used clinically. Mostly what they discovered was that those mental health practitioners relied on internalization-focused social influence tactics. This finding makes the relative lack of clinical research based on the dual-processing models of attitude change from social psychology particularly disconcerting. Houser et al. found that years of experience as a practicing psychotherapist was unrelated to the types of influence attempts participant practitioners reported making. On the other hand, a behavioral/cognitive-behavioral psychotherapeutic orientation was associated with greater reported use of persuasion and social influence tactics than other orientations. What makes research like this promising for the future is that it allows scholars to understand better the social influence practices in which clinicians engage, at least insofar as their self-reports validly portray their actual clinical practice. These self-reports, especially when coupled with research linking their self-reports with their observed clinical behaviors and with client perceptions of therapist social influence behaviors, have the potential to guide research, clinical training, and continuing education more effectively. For example, studies like this one may uncover social influence attempts that

clinicians engage in commonly but about which there is relatively little research. Any of these understudied but widely used tactics should become top priorities in the agendas of scholars who study clinical application of social influence behaviors. This is because it is important to determine whether these influence attempts are effective or ineffective in actual practice. In addition, it may be very useful to assess whether practitioners are using social influence approaches that have not been carefully studied scientifically, in which case they should be. It may prove useful to assess whether practitioners are using well-established and carefully researched social influence techniques, and if so, whether they are engaging in the best practices, based on the research on those techniques. Finally, assessing which techniques prove most effective in actual practice can provide useful feedback about theories developed through basic science and result in their confirmation, modification, or abandonment, depending on the findings.

A fourth promising future direction for social influence applications to clinical outcomes comes from a recent study of physicians' continuing education (Thase, Stowell, Berry, Mencia, & Blum, 2014). As part of their regular continuing education required for relicensure, a group of physicians volunteered to participate in a three-part performance improvement initiative to improve depression diagnosis and treatment practices. Those who completed the three parts showed major gains in the percentage of patients they screened for depression, the percentage they rescreened on a subsequent visit, and major gains in assessing whether patients were adhering to the prescribed treatment. What makes this promising is, like physicians, licensed psychologists are required to earn continuing education credits as a condition for relicensure, so the degree to which licensed psychologists effectively implement empirically supported social influence procedures with their clients could increase dramatically by adopting this approach to continuing education. One drawback in the study is that only 20 percent of those physicians who initially registered completed all three components, but that completion percentage could be increased dramatically by making receipt of any continuing education credit contingent on successfully completing all three parts of the performance improvement initiative.

A fifth important future direction involves an aspect of internalization that used to be known under the category "fear appeals" (e.g., Rogers & Deckner, 1975; Rogers & Mewborn, 1976; for a revised version of the theory, see Maddux & Rogers, 1983) but that now has evolved into the much broader scholarly area known as "communication of risk" (Arvai & Rivers, 2013). Given the effectiveness of fear appeals as persuasive tools, (despite some real limitations, see for example Dunwoody & Griffin, 2013), this area holds untapped potential for improving internalization of persuasive messages about mental health promotion and the alleviation of mental illness and for adding to the list of don'ts for clinical practice.

A sixth important future direction, also mentioned in the introduction to this chapter, involves focusing on theory as the Rosetta Stone that enhances communication between social influence scholars, whose research can benefit by real-world clinical application, and clinical practitioners, whose practices can benefit from accessible and relevant science (Heesacker & Lichtenberg, 2012). Scientists focus on research problems, not clients, whereas practitioners focus on clients, not science. Fortunately, both focus on scientific theory, so theory can serve as the common language uniting these two complementary groups in their pursuit of effective applications of social influence science.

A seventh direction, one also discussed in the introduction to this chapter, involves the oscillation between clinical practice, theory, laboratory research, and back to clinical practice (see Mortensen & Cialdini's, 2010, full cycle social psychology for a detailed description of this approach). This full-cycle approach is highly consistent with the federal funding emphasis on translational research (discussed earlier) and with federal priorities to enhance the degree to which federal funding meets the health needs of citizens. It also allows for teams of theorists, basic scientists, applied scientists, and practitioners to work together to address clinical applications of social influence theory and research.

As mentioned earlier in the chapter, research should be devoted to identifying the conditions under which normative feedback is and is not effective in influencing clinically relevant behavior. Existing research points to a number of promising leads, which were listed earlier. These leads must be explored and integrated in ways that enable normative feedback approaches to be more useful to practitioners and policy makers in improving clinical outcomes.

A ninth and final future direction was also mentioned earlier in the chapter. Alliance research and motivational interviewing research have both been plagued with definitional challenges that have created ambiguity regarding their effectiveness in improving clinical outcomes. So a future direction is for scholars conducting research in these two areas to meet to resolve these definitional challenges and to conduct research using agreed-upon conceptual and operational definitions wherever feasible, with the goal of clarifying conditions under which these approaches produce improved clinical outcomes.

## Author Note

I would like to acknowledge with gratitude the contributions of Elizabeth Lunior and Jordan Morris for their comments on an earlier draft, and especially Nicole Elimelech and Billy Palmer for their identification of relevant research and their comments on an earlier draft.

## References

Ackerman, S. J., & Hilsenroth, M. J. (2001). A review of therapist characteristics and techniques negatively impacting the therapeutic alliance. *Psychotherapy: Theory, Research, Practice, and Training*, 38(2), 171–185. doi:10.1037/0033-3204.38.2.171

Arvai, J., & Rivers, L., III. (2013). Effective risk communication. New York: Routledge.

Australian Institute of Health and Welfare. (2014). *Clinical intervention*. Retrieved August 2014, from http://meteor.aihw.gov.au/content/index.phtml/itemId/327220

Baer, J. S., Stacy, A., & Larimer, M. (1991). Biases in the perception of drinking norms among college students. *Journal of Studies on Alcohol*, 52(6), 580–586.

Barlow, D. H. (2010). The Dodo bird—again—and again. *Behavior Therapist*, 33(1), 15–16.

Barnett, E., Sussman, S., Smith, C., Rohrbach, L., & Spruijt-Metz, D. (2012). Motivational interviewing for adolescent substance use: A review of the literature. *Addictive Behaviors*, 37(12), 1325–1334. doi:10.1016/j.addbeh.2012.07.001

Begley, S. (2009). Ignoring the evidence: Why do psychologists reject science? *Newsweek*. Retrieved August 2015, from http://www.newsweek.com/why-psychologists-reject-science-begley-81063

Berkowitz. A. D. (2004). *The social norms approach: Theory, research, and annotated bibliography*. Retrieved August 2015, from http://www.alanberkowitz.com/articles/social_norms.pdf

Cacioppo, J. T., Claiborn, C. D., Petty, R. E., & Heesacker, M. (1991). General framework for the study of attitude change in psychotherapy. In C. R. Snyder & D. R. Forsyth (Eds.), *Handbook of social and clinical psychology: The health perspective* (pp. 523–539). New York: Pergamon.

Carey, K. B., Henson, J. M., Carey, M. P., & Maisto, S. A. (2010). Perceived norms mediate effects of a brief motivational intervention for sanctioned college drinkers. *Clinical Psychology: Science and Practice*, 17(1), 58–71. doi:10.1111/j.1468-2850.2009.01194.x

Carey, K. B., Scott-Sheldon, L. A. J., Carey, M. P., & DeMartini, K. S. (2007). Individual-level interventions to reduce college student drinking: A meta-analytic review. *Addictive Behaviors*, 32(11), 2469–2494.

Chaiken, S. (1980). Heuristic versus systematic information processsing and the use of sourse versus message cues in persuasion. *Journal of Personality and Social Psychology*, 39(5), 752–766. doi:10.1037/0022-3514.39.5.752

Chambless, D. L., & Ollendick, T. H. (2001). Empirically supported psychological interventions: Controversies and evidence. *Annual Review of Psychology*, 52, 685–716. doi:0066-4308/01/0201-0685

Cialdini, R. B. (1980). Full-cycle social psychology. In L. Bickman (Ed.), *Applied social psychology annual* (Vol. 1, pp. 21–47). Beverly Hills, CA: Sage.

Claiborn, C. D., Etringer, B. D., & Hillerbrand, E. T. (1995). Influence processes in supervision. *Counselor Education and Supervision*, 35(1), 43–53. doi:10.1002/j.1556-6978.1995. tb00208.x

Claiborn, C. D., & Hanson, W. E. (1999). Test interpretation: A social influence perspective. In J. W. Lichtenberg & R. K. Goodyear (Eds.), *Test interpretation: A science-practice integration* (pp. 151–166). Boston: Allyn & Bacon.

Cullum, J., O'Grady, M., Armeli, S., & Tennen, H. (2012). Change and stability in active and passive social influence dynamics during natural drinking events: A longitudinal measurement-burst study. *Journal of Social and Clinical Psychology*, 31(1), 51–80. doi:10.1521/jscp.2012.31.1.51

Cullum, J., O'Grady, M., Sandoval, P., Armeli, S., & Tennen, H. (2013). Ignoring norms with a little help from my friends: Social support reduces normative influence on drinking behavior. *Journal of Social and Clinical Psychology*, 32(1), 17–33. doi:10.1521/jscp.2013.32.1.17

Cumming, G. (2014). The new statistics: Why and how. *Psychological Science*, 25(1), 7–29. doi:10.1177/0956797613504966

DeJong, W., Schneider, S. K., Towvim, L. G., Murphy, M. J., Doerr, E. E., Simonsen, N. R., ... Scribner, R. A. (2009). A multisite randomized trial of social norms marketing campaigns to reduce college student drinking: a replication failure. *Substance Abuse*, 30(1), 127–140. doi:10.1080/08897070902802059

Del Re, A. C., Flückiger, C., Horvath, A. O., Symonds, D., & Wampold, B. E. (2012). Therapist effects in the therapeutic alliance-outcome relationship: A restricted-maximum likelihood meta-analysis. *Clinical Psychology Review*, 32(7), 642–649. doi:10.1016/j.cpr.2012.07.002

Dunwoody, S., & Griffin, R. J. (2013). The role of channel beliefs in risk information seeking. In J. Arvai & L. Rivers (Eds.), *Effective risk communication* (pp. 220–233). New York: Routledge.

Elliott, R., Bohart, A. C., Watson, J. C., & Greenberg, L. S. (2011). Empathy. *Psychotherapy*, 48(1), 43–49. doi:10.1037/a0022187

Fazio, R. H. (1990). Multiple processes by which attitudes guide behavior: The MODE model as an integrative framework. In M. P. Zanna (Ed.), *Advances in experimental social psychology* (Vol. 23, pp. 75–109). New York: Academic Press.

Flückiger, C., Del Re, A. C., Wampold, B. E., Symonds, D., & Horvath, A. O. (2012). How central is the alliance in psychotherapy? A multilevel longitudinal meta-analysis. *Journal of Counseling Psychology*, 59(1), 10–17. doi:10.1037/a0025749

Green, M. C., & Brock, T. C. (2005). Persuasiveness of narratives. In T. C. Brock, & M. C. Green (Eds.), *Persuasion: Psychological insights and perspectives* (2nd ed., pp. 117–142). Thousand Oaks, CA: Sage.

Greenson, R. R. (1965). The working alliance and the transference neurosis. *Psychoanalysis Quarterly*, 34(2), 155–179.

Hanley, T. R., & Reynolds, D. J., Jr. (2009). Counselling psychology and the internet: A review of the quantitative research into online outcomes and alliances within text-based therapy. *Counselling Psychology Review*, 24(2), 4–13.

Haverkamp, B. E. (2012). The counseling relationship. In E. M. Altmaier & J. C. Hansen (Eds.), *The Oxford handbook of counseling psychology* (pp. 32–70). New York: Oxford University Press.

Heesacker, M. (1986). Counseling pretreatment and the elaboration likelihood model of attitude change. *Journal of Counseling Psychology*, 33(2), 107–114. doi:10.1037/0022-0167.33.2.107

Heesacker, M., & Lichtenberg, J. W. (2012). Theory and research for counseling interventions. In E. M. Altmaier & J. C. Hansen (Eds.), *Oxford handbook of counseling psychology* (pp. 71–94). New York: Oxford University Press.

Heppner, P. P., & Claiborn, C. D. (1989). Social influence research in counseling: A review and critique. *Journal of Counseling Psychology*, 36(3), 365–387. doi:10.1037/0022-0167.36.3.365

Hettema, J., Steele, J., & Miller, W. R. (2005). Motivational interviewing. *Annual Review of Clinical Psychology*, 1, 91–111. doi:10.1146/annurev.clinpsy.1.102803.143833

Hewitt, J., & Coffey, M. (2005). Therapeutic working relationships with people with schizophrenia: Literature review. *Journal of Advanced Nursing*, 52(5), 561–570. doi:10.1111/j.1365-2648.2005.03623.x

Horvath, A. O., Del Re, A. C., Flückiger, C., & Symonds, D. (2011). Alliance in individual psychotherapy. *Psychotherapy*, 48(1), 9–16. doi:10.1037/a0022186

Houser, R., Feldman, M., Williams, K., & Fierstien, J. (1998). Persuasion and social influence tactics used by mental health counselors. *Journal of Mental Health Counseling*, 20(3), 238–249.

Hoyt, W. T. (1996). Antecedents and effects of perceived therapist credibility: A meta-analysis. *Journal of Counseling Psychology*, 43(4), 430–447. doi:10.1037/0022-0167.43.4.430.

Hruschka, D. J., Brewis, A. A., Wutich, A., & Morin, B. (2011). Shared norms and their explanation for the social clustering of obesity. *American Journal of Public Health*, 101(1), S295–S300. doi:10.2105/AJPH.2010.300053

Johnson, M. B. (2012). Experimental test of social norms theory in a real-world drinking environment. *Journal of Studies on Alcohol and Drugs*, 73(5), 851–859.

Kallgren, C. A., Reno, R. R., & Cialdini, R. B. (2000). A focus theory of normative conduct: When norms do and do not affect behavior. *Personality and Social Psychology Bulletin*, 26, 1002–1012. doi:10.1177/01461672002610009

Kazdin, A. E., & Durbin, K. A. (2012). Predictors of child–therapist alliance in cognitive–behavioral treatment of children referred for oppositional and antisocial behavior. *Psychotherapy*, 49(2), 202–217. doi:10.1037/a0027933

Kelman, H. C. (1958). Compliance, identification, and internalization: Three processes of attitude change. *Journal of Conflict Resolution*, 2(1), 51–60. doi:10.1177/002200275800200106

Kozar, C. J., & Day, A. (2012). The therapeutic alliance in offending behavior programs: A necessary and sufficient condition for change? *Aggression and Violent Behavior*, 17, 482–487. doi:10.1016/j.avb.2012.07.004

Kypri, K., & Langley, J. D. (2003). Perceived social norms and their relation to university student drinking. *Journal of Studies of Alcohol*, 64, 829–834.

Lambert, M. J., & Barley, D. E. (2001). Research summary on the therapeutic relationship and psychotherapy outcome. *Psychotherapy: Theory, Research, Practice, Training*, 38(4), 357–361. doi:10.1037/0033-3204.38.4.357

Larimer, M. E., Neighbors, C., Lostutter, T. W., Whiteside, U., Cronce, J. M., Kaysen, D., & Walker, D. (2012). Brief motivational feedback and cognitive behavioral interventions for prevention of disordered gambling: A randomized clinical trial. *Addiction*, 107(6), 1148–1158. doi:10.1111/j.1360-0443.2011.03776.x

Levenson, R. W, (2007). The future of the clinical science movement: Challenges, issues, and opportunities. In T. A Treat, R. R. Bootzin, & T. B. Baker (Eds.), *Psychological clinical science: Papers in honor of Richard M. McFall* (pp. 349–360). New York: Taylor & Francis.

Lewin, K. (1951). *Field theory in social science: Selected theoretical papers.* D. Cartwright (Ed.). New York: Harper & Row.

Lewis, M. A., & Neighbors, C. (2006). Social norms approaches using descriptive drinking norms education: A review of the research on personalized normative feedback. *Journal of American College Health*, 54(4), 213–218. doi:10.3200/JACH.54.4.213-218

Lilienfeld, S. L., Ritschel, L. A., Lynn, S. J., Cautin, R. L., & Latzman, R. D. (2013). Why many clinical psychologists are resistant to evidence-based practice: Root causes and constructive remedies. *Clinical Psychology Review*, 33(7), 883–900. doi:10.1016/j.cpr.2012.09.008

Lilienfeld, S. L., Ritschel, L. A., Lynn, S. J., Cautin, R. L., & Latzman, R. D. (2014). Why ineffective psychotherapies appear to work: A taxonomy of causes of spurious therapeutic effectiveness. *Perspectives on Psychological Science*, 9(4), 355–387. doi:10.1177/1745691614535216

Lundahl, B., & Burke, B. L. (2009). The effectiveness and applicability of motivational interviewing: A practice-friendly review of four meta-analyses. *Journal of Clinical Psychology*, 65(11), 1232–1245. doi:10.1002/jclp.20638

Luttrell, A., Briñol, P., & Petty, R. E. (2014). Mindful versus mindless thinking and persuasion. In A. Le, C. T. Ngnoumen, & E. J. Langer (Eds.), *Wiley Blackwell handbook of mindfulness* (pp. 258–278.). New York: Wiley.

Maddux, J. E., & Rogers, R. W. (1983). Protection motivation and self-efficacy: A revised theory of fear appeals and attitude change. *Journal of Experimental Social Psychology*, 19(5), 469–479. doi:10.1016/0022-1031(83)90023-9

Marshall, W. L., & Burton, D. L. (2010). The importance of group processes in offender treatment. *Aggression and Violent Behavior*, 15(2), 141–149. doi:10.1016/j.avb.2009.08.008

Marshall, W. L., Fernandez, Y. M., Serran, G. A., Mulloy, R., Thornton, D., Mann, R. E., & Anderson, D. (2003). Process variables in the treatment of sexual offenders: A review of the relevant literature. *Aggression and Violent Behavior*, 8(2), 205–234. doi:10.1016/S1359-1789(01)00065-9

McAlaney, J., & McMahon, J. (2007). Normative beliefs, misperceptions, and heavy episodic drinking in a British student sample. *Journal of Studies of Alcohol and Drugs*, 68, 385–392.

McFall, R. M. (1991). Manifesto for a science of clinical psychology. *Clinical Psychologist*, 44(6), 75–88.

McLeod, B. D. (2011). Relation of the alliance with outcomes in youth psychotherapy: A meta-analysis. *Clinical Psychology Review*, 31(4), 603–616. doi:10.1016/j.cpr.2011.02.001

McNeill, B. W., & Stoltenberg, C. D. (1989). Reconceptualizing social influence in counseling: The elaboration likelihood model. *Journal of Counseling Psychology*, 36(1), 24–33. doi:10.1037/0022-0167.36.1.24

Meehl, P. E. (1978). Theoretical risks and tabular asterisks: Sir Karl, Sir Ronald, and the slow progress of soft psychology. *Journal of Consulting and Clinical Psychology*, 46(4), 806–834. doi:10.1037/0022-006X.46.4.806

Messer, S. B., & Wampold, B. E. (2002). Let's face facts: Common factors are more potent than specific therapy ingredients. *Clinical Psychology: Science and Practice*, 9(1), 21–25. doi:10.1093/clipsy.9.1.21

Miller, W. R., & Rollnick, S. (2002). *Motivational interviewing: Preparing people to change* (2nd ed.). New York: Guilford Press.

Miller, W. R., & Rollnick, S. (2013). *Motivational interviewing: Helping people change* (3rd ed.). New York: Guilford Press.

Mischel, W., Shoda, Y., & Rodriguez, M. I. (1989). Delay of gratification in children. *Science*, 244(4907), 933–938. doi:10.1126/science.2658056

Moreira, M. T., Smith, L. A., & Foxcroft, D. (2009). Social norms interventions to reduce alcohol misuse in university or college students. *Cochrane Database of Systematic Reviews*, 8(3), CD006748.

Mortensen, C. R., & Cialdini, R. B. (2010). Full-cycle social psychology for theory and application. *Social and Personality Psychology Compass*, 4(1), 53–63. doi:10.1111/j.1751-9004.2009.00239.x

National Institutes of Health. (2013). *Funding facts*. Retrieved September 2014, from http://report.nih.gov/fundingfacts/fundingfacts.aspx

National Institute of Mental Health. (2014). *NIMH extramural research programs*. Retrieved September 2014, from http://www.nimh.nih.gov/about/organization/nimh-extramural-research-programs.shtml

National Science Foundation. (2010). *The role of the National Science Foundation in the innovation ecosystem*. Retrieved September 2014, from http://www.nsf.gov/eng/iip/innovation.pdf

National Science Foundation. (2013). *Congress completes action on FY 2013 appropriations*. Retrieved September 2014, from http://www.nsf.gov/about/congress/113/highlights/cu13_0409.jsp

Neighbors, C., Lewis, M. A., Atkins, D. C., Jensen, M. M., Walter, T., Fossos, N., & Larimer, M. E. (2010). Efficacy of web-based personalized normative feedback: A two-year randomized controlled trial. *Journal of Consulting and Clinical Psychology*, 78(6), 898–911. doi:10.1037/a0020766

Nisbett, R. E., & Wilson, T. D. (1977). Telling more than we can know: Verbal reports on mental processes. *Psychological Review*, 84(3), 231–259. doi:10.1037/0033-295X.84.3.231

Norcross, J. C., & Wampold, B. E. (2011). Evidence-based therapy relationships: Research on conclusions and clinical practices. *Psychotherapy*, 48(1), 98–102. doi:10.1037/a0022161

Pape, H. (2012). Young people's overestimation of peer substance abuse: An exaggerated phenomenon? *Addiction*, 107(5), 878–884. doi:10.1111/j.1360-0443.2011.03680.x

Perkins, H. W., Linkenbach, J. W., Lewis, M. A., & Neighbors, C. (2010). Effectiveness of social norms media marketing in reducing drinking and driving: A statewide campaign. *Addictive Behaviors*, 35(10), 866–887.

Perrin, P. B., Heesacker, M., Smith, M. B., & Pendley, C. (2010). Social influence processes and persuasion in psychotherapy and counseling. In J. E. Maddux & J. P. Tangney (Eds.), *Social psychological foundations of clinical psychology* (pp. 442–460). New York: Guilford Press.

Petty, R. E., & Cacioppo, J. T. (1986). The elaboration likelihood model of persuasion. In L. Berkowitz (Ed.), *Advances in experimental social psychology* (Vol. 19, pp. 123–205). New York: Academic Press.

Rivas, A., & Sheeran, P. (2003). Descriptive norms as an additional predictor in the theory of planned behaviour: A meta-analysis. *Current Psychology: Developmental, Learning, Personality, Social*, 22(3), 218–233. doi:10.1007/s12144-003-1018-2

Rogers, C. R. (1946). Recent research in nondirective therapy and its implications. *American Journal of Orthopsychiatry*, 16(4), 571–723. doi:10.1111/j.1939-0025.1946.tb05422.x

Rogers, R. W., & Deckner, C. W. (1975). Effects of fear appeals and physiological arousal upon emotion, attitudes, and cigarette smoking. *Journal of Personality and Social Psychology*, 32(2), 222–230. doi:10.1037/0022-3514.32.2.222

Rogers, R. W., & Mewborn, C. R. (1976). Fear appeals and attitude change: Effects of a threat's noxiousness, probability of occurrence, and the efficacy of coping responses. *Journal of Personality and Social Psychology*, 34(1), 54–61. doi:10.1037/0022-3514.34.1.54

Rozeboom, W. W. (1960). The fallacy of the null hypothesis significance test. *Psychological Bulletin*, 57(5), 416–428. doi:10.1037/h0042040

Safran, J. D., Muran, J. C., & Eubanks-Carter, C. (2011). Repairing alliance ruptures. *Psychotherapy*, 48(1), 80–87. doi:10.1037/a0022140

Scribner, R. A., Theall, K. P., Mason, K., Simonsen, N., Schneider, S. K., Towvim, L. G., & DeJong, W. (2011). Alcohol prevention on college campuses: The moderating effect of the alcohol environment on the effectiveness of social norms marketing campaigns. *Journal of Studies on Alcohol and Drugs*, 72(2), 232–239.

Sharf, J., Primavera, L. H., & Diener, M. J. (2010). Dropout and therapeutic alliance: A meta-analysis of adult individual psychotherapy. *Psychotherapy: Theory, Research, Practice, Training*, 47(4), 637–645. doi:10.1037/a0021175

Shirk, S. R., Karver M. S., & Brown, R. (2011). The alliance in child and adolescent psychotherapy. *Psychotherapy*, 48(1), 17–24. doi:10.1037/a0022181

Smith, M. L., & Glass, G. V. (1977). Meta-analysis of psychotherapy outcome studies. *American Psychologist*, 32(9), 752–760. doi:10.1037/0003-066X.32.9.752

Stoltenberg, C. D. (1986). Elaboration likelihood and the counseling process. In F. J. Dorn (Ed.), *The social influence process in counseling and psychotherapy* (pp. 55–64). Springfield, IL: Charles C Thomas.

Strong, S. R., & Matross, R. P. (1973). Change processes in counseling and psychotherapy. *Journal of Counseling Psychology*, 20(1), 25–37. doi:10.1037/h0034055

Suls, J., & Green, P. (2003). Pluralistic ignorance and college student perceptions of gender-specific alcohol norms. *Health Psychology*, 22, 479–486.

Thase, M. E., Stowell, S. A., Berry, C. A., Mencia, W. A., & Blum, J. (2014). A performance improvement initiative for enhancing the care of patients with depression. *Journal of Psychiatric Practice*, 20(4), 276–283. doi:10.1097/01.pra.0000452564.83039.69

Thombs, D. L., Olds, R. S., Osborn, C. J., Casseday, S., Glavin, K., & Berkowitz, A. D. (2007). Outcomes of a technology-based social norms intervention to deter alcohol use in freshman residence halls. *Journal of American College Health*, 55(6), 325–332. doi:10.3200/JACH.55.6.325-332

Vasilaki, E. I., Hosier, S. G., & Cox, W. M. (2006). The efficacy of motivational interviewing as a brief intervention for excessive drinking: A meta-analytic review. *Alcohol and Alcoholism*, 41(3), 328–335. doi:10.1093/alcalc/agl016

Walters, S. T., & Neighbors, C. (2005). Feedback interventions for college alcohol misuse: What, why and for whom? *Addictive Behaviors*, 30(6), 1168–1182. doi:10.1016/j.addbeh.2004.12.005

Wampold, B. E., Imel, Z. E., & Miller, S. D. (2009). Barriers to the dissemination of empirically supported treatments: Matching messages to the evidence. *Behavior Therapist*, 32, 144–155.

Wierzbicki, M., & Pekarik, G. (1993). A meta-analysis of psychotherapy dropout. *Professional Psychology: Research and Practice*, 24(2), 190–195. doi:10.1037/0735-7028.24.2.190

Westra, H. A., Arkowitz, H., & Dozois, D. J. A. (2009). Adding a motivational interviewing pretreatment to cognitive behavioral therapy for generalized anxiety disorder: A preliminary randomized controlled trial. *Journal of Anxiety Disorders*, 23(8), 1106–1117. doi:10.1016/j.janxdis.2009.07.014

Wilson, E. O. (2012). *TED Talk: Advice to young scientists*. Retrieved September 2014, from http://www.ted.com/talks/lang/en/e_o_wilson_advice_to_young_scientists.html

Zetzel, E. R. (1956). Current concepts of transference. *International Journal of Psycho-Analysis*, 37, 369–376.

# Social Influence and Health

Leslie R. Martin *and* M. Robin DiMatteo

**Abstract**

Early in the lives of children, parental influences are strong, and interventions targeting parents are essential to behavior change. In adolescence, peers emerge as critical additions to the influence of family members; their influence can support the growth and maintenance of positive health behaviors, or it can encourage unhealthy choices. Social groups continue to feature prominently in various ways throughout adulthood. A crucial role is played by supportive social networks in the improvement and maintenance of a wide variety of health behaviors, and the availability of normative information affects health choices. Health care providers hold a good deal of power in the practitioner–patient relationship and influence their patients toward health outcomes in a variety of ways. Finally, system-level influences such as public health programs, health-related media messages, and educational interventions can help motivate individuals toward ideal health behaviors.

**Key Words:** social comparison, social norms, modeling, health behavior, influence

We are social beings, influenced from our earliest days by those around us. Social influence is particularly important in the realms of health and health behavior. To date, a large corpus of research has shown that the health behaviors we carry out (or fail to accomplish) are shaped by our families, friends, communities, and the media; we look to these sources for information, inspiration, confirmation, reassurance, and motivation.

In 1959 John French and Bertram Raven described social influence as the change effected in an individual's beliefs, attitudes, or behaviors as a result of the action of someone else. This followed closely on Leon Festinger's (1954) description of his theory of the processes of social comparison (see also Suls & Wheeler, this volume). Much research has been done over the ensuing decades both on social influence itself and on the specific role that social comparisons play in shaping a wide variety of behaviors, including those that are relevant to health. In particular, the differential outcomes associated with upward versus downward comparisons have been of interest.

Upward comparisons are those in which the self is compared with someone who is in a more favorable position; in the realm of health, this might be a person who is more effectively managing her blood glucose, or who is able to run a mile in a shorter period of time. Downward comparisons, on the other hand, evaluate the self relative to someone who holds a less favorable position. In health terms, this might be someone who is more overweight or who has had less success in managing his blood pressure.

Of the two, upward comparisons are more effective for motivating changes (Bandura, 1997; Corcoran, Crusius, & Mussweiler, 2011; Taylor & Lobel, 1989). We strive to be like people we admire, and having the model of someone who is successfully engaging in positive health behaviors can encourage and foster our own success. Trying to improve one's health can sometimes be discouraging, however—it is easy to drift into negative moods and perhaps to feel like giving up after repeatedly succumbing to the temptation to have another dish of ice cream or to remain on the couch after supper rather than going for that walk. In this type of situation, downward comparisons can be useful because they are linked to more positive emotions (Buunk, Collins, Taylor, Van Yperen, & Dakof, 1990; Helgeson & Taylor, 1993; Wills, 1981). Comparing oneself to someone else who has poorer health or who is even less successful at making changes emphasizes the strides that one has already made, or the advantages that one has; these positive emotional states are incompatible with an "I can't do it, I might as well give up" attitude.

Neither form of comparison is ideal in all situations, of course. Data suggest that for individuals who believe that they have little control over outcomes, mood enhancement that normally accrues with downward comparisons is diminished (Buunk et al., 1990; Gibbons, 1999; Testa & Major, 1990) and even when downward comparisons do work to improve mood, they tend not to be potent motivators for change because they frame the challenge in terms of prior successes rather than in terms of one's future goals. In contrast, because they are focused on what might be achieved, upward comparisons tend to foster more ambitious goals (Collins, 1996; Croyle, 1992; Gibbons, 1999), and thus these tend to be the most useful in motivating all sorts of behaviors, including those related to health. But if our own progress toward an ambitious goal (influenced by the achievements of the person to whom we are comparing) seems to be stalled, discouragement can also result (Buunk & Ybema, 1997; Van der Zee, Buunk, Sanderman, Botke, & van den Bergh, 2000). Thus, it is important that comparisons be made to those who are perceived as being at least somewhat similar to us. If we use as comparators individuals who are much more accomplished, our deficits will be highlighted and our progress is likely to seem sluggish or nonexistent—neither condition is useful in motivating ongoing efforts toward goal acquisition.

Social comparisons play an important role in our learning of behaviors, habits, and skills at all ages. And, although the process of social comparison changes and becomes more sophisticated with time, even young children employ this strategy. Conformity can occur without an overt comparison (see Hodges, this volume), but comparisons between self and important adults often result in mimicry for children, as they imitate the grown-up behaviors they see and parrot the words they hear. Many a parent has expressed amazement at the sponge-like quality of a child as she or he repeats a word that was not meant to be overheard or copies an expression that was supposed to pass unnoticed. Thus, it is not surprising that health behaviors, both good and bad, have their earliest roots in the home, influenced by family members.

## Early Social Influences: Parenting and Family

The foundations of healthy (or unhealthy) behavior are typically shaped by parents and caregivers. Many health-relevant behaviors that are developed in childhood become fundamental aspects of one's lifestyle—for example, dietary habits or exercise regimens—and there is growing consensus that important individuals in children's lives should be incorporated into programs aimed at improving children's health (Davison & Birch, 2001). The habits and patterns that are developed in childhood, in turn, play an important role in the avoidance or development of chronic health problems such as cardiovascular disease or Type II diabetes. These lifestyle behaviors can be influenced either by direct instruction or by modeling (teaching by example) on the part of parents (Tinsley, 1992), and data clearly suggest that both the health beliefs and the health behaviors of children are influenced by parental efforts (e.g., Jones, Steer, Rogers, & Emmett, 2010). One review of studies published between 1980 and 2002 demonstrated that parental modeling and involvement in both exercise and healthy eating had significant and long-lasting (beyond adolescence) effects on children's behaviors and beliefs (Norton, Froelicher, Waters, & Carrieri-Kohlman, 2003).

Direct instruction and reinforcement are effective means of molding and strengthening healthy behaviors and minimizing unhealthy ones. Although modeling tends to be effective over an extended developmental period, rules and direct encouragement tend to be more effective for children than for adolescents (Pearson, Biddle, & Gorely, 2009).

In a large-scale community study of children, positive reinforcement for appropriate behaviors and monitoring of health-relevant behaviors were found to be associated with healthier eating and more exercise. On the other hand, parenting styles that were controlling in nature were found to be related to children's poorer eating habits (Arredondo et al., 2006). Similarly, a large cohort study found that encouraging healthy intake and physical activity were positively associated with energy balance and healthy body mass index (BMI).

Arredondo and colleagues also found, however, that the best approaches sometimes varied according to child characteristics (2006). For example, dietary monitoring and restriction were associated with desirable behaviors for children who ate normally but were less helpful for those who were characterized as picky eaters (willing to eat only a few food items) or as being always hungry compared with their peers (Gubbels et al., 2011). The picky or hungry children did respond well to efforts that encouraged healthy food intake instead of restricting undesirable foods. This may be because they were not being pressured to cut down on foods that they liked but rather were encouraged to expand their food preferences, thus focusing on gains rather than losses. The results with picky and hungry children illustrate the importance of tailoring early parenting practices to the characteristics of the individual child, consistent with theory on the development of health behaviors within families (e.g., Birch & Davison, 2001).

Parental modeling of healthy behaviors can also be quite powerful (Wrotniak, Epstein, Paluch, & Roemmich, 2005) and parental changes may predict similar changes in their children. For example, weight loss on the part of a parent has been shown to predict child weight loss (Wrotniak, Epstein, Paluch, & Roemmich, 2004). In this analysis of data from three family-based obesity intervention programs, parental weight loss was an independent predictor of child weight loss—that is, despite whatever other behaviors the children were engaging in as part of their weight-loss regimen, they were more successful if their parent was also successful. This suggests that modeling facilitates goal achievement by processes somewhat different than simply changing behaviors in the shorter term by restricting foods or requiring adherence to an exercise program. This idea is consistent with the conclusions of Pearson and colleagues (2009) whose systematic review suggests that learning by observation or by watching someone model a behavior tends to be effective even after the more direct methods of instruction, monitoring, and encouragement have lost much of their power.

The strength of parental influence is also illustrated by studies showing that interventions aimed at improving children's health behaviors might be most efficient when targeted specifically at parents, rather than at children or at parent–child dyads, which has in the past been the typical strategy. This type of parent-only intervention has been used to address problem behaviors such as tantrums, self-injury, phobias, and verbal aggression in children (Johnson & Katz, 1973), and one literature review compared interventions in which children only, parents only, or a combination were targeted. This comparison found that when parents were exclusively targeted as the agents of change for their overweight children, three elements were improved: the obesogenic environment, health behaviors, and children's weight (Golan, 2006). In fact, targeting of parents shows even better outcomes than when both children and their parents attend sessions together (Golan, Kaufman, & Shahar, 2006). The authors suggest that this may be partly due to the greater opportunity for indulgence and concession when more parties are involved in implementing changes, and they also posit that the lifestyle changes may feel more threatening to children (and they may be more likely to push back) when they are involved in this process that originates outside the family structure. Parent-only interventions are less burdensome and costly than more broadly targeted interventions (Golan, Kaufman, & Shahar, 2006; Janicke et al., 2009) and, although some studies show no differences between approaches that involve or do not involve children (e.g., Boutelle, Cafri, & Crow, 2011; Munsch et al., 2008), the data taken as a whole suggest that focusing solely on parents may be ideal because results appear equivalent or better, with lower cost.

## Social Influences in Adolescence: The Role of Peers and Friends

It has long been recognized that as children move into adolescence, the relative importance of peer groups for influencing some behaviors increases while the overt influence of parents tends to diminish (Berndt, 1979; Lau, Quadrel, & Hartman, 1990). Self-evaluations regarding weight, attractiveness, and competence involve a great deal of social comparison, particularly at this developmental stage (Eisert & Kahle, 1982; Jones, 2001; Mueller, Pearson, Muller, Frank, & Turner, 2010), and perceptions of the behaviors of their friends predict adolescents' own behaviors (Luszczynska, Gibbons, Piko, & Tekozel, 2004; Mueller et al., 2010). These perceptions have strong effects even when they are in error (Prinstein & Wang, 2005). The relative "pull" of family versus peers has, however, been shown to vary both by individual and by behavior type. For example, an early review by Glynn (1981) found that, for alcohol use, the influences of peer and family groups were almost the same; for most illicit drugs, the family's values were more important than those of peer groups;

and, for marijuana use, peers were most influential. More recent research substantiates that the degree of influence wielded by a given person or social group does, indeed, vary according to the behavior type and characteristics of the individuals involved and highlights the complexity of these associations. Regarding characteristics of the target adolescent, a recent review finds that social isolation seems to be a particularly important risk factor for initiation of smoking (Seo & Huang, 2012). With regard to the influence of others one longitudinal study of more than 2,500 adolescents indicated that parental expectations that their adolescent would not use alcohol not only predicted greater self-efficacy for avoiding alcohol but also less association with peers who used alcohol and lower self-reported use (Nash, McQueen, & Bray, 2005). Another analysis of family and peer influences, this time of alcohol, cigarettes, marijuana, and other illicit drugs in a sample of over 4,200 7th–12th graders, confirmed that peer influences are generally quite important, as are parental attitudes and sibling behavior, with parent–child attachment being more weakly associated (Bahr, Hoffman, & Yang, 2005). Interestingly, this study found that although parental attitudes and sibling substance use were related to the subject's use of illicit drugs, their effects seem to be mediated almost entirely by peers. Finally, a recent assessment of the relative importance of parent and peer influences on intentions to smoke cigarettes found that parents initially hold more sway, but as the adolescent grows older, there is a shift. Parental influence declines over time, while peer influence strengthens (Scalici & Schulz, 2014). Thus, parents would do well to discuss both risky and positive health behaviors with their children early and to provide as much guidance as possible in helping their children to select friends. These peers are likely to play an important role in influencing health behaviors—for better or for worse—and knowledge, a sense of self-efficacy for maintaining good health, and a set of like-minded friends may best facilitate long-term positive outcomes.

It is also prudent to note that not all data support the transition of influence from family to peer groups during adolescence. Researchers studying smoking behaviors in more than 3,800 6th–11th graders using a longitudinal design found different results from the standard cross-sectional design studies (Chassin, Presson, Sherman, Montello, & McGrew, 1986). Specifically, they found that peer and family influences on smoking initiation were not significantly different in magnitude from one another between 6th and 11th grade. That is, these researchers failed to find evidence for the often-identified shift in relative influence from parents to peers during this period of life. A recent review (albeit containing many cross-sectional studies) does substantiate the shift in influence from parents to peers (Mulvhill, 2014), but the literature as a whole highlights the great degree of complexity inherent in these associations. Other researchers also confirm that these associations are complex, with parental influences moderating those of peers, such as in the investigation of alcohol use during late adolescence (Wood, Read, Mitchell, & Brand, 2004) and the indirect, protective effects of positive parenting against adolescent smoking (Simons-Morton & Farhat, 2010).

Similar findings exist for positive health behaviors, such as physical activity and healthy eating. Significant others, including family members, friends, and classmates, were found to be important in shaping sports participation in a large sample of 10- to 15-year-olds, with peer influences being especially important for girls (Keresztes, Piko, Pluhar, & Page, 2008). A review extended the latter finding for both boys and girls, and demonstrated that overweight youth were more active when they were with friends (regardless of the weight of the friends) than when they were alone or with family, and that physically active friends/peers increased children's motivation to exercise (Salvy, Bowker, Germeroth, & Barkley, 2012). This peer influence on exercise may be especially relevant to overweight adolescents, as indicated by another study. This work showed that although motivation to exercise and the actual distance biked were somewhat greater for all adolescents when they were in the presence of a friend or peer, the associations were statistically significant only for those who were overweight (Salvy et al., 2009).

Another review also demonstrated the crucial role that friends play in determining the physical activity levels of adolescents (Fitzgerald, Fitzgerald, & Aheme, 2012) with researchers identifying a variety of ways in which peer groups might exert their influence. These ways include the presence of and support from peers, the understood norms within peer groups, and the quality of the friendships themselves. An additional review similarly demonstrated that peer groups exert a meaningful influence on both physical activity and dietary intake for children and adolescents and suggested that peer networks be involved in intervention efforts (Salvy, de la Haye, Bowker, & Hermans, 2012).

The importance of peer networks in enhancing adolescents' health behaviors is echoed in the recommendations emerging from a study of the eating habits of more than 2,000 adolescents in 20 different schools in the Midwestern United States. Significant similarities were seen within groups of friends in the amount of whole grains, vegetables, and dairy products consumed, as well as for whether breakfast was eaten. This research suggests that health professionals should be encouraged to engage the friends of adolescents in interventions designed to improve dietary habits (Bruening et al., 2012).

For young people coping with chronic health problems, incorporating peers and friends into the health management plan can be quite beneficial (La Greca, Bearman, & Moore, 2002). These researchers found that effective maintenance of medical regimens is fostered when young patients affiliate with peers who engage in healthy behavior. Healthy peer groups can create a supportive environment in which the child or adolescent can more easily adapt to the challenges of his or her illness. Thus, whether a young person is dealing with chronic illness, developing health-related habits, or making decisions about high-risk behaviors, peer and friend networks appear to play an important role in facilitating good decision making and engagement in positive health behaviors.

## Influences of Friends and Family in Adulthood

Social comparisons and peer behavior—real or perceived—are important not only to youth but also feature prominently in various ways throughout adulthood. As we shall examine later, the influence of peers can be harnessed to maximize positive health behaviors across all developmental periods.

The social influence of health-relevant behaviors often goes largely unrecognized by the individual, even as it is experienced. For example, social facilitation studies have often shown that more calories are consumed when an individual eats in the presence of others versus alone (e.g., de Castro & de Castro, 1989; Hetherington, Anderson, Norton, & Newson, 2006; Locher, Robinson, Roth, Ritchie, & Burgio, 2005), although some studies show that consumption is only increased when the others are familiar and not when the others are strangers (e.g., de Castro, 1994; Hetherington et al., 2006; Salvy, Howard, Read, & Mele, 2009). Most individuals are not aware of these changes in their eating behaviors.

The complexity of interactions between the social environment and behavior is highlighted, however, by impression management studies, which tend to show the opposite of what social facilitation studies find. The impression management studies suggest that individuals tend to decrease their food and/or calorie consumption in the presence of others (e.g., Roth, Herman, Polivy, & Pliner, 2001; Young, Mizzau, Mai, Sirisegaram, & Wilson, 2009), and this appears to happen most consistently among women who are eating with men. Researchers have used an "inhibitory norms" model to explain these seemingly contradictory sets of findings. They argue that when there are no clear signals of satiety, fullness, or satisfaction, individuals use social norms to determine when to stop eating. Consumption might increase or diminish depending upon the behavior of the comparison subjects and the desire of the individual to impress them; the behavior of others tends to suggest to the individual what his or her own behavior should be (Herman, Roth, & Polivy, 2003; Wansink, 2006).

We often take hints from those around us when we are searching for cues to aid everyday decision making on topics ranging from littering to energy use to food choices. For instance, in Cialdini, Reno, and Kallgren's now classic (1990) study, people were more likely to toss a flyer onto the ground when the area was already littered, indicating a social norm that littering was acceptable, than when the vicinity was trash-free. Similarly, women chose healthier snacks when healthy snack wrappers were visible, suggesting that other people had also chosen a healthy option (Burger et al., 2010); and energy use decreased significantly when people were told that they used more energy than did others living in their neighborhood (Schultz, Nolan, Cialdini, Goldstein, & Griskevicius, 2007). These tendencies are especially pronounced when we are unsure of how to act or truly do not know what option is best. But often social norms prove more influential than factual, objective information and operate even when we already know what we should do.

As an example, one study found that providing normative information on a simple sign ("Did you know? More than 90 percent of the time, people in this building use the stairs instead of the elevator. Why not you?") decreased elevator use by nearly 50 percent in a 1-week period (Burger & Shelton, 2011). Elevator use did not change at all when a sign with no normative data ("Did you know? Taking the stairs instead of the elevator is a good way to get some exercise. Why not try it?") was in place. When we think about health and the many small health-related choices made each day, taking the stairs is a good illustrator of a small-scale behavior that, cumulatively, might make a real difference in a person's fitness levels.

Consistent with data showing that social norms are used for decision making about individual behaviors, other studies illustrate that large-scale health outcomes are also linked to what those around us do. One finding that emerged from the Framingham Heart Study was that having a friend become obese during a given time period was linked to a 57 percent increase in the likelihood of an individual also becoming obese. Individuals were also more likely to become obese if their spouse (37 percent) or an adult sibling (40 percent) did (Christakis & Fowler, 2007). This study strongly hints at the importance of social distance (as opposed to geographic distance), because altering the former changed the magnitude of the observed associations but changes in the latter did not—that is, similarities in outcomes were greater between individuals who were socially closer (e.g., close versus casual friends) but not who were geographically closer (e.g., next-door neighbors versus those living across town). The authors note that because of the time lag observed, the unimportance of geographic distance, and the control of baseline weight, explanations involving shared environmental exposures or genes are less likely than social explanations, and they suggest that changes in social norms seem more likely to be explanatory than processes of imitation. The researchers also posit that although social networks appear to play a role in the obesity epidemic, these same social phenomena might be channeled in ways that promote healthy behaviors. The same social influence that draws individuals into obesity with their friends and families might be used to draw them into exercise and healthy eating along with the important people in their lives. This strategy relies not only on social norms but also on social support.

Indeed, many studies have demonstrated the crucial role played by supportive social networks in the improvement and maintenance of a wide variety of health behaviors, including adherence to medical treatments (DiMatteo, 2004a, 2004b); healthy eating (Emmons, Barbeau, Gutheil, Stryker, & Stoddard, 2007; Ralston, Cohen, Wickrama, & Kwag, 2011); and exercising (Emmons et al., 2007; Kouvonen et al., 2012), as well as positive health outcomes, including healthy aging (Thanakwang & Soonthorndhada, 2011), management of hypertension (Schmitz et al., 2012), and longer life (House, Robbins, & Metzner, 1982; Tucker, Schwartz, Clark, & Friedman, 1999). The efficacy

of incorporating social support and social connectedness into health interventions has also been demonstrated (e.g., Malchodi et al., 2003; Wing & Jeffery, 1999). The Framingham Heart Study, too, found that social influences apply not only to negative health outcomes (e.g., obesity) but also to positive behaviors—for example, a person's chances of smoking decreased by 67 percent, if his or her spouse stopped, and also diminished if a friend or coworker quit (Christakis & Fowler, 2008). The findings from the Framingham Heart Study are especially interesting because they suggest a blurring of the lines between two important forms of social influence: social norms and social support.

Social support is typically divided into the following subtypes: practical help (sometimes called "instrumental" or "tangible" support), informational support, and emotional support (Wills, 1984). Tangible support is concrete in nature—someone driving you to your doctor's appointment or giving you a ride to the gym so you do not miss your weightlifting class. Informational support, as its name implies, takes the form of shared information—someone recommending a safe biking trail or suggesting a new line of healthy snacks. Emotional support involves feelings and emotions—someone providing a listening ear and a shoulder to cry on, for example.

Social support takes different forms, and not all are equally beneficial when it comes to promoting health behaviors. For example, one study (Kouvonen et al., 2012) found that for those who were, at baseline, already reporting appropriate levels of leisure-time physical activity, greater emotional support was related to continuation of the active behavior. But emotional support was not helpful in getting those who were not getting enough exercise to become more active. This study also showed, however, that practical support was associated with maintenance and with improvement of leisure-time physical activity rates over time, both for the already-active and for the more sedentary. The researchers did not comment on why emotional support failed to improve activity levels for the inactive, but it seems likely that the emotional support simply served to reinforce whatever was currently being done. For someone who was already active, emotional support would be reinforcing, but for someone who was not active, the implicit message may have been accepting of the status quo (e.g., "You're fine just as you are, and you needn't change a thing").

An unsupportive network, not surprisingly, can be detrimental to the cultivation and maintenance of health behaviors. Intentionally or not, friends and family can enable and encourage bad habits or addictions, such as by continuing to buy sugary, processed desserts and storing them in cupboards shared with someone who is struggling to eat healthfully (Freeman, 2001; Martin, Haskard-Zolnierek, & DiMatteo, 2010). Unsupportive behaviors (sometimes called "negative social support") can also hinder coping, such as has been shown in patients with chronic obstructive pulmonary disease (COPD) who experience greater anxiety when they perceive that their social network members are insensitive or frequently let them down (DiNicola, Julian, Gregorich, Blanc, & Katz, 2013).

It is not only unsupportive actions by members of the social network that may be harmful; specific supportive behaviors can have unpredictable outcomes as well. This same study found that practical support predicted greater anxiety in COPD patients—that is, patients with more support were also more anxious (DiNicola et al., 2013). The authors suggest that although the association might be related to the relatively higher needs for support by patients who were more seriously ill (and relatedly more anxious), they speculated that the help patients received might also have served to highlight illness and dependence, thus increasing anxiety. Relatedly, a series of meta-analyses of partner support and smoking cessation found that when interventions to increase partner support were often ineffective and that when supportive partners provided "reminders" in the form of nagging or criticism, smokers were more likely to relapse and begin smoking again (Park, Schultz, Tudiver, Campbell, & Becker, 2002; Park, Tudiver, & Campbell, 2012; Park, Tudiver, Schultz, & Campbell, 2004). The authors do not speculate about the process, but it seems likely that the poorer outcomes might be due to the desire to reassert a sense of personal control (i.e., reactance).

Particulars regarding the most beneficial form of support also differ according to demographics such as age and socioeconomic status—for example, two studies, one of nearly 8,000 adults and another of nearly 1,000, found that older individuals were more likely to prefer doing physical activity with people in their same age group, whereas similar-age activity partners were less important at younger ages (Beauchamp, Carron, McCutcheon, & Harper, 2007; Burton, Khan, & Brown, 2012). Self-categorization, including concepts of being evenly

matched, not conspicuous, and able to relate to one another are all suggested as possible explanations for the observed differences. The larger study (Burton et al., 2012) also confirmed that low-income adults were more drawn to activities that were low-cost and offered benefit beyond exercise. This research highlights the importance of making physical activity affordable and multifunctional, particularly for lower income adults

Taken as a whole, these studies highlight the utility of tailoring health interventions so that they make use of social networks and support structures in ways that address the most pressing needs of particular groups or individuals.

## Social Influence in Health Care

Friends and families influence our health both purposefully and inadvertently; yet it is within the health care system itself that the most overt influence over health is attempted. Health care providers (e.g., physicians, dentists, nurse practitioners) are expected to instruct and perhaps persuade. Modeling is an essential element as well; patients look to their health professionals for clues to healthy behavior.

Patients' confidence in the advice and care they receive from their physicians has been shown to vary with the health of the physician himself or herself. For example, compared with patients of normal-weight physicians, those whose physicians are obese report less confidence in the health advice and illness-management counseling given to them (Hash, Munna, Vogel, & Bason, 2003). Similarly, a study in which participants were randomly assigned to groups and then asked to rate physicians described as normal weight, overweight, or obese indicated that people were less trusting of, and less likely to follow the advice of, overweight or obese physicians; this was true regardless of the weight of the participant (Puhl, Gold, Luedicke, & DePierre, 2013). This research suggests that a health care provider who does not model appropriate behaviors diminishes the influence she or he might have on patients. "Practicing what one preaches," in the form of modeling effective health behaviors, is important.

A health care provider's own health behavior tends to also predict the likelihood that he or she will actively promote better health in patients. Several studies have shown that physicians who are themselves healthier are more likely to counsel their patients about relevant health behaviors. For example, studies have found that physicians who exercised regularly and maintained a healthy weight were more comfortable counseling patients about healthy lifestyles than were those whose own lifestyles were less healthy (Abramson, Stein, Schaufele, Frates, & Rogan, 2000; Howe et al., 2010; Livaudais et al., 2005).

This pattern was also demonstrated in a study that assessed nearly 500 physicians and found that only 18 percent of those who were overweight or obese talked to their patients about losing weight. On the other hand, 30 percent of those with a healthy BMI did so. Those with a healthy BMI also had greater confidence in their own abilities to provide advice on diet and exercise, and they felt that personal modeling of healthy weight-related behaviors, including regular exercise, was important (Bleich, Bennett, Gudzune, & Cooper, 2012). Even health professionals whose personal behaviors do not represent the ideal should still counsel their patients about health lifestyles—they have expertise of various sorts, all of which can be important in helping patients to make good decisions, and they still have the ability to influence patients, although the data indicate that this ability is less than it might be if their personal behaviors more closely approximated their advice.

The concept of power has been important in health behavior—both research literature and practice—for a long time. French and Raven (1959) defined social power as the ability to exert social influence—that is, the ability to change the beliefs, attitudes, or behaviors of other people. They outlined six specific types of power, or ways in which these changes might be accomplished: (1) coercive power (derived from one's ability to withhold rewards); (2) reward power (derived from one's ability to provide rewards); (3) referent power (derived from one's ability to make others feel valued and accepted); (4) legitimate power (derived from one's position or status); (5) expert power (derived from one's knowledge and experience); and (6) informational (derived from the persuasiveness of the specific content or information shared) (Raven, 2010).

Information from a source that is deemed to have expertise on a particular topic carries more weight than the same information coming from a source that is perceived as less credible (Cialdini, 2008). The power to influence often comes because of an individual's knowledge and past experience (expert power), but health care professionals also use the other forms of power: coercive, reward, referent, informational, and legitimate. Referent power, in particular, is crucial when medical recommendations

need to be internalized by patients (Rodin & Janis, 1979) and is perhaps also especially relevant in situations where the health care provider's own health behaviors are less than ideal. In these cases, sharing personal struggles and identifying with the patient might help him or her to feel more accepted, thus empowering him or her to make lifestyle changes despite the lack of modeling on the part of the provider (Krupa, 2012).

Successfully influencing health behaviors using directives does not rely only on the expertise and power discussed earlier. Studies also show that messages are more persuasive when they come from someone who is well liked (Cialdini, 2008). We tend to like people who we perceive as attractive (Eagly, Ashmore, Makhijani, & Longo, 1991), with whom we are familiar (Zajonc, 1968), and who we perceive as similar to us (Byrne, 1971). Sharing some personal information (e.g., one's own challenging but successful struggle to maintain an exercise regimen) may help in the latter two areas: helping patients to feel more connected to and similar to the health care provider who is making recommendations (Martin et al., 2010).

Just as patients may be influenced in positive ways by the social processes noted earlier, expectations and biases may also negatively influence patient behavior. This tendency for expectations to become realities was outlined and labeled as the "self-fulfilling prophecy" phenomenon in the mid-20th century (Merton, 1949) and numerous studies have since demonstrated that expectations—both negative and positive—can be quite powerful (e.g., Madon, Jussim, & Eccles, 1997; Rosenthal & Rubin, 1978; Snyder, 1992). In cases where the provider likes the patient or feels confident that she or he can carry out the prescribed behavior, this is not problematic. But when clinicians hold negative perceptions about their patients, subtle cues that encourage those patients toward less ideal behaviors may be conveyed. When trust and satisfaction with the clinical relationship are lacking, patients are less likely to adhere to treatment recommendations (Bennett, Fuertes, Keitel, & Phillips, 2011; Hagiwara et al., 2013; Levesque, Li, & Pahal, 2012), but both satisfaction and health are greater when patients feel liked by their health care providers (Hall, Horgan, Stein, & Roter, 2002). Patients' trust and satisfaction levels, as well as the patient-centered behaviors displayed by their clinicians, have all been linked to the implicit biases held by clinicians (e.g., Cooper et al., 2012; Penner, Blair, Albrecht, & Dovidio, 2014; Penner et al., 2010).

These studies highlight how important it is to pay attention to all forms of social influence, even those that can be easy to overlook.

When it comes to goal setting, health professionals are ideally positioned to help patients identify targets that are both palatable and manageable. Research shows that when people think about their goals as steps toward learning (versus indicators of performance), they are more likely to stay engaged in their pursuit of those aims, even when they experience setbacks (Elliott & Dweck, 1988). Data also indicate that even small experiences of success, as well as perceptions of increasing task mastery, foster self-efficacy and encourage continued goal pursuit (Stretcher, DeVillis, Becker, & Rosenstock, 1986; Stretcher et al., 1995). Health professionals can not only assist patients in setting reasonable goals that have a high likelihood of success, but they can also aid the framing of those goals—that is, helping patients to view goal setting as an opportunity for learning and improving skills, instead of as a measure of their ultimate success. In this way, health professionals are able to be potent forces for health behavior change.

Health professionals may also be in a unique position to connect patients with appropriate support groups that can then influence their health outcomes in a variety of ways. In such groups, patients may experience multiple gains (Martin et al., 2010): emotional support to help them stay engaged in the process of self-care or behavior change; they may find practical advice and ideas for overcoming the obstacles they encounter; and they may be empowered as they help others who are struggling in areas where they have experienced success. Although the concepts of support groups and peer communities are not new, their movement into the digital realm is still in progress. These groups are varied—from discussion groups and chat rooms to newsfeeds and voice-activated systems; and they are often part of a complex system of care delivery. These methods have emerged recently, and there has not yet been much systematic evaluation of these virtual communities. One detailed review of outcomes associated with various sorts of e-groups concluded that while they do not appear to be harmful, neither do they seem to improve health outcomes (Eysenbach, Powell, Englesakis, Rizo, & Stern, 2004). Most of the studies included elements other than peer-to-peer support, and therefore it was impossible to determine whether intervention effects were due to the group or to some other element of the overall program. Another meta-analysis (this one focused specifically on depression as the outcome) drew similar conclusions and indicated that studies that were not as well designed (e.g., no control group) were more likely to find an association between the online support group and the measured outcome (Griffiths, Calear, & Banfield, 2009). Some studies have found that participation rates in e-groups is higher than with in-person groups (Alemi et al., 1996) and satisfaction also seems to be high (Hoey, Ieropoli, White, & Jefford, 2008), but links to other outcomes, including psychosocial, are inconsistent. Considering these factors, the best practice might be to have a variety of groups—of both types—available for patients, and for health care providers to help guide them to the environments that best meet their needs.

## Influence of Larger Social Systems

The focus thus far has been primarily on individual relationships, or social influence in relatively small groups. Larger societal systems, however, also influence personal behaviors, although not always as efficiently as we might guess. Public health programs aim to change health behaviors by educating and motivating people toward ideal behaviors. Educational interventions such as *5-A-Day for Better Health* (Frazao, 1999) and the *Nutritional Labeling and Education Act* (Marcus, Owen, Forsyth, Cavill, & Fridinger, 1998) have demonstrated moderate successes. Over a 5-year period the number of adults meeting the 5-a-day goal increased slightly, as did the number of adults who reported reading nutritional labels (French, Story, & Jeffery, 2001). There is no evidence, however, of a strong link between educational strategies such as these and large-scale behavior change in the population (Brownson, Baker, Housemann, Brennan, & Bacak, 2001).

Health-related media campaigns have historically received free time slots for their public service announcements (PSAs), but free access has diminished over time, and now it is common to have these sorts of informational and motivational messages funded by governmental agencies, nonprofit health organizations, or even for-profit providers. One of the early successes in this area was the Stanford heart disease prevention project in which communities targeted with intensive media campaigns showed improvements in cardiovascular health (Farquhar et al., 1977). This success fueled an increase in subsequent media campaigns, but their degrees of success have varied.

A review of mass-media health campaigns (Snyder & Hamilton, 2002) found that about 7–10 percent more people in target (versus control) communities change their behaviors and the changes are greater when adoption of a new behavior, rather than the cessation of an already-established behavior, is targeted. A subsequent review, utilizing both meta-analyses and other literature found an effect of about 5 percent in intervention communities (Snyder, 2007).

Because many mass-media campaigns are minimally effective (perhaps because they are too obvious in their attempts to sway perceptions or behaviors; Murphy, Hether, & Rideout, 2008), embedding of these messages into regular entertainment media is becoming more common, analogous to the "product placement" that has expanded dramatically over recent years. This approach was pioneered by Miguel Sabido of Mexico in the 1970s in an effort to improve adult literacy. Albert Bandura himself was impressed with Sabido's application of Bandura's social cognitive theory and the approach is now used around the world to educate people and connect them with community resources (Smith, 2002). One early example in the United States was the storyline for the television soap opera *The Bold and the Beautiful* in which one of the characters confided to his long-term girlfriend that he was HIV-positive. This episode, which had been planned in collaboration with scientists from the Centers for Disease Control and Prevention (CDC), was designed to challenge stereotypes associated with HIV and to encourage viewers to get tested. It was estimated by Neilsen that approximately 4 million viewers tuned in and received this message (Kennedy, O'Leary, Beck, Pollard, & Simpson, 2004), and calls to the National STD and AIDS Hotline increased dramatically following its airing in the summer of 2001. Subsequently, the CDC partnered with the University of Southern California's Annenberg School for Communication to form *Health, Hollywood, and Society*, which aimed to provide accurate information to television writers for embedding into storylines (Kennedy, Murphy, & Beck, 2004). *Health, Hollywood, and Society* contributes to hundreds of health-related storylines each year (Dutta, 2007). Because of their broad reach, and their appealing format, these types of social influences hold a good deal of promise; because of their nature, however, their specific impacts are challenging to parse in experimental studies and more study of the long-term effects of such campaigns is needed.

## Conclusion

The use of social influence processes holds a good deal of promise in fostering health behavior, in individuals as well as in populations. The influence of family members, friends, peers, and even perceived others can be harnessed to maximize positive health behaviors across all developmental periods. The specific effects of social support and social influence are, in some areas, challenging to determine precisely in observational studies; experimental studies are emerging to support the long-term effects of social influence, and more experimental intervention research is needed.

## References

Abramson, S., Stein, J., Schaufele, M., Frates, E., & Rogan, S. (2000). Personal exercise habits and counseling practices of primary care physicians: A national survey. *Clinical Journal of Sport Medicine, 10,* 40–48.

Alemi, F., Mosavel, M., Stephens, R. C., Ghadiri, A., Krishnaswamy, J., & Thakkar, H. (1996). Electronic self-help and support groups. *Medical Care, 34,* OS32–OS44.

Arredondo, E. M., Elder, J. P., Ayala, G. X., Campbell, N., Baquero, B., & Duerksen, S. (2006). Is parenting style related to children's healthy eating and physical activity in Latino families? *Health Education Research, 21,* 862–871.

Bahr, S. J., Hoffman, J. P., & Yang, X. (2005). Parental and peer influences on the risk of adolescent drug use. *Journal of Primary Prevention, 26,* 529–551.

Bandura, A., (1997). *Self-efficacy: The exercise of control.* New York, NY: Freeman.

Beauchamp, M. R., Carron, A. V., McCutcheon, S., & Harper, O. (2007). Older adults' preferences for exercising alone versus in groups: Considering contextual congruence. *Annals of Behavioral Medicine, 33,* 200–206.

Bennett, J. K., Fuertes, J. N., Keitel, M., & Phillips, R. (2011). The role of patient attachment and working alliance on patient adherence, satisfaction, and health-related quality of life in lupus treatment. *Patient Education and Counseling, 85,* 53–59.

Berndt, T. J. (1979). Developmental changes in conformity to peers and parents. *Developmental Psychology, 15,* 608–616.

Birch, L. L., & Davison, K. K. (2001). Family environmental factors influencing the developing behavioral controls of food intake and childhood overweight. *Pediatric Clinics of North America, 48,* 893–907.

Bleich, S. N., Bennett, W. L., Gudzune, K. A., & Cooper, L. A. (2012). Impact of physician BMI on obesity care and beliefs. *Obesity, 20,* 999–1005.

Boutelle, K. N., Cafri, G., & Crow, S. J. (2011). Parent-only treatment for childhood obesity: A randomized controlled trial. *Obesity, 19,* 574–580.

Brownson, R. C., Baker, E. A., Housemann, R. A., Brennan, L. K., & Bacak, S. J. (2001). Environmental and policy determinants of physical activity in the United States. *American Journal of Public Health, 91,* 1995–2003.

Bruening, M., Eisenberg, M., MacLehose, R., Nanney, M. S., Story, M., & Neumark-Sztainer, D. (2012). Relationship between adolescents' and their friends' eating behaviors: Breakfast, fruit, vegetable, whole-grain, and dairy intake. *Journal of the Academy of Nutrition and Dietetics, 112,* 1608–1613.

Burger, J. M., Bell, H., Harvey, K., Johnson, J., Stewart, C., Dorian, K., & Swedroe, M. (2010). Nutritious or delicious? The effect of descriptive norm information on food choice. *Journal of Social and Clinical Psychology, 29,* 228–242.

Burger, J. M., & Shelton, M. (2011). Changing everyday health behaviors through descriptive norm manipulations. *Social Influence, 6,* 69–77.

Burton, N. W., Khan, A., & Brown, W. J. (2012). How, where and with whom? Physical activity context preferences of three adult groups at risk of inactivity. *British Journal of Sports Medicine, 46,* 1125–1131.

Buunk, B. P., Collins, R. L., Taylor, S. E., Van Yperen, N. W., & Dakof, G. A. (1990). The affective consequences of social comparison: Either direction has its ups and downs. *Journal of Personality and Social Psychology, 59,* 1238–1249.

Buunk, B. P., & Ybema, J. F. (1997). Social comparison and occupational stress: The identification-contrast model. In B. P. Buunk & F. X Gibbons (Eds.), *Health, coping, and well-being: Perspectives from social comparison theory* (pp. 359–388). Hillsdale, NJ: Erlbaum.

Byrne, P. S. (1971). Evaluation of courses for general practitioners. *Journal of the Royal College of General Practitioners, 21,* 719–925.

Chassin, L., Presson, C. C., Sherman, S. J., Montello, D., & McGrew, J. (1986). Changes in peer and parent influence during adolescence: Longitudinal versus cross-sectional perspectives on smoking initiation. *Developmental Psychology, 22,* 327–334.

Christakis, N. A., & Fowler, J. H. (2007). The spread of obesity in a large social network over 32 years. *New England Journal of Medicine, 357,* 370–379.

Christakis, N. A., & Fowler, J. H. (2008). The collective dynamics of smoking in a large social network. *New England Journal of Medicine, 358,* 2249–2258.

Cialdini, R. B. (2008). *Influence: Science and practice* (5th ed.). Upper Saddle River, NJ: Pearson.

Cialdini, R. B., Reno, R. R., & Kallgren, C. A. (1990). A focus theory of normative conduct: Recycling the concept of norms to reduce littering in public places. *Journal of Personality and Social Psychology, 58,* 1015–1026.

Collins, R. L. (1996). For better or worse: The impact of upward social comparison on self-evaluations. *Psychological Bulletin, 119,* 51–69.6

Cooper, L. A., Roter, D. L., Carson, K. A., Beach, M. C., Sabin, J. A., Greenwald, A. G., & Inui, T. S. (2012). The associations of clinicians' implicit attitudes about race with medical visit communication and patient ratings of interpersonal care. *American Journal of Public Health, 102,* 979–987.

Corcoran, K., Crusius, J., & Mussweiler, T. (2011). Social comparisons: Motives, standards, and mechanisms. In D. Chadee (Ed.), *Theories in social psychology* (pp. 119–139). Oxford, England: Wiley-Blackwell.

Croyle, R. T. (1992). Appraisal of health threats: Cognition, motivation, and social comparison. *Cognitive Therapy and Research, 16,* 165–182.

Davison, K. K., & Birch, L. L. (2001). Childhood overweight: A contextual model and recommendations for future research. *Obesity Reviews, 2,* 159–171.

de Castro, J. M. (1994). Family and friends produce greater social facilitation of food intake than other companions. *Physiology and Behavior, 56,* 445–455.

de Castro, J. M., & de Castro, E. S. (1989). Spontaneous meal patterns of humans: Influence of the presence of other people. *American Journal of Clinical Nutrition, 50,* 237–247.

DiMatteo, M. R. (2004a). Variations in patients' adherence to medical recommendations: A quantitative review of 50 years of research. *Medical Care, 42,* 200–209.

DiMatteo, M. R. (2004b). Social support and patients' adherence to medical treatment: A meta-analysis. *Health Psychology, 23,* 207–218.

DiNicola, G., Julian, L., Gregorich, S. E., Blanc, P. D., & Katz, P. P. (2013). The role of social support in anxiety for persons with COPD. *Journal of Psychosomatic Research, 74*(2), 110–115.

Dutta, M. (2007). Health information processing from television: The role of health orientation. *Health Communication, 21,* 1–9.

Eagly, A. H., Ashmore, R. D., Makhijani, M. G., & Longo, L. C. (1991). What is beautiful is good, but . . .: A meta-analytic review of research on the physical attractiveness stereotype. *Psychological Bulletin, 110,* 109–128.

Eisert, D. C., & Kahle, L. R. (1982). Self-evaluation and social comparison of physical and role change during adolescence: A longitudinal analysis. *Child Development, 53,* 98–104.

Elliott, E. S., & Dweck, C. S. (1988). Goals: An approach to motivation and achievement. *Journal of Personality and Social Psychology, 54,* 5–12.

Emmons, K. M., Barbeau, E. M., Gutheil, C., Stryker, J. E., & Stoddard, A. M. (2007). Social influences, social context, and health behaviors among working-class, multi-ethnic adults. *Health Education and Behavior, 34,* 315–334.

Eysenbach, G., Powell, J., Englesakis, M., Rizo, C., & Stern, A. (2004). Health related virtual communities and electronic support groups: Systematic review of the effects of online peer to peer interactions. *British Medical Journal, 328,* 1166–1171.

Festinger, L. (1954). A theory of social comparison processes. *Human Relations, 7,* 117–140.

Fitzgerald, A., Fitzgerald, N., & Aheme, C. (2012). Do peers matter? A review of peer and/or friends' influence on physical activity among American adolescents. *Journal of Adolescence, 35,* 941–958.

French, J. R. P., & Raven, B. H. (1959). The bases of social power. In D. Cartwright (Ed.), *Studies in social power* (pp. 150–167). Ann Arbor, MI: Institute for Social Research.

French, S. A., Story, M., & Jeffery, R. W. (2001). Environmental influences on eating and physical activity. *Annual Review of Public Health, 22,* 309–335.

Farquhar, J. W., Maccoby, N., Wood, P. D., Alexander, J. K., Breitrose, H., Brown, B. W., Jr.,. . . Stern, M. P. (1977). Community education for cardiovascular health. *The Lancet, 1*(8023), 1192–1195.

Frazao, E. (Ed.). (1999). *America's eating habits: Changes and consequences.* [Department of Agriculture Information Bulletin AIB-750]. Washington, DC: US Department of Agriculture.

Freeman, E. M. (2001). *Substance abuse intervention, prevention, rehabilitation, and systems change strategies: Helping individuals, families, and groups to empower themselves.* New York, NY: Columbia University Press.

Gibbons, F. X. (1999). Social comparison as a mediator of response shift. *Social Science and Medicine, 48,* 1517–1530.

Glynn, T. J. (1981). From family to peer: A review of transitions of influence among drug-using youth. *Journal of Youth and Adolescence, 10*, 363–383.

Golan, M. (2006). Parents as agents of change in childhood obesity—from research to practice. *International Journal of Pediatric Obesity, 1*, 66–76.

Golan, M., Kaufman, V., & Shahar, D. R. (2006). Childhood obesity treatment: Targeting parents exclusively v. parents and children. *British Journal of Nutrition, 95*, 1008–1015.

Griffiths, K. M., Calear, A. L., & Banfield, M. (2009). Systematic review on internet support groups (ISGs) and depression (1): Do ISGs reduce depressive symptoms? *Journal of Medical Internet Research, 11*(3): e40.

Gubbels, J. S., Kremers, S. P., Stafleu, A., de Vries, S. I., Goldbohm, R. A., Dagnelie, P. C.,... Thijs, C. (2011). Association between parenting practices and children's dietary intake, activity behavior and development of body mass index: The KOALA Birth Cohort Study. *International Journal of Behavioral Nutrition and Physical Activity, 8*, 18–30.

Hagiwara, N., Penner, L. A., Gonzalez, R., Eggly, S., Dovidio, J. F., Gaertner, S. L.,... Albrecht, T. L. (2013). Racial attitudes, physician-patient talk time ratio, and adherence in racially discordant medical interactions. *Social Science and Medicine, 87*, 123–131.

Hall, J. A., Horgan, T. G., Stein, T. S., & Roter, D. L. (2002). Liking in the physician-patient relationship. *Patient Education and Counseling, 48*, 69–77.

Hash, R. B., Munna, R. K., Vogel, R. L., & Bason, J. J. (2003). Does physician weight affect perception of health advice? *Preventive Medicine, 36*, 41–44.

Helgeson, V. S., & Taylor, S. E. (1993). Social comparisons and adjustment among cardiac patients. *Journal of Applied Social Psychology, 23*, 1171–1195.

Herman, C. P., Roth, D. A., & Polivy, J. (2003). Effects of the presence of others on food intake: A normative interpretation. *Psychological Bulletin, 129*, 873–886.

Hetherington, M. M., Anderson, A. A., Norton, G. N. M., & Newson, L. (2006). Situational effects on meal intake: A comparison of eating alone and eating with others. *Physiology and Behavior, 88*, 498–505.

Hoey, L. M., Ieropoli, S. C., White, V. M., & Jefford, M. (2008). Systematic review of peer-support programs for people with cancer. *Patient Education and Counseling, 70*, 315–337.

House, J. S., Robbins, C., & Metzner, H. L. (1982). The association of social relationships and activities with mortality: Prospective evidence from the Tecumseh Community Health Study. *American Journal of Epidemiology, 116*, 123–140.

Howe, M., Leidel, A., Krishnan, S. M., Weber, A., Rubenfire, M., & Jackson, E. A. (2010). Patient-related diet and exercise counseling: Do providers' own lifestyle habits matter? *Preventive Cardiology, 13*, 180–185.

Janicke, D. M., Sallinen, B. J., Perri, M. G., Lutes, L. D., Silverstein, J. H., & Brumback, B. (2009). Comparison of program costs for parent-only and family-based interventions for pediatric obesity in medically underserved rural settings. *Journal of Rural Health, 25*, 326–330.

Johnson, C. A., & Katz, R. C. (1973). Using parents as change agents for their children: A review. *Journal of Child Psychology and Psychiatry, 14*, 181–200.

Jones, D. C. (2001). Social comparison and body image: Attractiveness comparisons to models and peers among adolescent girls and boys. *Sex Roles, 45*, 645–664.

Jones, L. R., Steer, C. D., Rogers, I. S., & Emmett, P. M. (2010). Influences on child fruit and vegetable intake: Sociodemographic, parental and child factors in a longitudinal cohort study. *Public Health Nutrition, 13*, 1122–1130.

Kennedy, M. G., Murphy, S., & Beck, V. (2004). Entertainment education and multicultural audiences: An action and research agenda. *Community Psychologist, 37*, 16–18.

Kennedy, M. G., O'Leary, A., Beck, V., Pollard, K., & Simpson, P. (2004). Increases in calls to the CDC national STD and AIDS hotline following AIDS-related episodes in a soap opera. *Journal of Communication, 54*, 287–301.

Keresztes, N., Piko, B. F., Pluhar, Z. F., & Page, R. M. (2008). Social influences in sports activity among adolescents. *Journal of the Royal Society for the Promotion of Health, 128*, 21–25.

Kouvonen, A., De Vogli, R., Stafford, M., Shipley, M. J., Marmot, M. G., Cox, T.,... Kivimaki, M. (2012). Social support and the likelihood of maintaining and improving levels of physical activity: The Whitehall II Study. *European Journal of Public Health, 22*, 514–518.

Krupa, C. (2012, April 2). Healthy physicians make better role models, research shows. *American Medical News*. Retrieved December 2012, from http://www.ama-assn.org/amednews/2012/04/02/hlsa0402.htm

La Greca, A. M., Bearman, K. J., & Moore, H. (2002). Peer relations of youth with pediatric conditions and health risks: Promoting social support and healthy lifestyles. *Journal of Developmental and Behavioral Pediatrics, 23*, 271–280.

Lau, R. R., Quadrel, M. J., & Hartman, K. A. (1990). Development and change of young adults' preventive health beliefs and behavior: Influence from parents and peers. *Journal of Health and Social Behavior, 31*, 240–259.

Levesque, A., Li, H. Z., & Pahal, J. S. (2012). Factors related to patients' adherence to medication and lifestyle change recommendations: Data from Canada. *International Journal of Psychological Studies, 4*, 42–55.

Livaudais, J. C., Kaplan, C. P., Haas, J. S., Perez-Stable, E. J., Stewart, S., & Jarlais, G. D. (2005). Lifestyle behavior counseling for women patients among a sample of California physicians. *Journal of Women's Health, 14*, 485–495.

Locher, J. L., Robinson, C. O., Roth, D. L., Ritchie, C. S., & Burgio, K. L. (2005). The effect of the presence of others on caloric intake in homebound older adults. *Journals of Gerontology Series A: Biological Sciences and Medical Sciences, 60*, 1475–1478.

Luszczynska, A., Gibbons, F. X., Piko, B. F., & Tekozel, M. (2004). Self-regulatory cognitions, social comparison, and perceived peers' behaviors as predictors of nutrition and physical activity: A comparison among adolescents in Hungary, Poland, Turkey, and USA. *Psychology and Health, 19*, 577–593.

Madon, S., Jussim, L., & Eccles, J. (1997). In search of the powerful self-fulfilling prophecy. *Journal of Personality and Social Psychology, 72*, 791–809.

Malchodi, C. S., Oncken, C., Dornelas, E. A., Caramanica, L.,Gregonis, E., & Curry, S. L. (2003). The effects of peer counseling on smoking cessation and reduction. *Obstetrics and Gynecology, 101*, 504–510.

Marcus, B. H., Owen, N., Forsyth, L. H., Cavill, N. A., & Fridinger, F. (1998). Physical activity interventions using mass media, print media, and information technology. *American Journal of Preventive Medicine, 15*, 362–378.

Martin, L. R., Haskard-Zolnierek, K. B., & DiMatteo, M. R. (2010). *Health behavior change and treatment adherence: Evidence-based guidelines for improving healthcare.* New York, NY: Oxford University Press.

Merton, R. K. (1949). *Social theory and social structure.* New York, NY: Free Press.

Mueller, A. S., Pearson, J., Muller, C., Frank, K., & Turner, A. (2010). Sizing up peers: Adolescent girls' weight control and social comparison in the school context. *Journal of Health and Social Behavior, 51,* 64–78.

Mulvhill, C. (2014). Parental and peer influences on adolescent smoking: A literature review. *Interdisciplinary Journal of Health Sciences, 4*(1). Retrieved December 2014, from ijhs2.deonandan.com/wordpress/archives/1760

Munsch, S., Roth, B., Michael, T., Meyer, A. H., Biedert, E., Roth, S.,... Margraf, J. (2008). Randomized controlled comparison of two cognitive behavioral therapies for obese children: Mother versus mother-child cognitive behavioral therapy. *Psychotherapy and Psychosomatics, 77,* 235–246.

Murphy, S. T., Hether, H. J., & Rideout, V. (2008). *How healthy is prime time? An analysis of health content in popular prime time television programs. A report by The Kaiser Family Foundation and The USC Annenberg Norman Lear Center's Hollywood, Health & Society.* Menlo Park, CA: Harry J. Kaiser Family Foundation.

Nash, S. G., McQueen, A., & Bray, J. H. (2005). Pathways to adolescent alcohol use: Family environment, peer influence, and parental expectations. *Journal of Adolescent Health, 37,* 19–28.

Norton, D. E., Froelicher, E. S., Waters, C. M., & Carrieri-Kohlman, V. (2003). Parental influence on models of primary prevention of cardiovascular disease in children. *European Journal of Cardiovascular Nursing, 2,* 311–322.

Park, E. W., Schultz, J. K., Tudiver, F., Campbell, T., & Becker, L. (2002). Enhancing partner support to improve smoking cessation. *Cochrane Database of Systematic Reviews,* (1), CD002928.

Park, E. W., Tudiver, F. G., & Campbell, T. (2012). Enhancing partner support to improve smoking cessation. *Cochrane Database of Systematic Reviews,* (7), CD002928.

Park, E. W., Tudiver, F., Schultz, J. K., & Campbell, T. (2004). Does enhancing partner support and interaction improve smoking cessation? A meta-analysis. *Annals of Family Medicine, 2,* 170–174.

Pearson, N., Biddle, S. J., & Gorely, T. (2009). Family correlates of fruit and vegetable consumption in children and adolescents: A systematic review. *Public Health Nutrition, 12,* 267–283.

Penner, L. A., Blair, I. V., Albrecht, T. L., & Dovidio, J. F. (2014). Reducing racial health care disparities: A social psychological analysis. *Policy Insights from the Behavioral and Brain Sciences, 1,* 204-212.

Penner, L. A., Dovidio, J. F., West, T. W., Gaertner, S. L., Albrecht, T. L., Dailey, R. K., & Markova, T. (2010). Aversive racism and medical interactions with black patients: A field study. *Journal of Experimental Social Psychology, 46,* 436–440.

Prinstein, M. J., & Wang, S. S. (2005). False consensus and adolescent peer contagion: Examining discrepancies between perceptions and actual reported levels of friends' deviant and health risk behaviors. *Journal of Abnormal Child Psychology, 33,* 293–306.

Puhl, R. M., Gold, J. A., Luedicke, J., & DePierre, J. A. (2013). The effect of physicians' body weight on patient attitudes: Implications for physician selection, trust and adherence to medical advice. *International Journal of Obesity, 37,* 1415–1421.

Ralston, P. A., Cohen, N. L., Wickrama, K. A. S., & Kwag, K. (2011). Social support and dietary quality in older African American public housing residents. *Research on Aging, 33,* 688–712.

Raven, B. H. (2010). The bases of power: Origins and recent developments. *Journal of Social Issues, 49,* 227–251.

Rodin, J., & Janis, I. L. (1979). The social power of health-care practitioners as agents of change. *Journal of Social Issues, 35,* 60–81,

Rosenthal, R., & Rubin, D. B. (1978). Interpersonal expectancy effects: The first 345 studies. *Behavioral and Brain Sciences, 3,* 377–386.

Roth, D., Herman, C. P., Polivy, J., & Pliner, P. (2001). Self-presentational conflict in social eating situations: A normative perspective. *Appetite, 36,* 165–171.

Salvy, S. J., Bowker, J. C., Germeroth, L., & Barkley, J. (2012). Influence of peers and friends on overweight/obese youths' physical activity. *Exercise and Sport Sciences Reviews, 40,* 127–132.

Salvy, S. J., de la Haye, K., Bowker, J. C., & Hermans, R. C. (2012). Influence of peers and friends on children's and adolescents' eating and activity behaviors. *Physiology and Behavior, 106,* 369–378.

Salvy, S. J., Howard, M., Read, M., & Mele, E. (2009). The presence of friends increases food intake in youth. *American Journal of Clinical Nutrition, 90,* 282–287.

Salvy, S. J., Roemmich, J. N., Bowker, J. C., Romero, N. D., Stadler, P. J., & Epstein, L. H. (2009). Effect of peers and friends on youth physical activity and motivation to be physically active. *Journal of Pediatric Psychology, 34,* 217–225.

Scalici, F., & Schulz, P. J. (2014). Influence of perceived parent and peer endorsement on adolescent smoking intentions: Parents have more say, but their influence wanes as kids get older. *PLoS One, 9,* e101275.

Schmitz, M. F., Gunta, N., Parikh, N. S., Chen, K. K., Fahs, M. C., & Gallo, W. T. (2012). The association between neighbourhood social cohesion and hypertension management strategies in older adults. *Age and Ageing, 41,* 388–392.

Schultz, P. W., Nolan, J. M., Cialdini, R. B., Goldstein, N. J., & Griskevicius, V. (2007). The constructive, destructive, and reconstructive power of social norms. *Psychological Science, 18,* 429–434.

Seo, D. C., & Huang, Y. (2012). Systematic review of social network analysis in adolescent cigarette smoking behavior. *Journal of School Health, 82,* 21–27.

Simons-Morton, B., & Farhat, T. (2010). Recent findings on peer group influences on adolescent substance use. *Journal of Primary Prevention, 31,* 191–208.

Smith, D. (2002). The theory heard 'round the world. *APA Monitor, 33*(9), 30.

Snyder, L. B. (2007). Health communication campaigns and their impact on behavior. *Journal of Nutrition Education and Behavior, 39,* S32–S40.

Snyder, L. B., & Hamilton, M. A. (2002). A meta-analysis of U.S. health campaign effects on behavior: Emphasize enforcement, exposure, and new information and beware the secular trend. In R. C. Hornik (Ed.) *Public health communication: Evidence for behavior change* (pp. 357–384). Mahwah, NJ: Erlbaum.

Snyder, M. (1992). Motivational foundations of behavioral confirmation. In M. P. Zanna (Ed.) *Advances in experimental social psychology* (Vol. *25*, pp. 67–114). San Diego, CA: Academic Press.

Stretcher, V. J., DeVillis, B. M., Becker, M. H., & Rosenstock, I. M. (1986). The role of self-efficacy in achieving health behavior change. *Health Education Quarterly, 13,* 73–91.

Stretcher, V. J., Seijts, G. H., Kok, G. J., Latham, G. P., Glasgow, R., DeVellis, B.,... Bulger, D. W. (1995). Goal setting as a strategy for health behavior change. *Health Education Quarterly, 22,* 190–200.

Taylor, S. E., & Lobel, M. (1989). Social comparison activity under threat: Downward evaluation and upward contact. *Psychological Review, 96,* 569–575.

Testa, M., & Major, B. (1990). The impact of social comparisons after failure: The moderating effects of perceived control. *Basic and Applied Social Psychology, 11,* 205–218.

Thanakwang, K., & Soonthorndhada, K. (2011). Mechanisms by which social support networks influence healthy aging among Thai community-dwelling elderly. *Journal of Aging and Health, 23,* 1352–1378.

Tinsley, B. J. (1992). Multiple influences on the acquisition and socialization of children's health attitudes and behavior: An integrative review. *Child Development, 63,* 1043–1069.

Tucker, J. S., Schwartz, J. E., Clark, K. M., & Friedman, H. S. (1999). Age-related changes in the associations of social network ties with mortality risk. *Psychology and Aging, 14,* 564–571.

Van der Zee, K., Buunk, B. P., Sanderman, R., Botke, G., & van den Bergh, F. (2000). Social comparison and coping with cancer treatment. *Personality and Individual Differences, 28,* 17–34.

Wansink, B. (2006). *Mindless eating: Why we eat more than we think.* New York, NY: Bantham Dell.

Wills, T. A. (1981). Downward comparison principles in social psychology. *Psychological Bulletin, 90,* 245–271.

Wills, T. A. (1984). Supportive functions of interpersonal relationships. In S. Cohen & L. Syme (Eds.), *Social support and health* (pp. 61–82). New York, NY: Academic Press.

Wing, R. R., & Jeffery, R. W. (1999). Benefits of recruiting participants with friends and increasing social support for weight loss and maintenance. *Journal of Consulting and Clinical Psychology, 67,* 132–138.

Wood, M. D., Read, J. P., Mitchell, R. E., & Brand, N. H. (2004). Do parents still matter? Parent and peer influences on alcohol involvement among recent high school graduates. *Psychology of Addictive Behaviors, 18,* 19–30.

Wrotniak, B. H., Epstein, L. H., Paluch, R. A., & Roemmich, J. N. (2004). Parent weight change as a predictor of child weight change in family-based behavioral obesity treatment. *Archives of Pediatrics and Adolescent Medicine, 158,* 342–347.

Wrotniak, B. H., Epstein, L. H., Paluch, R. A., & Roemmich, J. N. (2005). The relationship between parent and child self-reported adherence and weight loss. *Obesity Research, 13,* 1089–1096.

Young, M. E., Mizzau, M., Mai, N. T., Sirisegaram, A., & Wilson, M. (2009). Food for thought. What you eat depends on your sex and eating companions. *Appetite, 53,* 268–271.

Zajonc, R. B. (1968). Attitudinal effects of mere exposure. *Journal of Personality and Social Psychology, 35,* 151–175.

# The Expanding, Lop-Sided Universe of Social Influence and Law Research

Linda J. Demaine *and* Robert B. Cialdini

**Abstract**

This chapter explores "social influence and the law," which we conceptualize as consisting of three parts: (1) social influence in the legal system, (2) the legal regulation of social influence in our everyday lives, and (3) law as an instrument of social influence. Within each part, we identify the primary topics that psychologists have studied empirically and review the existing research. The chapter thus highlights the many and varied contributions of psychologists related to social influence and the law. The chapter also reveals a marked imbalance in the social influence and law literature—the vast majority of psychological research falls within the first part, despite the fact that the second and third parts capture equally or more important topics from both legal and psychological viewpoints. We end the chapter by explaining this uneven distribution of effort and urging psychologists to take a broader approach to social influence and the law.

**Key Words:** empirical legal studies, law and psychology, legal psychology, persuasion, persuasion and law, psychological jurisprudence, social influence

Law is, by its very nature, an institution of social influence. In its democratic form, law is a mechanism of social control for implementing challenging and sometimes conflicting goals such as stabilizing society, fostering individual freedom, and protecting members of vulnerable groups from powerful interests. Democracies achieve these goals through the most complex forms of social influence—those that impart to citizens a marked element of choice in their beliefs, attitudes, and actions rather than coerce them to predestined outcomes. By declining to control citizens through heavy-handed suppression, democracies permit nongovernmental forces to flourish, and these forces likewise establish and maintain social norms and societal values. Democratic law, then, is inextricably intertwined with social influence, both as a primary means of shaping behavior and as a check on other sources of social influence operating in public and private spheres.

There have been no attempts to conceptualize this universe of "social influence and the law." One

purpose of the current chapter is to offer a preliminary framework within which empirical research on social influence and law might productively be considered. Given the absence of a conceptual framework, there exist no overarching reviews of studies on the subject. A second purpose of this chapter is to employ our conceptual framework to highlight important experimental findings on social influence and law. We emphasize psychological research, because psychology, more than other disciplines, applies the scientific method in pursuit of understanding the topics of which social influence and the law is comprised. Our intent is to convey the current state of this research without reviewing it exhaustively.

We take an expansive view of social influence and the law. "Social influence" captures changes in our beliefs, attitudes, and behaviors induced by other persons. "Law" refers to the formal substantive laws that govern society and the legal process and procedures that implement them. Social influence and the law sits at the junction between these two subjects. Far from being a narrow, readily segmented area of inquiry, however, this review underscores that social influence pervades the law.

We place the topics of social influence and law into three distinct categories: (1) social influence in the legal system, (2) the legal regulation of social influence in our everyday lives, and (3) law as an instrument of social influence. While important discoveries have been made in each of these areas, the latter two literatures are relatively sparse. Psychologists have only recognized and devoted substantial attention to social influence within the legal system. Moreover, within the realm of social influence in the legal system, a select few topics have outshone all others (e.g., Williams & Jones, 2005). We end the chapter by briefly exploring the antecedents and consequences of the current imbalance of psychological research on social influence and law. Throughout the chapter, the focus is actual empirical investigations of social influence and law, not scholarship that merely theorizes how basic social influence research applies to legal issues. Also omitted are investigations of social influence and politics that do not directly implicate the law, although they overlap with social influence and law in some respects—for example, influence tactics employed in lawmakers' campaigns for office. We leave this area to the chapter dedicated to it (see Borgida & Fisher, this volume).

## Social Influence in the Legal System

Studies of social influence in the legal system address important factors that drive and, at times, derail legal decisions such as the passage of legislation, judicial rulings on the admissibility of evidence in anticipation of trial, and jury verdicts. We begin this section with the suggestibility of eyewitnesses recounting events underlying litigation and false confessions by crime suspects resulting from police interrogations, two topics that have undergone substantial, long-term, programmatic study. We next discuss juror decision making, several facets of which also have received considerable empirical attention. Finally, we relate the relatively scant research on judicial decision making and legislative decision making.

## Eyewitness Suggestibility

Eyewitness suggestibility studies investigate the ways in which eyewitnesses' memories of events that underlie litigation can be distorted by postevent information. Loftus revealed the potential influence of postevent information on eyewitnesses in a series of groundbreaking studies. In Loftus and Palmer (1974), for example, participants viewed several traffic accidents and estimated how fast the vehicles were going when the accidents occurred. To discern whether seemingly minor variations in investigative inquiries could alter eyewitness accounts, the researchers tested different verbs in the question they posed to participants: How fast were the cars going when they ["smashed into," "collided with," "bumped into," "hit," or "contacted"] each other? The phrasing of the question led to disparate speed estimates, ranging from a high average of 40.5 mph for "smashed into" to a low average of 31.8 mph for "contacted." In a follow-up study, the researchers investigated whether the verb actually altered participants' memories of how fast the cars were going or merely caused participants to report differing speeds while their memories of the events remained intact. Here, participants viewed a filmed car collision and estimated the cars' speed in response to an inquiry containing either "smashed into" or "hit." A week later, the researchers asked participants whether they saw any broken glass in the film (there had been none). Participants who received the "smashed into" inquiry were more likely to recall broken glass than were those who received the "hit" inquiry, indicating that postevent questioning actually changed their memories of the event.

These classic investigations of eyewitness accounts demonstrated that eyewitnesses' purported memories of events might actually be a combination of true memories and subsequently encountered information that merges with the memories. The studies ignited a firestorm of research on the malleability of memory for legally relevant information that continues to this day. This research investigates various types of postevent misinformation that could lead eyewitnesses astray, such as biased composition of lineups and suggestive instructions from law enforcement personnel. The studies also reveal some of the psychological mechanisms that underlie eyewitness misremembering—for example, eyewitnesses who are repeatedly shown a certain suspect during the investigative process might misattribute their enhanced familiarity with the suspect to having viewed him at the scene of the crime. Given these findings, the studies suggest potential remedies for minimizing the introduction of postevent misinformation and its effects on eyewitness accounts. Several recent works recount the empirical research literature on eyewitness suggestibility (e.g., Cutler, 2013; Lampinen, Neuschatz, & Cling, 2012).

## False Confessions

A large body of research investigates elements of police interrogations hypothesized to generate false confessions by innocent suspects. These studies focus primarily on the effects of questioning suspects for lengthy periods of time; confronting suspects with false evidence (e.g., that a fictitious eyewitness has identified them or that investigators found their DNA at the crime scene); and impliedly promising suspects leniency if they confess.

Drizin and Leo (2004) found that interrogations resulting in false confessions lasted 16.3 hours on average, approximately 14 hours beyond usual interrogations. These extended interrogations induce substantial physical and mental fatigue in suspects, which impairs their cognitive functioning and emotional regulation and thereby renders them more prone to falsely confessing.

Kassin and Kiechel (1996) simulated the police practice of presenting suspects with false evidence in order to encourage them to confess. In a purported study of reaction time, participants typed on a computer keyboard letters that a confederate of the experimenters read to them at either a slow or fast pace. Each participant was warned to avoid pressing the "ALT" key because this would supposedly cause the computer software to crash and the experimental data to be lost. When, during the experiment, the software stopped functioning due to no fault of the participants but the experimenter nonetheless accused the participants of pressing the forbidden key, every participant initially denied having done so. When a confederate then falsely claimed that she had seen the participant hit the forbidden key, however, 89 percent of participants in the slow-paced condition and 100 percent of participants in the fast-paced condition (who were less confident in their actions and therefore more susceptible to suggestion) signed a confession. This research and subsequent studies (e.g., Kassin et al., 2010) indicate that innocent suspects might falsely confess to committing crimes when confronted with fabricated evidence of their involvement.

Klaver, Lee, and Rose (2008) investigated the effects of interrogators' implicit promises to suspects that confessing will result in lighter punishment than will continued protestations of innocence. Within the Kassin and Kiechel (1996) reaction-time paradigm, participants were more likely to falsely confess when the experimenter normalized the act, termed it an accident, and blamed it on the computer. These results suggest that innocent criminal suspects might interpret police-offered moral justifications and face-saving excuses for the crime to be implied promises of leniency were they to confess. This, in turn, can decrease innocent suspects' resistance to falsely confessing. Implied promises of leniency thus can operate similarly to express promises of leniency, which courts view skeptically when determining whether a confession was coerced (Kassin et al., 2010).

Regardless of the precise factors that precipitate false confessions, these declarations often set in motion a pernicious chain of events within the criminal justice system. Police and prosecutors might consider a false confession to be confirmation of a suspect's guilt and therefore not investigate other suspects or discount exculpatory evidence (Kassin, 2012). False confessions also might corrupt the judgments of polygraph examiners, fingerprint experts, eyewitnesses, and other persons who are presumed to provide independent assessments of defendants' involvement in criminal activity (Kassin, Bogart, & Kerner, 2012). Finally, judges and jurors might be more inclined to find a defendant guilty when he has confessed to the charges against him, even when they believe the confession was coerced (Kassin & Sukel, 1997; Wallace & Kassin, 2012).

In sum, for decades, there has been a continual stream of studies investigates factors that increase the likelihood of eliciting false confessions from crime suspects and the consequences of false confessions within the investigative and adjudicative processes. Several reviews of this literature discuss these manifestations of social influence in greater detail (e.g., Kassin et al., 2010; Lassiter & Meissner, 2010).

More recently, psychologists have studied interrogations of suspected terrorists (e.g., Alison et al., 2014). This enterprise is conceptually related to traditional criminal interrogations but focuses on aiding intelligence-community interrogators in eliciting accurate and timely information from terrorist affiliates for use by national security personnel.

## Juror Decision Making

The factors that influence juror decision making constitute another popular area of psychological inquiry. Several primary issues include how jurors make sense of and use the voluminous, disparate, and conflicting evidence presented at trial; the role of inappropriate influences such as pretrial publicity, inadmissible evidence, and limited-use evidence on juror decision making, including the effectiveness of judicial instructions to disregard;

the relative persuasiveness of different types of evidence; methods attorneys might employ to minimize the influence that weaknesses in their clients' cases will exert on jurors; the degree to which trial attorneys' monetary requests influence the size of jurors' damage awards; and whether the verdict options that trial judges provide influence jurors' verdicts apart from the merits of the case. We address each of these aspects of the juror decision making literature below.

## Story Model

The most compelling description of juror decision making recognizes the persuasive power of narratives. In a series of studies, Pennington and Hastie (e.g., 1992, 1993) found that jurors construct stories about the events that underlie the case, and that these stories derive from three primary elements—1) the evidence and arguments presented at trial (Pennington and Hastie mentioned only evidence, but attorneys' arguments also naturally fall in this category), 2) jurors' knowledge of similar situations, and 3) jurors' general understanding of human behavior. Jurors ultimately arrive at verdicts by comparing the story that provides the greatest explanatory power of the evidence to the verdict options articulated by the trial judge. They place great weight on facts that fit their preferred story, draw inferences to fill missing gaps in the story, and downplay or disregard facts that contradict the story. While Pennington and Hastie focused on criminal trials, more recent research provides empirical support for the story model within the civil realm (Huntley & Costanzo, 2003). Studies of metaphor and other rhetorical devices provide substance to the story model framework. Research by Vasquez et al. (2014), for example, suggests that if prosecutors describe a defendant's actions in animalistic terms, jurors might view him as more likely to recidivate and therefore deserving of harsher punishment for the crime.

While the story model presents a general overview of juror decision making, it does not account for such extralegal influences as pretrial publicity, inadmissible evidence, and limited-use evidence on jurors' judgments. Rather, the model assumes that jurors incorporate only permissible evidence into their stories of the case. Pennington and Hastie (1993) acknowledge, however, that this assumption is probably more normative than descriptive, and empirical studies support the conclusion that jurors are often influenced by information not sanctioned by the formal rules of court.

## Pretrial Publicity, Inadmissible Evidence, and Limited-Use Evidence

### PRETRIAL PUBLICITY

A cardinal rule of trials is that jurors should base their judgments on information they hear and see in court. During voir dire, judges remove jury pool members who appear to be contaminated by pretrial publicity. If the contamination permeates the local jury pool, judges permit a change in venue. A meta-analysis (Steblay, Besirevic, Fulero, & Jimenez-Lorente, 1999) indicates that the judiciary's concerns are well founded; mock jurors who were exposed to negative pretrial publicity about a defendant or events at issue in a case were more likely to find the defendant guilty.

Several studies investigate methods for reducing the influence of pretrial publicity on jurors. Traditional measures, such as judicial admonitions to set aside this information, are generally ineffective (Studebaker & Penrod, 1997). More novel approaches to countering prejudicial pretrial publicity are rare. In one study, Fein, McCloskey, and Tomlinson (1997, Study 1) investigated the effects of causing jurors to question the validity and relevance of the pretrial publicity. They presented mock jurors with a criminal trial in which the defendant was accused of murdering his estranged wife and a male neighbor. Before the trial, some of the jurors read newspaper excerpts that incriminated the defendant. The excerpts suggested, for example, that the defendant's fingerprints were found on the murder weapon and an eyewitness placed him at the scene of the crime. Some of the jurors who read this incriminating information also read a newspaper article in which defense counsel questioned the information's validity and the motives of the press in publishing it. The attorney termed the pretrial publicity libelous, accused the media of omitting exonerating information in order to dramatize the story, and went so far as to suggest that the prosecution might have planted the information in order to inappropriately color public opinion. While all of the jurors were instructed to base their verdicts solely on the information presented at trial, those who encountered the pretrial publicity were more likely to find the defendant guilty unless they were induced to be suspicious of it.

### INADMISSIBLE EVIDENCE

Evidence is inadmissible at trial if the presiding judge deems it irrelevant, unduly prejudicial, confusing, misleading, unfounded, or contrary to specific public policy concerns (*Federal rules of evidence* [*FRE*], 402, 403; 2014). When jurors see or hear evidence that falls within these categories, the trial judge instructs them to disregard it in its entirety.

Many studies demonstrate the general inefficacy of traditional instructions to disregard (e.g., Kassin & Sommers, 1997; Thompson, Fong, & Rosenhan, 1981). A meta-analysis of the inadmissible evidence literature (Steblay, Hosch, Culhane, & McWethy, 2006) finds that instructions to disregard often fail to eliminate the impact of inadmissible evidence on mock jurors' verdicts. Moreover, instructions to disregard sometimes cause jurors to place greater weight on inadmissible evidence than they would in the absence of an instruction.

Given the generally unproductive nature of traditional instructions to disregard, researchers have tested alternative methods to remedy juror exposure to prejudicial inadmissible evidence. Diamond and Casper (1992) explored the effects of trial judges telling jurors the reasoning behind the instruction to disregard. In this study, an instruction that merely directed jurors to disregard the inadmissible evidence was ineffective, whereas an instruction that explained why jurors should disregard the inadmissible evidence negated its effects. These results indicate that some explanations underlying instructions to disregard can counter the influence of inadmissible evidence on jurors' verdicts.

In a study akin to their pretrial publicity work, Fein, McCloskey, and Tomlinson (1997, Study 2) investigated the effects of instructions to disregard that induce jurors to be suspicious of a trial attorney's motive in introducing prejudicial inadmissible evidence. Jurors who received a more-or-less traditional objection and instruction were influenced by the inadmissible evidence, whereas those who received a suspicion-inducing objection and instruction were not. The study suggests that jurors' suspicion regarding the introducing party's ulterior motives can eradicate the effects of inadmissible evidence. This type of instruction raises serious policy concerns, however. A judge who actively undermines the credibility of certain trial participants— for example, defense counsel—might violate litigants' right to a fair trial. Moreover, even when a suspicion-inducing instruction does not raise this constitutional concern, it might nonetheless remove trial judges from their role as objective arbiters of legal proceedings.

To effectively negate the effects of inadmissible evidence on jurors' verdicts while avoiding unwanted policy consequences, Demaine (2008) proposed that courts change their view of disregarding from forgetting to debiasing. Under this new approach to disregarding, courts would acknowledge that jurors cannot erase inadmissible evidence from their minds and recognize that jurors can correct for the biasing effects that this evidence exerts on their verdicts. The debiasing approach eliminates several concerns inherent to the traditional forgetting approach. For example, judges would no longer instruct jurors to undertake the cognitively impossible task of ridding their minds of the objectionable evidence or refuse to give an instruction to disregard on the grounds that doing so would only draw more attention to the objectionable evidence and thereby make it more difficult for jurors to forget the evidence. In an empirical test, Demaine found that jurors who received a debiasing instruction rendered a percentage of guilty verdicts indistinguishable from jurors who had not learned of the inadmissible evidence.

Taken as a whole, empirical investigations of inadmissible evidence suggest that judicial instructions to disregard are often ineffective but that, with careful wording and delivery, they can eliminate objectionable influences from jurors' verdicts (Demaine, 2012).

## LIMITED-USE EVIDENCE

In *Bruton v. United States*, the United States Supreme Court found that jurors cannot be expected to use the confession of a defendant when deciding his guilt yet disregard this confession when deciding the guilt of a co-defendant also implicated by the confession. The courts have not extended *Bruton* to other types of limited-use evidence (e.g., hearsay, prior convictions, or subsequent remedial measures) and cases (e.g., civil), however. Rather, the prevailing view within the legal system is that jurors can partially disregard all types of limited-use evidence except the confession of a co-defendant (*FRE* Rule 105).

Several psychologists have investigated this assumption.

Wissler and Saks (1985) tested the impact of prior conviction evidence on mock jurors' judgments of a defendant's credibility and culpability in two criminal cases. Jurors in these studies used the prior conviction evidence entirely contrary to the *FRE*—when the judge gave a limiting instruction, credibility ratings of the defendant were not influenced by evidence of a prior conviction, whereas judgments of the defendant's guilt were higher.

In the civil realm, Tanford and Cox (1987) found in a product liability case that a prior perjury conviction decreased a defendant's credibility with mock jurors, as predicted by the *FRE*. The perjury conviction also caused a higher percentage of jurors to find the defendant liable, however, potentially contrary to the *FRE*'s assumptions. Underscoring the possibility that limiting instructions might compound the inappropriate influence of limited-use evidence, the prior conviction had a stronger effect when the judge gave a limiting instruction than when the jurors merely decided how much weight to give it in deciding the defendant's liability.

Investigations by Severance and Loftus (1982) indicate that these unintended effects of limited-use evidence result at least partially from juror confusion regarding what precisely the limiting instruction directs them to do. Half of participants (52 percent) in one study and a third of participants (34 percent) in a second study misunderstood the Washington Pattern Instruction on the proper use of a prior conviction to impeach a testifying defendant. In these studies, 44 percent and 37 percent of participants, respectively, incorrectly applied the limiting instruction to the facts of the case. Clarifying the wording of the instruction led to only small increases in understanding and correct application (2.5 percent for understanding and 6 percent for correct application).

Taken as a whole, this literature suggests that limited-use evidence, in the form of a prior conviction, often exerts a strong, inappropriate influence on jurors' verdicts and that the traditional limiting instruction is unlikely to overcome this influence. In fact, the instruction can have an effect opposite that intended. Unlike with inadmissible evidence, researchers have yet to test nontraditional methods by which limited-use instructions might fulfill their policy objectives.

Similar issues arise when multiple defendants or multiple offenses are joined in one criminal case (*Federal rules of criminal procedure*, 2014). Research consistently demonstrates that jurors more often find a defendant guilty of a particular offense when they learn of evidence relating to at least one other offense (e.g., Greene & Loftus, 1985; Tanford & Penrod, 1984). The increase in guilty verdicts results most consistently from jurors' confusion regarding which evidence they should consider for which issues and negative inferences jurors draw from the limited-use evidence about the defendant. Limiting instructions in these studies were generally ineffective at eliminating the inappropriate influence. Although less studied, multiple-defendant trials would be expected to involve similar psychological processes and outcomes.

## TYPES OF EVIDENCE

A primary issue regarding admissible evidence—that is, evidence the judiciary deems appropriate for jurors to consider is that some types are more influential than others. Psychologists have investigated these differential effects primarily in the context of visually versus verbally presented evidence.

In Kassin and Dunn (1997, Study 1), the plaintiff claimed that her husband accidentally fell from a building at a construction site and the defendant insurance company was obligated to pay her the proceeds of the husband's life policy. The insurance company argued that the husband committed suicide, thereby voiding its obligation to pay. Mock jurors watched one of two versions of a 30-minute videotaped trial; one slightly favored the widow, whereas the other slightly favored the insurance company. Jurors who only saw these trials rendered comparable verdicts (the difference was a mere 8 percent). Some jurors also viewed a 10-second computer-animated re-enactment of the husband's death that corroborated either the plaintiff's or the insurance company's claim that had been made in the verbally presented evidence. This brief clip substantially altered jurors' verdicts, magnifying the difference between the pro-plaintiff and pro-defendant versions of the trial to 59 percent.

Douglas, Lyon, and Ogloff (1997) investigated the impact of a different type of visual evidence—graphic autopsy photographs—on mock jurors' verdicts in a criminal murder trial. The jurors read a 30-page trial transcript that included the medical examiner's description of the victim's body. Some of the jurors also saw three autopsy photos of the victim. These photos doubled, on average, the percentage of guilty verdicts, despite the fact that the trial transcript described the information the photos depicted.

This research suggests that visual evidence can exert a comparatively greater powerful influence on jurors (and perhaps other legal decision makers) than does its more commonly utilized verbal counterpart. Other studies indicate that confessions and eyewitness identifications also are quite influential (Kassin, 2014; Loftus, 2013).

## STEALING THUNDER

Cases that proceed to trial inevitably involve weaknesses on each side. These weaknesses might include undesirable characteristics of litigants, less than pristine witnesses, or ill-advised prior statements, for example. A fundamental question for trial attorneys is whether to allow opposing counsel to introduce these weaknesses to the jury or, instead, to take preemptive action, often referred to as "stealing thunder."

Williams, Bourgeois, and Croyle (1993) assessed the consequences of stealing thunder in a pair of studies. In the first study, mock jurors decided a criminal trial. Supporting the effectiveness of stealing thunder, jurors' probability-of-guilt scores were lower when the defense preemptively disclosed the defendant's prior convictions than when the prosecution initially presented them. The defense attorney experienced an increase in credibility following acknowledgment of the weakness, which resulted in the more favorable outcome for his client. The second study, involving a civil case, corroborated the findings of the first. In both studies, stealing thunder reduced the negative impact of the weakness on jurors' verdicts, by enhancing the credibility of the trial participant who employed the tactic.

Concluding that Williams, Bourgeois, and Croyle (1993) had placed a positive spin on the potentially damaging information, Dolnik, Case, and Williams (2003, Study 1) examined whether a positive spin is essential to stealing thunder or merely admitting a weakness is sufficient. The results indicate that trial participants can steal thunder without placing weaknesses in a positive light. Jurors in the stealing thunder–no framing condition rendered fewer guilty verdicts than jurors in the thunder condition, and the stolen thunder-framing condition fell between the two, differing significantly from neither. The researchers acknowledge, however, that while their particular framing of the weakness was not particularly effective, well-crafted framing could potentially outperform no framing. Curiously, in contrast to their previous studies, the relationship between stealing thunder and perceived guilt was not mediated by enhanced credibility of the acknowledging person.

The absence of credibility mediation spurred Dolnik, Case, and Williams (2003, Study 2) to investigate another potential mediator of stealing thunder—a change in the meaning of the revealed information. The researchers posited that stealing thunder can cause jurors to interpret the admitted weakness consistently with what they expect the affiliated party to be willing to reveal. Supporting this hypothesis, jurors in the stealing thunder–no framing condition judged the weakness to be less damaging than did jurors in the thunder condition. Credibility once again did not mediate the effect, perhaps because when jurors view the weakness as

less damaging, they give the person who reveals it less credit.

Dolnik, Case, and Williams (2003, Study 2) also investigated a method opposing parties might employ to counter stealing thunder—an accusation that the acknowledging party employed the tactic to manipulate the jurors into believing that he is more honest than they naturally would. Mock jurors' verdicts demonstrated, as in the earlier studies, that stealing thunder reduced the negative effects of damaging information. Informing jurors that the defendant had stolen thunder in an attempt to manipulate them, however, negated the tactic's benefit.

These investigations evidence the benefits of stealing thunder. They consistently find that stealing thunder at least partially negates the negative effects of weaknesses in the case on jurors' judgments, unless the jurors perceive the revelation to be manipulative as opposed to indicative of a forthright presentation of the case.

## DAMAGE AWARD ANCHORS

In civil cases, litigants generally seek monetary awards as compensation for their claimed injuries. These injuries can be economic in nature, such as medical expenses and lost wages, or noneconomic, which consist mainly of the "pain and suffering" that accompanies physical injuries. Economic damages translate relatively easily into monetary awards. In contrast, no specific dollar amount corresponds to noneconomic damages. To guide jurors in making noneconomic determinations, plaintiffs' attorneys propose substantial *ad damnums*—or specific monetary amounts—to compensate their clients, and defense counsel counter with correspondingly suppressed figures. Furthermore, plaintiffs' attorneys sometimes attempt to justify, or minimize, their *ad damnums* by breaking them down into small increments. This might take the form of a per diem proposal, for example, which suggests that a plaintiff's pain and suffering is worth a certain, relatively small amount per day multiplied by the days of suffering, which equals the requested *ad damnum*.

Marti and Wissler (2000) investigated the effects of *ad damnums* and defense counters on jurors' damage awards. Mock jurors awarded higher damages when the plaintiff's attorney offered an *ad damnum* versus merely presented the case without suggesting an appropriate amount of compensation for his client. Jurors' awards increased as the plaintiff's request increased, albeit not in proportion to the magnitude of the increased request. Defense counsel's attempts to counter the plaintiff's *ad damnum* were partially successful. When the defense countered with a comparatively quite low amount, the jurors rendered lower awards than when the defense offered no counter; in contrast, a higher counter was ineffective by this standard.

Marti and Wissler (2000) also investigated whether extreme *ad damnums* and defense counters might prove counterproductive (i.e., cause jurors to award less than they would without an *ad damnum* or more than they would without a defense counter). When the *ad damnum* was immense, jurors awarded less than when it was relatively moderate but still substantially more than when the plaintiff's attorney offered no *ad damnum*. The defense rebuttal evidenced a similar trend. The researchers suggest that the failure of extreme *ad damnums* and defense figures to produce counterproductive effects is attributable to the ambiguity inherent in assigning a dollar value to pain and suffering. In the absence of an objectively appropriate amount to compensate the plaintiff, jurors might view extreme requests as legitimate and therefore be unmotivated to reject them (Brehm & Brehm, 1981; Wilson & Brekke, 1994).

McAuliff and Bornstein (2010) investigated whether the form of a damage award request, as opposed to its amount, influences jurors' judgments. Mock jurors decided a negligence case in which the plaintiff sought compensation for two years of pain and suffering. The plaintiff's attorney offered one of four equivalent damage award recommendations—$10/hour, $240/day, $7,300/month, or a $175,000 *ad damnum*—or suggested no amount. The pain and suffering awards were larger when the attorney requested $10/hour or a $175,000 lump sum than when he requested $7,300/month or did not state an amount, and the $240/day recommendation produced intermediate awards. In other words, as the dollar amount in the numerator of the "per" conditions increased, jurors' awards decreased linearly; and the lump sum was as effective as the most effective "per" suggestion of $10/hour. A follow-up study revealed that these differential awards might have occurred because the jurors emphasized the dollar amounts attached to the "per" requests and perceived the larger dollar amounts to yield a larger award for the plaintiff even though the correspondingly larger time units rendered the awards equal.

These studies indicate that noneconomic damage award anchors can influence jurors' judgments independent of the evidence in a case. They

also indicate that the magnitude and form of the requests determine to a large degree the extent of this influence. A study conducted on actual jurors, without manipulating the *ad damnum* variable, suggests that, as with many psychological phenomena, a real trial context, with its greater complexity and variety of stimuli, might temper the persuasive power of these requests (Diamond, Rose, Murphy, & Meixner, 2011).

### VERDICT OPTIONS

Psychologists have recognized that jurors' decisions also could be influenced by the range of verdict options that judges provide. Jurors might acquit a criminal defendant, for example, if the only options are murder and acquittal and the jurors conclude that the defendant's blameworthiness falls short of murder. Jurors might be willing to convict the defendant if a lesser included offense such as manslaughter were also an option, however. Likewise, in the civil realm, jurors might find a defendant not liable for a plaintiff's harm if the plaintiff asserts only strict liability as opposed to also making the less stringent legal claim of negligence.

In a study of verdict options, Kelman, Rottenstreich, and Tversky (1996, Study 2) presented mock jurors with a homicide case in which the parties stipulated that the defendant had purposely killed the victim. The jurors' task was to determine what level of homicide the defendant had committed: special circumstances murder, murder, voluntary manslaughter, or involuntary manslaughter. Each juror was instructed on the elements of these four crimes, ensuring that they all possessed the same information when deciding the case. Some of the jurors were also instructed that the judge had ruled as a matter of law that special circumstances murder was not justified given the facts of the case. The other jurors were instructed that the judge had eliminated the involuntary manslaughter option. These different verdict options caused different verdict distributions. When the judge eliminated the involuntary manslaughter option, the majority of jurors voted for murder, whereas when the judge eliminated the murder with special circumstances option, the majority of jurors voted for voluntary manslaughter. The jurors gravitated toward a moderate, or compromise, verdict in each instance, and the legal charge corresponding to that verdict depended on the options available.

In a related vein, Greenberg, Williams, and O'Brien (1986) studied the effects of jurors considering the same verdict options—first-degree murder, second-degree murder, voluntary manslaughter, involuntary manslaughter, or not guilty—but in different orders. Jurors who were instructed to contemplate the options from harshest to most lenient rendered harsher verdicts than did jurors who were instructed to think about the options in the opposite order.

These studies support the idea that trial attorneys can influence jurors' decisions by careful selection of the claims they make, regardless of the substance of a case, and the corollary that judges should be mindful of the manner in which they present the verdict options to jurors.

## Judicial Decision-Making

While most legal decision-making studies focus on jurors, psychologists have begun investigating factors that influence judicial determinations. These judicial decision-making studies initially addressed two main aspects of the juror decision-making literature—inadmissible evidence and damage award anchors—and have recently investigated a broader array of topics.

### Inadmissible Evidence

Wistrich, Guthrie, and Rachlinski (2005) investigated whether judicial decisions are influenced by inadmissible evidence, which judges as well as juries should ignore when making judgments. In a test of several different forms of inadmissible evidence (a settlement demand, material protected by the attorney-client privilege, the sexual history of an alleged sexual assault victim, the prior conviction of a plaintiff in a personal injury case, information that the prosecution agreed not to introduce against a defendant pursuant to a cooperation agreement, the outcome of a search when determining whether probable cause existed, and a defendant's confession obtained in violation of his right to counsel), judges were inappropriately influenced by all but the outcome of the search and the confession.

Wallace and Kassin (2012) undertook a more narrow investigation—the effect of a defendant's confession on judicial determinations. Judges read a murder trial summary that contained either strong or weak evidence implicating the defendant and one of three confession conditions—high pressure, low pressure, or no confession. As would be expected, the judges more often viewed the defendant's confession as involuntary when it occurred under high pressure than low pressure (84 percent vs. 29 percent). Nonetheless, when the evidence in the case was weak, judges who learned of the high-pressure

confession were markedly more likely to find the defendant guilty than when there was no confession (69 percent vs. 17 percent). This finding indicates that high-pressure confessions might influence judicial determinations despite their questionable legal and factual validity, contradicting the Wistrich, Guthrie, and Rachlinski (2005) finding that judges ignore a criminal defendant's confession.

These studies, albeit preliminary, indicate that judges, like jurors, are often influenced by prejudicial inadmissible evidence to the detriment of the parties against whom this evidence is introduced.

### Damage Award Anchors

In a study of the effects of damage award anchors on judicial decision making, Guthrie, Rachlinski, and Wistrich (2001) gave judges a description of a personal injury lawsuit in which the defendant had seriously injured the defendant. In the no-anchor condition, the judges were asked how much they would award the plaintiff in compensatory damages. In the anchor condition, the judges learned that the defendant had moved that the case be dismissed because it did not meet the minimum of $75,000 for a diversity case. The judges ruled on this motion—which was meritless because the plaintiff had incurred damages far greater than $75,000—and rendered a compensatory damage award. Judges in the anchor condition (all but two of whom denied the motion) awarded 29 percent less on average than those in the no-anchor condition. In other words, the $75,000 jurisdictional requirement—an irrelevant figure in the calculation of the damage award—apparently influenced the judges' valuation of the case.

Guthrie, Rachlinski, and Wistrich (2009) replicated the anchoring effect in a wrongful termination of employment case. The researchers also tested whether requiring judges to explain the reasoning behind their compensatory awards, ostensibly for a reviewing body, can ameliorate anchoring effects. This attempted corrective failed to overcome the influence of the anchor on judges' valuations of the case—despite any increase in higher order thinking or concern with accountability engendered by the explanation—suggesting that anchoring effects can be fairly resistant to countermeasures other than perhaps a competing dollar amount (see discussion of damage award anchors in the section on "Juror Decision-Making," *supra*).

These initial studies of judicial decision making indicate that, although judges possess greater education and experience with legal decisions than the average juror, their reactions to environmental influences might be similar to jurors in many important respects. Subsequent studies explore an array of other potential extralegal influences on judicial decision making (Rachlinski, Wistrich, & Guthrie, 2013).

## Legislative Decision Making

Psychologists have generally forgone investigations of legislative decision making. Demaine (2009), however, investigated US legislators' practice of inviting celebrity entertainers (actors, musicians, and athletes, for example) to testify at congressional hearings on issues unrelated to their achievements. She found that celebrity entertainers testified before congressional committees about twice per month on average between 1980 and 2004, and that the frequency of celebrity testimony more than doubled between the 1980–1984 and 2000–2004 time periods.

To explain why celebrity testimony became an established part of the US legislative process, Demaine explored the psychology of celebrity appeal. She found that legislators' motives for calling celebrity entertainers are multifaceted and include, for example, the magnified attention that celebrity-affiliated issues receive from key players such as the media, the public, and fellow legislators; the opportunity for legislators to bask in the reflected glory of the celebrities; and legislators' personal fascination with celebrities.

Supporters of celebrity entertainer testimony deem the practice helpful, or at worst benign, under the presumption that celebrities merely bring attention to social issues and leave the substance of policy making to trained professionals. Demaine found, however, that the distinction between awareness and influence is mainly false. Legislators have limited time and attention, such that when they engage with celebrity entertainers' issues, they necessarily neglect other issues and constituencies. Moreover, 497 (98 percent) of the 507 celebrities who testified between 1980 and 2004 either proposed a solution to their issue or endorsed or opposed a solution that the federal government was contemplating. That is the celebrities did not merely bring attention to social issues but, rather, actively participated in substantive policy discussions.

Demaine also considered whether celebrity entertainers' participation in the lawmaking process fosters sound policy decisions. Only two of the 507 celebrity entertainer witnesses possessed formal education on the issues about which they testified,

and there was no evidence that the celebrities had received similar training in policy analysis. Demaine concluded that while formal education is not the sine qua non of quality testimony, it is an important factor when evaluating congressional witnesses' qualifications, and particularly the qualifications of unusually influential witnesses. Celebrity entertainers' lack of formal education combined with their extraordinary public appeal renders their involvement in the legislative process generally problematic.

In brief, psychologists have made great strides with several topics in the realm of "social influence in the legal system." They have learned much about eyewitness testimony, false confessions, and juror decision making; gained preliminary insights into how judges reach decisions; and recently begun exploring legislative decision making. While other topics on social influence in the legal system clearly exist, as do other social influence issues within the already explored topics, psychologists have vigorously (some would say relentlessly) pursued this area compared to the subjects that follow—the legal regulation of social influence in everyday life and law as an instrument of social influence. Few topics within these latter categories have been studied at all and rare is the topic that has received considerable psychological empirical attention, as the sporadic nature of the reviewed research will demonstrate.

## Legal Regulation of Social Influence in Everyday Life

Following World War II, psychologists conducted groundbreaking studies of powerful social influences in everyday life (e.g., Milgram, 1974; Zimbardo, 2007). They sought to understand how large numbers of people were persuaded to commit atrocities under Adolf Hitler's Nazi regime and how similar influences might operate frequently at less magnitude. Although these studies could have inspired sustained research activity that would foster effective and ethical government regulation of social influence, psychologists have left this area largely unpursued. This section represents our limited knowledge of social influences that the government currently regulates or that might be of sufficient magnitude to warrant regulation.

## Deceptive and Unfair Advertising

At the turn of the 20th century, Congress created the Federal Trade Commission (FTC) and tasked it with monitoring deception and other forms of unfairness in commercial advertising

(Federal Trade Commission Act). Since the 1970s, researchers have investigated myriad psychological issues that inform this regulatory framework. The studies explore children's and adults' vulnerability to deceptive commercial messages; the effectiveness of corrective advertising, which the government may mandate when it determines that an advertiser has deceived the public; and, more recently, the effects of direct-to-consumer advertising of prescription drugs on consumers and health care providers.

### Directed at Children

Wilcox et al. (2004) reviewed the psychological literature on children's vulnerability to advertising. These studies indicate that children under 4–5 years of age do not consistently differentiate television programming from advertisements. At 4–5 years, children generally distinguish between programs and commercials on fairly simple dimensions—for example, they find commercials shorter or funnier than programs. However, not until at least 7–8 years of age, and perhaps not until age 11–12, do most children attribute persuasive intent to advertising (see also Carter, Patterson, Donovan, Ewing, & Roberts, 2011). Kunkel and Castonguay (2012) point out that these studies might underplay children's vulnerability to advertising, as they often fail to discern whether children who recognize advertisers' persuasive intent also realize that this persuasive intent might cause advertisers to exaggerate or embellish product features.

Children thus process advertising claims more credulously than do persons with greater developmental maturity.

Researchers have considered ways to decrease advertising's effects on children. Buijzen (2007), for example, found that factual and evaluative interventions reduced the susceptibility of children aged 7–10 years to advertising's influence, whereas younger children received little benefit from the interventions. Other researchers have investigated children's responses to disclaimers and disclosures that advertisers include to render otherwise deceptive claims legally permissible. These studies indicate that young children generally do not understand commonly used disclaimers and disclosures (e.g., "some assembly required") and that rephrasing these statements in terms better suited to children (e.g., "you have to put it together") substantially increases their comprehension (e.g., Kunkel & Castonguay, 2012).

The literature on children's responses to advertising focuses on television commercials. Recent research comparing television commercials versus nontraditional advertising—such as movie and video game brand placement and product licensing—indicates that children possess an even less sophisticated understanding of the newer forms of advertising and are therefore less likely to view them critically (Owen, Lewis, Auty, & Buijzen, 2013).

### Directed at Adults

#### DECEPTION AND ITS EFFECTS

An illustrative study of the effects of deceptive advertising on adults (Olson & Dover, 1978) showed participants three different ads for a new brand of coffee at 4-day intervals and assessed their perceptions of the product compared to other participants who did not see these ads. Each ad included the same false claim about the advertised product—that the coffee had no bitterness when it was actually quite bitter. All participants then sampled the coffee and assessed its characteristics, in order to discern the degree to which exposure to the product counteracted any effects of the deception. Participants who saw the ads reported that the coffee was less bitter than those who merely rated the coffee's bitterness after tasting it, suggesting that the ads instilled a false belief about this product attribute. Further, these false beliefs drove purchasing behavior—participants who saw the ads were more inclined to purchase the coffee than were those who only tasted the coffee. Most intriguingly, the study suggests that consumers' false beliefs and corresponding intentions to purchase can persist despite their use of the product, perhaps because false advertising creates certain expectations or positive views of the product that consumers subjectively confirm.

#### EXPLICIT VERSUS IMPLIED CLAIMS

Whereas explicit advertising claims are generally straightforward, implicit advertising claims tend to be open to multiple interpretations. Shimp (1978), for example, investigated how consumers interpret incomplete comparisons of products. Participants reviewed a deodorant ad or an automobile ad, each of which contained an incomplete comparison. The car claimed to be "built better to give you more"; one of the deodorants claimed to help consumers "stay dryer." Participants completed these comparisons in the manner the advertisers intended, with positive product attributes.

For example, 53 percent of participants who viewed the car ad believed that the incomplete comparison might end with "luxury and sportiness," and 66 percent believed that the "stay dryer" ad might end with "than any other antiperspirant on the market." In fact, 28 percent and 64 percent of participants, respectively, mistakenly believed that the ad had directly stated these claims rather than implied them. This research suggests that consumers employ social conventions to finish incomplete comparisons in ways that render them potentially misleading.

Burke et al. (1988) focused on two common deceptive implications—expansion and inconspicuous qualification—and applied them to four product attributes in ads for ibuprofen-based pain relievers: headache and pain relief, side effects, low price, and speed of relief. For example, for side effects, the truthful statement read: "Fewer gastrointestinal side effects than aspirin"; the expansion implication read: "None of aspirin's annoying side effects"; and the inconspicuous qualification implication read: "None of aspirin's annoying side effects (causes fewer gastrointestinal side effects than aspirin)." Both implied claims created stronger beliefs on the attribute dimensions than did true claims or control conditions, which contained no information regarding product attributes. The same trend held for participants' reported likelihood of purchasing the products. The erroneous beliefs carried over, at times, to other product dimensions. For example, participants with a stronger belief in the drug's speed of relief more strongly believed that it was an effective pain reliever. Implied deception on one product dimension thus might color consumers' perceptions of other product characteristics.

PUFFERY

The FTC and courts permit advertisers to "puff," that is, to offer exaggerated opinions about a product or service that reasonable consumers recognize as false, and discount accordingly (Preston, 1996). Superlatives such as "the best" and "the finest," and other hyperbole, fall within this category.

Empirical studies suggest that puffery influences consumers (albeit whether the consumers are "reasonable" is a legal determination). Rotfeld and Rotzoll (1980), for example, assessed the degree to which participants believed puffery claims in ads for products such as aspirin, shampoo, and cold cream. Participants believed 40 percent of the

puffery claims, and this number rose to 49 percent for participants who reported that the ads had communicated the puffery claims, which provides greater assurance that they processed the puffery. These numbers obtained for a relatively highly educated sample. Persons with less education might be expected to view an even higher percentage of puffery claims as true.

## Corrective Advertising

The government periodically requires companies that have engaged in deceptive advertising to publish corrective advertising designed to leave the consuming public with a more accurate view of the product or service. Armstrong, Gurol, and Russ (1979) investigated the ability of a corrective ad to counter Listerine's deceptive claims that the mouthwash could prevent, ameliorate, and cure colds and sore throats. The corrective ad was attributed to either the Warner-Lambert Company, which produced Listerine, or the FTC. In both instances, the corrective ad decreased participants' beliefs in the false claims, and the effects persisted at least 6 weeks (the last experimental measurement) (see also Mizerski, Allison, & Calvert, 1980).

In a study of an actual corrective advertising campaign, consumers were less likely to intend to purchase the product (STP's oil additive) yet maintained their pre-campaign perceptions of the company and beliefs in the general efficacy of oil additives (Bernhardt, Kinnear, & Mazis, 1986).

These findings suggest that corrective advertising can decrease the attractiveness of deceptively advertised products or services while not overly punishing affiliated companies or inadvertently punishing other business firms in that market.

## Direct-to-Consumer Advertising of Prescription Drugs

Congress and the Federal Drug Administration (FDA) place stronger constraints on direct-to-consumer advertisements of prescription drugs (DTCA) than on ads for products that consumers are deemed qualified to purchase without a professional's approval. Proponents of DTCA argue that it educates consumers, thereby empowering them to take a more informed role in their health care. Critics assert that DTCA persuades consumers to request from physicians drugs that are medically unindicated or more expensive than equally effective generics.

Davis (2007) explored the possibility that DTCA provides consumers with an unrealistically positive view of advertised drugs, despite the FDA's requirement that DTCA strike a fair balance of their risks and benefits. The study focused on qualifying language that pharmaceutical companies use to make potential side effects appear less threatening to consumers: "If . . . may" ("If side effects occur, they may include . . ."), severity/length ("Side effects tend to be mild and often go away"), and discontinuation ("Few people were bothered enough to stop taking [the drug])." The qualifiers, individually and particularly in combination, caused consumers to believe that taking the drug would be a more pleasant experience and to be more inclined to request the drug from a physician.

Kim and Park (2010) found that DTCA emphasizing the potential costs of not taking the drugs is more effective than DTCA that focuses on the drugs' benefits, when consumers believe that they have limited knowledge about the drugs.

These studies suggest that DTCA's success (Donohue, Cevasco, & Rosenthal, 2007) is at least partially attributable to downplaying the risks of taking the drugs while highlighting the risks associated with not taking them, which motivates consumers to request the drugs from physicians. These requests, in turn, influence physicians' prescribing behavior (McKinlay et al., 2014).

## Fraud

The legal doctrine of fraud captures misrepresentations and concealments of facts upon which targets may justifiably rely. Fraud occurs in myriad environments and ways, all of which pit the ingenuity and resolve of the perpetrator against unsuspecting targets. Psychological research of these dynamics is limited, however.

Pratkanis and Shadel (2005) analyzed more than 300 audiotaped calls between fraudulent telemarketers and law enforcement personnel posing as laypeople. These recordings indicate that fraudulent telemarketers employ powerful influence tactics to convince their targets to act contrary to self-interest. For example, the telemarketers created for their victims a new social reality—a "wonderland of the mind" involving excitement and reckless abandon—that facilitated their acquiescence to the scam. They offered phantom dreams—things that targets desperately wanted but were normally unachievable—that detached targets from logical reasoning. They established relationships with targets, in which they were often trusted authority figures, friends, or dependents. And they convinced targets that the options they offered were the only ones available. The telemarketers also used several classic principles of influence, including social proof (communicating that many others are participating in the investment), self-generated persuasion (subtly convincing the targets to generate reasons for doing what the telemarketer wants them to do), scarcity (underscoring that the opportunity to achieve the phantom dream is fleeting), reciprocity (offering targets information, advice, or prizes so that they feel compelled to do something in return for the telemarketer), and commitment and consistency (reminding targets that they previously took some action or said something that indicated their commitment to the telemarketers' cause, such that to back out would reflect socially undesirable inconsistency in their behavior). The precise combination of influence tactics fraudulent telemarketers employ differs by target and scam (Pratkanis, Shadel, Kleinman, Small, & Pak, 2006).

Scheibe et al. (2014) found that discussing fraud with elderly persons who had previously been defrauded reduced their vulnerability to future scams, at least in the short term. Even following this intervention, however, almost a third of participants accepted without apparent reservation materials from a mock fraudulent telemarketer, underscoring the allure of these scams and the challenge of arming targets with means to resist.

Choplin, Stark, and Ahmad (2011, Study 1) investigated influence tactics that increase consumers' acceptance of problematic contract terms. Participants were asked to sign a consent form for a research study that contained a provision substantially different from previously provided information about the study. Those who questioned the problematic provision received one of three responses: (1) confirmation that the provision would be enforced (simulating a bait-and-switch scheme); (2) assurance that the provision would not be enforced—that the form was old and inaccurate (a plausible explanation); or (3) assurance that the provision would not be enforced—that the form contained the provision because that was the way it was drafted (a senseless explanation). A substantial number of participants (40 percent) in the bait-and-switch condition signed the consent form, and participants in the plausible and senseless explanation conditions were even more likely to do so (87 percent and 80 percent, respectively).

These results indicate that it can be fairly easy for fraudsters to convince targets to acquiesce to detrimental contractual provisions by first offering enticing terms. Given that the study participants were undergraduate college students, the results also underscore that young persons are vulnerable to at least certain forms of fraud.

## Undue Influence

Courts have long recognized the doctrine of undue influence, which governs cases in which one person alleges that a second person exercised such powerful influence over the first person that the first person lost free agency. Little research has investigated the circumstances that create this extraordinary influence, however.

The few existing studies focus on one context (recruitment and retention of research participants) and one form of influence (monetary inducements). Bentley and Thacker (2004), for example, assessed participants' willingness to engage in a high-risk (Phase I trial for a drug not previously tested on humans), medium-risk (bioequivalence study of a generic version of an already marketed brand name drug), or low-risk (salivary test of stress hormones) study for high ($1,800), medium ($800), or low ($350) payment. Higher monetary incentives increased participants' willingness to participate by relatively equal degrees at each level of risk, suggesting that they did not exert undue influence. A similar study (Halpern, Karlawish, Casarett, Berlin, & Asch, 2004) produced comparable results and conclusions.

## Implanted False Memories

Persons periodically claim to have recovered repressed memories of sexual abuse in their distant past. To investigate whether someone (such as a mental health professional) might implant in others (such as patients) a pseudomemory for an event that never occurred, Loftus and other psychologists expanded on earlier studies of the malleability of memory. Given institutional review board restrictions, they crafted experiments that tested whether mildly traumatic events could be falsely implanted in participants, following the logic that the results of these studies would provide empirical evidence to support or repudiate the prevailing presumption that recovered repressed memories are always actual memories.

In a classic study, Loftus and Pickrell (1995) investigated whether they could convince participants that they had once been lost in a shopping mall. Participants read descriptions of four events

from their childhood that a relative had purportedly related to the researchers. In actuality, three of these events came from the relative, whereas the fourth event was the fabricated lost-in-the-mall story. After reading a description of each event, participants wrote down what, if anything, they remembered about it. In two follow-up interviews, participants also reported as much detail as they could about the events. Ultimately, 25 percent of participants "recalled" being lost in the mall and provided details of the event. Subsequent studies involving variations of this methodology obtained similar results (e.g., Hyman, Husband, & Billings, 1995; Porter, Yuille, & Lehman, 1999).

This research suggests that some individuals who claim to have experienced trauma in their distant past might actually have been influenced by others to create a seemingly real memory of an event that did not occur. It also supports legal claims against mental health care professionals who negligently or intentionally implant false memories in their patients.

## Consent to Search and Seizure

The US Supreme Court has articulated an influence-based standard for determining when citizens' encounters with the police and their consent to police searches are protected by the US Constitution. If a reasonable person would have felt free to terminate the encounter or refuse the search, the citizen is deemed to have acted voluntarily such that there can be no Fourth Amendment violation (*Florida v. Bostick*, 1991). The standard has provoked much debate and some empirical inquiry.

Kagehiro (1988) investigated citizens' responses to variations in the phrasing of police requests to conduct warrantless searches. In all conditions, an officer knocked at the front door of a residence. Some participants were told that the officer asked permission to enter the premises to conduct a search, whereas others learned that the officer stated his desire to enter the premises to conduct the search. Moreover, some participants learned that the search would be warrantless, whereas others did not receive this information. Finally, participants took one of two perspectives—they were either the recipient of the police request or a third-party observer of the request.

The findings provide preliminary evidence that persons who interact with police and observers of these interactions, such as judges in suppression hearings, might view important aspects of the situations differently. Observers overestimated the degree to which recipients felt free to ask the officer to leave the residence, which suggests that legal decision makers could fail to grasp the coercive nature of police–citizen interactions as perceived by the average citizen. Observers also underestimated recipients' likelihood of requesting more information from the officer and of requesting that the officer leave the residence, indicating that legal decision makers might attribute the officer's request to accurate suspicions about illegal activities carried on by the residents. And observers who learned that the officer did not mention that the search would be warrantless believed that the officer had permission to search more of the premises than did the other participants, suggesting that legal decision makers might interpret a citizen's grant of permission to search more expansively than the citizen intended.

The legal regulation of social influence provides a rich array of important issues ripe for psychological investigation. Existing studies of these topics offer insights into how key business–citizen, citizen–citizen, and government–citizen exchanges operate, which, in turn, can inform the judicious use of government checks on unfairness and disparities of power within these exchanges. The relatively sparse and scattered nature of the topics subjected to empirical study and the generally small literature on most of these topics underscore the potential for substantial further development in this area.

## Law as an Instrument of Social Influence

Governments use law as a means of shaping citizens' behavior in desired ways, such that citizens' willingness to obey these laws is vital to the stability of society. Despite the importance of understanding law as an instrument of social influence, relatively few psychologists have investigated factors that support or undermine these efforts. Existing studies address the issue from three different vantage points: the degree to which citizens view legal authorities as legitimate and the law as moral, the human tendency to obey authoritative directives, and antisocial and prosocial influences operating in different social contexts.

## Legitimacy of Legal Authorities and Morality of Law

Governments rely on punishment as a means to deter illegal behavior, following the logic that citizens are likely to obey the law if infractions result in incarceration, a fine, or some other negative consequence. While the threat of punishment does prevent some illegal behavior, this approach has inherent disadvantages. It requires vigilant enforcement of the law, which is financially costly. The main form of punishment—incarceration—imposes social costs on individuals and communities through lost productivity and strained relationships. And some modes of enforcement, such as surveillance, place the government and citizens in a combative relationship, fostering citizens' distrust and resentment of government. Moreover, despite this immense investment, punishment exerts only a weak influence on citizens' compliance with the law (e.g., Tyler & Rankin, 2012).

Tyler (e.g., 2006a, 2006b; Tyler & Rankin 2012) therefore proposed an alternative approach for enhancing citizen obedience, based on internal rather than external motivations. His empirical investigations indicate that citizens who perceive legal authorities to be legitimate are more willing to cooperate with them and comply with legal decrees, and that governments gain legitimacy through employing legal procedures that citizens deem to be fair. Furthermore, citizens are more likely to follow laws that they perceive to align with their own moral code, such that governments exert greater influence on citizens' behavior when they frame public discussions of laws in terms that resonate with the target group's morality.

Psychologists also have empirically explored the concept of restorative justice, which, like legitimacy and morality, focuses on citizens' internal motivations to obey the law (Tyler, 2006b). Restorative justice was developed specifically to reduce recidivism, however, and centers on the reintegrative shaming of offenders through bringing them together with family, friends, and victims in an effort to convince them to take responsibility for their injurious acts and reconnect with their community (e.g., Braithwaite, 2002; Wenzel, Okimoto, Feather, & Platow, 2008). Several other, more narrowly conceived, empirically tested, psychologically driven programs designed to reduce recidivism also exist (e.g, McGuire, 2008).

## Obedience to Illegal Directives From Perceived Authorities

In a widely known series of experiments, Stanley Milgram (1974) investigated the extent to which ordinary citizens would harm another person at the behest of an authority figure. In a primary study at Yale University, participants met the experimenter, who was dressed in a lab coat, and a confederate of the experimenter, who pretended to be another participant. The experimenter explained that the purpose of the study was to discern the effects of aversive stimuli on learning. He then "randomly" assigned the participant to be the teacher and the confederate to be the learner, and introduced the teacher and learner to a shock machine (which, unbeknownst to the teacher, did not actually administer shocks). Each lever on the machine was labeled with the amount of voltage it would dispense (15 to 450 volts), and verbal descriptors put the voltage numbers in perspective (slight shock to XXX). The experimenter strapped the learner into a chair and attached wires through which the learner would receive increasingly powerful electric shocks from the teacher when the learner failed to correctly recite pairs of words that the teacher read from a script. During the memory test, the learner gave progressively more alarming responses to these shocks. When teachers expressed concern about the health of the learners and a desire to stop the study, the experimenter dictated otherwise with replies such as "The experiment requires that you continue" and "You have no other choice; you must go on."

All of the teachers in this study continued to 300 volts, and 65 percent administered the 450-volt, highest magnitude shock after the learner had screamed in agony and ceased responding. Subsequently tested variations in the experimental protocol—for example, conducted at a less prestigious location, with the experimenter dressed in everyday clothes, or with teachers instructing another person to administer the shocks rather than doing it themselves—resulted in more or less compliance with the experimenter's request.

While changes in human subjects protection policies since Milgram conducted these classic studies preclude their exact replication, a partial replication (Burger, 2009) indicates that persons might be comparably vulnerable today to committing illegal acts such as assault, battery, or even murder while under the influence of (perceived) authority figures.

## Antisocial and Prosocial Influences

A diverse array of powerful social influences can work with or against lawmakers' attempts to shape citizens' behavior. Psychologists have investigated some of these prosocial and antisocial influences, particularly as they relate to delinquency. These studies find, for example, that substance abuse prevention programs that address the social influences operating on youth are generally the most effective (e.g., Cuijpers, 2002). Similarly, the research indicates that antisocial peer influences play a pivotal role in adolescent gang membership (e.g., Gilman, Hill, Hawkins, Howell, & Kosterman, 2014). Taken as a whole, these investigations underscore that antisocial adolescent behavior is better understood and corrected when its considerable social influence origins are recognized.

To a lesser degree, psychologists have studied factors that increase the likelihood of successful crisis negotiations. Taylor and Thomas (2008), for example, analyzed transcripts of several actual hostage negotiations and found that police negotiators were more often able to diffuse situations when they matched their linguistic style to that of the hostage taker. Studies of this kind produce useful insights for influencing persons who are engaging in destructive illegal behavior, or threatening to do so, to accept a peaceful resolution to the situation.

More recently, terrorism gained the attention of psychologists following the September 11, 2001, World Trade Center attacks. Kruglanski and Fishman (2009) and Wilson, Bradford, and Lemanski (2013), for example, reviewed social psychological research that informs terrorist groups' recruitment and radicalization processes and effective counterterrorism approaches. These inquiries are useful to understanding, and thwarting, extremist thought and action.

Recognizing that laws are instruments of social influence underscores the importance of psychological empirical studies on factors that affect compliance. Research to date has produced thought-provoking findings on a few topics, but this conceptual territory is largely undeveloped and holds the potential for substantial future inquiry.

### A Reflection on the Social Influence and Law Literature

Some social influence and law topics— eyewitness testimony, false confessions, and juror decision making—are among the most heavily researched topics in the field of law and psychology. Moreover, a variety of other social influence and law topics, although researched through more circumscribed efforts or left uninvestigated to date, are central concepts within the law and psychology field.

The prominent place that social influence and law holds within the field of law and psychology renders previous critiques of the field relevant to our reflections on the social influence and law literature. The present chapter reveals that researchers continue to gravitate toward a few social influence and law topics, despite long-standing recognition that a broader approach to research is necessary if the field is to have a meaningful effect on the legal system. More than a decade ago, for example, Ogloff expressed the concern that "topics covered by legal psychology remain narrow and obscure from a legal perspective" (2000, p. 474).

Two primary considerations can explain the comparatively large allure of a small array of social influence and law topics. Haney (1993) noted that legal psychologists tend to investigate legal process over substantive law, which bolsters the appeal of eyewitness testimony, false confessions, and juror decision making, and engenders comparative disinterest in other topics. Legal process is easily translatable to psychological methods of empirical study, whereas substantive law can present greater methodological challenges (Haney, 1980). Moreover, whereas substantive law is rife with complexities and nuances that psychologists without formal training in the law can have difficulty mastering, legal process is more conceptually straightforward.

One might question whether the current skew in social influence and law studies merely reflects the presence of empirical questions within each area. In other words, perhaps "social influence in the legal system" is naturally richer in issues conducive to psychological study than are the "legal regulation of social influence in everyday life" and "law as an instrument of social influence." Theoretical reflection and research activity in these latter areas suggests otherwise, however. While psychologists shied away from exploring big legal questions, other disciplines moved into their intellectual territory. In recent decades, legal commentators have increasingly used traditional psychological research in their scholarship, and economists have informed legal issues with "behavioral economics." In both cases, much of this new literature addresses social influence (e.g., Kahan & Braman, 2006; Thaler & Sunstein, 2009). Law and psychology—and law and social influence, in particular—are, ironically, developing in significant ways without the benefit of psychologist-conducted research.

## Conclusion

Since the 1970s, when the modern law and psychology movement began in earnest, the empirical study of social influence and the law has been a centerpiece of the field. Legal psychologists have actively investigated social influence as it intersects with particular elements of legal procedure and, to a lesser degree, substantive law. This chapter offers a framework for conceptualizing "social influence and the law" and reviews existing empirical studies. The framework reveals that whereas some areas of social influence have flourished, many others have floundered. Attention that researchers have paid to certain issues has eclipsed other equally or more important and interesting issues. While much has been accomplished, there remains great potential for future discoveries. We hope that the present chapter motivates and facilitates them.

## References

Alison, L., Alison, E., Noone, G., Elntib, S., Waring, S., & Christiansen, P. (2014). The efficacy of rapport-based techniques for minimizing counter-interrogation tactics amongst a field sample of terrorists. *Psychology, Public Policy, and Law, 20*, 421–430.

Armstrong, G. M., Gurol, M. N., & Russ, F. A. (1979). Detecting and correcting deceptive advertising. *Journal of Consumer Research, 6*, 237–246.

Bentley, J. P., & Thacker, P. G. (2004). The influence of risk and monetary payment on the research participation decision making process. *Journal of Medical Ethics, 30*, 293–298.

Bernhardt, K. L., Kinnear, T. C., & Mazis, M. B. (1986). A field study of corrective advertising effectiveness. *Journal of Public Policy and Marketing, 5*, 146–162.

Braithwaite, J. (2002). *Restorative justice and responsive regulation.* New York, NY: Oxford University Press.

Brehm, S. S., & Brehm, J. W. (1981). *Psychological reactance: A theory of freedom and control.* New York, NY: Academic Press.

Bruton v. United States, 391 U.S. 123 (1968).

Buijzen, M. (2007). Reducing children's susceptibility to commercials: Mechanisms of factual and evaluative advertising interventions. *Media Psychology, 9*, 411–430.

Burger, J. M. (2009). Replicating Milgram: Would people still obey today? *American Psychologist, 64*, 1–11.

Burke, R. R., DeSarbo, W. S., Oliver, R. L., & Robertson, T. S. (1988). Deception by implication: An experimental investigation. *Journal of Consumer Research, 14*, 483–494.

Carter, O. B. J., Patterson, L. J., Donovan, R. J., Ewing, M. T., & Roberts, C. M. (2011). Children's understanding of the selling versus persuasive intent of junk food advertising: Implications for regulation. *Social Science and Medicine, 72*, 962–968.

Choplin, J. M., Stark, D. P., & Ahmad, J. N. (2011). A psychological investigation of consumer vulnerability to fraud: Legal and policy implications. *Law and Psychology Review, 35*, 61–108.

Cuijpers, P. (2002). Effective ingredients of school-based drug prevention programs: A systematic review. *Addictive Behaviors, 27*, 1009–1023.

Cutler, B. L. (Ed.). (2013). *Reform of eyewitness identification procedures.* Washington, DC: American Psychological Association.

Davis, J. (2007). The effect of qualifying language on perceptions of drug appeal, drug experience, and estimates of side-effect incidence in DTC advertising. *Journal of Health Communication, 12*, 607–622.

Demaine, L. J. (2008). In search of an anti-elephant: Confronting the human inability to forget inadmissible evidence. *George Mason Law Review, 16*, 99–140.

Demaine, L. J. (2009). Navigating policy by the stars: The influence of celebrity entertainers on federal lawmaking. *Journal of Law and Politics, 25*, 83–143.

Demaine, L. J. (2012). Realizing the potential of instructions to disregard. In L. Nadel & W. P. Sinnott-Armstrong (Eds.), *Memory and law* (pp. 185–212). New York, NY: Oxford University Press.

Diamond, S. S., & Casper, J. D. (1992). Blindfolding the jury to verdict consequences: Damages, experts, and the civil jury. *Law and Society Review, 26*, 513–563.

Diamond, S. S., Rose, M. R., Murphy, E. L., & Meixner, J. (2011). Damage anchors on real juries. *Journal of Empirical Legal Studies, 8*, 148–178.

Dolnik, L., Case, T. I., & Williams, K. D. (2003). Stealing thunder as a courtroom tactic revisited: Processes and boundaries. *Law and Human Behavior, 27*, 267–287.

Donohue, J. M., Cevasco, M., & Rosenthal, M. B. (2007). A decade of direct-to-consumer advertising of prescription drugs. *New England Journal of Medicine, 357*, 673–681.

Douglas, K. S., Lyon, D. R., & Ogloff, J. R. P. (1997). The impact of graphic photographic evidence on mock jurors' decisions in a murder trial: Probative or prejudicial. *Law and Human Behavior, 21*, 485–501.

Drizin, S. A., & Leo, R. A. (2004). The problem of false confessions in the post-DNA world. *North Carolina Law Review, 82*, 891–1007.

*Federal rules of criminal procedure*. (2014). Retrieved August 2015, from http://www.uscourts.gov/rules-policies/current-rules-practice-procedure

*Federal rules of evidence*. (2014). Retrieved August 2015, from http://www.uscourts.gov/rules-policies/current-rules-practice-procedure

*Federal Trade Commission Act of 1914*, 15 U.S.C. §§ 41-58 (as amended).

Fein, S., McCloskey, A. L., & Tomlinson, T. M. (1997). Can the jury disregard that information? The use of suspicion to reduce the prejudicial effects of pretrial publicity and inadmissible testimony. *Personality and Social Psychology Bulletin, 23*, 1215–1226.

Florida v. Bostick, 501 U.S. 429 (1991).

Gilman, A. B., Hill, K. G., Hawkins, J. D., Howell, J. C., & Kosterman, R. (2014). The developmental dynamics of joining a gang in adolescence: Patterns and predictors of gang membership. *Journal of Research on Adolescence, 24*, 204–219.

Greenberg, J., Williams, K. D., & O'Brien, M. K. (1986). Considering the harshest verdict first: Biasing effects on mock juror verdicts. *Personality and Social Psychology Bulletin, 12*, 41–50.

Greene, E., & Loftus, E. F. (1985). When crimes are joined at trial. *Law and Human Behavior, 9*, 193–207.

Guthrie, C., Rachlinski, J. J., & Wistrich, A. J. (2001). Inside the judicial mind. *Cornell Law Review, 86*, 777–830.

Guthrie, C., Rachlinski, J. J., & Wistrich, A. J. (2009). The "hidden judiciary:" An empirical examination of executive branch justice. *Duke Law Journal, 58*, 1477–1530.

Halpern, S. D., Karlawish, J. H. T., Casarett, D., Berlin, J. A., & Asch, D. A. (2004). Empirical assessment of whether moderate payments are undue or unjust inducements for participation in clinical trials. *Archives of Internal Medicine, 164*, 801–803.

Haney, C. (1980). Psychology and legal change: On the limits of factual jurisprudence. *Law and Human Behavior, 4*, 147–199.

Haney, C. (1993). Psychology and legal change: The impact of a decade. *Law and Human Behavior, 17*, 371–398.

Huntley, J. E., & Costanzo, M. (2003). Sexual harassment stories: Testing a story-mediated model of juror-decision-making in civil litigation. *Law and Human Behavior, 27*, 29–51.

Hyman, I. E., Husband, T. H., & Billings, F. J. (1995). False memories of childhood experiences. *Applied Cognitive Psychology, 9*, 181–197.

Kagehiro, D. K. (1988). Perceived voluntariness of consent to warrantless police searches. *Journal of Applied Social Psychology, 18*, 38–49.

Kahan, D., & Braman, D. (2006) Cultural cognition and public policy. *Yale Law and Policy Review, 24*, 149–172.

Kassin, S. M. (2014). False confessions: Causes, consequences, and implications for reform. Behavioral and Brain Sciences, 1, 112–121.

Kassin, S. M. (2012). Why confessions trump innocence. *American Psychologist, 67*, 431–445.

Kassin, S. M., Bogart, D., & Kerner, J. (2012). Confessions that corrupt: Evidence from the DNA exoneration case files. *Psychological Science, 23*, 41–45.

Kassin, S. M., Drizin, S. A., Grisso, T., Gudjonsson, G. H., Leo, R. A., & Redlich, A. D. (2010). Police-induced confessions: Risk factors and recommendations. *Law and Human Behavior, 34*, 3–38.

Kassin, S. M., & Dunn, M. A. (1997). Computer-animated displays and the jury: Facilitative and prejudicial effects. *Law and Human Behavior, 21*, 269–281.

Kassin, S. M., & Kiechel, K. L. (1996). The social psychology of false confessions: Compliance, internalization, and confabulation. *Psychological Science, 7*, 125–128.

Kassin, S. M., & Sommers, S. R. (1997). Inadmissible testimony, instructions to disregard, and the jury: Substantive versus procedural considerations. *Personality and Social Psychology Bulletin, 23*, 1046–1054.

Kassin, S. M., & Sukel, H. (1997). Coerced confessions and the jury: An experimental test of the "harmless error" rule. *Law and Human Behavior, 21*, 27–46.

Kelman, M., Rottenstreich, Y., & Tversky, A. (1996). Context-dependence in legal decision making. *Journal of Legal Studies, 25*, 287–318.

Kim, K., & Park, J. S. (2010). Message framing and the effectiveness of DTC advertising: The moderating role of subjective product knowledge. *Journal of Medical Marketing, 10*, 165–176.

Klaver, J. R., Lee, Z., & Rose, V. G. (2008). Effects of personality, interrogation techniques and plausibility in an experimental false confession paradigm. *Legal and Criminological Psychology, 13*, 71–88.

Kruglanski, A. W., & Fishman, S. (2009). Psychological factors in terrorism and counterterrorism: Individual, group, and organizational levels of analysis. *Social Issues and Policy Review, 3*, 1–44.

Kunkel, D., & Castonguay, J. (2012). Children and advertising: Content, comprehension, and consequences. In D. G. Singer & J. L. Singer (Eds.), *Handbook of children and the media* (pp. 395–418). Thousand Oaks, CA: Sage.

Lampinen, J. M., Neuschatz, J. S., & Cling, A. D. (2012). *The psychology of eyewitness identification*. New York, NY: Psychology Press.

Lassiter, G. D. & Meissner, C. A. (Eds.). (2010). *Police interrogations and false confessions: Current research, practice, and policy recommendations*. Washington, DC: American Psychological Association.

Loftus, E. F. (2013). 25 years of eyewitness science......finally pays off. Perspectives on Psychological Science, 8, 556–557.

Loftus, E. F., & Palmer, J. C. (1974). Reconstruction of automobile destruction: An example of the interaction between language and memory. *Journal of Verbal Learning and Verbal Behavior, 13*, 585–589.

Loftus, E. F., & Pickrell, J. E. (1995). The formation of false memories. *Psychiatric Annals, 25*, 720–725.

Marti, M. W., & Wissler, R. L. (2000). Be careful what you ask for: The effect of anchors on personal injury damages awards. *Journal of Experimental Psychology: Applied, 6*, 91–103.

McAuliff, B. D., & Bornstein, B. H. (2010). All anchors are not created equal: The effects of per diem versus lump sum requests on pain and suffering awards. *Law and Human Behavior, 34*, 164–174.

McGuire, J. (2008). What's the point of sentencing? Psychological aspects of crime and punishment. In G. Davies, C. Hollin, & R. Bull (Eds.), *Forensic psychology* (pp. 265–291). West Sussex, UK: Wiley.

McKinlay, J. B., Trachtenberg, F., Marceau, L. D., Katz, J. N., & Fischer, M. A. (2014). Effects of patient medication requests on physician prescribing behavior: Results of a factorial experiment. *Medical Care, 52*, 294–299.

Milgram, S. (1974). *Obedience to authority*. New York, NY: Harper & Row.

Mizerski, R. W., Allison, N. K., & Calvert, S. (1980). A controlled field study of corrective advertising using multiple exposures and a commercial medium. *Journal of Marketing Research, 17*, 341–348.

Ogloff, J. R. P. (2000). Two steps forward and one step backward: The law and psychology movement(s) in the 20th century. *Law and Human Behavior, 24*, 457–483.

Olson, J. C., & Dover, P. A. (1978). Cognitive effects of deceptive advertising. *Journal of Marketing Research, 15*, 29–38.

Owen, L., Lewis, C., Auty, S., & Buijzen, M. (2013). Is children's understanding of nontraditional advertising comparable to their understanding of television advertising? *Journal of Public Policy and Marketing, 32*, 195–206.

Pennington, N., & Hastie, R. (1992). Explaining the evidence: Tests of the story model for juror decision making. *Journal of Personality and Social Psychology, 62*, 189–206.

Pennington, N., & Hastie, R. (1993). The story model for juror decision making. In R. Hastie (Ed.), *Inside the juror: The psychology of juror decision making* (pp. 192–221). New York, NY: Cambridge University Press.

Porter, S., Yuille, J. C., & Lehman, D. R. (1999). The nature of real, implanted, and fabricated memories for emotional childhood events: Implications for the recovered memory debate. *Law and Human Behavior, 23*, 517–537.

Pratkanis, A. R., & Shadel, D. (2005). *Weapons of fraud: A source book for fraud fighters*. Seattle, WA: American Association of Retired Persons.

Pratkanis, A. R., Shadel, D., Kleinman, M., Small, B., & Pak, K. (2006). *Investor fraud study final report*. Washington, DC: National Association of Securities Dealers Investor Education Foundation.

Preston, I. L. (1996). *The great American blow-up: Puffery in advertising and selling* (rev. ed.). Madison: University of Wisconsin Press.

Rachlinski, J. J., Wistrich, A. J., & Guthrie, C. Altering attention in adjudication. UCLA Law Review, 60, 1586–1618.

Rotfeld, H. J., & Rotzoll, K. B. (1980). Is advertising puffery believed? *Journal of Advertising, 9*, 16–20, 45.

Scheibe, S., Notthoff, N., Menkin, J., Ross, L., Shadel, D., Deevy, M., & Carstensen, L. L. (2014). Forewarning reduces fraud susceptibility in vulnerable consumers. *Basic and Applied Social Psychology, 36*, 272–279.

Severance, L. J., & Loftus, E. F. (1982). Improving the ability of jurors to comprehend and apply criminal jury instructions. *Law and Society Review, 17*, 153–197.

Shimp, T. A. (1978). Do incomplete comparisons mislead? *Journal of Advertising Research, 18*, 21–27.

Steblay, N. M., Besirevic, J., Fulero, S. M., & Jimenez-Lorente, B. (1999). The effects of pretrial publicity on juror verdicts: A meta-analytic review. *Law and Human Behavior, 23*, 219–235.

Steblay, N. M., Hosch, H. M., Culhane, S. E., & McWethy, A. (2006). The impact on juror verdicts of judicial instruction to disregard inadmissible evidence: A meta-analysis. *Law and Human Behavior, 30*, 469–492.

Studebaker, C. A., & Penrod, S. D. (1997). Pretrial publicity: The media, the law, and common sense. *Psychology, Public Policy, and Law, 3*, 428–460.

Tanford, S., & Cox, M. (1987). Decision processes in civil cases: The impact of impeachment evidence on liability and credibility judgments. *Social Behaviour, 2*, 165–182.

Tanford, S., & Penrod, S. (1984). Social inference processes in juror judgments of multiple-offense trials. *Journal of Personality and Social Psychology, 47*, 749–765.

Taylor, P. J., & Thomas, S. (2008). Linguistic style matching and negotiation outcome. *Negotiation and Conflict Management Research, 1*, 263–281.

Thaler, R. H., & Sunstein, C. R. (2009). *Nudge: Improving decisions about health, wealth, and happiness* (rev. ed.). New York, NY: Penguin Group.

Thompson, W. C., Fong, G. T., & Rosenhan, D. L. (1981). Inadmissible evidence and juror verdicts. *Journal of Personality and Social Psychology, 40*, 453–463.

Tyler, T. R. (2006a). Restorative justice and procedural justice: Dealing with rule breaking. *Journal of Social Issues, 62*, 307–326.

Tyler, T. R. (2006b). *Why people obey the law*. Princeton, NJ: Princeton University Press.

Tyler, T. R., & Rankin, L. (2012). The mystique of instrumentalism. In J. Hanson & J. Jost (Eds.), *Ideology, psychology, and law* (pp. 537–573). New York, NY: Oxford University Press.

Vasquez, E. A., Loughnan, S., Gootjes-Dreesbach, E., & Weger, U. (2014). The animal in you: Animalistic descriptions of a violent crime increase punishment of perpetrator. *Aggressive Behavior, 40*, 337–344.

Wallace, D. B., & Kassin, S. M. (2012). Harmless error analysis: How do judges respond to confession errors? *Law and Human Behavior, 36*, 151–157.

Wenzel, M., Okimoto, T. G., Feather, N. T., & Platow, M. J. (2008). Retributive and restorative justice. *Law and Human Behavior, 32*, 375–389.

Wilcox, B. L., Kunkel, D., Cantor, J., Dowrick, P., Linn, S., & Palmer, E. (2004). *Report of the APA Task Force on advertising and children: Psychological issues in the increasing commercialization of childhood*. Washington, DC: American Psychological Association.

Williams, K. D., Bourgeois, M. J., & Croyle, R. T. (1993). The effects of stealing thunder in criminal and civil trials. *Law and Human Behavior, 17*, 597–609.

Williams, K. D., & Jones, A. (2005). Trial strategy and tactics. In N. Brewer & K. D. Williams (Eds.), *Psychology and law: An empirical perspective* (pp. 276–321). New York, NY: Guilford Press.

Wilson, T. D., & Brekke, N. (1994). Mental contamination and mental correction: Unwanted influences on judgments and evaluations. *Psychological Bulletin, 116,* 117–142.

Wilson, M. A., Bradford, E., & Lemanski, L. (2013). The role of group processes in terrorism. In J. L. Wood & T. A. Gannon (Eds.), *Crime and crime reduction: The importance of group processes* (pp. 99–117). New York, NY: Routledge.

Wissler, R., & Saks, M. J. (1985). On the inefficacy of limiting instructions: When jurors use prior conviction evidence to decide on guilt. *Law and Human Behavior, 9,* 37–48.

Wistrich, A. J., Guthrie, C., & Rachlinski, J. J. (2005). Can judges ignore inadmissible information? The difficulty of deliberately disregarding. *University of Pennsylvania Law Review, 153,* 1251–1345.

Zimbardo, P. (2007). *The Lucifer effect: Understanding how good people turn evil.* New York, NY: Random House.

# Social Influence in Marketing: How Other People Influence Consumer Information Processing and Decision Making

Amna Kirmani *and* Rosellina Ferraro

**Abstract**

Much of consumer behavior is socially based, involving public consumption of products, exposure to individuals or groups engaging in consumption, and discussions about products with family, friends, acquaintances, and strangers. We examine research on the effects of social influence on consumer behavior, focusing on articles from the top journals in the field. A large part of this work applies and expands on theories developed in the field of psychology; however, given the interdisciplinary nature of marketing, consumer research incorporates findings from other fields, including economics, sociology, anthropology, and communications. Some topics unique to consumer research include gift giving, brand community, and word of mouth. We close the chapter with a discussion of social influence research opportunities in the consumer behavior domain.

**Key Words:** social influence, marketing, consumer behavior, public consumption, consumer research, gift giving, word of mouth

Marketing involves exchanges between companies and consumers, companies and companies, and consumers and consumers. At the heart of marketing lies decision making about products, pricing, promotion, and distribution. Marketers attempt to persuade consumers to like their products and services, understand what those products and services mean, develop emotional connections with those products and services, and buy those products and services over and over again. Consumer behavior examines how consumers respond to these company decisions, as well as the types of internal and external influences that affect them. A large number of influences on consumers are socially based, as consumption involves public use of products, exposure to individuals or groups engaging in consumption, and discussion about products with family, friends, acquaintances, and strangers.

In some cases, consumer behavior research on social influence ran parallel to social psychology research, with researchers applying and extending theories developed by social psychologists. In other cases, concepts and theories unique to the discipline were developed. We discuss these various types of research in this chapter. Because social influence is so pervasive in marketing, we restrict this chapter to the specific consideration of social influence on consumer behavior. We seek to discuss interesting socially based effects that have had impact on the field and that are relevant to consumers' everyday functioning in the marketplace. Therefore, we restrict ourselves to articles appearing in the four most impactful marketing journals that publish consumer behavior work: the *Journal of Consumer Research*, the *Journal of Marketing*, the *Journal of Marketing Research*, and the *Journal of Consumer Psychology*. Furthermore, we consider decisions made by individuals, not those made by groups or organizations; thus, the focus is on consumer decisions rather than company decisions.

As a result, the unit of analysis is the individual rather than aggregates; this means, for instance, that advertising effects on individual consumers are included but not the effects of advertising on aggregate measures, such as sales or profits. Moreover, we exclude household decision making and consumer socialization because the literatures on these topics are so large that we cannot do them justice given the number of other topic areas we cover. We also exclude research focused solely on individual difference variables that have a social component, such as self-construal or self-monitoring, unless the contribution of the research is on a socially based consumption phenomenon. Finally, we focus on more recent research rather than earlier research from the 1970s or 1980s, unless the articles are seminal.

We discuss areas that are at the heart of social influence in psychology as well as topics that are unique to marketing. Given the range of topics and number of papers, we can only provide an overview of the relevant research. The chapter begins with a discussion of research on consumer persuasion, particularly source effects and persuasion knowledge, including resistance to persuasion. This is followed by a section on norms, focusing on normative influence and social norms affecting gift giving and uniqueness. Next, we examine reference group effects, including ethnic identity and brand-based identity. This is followed by a discussion of identity signaling, which has become a highly researched topic in recent years. The rest of the sections include social comparison, social presence, social contagion, and social networks. The section on social networks covers word of mouth, which is another highly researched topic in consumer behavior. We close the chapter with a discussion of social influence research opportunities in the consumer behavior domain. Many of these opportunities arise because of the advent of social media, which has prompted renewed interest in understanding the effects of the social environment on consumers. Social media allow people to disclose anything and everything about themselves to others. They allow people to follow and be followed by others, thus offering each other a view into their respective consumption activities. We discuss these and related ideas in the Future Directions section.

## Persuasion

Persuasion is the process of changing people's beliefs, attitudes, and behaviors. Because the goal of marketing is to persuade consumers to adopt products and services, persuasion is an essential focus of consumer behavior research. Marketers persuade consumers using numerous tactics, including personal and social influences. In this section, we discuss two important areas of persuasion research in consumer behavior: source effects and persuasion knowledge.

### Source Effects

Because of the importance of advertising and interpersonal persuasion to consumer behavior, there is a large literature on source effects. Source research considers the traditional dimensions of source credibility and attractiveness, particularly related to the influence of celebrity endorsers. Much of the early research was based on the elaboration likelihood model (e.g., Petty, Cacioppo, & Schumann, 1983), the heuristic systematic model (Eagly & Chaiken, 1993; Ratneshwar & Chaiken, 1991), or the cognitive response model (Greenwald, 1968; Sternthal, Dholakia, & Leavitt, 1978).

Because source trustworthiness is an important antecedent of persuasion, it is not surprising that trustworthiness has been examined in many different consumer contexts. In interpersonal bargaining situations, higher seller trustworthiness leads to higher buyer cooperation, particularly when the seller adopts a tough stand (Schurr & Ozanne, 1985). Untrustworthy sources lead to greater message elaboration, while trustworthy sources serve as a simple cue (Priester & Petty, 2003). A baby face spontaneously increases the trustworthiness of a company executive, leading to more favorable company evaluations (Gorn, Jiang, & Johar, 2008); this is particularly helpful when the company experiences a crisis.

Physical attractiveness has also been extensively investigated. Attractive salespeople are perceived as more skilled and treated more cordially by buyers (Reingen & Kernan, 1993). Stating the intent to persuade enhances persuasion for attractive or likable salespeople but hurts persuasion by unattractive or disliked salespeople, as the former are seen as less likely to have an ulterior motive (Reinhard, Messner, & Sporer, 2006). In the case of celebrity endorsers, initial research showed that an attractive celebrity endorser positively affects brand attitudes under low rather than high involvement (Petty et al., 1983). However, Kahle and Homer (1985) find that celebrity attractiveness also affects brand attitudes under high involvement when attractiveness is relevant to the product category. In this case, celebrity attractiveness is congruent with the brand.

An important perspective on celebrity endorsements was provided by McCracken (1986), who argues that the effects of celebrity endorsers go beyond simple source credibility and attractiveness. Rather, celebrities contain meanings or cultural associations that transfer to the brand and are picked up by consumers. The cultural meanings of the celebrity may include personality characteristics or other associations. For instance, Kirmani and Shiv (1998) find that source congruity can be based on celebrity associations rather than attractiveness. When a celebrity's image matches that of the brand (e.g., Clint Eastwood endorses a rugged watch), brand attitudes are positively affected under high but not low involvement. Under low involvement, celebrity liking rather than source congruity affects attitudes. These associations are different from expertise; i.e., Clint Eastwood is not an expert on rugged watches. Batra and Homer (2004) also find support for this meaning transfer model.

Research has also examined the effects of multiple celebrity endorsers and endorsements on attitudes. Multiple endorsements by a single celebrity reduce source credibility and thus persuasion (Tripp, Jensen, & Carlson, 1994). Rice, Kelting, and Lutz (2012) find that the effects of multiple celebrity endorsers and multiple endorsements by the same celebrity depend on the level of involvement. Under high involvement, multiple endorsers or endorsements result in more positive brand attitudes under high (vs. low) source congruity as the multiple endorsers and endorsements serve as strong arguments about the brand. Under low involvement, source congruity has little impact; multiple endorsers lead to more favorable brand attitudes while multiple endorsements decrease brand attitudes, suggesting that multiple endorsers are treated in a similar manner as are the number of arguments under low involvement.

Although the notion that celebrities have cultural meanings beyond those captured by traditional source dimensions (e.g., credibility, attractiveness, trustworthiness) is interesting, it is more difficult to generalize these meanings. Clint Eastwood's ruggedness is a celebrity-specific meaning, based on his acting roles; but ruggedness is not a theoretical construct. Thus, the challenge of the meaning transfer perspective is to come up with generalizations that can apply to multiple situations. For example, are there certain types of celebrity meanings that are more important than others?

## Persuasion Knowledge

Historically, consumer behavior researchers have focused on how persuasion affects consumers' decisions to buy products. A unique theory in consumer behavior, the persuasion knowledge model, turns the tables to take the perspective of the target (Friestad & Wright, 1994). The model asserts that consumers (i.e., persuasion targets) have theories about how marketers attempt to influence them, as well as theories about how people influence each other. For example, these theories may include the effects of source characteristics, the goals and tactics of salespeople, or strategies for coping with persuasion.

The persuasion knowledge model asserts that consumers move fluidly between the role of persuasion target and persuasion agent. Thus, consumers not only have theories about how marketers persuade them but also about how they themselves can persuade others, including salespeople. For instance, Kirmani and Campbell (2004) identify 15 strategies by which consumers cope with persuasion attempts. These strategies can be classified into two types of consumer orientations in dealing with interpersonal persuasion—seekers and sentries. Goal seekers try to use the marketing agent (e.g., a salesperson) to achieve their own personal goals; they might build relationships, directly ask for assistance, or otherwise approach the salesperson with requests. Thus, they attempt to persuade the agent to do what the consumer wants. In contrast, persuasion sentries are wary of agents; they might forestall the persuasion attempt or bring along a companion to protect them against the influence agent. Importantly, the relationship between the target and the agent affects the choice of strategy. Cooperative relationships lead to greater use of seeker strategies, while competitive relationships lead to greater use of sentry strategies. In addition, the orientation of the relationship (e.g., socially motivated vs. task-oriented) and dependency between the target and the agent also affect the use of strategies. For instance, sentry strategies are more likely when the target has low dependence on the agent or the relationship is task oriented. Finally, older consumers are more skilled in resistance than are college students because older consumers have greater experience dealing with persuasion attempts.

Persuasion knowledge may be activated in a variety of contexts, from advertising to interpersonal persuasion (see Campbell & Kirmani, 2008, for a review). Because persuasion knowledge requires higher order inferences about others' motives, its activation requires cognitive capacity (Campbell & Kirmani, 2000). However, when influence tactics are blatant and ulterior motives of the influence agent are salient, persuasion knowledge may be activated automatically. A salesperson will be judged as less sincere when ulterior motives are highly accessible; however, if ulterior motives are not accessible, the salesperson will be judged as less sincere only when cognitive capacity is unconstrained. Persuasion is reduced even if it is an acquaintance that is perceived as having a selling motive compared to a nonselling motive (Tuk, Verlegh, Smidts, & Wigboldus, 2009).

The persuasion knowledge model raises interesting questions about consumers' resistance to persuasion. According to the model, consumers recognize when marketers are attempting to persuade them. In addition, consumers have coping strategies that allow them to resist persuasion. This seems to imply an active, aware consumer and runs counter to other research that indicates that consumers overestimate their own abilities to resist persuasion, thereby falling victim to an illusion of invulnerability (Sagarin, Cialdini, Rice, & Serna, 2002). The obvious question is under what conditions consumers might fall victim to persuasion and when might they successfully recognize and resist persuasion. Although Campbell and Kirmani (2000) suggest two possible moderators (i.e., accessibility of ulterior motives and cognitive capacity), future research could investigate other conditions under which consumers may effectively resist persuasion.

## Normative Social Influence and Social Norms

Consumer behavior may be affected by expectations to behave in certain ways by other individuals or society more broadly. These influences may lead to conformity (see Hodges, this volume), which is a change in behavior to align with others' behavior or preferences (Asch, 1951). In this section, we discuss two drivers of conformity behaviors: normative social influence and the effects of social norms.

### Normative Social Influence

Normative social influence refers to the pressure to conform to the expectations of others, while informational social influence refers to the acceptance of information from others because it is correct (Deutsch & Gerard 1955). Burnkrant and Cousineau (1975) argued that prior consumer research had failed to distinguish between these two types of social influence, attributing

normative influence to situations in which informational influence may occur. They found that consumers tasting coffee based their evaluations on those of others; however, the underlying process was not identification or compliance, but internalization. In other words, informational rather than normative social influence was operating. Heeding their call, subsequent work has been more cognizant of the type of social influence (e.g., LaTour & Manrai, 1989; Wooten & Reed, 1998).

In order to measure consumers' tendency to conform to normative social influence, Bearden, Netemeyer, and Teel (1989) developed a 12-item scale called Consumer Susceptibility to Interpersonal Influence. The scale has two dimensions, susceptibility to normative influence and susceptibility to informational influence. The susceptibility to normative influence dimension has been used in several papers. Those high in susceptibility to normative influence are likely to avoid making negative impressions on others (Wooten & Reed, 2004); place greater value on socially visible goods (Batra, Homer, & Kahle, 2001); and engage in boycotts if others are participating (Sen, Gurhan-Canli, & Morwitz, 2001).

One aspect of normative social influence is the subjective norms component of the Fishbein model (Fishbein & Ajzen, 1975), which refers to the perception of what others think one should do (see Nolan, this volume). According to Fishbein and Ajzen, behavioral intentions are a function of both personal attitudes and subjective norms. During the 1970s and 1980s, there was a large stream of consumer behavior research testing the validity of these behavioral intentions models (Bonfield, 1974; Miniard & Cohen, 1979; Ryan & Bonfield, 1975). Research in the 1990s and 2000s continued to examine the effect of normative social influence across a wide range of phenomena. Bagozzi, Wong, Abe, and Bergami (2000) found that subjective norms affect behavioral intentions in a public context (i.e., when consumers eat with others) but not in a private context (i.e., when they eat alone). Fisher and Price (1992) found that normative social influence is important in predicting early adoption of new products. In their work, the significant effects of perceived visibility and superordinate group influence on expectations of normative outcomes are consistent with the general view that new products served as a basis for social identification and integration within social systems.

## Social Norms

Social norms refer to unwritten rules or standards of behavior held by a society. Social norms have been used to persuade consumers to engage in sustainable behaviors, such as water conservation, recycling, and composting. In a field experiment involving the reuse of towels in a hotel, Goldstein, Cialdini, and Griskevicius (2008) show that hotel guests conformed more to the norms of people who had previously stayed in that exact same room than to norms of other groups, such as other people staying at the hotel or other people related to them by social identity. However, in a similar field experiment, Schultz, Khazian, and Zaleski (2008) found no difference across these two types of normative messages. This calls for further research to address conditions under which different types of messages may be effective in this context.

Another area in which social norms come into play is gift giving. Gift giving is a social exchange process that is shaped by the norms of relationships and reciprocity (Belk, 2010; Belk & Coon, 1993). An important perspective on gift giving was provided by Sherry (1983), whose anthropological model of the gift giving process highlighted the importance of social relationships. According to his model, the relationship between the gift giver and the recipient drives all aspects of gift giving, including the motives underlying the gift; the size, quality, and cost of the gift; the timing of gift presentation; and the emotional reactions elicited. Subsequent research built on this model by identifying specific effects on social relationships. Following up on this perspective, Ruth, Otnes, and Brunel (1999) identify six effects on relationships ranging from strengthening (i.e., the gift increases the bond between the giver and recipient) to severing (i.e., the gift leads to termination of the relationship). The relationship effects of gift giving are relevant not only between giver and receiver but also to third parties (i.e., a nonrecipient) outside the dyad (Lowrey, Otnes, & Ruth, 2004). Gift givers sometimes involve a third party in selecting a gift for the recipient. Motivations to do so could involve gaining more information, verifying the gift, or improving the relationship with the third party (e.g., increasing closeness). Finally, cross-cultural differences in relationships affect gift giving. In Hong Kong, the term "gift" applies to exchanges between two unrelated individuals; as a result, the idea of gifting does not apply to family members, as the family is considered a sacred sphere that falls outside the realm of reciprocity (Joy, 2001).

Another aspect of socials norms that is important is consumers' desire to differentiate or diverge from others' choices. According to optimal distinctiveness theory (Brewer, 1993), individuals face opposing needs of assimilation and differentiation. Accordingly, consumers often engage in behaviors that allow them to express or restore uniqueness from others. For example, consumers engage in avoidance behaviors when distinctiveness concerns are heightened, such as when their product choices are copied by a similar rather than dissimilar other (White & Argo, 2011). Amaldoss and Jain (2005) found that demand for a product among consumers who desire uniqueness increases as its price goes up; that is, these consumers are willing to pay more for that uniqueness.

An interesting recent study indicates that consumers can satisfy the need for assimilation and differentiation within a single choice (Chan, Berger, & Van Boven, 2012). Whereas prior work examines choice as reflecting either assimilation or differentiation, Chan et al. examine how both processes can be satisfied within one choice. They demonstrate that consumers choose to assimilate with their in-group on one dimension (e.g., brand name) and differentiate on another (e.g., color). The key is that the assimilation attribute can serve as a signal of social identity (e.g., a brand), while the differentiation attribute might be a less popular variety within the brand. Since this is a single paper, it would be interesting to see whether these effects could be replicated with other types of choices.

Another example of the conflict between assimilation and differentiation comes from Ariely and Levav (2000). They examined how a person making a choice in a sequence with others making choices, such as when ordering in a restaurant, affects the management of goals in relation to the self and to the group. At the individual level, the goal is to satisfy one's taste; however, at the group level, the goals are self-presentation, minimizing regret, and information gathering. Choices made in a group context differed from those made in an individual context, with choices in the group context demonstrating self-presentational concerns in the form of uniqueness. Building on this research, Quester and Steyer (2010) show that the conflicting goals of individuality and conformity generate a curvilinear relationship between the number of people dining at the same table and product choice. When the percentage of the group selecting a product was small (i.e., <30 percent) or large (i.e., >85 percent), the individual tended to select another product; however, between those extremes, she was likely to select the same product.

The Need for Uniqueness scale (Snyder & Fromkin, 1977) has been used in much research examining consumer phenomena related to uniqueness. Simonson and Nowlis (2000) find that consumers high on the need for uniqueness make more unconventional product choices when they expect to disclose the reasons behind their product choices. Consumers are also less willing to provide positive word of mouth for publicly consumed products, but not for privately consumed products, as providing positive word of mouth encourages others to purchase the product, thereby making one's own possession less unique (Cheema & Kaikati, 2010). Because the generalized need for uniqueness measure has not shown consistent results in product choice behavior, Tian, Bearden, and Hunter (2001) developed a need for uniqueness scale specific to product choice, called the Consumer's Need for Uniqueness scale (also Tian & McKenzie, 2001). This scale captures counterconformity motivation, which arises when consumers feel too similar to others. Consumers high in need for uniqueness are less likely to rely on others' preferences (Irmak, Vallen, & Sen, 2010).

## Reference Group Effects

A highly researched consumer behavior area involves the effects of reference groups on consumer choice and evaluations. Reference groups refer to individual people (e.g., family member, friend) and groups (e.g., fraternity, sports team) whose opinions and tastes matter to the individual. Reference groups have a strong influence on consumer choice. In a seminal paper, Bearden and Etzel (1982) demonstrate that reference group effects on consumption differ by the type of social influence, whether the product is used in public or private, and whether the product is a luxury or a necessity. Based on the work of Deutsch and Gerard (1955) and Kelman (1961), they define three types of reference group influence: informational, which refers to seeking information from the reference group to make good decisions; utilitarian, which refers to using the reference group to gain rewards or avoid punishment; and value-expressive, which refers to having a psychological or symbolic association with the reference group. They find, for instance, that public luxuries, such as expensive cars, are subject to more value-expressive influence than are private luxuries, such as televisions.

The influence of reference groups can differ across cultures. In a comparison of respondents in the United States and Thailand, Childers and Rao (1992) found that different types of reference groups were important across the two countries. Whereas peers are more influential than families in the United States, the reverse is true in Thailand, a collective culture.

One of the reasons that reference groups so strongly affect consumer behavior is that products and brands can be associated with specific reference groups. Consumers are likely to connect with brands that are associated with member groups (i.e., groups to which they belong) as well as aspiration groups (i.e., groups to which they would like to belong) (Escalas & Bettman, 2003). Connection refers to overlap of the brand's associations with one's self-concept, thereby making the consumer feel closer or more attached to the brand. When the goal is to enhance the self-concept, consumers form connections with brands that are used by aspiration groups. When the goal is self-verification, however, consumers form connections with brands used by member groups. Moreover, consumers have stronger connections to brands that are associated with in-groups and weaker connections to brands that are associated with out-groups (Escalas & Bettman, 2005). Consumers are less likely to choose products associated with an out-group that they are motivated to avoid (White & Dahl, 2006, 2007).

The research showing the relationship between brands and reference groups is large and varied. One stream of research shows that consumers often choose to associate with groups based on wealth and social status. They may use large or prominent brand logos to associate with some groups and dissociate with others (Han, Nunes, & Dreze, 2010). However, subtle signals may be used as a means of communicating with those who have social capital and "are in the know" about certain brands (Berger & Ward, 2010). These subtle signals include, for example, extra buttons or superfine stitching that only people "in the know," and not the mainstream consumer, would recognize.

Another interesting stream of research shows that in order to boost their self-image as well make a positive impression on members of aspiration groups, consumers may tell lies about their purchases (Sengupta, Dahl, & Gorn, 2002). For instance, they may conceal that they have purchased an expensive product at a discounted price when paying full price would fit with the reference group's image; or they may conceal the fact that they have purchased the product at a regular price when it is important to be perceived as a smart shopper. Moreover, consumers are more willing to lie to people they know than to strangers in order to protect their self-image (Argo, White, & Dahl, 2006). The topic of lying in the consumer context can lead to interesting research questions, such as whether consumers' propensity to lie differs in an online (to a machine) versus a face-to-face context.

## Social Identity

The foregoing discussion highlights the notion that underlying reference group effects is people's perception of their social identity, which refers to the part of the self-concept that derives from membership in certain groups (Tajfel & Turner 1979; see Gaffney & Hogg, this volume). Social identity can be reflected by membership in various types of groups that are based on demographics, lifestyle, personality characteristics, or brand ownership. Two aspects of social identity that have been discussed extensively in the consumer literature are ethnic identity and brand-related identity.

Ethnic identity refers to membership in ethnic groups, typically minority groups. Briley, Shrum, and Wyer (2007) demonstrate that perceptions of whether minority group members are represented in advertisements depend on whether the observer is a member of that minority group; this seems to result from minority group members' intrinsic motivation to determine representation. As is true of social identities in general, Stayman and Deshpande (1989) find that ethnic identity is not just who one is but how one feels in a particular situation; that is, the effects of ethnic groups can be transitory and change with the situational context. Ethnic identity salience can occur because a person is in a numerical minority but also because of other factors that create feelings of being socially distinct, such as social class (Grier & Deshpande, 2001). Finally, Wooten (1995) finds that the extent to which a member of a minority group avoids stereotypical behavior depends on the relative size of the minority group.

Brand-related identity refers to membership in brand-based groups via ownership or love of a product. Muniz and O'Guinn's (2001) seminal paper introduces the idea of brand community, which captures the relationships among admirers of a brand. Examples of brand communities range from tight-knit, structured communities, such as the

Harley Davidson HOGs (Harley Owners Group), to more loosely based communities, such as Apple fans. These communities have characteristics of other social communities, such as shared consciousness, a sense of moral responsibility, and rituals and traditions. Brand communities serve to re-create and reinforce brand meaning, and evaluations of the brand are generally affected in a positive way by participation in a brand community. For example, Thompson and Sinha (2008) find that membership in the community increases the likelihood of adopting a new technology from that brand and decreases the likelihood of adopting a new technology from a competing brand.

Social influences within communities come through the relationships among members of the community (McAlexander, Schouten, & Koenig, 2002). Muniz and Schau (2005) show that brand communities can persist even after the brand is discontinued. They argue that elements of religiosity are played out in the context of brand communities. Strong relationships with brand community members enhance identification with the brand community, leading to further engagement and participation in the community (Algesheimer, Dholakia, & Herrmann, 2005). These relationships also increase brand loyalty and purchase behavior. Because of these positive outcomes, Schau, Muniz, and Arnould (2009) suggest that firms should encourage a broad array of practices among community members as a way to build engagement and positive feelings toward the brand and the community.

Brand communities can also have negative effects, however. For instance, communities exert pressure on members to conform to community rules and practices. Algesheimer, Dholakia, and Herrmann (2005) find that brand communities can influence members in a negative direction via normative pressures to conform, which may lead to reactance as consumers attempt to exert their personal freedom. Zhu, Dholakia, Chen, and Algesheimer (2012) find that participation in a brand community can lead to riskier financial decision making, as members have the perception that others in the community will help them and support them if the decision turns out poorly.

Communities are not limited to brands and do not require face-to-face interaction between members. Online, consumers can readily connect to communities devoted to product categories and ideas. Some research has examined social influence specifically within online communities. Virtual communities can create social capital in the form of knowledge and information relevant to the group (Mathwick, Wiertz, & de Ruyter, 2008); they operate on the social norms of voluntarism, reciprocity, and trust. Over time, members see the communities as family and are strongly influenced by community norms.

## Identity Signaling

A good deal of consumer research in recent years has focused on identity signaling, which refers to consumers' use of products and brands to convey who they (consumers) are to others. Based on work in both economics and psychology, identity signaling is similar to the notion of other kinds of costly signals. In the presence of asymmetric information, people incur monetary, social, or other types of risk to convey to others that they possess a valued attribute. For instance, they may invest money on education to convey to potential employers that they have the necessary intelligence to qualify for the job (Spence, 1973).

Identity signaling with brands works in the same way. Because brands contain cultural meanings and associations, they can be used to convey social status (e.g., a new Mercedes suggests wealth); traits (e.g., "I use Apple, therefore I am innovative"); and aspirations (e.g., a used Mercedes suggests the desire for a wealthy lifestyle). For example, choice of products with multiple capabilities may convey technological skills or openness to experience (Thompson & Norton, 2011). Interestingly, using a DVD player that has many features indicates to others that one is technologically advanced and skilled; however, when consumers anticipate having to use the product in front of others, they are less likely to adopt it.

Berger and Heath (2007) suggest that consumers' choices often diverge from others, not for uniqueness reasons, but because of identity signaling concerns. This is reflected in consumers' diverging from the majority choice in product domains that are used to signal identity, such as music preferences, but not in less symbolic domains, such as soap, where consumers opt for the majority choice. Identity signaling may lead consumers to engage in less risky health behavior if that behavior is linked to desirable identities (Berger & Rand, 2008). The reverse is also the case. The authors present anecdotal evidence from Stanford undergraduate students who stated that they avoided wearing helmets when riding their bicycles because graduate students, who are perceived as socially awkward, wore them. The authors go on to show that underage students consume less alcohol and eatery patrons select less fattening food when these behaviors are associated with avoidance groups.

Identity signaling also occurs online, where personal websites allow people to present multiple identities to friends and strangers (Schau & Gilly, 2003). The reasons for self-presentation on the Internet are the same as the reasons for self-presentation offline, namely, to create a positive impression of one's self to others. Consumers convey their identity to others through what they post, including their tastes in music, books, and brands, as well as through the technological complexity of the site. Personal websites may include feedback mechanisms for others to react to the poster. Unlike the offline context, where product choices are limited by income, online self-presentation allows consumers more freedom to convey identities through discussion or display of a broad range of products and services, whether or not they own them. Although this suggests that consumers may misrepresent their identities online, there is, to our knowledge, little research to confirm that this is the case.

Importantly, while consumers may use brands to convey a particular image, the observer may not always view doing so in a positive way. Ferraro, Kirmani, and Matherly (2013) examine the situation in which consumers try to gain attention via their brand usage, such as flaunting a Tiffany shopping bag. The authors show that observers infer that a consumer engaged in conspicuous brand usage is driven by an ulterior motive of impression management. For observers who are not highly connected to the brand, this conspicuous behavior hurts brand evaluations as their brand attitudes are fairly malleable and thus susceptible to influence. For observers who are highly connected with the brand, however, conspicuous brand usage by others does not affect brand evaluations. Their attitudes are strong enough to withstand such negative behavior by a brand user. These highly connected consumers are thus resistant to negative brand information.

## Social Comparison

Another important social influence on consumer behavior is social comparison, which is the act of making comparative judgments to others (Festinger, 1954; Kruglanski & Mayseless, 1990; see Suls & Wheeler, this volume). Consumers engage in social comparison as a way to evaluate and to reduce uncertainty about the self in consumption contexts (Moschis, 1976).

Upward social comparisons can result in negative affect or dissatisfaction because such comparisons can alter one's evaluation of the self or reduce self-esteem. For instance, satisfaction with one's own appearance was lower among those exposed to advertisements featuring idealized models because the comparison lowered feelings about one's own attractiveness (e.g., Richins 1991). Hafner (2004) shows that comparison to idealized models can lead to assimilation or contrast depending on the presence of social cues that trigger perceptions of similarities. Greater similarity results in more assimilation. In a retail environment, Dahl, Argo, and Morales (2012) found that comparison to an attractive customer using the same product leads to negative affect. Similarly, when customizing a product for oneself (e.g., designing one's own Vera Bradley handbag), comparisons to other consumer designers can lead to lower evaluations of one's own design (Moreau & Herd, 2010).

Downward social comparisons can also result in negative affect. Threats to self can arise from comparison to members of undesirable groups. These threats can be managed by contrasting from the comparison person(s). For example, consumers adjust away from the food choices made by a member of an undesirable group, such as an obese person (McFerran, Dahl, Fitzsimons, & Morales, 2010). Interestingly, Campbell and Mohr (2011) find a different pattern of results, whereby exposure to an overweight person leads to stereotype-consistent behavior as evidenced by eating greater amounts of food. However, this effect is attenuated when the behavior–stereotype link is made accessible, suggesting that assimilation does not occur when the undesirability of the group is salient. Another example of assimilation to an undesirable group was demonstrated by Shalev and Morwitz (2012), who found that seeing someone of lower status using a product triggers thoughts that one is out of the mainstream, which then leads to adoption of that product. These seemingly contradictory findings suggest that consumers will contrast away from undesirable groups when the negative associations of that group reflect back to themselves, but they will assimilate if those negative associations are not salient.

The phenomenon of "keeping up with the Joneses" is an outcome of social comparison. Social comparison can lead one to be impatient; wanting quickly what more fortunate others have (Hoch & Loewenstein, 1991). It can also lead to envy (Van de Ven, Zeelenberg, & Pieters, 2011), driving consumers to willingly pay a price premium for envy-eliciting products. According to Van de Ven, Zeelenberg, and Pieters (2011), benign envy (i.e., wishing for what another person has) leads to adoption of the product used by superior others, while malicious envy (i.e., ill will towards another person) leads to adoption of a different, but related, product as a means to separate oneself from those superior others. Relatedly, Sundie, Ward, Beal, Chin, and Geiger-Oneto (2009) find that envy may lead to schadenfreude, which refers to feelings of joy at another's downfall. In this case, consumers take pleasure when others using a status product experience a product failure. When an observer sees a consumer with an advantage (i.e., having a high-status product), this triggers an upward social comparison, which then generates envy and hostility. When that product fails, envy and hostility generate schadenfreude, and experiencing schadenfreude increases intentions to tell others about the failure.

## Social Presence

Social presence, which refers to the real or imagined presence of other people (see Seitchik, Brown, & Harkins, this volume), can affect information processing and choice. The "other" can be one person or multiple people.

The presence of others in consumption contexts may impact consumers because of self-presentational concerns. For instance, the real or imagined presence of others can create embarrassment for the consumer when she cares about what others think and purchase experience is low (Dahl, Manchanda, & Argo, 2001). Kurt, Inman, and Argo (2011) demonstrate that agentic consumers (in their research, men) spend more when they shop with a friend than when they shop alone, as they are trying to impress their friends. In contrast, communal consumers (in their research, women) are less concerned with impression management; they control their shopping in the presence of a friend. Finally, the likelihood of using coupons changes based on social presence, as consumers do not want to appear cheap to others (Ashworth, Darke, & Schaller, 2005).

Social presence can also affect consumption related to impulse purchasing (Luo, 2005), variety seeking (Ratner & Kahn, 2002), advertising response (Fisher & Dube, 2005), and charitable giving and volunteering (Garcia, Weaver, Darley, & Spence, 2009) via its activation of normative beliefs. For instance, consumers are more variety seeking in public than in private settings because they think that variety seeking is normative (Ratner & Kahn,

2002). Because expressing emotion when viewing an ad is inconsistent with the male stereotype and hence would be in violation of social norms, Fisher and Dube (2005) find that males' reactions to a stereotype-incongruent ad are more negative when in the presence of another male; however, no difference was found for stereotype-congruent ads. Finally, the effect of the imagined presence of others on charitable giving and volunteering is heightened if people perceive themselves to be the focus of a group's attention; in other words, more helping occurs when there is a feeling of public scrutiny as helping is the "right" thing to do (Garcia et al., 2009).

Social presence has also been considered in the context of crowds. Consumer behavior research has examined the influence of the presence of multiple people, creating a crowding sensation, on purchase behavior in a retail environment. However, the crowding literature is less about impression management or normative beliefs and more about feelings of control. Although crowding generally produces negative effects (Harrell, Hutt, & Anderson 1980), including decreased satisfaction with the shopping experience and decreased time spent shopping, these effects can be mitigated. For instance, Hui and Bateson (1991) find that giving consumers' perceived control reduces the negative effects of crowding by affecting perceived pleasure of the experience and desire to stay and affiliate with the retail establishment; and Machleit, Eroglu, and Mantel (2000) find that consumers' individual tolerance level for crowding affects satisfaction with a crowded shopping experience.

## Social Contagion

Research on social contagion (see Spears, this volume), which encompasses the spread of mood or behavior from one person to another (Lindzey & Aronson, 1968), highlights interesting consumer phenomena. It is distinct from conformity in that it does not result from social pressure but, instead, occurs via mere exposure to another person. Both behavioral mimicry and emotional contagion have been examined in consumer behavior research.

Being mimicked and engaging in mimicry has effects on preferences and consumption (Tanner, Ferraro, Chartrand, Bettman, & van Baaren, 2008). Tanner et al. find that consumers mimic the eating behavior of another person and this has an effect on their attitudes toward the food. Consumers who are mimicked by another person display greater positive attitude toward a product that is presented and

discussed by that other person, reflecting a salesperson–consumer interaction. White and Argo (2011) build on the behavioral mimicry literature to examine the idea of possession mimicry, which refers to imitation of another consumer's product choice. When people are aware that their product choices are being mimicked, concerns with distinctiveness lead to greater dissociation responses, including possession disposal intentions, recustomization behaviors, and exchange behaviors.

Emotional contagion is the transfer of emotion from one individual to another through physical mimicry. Positive emotional contagion that is generated through physical mimicry of smiling behavior generates positive attitudes toward a product (Howard & Gengler, 2001). Emotional contagion effects have also been shown in the context of charitable donations; people are more likely to donate when exposed to sad faces, which generates sympathy (Small & Verrochi, 2009). Ramanathan and McGill (2007) demonstrate emotional contagion effects in moment-to-moment evaluations of a video. Participants who were able to view the facial expressions of another person synchronously watching the same video exhibited greater convergence in evaluations than participants who were not able to view facial expressions. Although much of the research in this area attributes emotional contagion effects to mimicry of facial expressions, a different perspective is offered by Hennig-Thurau, Groth, Paul, and Gremler (2006), who argue that in a service encounter situation, emotion transfer occurs through an authentic display of emotion rather than physical mimicry. More research in this domain could explore the process by which emotional contagion occurs.

## Social Networks

Another important way in which social influence operates is via its spread across social networks, which reflect the social structure among a group of individuals (Barnes, 1954). Social networks have been studied in research on word of mouth effects, which deals with consumers' inclination to convey positive or negative information about a product to others. Because word of mouth involves consumer-to-consumer messaging, it is inherently a social phenomenon. There is a large literature in consumer behavior on the antecedents and consequences of word of mouth, and much of the research utilizes naturalistic settings rather than experimental manipulations to examine the phenomenon (see Berger, 2014, for a review). Whereas earlier research focused on face-to-face word of mouth, the advent of the Internet shifted the focus to online word of mouth.

The nature of the social ties within a social network can affect word of mouth. For example, Brown and Reingen (1987) find support for the importance of weak ties in the transmission of word of mouth across groups. Weak ties are those to whom one is distantly related, whereas strong ties consist of one's close network (Granovetter, 1973). Whereas weak ties are influential in terms of conveying information across groups, strong ties are more influential in terms of individual-level decisions. Frenzen and Nakamoto (1993) find that word of mouth flows through strong ties when information is costly, but through both weak and strong ties at other times.

Because marketers are interested in identifying individuals who will affect others' product adoption and usage, various types of influence agents in social networks have been identified. The earlier research in this area considered the characteristics of opinion leaders and how to identify them (Myers & Robertson, 1972). Opinion leaders and early adopters of a product tend to be experts, are highly involved in the product category, and occupy different positions in the social network (Kratzer & Lettl, 2009). Market mavens, on the other hand, are consumers who have general rather than product-specific knowledge of the marketplace through extensive shopping experience and who enjoy imparting this knowledge to others (Feick & Price, 1987). Individuals with high centrality in social networks are likely to be both opinion leaders and to be susceptible to interpersonal influence (Lee, Cotte, & Noseworthy, 2010). Watts and Dodds (2007) cast doubt on the importance of opinion leaders by showing, through simulations, that influence occurs because there are segments of individuals who are easily influenced, not because there are influencers who exert influence. However, others have found little empirical support for their framework.

As mentioned earlier, there is a growing literature on word of mouth that is specific to the online environment. Consumers read and see a variety of product information provided by others online, including product reviews, details about purchased items, and complaints. These sources of information may substitute for in-store salespeople or friends. As found in the face-to-face environment, online negative word of mouth is more influential than positive word of mouth (Chen, Wang, & Xie, 2011; Laczniak, DeCarlo, & Ramaswami, 2001) because of the negativity effect. However,

positive recommendations are more effective than simply providing product details (Cheema & Kaikati, 2010).

Some important differences exist between online and offline word of mouth. The one-to-one conversations occurring offline shift to many-to-many conversations online. As a result, ratings in online reviews are affected by the context, including the ratings of prior posters. Negative prior ratings lead people to post more negative reviews for impression management reasons or because of the salience of negative information (Moe & Trusov, 2011; Schlosser, 2005). Online word of mouth also differs in that a consumer might be one of many followers of one individual (e.g., a celebrity blogger) who comments on many products or services. Kozinets, de Valck, Wojnicki, and Wilner (2010) focus on the unique effects of community-based word of mouth effects. Similar to brand communities, the authors found that blogs have communal norms with which visitors are expected to conform; however, bloggers have to navigate mixed goals as they describe brands that have been provided to them as free samples while maintaining the trust of the community.

## Future Directions

The goal of this chapter was to provide an overview of the research on social influence in marketing. We touched briefly on a large number of articles to highlight the breadth of phenomena at work when consumers are processing marketing information and making consumption decisions. We now discuss future directions for social influence research. The technology available today (e.g., Internet, social media platforms, smartphones) affects the ways in which people interact with others in the face-to-face world and in the virtual world, fundamentally altering the nature of social influence. While some of the social influence theories apply in the new social world, they will need to be expanded upon, but new theories also need to be developed.

1. The lives of others are easily observable through social media. For example, via Facebook, a person can see the activities that someone engages in and the products that someone owns. A person may also share her financial or weight loss goals on websites such as stickK.com. The opportunity to do so has implications for the person posting the information and for the people observing the posts. How do observers react to seeing the entire contents of a person's life, especially when that life can be purposively

displayed to seem better than it actually is? Social comparison will be easily triggered when viewing people's online profiles, so there is the possibility for experiencing dark side emotions like envy, guilt, and embarrassment. On many social media platforms, people can actively seek feedback on what they have purchased by posting videos (e.g., YouTube) or photos (e.g., Instagram) of their purchases. While a person may do so for self-evaluation or for self-improvement, it still opens the person up to criticism from others. This raises interesting questions about why people seek out such opportunities and how others respond to them.

2. Having the opportunity to post the contents of one's life in various online outlets also raises interesting questions about what to disclose where. Pinterest is a platform where a person can take images, text, and video that she finds on the Internet and post it on her "pin board," which can then be shared with others. Users share pin boards related to home design, wedding plans, favorite activities, and so on. What types of selves do consumers reveal on Pinterest—the authentic self, the ideal self, or some other self? In contrast, Facebook may reflect a more realistic world about the day-to-day activities of a person. Do people have lay theories about which types of social media platforms reveal a more authentic self? Can a person create an ideal identity more freely in these environments than within the context of her face-to-face social environments with family, friends, and coworkers?

3. We briefly discussed brand communities earlier. Social media have an important role in the formation and operation of these communities. From a firm's perspective, marketers need to understand what value people get from participating in such communities. Brand communities are particularly important to the success of a brand because it is these members that advocate for the brand. From a theoretical perspective, additional research is needed to more completely understand the positives and negatives of being part of a brand community. For instance, firms are utilizing co-creation activities as a means of connecting and reinforcing the brand community. Co-creation refers to activities where consumers are collaborating with firms to build the brand, such as by creating advertising as part of a marketer-managed campaign, soliciting ideas for brand innovation, and designing product packaging. How can marketers construct effective co-creation campaigns that engage consumers and lead them to become brand ambassadors? What types of online co-creation activities lead people to "like" the brand on Facebook or share their efforts with friends and family? Dretsch and Kirmani (2015) are taking a lead in research focused on the role social influence has in the effectiveness of a co-creation campaign.

4. Some people desire to be influencers. As consumers post product reviews, and thereby reveal information about their purchases online, they become strategic marketers; in other words, they use persuasion knowledge to determine what to say, how to say it, and where to say it. Research by Chen and Kirmani (2015) finds that consumers utilize persuasion knowledge about where to post a review in order to maximize the chances that people will read it and comment. Future research can examine consumers' persuasion knowledge in contexts where the consumer acts as an influence agent.

5. Finally, a fascinating area of research examines the role of the computer as a social entity. The idea of human–computer interaction is not new, but it has expanded tremendously in recent years. Moon (2000) examined whether people treat computers as social actors and the implications for such an interaction for marketing research (see also Reeves & Nass, 1996). Moon finds that people divulge private information when the computer acts in a normative manner. Wang, Baker, Wagner, and Wakefield (2007) find that avatars, voices, and other social cues on online retail sites make the website appear more social; that is, the website is rated as more helpful and intelligent, leading to a more positive shopping experience for consumers. Further investigation into the social nature of technology is warranted. Can technological devices serve as surrogates for human relationships, or are there important differences between the two?

In short, there are numerous opportunities for further research involving social influence in marketing. We feel that over the next decade, much of that research will focus on the social environment as it is created and managed in the online environment.

## References

Algesheimer, R., Dholakia, U. M., & Herrmann, A. (2005). The social influence of brand community: Evidence from European car clubs. *Journal of Marketing, 69,* 19–34.

Amaldoss, W., & Jain, S. (2005). Pricing of conspicuous goods: A competitive analysis of social effects. *Journal of Marketing Research, 42,* 30–42.

Argo, J. J., White, K., & Dahl, D. W. (2006). Social comparison theory and deception in the interpersonal exchange of consumption information. *Journal of Consumer Research, 33,* 99–108.

Ariely, D., & Levav, J. (2000). Sequential choice in group settings: Taking the road less traveled and less enjoyed. *Journal of Consumer Research, 27,* 279–290.

Asch, S. E. (1951). Effects of group pressure upon the modification and distortion of judgments. In H. Guetzkow (Ed.), *Groups, leadership, and men* (pp. 222–236). Pittsburgh, PA: Carnegie Press.

Ashworth, L., Darke, P. R., & Schaller, M. (2005). No one wants to look cheap: Trade-offs between social disincentives and the economic and psychological incentives to redeem coupons. *Journal of Consumer Psychology, 15,* 295–306.

Bagozzi, R., Wong, N., Abe, S., & Bergami, M. (2000). Cultural and situational contingencies and the theory of reasoned action: Application to fast food restaurant consumption. *Journal of Consumer Psychology, 9,* 97–106.

Barnes, J. A. (1954). Class and committees in a Norwegian island parish. *Human Relations, 7,* 39–58.

Batra, R., & Homer, P. M. (2004). The situational impact of brand image beliefs. *Journal of Consumer Psychology, 14,* 318–330.

Batra, R., Homer, P. M., & Kahle, L. R. (2001). Values, susceptibility to normative influence, and attribute importance weights: A nomological analysis. *Journal of Consumer Psychology, 11,* 115–128.

Bearden, W. O., & Etzel, M. J. (1982). Reference group influence on product and brand purchase decisions. *Journal of Consumer Research, 9,* 183–194.

Bearden, W. O., Netemeyer, R. G., & Teel, J. E. (1989). Measurement of consumer susceptibility to interpersonal influence. *Journal of Consumer Research, 15,* 473–481.

Belk, R. (2010). Sharing. *Journal of Consumer Research, 36,* 715–734.

Belk, R. W., & Coon, G. S. (1993). Gift giving as agapic love: An alternative to the exchange paradigm based on dating experiences. *Journal of Consumer Research, 20,* 393–417.

Berger, J. (2014). Word of mouth and interpersonal communication: A review and directions for future research. *Journal of Consumer Psychology, 24,* 586–607.

Berger, J., & Heath, C. (2007). Where consumers diverge from others: Identity signaling and product domains. *Journal of Consumer Research, 34,* 121–134.

Berger, J., & Rand, L. (2008). Shifting signals to help health: Using identity signaling to reduce risky health behaviors. *Journal of Consumer Research, 35,* 509–518.

Berger, J., & Ward, M. (2010). Subtle signals of inconspicuous consumption. *Journal of Consumer Research, 37,* 555–569.

Bonfield, E. H. (1974). Attitude, social influence, personal norm, and intention interactions as related to brand purchase behavior. *Journal of Marketing Research, 11,* 379–389.

Brewer, M. B. (1993). The role of distinctiveness in social identity and group behavior. In M. A. Hogg & D. Abrams (Eds.), *Group motivation: Social psychological perspectives* (pp. 1–16). Hertfordshire, UK: Harvester Wheatsheaf.

Briley, D. A., Shrum, L. J., & Wyer, R. S., Jr. (2007). Subjective impressions of minority group representation in the media: A comparison of majority and minority viewers' judgments and underlying processes. *Journal of Consumer Psychology, 17,* 36–48.

Brown, J. J., & Reingen, P. H. (1987). Social ties and word-of-mouth referral behavior. *Journal of Consumer Research, 14,* 350–362.

Burnkrant, R. E., & Cousineau, A. (1975). Informational and normative social influence in buyer behavior. *Journal of Consumer Research, 2,* 206–215.

Campbell, M. C., & Kirmani, A. (2000). Consumers' use of persuasion knowledge: The effects of accessibility and cognitive capacity on perceptions of an influence agent. *Journal of Consumer Research, 27,* 69–83.

Campbell, M. C., & Kirmani, A. (2008). I know what you're doing and why you're doing it: The use of the persuasion knowledge model in consumer research. In C. Hugvstedt, P. Herr, & F. Kardes (Eds.), *Handbook of consumer psychology* (pp. 549–574). New York, NY: Psychology Press.

Campbell, M. C., & Mohr, G. S. (2011). Seeing is eating: How and when activation of a negative stereotype increases stereotype-conducive behavior. *Journal of Consumer Research, 38,* 431–444.

Chan, C., Berger, J., & Van Boven, L. (2012). Identifiable but not identical: Combining social identity and uniqueness motives in choice. *Journal of Consumer Research, 39,* 561–573.

Cheema, A., & Kaikati, A. M. (2010). The effect of need for uniqueness on word of mouth. *Journal of Marketing Research, 47,* 553–563.

Chen, Y., & Kirmani, A. (2015). Posting strategically: The consumer as an online media planner. *Journal of Consumer Psychology, 25,* 609–621.

Chen, Y., Wang, Q., & Xie, J. (2011). Online social interactions: A natural experiment on word of mouth versus observational learning. *Journal of Marketing Research, 48,* 238–254.

Childers, T. L., & Rao, A. R. (1992). The influence of familial and peer-based reference groups on consumer decisions. *Journal of Consumer Research, 19,* 198–211.

Dahl, D. W., Argo, J. J., & Morales, A. C. (2012). Social information in the retail environment: The importance of consumption alignment, referent identity, and self-esteem. *Journal of Consumer Research, 38,* 860–871.

Dahl, D. W., Manchanda, R. V., & Argo, J. J. (2001). Embarrassment in consumer purchase: The roles of social presence and purchase familiarity. *Journal of Consumer Research, 28,* 473–481.

Deutsch, M., & Gerard, H. B. (1955). A study of normative and informational social influences upon individual judgment. *Journal of Abnormal and Social Psychology, 51,* 629–636.

Dretsch, H. J., & Kirmani, K. (2015). Hearing their voice: When brand co-creation leads to social brand engagement. In C. Dimofte, C. Haugtvedt, & R. Yalch (Eds.), *Consumer psychology in a social media world.* London, UK: Routledge.

Eagly, A. H., & Chaiken, S. (1993). *The psychology of attitudes.* Orlando, FL: Harcourt Brace Jovanovich College.

Escalas, J. E., & Bettman, J. R. (2003). You are what they eat: The influence of reference groups on consumers' connections to brands. *Journal of Consumer Psychology, 13,* 339–348.

Escalas, J. E., & Bettman, J. R. (2005). Self-construal, reference groups, and brand meaning. *Journal of Consumer Research, 32,* 378–389.

Feick, L. F., & Price, L. L. (1987). The market maven: A diffuser of marketplace information. *Journal of Marketing, 51,* 83–97.

Ferraro, R., Kirmani, A., & Matherly, T. (2013). Look at me! Look at me! Conspicuous brand usage, self-brand connection, and dilution. *Journal of Marketing Research, 50*, 477–488.

Festinger, L. (1954). A theory of social comparison processes. *Human Relations, 7*, 117–140.

Fishbein, M., & Ajzen, I. (1975). *Belief, attitude, intention and behavior: An introduction to theory and research*. Reading, MA: Addison-Wesley.

Fisher, R. J., & Dube, L. (2005). Gender differences in responses to emotional advertising: A social desirability perspective. *Journal of Consumer Research, 31*, 850–858.

Fisher, R. J., & Price, L. L. (1992). An investigation into the social context of early adoption behavior. *Journal of Consumer Research, 19*, 477–486.

Frenzen, J., & Nakamoto, K. (1993). Structure, cooperation, and the flow of market information. *Journal of Consumer Research, 20*, 360–375.

Friestad, M., & Wright, P. (1994). The persuasion knowledge model: How people cope with persuasion attempts. *Journal of Consumer Research, 21*, 1–31.

Garcia, S. M., Weaver, K., Darley, J. M., & Spence, B. T. (2009). Dual effects of implicit bystanders: Inhibiting vs. facilitating helping behavior. *Journal of Consumer Psychology, 19*, 215–224.

Goldstein, N. J., Cialdini, R. B., & Griskevicius, V. (2008). A room with a viewpoint: Using social norms to motivate environmental conservation in hotels. *Journal of Consumer Research, 35*, 472–482.

Gorn, G. J., Jiang, Y., & Johar, G. V. (2008). Babyfaces, trait inferences, and company evaluations in a public relations crisis. *Journal of Consumer Research, 35*, 36–49.

Granovetter, M. S. (1973). The strength of weak ties. *American Journal of Sociology, 78*, 1360–1380.

Greenwald, A. G. (1968). Cognitive learning, cognitive response to persuasion, and attitude change. In A. G. Greenwald, T. C. Brock, and T. M. Ostram (Eds.) *Psychological foundations of attitudes* (pp. 147–170). New York, NY: Academic Press.

Grier, S. A., & Deshpande, R. (2001). Social dimensions of consumer distinctiveness: The influence of social status on group identity and advertising persuasion. *Journal of Marketing Research, 38*, 216–224.

Hafner, M. (2004). How dissimilar others may still resemble the self: Assimilation and contrast after social comparison. *Journal of Consumer Psychology, 14*, 187–196.

Han, Y. J., Nunes, J. C., & Dreze, X. (2010). Signaling status with luxury goods: The role of brand prominence. *Journal of Marketing, 74*, 15–30.

Harrell, G. D., Hutt, M. D., & Anderson, J. C. (1980). Path analysis of buyer behavior under conditions of crowding. *Journal of Marketing Research, 17*, 45–51.

Hennig-Thurau, T., Groth, M., Paul, M., & Gremler, D. D. (2006). Are all smiles created equal? How emotional contagion and emotional labor affect service relationships. *Journal of Marketing, 70*, 58–73.

Hoch, S. J., & Loewenstein, G. F. (1991). Time-inconsistent preferences and consumer self-control. *Journal of Consumer Research, 17*, 492–507.

Howard, D. J., & Gengler, C. (2001). Emotional contagion effects on product attitudes. *Journal of Consumer Research, 28*, 189–201.

Hui, M. K., & Bateson, J. E. G. (1991). Perceived control and the effects of crowding and consumer choice on the service experience. *Journal of Consumer Research, 18*, 174–184.

Irmak, C., Vallen, B., & Sen, S. (2010). You like what I like, but I don't like what you like: Uniqueness motivations in product preferences. *Journal of Consumer Research, 37*, 443–455.

Joy, A. (2001). Gift giving in Hong Kong and the continuum of social ties. *Journal of Consumer Research, 28*, 239–256.

Kahle, L. R., & Homer, P. M. (1985). Physical attractiveness of the celebrity endorser: A social adaptation perspective. *Journal of Consumer Research, 11*, 954–961.

Kelman, H. C. (1961). Processes of opinion change. *Public opinion quarterly, 25*(1), 57–78.

Kirmani, A., & Campbell, M. (2004). Goal seeker and persuasion sentry: How consumer targets respond to interpersonal marketing persuasion. *Journal of Consumer Research, 31*, 573–582.

Kirmani, A., & Shiv, B. (1998). The effects of source congruity on brand attitudes and beliefs: The moderating role of issue-relevant elaboration. *Journal of Consumer Psychology, 7*, 25–48.

Kozinets, R. V., de Valck, K., Wojnicki, A. C., & Wilner, S. J. S. (2010). Networked narratives: Understanding word-of-mouth marketing in online communities. *Journal of Marketing, 74*, 71–89.

Kratzer, J., & Lettl, C. (2009). Distinctive roles of lead users and opinion leaders in the social networks of schoolchildren. *Journal of Consumer Research, 36*, 646–659.

Kruglanski, A. W., & Mayseless, O. (1990). Classic and current social comparison research: Expanding the perspective. *Psychological Bulletin, 108*(2), 195–208.

Kurt, D., Inman, J. J., & Argo, J. J. (2011). The influence of friends on consumer spending: The role of agency-communion orientation and self-monitoring. *Journal of Marketing Research, 48*, 741–754.

Laczniak, R. N., DeCarlo, T. E., & Ramaswami, S. N. (2001). Consumers' responses to negative word-of-mouth communication: An attribution theory perspective. *Journal of Consumer Psychology, 11*, 57–73.

LaTour, S. A., & Manrai, A. K. (1989). Interactive impact of informational and normative influence on donations. *Journal of Marketing Research, 26*, 327–335.

Lee, S. H., Cotte, J., & Noseworthy, T. J. (2010). The role of network centrality in the flow of consumer influence. *Journal of Consumer Psychology, 20*, 66–77.

Lindzey, G., & Aronson, E. (1968). *The handbook of social psychology* (2nd ed.). Oxford, UK: Addison-Wesley.

Lowrey, T. M., Otnes, C. C., & Ruth, J. A. (2004). Social influences on dyadic giving over time: A taxonomy from the giver's perspective. *Journal of Consumer Research, 30*, 547–558.

Luo, X. (2005). How does shopping with others influence impulsive purchasing. *Journal of Consumer Psychology, 15*, 288–294.

Machleit, K., Eroglu, S., & Mantel, S. (2000). Perceived retail crowding and shopping satisfaction: What modifies this relationship? *Journal of Consumer Psychology, 9*, 29–42.

Mathwick, C., Wiertz, C., & de Ruyter, K. (2008). Social capital production in a virtual P3 community. *Journal of Consumer Research, 34*, 832–849.

McAlexander, J. H., Schouten, J. W., & Koenig, H. F. (2002). Building brand community. *Journal of Marketing, 66*, 38–54.

McCracken, G. (1986). Culture and consumption: A theoretical account of the structure and movement of the cultural meaning of consumer goods. *Journal of Consumer Research, 13*, 71–84.

McFerran, B., Dahl, D. W., Fitzsimons, G. J., & Morales, A. C. (2010). I'll have what she's having: Effects of social influence and body type on the food choices of others. *Journal of Consumer Research, 36*, 915–929.

Miniard, P. W., & Cohen, J. B. (1979). Isolating attitudinal and normative influences in behavioral intentions models. *Journal of Marketing Research, 16*, 102–110.

Moe, W. W., & Trusov, M. (2011). The value of social dynamics in online product ratings forums. *Journal of Marketing Research, 48*, 444–456.

Moon, Y. (2000). Intimate exchanges: Using computers to elicit self-disclosure from consumers. *Journal of Consumer Research, 26*, 323–339.

Moreau, C. P., & Herd, K. B. (2010). To each his own? How comparisons with others influence consumers' evaluations of their self-designed products. *Journal of Consumer Research, 36*, 806–819.

Moschis, G. P. (1976). Social comparison and informal group influence. *Journal of Marketing Research, 13*, 237–244.

Muniz, A. M., Jr., & O'Guinn, T. C. (2001). Brand community. *Journal of Consumer Research, 27*, 412–432.

Muniz, A. M., Jr., & Schau, H. J. (2005). Religiosity in the abandoned Apple Newton brand community. *Journal of Consumer Research, 31*, 737–747.

Myers, J. H., & Robertson, T. S. (1972). Dimensions of opinion leadership. *Journal of Marketing Research, 9*, 41–46.

Petty, R. E., Cacioppo, J. T., & Schumann, D. (1983). Central and peripheral routes to advertising effectiveness: The moderating role of involvement. *Journal of Consumer Research, 10*, 135–146.

Priester, J. R., & Petty, R. E. (2003). The influence of spokesperson trustworthiness on message elaboration, attitude strength, and advertising effectiveness. *Journal of Consumer Psychology, 13*, 408–421.

Quester, P., & Steyer, A. (2010). Revisiting individual choices in group settings: The long and winding (less traveled) road? *Journal of Consumer Research, 36*, 1050–1057.

Ramanathan, S., & McGill, A. L. (2007). Consuming with others: Social influences on moment-to-moment and retrospective evaluations of an experience. *Journal of Consumer Research, 34*, 506–524.

Ratner, R. K., & Kahn, B. E. (2002). The impact of private versus public consumption on variety-seeking behavior. *Journal of Consumer Research, 29*, 246–257.

Ratneshwar, S., & Chaiken, S. (1991). Comprehension's role in persuasion: The case of its moderating effect on the persuasive impact of source cues. *Journal of Consumer Research, 18*, 52–62.

Reeves, B., & Nass, C. (1996). *The media equation: How people treat computers, television, and new media like real people and places.* New York, NY: Cambridge University Press.

Reingen, P. H., & Kernan, J. B. (1993). Social perception and interpersonal influence: Some consequences of the physical attractiveness stereotype in a personal selling setting. *Journal of Consumer Psychology, 2*, 25–38.

Reinhard, M. A., Messner, M., & Sporer, S. L. (2006). Explicit persuasive intent and its impact on success at persuasion—the determining roles of attractiveness and likeableness. *Journal of Consumer Psychology, 16*, 249–259.

Rice, D. H., Kelting, K., & Lutz, R. J. (2012). Multiple endorsers and multiple endorsements: The influence of message repetition, source congruence and involvement on brand attitudes. *Journal of Consumer Psychology, 22*(2), 249–259.

Richins, M. L. (1991). Social comparison and the idealized images of advertising. *Journal of Consumer Research, 18*, 71–83.

Ruth, J. A., Otnes, C. C., & Brunel, F. F. (1999). Gift receipt and the reformulation of interpersonal relationships. *Journal of Consumer Research, 25*, 385–402.

Ryan, M. J., & Bonfield, E. H. (1975). The Fishbein extended model and consumer behavior. *Journal of Consumer Research, 2*, 118–136.

Sagarin, B. J., Cialdini, R. B., Rice, W. E., & Serna, S. B. (2002). Dispelling the illusion of invulnerability: The motivations and mechanisms of resistance to persuasion. *Journal of Personality and Social Psychology, 83*(3), 526–541.

Schau, H., & Gilly, M. C. (2003). We are what we post? Self-presentation in personal web space. *Journal of Consumer Research, 30*, 385–404.

Schau, H. J., Muniz, A. M., & Arnould, E. J. (2009). How brand community practices create value. *Journal of Marketing, 73*, 30–51.

Schlosser, A. E. (2005). Posting versus lurking: Communicating in a multiple audience context. Journal of Consumer Research, *32*, 260–265.

Schultz, P. W., Khazian, A. M., & Zaleski, A. C. (2008). Using normative social influence to promote conservation among hotel guests. *Social Influence, 3*, 4–23.

Schurr, P. H., & Ozanne, J. L. (1985). Influences on exchange processes: Buyers' preconceptions of a seller's trustworthiness and bargaining toughness. *Journal of Consumer Research, 11*, 939–953.

Sen, S., Gurhan-Canli, Z., & Morwitz, V. (2001). Withholding consumption: A social dilemma perspective on consumer boycotts. *Journal of Consumer Research, 28*, 399–417.

Sengupta, J., Dahl, D. W., & Gorn, G. J. (2002). Misrepresentation in the consumer context. *Journal of Consumer Psychology, 12*, 69–79.

Shalev, E., & Morwitz, V. (2012). Influence via comparison-driven self-evaluation and restoration. *Journal of Consumer Research, 38*, 964–980.

Sherry, J. F., Jr. (1983). Gift giving in anthropological perspective. *Journal of Consumer Research, 10*, 157–168.

Simonson, I., & Nowlis, S. M. (2000). The role of explanations and need for uniqueness in consumer decision making: Unconventional choices based on reasons. *Journal of Consumer Research, 27*, 49–68.

Small, D. A., & Verrochi, N. M. (2009). The face of need: Facial emotion expression on charity advertisements. *Journal of Marketing Research, 46*, 777–787.

Snyder, C. R., & Fromkin, H. L. (1977). Abnormality as a positive characteristic: The development and validation of a scale measuring need for uniqueness. *Journal of Abnormal Psychology, 86*, 518–527.

Spence, M. (1973). Job market signaling. *Quarterly Journal of Economics, 87*, 355–374.

Stayman, D. M., & Deshpande, R. (1989). Situational ethnicity and consumer behavior. *Journal of Consumer Research, 16*, 361–371.

Sternthal, B., Dholakia, R., & Leavitt, C. (1978). The persuasive effects of source credibility: Tests of cognitive response. *Journal of Consumer Research, 4*, 252–260.

Sundie, J. M., Ward, J. C., Beal, D. J., Chin, W. W., & Geiger-Oneto, S. (2009). Schadenfreude as a consumption-related emotion: Feeling happiness about the downfall of another's product. *Journal of Consumer Psychology, 19*, 356–373.

Tajfel, H., & Turner, J. (1979). An integrative theory of inter-group conflict. In W. G. Austin & S. Worchel (Eds.), *The social psychology of intergroup relations* (pp. 33–47). Monterrey, CA: Brooks/Cole.

Tanner, R., Ferraro, R., Chartrand, T. L., Bettman, J. R., & van Baaren, R. (2008). Of chameleons and consumption: The impact of mimicry on choice and preferences. *Journal of Consumer Research, 34*, 754–767.

Tian, K. T., Bearden, W. O., & Hunter, G. L. (2001). Consumers' need for uniqueness: Scale development and validation. *Journal of Consumer Research, 28*, 50–66.

Tian, K. T., & McKenzie, K. (2001). The long-term predictive validity of the consumers' need for uniqueness scale. *Journal of Consumer Psychology, 10*, 171–193.

Thompson, D. V., & Norton, M. I. (2011). The social utility of feature creep. *Journal of Marketing Research, 48*, 555–565.

Thompson, S. A., & Sinha, R. K. (2008). Brand communities and new product adoption: The influence and limits of oppositional loyalty. *Journal of Marketing, 72*, 65–80.

Tripp, C., Jensen, T. D., & Carlson, L. (1994). The effects of multiple product endorsements by celebrities on consumers' attitudes and intentions. *Journal of Consumer Research, 20*, 535–547.

Tuk, M. A., Verlegh, P. W. J., Smidts, A., & Wigboldus, D. H. J. (2009). Sales and sincerity: The role of relational framing in word-of-mouth referral. *Journal of Consumer Psychology, 19*, 38–47.

Van de Ven, N., Zeelenberg, M., & Pieters, R. (2011). The envy premium in product evaluation. *Journal of Consumer Research, 37*, 984–998.

Wang, L. C., Baker, J., Wagner, J. A., & Wakefield, K. (2007). Can a retail web site be social? *Journal of Marketing, 71*, 143–157.

Watts, D. J., & Dodds, P. S. (2007). Influentials, networks, and public opinion formation. *Journal of Consumer Research, 34*, 441–458.

White, K., & Argo, J. J. (2011). When imitation doesn't flatter: The role of consumer distinctiveness in responses to mimicry. *Journal of Consumer Research, 38*, 667–680.

White, K., & Dahl, D. W. (2006). To be or not be? The influence of dissociative reference groups on consumer preferences. *Journal of Consumer Psychology, 16*, 404–414.

White, K., & Dahl, D. W. (2007). Are all out-groups created equal? Consumer identity and dissociative influence. *Journal of Consumer Research, 34*, 525–536.

Wooten, D. (1995). One-of-a-kind in a full house: Some consequences of ethnic and gender distinctiveness. *Journal of Consumer Psychology, 4*, 205–224.

Wooten, D. B., & Reed, A. (1998). Informational influence and the ambiguity of product experience: Order effects on the weighting of evidence. *Journal of Consumer Psychology, 7*, 79–99.

Wooten, D. B., & Reed, A. (2004). Playing it safe: Susceptibility to normative influence and protective self-presentation. *Journal of Consumer Research, 31*, 551–556.

Zhu, R., Dholakia, U. M., Chen, X., & Algesheimer, R. (2012). Does online community participation foster risky financial behavior. *Journal of Marketing Research, 49*, 394–407.

PART 6

The Future

# The Future of Social Influence in Social Psychology

Kipling D. Williams *and* Stephen G. Harkins

**Abstract**

With notable exceptions, social influence has not played a major role in social psychology since the mid-1980s. The chapters in this volume, along with other developments, set the stage for a return of social influence to its once preeminent position. The chapters contribute to the renaissance of interest in social influence in a variety of ways. Some chapters show us that it is time to re-examine classic topics in the context of what has been learned since the original research was conducted. Others show how integrations/elaborations that advance our understanding of social influence processes are now possible. The chapters also reveal lacunae in the social influence literature, and suggest future lines of research. Perhaps the most important of these will take into account the change from traditional social influence that occurs face-to-face to social media-mediated influence that is likely to characterize many of our interactions in the future.

**Key Words:** social influence, social psychology, conformity, compliance, obedience, attitudes, influence sources, social identity, social comparison

It could be argued that research on social influence reached its high water mark in the 25 or so years following Asch's (1951) seminal work on conformity. Certainly there was more work done in the core areas of social influence, like conformity, compliance, and obedience, in this period than in any other. The same can be said about research in many of the other areas covered in this volume (e.g., social facilitation, social inhibition [e.g., bystander effect], deindividuation).

However, by the mid-1980s, interest in social influence had waned, corresponding with an increase in interest in social cognition over the same period, the leading edge of which was marked by work on attribution and person perception. This shift in interest can be seen in the marked decline in the use of behavioral measures, a hallmark of work in social influence, in the decade from 1976 to 1986 in research reported in the premier journal in personality/social psychology, the *Journal of Personality and Social Psychology* (Baumeister, Vohs, & Funder, 2007).

With the notable exceptions of the work of Moscovici on minority influence (reviewed by Butera et al., this volume), and Tajfel and Turner on social identity (reviewed by Gaffney & Hogg, this volume), social influence has not played a major role in social psychology since the mid-1980s. However, we believe that the chapters in this volume, along with other developments, set the stage for a return of social influence to the preeminent position it once held in social psychology.

The chapters contribute to this renaissance of interest in social influence in a number of ways. Some chapters show that it is time to take another look at classic areas in social influence. For example, as Burger points out in his chapter on obedience, few, if any, lines of research have had the shelf-life of Milgram's program of research, but despite its importance in the field, work in this area has not really advanced much beyond the original research. Burger describes a number of directions that work in this area can now take. For example, although direct replications of Milgram's paradigm are no longer possible, Burger (2009) has described a variant of the basic procedure that can be used in the original paradigm. He also notes that there are many settings in which people in authority give orders (e.g., supervisors, parents, elected officials), and examining the factors that determine whether people follow instructions from these sources would be of great interest. Also, instead of limiting our attention to the destructive effects of obedience, Burger suggests that studying situations in which obeying commands is beneficial (e.g., following instructions from medical professionals) would have practical as well as theoretical benefits.

We should also note that the behavior of obedience and the assumption that the source of the command is an authority have been inextricably linked since Milgram's seminal program of research. However, must they be so tightly linked? By defining obedience as something done in response to an authority, we necessarily preclude the question of when and whether people obey sources of similar or lower power status levels. It is not inconceivable to face a demand from an underling; however, this question currently is illogical to ask or examine if we insist that obedience can only be studied with the source as an authority figure. We encourage future obedience researchers to untether themselves from authority and, instead, use source power and status as independent variables worthy of investigation on their own.

Spears's chapter on deindividuation suggests that another look at this classic area of research is also warranted. He argues that the theory's central premise that "people lose their sense of self in the crowd and become more prone to mindless aggression, has not stood up well to closer empirical or theoretical scrutiny." However, he goes on to note that the tenets of the theory have not been tested under optimal conditions, and that advances in techniques for measuring unconscious states and processes made since the time of the original research now provide the opportunity for more definitive tests.

Other chapters contribute to renewed interest in social influence by showing how integration/elaboration that advances our understanding of social influence processes is now possible. For example, in another chapter on a social influence classic, conformity, Hodges proposes that our understanding of conformity would benefit from incorporating work from anthropology and developmental and cognitive psychology, as well as from considering forces that produce divergence as well as conformity. That is, instead of looking at conformity in isolation, this phenomenon should be considered within a broader context of social influence processes. Hornsey and Jetten's chapter on stability and change within groups not only represents a step in just this direction, but also an extension in that they suggest exactly how change occurs within the group (e.g., who seeks it; who is effective at it). In their chapter, Hales, Ren, and Williams contribute to our understanding of ostracism, an important topic in its own right, but also elaborate our understanding of conformity processes by showing exactly how normative pressure represents such a potent force in producing conformity effects. That is, Deutsch and Gerard (1955) argued for the role of normative pressure in producing conformity; Hales et al.'s work on ostracism identifies the source of this pressure.

Over the years, much has been made of the need for greater integration of personality and social psychology. Nezlek and Smith persuasively argue that the intersection of personality and social influence represents a place where such an integration could profitably take place. By bringing together work in a number of areas that rely on social inhibition processes (e.g., helping behavior, emotional expression), McCarty and Karau advance our understanding of social inhibition at a conceptual level, as well as suggesting new avenues for research. Seitchik, Brown, and Harkins describe a model that not only provides the basis for understanding social facilitation effects but also may allow for the integration of work on the effect of threat on task performance in many other domains (social loafing, goal setting, intrinsic motivation/creativity, achievement goal theory, and stereotype threat).

The chapters also reveal a number of lacunae in the social influence literature. For example, in his chapter on social influence and clinical intervention, Heesacker argues that "the most important future direction in this area is refocusing the efforts of social influence scholars back onto clinical applications of social influence theory and research." He notes that there is a wealth of basic research on the internalization process (e.g., elaboration likelihood model; Petty & Cacioppo, 1986), but next to none in clinical settings. Instead, a clinician-developed approach to internalization, motivational interviewing, has generated a great deal of work. According to Heesacker, it would make a great deal of sense to pit accounts from basic research against the motivational interviewing account in clinical settings.

In their review of social influence and the law, Demaine and Cialdini note that a great deal of attention has been devoted to the study of social influence in the legal system (e.g., eye witness identification; pretrial publicity), but very little has been directed toward the study of the legal regulation of social influence in our everyday lives (e.g., deceptive advertising; corrective advertising; consent to search and seizure) or to the law as an instrument of social influence (e.g., the legitimacy of legal authority and the morality of law). Because, as Demaine and Cialdini argue, the striking difference in the amount of attention paid to the three areas is not a result of differences in the number of empirical questions in or in the importance of these areas of research, these relatively ignored areas provide fertile ground for future research.

These are examples of some of the many ways in which the chapters of the volume can contribute to a renaissance of interest in social influence. Of course, the term "renaissance" suggests a renewal of interest in the topic. There are also topics in social influence that have little, if any, past but hold great promise in the future. For example, in their chapter in this section, rather than asking how we influence and are influenced by others, Sagarin and Henningsen ask how we resist influence from others. Unlike the other chapters, this chapter includes substantial input from research and theory on persuasion—in this case, resisting persuasion—primarily because there is surprisingly little literature on resisting social influence attempts aimed at eliciting behavioral responses. The authors acknowledge this gap and offer astute speculations as to how behavioral resistance might be similar to, or different from, attitudinal resistance, suggesting a number of areas for future research.

In a recent paper, Bohns (2016) describes another topic in social influence that has a promising future but little past: people's perceptions of their influence over others. She reports a series of experiments that show that people underestimate their ability to produce compliance with their requests, apparently because they fail to appreciate how difficult it is for the target of the influence attempt to refuse the request. She goes on to describe some factors that do (e.g., monetary incentives) and do not (e.g., request size) impact the underestimation-of-compliance effect.

Work on this underestimation process will be a welcome addition to the traditional focus of social influence research, but for the field to regain its prominence, it must also make a fundamental change. In the past, social influence research and applications have largely focused on face-to-face encounters. If not true already, we will soon enter a time in which people interact and influence each other through social media more than they do in person. There is a certain irony in the fact that the ebbing of interest in social influence was marked by the decline in the use of behavioral measures documented by Baumeister et al. (2007), but its renaissance may be characterized by more button-pushing, rather than a return to the behavioral measures of yesteryear. For example, major historical social actions have already occurred largely through the influence of social media (e.g., Arab Spring). As another example of the effects that can be produced by social media–mediated influence, as opposed to more traditional forms, the last chapter in this *Handbook* is a blog entry, "The Echo Chamber," by the singer, songwriter, author, and thinker David Byrne (formerly of the Talking Heads). Here Byrne engagingly spots important nuances that social media—Facebook, Instagram, Twitter—offer (or fail to offer) that significantly affect the process and direction of social media's special type of social influence. We could have peppered his blog with citations to existing research that spoke to his insights, but we chose to leave his piece unaltered. We think readers will be intrigued by his ideas, whether they agree or disagree with them. We hope to challenge future social influence researchers and theorists to bring what they know from the past to bear on what we are witnessing now with the rapid evolution of social media, to take us into the 21st century of social influence.

We close with reflection and a call for action. In our experience teaching social psychology for over 40 years (each), we know of no other topic that has garnered as much interest and enthusiasm among students as the research included in this volume on social influence. Students love behavioral measures; they are captivated by the findings of clever field studies that show surprisingly powerful effects with subtle tactics, and years later, these are the studies they remember. The cognitive revolution, in conjunction with statistical analyses that purport to discover psychological process, retarded the development of research and theory on social influence because intrusive measures searching for mediators of effects are ill suited for this type of research. Perhaps also contributing to the decline of high-impact social influence research is the fact that these studies often required the carefully controlled creation of dramatic situations, reenacted over and over again by skilled actors, in order to capture the psychological essence of the phenomena being studied. These procedures are much more difficult and time consuming than paper-and-pencil (or computer) methodologies. Perhaps if we consider the fact that social influence in the future will largely occur online, then we can conceive of both realistic and meaningful experiments that also happen to allow for more efficient means of data collection. As we trust is obvious to our readers, there are many new and important avenues of exploration in this domain. We hope that this volume will contribute to a resurgence of interest in research and theory related to social influence.

## References

Asch, S. (1951). Effects of group pressure upon the modification and distortion of judgments. In H. Guetzkow (Ed.), *Groups, leadership, and men* (pp. 177–190). Pittsburgh, PA: Carnegie Press.

Baumeister, R. F., Vohs, K. D., & Funder, D. C. (2007). Psychology as the science of self-reports and finger movements: Whatever happened to actual behavior. *Perspectives on Psychological Science, 2*, 396–403.

Bohns, V. K. (2016). (Mis)understanding our influence over others: A review of the underestimation-of-compliance effect. *Psychological Science, 25*, 119–123.

Burger, J. M. (2009). Replicating Milgram: Would people still obey today? (2009). *American Psychologist, 64*, 1–11.

Deutsch, M., & Gerard, H. B. (1955). A study of normative and informational social influences upon individual judgment. *Journal of Abnormal and Social Psychology, 51*, 629–636.

Petty, R. E., & Cacioppo, J. T. (1986). The elaboration likelihood model of persuasion. In L. Berkowitz (Ed.), *Advances in experimental social psychology* (Vol. 19, pp. 123–205). New York, NY: Academic Press.

# Resistance to Influence

Brad J. Sagarin *and* Mary Lynn Miller Henningsen

**Abstract**

This chapter reviews research on resistance to influence, active or passive processes that reduce the impact of a potential source of social influence. This chapter begins with a discussion of the antecedents of resistance: characteristics of the influence target (strong attitudes, demographics, and personality), perceived aspects of the influence attempt (manipulative intent, threats to freedoms), or counterinfluence messages from a third party (forewarning, inoculation, stealing thunder, the poison parasite defense, resistance to social engineering) that motivate resistance. The chapter proceeds to a discussion of internal mechanisms of resistance (counterarguing, bolstering initial attitudes, derogating the source, attributing negative affect to the message or source, attempting to correct for bias) and external mechanisms of resistance (interpersonal strategies of communicating resistance and issuing refusals) and concludes with a discussion of the consequences of resistance for attitudes and relationships.

**Key Words:** resistance, forewarning, inoculation, stealing thunder, counterarguing, refusals, politeness theory, boomerang effect

> Anyone can be made impervious to the most skillful propaganda if we reduce him to catatonic schizophrenia and anyone can, with a bare bodkin, be made forever free from influence.
>
> —*William McGuire*

As the heft of this volume will attest, social scientists have made substantial progress understanding the principles of influence—the mechanisms and tactics that we use to change others' attitudes and redirect others' behavior. This chapter is devoted to the other side of the equation: the question, vexing to practitioners of influence and intriguing to influence researchers, of why influence attempts so often fail.

In defining resistance, we draw on Gerald R. Miller's (1980) classic definition of persuasive communication, "any message that is intended to shape, reinforce, or change the responses of another or others" (Stiff & Mongeau, 1993, p. 4). Consistent with this, we define resistance as active or passive processes that reduce the impact of a potential source of social influence. Such sources include intentional persuasion and compliance tactics (Cialdini, 2009) as well as nonintentional pressures such as the mere presence or behavioral examples of others. We define the effect of resistance as the difference between (a) the attitudes or behavior of the influence target when exposed to the potential source of social influence without resistance, and (b) the attitudes or behavior of the influence target when resisting the potential source of social influence. In most cases, only one of these outcomes can be observed, of course—a dilemma Holland (1986) labeled the "fundamental problem of causal inference" (p. 947). That is, a participant in a study cannot be exposed simultaneously to both the resistance condition and the control condition (and sequential presentations of the conditions can elicit order effects). This is remedied in most instances through the use of randomized experiments in which different but comparable groups of participants provide each of the outcomes.

We exclude from our definition situations in which a target is never exposed to the persuasive communication. Thus, a person sent on a detour would not be considered to have resisted a billboard on the original route. In contrast, a person who successfully counterargues against an offending billboard would be considered to have resisted the billboard. In this case, the mechanism of resistance is counterarguing, and the result of resistance is the reduced or eliminated attitude change resulting from the counterarguing. Resistance does not need to be active, however. We include in our definition passive processes of resistance such as the structural resistance stemming from strong attitudes that run counter to a persuasive communication.

We begin with a discussion of the antecedents of resistance: characteristics of the influence target (strong attitudes, demographics, and personality), perceived aspects of the influence attempt (manipulative intent, threats to freedoms), or counterinfluence messages from a third party (forewarning, inoculation, stealing thunder, the poison parasite defense, resistance to social engineering) that motivate resistance (see Figure 25.1). We then discuss internal mechanisms of resistance (counterarguing, bolstering initial attitudes, derogating the source,

attributing negative affect to the message or source, attempting to correct for bias) and external mechanisms of resistance (interpersonal strategies of communicating resistance and issuing refusals). We conclude with a discussion of the consequences of resistance for attitudes and relationships.

As this list of topics reveals, the research discussed in this chapter differs in one important respect from the research discussed in previous chapters. Previous chapters focused primarily on influence tactics deployed to effect behavior change and other influence sources that impact behavior (e.g., conformity, obedience, social inhibition). This chapter, in contrast, also includes resistance to influence tactics deployed to effect attitude change (i.e., resistance to persuasion). We have included resistance to persuasion for three reasons. First, the major theories of resistance to influence were developed to explain resistance to persuasion. A chapter that excluded such theories would be ill-informed and incomplete. Second, many of the theories of resistance to persuasion also offer insight into resistance to compliance and other sources of behavioral influence. We highlight such research where it exists. Where it does not, we explore the applicability of the theories to resistance to compliance and other sources of behavioral influence. Third, we believe that resistance to compliance and other sources of behavioral influence offers a fertile and mostly unexplored territory for future research endeavors, and we hope that the inclusion of resistance to persuasion theories in this chapter will help to illuminate some of the potential directions.

## Target, Message, and Third-Party Antecedents of Resistance

In this section, we discuss factors that provoke resistance to influence. These factors include elements within the persuasive target such as

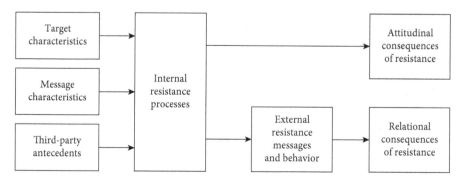

**Figure 25.1** Antecedents, processes, and consequences of resistance to influence.

preexisting strong attitudes and high levels of certain personality traits. They also include aspects of the message that can, possibly unintentionally, elicit resistance against that message. Finally, we review research on forewarning of an upcoming persuasive message and countermessages against an upcoming persuasive message that, if put into place prior to the receipt of a persuasive message, can lead to resistance against that message.

### Strong Attitudes

In *The Psychology of Attitudes*, Eagly and Chaiken (1993) define an attitude as "a psychological tendency that is expressed by evaluating a particular entity with some degree of favor or disfavor" (p. 1). Attitudes represent the valence or direction of an evaluation: John, a New York baseball fan, likes the Mets but dislikes the Yankees. But does John mildly prefer one team to the other, or does he love the Mets and loathe the Yankees? The intensity of this favor or disfavor is the attitude strength.

Attitude strength encompasses a variety of constructs, including the importance of the attitude, the certainty with which the attitude is held, public commitment to the attitude, the embeddedness of the attitude within a web of other attitudes, the degree to which beliefs support or oppose the attitude, and the accessibility of the attitude (Petty & Krosnick, 1995). Attitudes that are important, held with confidence, expressed publicly, connected to other attitudes, supported by beliefs, and accessed easily are theorized to be more resistant than attitudes that lack these characteristics (Petty & Krosnick, 1995).

Researchers have tested the resistance-enhancing effects of a subset of these constructs. Zuwerink and Devine (1996) had participants who favored allowing gays in the military listen to a counterattitudinal speech arguing against this position. Participants low in attitude importance were persuaded by the speech, reporting attitudes less favorable of allowing gays in the military. Participants high in attitude importance, in contrast, were less persuaded by the speech, with this resistance mediated through anger, irritation, and counterarguments (see also Jacks & Devine, 2000).

Kerr and MacCoun (1985) instructed mock juries to review nine case summaries and attempt to reach a unanimous verdict in each. Juries were randomly assigned to use either open voting or secret ballots during deliberations. For close cases decided by six- or twelve-person juries, open voting caused significantly more hung juries (juries that could not

reach a unanimous decision) than did secret ballots. Kerr and MacCoun (1985) attribute the results to public commitment: "Being publicly identified with a position may force early commitment to that position and make it difficult to change one's position without appearing inconsistent or irresolute" (p. 361).

Visser and Krosnick (1998) conducted a series of six studies that examined the relationships between age, attitude strength, and susceptibility to persuasion. Visser and Krosnick's first three studies demonstrated a curvilinear relationship between age and attitude change such that susceptibility to persuasion was lowest in middle age and higher at younger and older ages. Their last three studies then demonstrated a curvilinear relationship between age and three facets of attitude strength such that attitude strength was highest in middle age and lower at younger and older ages. The results across the six studies strongly suggest that changes in resistance to influence across the life span stem, in part, from parallel changes in attitude strength. As Visser and Krosnick note, however, their studies (and most other studies on this topic) have examined political attitudes, and it is possible that other attitudes such as food preferences might show different patterns of resistance across the life span.

Haugtvedt and Wegener (1994) presented participants with two sequential messages with strong arguments on opposing sides of an issue (senior comprehensive exams in Experiment 1; nuclear power in Experiment 2). Messages were either high in personal relevance (senior comprehensive exams implemented within a year at their university; nuclear power plants built in their own and neighboring states) or low in personal relevance (senior comprehensive exams at a distant university further in the future; nuclear plants in distant states) and presented in a random order. The study's results demonstrate that participants deeply processed messages with high personal relevance, and this deep processing led to stronger attitudes with greater resistance to the subsequent, opposing message. In contrast, participants appeared to shallowly process messages with low personal relevance, with this shallow processing leading to weaker attitudes that were vulnerable to the subsequent, opposing message.

Because strong attitudes are more likely than weak attitudes to guide behavior (Petty & Krosnick, 1995), compliance tactics aimed at causing attitude-discrepant behavior seem more likely to fail to the extent that the associated attitudes are strong. Kerr and MacCoun's (1985) work on mock jury decision making speaks most directly to this conclusion because their dependent variable is already behavioral (in that a vote on a verdict is an external, consequential action that might or might not reflect a juror's internal attitudes). In other cases, current research paradigms could be modified to include a behavioral dependent variable and an influence tactic designed to affect this behavior. Students facing the issue of senior comprehensive exams, for example, could be asked to sign a petition advocating for the implementation of the exams. Given that students for whom the issue is of high personal relevance resist changing their attitudes on the topic (Haugtvedt & Wegener, 1994), such students would presumably resist signing the petition as well.

### Demographics and Personality

In addition to age (discussed in the section on "Strong Attitudes"), researchers have identified a number of other demographics and personality traits associated with resistance. A meta-analysis by Rhodes and Wood (1992) found a curvilinear relationship between self-esteem and persuasion, with individuals with low self-esteem and individuals with high self-esteem showing greater resistance to influence compared to individuals with moderate self-esteem. Rhodes and Wood also examined the relationship between intelligence and persuasion, with individuals with high intelligence showing greater resistance to influence compared to individuals with low intelligence. Other research has found positive relationships between need for closure and resistance (Kruglanski, Webster, & Klem, 1993), argumentativeness and resistance (Kazoleas, 1993), and, in some circumstances, need for cognition and resistance (Haugtvedt & Petty, 1992).

One controversial question is whether there is a relationship between gender and resistance, with Pfau and Burgoon (1990) noting the longstanding belief that women are more susceptible to persuasion than are men. Consistent with this belief, Eagly and Carli's (1981) meta-analysis found a small overall effect suggesting that women are more easily persuaded than men. But their meta-analysis also revealed that this relationship is moderated by the gender of the researcher, with male but not female researchers tending to find a gender difference in resistance.

### Manipulative Intent

We dislike being manipulated. The perception that an influencer is attempting to manipulate the target will often motivate the target to resist. Early evidence comes from studies examining the negative-subject effect:

> Masling (1966) refers to the negative-subject effect as the "screw you effect." The evidence he provides for such an effect is an anecdotal report of one of Goldberg's (1965) subjects, who states that "she resented . . . brainwashing and attempts by psychologists to control the minds of other people. Consequently, I chose the tastes, because I knew you wanted me to pick the weights" (Goldberg, 1965, p. 897). The motivation for this behavior is, according to Masling, the subject's dislike in thinking that his or her behavior could be controlled by the experimenter. . . . The common theme running through these studies and speculations is that there is some manipulative intent on the part of the experimenter and the subject is aware of this fact. (Christensen, 1977, p. 393)

To test this, Christensen (1977) put participants through an intentionally manipulative experiment in which they copied telephone numbers after being told that "rapid performance was indicative of the obsessive-compulsive personality type" (p. 394). To highlight the manipulation, participants were subsequently told during debriefing that the procedure was not designed to test for obsessive-compulsive disorder. Rather, it was designed to make participants copy telephone numbers more slowly.

Participants in Christensen's (1977) study then volunteered for an ostensibly unrelated experiment involving a verbal conditioning task (all participants agreed to take part in the second experiment). Compared to control participants who had not experienced a prior manipulation, and compared to participants who had received instructions regarding manipulative experiments but had not personally experienced a prior manipulation, participants who had experienced a prior manipulation resisted the verbal conditioning. Results from Christensen's second experiment suggest that participants did not resist "because they are trying to screw up the experiment but because they do not like to feel as though they can be manipulated" (p. 398).

Research from a number of other domains supports the idea that we dislike being manipulated—a tendency that might have evolutionary roots due to the adaptive costs of falling prey to a cheater in a social exchange (see Cosmides & Tooby's, 1992, theory of an evolved cheater detection mechanism). Indeed, resistance to manipulation provides a rare exception to the otherwise powerful effects of compliments on liking (Cialdini, 2001; Jones & Wortman, 1973; see also Gordon's, 1996, meta-analytic finding of a curvilinear relationship between transparency of ingratiation and its effectiveness).

Finally, a number of studies have directly examined reactions to manipulative influence tactics. Campbell (1995) tested the impact of two attention-getting but potentially manipulative advertising tactics: mystery ads, in which the sponsoring brand is not revealed until late in the ad, and borrowed interest appeal ads, in which the focal, appealing aspects of the ad are not directly relevant to the brand. Mystery ads did not elicit perceptions of manipulative intent, but poor fit between the borrowed interest appeal and the advertised product did. Furthermore, increased perceptions of manipulative intent mediated the negative impact of this tactic on attitudes about the ad and brand.

Sagarin, Cialdini, Rice, and Serna (2002) taught participants to distinguish legitimate authorities (i.e., experts speaking within their areas of expertise) from illegitimate authorities (i.e., experts speaking outside their areas of expertise or actors dressed in the trappings of authority). Compared to participants in control conditions, participants who learned this distinction were more persuaded by ads containing legitimate authorities. Instilling resistance, however, required an additional step: a demonstration that participants were vulnerable to being fooled by ads containing illegitimate authorities. Participants receiving such a demonstration showed significant resistance to ads containing illegitimate authorities, with this resistance partially mediated by increased perceptions of manipulative intent (because attitudes were only measured once, it could not be determined whether attitudes were less changed or unchanged, or whether they showed a boomerang effect).

Certain compliance tactics feel manipulative, and if we do comply, we feel resentful doing so. An unwanted gift of a flower followed by a request for a donation, for example, likely leaves the target feeling manipulated even as the norm of reciprocity compels the target to comply (Cialdini, 2009). However, it also seems likely that this negative experience would motivate the target to resist next time. Future research that identifies which compliance tactics elicit perceptions of manipulative intent and

under what circumstances these perceptions motivate resistance would be of value.

### Threat to Freedoms

A great deal of what we know about resistance is the outcome of research on threats to freedom and reactance theory. Eagly and Chaiken (1993) refer to this line of research as the "best-known motivation theory of resistance to persuasion" (p. 568). Additionally, for decades, social influence researchers have evoked reactance as the mechanism for explaining failed social influence attempts or persuasive campaigns with unanticipated effects (e.g., Buller, Borland, & Burgoon, 1998; Henningsen, Henningsen, Jakobsen, & Borton, 2004, Ringold, 2002). In these instances, the receiver of a social influence attempt perceives that his or her freedom will be limited by compliance with the persuasive communication. The threat to freedom motivates the receiver to reinstate the lost freedom. Instead of influence occurring, the message is likely met by resistance in one of several forms: derogating the source of the message, enacting the opposite position as that advocated in the message (i.e., boomerang effects), or showing an attitudinal preference for the alternative that is being prohibited (Quick, Shen, & Dillard, 2013). When resistance occurs because of the threat to a receiver's freedom, psychological reactance theory (Brehm, 1966) provides an explanatory mechanism for resistance. In this section of the chapter, we review the tenants of psychological reactance theory and the current research advances related to the theory.

#### PSYCHOLOGICAL REACTANCE THEORY

Psychological reactance theory (Brehm & Brehm, 1981) rests on the foundation of four components: freedom, threats to freedom, reactance, and freedom restorations (for review, see Quick et al., 2013). Brehm (1966) asserted that behavioral freedoms are one of the crucial building blocks of psychological reactance theory. The theory is widely applicable to the study of resisting social influence; behaviors are the focus of theory.

The first component of psychological reactance theory is *freedom*. The term *freedom* applies to enacting a particular behavior but also to holding a particular attitude or emotional response (Brehm, 1966). To be valued, behavioral freedoms must be perceived by the individual (Dillard & Shen, 2005).

The second component of psychological reactance theory is *threat to freedom*. These threats are, essentially, any obstacle the individual believes would make it difficult to enact his or her behavioral freedoms (Brehm, 1966). Threats to freedom can come from impersonal events, including aspects of the environment like having a car problem, home repair, or sudden change in the weather (Brehm, 1989). More often, when persuasion scholars investigate psychological reactance theory, the threat to freedom comes in the form of a persuasive message (e.g., Quick & Considine, 2008; Rains & Turner, 2007). The message is a form of freedom imposition on behalf of the persuader. The attempt at social influence itself triggers the perception that the receiver's freedom could be lost.

Threat to an individual's freedom creates aversive motivation to reinstate the lost freedom (Brehm & Brehm, 1981). That motivational state is *reactance*. Brehm and Brehm describe reactance as the motivational arousal that leads a person to attempt to reinstate his or her lost freedom. According to the theory, the greater the importance of the threatened freedom, the greater the magnitude of reactance that is aroused by the threat to freedom (Brehm, 1966). Brehm and Weinraub (1977) reported that as the attractiveness of the threatened freedom increases, so does the aroused reactance. The crux of the theory is that reactance is the motivational state that inspires individuals to perform cognitive or behavioral work to reinstate their lost freedom.

*Freedom restorations*, then, are the final building block of psychological reactance theory. According to Quick et al. (2013), direct restoration "involves doing the forbidden act" (p. 168). Direct restoration involves a behavioral outcome that is consistent with other outcomes in social influence research. Indirect forms of freedom restoration would include denying the threat exists (e.g., Worchel & Andreoli, 1974), showing greater liking for the prohibited choice (e.g., Hammock & Brehm, 1966), or derogating the persuader (e.g., Worchel, 1974). These indirect forms parallel the attitude outcomes in many persuasion studies. In the case of both direct and indirect restoration, reactance motivates the individual to want to reject or refuse the social influence attempt. In extreme instances, the result may be a boomerang effect (i.e., changing attitudes in the opposite direction of the position represented in a message or influence attempt).

## REFINING REACTANCE RESEARCH

Psychological reactance theory offered a theoretical framework for investigating resistance to influence for almost 50 years. Over the decades

of reactance scholarship, the theory has received a great deal of replication and refinement (Quick et al., 2013). For example, Jonas et al. (2009) have established that that there is a cultural bias in reactance. In their studies, Jonas et al. report that collectivistic cultures evidence less reactance when freedoms are threatened in comparison to individualistic cultures.

In the communication discipline, the refinements in reactance research have addressed the measurement of reactance (for review, see Quick et al., 2013; Rains, 2013). Dillard and Shen (2005) argued that psychological reactance theory was constrained in utility by the conceptualization of reactance as an unmeasurable variable within the theory. Essentially, their argument is that reactance is the key mediator between threats to freedom and freedom restorations. If the mediator is not measured, the theory has less utility for researchers. Central to Dillard and Shen's argument, Brehm and Brehm (1981) asserted "reactance has the status of an intervening, hypothetical variable" (p. 37). Dillard and Shen's research demonstrated that reactance can be measured as an intertwining of anger and counterarguing.

This line of research has been generative of research in the communication discipline (e.g., Miller, Lane, Deatrick, Young, & Potts, 2007; Quick & Considine, 2008; Quick & Kim, 2009; Rains & Turner, 2007). Not all of the scholarship has specifically investigated the intertwined model. A sufficient pool existed, though, for a meta-analysis on the intertwined model (Rains, 2013). In the meta-analysis, other possible operationalizations of reactance are tested against the intertwined model. The other possible models (i.e., dual-process, linear affective-cognitive) did not fit the data as well as the intertwined model. The original Dillard and Shen (2005) study, direct comparisons in research (e.g., Rains & Turner, 2007), and the meta-analytic findings all suggest that reactance can be measured (Rains, 2013). When represented as an intertwined combination of anger and counterarguments, reactance serves as a mediator between threats to freedom and attitude change.

## REACTANCE AND COMPLIANCE

Psychological reactance theory (Brehm & Brehm, 1981) presents an effective theoretical framework for investigating resistance to social influence. Compliance tactics may easily present a receiver with a message that threatens the receiver's sense of behavioral freedoms. In the process of resisting the influence attempt, reactance may motivate reinstatement of lost freedoms through a number of direct or indirect restorations. For example, foundational research on reactance involved children selecting between toy options (e.g., Brehm & Weinraub, 1977); playing with a toy is a direct, behavioral restoration of freedom. Future research might investigate compliance tactics like the bait-and-switch technique to determine if reactance occurs when an appealing alternative is exchanged with a more costly, less attractive option. It is plausible that many compliance tactics could evoke reactance in the intended target of persuasion.

## Forewarning

Forewarning occurs when persuasive targets learn of the intent of the persuader prior to message exposure (McGuire & Papageorgis, 1962). In these instances, the receiver has the opportunity to defend his or her beliefs and develop counterarguments prior to receiving a persuasive message. The initial supposition from the forewarning literature was that "forewarned is forearmed" or that forewarning would lead to resistance (e.g., McGuire & Papageorgis, 1962). That supposition, however, was not universally supported in investigations of forewarning. In this section of the chapter, we describe the early literature on forewarning and the subsequent meta-analysis (Wood & Quinn, 2003) that provided clarity to this body of scholarship.

In their investigation of forewarning, Freedman and Sears (1965) found that forewarning conferred resistance to a persuader's message. In their study, high school students were surveyed about their attitudes toward teen driving. Perhaps not surprisingly, the attitudes that the high school students reported favored unrestricted teen driving. After a few weeks, the high school students were then exposed to a speech against teen driving with some participants being forewarned ahead of time about the title of the message (i.e., "Why Teen-Agers Should Not Drive."). The results of the Freedman and Sears's study indicated that forewarning reduced the persuasive effects of the speech. Those participants who were forewarned about the message content were more resistant to the message than those who did not receive forewarning.

Contemporaneously, research was also being conducted by McGuire and Millman (1965). In their study, published within months of Freedman and Sears (1965), McGuire and Millman reported quite different results. McGuire and Millman presented participants with messages on issues (i.e., emotional or technical) that were pretested to ensure that participants would disagree with the position in the advocacy. Participants were forewarned about some of the content of the messages that they would read. In McGuire and Millman, forewarning had no effect on participants' responses to the persuasive messages. Forewarning did have an effect in the processing of emotional issues. In those contexts, forewarned participants reported more favorable attitudes toward the issue than those who were not forewarned. Forewarning caused an anticipatory shift toward the position in the persuasive message.

As was stated in an early review of the forewarning literature (Cialdini & Petty, 1981), the research testing the effects of forewarning showed complicated, sometimes contradictory findings. That was, most likely, partly because of the diversity of the studies investigating forewarning. For example, forewarning research varied in method (i.e., use of personally relevant topics or messages with a more general stance), timing of the measured effect (i.e., whether attitudes were measured before or after hearing a persuasive message), and outcomes (i.e., if the study reported increased resistance or acquiescence). Wood and Quinn's (2003) meta-analysis helped to clarify some of the complexity.

Wood and Quinn (2003) separated forewarning studies into two groups. Included in the first group were studies that measured attitudes after forewarning but before participants received a message. Included in the second group were studies that measured attitudes after participants received forewarning and received a persuasive message. The results of the meta-analysis indicate that timing matters. Wood and Quinn reported, "When attitudes were assessed prior to the appeal, forewarning generated shifts toward the source's impending position" (p. 131). The results from this set of analyses supported McGuire and Millman's (1965) findings. In contrast, Wood and Quinn asserted "Warning recipients of an impending appeal proved to be an effective resistance technique when attitudes were assessed following the appeal's delivery" (p. 134). Forewarning may trigger scrutiny of the message or, perhaps, self-inoculation. Additionally, consistent with Freedman and Sears (1965), Wood and Quinn found that more resistance occurs in situations that are personally relevant to participants.

Wood and Quinn (2003) also reported results related to cognitive processing of persuasive messages and forewarning. They found that distraction tends to reduce the amount of resistance, but thought-listing bolsters resistance when forewarned.

The implication is that forewarning can change the care and detail of message scrutiny during message processing. When a person has received forewarning of persuasive attack, the topic is personally important, and the person is able to attend to the message, forewarning will lead to message resistance after a message appeal. When a person has been forewarned of a message that is not particularly personally relevant, he or she will shift in the direction of the advocacy prior to receiving the message.

## FOREWARNING AND COMPLIANCE

The early research in the effects of forewarning has focused, primarily, on the attitude change associated with forewarning. In these instances, participants are forewarned that they are going to be persuaded or forewarned of the persuasive intent of the influencer. In many cases, however, people know that they are going to be persuaded and that the influencer is going to attempt social influence. For example, when a person buys a car at a car dealership or serves on a jury, she knows that the salesperson or lawyer is going to attempt to influence her. In this type of situation, forewarning of persuasive intent may not accomplish much resistance. Instead, what may function to effectively nurture resistance in these cases is to understand more about influence tactics that may be at work.

Framed in Cialdini's (2009) social influence principles, Cialdini, Sagarin, and Rice (2001) studied the effects of training individuals to recognize the use of real versus unethical authority. In their studies, participants became more resistant to the use of false authorities when they were provided with tutoring and information about the use of the social influence tactic. Although the study focused on one of Cialdini's (2009) social influence principles, this type of effect may be manifest in the other principles as well. Essentially, instead of being forewarned of persuasive intent, the operating forewarning may be to understand that social influence is going to be present and developing a vocabulary and repertoire for resisting these types of tactics. Future resistance research could investigate training methods for other social influence tactics.

## Inoculation

Inoculation theory boasts a 50-year tradition in the literature on resistance (Compton, 2012). Operating according to the analogy of biological vaccinations, inoculation attempts to confer resistance against attacks on attitudes (McGuire 1961, 1964). In biological systems, inoculations protect an individual by exposing the human body to a weakened, often inert, dose of a virus. An individual's immune system then is able to develop antibodies that defend the individual against exposure to the infecting agent in the future. For example, to defend against the flu, an individual gets a flu shot with weakened doses of the most likely flu viruses for the season. If an individual is then exposed to the flu, he or she should have protection from contracting the flu virus.

McGuire (1964) argued that attitudes operate in analogous ways to biological systems. He argued that individuals can have their attitudes attacked by persuasive messages. To protect existing attitudes from attacks, the attitudes could be inoculated by exposure to a weakened, often refuted, version of the attacking message ahead of time. That process is called refutation preemption. McGuire asserted that the inoculation message should provide the individual with natural cognitive defenses against the future attack.

McGuire's (1964) original tests of inoculation theory tested attitudes that were referred to as "cultural truisms" such as the importance of frequent tooth brushing. These cultural truisms existed, according to McGuire, in untested cognitive environments. In other words, the truisms tended to be believed but rarely challenged. According to Papageorgis and McGuire (1961), inoculation requires the key elements of threat and counterarguing. Threat signals to the individual that he or she is vulnerable to attack and provides motivation to the person to defend his or her attitude (Pfau et al., 2006). Counterarguing is the process that individuals use to resist; the person raises and then answers challenges to his or her existing attitude (Pfau et al., 2006).

In his early series of experiments, McGuire (1964) compared the efficacy of three types of messages: refutational-same, refutational-different, and supportive treatments. Refutational-same messages "raise and refute the same arguments that are later used in the attack message" (Compton, 2012, p. 221). In contrast, refutational-different messages "raise and refute novel arguments, not included in the attack" (Compton, p. 221). Supportive treatments are proattitudinal messages that offer reinforcement for an existing attitude. In biological terms, refutational-same messages inoculate against the flu by exposing an individual to a weakened version of the flu. Refutational-different messages inoculate against the flu by exposing an individual to a weakened version of chicken pox. Supportive treatments prevent the flu by getting the individual vitamins, a healthy diet, and enough sleep. In McGuire's (1964) experiments, both types of refutational defenses outperformed supportive treatments at defending existing attitudes against future attacks. The biological metaphor breaks down a bit in research findings; the most effective defenses would be the ones analogous to the flu inoculating a person against chicken pox, which is not possible in biology.

## INOCULATION AND COMPLIANCE

Although the original framework for inoculation theory was focused on attitudes, inoculation theory has generated a large body of scholarship in both laboratory and applied settings (Compton, 2012). Many inoculation studies are directly applicable to the study of social influence. Inoculation research has been applied to health topics such as smoking (e.g., Pfau & Van Bockern, 1994; Pfau, Van Bockern, & Kang, 1992) and underage alcohol consumption (e.g., Godbold & Pfau, 2000). Inoculation messages confer resistance to attack messages in political campaigns (Pfau & Burgoon, 1988; Pfau, Kenski, Nitz, & Sorenson, 1990), though the effects may be qualified by political party affiliation (Pfau, Park, Holbert, & Cho, 2001). Inoculation has been applied to economic decisions such as college students resisting credit card marketing strategies (Compton & Pfau, 2004) and advertising claims (Pfau, 1992). It is noteable that a majority of the studies reflect social influence attempts rather than simply attitude change. A complete review of the areas of application is beyond the scope of this chapter but may be found in Compton (2012) and Compton and Pfau (2005).

## THEORETICAL SPECIFICATION
## IN INOCULATION THEORY

In addition to focusing on contexts that expand the scope of inoculation theory application, recent research has attempted to fine-tune the theoretical mechanisms of the theory. The research tends to implicate three areas: the role of affect, the nature of threat, and timing.

Much of the foundational literature in inoculation theory focused on the cognitive features of the theory (Wigley & Pfau, 2010). Emerging scholarship on inoculation suggests that resistance is also an affective experience (e.g., Pfau, Szabo, et al., 2001). For example, Pfau et al. (2009) compared the effectiveness of cognitive, affective-positive, and affective-negative inoculation messages at conferring

resistance. In their study, they investigated resistance by measuring threat, issue involvement, counterarguing, and cognitive associative networks. They reported that affective-negative messages tended to be the most effective form of inoculation treatment. Compton (2012) argues that inoculation appears to make people less fearful but angrier about the topic. Additional research on the affective processes within inoculation should shed further light on this aspect of the theory.

Inoculation research has also attempted to better understand the role of threat in the theory. Compton and Pfau (2005) argued that most of the inoculation research induces only moderate levels of threat. Threat, though, is a necessary precondition of inoculation (Compton, 2012; McGuire, 1964). Research has investigated whether language intensity can raise the perception of threat (Pfau et al., 2010). The operating presumption is that greater threat should lead to greater resistance. That relationship was not supported in a recent meta-analysis (Banas & Rains, 2010). Although threat is a necessary precondition of inoculation, the role of threat in the process of inoculation merits future investigation.

One of the final lines of research on inoculation relates to the timing of inoculation messages and subsequent attack messages. In biological systems, an organism requires some lag in time between an inoculation and subsequent exposure to the infecting virus. If exposed to a virus immediately after an inoculation, the immune system would not have enough time to build up antibodies for the virus. In inoculation theory, however, many of the early studies exposed participants to attitudinal inoculations and immediate (i.e., a few seconds or a few minutes) attack messages (e.g., McGuire, 1961). Recent inoculation research has attempted to investigate what the optimal timing is between inoculation messages and attack messages. In their meta-analytic review, Banas and Rains (2010) hypothesized that there would be a curvilinear relationship between inoculation and resistance such that resistance would be highest at moderate time delays and lowest at the shorter and longer time spans. The meta-analysis did not support the proposed curvilinear hypothesis. Instead, the results indicated that inoculation conferred similar levels of resistance immediately and for about 13 days after exposure to the inoculation message. Resistance effects decayed after that point. The role of time in resistance, though, is an interesting question, and it opens up a possible avenue for future scholarship.

## Stealing Thunder

According to Williams, Bourgeois, and Croyle (1993), stealing thunder consists of "revealing negative information about oneself (or, in a legal setting, one's client) before it is revealed or elicited by another person" (p. 597). Thus, stealing thunder is an attempt to blunt the impact of negative information by preemptively releasing the information (Claeys, Cauberghe, & Leysen, 2013; Dolnik, Case, & Williams, 2003; Howard, Brewer, & Williams, 2006; Williams et al., 1993). Williams et al. tested the effectiveness of stealing thunder in two studies: the first examined responses in a criminal trial, the second examined responses in a civil trial. In the first study, participants read or listened to a trial in which the defendant was accused of assault. In the "thunder" condition, the prosecuting attorney informed the jury that the defendant had two prior convictions for the same crime. In the "stolen thunder" condition, the defense attorney raised and downplayed the same information. In the "no thunder" control condition, the prior convictions were never mentioned. Ratings of guilt were lowest in the "no thunder" condition—clearly it is better if negative information never comes up at all. But stealing thunder significantly reduced the impact of the negative information. Further analyses suggested that stealing thunder increased the credibility of the defense attorney who revealed the information, and that this increased credibility mediated the effects of stealing thunder on ratings of guilt. The second study replicated these effects with a civil trial in which an expert witness for the plaintiff stole thunder by acknowledging that he had previously testified on the opposite side of the issue. As with the criminal case, stealing thunder significantly reduced the impact of the negative information, with the effect mediated by increased credibility.

Subsequent research has identified a number of mediators and moderators of stealing thunder. Dolnik et al. (2003) found that stealing thunder was effective even without downplaying the importance of the negative information and whether or not the opposition also mentioned the information. Furthermore, in Dolnik et al., stealing thunder appeared to operate by changing the meaning of the negative information (rather than by increasing the credibility of the person raising the information). Finally, Dolnik et al. identified a method by which the opposition could undermine the effectiveness of stealing thunder: by accusing "the defense of trying to manipulate the jury" (p. 277)—a technique that highlights the resistance-enhancing effects of perceptions of manipulative intent. Additional research suggests that stealing thunder operates via the peripheral route by increasing the peripheral cue of source credibility (Howard et al., 2006) and that organizations facing a crisis can reduce the reputational impact of the crisis by releasing negative information themselves rather than waiting for other parties to release the information (Arpan & Pompper, 2003; Arpan & Roskos-Ewoldsen, 2005; Claeys & Cauberghe, 2012; Claeys, Cauberghe, & Leysen, 2013; Wigley, 2011).

## The Poison Parasite Defense

The poison parasite defense is a method of instilling resistance to deceptive persuasive messages by incorporating elements of those messages into countermessages (Cialdini et al., 2015). Cialdini et al. (2015) coined the term to refer to "a technique that consists of two elements, one poisonous (strong counter information) and one parasitic (associate links between one's counter claims and the rival position)" (p. 1). The defense was designed for situations in which the persuasive opponent has a greater ability to expose targets to his or her persuasive message but in which the opponent's message is misleading or deceptive. To counter this, the poison parasite defense (a) highlights the misleading or deceptive aspects of the original message and (b) incorporates elements of the original message into the countermessage so that additional exposures of the original message will make the countermessage salient.

Cialdini et al. (2015) tested the poison parasite defense in three studies, two involving a political campaign against an incumbent who misrepresents his credentials as a pro-education candidate, and one involving a corporation that misrepresents itself as protecting the environment. In both cases, the poison parasite defense presents counterinformation that undercuts the claims of the original messages, and it places this counterinformation within a visual context that contains many elements of the original messages. Compared to messages that contained the same counterinformation in a visually dissimilar context or to messages that contained derogation without counterinformation, the poison parasite defense instilled significant resistance against the original message, and this resistance persevered against repeated exposures to the original message.

## Resistance to Social Engineering

With the increasing amount of important (and exploitable) information kept online, gaining illicit access to this information is becoming an increasingly profitable enterprise. The use of persuasive tactics—typically in a deceptive manner—to gain access to such information is called "social engineering." According to Mitnick and Simon (2002), "Social engineering uses influence and persuasion to deceive people by convincing them that the social engineer is someone he [or she] is not, or by manipulation. As a result, the social engineer is able to take advantage of people to obtain information with or without the use of technology" (p. iv).

Muscanell, Guadagno, and Murphy (2014) and Sagarin and Mitnick (2012) analyze a range of social engineering tactics using the perspective of Cialdini's (2009) six principles of influence (i.e., reciprocity, commitment and consistency, social proof, liking, authority, and scarcity) and offer recommendations for individuals and organizations seeking to protect themselves against social engineering attacks. Muscanell et al. recommend the use of resistance strategies proposed by Cialdini (2009). In general, these strategies involve the attempt to circumvent the cognitive heuristics that often drive our decision making (e.g., if one feels the arousal and panic that often accompany a fleeting opportunity, one should calm down before making a fast, scarcity-fueled decision).

Sagarin and Mitnick (2012) recognize the benefit for organizations and individuals to learn about Cialdini's (2009) principles of influence and Cialdini's recommendations for defense against the illegitimate use of these principles. But Sagarin and Mitnick note that "In many cases . . . the principles appear legitimate within the context of the social engineer's deception" (p. 34). Instead, Sagarin and Mitnick recommend a resistance strategy based on (a) a perception of personal vulnerability to social engineering attacks (without which people might not see the need to develop resistance; Sagarin et al., 2002), (b) an understanding of what types of actions can put a person or an organization at risk (e.g., most computer users understand the risk of opening an .EXE file, but many do not realize that. PDF files can also contain malicious code), and (c) a set of tactics for refusing inappropriate requests (e.g., scripts that allow a person to say "no" to an inappropriate request without violating politeness norms; Sagarin and Mitnick [2012] offer an example that might have helped a target fend off a social engineering attack: "Surely, as a

fellow Motorola employee, you agree that the security of our computer systems is paramount? Great. Then you will understand why we cannot give out our SecureID token code or PIN over the phone," p. 37).

The recommendations of Muscanell et al. (2014) and Sagarin and Mitnick (2012), and, indeed, many of the resistance-enhancing recommendations of Cialdini (2009), have yet to be tested empirically. Such tests could be of great theoretical and applied value.

## Internal and External Mechanisms of Resistance

In this section, we review the internal and external mechanisms by which people resist influence attempts. Internal mechanisms include counterarguing, bolstering initial attitudes, derogating the source, attributing negative affect to the message or source, and attempting to correct for bias. External mechanisms include interpersonal strategies of communicating resistance and issuing refusals.

### Internal Mechanisms

The dual-process models of persuasion, the elaboration likelihood model (Petty & Cacioppo, 1986) and the heuristic-systematic model (Chaiken, 1986), provide a useful framework for understanding a number of internal mechanisms of resistance. According to these models, when a persuasive target has both the motivation and ability to think deeply about a persuasive message, the key mediator between reception of the message and persuasion is the set of idiosyncratic thoughts that the target has in response to the message (Petty & Cacioppo, 1986). Persuasive messages that elicit favorable, message-supportive cognitive responses are likely to succeed in influencing the target. Persuasive messages that elicit unfavorable cognitive responses such as counterarguments are likely to fail. These models thus inform a number of internal mechanisms of resistance, including counterarguing, bolstering initial attitudes, derogating the source, attempting to correct for bias, and, arguably, the attribution portion of attributing negative affect to the message or source. Although some of these mechanisms likely involve effortful cognitive processing (e.g., counterarguing), not all do. As Wegener, Petty, Smoak, and Fabrigar (2004) note, persuasive targets use both effortful and noneffortful (or thoughtful and nonthoughtful) processes of resistance. For example, in describing the impact of current attitudes on resistance, Wegener et al. (2004) explain:

When motivation and/or ability are lacking, attitudes can be used rather directly to reject (or, for some people, accept) the message advocacy. In such settings, the pre-message attitudes are not providing a strong guide for active resistance processes, such as counterarguing. When motivation and ability are higher, however, pre-message attitudes guide information processing, resulting in more negative cognitive response to the message when pre-message attitudes are more negative toward the advocacy. (p. 25)

Thus, processes of resistance vary in the extent to which they depend upon cognitive resources, and the same elements that determine whether persuasion occurs via effortful or noneffortful processing—motivation and ability—likely determine the types of processing responsible for resistance.

Counterarguing is a frequently used, unfavorable cognitive response to a counterattitudinal persuasive message. Counterarguing is cognitively demanding, however, and can be disrupted by distraction. In an early demonstration of this effect, Osterhouse and Brock (1970) presented undergraduate participants with a counterattitudinal message advocating a tuition increase at their university. Participants distracted by a competing task (vocally responding to a series of flashing lights) produced fewer counterarguments and were more persuaded by the message. Subsequent research has established the role of counterarguing in resistance (e.g., Petty & Cacioppo, 1979) and demonstrated that counterarguing is not only cognitively demanding but also ego depleting (Wheeler, Briñol, & Hermann, 2007).

Persuasive targets can also resist persuasive attacks by bolstering their initial attitudes. Lydon, Zanna, and Ross (1988) exposed participants to a persuasive message that changed the target attitude and then instructed participants to recall behavior relevant to this newly changed attitude. Participants were then exposed to a countermessage that attacked the newly changed attitude. Compared to participants who had recalled irrelevant behavior, participants who had bolstered their initial attitude by recalling attitude-relevant behavior showed increased memory for the original message and reduced memory for the countermessage.

Targets also resist persuasive attacks at times by derogating the source of the persuasive message (Tannenbaum, Macauley, & Norris, 1966) and by attributing negative affect to the message or source (Cacioppo & Petty, 1979). Zuwerink and Devine (1996) demonstrated source derogation and negative affective response in two studies in which participants heard a counterattitudinal message on a topic of either high or low personal importance. Participants for whom the topic was personally important resisted the message, in part by having unfavorable, affectively charged thoughts about the source of the message.

Targets can also resist persuasive attack by attempting to correct for factors that they believe might bias their attitudes (Wegener et al., 2004). Insight into this process is provided by Wegener and Petty's (1997) flexible correction model, which specifies that people use naïve (and also possibly incorrect) theories of what might bias their attitudes when attempting to correct for bias. This process can lead to resistance if the attempt at bias correction works against the persuasive message or to greater persuasion if the attempt at bias correction works in favor of the persuasive message. Wegener et al. (2004) illustrate these dual possibilities in the context of the effects of mood on persuasion:

> If a person believes that positive moods make perceptions unduly positive, then realizing that one is in a positive mood could actually make one's judgments less positive (e.g., DeSteno et al., 2000). If, however, a person believes that the same positive mood makes judgments unduly negative, as they sometimes do (e.g., Dermer, Cohen, Jacobsen, & Anderson, 1979), then realizing that one is in a positive mood could make the person's judgments even more positive. (p. 29)

Finally, in an intriguing demonstration of the myriad ways that people attempt to protect important attitudes, Ahluwalia (2000) polled Clinton supporters at key moments during the Clinton-Lewinsky scandal. After Clinton's admission of an "inappropriate relationship" with Lewinsky, Clinton supporters defended their attitudes primarily by rejecting the validity of the negative information. Later, the release of the Starr Report undermined the effectiveness of this resistance strategy, and Clinton supporters began to perceive Clinton as less honest. In response, supporters reduced the importance of honesty relative to Clinton's other positive attributes. Throughout the process, Clinton supporters also minimized the impact of the negative information. In contrast to other voters who generalized Clinton's reduced honesty to a number of other attributes, Clinton supporters generalized Clinton's reduced honesty to only one other attribute: morality.

Clearly, resistance to compliance operates, in part, via internal processes, and it seems likely that the same processes that facilitate resistance to persuasion (e.g., counterarguing, bolstering initial attitudes, derogating the source, attributing negative affect to the message or source, and attempting to correct for bias) might also facilitate resistance to compliance. Because resistance to compliance often requires socially uncomfortable refusals (see the following section), these processes might need to yield particularly compelling rationales for resistance. Future research that identifies the mediating processes of resistance to compliance would be of both basic and applied value.

## Resistance Messages and Refusals

In addition to mustering internal processes of resistance, targets attempting to resist influence must also navigate the interpersonal process of refusing the request. Within the scholarship on resistance, a number of resistance and refusal typologies have been constructed (for review, see Ifert, 2000). The goal of this section of the chapter is to provide an example of message typologies as well as the critiques and alternatives of this approach.

### MESSAGE TYPOLOGIES

In the extant resistance message typology literature, two common types of typologies appear. In the first set, a general typology is offered that tends to be free from situational constraints in the typology's conceptualization. In the second set, the typology is derived to acknowledge the unique aspects of context of persuasion. An example of the former was presented by McLaughlin, Cody, and Robey (1980). Derived from research on conflict, McLaughlin et al. defined five strategies for resistance: (a) nonnegotiation (i.e., direct, unqualified refusals), (b) identity management (i.e., acting incompetent), (c) justifying (i.e., providing the persuader with reasons for noncompliance), (d) negotiating (i.e., the refusing party offers a counter proposal to the persuader), and (e) emotional appeal (i.e., using strategies that trade on the persuader's feelings for the refusing party). Typologies of this nature are meant to provide a list of messages that are available to a refusing party in the face of any number of persuasion strategies (Ifert, 2000).

In a review of the general typologies of refusals, Ifert (2000) noted that many of the typologies share commonalities. For example, strategies such as withdrawal of the refusing party or deceiving the

persuader are represented on most of the general resistance message typologies.

The alternative to general resistance message typologies are situationally derived typologies. For example, in examining adolescent responses to offers of drugs, Alberts, Miller-Rassulo, and Hecht (1991) provided four refusal strategies: (a) simple no (i.e., just saying no without offering an explanation), (b) no with an explanation (i.e., saying no but also providing reasons), (c) deception (i.e., lying or pretending to engage in the behavior the persuader suggests), and (d) leave (i.e., the refusing party exits the situation). In current use (e.g., Pettigrew, Miller-Day, Krieger, & Hecht, 2011), this typology has come to be known as the "REAL typology" (i.e., refuse, explain, avoid, and leave). This type of message typology reflects the situation in which it was constructed: refusals of offers for alcohol, tobacco, and other drugs. Typologies of this sort are ecologically valid for the type of situation in which the typology was grounded. Indeed, Hecht and Miller-Day (2009) constructed an antidrug intervention on the basis of the REAL typology.

As is the case with drug resistance typologies, many of the resistance typologies that are situationally grounded have important implications for that particular context. Motley and Reeder (1995), for example, conducted research on resistance messages employed by heterosexual women in sexual situations. Motley and Reeder concluded that many of women's most commonly used resistance strategies were misunderstood or misinterpreted by men. The important nature of these contexts (i.e., adolescent drug resistance and sexual communication) shows the importance of contextually derived strategy typologies.

Strategy typologies, however, are not without their flaws. Kellermann and Cole (1994) provide a detailed critique of the compliance message typology literature. Ifert (2000) notes that resistance typologies have evolved in the same way that compliance message typologies have developed. Many of the same failings outlined by Kellermann and Cole evaluating compliance typology research are also failings that are evident in resistance typology studies. For example, scholars who develop typologies tend to ground them in a specific context, making generalization of the typology to new contexts problematic. In addition, typologies label similar strategies with different titles, making it difficult to make generalizations across studies.

An alternative to resistance message typology construction is to investigate theoretical approaches to refusals. Two theoretical frameworks, politeness theory (Brown & Levinson, 1987) and constructivism (e.g., O'Keefe & Delia, 1979), have provided an alternative perspective in the generation of messages that refuse a persuader's goal.

## POLITENESS THEORY AND REFUSALS

Politeness theory is based on the notion that all people have two forms of face needs: positive face and negative face (Brown & Levinson, 1987). Positive face refers to a person's need for approval for social role characteristics that are relevant to the context (Brown & Levinson, 1987). For example, a graduate student may hope to possess the attribute of being well read. When an advisor compliments the student's breadth of reading, the compliment bolster's the graduate student's positive face. If the same graduate student were competing in a game of Halo, affirming the graduate student's breadth of reading might undermine the graduate student's positive face if the irrelevant compliment is seen as implying that the relevant skills are not worthy of praise. Negative face, on the other hand, references the individual's need to be unimpeded toward his or her goals (Brown & Levinson, 1987). This type of face is an imperfect parallel to the need for autonomy or independence. As an example, people often feel frustration when traffic closures delay their travel. These closures reflect an obstacle to pursuing the goal of commuting on time or traveling at the pace the person hopes to travel.

In all interactions, there are four possible face threats that may occur: the speaker's positive face, the speaker's negative face, the hearer's positive face, and the hearer's negative face (Brown & Levinson, 1987). In the context of a refusal, the speaker is likely to be the person who is making a request and the hearer a person who is refusing. Researchers in communication have argued that more than one face threat may occur in interactions (Wilson, Aleman, & Leatham, 1998). Additionally, the situational constraints of the context and relationship implicitly define the nature of the face threat (Wilson et al., 1998).

Johnson and her colleagues (e.g., Johnson, 2007, 2008; Johnson, Roloff, & Riffee, 2004a, 2004b) have used politeness theory to describe the nature of refusals in interactions. For example, Johnson et al. (2004a) establish that more than one type of face can be threatened when a refusing party thwarts the persuasive attempt of the persuader. Furthermore, Johnson et al. (2004b) argue that request messages from persuaders are created in anticipation of the obstacle to compliance that the receiver might use to resist. The theory, then, explicates a series of message strategies that can be used as resistance messages. The theory also provides mechanisms to connect resistance messages to constructs in the theory such as positive and negative face.

## CONSTRUCTIVISM AND REFUSALS

Research in constructivism has also shown promise with respect to accounting for variation in messages that are used to resist influence. The principle of constructivism is that people differ in their depth and breadth of thinking about topics, including effective social interaction (i.e., cognitive differentiation) (Delia, 1977). For any construct or topic, the greater the cognitive differentiation, the greater the depth and breadth of categories that a person uses to evaluate the construct (O'Keefe, 1988). For example, a person low in cognitive differentiation may see a job interview as an attempt to get a job. A person high in cognitive differentiation may frame his or her perception of a job interview in terms of his or her goals, the goals of the interviewer, the goals of the corporation, the research that the person needs to do prior to the interview, and so forth. The person lower in construct differentiation has a more basic, simplistic perception of the social context in contrast to the person higher in differentiation. In interpersonal contexts, higher cognitive differentiation is associated with a better understanding of the situational demands of the context and needs of the other person (Burleson & Rack, 2008). Cognitive differentiation is associated with the production of more effective and appropriate messages (O'Keefe, 1988). This association also has been demonstrated in the context of refusals (Kline & Floyd, 1990). The greater the cognitive differentiation, the better able a target of persuasion is at constructing effective refusals that address the concerns of the requester.

## SUMMARY OF REFUSALS

Both theoretical approaches (i.e., politeness and constructivism) provide advantages for scholars of refusal messages. Specifically, the theoretical approaches are broader and adaptable to a greater number of possible contexts. The message typologies tend to be specific in focus. Another advantage of the theoretical approach is that it offers a mechanism for explaining the precursors and/or effects of refusal messages. From a politeness theory perspective, effective refusals redress threatened forms of face in interaction. From a constructivist perspective, the refusal messages that reflect greater cognitive differentiation are more effective. The goal of the research on refusal messages, whether context based or theoretically derived, is to provide a set of messages that receivers of social influence use to resist attempts at compliance.

## Consequences of Resistance

The most obvious consequence of resistance is that the target remains unmoved, and attitudes and behavior remain unchanged by the influence attempt (or, more precisely, the target remains less moved, unmoved, or, in the case of a boomerang effect, moved in the opposite direction of the influence attempt). But the process of resistance might, nevertheless, leave a trace on the target or on the target's relationship with the influencer. This section reviews research on the consequences of resistance—the effects of resistance on the target's attitudes and behavior, and the effects of resistance on the relationship between the would-be influencer and the target of influence.

### *Effects on Attitudes*

As noted earlier in this chapter, extensive research supports the idea that attitude strength increases resistance to influence. In an intriguing program of research exploring the reverse relationship, Tormala and Petty (2002, 2004a, 2004b) have demonstrated that successful resistance increases attitude strength and attitude-relevant behavioral intentions. Tormala and Petty (2002) theorized that "When people perceive that they have resisted persuasion successfully, they might infer that their attitude is correct, or valid, and thus feel more certain about it" (p. 1298). In Tormala and Petty's (2002) first experiment, participants were informed, based on random assignment, that an upcoming persuasive message would contain either strong arguments or weak arguments (all participants actually received the same message). After successfully resisting the message, participants who believed they had resisted a strong attack reported significantly greater attitude certainty compared to participants who believed they had resisted a weak attack. Tormala and Petty's (2002) subsequent experiments demonstrated that (a) only successful resistance increases attitude strength; participants given false feedback that they had failed to resist the message did not increase their attitude certainty, and (b) newly strengthened attitudes showed greater resistance to a subsequent persuasive attack and a stronger relationship between the attitudes and corresponding behavioral intentions.

Subsequent research demonstrated that the effects of resistance on attitude certainty only occur under conditions of high elaboration (Tormala & Petty, 2004a) and only when the message comes from a source high in expertise (Tormala & Petty, 2004b), suggesting that the increase in attitude certainty occurs via a metacognitive process of targets reflecting on the implications of successful resistance on their own attitudes. Source trustworthiness, in contrast, appears to create a different pattern of moderation, with successful resistance showing the greatest increase in attitude certainty when the message source is low in trustworthiness and the target is under low cognitive load (Lemanski & Lee, 2012).

Does successful resistance ever move the attitude away from the direction of the resisted message? That is, does a failed persuasive message ever cause a boomerang effect? Boster and colleagues (2010) tested this by attempting to create the worst possible persuasive message: a (depending upon condition) insulting, reactance-inducing, low-credibility message with weak arguments that proposed that the participants' university become a satellite campus of a rival state university. Across conditions, targets showed a significant boomerang effect, with their attitudes moving modestly but significantly away from the position advocated by the message. Indeed, certain reactance-based phenomena (e.g., instructions not to play with a toy leading to increased play time with that toy) could be seen as a boomerang effect on behavior.

As noted earlier, strong attitudes are more likely to guide behavior. Thus, in situations in which resistance strengthens attitudes, resistance is also likely to strengthen attitude-consistent behavior.

### *Effects on Relationships*

Little research on resistance directly informs the relational consequences of resisting a relational partner's influence in ongoing, intact relationships. Two lines of research from interpersonal communication scholarship may offer some insight, though, into the way that resistance affects the dynamic of relationships.

The first body of scholarship about resistance relates to resisting a partner's sexual advances in a romantic relationship. This research suggests that men and women, in heterosexual interactions, may not share the meaning of sexual resistance messages (Motley & Reeder, 1995). Motley and Reeder's research began as an attempt to make sense of sex differences in perceptions of sexual resistance, but current research (e.g., Bevan, 2003) has extended the scope of sexual resistance research to include relational outcomes of sexual resistance.

Consistent with findings of Metts, Cupach, and Imahori (1992), Bevan (2003) reported that resisting a long-term dating partner was perceived as a greater expectancy violation and more negative than rejecting a cross-sex friend. The study also demonstrated that using explicit resistance messages (e.g., saying "no") was perceived as more consequential to the relationship than using indirect resistance messages. Bevan's findings are consistent with research by Afifi and Lee (2000). Afifi and Lee assessed the dynamics of sexual resistance when persistent attempts followed an initial refusal. Afifi and Lee found that as a requester persisted in making sexual advances, the resisting party increased the directness of the sexual resistance refusal messages and used more face-threatening refusal messages to resist. Sexual resistance research indicates that extant relationships navigate the effect of request resistance long after the initial resistance.

A second line of scholarship also suggests that continued resistance may damage ongoing relationships: serial arguments research (Johnson & Roloff, 1998). Serial arguments are recurring conflicts between two individuals (Johnson & Roloff, 1998). The conflict may, in some senses, parallel persuasion. In many respects, serial arguments reflect repeated attempts at persuasion and repeated resistance. Serial arguments research shows that episodes of serial arguments occur in a wide variety of contexts such as in romantic relationships (e.g., Wright & Roloff, 2015), in families (Bevan, 2010), and in classrooms (Hample & Krueger, 2011). As a result, the serial argument literature may have broader applicability than the sexual resistance scholarship to identifying the long-term consequences of resistance within a relationship.

Several studies indicate that relationships suffer when serial arguments persist (Bevan & Sparks, 2014; Johnson & Roloff, 1998; Reznik & Roloff, 2011). Serial arguments may cause mutual hostility and even lead to relationship termination. Emerging scholarship from this literature also indicates that individuals in the relationship may have health-related outcomes from serial arguments. For example, Reznik, Miller, Roloff, and Gaze (2015) reported that young adults who experience serial arguments with their parents report health-related disruptions to their daily lives and routines because of the stress of the serial arguments. Malis and Roloff (2006) and Bevan and Sparks indicate negative health perceptions like trouble eating, difficulty

sleeping, and anxiety are related to the nature of serial argument episodes in a romantic relationship. By analogy, the research on serial arguments indicates that repeated resistance in a relationship may affect cognitive perceptions of the relationship, the health of the individuals in the relationship, and the ultimate stability of the relationship.

One avenue for future research in resistance, then, should be to investigate the effects of resistance in relational contexts. The presumption from the sexual resistance and serial argument literatures indicates that repetitive, important resistance influences the individuals within a relationship and the relationship itself. One line of research that demonstrates both the impact of resistance on relationships and the persuasive power of resistance is Czopp, Monteith, and Mark's (2006) research on confronting stereotypes and prejudice. Across three experiments, White participants were confronted by a confederate after being induced to make "stereotypic inferences about Black individuals" (p. 784). Although confronted participants evaluated the confronter negatively, the confrontation succeeded in reducing subsequent stereotypic responses and self-reported prejudice.

## Conclusions

The research on resistance to influence is a diverse, interrelated body of scholarship. Some of the research dates among the early foundations of social influence like reactance (Brehm, 1966) and inoculation (McGuire, 1961). Other research lines such as the research that indicates that resistance may cause attitude strength (e.g., Tormala & Petty, 2002) offer 21st-century perspectives on the mechanisms related to resistance. In this chapter, we offered an overview of the lines of research that inform scholarship on resistance to persuasive communication. From this chapter we would draw two general conclusions. First, many avenues of resistance research are still available for pursuit. Second, as *Divergent* author Veronica Roth would say, "Resisting is worth doing."

## References

Afifi, W. A., & Lee, J. W. (2000). Balancing instrumental and identity goals in relationships: The role of request directness and request persistence in the selection of sexual resistance strategies. *Communication Monographs, 67*, 284–305. doi: 10.1080/03637750009376511

Ahluwalia, R. (2000). Examination of psychological processes underlying resistance to persuasion. *Journal of Consumer Research, 27*, 217–232.

Alberts, J. K., Miller-Rassulo, M. A., & Hecht, M. L. (1991). A typology of drug resistance strategies. *Journal of Applied Communication Research, 19*, 129–151. doi: 10.1080/00909889109365299

Arpan, L. M., & Pompper, D. (2003). Stormy weather: Testing "stealing thunder" as a crisis communication strategy to improve communication flow between organizations and journalists. *Public Relations Review, 29*, 291–308.

Arpan, L. M., & Roskos-Ewoldsen, D. R. (2005). Stealing thunder: Analysis of the effects of proactive disclosure of crisis information. *Public Relations Review, 31*, 425–433.

Banas, J. A., & Rains, S. A. (2010). A meta-analysis of research on inoculation theory. *Communication Monographs, 77*, 281–311. doi: 10.1080/03637751003758193

Bevan, J. L. (2003). Expectancy violation theory and sexual resistance in close, cross-sex relationships. *Communication Monographs, 70*, 68–82. doi: 10.1080/715114662

Bevan, J. L. (2010). Serial argument goals and conflict strategies: A comparison between romantic partners and family members. *Communication Reports, 23*, 52–64. doi: 10.1080/08934211003598734

Bevan, J. L., & Sparks, L. (2014). The relationship between accurate and benevolently biased serial argument perceptions and individual negative health perceptions. *Communication Research, 41*, 257–281. doi: 10.1177/0093650212438391

Boster, F. J., Carpenter, C., Shulman, H., DeAngelis, B., Shaw, A., & Manata, B. (2010). *In search of the elusive boomerang effect*. Paper presented to the National Communication Association Convention. San Francisco, CA. November 16.

Brehm, J. W. (1966). *The theory of psychological reactance*. New York, NY: Academic Press.

Brehm, J. W. (1989). Psychological reactance: Theory and applications. *Advances in Consumer Research, 16*, 72–75.

Brehm, S. S., & Brehm J. W. (1981). *Psychological reactance: A theory of freedom and control*. New York, NY: Academic Press.

Brehm, S. S., & Weinraub, M. (1977). Physical barriers and psychological reactance: 2-year-olds' responses to threats to freedom. *Journal of Personality and Social Psychology, 35*, 830–836. doi: 10.1037/0022-3514.35.11.830

Brown, P., & Levinson, S. C. (1987). *Politeness: Some universals in language usage*. Cambridge, UK: Cambridge University Press.

Buller, D. B., Borland, R., & Burgoon, M. (1998). Impact of behavioral intention on effectiveness of message features: Evidence from the family sun safety project. *Human Communication Research, 24*, 433–453. doi: 10.1111/j.1468-2958.1998.tb00424.x

Burleson, B. R., & Rack, J. J. (2008). Constructivism theory: Explaining individual differences in communication skill. In L. A. Baxter & D. O. Braithwaite (Eds.), *Engaging theories of interpersonal communication: Multiple perspectives* (pp. 51–63). Thousand Oaks, CA: Sage.

Cacioppo, J. T., & Petty, R. E. (1979). The effects of message repetition and position on cognitive responses, recall, and persuasion. *Journal of Personality and Social Psychology, 37*, 97–109.

Campbell, M. C. (1995). When attention-getting advertising tactics elicit consumer inferences of manipulative intent: The importance of balancing benefits and investments. *Journal of Consumer Psychology, 4*, 225–254.

Chaiken, S. (1986). The heuristic model of persuasion. In M. P. Zanna, J. M. Olson, & C. P. Herman (Eds.), *Social influence: The Ontario Symposium* (Vol. 5, pp. 3–39). Hillsdale, NJ: Erlbaum.

Christensen, L. (1977). The negative subject: Myth, reality, or a prior experimental experience effect? *Journal of Personality and Social Psychology, 35*, 392–400.

Cialdini, R. B. (2001). *Influence: Science and practice* (4th ed.). Boston: Allyn & Bacon.

Cialdini, R. B. (2009). *Influence: Science and practice* (5th ed.). Boston: Allyn & Bacon.

Cialdini, R. B., Petrova, P. K., Demaine, L. J., Barrett, D. W., Sagarin, B. J., Rhoads, K. L., & Maner, J. (2015). *The poison parasite defense: A strategy for sapping a stronger opponent's persuasive strength*. http://mba.tuck.dartmouth.edu/pages/faculty/petia.petrova/working_papers.html

Cialdini, R. B., & Petty, R. E. (1981). Anticipatory opinion effects. In R. E. Petty, T. M. Ostrom, & T. C. Brock (Eds.), *Cognitive responses in persuasion* (pp. 217–235). Hillsdale, NJ: Lawrence Erlbaum Associates, Inc.

Cialdini, R. B., Sagarin, B. J., & Rice, W. E. (2001). Training in ethical influence. In J. M. Darley, D. M. Messick, & T. R. Tyler (Eds.), *Social influences on ethical behavior in organizations* (pp. 137–153). Mahwah, NJ: Lawrence Erlbaum Associates.

Claeys, A.-S., & Cauberghe, V. (2012). Crisis response and crisis timing strategies, two sides of the same coin. *Public Relations Review, 38*, 83–88.

Claeys, A.-S., Cauberghe, V., & Leysen, J. (2013). Implications of stealing thunder for the impact of expressing emotions in organizational crisis communication. *Journal of Applied Communication Research, 41*, 293–308.

Compton, J. (2012). Inoculation theory. In J. P. Dillard and L. J. Shen (Eds.), *The persuasion handbook: Developments in theory and practice* (2nd ed., pp. 220–236). Los Angeles, CA: Sage.

Compton, J., & Pfau, M. (2004). Use of inoculation to foster resistance to credit card marketing targeting college students. *Journal of Applied Communication Research, 32*, 343–364. doi: 10.1080/0090988042000276014

Compton, J., & Pfau, M. (2005). Inoculation theory of resistance to influence at maturity: Recent progress in theory development and application and suggestions for future research. In P. J. Kalbfleisch (Ed.), *Communication yearbook* (Vol. 29, pp. 97–145). Mahwah, NJ: Erlbaum.

Cosmides, L., & Tooby, J. (1992). Cognitive adaptations for social exchange. In J. H. Barkow, L. Cosmides, & J. Tooby (Eds.) *The adapted mind: Evolutionary psychology and the generation of culture* (pp. 163–228). New York, NY: Oxford University Press.

Czopp, A. M., Monteith, M. J., & Mark, A. Y. (2006). Standing up for a change: Reducing bias through interpersonal confrontation. *Journal of Personality and Social Psychology, 90*, 784–803.

Delia, J. G. (1977). Constructivism and the study of human communication. *Quarterly Journal of Speech, 63*, 66–83. doi: 10.1080/00335637709383368

Dillard, J. P., & Shen, L. (2005). On the nature of reactance and its role in persuasive health communication. *Communication Monographs, 72*, 144–168. doi: 10.1080/03637750500111815

Dolnik, L., Case, T. I., & Williams, K. D. (2003). Stealing thunder as a courtroom tactic revisited: Processes and boundaries. *Law and Human Behavior, 27*, 267–287.

Eagly, A. H., & Carli, L. L. (1981). Sex of researchers and sex-typed communications as determinants of sex differences in influenceability: A meta-analysis of social influence studies. *Psychological Bulletin, 90,* 1–20.

Eagly, A. H., & Chaiken, S. (1993). *The psychology of attitudes.* San Diego, CA: Harcourt Brace & Company.

Freedman, J. L., & Sears, D. O. (1965). Warning, distraction, and resistance to influence. *Journal of Personality and Social Psychology, 1,* 262–266. doi: 10.1037/h0021872

Godbold, L. C., & Pfau, M. (2000). Conferring resistance to peer pressure among adolescents: Using inoculation theory to discourage alcohol use. *Communication Research, 27,* 411–437. doi: 10.1177/009365000027004001

Gordon, R. A. (1996). Impact of ingratiation on judgments and evaluations: A meta-analytic investigation. *Journal of Personality and Social Psychology, 71,* 54–70.

Haugtvedt, C. P., & Petty, R. E. (1992). Personality and persuasion: Need for cognition moderates the persistence and resistance of attitude changes. *Journal of Personality and Social Psychology, 63,* 308–319.

Haugtvedt, C. P., & Wegener, D. T. (1994). Message order effects in persuasion: An attitude strength perspective. *Journal of Consumer Research, 21,* 205–218.

Hammock, T., & Brehm, J. W. (1966). The attractiveness of choice alternatives when freedom to choose is eliminated by a social agent. *Journal of Personality, 34,* 546–554. doi: 10.1111/j.1467-6494.1966.tb02370.x

Hample, D., & Krueger, B. (2011). Serial arguments in classrooms. *Communication Studies, 62,* 597–617. doi: 10.1080/10510974.2011.576746

Hecht, M. L., & Miller-Day, M. (2009). The drug resistance strategies project: Using narrative theory to enhance adolescents' communication competence. In L. R. Frey & K. N. Cissna (Eds.), *Routledge handbook of applied communication research* (pp. 535–557). New York, NY: Taylor & Francis.

Henningsen, D. D., Henningsen, M. L. M., Jakobsen, L., & Borton, I. (2004). It's good to be leader: The influence of randomly and systematically selected leaders on decision-making groups. *Group Dynamics: Theory, Research and Practice, 8,* 62–76.

Holland, P. W. (1986). Statistics and causal inference. *Journal of the American Statistical Association, 81,* 945–960.

Howard, M. V. A., Brewer, N., & Williams, K. D. (2006). How processing resources shape the influence of stealing thunder on mock-juror verdicts. *Psychiatry, Psychology and Law, 13,* 60–66.

Ifert, D. E. (2000). Resistance to interpersonal requests: A summary and critique of recent research. In M. Roloff (Ed.), *Communication yearbook 23* (pp. 125–161). Thousand Oaks, CA: Sage.

Jacks, J. Z., & Devine, P. G. (2000). Attitude importance, forewarning of message content, and resistance to persuasion. *Basic and Applied Social Psychology, 22,* 19–29.

Johnson, D. I. (2007). Politeness theory and perceived competence of conversational refusals: Association between multiple face threats and perceived competence. *Western Journal of Communication, 71,* 196–215. doi: 10.1080/10570310701518427

Johnson, D. I. (2008). Modal expressions in refusals of friends' interpersonal requests: Politeness and effectiveness. *Communication Studies, 59,* 148–163. doi: 10.1080/10510970802062477

Johnson, D. I., Roloff, M. E., & Riffee, M. A. (2004a). Politeness theory and refusals of requests: Face threat as a function of expressed obstacles. *Communication Studies, 55,* 227–238. doi: 10.1080/10510970409388616

Johnson, D. I., Roloff, M. E., & Riffee, M. A. (2004b). Responding to refusals of requests: Face threat and persistence, persuasion and forgiving statements. *Communication Quarterly, 52,* 347–356. doi: 10.1080/01463370409370205

Johnson, K. L., & Roloff, M. E. (1998). Serial arguing and relational quality: Determinants and consequences of perceived resolvability. *Communication Research, 25,* 327–343. doi: 10.1177/009365098025003004

Jonas, E., Graupmann, V., Kayser, D. N., Zanna, M., Traut-Mattausch, E., & Frey, D. (2009). Culture, self, and the emergence of reactance: Is there a "universal" freedom? *Journal of Experimental Social Psychology, 45*(5), 1068–1080. doi: org/10.1016/j.jesp.2009.06.005

Jones, E. E., & Wortman, C. (1973). *Ingratiation: An attributional approach.* Morristown, NJ: General Learning Corp.

Kazoleas, D. (1993). The impact of argumentativeness and resistance to persuasion. *Human Communication Research, 20,* 118–137.

Kellermann, K., & Cole, T. (1994). Classifying compliance gaining messages: Taxonomic disorder and strategic confusion. *Communication Theory, 4,* 3–60. doi: 10.1111/j.1468-2885.1994.tb00081.x

Kerr, N. L., & MacCoun, R. J. (1985). The effects of jury size and polling method on the process and product of jury deliberation. *Journal of Personality and Social Psychology, 48,* 349–363.

Kline, S. L., & Floyd, C. H. (1990). On the art of saying no: The influence of social cognitive development on messages of refusal. *Western Journal of Speech Communication, 54,* 454–472. doi: 10.1080/10570319009374355

Kruglanski, A. W., Webster, D. M., & Klem, A. (1993). Motivated resistance and openness to persuasion in the presence or absence of prior information. *Journal of Personality and Social Psychology, 65,* 861–876.

Lemanski, J. L., & Lee, H.-S. (2012). Attitude certainty and resistance to persuasion: Investigating the impact of source trustworthiness in advertising. *International Journal of Business and Social Science, 3,* 66–75.

Lydon, J., Zanna, M. P., & Ross, M. (1988). Bolstering attitudes by autobiographical recall: Attitude persistence and selective memory. *Personality and Social Psychology Bulletin, 14,* 78–86.

Malis, R. S., & Roloff, M. E. (2006). Demand/withdraw patterns in serial arguments: Implications for well-being. *Human Communication Research, 32,* 198–216. doi: 10.1111/j.1468-2958.2006.00009.x

McGuire, W. J. (1961). The effectiveness of supportive and refutational defenses in immunizing and restoring beliefs against persuasion. *Sociometry, 24,* 184–197.

McGuire, W. J. (1964). Inducing resistance to persuasion: Some contemporary approaches. In L. Berkowitz (Ed.), *Advances in experimental social psychology* (Vol. 1, pp. 191–229). New York, NY: Academic Press.

McGuire, W. J., & Millman, S. (1965). Anticipatory belief lowering following forewarning of a persuasive attack. *Journal of Personality and Social Psychology, 2,* 471–479. doi: 10.1037/h0022486

McGuire, W. J., & Papageorgis, D. (1962). Effectiveness of forewarning in developing resistance to persuasion. *Public Opinion Quarterly, 26,* 24–34. doi: 10.1086/267068

McLaughlin, M. L., Cody, M. J., & Robey, C. S. (1980). Situational influences on the selection of strategies to resist compliance-gaining attempts. *Human Communication Research*, 7, 14–36. doi: 10.1111/j.1468-2958.1980.tb00548.x

Metts, S., Cupach, W. R., & Imahori, T. T. (1992). Perceptions of sexual compliance-resisting messages in three types of cross-sex relationships. *Western Journal of Communication*, 56, 1–17. doi: 10.1080/10570319209374398

Miller, C. H., Lane, L. T., Deatrick, L. M., Young, A. M., & Potts, K. A. (2007). Psychological reactance and promotional health messages: The effects of controlling language, lexical concreteness, and the restoration of freedom. *Human Communication Research*, 33, 219–240. doi: 10.1111/j.1468-2958.2007.00297.x

Miller, G. R. (1980). On being persuaded: Some basic distinctions. In M. E. Roloff and G. R. Miller (Eds.), *Persuasion: New directions in theory and research* (pp. 11–29). Beverly Hills, CA: Sage.

Mitnick, K. D., & Simon, W. L. (2002). *The art of deception*. Indianapolis, IN: Wiley.

Motley, M. T., & Reeder, H. R. (1995). Unwanted escalation of sexual intimacy: Male and female perceptions of connotations and relational consequences of resistance messages. *Communication Monographs*, 62, 355–382. doi: 10.1080/03637759509376367

Muscanell, N. L., Guadagno, R. E., & Murphy, S. (2014). Weapons of influence misused: A social influence analysis of why people fall prey to internet scams. *Social and Personality Psychology Compass*, 8, 388–396.

O'Keefe, B. J. (1988). The logic of message design: Individual difference in reasoning about communication. *Communication Monographs*, 55, 80–103. doi: 10.1080/03637758809376159

O'Keefe, B. J., & Delia, J. G. (1979). Construct comprehensiveness and cognitive complexity as predictors of the number and strategic adaptation of arguments and appeals in a persuasive message. *Communication Monographs*, 46, 231–240. doi: 10.1080/03637757909376009

Osterhouse, R. A., & Brock, T. C. (1970). Distraction increases yielding to propaganda by inhibiting counterarguing. *Journal of Personality and Social Psychology*, 15, 344–358.

Papageorgis, D., & McGuire, W. J. (1961). The generality of immunity to persuasion produced by pre-exposure to weakened counterarguments. *Journal of Abnormal and Social Psychology*, 62, 475–481. doi: 10.1037/h0048430

Pettigrew, J. Miller-Day, M., Krieger, J., & Hecht, M. L. (2011). Alcohol and other drug resistance strategies employed by rural adolescents. *Journal of Applied Communication Research*, 39, 103–122. doi: 10.1080/00909882.2011.556139

Petty, R. E., & Cacioppo, J. T. (1979). Effects of forewarning of persuasive intent and involvement on cognitive responses and persuasion. *Personality and Social Psychology Bulletin*, 5, 173–176.

Petty, R. E., & Cacioppo, J. T. (1986). The elaboration likelihood model of persuasion. In L. Berkowitz (Ed.), *Advances in experimental social psychology* (Vol 19, pp. 123–205). San Diego, CA: Academic Press.

Petty, R. E., & Krosnick, J. A. (Eds.). (1995). *Attitude strength: Antecedents and consequences*. Mahwah, NJ: Lawrence Erlbaum Associates.

Pfau, M. (1992). The potential of inoculation in promoting resistance to the effectiveness of comparative advertising messages. *Communication Quarterly*, 40, 26–44. doi: 10.1080/01463379209369818

Pfau, M., Banas, J., Semmler, S. M., Deatrick, L., Lane, L., Mason, A., Craig, E., Nisbett, G., & Underhill, J. (2010). Role and impact of involvement and enhanced threat in resistance. *Communication Quarterly*, 58, 1–18. doi: 10.1080/01463370903520307

Pfau, M., & Burgoon, M. (1988). Inoculation in political campaign communication. *Human Communication Research*, 15, 91–111. doi: 10.1111/j.1468-2958.1988.tb00172.x

Pfau, M., & Burgoon, M. (1990). Inoculation in political campaigns and gender. *Women's Studies in Communication*, 13, 1–21.

Pfau, M., Compton, J., Parker, K. A., An, C., Wittenberg, E. M., Ferguson, M., Horton, H., & Malyshev, Y. (2006). The conundrum of the timing of counterarguing effects in resistance: Strategies to boost the persistence of counterarguing output. *Communication Quarterly*, 54, 143–156. doi: 10.1080/01463370600650845

Pfau, M., Kenski, H. C., Nitz, M., & Sorenson, J. (1990). Efficacy of inoculation messages in promoting resistance to political attack messages: Application to direct mail. *Communication Monographs*, 57, 25-43. doi: 10.1080/03637759009376183

Pfau, M., Park, D., Holbert, R. L., & Cho, J. (2001). The effects of party- and PAC-sponsored issue advertising and the potential of inoculation to combat its impact on the democratic process. *American Behavioral Scientist*, 44, 2379–2397. doi: 10.1177/00027640121958384

Pfau, M., Semmler, S. M., Deatrick, L., Mason, A., Nisbett, G., Lane, L., Craig, E., Underhill, J., & Banas, J. (2009). Nuances about the role and impact of affect in inoculation. *Communication Monographs*, 76, 73–98. doi: 10.1080/03637750802378807

Pfau, M., Szabo, E. A., Anderson, J., Morrill, J., Zubric, J., & Wan, H. H. (2001). The role and impact of affect in the process of resistance to persuasion. *Human Communication Research*, 27, 216–252. doi: 10.1111/j.1468-2958.2001.tb00781.x

Pfau, M., & Van Bockern, S. (1994). The persistence of inoculation in conferring resistance to smoking initiation among adolescents: The second year. *Human Communication Research*, 20, 413–430. doi: 10.1111/j.1468-2958.1994.tb00329.x

Pfau, M., Van Bockern, S., & Kang, J. G. (1992). Use of inoculation to promote resistance to smoking initiation among adolescents. *Communication Monographs*, 59, 213–230. doi: 10.1080/03637759209376266

Quick, B. L., & Considine, J. R. (2008). Examining the use of forceful language when designing exercise advertisements for adults: A test of conceptualizing reactance arousal as a two-step process. *Health Communication*, 23, 483–491. doi: 10.1080/10410230802342150

Quick, B. L., & Kim, D. K. (2009). Examining reactance and reactance restoration with Korean adolescents: A test of psychological reactance within a collectivist culture. *Communication Research*, 36, 765–782. doi: 10.1177/0093650290346797

Quick, B. L., Shen, L., & Dillard, J. P. (2013). Reactance theory and persuasion. In J. P. Dillard and L. Shen (Eds.), *The SAGE handbook of persuasion: Developments in theory and practice* (2nd ed., pp. 167–183). Los Angeles, CA: Sage.

Rains, S. A. (2013). The nature of psychological reactance revisited: A meta-analytic review. *Human Communication Research*, 39, 47–73. doi: 10.1111/j.1468-2958.2012.01443.x

Rains, S. A., & Turner, M. M. (2007) Psychological reactance and persuasive health communication: A test and extension of the intertwined model. *Human Communication Research*, 33, 241–269. doi: 10.1111/j.1468-2958.2007.00298.x

Reznik, R. M., Miller, C. W., Roloff, M. E., & Gaze, C. M. (2015). The impact of demand/withdraw patterns on health in emerging adults' serial arguments with parents. *Communication Research Reports*, 32, 35–44. doi: 10.1080/08824096.2014.989973

Reznik, R. M., & Roloff, M. E. (2011). Getting off to a bad start: The relationship between communication during an initial episode of a serial argument and argument frequency. *Communication Studies*, 62, 291–306. doi: 10.1080/10510974.2011.555491

Rhodes, N., & Wood, W. (1992). Self-esteem and intelligence affect influenceability: The mediating role of message reception. *Psychological Bulletin*, *111*, 156–171.

Ringold, D. J. (2002). Boomerang effects in response to public health interventions: Some unintended consequences in the alcoholic beverage market. *Journal of Consumer Policy*, 25, 27–63. doi: 10.1023/A:1014588126336

Sagarin, B. J., Cialdini, R. B., Rice, W. E., & Serna, S. B. (2002). Dispelling the illusion of invulnerability: The motivations and mechanisms of resistance to persuasion. *Journal of Personality and Social Psychology*, 83, 526–541.

Sagarin, B. J., & Mitnick, K. D. (2012). The path of least resistance. In D. T. Kenrick, N. Goldstein, & S. L. Braver (Eds.), *Six degrees of social influence: The science and practice of Robert Cialdini*. New York, NY: Oxford University Press.

Stiff, J. B., & Mongeau, P. A. (1993) *Persuasive communication* (2nd ed.). New York, NY: Guilford.

Tannenbaum, P. H., Macauley, J. R., & Norris, E. L. (1966). Principle of congruity and reduction of persuasion. *Journal of Personality and Social Psychology*, 3, 233–238.

Tormala, Z. L., & Petty, R. E. (2002). What doesn't kill me makes me stronger: The effects of resisting persuasion on attitude certainty. *Journal of Personality and Social Psychology*, 83, 1298–1313.

Tormala, Z. L., & Petty, R. E. (2004a). Resistance to persuasion and attitude certainty: The moderating role of elaboration. *Personality and Social Psychology Bulletin*, 30, 1446–1457.

Tormala, Z. L., & Petty, R. E. (2004b). Source credibility and attitude certainty: A metacognitive analysis of resistance to persuasion. *Journal of Consumer Psychology*, 14, 427–442.

Visser, P. S., & Krosnick, J. A. (1998). Development of attitude strength over the life cycle: Surge and decline. *Journal of Personality and Social Psychology*, 75, 1389–1410.

Wegener, D. T., & Petty, R. E. (1997). The flexible correction model: The role of naive theories of bias in bias correction. In M. P. Zanna (Ed.), *Advances in experimental social psychology* (Vol. 29, pp. 141–208). Mahwah, NJ: Erlbaum.

Wegener, D. T., Petty, R. E., Smoak, N. D., & Fabrigar, L. R. (2004). Multiple routes to resisting attitude change. In E. S. Knowles, & J. A. Linn (Eds.), *Resistance and persuasion* (pp. 13–38). Mahwah, NJ: Lawrence Erlbaum Associates.

Wheeler, S. C., Briñol, P., & Hermann, A. D. (2007). Resistance to persuasion as self-regulation: Ego-depletion and its effects on attitude change processes. *Journal of Experimental Social Psychology*, 43, 150–156.

Wigley, S. (2011). Telling your own bad news: Eliot Spitzer and a test of the stealing thunder strategy. *Public Relations Review*, 37, 50–56.

Wigley, S., & Pfau, M. (2010). Arguing with emotion: A closer look at affect and the inoculation process. *Communication Research Reports*, 27, 217–229. doi: 10.1080/08824091003737901

Williams, K. D., Bourgeois, M. J., & Croyle, R. T. (1993). The effects of stealing thunder in criminal and civil trials. *Law and Human Behavior*, 17, 597–609.

Wilson, S. R., Aleman, C. G., & Leatham, G. B. (1998). Identity implications of influence goals: A revised analysis of face-threatening acts and application of seeking compliance to same-sex friends. *Human Communication Research*, 25, 64–96. doi: 10.1111/j.1468-2958.1998.tb00437.x

Wood, W, & Quinn, J. M. (2003). Forewarned and forearmed? Two meta-analytic syntheses of forewarnings of influence appeals. *Psychological Bulletin*, 129, 119–138. doi: 10.1037/0033-2909.129.1.119

Worchel, S. (1974). The effect of three types of arbitrary thwarting on the instigation to aggression. *Journal of Personality*, 42, 300–318. doi: 10.1111/j.1467-6494.1974.tb00676.x

Worchel, S., & Andreoli, V. A. (1974). Attribution of causality as a means of restoring behavioral freedom. *Journal of Personality and Social Psychology*, 29, 237–245. doi: 10.1037/h0036012

Wright, C. N., & Roloff, M. E. (2015). You should just know why I'm upset: Expectancy violation theory and the influence of mind reading expectations (MRE) on responses to relational problems. *Communication Research Reports*, 32, 10–19. doi: 10.1080/08824096.2014.989969

Zuwerink, J. R., & Devine, P. G. (1996). Attitude importance and resistance to persuasion: It's not just the thought that counts. *Journal of Personality and Social Psychology*, 70, 931–944.

# The Echo Chamber

David Byrne

Not too long ago some friends were asking each other, "How are Trump supporters so seemingly unaware of his lies and bullshit, and the ridiculousness of many of his positions and ideas?" (His claim that he "watched in Jersey City, New Jersey, where thousands and thousands of people were cheering" on 9/11 comes immediately to mind.) Lately it seems that anything that contradicts a passionate belief has become invisible.

The avoidance of a "reality-based community"—as the Bush advisors derisively called it[1]—is truly puzzling, but the other reasons why folks are drawn to Trump and others like him are, in my opinion, pretty clear. One reason why folks on either side of the party line are angry with how things stand is that both sides sense that Congress is beholden to the money of special interests and consequently the voice of the people goes unheard. Democrats might blame the Koch brothers and I'm sure that conservatives blame some outside influences, too. The decision to bailout the banks doesn't sit right with some, and others feel that the government wants to regulate their private lives.

The article "Why are Americans so angry?"[2] from the BBC provides "five reasons why some voters feel the American dream is in tatters": the economy, immigration, Washington, America's place in the world, and existing as a divided nation. And here is a link to the Pew Research Center article, "Beyond Distrust: How Americans View Their Government"[3], from which a lot of the figures in the BBC article were taken.

According to a study[4] by Nobel Laureate Angus Deaton and Anne Case, white middle class men may be killing themselves due to an increase in pessimistic outlooks concerning their financial futures. My guess is that the middle class senses the end of the American dream and that white middle class Americans are experiencing a lack of mobility and

opportunity in the economic spheres where they were previously the privileged and entitled majority.

Americans feel disenfranchised—that the government isn't responsible to the people and instead only responds to the wishes of special interests. In my opinion, the latter is not just a feeling, it's true. Add to that the feeling of impotence—that traditional remedies and corrections aren't effective anymore—and you have a pretty explosive cocktail. This probably drives a lot of Sanders supporters, too, though my bias leads me to assume that Sanders isn't propagating outright lies and misconceptions—he's actually addressing issues and not simply massaging his ego and building his brand.

That anger explains a lot, but the question still remains: how do folks continue to ignore facts? How have people's viewpoints become so insular and isolated that any contradictory information never even penetrates the bubble? How did we get to a point where dialogue is impossible? And I'm not just referring to this presidential race, but to many other areas of discussion as well. Am I imagining this or has the echo chamber, where one only hears what one agrees with, expanded in scope and at the same time had the effect of increasing that anger and the inability to have a dialogue?

It's been suggested that social media has a big hand in this increase in insularity. By its nature, a social network is adept at creating in-groups that share similar likes and opinions. Like many people nowadays, followers of Trump (and other candidates) often get their news from social media platforms like Twitter and Facebook—which allows users to post articles and video from other sources. (TV is a big source of information, too, but then folks still gravitate to shows that project familiar and agreeable point of views.) The problem with Facebook and Twitter is that those platforms mostly present a point of view that you already agree with, since you only see what your "friends" are sharing. We all do this to some extent—your friends share news with you and presumably many of your friends share your viewpoints. The algorithms built into those social networks are designed to reinforce this natural human tendency and expand upon it—if you like this, you'll like this. The networks reinforce your existing point of view in order to give you more of what you like, as that will make you happy and keep you on the network—and, in turn, more ads can be accurately targeted your way. You remain blissfully happy "knowing" or, rather, believing, more and more about less and less. Add that algorithm to folks' natural inclination to seek points of view that confirm existing biases and you've got a potent combination. Once you've surrounded yourself with only one point of view, soon that point of view is all you hear.

That is why, a friend argued, Trump supporters are immune to criticism and to the exposure of his lies and false accusations: for the most part these algorithms and subsequent self-censorship make it so that they never see anything but what they already agree with. As often happens when groups of like-minded individuals discuss something, the result is that their points of view are not only reinforced but also become more extreme. Cass Sunstein describes this phenomena in his article, "Deliberative Trouble? Why Groups Go to Extremes"[5]:

> Like-minded people engaged in discussion with one another may lead each other in the direction of error and falsehood, simply because of the limited argument pool and the operation of social influences. . . . The point also bears on the design of deliberating courts, legislatures, and regulatory agencies. Above all, an understanding of group polarization helps explain why like-minded people, engaged in deliberation with one another, sometimes go to astonishing extremes and commit criminal or even violent acts.

This is a natural human tendency, and social media seems to encourage it. By design. In order to keep the eyeballs happy and people on the site, the news is filtered—you get fed content on subjects and people you have previously expressed interest in. The algorithm uses that information to find more articles, images, etc., that pander to your likes. You are an increasingly happier viewer as you see more of what you like.

Below is a selection from an article[6] in *The Guardian* by Iran's "blogfather", Hossein Derakhshan. His blogging was, some years ago, very effective as a voice of protest and resistance—so much so that he was imprisoned for six years and only recently released. But now he senses that the web landscape has changed and voices like his don't penetrate as much:

> Instagram – owned by Facebook – doesn't allow its audiences to leave whatsoever. You can put up a web address alongside your photos, but it won't go anywhere. Lots of people start their daily online routine in these cul-de-sacs of social media, and their journeys end there. Many don't even realise they are using the internet's infrastructure when they like an Instagram photograph or leave a comment on a friend's Facebook video. It's just an app. But hyperlinks aren't just the skeleton of the web: they are its eyes, a path to its soul. And a blind webpage, one without hyperlinks, can't look or gaze at another webpage – and this has serious consequences for the dynamics of power on the web.

Wael Ghonim, who is credited with helping to launch 2011's Tahrir Square revolution via his anonymous Facebook page, laments the state of things today via *The New York Times* article "Social Media: Destroyer or Creator?"[7]:

> We tend to only communicate with people that we agree with, and thanks to social media, we can mute, un-follow and block everybody else. Five years ago, I said, "If you want to liberate society, all you need is the Internet". Today I believe if we want to liberate society, we first need to liberate the Internet.

We would like to think of the web at a place of pluralism—a place where many voices, often at odds with one another, can be heard. A place of diversity. A place to find out what wonderful and unexpected stuff exists that is different than anything and everything you already know. It seems that may have been true with net 1.0, but as market forces increasingly take effect, the diversity of voices, while it still exists, is now so filtered and targeted that you may only hear echoes of what you already believe. It's human tendency—further complicated by the fact that doing so funnels lots of advertising dollars into the pockets of big corporations.

Here's[8] a review in the *New York Review of Books* by Jacob Weisberg of some recent books on this and related phenomena. He writes:

Some of Silicon Valley's most successful app designers are alumni of the Persuasive Technology Lab at Stanford, a branch of the university's Human Sciences and Technologies Advanced Research Institute. B.J. Fogg calls the field he founded "captology," a term derived from an acronym for "computers as persuasive technology." It's an apt name for the discipline of capturing people's attention and making it hard for them to escape. Fogg's behavior model involves building habits through the use of what he calls "hot triggers," like the links and photos in Facebook's newsfeed, made up largely of posts by one's Facebook friends.

A successful app, [Nir Eyal] writes, creates a "persistent routine" or behavioral loop. The app both triggers a need and provides the momentary solution to it. "Feelings of boredom, loneliness, frustration, confusion, and indecisiveness often instigate a slight pain or irritation and prompt an almost instantaneous and often mindless action to quell the negative sensation," he writes. "Gradually, these bonds cement into a habit as users turn to your product when experiencing certain internal triggers."

Facebook's trigger is FOMO, fear of missing out. The social network relieves this apprehension with feelings of connectedness and validation, allowing users to summon recognition....checking in delivers a hit of dopamine to the brain, along with the craving for another hit. The designers are applying basic slot machine psychology. The variability of the "reward"—what you get when you check in—is crucial to the enthrallment.

ISIS and other radical organizations take advantage of this web-based phenomena as well. They too target folks' passions—videogames, for example—and their frustrations. Many of their recruits were not previously angry or radical, but social media allows all sorts of entities—the good and the bad—to tap into our latent feelings. This article[9] in *Teen Vogue* describes just how ISIS uses social media to recruit American teens.

So what can be done? The article "Terror on Twitter: How ISIS is taking war to social media—and social media is fighting back"[10] outlines some ways of mitigating the attraction of terrorist websites and ISIS's presence on the internet at large, including banning jihadist content and ISIS users, counter-recruiting via target advertising and hackathons, and gathering counter-intelligence from the outside and in.

But that's just focusing on ISIS. What about local politics? Aren't issues of race and immigration similarly ramping up in the U.S. (and elsewhere) into intolerant screaming matches? How do you encourage tolerance and open-mindedness while promoting exposure to diversity of opinion? It's an old question... As Alexander Hamilton wrote in *The Federalist Papers* of 1788, "The differences of opinion, and the jarring of parties...often promote deliberation and circumspection, and serve to check excesses in the majority." Further to that point, from philosopher John Rawls:

> In everyday life the exchange of opinion with others checks our partiality and widens our perspective; we are made to see things from their standpoint and the limits of our vision are brought home to us. . . . The benefits from discussion lie in the fact that even representative legislators are limited in knowledge and the ability to reason. No one of them knows everything the others know, or can make all the same inferences that they can draw in concert. Discussion is a way of combining information and enlarging the range of arguments.

Easy for Hamilton and Rawls to say, and for Sunstein to advise similarly as to group decision making (i.e., allow for dissenting views, limit the power of the leader, etc.). But what about in our day-to-day lives? What about the folks who will never hear that Trump is full of shit when he says he self-finances his campaign? See no evil hear no evil.

I'm probably as guilty as anyone, though I do scan about four to five different news sources during my daily browsing. While none of them are presented to me via a social media feed, the newspapers themselves are skewing more and more towards likable headlines, topics and subjects. Am I then supposed to force myself to read the *Post* and watch Bill O'Reilly from time to time?

Seriously though, some of those news outlets do skew towards opinions that are not reinforcing my pre-existing beliefs (the *Financial Times*, for example). So perhaps I have tempered some of my knee jerk reactions in some issues. But still.

I'm going to suggest that cycling or walking around in different neighborhoods gives one a slightly more face-to-face view of the diversity of humanity, especially here in New York. I love writing songs from different characters' points of view—characters who are often saying things I would never personally say, but whose shoes I can put myself, sometimes.

Like most people, I gravitate to others who probably share many of my viewpoints. . . but not always. If it's not already been filtered and combed through, sometimes we discover that friends hold some surprising viewpoints. And because they're friends—or at least because I respect them—I'll take those ideas on board, for a little while at least.

## Notes

1. http://www.nytimes.com/2004/10/17/magazine/faith-certainty-and-the-presidency-of-george-w-bush.html?_r=1
2. www.bbc.com/news/magazine-35406324
3. http://www.people-press.org/files/2015/11/11-23-2015-Governance-release.pdf
4. https://www.nytimes.com/2015/11/03/health/death-rates-rising-for-middle-aged-white-americans-study-finds.html?_r=1
5. http://www.yalelawjournal.org/essay/deliberative-trouble-why-groups-go-to-extremes
6. https://www.theguardian.com/technology/2015/dec/29/irans-blogfather-facebook-instagram-and-twitter-are-killing-the-web
7. https://www.nytimes.com/2016/02/03/opinion/social-media-destroyer-or-creator.html?_r=0
8. http://www.nybooks.com/articles/2016/02/25/we-are-hopelessly-hooked/
9. http://www.teenvogue.com/story/isis-recruits-american-teens
10. www.popsci.com/terror-on-twitter-how-isis-is-taking-war-to-social-media

# INDEX

Note: Page references followed by a "*f*" indicates figure.

## A

ability self-assessment, proxy model for, 74, 75
accidents, local dominance and, 81
accountability, 94, 279, 292–93
  anonymity and lack of, 289
  cues manipulation, 287
acquisitive and protective goals, 61–62
active deception, 18
active minorities, 332, 334
*ad damnum* monetary amounts, in damage awards, 401–2
adolescents
  deviance and risk-taking behavior of, 271
  health behavior and peers of, 8, 383–85
  working alliance with, 369
adults
  deceptive and unfair advertising directed at, 405–6
  health and social networks of, 8, 385–87
  inhibitory norms model for, 385
adverse outcomes, in Milgram's obedience research, 17
advertising
  deceptive and unfair, 404–7
  gender influenceability and, 43–44
affect as information model, 249
affect-cognition priming model, 76–77
affective deviants, ostracism of, 209
affective reactions, 80, 245
  in EASI, 241–42, 249
  of emotional expressions, 7, 240–41
  expectancy violations negative, 243
  persuasion and, 246
affective responses, in social comparison, 77
afterimage effect, 324
agency
  of females, 35–36
  gender and, 33–35, 38–39
  of males, 36–37, 38
agenda, in self-identification theory, 222
agentic state theory, of Milgram, 138–39
agents of social influence
  emotions as, 250–51
  social norms as, 149–56

theory and emotions, 7, 237–52
aggression, 205, 279, 291
  anonymity relation to, 282–83
  deindividuation and self-awareness, 284–88
  individuation and deindividuation cues, 286–87
  ostracism production of, 207, 212–13, 214
  reduced self-awareness and, 284–88
agreeableness, 246, 308
agreeing dynamics, 93–95
agreement patterns, in Asch's dilemma, 92
AIM theory, 249–50
alignment, 87, 88
  conversational, 96, 100
  descriptive and injunctive norms, 152–53, 154, 159
alliance ruptures, 368
Allportian trait-based approach, to personality, 54, 64–65
alone/evaluation condition, 186–88
ambiguity and uncertainty, 169, 170
ambivalent arguments, 321–22
analogue studies, 362
anger, 238, 241, 247
  conformity, happiness and, 248, 250
  core relational themes of guilt and, 251
  of Cyberball, 208
  EASI theory on, 248
  verbal expression, interpersonal effects of, 244
anonymity, 279, 290
  aggression relation to, 282–83
  antisocial behavior from, 285
  CMC use and, 291, 293–94
  in deindividuation, 176, 286
  diffusion of responsibility and, 176
  identifiability and, 281–82, 286, 289
  inhibitions and, 283
  lack of accountability and, 289
  privacy and, 22
  SIDE model and, 293
antagonistic power relation, 320
antecedents, in resistance to influence, 438*f*

anticompliance, 94
anticonformity, 87, 89, 90
antinormative behaviors, 294–95
antisaccade task, 194, 195
antisocial behavior, from anonymity, 285
antisocial influence, law literature and, 410–11
applied research, ethical issues in, 23
appraisal theories, on discrete emotions and happiness, 241
aptitude tasks, 330
arousal, 169, 190, 323
  dominant responses and, 184
  prepotent dominant responses and, 196
  social loafing reduction of, 176
Asch, Solomon, 55, 91–92, 94, 95, 205, 211, 300, 340, 433
Asch paradigm, conformity and, 55, 205, 211, 300, 340, 433
Asch's dilemma, 94, 95
  attribution account, 91
  dissent in, 91, 92
  divergence and convergence in, 91
  moral epistemology account, 91–92
  social identity theory, 92
assimilation, 71, 419, 423
  contrast and, 77–80
  downward, 81
  proxy model and, 78
  upward, 78
asynchrony, 99
attentional focus manipulation, 288
attitude, 4
  -behavior relation, MODE on, 369–70
  interpersonal effects formation of, 247
  intrapersonal effects formation of, 246
  personal relevance and stronger, 154
  resistance to influence and, 439–40, 448, 451
  vested, 330
attitude change, 317, 325, 327, 328, 333
  counterarguing and, 438
  ELM and, 369
  inducement, in ingroup minorities, 269
  research, 374
attractiveness, 120–21, 416
attribution account, 91

## S

salient behavior, 365, 366
SAM. *See* selective accessibility theory
scarcity, 5, 107–10
schisms, 333
selective accessibility theory (SAM),
  78, 79–80
selective targets, in ostracism, 6
  affective deviants, 209
  black sheep effect, 210, 266, 301
  burdensome individuals, 210
  disagreeable individuals, 209
  fairness principle violation, 210
  low-contributing others in group, 209
  symbolic threat to group identity, 210
selectivity, 100, 209–10
self, 219
  associated information about, 230
  beliefs of, 223
  defined through group, 265, 290
  favorable image of, 228, 230, 232
  group and understanding of, 259
  positive automatic, 226, 229
  uncertainties relating to, 262
self-abasement, as social influence
  tactic, 60
self-awareness, 279
  aggression and reduced, 284–88
  deindividuation from group loss of, 176
  public compared to private, 287–88
self-categorization
  referent informational influence, 261–
    62, 272, 290
  social comparison role in, 261
  social identity and, 7, 260–63
  uncertainty-identity theory, 262–63
self-categorization theory, 153, 259, 262,
    283, 289
  on group polarization, 270
  on majority/minority influence, 326–27
  on psychological groups, 340
self-construal, influence relationship
    and, 64
self-depreciation, 224
self-descriptions
  cognitive resources and, 225–26
  critical assessment, 229–33
  cued knowledge activation and,
    228–29, 231
  explicit, 226–27
  positive bias for, 226–27
Self-Determination Theory, 54, 62
self-distraction, 207
self-efficacy, in transformational
    leadership, 349
self-enhancement, 5, 71, 72, 73
self-evaluation, 71, 187
  in social comparison, 72, 73, 82–83
  threat, 194, 195, 423
self-identification theory, 221–22
self-other comparisons, 78
self-perception process, in FITD, 116
self-positivity, implicit, 226, 227

self-presentation, 6, 232. *See also*
    automatic self-presentation
  acquisitive and protective goals, 61–62
  background, 222–23, 231
  cognitive resources and, 224–25, 231
  concerns of, 172–73
  controlled, 220, 224–29, 231
  evidence for automatic, 223–29, 231
  fitting in compared to standing out, 61
  foreground, 222, 231
  habitual, 227, 228, 229–31
  identity and, 219, 221–22
  of introvert and extrovert
    identity-images, 225
  involving strangers or friends, 224
  Milgram's obedience research and, 139
  misconceptions about, 219–20
  positive self-representations, 228
  routine, 229
  self-identification theory, 221–22
  self-regulatory resources during, 227–28
self-presentational model, of social
    anxiety, 170
self-promoting identity-images, 224
self-regulatory resources, during
    self-presentations, 227–28
self-schema, 225, 228
severe deception, 19, 20
shared distinctiveness, 78
SIDE. *See* social identity of
    deindividuation effects model
silent treatment, as social influence
    tactic, 59
similarity, 5, 98, 107, 120–23
  direction of comparison factor, 77
  related attributes hypothesis and, 73–74
  SAM cognitive search for, 78, 79–80
simple tasks, in social facilitation, 6
simulations, 20
situational factors, for diffusion of
    responsibility, 171
situational variables, in Milgram's
    obedience research, 142
  FITD effect, 140–41
  information sources, 141
  responsibility removal, 141
social anxiety, self-presentational model,
    170, 173
social change, 267, 318
social communication theory, 72
social comparison, 3, 8, 71, 84, 329, 381
  affective responses in, 77
  assimilation and contrast back on
    range, 77–80
  contrast, 76–77
  downward comparison and, 72
  evaluhancement exceptions, 80–81
  frog pond effect, 82
  future research on, 83
  group polarization and, 269–70
  local dominance and, 81–82
  in marketing, 422–23
  opinion comparison, 75–76

proxy model, 74–75, 78, 80
  rank-order paradigm, 72, 74
  related attributes and similarity, 73–74
  related social influence
    phenomena, 82–83
  role in self-categorization, 261
  self-enhancement in, 72, 73
  self-evaluation in, 72, 73, 82–83
  across social networks, 83
  successive, 83
  upward comparison and, 72
social comparison theory, 5, 7, 261, 381
social compensation, 211
social conflict, 319
social contagion, 424
social context
  minority group influence in, 268–69
  risky shift paradigm, 270
social contract theory principles, 27
social cryptomnesia, 332–33
social dilemma task, 210–11
social disapproval behaviors, 6, 168
social distance, 386
social dynamics, of groups and
    individuals
  convergence and divergence in, 93–96
  cross-cultural issues, 5, 91–96
social engineering, resistance to, 447
social environment, cues in, 230
social exclusion, 205, 208, 209, 212, 301
social facilitation
  alone/evaluation condition, 186–88
  coaction/evaluation condition, 186–88
  cognitive interference, 188
  dominant response and, 184,
    186, 189–90
  drive interpretation of, 184
  evaluation effects tests, 186–88
  focus of attention and, 188, 190
  history of, 183–85
  mediator of effects, 6, 188–89
  mere effort account, 189–96
  mere presence tests, 185–86
  molecular task analysis, 6, 183–200
  motivated task performance, 3, 6, 62,
    175–76, 188–89, 199–200, 211
  social inhibition compared to, 174–75
  TIPPR, 196–99, 197f
  withdrawal of effort, 188, 195
  working memory deficit, 188
social force field model, 94
social harmony
  agreeableness for, 246
  leadership and, 246
social identity, 3, 259, 273–74, 339
  brand-related identity, 421–22
  deviance and marginalization, 266–67
  ethnic identity, 421
  extreme group norms, 269–72
  leadership, 263–66
  marketing and, 421–22
  minority influence, 267–69
  self-categorization and, 7, 260–63